MANUAL OF PRACTICAL CHURCH WORK

MANUAL

of

Practical Church Work

LUTHERAN PRESS

Publishers

1819 BROADWAY

New York 23, N. Y.

First Edition, December, 1942
Second Edition, May, 1943
Third Edition, March, 1944

Note: *Change of Address*
LUTHERAN PRESS
1819 Broadway, New York 23, N. Y.
Not "239 West 28th Street" *as given
on some pages*

Preface

For the past twenty-five years the AMERICAN LUTHERAN Magazine has published practical plans for the building of the Kingdom, plans which since have proved successful. Thousands of readers profited by utilizing these practical suggestions in their home congregations. When asked by brother pastors where they procured their ideas, many replied: "The AMERICAN LUTHERAN." Oftimes they would mention some past number as being particularly valuable and many would write in to our office for a copy. As the years passed, repeated requests came in for back numbers which could not be filled. Certain pastors asked us to print a detailed index which could be used by those who had saved their back issues.

In order to meet this request for an index, and also the need for a reprint of valuable back numbers, it was decided to make a selection of the most popular articles, proved over a number of years to be practical, and publish them in book form by the offset process.

This project was found to be more difficult than anticipated. Every article selected had to be carefully cut and mounted. Readers may find certain pages resembling a pasted scrap-book, and others which carry articles referring to some past event. In editing the book it was impossible to eliminate all past dates. It was felt, however, that the pastor who purchases the "Manual of Practical Church Work" will care little where the scissors cut as long as he can find therein some practical help for a more efficient operation of his church.

This much we know. Preachers will find little theory in this book. Hard working pastors, successful in saving souls, have written the articles used in our "Manual." Thousands of pastors have read and tested the ideas as they appeared in current issues. This "Manual of Practical Church Work" gives an accurate idea as to the contents of the monthly AMERICAN LUTHERAN Magazine.

Our one large purpose in editing the "Manual of Practical Church Work" is to make the choice of these time-tested ideas easily available to churchmen everywhere. Especially do we have the hope that this volume will serve in a wonderful way the young men recently graduated from theological seminaries. God has blessed our AMERICAN LUTHERAN Magazine in the past. In His grace He will provide the blessing to those who prayerfully utilize the "Manual of Practical Church Work."

This book is dedicated to the building of the Kingdom

Topical Index

MANUAL OF PRACTICAL CHURCH WORK

A Working Plan for a Greater Efficiency in the Church

In this working plan, submitted with the hope that it may offer some helpful suggestions, the external set-up of the local congregation has been approached from the point of view of the visitor, who offers both an opportunity and a responsibility.

I. REACHING THE PUBLIC

a. Newspaper publicity.

The church's invitation to a community can be most effectively extended through the newspapers. The columns of the community, and, if possible, metropolitan, newspapers ought to carry the Lutheran name regularly. Failure in this means, at least potentially, the loss of many a prospective visitor and eventual member.

Hints for successful newspaper work: Announcements must not be cut and dried. Sermon topics, music, activities in the church must be given. Whenever occasion invites, the great festivals of the church, patriotic events, special services, District and Synodical celebrations — g i v e the newspaper a "Story."

b. Signs and road-markers.

Direction signs are courtesies extended the prospective visitors. Signs must never be unsightly, amateurish. No pastor has the right to influence the public as to the Lutheran church by a cheap looking sign. The Lutheran church, often regarded as foreign and provincial, can afford to make only one impression: The best possible.

Signs should read:

TRINITY
LUTHERAN CHURCH
→
Two Blocks

II. APPEARANCE OF CHURCH BUILDING AND GROUNDS

Twenty visitors, let us say, have decided to attend your service. An impression, good or bad, is inevitable. They came without bias, at least we think so. Any impression they get you must give and convey. This requires a sympathetic understanding of the visitor's point of view.

a. The general appearance of the

church will create the first impression. The church need not be a cathedral, but it must be neat, prim, clean. Uncut, dry lawns, untrimmed hedges and shrubs, unpainted buildings, broken windows—all this is noticed by the visitor, and indelibly impressed upon him, although we, through frequency of association, do not even notice these repelling things. The building and furnishings ought to be regarded as an humble effort on the part of God's followers to pay Him tribute and homage in the most solemn manner we can afford and devise.

No church can be excused for allowing the church building and grounds to remain unsightly. Members can easily be led to become proud of the appearance of their worship home.

b. The bulletin board, or wayside

pulpit, is important in determining impressions. Slogans or sermon subjects should be thought-provoking, not laughter- or ridicule-provoking. Bulletin board sentences should have dignity and should appeal to intelligence.

Wrong (actual cases): "What Is the Price?" "Where Do We Go from Here?"

Right: "Heaven's Cures for Earth's Cares." "Human Attainment or Divine Atonement—Which Shall it Be?" "Are You a Christian or Merely Religious?"

The first sermon subjects are too vague, too general, uncertain, hence of little value.

III. ENTERING THE CHURCH

Every visitor is a guest whom the congregation, as host, owes certain courtesies, the absence of which will mark the congregation as boorish, un-American, careless. The following has worked out successfully.

a. Reception Committee.

The visitor is ready to enter the church. He wonders, Will the church be friendly, inviting, or cold and repelling? The visitor must not be allowed to run the dreaded gauntlet of (1) wondering where to go, (2) being gawked at, (3) finding his own way, (4) being entirely neglected.

Let the reception group of two or three, at least one, be stationed in the narthex to welcome visitors. It is far better to extend this courtesy when the visitor enters than to wait until he leaves. Let him feel at home from the start. From the very start let him feel that here is Christianity exemplified in courtesy.

The reception group must be carefully chosen and trained. Like the ushers, these individuals must be neatly dressed and well-spoken.

Addressing the visitor: "Good morning, are you a visitor? We are certainly glad to see you. Will you please sign this guest-card or our guest-book for visitors? An usher will show you to your place. I hope you thoroughly enjoy the service."

Note: Visitors from the neighborhood will receive a letter from the pastor. See model attached.

b. The Sunday calendar or bulletin.

The visitor will enjoy nothing more than to receive further directions for the hour of worship. Unless he receives guidance, he will be confused as to the Order of Service, local customs, etc. Our Lutheran Liturgy, hymns, customs, differing greatly from many other churches, call for explanation.

IV. THE DIVINE SERVICE

"Fellow-citizens . . . of the household of God" in their holiest exercise and experience. Nothing haphazard, slip-shod, has a place here. Only the best is good enough.

An organ prelude of ten minutes offers opportunity for prayer and preparation; also checks tendency of members to remain outside until the last minute.

The congregation must feel that every detail of the service has been carefully worked out. The service must not vary greatly in length.

The selections of the organist ought to be carefully correlated to the theme of the day. Let the church provide the organist with a number of good books of organ music. Light, breezy solo effects should be avoided.

The choir will enhance the effectiveness and atmosphere of the worship hour by the rendition of a simple chorale far more than by crude rendition of difficult anthems.

V. USHERS.

Ushers should be identified by lapel-flowers, or in some other way. They must be friendly, congenial, courteous, neatly dressed, alert. The duties of the usher should be specifically stipulated in a written form. They should know (1) At what point to admit strangers, (2) How to handle the case of a disturbing child, (3) How to watch ventilation, (4) What emergencies to expect and be prepared for.

VI. OTHER PROBLEMS RELATED TO THE SERVICE.

a. Flowers in the sanctuary.

Instead of constantly fearing that some well-meaning member will in the last minute before service bring in flowers, have a committee in charge of placing and arranging flowers. A local nursery, or an Altar Guild in the church may provide well-chosen flowers for the altar-vases. Flowers should never be placed upon the altar but upon the retable of the altar.

b. Nursery for small children.

Neatly printed removable signs may designate the rear pews as reserved for parents with small children. When children become a disturbing element, parents will welcome a nursery which a committee from the Ladies' Aid will readily maintain.

VII. AFTER THE SERVICE

The pastor ought to welcome the opportunity to greet his members and meet visitors. It is a good plan to have a number of members standing near the pastor so that a cordial contact can be made with all visitors.

VIII. OTHER PHASES OF THE CHURCH PROGRAM.

a. The Sunday School.

The importance of the Sunday School deserves a serious evaluation in our circles. Every member of the school must feel that a carefully outlined program has been prepared. Some one should be appointed to welcome visitors and new members. The opening service must not be cold, formal. Hymns may be introduced by hymn-stories, by correlating them to the theme of the day or by reference to their content. Nothing will so arouse loyalty, appreciation, interest, as calling upon various classes to furnish special features (mission stories, hymn-stories, Bible-verse sketches, recitations). Love for the divine service of the church, interest in church attendance can be engendered by conducting a fully appointed children's service in the church at regular intervals of five or six weeks, also by giving a report each Sunday of the church attendance.

b. Ladies' Aid, Men's Club, Young People.

All societies of the church must have a worthy, purposeful program. The spirit of unity will be fostered in the degree that interest is aroused in the activity which forms the essence

of union. How to make the best profit on the church-dinner, what prizes to give to the winning player, etc.—these are things that engender strife because opinions vary greatly. Discussion upon worthy themes, How Can We Make the Most of the Lutheran-Hour Opportunities? What Can We Do to Promote the Reading of Good Literature? How Can We Place the Lutheran Witness Into Every Home? How Can We Form a More Vital Contact With Our Foreign Missionaries? What Are Essentials of Home Happiness? How Can We Assist Our Institutional Missionary? etc.—this builds the spirit of unity.

FORM LETTER

Date..............................
Dear..:

We were highly pleased to have you present with us in.........................Church last Sunday.

Your presence would indicate to us that you hold in prayerful esteem the abiding values of the Kingdom of God, the Saviour, His Bible and Church. They who seek this righteousness shall have all other things added to them. That is the Saviour's promise.

We know from experience that people like to use their own judgment in selecting their church-home. Therefore, may we simply express to you a hearty and sincere welcome. (Add a concluding paragraph.)

(Several congregations are using the following outline in printing the order of service.)

Key to the Morning Service

PART I. THE PREPARATION. (May be omitted when there is a special Preparatory Service for Holy Communion.)

a) The Invocation of the Holy Trinity.

b) The Confession of Sins (taken from Hebrews 10:22; Psalms 124:8 and 32:5).

c) The Declaration of Grace (taken from John 3:16 and 1:12, and Mark 16:16).

PART II. THE WORD CHANTED.

a) The Introit. (The Beginning of the Service Proper, consisting of an Antiphon, one or more verses from the Psalms or other parts of Scripture and the Gloria Patri. The different Introits for each Sunday and Holiday are found in the Hymnal right after the Order of Evening Service.)

b) The Kyrie. (From Psalm 51:1; Matthew 9:27 and 15:22. Not another confession of sin, but a prayer for the removal of all misery and suffering in the world.)

c) The Gloria in Excelsis. (From Luke 2:14 and other parts of Scripture. Another Hymn of Praise, as 261, 74, or 68, may be sung as the Gloria; see Hymn Announcements.)

PART III. THE WORD PROCLAIMED.

a) The Salutation ("The Lord be with you, etc.").

b) The Collect. (A short Prayer. The Collects are found in the Hymn Book right after the Introits for the day.)

c) The Epistle followed by the Hallelujah. (A Hymn by the Congregation or an Anthem by the Choir may be sung after the Hallelujah. See Hymn Book.)

d) The Gospel followed by "Praise be to Thee, O Christ." (The "Glory be to Thee, O Lord" before the reading of the Gospel may be, not shall be, said or sung, says our Liturgy, and is omitted in our church.)

e) The Creed. (The Nicene Creed at Festival and Communion Services, otherwise the Apostles' Creed. In our church the congregation is seated during the reading of Scripture, but at the words, "Here endeth the Gospel," the Congregation shall stand up and make its Confession of Faith standing.)

f) The Sermon. (The Climax of the Service, followed only by the words, "The peace of God, etc.," or words of similar import.)

PART IV. THE WORD RECEIVED.

a) The Offertory. (The Offertory in the Hymn Book is from Psalm 51, but "any other suitable Offertory may be used," any short hymn containing the response of the congregation to the sermon.)

b) The Gathering of the Offerings. (The placing of the Offerings on the Altar is symbolic and scriptural. See Deuteronomy 26:4.)

c) The General Prayer (including Special Intercessions, concluded with the Lord's Prayer prayed in unison).

d) The closing Hymn.

e) The Benediction.

If there be Communion we have a fifth part:

PART V. THE WORD INDIVIDUALIZED.

a) The Preface with the Salutation and Sursum Corda ("Lift up your hearts").

b) The Sanctus ("Holy, holy, holy"), followed by Benedictus Qui Venit ("Blessed is He that cometh").

c) The Exhortation (usually omitted when there is a Preparatory Service).

d) The Consecration of the Sacramental Elements.

(1) The Lord's Prayer.

(2) The Words of Institution.

(3) The Peace ("The peace of the Lord be, etc.").

e) The Agnus Dei ("O Christ, Thou Lamb, etc.").

f) The Distribution with accompanying Hymn.

g) The Post-Communion:

(1) The Nunc Dimittis ("Lord, now lettest, etc.").

(2) Versicle and Collect of Thanksgiving.

(3) The Parting Salutation and Benedicamus.

h) The Benediction.

Silent Prayers

For the beginning of the service:

"Lord Jesus, bless the pastor's word
And bless my hearing too,
That after all is said and heard
I may believe and do. Amen."

Or:

"Lord, open Thou my heart to hear,
And by Thy Word to me draw near,
Let me Thy Word still pure retain,
Let me Thy child and heir remain.—
Amen."

At the close of the service you may pray:

"Grant, O Lord, that Thy Word may
abide in my heart,
That I may receive its blessing,
To Thy glory and my salvation.—
Amen."

DO YOU KNOW THE ANSWERS TO THE QUESTIONS?

1. Where do I come from? Am I just an accident of biology or am I a purposefully created creature?

2. Why am I living? Is it just to eke out a physical existence or have I a definitely assigned place to fill?

3. Is there a God? What is He? How is He? Does He know me? What is His disposition towards me?

4. Where am I going? Is there a heaven? Is there a hell? Am I just a creature of the hour or am I immortal?

5. What is sin? Is it just an excusable weakness or is it a damnable transgression of divine law?

6. What is death? Why is death? Why am I afraid of death? Is it a normal termination of life or is it a curse?

7. Has God revealed Himself to man? Is the Bible His Word? Is it reliable? Can its inspiration be proven?

8. What does the Bible teach regarding God and regarding man and their mutual relationship?

9. Is the Church a necessary institution? Has it something that I need? Has it an answer to the questions of my heart?

10. Is Jesus Christ the Son of God or is He merely an extraordinary man? Does it make any difference what I believe regarding Him?

11. Can I find peace and happiness in life and can I acquire a cheerful fortitude in the face of death?

A SATISFACTORY ANSWER

must be found for questions as these by every thinking person. We believe we have the answer and we therefore invite you to attend our course of lectures.

The following facts are to be noted regarding this lecture course:

1. The course covers twelve weeks, with lectures every Friday evening at 8:00 p.m. at the Parish House of the church.

2. The course begins on **Friday, September 25th, at 8:00 p.m.**

3. The prime purpose of the course is to prepare adults for church membership, but it is to be noted that attendants may consider the course purely informative and are under no obligations to join the church.

4. No memory work is required. The lectures are informal and the discussional method is encouraged.

5. The course involves no expense. A little text-book will be furnished free.

6. Regularity of attendance is expected. The short course means a compression of material and absence means a serious break in the course's continuity.

7. The course is also open to such as have already been confirmed in the Lutheran faith and desire to refresh their knowledge of the tenets of Christian religion.

8. Previous registration is requested. Kindly use the rear page of this folder for your enrollment and place it in the collection basket or send it to the church office.

Remember that the date for the class's first session is **Friday, September 25th.**

Summer Slump Advertising

The suggestion that the Outdoor Advertising done by means of the 23 feet Lutheran Posters during Lent be continued during the spring and summer months has come to us from all directions. The majority of the congregations which used this means of highway advertising report excellent contacts, "we had a number of people worship with us, who responded to our poster invitation" writes one pastor, another writes "our people liked the poster, and I am glad to say we secured the membership of an entire family through contact made by the poster."

The following imprints are suggested for Spring and Summer display:
SAINT MARK'S LUTHERAN CHURCH
Broadway & 42nd St.
BIDS YOU WELCOME TO ALL ITS SERVICES
and here is another suggestion,
IMMANUEL LUTHERAN CHURCH
Lexington Ave., at Main
INVITES YOU TO WORSHIP WITH US NEXT SUNDAY
Services 8:30 and 11 A.M.

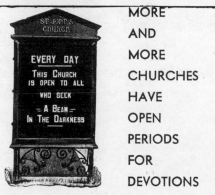

MORE
AND
MORE
CHURCHES
HAVE
OPEN
PERIODS
FOR
DEVOTIONS

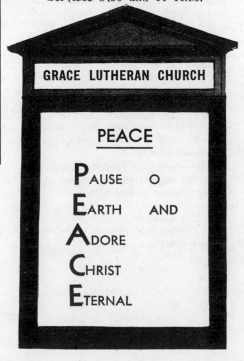

GRACE LUTHERAN CHURCH

PEACE

Pause O
Earth AND
Adore
Christ
Eternal

Church Plan for the Season

FALL, 1934 to SUMMER, 1935

Submitted to the Vestry by the Pastors and several Committees

BELIEVING that the continued success of our church has been due in the past and will be due in the future largely to a well-planned program, the pastors are submitting for the information of the Vestry their plans for the coming season, together with several suggestions that call for vestry action. The suggestions of the Finance Committee and the committee for the celebration of the forty-fifth anniversary of the church are also herewith submitted.

SERVICES

We are glad to report that in our opinion the double morning service arrangement has been a great success and has very appreciably increased the morning church attendance. A moderate estimate, based on the socalled loose collection, would place the increased attendance per Sunday at the figure of from 150 to 200 additional people.

The institution of an additional communion service every month has brought about a greater regard for the Sacrament and a very appreciable increase in the number of communion participants.

The evening service causes us grave concern. In spite of its disregard on the part of most of our members, it is still proving itself a valuable missionary institution. The Pastors will endeavor to create a greater interest in the service by announcing attractive series of sermons. One series will be entitled "Pen Pictures of the Prophets," and will be along practical lines, applicable to the problems of the day. It is also intended to reintroduce, perhaps for one Sunday evening of the month, the hymn services which proved so popular several years ago.

SPECIAL SERVICES

(Harvest Home)

We suggest that due to the particular physical need which will again be prevalent this winter, Harvest Home be once more celebrated. We suggest as the date, Sunday, September 30th.

We suggest that a card or letter be sent out previous to the festival, asking for a general participation in the collection of foodstuffs.

We suggest that after a sufficient supply of foodstuffs has been retained for family relief, the remainder be donated to the Home of the Children's Friend Society.

(Bible Anniversary)

We suggest that the 400th anniversary of the appearance of Luther's Bible translation be celebrated in connection with the Reformation Festival on Sunday, October 28th. (The joint celebration of the St. Paul churches will be held at the Auditorium on Sunday afternoon, October 14th.) Other plans for a suitable observance of the anniversary are presented in another part of this document.

(Evangelism (Mission) Sunday)

We suggest:

1. That the observance of the day be held on Sunday, November 11th, with the local pastors preaching at both services.

2. That informative letters, together with special offering envelopes be sent to all the communicant members of the church.

3. That the proceeds of the collection be devoted to the treasuries of Synod.

(Christmas and New Year Services)

We suggest that in regard to the Christmas and New Year services no change be made.

LENTEN SERVICES

We suggest:

1. That provisions again be made for a daily Lenten Self-Denial offering.

2. That an additional service be held during Holy Week on Wednesday evening with the celebration of Holy Communion.

3. That the Communion in connection with the Good Friday service be omitted.

4. That a Communion service be held in connection with the early service on Easter day.

EDUCATIONAL WORK

Conditions of the day demand that the Church become more and more an educational institution. A well-informed and soundly-trained laity is a necessity. The Pastors will in the coming season lay much stress upon the educational features of the church.

1. The Sunday School

The Sunday School Board is constantly endeavoring to increase the efficiency of our school.

Regular meetings of the staff are held every month, and at every meeting the educational feature is predominant. The Pastor at these meetings will again lecture on "The Social Background of Jesus."

The Twin City Sunday School Teachers' Institute will again be conducted for the benefit of those who wish to be trained as teachers.

The Pastors intend to conduct a persistent campaign for the development of the adult classes of the school.

In accordance with the church's suggestion, names and addresses have been furnished by the United Charities of families in the Pleasant Avenue district leading into the downtown section of the city. The church spoke of possible bus service to this locality. The names furnished by the United Charities call for a systematic visitation to determine the feasibility of establishing bus service. Neighborhood conditions seem to demand male adult visitors. We suggest that a sub-committee of the Vestry be appointed to superintend this visitation. This work should be done at once.

2. The Confirmation Classes

The children's classes preparatory to confirmation will be conducted as usual on the afternoons of Mondays, Wednesdays, and Fridays from the end of September to Palm Sunday and possibly later.

Several classes for adults will be organized to meet on Friday evenings in the parish house.

3. The Thursday Evening Bible Class

The Thursday Evening Bible Class will be conducted by the Junior Pastor. The lecture subjects will be announced in the near future.

THE CHURCH SOCIETIES

The educational work in our church societies has been growing in popularity and importance. The two Walther League groups are reorganizing along the "New Deal" plans suggested by the International League. The two objectives of education and service will be stressed. Both organizations have two meetings each month. In order to show the diversity of the work done, the program of both Leagues are appended.

Senior Walther League:

Sept. 11   Reorganization. Convention Reports.
Lecture: "The Function of Church Organizations" Pastor Paul Lindemann

Sept. 25   Discussion: "Stewardship and My Income"
(A study of the stewardship of money with charts and graphs.)

Oct. 9   Lecture: "The Liturgical Movement" Pastor Herbert Lindemann

Oct. 23   Lecture: "The Church and Penal Institutions" The Rev. Roy Olson, chaplain at the prison at St. Cloud (Open meeting for all members and friends of the church).

Nov. 13   Lecture: "The Romance of the English Bible." Pastor Paul Lindemann

Nov. 27   Lecture and Discussion: "St. Augustine" Pastor Herbert Lindemann (Beginning a series of lectures on the Church Fathers)

Dec. 11   Debate: "Resolved that All Money-making Schemes for the Benefit of the Church are Detrimental to its Interests."

Jan. 8   Lecture: "How the United States Became a Protestant Nation", Pastor Paul Lindemann

Jan. 22   Lecture: "The Devil-Worshipers of Kurdistan" Dr. A. C. Piepkorn (Open meeting)

Feb. 12   Lecture: "The Real Conflict of the Civil War" Pastor Herbert Lindemann

Feb. 26   Lecture and Discussion: "St. John Chrysostom" Pastor Herbert Lindemann (Second of the series of lectures on the Church Fathers)

March 12 Lecture and Discussion: "The Religion of the Lodge"

March 26 Lecture and Discussion: "Is Capitalism Christian?" Rev. E. B. Glabe   (Open meeting)

April 9   Lecture: "Are the Rules of Morality Fixed?" Pastor Paul Lindemann

April 23 Activities Contest

May 14   Annual Banquet

May 28   Discussion: "The Church and Politics" (A timely topic on which we want a general expression of opinion)

June 11   Lecture: "St. Ambrose", Rev. Herbert Lindemann (Third of the series of lectures on the Church Fathers)

Junior Walther League:

Sept. 3   Reorganization and Convention Reports

Sept. 17 Discussion: "Enjoying Church Work"

Oct. 2   Lecture: "St. Augustine", Pastor Herbert Lindemann

Oct. 15   Discussion: "The Church and Entertainment"

Nov. 6   Lecture: "How Did We Get Our Bible?"

Nov. 20   Debate:

Dec. 4   Lecture: "The Various English Bible Translations" Parents' Night; Social, Pastor Paul Lindemann

Dec. 18   Discussion: "Christian Customs" Christmas Social; White Christmas

Jan. 1   Lecture: "St. John Chrysostom", Pastor Herbert Lindemann

Jan. 15   Discussion: "The Attitude of Young People Toward Intoxicants"

Feb. 5   Lecture: "The Church and the Individual" Pastor A. E. Frey

Feb. 19   Debate:

March 5   Lecture: "St. Ambrose", Pastor Herbert Lindemann

March 19 Activities Contest

April 2   Stereopticon Lecture: "The Suffering Savior"

April 16 (Holy Week) Lecture: "The Cross in Christian Usage", Pastor Herbert Lindemann

May 7   Reception for Confirmation Class. Social

May 21   Lecture: "What is Culture?" Pastor Paul Lindemann

June 4   (Election of officers), Discussion: "The Church and Politics."

June 18   Ice Cream Social

Courses of lectures have been prepared for the Ladies' Aid Society and the Cotta Guild. The Men's Club arranges its own program.

Leadership Training

Under the auspices of the Twin City Walther League a course in church leadership will be conducted. A program is now being prepared. The meeting place has not yet been determined.

Children's Choir

In order to foster a taste for good music, to interest in the church a group of children, and to furnish music, particularly for the early service, it is suggested that a children's choir be organized under the direction of the Junior Pastor and Miss Rast.

Orchestra

Efforts will be made to enlist also the musical talent of the church in the foundation of a church orchestra. The success of this project depends on the finding of a competent director.

Voters' Meetings

The lectures on "The Religious Bodies of America" will be conducted at the meetings of the Voting Members, if so desired.

PUBLICITY AND PRINTING

1. The Pastors suggest that the church resume regular weekly Saturday evening ads, at least in the Dispatch. In order to make the ad stand out, it is to be preceded by a two- or three-line sermonette.

2. We suggest that the Senior Walther League be permitted to place new signs at the intersections of Dale and Selby, Dale and Rondo, and Dale and University.

3. The Senior Walther League intends to place copies of the Redeemer Record in the libraries of Macalester College, Hamline College, and the University of Minnesota Farm School.

4. The same League also intends to place a framed church ad in the St. Paul Bus Station.

5. Copies of the Redeemer Record will again be placed in the racks of the Y. M. C. A., the Y. W. C. A., and in as many hotels as will receive them.

6. Window advertising will again be used for advertising the Lenten services and also the Christmas services.

7. The tract and magazine rack has proven a great help and is widely used. It will again be featured in the coming season.

8. The penny gospels on the table in the narthex have been much in demand. They, together with other suitable literature, will again be offered for sale. The same is true of the Walther League Messenger and the American Lutheran.

9. We have for quite a number of years been lacking a folder for new members, setting forth the duties of membership. We suggest that such a folder be printed. The manuscript is ready.

10. We believe that much printing expense could be saved if the church had a mimeograph machine. Much of the work of the church, such as financial reports and any matter covering more than a page, must be sent out for mimeographing. The same is true of material for the Bible classes, church societies, lecture courses and music. We suggest that the Ladies' Aid Society be encouraged to purchase such a machine. The multigraph is good for only a limited kind of work.

Visitation Day

Open house on part of the Sunday School. Invite the parents. Ask the officials of the congregation to sit in. Perhaps some extra music and a few special songs. Advertise this service as a means to acquaint the older folks with the splendid work of the Bible School.

Christian Fellowship Dinners

ELMER A. KETTNER

A SECTARIAN minister recently complained to me, "The clatter of dishes in my church is drowning out the sweet sound of the gospel." Certainly we don't want such a situation to arise in our congregations. Most of our people are convinced that the church ought to raise money for its support by voluntary contributions. Probably, then, many readers are looking for an article on the subject: "How To Avoid Church Suppers," rather than a good word for them. However, it is generally agreed that social gatherings in the church have their place, if they can be kept in their place. Anticipating a blast of adverse criticism, we venture to relate our experience with a novel method of conducting a series of church suppers which we called "Christian Fellowship Dinners." Sounds good, doesn't it?

It came about in this way. We always have a long list of prospects for church membership. It is impossible to keep up with the list, calling on all prospects, and following up the calls repeatedly. New faces appear in the church service every Sunday. These people go home week after week without meeting our members or becoming acquainted with them. How shall we get these people to know our members? That is a real problem. In a church that is not growing this difficulty would not exist. Pastors of such churches may as well stop reading here.

We had another problem. Our ladies were putting on one church supper a year. It was suicide for them to try to handle 180 people in a social hall that was meant to accommodate 60. Somehow these two problems bumped together in our mind and united in a happy solution.

Why not have a church supper every month, and take care of a small group which could be regulated in size, so that there would be room to move about and opportunity for introductions and conversations? It seemed worth a trial.

We found one willing soul, one of our men, who had been a chef in a hotel, and who agreed to put on the first dinner with the help of two others. The girls of the Junior League were delighted to act as waitresses. We mimeographed 40 tickets, made out a list of all members and prospects, divided the list into four parts, secured four ladies to act as "table hostesses," and in return for the honor gave them each ten tickets and one-fourth of the total list

of names. The hostesses were to contact only those whose names appeared on their lists. They were to invite these to be guests at their table (at 40c each!).

The evening for the first dinner came. Thirty-eight of the forty invited guests appeared. It was not a banquet, but a simple meal such as might be served in the average home. For once the mothers had a rest! The table hostesses introduced their guests to each other at the table. In the course of the evening everyone in the group had an opportunity to meet everyone else. For Christian fellowship we used community singing. Between hymns and songs we read and discussed a list of questions pertaining to religion, which we took from our files, questions which people had asked us within the last six months. Before bidding our guests adieu we announced the plan of Christian Fellowship Dinners. We would have one on the last Wednesday of every month.

But how could we? No one had volunteered to prepare the food for the next dinner! We had scarcely expressed the fact when one of our guests volunteered. We would pay for the food, we said, if she would keep the cost down to 40 cents and prepare for forty people. Were there four women present who would act as table hostesses? No, there were not! But there were three women and one man! Why not? We gave each one ten tickets and a list of sixty potential guests, to whom the tickets were to be sold. It sounded easy. It was easier than it sounded. We had to refuse requests for tickets. There were only forty for sale.

So our Christian Fellowship Dinners have gone on from month to month. They are still as popular as ever. We don't make money on them. We don't expect to. No one has to work very hard. No one has to serve more than once a year. No organization is needed to sponsor the affairs. They carry themselves along from one month to the next. Dinner is served from 6 P.M. to 7 P.M. From 7-8 P.M. there is fellowship. Our guests can get home early, or even keep a "previous engagement" if necessary. Little groups of newly-made friends often go to some home after our hour of fellowship to spend the rest of the evening. The pastor has had a chance to speak to all the newcomers.

What do we do between 7 and 8 P.M.? Some time is needed for introductions. These are interspersed with singing. The hostesses for the following dinner must

be appointed. In addition to this we use the "Question Box," asking all those present to contribute to the interest of the following program by submitting one question. Each time we read the question which we will discuss the following month. Sometimes we have a motion picture of synod's work. A stereoptican helps present an interesting Bible lecture. We have had some hymn study, discussing the authors, composers, the music and the words of familiar hymns. The program varies.

Our people do get acquainted, sometimes not without a little embarrassment. A comparative stranger volunteered to be a table hostess. She took her list and began calling the people on the phone in succession. Finally, she phoned one of our young bachelors and asked him whether he and his wife would like to attend the next dinner. She was politely informed that he would be delighted, if in addition to the dinner, she would furnish the wife. I suppose she blushed! But by the time she had sold her tickets, she knew the people on her list better than she would have known them in a year's time otherwise.

Whether Christian Fellowship Dinners are just glorified church suppers or periods of Christian education and fellowship depends largely on what the pastor and his committees make them. They need not drown out the sound of the sweet gospel.

A NEWSPAPER MAN'S TRIBUTE TO THE RELIGIOUS PRESS
By William T. Ellis
Foreign and War Correspondent; Newspaper Syndicate Writer

For nearly half a century, my life has been chiefly devoted to reading and writing. My calling has made me an addict to secular periodical literature; yet every week I have also perused carefully several religious papers.

Now, looking back, I want to bear tribute to the value of these religious publications. They have been a large part of my education. Through them I have got a continuous picture of life in its more serious aspects. They have kept me "au courant" with the religious movements of the world. Their editorial and contributed articles, their quotations from the wise of all ages, and their good poetry, have entered largely into my literary inheritance.

Best of all, the religious press has continually fertilized my spiritual life, giving me a ceaseless awareness of the things of God. Without the corrective of these to my constant newspaper reading, I am sure that my own outlook would have been materialized and distorted. Times beyond count I have met God in the pages of the religious press.

An Interesting Experiment

Testing one's religion is always interesting!

To see the *practical religion* of a congregation put to the test should be most inspiring.

Every year when the financial roll call of our congregation is made, the attitude of our people over against God is tested, whether they admit it or not. For it is Christ who declares in Luke 12, 34: "For where your treasure is, there will your heart be also."

The gift of the individual donor is not made public. We feel that God and the donor know, however, as to how the test has been met.

Folks who refuse for any reason to support the Lord's work, should remember that all excuses must eventually be made to God who knows whether or not they will stand.

But it is easy to give money. Merely to make a contribution and tell God that we have done our full duty is taking the easiest course possible.

Therefore this year, we mailed to our communicants a questionnaire entitled "We Pledge Ourselves to God," which offers to enlist *not the money* but the time and talents of our people in the service of God's Church. People who have said: "I cannot give money at this time, but I would like to help," have in this questionnaire *an opportunity to help God which they cannot evade.*

It will be interesting to see how many people will persist in the "do nothing for God" policy. It will be interesting to see how many folks will wish God to help them, will expect the church and the pastor to serve them, and yet refuse to serve God in any capacity.

We believe that our endeavor to bring joy to our members in *this opportunity of serving Christ with our lives* is an experiment which will be followed with the closest interest by the Christ Who is sitting at the right hand of God in Heaven.

WE PLEDGE OURSELVES TO GOD

GOD EXPECTS IT. He has the right to say: "*You* belong to My Church. There is much work to be done in My Church. As your Master I expect *you* to do this for *Me*. Sometime I shall ask you for a report."

The easiest way, of course, is to contribute our money, and then say to Jesus: "My contributions have taken care of my part of the work."

Some folks are so busy they cannot say anything else. As one business man of St. Mark's put it: "I realize that it is my duty to serve God in my Church. But my business will not permit me. I must be content in giving a bit more money than the average, and hope that in this way I do my duty."

Others are more fortunately situated. They wish to contribute their share. But they also have time to serve personally. To help those who are anxious to serve we enclose the following list of "opportunities." We know that those who serve God in person, are also as a rule some of our most happy and contented members. FIND YOUR PLACE. Try doing Christ's work personally.

OPPORTUNITIES FOR HELPING CHRIST IN HIS CHURCH

1. Help pastor to introduce strangers after services and by visiting them in their homes............ ( )
2. Visit prospects with the object of bringing them to church .... ( )
3. Visit sick or unfortunate...................... ( )
4. Help chaperone hikes of young people.......... ( )
5. Canvass from house to house for new church prospects .... ( )
6. Help coach young people's athletic teams....... ( )
7. Serve as Big Brother or Big Sister for orphan ( )
8. Help in Choir, Sunday School or society........ ( )
9. Serve as speaker before societies on certain subjects .... ( )
10. Work under auspices of Lutheran Inner Mission in hospitals .... ( )
11. Help out sick mothers in care of children and household .... ( )
12. Offer automobile for taking shut-ins to church and for rides .... ( )
13. Repair and make gifts for poor at Christmas time ( )
14. Volunteer as stenographers to pastor on certain evenings .... ( )
15. Help fold Messengers and church literature for mailing .... ( )
16. Help House Committee in making small repair jobs at church................................. ( )
17. .... ( )

(Specify any work you choose to do)

"I have checked the work which I would like to do for Christ. You may call upon me when I am needed."

Name ....

Address ....

Telephone ....

St. Mark's Messenger

SATAN'S BROMIDES

Administered in the Average Church Meeting

1. "Our people are doing all they can financially."
2. "We have peculiar local conditions."
3. "The times are hard."
5. "The pastor talks too much of money matters."
6. "Charity begins at home."
7. "If we drum for money too hard, the people will not come to church."
8. "The old system has worked pretty good; why change?"
9. "We have a building program on, therefore Synod must wait."
10. "The envelope system is just a new-fangled idea."
11. "We had better go easy because there is a lot of talk going around."
12. "They say."
13. "I have heard that Mr. So-and-So is already complaining."
14. "Our former pastor said."
15. "The other churches are doing less than we."
16. "This has been a custom here for many years."
17. "The people are used to the old way."
18. "We cannot afford to offend."
19. "Our people are poor."
20. "The whole scheme is legalistic."
21. "I move the matter be tabled."
22. "Perhaps when things pick up more we can go ahead."
23. "We cannot afford to experiment."
26. "Let's play safe."
27. "We have to cut down somewhere."
28. "If everyone does just a little."
29. "Let all give their 'mite'."
30. "The time is no ripe."
31. "Our present situation does not allow."
32. "Let us not have too many changes."

Vacation does not mean that we ask the Lord to vacate the premises of our heart for the summer season.

* * *

Stewardship is primarily spiritual. Its great objective is character. It is the principle on which daily life must be organized in order to be fully Christian.—*Luther E. Lovejoy.*

The Church and Its Members

O. A. GEISEMAN

THESE STUDIES are not intended to serve as a new and comprehensive volume on pastoral theology. Hence we make no pretense of covering the entire field of the church's work with its people. We are merely striving to emphasize some things which we believe to be of particular importance in the urban church and which in our humble opinion need to be set forth with special emphasis in this transition period in which our church now finds itself.

RELIGIOUS EDUCATION

The very first thing which we should like to point out as an exceedingly important factor in our organized congregational work of today is religious education. Our previous studies have shown how the home influences, the face to face behavior controls, which played so important a part in human society in the past are lacking in a very large degree in our modern urban society. We have also seen how great and influential agencies such as well nigh universal education, the press, the moving picture theatre, the radio, and the frequent contacts of man with man in urban life tend to build up universal thought patterns which are hopelessly out of harmony with the requirements of Christian doctrine and Christian life. All of this means, if it means anything at all, that the person of today who is living in the large city finds himself engaged in a more difficult struggle for the preservation of his Christian faith and Christian morals than was true in a simpler form of life. It also means that a mere corporate type of Christianity which never has been satisfactory and adequate is even less so today. Should the modern Christian come safely through his earthly pilgrimage and reach the goal of life, then it will be absolutely essential that he be so thoroughly influenced and instructed and indoctrinated as to make it possible for him with the help of God's Holy Spirit victoriously to resist the dangers and temptations which dog his every step. This means that we cannot be too diligent in giving to our members, particularly in the days of impressionable youth, the finest kind of religious education which it is possible to give, and to extend this systematic effort throughout the entire life of all the members. The beginning should, of course, be made in the individual home so that fathers and mothers once again become more conscious of their parental responsibilities in the religious training of their children; but we dare not forget that the Lord has also commanded this particular task to his church.

This is a fact which many seem to overlook. Not a few of our people have come to believe that the maintenance of church schools is no longer as necessary today as it was in the earlier day when our preaching was done almost exclusively in a foreign tongue. We can do no better than to invite all those who hold such a view to look about them and to see how bitterly inimical the world is in which we find ourselves, and thus to realize that no efforts which we may put forth will be too great for the actual needs of the day. All of this means, of course, that we ought without delay give this aspect of our church's work our immediate and most careful thought. We ought seek to develop such religious day schools as we have into exemplary institutions of their kind. We ought earnestly and prayerfully consider the establishment of such an institution wherever it does not exist and where conditions at all make its existence possible.

We must, however, not make the mistake to suppose that we have met our obligations when we support an institution like the school merely for the sake of the institution. We ought rather see it as merely one factor, a very important factor to be sure, but still only one factor in the wider program of religious education. In addition to the home and the school we ought reach out for every other facility which our conditions may afford in order to attend unto the indoctrination of our people.

We ought strive to improve and develop our Sunday Schools, arrange for Saturday and vacation Bible schools. Instead of deliberately passing by the children of such parents who do not see the value of a Christian day school where it does exist earnest attempts ought be made either to try and gain such children who are attending public schools for hours of religious instruction during regular school time, or as the Jews have done for many years, meet with them in special classes after school hours. Long before they reach the age when they are especially instructed by the pastor and prepared for the responsibilities of Communicant membership with the church. Then, too, as already stated, we ought not to limit our view in the matter of religious education only to the days of early youth, but we ought develop comprehensive programs which include Bible studies and the presentation of educational topics for the various organizations within the church. Only then when we give this phase of our work with the members of the church such attention as it deserves and demands will it be possible for us to escape the sad conditions prevailing in many Protestant groups because they have neglected to thoroughly instruct their members. Here, too, we should like to speak a word for Christian secondary schools, colleges, and for the wider use of existing synodical institutions for the education of the laity. Anyone who is not entirely oblivious of the spiritual and moral dangers inherent in modern urban life ought recognize the value of such institutions, deeply lament the fact that they are so sadly lacking in our circles, and enthusiastically give support to such secondary and higher schools as do exist to the end that they may function in a most effective way.

THE MINISTRY

We should also like to point out some things which we believe to be demanded by the conditions of the new day in the modern ministry. It is our humble opinion that it has never been more important for the Christian minister to study and to busy himself with good and instructive books than it is today. To be sure the less one studies the less one is likely to feel the need thereof, for the less one knows the more able does one feel to meet any exigencies which may arise. Surely, we of the Lutheran church who look back upon a spiritual ancestry as represented by the fathers of our church who were able and carefully trained scholars ought be inspired by the high standards of scholarship which they held. The history of the church also teaches us that the Lord invariably placed well trained men like Moses, Paul, or Luther into strategic places of leadership. This ought impel us to make the most of our God-given capacity for spiritual and intellectual growth. It ought drive us despite the many unavoidable interruptions and the oft broken plans to find time and opportunity for study.

Were one to ask, "What should be studied?" our immediate reply should be, first, foremost, and above all things, the sacred Scriptures, and these, for richest rewards, in the original languages. It is extremely difficult, if not quite impossible, to recapture the full flavor, the amazing beauty, the life and sparkle of individual Biblical books unless this is done. It would be quite impossible even to imagine any expenditure of time and effort which could prove more productive of rich fruits, than a careful exegetical study of the Biblical books in the original made with the aid of a good lexicon, a good grammar, and a number of scholarly linguistic commentaries. No matter how many new sciences may make their appearance and how fascinating the study of them may be, this is, after all, the first prerequisite for an efficient ministry. Naturally, such direct searching of Holy Writ will be supplemented by other studies which contribute to an enhanced ability clearly to preach the truth, to warn against evil and error, and to give an improved understanding of the world in which we live.

Diligence in the matter of study will be increasingly demanded and required as the cultural level of our membership rises. We dare not forget that the days are gone forever in which the minister is the only one in the congregation who has enjoyed a college training and a pastor with a woefully limited horizon will soon enough discover that he is losing the interest and the respect of his people, especially of those who have gained a broader outlook upon life. The question is not whether this ought so to be, the fact remains that it is so, and it is for us to face realities.

PREACHING

The chief public service of a minister is today, as it always has been, that of preaching the Word. Good preaching requires more than just enough words to fill in twenty-five or thirty minutes in a public service even though these words cannot be questioned as to their orthodoxy. Orthodoxy is, of course, an inescapable requirement, but it is not the only requirement. Our sermons must have life and power. Should this be true then it will be necessary for the preacher first to recapture that meaning of any given text which it was originally intended by the inspired writer to have for the readers to whom it was first addressed. The proper treatment of any given text requires that it be seen against the background of that day in which it was first used. It is so we must present it to our hearers in order that they may also see it as a truth and teaching of God and grasp its real meaning and significance. Then having done this we must relate the message of that text to the lives of our hearers. Needless to say, this is a matter in which our sermons only too often fall short of their real purpose. We are inclined to preach as though Christian doctrine had no relationship to life. We forget that our people are living in a real world, facing real problems, perplexed by real questions, and that it is our duty and task to show them how the Word of God is to function in their daily lives, and how the eternal truths are to be applied to their own hearts and their own souls. This presupposes that the preacher possesses a sympathetic understanding of his people and their needs.

Perhaps it will also not be entirely amiss to remind ourselves that our members are human and that we ought spare them every unnecessary torment while listening to us. The pastor of today facing a modern and educated congregation finds himself in a position quite different from that of a pastor in an earlier day when members seldom if ever heard public speakers outside of their own minister. The radio of today makes it possible for our people to hear the country's most brilliant orators on almost every conceivable subject. They are being trained if in no other way then at any rate by this modern invention to become more fully appreciative of beautiful language, careful organization of thought, and an able and fluent presentation. They are being taught to evaluate more critically the sermons and public addresses of their own minister. All of this ought make us realize that the requirements of the ministry are rising and that we cannot give too much thought and attention to the careful preparation and able presentation of the Savior's glorious Gospel.

PASTORAL WORK

Beside his duties as a preacher the modern minister must also have an intelligent appreciation of his responsibilities and duties as a pastor and shepherd of immortal souls. Modern urban conditions which make for exceedingly difficult and complex lives on the part of our church membership demand an endless amount of pastoral work. It is not merely a question of calling on the aged, the sick, the backsliding, and the new prospect. It is in large degree also a problem of straightening out tangled lives, advising the troubled and perplexed, and remaining constantly in the closest possible relationship with every member of the church. This is a difficult task, to say the least. It cannot be accomplished by house calls alone. The pastor of the average urban church will find his time so occupied with meetings that he will have but very few evenings at his disposal in which he can make calls. If he calls only by day he is almost bound to miss the wage earners in the home and to find only the wife and mother. Hence other means and methods must be used in order to reach the bulk of the membership and to establish personal contact with them. We believe that every meeting within the church whether it be that of the voting members, the young people, the men, the ladies, or a group gathered about a banquet table or an audience appearing for an evening's entertainment, ought be grasped in order to seek out those individuals who ought be personally spoken to. Here within close reach one can often contact persons whom it would otherwise be difficult to find. It is also our opinion that conscious effort ought be made to so train the members of the church that they will come to the pastor's study for private consultations, and there discuss with him such problems and difficulties as they may have. We regard the time of Communion announcement as providing the very finest kind of a situation in which such consultations may take place or in which at any rate definite appointment for such consultations may be made. We have frequently been astonished to learn from the published bulletins of large congregations how little time is allowed for Communion announcement. We have seen instances in which congregations with a thousand and more members were given but one or two hours of time in the afternoon or evening of some given day in which to appear for the purpose of announcing their intentions to come as guests to the Lord's altar. We believe that many a pastor could save himself many hours of time, much needless travelling if he were to allow a longer period for Communion announcement and train the members to avail themselves of this occasion as an opportunity for conferring with him. Frequently it is possible also to make calls successfully at an appreciable saving of time by using the telephone which is ever ready on one's desk.

But no matter how much effort the pastor may put forth by way of keeping in close touch with his people it is our opinion that his efforts must for the finest kind of work be greatly supplemented through the assistance of lay-workers. Life moves on with a terrific speed. Sometimes radical and violent changes take place in the lives of people just over night. Hence arrangements ought be made that someone of the church gets into every home of the congregation at reasonably frequent intervals. Here it is important either to have a large number of elders or, as we personally prefer, a well trained stewardship committee which operates under the direction of an earnest and conscientious chairman and which makes regular reports on the members within the territory of any given worker. The members of such a committee serve not only in the every-member-canvass and in the follow-up of delinquent contributors, but they also interest themselves in the spiritual life of the individual families and in the degree to which these families actively participate in the life and program of the church's work. They solicit the children for school and Sunday School, encourage the young to become members of the young peoples' organizations, urge the men to attend voting members meetings, invite men and women to join the men's club or the ladies' society, and wherever necessary work for a more regular church attendance and greater faithfulness in the use of Holy Communion. Such a distribution of the task greatly relieves the pastor and offers appreciable assistance in what would otherwise seem like a very forbidding task. The work of the stewardship committee ought then again be supplemented by the services of special committees elected or appointed by various groups within the congregation. The young people, the men's club and the ladies' society ought have carefully selected membership and visiting committees who periodically call on those who are to be solicited for membership in these groups and who receive from the pastor a list of those who are ill so that they may visit them. When the work is so organized, the chances of neglecting certain members or of failing to contact them just at critical times are reduced to a minimum and one is at any rate afforded the comfortable feeling that important duties are not being too sadly neglected.

DIVINE SERVICES

We have already spoken of the importance of the sermon. We dare not entirely ignore the significance and value of a truly beautiful and impressive service. As the cultural standards of our people rise and their taste for that which is beautiful becomes more fully cultivated they will also increasingly demand beauty in the house of God and in the hour of worship. While we do not profess to be able to speak with the least bit of authoritativeness on this subject, we do believe ourselves to be sufficiently competent in the matter to say that a service conducted in a slovenly manner and music which would ruin the disposition of the deaf can so completely disturb the devotion of a congregation as to greatly interfere with the effective preaching of the Word. We believe that the members and friends of the Society of St. James are rendering a valuable service to the church by bringing this matter so forcibly to our attention particularly at this time when souls of men, tragically disillusioned by the break-down of a materialistic philosophy, are turning once again to things that are beautiful in order to gain some joy and satisfaction from life. This desire for the beautiful has gripped also our people and we ought receive with appreciation the splendid studies which are being made of the various parts of our Lutheran liturgical services to the end that we may in a sanely and well balanced way use thereof whatever may assist in the beautification of our services.

ORGANIZATIONS

A further factor to which a great deal of time and thought must be given in our regular congregational work today is presented by the various social organizations within the church. Some seem to view young people's societies, men's clubs, and ladies' organizations as but necessary evils which perhaps must be tolerated as a concession to the spirit of the day, but which in no wise are to be cultivated and developed into worthwhile undertakings. Frankly, we cannot share such an attitude. When we consider the amount of leisure time at the disposal of the average American, when we remember the frantic efforts which are being made by a grasping and greedy world in order to have men and women, young and old devote their time, their interests, and their money to such pastimes as it stands ready to provide, then we cannot but conclude that the average urban church ought recognize the important place which such organizations may well fill in the life of the congregation's members. It is our opinion that such organizations should not only be tolerated but that they should be systematically and carefully cultivated, and that they should be provided with well balanced programs which will prove so attractive and inviting as to draw in the largest possible number and to prove most beneficial to those who are drawn in. The programs ought be of such a character as to contribute to the development of the spiritual life of each individual, to increase the abilities of the members to be of service to the church, and to foster a finer spirit of Christian fellowship among the brothers or sisters in faith. It may be necessary to organize a variety of organizations in order to meet the different interests of the various members, and naturally each organization which finds a place within the church will require a certain amount of the pastor's time and thought. It will soon prove to be a physical impossibility for him to attend all of the meetings of all the groups. Here again then it will be important to select and train able and conscientious leaders who will work in closest cooperation with the pastor and who will grasp and accept the ideals and common objectives for which all should strive. Where this is done it will be possible to carry through a rather ambitious program of organizational work and to have the activities of all of them dove-tail in such a way as to promote most effectively the one great task for which the church of Christ exists, that is to say the salvation of souls, the improvement of life and character, and the extension of God's kingdom here on earth.

Gleanings From Wide-Awake Churches

Bus service for Sunday School pupils in outlying districts has been instituted by quite a number of churches. Bus companies seem to be willing to quote very low rates for such service.

A western church has regular Sunday automobile accommodation for the nurses of the city hospital, where rules of punctuality make dependence on street-car service inadvisable.

Another church makes practical use of the gardens of its members by asking for floral contributions to be delivered at the church on Sunday mornings and distributed on Sunday afternoons among the sick.

Many city churches are making use of the school police system to insure the safety of the Sunday School pupils at dangerous street intersections. These youthful policemen are commissioned by the city and have the same standing as public school police.

The practice of sending multigraphed copies of the pastor's Sunday sermon to the sick and shut-ins is growing. The most gratifying results are being reported.

Some of our churches are running attractive standing headings on their weekly church announcement sheets. These headings are usually in the form of cuts. Some have their cuts printed on a year's supply of the sheets used for mimeograph or multigraph purposes. Others use a standing multigraph cut.

One church makes the suggestion that, unless the Sunday announcement sheet is crowded, the text of the choir anthem be printed out in full. If the choir number has been carefully selected and is in harmony with the sermon, such an arrangement will enhance the value of the service.

Some churches have installed a blackboard in the choir room, which records the number of the processional hymn and the title of the choir selection for the day, thus eliminating the possibility of confusion.

In order to help eliminate the need for oral announcements, a western church has installed three indoor bulletin boards in different sections of the church building. The boards are home made. Compo-board, green felt and ordinary moulding furnished the materials.

An eastern church sends out weekly printed post-cards giving the sermon topic and other features of the service. It sounds expensive but no doubt the investment pays. The church in question has a reputation for sustained vigor.

A number of churches include suggestions for daily Bible readings in their weekly church bulletins. The passages are carefully selected and arranged. There is no doubt that such an arrangement stimulates daily use of the Bible.

In a certain church the cost of the weekly bulletin is borne by one member. The bills are sent by the printer directly to his home. Only the printer and the pastor know who the donor is. This example of modest and practical helpfulness is worthy of emulation.

The women of some churches use the tattered and discarded hymnbooks for making little booklets of perhaps eight or twelve pages, containing hymns clipped from the old books and interspersed with brief prayers. These little home-made hymnbooks are embellished on the outside cover with a little biblical picture. The leaves are bound together with narrow ribbon or ornamental cord. The booklets are used for distribution among the sick in hospitals.

Planning For Summer Months

IT was Easter Monday morning. Pastor Winsome was seated at his study desk. He had just entered the names of the Holy Week and Easter communicants in St. Paul's communion register. While engaged in this labor of love, scenes from St. Paul's "most fruitful Lenten and Easter Season" flashed across his mind. How God's powerful Word had gripped the hearts again! What a joy it was to break the Bread of Life and offer it to hungry souls! What a privilege it was to be an ambassador of the Living Christ! —His people had climbed to new heights with him. He must do his utmost with God's help to keep them there and to help them to go forward in these days of blessed opportunity.—He had called a special meeting of his Church Council for that evening. He would review again the plan he had prepared for their considera- tion.—A long, and perhaps trying, summer was in the offing. Easter was very early and after Pentecost would come the long, lean summer with its June, July, August and September—a most trying season for the Church, especially this year.—He would caution his Church Council not to grow weary. Together they would plan for St. Paul's "most fruitful summer season" and the enrichment of the congregation's life.—After carefully perusing and arranging his notes Pastor Winsome prepared the following plan:

1. *Church Services*
   a. Regular Services of Worship throughout the summer.
   b. The continuation of evening services through June.
   c. A series of special sermons (anniversaries of church societies, parents, sponsors, aged and shut-ins).

2. *Visitations to Promote and Stimulate "The Christian Life"*
   a. Prospective members who have been stirred during Lent, but have not been won. A careful follow-up will be rewarded

   with encouraging results. Invite these to enroll in the Pastor's Church Membership Class. Earnest and persistent efforts in this direction will mean a great Pentecost harvest.

   b. The unemployed among the members, many of whom re- main away from the services because they find it impossible to fulfill the pledges they made for the support of the Church. Woo them to the worship they so sorely need.

   c. Children of the parish, and others who are not receiving religious education, for enrollment in the Summer Vacation Church School.

   d. Inter-society, conducted by the various societies in the con- gregation.

3. *Congregational Family Gatherings*
   a. To welcome the new members to share in the work and worship of the congregation. A great help in assimilating and absorbing.

   b. To honor the sons and daughters of the congregation who this year graduated from grammar schools, high schools and higher institutions of learning.

   c. To celebrate the congregation's birthday. This will assist in keeping hearts firmly knitted and cemented.

   d. To study the current issue of the Minutes of the Synod. This can be made intensely interesting. What a story the Church has to tell!

4. *Districting the Congregation,* and appointing district leaders to look after the spiritual interests of the members in their district, with the major effort spent with the luke-warm, and also inviting the new comer, the stranger and the careless to the services.

5. *Organization of a Church Workers' Conference,* where the work of the congregation is discussed, and, what must follow, is distributed.

6. *Exchange Visits* with neighboring Lutheran congregations, under the auspices of the Luther League, Choir, Sunday School Teachers' Association, Brotherhood, Ladies' Societies, etc.

7. *Engaging the Unemployed in the Congregation* to make needed improvements on the church property, such as brightening up the rooms, planting shrubbery, etc.

8. *Vacation Plans*
   a. Winning some of the workers in the congregation to attend Summer Assemblies, Church Workers' Conferences or Lead- ership Training Schools.

   b. The "best ever" church picnic, built up around the Church School, in co-operation with all of the societies in the congregation.

   c. An "Appreciation Outing" for the Church Choir.

   d. A Brotherhood outing, with the "Little Brothers" as the guests of honor.

9. *Objectives for the Fall and Winter Work,* growing out of the efforts of the Summer.

—From *The National Lutheran.*

Report Cards

REDEEMER LUTHERAN CHURCH
BRONX, NEW YORK CITY

Report for....................   Term 19......to 19......
Class..................

.......Excellent; ....Good; ....Fair; .... Unsatisfactory; ....Failure

MONTH	Effort	Memory Work	Class Work	Bible Work	Times Absent Class	Times Late Class	Times Absent Sunday School	Times Absent Public Worship	Signature of Parent or Guardian

Pastor..............

Monthly or quarterly report cards have always been used in the day school. Some Sunday Schools have also introduced them.

They have also been introduced into some Sunday School with success. Where teachers are capable of fair and accurate grading a great deal of benefit might be derived from their use.

Such report cards will be found especially useful in the con- firmation class. A general report card should be printed which may be used for confirmation class, Saturday or week day school, vacation Bible school, or Sunday School.

If the name of the church, columns for grades, space for the pastor's or teacher's signature, and space for "Class" are printed such cards may be used from year to year and will not be found very expensive. Items which may appear in the columns for grad- ing are Effort, Memory Work, Class Work, Bible, Conduct, Absent, Tardy, Absent Sunday School, Absent Public Worship. Several blank columns should also be included. There will of course be a space for the singnature of parent or guardian each month or term.

A church in Iowa publishes in its very neatly mimeographed weekly bulletin the church service and Sunday School attendance figures of the previous Sunday. The count is accurately taken and reported. The practice no doubt has not only an information but a stimulating effect.

Some weekly bulletins list in their proper place only the words: "The Sermon." Others have the better custom of listing the pastor's theme and the text. The mentioning of the text seems valuable, since it enables the members to refresh their unreliable memories at home.

Ministerial Ethics

THE Rev. Dr. Gould Wickey, executive secretary of the Board of Education of the United Lutheran Church, in his lectures at the theological seminaries of that body, has presented a "code of ethics for ministers," which has been received favorably with requests for wider circulation. The code, as Dr. Wickey presented it, is outlined as follows:

A—VIRTUES

1. *Passion of God*

Constant consciousness of God's presence and grace, thereby securing calmness of soul, cheerfulness of mind, and poise of self.

2. *Passion for Character*

Purity of life, since immorality produces physical, mental and spiritual degeneration.
Discreet in conversation.
Carefulness in dress and manners.

3. *Passion for Truth*

Desire to possess all the facts, tho conscious of the limitations of the human mind.
Moved by the two rules: Thou shalt not lie, and Let the truth be known.

4. *Passion for Righteousness*

Courageous in periods of trials and persecutions.
Unrelenting in opposition to evil.
Strict business standards in financial matters.

5. *Passion for Service*

No laziness—every day an honest day's work.
Willing to give extra service.
Serving all without partiality.

6. *Passion for Souls*

Conscious that there is
Something to be saved—
Something to be saved from—
Something to be saved by—
Something to be saved to.

B—DUTIES

1. *To Self*

Maintain one's health—Mens sana in corpore sano.
Secure the best scholastic training, and keep up studies when in the pastorate.

2. *To Parish*

No special calling places—all homes whatever their condition need pastoral oversight.
True to confidential conversations and communications.
Willing to give service whenever called.

3. *To Community*

All unchurched souls to be sought, whatever their financial and social standing.
Perform the duties of a citizen.
Interested in community progress.

4. *To Fellow-ministers*

Courteous—Love one another.
Acknowledge any indebtedness in serman material.
No unjust criticism or competition.
Rejoice in one another's success.

5. *To Denomination*

Loyalty to creeds, doctrines, and liturgy.
Obedient to superiors, in so far as they are correct.
Enthusiastic for its progress—be a booster.

6. *To the Profession*

Maintain its dignity and standards.
Protect its reputation.
Inspire others to enter.

Suggestions for Fall Work

Institute a Sunday School Teachers' Training Course. In localities where there are several churches this may best be done jointly. For suggestions as to curriculum and management address the American Lutheran Publicity Bureau.

Arrange for a local mission program along the lines suggested by the Synodical Press Committee in its proposed Anti-Modernism Campaign. If you have mislaid your handbook, write to the American Lutheran Publicity Bureau for another copy.

If you have no tract rack, install one at once. Have a handy man in the church make one according to plans which the Bureau can furnish. Get a rubber stamp to mark all tracts with the name of your church.

Use the Reformation Festival for a stirring presentation of the sound Scriptural principles of Lutheranism over against the uncertain, faltering claims of modernism. Let the pope alone for once.

Make arrangements for a thorough canvass of your neighborhood with an effective follow-up system. The Publicity Department of Synod with offices in Concordia Publishing House furnishes all canvass paraphernalia free.

Persuade your church officers to subscribe to the American Lutheran, or have the church place a blanket subscription for them. They will profit by its practical suggestions.

Inject the spirit of hope and optimism into your parish paper. The depression must not be permitted to affect the spiritual life of the Church.

Send out a letter to all the members of the church, reminding them that the summer recess is over and summoning them to immediate service. Do not let the summer let-down drag on into October.

A certain layman in a town of New York State is using the tire cover on the rear of his car for the advertisement: "You Need the Church; the Church Needs You." The novel idea suggests wider development. Tire covers are now being used for publicity purposes by garages, summer resorts, dance halls, etc. A dignified church ad used by all the members of a local church would be effective.

A mid-western pastor occasionally uses a picture on his outdoor bulletin board to illustrate the coming Sunday sermon. The idea is attractive. Most bulletin boards are so constructed as to make the insertion of a picture a simple matter.

Some churches are adopting the laudable custom of embodying the full text of the choir selection in the printed order of service, especially on festival occasions. If the choir number is well selected and in harmony with the rest of the service, this arrangement contributes to the devotional spirit of the congregation.

During the garden flower season a certain church asks its amateur gardeners to bring bouquets to the church not only for the altar but especially for the benefit of the sick. A group of volunteers delivers the flowers to a list of sufferers furnished by the pastor. Usually enough flowers are on hand to supply seven or eight bedsides with generous donations. A suitable card is enclosed, designating the church as the donor.

Stewardship is the heart of Christianity. God is counting upon all we have for His work, for we are His stewards. He does not want us to waste our TIME, LIFE, TALENTS or POSSESSIONS.
—*Lutheran Herald.*

* * * *

Hints on Leadership Gathered from Various Sources

I TRUST that all of us are ambitious to become leaders in our various spheres. If we have not that ambition, we should have it. Every sincere Christian should want to be a leader for Christ—not for his own glory or honor or prestige—but in order that he might in a larger official capacity do larger things for his God.

Remember, that the more valuable we are, the more good we can do. In warfare it has always been the part of good military strategy to kill off the officers first. If an army is without officers, it will fall into a disorganized mob.

Satan uses the same strategy. He is always trying to take away from the Church of Christ the Christian Leaders. Any Church which lacks the right kind of leaders can do little in an organized way against the will of Satan.

There are many secrets of leadership. But the first and foremost is the psychological element. The leader must have interest in his work before he can expect to lead successfully. If he accepts an office merely as a matter of form, he will only coast along and fail to climb the hills.

Take the chassis of an automobile, give it a push, and it will coast along on even ground—or down hill for a while. But when it comes to a hill or to a mudhole it will stop! What is the matter? It has nothing to push it, and nothing to pull it.

To make that automobile chassis really *go* you must install a motor, a motor which works, and then when that car comes to a hill it will not stop but climb higher and higher until it reaches the top. If it comes to a mud hole with chains on the wheels, the powerful engine will quickly pull the car through the sticky mud on to solid ground again.

Many leaders are like that. Some are only an empty chassis. They have been carelessly put on the ballot of the society and elected as a matter of form. They are figuratively and actually given a shove into church work and as long as things are coasting along on even ground the empty chassis keeps going, but when it comes to a difficulty—to a hill of church work, it stops. What is the matter? There is nothing to push that leader over the difficulty.

When there is a bit of mud encountered in the form of a disagreement of members, again this leader stops. He has not the power to surmount difficulties of leadership. What is the reason? Because he does not have a motor inside of him, a motor of genuine interest· in his work which gives him the strength to pull through distressing difficulties.

The first prerequisite of a leader is that he must be interested in church work. And that presupposes that he must be interested in Christ. If a leader is sufficiently interested in His Christ and His Church why he will not stop at anything—he cannot stop for anybody. The "Christ Interest" in his heart is so powerful that it pushes him over any hill of difficulty and through any kind of mud of disagreement in order to reach the goal.

Therefore, in training yourself to be a leader—in training someone else to be a leader, remember the first prerequisite is that you must place a "motor" inside of you—a motor of interest and enthusiasm for Christ. If you are not interested in working for Christ, don't take the job. Let someone else take over the leadership who will welcome difficulties and still make a success.

Of course, I would not have you think that the moment this motor of interest is placed in your heart that then there is nothing more to be done,—that immediately you are a finished leader. No, indeed, here are many basic factors of character which should be taken into consideration.

First of these are COMMON SENSE AND INTELLIGENCE.

Common sense means good, sound, ordinary intuitions which are supposedly common to all mankind, nothing to do with knowledge although much aided by :

INTELLIGENCE—Common sense implies intelligence, that relatively rare quality of being able to pick and choose between various positions. People, who move usually in one rut of life,—and when accident of life suddenly thrusts them into other circumstances necessitating other decisions—find themselves wholly at sea and unable to choose the right way,—certainly are not intelligent.

And I might say that in this connection—that whenever certain critical matters come up for decision that THE COMMON SENSE THING TO DO IS ALWAYS THE RIGHT THING TO DO. That society officer who does not show a charitable attitude toward others, who insists on hard, unyielding justice, who refuses to soften his judgment with tact and Christian love, who enforces the letter of the law rather than the spirit of the regulations is neither following common sense nor the teachings of Our Saviour as told in His Sermon on the Mount.

SIMPLICITY—the ANTITHESIS OF AFFECTION. A leader who is affected—is no leader. Remember, that no job, or position, or what you might care to call it, can ever make us one whit better than other men. The only thing which can do that is man's own character. And, surely, to have character one must avoid the superiority complex!

SENSE OF HUMOR is very valuable in conducting meetings, large and small. In one of the large congregations of our synod a chairman presides over the voting body meetings, elected to do so particularly because of his sense of humor. Whenever a question caused a great deal of discussion which became warmer and warmer until finally some of the opposing speakers became excited, and different men were getting angry at each other over nothing, then the chairman would bring out some humorous incident about the matter which would cause them all to have a good laugh. After the entire assembly had indulged in a smile they would settle back in their seats, think how foolish they had been and forget all about their anger. The members continued to be the best of friends, the matter was settled very easily—all through the aid of humor. Of course, it is unnecessary for me to add that if a leader of a meeting loses his temper, and breaks up the meeting he is a disgrace.

JUSTICE—A leader MUST BE JUST from a viewpoint of pure leadership policy, if not from moral motives. Nothing rankles subordinates more than the fact that their leaders have been disloyal to them. The moment the idea gains a foothold in the society that the leader is showing partiality, everything is lost.

ENERGY—We advocate the energy which is catching. The right kind of a leader will not always say *"You* go do this *you* go do that," but *"let us* do this." If the leader of a group shows energy in putting over a certain movement—the other members will catch the spirit and aid the matter along. But remember that not only is energy catching, but unfortunately the "lack of energy is catching" likewise. If the leader does not show any interest about a certain matter certainly one cannot expect his followers to be filled with enthusiasm.

PERSEVERANCE—In the beginning of our discussion we emphasized the fact that every officer—in order to lead—must have enthusiasm. The word enthusiasm comes from ("en theos" —to be filled with God). But let us remember that short-lived enthusiasm never gets you anywhere. The early Christians were able to do great things only because they were "filled with God." What if the disciples who showed a great deal of enthusiasm at Pentecost Day had stopped there and had not persevered? Humanly speaking it would have been a comparatively short time before all of their hearers would have forgotten their admonitions and would have forgotten Christianity. Only because that spirit of the Holy Ghost gave to the first disciples a lasting spirit of real enthusiasm, did they persevere and succeed in their work. Remember, that there are plenty of fine starters in this world, but good finishers are few. Also remember that it is not the "starters" but the "finishers" who succeed. Any officer who wishes to call himself a leader should never become "fed up" with his job.

And in this connection we might advise all leaders "never to start anything which they cannot finish." Whenever you begin a new piece of work, you are making a promise with yourself—making a promise that you will see it through to the finish. If the work is not completed, then that promise to yourself has been broken, and one's strength of character has been weakened thereby. All great accomplishments of life have been made by perseverance under obstacles and not by sudden spurts.

FAITH—Faith in the worthiness of your task is absolutely necessary. "Without Faith ye can do nothing" applies especially to leadership. The secret of the traveling salesman—i.e. if he believes in the worthiness of his article he can talk for it with an earnestness which is convincing—applies to society officers in pushing projects of church work. First convince yourself of the worthiness of the task before you try to talk.

WORRY—Is the negative of faith in God. Of all the profitless occupations of the human mind, worry stands supreme as the most useless and foolish. Most of the things which we worry about never happen. To those afflicted with this malady we would recommend the words of Christ as found in Matthew 6.

HONOR—We mean not only the code of the letter of the ten commandments. You can keep commandments outwardly and yet be most dishonorable. They must be kept in the spirit. That leader has no real code of honor who assumes credit for work which has been done by others in the society. For a leader to neglect mention of assistance received from members in accomplishing a certain result is to belittle what others have done and to assume the credit unhonorably. This brings us to

LOYALTY—Of course, leaders expect that all lay members of societies and congregations should be loyal to superiors. They have a right to expect that much. This is "loyalty up" but the leader should never forget that loyalty is bi-directional,—sort of a perpendicular virtue—which cannot run up, unless it also runs down. Superiors owe quite as much loyalty to their subordinates as these latter owe to them. In a broad way, this is the great secret of leadership, to bind men by the ties of respectful, affectionate loyalty, so that they will follow the leader through prosperity and adversity, pursuing the ideal put before them.

Other minor hints might be mentioned.

A leader must always be a gentleman or lady in the true sense of the word.

He must have tact—a subject in itself for a lecture.

Courtesy and good manners are children of tact. A leader should never be so pressed for time but that he can be courteous.

Gentleness, together with firmness.

The leader must have dignity, but never think of his dignity.

Courage is necessary. Cowards do not follow cowards. It takes real courage to face the problems of society leadership.

An official Pollyanna who fools himself into believing that everything is going well with his leadership because he has not the moral courage to look things squarely in the face is guilty of moral cowardness and ethical laziness. With this thought we would close and ask leaders to take courage and face not only the problems of their society, but the problems of themselves. Check over your own character, and see if you are really fitted to be a leader. Have the courage to examine yourself, not with the idea of finding your good points, but your weak points and how you can overcome them. Be honest with yourself.

I am a Preacher

I AM a preacher. I am very poor. My wife seldom buys a new coat. My children are not able to go to college. Some of my cultured friends smile superciliously when the subject of my profession comes up. Some people in my church prefer to pay little or no attention to me. They say I know nothing about life. Some of my young people who have spent a few hours in a college classroom laugh when I talk about the modern world. I am not supposed to know very much. I am not as young as I once was. Some of the deacons have been hinting that they would prefer a younger man who has no theme and parts in his sermons and tells stories. Some of the ladies would like me more if I could balance a tea cup gracefully. A committee of my young people came to me a few days ago and asked if they could conduct a dance in the basement of the Church. The orchestra would be just below the altar. Some of the businessmen in my church claim that I know nothing about finances—I who have reared a family on a thousand dollars a year. Out in the world I am considered just a little queer and old fashioned.

I am a preacher. I am one of the greatest line in the history of men. My fathers in God were Isaiah and Jeremiah, Peter and Paul, Luther and Walther. My line reaches back beyond the Cross to the days before the flood came over the earth. Only because of the Church I serve and the Word I preach does God permit the world to roll on its way. I have watched men step quietly through the last gate because I had been permitted to show them the way. There are men and women, and children too, before the throne of Heaven today who are my children. They are there because God let me bring them there. The saints of the Church are my joy and the sinners are my burden. I am an ambassador of the King of kings. My lips are among the few left in the world that speak truth. I, almost alone among men, deal day after day with eternal things. I am the last echo of a far voice that forever calls men Home. I am the hand of the Bridegroom, the shadow of the Cross, the trumpet of the King. Neither obscurity nor unpopularity can rob me of my glory. It is not my own, but the reflected glory of Him Whose free and happy slave I am. I am a driven man. I must preach faith in a world that disbelieves, hope in a time that has no hope, and joy in an hour that knows only sorrow. I am at home in a tenement house or in a mansion because my home is neither. I and my people alone stand between the world and destruction. The flames on my altar will not die and the lights in my sanctuary will not be quenched by flood and storm. I am a preacher—and, more than ever, glad of it.

———————————

When church members "knock," their spiritual machinery is out of order.

The Mission of the Home Church

OSCAR E. FEUCHT

THOSE who have studied the mission field in America have for years advocated the adoption of a policy and the organization of a program that would be adequate to the needs. Home missions has so many ramifications and is so vital to the existence of the church that even a brief survey is overwhelming in its effect on the student. In quick succession the student is awe-struck with its magnitude, inspired by its magnificence, and finally heart-sick over the general lack of understanding for work of such importance. While in other undertakings there were plan, purpose, and organization there seemed to be only a few voices that championed and properly evaluated home missions. It was left to take care of itself. And yet no work of the church can approach it in importance or magnitude. What rejoicing there must be in the hearts of these students of home missions at this time when district and synodical boards and a special committee on missionary expansion come forward with a flood of material and plans for the advancement of missions in the homeland. God grant that this movement will create a new mission morale, needed perhaps more than anything else in synod. In reality it is simply an awakening of the Christian's sense of Gospel stewardship. And perhaps it is just another fruit of greater stewardship teaching.

Mission of the Home Church

In addition to the home mission of the church there is also the mission of the home church. In opening up new mission stations in our cities we are likely to forget the expansion work that should be done by the local congregation. It is already organized. It need not wait for a candidate to occupy the field. It is already in the field. Already it has contacts numbering ten times its communicant membership. It has built up a reputation. It has done some publicity work. It already has a church plant. Are we overlooking the mission of the home church? What expansion program does your congregation have? What subjects are chiefly discussed at your elders' or voters' meetings? How much personal work are the officers doing? the congregation members? Is every undertaking of the congregation keyed to mission work? Is your machinery geared to the road of missions? Or is your congregational machinery in operation chiefly to keep the congregation solvent? to take care of the ninety-nine in the fold? to keep up some institution like the school? to take care of the sick? or to "make" the synodical budget?

While the congregation is engaged in some purely selfish endeavor the souls of the community are being lost. While the discussion turns about raising next month's budget, or painting the parsonage, or deciding just which way the church gate is to swing, one congregational meeting after another passes into the irretrievable past and the really important work of the church is either crowded into the last few minutes or is not taken up at all. Nor can the mission work that should have been done be made up. What is more, generations to come will pay a tremendous price for this neglect. Its cost will be both spiritual and financial.

If congregations fully accepted the mission God has given them there would be a different story to tell at their twenty-fifth anniversaries. One pastor would not be serving a large congregation without the proper assistance. Churches would see to it that their work is duly organized and fully provided for. The first Christian congregation at Jerusalem had a right conception of its mission at home. It had more than 3,000 members, who were served not by one but by twelve pastors. And yet these ministers were unable to do all of the work. They called the multitude together to select seven elders. The entire membership was so active that the city was filled with the Christian doctrine.

We are doing less actual mission work (converting the unbelieving) than we often think we are. What if every congregation in synod were to adopt a missionary expansion program? Each year it would put on that program the winning of a certain section of its community. The whole membership would be educated in personal evangelism. A mission consciousness would be developed like that in Korea where a person's Christianity is doubted until such a time that he has brought some other soul to the Saviour. Mission study classes would be organized and actual case work done. These missionary members would "Go to God for the sinner" and then "Go to the sinner for God." They would not give up a field until all possibilities had been exhausted.

The Pastor's Time

Beginning with the pastor, how much time does the church require of him to serve its members with spiritual food? There are two or three sermons to preach every Sunday in probably two languages. He also teaches one or two Bible classes each week. There are many funerals. The routine work of the congregation is left to him. Often it is necessary that he push every endeavor through to the finish. Most of his time is used for the edification of the saints. There isn't much time to get strangers into the church. The sermons are largely soul-building sermons and not soul-winning sermons. They are scrupulously evangelical and doctrinal; and rightly so. But are they also evangelistic? The work keeps the average minister in such close contact with the converted that he is usually thinking of their needs and not of the trend of mind of the unconverted.

Even the home missionary with a small congregation has his difficulties. When he begins his work he is chairman, deacon, secretary, treasurer and perhaps janitor. As he gets men to fill these positions and other committees these must be trained. He has to be eyes and ears and lips for many of them for some time. This pastor gives his Sunday-school teachers a training course. He has pastoral and sick calls to make regularly. His Juniors have been the object of much labor and prayer previous to their confirmation. What right has he to leave them adrift between the safe land of the Christian home-life of childhood and the ship of active church work in the sea of life's greatest danger-period. The senior young people need the pastor's leadership also. They are not merely the church of tomorrow, they are the strength of the church today. The Christian day school will call for much attention. In fact it may require his presence in the school room five days a week. Then there are confirmation classes for children and adults and the Saturday religious school. The vacation Bible school will require fully six weeks of his time. If at the same time he does work for the Walther League at large probably two months of the year are devoted to young peoples' endeavors. And yet who will assert that this important church work can be done without theologically trained leadership? The finance committee, the congregational board of Christian education, the church council, the parish paper, the mailing list, the parish reports (one missionary made no less than eight in January), the Junior council, the Bible class council, publicity work, all come in for a good share of the missionary's time. In addition there are the church services, the hospital services, lectures, conferences, conference papers. Thus it happens that the busy city pastor who is in the largest mission field in America and can daily reach ten times more people than the country minister may have some forty activities outside the missionary visitation.

Assigning the least possible time to these activities the pastor finds that he has 164 hours of work scheduled for a week that has only 112 waking hours in it. And that includes only eight hours for calling and reduces many worth while activities to a woeful minimum. It does reserve one hour a day with the Bible.

Results Lacking

The result is that even in a small community of a large city he does not measure up to his own ideals of a missionary. Canvasses are started but the more important follow up work is never completely and systematically done. By the time he gets to the last cards the information is antiquated. A new canvass is launched. He resolves that it shall have the right of way. He has little clerical assistance. Much time is spent in sorting and routing the cards. Then some other endeavor calls for immediate attention. In a piece-meal fashion he takes up the cards in his spare moments. He would like to make the calls like a salesman with some semblance of system. He would like to ring those door bells periodically. He would like to enter some homes as regularly as the meter-reader for the gas company. He is thoroughly convinced that "A house-going pastor makes a church-going people." He knows that thousands are hiding from God and must be looked up. He is certain that hundreds will never be gained for Christ's kingdom if they are not won by this house-to-house, person-to-person method. There is no use starting the Vacation Bible School without a canvass. Much of the preparatory work rests on the pastor. At last there are only three or four days left for the canvass. Finally he does manage to call on 200 parents of the neighborhood. But there are 2000 in the community served by his church! Nearby is a large, new home district. There is no church in its center, although there are several on its borders. The church that enters the homes is likely to get the children. New houses are erected constantly. Every new resident should receive a letter from the church and a personal call. Each September another systematic canvass of the 2000 homes should be made in the interest of the Sunday School. The pastor knows that the program offered by his church is superior to that offered by many other churches in the field. What shall he do about it? They seem to be getting the large Sunday school enrollments.

A personal call should be made within a week or ten days after a visitor has appeared in the church service. Some Sundays there may be as high as forty non-members in the service. Not all of them will need a call but perhaps half of them should be given the courtesy of a personal visit. Then there is the work among the non-member Lutherans. The pastor has cards for 96 of them. They are not affiliated with any local church. Some have drifted for a long time and need special attention. He feels that this work is important so that the efforts expended by the church upon these people shall not have been in vain. His church needs strength at once for its program. He follows up these Lutherans. There is hardly anything else to do in this matter. This work alone could occupy most of the time he has for calling. But what about those 2000 homes in the community?

From a Missionary's Report

This situation is aggravated by the fact that the minister has only two afternoons and one or two evenings a week for missionary calling. He has only one night with his family and that is Saturday night. He tries to be a good steward of his time but often at the close of day learns, to his regret, that certain hours were spent uneconomically. With the failings common to us mortals he finds at the end of the year that he has made 1200 calls. Many of these were pastoral and sick calls. Many are duplicates. That is, there may be as high as six calls on one family or person. Then what about those 2000 homes in the community?

Here is an actual record taken from a home missionary's report for the year 1930: Meetings attended 211, hours of religious instruction given 227, Bible classes conducted 92, sermons preached in the congregation 97, sermons preached elsewhere 9, sermonettes preached at a local hospital 147, lectures and addresses given elsewhere 16, topic and missionary discussions led 51, bulletins or parish papers edited 24, articles written for church papers 8, conferences attended 23, calls made 1186. In addition he has addressed almost every business meeting of the voters' assembly, Ladies' aid, and Walther League, served on several extra-congregational committees, taken an active part in the charity work,

and lived in close company with his telephone. And now where do the pastor's general reading, special study, and filing come in?

Can a congregation grow adequately and work its community as thoroughly as God expects it to do when the pastor's time is so occupied? How much actual mission work can such a pastor do? The church will grow from within, but how much can it grow from without? Mind you this pastor is not exactly "serving at tables." He uses very little of his time for social events. His friends come seldom to see him because he is always too busy. His church program is educational throughout. Even his young people find no time for play-practise. He does some work for the church at large. Should he refuse it? If this were a common practise would the kingdom of God prosper as it should? Did Paul do work in the church at large?

You see then that the mission of the home church will never be accomplished through the efforts of the pastor alone. It will not be achieved with a few committees. Nothing short of personal evangelism on the part of the whole congregation can fulfill the missionary obligations of the home church. But let us get back to the pastor.

He realizes that now is the time to build up the congregation. A larger membership will mean more people of the community won, larger adult membership classes, a larger Sunday school, a greater Bible class, financial independence, the church debt retired, more money for world-wide missions, the beginning of a Christian day school, if none already exists, more strength for united work with other churches of the same faith, larger returns to the synodical district for efforts and money expended in starting the mission, and an encouragement to other home mission projects. And yet many of these aims are selfish. The real reason for redoubling our missionary efforts at home is the ingathering of souls, not numerical strength, not financial power, not a new church building, not the making of a name, but the deep-seated conviction: all men are sinners; as such they are going head-long into damnation; Christ alone through His substitutionary death saves; we have that Gospel of the Crucified Lord. Back of the pastor's missionary expansion program is the passion for souls. That is the controlling influence of his life.

A Missionary Working Program

Having made this study the missionary owes himself and the kingdom of God a reconstruction of his working program. He will weigh everyone of his activities with the counterbalance of "missionary value." He will find himself asking the question: Is this vital to the cause of missions? Will it help save souls? He will decline to serve in certain capacities. He will assign to others duties he had long kept for himself. He will ask the congregation to adopt a program of missions for itself. His elders will not merely post the hymn numbers and ring the church bell. Thenceforth they will be assigned missionary prospects. The pastor will measure his day's labors not only by the preparations he has made for the flock or by the guidance he has given the ninety and nine but by the rescue work he has done for the lost sheep which he sought as the undershepherd of Christ. He will receive the names of prospects with eagerness. He will regard it a privilege to get acquainted with everyone in any circle in which he may find himself. He will not disdain to take time from his Saturday afternoon sermon preparations to make a missionary call. He will keep in mind that a sermon of simple straight-forward language containing a forceful presentation of the way to salvation preached to a large audience with a liberal sprinkling of the unchurched in it will produce greater results than a homiletical masterpiece delivered to a half filled church. In other words he will pay as much attention to getting the people there as to the preparation of the message. He will come late perhaps to committee meetings because he has used the fore part of the evening to visit the men in their homes. He will combine meetings as much as possible in order to gain another night for calling. He will not let the weather interfere with his calling. In fact he is thankful for a rainy day for it serves his purpose best. He would rather spend two hours with a soul in distress than with a half dozen friends who are safe in the ark of the church.

The "Undermanned" Congregation

But what missionary calling can a pastor do who has more than 500 communicant members under his spiritual care? How can a single pastor serve 800 or 1000 members efficiently? It is impossible to keep in touch with the spiritual life of each member. As a result conditions develop in the homes and in the congregation that greatly undermine the spirituality. Some people are going through a crisis which will determine their status probably the rest of their lives. If they are not given pastoral attention they either fail to become stewards of their time, energies, money and the Gospel, or they are entirely lost to the church. If such, a pastor has more than enough to do to take care of the 1000 souls that are written opposite his name in God's records, how can he be expected to do missionary work? And yet has he no obligation over against the unchurched of his community? Shall many of them forever be deprived of Bible instruction and eternal happiness just because he has been too busy and the congregation provided no help? What about the 2000 unchurched? The large congregation that is "undermanned" is one of the major problems of our synod. It has lost sight of the mission of the home church.

The Pastor as Student

The pastor is a student. He must remain a student. The pastor has an office. It should be an efficient office. Letters should be answered with some degree of punctuality. The work that is referred to the pastor should be attended to before the next voters' meeting. The immense amount of material received at the desk should be filed and not allowed to pile up. At the same time there is a danger that the pastor becomes a good desk man, or a good sermonizer, at the cost of being a good pastor and missionary. There is witnessing for Jesus to be done outside of the pastor's study and the four walls of the church. In fact the unchurched come neither to the pastor's study nor to the church service of themselves. It is a mischievous error to think that the sermon can do all of the pastor's missionary work or to conceive of the ministry as a swivel-chair job. The one should be done and the other not left undone. The missionary pastor will hold to visiting hours as rigorously as to study hours.

Pastoral Assistance

But how get both done? By getting the right kind of assistance. Why should the pastor do all the odd jobs around the church just because he is footloose? Why should he look after details that laymen can do as well? It will pay the pastor to prepare detailed regulations for officers and work-schedules for committees so that he himself has more time for the vital things of his ministry. A number of years ago a layman traveled through one of our synodical districts. He was shocked to find many pastors doing trivial things which others should have been doing. The missionary pastor will not waste the odds and ends of time. He will list his activities of a single month, rearrange the list according to the respective importance of the items, and then drop such things as are really not vital for the life of the church and the salvation of souls. He will organize his desk to avoid lost motion. If the congregation cannot supply a stenographer, members of the church with a business training can be called in to help with the correspondence and the purely mechanical work. Or a small sum can be set aside for clerical help that is used from time to time. A good rule for the mission-minded pastor is: Do nothing someone else is supposed to do unless it is very urgent or vital. Do nothing that some member can do as well or nearly as well as you can do. Then create a sense of stewardship that makes these members willing assistants. The pulpit will do well not merely to supply indoctrination and inspiration but also definite tasks for the exercise of the Christian faith. It will pay to assign some missionary work to each member. What folly to fan the flame of missionary enthusiasm to white heat and then provide an outlet for that enthusiasm. "Impression without expression results in depression." (Phil. 4,17). The church gains doubly when work is divided. The pastor gains time for mission work. The members develope into missionaries.

More Full-Time Workers

But why not cross off of the budget all of the unessentials and get more full time workers? Out in the middle west we have a congregation that in the course of twelve years grew from 104 to 492 communicant members. Some years ago the pastor announced that when the sum of 900 was reached not another soul would be admitted to the congregation, if he could have his way about it, until additional help was supplied. Recently five suggestions were made to relieve this situation. A thorough survey made by pastors and church councils in every congregation should result in hundreds of requests for assistant pastors, Christian day school teachers, directors of religious education, parish deaconesses, parish visitors, stenographers or other full time workers. No congregation has the right to use its pastor for menial tasks when hundreds of souls are to be won. It is sheer folly to pay a pastor with a specialized training a professional salary (?) for things a common typist can do as well or better than he can.

When a business firm gets an increase in business, it installs another desk and hires another salesman. But when the church's business increases a few workers are loaded down to the breaking point and the rest of the prospective "business" is permitted to slip through the fingers of under-organization, inefficiency, small faith, little vision, and missionary indifference.

The mission of the home town church like the home mission of the church is to save souls. Our home mission will be carried on along the far-flung battle-line where about 900 missionaries are stationed. Their chapels of today will be our strong churches of tomorrow. But the most economical home mission work will not be done at the 1,558 stations where our home missionaries are now at work, nor in the new fields that are to be occupied, but by the several thousand congregations that are no longer classed as mission churches. Whether it will be done depends entirely on the measure in which our churches will see their mission obligation at home. It will depend on seeing and working for the potential congregation in the community and not merely for the visible flock represented on the church records. In order to do this the missionary pastor will make every ounce of effort count in some way for the conversion of those who do not acknowledge Christ as their personal Saviour. After a pastor has found the true Bible doctrine the question he must answer above all other questions is: how can I apply this doctrine to the hearts of the most men? or to put it in other words: how can I keep my work vital?

Favorite Texts of Famous Men
Mid-Week Messages
Broadway Methodist Church

The Text from Which John Bunyan Preached to the Multitudes. —John 6:37

The Text That Saved William Cowper from Suicide. —Romans 3:24, 25.

The Text That Made Martin Luther the Hero of the Reformation. —Romans 1:17

The Text That Comforted the Troubled Soul of John Wesley. —Mark 12:34

The Text That Made David Livingstone a Missionary. —Matthew 28:19, 20

The Text To Which John Knox Anchored His Soul. —John 17:3

The Text That Gave William Carey a World Vision. —Isaiah 54:2

The Text That Made William Penn a Conqueror. —I John 5:4

The Text on Which Michael Faraday Staked Everything. —II Timothy 1:12

Volunteer Help

THE MODE of human life in our rapidly moving age is vastly different from what it was a generation or two ago. The Church has not escaped the influence of an immeasurably speeded-up age. Congregational life, especially in large cities, has become inordinately complex. The office of the ministry is making demands, both mental and physical, such as our clerical forefathers never knew. Three or four decades ago ministerial life was comparatively simple. One service on Sunday, a few catechetical classes, a meeting or two each week, the regular routine of calling and the keeping of simple records constituted the program of the average pastor. The local church still bulked large in the social life of the people. Under the pressure of a new age the up-to-date church has been compelled to augment and widen its activities. Intensive organization has become necessary. The educational program demanded expansion. Bible classes and study groups had to be organized. The various church societies needed specialized attention. The young people's problem became acute. The business affairs of the church called for better systematization. With the disappearance of materialistic and linguistic barriers mission work had to be intensified and modernized. Canvasses and neighborhood visitations became necessary. Sunday School work developed. Teachers had to be trained. Advertising had to be resorted to. Parish papers and Sunday bulletins came into vogue. Saturday schools and periods of weekday instruction and vacation schools were added to the educational set-up. Multigraphs, typewriters, mimeographs, addressographs, filing cabinets and the like appeared in the pastor's study. As a matter of fact, that old term "study," denoting a retiring place for quiet and prolonged meditation, began to be known as the "office." More and more the pastor's time began to be usurped by the multiplying technical details of his manysided labors. Naturally the time for the all-important spiritual phases of his office became more and more constricted. The executive began to replace the minister, the manager began to take the place of the preacher.

A modern church is a complex and highly organized business. Unfortunately the whole business with all its ramifications has in most cases been left in the hands of the pastor. Some churches have indeed employed secretaries and executives, but ordinarily the financial status of the church precludes any salaried position outside of the pastor and perhaps the parochial school teaching force. But the average pastor needs help. We should be relieved of the numerous tasks of a clerical character which his position involves. The keeping of records and files, the mailing of literature, the production of mimeographed material and the like, can and should be done by volunteer lay helpers in the church. A good stenographer and typist is a godsend to a busy pastor. Even some of the routine calling can be delegated to lay assistants. Of course, the business affairs of the church should be handled by the laymen.

The pastor should be free to devote much of his time to intensive study and to the specifically spiritual aspects of his ministry. The inordinate amount of time which he is oftentimes compelled to devote to mechanical details is bound to reflect detrimentally on his work as a spiritual leader. His sermons will become shallow and superficial. His class and lecture work will lack the necessary preparation. His intellectual and spiritual growth will be stunted. He will in the course of time become an ecclesiastical jack-of-all-trades.

A TRIBUTE TO CHURCH WORKERS

If the Church is to function efficiently a large amount of work must be done. Most of this work is done without any remuneration. The love of Christ constrains Christians to serve Him through serving His Body, which is the Church.

The Atlantic District of our Synod, for instance, has only two paid workers. Officers, directors, visitors, committee members, busy pastors and laymen all of them, take time which they can ill spare in order that the affairs of the District be properly carried on.

Every congregation duplicates in miniature this picture. Usually beside the pastor there are only two other workers who receive a salary, the organist and the sexton. Working with these there may be dozens—the number depends on the size of the congregation—who have consecrated their time and their talents to the service of the Church.

The duties that must be discharged are varied and numerous. All of them require time and thought and faithful application, some more, some less. We might think of Sunday School workers, choir members, financial officers, society leaders. Some are known, most of them labor and their names never appear on any official report. But whatever their tasks and whatever the amount of publicity they get, their labors of love are an important item in the program of the Church. They know that by a faithful performance they help the cause for which the Son of God became a man and laid down His life. Men may neither acknowledge nor praise it, but the Saviour is fully aware of all that they are doing and the reward He has in store for them will far exceed their highest expectations.

We have written these paragraphs because at this time of the year in most congregations a new set of officers is installed. That ceremony calls the attention of the congregation to the men who are entrusted with the conduct of its affairs. They should receive the loyal cooperation of the congregational rank and file. At the same time we must not forget that there are many other helpers who are not publicly installed. For them too let us give thanks to God and pray that they may receive grace from on high faithfully to do their duty. MY CHURCH.

The Long-Range Plan

CLAUDIUS S. KULOW

THE English Lutheran Church of Our Saviour, Brooklyn, N.Y., under the capable leadership and foresight of its pastor, Rev. Erwin Kurth, has put into operation a well-prepared and co-ordinated program for church activities which we feel offers much in the way of suggestion and adaptation to congregations desirous of a unified scope for co-operative leadership.

Pastor Kurth, like many church workers, has felt that too often there has been an over-lapping of activities or they have gone to the other extreme and there has been a lack of meaningful objectives—each group only laboring for its own desired goals. In solidifying all the stray ends of varied programs, Pastor Kurth has carefully outlined his suggestions on seven pages of legal-size paper, mimeographed them and distributed the same to leaders of his parish. The resultant not only calls forth aims and objectives for one year, but serves as a set-up for activation over a period of four or five years. Indeed, we feel that some of the aims of the "long-range" plan will become a definite method of direction for many years to come.

The Program of the Church

With the motto "Plan the work—work the plan," the general aim is three-fold: (1) To work towards the growth of the congregation; (2) To improve and modernize the church plant as a spiritual work-shop; (3) To co-ordinate the efforts of church organizations so that all have a common goal.

The growth of the church is to be spiritual, numerical and financial. This challenge aims to evoke increased church and communion attendance, the cultivation of the devotional life, intensified religious instruction and personal service in some phase of Christian work. For the church to grow numerically there must be a program of conservation, reclamation and personal evangelism, whereas the general financial aim will be the dissemination of inspirational information, the emphasis of the stewardship life, the inculcation of improved methods of church finance, the integration of budgetary efforts of all church societies, and the increase of contributions for missions, charities,

and home purposes.

After a check-up of the church plant, the needs are not presented to the congregation in an abstract manner. The church is to be pointed up, the interior re-decorated, art windows re-leaded, new lighting fixtures installed, a rheostat purchased, the organ and chimes amplified, and there is a need for new landscaping, hymnals, carpets, and office equipment. Needless to say, all this will not be done at once. But, at least, the church knows its needs and knows where it is going in this respect.

Societies Work Together

In order to interest the church organizations in the above plan, Pastor Kurth does not overlook the necessity of discussing with the society leaders their responsibility in delegating work to others, in seeing that committees function, and in sponsoring worthwhile meetings and activities. After stressing the fact that each society has only three basic objectives—Christian Knowledge, Service and Fellowship—the leaders discuss questions such as: What is being done to make your society's program more attractive? What does your group hope to accomplish within the next five years? Are you moving toward set goals of attainment? Are your meetings stereotyped, monotonous, indifferent? Are we envisioning greater things?

How refreshing to find such questions occupying the floor instead of the usual trite: "What kind of an affair shall we run? What kind or entertainment and food shall we provide for the next meeting?" Instead, each society is to help the Church realize its "long-range" program.

To Hold—To Win

In a large city church the turn-over is usually quite large. Hence there is no standing still in organizational life —it is either a case of "go forward" or you "go backward." The organizations of the church must constantly strive (a) To hold what they have; (b) To gain new members.

To hold regular members the long-range program provides for visitations to sick and delinquent members, also the bringing of cheer to the distressed, poor, bereaved, aged. The person who for many years was active in a society,

but now because of illness or infirmity can no longer be present at meetings, certainly deserves to receive the consolation afforded by the bonds of Christian fellowship.

The agenda of the societies also provide for a regular effort in recruiting new members with a stress on personal contact and friendliness.

Increasing Church Attendance

The church anticipates, in its five year plan, a full church on ordinary Sundays with two services on festival days. How can this be done? Pastor and leaders discuss the following questions among others: The Duty and Privilege of Worship; Deepening the Spiritual Life of the Individual; Praying People into Church; Better Sermons; A Devotional Atmosphere; Congregational and Choir Music; Orderliness in the Service from the viewpoint of officiant, ushers, council, people and children; A Spirit of Friendliness to Strangers and the Glad-Hand Committee; Visitation of Delinquents and Prospects; Larger Youth Choirs; Revival of the Family Pew; Mechanics of the Service—light, heat, ventilation; Special Services; More Effective Publicity; Overcoming the Summer Tail-Spin; Greater Personal Service on the Part of the Church to Members and Community; Young People's Vespers.

Young People

The long-range plan does not lose sight of the youth of the church. It aptly co-ordinates many features of the Walther League program. Confirmation Classes are to have sponsors; six young people's vespers, an annual banquet and a corporate communion will be provided; the young people's Bible Class is stressed and opportunity is afforded for service and participation in choirs, week-day religious school, Sunday School, Kingdom Work and on the staff of ushers. Rather detailed programs are outlined for an entire year for young people's meetings with an endeavor to make certain events recurrent and therefore traditional, e.g. Loyalty Month, Personal Evangelism, Unite the Youth, etc. Such a set-up affords opportunity for annual improvement on the basis of past experiences.

An Integrated Budget

With respect to a unified budget for societies, Pastor Kurth writes: "For years our societies have nobly remembered with gifts of money, eleemosynary institutions and endeavors. Thousands of dollars have been spent for others. All this is as it should be. Charity begins at home but does not end there. We have never yet tried to train our people to be selfish, but have always encouraged the giving of money to 'outside purposes' and shall continue to do so. Next year is the fortieth anniversary of our church and I think it proper that all societies concentrate on remembering the church with special gifts. At a Fall meeting each society can fix the amount to be given." Then, in a joint meeting of the United Societies the integrated budget is established with questions like the following answered: Which are the causes we wish to remember? Who wants to remember these? To what extent? For instance, if the Ladies Aid says, "We are particularly interested in Bronxville" the other groups will say, "Fine, then we shall stress some other endeavor." If the Sunday School says, "We are particularly interested in remembering the — ALPB with a special offering," the others will accede to their request. In other words, there is to be no overlapping. Moreover, all special appeals become part of the unified budget. Furthermore, there is given a proper evaluation to the need in its relation to the parish.

One of the features of the long-range plan is that it overlooks no phases of the church's work. Men's work, music programs, service enhancements, synodical endeavors, publicity—none are lost sight of. Pastor, vicar, choir director, council, ushers—all have their program for some time to come. The economy of time effected in planning the work thus saved can be devoted in the future to the even more important "working of the plan."

In summarizing, the chairman constantly keeps the following ten criteria before his leaders:

1. What does it mean?
2. Whom does it benefit?
3. Is it in the interest of all? Fair and just?
4. Will it antagonize any group?
5. Will it work under AVERAGE leadership?
6. Is it a reduplication of any other effort?
7. Will it push aside other more important work?
8. What will it cost? Is it worth the effort?
9. What are the dangers connected with it?
10. Is it in keeping with Scripture and the policies of Synod and our Church?

Interesting, too, as a standard by which to judge the plan, are the eight "izes" with which Pastor Kurth concludes his splendid detailed plan which we have sought to summarize for the readers of the AMERICAN LUTHERANS.

1. Scrutinize—"Take stock." Examine and re-examine.
2. Advise—Take counsel with those familiar with the particular line of work.
3. Organize—The effort must become directional, moving towards well-defined objectives.
4. Deputize—Others must be entrusted with sharing of burdens.
5. Energize—Inspire, encourage, "enthuse."
6. Supervise—Carry the task thru to completion.
7. Realize—Evaluate the results.
8. Recognize—Give credit where credit is due.

The Congregational Rally

CHARLES D. WOHLTJEN

In many churches where services are held Sunday mornings and evenings, especially in different languages, it so happens that some communicant members of the same rarely meet. Holding no membership in one or the other of the many organizations in the Church, it is self evident that they are strangers unto themselves, and if by chance they should meet at Divine worship, it would not be surprising were one to greet the other as a casual visitor and extend an invitation to come and join the church. This embarrassing circumstance has, no doubt, occurred to many, especially such as hold the office of deacon.

The congregational rally offers an opportunity to all members to meet each other and create a good fellowship which will show results in the work of the church sooner or later. But while the rally serves this very good social purpose it can also be the valuable means of bringing to the congregation the more important message relating to some particular phase of Lutheran church work and help to instill in the hearts of those present an earnest desire to promote the Master's work. This is by far the main reason for the rally.

Rallies may be arranged periodically—say three times a year, and might be sponsored by the Walther League Society as part of its educational program. An appropriate time is in September when there is a resumption in church work which has been permitted to lag during the summer vacation period. Then, too, about Thanksgiving time, when one is reminded of the benefits that God has bestowed and then, again directly after Easter, when the glorious message of the resurrection has been proclaimed.

An outside speaker on missions, hospice or Bible study may be secured through the agency of the Lecture Bureau of the District, and in this way the members of the congregation are made acquainted with all phases of church work. What a vast amount of information can be disseminated in this manner—our work in the mission fields, foreign and domestic, the work among the poor, the sick, the unfortunates in the cities; hospice work and many charitable endeavors; the needs of the orphanages, hospitals and homes for the aged and infirm; church publicity and numerous other activities of the church. A concrete example might be cited. In one congregation the work among the Indians in this country was little known and appreciated. Mr. Sam Miller then lectured at a congregational rally and overnight this important work and its needs were brought close to those members who heard him, and as a result, contributions, donations, and general interest toward Indian Mission work showed a marked increase.

True enough, our church papers and bulletins treat of mission and benevolent purposes in great detail, but the spoken word, especially from the lips of the trained worker, goes very much farther and creates a greater impression than the printed article, no matter how well written.

The congregational rally bent on bringing together not only twenty or twenty-five members of an organization of the church, but rather a great number of communicants for the furtherance of better acquaintanceship, provides a fair sized audience, which in itself is an incentive to the lecturer.

An open forum discussion should follow the lecture and questions invited. In this way many an individual can satisfy himself with regard to any misconception he may have of this or that phase of church work.

Sufficient publicity should be given to insure a good attendance. A well-worded letter of invitation should go forward to every household or every member of the congregation. Then, too, the columns of the parish paper should be used to good advantage and announcements made at services.

A practical program for the evening is herewith suggested:
a. Devotional exercises led by pastor
b. Introduction of speaker by president of Walther League Society or other organization conducting rally.
c. Lecture
d. Open forum discussion
e. Closing with Lord's Prayer
f. Community singing and serving of refreshments.
g. Informal talks

During the social hour following the inspirational lecture, the committee in charge should assist congregational members to become acquainted with one another, and especially to welcome strangers and make them feel at home.

A Book Store Operated By The Men's Club

JOHN PIEPKORN

WHY SHOULD THERE BE A MEN'S CLUB or Society in a Lutheran Congregation? If its purpose is to foster sociability and good fellowship only the congregation had better discourage the establishing of a Men's Club. Yes, if there is a Men's Club within your congregation now it will either soon dissolve for want of a real purpose or it may function in a way detrimental to the spiritual life of the congregation itself. The only justifiable existence or continued existence of a Men's Club is, if it is devoted to promoting or extending the work of the congregation to build a better Zion and winning souls for Christ. Of course, as Christian brethren we want to be sociable, we want to be good fellows; but to do this over a card table or through bazaars or phases of activity along these lines does not require to be a member of a Christian congregation whose only duty is to preserve the spirituality of its members to and to spread the true saving Gospel for the edification of its members in matters that pertain to the soul rather than to the flesh and to glorify God. Then what should be the aims and object of a Men's Club in a Lutheran congregation? The writer does not claim to be able to lay down the only rules and regulations that really make the existence of a Men's Club worth while according to his own ideas, but we all agree that in order to accomplish the things that our Lord wants us, as Christians, to accomplish we must not cater to such things that the world indulges in for pastime or to raise funds.

Here is a Men's Club in Bethany Congregation, Milwaukee, Wis., that has existed for more than ten years and is as active today as it was when first organized. One of the goals of this Men's Club is to canvass the neighborhood to ascertain the religious affiliation of people living in its territory and if such are found, and such are found, that have no congregational connection or are backsliders of the Lutheran faith, all information regarding such people is obtained by the visitor and the pastor of the congregation then follows up the names of such people. A list of youngsters not belonging to any church is also prepared and an effort is made to gain them for the Christian day school or for the congregational Sunday School. It is true that every member of the Men's Club is not able to participate in this work of personal evangelizing. To do such work requires courage of a peculiar nature with which every member is not endowed, but if such members who have the courage and make-up, and there are always a goodly number of them, will take active part in such efforts, there is not only a great deal of personal satisfaction to have helped gain a member for Christ's Kingdom but there is also the satisfaction to have done his duty, as a Lutheran church member, not only to be concerned about his or her own salvation but to have been instrumental to have gained a member for the church. A canvass like this was conducted in Bethany many years ago and as those who had participated gathered on a subsequent evening to discuss the experiences met with, a great deal of joy prevailed and everyone was happy to have devoted some time to such most important work. For instance, the writer recalls that his partner visitor or canvasser was a recent convert to the Lutheran faith. After we had gotten to the territory allotted to us and we were about ready to ring the door bell, he said, "What will you say when the people answer the door bell and ask you what do you want?" and no sooner had the door bell been pressed when the occupant of the home appeared at the door and wanted to know what was wanted, and it was explained that we were members of Bethany Congregation located on N. 38th and West Lloyd Streets, that we were making a canvass of the neighborhood and that if he would tell us whether or not he had any religious connection, or no religious affiliation, we would note it on our report; and the answer came, "I am a Roman Catholic but I surely admire your church members who take enough interest in their neighbors to inquire about such an important matter, and a congregation whose members are willing to spend a Sunday afternoon for that purpose surely is and will be blessed spiritually. I wish members of our church could be induced to make a similar canvass." Just how many names were turned in the writer does not recall, but as a result thereof several families were located whose children had not been baptized and subsequently these children were brought to the church through Holy Baptism. If every congregation in our synod had a Men's Club to conduct such a canvass in its neighborhood once in two years, there is no one in the Lutheran church who would not admit that such efforts would bring results and that members would be gained for the church and God's Kingdom.

Bethany's Men's Club also conducts a "Book Store." The custodian of this book store is a member of the Men's Club. In our case it is the custodian of the congregational property, in other words the janitor. Such book store contains a fine display of books produced by the Concordia Publishing House. A sample of many of the best books are always on display, and, by the way, the "sample line" is carried in a wall display case with glass doors and the books are so displayed that the member coming to the basement hall is attracted by such display. Often you will find a congregational member doing "window shopping" when the librarian is absent. The latest Concordia Publishing House catalog is always handy and prospective buyers of books can order from this catalog. The Men's Club is exclusively responsible for maintaining this book store in Bethany Congregation. Seasonable greeting cards are also sold. The members of Bethany, young and old, man or woman, is continually urged to patronize the Men's Club Book Store. The pastor very often speaks special words of encouragement to give "good books" for gifts. Every time there is anything doing in the basement hall the manager of the book store is present offering the wares that are for sale, taking orders for the requirements of Bethany's members and making delivery of the purchase when desired. On special occasion the manager is at work in the main hall to the church auditorium showing the "goods," books, booklets, tracts, Church Annual, Synodical Reports, and what have you. The sale of good books is the principal object. You may ask, "How many books do you sell each year through this Men's Club Book Store?" For the past eleven years the volume of sales aggregates the sum total of $1,970.37, or an average of $180 yearly. During 1930 the total sales were $37, the highest for any one year, while during 1933 the sales dropped to $61.63. Will anyone dare to say that Bethany Men's Club is not doing a God pleasing work? Just imagine the many good books found in the homes of Bethany members, books that would not be there if the Men's Club Book Store was not in existence. We do not want to brag, we do not know of any congregational Men's Club doing what we are doing, we hope there are many more, but we do feel that we are doing "a good job," a job that we are proud of and the benefits of which redound to the benefit of the congregation in particular and to the church in general.

How to Acquire and Read Books

ALFRED KLAUSLER

THE OLD-TIME MINISTER'S study was generally known for its ceiling-high bookcases filled with books of every conceivable sort. Stepping into such a room and atmosphere one could rightfully expect good, solid talk on subjects ranging from Thomas Aquinas to the implications of the Industrial Revolution. How the old-time ministers managed to acquire such voluminous libraries is something of a mystery. The fact stands that they did build up genuine libraries.

Perhaps it is a modern trend with many present-day ministers that the acquiring, not to say reading, of books is regarded as a discommoding fact; a library being considered merely as something to clutter up the home, a dust accumulator of the first order. There must be hundreds of modern pastors who have discovered, perhaps after it was too late, that one cannot survive intellectually, yes, and spiritually, if there is no regular acquiring and reading of books.

Books that a pastor should own, or at least read, pour from the presses endlessly. The pastor reads glowing reviews of books on psychiatry, history, literature, religion, sociology and biography. He would like to own the books. They cost money. That minister is rare who can spend $10 a month on his library. He would like to borrow the books from the local public library. If he lives in a rural community, there may not even be a library. He must live in a fairly large metropolitan center if he wishes to read books that concern himself and his profession.

Last winter, eight ministers organized a circulating library with dues set at one dollar a quarter per member. After twelve months of organization we have been able to spend approximately $40 for books. We have bought and read some twenty-five current and not-so-current books. Many of us have again learned the nature and value of systematic reading. If you wish to obtain full value from your dues, you have just two weeks in which to read a book! Buying books in this way and of this sort has also given the individual an opportunity to acquire for his private library books of a more technical sort, such as commentaries, dictionaries, grammars and dogmatics that a group could not consider profitable buying. Or else he may devote his book-budget money in building up a certain phase of his private library.

This year we held our first auction of the books acquired during the first three quarters. Those unable to be present at the auction are entitled to enter sealed bids. The sum realized from the auction was added to the library fund. Only members are entitled to bid. In addition money is realized from fines. No book is to be kept over a period of two weeks. After that a minimum fine of 10c. a week is charged to the overtime borrower. Naturally, the librarian must enforce these rules. He also does the buying, the arranging of the schedule for each book and the keeping of the accounts.

Here are the titles we purchased the first four quarters:

LUTHER AND HIS WORK: *Clayton*
THE SYSTEMATIC STUDENT: *Rossin*
AUTOBIOGRAPHY OF G. K. CHESTERTON
TYPES OF PREACHERS IN THE N. T.: *Robertson*
CHRISTIAN FAITH IN THE MODERN WORLD: *Machen*
VARIETIES OF CHRISTIAN EXPERIENCE: *Norborg*
THE CHRIST OF THE LOGIA: *Robertson*
CARDINAL IDEAS OF JEREMIAH: *Jefferson*
PSYCHIATRY AND MENTAL HEALTH: *Oliver*
GERMANY'S NEW RELIGION: *Adam*
VIRGIN BIRTH: *Machen*
WAY OF A MAN WITH A MAID: *McCartney*
PERSONAL EVANGELISM: *Knock*
RETURN TO RELIGION: *Link*
MORAL MAN AND IMMORAL SOCIETY: *Niebuhr*
IN THE STEPS OF ST. PAUL: *Morton*

U. S. LOOKS AT ITS CHURCHES: *Fry*
ROME STOOPS TO CONQUER: *Barrett*
ORIGIN OF RELIGION: *Zwemer*
ART OF MINISTERING TO THE SICK: *Cabot-Dicks*
QUEST FOR HOLINESS: *Koeberle*
PILGRIM PAUL: *Eickmann*

Every book in this list was chosen by majority vote. About two weeks before the beginning of a new quarter and before the dues for that quarter are remitted to the librarian, each member sends in his nominations of titles. The librarian prepares a ballot of the nominations. Then the ballot is circulated. Those books having the majority votes are purchased. Some of the above books, as will be noted, are of the flashy type, some almost distinctly non-theological; some are old and are appearing as reprints. Many are titles one would not place in a permanent private library. But at least the member has the opportunity to read books that are being talked about, books that may have an influence on contemporary trends, books that may perhaps give a new approach to certain problems.

This system of buying books is, undoubtedly, used in many other parts of the church. It is recommended especially where a group of pastors may live in a sparsely settled country or where there is no large library. We do not claim the idea as original. In fact, the plan is modeled after the North Dakota Missouri Slope Pastoral Conference circulating library. This library has been in existence many years and has built up an enviable reputation. It is worth noting that this library, so Rev. L. T. Wohlfeil informs me, buys not only ordinary run-of-the-mill theological books, but also books ranging from analyses of the New Deal philosophy to the continental European publications in theology, history and biography.

No library of this kind can be a success unless (1) the membership is limited to a maximum of ten members within a conference circuit; and (2) the rule of two weeks' rental is observed. When a pastor is called from a circuit and is thus unable to attend auctions, he loses his membership. However, he is entitled to enter his bids on all books purchased during the period of his membership. Any group of pastors using this system, or some similar kind, can soon rediscover, without violently disturbing the family budget, the zest and stimulus that comes from systematic reading and contact with other men's ideas.

* * * *

Luther is the greatest man born to humanity since time began.
—Simon Wolf.

* * * *

Propagating the Gospel Through the Printed Page

A Lutheran minister relates how he recently read that the American Association for the Advancement of Atheism conducts its propaganda mostly through leaflets which its finds cheapest and most effective. At the same time it regards the American Tract Society as its greatest and most formidable opponent. Just as when the burglar admits that the small dog in the house is his greatest danger, we have there the best evidence for the value of a good watch dog on the premises, so this admission on the part of the atheists offers indisputable proof of the value of printed evidence for the truths of Christianity. Pastors, as a rule, should be doing much more than is being done in the way of disseminating tracts and leaflets, (and Synod would probably be well advised in setting apart more money for this purpose than it has done in the past.) Books are, as a rule, too expensive to permit of wholesale free distribution, but leaflets can be produced at a low cost and should be available to all at a small price, so that those willing to distribute them incur no large expenditure.
—*Australian Lutheran*

Pastoral Evaluation of Sickness

C. A. BEHNKE

WHAT SPIRITUAL VALUE can there be in a physical condition that is associated with pain, sleeplessness, emotional conflicts, unpleasant smells, and ultimately with defeat through death? Certainly a pastor will pray for the recovery of the patient and use the resources of religion to enable him calmly to bear his affliction. He will also, whenever necessary, render such social service as will remove economic worries and provide pleasant diversion during the lonely hours of a protracted confinement Better still, if he is progressive, he will draw on the recent discoveries of medical science and psychology to develop in the patient mental attitudes that tend to cure diseases having their origin in the personality and aid in more successfully combating others of an organic nature. This is about the extent of a pastor's service in the sick room."

A WRONG APPROACH

It is, if the writer on pastoral technique hastens to give his readers assurances such as, "The conception of the ministry as a life of 'saving souls' by pulling them back from the brink before they plunge to their doom, involves beliefs which we do not hold."—"For good or ill the hell-fire-and-damnation conception of death has pretty much gone by the board in the Protestant Church today and we are among those who wish to pronounce a hearty "Amen" to its going." It is that also when another, trying to bring about "a constantly increasing cultural and practical co-operation between physician and pastor," refers to certain biblical truths as "legend" and "superstition" and groups "Judaism, Christianity and Islam" as equally authoritative.

But what about the pastor who in theory accepts the Bible as the sole source and guide of his religious faith and practice, who has enriched his library with outstanding books on Christian pastoral theology, whose hymn book glows with great hymns that take us into the inner recesses of a soul trying to function within a sick body. Surely, he cannot fail to properly evaluate sickness.

Yet certain practices indicate that some do. When a pastor starts out on his round of sick calls with a set meditation and a fixed prayer and reads them to all of his patients, regardless of age, type of illness, degree of Christian intelligence, presence or absence of mental, resp. spiritual difficulties, he can hardly be following in the footsteps of the Savior-Pastor whom Matthew Arnold describes in the following lines:

"He took the suffering human race,
He read each wound, each weakness clear,
He struck His finger on the place
And said, 'Thou ailest here and here.'"

What are the spiritual possibilities in the sick room? Merely those of psychotherapy, mental healing? We do not discount the healing power of sound attitudes. To "cleanse" the mind of unpleasant memories of the past, to inspire it with dynamic faith for the present and future, is of decided value in the battle against physical ailment. Dr. Crile of the Cleveland Clinic says: "When a man fears, he does not fear with the mind alone, but every cell and tissue of his body fears." The implications of this statement are apparent.

We have seen the therapeutic effects of a Christian faith in neurotics, people of morbidly introvert tendencies. They learned to shift the focus of attention from themselves to Him "from whom cometh our help." Selfishness gave way to sympathetic interest in their fellowmen. As a result, the patients were "cured" of their physical and mental distresses.

In organic diseases we have repeatedly witnessed recoveries that could not be explained entirely by physical processes. In dealing with mental cases, border-line type, manic-depressive, schizophrenic (dementia praecox), paranoic, and even paretic, we have time and again marvelled at recoveries or improvement. Physicians and psychiatrists, recognizing the value of "religion," have repeatedly called us to minister to their patients, because there are "vital areas in the personality" which they could not reach.

But these are by-products of a treatment that dare not be satisfied with physical results. For what shall it profit a man if he gain perfect health, and yet loses his soul?

Nor will sound pastoral practice merely try to substitute for fear, worry, depression, spiritual attitudes known as quietness, courage, peace. This can be done without the aid of the Gospel. A strong personality, skillfully using the art of suggestion, beautiful prayers, or hypnosis, may produce a mental condition, even in the face of death, which cannot readily be distinguished from the "peace" which our Savior gives.

Medical science tells us that because a person feels well he is not necessarily well. Dr. Cabot offers the following incident in proof. "An elderly man, sixty-four years of age, with a ruddy, fresh complexion and white hair, stepped off the corner of a street without looking where he was going, was struck by an automobile and fatally injured. He was brought to the Massachusetts General Hospital and died within an hour. His wife came soon after, and when we asked her about him, she declared that he had never been sick in his life. He was a bartender, a local politician, a most active person both in mind and body. I was present at the autopsy on his body, and this is what we found: (1) Cirrhosis of the liver, with all the blood going around by a new set of roads above and below his liver. (2) Healed tuberculosis of both lungs. (3) Chronic kidney trouble. (4) Hardening of the arteries and compensatory enlargement of his heart." Here was a man who "felt well," while four fatal diseases were at work within.

Similarly superficial pastoral care may enable a patient to feel well, to exhibit quietness, courage, and peace, while within the soul the disease of sin moves toward eternal death. Religion then becomes an anodyne or a sedative, which keeps the patient in blissful ignorance instead of a cure.

A RIGHT APPROACH

In treating an individual who as yet is not a Christian the pastor must aim at more than surface emotional expressions. He must reach the source of his being, his immortal soul. He must bear in mind that his condition does not merely require a little psychological tinkering, but a thorough overhauling, a change so complete that our Savior says to Nicodemus: "Except a man be born again, he cannot enter the kingdom of God." He must therefore lead the patient to the source of the new birth given by Jesus in the immortal words, "God so loved the world, that He gave His only begotten Son, that whosoever believeth in Him should not perish, but have everlasting life."

The "new man," however, comes into being as an infant. He needs to grow. Pastoral care, therefore, requires that the child be placed on a nourishing, balanced diet offered to us by the "Bread of Life." The infant will try to walk. But in the effort he will stumble and bruise himself, even seriously incapacitating himself for a while. The pastor will pick him up, apply the "balm" to the wounds, and offer such support and guidance as may seem necessary. As the infant matures, he will aim more fully to play the part in life which God has assigned to him as a steward of his physical mental and spiritual gifts. Sound pastoral practice will also give to this phase of spiritual life due consideration.

Approaching the sick room with these principles in mind, what are the spiritual possibilities to be found there? In the instance of the unchristian, removed from the distracting struggle for existence to the solitude of the bed where he lies on his back with his eyes directed upward toward his Maker whom he must one day meet face to face, it may mean forgiveness, the beginning of eternal life reaching its climax in heaven.

SICKNESS MAY MEAN GROWTH

For the patient who already is a Christian sickness may mean growth. Largely removed from the routine and forms of religion, thrown "upon his own resources" a large part of the time, he may under pastoral guidance "work out in experience" some of the vital truths which he has previously learned in theory and glibly recited and sung in public worship, such as, "God loves," "God forgives for Jesus' sake," "God hears prayer," "all things must work together for good to them that love God." He may in spirit pause under the cross and evaluate the power of the crucified Savior "to save to the uttermost." He may there find a partial answer to mystifying questions arising from his present experience. He may learn not only to submit to the will of God, but to be "more than a conqueror through Him that loved us." Within the framework of permanent physical handicaps he may build a life noteworthy for faith and achievement.

Such a life will not be self-centered. The mental focus will not be upon sickness and distress, but upon Christ, love, divine purpose. As a consequence, he will not be a whimpering defeatist who becomes "a pest" through his frequent, unreasonable demands upon the time and service of nurses and attendants. Instead he will be appreciative, co-operative, and otherwise lighten the burden of those who serve him in his efforts to regain health.

While isolated the patient may rise to a level from which he gains a better perspective of life. There will be a change in values and resultant emphasis upon life's interest. He may learn "to seek first the kingdom of God and its righteousness" and subordinate all other activities to this supreme purpose. Life hitherto has seemed more or less empty. He may learn to fill it with a rich service toward God and his fellowmen.

Sickness may give to him an appreciation of friendship. He discovers that others do care. The flowers and cards which they send, their visits, and other manifestations of love are ample proof for it.

Having suffered, he is able to understand better than before the meaning of pain, sympathy, divine comfort. When he returns to normal life, it may be with a broader and deeper sympathy and the ability to comfort others "with the comfort wherewith he has been comforted."

In the event he is called to pass through "the valley of the shadow," death will not spell defeat, but victory. He will "not see death," but looking beyond the valley to the better pastures on the other side, he will cheerfully commit himself to the guidance of the Shepherd who on Good Friday traveled "the way of all flesh" and returned on Easter Sunday with the divine assurance, "Where I am, there shall also my servant be."

MEMBERS OF THE FAMILY

There are also spiritual values in sickness for the members of the family in whose home the pastor ministers, for the patients occupying adjoining beds in the hospitals, for nurses who may be standing by while the pastor offers spiritual comfort and guidance. The words spoken, the sacrament administered, the inspiration that comes from the patient who responds to spiritual treatment, the personality and the faithful service of the pastor, may and frequently do prove a rich source of spiritual blessings to those who are in attendance.

THE PASTOR BENEFITS

Last, but not least, the pastor himself is a preferred beneficiary of the sick room. He is more than compensated for what some consider a disagreeable phase of their pastoral service. His experiences with the sick may immeasurably strengthen his own faith. The sick room may also be a laboratory in which he becomes more fully acquainted with human nature as it actually is. As patients unburden their souls, he gains an insight into life such as no book on psychological or social pathology could give him. He learns to know their weaknesses, their strength, their struggles, their defeats, their virtues, their needs. He sees the power of the Gospel at work upon the complexity of the soul.

As a result, his ministry cannot be a profession by means of which he earns a living, but a real service rendered to real needs. His sermons will not be a collection of beautiful phrases dealing with religious truths in the abstract, more or less unrelated to life, but the outpouring of a heart reflecting the love of Him, who is love personified, and yearning to bring the full saving power of the Savior to bear upon all who hear him.

Such devoted service directing the realities of the Gospel to the realities of life will frequently also create between pastors and members "ties that bind," friendships which infinitely surpass in value other satisfactions that may come in the course of the ministry.

KNOWING THE PATIENT

HE as a pastor had often ministered to the sick. Now he was a patient himself. Pain had taken possession of his normally robust physique and threatened to master his virile personality. Then followed wanderings through strange places of the spirit as he for the first time in his life consulted a physician; meekly answered pertinent and seemingly impertinent questions; was fluoroscoped, x-rayed, tested; then for several days anxiously awaited results; was stunned by the almost brutally frank verdict that a major operation was the only way out; took inventory of his financial assets and prospective liabilities; several days later arrived at the hospital; there exchanged a neatly tailored suit for an inverted, abbreviated nightgown; was medicated and otherwise conditioned for surgery; drowsily awaited the arrival of an ominous-looking attendant who nonchalantly wheeled him into a room in which daylight seemed to have outdone itself; was surrounded by ghost-like figures, and a few moments later felt a peculiar whirl in the head as he was wafted into the dark oblivion of anaesthesia.

Somehow sickness now acquired for him a new meaning. Before this he, at times, had regarded sick calls as an intrusion upon his carefully constructed schedule. He had not minded them otherwise. He had generally found it rather easy to speak to the sick of sin as the ultimate cause of suffering; of the Savior as the all-sufficient answer to the problem of sin; of the sovereign, benign will of God; of the purifying, invigorating power of the cross when patiently borne; of the transcendant glories of heaven as outweighing our light afflictions. He had, however, been unable to understand why everybody, especially professed Christians whose lives had been deeply rooted in the fertile soil of divine truth, did not always readily respond to the comfort he so generously dispensed.

Now, as he slowly emerged from distressing post-operative effects, he tried to observe the workings of his own soul while under the stress of illness. He occasionally engaged in brief conversations with men in adjoining beds and listened to remarks which were almost shouted by occupants of outlying beds to each other. He began to know men, not as they appear to be in their usual approach to the pastor, but as they actually are when temporarily stripped of the veneer of civilization and the formal supports of organized religion.

He watched nurses as they flitted about, performing some of the most disagreeable tasks with amazing cheerfulness. In the stillness of the night, when semi-darkness cast a merciful veil over the suffering figures peacefully resting in the depths of medicated sleep or tossing about restlessly, he saw the night nurse as she periodically made the rounds with a small flash light in her hands. He thought of Longfellow's immortal lines:

> "Lo! in that house of misery
> A lady with a lamp I see
> Pass through the glimmering gloom
> And flit from room to room."

She brought to memory Mrs. Theodore Fliedner and Miss Gertrude Reichard of Kaiserswerth, their famous disciple, Florence Nightingale, the heroine of the Crimean War, who lifted the nursing profession to new heights, and others.

Yet not all nurses were alike. Some were rather impersonal, though professionally efficient. Others, however, transformed the atmosphere. They were deeply interested. They seemed to understand. They inspired hope and cheer.

In the morning he observed doctors as they greeted nurses, studied charts and then called on patients. Being in a meditative mood, he called to mind the history of medicine as he knew it from his extensive reading. He thought of Hippocrates, Galen, Harvey, Koch, Virchow, Mackenzie, Roentgen, Curie, Trudeau, Pasteur, Lister, the Mayo brothers, Kelly of John Hopkins, and others. What a heritage and source of challenge for the medical profession! Was the poet thinking of them when he wrote:

> "All you had you gave
> To save mankind—yourselves you scorned to save."

Yet there was a striking difference in doctors as he saw them. Some appeared to be interested in the disease only and offered little or nothing to the anxious, frightened mind of the sufferer. Others did much more. They gave of themselves, their sympathetic personal interest, their calm courage, their hopefulness.

After most of the physicians had left, he saw pastors enter the room. Once more his mind reverted to the past. Before his mental eye there moved the model pastor, our blessed Savior, on His memorable mission of mercy to the sick. Incomparable devotion coupled with a profound understanding of the conflicts and needs of the sick glorified His service to the distressed. Others tried to follow in His steps. But who were they? History had carefully preserved the names of eminent theologians and preachers. Pastors as such, however, were largely lost in the crowd. Yet memory yielded names such as Paul Gerhardt, Johann Heermann, Lassenius, Wyneken, Herzberger, Wambsganss, and others.

Against this background he viewed the pastors calling on the sick. The first to make his entry was the hail-fellow-well-met type. He breezed to the bedside of a patient, offered a few wise-cracks, a funny story or two, and then left. One of the other men ventured the compliment, "He is a swell fellow. You'd never guess he was a minister."

A striking contrast was the next pastor whose every move seemed studied. His smile, his greeting, his conversation, his prayers were a la Hoyle. He appeared to be obsessed with the fear that he might step out of character. Under his treatment the patient in self-defense withdrew into a shell and acted as though he were greatly relieved when the pastor had vanished.

Some time later another pastor dropped in. He seemed to understand. His patient apparently was enjoying the visit. But why did he "have to spoil it all" by reading from a book instead of blending his pastoral treatment in with the conversation?

There followed the noon meal, a brief rest period and the afternoon visiting hour. Then still another pastor called. There was something wholesome about him. One instinctively felt drawn toward him. Pastor and patient were genuinely pleased to see each other. Occasionally both smiled. They became deeply serious. Both bowed their heads for prayer. It all was so natural, so effective. When the pastor left, echoes of his own dynamic faith and radiant personality lingered in the patient.

About a week later the pastor-patient returned to the parsonage. Inspired and broadened by an incipient vision of the possibilities of pastoral care of the sick, he during convalescence re-studied text books and notes which might aid him in his search for a larger evaluation of sickness.

As he read, he discovered that the blame for his more or less ineffective ministry to the sick could hardly be charged to the text books. Yes, there it was. Dr. Walther suggests that a theological student visit hospitals, in order to become better acquainted with the inner life of the sick and to master innate revulsion against disagreeable smells and sights. Seidel writes: "One can readily see that it is not feasible to treat all sick alike, and that it is not sufficient for the pastor, as is frequently done, to read something from the Agenda, but that a pastor prove himself a physician who knows the illness of each and understands how to apply the proper remedies." Olearius recommends that a pastor in his "explorations" seek to determine "the nature of the disease, whether and when it will permit lengthy conversation, whether it will soon terminate in death or grant the patient ample time to set his house in order, whether or not it leaves the mind clear and unconfused, and whether his remarks and activities are traceable to his illness or to the usual trend of his mind."

Why had he failed to notice it before? Perhaps he had been so busy endeavoring to realize his dream of becoming a forceful pulpit orator and an efficient pastoral executive that he had largely overlooked one of the most potent phases of his ministry. He now wished to make amends by assembling his experiences while on the "inside of sickness."

"What transpires within the soul of the patient?" he asked. "What are his reactions to physical distress and discomfort? What are the needs to which I as a pastor ought to minister?"

Apparently he is trying to force his way into a hopeless maze of mental conditions and processes. Sickness has outgrown the simple classification of the past and called into being a dictionary of more than forty thousand terms. It brings to mind such ailments as measles, scarlet fever, appendicitis, infantile paralysis, fractures, tumors, cancer, pneumonia, tuberculosis, diabetes, arthritis deformans, arterio sclerosis, cerebral hemorrhage, and many others. Since it involves not only the body, but also the inner life, a larger grasp of it takes into consideration such vital factors as age of the patient, heredity, environment, training, occupation, and temperament. Apparently the pastor is doomed to defeat before he starts. But is he?

The average physician has been so trained that it becomes second nature to notice the pupils of the eyes and the color of the skin, to note how patients walk and whether they puff on exercising. Several years ago members of a committee waited on a prominent public official. After an extended interview they left. Walking through the corridors, one called him "brilliant," another "a genius." A physician alone disagreed. "The man," he ventured, "is on his way to insanity." Later events proved that he was correct. He had studied the man's eyes.

Similarly an observant pastor, as a result of study and experience with the sick, may sense the mental and emotional life of the patient. Balzac, who in his stories enters deeply into the inner recesses of many people, relates that in walking through the streets of Paris he frequently absorbed the personalities of passersby "through his skin."

For purposes of intelligent pastoral treatment we suggest a threefold division of reactions: 1. those which are superficial; 2. those which at least in part are of a physiological origin; 3. those which often require special attention on the part of the pastor.

There are emotions that are largely on the surface. A normally balanced patient is "blue" or irritable. This may be due to a restless night, failure to receive mail or company, hypos and intravenous injections, imaginary or real grievances against nurses or physicians. A congenial pastor, radiating strength and cheer, will soon dispel such feelings by force of his own example.

The source of the second group is to a great extent found within the physical organism. Christian Science would trace every human ailment to a diseased imagination, while a materialistic psychology with equal confidence assures us that every emotional reaction is the product of bio-chemical composition and changes of the body. As a matter of fact, however, the truth lies somewhere between the two extremes. At best we can merely say at this stage of our knowledge that the mind influences the body and the body the mind. How does this work out in the sick room?

The pastor finds a patient listless, seemingly indifferent to his ministry of comfort. He may diagnose his attitude as spiritual apathy and obtuseness, while in reality the person may be in a stuporose condition, due to some drug administered by the nurse under orders of the attending physician.

The patient may be groaning in the depths of depression. This may be of psychic origin and thus demand special pastoral and, perhaps, psychiatric treatment. Or it may be a concomitant of abdominal ailments, the gout or diabetes. Physico-chemical alterations, toxic substances circulating in the blood-stream, profoundly influence the emotional tone.

Perhaps the patient is worrying about having committed the unpardonable sin. The pastor prayerfully brings to bear the most comforting and enlightening passages of the Word of God. But he fails to make any appreciable progress. As a matter of fact, however, the mental conflict may be of a physical origin. We have known arterio-sclerosis patients who for weeks were terrified by the haunting conviction of having sinned against the Holy Ghost and then cleared up shortly before death with the peace of God once more in control of their spiritual life.

Again, a patient whom we previously had regarded as basically happy seems to have collapsed emotionally. He has become self-centered, complaining, manifests mild delusions of persecution and underestimation by others. In reality, however, he may be suffering from extreme fatigue. Medical care and rest usually will restore the emotional balance of such a person.

In treating reactions of a physiological origin, however, a pastor should bear in mind that the body may condition, but does not always compel the level and trend of the "psyche." A strong faith may enable a patient to rise above the most distressing ailments and "be more than a conqueror through Him that loved us."

A third group of mental reactions are those which may call for both general and specific pastoral ministration. No Christian physician of souls can afford to ignore them or treat them lightly.

The first and most important of these, from a pastoral standpoint, is a sense of guilt. C. E. A. Winslow, Dr. P. H. of Yale University, writes: "In the home of a Spanish peasant, one may find a pot of what is called 'olla Podrida.' Each day this pot receives contributions from the food uneaten at meals, and each day it is brought to a boil and used as a source for savory, if ambiguous, soup. The pot is never emptied, and if stirred incautiously, it reveals strange and disturbing relics of the past. Such an olla podrida is the subconscious mind." The patient, harassed by intense pain, sleepless nights, economic loss, accumulating bills, the prospect of death, "stirs it up" as with cumulative force as he is haunted by such questions as "Why? Why go I mourning? Why hast Thou forsaken me? What have I done to deserve this?" He then rightfully looks to his pastor for sympathetic understanding and relief.

Fear is another companion of illness. Man instinctively dreads the unknown. He is afraid of medical tests, medication, the anaesthetic, the operation, and the post-operative effects. As the disease progresses, there may be fear of the prognosis. What will it be: invalidism or freedom to again work and play, recovery or death? In the event of approaching death, there may be dread of the inescapable judgment before the throne of God or the leaping into the dark unknown. Such a patient requires a generous measure of the message of love "that drives out fear."

Sickness often makes a person lonesome. It takes away the companionship of relatives and friends, of his daily occupations and his usual habits. In spite of a well-organized hospital routine, designed to interrupt the monotony and to distract, there is ample time for the sickening feeling of being alone, focussing attention upon real or imaginary difficulties, exaggerating them, intensifying emotion. Conrad, in "Chance," gives us a remarkable insight into the psychological processes of isolation in a prison and and its reactive effects. Some of it is true of the chronic patient, confined in his home or an institution. "There is something which is preserved by prison life even better than one's discarded clothing. It is the force, the vividness of one's sentiments. A monastery will do that, too; but in the unholy claustration of a jail you are thrown back wholly upon yourself. . . . The people outside disperse their affections; you hoard yours, you nurse them into intensity. What they let slip, what they forget, in the movements and changes of free life, you hold on to, amplify and exaggerate into a monstrous growth of memories. They can look back with a smile at the troubles and pains of the past, but you can't. Old pains keep on gnawing at your heart, old desires, old deceptions, old dreams assailing you in the dead stillness of your present—where nothing moves, except the irrecoverable moments of your life."

Worry, "one of the major diseases of civilization," is closely allied to it. What is there in sickness to cause anxiety? Humanly speaking, plenty. It may be the mounting medical expenses. Can he meet them? How long will it take until he is "out of the red"? It may be the ability of the family to manage during his or her absence. It may be undue interference on the part of relatives. It may be rumors questioning the fidelity of the wife, resp. the husband, during a prolonged absence from home. In certain illnesses such as tuberculosis it may mean occupational readjustment. In case of invalidism it may be the possibility of becoming dependent upon others for support.

In some instances the outlook of the patient is blocked by the feeling of frustration and futility. Life's plans have collapsed or, at least, seemingly so as a result of illness. The nature of the disease foreshadows "premature" death. Or the patient has arrived at that stage of life when it appears to him that "memory is the only friend that grief can call its own."

What a variety of reactions provide the setting for sickness! The poet knew something about it who wrote:

"Surrounded by unnumbered foes,
Against his soul the battle goes."

The patient looks to the servant of the Master of Gethsemane for help. Does he understand? Does he know how to minister to his needs?

AT EVEN, when the sun was set, they brought unto Him all that were diseased, and them that were possessed with devils." Imagination struggles in vain to recapture this immortal scene from a distant past: the setting sun gathering, as it were, his transcendent glory into a sublime focus and then giving way to the Light of the World as He concentrates His healing power upon human distress. It all seems so elusive.

It emerges, however, into a present living reality when Christian pastors, profoundly conscious of their solemn responsibility and immeasurable opportunities, actually function as personal representatives of the healing Savior and bring to bear their Christ-given powers upon human suffering in its varied setting and expression.

It is comparatively easy to rise to ethereal enthusiasm when touching upon a phase of Christian life that so deeply grips the sympathetic interest of a person who has caught the spirit of our Savior's commendation, "Inasmuch as ye have done it unto one of the least of these my brethren, ye have done it unto me." But to really "heal, raise from the dead, free from demoniacal possession, to cause a patient to rise and walk," is a task that will prove a constant challenge to the conscientious pastor throughout his ministry.

The process through which this is done is called pastoral technique. This does not mean that one can reduce the task to a set of simple or complex rules which may be uniformly applied as a mathematical or chemical formula. It does imply, however, that in general a pastor may and should have a working plan, adapted to his own personality and ability and adaptable to the needs of those to whom he ministers.

Pastoral technique is primarily a matter of spirit. Effectively representing the healing Savior at the sick bed, above all, requires a strength of faith and character which reflects that of the Great Physician. Plato excluded from his Republic "those men, always occupied in dreaming of imaginary sufferings, having lost all aptitude for the arts and sciences, incapable of understanding and meditating." In the realm of human misery there is scarcely room for the pastor who spiritually exudes an atmosphere of defeatism because he himself is unable to say, "I know whom I have believed," or because he is more or less habitually depressed. The healing influence of the pastor ought to be felt before he begins his conscious ministry. There ought to be in him a humble virility of faith and its expression that is contagious to those whom he serves.

Closely allied to it, yes, an integral phase of it is sympathetic understanding, born in the shadows of Gethsemane and at the foot of Calvary's cross. Some physicians develop an uncanny skill in diagnosis, almost amounting to intuition. A pastor may, in the course of time, learn to sense and in his own heart feel what is transpiring within the storm-tossed soul of the sufferer. His approach, his conversation and his prayers will thus awaken within the sick a feeling of confidence as they realize that he understands and suffers with them.

It is said that Tennyson and Edward Fitzgerald were once looking at portraits of Dante and Goethe. "What is there in the face of Dante which is not in the face of Goethe?" asked Fitzgerald. "The divine intensity," replied Tennyson. That is the essential difference between the pastor who visits the sick as a matter of professional obligation and routine and one who is impelled by the consecrated and constraining love of Christ. That is largely also a difference between an ineffective and an effective pastoral technique.

An indispensable requisite of a healing ministry is also a mental and spiritual working equipment. A pastor ought always have at his disposal surgical instruments that will enable him to cut into the consciences of the indifferent and self-righteous, Bible passages such as, "There is not a just man upon earth that doeth good and sinneth not." "All have sinned and come short of the glory of God." "Cursed be he that confirmeth not all the words of the law to do them." His kit ought to contain such therapeutic balm for sin-wounded souls as, "God so loved the world that He gave His only begotten Son, that whosoever believeth in Him should not perish, but have everlasting life"; "The blood of Jesus Christ his Son cleanseth us from all sin"; "Come now and let us reason together, saith the Lord; though your sins be as scarlet, they shall be as white as snow; though they be red like crimson, they shall be as wool." Whenever necessary, he ought to be ready to inject into anaemic souls such spiritual elements as, "Underneath are the everlasting arms of God"; "Fear thou not; for I am with thee: be not dismayed; for I am thy God: I will strengthen thee; yea, I will help thee; yea, I will uphold thee with the right hand of my righteousness." To those who share the crucified Savior's complaint of being forsaken of God he will offer such choice assurances as, "Zion said, The Lord hath forsaken me, and my Lord hath forgotten me. Can a woman forget her sucking child that she should not have compassion on the son of her womb? Yea, they may forget, yet will I not forget thee. Behold, I have graven thee upon the palms of my hands." He will transform the sick room into a house of God, a gate of heaven, by telling of Jacob's memorable dream in the wilderness. Called to the bedside of one who is about to undergo a serious operation, he will re-echo the faith reviving assurance of Him whom he represents: "Fear not: for I have redeemed thee, I have called thee by thy name; thou art mine. When thou passeth through the

waters, I will be with thee; and through the rivers, they shall not overflow thee; when thou walkest through the fire, thou shalt not be burned; neither shall the flame kindle upon thee." He will direct the patient's attention away from his own distress to the source of help by praying with him the 121st Psalm. If the sick person, like Asaph, is grappling with the baffling problems of life, he will offer partial, but satisfying enlightenment as found in such divinely inspired statements as, "What I do thou knowest not now; but thou shalt know hereafter"; "We know that all things work together for good to them that love God"; "Behold I have refined thee, but not with silver; I have chosen thee in the furnace of affliction"; "He that spared not His own Son, but delivered Him up for us all, how shall He not with Him also freely give us all things?" He will lighten the burden of those who are groaning under economic burdens with, "Cast all your care upon Him, for He careth for you"; "Seek ye first the kingdom of God, and His righteousness; and all these things shall be added unto you." To the dying he will offer, not an anaesthetic or anodyne, but something that will remove the blinding cataract from his mental eye so that he may see Him who has said, "I am the Resurrection and the Life; he that believeth in Me, though he were dead, yet shall he live; and whosoever liveth and believeth in Me shall never die"; "Because I live, ye shall live also." The gratitude of the convalescent he will resolve into such prayers as, "Bless the Lord, O my soul, and all that is within me bless His holy name; bless the Lord, O my soul, and forget not all His benefits." As the cured is about to leave for home, there should be opened to him a larger perspective of the purpose of redemption, revealed by the inspired writers in such gems of truth as, "He died for all, that they which live should not henceforth live unto themselves, but unto Him which died for them and rose again"; "We are His workmanship, created in Christ Jesus unto good works which God hath before ordained that we should walk in them."

This equipment of the pastor may be enlarged by further prayerful study of the healing Word of God which offers on practically every page some statement, phrase, or example, which may be effectively applied to some or all the needs of the sick. Particularly is this true of the Psalms, Isaiah, the four Gospels, Romans 8, 2 Cor. 4 and 5, Hebrews 11.

The service of the pastoral physician will also be enriched through ready use of outstanding hymns. We mention but a few:

Just as I Am; Rock of Ages; Come Follow Me, the Savior Spake, Verses 1 and 2; Savior I Follow On, Verses 1 and 4; My Faith Looks Up to Thee; My Jesus as Thou Wilt; What a Friend We Have in Jesus; If Thou But Suffer God to Guide Thee, 1-4; Dear Refuge of My Weary Soul; I Fall Asleep in Jesus' Wounds; I Know That My Redeemer Lives; Abide With Me, first and last verses; Jesus Lover of My Soul, 1 and 2.

Now let us observe a pastor, thus or similarly equipped. He begins with prayer for the guidance of the Holy Spirit. The potentialities and corresponding difficulties of his task make this mandatory.

He then carefully studies his list of sick as to urgency and geographical location, in order to determine his route and schedule. If he, following the advice of some writers on poimenics, makes notes concerning previous interviews with patients, he will consult them. If not, he will at least from memory form a mental picture of the spiritual status of the individual patients and his course of pastoral treatment, in order that "the cure of souls" may be progressive in purpose and effect. In his mental kit he may then include a summary of last Sunday's sermon for shut-ins and chronics, and several pertinent Bible passages and hymns about which he expects to build his pastoral service to others.

The time of making calls depends on several factors as emergency, number of visits, and the distances to be covered. The pastor who reserves the morning hours for study, need hardly be warned to usually avoid the early hours when nurses and attendants are busy with medications and arrangement of bed and room. In the afternoon and evening it is also advisable to shun the larger wards during the regular visiting hours, if one is not to compete with company, noises and interruptions.

If not known at the hospital, it is well for the pastor to introduce himself at the information desk, even though he can somehow get by without a ticket, in order to let the hospital know that some "Protestant ministers" do visit the sick, and to facilitate future admission and activity.

If possible, he ought tactfully to learn something about the patient's condition from relatives or attendants. The information thus acquired may determine his pace and method in dealing with one who is not a professed Christian. It may furnish the key to the patient's mental reactions and their causes, whether superficial, physical or spiritual. It may indicate how long the pastor may effectively stay. If a patient is just emerging from anaesthesia, if he is nauseated, if "it hurts him to talk", if he has just had a "hypo to put him to sleep", a pastor's course is obvious. If on the other hand, the patient is "feeling fine", if he "is anxious for company", the pastor may remain longer, combining sociability with pastoral treatment, being careful, however, not to be led so far afield that it is next to impossible to fulfill his pastoral obligation.

Entering the room of the sick, the pastor ought to leave behind his own troubles, no matter how much his own heart may be aching because of serious illness in his home, recent personal losses, or parish difficulties. His task is to relieve and remove, not to increase, the burdens of those whom he is to serve. He should be ready strongly to face human misery no matter how distressing. A physician was once asked how it was possible for him to see what he saw without breaking down physically and mentally. He replied: "I think not of the disease, but of the cure." If a pastor likewise will focus his attention, not upon the pathetic physical misery, but upon the potential spiritual triumph over it, he will be equal to any situation or emergency that may confront him.

At the time of making his calls he may be under severe mental pressure because of an overcrowded schedule that demands plan plus speed. But he must give no evidence of it while with the sick. Otherwise the latter will feel uneasy and restrained. If a pastor must hurry, let him "step on it" after he has left the sick room. But while there, he must be calm and as cheerful as the situation will permit, concentrating his undivided interest upon the person whom he as the Savior's representative has come to serve.

If the patient appears nervous, depressed or frightened, he ought to try to discover its cause. The emotional reactions may be superficial, due to sleepless night, disappointment or some real or imaginary grievance against the doctor, the nurse, a relative or friend. They may be concomitants of the disease. Or they may be traceable to a sense of guilt, fear concerning the outcome of the ailment, economic worry, or lonesomeness. A sympathetic approach may induce him to talk.

When he does, the pastor ought to be prepared to listen. Troubles have accumulated in the solitude. He has tried to repress them. But they refused to be shackled. They threaten to unbalance him. Toxic in effect, they poison his personality. A "catharsis" becomes necessary. He therefore is compelled to unload to someone who understands and is interested, if he is to regain spiritual and mental health.

This is true, in particular, of a deep sense of guilt. Some psychiatrists attribute great therapeutic value to the Catholic confessional. But a former Catholic priest, now an analyst, writes: "Catholic confession is too coercive in character to be a health-giving mode of release." The contemporary cult of "Buchmanism", perhaps, owes its power to the fact that it centers in voluntary confession.

When listening, however, the pastor must avoid being censorious. To bear down with the lightning and thunder of Sinai may drive the patient into a defensive, repressive silence. The fact that he is anxious to make a confession usually indicates some degree of penitence. He may require a broader knowledge of his guilt. He may be grieved over the consequences of his sin rather than over the sin itself. But whatever the nature of the penitence, he needs a listening that understands and will wisely, albeit firmly, lead him to the cross.

Listening may also give the pastor insight into the life of the sick person. If he is to minister intelligently, if he is to begin at the point at which the patient is, he must at least approximately know his present spiritual status.

When a patient talks he may thereby solve his own problems. Inner resources, stored up in childhood and youth, such as Bible passages, hymns, the Christian example of relatives and friends, are aroused from dormancy and come to his aid. Time and again the sick thank the pastor for "what he has done for them", when in reality he has done no more than wisely listen and occasionally direct, as the person drew upon unsuspected sources of enlightenment and strength within his own being.

In the event of special spiritual treatment the pastor must begin on the level of his patient. He is a shepherd who leads, a guide who accompanies. Conceit alone will permit him to view his task as that of pulling his patient up to his own imaginary level.

It is likewise important that he speak the language of the patient. If the latter is a child, he ought to think and speak as a child at its stage of development. If he is a person of limited education, he will "observe his mouth", as Luther suggests, and speak in a tongue that will put him at ease, rather than one that will force him into an oppressive inferiority complex. If on the other hand, the patient is well educated, he will convey to him the all-important facts of sin, divine grace, the purposes of affliction and the larger perspective and service of a redeemed soul in terms that will not insult his intelligence.

Sound pastoral technique also offers a large place to prayer. Dr. Hyslop of Bethlehem Mental Hospital, London, writes: "As one whose whole life has been concerned with the sufferings of the human mind, I believe that of all the hygienic measures to counteract depression of spirits and all the miserable results of a distracted mind, I would undoubtedly give first place to the simple habit of prayer."

To serve a definite pastoral purpose, the prayer at the bedside must be the outgrowth of the conversation or what a discerning pastor has sensed. Any pastor who can really preach, can render this service. He learns it from his own daily communion with God. As the priest of his own household he at the family altar prays with and for his family. Dr. F. Pieper also suggests that he resolve his daily Bible readings into appropriate prayers. Out of these practices there ought to grow the art of praying at the bedside of the sick without the guidance of a prayer book.

This does not preclude the advisability of having a prayer or two in reserve in one's own mind for emergencies. Otherwise he may find himself tongue-tied when awakened in the middle of the night or called from some task that left him mentally fagged.

What are the vital needs to be expressed in pastoral prayer with the sick? Confession of sin; faith; physical recovery, subject to divine discretion; gratitude, patience, submissiveness in case of prolonged illness or invalidism; God's blessing upon family, the physician and attendants; a renewed and larger life; intercession for others in distress; the work of God through the church.

The sacrament of Holy Communion is another invaluable asset of pastoral service. It is not primarily "a last rite", a religious act immediately preceding death, but a "supper" instituted by an all-wise Savior to strengthen the faith and promote Christian life. It ought to be celebrated "oft" in the case of lingering illness.

The economic or personal situation of the sick may require social service. Extreme poverty, unemployment, domestic difficulties, friendlessness and the resultant lonesomeness dare not be overlooked. Wherever possible the material and personal resources of the church ought to be placed at the disposal of the sick. In other instances the pastor may have to serve as intermediary between the patient and some social agency.

The number of visits to be made ought to be determined by the physical and spiritual condition of the patient as well as by the work load of the pastor. Special situations may require daily ministrations, while shut-ins and chronics may be adequately served with one call a week.

If the physician confidentially informs the pastor that the patient will not recover, what then? Shall he break the news to the latter? There may be exceptional cases in which this may be advisable. The sick person is stubbornly or indifferently unresponsive to pastoral treatment. He needs to be shocked into his senses. Or, perhaps, his financial affairs are in a muddle; he alone can satisfactorily straighten them out. Or he has failed to make a will, with prospective litigation among members of the family as a result. A word of warning, suggesting the possibility, if not probability, of death will be in place.

As a general rule, however, it is extremely unwise to act as the spokesman of the attending physician. They are good, mediocre and inefficient doctors. But even if the physician is exceptionally able, he still may be in error. As a result it would be a trifle embarrassing later to meet the patient whom one in seriousness had informed that he could not possibly get well. Last, but not least, why offer prayers of recovery if their efficiency is to be limited by medical pronouncements?

Certainly every illness, no matter how slight, and every surgical operation, whether termed major or minor, contains the element of danger. It is a prophet of ultimate death. Wise pastoral guidance will always bear this in mind and be influenced by it in ministering to the sick.

When, humanly speaking, death is impending, when the patient is visibly disintegrating and growing weaker, the pastor ought ordinarily limit his ministry to brief, pertinent Bible passages and hymns, preferably those that are well known, and prayer. At what point the mind fails to grasp, cannot be deter mined. Patients who, as a result of a stroke, may forget most recent happenings, may be able to join in the extem poraneous recitation of long hymns such as, "O Haupt voll Blut und Wunden." Incipient or sustained coma may be broken by such familiar gems as, "Christi Blut und Gerechtigkeit", the 23rd Psalm or the Lord's Prayer.

If the pastor is present when the patient is about to begin his passage "through the valley of the shadow of death", a prayer commending him to the merciful guidance and care of the Redeemer, and the benediction may bring invaluable comfort to the patient and members of the family.

The latter should not be overlooked, especially in cases of critical or fatal illness. They suffer with the patient and, therefore, require comfort and strength. Wise pastoral evaluation may also enlarge their spiritual vision and service.

Much more may be written upon the subject. But enough has been said, we hope, to at least faintly intimate the possibilities of consecrated, enlightened pastoral service to the sick. A growing pastor, a growing congregation, a growing heaven will be the result.

Institutional Mission-Work Among the Sick

ERWIN KURTH

TWENTY-SIX years ago institutional mission-work was systematically begun in our church when a number of Saint Louis congregations called the Reverend F. W. Herzberger to devote his whole time and strength to mission-work, especially in the public charity institutions.

Since that time, many of the larger cities have followed suit. Chicago, New York, Buffalo, Cincinnati, Cleveland, Indianapolis, Detroit, Milwaukee, Saint Paul-Minneapolis, Los Angeles, and San Francisco have engaged the full time service of one or two missionaries, and, in some cases, of a woman worker besides.

In addition, quite a number of our pastors have taken over the extra work of ministering to the spiritual needs of the sick, the poor, and the afflicted in near-by institutions. In Minnesota, for instance, there are eleven pastors who, besides serving their congregations, serve a total of fifteen Sanatoria, Reformatories, Industrial Schools, Insane Asylums, or Poor-Houses.

If statistics were available, it would be interesting to note how many institutions of our land might yet be served if more of our pastors would be willing to "take the time" to do this most blessed work. Of Sanatoria alone there are 700 in the United States with over 67,000 beds for tubercular patients. Twenty years ago there were only 100 hospitals and sanatoria for the treatment of tuberculosis, with about 10,000 all told. What a mighty missionary opportunity is ours, alone among the tubercular patients. Whenever we of the younger generation are inclined to lament over the glorious opportunities which our forefathers are supposed to have passed by, it were well for us to remember "the field white unto the harvest" in the numerous public institutions of our land. So "Hats off to the past; coats off for the future."

For those pastors who are located near a public institution and are interested in doing work there this article is written. The writer does not claim to be a past master at the art, nor to have any wider experience than that which can be gathered in sanatoria, hospitals, and poor-houses; but, since he has been requested to write what he knows, and no more, and since the AMERICAN LUTHERAN is to serve as a clearing-house for ideas, he makes bold to present whatever ideas he has on how to start and carry on mission-work in public institutions.

HOW TO START

The first, and perhaps the greatest, difficulty about institutional work is the start. The unknown ever intimidates. Human nature shrinks from beginning whatever is strange and different. Not having done work of that kind before, the average son of Adam will hesitate about entering upon it. "Am I cut out for it? Have I the gifts, the tact, a pleasing manner of address? Will I be able to say the right thing to the right person at the right time?" These thoughts will come and, if they are allowed to linger too long, they will fill the heart with faintness. Away with them! They belong to the future; the future will take care of them. Your concern for the present is: "Do I really want to start?" If so, then make up your mind to the fact that there is no better way to start than to start.

All right then; how? The first thing would be to find out what ministerial work is being done in the institution. If nothing, or very little, your course is clear. Go to the superintendent, inform him who you are and what you want, that you would like to hold a service soon, just a short service, with a Gospel sermon, to comfort and strengthen the patients. Would he give his permission? As a rule, you will find him right willing to comply with your request, especially so, if he knows that you will conduct your service in a soothing and solemn way and actually do the patients some good.

On the other hand, if you think that you are not wanted, make yourself wanted. Work for an opening and create a demand for your services. Perhaps on this wise: Visit some of the Lutheran patients who have been referred to you. Do this, of course, during the regular visiting hour, so that no objection can be raised. Then make the acquaintance of others in the same ward. If they have no pastor visiting them and desire your ministrations, make it a point to see them regularly, especially when they have been transferred to another ward, floor, or building. There you can repeat the process and learn to know still others, and so on, until by and by you are pretty well known all over the place. The chances are that they will soon ask to hear you preach, and when the authorities find out that the patients themselves want to hear you, they will gladly permit you to hold your services.

HOW TO CONTINUE

The *sermon* is the most effective way of bringing the Gospel to the greatest number of people with the least expenditure of time and effort, and therefore the institutional worker will endeavor to arrange as many preaching services as practicable. No hard and fast rule can be laid down as to the number. Much depends upon the size of the institution, the number of other services held, and the church preference of the inmates. The writer, for instance, has a monthly schedule according to which he preaches twice in one institution, namely, upon every second and fourth Wednesday afternoon, and eight times in another, that is, seven times on as many floors and once in the chapel. Two services are conducted in rapid succession on the same Thursday evening, during the visiting hour, between seven and eight-thirty o'clock, each service lasting about forty minutes. The service in the chapel is conducted on a Sunday evening, for the benefit of the hundred or more that attend and the unseen hundreds who do not attend but listen in over the radio.

Referring to the sermon proper, we should suggest, in passing, that its contents be not too heavy; for not a few of the hearers are woefully lacking in a knowledge of even the fundamentals of the Christian faith. The style must be simple; otherwise some person might venture a question similar to the one that was put to us when, after a sermon in which we had preached on the theme "Prudence," a man inquired: "Say, Reverner, was prudence a man or was he a woman?" Polemics, sob-stuff, and a constant reminding the patients of their condition, are to be carefully avoided. The true Lutheran sermon has for its underlying theme the old but never antiquated doctrines of the Law and the Gospel, and when these are presented in a pleasing and convincing manner they will produce the desired results, that of engendering repentance and faith, and dispensing the peace of God which passeth all understanding.

THE WORKER'S EQUIPMENT

Next in importance to the sermon is *bedside ministration*, such as visiting the sick, comforting the dying, instructing candidates for Baptism, preparing for confirmation, and distributing the Lord's Supper. This work is indeed an art, and, like every other art, must be cultivated. To do this work successfully the missionary must have the proper equipment. He can gain the proper equipment only through study and prayer. The work that he does at his desk will in a large measure determine his success in the sick-room. For one thing, he will be a student of doctrinal theology, so that at any time he can give a reason for the belief that is in him. He will also study books like Walther's "Gesetz und Evangelium" or Bente's "Gesetz und Evangelium," since no more frequent demands are made upon him than to rightly divide the Law and the Gospel. He will furthermore acquaint himself with other religions, theories, and fads, like evolution and faith-cure, so that he can hold his own in an argument. And finally, he will devote the choicest moments of his study-period to a preparation of that message which is to serve as a medicine for his sin-sick patients. In this preparation he may be aided by books like "The Lord Thy Healer," J. Sheatsley; Starck's "Prayer-book"; "The Pastor in the Sick-room," C. Abbetmeyer; or Herzberger's "Family Altar."

CARD INDEX

Some sort of system is necessary to facilitate the worker in making his round of visits, and keeping tab on the patients. After a complete list of Lutheran patients has been secured from the social worker or the office, the names are entered into a book, or, which is preferable, upon three by five inch cards and the information recorded thereon as it is obtained. The cards may provide for the following information:

Name:

Room:
Religion:
Visits:
Communed:
Disposition:

The reverse side is reserved for remarks. The cards are kept in an oak tickler and arranged according to the floors.

The work of keeping them up-to-date may be entrusted to a nurse or an obliging patient.

DO-S AND DON'TS FOR THE SICK-ROOM

1. Enter the sick-room with the doctor's permission. Enter quietly and softly, with a bright face, and a neat, tailored appearance.
2. Get down to business as soon as possible. Know what you want to say, then say it. Don't dawdle away time in light conversation or lengthy argumentation.
3. Read, explain, apply the Word of God. Append a prayer. Don't read your message out of a book, nor the prayer either.
4. Don't open your religious talk with questions like these: "Are you saved?"—"Are you a Christian?"—"Did you come to Jesus?" "Are you prepared to die?" These questions have been asked too frequently and have lost their savor.
5. Don't speak too much or too solemnly about religion and death. Don't worry them with a dissertation about dying.
6. No matter how emaciated the sick may be, express no surprise. Don't speak discouraging words. Not like the pastor who said to a girl-patient: "Do you know, I find it awfully hard to make sick-calls. I'd rather preach three times than make one sick-call. It always makes me feel so sad." After a little while he ventured the statement that "in all of his experience he did not know of one single real cure" of the sickness that she had succumbed to. That girl would liked to have cried her eyes out.
7. Study each individual case and apply the Word of God accordingly. The minister is a physician; as such, he must correctly diagnose the case and prescribe the right medicine.
8. Don't stay too long. Even if the sick one urges you to stay, don't do it.
9. Find the way of approach to every person's heart. If it lies by way of his stomach, use that way. Have the ladies of the congregation help you, by providing jams, jellies, preserves, sauce, or clothing.
10. Leave something as you go away, your card, a tract, or at least a cheerful remembrance.

TRACTS

Tracts are very helpful and should be distributed with lavish hand. The missionary may procure any number of them free of charge or for a nominal sum. Whatever expense is incurred can be borne by some organization of the church or, as a last resort, by the Mission-Board of the District.

We deem it advisable for the missionary to place his name, address, and telephone number upon every tract. It helps to advertise him and enables the patients to summon him quickly in times of distress. A rubber stamp, procurable for a dollar or so, very well answers the purpose.

PRAYER FOR PERSONAL PREPARATION

Ministering to the sick in an institution is indeed a difficult work. The missionary comes in contact with men and women from all walks of life, from the highest to the lowest, from the keenest to the simplest, from the most responsive to the most resentful. Great discernment and tact is needed to apply the Word aright to fit each individual case. In this the missionary needs strength from above. He needs the enlightenment of the Holy Spirit. And for these gifts he must wrestle with God in prayer.

Prayer puts the missionary in mind of his high calling and sets vividly before him what he must accomplish, as the ambassador for the King of kings. He must dispense peace to the troubled, comfort the stricken, convict the gainsayers, and guide the wayward back to the way that leadeth over Calvary to the plains of peace. And with this purpose clearly set before him, his visits are not apt to degenerate into mere social calls.

Prayer also inspires with confidence. After having asked the Master to aid him in His work, the missionary can sally forth to his difficult duty with the blessed assurance: "We too shall win in the end: Jesus and I."

"EFFECTIVE PREACHING"

ARTHUR BRUNN

THE Church Council was meeting. It so happened that the offering on Thanksgiving Day was considerably larger than it had been last year. A number of explanations were offered. "Let me tell you, brethren," said Deacon W., "let me tell you why the offering was so large. Something happened during that sermon." Deacon W. believed that the sermon had something to do with the larger offering.

Whether Deacon W. was right in this instance or not does not matter much. But this does matter, that he believed that something happened in consequence of a sermon. When something happens in consequence of a sermon you have effective preaching. If nothing happens then we might as well quit preaching. The thing that is to happen may not always be on the surface. It may not always be counted out in dollars and cents. Hearts must be touched. Faith must be strengthened. The inner life must be nourished. The wayward must be aroused. The indifferent must be shaken. Something must happen or preaching is ineffective.

Something will happen. The message which we preach is the gospel, the power of God unto salvation. Where there is not gospel preaching there can be no effective preaching. We mention this only in passing, lest somebody think we are going off on a tangent.

Preachers being what they are and congregations being what they are, they can do much to make even gospel preaching ineffective.

Probably it will be well once again to emphasize the importance of preaching. There is danger that both pastors and congregations forget that the chief business of the preacher is to preach. In the multiplicity of pastoral work, in the demands upon the time of the pastor, there is great danger that both the pastor and the congregation lose sight of the fact that no matter how pressing other duties may be, there is just nothing which dares to interfere with the preaching work of the preacher. Pastors and congregations who forget this will do much to make for ineffective preaching.

Effective preaching requires two things, preparation and delivery. Effective preaching is something that needs to be learned. Some preachers have native ability above others. If there is no native ability at all, the preacher had better give up his effort to develop

something that does not exist. However, let no one be discouraged. Wonderful results can be obtained by constant application and care and training. Remember Helen Keller. Every handicap ought to be a challenge. On the other hand let no one imagine that a diploma from the seminary is the only preparation required for effective preaching. If a preacher does not grow in his preaching ability there is something wrong somewhere. Most probably the preacher is neglecting his preparation. No, we do not mean the preparation for that sermon next Sunday. We are thinking of preparation in a much wider sense of the word.

There is just nothing that a preacher does, reads, hears, sees, observes which he must not in some way try to press into the service of his preaching. A preacher must continually be preparing himself to become a better preacher. He must have a very wide acquaintance with his Bible. That is basic. It ought hardly be necessary even to mention that. A preacher ought to be so well acquainted with his Bible that when he is preparing a sermon on a given text or on a given topic, related texts, stories, examples, applications, thoughts, words, phrases come running to him from all over the Bible. Everything a preacher reads, and he ought to read much, must be read from the viewpoint of the preacher. Every parish visit ought in some way help to develop his preaching ability. Every contact he makes ought to furnish something for the preaching development of the man in the pulpit. These are some of the things we think of in connection with preparation. "Stop—Look—Listen." That ought to be the watchword of every preacher.

Then of course comes the preparation for that specific sermon which must be preached next Sunday. Every preacher has some homiletical material in his library. It is essential equipment. The preacher must see what others have been doing. He must learn from others what not to do. He must take over, if you please, some thoughts, phrases, expressions from others. But he must not do that when he is preparing that sermon for next Sunday. Next Sunday it must not be the Rev. Doctor So and So who is going into the pulpit, but the preacher himself. And so in preparing that sermon for next Sunday we suggest that the homiletical material be kept under

lock and key. Take your text. Take a good exegetical commentary which will lead you into the niceties of your text without any thought of that sermon which is in the course of preparation. Whip the thoughts of the text into shape. YOU are preaching, not some one else.

You are preaching to a very definite congregation. You know the needs and requirements of your congregation. You know the weakness and the strength of your congregation. You just can not take a sermon which was preached three years ago out in Oklahoma and preach it to your congregation in Alabama. It will not fit. You may be giving your congregation stones instead of bread. Why preach on the dangers of youth in an old people's home.

So in the preparation for that sermon next Sunday the preacher will remember that he is going to preach himself, that he is going to preach to a very definite group to which no one else can minister as well as he can because he knows exactly what that group needs.

That reminds us of another important item in the preparation of your sermon. Do not preach generalities. There is not much sense in preaching about the wickedness in the wide, wide world. Preach about the wickedness among the people who are going to hear your sermon next Sunday. There is not much sense in preaching about the general neglect of spiritual things in the wide, wide world. Preach about the neglect among the people who are going to hear your sermon next Sunday. Do not lose yourself in generalities. People may marvel at your general knowledge of the situation in this world. The effect of your sermon may be that people will compliment you on your great learning. But that is not the effect you are looking for in your preaching.

Some time ago an inquiry came about a preacher who happened to be a candidate for a vacant pastorate. One of the questions submitted was, "Does he use a manuscript?" Pray God, that your preacher uses a manuscript. There are very few men who have the mental equipment to preach Sunday after Sunday and year after year to the same congregation without writing out carefully what they are going to say. There are some few who can do that sort of thing. Generally speaking the men who think they can do that sort of thing are the men who are least equipped for it and the men who could do that would hardly dare to do it. "Does the preacher use a manuscript?" Pray God that he does. It is a different question where he uses it, whether he uses it in the study or whether he has his eyes glued to it in the pulpit.

Preparation for the sermon requires that the preacher vary his approach, his style, his language. He must not get into a rut with his preaching, so that when he has started a sentence half of the congregation can finish it for him. The preacher must avoid pet words, pet phrases. He will undermine the effect of his preaching.

"Have you finished your sermon for tomorrow?" asks the good wife. Have you? When is a preacher finished with the preparation of his sermon? Not until he steps into the pulpit. Not a moment earlier. By that time however the preparation must be so complete that nobody sees or senses it. The best dressed woman is the woman who attracts no attention. Her clothes must be part of herself. The best preparation is that preparation which attracts no attention. Like a woman's dress, so the preacher's sermon must have become a part of himself. The sermon must sound like the spontaneous outpouring of a soul.

Then comes the delivery. That is essential to effective preaching. And again your delivery must be so natural that it attracts no attention. Do not imitate some great preacher. Be yourself. YOU have something to say to your people. Open your mouth and say it so that your people will understand you. The greatest compliment that can be paid to a preacher is that the children of the church hang on his lips. If the children can understand you, you may rest assured that the fathers and mothers also know what you are saying. Avoid big words when you can use little words. Do not imagine that you must repeat again and again just because your sermon is supposed to last half an hour. Probably your sermon would be more effective if you would preach fifteen minutes.

The story is told of one of our well-known fathers, that when he came to a new charge he preached only 15 minutes. By and by some of the deacons complained about the shortness of the sermon. Why they could hardly make themselves comfortable when the preacher said "Amen." So the good old pastor asked what the sermon of the day had been. The poor deacons were hard put. Finally they confessed that they did not exactly remember. "You see," said the wise preacher, "I am still preaching too long."

The other day we inquired into the preaching of a certain pastor. We were told, "He is a fine preacher, he preaches 45 minutes."

The effectiveness of a sermon does not depend upon the time consumed. Remember Lincoln's Gettysburg address!

There are so many other things which play a vital part in the delivery of your sermon. Don't yell in the pulpit. People do not want to be yelled at. Don't whisper as though you had a secret which nobody should hear. Watch the hymns you choose. Watch the organist. Don't let him rouse the dead with an open diapason when he ought to be using the dulciana. Don't let that choir shriek so that the rafters will shake. Some time ago visitors attended a strange church. They reported that the choir came out of a side door, marched down the side aisle in single file, half of them disappeared and went up into the gallery, the other half marched down the center aisle and occupied the front pews. The pastor came out of another side door and sneaked up on the altar platform. His preaching gown was awry. The surplice needed laundering. The service was run through as though it was just another thing that had to be done. By the time the preacher got into the pulpit these people had seen so much that disturbed them, that they could not even listen attentively to the sermon. Watch that sexton so that the spider spinning his web will not attract the attention of the people. Watch the ventilation. It will kill your best effort if the air is so thick that it can be cut with a knife. Neither will women pulling their fur collars around their necks because they are cold help to make an attentive audience. Don't permit anything in your church which will make ineffective a sermon over which you have travailed for 25 years. Everything in the church must be set so that when the preacher steps into the pulpit everybody is keyed up to listen. An effective sermon can not be preached amid disturbances of all kinds.

Effective preaching—what a topic! When you have done your very best, you will still tremble at your inefficiency, if your preaching is really effective. You will know and understand that God alone can make effective preachers. But let neither the preacher nor the congregation do anything which will make God's efforts ineffective.

"EFFECTIVE PREACHING"

LAWRENCE ACKER

"THERE IS nothing wrong with Lutheran preaching. It is very effective. It must be effective because Lutheran preachers preach the Bible, the whole Bible and nothing but the Bible. And God's Word never comes back void. I see no need for you to write an article on 'Effective Preaching.' It is not the preaching that is at fault, it is the worshippers. They have heard Lutheran preaching so long that they no longer appreciate the good things offered in a Lutheran sermon. Like the Israelites in the wilderness they reject the manna of God's Word brought them by a Lutheran preacher and say 'Our soul loathes this light bread.' What they now want is something different, something new. What THE AMERICAN LUTHERAN needs is an article in which the readers are informed that the reason why Lutheran preaching is sometimes ineffective is to be found with the worshipers and not with the preacher."

The one who wrote these words must be listed as an extremist. We dare not say that all Lutheran preachers preach good sermons! There is Lutheran preaching that is not effective and the fault lies with the preacher.

I

One reason why some preaching is ineffective is that preachers preach above the heads of the hearers. As I read printed sermons, as I hear sermons preached, I become convinced that many preachers are searching their dictionary to find big words with which to clothe the thoughts of their sermons. One is inclined to excuse the graduates entering the active ministry when they continue to use classroom language, but what shall we say when a minister, having served a congregation for five, ten or more years, refuses to get down to the level of his people. There were days when worshipers were awed into wonder as they listened to their preacher deliver sermons in which one jawbreaker outdistanced the other in length of syllables. I still remember the story often told by my sainted mother. A dear friend informed her one day that he had heard a great preacher preach a wonderful sermon. When mother asked wherein the greatness consisted the friend remarked that he really did not know what the preacher was talking about, but that any person who could use as many big words as he did must be a great man and his sermons must be wonderful sermons. Many preachers today must still be living in horse and buggy days, for they still believe that people come to hear them because of the big words they use. I disagree with them. My pastoral experience covering more than 25 years has encouraged me to teach younger brethren the lesson taught me by the sainted Pastor F. Leimbrock. Soon after I arrived in San Diego, California, to serve as student assistant in The Trinity Lutheran parochial school, Pastor Leimbrock invited me to preach regularly every two weeks, either in San Diego, or in one of the several neighboring cities where he had organized mission congregations. Accepting the invitation I occupied his pulpit the very next Sunday and he sat among the worshipers. At the close of the service he invited me to dinner the following Wednesday and asked me to bring along the manuscript of the sermon I had just preached. Even if I no longer had the manuscript with the many penciled notations made by "my beloved San Diego Bishop," I could never forget the lesson he taught me regarding the use of plain, simple language. As he read my manuscript he jotted down on a sheet of paper 72 words that he felt the audience did not understand. To prove to me that the average worshiper did not know what the words meant, he asked the pupils of the seventh and eighth grade the following day to give the meaning of twenty words chosen at random from the list. And then a few nights later members of The Walther League were asked to give the meaning of about forty words on the list. Was I surprised when I saw the examination sheets! The answers convinced me that Pastor Leimbrock was right in urging me not to use language far above the heads of the people. Then and there I decided to preach in the language of the people, to use such plain language that even a small child could understand me, and to keep out of my sermons, if possible, all words with four or more syllables.

It is one thing to make a promise; it is another thing to keep it. It was not an easy matter to keep the promise I made to myself in San Diego. As I recall the first years of my ministry, I see myself sitting at my desk. On the one side is that very large book by Francis A. March, containing thousands upon thousands of words and expressions so arranged that within several minutes a person can find listed just what one needs to express exactly a given idea, a book whose binding I have worn through twice in twenty-five years. On the other side are the German-English and the English-German dictionaries by Schmidt, Fluegel and Tanger. Before me lies my Sunday sermon. I have spent many hours preparing it, have tried my best to get proper thoughts arranged in logical order. But before I preach it, I want to polish it, especially do I want to simplify the language. And so I am really rewriting the sermon. Every time I come to a word with four or more syllables, I try to find a shorter word or a plain expression for that "big word."

Every time I find an expression that does not register with my wife, I search for a simpler word or expression which she understands. Again and again I spend five and ten minutes rewriting just one sentence, trying to clothe its thoughts in words the every-day person can understand. Sometimes an hour or two are used to remove from one paragraph in that sermon the words that darken its thoughts; then I rewrite that paragraph in the plain language of the plain people. Again and again it happened that the time used in preparing the content of the sermon was short when compared with the time used to have the sermon clothed in words as plain as those of the 23rd Psalm. Yes, it was hard work, very hard work.

But I have no regrets. I know it was time well spent. I now always use in my preached sermons a language of which one person writes that "it is understandable by the least educated, yet inoffensive to those of more than average intelligence." It has become a habit with me to avoid big words. And I know that people like sermons preached in plain language. When an aged German mother, who has learned all her religion in the German language, tells me that she sees no need for German services in my church because she can understand my English sermons just as easily as sermons preached in German, then I thank God that He permitted me to be for two years a pupil of the sainted Pastor Leimbrock of San Diego, California. When lay people, who whisper into my ear that they never entered the seventh grade, come to me and with a pressure in their handclasp emphasize their statement to the effect that they enjoy listening to my sermons because they know what I am talking about, then I thank God that He made me ready and willing during the early years of my ministry to learn how to speak the language the common people speak. And just a few days ago a sick mother told me that her nine year old daughter had come home from church services and had told her "everything the preacher had said in his sermon, even mentioning several of the examples used." Mr. Editor, it was Moody, The Chicago evangelist, or Spurgeon, the great English preacher, who once said that when your preaching holds the attention of the children, you can begin to believe that you are preaching effectively.

II

Out near Arrowbear, California, I recently met Pastor Walter Troeger of Santa Monica, California. Attending the opening service of The 1939 Southern California Walther League Summer Camp, he and his family remained to become acquainted. Soon we were doing what preachers do when they get together, we were "talking shop." I have never heard Pastor Troeger preach, but I have read with much joy and lasting benefit his sermon sketches printed in magazines for preachers. I do know persons who have heard him preach more than once. They tell me that his sermons "are just full of examples from everyday life," that in his preached sermons there are many more illustrations than in his printed sermon outlines.

There are many more preachers like Pastor Troeger. There should be more than there are. Every preacher ought do what Pastor John Kaiser of Leigh, Nebraska, has been doing for many years and is still doing. Just recently Pastor Kaiser told me that during the past twenty years he has collected hundreds of illustrations, indexed them properly, and uses them as windows for his sermons. When he prepares a sermon and comes to a point he does not want his hearers to forget, he opens his file of illustrations, selects that heading under which the point he wishes to drive home might be found and soon he has several suitable illustrations. As one listens to him tell how he collects and how he uses illustrations one can easily understand why his sermons are so rich with short stories, stories that assist the hearer in understanding better the preached Word of God, stories that linger in the memory of the hearer and help him to remember the sermon.

If every preacher would do as Pastor Kaiser does, would preach as Pastor Troeger does, he would soon learn that his preaching is effective. People like that kind of preaching. People living when Jesus did liked preaching in which teachings were made plain to them by means of stories and examples. Any Bible reader knows that the common people heard Jesus gladly and one reason why they listened closely to every word He spoke was that He preached as their religious leaders never preached. Jesus told stories, Jesus used examples of the everyday life they lived, Jesus made His point clear and then drove it home by referring to incidents and happenings in the world they were then living in. It is any wonder that the preaching of Jesus is effective? And why, may I ask, was Luther a preacher whom the common people wanted to hear? Why was the church full when Luther preached? One reason was that Luther's sermons were not dry. Some years ago I heard Dr. Dallmann of Milwaukee say that Luther did not preach as he taught in the university. Had Luther taught the people as he taught the students, I wonder if he would have been as popular as he was, I wonder if his preaching would have been as effective as it was. I do not know Luther's life as well as I ought, but I am wondering whether I am saying too much when I declare that Luther was an effective preacher also for this reason that his sermons abounded with proper anecdotes, stories and illustrations.

Mr. Editor, soon after I accepted your offer to write this article I mailed a letter to several Omaha Lutheran lay people asking them to tell me what they think effective preaching is. All of them answered and all of them had something to say about illustrations. One writes: "subject matter should be made interesting with sufficient illustrations and anecdotes." Another stated that a preacher should "use illustrations which linger in the memory and which might serve as a handle with which to grab hold of the sermon thoughts for later use." And as I turn to the third letter I read: "Some sermons I have heard consisted only of definitions. I like sermons with homely illustrations and examples. An audience will listen and learn when the preacher relates a personal experience, such as an observation on a trip, a conversation with a dying Christian, the confession of one whose life was misspent." And if I might add one more, let it be a statement copied from the letter of a young lady who wrote: "I like a doctrinal sermon, I like a sermon in which the text is explained, but I don't like these sermons when they have no local color or atmosphere, when they are just full of facts that are as dry as the reading of The Constitution of The United States." Other quotations could be added, all of them in the same vein, all of them urging the preacher "to enliven his sermons with human-interest stories." Now, no one can make me believe that these Omaha Lutherans are different from other Lutherans. When they tell you that they like homely illustrations in a sermon they are voicing the views of thousands of churchgoers and are forcibly driving

home the truth that the Christians today are very much like the Christians in the days of Luther and in the days of Jesus Christ. Christians today will go out of their way to hear a preacher who helps the hearers to understand by using proper illustrations. To prove my point, may I cite a recent experience made by Pastor A. R. Kretzmann of Chicago? As I put the finishing touches on this manuscript, he is in Omaha delivering a series of lectures to The Omaha Lutheran Sunday School Institute. He spoke for eighty minutes before a group of young people on a Sunday afternoon and when he finished many were wishing that he would continue. That same evening he lectured for almost ninety minutes to a larger group and many wanted him to "keep on talking." Twenty-four hours later he was scheduled to deliver another lecture. That would be Monday evening. All of us were agreed that it was a bad night and were quite positive that not many persons would attend the lecture. What a surprise awaited us. More than were present on Sunday afternoon or Sunday evening were in their chairs when the time came for him to speak and for another sixty minutes he lectured. And all listened attentively. Why? Let someone answer for me. She said: "What I like about that man is that he can tell stories which make it impossible for you ever to forget the lesson he is teaching us. And that is what all the others like about him. We have this fine crowd this evening because all day long today we told all we saw that they should come this evening and hear this man who uses the language we daily use and who explains his teachings with such human interest stories that you cannot forget them even if you wanted to."

III

Before me lies a book of sermons. The author informs me that these printed sermons were preached in his church, located somewhere in that section of our beloved country which Mencken once branded The Bible Belt of America. The sermons are of the average length, none of them covering more than nine pages, most of them about six pages long, all of them printed with eight point type on a page measuring about 6 x 9. At random I choose a sermon. It is seven pages long. I read it. I read it once more because there is something about that sermon that appeals to me. The author has an unusual gift. He can explain the text; he can bring forth from the text thoughts that one did not think could be found in it. I like that sermon and yet—there is something wrong with it. I feel that something is missing,

something that must be there before it could be called a good sermon. But what is missing? At first I cannot detect it. The power of this author to explain a text is so much to my liking as to cause me to forget that a good sermon consists not only in a fine explanation of the text but also and especially in the proper application of that text and its explanations to the persons addressed. Gradually, however, it begins to dawn upon me that the one thing this sermon, as well as many others in the volume, woefully lacks is application. You will probably not believe me, but I speak the truth when I tell you that of the seven pages on which the sermon I selected at random was printed, only one-half page is devoted to application. Think of it! Six and one-half pages to explanation, one-half page to application.

There are many sermons preached these days that do not get under the skin of the hearers because they are preached BEFORE the hearers and not TO them, or, if they are preached TO the people, it is done in such a general way as to make the hearer feel that he is not meant. Let me not be misunderstood. I do not condemn the preacher who preaches BEFORE the people. We must have preaching telling us what to do and what not to do, telling us there is salvation in none other than in Christ Jesus. Such preaching is good for the people. They learn to know their Bible better; they grow in the knowledge of our Lord Jesus Christ. And so I would be the last to say that we are having too much of that preaching which just explains the text. I believe, we should have more of it. On the other hand, I do maintain that we do not have enough preaching TO the people. We need more preachers who by their sermons prove they subscribe to the statement that "the sermon begins where the application begins." We need more preachers who really believe the greater number of their hearers are like Daniel Webster who once said with emphasis "when a man preaches to me, I want him to make it a personal matter." We need more preachers whose sermons will induce the hearers to say: "Pastor, it seems to me you are preaching your sermons just to me. As I listen to you I forget all about all the other people in church. I feel that your words are meant for me only; I feel that you are correcting my faults, instructing me how to walk worthily before God, urging me to repent of my sins and persuading me to accept Jesus as my personal Savior."

You are shipping oranges to California when you state that "the hardest part of sermon-making is to apply the text properly." To apply the text is very

Effective Preaching

hard for some preachers for the reason that they do not rub elbows with the man on the street and do not get close to the hearts of those persons over whom the Holy Ghost has placed them as overseers. They can tell you of the sorrows and sadnesses, the joys and happinesses of The Saxon pioneers; they are well acquainted with the peculiar problems confronting the Christian Church when Luther lived, but they know so little about the heartaches and headaches of the people who live today. And preachers who believe that the Lutheran motto selected by THE AMERICAN LUTHERAN years ago, should be changed to read "A Changeless Christ for a Changeless World," will find it very hard to apply the text properly.

But now there are some preachers who are seen not only on Sunday when they are in the pulpit, but also on week days when they go out among the people. Such preachers soon learn to know what the spiritual needs of their people are. And yet there are a few of these preachers who find it hard to apply the text properly. Why? They know on which side their bread is buttered and they fear that if they step too hard on certain pet sins, not only the butter but even the bread will be taken away from them. And so they close one eye, they say nothing, what they could say they leave unsaid, because they do not wish to endanger their daily butter-bread. Their sermons are worthy of study only by those who want to say something yet do not want the hearer to feel that God means just him and not the one sitting next to him in church. But such preachers who do not want to say what God wants them to say, who refuse to apply the text properly, are they really God's messengers? What God thinks of them may be found in Isaiah 56, 10; God calls them dumb dogs.

And once more let me say that applying the text is very difficult because so many preachers preach so seldom to the heart but mainly to the head. I am not so foolish as to deny that the ministry is a noble calling; I will readily agree with anyone who says that the work of shepherding God's flock on earth is a very, very important work. But when a preacher begins to think that because of his high calling he is so much holier than the people who called him as their pastor, that he need not preach to himself the message he is preaching them, then his preaching will be head preaching only, and not the head-and-heart preaching it should be. And at the risk

of making myself an outcast even among my friends, I am going to be so bold as to declare that there is not enough head-and-heart preaching heard in our circles. There is plenty of head-preaching. I know that to be true, not so much because of the preaching I have heard but especially because of the remarks made by such who travel all over our country and whose judgment I value very highly. What they say agrees with the traveling salesman who wrote me years ago "that because our Lutheran Church was born in a university, almost all of us are compelled to listen to a recitation of doctrinal truths delivered in an academic manner." Now I know this traveling salesman did not condemn the Lutheran ministers because they preach bread and butter sermons, as one of my friends describes doctrinal sermons. Thousands of worshipers are happy that our Lutheran ministry is still determined to know among the people nothing save Jesus Christ and Him Crucified. Their hearts overflow with thankfulness when they hear our Lutheran ministry preach sermons which tell the people what they must do to be saved and how they may cleanse themselves from all filthiness and let their light shine before all men. But worshipers do bitterly complain that some sermons are like sounding brass and a tinkling cymbal, that though the sermons are correct "as to form, sound as to homiletics, logical in construction, perhaps beautiful in style, eloquent as to delivery," they are still as cold as ice. Why is that? Is it because the preachers so frequently say not what they really feel, but what they think they ought to feel and are without success trying to feel? I believe it is because the sermons came only from the head and not from the head and the heart. Please, do not misunderstand me. I am not pleading that our ministers preach like Billy Sunday; nor am I in favor of a sawdust trail leading to a mourners' bench. I am not urging that we reject all head sermons and have only heart sermons; I am pleading that we put a heart into the head sermons we preach. The poet has rightly said:

"'Tis not enough that what you say is true;
To make us feel it, you must feel it, too.
Show yourself warm, and that will warmth impart
To every hearer's sympathizing heart."

And there will be warmth in our sermons if we love our God with all our heart and again and again recall what He has done to save us. There will be warmth to our sermons if our hearts are filled with an intense desire to tell others the good news that God so loved the world that He gave His only begotten Son. There will be warmth to our ser-

mons if we preachers will remember that the reason why people come to church is not because they want to know what the preacher thinks about this or that, but because they desire to know what God has to say about it. And they want the preacher to say it as though God himself were speaking. Many hearers today are like the sailor, who, when he was asked what good preaching is, replied: "When a man takes something warm out of his heart and shoves it into mine, I call that good preaching." Do you agree?

I have said enough. Probably I have said more than I should have said, but what I have said has come from the heart of one who is very much interested in the betterment of Lutheran preaching.

FOR DAILY USE AND IN PLACE OF GENERAL DOXOLOGY ON SUNDAY

Lord, while for all mankind we pray,
Of every clime and coast,
Oh, hear us for our native land,
The land we love the most.

Oh, guard our shores from every foe,
With peace our borders bless,
With prosperous times our cities crown,
Our fields with plenteousness.

Unite us in the sacred love
Of knowledge, truth, and Thee;
And let our hills and valleys shout
The songs of liberty.

Here may religion, pure and mild,
Smile on our Sabbath hours;
And piety and virtue bless
The home of us and ours.

Lord of the nations, thus to thee
Our country we commend;
Be Thou her Refuge and her Trust,
Her everlasting Friend.

ZION LUTHERAN CHURCH
NW 9th & Walker, Oklahoma City.

HOW TO BEHAVE IN CHURCH

Thou shalt not come to service late,
Nor for the Amen fail to wait.
Thy noisy tongue thou shalt restrain
When speaks the organ its refrain.

But when the hymns are sounded out
Thou shalt lift up thy voice and shout.
The endmost seat thou shalt leave free,
For more must share the pew with thee.

The off'ring plate thou shalt not fear,
But give thine uttermost with cheer.
Unto thy neighbor thou shalt bend
And, if a stranger, make a friend.

An Organized City-Wide Program for the Alleviation of Distress Caused by Unemployment

THE SAINT PAUL PLAN

By A E. Frey

THE BILL of American private social work even in normal times has become gigantic. The estimate is that in our country as much as two billion dollars was spent annually on philanthropic activities. A large percentage of that vast sum was used for feeding, housing and to clothe the needy. But that was in normal times. Now unemployment has brought dire need. With eight to ten million people out of work the need has become intense and the suffering beggars description.

The vitally important question throughout our land is: "What can be done to alleviate suffering?" There are three main sources from which relief will come: the churches, the private relief agencies, who pool their funds, and the public relief agencies. The bulk of relief is swinging to the latter and they are tax-supported. And that is not a necessarily healthy trend.

In Saint Paul relief is dispensed in a small way by churches, the chief relief through private sources comes from the United Charities, the Catholic Charities, and the Jewish Welfare Association. These are the three main organizations supported by the Community Chest. The third relief agency is the Public Welfare, which is county-wide and tax-supported. Of the three field agencies the United Charities is by far the largest. It is in this agency that the Lutherans are particularly interested. The United Charities pay the rent, the gas and electricity, provide clothing, make investigations and render service of adjusting affairs, in this manner often preventing public dependency. The Public Welfare pays for fuel and food. But there is close cooperation between private and public relief agencies.

The ideal from the viewpoint of the Church is that the churches take care of all people in need of physical relief in addition to providing spiritual care. But except in a few instances, under most favorable conditions, the individual congregations cannot give intelligent and sufficient aid. Especially is this true in the cities. And in times of stress, as we are having now, that surely is not possible in the vast majority of cases. Which congregation has an "Armenkasse" or a Poor Fund, supplied with sufficient money to meet the present need of relief? The pastors lack the time, the funds and the training of successful relief work on a large scale. Their spiritual work would suffer, even though they might have the available funds and the training for intelligent investigation and wise distribution. And if a pastor would have a trained case worker to assist him and would handle the relief work intelligently under the present abnormal conditions of unemployment, what could he and his congregation do about the unattached group, the many unchurched needy people who might be real missionary material?

Some social workers, especially the leaders among them, recognize the need of the Church's help. There are exceptions, of course. Workers and leaders of the extreme liberalistic type sometimes assert that art, literature and music are sufficient to provide a so-called emotional outlet. But many thinking social workers realize that these are not sufficient. They realize first of all that relief agencies do not give satisfactory service by providing only cold relief, that it is not sufficient to keep people's stomachs satisfied and to have their agency be a machine to dispense relief at the lowest possible cost. They are convinced that individual guidance is needed and that the Christian Church is an agency which can contribute largely to this. In a general way they are ready to grasp opportunities which will help develop individual people and promote in them a cheerful attitude toward life and a closer relationship to the Church of their choice.

As we see it, the Church has two chief duties, the spiritual and the physical care of its people. The spiritual care is its own individual obligation. No organization can be of help to her in that field. She has and uses the means of grace. But in the field of rendering physical relief the church is not alone.

Whether motivated by common human sympathy or moved by the thought of self-defense, civic agencies and public groups dispense relief. If the Church can do a better job of its physical relief work by availing itself of the organized trained social case method and study and help influence the whole welfare program, and in addition, contact many unchurched people, why should it not try to do this? These are the thoughts underlying the

SAINT PAUL PLAN

We have a Lutheran Emergency Relief Committee, consisting of seven pastors representing all the Lutheran groups of our city and county. As a first effort these seven men were appointed by their respective conferences to study the question of physical relief for Lutheran people. Our folks had contributed to the Community Chest in their annual drives and we wanted to learn whether the needy among the Lutherans were receiving sufficient help. The original plan was to establish a downtown central office, employ efficient and trustworthy workers, who would investigate the different cases of need among Lutherans, and arrange for proper relief.

In consulting with the officials of the Community Chest and those of the United Charities, especially, it was found that this plan would not be practicable under prevailing local conditions. A new plan was studied and accepted. It is different from other known plans in use. Our Committee decided to appeal to the Lutheran people to designate their Community Chest contributions to *Lutheran Emergency Relief*. A trained Lutheran case worker was recommended to the officials of the staff of case workers but also to be the Lutheran Case Consultant. In the several district offices of the United Charities there are Lutherans among the regular case workers doing general case work, but who, because of their religious training, have a better understanding of the problems of Lutheran families. This was carried out. We were fortunate in securing Miss Emma V. Jensen as the Lutheran Case Consultant. She has brought understanding help to our work and the pastors are convinced that we have an able and Christian worker. What has helped our program very much is the attitude and cooperation of the General Secretary of the United Charities For one year the Committee has met bi-weekly and these meetings have been attended by the General Secretary and our Lutheran Case Consultant. Much time and thought has been given to devise ways and means of assuring adequate relief to all needy deserving Lutheran families. In addition, we have emphasized the plan of referring unchurched Lutheran families and individuals to one or the other Lutheran Churches, depending on former connection, nationality, etc., as well as discussing with the respective pastor the cases of needy families already known to him and belonging to his congregation or who attend his services.

The scope of physical relief given to Lutheran families by the United Charities is interesting. The records of our Lutheran Case Consultant show that more than eight hundred (800) families have received relief since December 15, 1931, and of these four hundred and sixteen (416) are now on the active list and receiving aid. This list refers only to families in which both husband and wife give their religion as Lutheran and not to instances of "mixed marriages." It should also be understood that the list does not include the many Lutheran families receiving help from the Board of Public Welfare, the tax-supported public relief agency of our county. The check-up of this list has not been obtained, as their records did not include details of church connection. It is hoped that this can be corrected.

As to definite progress and results of our endeavor, we can report that a number of Lutheran families have been definitely reconnected with their church and have been spiritually strengthened. As an example, let me mention only one of several cases.

PLEASE TURN TO PAGE 38

Putting the Lay People to Work as Assistants in Institutional Work

A. E. FREY

MEMBERS of this Conference are engaged in ministering to sick and unfortunates in the public institutions throughout our state of Minnesota. Some of us devote a part of our time to this blessed work, others devote all their time and energy to the work of soul-saving in institutions and the follow-up work in homes. Who of us has not found that this field affords wonderful opportunities to be of real spiritual help to those coming under our care? Although this field of pastoral labor also has peculiar difficulties, who has not felt amply rewarded when he was enabled to bring God's Word to a person who was formerly indifferent but as a patient or as an inmate is more approachable and finally, by the power of the Holy Spirit, finds peace in the Redeemer Jesus Christ! Who of us has not had the inexpressible joy of hearing words of gratitude come from the lips of a suffering patient or felt the pressure of a dying person's hand giving eloquent expression of thanks? And those of us who serve in institutions where people are confined for their misdeeds have heard words of apparently sincere repentance from people who have seen the error of their ways and who reveal and profess a sincere desire to walk in ways pleasing to God and man. What satisfaction there is to serve such people with the one means which can change the heart of sinners, namely, the Word of God.

In serving these various types of people in institutions there are some duties which we must perform ourselves. We cannot delegate the preaching, the administering of the sacraments, the individual pastoral care to some member of our congregation, or our Ladies' Aid, or a Walther Leaguer, or any volunteer worker. On us rests the duty and we ourselves must perform it conscientiously and properly. While it is true that the preaching, the instruction of classes, the confirmation, the administering of the sacraments, the individual pastoral care are the most important duties among patients and inmates, there are numerous opportunities to use the consecrated helpers available as volunteer workers. Such opportunities for service are:

Singing to beautify our institutional services;

Assisting invalids to attend the services;

Visiting shut-ins and reading to them; same to incurables;

Teaching in the Sunday school at the institution;

Singing in the corridors or wards, where permissible;

Befriending a stranger and lonesome patient, making such a person the special charge of an individual volunteer;

Providing the institutional worker with funds to purchase tracts, New Testaments or penny Gospels or prayer books;

Providing a supply of usable clothing for the worthy needy, where such opportunities exist;

Entrusting a list of patients for visiting purposes to consecrated volunteer visitors, provided they have received from us proper directions as to conduct in public institutions, observing of rules, proper approach of people to be visited, what to avoid, etc.;

Remembering people at Christmas or Easter or on birthdays;

Assisting the institutional pastor with clerical work, such as notices, preparing and sending of programs, etc.

Perhaps there are a few of us who can use volunteer workers for all these purposes, but I can hardly conceive a field where volunteer workers can not be used for one or the other activity. They must always work under the direction of the missionary and be responsible to him. Unless properly guided they can become a hindrance instead of a help. For that reason we must keep them under proper direction and do it in a tactful manner.

A FEW PRACTICAL HINTS

Permit a few practical examples of telling our people what to do and what not to do. This refers especially to visiting in institutions.

The authorities in an institution are supreme. Their rules and regulations are to be scrupulously observed. If visitors must have a pass, let not our people consider themselves exempt from that rule. At first they may be able to secure a pass for visiting only one patient. Later they must be able to get a so-called "general pass." With the assistance of the missionary this usually can be done, especially if it can be shown that the visitors are not of the revivalistic, emotional type.—If the visiting hours are from 2 to 4 o'clock, let our volunteers conform to that rule. They will soon outwear their welcome if they do not. Let us remember that the nurses have many duties to perform and must do many of these duties after visiting hours. Visitors are a hindrance to them after the visiting hours and the nurses will soon frown on their work.—We had that experience recently. A supervisor complained that a group of volunteer visitors were continuing their visits after the close of the visitors' hours. We were fortunate to be able to say that they were not of our group. She told me that she had complained to the superintendent of nurses and had received instruction from her to send the next offenders to her office.

Teach your volunteer visitors not to visit too long. Twenty minutes should be sufficient as the maximum. Sometimes five minutes are too long. A certain tuberculous patient told me recently that a church visitor had remained in her room a full hour. As she was an advanced T.B. patient she was worn out by that visit. I know of many cases where patients have feigned sleep when they saw certain volunteer workers approaching their rooms or beds, because they were not refreshed by their visits but rather were bored by the same.

Instruct your visitors to tactfully avoid listening to complaints about the care, the attention, the food they receive in the public institution. If they are not satisfied they should complain to the proper authorities and not to volunteer workers. And let not our volunteer workers broadcast these complaints. They may not be true. We heard of a case in a hospital where one visitor carried gossip from one bed to another and embittered the first patient she had visited.

Our volunteer visitors should be told not to give medical advice to patients. That is perhaps the quickest way of closing the doors of the hospital to their work. It takes an able physician to diagnose a case and here a stranger, unable to tell the difference between truth and fiction in the patient's account of real or imaginary symptoms of this or that ailment, wants to give information. Let them not give any kind of advice, except that the patient obey the physician's orders. A T.B. specialist recently told his patients that often our relatives and friends are our worst enemies when giving advice. Do not let them relate instances of sickness among their own relatives, mothers, grandmothers, aunts, etc.

Instruct your volunteer visitors not to bring food to patients without the consent and knowledge of the proper authorities. Great harm may be done to a patient by providing him or her with food. Many of them are on special diets.

Our visitors and also our singers are never to be boisterous in an institution. Loud laughing and disturbing talking are most unwelcome. The sincerity of the visitors and singers may easily be questioned, too. Tell them to be natural. Tell them to come with a smile and not with a foolish grin.

Since volunteer workers can easily do more harm than good when visiting in institutions unless they are properly directed, we suggest that they be trained for Personal Service. Our method has been to invite the interested women to form a class for Personal Service. They met every two weeks for a series of informal lectures, ten in number. Every member of the class was supplied with a mimeographed copy of the lecture outlines. Pastor H. F. Wind, our city missionary at Buffalo, has prepared a set of practical outlines. We were guided by these in preparing ours.

WHERE ARE WE TO SECURE VOLUNTEER WORKERS?

In every congregation there are people who can be used for this work. Perhaps we have only a few good people available, but they may make up in quality, adaptability and consecration for a large number of people who are willing but unadapted for the work. A very few real workers who do not give up after a few visits or opportunities of other service are better than a large group of workers who are difficult to control or who do the work for the thrill there may be in it.

We think first of all of our Ladies' Aid Societies. Should it be impossible to find a group of such women ready to take an active part in our missionary endeavor in an institution of their own town or city? What a blessing it would be if we could enlist the interest and whole-hearted support of a Ladies' Aid Society of our congregation! Not all could and should be visitors. Not all could or would be singers. We could divide them into committees and use the women for the work for which they are adapted. We would have the singers, the sewing committee, the visiting committee, the welfare and clothing committee, etc.

We think of our Young People's Societies. Perhaps we can enlist the entire organization to take an active interest in the missionary opportunity in some institution. Here again we must carefully choose our workers for their special duties. We will find them especially willing to serve their Lord by singing for the patients or inmates. But we may also find able Sunday school teachers, or a few cheerful persons—not the giddy kind, however,—who would be adapted for visiting certain patients.

We think of a Men's Club in this or that congregation. Should it be utterly impossible to gain the interest of such a church organization to show active interest in institutional mission work? Should they not be willing to serve men in the institution? Should we not be able to win singers for the work? Should they not be ready to give the use of their automobiles and serve as drivers for taking aged inmates, or crippled people for an occasional auto ride? What a diversion they would bring to the patients who are unable to go about in the out-of-doors. What pleasure they would give themselves by serving unfortunate people!

It may be impossible to enlist an entire organization as the Ladies' Aid Society, the Y.P.S., the Men's Club, for this work. Why not start a missionary group? Even though it consist of only a half dozen workers, these can be of outstanding help in our particular institution. It can be done. It has been done.

HOW CAN WE WIN THEIR INTEREST AND ACTIVITY?

To win the interest of our people for active participation in missionary work we must give them information. Picture the field in which you work. Describe individual cases. Bring proof of the saving power of the Gospel in our day. Show the incidents in which lay people have rendered real service in that institution. Do not generalize too much but give specific cases, without mentioning names of patients and workers. Our people will become interested. Information begets interest and incites them to real activity. Then give our people something to do. Give them duties which they really can perform and keep them at these duties. Do not fail to recognize their help and make mention of their good work. Above all, show that the service they render to the least of the people, they render unto the Lord. Show that charity is a requisite of true discipleship.

In the Twin Cities Mission we have had the valuable help of the women. We have two Women's Auxiliaries, one in St. Paul, the other in Minneapolis, with a combined membership of 1000. The membership of each consists of women communicant members of congregations with Synodical Conference connection. They have their constitution, which limits their activities to the field of City Mission and endeavors to avoid infringing on congregational rights and activities. In the monthly meeting of the St. Paul Auxiliary, and in the bi-monthly meeting of the Minneapolis Auxiliary, we open with brief devotional exercises, have the minutes of the previous meeting read and then hear the reports of the Standing Committees. Such committees are:

Visiting Committee, which systematically visit patients;

Welfare Committee, which sews and mends, supplies usable clothing, food, milk, etc., in case of emergency;

Music Committee, which provides vocal and instrumental music for regular services, also for corridor singing (song services) and programs at Christmas and Easter and for the annual party in October at the Country Home. We have in one city a Ladies' Mission Trio, consisting of ladies of the Auxiliary preparing themselves for regular or emergency singing in the interest of City Mission.

Membership Committee, whose duties are to gain new members for the Auxiliary and also to keep after the renewals.

After the report of the various standing and possibly some special committees, the institutional missionaries and the women welfare workers render their reports. Brief statistics on the activities of the previous month are rendered, such as services, hearers, bedside visits, home visits, baptisms, confirmations and communions, private and general. The most important items related, however, refer to specific instances, such as particular proofs of the power of the Gospel, or unusual difficulties of approach, or evidences of real gratitude, etc. Through these reports of incidents we have held the interest of our good women.

ORGANIZED CITY-WIDE PROGRAM *from p.36*

The family consists of four members. The father and mother are now attending services regularly in one of our Missouri Synod churches; one son has been confirmed after a full course of instruction, and the second child is in the new class of catechumens in the same church. — — — Another encouraging development is that the entire staff of the United Charities has come to appreciate the spiritual ministration of the church in the rehabilitation of families and of individuals. Furthermore, the members of the staff are anxious to learn more about the spiritual help obtainable from the churches. Thus at least some of the non-Lutheran workers on the staff are gaining a new viewpoint of the far-reaching help the Churches can render.

We have used *volunteer* lay workers to gather religious information from families listed as Lutherans. This was important to learn about the prospects for reconnection with some church and through the Lutheran Case Consultant refer favorable cases to the proper pastor and church. We now have a permanent and smaller group of such volunteer workers who are becoming more proficient and dependable. Thus the important link of contacting for reconnecting families with a Lutheran church is being simplified and improved.

The question may be raised: What is there under this plan for the individual congregation and pastor to do in the way of physical relief for their own people? Our answer is: The Lutheran Emergency Relief Committee, our Lutheran workers and the officials of the United Charities earnestly endeavor not to infringe on the rights and duties of the pastors and the congregations in helping their needy Lutheran families. The pastors and the congregations are not encouraged to discontinue the giving of aid. They are urged to restrict such help to the cases where it does most good, where they know the situation well. For example, there may be old folks not in dire need but who appreciate extra attention. Or there are cases where a family has become financially embarrassed through the death of one of its members or through business reverses.

In furnishing usable clothing for the needy, two clothing centers have been established, the one of the Synodical Conference group is in a Saint Paul office building and under the care and direction of the Welfare Committee of our Ladies' City Mission Auxiliary. Many hundreds of articles of clothing and bedding have been distributed among needy Lutheran people. Just now the supplies are being increased to meet the demands of the coming winter. This, then, is the Saint Paul Plan of an Organized City-wide Program for the Alleviation of Distress Caused by Unemployment:

The Small Pastoral Conference—I. The Balanced Program

HERBERT M. DAENZER

Introductory

The Pastoral Conference in our Lutheran circles is, humanly speaking, that agency by which we are assured of continued orthodoxy and scriptural practice in the church. It is primarily our postgraduate course in Theology. It is also an excellent means for the promotion of good will and fellowship among the pastors. Anything, therefore, that will serve to keep this institution upon a high plane of efficiency serves a most important cause.

It is the humble intention of the writer to have this essay serve in this capacity, with particular reference to the Circuit Pastoral Conference, and with brief reference to the One-day Conference or Winkel Konferenz. He would then with your indulgence describe the most effective methods in use here and there in our church, according to information which he has lately gathered with the knowledge of the respective Visitors from about two score circuits in the United States and Canada.

This inquiry revealed the fact that a few conferences use certain excellent methods not found elsewhere. This very information has been requested by a number of Visitors and secretaries, and so it is herein made available to anyone interested. The themes used in this essay were supplied by the conference secretaries, and the principles discussed in Section I *are in use* at one place or another, so that the writer is just an agent in their general dissemination. They are presented especially under this section, The Balanced Program.

The Need for Balance

What are the elements of an efficient circuit pastoral conference session? The well written essay which exhausts its theme is of course the prime requisite. But the essay is not concerned so much at this time. But even in spite of their excellent papers occasional sessions fail to accomplish what they might. Something is missing, and that something often is balance.

To gain the intended benefit from our circuit conferences we must have the theological material well balanced. And balance in Theology may only be attained by a proportionate treatment of *all* of its component parts. It is obviously important that in this discussion we have before us a chart of the departments in Theology (see below), because it naturally weighs heavily in this essay.

Theology

A. Exegetical Theology
    Philology and Exegesis; Isagogics; Hermeneutics.
B. Historical Theology
    History (Sacred and Church); Archeology.
    Symbolics; Confessions; History of Dogma.
    Patristics.
C. Systematic Theology
    Dogmatics; Apologetics and Polemics.
    Moral Philosophy and Ethics.
D. Practical Theology
    Pastoral Theology; Church Polity.
    Catechetics; Homiletics; Diaconics and
      Evangelistics.
    Liturgics; Church Music; Hymnology; Heortology.
    Christian Art and Architecture.

The 474 themes which have been compiled reveal the following proportion for each of the four departments, the sermon for criticism not included:

    A. Exegetical Theology .... (94) 20%
    B. Historical Theology .... (82) 17%
    C. Systematic Theology.........(143) 30%
    D. Practical Theology...........(156) 33%

Such a general chart can do little except indicate the neglect of the department of Exegetical Theology, and so the following is appended to show the attention given to the individual branches.

	Essays		Essays
Greek Exegesis	59	Phil. and Ethics	30
Hebrew Exegesis	21	Pastoral Theology	70
Isagogics	10	Church Polity	4
Hermeneutics	4	Catech. and Educ.	34
History	58	Y.P. Work	7
Archeology	3	Homiletics	15
Symbolics	10	Missions and Publ.	15
Confessions	10	Christian Art	0
History of Dogma	1	Architecture	2
Patristics	0	Liturg. and Hymns	8
Dogmatics	79		
Apol. and Polemics	34	Total	474

The Centennial and the intersynodical situation are represented by a goodly number of essays. Hebrew exegesis is specifically reported by only one-third of the conferences. And German essays comprise 6.5% of the total.

In Pastoral Theology the majority of essays deal naturally with the customary subjects as Matthew 18, burial, dancing, etc. But the other everyday problems of the pastor (social, rural, urban, racial, and educational) receive surprisingly little attention. The personal observations of one pastor who comments, "They (the essays) are too unrelated to our work at hand," appear to be quite correct with the exception of but few conferences. Comparatively few circuits give attention to balance.

Effecting Balance in the Program

In creating balance we effect proper proportion among the elements involved, in this case the four departments of Theology. But not all departments are equally difficult or extensive, and so a snap judgment of using the proportion 1-1-1-1 (for the two day circuit session) bears inquiry. Let us survey the four departments briefly from this angle.

Exegetical Theology treats of "the proper exposition and elucidation of Scripture including auxiliary studies." Luther urged that our love for the Gospel should determine our study of biblical philology. Doctrine rests upon thorough philology and sound exegesis, and so "Exegetica est regina." The branches in this department are fairly heavy studies and thus lend themselves best for essays read in morning sessions.

Historical Theology tells us of the experiences, the work, the confessions, and the extant antiquities of "that communion which appeared on earth as a result of the Saviour's work" of both the Old and New Testaments. The first two branches are less heavy studies, while the third (Symbolics, etc.) and portions of the fourth are practically Dogmatics.

Systematic Theology presents the truths of the Christian religion as a system "in their connection and mutual relation", vindicating these truths and opposing error. This department is of the highest importance, which importance is also mirrored in the frequency of its treatment. It requires very close attention and thus lends ifself best for morning sessions.

Practical Theology includes "everything that belongs to church activity". This department is very extensive and no branch may be ignored. In fact the writer is tempted to give this department a larger proportion than he does and much could be said in its defense. But after all right principles will make for right practice, and so Exegetical Theology should remain on a level with Practical. Is Exegetical Theology the source of scriptural truths, then Practical Theology is their external expression. And since these truths may be set aside by an anti-scriptural practice, this entire field in all of its branches by no means may be regarded as of little importance. Historical and practical essays are usually read in afternoon sessions.

On the basis of the foregoing the writer would rate the four departments as follows: A-10, B-7, C-10, D-10; or A 27%, B 19%, C 27%, D 27%; or roughly the proportion 2-1-2-2. But since this practical proportion 2-1-2-2 is not sufficiently exact, we are compelled to alternate some departments to maintain a general balance, especially also since conferences use anything from 2 to 9 essays for a two day session. The following work chart rests on this fact. Try the suggested proportions in rotation and give neglected branches better representation.

    (a) for 5 essays: 2-1-1-1, 1-1-2-1, 1-1-1-2
    (b) for 6 essays: 2-1-2-1, 2-1-1-2, 1-1-2-2
    (c) for 7 essays: 2-1-2-2, 2-2-1-2
    (d) for 8 essays: 2-2-2-2, 3-1-2-2, 2-1-3-2, 2-1-2-3
    (e) for 9 essays: 3-2-2-2, 2-2-3-2, 2-2-2-3

Accordingly the bi-annual or annual circuit pastoral conference, in session for two days, ought conclude from five to eight, or nine, brief essays. This number may appear excessive. And it is when essays require more than 1½ hours each. But few essays for the small circuit conferences need contain more than 5,000 words with a reading length of 60 minutes. Longer ones ought to be exceptional, depending on the amount of necessary material. Verbosity not only fails to lend dignity to essays but it is also a poor substitute for logical and authoritative argumentation. Brevity is even more so today the soul of wit. But there is another reason for less lengthy papers. Every pastor should be permitted to write one conference essay annually. The regular practice of writing an essay which must be clear, logical, and concise, and the necessity of revising this essay again and again to achieve smoothness and hard hitting rhetoric will be of priceless value in his sermon writing. Furthermore, the small or large number of members of the circuit determines of course to some degree the number of essays that ought to be concluded within a specified time; but the circuit which finishes only three papers in two days is working at less than 50% efficiency. According to their whole character essays will be limited to 30, 45, 60, or 90 minutes.

Essay committees are with increasing number mimeographing a list of the assigned papers and sending a copy to each conference member. At times they also specify the rotation of the essays to provide variation. But every committee knows that it is a far cry from a mimeographed balanced list to a concluded list. And here is the rub.

Maintaining Balance Consistently

(a) By the creation and stimulation of interest.

When the committee has finally mailed the programs it can do little more than hope for the best. And this hope need not fail of accomplishment if, for one thing, essayists are interested in the theological field with which their essays deal. At times essayists ask for themes that have to do with a different department. An essayist who is interested in his theme will naturally work much harder than one who is not, and he will unquestionably have his essay promptly ready instead of permitting it to "age" for a year or two.

But just this creation and stimulation of interest appears to be a widespread problem. "How do other conferences succeed in holding interest?" one pastor asks. And the answer comes from the S.W. Minnesota Circuit, comprising 26 pastors. This circuit has solved this vexing problem by a method that deserves more than passing interest, since it creates and stimulates the necessary ambition. It appears below in condensed form.

The Southwest Minnesota Conference Method
By the Rev. C. Bramscher, Alpha, Minnesota

(1) Each conference member specifies the department in which he is particularly interested and prefers to study.
    His conference essays deal with this department.
(2) This method reveals abilities in men never suspected.
    It promotes interest in study and in conference essays.
    It aims to give each man a special life study.
    It facilitates the treatment of all fields of Theology.
(3) The Essay Committee acts as the balance wheel.
    Normally several men work in certain fields in complementary fashion; one has cont'd exegesis, the other unit exegesis. Etc.

This method appears sound, no matter from what angle it is studied, and it is worthy of general adoption. The writer has asked Pastor Bramscher to describe this system in detail and to cut a stencil. Kindly enclose postage with your request for a copy.

(b) By the use of a timed schedule.

There is probably no better way to maintain the originally planned balanced program than via the observance of a timed schedule. For one thing it eliminates the interest killing practice of carrying ordinary essays over two and even three sessions. The sessions of District Synods have amply attested the feasibility and expediency of such an arrangement. And after a few trials the Essay Committee will have learned how much time is advantageously consumed by discussion. Have the essay read in definite sections and divide the time for discussion accordingly. Normally the well written essay which exhausts its theme and the amount of discussion are inversely proportional.

A number of circuits are beginning of late to print or mimeograph experimentally such timed schedules and reveal no intention of returning to previous methods. The writer has sample schedules of the Freistatt Circuit in Southwest Missouri, the Effingham Circuit in Illinois, and the Southwest Circuit in Kansas. The balanced program is not a matter of mere theory, and the use of timed schedules is actually practiced and is working out in a satisfactory manner. If you wish to save yourself much experimentation, write for copies of 1939 spring conference schedules. Such may be obtained from the Rev. J. Grapatin of Monett, Mo., and from the writer. The name of the secretary of the Effingham Circuit is not known to the writer. Kindly enclose postage.

Suggestions for Essay Committees

1. Type or write theme, carefully defined, for every essayist.
2. Add explanatory or limiting notes. Suggest general time limit.
3. Present themes with choice of essayist to conference for approval.
4. Send out reminder cards after 60 days.
5. Inquire exact length of essays six weeks before conference.
6. Ask the Visitor, Secretary, and Pastor loci for announcements.
7. Mimeograph schedule; send out two weeks before date of conference.

Other Suggestions

Let the criticism of the sermon for criticism be prepared previously by another pastor to be delivered after the sermon has been read.

Have the questions in casuistry handed to the secretary in writing. A Committee on Casuistry will report toward the end of sessions.

Ask the essayist of an extensive paper to mimeograph outlines to facilitate understanding and attention.

An interesting and profitable item: Current events which influence the work of the church and of the ministry. These 15 minute essays are to be delivered as occasions of sufficient importance arise. Choose essayist carefully.

Sample Timed Schedule
Circuit Pastoral Conference, Location, Date

	A.M.	P.M.
Tuesday, November 7	9:00—12:00;	1:30—4:30
Wednesday, November 8	9:00—12:00;	1:30—3:30

Tuesday

A.M.

9:00— 9:30 Devotion, Preliminary business.

9:30—11:00 Exegesis on Matt, 7,15 and Rom. 16,17 (1 hr.) ....(essayist)
(Discussion 30 minutes)

11:00—12:00 The evil of religious confusion resulting from the practice of mixed marriages (45 min.).....(essayist)
(Discussion 15 minutes)

P.M.

1:30— 1:40 Devotion (Minutes).

1:40— 3:00 Historical essay on the Samaritans (1 hr.) ....(essayist)
(Discussion 20 minutes)

3:00— 3:10 Recess.

3:10— 3:30 Official matters, by the Visitor.

3:30— 4:00 Our practice over against the excommunicated who continues to attend our services (20 min.)...(essayist)
(Discussion 10 minutes)

4:00— 4:30 Catechesis on Q. 208: What Is Prayer? ....(essayist)

Wednesday

A.M.

9:00— 9:15 Devotion (Minutes).

9:15—10:15 Scriptural definition of False Prophet (40 min.) ....(essayist)
(Discussion 20 minutes)

10:15—10:45 Report of Committee on Casuistry ....(Com. Chr.)

10:45—10:55 Recess.

10:55—12:00 Relation of the doctrine of the invisible church to fraternal relations with other Christian church bodies (50 min.) ....(essayist)
(Discussion 15 minutes)

P.M.

1:30— 1:40 Devotion (Minutes).

1:40— 2:20 Sermon for criticism on Eph. 4,3-6.(essayist). Criticism, previously prepared, delivered ....(essayist)

2:20— 3:00 Book review, "The Christ of the Indian Road" ....(essayist)

3:00— 3:20 Current Events (inter-synodical). (essayist)

3:20 Minutes, Closing Devotion.

Special announcements by Pastor loci, Visitor, secretary.

II—The Unified Program
HERBERT M. DAENZER

Introductory

The Unified Program represents a type of program in which an inner relationship exists among its various component themes. The limits of this relation are defined in such a manner that the elements involved complete a scheme which appeals to one's esthetic sense and so effect harmony. But harmony in a conference program must of course justify its existence.

The basic reason for the harmonious character of the essays rests on the importance of gaining a cumulative effect. The well known "Steter Tropfen." The relentless impact of papers treating different but complementary aspects of the same subject will produce an indelible impression on all who are subjected to such a program. This constitutes the main purpose and one of the chief benefits of the Unified Program.

Many pastors undoubtedly prefer a type of program in which the essays are entirely unrelated, since it provides them with a great latitude in variety. But other pastors prefer variety within narrower limits. This matter is beyond argument. It is fruitless to censure anyone's personal preference.

Harmony As Now Applied

The principle of harmony is being applied successfully in the field of education. Educators have made efforts to weld the various school subjects together into a harmonious scheme known as the Unit Method. And its practical value is observed in schools where it is employed by expert teachers.

Furthermore, the principle of harmony is regularly applied by our pastors on Sundays, observable particularly on festivals. But also on the average Sunday, say the fifth Sunday after Easter, the text harmonizes with the topic of the Sunday which is Prayer. Hymns are selected that not only mark a progression of thought but that agree with the sermon. The collects and general prayer also conform to the theme for the day. Choir and organ selections should also have the same general character. This inner relationship of the different elements of the service provides both esthetic excellence and dignity. There is harmony with a purpose.

But can this principle also be applied to conferences? The fact is that the Unified Program is not unknown in this field. But it is used chiefly for Teachers' Conferences, Mixed Conferences, and conferences of our Associated Lutheran Charities. In 1938 a circuit pastoral conference planned an all-Centennial program for the fall of the year. But due to unforeseen circumstances the whole program could not be exhausted as projected. This program is given below.

Southeastern Circuit Conference (English)
(Special Centennial Topics)
The Founders of Synod as Scholars and Theologians
The Founders of Synod as Preachers
The Founders of Synod as Men of Piety
The Founders of Synod as Missionaries
The Founders of Synod as Musicians

Is There a Place for the Unified Program?

By reason of its very character this type of program permits the treatment of weighty problems and vital issues in all of their main phases at one time. In the customary type of program these are spread over a number of widely separated sessions and their relationship is lost sight of. As a matter of fact the vital issues which are before the church from time to time are ignored altogether too much. And still who would not like to have in his file seven or eight essays that deal thoroughly with the chief points, for instance of Church and State?

The use of the Unified Program represents the treatment of Theology from a new approach; but the success of this type of program in other conferences should give assurance that it is not unproductive of favorable results in the small pastoral conferences also. And these results may be realized, if a method to construct unified programs has been evolved, which is suited to Theology and logically sound. But is there such a method? Instead of one there are two such methods, the Topical Method and the Dogmatical Method.

The Topical Method

According to this method one chooses a properly bounded topic and lists under it such themes which are related to it. In practice the topic itself will usually undergo a series of revisions for proper limiting, and some of the themes will be too loosely related to the topic. Redefining of themes, combining several into one, and the discarding of others will be the ordinary experience. The remaining themes, possibly a score in number, will be divided according to the four theological departments, and from this fund a well rounded program of about seven themes may be arranged in which sameness and overlapping are avoided. The sample program given below illustrates these points.

Unity vs. Unionism

A. Exegesis on 2.Kings 5,15-19
   The Scriptural definition of False Prophet
B. Historical essay on the Samaritans
C. Relation of the doctrine of the invisible church to fraternal relations with other Christian church bodies
   The evil of religious confusion resulting from the practice of mixed marriages
D. Our practice over against the excommunicated who continues to attend our services
   Catechesis on Question 208, "What Is Prayer?"
   Book review, "The Christ of the Indian Road"
   S.S. demonstration, "Returned exiles rebuilding the temple"
   Sermon for criticism on Eph 4,3-6

The Topical Method may be employed to treat (in such group form) a great number of subjects. But it lends itself especially well for conference programs for problems of wide scope, vital issues, important occasions, and church anniversaries.

The Dogmatical Method

If pastoral conferences should intend to follow unified programs as a matter of general practice, it is evident that for the average session a different method ought to be employed. And since conference sessions have the prime purpose of providing a systematic post-graduate course in theological science, it is logical to construct programs upon limited sections of our Christian Dogmatics or of our synodical catechism.

Christian doctrines all have "sedes doctrinae", and these ought regularly receive exegetical treatment. Sacred and Church History are full of varied references to and aberrations from these doctrines. And church practice rests on doctrine or on the subjective opinions added to or replacing doctrine.

The use of the Dogmatical Method accordingly should provide one with a sufficiency of varied material in all four theological departments; but it will be considerably more difficult to obtain a variety of themes for the Unified Program than for the customary type. It will require extensive study and searching in reference works of all kinds.

Let us for example select "Holy Scripture" from our Dogmatics, Question 5 in the catechism, and on this general theme select related essays. The type of program which the writer has in mind may be illustrated as given below.

Holy Scripture

A. Exegesis on Psalm 19
   Variant readings; origin, influence, and relation to Inspiration
B. The cause of the rise of the Jewish nation
   Substantiation of the deluge by archeology
C. Scriptural authority vs. that of tradition and "papal infallibility"
   The chief error of all non-Christian sacred books
D. In what manner does the influence of the doctrine of inspiration cause Lutheran preaching to be distinct?
   Catechesis on Questions 1-6
   Orthodoxy and heterodoxy in hymns on "God's Word"
   Sermon for criticism on Hebrews 5,1-14

The Gathering of Material

Because of the character of the Unified Program the gathering of the material is of necessity not a hunting for new themes but a systematic search for themes that are related to a certain subject. And this complicates matters. The following procedure ought, however, give assurance of satisfactory results (list all source material, by the way):

1. Read up on the subject in your Dogmatics; also in heterodox books.
2. Look up Eckhardt's Real-lexicon on related subjects.
3. Look up the subjects in Religious Encyclopedia and Bible Dictionary.
4. Check through your Isagogics in suggested portions.
5. Subscribe to magazines on Archeology, Religious Digest, etc.
6. Study indices to Luther's Works, Pastoral Theology, Lutheraner, Lutheran Witness, C. T. Monthly, Lehre und Wehre, etc.
7. Reserve necessary envelopes in your file.

"Compel Them To Come In," Luke 19, 23

P. L. BORNHOEFT

TO reach out to the new-comer in a city is the duty of the church. These are to be found. How?

There is a congregation in Cedar Rapids, Ia., Trinity Lutheran, of the Missouri Synod, which makes it a point to welcome the new-comer. The Guide and Credit Bureau of the city issues a weekly bulletin with all the names and addresses of the new-comers in the city. The publicity committee mails to each new-comer a letter as follows:

TRINITY EVANGELICAL LUTHERAN CHURCH
CEDAR RAPIDS, IOWA

Dear Friend:—

We welcome you to Cedar Rapids and trust you will soon feel at home in our city.

We all love and cherish our home where our family dwells and where kindness and sunshine welcome us after a toilsome day. The word "home" means rest, peace, happiness. You have perhaps left a dear home and now find the city a cold place, because of dear friends far away. Soon you will be readjusted and the new home will be a real home again. Your door will be a harbor which shuts out the world of strife—when it is your home.

Our homes are only temporal abodes; they are to be a preparatory place for the home above—heaven. The door of our home is ever to remind us of the door to heaven, which is Christ. He declares: "I am the door." Here our families often gather for a reunion; will we meet in our grand reunion in heaven? This is what we are living for.

It is our duty as well as our pleasure to make you feel at home in Cedar Rapids and thus we invite you to our place of worship, Trinity Lutheran. We are always pleased to welcome new-comers. Let us link your home with our church-home, provided you are not affiliated elsewhere, and let us, as friends, gather in faith around Him of Whom we sing "The best friend to have is Jesus."

Again we welcome you to Trinity Lutheran.

Sincerely yours,

P. L. BORNHOEFT,
Pastor

When the visitor looks up the church and attends the services, it is the practice of this particular pastor to extend a welcome to all visitors from the lectern after he has made his announcements in this wise: "We bid all our visitors welcome to Trinity Lutheran. The doors of this church are open to every one. If you are without a church-home, Trinity Lutheran welcomes you." The personal welcome extended *before* the sermon puts the visitor at ease and it is likely he will come again. In this church he does come again.

As the service closes, the congregation singing the last verse gives the pastor a chance to shed his gaion and make his way to the front of the church to shake hands with all as they file out. As the new-comer or visitor passes the minister he is given a special welcome and is requested to enter his name in the registration book, which is found on a small desk in the vestibule of the church. A neatly framed placard with two arrows pointing downward to registration book reads: "Visitors Please Register." As high as 20 names have been entered on a Sunday. These new people receive a letter during the week which reads as follows:

TRINITY EVANGELICAL LUTHERAN CHURCH
CEDAR RAPIDS, IOWA
Cedar Rapids, Iowa

Dear Friend:—

We are pleased to have had you as a visitor in our services at Trinity Lutheran. We herewith invite you to come again.

Christian religion is a tonic which is administered through the Word of God to rejuvenate our soul and spirit. It helps us to go on with our problems in life. It assists us to live our life joyfully, regardless of its reserves. Religion was not intended by our Savior Jesus Christ to make us morose

and melancholy, but to instill the note of rejoicing. "Rejoice in the Lord alway and again I say rejoice."

Our house plants are much refreshed by a light rain. The pores are opened and the fresh green is restored. Your soul needs the refreshing rain of the Word of God. Your spiritual life will be refreshed, helping you to smile. The influence of the Gospel will help you to see that life is worth living. You will have a different outlook. Life will be different; people will be different; your home environment will be different; your problems will be different, seeming much lighter because you are different. It is all different because you have learned to say: "My faith looks up to Thee, oh Lamb of Calvary."

We were not created to pine our life away in seclusion. "It is not good that man should be alone." We need the contact of our friends. We invite your family to attend our "Family Club," which meets on the last Friday of every month at 7:45 p.m., in the Church Assembly Hall, Third Avenue and Fourteenth Street West. May we welcome you at our services again.

With kind greetings,

THE WELCOME COMMITTEE,
Chairman

The publicity committee, of course, mails out these letters. In the week following, or later, the pastor makes his call. In case he does not find the people at home he leaves not just a calling card, but a welcome to Trinity Lutheran card.

Does the stranger come? Since July the registration book has been in use and to date, Nov. 17, 1929—281 new-comers and visitors entered their names.

Do people come to the adult catechumen class? They do. And when they come they are presented with Dr. Dallmann's Catechism For Very Busy People. The catechetical method is used—not the lecture method, for it is only by the former that a real benefit is gained. Thus this congregation compels them to come in.

Following Up Newcomers After They Have Left Our Church Doors

F. P. WILHELM

WE gladly comply with the request to write a few lines on a follow-up system introduced some time ago in a mission congregation in New York City. In the mission in question there are newcomers almost every Sunday, sometimes quite a number.

In all follow-up work much valuable time is lost if the addresses given on follow-up cards are not thoroughly reliable with regard to spelling of names, correctness of street and apartment numbers, whether the person to be visited is a Mr., a Mrs., or a Miss, etc.

Most of these difficulties are overcome by the use of a church guest book. Ours is a well bound book, worthy of the purpose it serves. Lying open upon a stand near the entrance of the church, with pencil ready for use and a sign reading: "Please enter your name in our Guest Book," it catches the eye of newcomers. In some instances they comply and enter their names and addresses. But the chief purpose of the sign is to prepare strangers for the request, usually made after the close of the service, that they give us their names and addresses. Our ministers know that especially in large cities people not infrequently are quite unwilling to give their addresses. They do not wish to be followed up, for many different reasons. Some wish to slip into the church unnoticed and to slip out in the same manner. They do not wish to be spoken to, neither by the pastor nor by anyone else, much less do they wish to be asked for their names and addresses. But these are, after all, rather the exceptions. Most first-timers, no matter who they are or where they come from, greatly appreciate a friendly greeting by someone, either by the pastor, or by the members, or, better still, by both.

In our case, the pastor after the service is always at the church door, chiefly for the purpose of greeting strangers and securing their addresses for future missionary or other friendly and helpful calls. The regularly appointed guest book secretary, in our case one of the deacons, who by this time has gained considerable experience, is standing at the foot of the stairs near the exit doors of the building. The pastor standing at the top of the short stairway calls down to the secretary: "Mr. R. these two young ladies, both from Atlanta, Georgia, will be glad to have you enter their names and New York City addresses in our guest book," or "Mr. Secretary, this is Mr. Miller and his young daughter, both of Inwood. Mr. Miller lives in your neighborhood. Please introduce yourself. In making the entry please do not fail to give the apartment,—eighty families, you know, live in 120 Vermilyea Avenue, or, "Here are two new neighbors who, I think, will be glad to enter their names in our guest book, or have you enter them," etc.

We avoid using the word stranger, as much as possible, especially in the hearing of the people. There is something cold in the sound of the word. What we desire to do is make them feel that they are not strangers, and having attended one of our services they are, indeed, no longer strangers.

Most first-time follow-up calls are made by the pastor, but some are assigned to members, especially, too, the second-time calls. Women with some missionary experience and the love of the Savior in their hearts make excellent church visitors. Calls upon young people, again mostly the second-time calls, are as a rule assigned to young people, mostly to Walther Leaguers, calls upon men to men.

As practical helps we use follow-up cards. The following is written (later on it is to be multigraphed or printed) upon 3" x 5" index cards:

Record of Visits

Date................

Dear Fellow Worker:

Please visit as soon as possible ....

Name ....

Address ....

Reason and purpose ....

and report to the pastor, soon, please. Thanks in advance!

Pastor.

Report on visit ....

Date of visit ....Visitor.

If the result is good the regular mailing address is written on the unused side of the card, and it is, with all the information on the reverse side intended for later visits, added to the mailing list. If the results do not as yet warrant the adding to the mailing and visiting lists, the card is filed under "mission material," for future visits.

In conclusion, we add a suggestion. We suggest a return post card, to be used in continuing follow-up work, containing the following wording:

"Faith cometh by hearing, and hearing by the word of God."—Romans 10, 17.

..........................19......

M....................

I desire very much to have you go to Church with me this coming Sunday. The service begins at .... A. M. P. M.

I shall be glad to call for you at your home about ....

Will you go? Sincerely yours,

INVITATION

"Enter into His gates with thanksgiving, and into his courts with praise: Be thankful unto Him and bless His name."

..........................19......

M....................

Dear friend:

I shall be glad to go with you. Please call for me at

....

Sincerely yours,

REPLY

(These cards are obtainable from the Lutheran Press, 239 West 28th Street, New York, at $1.00 per hundred.)

The most important part of mission work is the right kind of follow-up work. It is at this point where we often "fall down." We ask our brother pastors and other fellow workers whether this is not the case. One of the reasons is that follow-up calls are more difficult and often more discouraging than first-time calls, house-to-house canvass calls and other similar calls.

The news service of the National Lutheran Council reports the following interesting experience:

ONE PASTOR'S SUCCESS SECRET

Several years ago a young man in seminary founded a congregation in a small community suburban to New York City. He served the congregation faithfully and eagerly for nearly six years, erecting a fine church edifice and establishing the Lutheran Church firmly in a rapidly growing section now quite populous. Much of his success was due to cordial relationship maintained with the newspapers and through them with the general public. When he left to accept his second charge in another city, editors of two newspapers in two neighboring cities wrote him their "regrets." One of them wrote:

"It has been a pleasure on my part to cooperate with you and your church. I wish that every individual and organization were as easy to work with. Please accept my personal wishes for your continued success in your new field. We shall be glad to receive news items concerning the activities there which would interest your friends here."

The other wrote: "On the eve of your departure from ...., which is a source of regret to me, may I not say that during your stay at .... Church, your cooperation with this paper has set a standard never before equaled by any minister in our field. Newspapers and newspaper men are human, a fact not always taken into consideration by those outside the profession, and we do, quite often, as we would be done by when one like yourself cooperates with well prepared, adequate and promptly supplied copy, the doors and the arms are opened wide. Feeling that the press and the church should stand shoulder to shoulder for the things that are best and against the things that are bad, it is a pleasure to me to find a minister willing to come half way. They are extremely rare." The pastor had never met in person the editor who wrote this letter. The publicity which appeared featured the great work of the Church of Christ and told its story in a fashion which fascinated the reading public.

LUTHERAN TENT SERVICES

J. W. Behnken

The Mission Society of Missouri Synod Lutheran Churches in Houston, Texas has hit upon a plan to start new missions which may be of interest to the readers of the American Lutheran. First of all they look about to find a part of the city in which a church might be located. The people of the mother church who happen to live in that part of the city are then urged to form the nucleus of the new mission. Next the district is canvassed for Sunday School children. If this meets with any success a Sunday School is started in temporary quarters, a hall, a school auditorium, or even a private home. Then the Mission Society appeals to the District Mission Board to call a missionary for the field. As soon as notice is received that the missionary is coming, preparations are made to give proper publicity to this fact.

The reader perhaps thinks by this time that there is nothing unusual about this method, for the same thing is done in many other places. But when I tell you now in what these preparations for proper publicity consist you will agree that the method is somewhat out of the ordinary in our circles, in fact so much out of the ordinary that some well meaning brother has felt it necessary to warn against the "modernistic" tendencies of the people in Houston. Before I enter upon an answer to charges which are made against this plan I must tell you what the plan really is.

The Mission Society rents a tent large enough to provide seating room for about 300-400 people. Then it secures some rough lumber to fix rough benches. Of course, a committee arranges for topics and speakers for the services, another committee sees to it that the services are properly advertised by placing large signs at prominent street corners in the section where the services are to be conducted, by distributing handbills which announce all of the topics to be discussed and the speakers who will deliver the sermons, by furnishing the newspapers with proper material to give due publicity to the services to be held, etc. Another committee solicits free will offerings from our Lutheran people to defray the costs of the undertaking. All members of the Society begin to talk and to work for the success of the services. Of course, the matter is taken to the Lord in prayer both by the individual members as well as by the Society in its meetings and by the congregations at the time when announcements are made.

Such Tent Services have now been held twice, two consecutive years. At every service there is a goodly amount of singing by the congregation. A chaplain, who has charge of the services, who also introduces the speaker for the evening, leads the singing. The hymns used are taken from the Sunday School Hymnal. There is a reading of an appropriate Scripture lesson, after which all are asked to join in the confession of the Apostles' Creed. There is always a special selection of music, either choir or quartet or duet or solo. Of course, the kernel of the whole service is the sermon, which deals with *fundamental* or practical matters. Just by way of example the list of topics for the services which were held this year from Sept. 15th to 26th every night excepting Saturday might be mentioned:

"The Book of Books"
"What Think Ye of Christ"
"Faith or Works?"
"Hell—What Is It?"
"Almost Persuaded"
"Come Thou with Us and
     We Will Do Thee Good"
"   "

"Too radical a departure," "Too much like a revival," "Too sectarian" are some of the comments. We admit that the idea originated when the writer attended a revival meeting. But are we going to condemn every method which is employed successfully by others? Does the mere fact that others do it make it wrong? Must we not admit that many are drawn to services at a tent who cannot be persuaded to attend services held at church? If you are in doubt about this, just try it. Are not the sermons which are delivered, the hymns which are sung, in fact the whole service which is conducted soundly Lutheran? Did not some of our forefathers meet for services in lodge rooms, dance halls and the like when they could find no more appropriate place? Is it wrong then to meet under a tent? Is it wrong to bring people under the influence of the Word of God and perhaps give them the start to go to services regularly in such a manner simply because sectarians use tents for sensational revivals, sensational methods, sensational sermons and have their "saw dust trails," "mourners' benches," etc?

Such services are certainly good means of publicity. If the handbills are distributed, the large signs are erected and other publicity employed, the services will become well advertised. Many will attend the services who could not be persuaded to come into a Lutheran Church building. They will take home a far different impression of the Lutheran Church services than they entertained before this. The very fact that the Lutheran Tent Services are so different from the revivals which play so much upon the emotions of people causes such people to notice the difference. They tell you that they do. Again, some comment upon the fine order during the services, the good conduct of the young people, even the fine behavior of the children who attend. They may not name it so, but they realize that the Lutheran service is something solemn in which every respect is given the Word of God. They notice also that the Lutheran Church insists upon the preaching of the Word of God in all of its truth and purity. What they notice they tell unto others. They help to advertise. They bring others with them. They urge people to "come and see." The result of all of this is that there is hardly a person in the community where the mission is started who does not know that we are in the field.

Such services help the missionary who is working in the particular field. He should be present at the services and be introduced publicly to the audience. Before and after the services he has opportunity to meet the strangers. Thus he can get acquainted with many who will readily know his purpose in speaking to them and will manifest an altogether different attitude toward him than if he sought to get acquainted with them at their homes. When later the missionary makes calls at such homes he finds people whom he knows and who will welcome him because they know him as a missionary and need not fear that he is a book agent or some other sort of solicitor. Such people in turn will help him to get acquainted with others who are not going to church, who are not sending their children to Sunday School etc. In short the missionary is given opportunity to get a mailing list of reasonably good prospects.

Such services are good for our own people. Since the sermons will naturally be such as to urge people to accept Christ and to acquaint them with true Bible doctrine, they will inspire our own people to greater missionary activities. They will help to arouse Lutheran consciousness within them. But above all such service will give them an opportunity to do something for their Lord and for their Church. There are many details which must receive attention. These are placed into the hands of laymen, who thus learn to do some active work for their Church. The venture offers them an opportunity to speak to others, to invite them to the services, and thus to do some personal mission work. It helps them to become not merely church-goers but also missionaries, not merely faithful benchwarmers but also active church workers, not merely satisfied church-members but also enthusiastic soul-winners. The writer feels that we Lutherans need to devote more thought to this phase of church work. We should offer more opportunities to our people for personal mission work and show them how to go about it. To be sure we need the preaching of God's Word to win souls. But we need to have more Philips who will tell the Nathanaels: "Come and see." We need Samaritan women who will leave their waterpots to tell others: "Come, see a man, which told me all things that ever I did: is not this the Christ?" We need more and more people who will not merely "come and see" but also "go and tell." Upon the personal mission work of our Lutheran church members much of the success of our Home Mission work will depend. Let us then put our people to work. Let us train them for the work. Let us give them opportunities to work. They will surprise us with their willingness and their ability.

An Evangelistic Visitation Campaign

FRED H. LINDEMANN

EVANGELIZATION is not something that can be done effectively only in spasms, in fits and starts. It dare not be a spasmodic effort, extending over a week or two, to be laid on the shelf again for the remainder of the year. The work which Christ has commanded is to be done constantly and persistently, throughout the year. When a campaign is suggested in this article the thought is not that this is to be an isolated effort. It must be remembered that in a previous article it was stated that we are facing a peculiar situation and condition and a campaign of visitation is to deal with this situation. Our people are laboring under the mistaken idea that they can not do personal mission work, that it is impossible for them to do the kind of work which has proved itself to be so effective at Christ's time, in the early Church, and whenever it has been undertaken since. Our problem is to convince our people that they can employ the personal method effectively, to demonstrate to them that Christ can do just as much through them today as He did through others centuries ago. So a campaign is proposed for demonstration purposes. When the campaign is over and our people have learned that everybody is able to do this work, it will not be necessary to organize another such effort. Rather the life of the congregation will be one continuous, uninterrupted campaign for Christ and souls. People who have once realized and felt the marvelous power exercised through them, who have learned to know the satisfaction and exultation that comes with the exercise of that power within them, will never cease to campaign for Christ. The rest of their life will be one continuous campaign.

So to demonstrate that all who have learned to know Christ can do personal work successfully and effectively a campaign is organized. The first requirement is a list of prospects. This is not to be a canvass of the neighborhood. The names and addresses of the people to be visited are written on cards. Surely every pastor has a list of prospects. There are the parents of children in the Sunday school, members of families who are not identified with the church, people whom we have met at baptisms and funerals and other occasions. It ought not be difficult to prepare a lengthy list of prospects. The fact that the pastor has already approached these people, perhaps frequently, should not deter us from placing them on this list. The fact that it was the pastor who made the previous visit perhaps robbed that visit of fifty per cent. of its effectiveness, because the pastor is supposed to make such visits, they are looked upon as more or less professional. But we are planning to send some tired business man to make the next visit, some man who could have no possible interest in giving up his evening but to win the prospect. The fact that the visitor is not a pastor will impress.

The next requirement is a number of people to act as visitors. It is suggested that they be enrolled privately rather than by asking for volunteers. If we ask for volunteers we will have the same people come forward whom we are accustomed to see in every endeavor, that little band which always does the work. But we are engaging in an endeavor which is to demonstrate the ability of everybody to do a certain work. This demonstration will lose in effectiveness on the congregation as a whole if only experienced workers are engaged. We need at last some who have never taken a prominent part. We also need the timid, backward man and woman. We want some who find it impossible to speak fluently, who can speak only haltingly. We want every kind of people. So we had better choose them and enroll them privately. We will probably meet with horrified refusals. The inevitable "I can't do that" will be heard constantly. To overcome this hesitancy it will be necessary to say that any visitor is at liberty to withdraw at any stage of the undertaking, before the first visit is made, after the first visit, any time. It is wise to assure these timid ones that you will not hold it against them if they withdraw. Never shall a word be lost about it. It is safe to make such an offer and promise because when once the campaign is under way no visitor will withdraw. It is then that the Holy Spirit gets busy, men and women are fascinated by the power which they are exerting,

they feel that supreme satisfaction which comes to all who truly follow Jesus, the inner joy which the Master has promised. Our visitors will return hilariously happy and exclaim with the disciples of old: "Even the devils are subject unto us in thy name!" To assure efficiency it will be best to ask all visitors to sign a card stating that they will attend all meetings and to give every evening of one week to this work.

With this preliminary work done there follows a period of preparation and instruction for the visitors. This might extend over a week with a meeting every second evening. With the beginning of this week every other activity in the church comes to a complete standstill. All other meetings are dropt, nothing is permitted to interfere. Aside from the fact that this interruption of the usual activities will assure the attendance of every visitor it serves to impress the whole congregation with the importance of the work to be undertaken.

The following Sunday the week of actual visitation will be ushered in by a special prayer and consecration service. It is vital that our endeavor be brought to the attention of every member, for we are giving a demonstration and this demonstration will be lost upon every one who does not see it. In this service the visitors will be commissioned and the congregation asked to spend the week in prayer for the success of the campaign.

In the afternoon of this Sunday the final meeting with the visitors takes place. They will gather for a few words of encouragement and for prayer. It is at the close of this meeting that the breaking point is reached with most visitors' nerves and courage. So we must insist most strenuously that they go from their chair in the meeting directly to the first house to be visited. They must not pause a moment, they dare not stop to talk with their best friend. The object is to have them push the first doorbell and make the first visit before their courage breaks.

And now follows a week of intensive work. The visitors go out in pairs, never alone, in order that one may supplement the other. Jesus had excellent reasons for sending out the Twelve and the Seventy by two and two. The purpose of the visit is to have the prospect put his signature on a card stating that he acknowledges Christ as his Master and Lord, is willing to conform his life to his Master's will, to this end will identify his person with Christ's institution, the Church, and will on a stated day present himself to be accepted as a member. It is vital that the visitors leave the prospect at least as kindly disposed toward the Church as he was when they came. They must never offend, they must never become abusive. They must leave the door open for the next visitor if they should prove unsuccessful in procuring that signature.

A big feature of the week's campaign is the visitors' supper every evening. Our workers come directly to the church and are not to go home when they return from their daily occupation. These suppers with all present mean much. Let us imagine a man who has had no success on the previous day and is on the verge of withdrawing. He happens to sit next to a man who has had one or two or three cards signed. It may happen that the successful visitor has not the gifts and personality and ability he knows himself to have. He will tell himself that if his neighbor was able to succeed he can do it too. These meals serve to encourage and stimulate. It is well to have a few state briefly some encouraging experience. After a short prayer and a few inspiring words by the leader the visitors go out again.

If the campaign is of only one week's duration the following Sunday or perhaps the second Sunday, if preferred, can be made to be a red letter day. The service will never be forgotten. Let us say that twenty-five teams have been sent out and each team should have gained only one soul. Yet by having the visitors lead their one convert into the chancel we have seventy-five people massed before the congregation. Each convert is welcomed personally and by name. It is not possible for us to accept a member by a handshake. If he has been confirmed in his youth he may be welcomed and invited to partake of Holy Communion with us on the following Sunday. People in need of instruction may be welcomed and invited to join the adult class which is to be organized during the week.

The campaign may be closed with a social arranged in honor of the new members to give them an opportunity to become acquainted. This is often considered unnecessary, but it offers the only occasion to have them meet their new brothers and sisters. And let us not forget that we are out to impress the whole congregation, we are after a certain psychological effect. So make the welcoming social a big affair.

It must be understood that the appeals to be used by the visitors are such and are used so as not to offend. An opening must be left for another visit by a different person. One appeal should be used only in the rarest case and that is the one so popular with some preachers years ago, the appeal to escape the wrath to come and damnation. The only thing against it is that it is not successful in the majority of cases, and that is sufficient reason why it should not be used. Furthermore, we are not out to scare people into identifying themselves with the church. Should we find that death has very recently entered the home it may be well to exhort that preparation be made for the Hereafter. Here death has recently made the other world seem very near and an appeal to be sure of that world may succeed.

By and large we will find that the people we are dealing with may be classified under two heads, such as at one time were members of some church or still consider themselves members of a church not in our community, and such as were never members anywhere. The first thing to do in every case is to announce our errand and try to enter the home. If we are not invited upon stating our reason for coming we will say: "We will take but a few moments of your time. May we please come in and go over the matter with you?" The next thing would be to ask: "Have you ever been a member of any Christian church?" If he was a member in some other place we might say: "Give us the information and our pastor will send for your letter of transfer." Never ask them to send for it or ask any questions which might admit of the possibility that there are two sides to the matter of church transfer. Sentimental reasons may cause the man to hesitate. Suggest that the pastor back there at the old church will be glad to have them be active in the cause of the Church in their community. He may have felt that they cherished his membership back there, when as a matter of fact, any pastor feels that is doing a person the very best service by getting him related to the church in the community where he lives. This argument usually brings his permission to get the transfer.

If we find that the man has never been a member of any church, we proceed by asking some direct questions to discover just what his attitude is toward Christ and the Church. If his attitude is friendly, we insist in a tactful, gracious manner, to get an immediate decision. Is he willing to accept Jesus Christ as his Savior, and to confess Him as his Lord and Master? Does he receive and profess the Christian faith as contained in the New Testament? Does he realize what is Christ's attitude toward the Church, His Bride? Will he help carry out Christ's entire program? Will he unite with the church and will he present himself for membership upon a definite Sunday? If we find that he is more difficult to win than we supposed we make one of several appeals.

There is the appeal to conscience. Every man knows the difference between right and wrong. So we would ask a father: "Would you like to live in a community where there were no schools?" and remind him that our schools are the product of the Christian Church. "Would you care to live in a community where there was no system of jurisprudence?" and suggest to him that this has many protective features which have been fostered and nurtured in the Christian Church. And so we would continue to mention every feature of our civilization, hospitals, institutions, everything he enjoys. Then we would directly and frankly impress him with the fact that he is demanding a certain kind of social environment, which is in a real sense Christian, in which to live and rear his children; that this demand makes him mutually responsible with every other person in the community who makes a like demand; that

just at present he seems to be assuming that somebody else will carry his religious responsibility; that this really is not the thing he would choose to do when he realizes that he is doing it. We will indicate to him that the only way to perpetuate any institution is to invest personality in it. We will ask him if he does not think it perfectly fair to expect him to put his life into the Church if he desires the continuance of the kind of environment which he now demands in the community.

If we are dealing with a youth we will attempt to persuade him that he is not using his time and talents properly and ask him if he is not preparing himself for some really constructive and altruistic purpose in the world, whether he is using his physical strength, his mental ability, and the influence of his personality for the purpose that God intended, whether he is really fair to himself, to others, and to his Heavenly Father.

Another appeal is that for a Christian home. This is a tender and beautiful appeal. It is almost unfailing when, with a little child on our knee, we ask father and mother if they would not do anything on earth that is possible and legitimate to secure the spiritual and moral standards of the little one. If there are children present, we start with them, beginning with the smallest who can intelligently answer our questions. We next take the older and then the mother and only last the father. This is undoubtedly the best method. It might be argued that if we gain the head of the house we have gained all, but the same is true if we do not gain him. If we fail to gain him when we approach him last, we have the rest of the family. And our successful beginning is assured if we approach the little ones first.

Naturally our visitors will have to meet many objections. Some of these can be anticipated and discussed during the preparatory period. One of these is: "I will think it over." We must discover whether the man saying this is just trying to dodge the appeal, or whether he really does desire time for further consideration. Nine times out of ten he is simply attempting to postpone his decision. He has thought it over and now is the time to act upon the thing he already believes. If he is sincere in his wish for further consideration we make a definite date for a return call.

If our prospect says: "WE may move," we tell him that this is a good reason why he should make his Christian decision. He ought to declare for Christ in his old community so that his acquaintances may know of it. A transfer is readily made if he should move after that. There are many families on the verge of moving all the time.

Another prospect might say: "There are too many hypocrites in the Church." We will admit it frankly. The Church is subject to the same weaknesses as any other human institution. The question, however, is not a responsibility for the inconsistency, weaknesses, and sins of some in the Church, but his own responsibility for his religious obligations. The question that faces him is whether religion is important to him, whether he believes in the reality of Christ, whether he should actually confess his faith in Jesus Christ as his Savior, whether he can be true to Christ and stay outside of the institution that Jesus loved so much and made the instrument of His will. We are not responsible for the other man's failure. We are responsible for our influence and for the perpetuation of the Christian Church, if we believe in the superiority of Jesus as a religious leader.

Again the question might be put to us: "Can I not be good without joining the Church?" This really is not the question at all. We are not particularly interested in just how good a person can be outside of the Church. But if a person is good outside of the Church, he should immediately thank the Church for his goodness. Every moral standard he has, was either made and then lifted up by the Church, or else it was found and filled full of life and significance by it. He has received what he has of morality because others were willing to perpetuate a religious environment and the Christian Church. Surely he will be willing and glad to pass on to posterity the things that he has received by putting his life in the Church. If he is really a good man he will meet Christ's attitude and accept it as authority.

My Assistant Missionaries

PHILIPP LANGE

GOD WANTS EVERY Christian congregation to be a center of missionary activity. It dare not be satisfied with the regular routine service of the Lord's Day, a session of the Sunday school, and perhaps a poorly attended midweek service. It must make a definite and systematic effort, through an efficient and willing force, to reach out into the masses surrounding its place of worship, that it may discover their spiritual needs and furnish the required relief.

Why should not a church in the midst of a teeming population be a hive of activity all the while, week days as well as Sundays, making use of every legitimate gospel means to win old and young for Christ and for eternity? Why should it not have, besides its pastor, a host of volunteer helpers to come into personal touch with, and to do individual work among those who are in the immediate neighborhood and who most need such effort? What great results could be accomplished if every member of all our congregations would realize that it is his or her duty as well as that of the pastor to seek and win erring souls. It is true that the pastor has been called to the congregation to visit the unchurched, but he is greatly handicapped in his mission labors if his parishioners are not mission-minded, if they will not assist him in this very important and most productive department of church service.

A volume of sermons by Sam Jones contains a picture illustrating one of his famous perpetrations. A preacher, emaciated, underfed and threadbare, is struggling between the shafts of a long wagon that is loaded up with the whole church, steeple and back-steps, the entire congregation plus an assortment of hangers-on. The preacher is doing all the pulling and the others are doing all the riding. There they are—laughing, talking, smoking, reading, necking, scrapping, some of them sound asleep, some of them enjoying the scenery, some of them not enjoying anything, and all of them often crying out, "Get up! Move faster!" The picture is true to life in many of our congregations, especially with reference to soul-winning work.

Every member of the congregation—an assistant missionary. That is our ideal and perhaps some day the ideal will be realized, but it is not being realized today, and I am dealing not with the future but with the present. My assistant missionaries are the assistant missionaries of every mission-minded pastor.

1. *My assistant missionaries are filled to overflowing with love for lost souls.* God has stirred them to a sense of their duty in this respect. They are not carelessly drifting along in their church life, unconcerned about souls around them. They have a burning love for immortal souls. Love begets action. When men love they begin doing things. If I can get the members of my congregation to a point where they love souls as they should, a mission revival is sure to follow. Love knows no restraint. Those who brought the man to Jesus on a cot and let him down through the roof undoubtedly loved the man. They had all sorts of obstacles to encounter, but they were determined to get this poor cripple to Jesus, for they knew He could give the needed help. When this love gains proper headway in my congregation, then souls are being brought to Jesus. Love knows no impossibility. A great number of men were entombed in a coal-mine, and great crowds gathered to help clear away the earth and rescue the miners. An old, gray-headed man came running up, and, seizing a shovel, began working with the strength of ten men. Some one asked to relieve the old man. "Get out of the way," he cried, "I have two boys down there." My Christian workers, whose hearts throb with love to Christ, will exert themselves to the utmost to rescue from sin those who have been purchased by His blood.

2. *My assistant missionaries are those who pray daily and fervently for their pastor.* They know that he needs the intercessions of his people, that he may be fully equipped to reach and win the erring and lost, and to be ever courageous and hopeful in the face of bitter disappointments and repeated rebuffs. They know what the prayers of saints meant to the great missionary Paul. He was a most gifted student. He was inspired to write more epistles than any other. God appeared to him in visions, saying, "Fear not, for I am with thee!" In eloquence he could stand by the side of the greatest orators of ancient or modern times he was a master in the field of debate. Yet this very man begged those to whom he ministered to pray for him and was greatly encouraged and strengthened by the prayers of others.

My assistant missionaries pray also for themselves that God would direct their mind, give them the right words to speak, help them choose the proper tactics in winning a soul. They cannot hope to be successful in their mission endeavors if they have not learned to pray God that when they address their churchless neighbor he might see the error of his way, break away from the grip of sin, cry penitently for deliverance, and that when he hears the gospel he may be eager to accept the same and to be saved through the same.

What spiritual triumphs the early Christians witnessed; but the secret of it all was that "they continued steadfastly in prayers." Why is it that today many of our church members have so little courage and so little power to win others to Christ? They neglect prayer. Nothing is more essential to evangelistic work than prayer. Prayer will generate a spiritual atmosphere in the individual life. The prayers of many will generate a spiritual atmosphere in a community. In answer to prayer the Holy Spirit will produce such fervid conviction of sin that sinners will cry out, as on the day of Pentecost, "Men and brethren, what shall we do?" My people that have attended Christ's school of prayer and have learned the paramount lesson of giving themselves continually to prayer can sometimes accomplish more on their knees than on their feet.

3. *My assistant missionaries personally approach the churchless man and call his attention to the needs of his soul.* There is no greater crime committed by men than to have truth in their possession and refuse to pass it on. The world demands that its men of great wealth shall use such wealth in a benevolent spirit. A physician who knew a complete remedy for tuberculosis but refused to reveal it would be branded as public enemy number one of human society. The world needs a message of God more than it needs money or physical healing. Many sinners will never hear and accept the message of salvation unless delivered by the lay members of the church. Countless numbers never go to church; never read the Bible; never pray. My parishioners are in duty bound to make the community in which they live less ungodly, and the only way they can do it is to reach the hearts of the ungodly, and point out to them the error and folly of their ways. They realize that personal work is required, that personal testimony is necessary. They go out after that individual sinner, who has never repented of his sins and professed faith in Christ, or who has drifted away from the church and needs to be aroused from his sleep of carelessness and be brought back on the path of salvation. They speak to him directly and plainly about his responsibility to God, warn him to flee from "the wrath to come," and plead with him to come to the foot of the cross and accept Him who alone can save him from the wrath of God and eternal perdition. They invite him to accompany them to the services of their church. Once there, they will see to it that the newcomer

meets quite a few of the members, in order that he may feel at home in the house of the Lord. They will, if necessary, pilot him through the order of the service that he may participate in the liturgy and singing of the hymns. After the service they converse with their neighbor about the sermon that has been delivered and about church life in general to discover how he stands on the entire religious question. And they keep their pastor in close touch with the situation that they may work together on the case to final success.

4. *My assistant missionaries assist me by distributing the printed word.* The circulation of tracts and other publications will help to advertise the Christian religion. Other denominations have realized this before we Lutherans have. They have been "tracting" the country for many years. Not a few sinners have attributed their conversion to the reading of some piece of Christian literature. It may have been but a little leaflet, yet the Holy Spirit used it to awaken the sleeping conscience and to arouse the prodigal to arise and seek an injured Father's face. My colporteurs are furnished with a new supply of literature every month. There is a tract fund in the congregation which provides all necessary printed material. And thus not only the pastor but also the lay members are able to accomplish something for God and His church. It makes no difference to God how a soul gets in touch with the gospel message, whether through the spoken or through the printed word, so long as he gets the message and learns the way of salvation.

An agent of the American Tract Society relates the following: "A man on a canal-boat received a tract, but to show his contempt for the tract and its giver, took out his penkife and cut it up into fantastic shapes. Then he held it up to the derision of the company. In tearing it apart, one of the pieces clung to his knee. His eyes were attracted by the only word on it—"eternity." He turned it over, and there was the word "God." These ideas remained in his mind. He tried to laugh them off, then to drink, to play cards in order to banish them. But they still clung to him, and plagued him till he sought God and preparation for eternity."

5. *The daily life of my assistant missionaries is such as does not repel but rather draws people to their religion.* The church of Christ is much like an illustrated magazine. When people pick up such a magazine they very often do not read the printed matter or, at least, not very much of it, but they always look at the pictures; so in church the preacher's sermons are the printed words, and the pictures are the living men and women who form our churches, and outsiders may not come to hear the preacher of the word, but they always consider and criticise the lives of the members.

A life of piety is most essential in the work of personal testimony. Only pious missionaries can be trusted to report truly their religious experiences; therefore any lack of character disqualifies them as reliable witnesses. Their testimony concerning the truth of Christ's gospel and their effort to convince others of the veracity of their statements are not valid or effective unless their life prove the facts of their Christianity. I know of a few cases, in which a churchless person had been won for the church and then was shocked by the lives some of the church members were living, and was tempted to leave the church in great disappointment, and the pastor had to put forth special efforts to retain the membership of the offended convert. There are such professed Christians in all of our congregations who actually drive people away from the church instead of drawing them to Christ and the church. Sometimes this is done by careless attitude towards the church, sometimes by ungodly conversation, sometimes by disreputable business methods, by covetousness and avaricious-

ness, sometimes by social pride. Great is the influence of the Christian who is known to be pure in life, honest in business, sincere in church affiliation. He is by his outward deportment, by his daily conduct, a great assistance to me in winning and keeping sin-hardened and skeptical sinners.

6. *I have another group of assistant missionaries who supply me every week with the addresses of people that have moved into their neighborhood.* Occasionally they lack the courage or the time to approach strangers on the subject of religion, or they may have been unsuccessful in their efforts to persuade them to mend their churchless ways. Whenever that is the case, they keep me informed regarding these families that have taken up their residence in their block, and of whom they may know that they are without church affiliation, and perhaps eager to become better acquainted with the teachings and principles of the Lutheran church. They hand these "leads" to me at the close of the Sunday services, at the meetings during the course of the week, or mail them to me. They render some such report as follows: "Pastor, go up to the north east corner of N. 30th and W. Walnut Street and get the Smiths. I have it all clinched for you. All you need to do is to go. They are expecting a call from you." Blessed is the man in the ministry who has such experiences!

A Sectarian man informed me by telephone, while I was dictating this very paragraph to my typist, that a person of eighty-five years living next door was critically ill. He knew that last summer I had made a canvassing call at this home, and that that neighbor needed spiritual care. On the evening of that same day I stood between an immortal unprepared soul and eternity, and spoke the words that, by the grace of God, lead unto repentance and salvation. An example of a non-Lutheran worthy of emulation!

7. *Five of my most efficient assistant missionaries constitute a mission committee,* whose duty it is to make a careful study of the need of and the opportunities for personal work, to plan and prepare all mission canvasses, to provide the necessary publicity material, to irradiate religious earnestness and contagious enthusiasm, to keep this missionary fire burning among all groups of the parish, and to secure just as large a number of members as it possibly can to assist in the visitation of the unchurched.

The secretary of the school board is a member of the mission committee and furnishes at every monthly meeting the names and addresses of the children that have been enrolled in the Christian school. My faithful assistants call on the parents of these children within one or two weeks. They find these people, as a rule, most responsive to their call and message. Many of them have not been coming into the church for want of this very invitation. Others require but a small measure of urging. Here is a field that reveals a new world to those who will seek these open doors of opportunity. It is the point of least resistance and greatest promise in leading to full church membership parents who are interested enough in their children to help them enter and attend a church school.

8. *My assistant missionaries are, finally, those who realize that for too long a time they have been depending upon the evangelistic work of their soul-thirsty pastor, and that it is high time that they as the rank and file of church members begin to understand that the Lord is depending upon them to do their part in this God-given task.* They are willing to unite, under the direction of the mission committee, in a joint systematic effort to canvass the territory of their parish. Upon the committee's request they place their signature upon the Canvassing Agreement Card, having been assured that wherever church members have attempted to do this service, they have had phenomenal success. They are present at the preliminary meetings at which the various phases of the undertaking are discussed and all necessary instructions are given.

They receive their supply of folders and questionnaire cards. In order to apportion the territory correctly among the workers a map is used, upon which the entire area to be covered is delimited by drawing boundary lines. When this area has been set off on the map it is sub-divided into sections which may be numbered. The streets in each section can then be listed. Care must be taken to preserve as nearly as practicable equality in the amount of territory in each section. The canvassers are now allotted their districts by section numbers, and the map with the list of workers will reveal the identity of anyone canvassing any street in the territory. After this portion of the work has been completed the canvass proper is held within a specified time. The cards, carefully filled out, are returned to the committee and the results of the endeavor are classified and filed. My fellow-laborers then assist me in the personal follow-up work, which consists in repeated visits to all prospects and is continued until the next house-to-house canvass is conducted.

My assistant missionaries do not labor in vain. A considerable number of accessions are received into the congregation every year as a result of personal service. The whole congregation is quickened by the mission spirit which has thus been created. Contributions for the cause of home mission increase. Most gratifying is the spiritual growth of the workers themselves. Their own faith is strengthened by every attempt at conversation for Christ. They have learned that sometimes when they are obliged to retire discouraged after a personal chat with someone whom they have been trying to point to Christ, their efforts have not been in vain. The results of faithful work will appear in God's good time. That may not be till the judgment day. Then it will be known how God has used feeble attempts on the part of lay laborers to serve Him.

Commissioning Service

FOR USE IN SETTING APART MEN FOR THE EVERY MEMBER CANVASS

FEAR the word of God as recorded in St. Luke 10:1-2. Now after these things the Lord appointed seventy others, and sent them two and two before his face into every city and place, whither he himself was about to come. And he said unto them, The harvest indeed is plenteous, but the laborers are few; pray ye therefore the Lord of the harvest, that he send forth laborers into his harvest. Also in Acts 13:2,3. And as they ministered to the Lord, and fasted the Holy Spirit said, Separate me Barnabas and Saul for the work whereunto I have called them. Then, when they had fasted and prayed and laid their hands on them, they sent them away.

Dear brethren: You have been asked to make a visitation in this congregation in the interest of the upbuilding and extension of Christ's Kingdom. I ask you, therefore, in the presence of the assembled congregation whether you are now ready and willing to carry out the instruction given you, depending upon the gracious help of God? If so, then answer, I AM.

In accordance with the Scriptures which you have heard, I, as pastor of this congregation, do now commission you to visit among the members and friends of this congregation, soliciting for greater loyalty, liberality, devotion and consecration, that Christ's Kingdom may be advanced among us and that this congregation may become a greater power in the world's evangelization. Go, then, in His name, and may the Holy Spirit direct you in presenting the claims of Christ's Kingdom and abundantly crown your labors with success. Go in the Saviors name and for His glory. Amen.

Then shall the congregation be addressed as follows:

And now, brethren and friends of this congregation, as we are setting these men apart for this definite service, I ask that you receive them kindly and sympathetically. They are your brethren and workers together with God. Prepare yourselves thoughtfully and prayerfully that you may give a prompt and favorable answer to their questions and requests.

To this end let us arise and unite in prayer to Almighty God for His blessing upon them and us, in the work we are undertaking.

Let us pray.

Then shall follow a brief prayer of definite petitions.

Go then, in the name of your Lord and Master and do your utmost to promote His Kingdom.

Protestants　　　　*Roman Catholics*　　　*Jews*

Each Figure Represents Five Million Souls — The Challenge of Seventy Million

© RES. DIV., NAT. EDUC. ASSN.　　*Unchurched*

Handling a List of Prospects

HAVING built up a list of the 592 unchurched, families in our community which had no church connections (this was done through the Atlantic District canvassing system) our next step was to get these people favorably inclined toward our church before approaching them with a personal invitation to attend.

A series of five stories was prepared, and one letter sent every two weeks. This letter was multigraphed on a high grade bond paper, having no letter head nor customary closing greeting.

The story was based on the curiosity appeal. No attempt was made to preach or to explain any of the statements made in the story or in the "moral" attached to the story. The purpose of the letter was not even to get these people to come to church: merely to get them interested in the church, or curious to know more about the church which dared claim it could make people happy.

Follow up work showed that 92% o tfhe women who received these stories actually read and remembered some incident from them; while 65% of the men perused them.

The real work was done through personal follow up calls after the conclusion of this campaign. There the attempt was made actually to get these people to come to church and under the hearing of the Word which could bring them the promised happiness.

The first result of this advertising was the increase in Sunday School enrollment by 118 children, with slow but steady increase in church attendance.

NEW! A Series of Stories About "Untouched Treasures"

1—The Ships of the Norsemen

Long before Columbus was born the Norsemen were sailing the seven seas to make raids upon lands which were unknown to other men. Legend tells of Norse treasure ships laden with stolen ivory and gold which wandered too far North only to be frozen fast in the ice. The crew died; the ships became encased in ice; there they remain even today—perfectly preserved!

Someday an Artic explorer may find these untouched treasures and become wealthy beyond his wildest dream.

One of the greatest of the untouched treasures of today is happiness. Elusive. Yes, not even understood by the majority of people today.

If you are interested, perhaps we can furnish a clue or two in your quest for the untouched treasure which is rightfully yours. Come any Sunday morning at 10:30 A.M. The place? St. John's Lutheran Church, located at Willis Avenue and Princeton.

2—Gold in the Sands of the Sahara

Scientists claim that there is millions of dollars worth of gold in the sands of the Sahara. But it will remain one of the great untouched treasures of the world until someone discovers a profitable method of extracting the gold from the sand.

A life of luxury awaits the man who finds some new and inexpensive method of extracting the gold.

Strange paradox, when you think of it: the most precious thing in life is very well known, yet just as difficult to get at for most people as this gold in the sand of the desert...Happiness!

We believe that we can help you find the road to happiness. Don't you think it would be worth your time to drop in some Sunday morning at 10:30 and see what we have to offer? The place? The Lutheran Church on Willis Avenue, corner Princeton Street.

3—The Lost Continent of Atlantis

Legend tells of a lost continent and a race of people known for their art, their men of science, and their wealth. It seems that this continent was undermined by the sea, and some volcanic disturbance caused the entire continent and all its people to sink far beneath the waves.

Somewhere on the bed of the sea lies this continent, with all of its treasures, untouched, awaiting the day of its discovery.

You and I will not be the discoverer of this lost continent, but there is another untouched treasure that is within our reach. This treasure is happiness. But seldom is a treasure found without diligent search. And half the search is knowing where to look.

St. John's Lutheran Church, Willis Avenue at Princeton, claims that it can help you in your search. Why not drop in some Sunday morning at 10:30 and see what they have to offer?

Map of WILLISTON PARK, L.I. Present Location of St. John's Lutheran Church, corner Willis and Princeton, (marked X on map)

4—The Gold of Ophir

King Solomon and Hiram of Tyre sent a navy to Ophir to obtain gold, silver, jewels, and sandalwood for the building of his great Temple at Jerusalem. And although it toook this navy three years to make the trip, the amount of wealth gained was so great that 100 years later another king of the Jews, named Jehoshaphat, attempted to imitate the enterprise. His ships were wrecked, but some think they sank because they had been overloaded with gold and silver by their avaricious captains.

In the past few years several ships which sank during the late war were reached and their treasures recovered. Perhaps some of the treasure ships of the past will again be located and their golden cargoes brought back to the use of man.

THE TEN COMMANDMENTS IN RHYME

I am the Lord thy God, saith He,
And thou shalt worship only Me;
Take not My holy name in vain;
Nor dare the Sabbath-day profane;
Obey your parents, lass and lad:
Kill not, nor hate, it's just as bad;
In tho't, in word, in act be clean;
Steal not, for thou of God art seen;
Of no one say an unkind word;
Nor covet, Always love the Lord.
—Author Unknown.

The Kingdom Workers

*(A Practical Plan for Missionary Work Within
the Congregation Which Will Work)*

Dr. J. W. Behnken, President of the Missouri Synod, in addressing the Pastoral Conference of the Atlantic District held in New York City during the last week of September, appealed for an intensified Home Mission Program. President Behnken emphasized not only the raising of funds for home mission expansion but especially greater missionary activity within the individual congregation. The pastors were urged to preach not only the doctrine of Justification, but also that of Sanctification.

In the discussion which followed "The Kingdom Workers" of the Lutheran Church of Our Saviour, Brooklyn, N. Y., was recommended to the attention of the brethren. The *American Lutheran* after an interview with Pastor Kurth and a detailed examination of the various details of the plan is happy to recommend it to our readers.

THE KINGDOM WORKERS

NAME
We are pledged to do everything in our power to advance the Kingdom of the Christ. Therefore the name—"The Kingdom Workers."

SET-UP
The parish is divided into ten districts. Over each district a captain is placed. If the district is numerically large, the captain will divide the district into sections and place an assistant over each section. Each worker should be in charge of about twenty homes.

GENERAL OBJECTIVE
Our purpose in general is to work for the advancement of Christ's Kingdom. We do this:
1. By interesting ourselves in our own members (Conservation, reclamation).
2. By interesting ourselves in the unchurched.
3. By interesting ourselves and others in mission-work, at home and abroad.

THE WORKERS' MOTIVES
1. The joy of salvation. You know what Christ means to you.
2. The desire to serve him. Love for Christ. "Come"—"Go."
3. The desire to serve man. Love for man. A passion for souls.

THE WORKERS' PREPARATION
1. Prayer for the blessings of the Holy Spirit, without whom we can do nothing. Pray for ourselves and for those on your list. Do this daily. Depend on God's guidance.
2. Bible-reading.
3. Study-groups.
4. Actual experience.

SEASONS OF WORK
Though we shall be at work steadily, yet there are certain times when we shall do intensive work, as, for instance, during
September—The church must get back to work early in the season.
November—To build up our list of prospects.
The first invitation to the Lecture Course of February.
Arouse interest for the Advent season.
Possibly, broach the question of stewardship.
Pre-Lent—The big missionary campaign for members in the Adult Lecture Group. Announcement appertaining to Lent. Incidentally, the distribution of the Lenten banks.

SPECIFIC AIMS, March 21-April 13, 1935
TO VISIT EVERY ONE, MEMBERS AND NON-MEMBERS
PURPOSES IN CALLING ON OUR OWN MEMBERS—
1. To manifest that the church is interested in them; to knit closer the bond of fellowship; to be of service to our people, wherever needed.
2. To make our people a church-going people. Though the pastor and the Council make calls for this purpose, yet, what with our growing congregation, it is physically impossible to do justice to this important work. "I'll see you in church," is one message you are to leave. Look for them in church, greet them. If you miss them two or three weeks, call on them again. Do this of your own accord. Whereas the pastor cannot keep track of the attendance of 700 people, one worker can keep track of 20 or more.
3. To remind them that we shall have five celebrations of Holy Communion during April, namely, on the first Wednesday evening of April, and then, four times during Holy Week, on Wednesday, Maundy Thursday, Good Friday, and Easter morning. It is encouraging to know that the average attendance per communicant for for the year is 3.5. Saddening, however, to think that 106 members did not receive the Blessed Sacrament last year at all. The Sacrament is the pearl and gem of the Church, a legacy of grace which the Saviour has left us. We should go often, prompted by our need, and the joy and strength it imparts.

BORN	AT	BAPTIZED	AT	PASTOR	CHURC
CONFIRMED		AT		BY PASTOR	
RECEIVED	MODE		WITHDRAWN	MODE	
REINSTATED				CHURCH RECORD	

COMMUNION RECORD **MEMORANDA**

1	2	3	4	5	6	7	8	9	10	11	12	YEAR	TOTAL	1	2	3	4	5	6	7	8	9	10	11	12	YEAR	TOTAL	VISITOR:

REMARKS

ACCOUNT NO.	NAME		ADDRESS	PHONE

4. To get the **names of prospects.** "Do you know of any unchurched adults? Any children without a S.S.? Will you bring these to church, or shall we make the call?" In either case, take the name and address of the prospects. Our church, if it so please God, will go way over the 700th membership-mark in this year. Naturally,

we have our losses too. If we want to forge ahead, we must be everlastingly at work. We have an advantage which other congregations have not: We have able and willing workers. But the workers must have names of people on whom to call. Therefore, ask the members whether they know of any one who is not attending a church.

5. Find out why the **other members of the family** do not belong to our church. (Record all information, but do it after you visit) Seek to win them. Pray for them. Invite them to church and to attendance upon the **Adult Lecture Course.** It may take years before you win certain ones, but stick to it. God has promised that his Word shall not return unto him void.

6. In the course of the visit you may ask, with a smile, "whether they had any trouble getting their **Lenten banks** together?" If so, offer to set up the bank. In either case, improve the opportunity by telling them of the needs of the Kingdom, at home and abroad. This is a topic worthy of a Kingdom Worker, for the Biblical fact is that the Head and Bishop of the Church, Jesus Christ, expects his people to be willing to help towards the extension of his Kingdom.

Our own treasury shows a deficit of over one thousand dollars. During March the treasurer needs $1600 to meet all current bills. Besides this, we owe Synod a moral debt of $2000. If our people are informed, they will do more than they have done. You give the information that begets inspiration.

7. To encourage **Prayer and Bible-Reading.** Those who are members of the H.D. should be encouraged to read their lesson outlines. Call the attention of the others to the course outlined in the Bulletin, "Fifteen Minutes with God."

8. Occasionally, mail tracts, or the Sunday Bulletin to the absentees, with a note, "I missed you last Sunday and Wednesday. Hope to see you on Wednesday."

9. Keep an **exact record** of your visits, the date, the information gathered, etc., and add to it after each visit. Don't lose the records, they are invaluable.

10. To be a Kingdom Worker means consecration and work. But it is the most glorious work earth has to offer. It is only by this kind of work that the Church justifies her existence. This is THE work of the church. You may drop other kinds of work without loss, but

to drop this kind of work means a loss to you in spiritual experiences, rich and many.

There are diversities of gifts and capacities of work. Some have more time than others. If you cannot take over twenty homes, take over ten, or five, or three, or one. But whatever your assignment, do it well.

PURPOSES IN CALLING ON PROSPECTS

1. **To make the contact.** Be a friend. Take a real interest in the person. Also in the children. Don't overlook the men.
2. **To invite them to church.** Sunday or Wednesday. Many people can easily arrange to come on Wednesday, whereas they give excuses for not being able to come on Sunday.

Tell the parents we are glad the children are in the S.S., that the religion which is good for the children is good for the grown-ups too, particularly the men: that as believers in God we should worship God. No one would care to live in a community which had no church. The best insurance against having the children go wrong is to make Christians out of them. But parents should set the example. The time will come when the children will grow up and the parents can no longer say, "You go to church." The youngster will say, "Why don't you go?" To the boy, the father is a hero. Now, no father has the moral right to set a bad example for his son. Parents should go to church, for their children's sake. Not only that, but also for their own sake. They need God and Christ and the ministrations of the church. Hearing a sermon on the radio is not sufficient. Christianity is more than listening to a sermon and music, it is living the life and influencing others to embrace Christ. You can't get the Blessed Sacrament over the radio.

We do have time for church. If we haven't time, we must take time. The soul is more important than the body. We should be wiser than the squirrel which provides against the storms of winter. Let's be sensible and prepare against the future which is sure to come. Let us be ready to face eternity. If we are ready, we have Christ; and only then.

"Going to church won't make me a Christian!" It may at that. One thing is certain, "Every Christian will go to church. Love couples him."
compels him."
show you the order of service," etc.

3. Get information regarding the status of every member of the family. Get this accurately. Ask regarding each one whether baptized, confirmed in the Lutheran Church, where and when member last. Tell them about the Adult Lecture Course which will start on the Thursday after Easter, April 25th, at 8:15 P. M., in the church. A series of eight lectures. Under no obligation, neither to the pastor nor to the church. We exert no high-pressure salesmanship methods to have them join against their will. We do not hound them to death.

If, after the course is over, they decide not to join the church, we do not press the matter any further. However, if they decide to join, we shall be happy to receive them. There is nothing about the Course to embarrass any one. I ask no questions, nor do I give examinations. I lecture. In simple language I set forth the great teachings of Christianity. All they have to do is to attend, listen, think it over, and after the course is done, make up their own mind what they intend to do.

Let us work hard towards another large Adult Group.

4. Ask them whether they know any unchurched people in the community. "Are there any relatives or friends of yours in this neighborhood that do not go to any church at present?" If so, take the name and address, and make the call immediately. Remember to get

the children for the S.S.
5. **Persevere.** You are dealing with people of "flesh", and Jesus said, "The flesh is weak." It takes a whole summer to produce certain flowers. Be patient. Don't expect too big results at once. Remember, it is up to the Holy spirit to work conversion.
This type of work is exceedingly interesting and most gratifying.
At first you may be a little nervous about it, but just speak a little word of prayer as you ring the bell, and you will feel the strength coming into your soul. Don't worry about any prepared speech and argument. The Spirit will give you utterance. "O Lord Jesus Christ, by Thy Spirit tell me what I should say. I am doing Thy work, therefore I look to Thee for help. Be with me, for thy name's sake. Amen."

AS REGARDS THE VISITS

These are to be short, ten or fifteen minutes in duration (unless the person has a real spiritual problem.) Get down to business immediately. State the purpose of your visit frankly. Don't stall for an opening, but state right away why you have come. "The king's business requireth haste."
Don't let yourself in on gossip. Shun it like poison. If some one has a complaint to make, don't side in with that person, for you have heard only one side. Listen to the complaint objectively, without giving an opinion or passing judgment, and say that you will go to the other party and state the complaint and do everything in your power to remove the cause.
It is best not to drink coffee. It drags out your visit too long, which is waste of time and there is always the danger of gossiping over the coffee-cup. You know how it is.

"SEE IT THROUGH"

You are supposed to be trained workers. As such, you will draw on your own initiative and resources to "see your particular work through." We stand ready at all times to aid you with advice and suggestions. At times it may even be necessary for the leader or pastor to make a call. But, as a general thing, we expect you to follow-up your work and see it through to the blessed end. Whether you have one assignment or ten or twenty, do your part, finish your task. And thus, by all of us working in our little section, bringing in one, two, or more, we shall, by the grace of God, show such results as will cause the angels in heaven to rejoice. Through the united and faithful efforts of the Kingdom Workers, the Kingdom of God and of his Glorious Son shall be advanced.
WE GO FORWARD IN THE NAME OF THE FATHER AND OF THE SON AND OF THE HOLY GHOST.
AMEN.

Rev. Erwin Kurth.

It is obvious to any church worker of experience that the above plan—or for that matter any plan—will not work unless the pastor as the leader of his people attends to the necessary details which make theoretical directions operate. To discover the secrets as to what made this plan work was the purpose of our interview with Pastor Kurth. Inspired by him we offer the following suggestions:

1. Take a large local map of the community, place it upon beaver board, shellac it, and use varied color pins to mark the location of members, Sunday School families, and prospects. This may be divided into approximately 10 districts. A "captain" should be placed over each district. Each captain should have several people working under him so that approximately not more than twenty homes would be allocated to each Kingdom Worker. Women as well as men should be enlisted. The success or failure of the entire venture depends on the key men selected as captains over the entire group.

2. The Filing System. In order to make the Kingdom Worker's plan effective, the pastor must have at his disposal a filing system which is constantly up-to-date. We suggest the cardex system for the communicant membership of the congregation (see reproduction of sample card). The visible name reference is invaluable to the busy pastor in checking communions and other information. In addition there should be a master file of the prospect list. The information concerning prospects need not be voluminous, but should contain name, address, church antecedents, children, and a space entitled "Remarks." Almost every prospect presents a different problem, and there-

3. In addition to the cardex system for the communicant members and the master file for the prospects, the pastor should have a loose leaf book for his pocket, entitled "Street Guide." In this book he would have the names and addresses of all members and prospects listed according to streets so that when he goes out for an afternoon's visitation, all the preparation necessary is to slip the book into his pocket and go forth. When he comes home with a new prospect gathered from his visiting, a wedding, funeral, or any other contact, *before* he sits down to his meal he would go to the master file and drop in the necessary card.

4. It is important that the pastor definitely announce the date for the beginning of a new adult class long in advance. But it is best to have the campaign of visitation by the Kingdom Workers last over a period not to exceed four weeks. Say if

the adult class is to begin on Feb. 22nd, the workers would carry on their visitations for a period of three weeks previous, and if their prospects did not show up for the adult class lecture on Feb. 22nd, they would have the week until the 29th to gather in the stragglers. After Easter, it is suggested that a period of four day visitation be made on Monday, Tuesday, Wednesday and Thursday of Easter week for the last spring class which may begin the second week following Easter. The visitation after Easter will be found to be comparatively easy as all details of the various prospects will already be familiar to the Kingdom Workers from the pre- Lenten visitation.

5. But there is one very im- portant phase of this congregational missionary plan which dare not be overlooked. The pastor must visit practically every individual personally whom he would list as a prospect for his Kingdom Workers. And the pastor must make this visitation far in advance. For a February adult class we suggest that he use the months of September and October for a personal visitation to his entire membership. One pastor publishes the names of those whom he will call upon during the week in his weekly bulletin as a measure of self-discipline compelling him to make the number of visits planned, and to prepare his people for his visit. In this visitation the pastor would lay the ground-work for the coming adult class campaign. Each visit need not last more than ten to fifteen minutes. But in every home the pastor should speak of church and communion attendance of the regular members, of their prayer-life, Bible Study, and their responsibility as Disciples of Christ in gathering other disciples as followers of Jesus. To non-church parents of all Sunday School children he would naturally explain the adult class and give them a general invitation to attend.

Where he encounters a family which has drifted from church for a long time but are still nominal Lutherans, it is well to enroll them in the adult class so that their knowledge of the Christian fundamentals may be renewed and their zeal be re-awakened in the cause of the Master. If the pastor walks into every home, not with the purpose of making a social contact but with a definite spiritual objective in mind, the effort would be most thoroughly worth while as measured by church attendance, Bible reading, prayer life in the home and devotion in the church service.

Our System of Visitation

God arranged that parents should supervise their children and guide them aright. Many parents neglect this their duty. The Church must lovingly take these children in hand, especially after confirmation, and watch over their souls.

With a congregation numbering 750 communicant members it is impossible for the pastor to devote the time and strength which is required for this persistent sort of work. Therefore the congregation has elected elders to assist him in this taxing, but glorious work.

It is a hard thing to train character. But persistent effort, graced by the blessing of God, can accomplish it. This year we shall give to each "weak" member personal and steady attention, in the hope that such ceaseless attention, given throughout the year, will at last establish a habit, and the good habit form the character.

So then, our new plan is: Each Councilman is to be an "ELDER" over a certain number of members.

As much as in him lies, he will seek to get these persons to function as Christians should, and that is, to attend church regularly, at least once a week; to attend the celebration of the Lord's Supper at least four times a year; to be Bible readers, to have family devotions or daily prayers; to become acquainted with, and vitally interested in, the Church's program of world evangelization (through reading of the Lutheran Witness, the American Lutheran, tracts, etc.); to become generous in the support of the Lord's work, by giving time, talents, and money to the Kingdom. (Stewardship and Tithony.)

The Elder will remember the people in his daily prayers; he will visit them in love, with the definite intention of helping them to the life more abundant; he will look for them at church and at the Lord's Table; he will greet them at services and, if feasible, introduce them to other members; occasionally he will send them the Sunday bulletin or other literature; he will perseveringly seek to get them to function and live as Christians and stewards of God.

That is the new plan, and yet how old! It is a plan that goes back to the old principle of "'Love the Brotherhood."

The success of the plan depends: 1. Upon God's blessing; 2. Upon our consecration to Christ and our willingness to serve faithfully; 3. Upon our love for the brethren.

The New Resident

THE Church, in the very nature of the case, should be the first to welcome the new resident to the community. The Spirit of the Christian faith is friendly and the Church should be genuinely concerned about the welfare of the new neighbor. We are confident that more pastors and mission committees would contact every new resident in their communities, if it were less troublesome to keep informed about vacancies and rentals in any given area. A number of methods have been employed to obtain the names of new residents. In some cases the Chamber of Commerce has been helpful. The co-operation of the real estate agents was successfully sought in one community. In another the Gas Company provided a list of residents. In one congregation the deacons and elders were individually assigned portions of the city, over which to keep an alert watch.

A recently developed advertising service in suburban communities, known as "hostess service," is the best source of information we have found.

A hostess, with an unusually complete list of new residents, represents a group of merchants and personally calls to recommend the products of her patrons and leaves informative literature. Each merchant represented receives a list of names with general information about each appended.

Such merchants are usually happy to allow the Church to make a copy of these lists. Most "hostess services" are glad to give permission for the use of the lists by the Church.

Having a list of new residents, the best approach is by letter-of-welcome and a follow-up call by the pastor. The following letter has been successfully used.

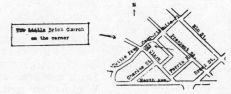

A FRIENDLY NOTE TO OUR NEW NEIGHBORS

It is a pleasure to welcome you to your new home. You will find Westfield an ideal place to live. Our town seldom fails to impress,—there are so many things that appeal to the newcomer. We hope you will find many friends among our towns-people, and if we can contribute to the number of friendly contacts and pleasant associations which you make, we shall be most happy. In this spirit Redeemer Lutheran Church sends you a cordial greeting.

If you are connected with one of the locally represented denominations, you will be interested in the information published in the church notices of The Westfield Leader

If you are not connected with any church, we bid you welcome to the services of the Lutheran Church,

The Reverend Walter A. Reuning, Pastor of Redeemer Church, will deem it a privilege to meet you at your door in the near future. Should information of any kind be desired, please feel free to telephone the pastor,

Serving in the name of Christ, the Savior.

Various Appeals to the Unchurched

1. *You Say You Believe the Christian Religion;* the majority make that claim; the Christian religion is here to stay; it has proved its worth; a help to mankind; see the churches in the world; millions believe it; in that claim you do well but it must not stop with a claim; a person does not really believe a thing to be true until he shows that faith by action: church going, etc.

2. *You Believe in Christ* that is well. Christ is world's greatest teacher; no other person like Him; even unbelievers have placed Him at the head of list of great men. Christ is true Redeemer all the prophecies in Him fulfilled (dozens of them), His miracles, doctrines, have lived for 1900 years, His resurrection proves Him more than a man, true God, His love supreme, His sacrifice unequalled, He saves from sin anyone who comes to Him, You say you do not deny Christ you believe in Him, very well then remember He said: "He that confesseth me before men Him will I also confess before my Father—and whosoever denieth me—him will I deny—" Matth. 10,32f. Can a person confess Christ and yet have nothing to do with Him, with His Word, with His Church? He that is of God heareth God's Words.

3. *You Accept the Bible* as the Word of God it is the world's greatest book; any other book like it? 30 million copies sold each year; Translated into 900 languages it has comforted more people than any other book. If it were a "fake" would it have fooled some of the greatest minds of earth these many years? It is well that you accept the Bible. Inspired! But does a man really believe the Bible if he seldom reads it? Never wants to hear it preached? Gives more time to novels and newspapers? Can a man believe the Bible and yet refuse to follow it? You believe the Bible the Bible says: Hear the Word of God and keep it, the Bible tells us the Church was established by Jesus; that men are to hear the preaching of the Gospel.

4. *The Church is God's Ordinance.* He established it in Old Testament and New Testament. Jesus spoke of His Kingdom repeatedly; He prepared 12 apostles to build the church on earth, and said that church should not perish from the earth; that He would be with the church always. To despise, neglect, or be indifferent to the church is to be indifferent to Christ's ordinance and hence to Christ. Do you think it possible to be true to Christ and the Bible outside of the church?

5. *The Apostles Knew of No Salvation Outside of the Church.* God through the church has kept the Bible and Christ before the world; without Christ world would be lost; you would be lost; the first Christians thought it impossible to be a Christian without being a church member and church goer. To those who refuse the Word, God says: "Because thou hast rejected knowledge I will also reject thee." What does Jesus teach in the parable about those who always have excuses? Luke 14, 15-24.

6. *The Church is the Most Helpful Institution on Earth.* In times of sickness, death, and sorrow it is there to help you: it extends charity to the poor, it takes an interest in the children, and spends many hours to bring them up as good people, and believers in Christ, in this the church helps fathers and mothers; think what it has done for the children of the world. The church helps you with counsel, advice, instruction, guidance, on the greater matters of life, it helps you get a clean conscience, forgiveness, inward peace such as no money can buy, it warns you against inward and danger. Would you refuse a man who wanted to warn you of an approaching automobile, or a bank failure?

7. *There are Some Things About the Bible and the Church which You Do not Fully Understand;* it may be a matter fully decided in Scriptures but you have never seen the verse that explains it, the Church is there to show it to you, it clears away doubts; it helps you understand your Bible, it answers your questions, things of the church and Bible are in full harmony, if you don't see this harmony it is because you do not know all of the Bible, the Church through Bible classes, sermons, etc., helps you overcome difficulties. You never will get satisfaction unless you read the Bible and go to church to hear the Bible preached. Every sermon has something in it to help you better understand Christ's gospel.

8. Every man has asked himself *the Questions: Where Am I From? What Am I Here For?* Only to slave and have trouble? *Where Am I Going?* Does death end all? Have I a soul? Is there sin? Is there a hereafter? Is there a hell? Life is more than meat and drink and house and clothing. Are you ready for death? Do you think there is going to be a judgment? Is it foolish to prepare for eternity? The church through the Bible answers the greatest questions about life. You can get the answer nowhere else. Any animal can live. Only a thinking man knows why he lives. Don't just live. Know why you are living?

9. *The Christian Home is the Gift of Christ and the Church* to the world. Think of the homes where hate, quarrels, envy, jealousy, cursing, evil actions, words, thoughts are everyday occurrences: from such homes dissatisfaction, vice, crime, unruly children come. Show its relation to divorce; reform schools; business failure; unreliable workmen; thieves; evil neighbors; etc. Then think of Christian home where harmony prevails, daily Bible reading, prayer, love, kindness, virtue, good works, kind deeds, reliable, trustworthy, fine families of God-fearing children; The church produced the Christian home not the unbelieving world; can the church be wrong when it produces the finest fruits of the nation; Christian home? Has philosophy or science or education produced anything like them?

10. *Un-Christian Countries are Far Behind Christian Countries:* Would you want to live in a churchless town ruled by infidels? Are the jails filled with church people or unchurched people? Do we need expensive law enforcement (high taxes) because of the devout Christians that are in the world? Who fills the reform schools? Church gave us hospitals? Popular education? Liberty of conscience, of speech, of religion! Compare conditions in a Christless land. All of our presidents have said that the Bible and Christianity will do more for prosperity than law or any other factor. Why then despise the very institution that helps you?

Note: Also make such appeals as; your conscience; sin is worse than pneumonia; church gives you the well-rounded out life God intended for you. Church gives lasting pleasures and joy, etc.

Estimates of Luther

L UTHER WAS NOT THE ONLY LEADING REFORMER of his day, but also a scholar of great merit. The names of the Roman popes of the sixteenth century are known to very few; Charles V is but a shadow on a printed page, but Luther is still a potent presence in this twentieth century, strengthening men for duty whatever they are, and summoning them to perform duty, solely in view of their responsibility to God and with fullness of faith to Him."—Rev. Wm. H. Roberts, D.D., LL.D. (Presbyterian)

* * * *

"The world is a freer place to breathe in, a better place to work, the place of a larger opportunity and a more confident hope because of what was done and suffered in the nations of Europe as a consequence of Luther's following of his own conscience from step to step along the Reformation way. Even the Roman Catholic Church in its sloughing off of follies and excrescences is today more clean and free and strong because of the Reformation. With the too-reluctant giving up of acknowledged worldly control, the spiritual life of the Roman Church has been purified. Rome owes much to Luther."—The Congregationalist.

A Word About Canvassing

LOUIS HENZE

THERE never was a time in the history of our Synod when there was so much canvassing. The word "canvass" has come to mean something. It is the first step toward aggressive mission work to win the great American unchurched public.

A canvass in the true sense of the word should be nothing more than fact finding. It is designed to secure correct data on the churched and unchurched in a given community. On the basis of the fact finding the unchurched are to be followed up, visited.

To secure correct data, or the true facts, relative to the church affiliation, or the lack of any affiliation, of every man, woman and child in the territory to be canvassed is the real task of the canvasser. Correct data—here is where most canvassing falls down. A canvass will be only as good as the canvasser. He must know his job.

In the course of years we have had the opportunity to investigate various systems of canvassing and the various kinds of canvass cards that have been used. We have had the opportunity to talk to canvassers and to discuss their problems with them. By far the greater number have succumbed to the pitfalls of canvassing and by far the greater number believe that they have fallen short of the objective—correct information.

Not to secure correct information means something. It means much. It means that souls which may be won for Christ will be passed by and left in darkness. Or it means that where canvassing is done in connection with a survey of a community to investigate the possibilities of opening a new mission, the community will be passed by as one that holds little or no prospects for the establishing of a church.

To our knowledge there is only one way to secure correct information in canvassing. By years of experience we have come to know that the canvasser must use a certain type of questions which will get the true facts. These questions must be so designed that people unknowingly contradict themselves. To a trained canvasser it means nothing when the lady at the door says, "We are all Methodists." The fact is that very often those referred to by "me" have lost all church connections and are prospects to be followed up.

The other factor that plays such a vital part in canvassing for correct informa-

tion is the businesslike way in which it is done. It must be done as a church census and strictly carried out as such. The canvasser must be aware of the necessary psychology back of his difficult task, put himself in the mental attitude of taking a church census and carry that atmosphere about with him. It makes all the difference in the world whether he goes up to each home as if it were his own, unhesitatingly gives the door bell a real healthy ring, stands before the door with an air of authority expecting information, or whether he hesitatingly looks over the house as if he never saw one before, and when the door is opened expects a madman to attack him. We have learned by experience that it does not pay to be over-polite, make explanations and then ask questions—personal questions. We have found that it does pay to be businesslike, impart to the party at the door the air of authority and expectancy, to ask your personal questions quickly but thoroughly and to end the interview with a word of thanks and start for the next door.

At this point we would again like to remind the reader that we are merely securing facts, that we are not attempting to talk religion, that we are separating the church from the unchurched in a given community, securing prospects to be followed up. It is a mistake to canvass and to try to do follow up work at the same time. The canvasser will not canvass properly nor do his follow up as it should be done if he tries to combine both. People, as a rule, do not die over night, nor immediately leave the community. There will be time to visit those that are to be visited, and at that time the canvasser or some other party will be more fit to make the right approach and prepare the way for a vital message.

Armed with a set of questions designed to get at the truth and going about the task of canvassing in a businesslike way, a trained canvasser should obtain ninety per cent correct information after two or three weeks of experience in the field. We herewith present a set of questions that have been tested and proven by years of experience. These questions are designed to be used in connection with the canvassing card presented with this article. Many modifications and improvements will immediately come to the reader's mind. Unless you have spent real time and thought

on canvassing and actually worked in the field do not be too hasty to make changes. Pitfalls are everywhere. It seems to be a fine improvement on the question set forth to ask, "How many children of Sunday School age in the family?" Instead of, "How many children below fourteen years of age in the family?" People of Roman Catholic background who are no longer affiliated with their church may have children below fourteen years of age in their family, but if they were asked about children of Sunday School age the answer may be "no," because they still think of *their* children not in terms of Sunday School, but in terms of the children's mass. And so innumerable pitfalls on improvements may be cited. Use the questions as advocated.

1. "I'm taking the church-census: does this family go to any particular church?" (The instant the door is opened.)

2. "How many children below 14 years of age in this family? Do they go to Sunday School regularly?"—Check-question where attendance is claimed: "Which Sunday School?"

3. "Where do the men of the family go to church?"—Check-question where church connection is claimed: "Is he (they) a *regular* member or does he just go there *once in a while?*"

4. "Where do you go to church?"—Check-question when church connection is claimed: "Are you a *regular* member or do you just go there once in a while?"—Check-question when regular membership is claimed: "What is your minister's name?"

5. "What's the family name? The initials?" "Oh yes, those children—what are their ages?"

These questions are all that are necessary. They are questions which, with a little experience, will place men and women in one of four categories: they are regular members, attend a church but are not members, unchurched former members, or totally unchurched. And the children in a family either attend a Sunday School or they do not. And that is all the information we want. People, in general, gladly give this information, and we heartily agree with them when they refuse to give their telephone number, or perhaps their pedigree.

It is well to note that these questions get the party at the door to give information about others first. Should a man

ADDRESS:						
FAMILY NAME:						
Sunday School Prospects: How Many?		Ages?				
Not at Home.						
Vacant House:						
Refused:						
CHECK ALL INFORMATION (√)						
DENOMINATION		Regular MEMBER (Not a Member)	Attends (Not a Member)	UNCHURCHED (Former Member)	Regular MEMBER (Not a Member)	Attends (Not a Member)	UNCHURCHED (Former Member)
		M E N			W O M E N		
Lutheran: Our Synod	1				1		
Lutheran: Other Synods	2				2		
Baptist	3				3		
Catholic	4				4		
Christian Science	5				5		
Congregational	6				6		
Episcopal	7				7		
Evangelical	8				8		
Jewish	9				9		
Methodist	10				10		
Presbyterian	11				11		
Reformed	12				12		
Unitarian	13				13		
Sects: All-Others	14				14		
Totally: UNCHURCHED	15				15		

Canvasser's Signature

(USE OTHER SIDE FOR PERSONAL NOTATIONS OR REMARKS)
L. P. NO. 107—PRINTED IN U.S.A.

Canvass Card No. 107

All the data to be gathered require only checkmarks. Very time-saving and convenient.

Size of Cards, 3 x 5 inches.

Price:

100	$ .50
500	2.25
1000	4.25

Postage extra

come to the door question No. 3 and No. 4 are reversed. People do not like to answer questions about themselves but do not mind talking about others. The proper approach is to have the lady at the door not talk about herself but about her children. Under question No. 3 should she in any way imply church connection for her husband, experience has shown that if the canvasser asks his check-question, "Is he a regular member or does he just go there once in a while?" and especially if there is the shadow of a grin on his face, she will tell the real truth about her husband.

The trained canvasser will disregard the information given in answer to question No. 1 and merely pretend to make a note of it on the card. The first answer seldom means anything as subsequent questioning will reveal. If, however, after asking question No. 1 the information is immediately given that neither husband nor wife attend any church, further questioning is unnecessary after checking up on the children

with question No. 2. The canvasser will certainly not be satisfied with the answer, "We are all Baptists," or something similar, but he will continue with the questions as such and emphasize check-up questions under No. 3 and No. 4.

No experienced canvasser will seek to secure information on a family not at home by asking information about that family from the party next door. Nor will he accept information about father and mother from a child. No canvasser has completed his job until he has retraced his steps and covered the not-at-homes.

What to do with the men and women who refuse information, or refuse to come to the door, is the real test of a good canvasser. The party who calls from back of the door, "Nothing to-day," or, "Not interested" and the like, must be dealt with. The canvasser must know how to handle such cases. He will immediately ring the door bell again and disregarding the fury with which the party opens the door ask his questions with an air of authority as though nothing unusual had happened. It is not unusual for the housewife to be upstairs making beds in the morning when the canvasser rings her door bell. And it is not unusual for her to go to the window and call down, "Who's there, what do you want?" A good canvasser will not try to explain his business from the steps below, but without hardly looking up he will answer firmly, "Church census come down here!" And they usually do if the sound of his voice has a ring of importance. And isn't church canvassing important? These and many more incidental problems connected with canvassing will not faze the real canvasser, but he will know how to deal with each case as just part of the day's work.

All canvassing should be conducted wherever possible by permission of the Police department. Such permission will usually be granted in writing and it is well to request it in writing if it is only given by consent. In many towns and cities throughout the east, canvassing must be done by permission of the Police department, without which canvasses cannot be carried out and the custom

has grown in most communities. Armed with a police permit, the canvasser feels secure and he can immediately clear himself of any complications when held as a suspect, as has happened more than once, that he is the suspicious character responsible for the epidemic of house-breaking that has been going on in the community. And when people vent their ire on him for annoying them or taking offense at his personal questions, it makes a canvasser feel mighty good to produce his permit, to soothe the ruffled waters and to quickly get his questions answered with the magic word "police."

This then is a word about canvassing. If you will now take a glance at the card used in the canvassing system herewith advocated, you will notice that it has been devised to tabulate and make a record of the information secured. No writing is required beyond the name and address. The data secured on each individual is done by check, and the numbers on the card are merely to guide the canvasser's hand. We know of no better canvassing card. These cards may be secured from the American Lutheran Publicity Bureau, 1819 Broadway, New York City.

An aggressive missionary will know his community. He will have the data on every man, woman and child within the sphere of activity of his church. The same applies to every pastor. There will be no need to publicize that we have opened a church in "X" and kindly inform "me" if you know of people who have moved to "X." The canvass and recanvass of "X" will tell who lives in "X."

Aggressive missionary boards will know by survey and canvasses what the mission possibilities are in the territory under their jurisdiction and the data revealed by the canvassing connected with the surveys will reveal where the real missionary opportunities are and the cream of these opportunities will be selected for establishing our mission churches. The money spent on trained canvassers to do the work will be money well spent.

Non-Attending Church Members

DO the members of our churches attend the church services with any degree of steady regularity? A question like this is apt to elicit various hasty, ill-considered answers, based not on actual figures but on the temperamental reactions and indefinite impressions of the one volunteering an answer. Most congregations do not keep an accurate attendance record and the guess of the pastor or deacons as to the number of people in attendance, based perhaps on the seating capacity of the church and a cursory estimate of the audience, has always proven unreliable and usually over-optimistic. A clerical friend of ours boasted for years that he in his church ran regularly an average attendance of six hundred people. Presuming on our friendship, we persistently disputed his claim and insisted on an accurate count over a period of two months. To our friend's discomfiture and amazement the count showed a Sunday average of 349 attendants. Again and again we find churches packed to the doors Sunday after Sunday to the self-satisfied gratification of pastor and people, and then find out that the church has a seating capacity of four hundred with a membership of eight hundred communicants. Not long ago one of our deacons boasted: "Pastor, there is one thing about our members, they are regular church attendants." We disputed his claim to his great astonishment, for the ushers had carried chairs that very Sunday. We pointed out that our church had a seating capacity of about one thousand, that by our method of counting 203 strangers and visitors and 102 unconfirmed children had attended the service. We had all told 1103 communicant members. The attendance that morning had been 1045, which meant that 363 of our members had not been in church. A church that keeps an accurate count of its attendance is bound to experience some startling revelations. Rough estimates are misleading and dangerous. The vast majority of our churches, especially in the cities, have a larger number of non-attending church members than they realize. Large memberships with small places of worship are drifting along complacently, misled by crowded services. Congregational missionary activities are being curtailed because of inadequate facilities to take care of any more membership accessions. The American Lutheran recommends to all our churches a careful survey of the facts. The depressing revelations that are bound to result will in the end have only wholesome reactions.

THE REASON WHY

In a recent article by Dr. William Judson Hampton, appearing in "The Presbyterian," an explanation of the above mentioned condition is ventured. Dr. Hampton adduces first of all a number of figures to substantiate his claim that many Protestants do not attend church. He claims, for instance, that 32% of church members never attend the services of the church. We believe that we are safe in saying that this figure does not hold good in Lutheran circles, where disciplinary measures in connection with non-attending church members are at least in a measure applied. But also in our Church we dare not close our eyes to the fact that a really astonishing percentage of our members is not in regular attendance at the Sunday services. Dr. Hampton mentions the poll made in a Michigan high school where the question was put to 325 pupils as to whether or not they had attended church services on the previous Sunday. Only 14 pupils had attended. In endeavoring to lay his finger upon the chief cause of this widespread delinquency, Dr. Hampton quotes Judge C. T. Crane of the New York Supreme Court, who believes that the trouble is largely with the home and who claims that the absence of children from the services of the church is not only a grave danger but a positive tragedy. He states that there are 500,000 children from Protestant homes in New York City absolutely without any religious instruction. Dr. Hampton continues, "Other large cities could no doubt point to an equally appalling condition. By law we kick the Bible out of our public schools and after the law has laid its mailed hand on the shoulders of youthful offenders and they find themselves behind prison bars, the church comforts itself with the thought that it has placed a Bible in every cell. . . . Prevention is better than cure. If the Bible possesses curative values, it also prescribes some wholesome preventive measures. It is far better that our children be taught to 'Remember their Creator in the days of their youth' than for the church to underscore with red ink the words of Holy Writ in prison cells, 'The way of the transgressor is hard.' "

There is no doubt that Judge Crane is right. There has been a growing delinquency in our midst in bringing the children into the house of God. We are absolutely out of sympathy with the special "children's church," where the minister offers the children of the Sunday School a denatured and enervated and expurgated edition of the regular church service, with a wishy-washy sermonette and trite sentimentalities, and then permits them to wend their way homeward. Dr. Hampton properly regrets the passing of family worship in the family pew. He regrets that children no longer sit with their parents. He points out that old and middle-aged men of church-going habits almost invariably formed the habit of church attendance in childhood, trudging to church with their hand in that of father or mother. Dr. Hampton says, "It is a regrettable fact that the experience is only a precious memory. The family pew with the children present is practically a dead letter. Horace Bushnell once said, 'Two methods of growth should be observed by every church; growth by conquest from without, and growth by population from within.' The father and mother represent the crux of the whole problem. If parents would assume a different attitude toward their children, we would not have childless churches." There are, of course, other reasons for the irregular attendance of church members, but we believe that the one mentioned by Dr. Hampton is worthy of our most serious consideration. Our own churches are everywhere confronted by the problem of having at least the older children remain for the church service when the Sunday School is dismissed. The maintenance or reestablishment of the family pew is also a subject for very serious discussion in our various churches.

Early Fall Attendance Campaign

AUGUST F. BRUNN

AFTER THE VACATION SEASON it is often difficult to build up good attendances, early in the fall season. Frequent absence has dulled the conscience; and many a vacation has had its blighting effect upon the soul, leading away from Christ. An effort may be necessary to win the soul back to loyalty. For this reason, an earnest appeal for a new start in regular church-going, soon after the vacation months, is usually effective, and well received.

The messages here printed, on a good white card 4¼ by 5¼ with matching envelope, were sent to the entire mailing list, the week following the Sunday School Rally Day. Card A was sent to all members, one to each communicant in the family, with his name written in as the salutation; the whole family's cards were enclosed in one envelope, sealed. Card B was sent to the prospect list, with names similarly written in. Card C was mailed a week later, to members who did not respond, and to absentees on following Sundays.

Writing in each person's name, each on a separate card, brought the message to everyone's attention; using a good white card, of an odd size, made the message seem important. The same wording mimeographed, on ordinary paper, would not have produced a like effect.

Naturally the campaign must be supported by other appeals for regular attendance, on the church calendar, at the services and meetings, and in particular by visiting those who do not appear after the second printed card. An attendance record of all communicants, for which one may use quadrille paper, is very helpful in this. The weekly perusal of this list, to mark present those the pastor or the ushers remember seeing at the door, will soon indicate who has not "come back", and needs special attention.

With such an effort the demoralizing effect of summer church attendances is soon overcome, and the congregational machinery put into full motion before too many weeks of the fall season have passed. The plan has worked, and perhaps you will want to try it.

"We are the Lord's"

Dear Charles,

In the name of Jesus, Whom you profess to love, and as one deeply concerned about your well-being:

Will you now make a new start, in loyalty to Christ?

Beginning this Sunday, which is our Congregational Rally Day, will you sincerely pledge your devotion to the Lord, by attending church every Sunday?

You cannot take this lightly. Everything is at stake. Your own faith, which will starve without week-for-week nourishment as God has ordained it. The faith of your fellow-believers, who are saddened by your absence, for they need the strength of your example. And the whole world about you loses, whenever Christ does not appear supreme in your life.

When may we prove more sincerely that we are the Lord's, than on Sunday morning? While others think of their ease, or pleasure, or company, or chores, it is for us to show that Christ comes first in our lives. Church-going is the test of our faith, whether we serve God, or self.

I pray that God may help you give the right answer. Pledge yourself anew to Him Who has redeemed you. Say with us now: "Thee will I love, my Saviour, and Thine will I be, here and in eternity!"

In His Name, and for His Honor,

AUGUST F. BRUNN, Pastor.

Congregational Rally Service,
Sunday, Sept. 26th, at 9:30 A.M.

Card "A", to all communicants

"Blessed are they that hear the Word of God, and keep it."—LUKE 11, 28

Dear Mr. Jones,

You are among the friends of our church, and have gladdened our hearts by worshipping with us. You believe in the Christ we serve, and we count you among our fellow pilgrims on the way to Life.

In His name we extend this sincere plea to you, as we enter this new season: that you join us in our regular worship each Sunday morning.

So much is at stake. There can be no real peace and happiness for us, nor for our strife-torn world unless we withstand the inroads which our modern life makes upon that divinely ordained hour each week, when men should draw away from self and others, to look upward for guidance and spiritual strength. With our emphasis upon material comforts and progress, we dare not starve our souls. Else we shall destroy ourselves, and lose all.

For the deepening of your faith in God and man, the joy of forgiveness, and a more abundant life, and for the encouragement of others in following the Master, will you not make it anew the habit of your life, to join in public worship on the Lord's Day?

We invite you to make St. Paul's your church home, and upon the entrance to each new week to unite with us, in praise of Him Who has so wondrously loved us, and Who yearns for His children to receive His life-giving Word.

"Come thou with us, and we will do thee good!"
For your well-being, and in His Name,

ST. PAUL'S LUTHERAN CHURCH
OF AMITYVILLE
REV. AUGUST F. BRUNN, Pastor.

Sunday Service, 9:30 A.M.
Sunday School, 10:45 A.M.

Card "B", to non-members

"Blessed are they that hear the Word of God, and keep it."—LUKE 11, 28

Dear Friend,

The service was most inspiring last Sunday, but for the absence of those of our brethren who could not be with us.

We missed you, dear friend, and the testimony your worship would have meant to us and others. And we are sorry you could not share with us the peace and joy God afforded us.

As a fellow-member you are close to us, and we depend on you for strength and encouragement. It always matters whether you are with us, whenever we unite to worship our great Saviour.

Will you gladden our hearts, and make it an unfailing habit to lift your heart with us each Sunday, to the Giver of all grace? Oh let us prove our love to Him, and to each other!

Come this Sunday. We need you. You need the Word. Come!

In the Name of your brethren, and of Christ,

AUGUST F. BRUNN, Pastor.

Card "C", follow-up of members

Training Children In Church Attendance

FRED H. LINDEMANN

A MAN, IF HE GROWS WISER as he becomes older, stops giving advice freely when he grows old enough to speak from experience in the matter. Before he has learned enough from experience to give advice, his counsel is not worth heeding. After he has had sufficient experience to give sound advice, he knows that he is wasting his breath, and tells stories. So in approaching the problem of preventing children from going home after Sunday school without attending the service of the congregation, no advice shall be given. At the request of the AMERICAN LUTHERAN a story shall be told. If there is anything worth imitating in it, the wise will find it and put it to good use. All others may now turn to the next article. There is nothing here for them.

Introductions are frequently trite. So the subject shall be introduced with the rather trite observation that children cannot be expected to do something after confirmation which they have not learned to do before. If a child has not acquired the habit of regular church attendance before confirmation it is vain to hope that at the moment of reception into membership a complete change of habit may take place and that this change be lasting.

How can children be trained to attend services when the parents never or seldom attend and are utterly indifferent? One can say that the child should be trained in the home and by the parents and wash his hands of the problem. But that does not train the children. Perhaps we have indifferent and unchurched parents today because the Sunday school assumed this attitude a generation ago. If the home functioned ideally, there would be no need of Sunday schools. For the school to teach the Third Commandment in theory only and not to insist upon the practice and to train in the doing, is folly. So the school and the church have a responsibility here.

But it is time that the story begin. Once upon a time there was a pastor who discovered to his horror that in his confirmation class of fifty-four children forty-eight came from totally unchurched homes, five had a mother who was connected with the church, and one lone child ever saw both father and mother in the house of God. Some of these parents would no doubt be won in the course of time, but something had to be done about the children at once. During the two years of instruction preparatory to confirmation regular church attendance was insisted upon and a careful record kept. But the pastor resolved that never again would he gather a class which consisted of children who had attended church only on rare occasions. The habit of attendance must be formed before the age of twelve. Children who are ripe for instruction which is to prepare them for membership in the church must be regular churchgoers before they enter the class.

Local conditions suggested a partial solution. The Sunday school met in two separate buildings, the intermediate department in the basement of the church, the junior and primary departments on different floors of the parish house. Children from eight to ten years were instructed in the parish house and transferred to the intermediate department in the church basement at the age of ten years. Before promotion the following letter was sent to the parents:

"Your child is ready to be transferred to our Intermediate Department. The children in this department are required to attend church services after the hour of instruction in the school. For the sake of the common good and general welfare we must insist that all attend church regularly. We endeavor to train the children so that they become faithful churchgoers later in life.

"Naturally, the cooperation of the parents is necessary to have the child attend the morning worship after school. To assure us of this cooperation we ask that the parents sign the inclosed card which is to be handed to the superintendent of the department. Upon receipt of the signed card the child is promoted.

"Permit us to suggest that the parents of our children cooperate with us also in that they give the children the example of faithful and regular attendance upon the services in God's house, either in the morning or evening. You may be sure of a hearty welcome. We need the help of the parents in training the children to become God-fearing men and women who hear God's Word during their whole life whenever opportunity offers."

The inclosed card to be signed by the parents read as follows: "Gratefully acknowledging the sincere efforts of officers and teachers to train my child in the way of the Lord, I cheerfully give my consent to the transfer into the Intermediate Department with the understanding that attendance upon the morning service be included in the course. I will do all in my power to encourage regular attendance upon divine service after the Bible school."

It worked. No child was transferred to the intermediate department until the card was signed and returned. When parents refused to sign, the child found itself a solitary remnant of the class which had been transferred into the other building. A tearful, perhaps stormy interview at home resulted in the signing of the card within a week or two. In the goodness of his heart the superintendent then made an "exception" and transferred the child after the set date for promotion.

After a few years the entire intermediate department was definitely committed to regular church attendance. At the close of the instruction period, which was lengthened to an hour and ten minutes, the teacher led the class up into church. To teach the proper attitude of worship, the teacher sat with the pupils throughout the service.

If any parents believed that there was sufficient reason for the child's going home after Bible school without attending church on that particular day, a written and signed excuse had to be brought. This was handed to the teacher, who discussed the matter briefly, stated God's opinion and admonished if necessary. After the close of school the superintendent examined each excuse and dealt with each individual before permitting him or her to leave by a door other than that used when entering church.

In the meanwhile the teachers led their classes up a flight of stairs. At the top was a door leading to the street. An usher was stationed at this door. Why? Well, even in those days the spirit may have been willing but the flesh often was weak. Some child might have been tempted to slip through the wrong door by mistake. The usher was just a silent reminder that the door to the left was the one for which the children were looking.

No, the arrangement was not perfect. There were always a few children who brought written excuses. The reasons given for wanting the child to come home after school were not always valid in the light of God's Word. But something was accomplished. Parents grew tired of writing excuses. Perhaps the visits of the superintendent had something to do with it too. He called whenever the excuses became frequent and reminded the parents of the card they had signed.

The Gospel in the Open Air

AMBROSE HERING

WHAT YOU SAID is true. He saves and He keeps. I am over eighty-four, have buried my wife, two grown children and a daughter-in-law. In the past several years I have lost everything but Him."

The remark was made to me yesterday immediately after our Lutheran open air service in Madison Square, New York City, by a stranger of fine personality and rather gracious manner. It appeared evident he was lonely and in need of someone with whom to share his thoughts and emotions.

As the conversation continued it came out that he is on relief, enough to eat and live in a better-class lodging house (if there are such). While he appeared clean and indeed dignified, his clothes were shabby and he missed the concern of thoughtful loved ones. His only complaint was that the men on the park benches and in the lodging houses are so raw and vicious. His treasured fountain pen and watch had been stolen from him and he very clearly did not fit into the surroundings to which the depression and misfortune had consigned him.

He was plainly happy in his Lord. Believed and trusted. Daily grace he found sufficient. He had attended some of our services toward the end of last summer's season but had forgotten the hour and so in vainly looking for us recently he had concluded that there was no park preaching this year. Now he was comforted.

Why They Don't Attend Church

In his economic and religious background this man is of course superior to many we meet in our open air preaching but he does nevertheless represent a type, growing in numbers; men, and some women too, generally past middle age, discarded by industry, living on small savings, odd jobs or on relief and sleeping in crowded, unsanitary and often morally filthy lodging houses. During the day the park benches represent home to them.

These folks do not come to our churches for worship. In their better days many of them did. Now that they find themselves on a lower standard of life and respectability they feel the church is no longer for them. They cannot contribute, they haven't the proper clothing and they do not want the facts of their circumstances generally known. Moreover their surroundings are not conducive to any growth in Grace. Atheistic literature confronts their minds and militant hate and class agitation envelopes them.

They read in the daily press of churches closed for the summer and prominent preachers off to Europe so they easily conclude that after all perhaps the Communists are right,—"when your money is gone the church has no more use for you." They see pictures of beautiful churches dedicated in attractive suburban districts while in the congested area where they find shelter churches either are marked "for sale," abandoned or old and seldom opened.

If our Lutheran Church is going to minister to these discarded hosts, who comprise the major group of the approximately ten million still unemployed in this country, we will have to prove the sincerity of our words by more positive means. Here in New York City as well as in a number of other places we are finding that these multitudes will generally recognize the voice of the Good Shepherd when it meets them where they are.

Yes, He Will Pray for Us

My new friend of yesterday did not need to be invited back. We were on his own ground and he felt at home. Indeed, he expressed his gratitude for this evidence of interest on the part of the Church. To my invitation to help us, he replied: "yes, well I can pray—that's something I can do."

Since the middle of May Lutheran preaching services have been conducted every Monday and Friday at 12:30 P. M. On other days of the week the general committee of the New York Federation of Churches has charge of the meetings. The New York Bible Society is donating the Bible sections which are handed out to those who promise to read them. The following languages beside English have been asked for most frequently: Italian, German, Swedish, French, Yiddish, Hebrew, Russian, Dutch, Slovak, Spanish, Norwegian, Hungarian and Chinese.

Contrary to the long standing practice of the City Government permission has been granted, this year and last, to conduct these services right on city park property. It is doubtful if a better site for open air evangelism exists in the city than under the big elm tree besides the Northern Flower Circle of Madison Square Park. The largest attendance this year was over 400 early this week. The general average is about 100; most of whom stay for the greater part of the forty-five minutes of the service.

Our greatest need is for a larger number of effective preachers. Choirs, soloists and cornetists, were they available, could be very helpful. Personal workers and lay speakers, a personnel resource which our great Church, in terms of its principles and its practice, should produce in greater abundance, are also needed.

We Preach Christ

What the real explanation is I do not know but so far this season we have not been disturbed by atheists, Communists, Jews or "hecklers." Our audience is sympathetic and interested. Probably our enemies have decided to let us alone. As a matter of policy we do not condemn. We preach Christ and Him crucified. Messages are direct, simple and short. We appeal to common sense and fair play. We remind folks of mother's prayers and mother's faith. "Go back to your home church, if you haven't any, the Lutheran Church is here today to bid you welcome. Study her way of salvation and see if she does not offer you what you need.

What about results? We have frequent questions and inquiries about matters of faith, Bible truths, location of churches, preachers, doctrine, attitude of the church on modern social questions, personal morality, war, race relations, etc. We make it a point to refer inquiries to pastors who are specially interested in such work or known to the inquirer. Some we follow up ourselves as far as we can. However, it must be stated that the results in church accessions have not been extensive. This is partly due to the wide gaps between the church and the masses and the general absence of positive hospitality to strangers in so many Lutheran congregations especially in downtown churches. Formerly we printed a special program announcing the Inner Mission Society, the preachers, a Scripture lesson, a personal prayer, several hymns, a short sermonette and a brief statement about the Lutheran Church. The past three years our lack of funds made this impossible.

Open Air Preaching Nothing New

Were it necessary a great deal might be said in support of open air preaching. We find the practice in the Old Testament. The only recorded sermon we have of our Saviour was an open air message. The early fathers preached in the open and the great evangelists have followed them. In the Lutheran Church our city missionaries have for years preached in hospital wards, shops, lodging houses, ships, prisons and almshouses. Open air preaching is really a part of the modern missionary movement to carry the Gospel to the lost and unchurched where they are.

While home mission has its problems of rent, light and property, open air work involves no rentals, no light bill, no sexton fees, no ventilation difficulties and no ushers. Many who are averse to attend an indoor meeting will stop to listen to an open air speaker no matter who is or what he affirms. All that is needed to begin is—Faith and Zeal. As of old, so today—"how can they hear without a preacher." It is up to us preachers.

Summer-time Mission Publicity Through the Open Air Service

THE Church's mission duty is continuous. Even summer time and vacation time are not to be considered as times of complete surcease from missionary effort in the home field, as little as in foreign fields.

But mission work during the hot and languid summer months is, in most congregations, especially in city churches, difficult and discouraging. The schools are closed, even some Sunday schools. Most children are gone. Evening services are dropped. People flock to the country, to mountains and seashore, where, as a rule, no Lutheran churches are found. Automobiles filled with week-enders clog the highways on Saturdays and Sundays.

And yet church work dare not cease. On the contrary, just because of the condition described church workers are beginning to ponder whether church publicity and certain phases of summer time mission work should not be intensified or given new forms. As the habits of our people, due to the automobile, the spread of the outdoor life and summer camp idea, are changing church workers are asking whether new forms of Gospel publicity and summer time mission work should not be sought to meet these new conditions. If our people go to the country, in ever-increasing numbers, should not the church go with them, or direct them, so that both will meet when the destination is reached? And if people from the country, also in increasing numbers, visit the city, should not the city churches be ready to receive them?

And there have been definite and tangible results. We mention only two with which we are familiar here on the Atlantic Coast, Luther Day in Asbury Park and Ocean Grove, and the splendid work done in Lutherland.

For several years back largely attended and therefore inspiring Luther Day services arranged by a local committee in conjunction with the American Lutheran Publicity Bureau have been held in the large auditorium in Ocean Grove, N. J., which adjoins Asbury Park, both facing the Atlantic Ocean. Many non-Lutherans attend these impressive Lutheran services with their strong message and glorious choral singing.

On a very much larger scale summer time mission work and Lutheran publicity work is carried on in the new Lutheran summer colony in Lutherland, Pocono Pines, Pennsylvania, with its well attended devotional services every morning, its daily lectures on all manner of church work and mission work, its very well attended Sunday morning services held in a large assembly hall and its inspiring Sunday evening sunset services held on the shores of a beautiful inland lake.

And thus both Asbury Park and Lutherland are answers to the question, How can new forms be added to our summer time mission and Lutheran publicity work? And doubtless many similar answers are given in our church in many different parts of the country. We are glad to note that the Walther League wayside church signs are reported as being productive of good results.

One other answer to the question of summer time publicity work is to be given in this article, viz., through the open air service. The undersigned has been repeatedly requested to describe the open air services conducted for four years past by Messiah Evangelical Lutheran Church, a mission congregation of the Atlantic District, located in the northern part of old Manhattan Island. Reluctantly we consented, for it is summer time.

1. *Publicity Value.* Open air services have real publicity value. They create a new occasion and furnish an admittedly good reason for using printer's ink and flooding the entire section of the city from which the congregation draws its mission material with circulars announcing the services. The name of the Lutheran Church and of Messiah Church is brought to the attention of people who have never heard of either—Jews and Gentiles alike. Not a few Jews attend our services or at least listen to our sidewalk talks, or else listen from their third, fourth or fifth story windows. Lay workers, mostly mothers and their children of school age, have covered the entire northern part of Manhattan Island by placing the circulars, gotten out as attractively as we know how, into the mail boxes, or, where this was not permitted, slipping them under the doors of the apartments. The entire territory of Messiah Church is built up with five- and six-story tenement or apartment houses, occupied by average middle class people. The circulars are printed in such a way that the set-up can be used for posters which are placed into the store windows of the neighborhood.

The exceptional publicity value of outdoor services is also evidenced by the fact that even the large daily New York City newspapers are willing to print our announcements and write-ups sent them through the office of our American Lutheran Publicity Bureau and that they send representatives to photograph the assembly, or parts of it, for publication in the photogravure section of their Sunday editions. The New York *Times* in their Sunday photogravure pictorial section brought excellent pictures of the services, with well-worded captions, both in June and in July, 1929, one of the pictures being a time exposure of the entire assembly and the other a flashlight of the vested boys' choir and the clergy. Non-Lutherans have been brought to our services through these pictures.

The open air service also creates an occasion and furnishes a reason for displaying all manner of signs, signs so large and loud that even the sign-surfeited New Yorkers take notice and read them. For this year a sign eighteen feet long and four feet high was painted by a Japanese artist who is a faithful member and one of the most active deacons of the congregation. It was placed against the brick wall of the Church House shown in the cut, directly above the six doors that lead from the chapel located on the second floor, out to the balcony, which was built to serve as the pulpit for the outdoor services. The top floor contains the parsonage and the lower floor the large room used for the main Sunday school, Catechism classes, meetings, etc. To state, in passing, why the Church House is set so far back from the street, on the rear fifty feet of the lot measuring seventy-five by a hundred and fifty it is because it is hoped that some day this building will house a Christian day school and that the church proper and later on perhaps a parsonage can be built up near the street. Until that time comes the fine large property of Messiah Mission purchased four years ago at a bargain price is to be used for open air services and, of course, also to furnish an attractive and worthy setting for the present Church House.

2. *The Place.* Messiah Church is thankful for having a place so well suited to open air services. Without a suitable place open air services are not likely to succeed. In some instances they are held on the steps leading from the church doors down to the sidewalk. Just as we began to write, the following came to our desk in a bulletin sent through the mails:

*"Open Air Pulpit
"Conducted from May to October*

"Daily at 12.30 p.m. (except Saturday and Sunday) from the steps of the Marble Collegiate Church on Fifth Avenue (Reformed) a gospel message by trumpet, song and sermon is given to the passing throngs and people are urged to stop sinning and accept Jesus as Savior and guide. This service is maintained jointly by the Marble Collegiate Church and the New York Federation of Churches."

This service is more in the nature of what Messiah Church calls her "Sidewalk Talks" which precede and follow the main open air service and of which we shall speak later on.

Outdoor services were begun by Messiah Mission four years ago, two years before the present church house was built, immediately after the ground was purchased. The third service held is shown in the picture. In anticipation of a possible purchase débris by the truck load had been removed by the young people, shrubs and flowers planted and a tennis court constructed. Today the people of Messiah Church are planning and working to make the setting of the open air as well as of the indoor services more and more attractive, all, of course, for the Gospel's sake. Permission has been secured from the owners of adjoining buildings to fasten and then drop from the top of the buildings open mesh wire for the purpose of running up non-clinging flower-bearing vines. The inexpensive mesh wire fence that encloses the property will also be beautified by all manner of vines judiciously placed.

3. *Lighting.* The beauty of the setting for the services, most of which are held at night time, is enhanced by floodlighting the

grounds as well as the building by concealed lights. One light of only sixty watts in a reflector placed on the wire arch surmounting the entrance to the grounds, flood-lights the entire front of the building in such a manner that the lettering on the large sign described above, but not shown on the picture, is legible from automobiles passing upon the street. The cross on the top of the building, a common wooden cross painted white, taken for marble by most who see it, is floodlighted by two or sometimes three small bulbs concealed in a copper box at the base of the cross. This cross is floodlighted every night of the year, up to eleven or twelve o'clock. Seen from the street, it silhouettes against the nightly sky and not, as the photograph shows, against the buildings in the rear. The open air services viewed from the street,

and especially from the windows or roofs of the buildings across the street, present a picture of rare beauty.

4. *The Time.* Our open air services are not held during the week, but only on Sunday nights, and so far only once a month. More many be added later on. These are, of course, extra services, held in addition to the two morning services and the Sunday school between the two services, conducted every Sunday of the year. The main open air service begins at 8.30 p.m. It is preceded and followed by sidewalk talks of half an hour each. The pastor of the congregation and an outside pastor take turn about, speaking five or eight or ten minutes each. Questions are invited. They must have some relation to the subject of the talk. The subjects of the last two services were, "Only two religions, 1, the religion of works; 2, the religion of grace," and "Is it true that one can be a Christian without going to church?"

The New Church House, Showing Garden and Open Air Service

The position taken by the speakers is on the sidewalk, before the bulletin board shown in the picture. Benches covered with a rug and a velour cover thrown across the wire fence for a background form the wayside pulpit. The subject of the talk is displayed on a special sign.

These sidewalk talks are a new feature added this year. We regard them as an experiment. So far they have been satisfactory. The people give us a respectful hearing. Few questions have been asked thus far. We should be glad to hear from other congregations that have gathered experience along these lines.

Open air services during the winter season have not been attempted thus far, but for years we have had open air congregational singing with instrumental accompaniment at Christmas, Easter and Pentecost, with good results. And this year experiments have been made with occasional open air morning services during the late spring and early summer.

5. *The Scriptural Precedent.* Some forms of street or sidewalk preaching have been frowned upon in our Lutheran Church, and rightly so. But if these services are properly conducted, and especially if their message in its entirety is of God, they are quite in accord with scriptural precedent. The greatest open air and wayside preachers of all times and ages were none other than Christ Himself, John the Baptist, the apostles and evangelists in the New Testament and the prophets in the Old Testament.

And today men who continue in the words of Jesus, men with a message, the Gospel message, voiced forth in a language and in a manner of presentation which the people who make up our city audiences can understand, men who rightly divide the word of truth, who have learned the art of preaching both the law and the gospel in their proper proportion, men whose souls are fired with the love that flowed forth on Calvary, with love like that of Paul, who was willing to be accursed from Christ for his brethren, his kinsmen according to the flesh, like that of Moses, who was willing to be blotted out of God's book that Israel might not be destroyed—not a love alike in degree but a love alike in kind—are today the preachers that are needed for all preaching and especially, too, for open air preaching in our cities, large or small, east and west, and north and south.

A necessary outward qualification is a voice that carries, and in our case a voice that is able to overcome the noises caused by many automobiles passing by on a hundred-foot street, two blocks from uptown Broadway. All these years we have been fortunate in enlisting the active interest and cooperation of brother pastors who in a very satisfactory manner "filled the bill" as open air preachers.

What we are in sore need of, however, is a loud-speaking or amplifying system, not for the people seated within our enclosure, but to reach the people standing in large groups out on the street and the people across the way and up and down Sherman Avenue and other nearby streets, but upon inquiry we find that the price of a good installation of this kind would run into three figures, and that is, of course, beyond the means of a small debt-laden mission congregation. Here, too, we would invite the suggestions of such as have had experience along these lines.

6. *Music and Singing.* The congregational singing is accompanied by a piano and this year by a small, newly formed band. Last year two paid trumpeters served our purposes very well, but their charges were so high that we felt that a subsidized mission must try to furnish its own music, even though in the beginning it might fall short of what we should like to have.

Choirs of sister congregations were always found willing to serve us during June and September, but during the months of July and August we must rely entirely upon our own boys' choir. Boys' voices, beautiful as they are indoors, do not carry as well as adult voices out in the open air, especially if there are unfavorable wind currents. Excellent vocal soloists and also a few instrumental accompanists placed themselves at our disposal ever since we began our outdoor services. As long as we had no professional accompanists to pay, the collections taken at the services about covered the expenses.

Is it not possible that in smaller centers of population the open air service idea would work our equally as well as, if not better than, in the large cities?

Orphan Dinner Guests

FROM the congregation at Omaha, Nebraska, served by Pastor Lawrence Acker comes an excellent suggestion. In a form letter mailed to his people we read, "We are happy to announce that children of the Lutheran Orphanage in Fremont will be our guests next Sunday morning. Our members will call for the youngsters and in the afternoon return them to the institution. A Sunday meal at our homes and a sightseeing tour are included in the program of the day."

The visit of the children is combined with the annual Harvest Festival. The church is appropriately decorated with fall flowers, foliage, etc. Food stuffs and other material from soap to bacon and sausage was collected for the orphanage. On the late afternoon of the designated day not only a caravan of automobiles with happy children bent its way homeward, but also several loads of food supplies, etc.

In larger cities this plan could be worked by having a delegation of six or twelve visit the larger congregation on Harvest Home Sunday.

Meeting A Home Missions Problem

LOUIS HENZE

IT IS ONE of the paradoxes of our organized church work that we usually turn over the most difficult work to the men least fitted for it. We have always thought of mission work and church extension in terms of newly ordained candidates. It is a fact that candidates for the ministry are the men usually called into the subsidized work of the church, and that the subsidized work of the church more and more requires special talent.

Right here let it be said that we in no wise wish to infer that candidates ought not to be called into the mission field, nor do we wish to devalue their work. Many candidates bring into service an asset which older men do not always have: a freshness and youthful exuberance which directed into the right channels have real value. We are heartily in favor of using candidates for mission work provided they are given constructive preliminary training before taking over a major mission opportunity.

We are here calling attention to a factor which we deem of vital importance to an aggressive home missions program: the need of building up a corps of experienced home mission workers. We must train and develop men who will make the task of home missions their life's work. This means that such men must not only be trained for efficient service, but that they must also be retained for continued service.

The task of home missions has changed with the language transition of our church. It is no longer primarily the task of gathering in the unchurched Lutherans. It is no longer the task of planting churches on a receding frontier. We must accept the fact that we must start churches to reach the unchurched in competition with other church bodies and that the criterion for placing a missionary in a community is not how many Lutheran families are located there, but how large is the unchurched population.

Under such circumstances our subsidized work must be done by men of the best caliber and by men who are specialists in their field. Such men must know the fundamental principles necessary for such work and be able to apply them to their particular field of endeavor for successful work. They must know what it is all about. This can be gained alone by experience, but that experience must be utilized again and again in the expansion program of the church.

This will do away with much of the experimental features of home mission work. How often has the church started to subsidize work in a given field as a "noble experiment." The church kept its fingers crossed, so to speak, and hoped for the best. All too often that hope cost the church real money. The church cannot afford to experiment in its mission fields. It is safe to say that many of these "noble experiments" failed due to a lack of experience on the part of the worker.

For some years we have been trying to build up a corps of experienced men in the Atlantic District for the task of home missions. This has been made possible by a District that has had the vision to accept and put into operation policies and factors that are vital to the attempt. We shall just mention one which is of utmost importance. It has done away with a rigid salary level for pastors of subsidized congregations and missionaries-at-large. All too often men in the subsidized field accepted calls to self-sustaining congregations for no other reason than a larger salary. Not because the salary in itself was an inducement, but with a growing family the missionary could not do his best work under the financial worries of a salary to which he was doomed, so long as he served in the subsidized field. In this way District Mission Boards have lost and, we believe, still lose their most talented men. In fact, it is usually the successful men who receive the calls. Every time an experienced missionary is called out of the subsidized field, it has cost the church money, far more than a better salary would have cost the District. A flexible salary scale is vital to a program designed to retain men in a field which more and more is becoming a highly specialized branch of church work. Better salaries to retain experienced men in the subsidized field is, in the final analysis, economy.

This factor more than any other has helped us to retain experienced men in the field of home missions. What that means we shall try to point out by taking the reader over the program of a missionary-at-large in recent years. This man is primarily engaged in the opening of new fields. His task is to guide the subsidized group to a certain stage of development and then he is succeeded by a permanent pastor. Next to starting in the right place and with the right man, there is nothing more important than to get the new congregation off to the right start, and that means to function from the very beginning with the right principles and with correct attitudes toward those who are supporting the work. In this respect alone the work of such an experienced man is eminently worthwhile. This particular man, whose program we wish to outline, spent one year with our District engaged in the detailed survey work of that year. Toward the close of the year he took charge of a field which was judged to be open for a major endeavor in the light of the mission opportunities of Greater New York. He stayed in this field almost one year. At the end of that period the congregation numbered more than two hundred souls and close to a hundred communicant members. A fine piece of property had been secured without outside financial aid, and preliminary steps were underway for a building project. Today under a successful successor the congregation numbers close to four hundred souls with a Sunday School enrollment of more than two hundred.

The second endeavor of this missionary-at-large was in a community of about 20,000 inhabitants within the Greater New York area. Lutheranism had failed in a previous attempt to gain a permanent foothold in this field. At the close of one year's intensive follow-up work of the canvass, the work was permanently established, property had been secured, a modest chapel erected and the groundwork laid for a permanent pastor. This field today is in a flourishing condition.

Last year the missionary-at-large opened another field in the Greater New York area. Not a single soul wanted the mission, but we had the large unchurched population which needed us. Intensive follow-up work after recanvassing the field had its results and today the mission ministers to about three hundred souls, numbers slightly more than a hundred communicant members, and has a fine Sunday School enrollment.

In all these fields no borderline methods were used to get established. There was no commercialism of any kind. The subsidized group was guided to support its work solely on the New Testament plan. People were accepted into membership after long periods of informal talks preparatory to communicant membership and, we believe, joined the respective church on conviction. That the work did not center around a personality is attested by the fact that in each case the missionary-at-large was followed by the permanent pastor without any difficulty or harm to the work. It may be said to the credit of these groups that they realized the importance of the work which the missionary-at-large was doing, and he left each group with its blessing.

We believe that this given sample of the work of a missionary-at-large shows that it is successful work—successful not because he played a part establishing three congregations, but judging the work solely as it should be judged, in terms of effectively reaching the unchurched. There is room for more men who will do this type of work. It is nothing new. It has been done before. We call your attention to it, upon request, because it is a necessary fac-

tor in an aggressive home missions program and which deserves more consideration by the church-at-large. It is, at the same time, an argument for the building up of a corps of permanent home mission workers.

There are those perhaps who look upon all this as a high pressure method of doing things. We fail to see any high pressure. It is simply doing rather successfully what we are always trying to do by means of our missionary agencies: bring Christ to the unchurched. There may be those who are dubious about instilling a Lutheran consciousness in a group of newly gained unchurched. We have heard the thought expressed. God, however, did not tell us to instill a Lutheran consciousness. He told us to preach the Gospel. We believe in its power. There are those perhaps who look upon all missionary agencies of a specialized nature as an overhead expense. God give us more overhead expense, if this is what it may legitimately be called.

This article, in conclusion, may seem to be but a cold analysis of a missionary problem. The writer, nevertheless, is keenly aware that human energy and ingenuity cannot accomplish supernatural and divine work, and that our missionary agencies can only be instruments of the Holy Spirit. With His directing, however, we can be better instruments and more efficiently used for His great purposes.

Adult Class Appeal

HERE is another invitation to join the adult class as it appeared in a parish paper.

A STANDING INSTITUTION
(A word to such as have no church connection)

Throughout the year the pastor conducts a lecture class for such as desire to inform themselves on the doctrines and principles of the Lutheran Church. Incidentally attendance at this class prepares for church membership, although the attendant assumes no obligations whatsoever by listening in. The course consists of about twelve lectures, held on Friday evenings from 8 to 9 o'clock. The next class will be organized on Friday evening, January 16th.

If you are unchurched or if you desire to acquaint yourself with the fundamental doctrines of Lutheranism, you are urgently invited to attend these lectures. You do not become obligated in any way to join the church. There are no memory assignments and no expenses. Just sit in. Any steps towards church affiliation must come from you.

You ought to be informed regarding the teachings of the Church. You ought not be satisfied to believe and repeat parrot-like the woefully perverted, incomplete and garbled conceptions of the Church as they are peddled by some misinformed and prejudiced detractor. Get first-hand knowledge.

You need the Church! We say this without any apologies or reservations. You have no right to permit the questions of your heart to go unanswered. You have no right to trifle with your soul. Eternity is long and you can afford to take no chances with it.

Join the class. The first lecture is on Friday, January 16th.

The Organization of Mission Study Groups
By G. A. KUHLMANN

ALTHOUGH REPORTS INDICATE that the general response in the present Missionary Forward Movement has been satisfactory, still the importance of the missionary responsibilities of our church warrants careful consideration of all possible channels through which we may effectively accomplish the missionary task which has been assigned to us. In our efforts to disseminate missionary information, we have, as a church body, been presenting the missionary problems to the entire congregation or to the entire membership of the larger organizations of the church, such as the Sunday School, the Ladies Aid, the Men's Club, the Walther League, etc. In the educational program of each of these organizations mission study has played an important part, and every member has thus been touched in the regular contacts of the pastor and teacher.

But the question nevertheless arises: Could we perhaps increase our results, if we would add to this "blanket" mission study a system of more intensive study of mission problems among smaller groups of those who are deeply interested? Could we utilize more fully the talents of our people, if we would each year organize groups of those who are especially interested in missions for more intensive training courses?

The formation of mission study groups within the membership of the various organizations of the church may at first thought seem superfluous and a tendency to clutter up the daily program of the pastor. A further explanation is therefore in place concerning the organization of mission study groups with sufficient flexibility of membership to avoid the cluttering effect that might be anticipated.

In the first place the mission study group is not a permanent organization and remains organized only so long as it is doing intensive work on a definite missionary project. Since members of various organizations are already grouped in natural divisions because of their common interests, more effective work will probably be done, if the members of the mission study group are all volunteers from the same church organization, such as the Ladies' Aid, the Walther League, the Men's Club, or the adult section of the Sunday School.

The mission study group should be small. Its membership should not exceed eight or ten persons. With more than ten members, the opportunities for discussion by each member become limited. To do the best work, the leader and the members should be in close personal touch, so that the atmosphere will be thoroughly informal and each individual will feel free to express his opinions and impressions, and to discuss the questions and problems in his mind.

The group should meet weekly for a course ranging from five to ten sessions, the number of sessions depending upon the material to be studied. The actual duration of the sessions will probably not exceed an hour and a half. Even "busy" people can usually find time for eight or ten such meetings each year. The entire course, rather than the session, is the unit. The series of meetings may begin at any time, but should be so arranged as to avoid interruptions by holidays or special services. The group organizes for a definite piece of work, meets independently of the larger organization from which it has drawn its members, and should be dissolved when the course is completed. If the members wish to take up another course, it is best to leave an interval of time between courses.

Suitable meeting places can easily be found for such a small group. Preferably the group should have access to blackboard space and to large wall maps. Care should, however, be exercised to avoid a formal classroom attitude.

MAIL ADVERTISING FOR THE LOCAL CHURCH

O. H. PANNKOKE

There is a difference between direct and indirect advertising which the careful advertiser always keeps in mind. Indirect advertising is addressed to people in general regardless of the interest which they may have in the matter presented. Such is the advertising in newspapers, through bulletin boards and throw-cards. Direct advertising is addressed to individual prospects likely to respond to the appeal. Letters are direct advertising. There is no choice between the effectiveness of direct and indirect advertising, just as there is no choice between the driving force of a rifle bullet and the scattering effect of buckshot.

A good letter, first-class mail, costs five cents. A personal visit costs between one and three dollars. A pastor can send any number of letters. He can make only a very limited number of calls. From the standpoint of economy of time and effort the mails are a necessity for effective parish work.

A number of functions suggest themselves for mail-advertising for the church; building up attendance for the regular services, for special services; gaining members for the various societies; enlisting new members; obtaining financial assistance; suggesting specific work to be done for the church.

In thus suggesting "functions" for mail-advertising, the advertising is saved from hopeless, ineffective generalities. A letter with no clear object is like a dreamer. You don't know just what he is after, and feel uncomfortable in his presence. Find out what you want and then in clean, precise, unmistakable language say it.

In mail advertising six elements must be considered: the lists, the approach, the contents, the outward form and appearance, the enclosures, the following.

The importance of good lists cannot be emphasized too strongly. That means in the first place accurate lists. A misspelt name, a slovenly address are an immediate prejudice to an otherwise good letter. In the second place, lists must be grouped according to their interests. A congregation is a unit. But in that unit are represented every variety of interest and activity and the strength of an appeal lies in its aptness to reach the person addressed.

Lists of prospective new members are most difficult to obtain. The average pastor, however, finds no greater difficulty than the average business man. Business men pay up to three and more dollars for one good name and they are ceaselessly at work to add to their lists.

The first source to obtain names of prospects are the members themselves. A regular form for that purpose ought to be standard equipment of an active church and by letter and word of mouth the members from time to time ought to be asked to coöperate.

The second source is the Every Member Canvass. Names of prospective members are and must be one of its most important by-products and canvassers must be impressed with the importance of receiving this information.

A house to house canvass from time to time is the next means of adding to the mailing list.

Something that has never been tried is "coupon" newspaper advertising, that is, church announcements in the newspaper with a coupon attached asking for a reply and offering literature. Correspondence schools build up their mailing lists entirely by this method. It would be splendid if it were tried for the church to test its value and work out an effective method. The writer would be happy to coöperate in such an effort in order to test the method.

The approach in a letter is the salutation and the signature. Shall it be a sealed or an unsealed letter, first or second-class mail? The question is determined by asking, "Do the people read second-class mail, and is the communication worth a two-cent stamp?" With very few exceptions, the answer will mean a sealed two-cent stamped letter. That means the letter opens with the personal salutation and closes with a personal signature. Saving one-cent stamps is good where it can be done. It is waste where it will weaken an otherwise good appeal.

Who shall sign the letter? The person who has most influence with the addressed. Here lies the real strength of mail advertising. An unknown signature means nothing. A known signature stands for the personality which it represents.

Next to the approach come the contents of the letter. There must be in a good letter at least an appeal, a specific application and the instruction for action. In spirit and make-up it ought to be concrete, sincere, winning or persuasive, and vivid.

For instance, a letter for a Young People's Society should begin with a description of the advantages of being part of such an organization. It should then make the specific application: "You will enjoy to be associated with them." It should close with instruction for action. Such instructions are valueless if they are general and vague. "Join us," means nothing as an action appeal. "Our next meeting is held on Tuesday. We would like to see you there" is definite and to the point.

The specific action appeal is the most important part of the letter. The Tories believed that information is sufficient to lead to action, and H. G. Wells is bravely spreading again the age-old folly. If that were true Christ and Christianity would have been superfluous. Every sinner who has ever been damned has known the right but chose the wrong. Information which does not bring a strong plea for action is not advertising. It is day-dreaming.

The outward form and appearance in mail advertising is the same as the care in dress and appearance of the salesman. A slovenly salesman is not a good recommendation for his firm. A slovenly letter is not a good recommendation for a church. The paper, letterhead, letter and address are the elements making up the outward form. A letter ought to look distinctive as well as dignified. For important communication a good bond paper gives an air of quality that has its effect. On the letter head ought to be printed only the information necessary to identify the institution which sends the letter and it ought to be set up in single, harmonious type. If there is a good distinguishing mark which can serve as a trade mark for a commodity, to identify the church, that may be printed on the letterhead. For instance, "the oldest Lutheran Church in America."

Appropriate enclosures strengthen a letter. But— they must be appropriate to the contents of the letter. In a plea for church attendance a tract against dancing would be out of place; one on the Third Commandment would not. In a more elaborate mail campaign it is well worth the effort to get a series of folders to go with the successive letters. But don't stultify yourself by stating in your letter: "Enclosed you will find." The letter is your big, effective gun, not the folder. Furthermore, a host of different enclosures distracts and leaves a person bewildered.

Finally, the follow-up: Most men who use the mails think in terms of a single letter and are disappointed if the replies do not come as they expect. That is wrong. A single letter will sow the seed and lead some to act, a follow-up letter will bring more; a second follow-up will bring still more. Mail efforts ought to be conceived in series of five, the first four communications two weeks apart from each other, the last one seven days after the fourth. The first letters ought to contain more information, the last concentrate more on the appeal to action.

A mail effort is spent after two weeks. Experience has conclusively proven that. The writer has frequently worked with men who did not believe this to be true, only to see the return mail stop after two weeks as though stopped by a magic hand. The effort was spent. Another effort was needed to start action again.

Ceaseless and merciless testing is the secret of successful advertising. The dashed off letter may look fine the moment it is written. After two days it will show many threadbare, weak spots that must be strengthened. Try out a letter or a folder on a few people of judgment. It often saves money and prevents disappointments.

When letters are sent a tabulated report ought to be kept as to the actual results obtained by them. That is the only way to learn. Advertising is not proven by theories and arguments. It is proven solely and alone by results.

A Successful Postcard Campaign

Since January 1, 1940, Pilgrim Church of Lakewood, Ohio, a suburb of Cleveland, has conducted an extraordinarily successful one-cent postcard campaign designed to increase Church attendance and to maintain general interest in parochial projects and organizations. The text is prepared weekly by the pastor, the Rev. Karl H. Ehlers, and mailed on Wednesday evening to the printer in Lorain, thirty-five miles away. The printing is completed on Thursday, and the cards remailed in time to reach the addressees on Friday morning. A two weeks' supply of cards, pre-addressed on the parish's hand-fed Addressograph, is forwarded to the printer every fortnight. A week's mailing costs $3.50: $2.50 for 250 postcards and $1.00 for imprinting. The time required for addressing averages thirty minutes a week.

The membership of Pilgrim Church has been stabilized in the neighborhood of 500 communicants. For the period 1932-1939 the Sunday morning congregations had averaged between 273 and 302, gaining slowly. The 1940 average for the first six months was 347; the January to June average in 1939 was 308. The total Church attendance for the first half-year of 1940 was 11,003; for the same period in 1939 the figure stood at 9841. Thus 1940 shows a gain of 1,162 worshipers, or more than 12 percent.

The text of sample card is presented herewith.

During Holy Week:

"Dear Friend: 'Come, let us feast this Easter-day on Christ the Bread of Heaven!' So sang Luther long ago; so we sing still. The flowers may not yet be blooming, but the Sun of the Soul is shining. Come early! Last year 600 worshiped with us. But we have always found room for all. Bring your friends. Subject: 'AN EASTER CELEBRATION PLEASING TO CHRIST.'—Holy Communion Thursday at 8 p.m. Announce in the half hour preceding. No 'phone announcements, please! A sermon of interest to all. Those not communing will be dismissed early.—Good Friday service at 8, with sermon by Prof. W. G. Polack, Concordia Seminary. It will be a pleasure and a privilege to hear this distinguished clergyman.—Offering for missions by special Lenten sacrifice envelope on Good Friday; by Easter envelope Sunday. Yes, we believe in giving you many opportunities to become rich in God and good works.—Sorry to hear our boys and girls lost their basketball games Saturday, our boys' first loss in second half. Next game March 31, Mt. Olive, 2:15.—Noonday services Engineers' Hall, 12:20-12:50, your pastor speaking Good Friday. Attend with friends. Vestry March 25, 8."

My dear Miss G.

Birthdays are gala days. They stand out in our lives as "red letter" days. A Christian reflecting on the mercies of God and His blessings transforms them into festivals of praise and thanksgiving. May your birthday be both a holiday and a holy day!

Such an anniversary answers the question: "Is life worth while?" God gave us life. He extends our days for a purpose. We are His children, His stewards. Let us make the most of our lives, of our opportunities that present themselves day by day, so that our lives may abound to the welfare of His Kingdom, to the service of our fellowmen and to His glory!

God grant that yours is that abundant life!

Very faithfully your Pastor,

Weekly Lenten Post Card,

No. 1

"Behold, we go up to Jerusalem!"

We are again making the journey with Jesus in our Lenten meditations. Surely, the Savior wants every one of us to go with him. Every portion of the Passion Story should have our whole-hearted devotion.

Follow Him, then, all that mournful way from Olivet to Calvary. Attend every Lenten service. And gain the blessings of His wondrous cross.

No. 2

"Not my will, but thine be done."

Thus our adorable Savior prayed on the eve of His death. The answer to that prayer would bring agony, suffering, and death. He loved us and suffered all to redeem us.

Lent calls us to do His will. Lest we grow weary in serving Him, let us remember Gethsemane and pray with our Lord: "Thy will be done."

No. 3

"What shall I do then with Jesus which is called Christ?"

This question of Pontius Pilate demands an answer. Shall we love or despise, accept or reject Jesus? One or the other it must be.

May your answer be: I will have Jesus as my Savior and King, my Lord and my God.

Come and claim Him as your own on Calvary.

No. 4

"If I wash thee not, thou hast no part with me."

How necessary for us to accept Jesus as our Savior! He redeemed us with His holy, precious blood.

We are so prone to forget what He has done for us. He therefore reminds us again: "If I wash thee not, thou hast no part with me."

May He share with us that life of service which climaxed in His death on the cross.

No. 5

"Art not thou also one of this man's disciples?"

Peter thought he was a disciple, but he denied his Lord. Are we disciples? Do we follow distantly or do we walk in the Savior's company? Do we accompany Him weekly in the Lenten meditations? Do we identify ourselves with Him and His work?

Let us confess Jesus before men. Then He also will confess us before His heavenly Father.

No. 6

"And when he was come into Jerusalem, all the city was moved, saying, Who is this?"

Here is life's most important question: Who is Jesus Christ? The answer of this question decides the weal or woe of every person.

Jesus is again passing through town and hamlet during this Lententide. May we learn to know Him. When, then, the final question is addressed to us: "Who is this?" the answer will come from the depth of our heart:

He is my Redeemer, my Lord and my God.

No. 7

"Put off thy shoes from off thy feet, for the place whereon thou standest is holy ground."

So God called to Moses out of the Burning Bush.

We are entering Holy Week. The Christian Church pauses to contemplate the death of the Son of God. "Put off thy shoes." Take time to meditate. Ponder, O child of man, on the price paid for your redemption.

The Savior walks the way of sorrows. He dies, but He will rise again and show forth the victory.

May we be counted worthy to share in His triumph.

No. 8

"Let us also go, that we may die with Him."

Devotion and loyalty are here combined in matchless beauty. Death with the Lord is preferred to life without Him.

Good Friday calls us to an exercise of faith. We are to ascend Calvary with Jesus, stand beneath the cross and behold the death of the Son of God. His death will be our death if we believe that He died in our stead. If thus by faith we have died with Him, we shall also live with Him.

Let us also go!

LOCAL CHURCH PUBLICITY SYSTEMATICALLY CONDUCTED

J. F. E. NICKELSBURG

The many letters received at the office of the Publicity Bureau, asking for printed matter which might be helpful to successfully conduct local publicity, would indicate a new and greater interest in this important phase of church work.

This article has been written to present a working plan, by which a congregation, whether small or large, in a city or town, blessed with unlimited funds or "just breaking even," can do efficient publicity work. Study the chart below and after you have carefully read it, perhaps twice, then read the explanatory remarks.

The Presentation

The matter of more systematic publicity and advertising in the interest of the congregation is discussed in the meeting of the Church Council. The Pastor or some interested layman should be prepared to submit facts and figures showing the need of better publicity methods. The Council recommends to the voting body the adoption of the chart.

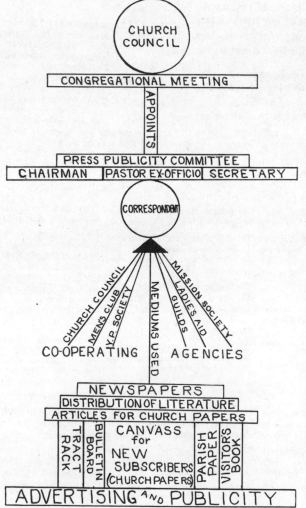

The Adoption of the Scheme

At a meeting of the voting members the recommendations of the Council are discussed and the Press or Publicity Committee is appointed or elected.

For efficiency a committee consisting of two men from the voters, a young lady from the Young People's Society, preferably a stenographer, the Pastor (ex officio).

The Press or Publicity Committee

Committee organized by the selection of chairman, secretary and correspondent. Each active member of the committee holds an important office.

The Chairman presides at the meetings and represents the committee at the meetings of the congregation and church societies. The Secretary keeps minutes of the Committee's sessions and receives all correspondence.

The Correspondent types and sends out all news material prepared by the committee, releases to the societies' bulletins, etc., etc.

Co-operating Groups

The Church Council, the voting body and every society within the congregation appoints one of its members as its representative to keep the Press Committee informed of "What is going on."

This person sends to the secretary of the Press Committee written reports of the society's activities, calendar of its coming events and all information of news value.

Mediums Employed

Newspapers. The Press Committee meets weekly and prepares for the local press a write-up of the activities of the church. The announcements of the Pastor (services, meetings, etc.), the reports of the societies, news items from the school, national and district synodical matters, excerpts of the pastor's sermons, etc., etc., are some of the material considered for copy. After the committee has prepared its line-up, the correspondent types one copy for each paper.

Paid Advertising. If the congregation inserts paid advertising, a carefully edited advertisement is drawn up, submitted to the pastor for approval, and then sent to the newspaper office with note attached: "St. John's Church will appreciate publication of its news story sent to the Editor. Thanks."

Lutheran Literature. The Press Committee from time to time secures a supply of Lutheran tracts, pamphlets, church papers, etc. These are distributed at the close of all services, meetings, etc. Members are urged to leave this printed matter in the neighborhood stores, offices, etc. The Tract Rack is kept well stocked and titles changed from time to time. The sick, infirm and older people are supplied with reading material and kept in touch with the church. The pupils of the schools are organized for a house-to-house distribution of the church's announcements, etc.

Bulletin Board. The best church sign is the bulletin board with the movable letters. These permit a weekly or bi-weekly change of the message and as a "Wayside Pulpit" proclaim the word to saint and sinner, by day and by night, in bad and in good weather. The Press Committee should have several good books with an ample selection of suitable and usable sentence sermons and pithy sayings, mottoes, slogans, etc. Since books of this kind contain much which a Lutheran Church cannot use, the committee should carefully mark all the approved sentences and then change its board at least once each week. The committee may appoint one person outside of its membership to have charge of the board and do the

PLEASE TURN TO PAGE 70

Vest Pocket Kodak Snapshots—A Church Publicity and Award Program

HERMAN BIELENBERG

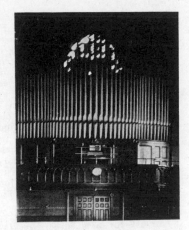

LAST YEAR our Sunday School staff originated and put into successful operation a novel award for stimulating attendance of pupils at church and Sunday School. In previous years we had awarded Bibles, Prayer Books, and religious pictures and wall mottoes, and found that they served the double purpose of increasing attendance and of introducing sound Christian literature into the home. Our Sunday School attendance, and also the attendance of children at the services of our church, has increased over 100% during the last decade.

**Church Fotos
Are Splendid
Publicity Helps**

**Church Fotos
Remind Confirmands
of Their
Religious Vows**

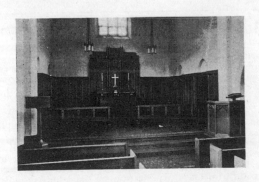

(Above pictures are not the ones used by Pastor Bielenberg but are only offered as suggestions)

Our most successful plan, one that appealed to young and old alike, was the awarding of a small photo album (about 6x8 inches) and a series of miniature photos. Beginning on Rally Day we offered the small photo album to each pupil who had perfect attendance at church and Sunday School for 15 consecutive Sundays. Following that we awarded a small photo each Sunday. Only the pupils who had won their album were eligible for the photos.

The pictures included various views of our church, the Pastor and his wife, the Sunday School classes, the teachers and officers, the choirs of the church, and also various interesting scenes in and about Oil City. Then we added a series of views designed to call attention to Synod and its work, which included the Seminary, the various institutions and views of our missionaries and their work.

Our albums in the hands of enthusiastic pupils have been a very effective publicity medium, for the children delight in showing their albums to visitors. In this way our church, its work and its facilities are brought to the attention of many people who otherwise might know little of it.

My photographic hobby has come in handy in this case. I have done most of the picture snapping personally. Certainly anyone with ordinary knowledge of photography can take pictures here and there. The cost can be reduced by having a number of pictures affixed to a sheet and copied, printed on one print, then cut up into smaller pictures. The cost is as low as an award Bible. Looking at it from a hard-boiled financial standpoint, it has paid for itself in increased contributions.

In laying claim to originality in the above plan, we wonder whether anyone anywhere has tried it before.

LOCAL CHURCH PUBLICITY *from P. 68.*

actual work, but the committee shall have complete authority to say what is to appear. (In some places the pastor prefers to have personal charge of the bulletin board. Where this is the case, the committee acts in an advisory capacity and helps the pastor to find suitable material.)

Parish Paper. The Pastor is Editor of the Parish Paper. The members of the Press Committee are associate editors and with the Pastor comprise the Editorial Committee. Brief news items make the most interesting and most carefully read parish papers. Too many clipped items make a "stale" paper. Dates, all financial reports, routine matters are necessary, but they must be presented in an attractive form. Use cuts; an illustration arrests attention and "sells the idea." Box an important news item or announcement but don't have the printer place a rule around everything. If your parish paper carries "ads," take a personal interest in having the merchants patronized by the members. Watch your advertisements. If Wm. Schneider advertises "Useful Holiday Gifts" two months after Christmas call at his store and ask him for new copy for St. John's Messenger and thank him for his favorable consideration of your paper as an advertising medium.

Miscellaneous. If the congregation decides to have a canvass for new subscribers to the church papers, send for bundles of sample copies. Insert a subscription blank (obtainable from publishers) in each paper. Divide your parish into districts. Send out canvassers in groups of two. They should be familiar with ten good reasons "why in every Christian home there should be at least two church papers" and "why every Lutheran should read his church paper regularly."

Visitor's Book, kept in the vestibule or reception room. Strangers should be asked to register their names and addresses in this book. The visiting committee is instructed to "follow up" and visit these people, or, if out of town visitors, to mail them from time to time the church's literature.

Last but not least, the American Lutheran Publicity Bureau stands ready to co-operate with every Press and Publicity Committee in its work. Send for a package of church printing samples, supply of tracts, suggestions for news articles, back numbers of the AMERICAN LUTHERAN with articles pertaining to publicity work, etc.

BLOTTERS FOR CHURCH PUBLICITY
J. F. E. NICKELSBURG.

Blotters are fifty per cent advertising and fifty per cent utility, a medium then of one hundred per cent inherent advantage. Blotters may be used for the same purposes as regular cards or folders, i. e., general distribution, house visitations, special announcements, etc., etc. A retail store merchant will often permit a supply of blotters "to be laid on the showcase, free for the taking" when he would refuse the ordinary supply of cards. A blotter is a handy thing around the house; therefore when another form of announcement is often thrown away after the first reading, the blotter is preserved for a length of time. Of blotters it is said, "they give mental impressions from each printing impression."

Blotters are ideal for church advertising purpose They may carry the announcement of the regular services, with name of church, pastor, etc., or bring th advertisement of a special service, lecture or social even A popular size, one that will permit insertion in th regular commercial envelope, is 3¼ x 6¼ inches. On thousand of these well printed will cost less than $5.00.

In making up your copy include, if possible, a smal cut of your church or school or a plain ornamenta design, such as a cross, etc. An illustration of some kind will add to the attractiveness of your medium.

Your distribution plans should include the public libraries, Y. M. C. A. and Y. W. C. A. reading rooms, hotel and hospice writing tables, post offices and substations at drug stores, etc., information bureaus in department stores, railroad stations, etc.

Sunday Schools will do well to provide the pupils of the neighboring public school with a blotter advertising the fact that boys and girls having no connection with any Sunday School will always find a hearty welcome at Such and Such Lutheran Sunday School.

Suggestions for Blotter Advertising

In carrying on house-to-house canvass work it is always advisable to leave some appropriate piece of printed material. No matter how cheery the smile and how appropriate the spoken word, the people are prone to forget unless they have something visible to remind them. This applies to canvassing for parochial schools as well as for church attendance. We herewith reproduce two pieces of printed matter which are appropriate in effective parochial school publicity.

" . . . reason and experience both forbid us to expect that national morality can prevail in exclusion of religious principle.—*George Washington, Farewell Address.*

Religion Is an Essential Factor in Education
Zion Lutheran School
EAST BOWERY STREET   AKRON, OHIO

CHARACTER IS HIGHER THAN INTELLECT" — EMERSON

ZION LUTHERAN SCHOOL
HIGH AND BOWERY STREETS
AKRON, OHIO
GEO. G. ARKBAUR   P. 9931-J

SPIRITUALITY IN TEACHING CATECHISM *from p120*

By making confirmation the subject of much prayer and private heart-to-heart discussion with those to be confirmed we can do much to correct the false impressions prevailing in this matter and the false emphasis that is so often placed upon mere intellectual fitness for confirmation.

V

Then the instructor himself must also *look well to his own spiritual life.*

Only a true Christian after the heart of God is a proper instrument of the Holy Ghost in the work of saving souls. "Unto the wicked God saith, What hast thou to do to declare My statutes or that thou shouldst take My covenant into thy mouth? seeing thou hatest instruction and castest My words behind thee."

The teacher of religion must have seen and tasted that the Lord is good, if he would commend His grace to others. He must be filled with love to Jesus Christ, for the Master asked Peter, "Lovest thou me?" before He commissioned him to feed His sheep and lambs. He must be fervent in spirit, as it is said of Apollos: "Being fervent in spirit, he spake and taught diligently the things of the Lord." His yearning for human souls must be like a burning thirst, driving him almost frantic, as it were, and causing him not to be satisfied until his thirst is quenched. He must also regularly intercede before the throne of grace for every one of his little charges. In short, the teacher of religion, whether in the home, church, school, or Sunday school, must be in a state of grace, making constant use of the means of grace and leading a life of prayer.

If he who endeavors to teach others the religion of the Bible is himself a very spiritual person, whose heart has been baptized into the heart of Jesus Christ, he will quietly but effectively impress the stamp of his personality upon those whose lives he is molding by his teaching and example. As the stone mason breaks his stones, he will be better able to break the stony hearts of men, the more he works upon his knees. And that is the sacrifice best pleasing unto God, namely, a broken and a contrite heart.

A Harvest Home Decoration

The accompanying picture portrays the sanctuary as it appeared at the Harvest Home Festival held at the Lutheran Church of the Redeemer of St. Paul, Minn. The central decoration is the life-size figure of Christ in the midst of artistically arranged sheaves of grain interspersed with autumn leaves. The grain decorations for the most part were secured from the florist of the State Fair Grounds, who had reserved them for the use of the church after the Fair had been concluded. The figure of Christ was reproduced from a small reproduction of the celebrated Thorwaldsen picture and was enlarged to life size by a photographer of the congregation. The figure was placed upon ordinary comport board and was then cut out and appropriately tinted. It was mounted on a simple standard to hold it erect and then formed the center of the whole decorative scheme. Almost any church can reproduce the effect with the expenditure of a little taste and time.

Christmas Publicity in the Sanctuary

WE are bringing in this issue of the American Lutheran a plan for the decoration of the church sanctuary at Christmas time. In the accompanying illustration the decorative means were home-made Christmas garlands, southern smilax, and various sizes of Christmas trees. The Christmas tree adornment consisted of silver tinsel and asbestos wool. Little flakes of this asbestos wool were also sprinkled over the Christmas garlands. The accompanying picture does not bring the large Christmas tree, which stood to the right of the sanctuary and which also was unadorned except with tinsel and asbestos wool. We bring this illustration with the hope that it may be of help to the decorating committees at Christmas time.

Open Church

"CATHOLIC churches are open to people who wish to enter for devotion. Why do not Lutherans open their churches for devotion and prayer during the week?"

One has a difficult time answering the above question. A butcher or banker who invests thousands of dollars in a building, and then opens it for business a few hours on a single day of the week, would be considered a poor business man. In order to make factory buildings and equipment pay large dividends, the shrewd manager operates three eight-hour shifts. In meeting the present war demands the buildings are never closed.

Is it not reasonable that churches which wish to realize the largest dividends for Christ from their physical equipment utilize such equipment to the fullest extent? Is there any good reason why Lutheran churches should not be open during the week for meditation and prayer?

It can be done!

It is being done!

We know of one church in the metropolitan area of New York City which has had its doors open every day of the week since October, 1941. The results have been gratifying. One little lady (a stranger who has never revealed her name) has slipped in quietly every day rain or shine since the church was opened. Likewise every evening a man who remains unknown to the attendants, enters the church for his period of prayer and quiet meditation. An average of one hundred persons, some members, some strangers, per week were counted. This is not a large number. But somehow we feel that God is not interested in large numbers. We think of Hannah, the mother of Samuel, who was able to draw near to God in the privacy of the tabernacle at Shiloh. What a blessing to Hannah that her church was always open for devotion. We believe that especially in this day when modern living conditions provide so little privacy in the apartment home, that there are many burdened hearts which seek a place where they can meditate and pray to their God without interruption. Amidst the present sorrows of war the quiet peace found within the church's walls may help to bring healing and comfort to many a wounded heart.

It is only natural that the church on every week day as well as every Sunday is the ideal place to meditate and worship.

It is only natural that the altar, the stained glass windows, the symbolism in the carved woodwork preach a helpful message to all who enter.

Of course there are problems. The church must be partially heated right through the winter season. But this expense in turn pays unexpected dividends. In the first place those who enter for private meditations will almost always leave a contribution in the alms box on their way out. One Christian neighbor who noticed the fact that the Lutheran church was open for meditation and prayer was so impressed with the fact that the church was doing the work of God every day of the week, that even though he himself did not use the church during the week, and was not a member, gave the church a donation of $100.00.

"Open Church" should be properly supervised. The church in New York places a neat sign on the front door: "OPEN for Meditation and Prayer—1 to 5 P.M." During those hours various ladies volunteer to stay in the church for two hour shifts. They themselves come for prayer and meditation. They watch over church property and use the extra time in sitting and knitting for the Red Cross, or performing some slight task about the church. They do not embarrass strangers with questions, but are always ready with a welcoming smile to answer questions within their ken. They make appointments with the pastor for people who seek additional information.

Recently one of the ladies noticed a stranger hesitating outside the church. She went out and invited her to enter. The result was a family won to the church and a child for Sunday School. This one incident alone repaid all of the expenses and sacrifices.

Sacrifice? Of course there is an element of sacrifice. We expect that. Whenever Christ offers any opportunity for victory He assumes that the disciple is willing and anxious to take up the cross. And the sacrifice in the case of the Open Church is definitely worth while.

An Open Church

The September meeting of the Voters resolved to keep the church open all week for the benefit of those of our members and the casual passers-by who would desire to enter for a few moments of prayer and meditation. There are many people who feel disturbed and distressed by the buffetings of life and weighted down by the burdens of their personal trials and problems who would welcome an opportunity to compose their hearts and spirits in the peaceful atmosphere of God's house, away from the distracting influences of their everyday life. There seems to be reason to the argument that the house of God with its beautiful appurtenances should be at the disposal of the people steadily and not only during the formal services on the Lord's Day. It is contended that the casual stranger, passing by in spiritual distress and perplexity, and seek to regain his spiritual balance.

The idea of a church that is open all week is not a new one even in Lutheran circles, although it is only of late that the practice is attaining widespread popularity. Many of our Lutheran churches are now open all day and the oft-mentioned fear of vandalism, disorder and theft does not seem to have materialized. During our vacation days we heard of a church where children, particularly those of confirmation class age, make it a practice to stop at the church for their morning prayers on the way to school. We wonder how the idea of a church open during the week appeals to our people. Naturally we do not expect the place to be overrun with people. Perhaps days will pass without anyone making use of the privilege of private devotion in the house of God, but personally we believe that such privilege should be provided. What do you think?

The Redeemer Record.

The Weekly Parish Paper

EDGAR F. WITTE

The purpose of the parish paper is threefold. It is a reporter keeping the members informed of past events and happenings in the life of the congregation. It is a publicity agent bringing news of the future plans of the church and enlisting support for its program. It is a missionary bearing the invitation of the congregation to the unchurched and creating interest in the Kingdom in the hearts of those who are as yet indifferent to the claims of Christ. If the first purpose is the only objective the congregation has in publishing a parish paper, if its only desire is to keep the members of the congregation posted in regard to happenings during the preceding month, then the monthly parish paper is ideal. But if the congregation desires a wider sphere of usefulness for its parish paper than that which is imposed by the narrow limits of post mortem publicity, then the weekly parish paper is the only solution of the problem.

The average life of a parish paper is less than a week. This is true no matter how well edited or how elaborate the paper may be. If the parish paper recommends itself to the reader by the loftiness of its thought and the beauty of its typography the saving remnant of the congregation will carefully peruse it from cover to cover and then tenderly file it away in some dusty nook where, in common with other good things, it awaits the final consummation of all things earthly. The average church member will read the church notes and then let the paper lie upon the floor next to the davenport or upon the table of the living room where it is gathered up the next day by the thrifty housewife and put away with other papers and finally finds its way back to the church of its origin when the Ladies' Aid holds the annual paper sale to pay for the new church. The monthly paper is very effective as a publicity and missionary agent for all events that transpire within a week after its publication; but for the remaining three weeks of the month its effectiveness is almost nil. Most pastors recognize this weakness, yes, admit it, by augmenting their monthly parish papers by pulpit programs, throw-aways, circular letters and the like. The weekly parish paper serves the purpose of all these and is effective for every week of the month. As a publicity agent and as a missionary it is at least twice as effective as the monthly, and, in the minds of many, four times as efficient. Even though it shares the fate of many parish papers and is just glanced at and thrown away it has served its purpose. It has called to the mind of the reader the events of the coming week, it has brought the program of the church to notice, it has extended the invitation of the church. And next week when it is gone and forgotten there will be another paper to take its place and carry on the good work.

This brings to mind another great advantage of the weekly parish paper, the accumulative publicity value of the paper. Advertising men tell us that a thing must be said at least three times before there is any certainty that it has been brought to the attention of the public. The weekly parish paper enables the congregation to do this. Where the monthly paper will announce a given event or contemplated course of action but once, the weekly can call attention to these things three or four times during the weeks immediately preceding. This is a great advantage. The repeated announcement of an event is bound to reach more people and fasten the idea more firmly in their minds than a single announcement such as is possible in a monthly paper. It is the constant drumming that gets the hearing. Even such novices in the field of publicity as the clergy will sense this. This accumulative publicity value will be especially appreciated wherever the congregation embarks upon an extensive program, a membership drive or a stewardship campaign. The weekly keeps the matter before the people constantly, it pounds the one theme again and again, presenting now this angle and now that, until the soil is thoroughly prepared and the greater part of the membership enlisted in the effort at hand. A monthly paper cannot do this. Too long a time elapses between issues.

Another advantage of the weekly is its timeliness. It gives the publicity to an event when you want it, before and not after. No doubt it is very interesting to read that a good time was had by all at the recent ice-cream social and the ladies raised enough money to buy the pastor a new gown; or that a capacity crowd attended the service in which the cornerstone of the new church was laid and that the collection almost paid for the thing; but as publicity such information is a total loss. The purpose of the parish paper is to arouse interest in coming events so that they will be well attended and adequately supported. It is to be a missionary going up and down in the city telling not about the "wonderful crowd we had last Sunday" but about the good things in store next Sunday so that people will be interested and come and souls be won for the kingdom of Christ. The monthly parish paper does this very well the first week of the month, or in whatever week it may be published; but the weekly does this week in week out. If it is effective to invite people once to the services of the church, is it not more effective to invite them four times? But we are speaking of timeliness. It often happens that an emergency arises, or that a special service is held, or program adopted after the monthly has gone to press. Before the next issue is published the event is over. It is here that the weekly rises to the occasion. No matter how hurried the arrangements are, the weekly parish paper will carry at least one notice, and sometimes even two or three, advertising the event and creating interest in the proposed action. Pastors will find this feature of the parish paper of indispensable value as they become accustomed to its usefulness.

Most pastors, no doubt are aware of the marked superiority of the weekly parish paper over its more elaborate brother, but are deterred from adopting it because of fancied drawbacks. Foremost among these in the minds of most is the cost. This is not as insurmountable as it appears. In the first place the weekly parish paper need not be and by rights should not be as elaborate as the monthly. Where the average monthly is eight or twelve pages the weekly need only be four pages, because in the aggregate it has more pages per month than the monthly. The four page weekly gives one at least sixteen pages of publicity and kindred matter per month as against the eight or twelve pages of the monthly. However, a four page paper can be printed for about one third the cost of an eight page paper, the cost of binding and stitching being eliminated so that the cost of the weekly over and above the monthly for the entire month is but one third or perhaps one half more, depending upon the printer. But this does not tell the whole story. Granting for sake of argument that a weekly will cost twice as much as a monthly paper there are added savings which cut this difference down considerably. There is first of all the elimination of all pulpit programs, throwaways, and to a large extent, of circular letters. The weekly makes these unnecessary because it serves the same purpose in a much better way. It is not handed to the individual as he goes out of church on Sunday morning, when he is busy talking to his friends or anxious to be on his way home. It is mailed to him in his home where he has time to read it at his leisure. Where the congregation is in the habit of re-enforcing its monthly parish paper with the added publicity just mentioned, the elimination of this expense will make up the most of the additional cost of the weekly.

Then there is another great saving that the weekly makes possible. Weekly parish papers can be mailed in the city of their publication at second class rates. Pastors of wide experience in church publicity will agree with the statement, that the only real effective use of the parish paper as a publicity medium and a missionary agent is to mail it to the homes of the individuals one desires to reach. To hand out a parish paper after the service is a most nonsensical proceeding. It reaches only the member who is present in the service, who has already been reached by the pulpit announcement. It does not reach the slack member who is in most need of a parish paper, and it does not reach the prospective member, the unchurched and the missionary material to whom it should bring a message above all others. The only effective way is to mail the paper so that it comes to the attention of the individual the day before the Sunday service and not after the service is over. Granted this, it will cost $7.50 to mail five hundred copies of a monthly paper each issue. It costs eight cents to send the same number of weekly papers, or thirty-two cents a month, a saving of over seven dollars on this one item. This and the saving occasioned by the elimination of miscellaneous publicity matter will more than offset the added cost of a weekly. Where the paper is dependent upon advertising the weekly can be published at even less expense to the congregation than the monthly because of a greater income from advertising. Ads appearing four times as often certainly should sell for at least twice as much, unless the congregation has been in the habit of charging all that the traffic will bear. There was no difficulty in doubling the rates when the writer's paper went on a weekly basis. Where the congregation can afford to do so, however, it will do well to eliminate all advertising from its parish paper. Advertising is to be tolerated only where it means the difference between life and death for the paper.

Another difficulty may be the labor involved. This is not so formidable. Naturally one is held to schedule. When Monday morning arrives one must sit down and turn out the copy for the week's issue. And if one is wise one will do this with the pen rather than with the scissors. But this is a good bit of routine that enables the preacher to start his week right and get down to business without frittering away a lot of precious time. The rest of the work can be cut down to a minimum. The writer's experience may be helpful. An arrangement was made with the printer to send the copy direct to the typesetter who in turn mails the editor a proof at the time the composition is sent to the printer. The proof is corrected by phone and the issue is delivered to one of the church members who has the mailing in charge. The first glimpse of the new issue is received by the editor when the mail man brings it to his door. Some mistakes are bound to occur, but these are not frequent enough to be taken into consideration. A few hours Monday morning, therefore, will be all that is required to edit and publish a weekly parish paper. If this duty will relieve the house broken pastor from the task of helping with the family washing on Monday morning, why that is added gain. The correcting of the proof takes but a few minutes.

The limited space of a four page weekly may also be an objection to it. This of course can be overcome by those who care to go to the expense by adding more pages, though four pages without advertising should give even the most verbose ample room for his talents. However, the limitation of the weekly is more of a help than a handicap. If it will serve to exclude the dross of excess verbiage from parish papers and eliminate the pious but often impossible stories which serve so many papers as fillers and padding it will be an undisguised blessing.

The second class mailing rates also impose several conditions which may appear to make the weekly parish paper impossible for the average congregation, as the weekly is not economically possible without this privilege. In applying for this class of rates the congregation is required to fill out an application blank which can be had at the local post office. The first requirement is that the paper have a bona fide subscription list. This does not, as its seems, propose an insurmountable difficulty. It is met by including this phrase upon the yearly pledge card, "Of this amount fifty cents is to be set aside for subscription to the *Pilgrim*." One subscription per family is then listed as a subscription paid by subscriber, and the rest of the subscriptions, with permission of the members, are listed as subscriptions paid for by others, and the copies are mailed to prospective members. The same result may be obtained by including an envelope for the subscription to the parish paper along with the regular weekly envelopes. This, however, will not be as effective in obtaining subscriptions from every member as the other method. A sample pledge card, of course, must be forwarded to Washington, along with the application. The government allows exchanges and copies to advertisers and also a certain percentage of free copies, not to exceed 25% of the paid subscriptions. A congregation of five hundred members should have no difficulty in obtaining a permit to mail 750 copies a week, which should be ample. Once the permit is granted one may add copies as one desires. There is no check on the number of copies mailed, though of course, common ethics will dictate that the proportion of free copies to paid copies be kept at the ratio the government requires. Another thing may be mentioned here, and that is that paper must be issued regularly as stated on the mast-head. There can be no skipping of an issue when work presses and publishing a double issue next week. If no papers are issued in the summer months this fact can be noted upon the mast-head and the issues omitted, but all other issues must appear on schedule.

The only other regulation that may occasion the editor some difficulty is the one requiring that half of the printed matter be of more than parochial interest. The object of this regulation is to exclude bulletins and announcements from the second class privilege. The government's interpretation of this is broad enough, however, that there should be no difficulty in meeting it. Any article that does not deal with a specific event in local church will pass. Articles dealing with church attendance, Christian giving, Holy Communion, synodical news, news of the congregation that is of more than local interest are acceptable. This gives the editor a wide range and will enable him to publish his paper without being hampered by this regulation.

Other regulations are that the subscription price, the place of publication, and the notice of second class privilege appear in every issue. Four to five weeks are generally required before the application is acted upon. In the meantime the congregation is required to deposit enough postage to guarantee the payment of regular rates in case the application is not granted. This is later refunded or may be left on deposit to pay the second class rates. The practice is to pay the yearly amount in advance, which amounts to from three to six dollars, depending upon the number of copies mailed. The rate is one cent a pound. When the issue is ready for mailing it is brought to the post office or substation and weighed-in there. The central office is then notified and the amount of postage is deducted from the deposit. The service is excellent. In fact it gives the parish paper the same service as first class mail. The writer's paper is mailed and distributed at a substation in the neighborhood, and it has happened that his copy has reached home before he did. The paper is always delivered in the neighborhood on the day of mailing.

In conclusion a fact may be mentioned which alone makes the issue of a weekly parish paper indispensable to the busy city pastor. The post office sends the editor of the weekly paper that is mailed at second class rates a written notice of all changes of address. Within one or two weeks after the change is made notice is sent. In a large congregation where there is a great deal of moving about, this service is priceless, and is given free of charge to the publishers of weekly parish papers.

I need not add that good printing, a good quality of paper, a frequent change of the appearance of the paper by the use of various colored inks or paper or cuts is as essential to a successful weekly as to a monthly. Given these things, the same editor with the weekly parish paper is bound to be successful in keeping his members informed, in enlisting their support for the program of the church and in interesting the unchurched in the kingdom.

Some Parish Paper "Do Nots"

THE parish paper has become an established factor in our modern congregational life. It may be a very valuable factor in maintaining and fostering a church's welfare or it may represent a waste of time and money and may even be a congregational detriment. In order that certain flagrant mistakes may be avoided, we reiterate certain points of warning.

1. Do not choose any old printer who happens to quote the lowest price and whose low figure is reflected in his cheap and slovenly work. A church paper should reflect neatness and dignity.

2. Do not try to economize by choosing the lowest grade of paper. A parish paper represents the church and is to typify its characteristics, and no church wants to advertise itself as coarse or flimsy.

3. Do not make your paper an outlet for your spleen or significant of a torpid liver. Avoid personal attacks or insinuations. You are taking an unfair advantage of the person or organization you are criticizing.

4. Do not let your paper reflect pessimism and discouragement. If you have the blues, lay your pen aside and wait until you have returned to normalcy. Printed gloom can do no possible good.

5. Do not fail to inject the spirit of optimism and hopefulness. A parish paper that adopts a defeatist policy is a destructive rather than a constructive influence. Help your readers to visualize a certain attainable ideal. Hitch your editorial wagon to a handy star.

6. Do not shirk the work of writing timely, original articles. Everything worth while demands a price, and a good parish paper demands the price of hard, conscientious work. Unless it reflects painstaking effort it frustrates its purpose.

7. Do not become a clipping fiend. The use of a clipped article must show a definite purpose and must not be evident as a lazy man's last resort. A paper that is filled with the products of others lacks individuality and wields little influence.

8. Do not fail to give credit to the source from which you have clipped. To present another man's product as your own is not only unethical but dishonest. If you sail under false colors you will eventually be discredited.

9. Do not fail to read proof carefully. Your paper may be modest but it should be correct. Nothing is more irritating to the reader than persistent typographical carelessness. Trust no printing office for your proof-reading.

10. Do not rush your printer. The publication of your paper is not to be a hectic last-minute job. Start your work in time. The best plan is to work according to a carefully observed schedule.

11. Do not have uncertain and varying dates of publication. Have a fixed date of publication and adhere to it religiously. Statements like "Owing to unavoidable circumstances the appearance of our paper has been delayed" evoke knowing smiles of skepticism and in most cases they are deserved.

12. Do not be afraid to give credit and praise where it is due, but do not get gushy. Honest expressions of appreciation for faithful work on the part of some church member or organization is proper and will prove a good investment.

13. Do not let your "ego" obtrude. A parish paper is not to be a parade ground for ministerial vanity and a court of appeal for appreciation. It is to serve the church and not the pastor.

14. Do not sentimentalize in your "personal messages," and cut out the endearing adjectives. These "personal messages" are a dangerous business anyway. If you must have them, be cordial without slopping over.

15. Do not accept questionable ads. Your readers naturally construe the appearance of an advertisement in your paper as an endorsement of the product advertised. The acceptance of an ad is the assumption of a responsibility.

16. Do not fail to use your paper as an agency for boosting synodical projects. Some parish papers are glaringly provincial and foster a spirit of congregational narrowness and selfishness.

17. Do not publish long articles. In our day longwinded statements are read by very few. The publication of continued articles running over several issues is of questionable value. Be concise. Break up your longer articles into headed paragraphs or, better still, throw them away.

The Advantages of the Weekly Bulletin
RUDOLPH S. RESSMEYER

THE purposes served by the weekly "Bulletin" handed the worshipper each Sunday as he enters the church are many and various.

Printing the order of service with hymn numbers and page numbers, where the liturgical parts may be found, helps to make it easy for the visitor to find his way through the service and eliminates the announcing of the hymns and location in hymnal and the order of service.

The printed announcements of society meetings and functions, socials and suppers, entertainments and hikes, does away with injecting into the worship these rather trivial and material and distracting things, usually so foreign to the spirit of devotion and worship that should permeate the entire service.

Certain matters may be brought to the attention of the members each week for a longer period than if verbal announcement has to be made—the correcting of some evil practice—the supporting of some cause. Just a few lines each week will help materially to reach the desired end.

Items of interest concerning synodical matters and local church work may readily and profitably be brought to the attention of the members.

The Sunday evening sermon topic, the subjects for the following Sunday's sermon may be printed and some thoughts given regarding the subject.

On special occasions the hymns may be printed out, as, for instance, for Palm Sunday, Easter and Christmas, and at times the size of the "Bulletin" may be increased to six pages to take care of the annual reports of the pastor, treasurer and societies.

There is often much waste space—especially when the last page contains week after week, for fifty-two weeks, the names of congregational and society officers. At a small additional cost the last page could be devoted to daily Bible readings or meditations, which would aid our people in their private devotion.

Information for the pastor concerning the sick, change of address, names of visitor can be more readily obtained when a little printed form is given where a person may fill in his name and check the information he wishes to convey.

Some churches have had extra copies of the weekly "Bulletin" printed for distribution in the neighborhood or in hotels on Saturdays.

The aggressive pastor will undoubtedly find many other uses to which the "Bulletin" can well be put, as, for instance, a weekly prayer or a short extract of a sermon.

PAID NEWSPAPER ARTICLES
R. S. RESSMEYER

Some ten years ago, if you remember, the sermons of Russell appeared as paid articles in the newspapers throughout the country. At that time the writer thought that if this false prophet uses this splendid means for bringing his teachings to the attention of as many people as possible then surely our Lutheran Church, which has the Word of God in all its truth and purity and the Gospel of Jesus Christ in all its beauty and power, should use this means for bringing the truths of Scripture to the notice of as many people as possible, especially when we remember the command of the Master, "Go into all the world and preach the gospel to *every creature*."

It may or may not be known to you that the American Lutheran Publicity Bureau has recently taken up this kind of publicity and before that time individual laymen supported, and in some cases very liberally, this great undertaking.

Last year paid articles on fundamental teachings appeared in New York, Chicago and Newark, N. J., papers with the result that fourscore and more requests for literature were received.

One Episcopalian rector in New York wrote that one of the articles impressed him most favorably and he requested 1000 copies for distribution in his parish. A Chicago lawyer wrote that one of the articles created new interest in him in Luther and the Reformation and he requested the Bureau to recommend to him recent works on the subject.

The *Moody Bible Institute Monthly* printed this editorial in August of 1921. "Luther-America, this title of a large advertisement in the Chicago dailies last winter, strongly impressed us, and we have waited an opportunity to mention it editorially. It was put forth by the Lutheran Publicity Bureau (Missouri Synod) not in the interest of any single parish but the whole denomination. And yet back of it was the praiseworthy desire to bear witness to true Americanism, and also to pure and undefiled religion as revealed in the Word of God. . . . it was well worth the effort and heartened us all. . . . God be praised that in these dark days of apostasy we have a body of Christians as strong and influential as the Lutherans, who boldly and unitedly express themselves in that form of doctrine which was delivered unto us. (Rom. 6:17.)"

Who can estimate the good that can come to the souls of men through this sowing of the seed of God's Word in articles of this nature? Supposing that the newspaper in your town or city has a circulation of 50,000 or 100,000, and say that only ten per cent read that article, you are preaching God's eternal Truths to 5000 or 10,000 people, the majority of whom you would not reach otherwise.

If God's promise is true that His Word does not return unto Him void, but that it accomplishes that which He pleases and prospers in the thing whereto He sent it, then we know that this sowing of the seed through paid articles in the daily papers is not in vain.

In 1922 articles have appeared in the *Harbor Beach Times,* in New York, Baltimore, Buffalo and Fort Wayne papers. In Harbor Beach the congregation paid for the article, in New York the American Lutheran Publicity Bureau, in Buffalo two insertions were paid for by the Walther League, in Fort Wayne each day during Holy Week articles were inserted by the Fort Wayne Council of the American Luther League, in Baltimore, Emmanuel Sunday School paid for six articles.

Could not your society or Sunday School contribute toward the insertion of such articles in your local paper? The A. L. P. B. will gladly furnish the material. A way of bringing the Gospel to others.

There is only one thing in this world that can save the souls of men, that is the Gospel of Jesus Christ. We have this gospel. Now let us not keep the light of the gospel under a bushel, but let us use every means and every agency to bring this great message of life to those who know it not.

Crosses on Church Steeples Humanity's Traffic Signals

Crosses on church steeples are traffic signs directing humanity in the right direction along the highway of life.

They are the moral sentinels of every community, watching the coming and going of the people.

They see them leave home on Sunday morning. As they come nearer and nearer, the steeples hope that they will stop at some church door. Some do. More do not, passing with no regard for the cross that points the way.

Steeples may have a radio of their own. They know to which church we belong, or should belong. Seeing us start, they can signal to each other that we are on the way. Many never arrive.

High in the air the cross sweeps the landscape with its watchful eye and sees our destination. No matter where we go, or how far, we are seldom out of sight of a cross. Friends may not know where we are, and we may not want them to know. But the cross knows, and in many cases is sorry.

Heed the cross on the steeple which is a guide to the people, and remember that it is never wrong. It represents a Man who thinks of us every minute of every day. Sometimes we do not think of Him in months.

Sunday is a good time to heed the appeal of the cross and renew an acquaintance which may have been long neglected.

—The Reading (Pa.) Eagle

"Lutheran Information"

AUGUST W. BRUSTAT

EVERY CHRISTIAN knows that he is to be a witness for Jesus. Every Christian will, through the channel of his personal life, lips, actions, personality and character convey to others the good news of salvation in Christ Jesus.

But the Christian also knows that witness-bearing has world-encircling implications. And so in addition to his personal testimony and prayers he will support with his liberal gifts the world-program of the Church. Through the agency of Synodical and District Boards and Committees the Christian will by proxy witness for Jesus to the four corners of the earth.

But even in the circumscribed communities in which we live, and in which we personally witness, many are still to be contacted with the Gospel. How can we effectively reach these people?

Everybody Reads the Paper

Among other means which have been utilized, e.g., tracts, the radio, etc., another means at our disposal is the daily or weekly NEWSPAPER. But we do not mean the "usual" announcement of church services, for experience proves that very few read such announcements in the newspapers.

We would suggest a PAID ADVERTISEMENT containing some fundamental doctrine of the Lutheran Church, carried weekly over a period of several months or a year in a respectable newspaper with a far-reaching circulation. This advertisement might be made the project of some mission-minded individual, one or more of a church's organizations, or the local

congregation itself, or a group of congregations in the area covered by the newspaper.

The American Lutheran Publicity Bureau inaugurated such a paid "ad" series of doctrinal presentations in Nassau County, Long Island—a territory suburban to New York City. The "ads," as per sample, appeared for fourteen consecutive weeks in the lower right hand corner of page two, in the Saturday issue of the *Nassau Daily Review-Star*. The paper covers more than a score of villages and towns, and has a circulation of about 75,000. The cost per issue was

$10.08.

The articles were entitled as follows:
1. A Bit of History
2. The Conference at Worms
3. Some Reformation Blessings
4. More Reformation Blessings
5. The Lutheran Church and the Bible
6. Man
7. I Believe in God
8. Who is Jesus Christ?
9. What is a Christian?
10. What is the Church?
11. The Church and State
12. Why Wear the Cross?
13. Why Lent?
14. What is Man's Destiny?

The Results

What were the results of this experiment? 168 replies reached the offices of the Bureau, an average of 12 letters per issue.

Here is a sample letter.

"Enclosed please find 30 cents for which please send me the devotional booklet you offer, "The Candles of God." Your articles in the newspaper are such inspirational reading and offer such food for thought. They have been such a God-send to me while lying here in bed going on three months now. Your messages are such a wonderful comfort to me. I thank you. Gratefully, Mrs. G.S. —Valley Stream, L.I.

Here is a word from a pastor. "Your ads have been great. Hope others have seen fit to sponsor an issue or two. Our Church cannot do much right now but we trust the enclosure will assist in this worthy effort." Rev. R.H.R., Long Beach, L.I.

And here is one of several letters sent

Lutheran Information

WHAT IS MAN'S DESTINY?

Men have offered many unsatisfactory answers to the vital question: "What is man's destiny?" Labor answers: "Shorter hours, better living conditions, increased wages." Industry answers: "Greater industry, greater production." Capital answers: "More money, greater profits."

But there is only one satisfactory answer. Man's destiny is union with God, reconciliation with God. Man's destiny is to become one with God.

Is not man one with God now? No, he is not. Man has left God, has separated himself from God, has placed a barrier between himself and God. Sin is the barrier that has separated man from his God.

How then can man accomplish his destiny of union with God? The truth is that man cannot of himself or by any efforts of his own return into fellowship with God. God Himself has provided the means whereby man can again be united with God. That means God provided through Jesus Christ, His Only-begotten Son. By His death on the Cross, Christ removed the barriers that man's sin had erected, and bridged the gap between heaven and earth. The Cross brought us back to God.

Scripture says: "For Christ has once suffered for sins, the just for the unjust, that He might bring us to God." I Peter 3:18.

Therefore, "whosoever believeth in Him should not perish, but have everlasting life." John 3:16.

Listen to the LUTHERAN HOUR, Station WHN, every Sunday, 6:00 p.m.

A special Lenten devotional booklet "Our Lord's Passion" will be sent free of charge to anyone requesting it. Address your request to the sponsors of this column:

The AMERICAN LUTHERAN PUBLICITY BUREAU

ROOM 812—E. N

1819 Broadway, New York City

These articles appear in this newspaper every Saturday

---

directly to the newspaper office which was subsequently published in their colums:

MRS T . . . ENJOYS LUTHERAN ARTICLES

Editor, *Nassau Daily Review-Star*:

"What fine articles are appearing in your paper sent by the American Lutheran Publicity Bureau. The latest one, 'I Believe in God' makes it so plain, that it isn't what we think is true, but what the Bible, the inspired Word of God says is true . . . "

Mrs. F.G.T. . . . ,Rockville Centre, L.I.

Does It Pay?

As a result of these doctrinal advertisements a request came into the Bureau from a resident of Hempstead, L.I. who had studied for the Roman priesthood. He asked that a Lutheran pastor visit him to discuss Lutheran doctrine. A nearby pastor was sent. And the result? Two former Romanists were recently received into membership in one of our churches. And who knows how many more were by these articles strengthened spiritually, or led to attend a Lutheran service, or even brought to Jesus. Does it pay? Does it pay?

The A.L.P.B. has now branched out and is conducting a similar experiment in Westchester County, N.Y. But while returns are promising it is too early to tabulate results.

The Bureau stands ready to render this paid "ad" service to any newspaper in the country. We hope individuals with a mission-minded vision, or church societies, or individual congregations or groups of congregations will take up this suggestion of circulating our doctrinal position through the agency of the nation's newspapers so that many who might otherwise never hear these truths may read and live.

Send Us the Following Information

To get this service follow these steps

1. Contact the newspaper office with the printed sample and ask the cost of such advertising.

2. Enlist support for the project for a definite period of weeks from individuals, societies or congregations.

3. Send this information together with the name and full address of the newspaper office to the Bureau, remit the cost, and we will do the rest.

May the spirit of missionary enterprise impel us to inaugurate a crusade of doctrinal publicity in the pewspapers of America that will show the nation's millions that there is a Bible Church which will be heard.

Preaching in Print or EffectiveChurch Advertising

FIVE years ago last July our local newspaper changed hands. We had come to the office of the newspaper with our usual weekly "Church Notice." We introduced ourselves to the new editor and had a friendly talk. During the course of our conversation we suggested that even as other columns (editorials, politics, society, sports, and others) were run regularly, perhaps some column for the Christian reading public might regularly be offered. The suggestion was favorably received and we were asked to edit such a column. He assured us that if the response warranted it, the column would be continued. It has continued now for over five years, of course without any cost to our congregation.

At the request of many of the brethren for information regarding this newspaper project we submit a brief analysis.

Headings

Our original heading ran this way:

SERMON OF THE WEEK

By THE REV. A. W. BRUSTAT

The Rev. A. W. Brustat preaches at the Lutheran Church of Our Saviour, Jefferson and Willis Avenues, Mineola, every Sunday at 10:45 a.m. Sunday School is conducted at 9:15 a.m. Studies in the Gospel of St. John are conducted every Sunday evening at 7:30 p.m.

Later on it took this form:

SERMON OF THE WEEK
By
REV. A. W. BRUSTAT
Pastor, Lutheran Church of Our Saviour, Mineola

THE SACRIFICE OF CHRIST

And for the last year it has taken the following form, and with it we submit a sample column to indicate the approximate length of the weekly

article and its general set up.

Religion Today

1. Golden Text
2. Thought For The Week
3. Personality of Jesus
4. Universality of Christianity
5. The Teachings of Jesus
6. Jesus' Touch

---

by THE REV. A. W. BRUSTAT
Pastor Lutheran Churches
In Mineola and Westbury

1. "Let your light so shine before men, that they may see your good works, and glorify your Father which is in heaven." Matthew 5:16.

2. "If a Jew gave one tenth of his income under the Law, for a Christian to give less under Grace is a disgrace."

3. Note the dynamic personality of Jesus, who in prophecy is called "The Wonderful" by Isaiah. Recall that the age in which Jesus lived was an age of Jewish traditionalism, conceit and bigotry. It was an age of Caesarean imperialism, selfishness, brutality and idolatry. Yet despite all this, Jesus of Nazareth is earth's solitary ideal, time's transcendent miracle. He broke all apparent laws of heredity. He was a tremendous exception to the law of environment. You can account for Plato, he sat at the feet of Socrates. You can account for Cicero, he was trained in the statutes of the twelve Tables. You can account for Newton, he pondered in the cloisters of Cambridge. But how will you account for Jesus, who never argued with Socrates, never strode with Cicero by the golden Tiber, never meditated with Newton by the rippling River Cam. How does it happen that Jerusalem with her Temple, Egypt with her Heliopolis, Athens with her Academy, Rome with her Forum, France with her Sorbonne,

Germany with her Heidelberg, England with her Oxford, and America with her Harvard, have never produced the peer of Jesus, never produced a single graduate that could even dimly compare with Jesus of Nazareth?

4. Glance at the universality of Christ's religion. All other religions are, comparatively speaking, more or

less local and topographical. For example there is the Priest religion of Egypt; the Hero religion of Greece; the Empire religion of Rome; the Brahma religion of India; the Buddha religion of Ceylon; the Islam religion of Arabia. But Christianity is the religion of mankind. Baal was Phoenician; Osiris was Egyptian; Apollo was Grecian; Mars was Roman; Zoroaster was Persian; Confucius was Chinese; Guatama was Indian, and Mohammed was Arabian. But Jesus is the Son of Man. He is universal. And therefore His religion is the religion of the sons of men; equally suited to black and white, to cultured and ignorant, to high and low, to rich and poor, to philosophers and novices, to young and old, to patriarchs and children, to mountaineers and lowlanders, to landmen and seamen.

5. For 1900 years the teachings of Jesus have been sweeping across the nations like a whirlwind. Jesus conquered Europe and changed its name to Christendom. He entered China and the binding of feet stopped. He passed through India and the suttee fires went out. He stopped in Africa and savages were transfigured. He visited the Islands of Oceania and cannibalism fled before the onward march of Christian civilization.

6. Note how everything touched by Jesus received eternal value and everlasting adoration. The Cross, the ugliest instrument in the world, made so by Roman cruelty and hate, is glorified because it bore His body in the agony of death. Nazareth, the despised city of Galilee, being the scene of His childhood, becomes one of the sacred places of the Holy Land. Poets have sung praises to the "Little town of Bethlehem," because He was born there. And not a spot on earth is more attractive than the Sea of Galilee. His place of burial is sought by thousands, and the Garden of Gethsemane has a place in human hearts that will abide forever. Jacob's well is immortalized because He rested here and gave the Water of Life to a thirsty soul. And the least and lowest Individual is lifted out of obscurity and crowned with immortality by identifying himself with Jesus by word and deed.

This Jesus is your heaven-sent Redeemer. He died on the Cross to wash away the crimson stains of your sin and reunite you with God. Believe Him, accept Him, worship Him and serve Him, and be assured of a place in glory.

Attend Church every Sunday!

Another possible heading might be:

GOSPEL TALKS

By

REV. A. W. BRUSTAT

Pastor, Lutheran Church of Our Saviour, Mineola

THE ATONEMENT

A Positive Approach

Such a newspaper column, we believe, should always be positive in its approach, never negative. It would be a sad mistake for instance to denounce other church bodies. The positive message of Christianity should rather be presented and the public be permitted to draw its own conclusions. It would not be possible to retain such a newspaper column for long if it were used as a polemics forum.

List Paragraph Heads

For a streamlined age we feel that the column should be broken up into short, pithy paragraphs. This can be done even when a sermon digest is used as in the sample column printed here. This makes it much more readable and attractive. A long, unbroken column may be overlooked entirely or read cursorily and much of its value lost. But if broken up into sections with a special heading for each section it is more likely to be read and more easily digested.

"Know Your Bible"

Some two and a half years ago we approached our editor with another suggestion. The public ought to be better acquainted with the Bible itself and a column entitled "KNOW YOUR BIBLE" consisting of ten Bible questions, the answers appearing on another page of the newspaper, might be a real asset to the newspaper and a help to those who desired to study the Bible. Again our editor was willing to try it and so a second religious column developed in our local weekly newspaper.

A sample follows:

Know Your Bible

CAN YOU ANSWER THESE QUESTIONS?

By THE REV. A. W. BRUSTAT
Set 86

1. Give the name of the priest who did not need to offer sacrifice for his own sins?
2. To whom was the command given: "Follow me and I will make you fishers of men"?
3. What beggar was laid at a rich man's gate?
4. What is the name of the first wood mentioned in the Bible?
5. Who delivered Joseph from the hands of his brethren?

(Answers to these questions will be found below.)

Bible Answers

By THE REV. A. W. BRUSTAT
Set 86

1. Christ, because He was sinless. Hebrews 7:22-27.
2. Simon Peter and Andrew. Matthew 4:19.
3. Lazarus. Luke 16:20.
4. Gopherwood. Genesis 6:14.
5. Reuben. Genesis 37:21.

Is It Worth While?

The question may be asked: Do people read these religious columns in the newspapers? Are they worth while? We are convinced that they do. We are informed by the editorial office of the newspaper that when on occasion the column was inadvertently omitted a flood of inquiries from the reading public came in either by mail or phone. We are further informed that it is regularly read by shut-ins, the sick and the reading public in general. Sunday School teachers from other churches in town have told us they use the material in both columns regularly with their classes. A Presbyterian women's group in town uses the RELIGION TODAY column for their discussion group and the KNOW YOUR BIBLE for their Bible study project.

But let the editor himself tell the story. On May 22, 1937, the following unsolicited item appeared in our local newspaper under the caption: "Biblical Column Commended by Local Pastor," from which we quote: "To date ten sets of questions in the "Know Your Bible" column have been released in this publication by the Rev. A. W. Brustat, religious editor. One hundred questions on the Bible have been submitted to our readers. The results of this venture and the interest it has aroused in the community is fascinating. We submit some of the results as narrated by our readers.

"A pastor of one of the Williston Park churches reports that the members of his Bible Class clip the questions and answers from the newspaper every week and they are reviewed and studied when the class meets.

"A mother of three small children pastes the questions and answers into a scrap book and teaches her children the answers to at least one of the questions every day when the children retire for the night. This is in addition to their evening prayers.

"A resident of Hempstead, passing through Mineola on his way to work, stops at a local newsstand every Thursday morning for the Mineola News-Sun, and clips the sermons and Bible questions and answers for his scrap book.

"When in a recent issue of the 'Westbury Home News' one of these religious columns was omitted for lack of space, a resident of Westbury sent in for a copy of that week's issue of the Mineola paper because as she said: 'I don't like to miss any of these articles.'

"These are some of the more interesting results and reports made so far. The editors would appreciate it if you would report similar information.

"If the ten questions and answers of the KNOW YOUR BIBLE column were studied every week for one year it would give the Bible student a knowledge of 520 Bible questions. We feel this to be a splendid way of gaining knowledge of the greatest book in the world."

To us these columns have been an opportunity of preaching in print and thus proclaiming through another medium the everlasting Gospel of our crucified and risen Saviour. Through it many visitors have been led to our Church. Some of our recent converts came to us through this medium. Some of them may not have been won for Christ had it not been for these religious columns in the newspaper.

Application for Membership Form

The Application for Membership form is suggested for the church which is looking for a systematic method of keeping records and enrolling new members. On one page which fits the standard 3 ring notebook is combined the pedigree of the applicant, together with a convenient office record which will tend to systematize the routine of accepting new members.

There is an advantage to having every new member of the church sign such an application, be he a member of this year's confirmation class, or a new member who is being accepted on the basis of a letter of transfer: the new member is asked to sign a document which reminds him of his spiritual and physical obligations over against his church.

Likewise for the pastor there is the safeguard that all necessary steps will be carried out: the pastor is reminded, under the portion marked "Office Record" to see that the name of the new member is at once placed on the church's mailing list, that the secretary and treasurer are notified (and envelopes handed out), that the communion record is filled out, and that this new name finds its place in whatever filing system is kept.

This new form becomes a one-page biography of the new member which effectively covers every department of the church involved in the reception of that new member.

Incidentally the line in the Office Record which reads "Membership Certificate issued" refers to the growing custom of many churches to issue a certificate of membership to each new member —it makes their membership more tangible to them.

Application forms may be ordered from the Lutheran Press, 1819 Broadway, New York City, at $2.00 per hundred (punched for the 3 ring, 8½ x 11 notebook) Information on Church Membership certificates on request.

Application for Membership
Concordia Lutheran Church
Bronxville, New York

1. In applying for membership in this church, I again confirm and confess my faith in my Lord and Saviour, Jesus Christ.
   Through membership in this Church I seek to attain to a closer partnership with Christ, my Lord, through diligent use of the Sacrament of Holy Communion, and through regular attendance at the services in His House.

2. I recognize that "faith without works is dead"—therefore I shall do all in my power to show my love for Christ, my Lord, by living my Christianity, by Christian service in carrying out my part in the church's program, and in properly supporting my church with a proportionate share of my income.

3. My full name is..

4. My address is...City..................

5. I was born at (City and State only)...................................

6. I was Baptized at (City and State).....................................

7. I was confirmed at: (Name of Church—City and State)..........

8. The last church in which I held membership was the: ....
....

9. If married, give city and state where ceremony was performed: ......
....

10. I understand that this Church is operated on the New Testament Plan of Free Will offerings, and that it has *no* other source of income. I shall, therefore, give as God has prospered me, weekly and regularly, through my church envelopes, for which I herewith apply.

(Signed) ....

OFFICE RECORD

Application Received...............	Other requirements fulfilled...........
Letter of Transfer...................	Communion Record........................
Stencil checked......................	Membership Certificate issued..........
Secretary and Treasurer notified........	(privately) At Service........
	Cards in Master File....................

Form No 507

Little-Town-Stuff

ARTHUR E. NEITZEL

SOMEHOW that expression, "little-town-stuff" has lost its sting for the writer of these lines. After all, there is something intensely human about most of those things which are classed under that head. And surely the preacher, especially the preacher who is called by God to labor in the small town, and who with St. Paul is to be all things to all men, ought not to share that spirit which looks with disdain, not to say aversion, upon people merely because they are given to ways, which by the "big town folks" are called "little-town-stuff." On the contrary, he ought to accommodate himself as far as possible to the way of thinking and doing which characterizes the people among whom he is a messenger of the Gospel. And in many respects this way of thinking and acting offers the pastor in the small, rural village many an advantage over those who are ministers in the large cities. This is true especially also in that line of church work which is so efficiently and effectively sponsored by THE AMERICAN LUTHERAN, church publicity.

There is in most any village of any considerable size a print shop where the pastor can have his printing done just as he wants it. The concern is usually not rushed with work and can give the pastor all the time he needs. The owner needs all the business he can possibly get and he is willing to accommodate the pastor in any way, and will provide him with any number of proofs. And the pastor will find prices cheap. I make the bold statement that the local, small town printer will give quality work at a much lower price when it comes to printing parish papers, for example, than any of these syndicate companies which are at present advertising. The writer has compared them. He gets his parish paper printed at the rate of $1.50 per page (6x9 in.) for the first 150 copies. Aside from this, it is a rather poor policy for the church to ignore home-town merchants in a small town. Moreover, the pastor is not compelled (or should I say tempted?) to use syndicate material in order to keep expenses down. And syndicate material, even at its best, is of too general and impersonal a character.

But the best publicity advantages which the little town, or the country and farm district for that matter, presents, is newspaper publicity. Every town of any size has its own weekly (sometimes also weakly) newspaper, and, if not, there is another town not far away, perhaps the county seat, which supplies the local news. Either one of them will tell all about John Jingo being a business visitor at Rubberville (he bought a pair of trousers) and all about————, but I believe I can see many of the brethren beginning to smile. You see, that's little-town-stuff, and many of them don't "believe in it." The question with them is, "Is it worth while?" But why not? "Well," they say, "the rural weekly has so few subscribers." What of it? A few are some. And just how many are a few? In comparison with the large city papers the subscription list of the small town paper is small indeed. But how does the subscription list of your little paper compare with your average Sunday audience? I don't know for a certainty, but I can scarcely imagine that a paper can exist with less than 500 subscribers. It is estimated that on an average each paper is read by three people. That would give you an audience of 1,500. That's quite a crowd, a crowd worth reaching.

But will the people read the things which I have put into the small paper? Is the village weekly read by the people? Or do they only keep it from local patriotism? You can be assured that on the average a greater percentage read the small town papers than the large city papers. The city paper is so large and comes so frequently that many merely page through it and then put it on the pile for the rag man. But when the *Weekly Blurb* comes it is read from cover to cover; it stays around for nearly a whole week; much of it is read for the second time. Everybody wants to know what everybody else is doing, where so and so went when they saw him "gittin on the train" and what for, who "growed the bigist ear o' cawn," and whether anyone "is butcherin yit." For everyone knows everybody, including the preacher. And when that preacher writes, you can be sure that most people will read that. Small town and country folks as a

rule have more time for religious thought. And even the enemies of the church will want to read "what that there fool preacher has got to say this week." The writer is speaking from experience. His weekly sermonettes are talked about. His parishioners look forward to them. They are the subject of conversation when the Ladies' Aid of the Christian Church meet. People stop him on the street and remark about them. Sectarian preachers have tried to imitate them, but for some reason could not stay in the race.

But—will the publisher-editor print our announcements? Yes, as a general rule he will. He will be anxious to. The writer has thus dealt with five editors, and they always accepted his weekly notes without hesitancy. Of course the minister must always put his name to his announcements, thus clearly declaring to the public that these are his and not the editor's views. If he does that he is almost certain of breaking into print. The editor will want his announcements. In the first place, it will help fill his paper with local matter of which generally so little is available. In the second place, if the articles are really worth while they will serve him much better than syndicate articles of that nature which are sometimes found in such papers and will cost nothing; and people will compliment him on them. Above all, he knows that he is thereby accommodating a goodly number of his readers, the Lutherans, many of whom will mention it to him if these church notes fail to appear for a week or two. Thus in every way it is advantageous to him to print the announcements of your church. Almost every rural paper has a column for church news. Many small town editors bitterly complain right in the columns of their paper that the preachers do not co-operate with him in filling it.

How much will it cost? Nothing. This service is free. You can have a good share of space, although it pays not to use too much of it. In return for this service the pastor can and should do the editor many a favor. He can provide him with many a news item, call his attention to good articles which he has read, e.g. on the value of advertising, on buying at home, improving the town, etc. This will be greatly appreciated. And do not forget that he wants to know when you go to conference and what for, when you attend synod and what you do there, when you preach at mission festivals, anniversaries, etc. All these things he considers favors. An occasional ad. for a special series of services, which will cost you very little, will be highly appreciated. Writing your announcements carefully or, better, typewriting them, and turning them in regularly and early will also please him greatly. All these things will help to make him your friend.

What kind of announcements shall I write? Let it be said that it is not enough to announce time and place of the Sunday School and services. The writer has a mania for small town papers and looks through every one he gets hold of. The "Church News" column generally reveals that the Lutheran Church is not represented. Many of our pastors utterly ignore this grand opportunity. In most of the cases where the Lutheran Church has a place in these columns they are so arranged that they need not be changed from week to week, and sometimes are not even changed when the Church has changed her program. The following is a sample:

ZION EV. LUTHERAN CHURCH
AMOS J. JONES, *Pastor*
Sunday School at 9:45 a.m.
German services at 10 a.m.
English services at 7:30 p.m.

Now there is some publicity value in that if the announcement is correct and not out of date. But what opportunities that Church is missing! Here is a chance to tell what our Church stands for and to publish the Gospel, a chance to bring the news of salvation to some hearts which otherwise would not be reached. It should not be neglected. A church announcement for the rural weekly might be made up something as follows:

First of all, the name of the Church should be given in full. Write or typewrite it with all capitals. Then beneath the name should follow in parentheses the slogan of the Church. It should be distinctively Lutheran, i.e., distinctively Biblical. Do not let anyone persuade you to use anything as trite and stale and punchless as "Follow the Crowd to First Church." Chances are that will lead to disappointment anyway. There is nothing definite about that. The same is true of these slogans: "We Aim to Put the Cross in the Sky"; "Meet the Missionary Command With Grace Church"; "Pilgrim Church Saves You and Helps You Save Others"; "Drop Your Task and Commune With God." All of these say nothing. And don't let anyone tell you that "The Bible Church"; "We Preach Christ Crucified"; and similar slogans are not distinctively Lutheran. They are. They apply to the Lutheran Church as they do to no other, and in the strictest sense. The Bible is our only foundation, the cross of Christ our only glory. And you will have abundant opportunity to demonstrate this in your weekly sermonettes. The AMERICAN LUTHERAN has recently had some fine little articles which brought home the much overlooked fact that we are to advertise our ware, our message, the Gospel and not primarily the Church. Let us remember that also for our slogans. After the slogan should follow the name of the pastor. This is necessary for the reason stated above. This much goes to make up the heading.

Thereupon should follow the announcements. These should be given in short, snappy sentences and should not be cluttered up with any unnecessary remarks. They should stand out boldly. They should include: time of Sunday School and Bible Class, time of morning service or services with announcement of sermon theme, time of evening service and sermon subject, celebration of Holy Communion, services preparatory to Holy Communion, time and place of registration for Holy Communion, voters' meeting. Time and place of society meetings are better put into the paper at another place as a news item, as social events. Let the society secretary attend to this. These elements really mar the Church notes. The same is true of the report of the voters' meeting and other things. In the small paper you don't need news to get into the Church announcement column. If the interior of the church has been or will be decorated, if the pastor has a new gown, if new church furniture was bought, that should go into the paper, to be sure. The editor wants that. But it doesn't belong in the "Church News" column. It will serve its purpose best somewhere else, and you will save your space for something more important. After the announcements should follow the sermonette.

How long should the sermonette be? As short as possible. There's an art in brevity. And that is the hardest part in preparing sermonettes, to say something, to really say something, and avoid all false impressions, in a few words. The sermonette should be from 200 to 300 words long. Longer ones are permissible and even desirable at times. But in general the rule should apply: the shorter the article, the more certain it is of being read.

What shall I write on? Almost any Biblical subject. The writer began with subjects such as "Church-going," "Preparing to Meet God," "The Necessity of Salvation," but soon found that people desired Scriptural light on almost any subject. He has found it good practice at times to write short headings, e.g. "Grace," "Truth," "Sin," "Eternal Life," "The Christian," "Peace," "Preparedness," etc. The opinion prevails that these articles should not be "preachy." That is a mistake. A sermonette is a short sermon. It should be a sample of the kind of preaching people will find if they attend the services. Bible passages should be quoted in substantiation of every statement that might possibly be challenged. The people of every and no religious persuasion will then soon realize that here is a real "Bible Church," and that the Lutheran Church is not just one of the sects. The sermonette should not make the impression that the writer is carrying a chip on his shoulder. They should not be polemical in the sense that they invite controversy or cast flings at other churches. At the same time they should be a fearless confession of the truth and should not "beat about the bush." By bold presentation of the truth they may denounce modernism and unbelief in the plainest terms. Such fearless honesty and open-facedness, especially when it bears all the marks of being deeply interested in the welfare of immortal souls, will arouse admiration rather than anger.

The sermonette should not contain material about the Augsburg Confession anniversary. This will be better at another place in the paper and can be written up as a news item. (The writer's

experience is that clip sheets handed to the editor are often not used, but if the same matter is written over by the minister it will readily be set up and printed. In doing that a little local color may be added.) All necessary announcements in regard to such a celebration should be made in the Church News column under the announcements proper, but the details and importance and meaning of the event should be given in a separate article, which, in most cases, will receive front page space.

Quotations from Luther and other sources, even the confessions, should be used, if at all, very carefully, so as not to make the impression that such sources had the same authority in our Church as the Bible. People have that impression, and it is to be feared that we have helped to form it. Human arguments for the importance of the Church may be used, and temporal advantages of the Church may be pointed out, but it should be made plain that these are not THE reasons for the Church's existence nor her best talking points. Above all, the Gospel should be preached and the way of salvation pointed out.

When shall I write them? By all means, not five minutes before it is time to go to press. This matter is earnest and serious and needs thoughtful and prayerful consideration. It is not a side issue. It is a vital matter. These articles should be written far in advance of the time when they will be needed. Excerpts from the Sunday sermon may be used. Other sources should be consulted. If you read something that makes a lasting impression on you, pass it along. It may have the same effect on others. Sometimes thoughts are suggested, sometimes striking sentences, and sometimes whole sermonettes. For this purpose the AMERICAN LUTHERAN is invaluable. Get out your old copies and look them over. There is many and many an article which will serve you well along this line. Editor and contributors will be only too glad if you can use what they wrote to the advantage of your Church, for the glory of the Savior, and for the salvation of souls. In fact, they wrote much of what the AMERICAN LUTHERAN contains for that purpose. The writer has made abundant use of it and would not think of offering an apology. He keeps a box on the desk in which he places clipped articles or slips of paper on which he has written the name of the source and the page where he has found a suggestion or a suitable article. In this box he also places sermonettes which he has written and doesn't need at present. Whenever he is at a loss what to write or is short of time, he consults that box, and thus it is never necessary to dash off something in a hurry which may have little value. The pastor must set himself a high standard in this matter and should never lower it. If one or two of his articles become stale and dry, the chances are that people will lose interest and quit reading them.

So let us not overlook and neglect the opportunities which the small town paper affords. Here is a glorious opportunity to preach the Gospel. It costs us nothing. It takes but little effort. And the good it will do will be revealed in eternity, if not now. This assurance we have, it shall not be in vain. (Isa. 55,10.11.)

* * *

A preacher who wanted to vividly illustrate a sermon on evolution recently took a monkey into the pulpit. He at least proved an intimate relationship with his partner.

* * *

✝ *Your pastor was here to-day to make a pastoral visit. If you desire that he call again, kindly let him know. Tell him at church next Sunday that you found this card.*

"Faith cometh by hearing, and hearing by the word of God." Romans 10:17.

Faithfully,
Your Pastor

Newspaper Campaign Mentions 310 Individual Churches

Series of Four Maps Gives the Location of Each Church in Metropolitan District at Small Cost to Each

Three hundred and ten Lutheran churches in New York and vicinity recently ran a series of newspaper advertisements which were interesting in that, in spite of the large number of contributing members to the campaign, each member received individual mention and was able to attract the attention of the group it desired to interest.

These advertisements, which appeared in the New York *Times,* were in the form of a series of maps. One, for example, was a map of Northern New Jersey and Staten Island. On this map were marked a number of crosses to indicate each Lutheran church in its proper geographical location. Beside each cross was printed the name and address of the church or churches and the name of the town in which they are located.

"The use of the cross as a marker for the locations of the churches in the advertisements was quite fitting," declared J. F. E. Nickelsburg, business manager of the American Lutheran Publicity Bureau, which sponsored the campaign, "for the cross may well be said to be the church's trade-mark."

A tie-up with this use of the cross was also made in the copy which accompanied these maps and which read: "Find Your Lutheran Church in New Jersey by the Sign of the Cross"

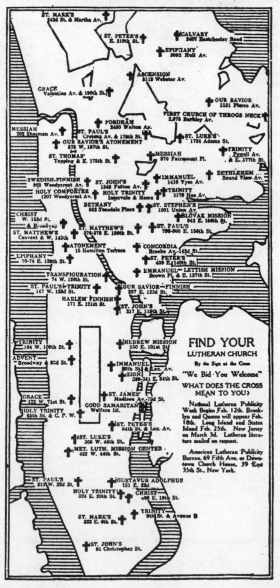

and "What Does the Cross Mean to You?"

Four maps constituted the series in this campaign and were run in succeeding Saturdays to mark the churches in the various sections around New York. The size of the maps varied somewhat but they were approximately six inches square. The number of churches indicated by crosses on each map ran from over forty to more than sixty.

The opportunity of naming so many churches naturally spread the cost of the advertisements over a great number of contributing churches. The cost to each church was only $3. Inasmuch as most churches have not a great deal of money to spend for advertising purposes, this economy was an attractive feature of the campaign.

Then again, by the use of the map, each church was able to attract the attention of those in its own district, for a natural curiosity would lead the reader to notice what church in his vicinity was marked. A footnote in one of the advertisements told what maps had already appeared and gave the dates of the maps to appear subsequently. Thus the campaign also benefited the whole Lutheran organization by the dominating space on the religious advertising page which the co-operation of so large a number of churches made possible.

This campaign is to be suggested by the American Lutheran Publicity Bureau to its churches in other parts of the country.

The task of getting all the churches to enter into this co-operative effort was not difficult since the individual charge was so small that many of the churches were lined up by telephone and by mail.—*Printers' Ink.*

An Admirable Example of Group Advertising

WE print the reproduction of a full page advertisement which appeared in the "Daily Star" of Queens Borough, New York City, because we think it worthy of emulation in other Lutheran localities. There are several reasons why we like the "make-up" of this advertisement.

We like the message. It is a message written by a person who knows how to attract the average newspaper reader. When the careless man of the world starts to read it, he will continue. He is interested in the message, for the simple reason that the message is intended especially for him and for others like him. Many of our well meaning Lutheran Churches word their advertisements for the theological professor.

We like the dignity. The names of the churches are not spread out over the entire page and a few inches given to God. Christ holds the center of the page and the center of the reader's interest. The valuable white space in the corner and on both sides of the cut is paid for by valuable dollars. But it is worth it. It is impossible to clutter up space with reading matter and yet preserve dignity. Leading houses on Fifth Avenue which cater to the elite know the value of white space.

We like the idea of advertising the necessity of salvation. Merely advertising the church, its modern bowling alleys and comfortable pews, is advertising wasted. Whereas in advertising the message of salvation, the advertiser is not only benefiting himself, but his Christ, the head of the Church.

We would also remind the pastor that newspaper advertising is financially economical. A Bronx Church paid Twelve Dollars for a single sermonette insertion in a New York paper of 130,000 circulation. If we stop to think, the mere printing of a tract to the number of 130,000 would cost considerably more than twelve dollars. Added to this would be the huge expense of postage or carrier service to the individual home. And in addition the sermonette appears in the newspaper where it is read. Whereas if the tract alone were handed to the unchurched in all probability it would be cast aside.

This advertisement paid in dollars and cents. The full page advertisement in question cost $165.20. However, when the expense is divided among twelve congregations the individual church's cost comes to but $13.76. The filled churches on the Sunday following the advertisement proves that it brought results. If it pays in dollars and cents, then cert ainly it should pay in incalculable values of eternal souls.

Telephone Stillwell 6600   THE DAILY STAR, QUEENS BOROUGH, SATURDAY EVENING, FEBRUARY 26, 1927.   Telephone Stillwell 6600   Page Nine

BAYSIDE
Redeemer Lutheran Church
Pastor Walter E. Schwolert
Bell and Lamartine Avenues
Midweek Lenten Services Wednesdays
At 8:15 P. M.
Sunday Services at 10:30 and 7:45
Sunday School at 9:15 A. M.

COLLEGE POINT
St. John's Lutheran Church
Pastor Arthur H. Halfmann
Sixth Avenue and Fourteenth Street
Lenten Services Sunday Evenings
At 7:30
German Wednesdays at 8 P. M.
Sunday Mornings at 8:45
German at 10:45
Sunday School at 9:45 A. M.

CORONA
Emanuel Lutheran Church
Pastor Emil Holls
104th Street and 37th Drive
Midweek Lenten Services Wednesdays
At 8 P. M.
Sundays Mornings at 11
German at 8:30
Sunday School at 9:30 A. M.

ELMHURST
Bethany Lutheran Church
Pastor B. V. Skov
48th Avenue and 91st Place
Midweek Lenten Services Wednesdays
At 8 P. M.
Sunday Services at 10:45 A. M.
and 8 P. M.
Sunday School at 9:30 A. M.

FLUSHING
St. John's Lutheran Church
Pastor C. George Kaestner
Percy St. (147th), near Beech St.
Lenten Services Friday at 7:45 P. M.
German Wednesdays
Sunday Mornings at 9:45
German at 10:45
Sunday School at 9 A. M.

LONG ISLAND CITY
Grace Lutheran Church
Pastor Walter M. Degenhardt
Wolcott Avenue, between 2nd and
4th Avenues
Midweek Lenten Services Wednesdays
At 8 P. M.
Sunday Services at 11 A. M.
and 8 P. M.
Sunday School at 9:30 A. M.

LONG ISLAND CITY
Trinity Lutheran Church
Pastor Fred H. Lindemann
31st Avenue and 37th Street
Lenten Services Thursdays
At 8:15 P. M.
German on Wednesdays
Sunday Services at 10:45 A. M.
and 7:45 P. M.
German at 9 A. M.
Sunday School at 9, 10, 10:45
and 2:15

REGO PARK, ELMHURST
Lutheran Church of Our Savior
Pastor B. V. Skov
61-22 Booth Street
Lenten Services Thursdays at 8 P. M.
Sunday Mornings at 9:30
Sunday School at 10:45 A. M.

THOMSON HILL
Golgotha Lutheran Church
Pastor C. W. Jacobs
4510 Heiser Street, near Queens Blvd.
Midweek Lenten Services Wednesdays
At 8 P. M.
Sunday Mornings at 10:30
Sunday School at 9:30 A. M.

WHITESTONE
Immanuel Lutheran Church
Pastor Henry C. Wolk
21st Street near 8th Avenue
Midweek Lenten Services Wednesdays
At 8 P. M.
German on Fridays
Sunday Services at 11 A. M.
and 7:45 P. M.
German last Sunday of Month
At 11 a. m.
Sunday School at 10 A. M.

WINFIELD
St. Jacobus Lutheran Church
Pastor Frederick E. Tilly
43rd Avenue and 72nd Street
Lenten Services Sunday Evenings
At 7:30 P. M.
German Wednesdays at 8 P. M.
Sunday Mornings at 8
German at 10:45
Sunday School at 9:45 A. M. and
2 P. M.
German at 9:30 A. M.

WOODSIDE
Christ Lutheran Church
Pastor Henry F. Bunke
58th Street, near Broadway
Lenten Services Fridays at 8 P. M.
German on Wednesdays
Sunday Mornings at 10, German at 11
Sunday School at 9 A. M.

Is It Nothing to You?

Are you among the preoccupied crowd that rushes heedlessly by the Savior year after year? Can you afford longer to neglect the vital issues of life? What is life? Why are you here? Where are you going? Are you created merely for this brief, restless existence here on earth, to live your short span of life and then cease to exist? When death comes, what then? Are you ready to meet your God? The man or woman who puts these questions off and lives on with thoughtless abandon from day to day is gambling with eternity.

Do not try to choke your conscience. It is the best friend you have. Let it speak. Do not try to silence it with the argument, "I am all right. I am doing the best I can. I am doing no wrong. I am living a decent, honest, upright life. I am ready to meet God without the ministrations of the Church."

The God whom you must meet sooner or later says: "All our righteousnesses are as filthy rags." "There is none that doeth good, no, not one." "Ye shall be holy, for I, the Lord, your God, am holy." "If we say we have no sin, we deceive ourselves and the truth is not in us." Remember, God demands perfection in thought, word and deed.

Remember also that sin is damnable. "The soul that sinneth it shall surely die." Your sins will testify against you unless they are removed. You need a Savior. Your greatest problem in life is not solved until you have found Him. You are not ready to die unless you have found peace in Him. He says: "I am the way, the truth, and the life; no man cometh to the Father, but by Me." "Believe in the Lord Jesus Christ and ye shall be saved."

What are you going to do about it? Your whole life is misspent unless you make provisions for a blessed eternity. Are you trifling with your soul's salvation? Do not argue, "I am just as good, and even better, than many church people." Perhaps you are. But your argument is wrong. Both you and the church member are sinners in need of salvation. The sincere church member has found his Savior while you have not. That is the difference.

We are talking to you straight from the shoulder because we have something you need, and we are really desirous to offer its blessing to you. It is nothing strange or new. It is as old as time. It is the Gospel of the crucified Redeemer, the old story of man's sin and God's pardoning grace, the "sweetest story ever told," the solution of all man's problems.

Is that "old-fashioned"? But so is man's sin. Modern man with all his advancement in knowledge and all his achievements in many fields of human endeavor is not inherently different from his forefathers. He is still a sinner and still needs a Savior. He still dies and faces the great issue of eternity. To this day the Word of God alone gives satisfactory answer to the anxious questions of the heart.

Wake up, friend, and get busy with the main business of your life. Come to church! We cordially invite you. If you have drifted away, use the Lenten season to come back. If you have never been connected with a church, come and give its message a hearing. Whatever you do, stop drifting and give serious thought to your own soul's needs.

Reprint of Full Page Group Advertisement of Lutheran Churches in Queens, N. Y.

Copy for Newspaper Advertising or Sermonettes

A Changing World

WE are living in a rapidly changing world. Our life is vastly different from that of our fathers. Science and invention have revolutionized our methods of living. Education has broadened our culture. But the fundamental needs of man have not changed. Man lives and sins and dies just as he did ages ago. All the wisdom of the world has no answer to the anxious questions of his heart regarding God and eternity. All cultural advancement has not been able to eliminate or even to curtail his sinning. His elemental need is today, as it has ever been, for a Savior. Nothing else can satisfy. Nothing else can bring him peace of heart. "There is salvation in none other and none other name given among men whereby we may be saved" but that of Jesus Christ. Amidst all the changes of the world He everlastingly remains unchanged.

You are invited to hear Him proclaimed at:

_____

_____

Man and God

IF MAN would only stop trying to make God fit into the narrow confines of his reason! Man is actually trying to make God instead of realizing that God has made man and has revealed all that man needs to know about God in His holy word. That God in His essence and in His methods cannot be completely understood by man is reasonable and natural. Man does not even understand much about himself nor about the physical world round about him. How then can the finite grasp the infinite? Let man stop trying to rationalize God and simply accept God's revelation regarding Himself. In his present-day perplexities man sorely needs this revelation.

Hear God revealed at:

_____

_____

The Church Is Needed

THE WORLD cannot get along without the Church and the influence it exerts upon all the phases of human life. All the benevolent and charitable activities of man, all the wide-flung ramifications of social service reflect the influences of Christian religion. In countries untouched by the gospel of Christ, spiritual and physical reconstructive efforts of man in behalf of his fellow-man are unknown. The world today would be flooded with uncontrolled viciousness if it were not for the curb of Christian religion. Few men today would want to live in a community where there are no churches. Why not interest yourself in this vital institution of the Church? Why not find out what it stands for and whether or not you need it in your life?

You are invited to meditate with us at:

_____

_____

The Cardinal Doctrine of the Scriptures Stressed by the Lutheran Church

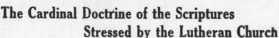

The cardinal doctrine of the Scriptures, stressed and emphasized by the Lutheran Church, is the doctrine of justification by faith. To justify means to make just, to acquit because another has paid the penalty. Jesus paid the sin-penalty with His blood when He died on the cross. Those who accept or believe that Jesus Christ died for them are acquitted and saved, justified by faith "without the deeds of the law." Rom. 3. 28.

The Bible and the Lutheran Church

The Lutheran Church teaches and believes that the Bible, word for word, is inspired by God and therefore the sole authority and rule of faith and life of the Christian and the final court of appeals in all things pertaining to Christian Doctrine and of life. The Bible therefore must be accepted word for word without a mental reservation.

NOTE: Editors welcome the cooperation of Pastors to make the Church News page as interesting as possible. If you cannot afford to insert paid advertising, offer your local newspaper material of this kind.

Church Printing Samples

Packages which contain fifty or more pieces of printed matter, announcements, programs, pulpit cards, folders, etc., etc. These samples will aid you to plan and prepare attractive advertising material. Write for package of Church Printing Samples and be sure to send twenty-five cents in silver or stamps for packing and postage.

Parish Papers

We have made up packages of various styles and sizes of parish papers, weekly calendars, etc., etc. Those that now have or those that plan to start a parish paper will find these samples helpful for ideas as to type, layout, illustrations, etc., etc. Write for Parish Papers, enclosing twenty-five cents for packing and postage.

Stock Electrotypes

Printed matter embellished with beautiful illustrations is never laid aside. Cuts arrest the attention of the readers and prompt reading of the message. The costs of cuts are paid for by results. Send for our illustrated catalog of stock electrotypes. Enclose ten cents for postage.

Stock Folders

These are different in size, average about 6 x 9 in.

NOTE—We list subjects for all seasons of the church year, so that a complete list may be available for ready reference, to place your church publicity for the year.

All Listed Below are Colortypes

1. Reni: Ecce Homo.
2. Hoffman: Gethsemane.
3. Plockhorst: The Women at the Grave.
4. Fuerst: The Resurrection.
5. Da Vinci: The Lord's Supper.
6. Plockhorst: Christ Blessing Little Children.
7. Plockhorst: Glad Tidings.
9. Ebbinghaus: The Institution.
10. Ittenbach: The Crucifixion.
11. Deschwanden: He Is Risen.
12. Christ's Triumphal Entry.
13. Klagstad: "My Master."
15. Martin Luther; a wonderful folder.
16. Luther Posting the 95 Theses.
18. Plockhorst: The Good Shepherd.
20. Harschaar: Christ, the High Priest.
22. The Disciples of Emmaus.
23. Luther at Coburg.
25. Christ Knocking at the Door.
26. The Holy Sepulchre.
27. The Marriage Feast.
28. It is Finished.
29. The 12 Years' Jesus.
30. The Great Sinner.

PRICES: The prices for these folders are made as low as possible for good stock and workmanship. 100 folders, $1.50. No discount; postage or express extra.

These Printed in a Rich Brown

3. Lenten design, Da Vinci, The Lord's Supper.
4. Lenten design, Hoffman, Gethsemane.

5. Lenten design, Reni, Ecce Homo.
6. Easter design, Plockhorst, He is Risen.
8. General design, Plockhorst, Christ the Good Shepherd.
9. Lenten design, Lingner, The Crucifixion.
12. Raphael, The Sistine Madonna.
16. Plockhorst, Abide With Me.
17. Deschwanden, Behold I Stand at the Door.
18. Harschaar, Jesus Only.
19. Christ and His Disciples on the Way to Emmaus.
20. The Lost Sheep.
21. Easter Dawn.

Price, per 100, $1.40; postage extra

* * *

The Lutheran Press

The Lutheran Press, 229 West 28th Street, New York, has advertising and publicity material in the form of stock folders, announcement cards, electrotypes, poster and window cards, etc., etc. Some of the material is listed below:

Car Sign or Window Cards, No. 19270

Size 21 x 11 in., regulation size for Street Car, Subway and Elevated. Printed in 3 colors on 5 Ply Car Sign Board.

Set consists of 6 Cards, one for each week of Lent. General Make-up same on all, but wording different on each.

Panel at bottom left blank for local imprint as illustrated below.

Most effective way for advertising regular and special Lenten Services.

Price per set of 6 Cards	60c
10 sets	$ 5.00
25 sets	10.00

Postage extra

The Texts on the other five show cards are as follows:

The BIBLE Teaches
ALL MEN ARE SINNERS

"For all have sinned and come short of the glory of God"

Therefore the Lutheran Church Teaches:
YOU HAVE SINNED

The BIBLE Teaches
THAT SIN CONDEMNS

Wherefore, as by one man sin entered into the world and death by sin; and so death passed upon all men, for that all have sinned

Therefore the Lutheran Church Teaches:
SIN CONDEMNS YOU

The BIBLE Teaches
MAN CANNOT SAVE HIMSELF

For by grace are ye saved through faith; and that not of yourselves: it is the gift of God: Not of works, lest any man should boast.

Therefore the Lutheran Church Teaches:
YOU CANNOT EARN SALVATION

The BIBLE Teaches
DIVINE CREATION

So God created man in His own image, in the image of God created He him.

Therefore the Lutheran Church Teaches:
GOD CREATED YOU

The BIBLE Teaches
WORLD REDEMPTION

For God so loved the world, that He gave His only begotten Son, that whosoever believeth in Him should not perish, but have everlasting life.

Therefore the Lutheran Church Teaches:
CHRIST IS YOUR REDEEMER

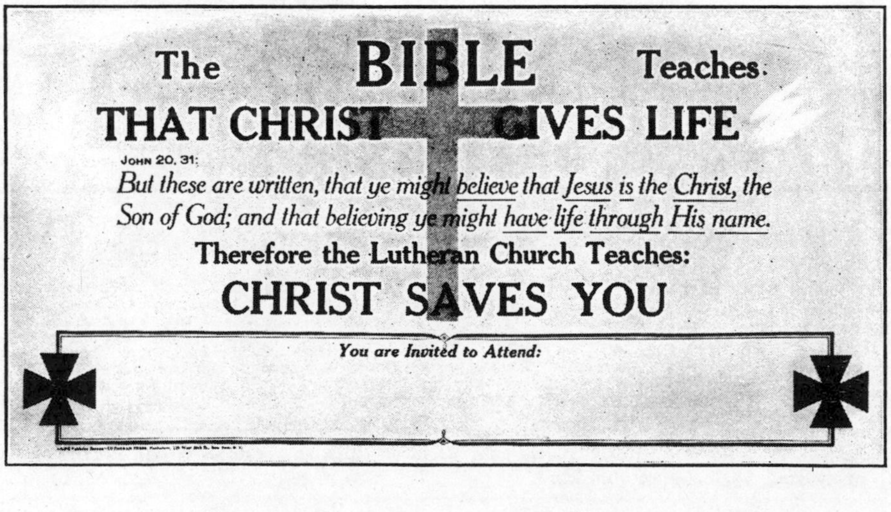

Car Sign or Window Card, No. 19280

Size 21x11, printed in red, black.

The text is as follows:

YOU
—have sinned
—need a Saviour
—have no Saviour but
CHRIST
"Come and See"

Panel for Imprint

Only One Text

Price	10 Cards $1.00	Price 50 Cards	$3.50
Price	25 Cards $2.00	Price 100 Cards	$6.00

Special Line of New Folders

Price given is per 100, postage extra

30-0.	"The Nativity"	6x9½	$1.40
31-0.	"The Nativity"	6¼x3½	.85
32-0.	"The Good Shepherd"	6¼x9½	1.40
32A-0.	"The Good Shepherd"	3½x6¼	.85
10A-0.	Christ on the Cross	6¼x9½	1.40
10B-0.	Christ on the Cross	4x8½	1.00
10C-0.	Christ on the Cross	6¼x3½	.85
11-0.	Ecce Homo	6¼x3½	.85
12-0.	Head of Christ	6¼x3½	.85
20-0.	"He is Risen"	6¼x3½	1.00
20A-0.	"He is Risen"	6¼x9½	1.60
21-0.	The Lord is Risen Indeed.	6¼x3½	1.00
21A-0.	The Lord is Risen Indeed.	6¼x9½	1.60
22-0.	Mothers' Day	6x3½	1.00
23-0.	"Open Church Door"	6x9	1.50
24-0.	"Open Church Door"	4¾x7¾	1.00
25-0.	"Open Church Door"	6¼x3½	.85
26-0.	Dr. Martin Luther	6x9½	1.40
34.0	"Christ in Gethsemane"	6¼x3½	.85
35-0.	Ascension	6¼x3½	.85
36-0.	"The Child's Friend"	6¼x3½	.85
	Christmas Hymns, 9 well-known Carols		1.00
	Hymns for Lenten Devotion, 17 Hymns for Lenten Services		1.00
33-0.	Announcement Cards, 5¼x3½, with National, Church and Luther Emblem combined, white, red and blue border		1.25
33-0.	Envelope to match, with red border		1.00
33-0.	Envelope to match, without red border		.75

The above folders are suitable for Parish Paper covers, programs, announcements, programs for special occasions, anniversaries, church dedications, etc., etc. No free samples. Requests for samples can only be filled if stamps are enclosed with letter.

Order direct from Lutheran Press, 229 W. 28th St., New York.

The **BIBLE** Teaches THAT CHRIST GIVES LIFE

John 20. 31:

But these are written, that ye might believe that Jesus is the Christ, the Son of God; and that believing ye might have life through His name.

Therefore the Lutheran Church Teaches:

CHRIST SAVES YOU

You are Invited to Attend:

National Lutheran Publicity Week

Joint action creates enthusiasm and spells success. The call of the official Press Committee of the Missouri Synod to observe the week of February 12th to 19th, 1928, for simultaneous publicity and advertising should meet with general favor and sincere efforts should be made by congregations and societies for full cooperation. Publicity for the Biblical principles of the Lutheran Church, publicity for her doctrines and practices and her glorious history!

"The Lord gave the Word; great was the company of those that published it."
Psalm 68, 11

We insist that our Lutheran people have no right to boast of themselves. However, we likewise insist that the Lutheran Church as well as all Lutherans have a right to boast of the Biblical principles for which we stand. In fact, we would not be true disciples of our Lord, unless we proclaimed far and wide, loud and long, those principles of Lutheranism which are founded upon His teachings. Any Lutheran who hangs his head in unjustified shame, and is afraid to present his Church as a Bible Church, certainly cannot be classed as a sincere follower of Our Saviour.

Christ commanded that we should let our light shine. We feel that all Lutherans have a light which is shining. But the tragedy is in *where* it is shining. Too often we find it hidden under a bushel, we make sure that no man can see it. Let us follow the precept of our Master and place it upon a high candlestick in this world, where it can be seen of all men.

Let us have Lutheran Biblical Publicity every day throughout the year. But in order to prepare for the missionary opportunities of Lent; in order that we might make a greater impression upon the general public by a concerted effort, let there be a general cooperation throughout the country in carrying out the second annual NATIONAL LUTHERAN PUBLICITY WEEK.

The International Walther League Convention, St. Louis, Mo., July, 1927, and a number of District conventions of the Missouri Synod, as well as many individual societies, have endorsed the idea of a Publicity Week, pledging whole-hearted support.

"Publish and set up a standard; publish and conceal not."
Jer. 50, 2

COOPERATION

Concordia Publishing House

An excellent assortment of tracts and pamphlets are listed in the catalog (Pages 471-474) of Concordia Publishing House, St. Louis, Mo., suitable for wide distribution during Publicity Week. One especially suited for distribution is: "What Lutherans Teach'" sold at $1.50 per 100.

A special folder has been published which lists groups of books suitable for placing in public libraries, reading rooms and congregational libraries. Send for this folder and then place these books where the general public may read them.

"Ye shall be witnesses unto Me both in Jerusalem and in all Judea and in Samaria and unto the uttermost part of the earth."
Acts. 1, 8

The American Lutheran Publicity Bureau

The American Lutheran Publicity Bureau has passed a resolution recommending National Lutheran Publicity Week to all Lutheran congregations, and has pledged financial support for the carrying out of the undertaking. Since at the present time there are no funds available in the Synodical Treasury to pay for the printing and postage expenses incurred in connection with this week, the Syodical Press Committee gratefully accepted this offer of cooperation, and suggests that our Lutheran congregations remember the American Lutheran Publicity Bureau with a financial donation. The offerings gathered during the special service of National Lutheran Publicity Week may well be devoted to this purpose.

Besides paying the necessary expenses of the Synodical Press Committee, the American Lutheran Pulbicity Bureau is offering her offices, her office equipment and entire staff to aid in making National Lutheran Publicity Week a success. Professional advice and suggestions for the solution of any publicity problem will be furnished by the staff of the A.L.P.B. to any person making inquiry.

Millions of tracts have been published and distributed by the A.L.P.B. during past years as their contribution to the cause of Lutheran Publicity. For National Lutheran Publicity Week, February 12th-19th, they have reprinted one million tracts. The following tracts may be ordered free of charge while the supply lasts:

Rock of Ages	You and Your Boy
Eternal Life and Where to Find It	The Church's Claim Upon Men
Repentance	What Is the Business of the Church?
Amusements	Jesus the Great Physician
The Devil's Grip	The Glories of the Lutheran Church
The Great Problem of Sin and Its Solution	Christian Giving
Am I Converted?	The Forgiveness of Sins
Christ Crucified	When Jesus Came Into My Heart
Sanctification	Salvation
Family Worship	Holy Communion
Mission Work	The Ambassador's Message
Christianity	Helpless Man
My Church	Sin
The Bible Church	Suffering for Us
Why Go to Church?	The Light of the World
Where and How to Pray	Marvelous Savior
This Do! How Often?	Des Glaubens Fruechte
How to Join the Lutheran Church	Kirchengehen
What the Lutheran Church Stands For	The Lutheran Church

> Special Tract for Lent
> OUR LORD'S PASSION, 20 pages
> Lavender Cover, $2. per 100

K F U O

The Lutheran Laymen's League has arranged for a special program to be broadcast daily   The Rev. H. H. Hohenstein. director of the station, appeals to all Lutherans to call these features to the attention of the radio listeners so that these messages may receive nationwide reception. Ask your frinds and neighbors to tune in on KFUO.

The Walther League

The central office of the International Walther League is giving wholehearted support and cooperation to the Lutheran Publicity Week idea. A special folder brimful of ideas has been issued which will be mailed to all societies. If you have not received this folder, drop a line to the Chicago office and a supply will be sent to you for your young people's work.

"I will publish the name of the Lord. As one be ye greatness unto our God.
Deut. 32, 1-3

In directing National Lutheran Publicity Week, the Synodical Press Committee expects the full cooperation of the following:

I—1. Pastors
   2. Congregations
   3. Sunday Schools
   4. Mission Societies
   5. Ladies' Aid Societies
   6. Men's Clubs
   7. Young People's Societies

II—1. Conferences
   2. Institutions
   3. Local Press Committees

GENERAL PLAN

1. *Newspapers:*

a) Group advertising of Lutheran Churches. (Paid advertisement with gospel message surrounded or followed by list of local churches. See illustration in AMERICAN LUTHERAN, April, 1927, page 8.) News copy of congregational activities. (Items of interest which the editor of local paper will be glad to insert as church news.)

b) Use the clip sheet sent out by the Synodical Press Committee. The articles contained therein have been written up to appeal to the newspaper reading paper public.

c) Use paid sermonettes in newspapers. (A 2c stamp to the American Lutheran Publicity Bureau will bring twenty sample sermonettes suitable for newspaper publication.)

2. *Church Publications*

a) Lutheran periodicals of national circulation. (We are glad to announce a general spirit of wholehearted cooperation of the various editors of our Lutheran publications. This will be carried out by special articles, illustrated articles and editorials.)

"I have taught you publicly and from house to house."
Acts 20, 20

b) A clip-sheet has been prepared which will be mailed to all of our pastors with matter suitable for parish paper publication. Print an extra number of copies for distribution to the unchurched.

3. *Radio*

a) Station KFUO in St. Louis in the middle west, WRNY in New York City, and other stations which are regularly broadcasting Lutheran services will take special notice of National Lutheran Publicity Week effort.

b) Churches in every larger center, where a radio station is available should try to get on the air for as much time as possible. In offering his services, it might be well for the local pastor to plan a complete Lutheran musical program. For instance in using musical numbers by Bach, it should be mentioned that Bach was a Lutheran. Other Lutheran composers might be featured. In short every opportunity should be taken to inform the general public of the Lutheran achievements.

4. *Public Libraries and Reading Rooms*

a) Placing of Lutheran books. (Read article in AMERICAN LUTHERAN, January, 1926. Write to Concordia Publishing House for pamphlet listing suggested books and for prices.) Try the following suggestions:

1) Go to your local library and examine the books on the shelves and index cards. Note the titles lacking.

2) Get acquainted with the librarian and have a frank talk together. Explain that you wish to cooperate with the library in bringing the book collection of the religious department to a higher state of perfection. Suggest that books of the Bible should be purchased from library funds while books dealing with purely Lutheran fields might be furnished by your own church. Get the librarian's promise to accept the gift of Lutheran books and place them on the shelves should you furnish them free of charge.

3) Get the Walther League or any other society or individual to provide the necessary funds for purchasing the important Lutheran books which the pastor would select.

4) Create the Demand. As the librarian of the New York Public Library told the writer, "We will be glad to place any reliable book upon our shelves, providing you can prove that there is a sufficient demand for it. . . ." It is the pastor's duty to help create that demand among his people.

b) Place Lutheran periodicals in public reading rooms. (The *Lutheran Witness*, the AMERICAN LUTHERAN, and the *Walther League Messenger* may be placed in any library or reading room at the special club rate of $1.80 per year for the three publications.)

c) Display of Lutheran Books. (Request book stores and libraries to make a special window display. Send in photographs of original settings to the American Lutheran Publicity Bureau.)

4. *Distribution of Literature*

a) Lutheran tracts. (These supplied free by the American Lutheran Publicity Bureau, a policy made possible through the Free Tract Fund. Excellent tracts may also be purchased from the Concordia Publishing House.)

b) Gospels. (These supplied by the American Lutheran Publicity Bureau at $1.00 per hundred, plus postage.)

c) Church Papers. Procure extra copies of the *Lutheran Witness*, the AMERICAN LUTHERAN, the *Walther League Messenger*, as well as your local parish paper, and distribute to

parties who would read them.)

d) Subscribe to one or more of the above Lutheran periodicals for one of your friends, who possibly in this way may become interested. In just such a manner many church members have been won.

e) Order bundle copies of the Super-Tract Number, February, 1928, of the AMERICAN LUTHERAN for mass distribution at Lutheran Publicity Week Services and during the Lenten Season. The issue will contain 32 pages and can be had at the special rate of $5.00 per hundred. Sample copy 10c.

6. *Hotels, Railroad Stations and other Public Places*

a) Directory Advertising.

(See article on Hotel Directory Advertising in this issue of the AMERICAN LUTHERAN.)

b) Show-Card or Poster. (Use original ideas and draw up a poster to suit your own needs. See cut of poster issued by Lutheran Press at cost. Price for series of six, 60 cents. A new poster by the Lutheran Press which can be used for National Lutheran Publicity Week, as well as for the Lenten Season may be had at $.95 for twelve, $1.75 for 25, $6.00 per 100, postage extra.

c) Distribute invitation cards of church. (Send for free samples from the American Lutheran Publicity Bureau and have local printer get up something attractive.)

"And the gospel of the Kingdom shall be preached in all the world for a witness unto all nations." Matt. 24, 14

PERSONNEL

(A) *Pastors*

1. Preach a special topic on the duty of Individual Evangelism. (See article, Personal Evangelism, this issue.)

2. Arrange to conduct a Lutheran service over the nearest radio station. (Lutheran hymns, Bach music, etc., as outlined under section "Radio".)

3. Address Sunday School Children in morning session on "Why you should be proud that you are Lutheran Children."

4. Address Parochial School Children on a similar topic, and have different scholars write essays on topic, "Why we are glad that we have the privilege of attending a Christian school."

5. Conduct a Mid-Week lecture on Lutheran Doctrine and Practice. (This Mid-Week lecture to be principally for unchurched who are unacquainted with our church. May also serve to awaken the community to the fact that Lent begins on the following Wednesday. Advertise the fact that you will conduct a question box and will be glad to explain anything concerning the stand of the Lutheran church in doctrine and practice.)

6. Cooperate with our Lutheran ministers in the locality in regard to carrying on a week of Evangelistic Services.

Get together with your brother pastors upon the subject of group advertising in the newspapers.

7. Send out a series of letters "Selling the Gospel." (A series of letters written by an expert on mail campaigns is available for any one writing to the American Lutheran Publicity Bureau. 50c per sample set.)

8. Supervise Lutheran Publicity in local field.

   a. Write article for local newspaper.
   b. Draw up paid avertisement for newspaper.
   c. Speak to various church societies during week on various topics furthering Lutheran evangelism.
   d. Direct house-to-house visitation campaign and follow up prospects during the next week.

"Because I will publish the name of the Lord; ascribe ye greatness unto our God." Deut. 32; 3

(B) *Church Societies*

1. Walther League Societies.

a) Walther League Societies to carry out as many of the suggestions of the special Walther League pamphlet for National Lutheran Publicity Week as possible. Report your efforts and successes not only to Walther League Headquarters but also to the Synodical Press Committee at 69 Fifth Avenue.

3. Men's Club to arrange for special speaker who will treat of the history of the Lutheran Church in America. (See historical articles by Karl Kretzmann in issues of the AMERICAN LUTHERAN for the past year.)

4. Ladies Aid Society to arrange for slide lecture concerning negro missions, foreign mssions, institutional work of any kind. (A complete list of slides on above subjects may be had from the educational department of the Walther League.)

5. ALL SOCIETIES TO CONSIDER ONE OF THE FOLLOWING TASKS:

a. House to House Visitation.

The week before Lent is the psychological time to approach the unchurched. See list of avaliable tracts published by the A.L.P.B. elsewhere in this issue. House to house visitation has also been made one of the features of the Systematic Mission Endeavor carried on for a number of years by Walther League Societies. Excellent study material and helps for canvassing can be obtained by writing to the Educational Secretary of the Walther League. See article, "How to Conduct a Missionary Canvass," by O. Feucht, page 7, this issue.

b. Assist pastor in placing series of six posters advertising Bible Doctrines regularly in various store windows; pay for placing them on the passing street car or bus. See poster cut and description of various Bible texts on another page.

c. Assist pastor in sending out series of letters. (See section A. 7.)

d. If the church has no bulletin board—buy one.

If the church has a bulletin board—assist pastor in thinking up striking sentence sermons for period of Lent.

e. Buy tract rack for home church.

f. Pay for placing church address and time of services on Local hotel directory. (See AMERICAN LUTHERAN, January, p.   .)

g. Help to pay for inserting sermonettes regularly in local newspaper. (See section 1. c.)

h. Insert paid ad in local paper advertising Lutheran special service or lecture.

i. Place books and magazines in public library and reading rooms. (See section 4.)

j. Where practical, place tract racks in local depots, stores, etc.

k. Help pastor in campaign for Lutheran church paper subscriptions.

l. Cooperate with pastor in dressing up a store window as a Lenten Display. (Ideas for same may be had from the January issue (1926) of the AMERICAN LUTHERAN.) The poster and Bible text in the window should be changed every week, and an entirely different display with Easter lilies prepared for Easter.

The Educational Program of the Lutheran Church

The Missouri Synod of the Lutheran Church believes in an educated ministry. Therefore Concordia Seminary, St. Louis, insists that each candidate entering the ministry take a classical course at high school, a junior college course and a three-year theological course.

Every student entering Concordia Seminary—the theological school—must have a working knowledge of at least two modern languages and a reading knowledge of Latin, Greek and Hebrew.

The Missouri Synod has ten preparatory schools at which young men desiring to prepare for the ministry receive their preparatory schooling, free of charge, the Synod paying for the tuition and the upkeep of the institutions. At these schools are enrolled at present 2504 students, who have as their goal the ministry in the Lutheran Church.

Valparaiso University, Valparaiso, Ind., since September, 1925, is under the control and supervision of an educational society of the Missouri Synod.

The Doctrine of the Church and the Lutheran Church

The Christian Church is made up of the whole number of all believers and is not limited to one individual church denomination. A Christian is one who believes that he is saved from his sin solely and alone by Jesus Christ who, through the shedding of His blood, has made a vicarious and complete atonement for all sin, inherited and actual. Even in a church body in which error and false doctrine is taught, Christians can be found. They are Christians by God's grace in spite of these errors.

A congregation and a church body which does not teach and confess the Trinity and the atonement is not Christian.

The Deity of Jesus Christ

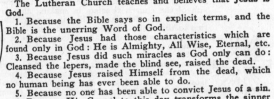

The Lutheran Church teaches and believes that Jesus is God.

1. Because the Bible says so in explicit terms, and the Bible is the unerring Word of God.

2. Because Jesus had those characteristics which are found only in God: He is Almighty, All Wise, Eternal, etc.

3. Because Jesus did such miracles as God only can do: Cleansed the lepers, made the blind see, raised the dead.

4. Because Jesus raised Himself from the dead, which no human being has ever been able to do.

5. Because no one has been able to convict Jesus of a sin.

6. Because His Gospel to this day transforms the sinner into a saint.

KFUO—The Gospel Voice of St. Louis

KFUO is the broadcasting station owned, controlled and supervised by Concordia Seminary of the Lutheran Church, Missouri Synod. The great purpose and aim of this station is to send out into the world the Gospel of Jesus Christ in its truth and purity, adhering to the Word as it is found in the Bible, the unerring and inspiring revelations of God.

Those who operate and support KFUO believe that the Gospel of Jesus Christ is the only means by which men can be converted and saved, by telling man that he is a sinner who must be cleansed by the blood of Jesus Christ.

KFUO is known throughout the length and breadth of our country as "The Gospel Voice" and broadcasts daily its messages of hope and salvation.

The Missionary Activities of the Missouri Synod, Lutheran Church

The Missouri Synod of the Lutheran Church carries on mission work at home and abroad. At home among the Negroes and Indians, and also the deaf-mutes. The Synod also carries on very extensively its missionary activities among the unchurched of this country, especially in the rural districts of the West and Northwest. Abroad the Synod does mission work in so-called Christian lands: Brazil, Argentine, Isle of Pines, Hawaii, Mexico, France, Germany, England, Denmark, etc.

The Missouri Synod's work in heathen lands is centered in India and China. The Synod has 835 missionaries in its various missionary fields—out of every three ministers in the Church, one is a missionary.

The Missouri Synod—Lutheran Church

The Missouri Synod, officially incorporated as the Evangelical Lutheran Synod of Missouri, Ohio and other States, is one of the largest Lutheran bodies in America, numbering more than one million souls and having congregations in almost every State of the Union, also in Canada and South America. This Synod is affiliated with the Synodical Conference of North America, which forms the largest Lutheran body in this country. The Missouri Synod is likewise affiliated with the independent Synods of Denmark, Finland, Germany, France, Australia and New Zealand.

The Missouri Synod is divided into twenty-six districts, covering the United States, Canada and Brazil.

Outward Reformation vs. Regeneration of the Heart

Man cannot be made good, much less righteous and just in the sight of God, by laws enacted by the state. The state can only attempt to keep order outwardly by laws and penalties of fines and imprisonment. Laws cannot change the heart of sinful man.

Man is made righteous and just before God through the re-creation or regeneration of the heart, which is brought about by the Holy Ghost through the preaching of the Gospel of Jesus Christ.

Concordia Seminary

Concordia Seminary is the outstanding theological institution of the Missouri Synod of the Lutheran Church. This institution was founded in 1839, in Perry County, Missouri, in a small log cabin, by the Saxon immigrants of Lutheran persuasion, coming to America. The institution has a full university charter. In 1850 it was moved to St. Louis, on South Jefferson Avenue. The first addition to this rapidly growing institution was made two years later, in 1852. Further additions were made in 1858, 1875, 1883 and 1907. In 1920 the Missouri Synod resolved to relocate the present institution. This was done and in 1926 the New Seminary, west of Forest Park, was dedicated. The present enrollment of Concordia Seminary is 380. Concordia Seminary is the largest denominational theological seminary of its kind in this country.

The Gospel of Social Service—No Gospel

The gospel of social service declares that the mission and aim of the church consists in making the community and the world a better place to live in, giving little or no attention to the soul's salvation after death. This gospel believes that all is well with man as long as he is outwardly respectable and lives amid sanitary and wholesome environments.

The Gospel of Jesus Christ is the glad news that Christ died for our sins. Therefore the chief purpose of Christ's Gospel is the saving of the soul from eternal damnation, showing that his soul must be cleansed through the blood of Jesus Christ.

Faith in this Gospel of Jesus Christ, regenerating the heart, affects the life of the believer in such a manner that he is transformed into a better citizen and a good neighbor.

The church which preaches only the gospel of social service has no gospel at all, as it offers no forgiveness and hope of eternal life.

Sanctification Through the Holy Ghost

Man is saved by grace without any merit or worthiness on his part. Man cannot save himself because he is spiritually dead in trespasses and sins.

The Holy Ghost through the Gospel creates faith and love in the heart of man. Having thus been brought to faith in Christ, the believer serves no longer sin but Christ whom he loves. By these good works, which the Christian does out of love to Christ, he does not to save himself but proves to the world that he is a saved child of God.

Good works are a fruit and evidence of the Christian's saved and consecrated state.

God's Plan of Salvation

God's plan of salvation as revealed in the Bible and taught by the Lutheran Church:

1. Man is a sinner and therefore worthy of death. "The soul that sinneth, it shall die."
2. Man cannot save himself, neither by his good works nor by his character. Eph. 2:8,9.
3. Jesus in our place and for us made full payment for all our sins by shedding His blood on the cross. I. Pet. 1:18, 19.
4. Man must accept this Jesus, God's Son come into the world, by believing in Him as his personal Saviour.

The Means of Grace and the Lutheran Church

Jesus Christ has given His Church as a means of grace the Gospel and the Sacraments: Baptism and the Lord's Supper. A means of grace is a means or way by which God's grace is offered and conveyed to the sinner, who, accepting this grace is forgiven, finding peace with God, and saved. These means of grace, the Gospel and the Sacraments, are the only ones by which the heart of man is regenerated and by which the sinner becomes a believer.

The Church and the State

The Lutheran Church teaches and believes that the church and the state are two distinct and separate organizations with separate and distinct spheres which should not interfere with one another. The church is to show man the way to life through faith in Christ, by the preaching of the Gospel. The state is to keep order in this world endeavoring to enable man to live in peace and, within the law, perfectly free.

The state guides its people, the citizens, both Christian and non-Christian, by natural, civil and economic laws; the church guides and directs her people, the Christians, by spiritual laws laid down in the Bible.

The state must not dictate to the church, neither must the church insist that the state enforce the church laws upon non-Chrisian citizens. The church has no jurisdiction over those who do not profess to be her members.

The Atonement and the Lutheran Church

The Lutheran Church teaches and believes with the Bible that man is saved solely and alone through the Atonement of Jesus, that is, that Jesus Christ, the sinless Son of God, took upon Himself our sin and in our place and for us, by the shedding of His blood, made full, complete payment for all our sins and thus reconciled us to His Father. Believing this, the sinner is acquitted and saved.

The Cardinal Doctrine of the Scriptures Stressed by the Lutheran Church

The cardinal doctrine of the Scriptures, stressed and emphasized by the Lutheran Church, is the doctrine of justification by faith. To justify means to make just, to acquit because another has paid the penalty. Jesus paid the sin-penalty with His blood when He died on the cross. Those who accept or believe that Jesus Christ died for them are acquitted and saved, justified by faith "without the deeds of the law." Rom. 3, 28.

The Lutheran Church—A Singing Church

The Lutheran Church is a singing church, praising God with songs and hymns. One outstanding feature of a service in a Lutheran Church is the congregational singing. Martin Luther restored the hymn to the church.

The best known hymn of the Lutheran Church is Martin Luther's great hymn—A Mighty Fortress Is Our God. This hymn has been translated into more than 163 languages and dialects, and is found in the hymn book of practically every Protestant denomination.

The Bible and the Lutheran Church

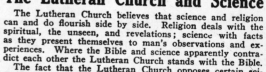

The Lutheran Church teaches and believes that the Bible, word for word, is inspired by God and therefore the sole authority and rule of faith and life of the Christian and the final court of appeals in all things pertaining to Christian Doctrine and of life. The Bible therefore must be accepted word for word without a mental reservation.

The Lutheran Church and Science

The Lutheran Church believes that science and religion can and do flourish side by side. Religion deals with the spiritual, the unseen, and revelations; science with facts as they present themselves to man's observations and experiences. Where the Bible and science apparently contradict each other the Lutheran Church stands with the Bible.

The fact that the Lutheran Church opposes certain scientific theories which are not even universally accepted by scientists, cannot be construed as opposition against true science.

Lutheranism and Americanism

The Missouri Synod of the Lutheran Church is not an institution transplanted to this country from a foreign shore, but is a native of this continent. It is as independent as the United States. Lutheranism was well established in North America at the dawn of the American Republic and has always insisted upon the separation of the Church and State.

Organization of the Lutheran Church

The Lutheran Church of the Missouri Synod has a congregational form of government. The congregation is supreme. The congregation calls its pastor and grants him permission to accept another call. These sovereign and free congregations have organized into a Synod subscribing to the unaltered confessions of the Lutheran Church. Synod acts only in an advisory capacity and none of its resolutions are binding upon the congregations without their consent.

The Lutheran Church, Missouri Synod, has a democratic form of government and has at no time been transplanted, supervised or directed by a European Lutheran Church.

The Lutheran Church— Not Luther's Church

The Lutheran Church is not built upon Martin Luther nor any personal and private teachings of Martin Luther, but upon the Word of God as revealed in the Bible. Luther did not found or create a new religion but restored to its purity the Gospel of Jesus Christ.

Luther annunciated no new doctrine or teaching, but stressed the old Bible Truths, especially the supremacy and authority of the Scriptures and justification by faith.

Newspaper Sermonettes

Many of our Lutheran men throughout the country are doing excellent things in newspaper publicity. Due to lack of space it is impossible for the *American Lutheran Magazine* to reprint even a small portion of the clippings which are received for our files. We do believe, however, that our Magazine is justified in reprinting the following sermonettes by Pastor P. M. Freiburger of Billings, Montana. While conceived and used for local purposes, we believe that many of our men will be helped by this material in drawing up their own newspaper sermonettes.

We quote from Pastor Freiburger's letter:

"For more than five years and up to the present, I have managed to get local papers to run stuff for me, getting weekly publicity. Rather than run a sermon, even in excerpt, I thought of the idea to use a regular story-sermonette according to the church season, not too long, but still long enough to drive home at least one thought. This would be run separately or usually in connection with my regular announcement for next Sunday's services.

"Have been surprised at the reaction, and am more than convinced that it is good Gospel and Church publicity.

"I believe in publicity with a vengeance, especially when I can get it the Scotch way; as a rule it is the only way for us preachers with congregations slow or definitely opposed to see the necessity of PAID advertising."

A CHANGELESS CHRIST FOR A CHANGING WORLD

Is the Gospel of the Bible out of place in our age of progress and enlightenment? The ox cart, the goose-quill, the pine torch have been discarded, and some people conclude, therefore, that the old Gospel religion of Christ and Him Crucified and Risen, must also be replaced by something that is modern, up-to-date.

This, however, is a wrong conclusion, a fatal mistake. The mere circumstance of age does not argue against usefulness. A drink of water today will quench the thirst as well as it did when Moses brought forth water from the rock. Exodus 17.

Even so the Gospel of the Bible is as useful today as it was centuries ago. The only soul-satisfying and soul-saving religion is still that of the Bible with its changeless Saving Christ inviting a changing lost world: Come unto Me all ye that labor and are heavy-laden, and I will give you rest. Matt. 11:28.

To give up this Gospel for something new or modern means to sink back into heathenism, clothed only with the thin veneer of present-day culture and civilization.

The old, yet ever new Gospel of Christ is the only message of salvation through the sin-atoning blood of Jesus, the Redeemer of sin-cursed and death-doomed mankind.

Therefore, even today it is a necessary and saving truth that whosoever believeth in Him shall not perish, but have everlasting life. John 3:16.

CHRIST, THE SON OF GOD

"Thou art that Christ, the Son of the Living God." John 6:69.

All the world is agreed that Jesus was a true man. Even agnostics and atheists laud Christ as the great examplar of righteousness.

But the Jesus of the Bible is not only a true man, great and good. He is also the exalted Lord, the Son of the Living God.

Christ is true God.

For making this assertion and claim the Jews of His time condemned Him to death.

And Christ, the Son of God, even today is a rock of offense, worthy only of rejection. But God says:

"He that honoreth not the Son, honoreth not the Father which hath sent Him." John 5:23.

Jesus, the God-Man, is the heaven-sent and divinely-appointed Savior of all mankind. Christ came into the world to save sinners. I Tim. 1:15.

"And He is the only Savior. Neither is there salvation in any other." Acts 4:12.

Jesus, the God-Man, is also the only all-sufficient and efficient Savior. "In whom we have redemption through His blood, the forgiveness of sins." Eph. 1:7.

For this reason the Bible says: "He that believeth on the Son hath everlasting life; and he that believeth not the Son shall not see life, but the wrath of God abideth on him." John 3:35.

"Therefore, believe on the Lord Jesus Christ, and thou shalt be saved." Acts 16:31.

GOD'S CHRISTMAS MESSAGE

Have you heard God's Christmas message to you and all sin-cursed humanity? It reads: "Fear not, for behold, I bring you good tidings of great joy, which shall be to all people. For unto you is born this day in the city of David (Bethlehem) a Savior, which is Christ the Lord." Luke 2.10.11. God's Christmas gift to the world is: "Unto us a child is born, unto us a Son is given." Isa. 9:6. "For God so loved the world, that he gave his only begotten Son, that whosoever believeth in Him should not perish, but have everlasting life." John 3:16.

We preach Christ Jesus; The Savior of mankind, the deliverer from sin and eternal damnation.

"CHRIST—THE BREAD OF LIFE"

Jesus says: "I am the Bread of Life."—John 6:48.

True to the earthly origin of their bodies, most men "labor for the meat that perisheth" trailing their lives like low vines along the ground to the dreary and weary tune, "What shall we eat, what shall we drink, wherewith shall we be clothed?"

True to the heavenly origin of their souls some men also seek God, if haply they might feel after Him and find Him. But man of himself cannot find the true God. Even the highly cultured city of the ancient world by wisdom knew not God. Athens publicly and officially proclaimed its ignorance by building an altar "To the unknown God." Acts 17.

Man cannot of himself satisfy his soul-hunger with the bread of life—cannot find God, dwelling in the light which no man can approach unto, whom no man hath seen, or can see. And yet, we can know God—since Christ, Jesus, the Son of God, hath declared Him.

Are you vainly groping in darkness for satisfying food for the soul? Then accept Jesus, the God-sent Redeemer from sin and damnation, as your loving Savior. Christ graciously and generously offers and conveys Himself to you as the Bread of Life. He that believeth on Him shall not perish, but shall have everlasting life." John 3:16.

FREEDOM

"If the Son shall make you free, ye shall be free indeed." John 8:36. Man's persistent striving for freedom, civil, social, religious, has not been in vain. Despotic dominion has been replaced by popular forms of government. Serfdom has almost everywhere been abolished. Religious liberty is one of the fundamental principles of our constitution. But in spite of all evident progress and advancement, man today, as ever, is held in the most shameful spiritual slavery. Man by nature is the slave of SIN. And by his own efforts and power he is not able to loose himself from the fetters of this thraldom. For all are sinners; and "whosoever committeth sin is the servant of sin." John 8:34. To deliver man from this degrading slavery "God sent forth His Son, made of woman, made under the Law, to redeem them that were under the Law." Gal. 4:4,5. His vicarious fulfilling of the Law, by His atoning suffering and death, He ransomed us from the bondage of sin. For in Christ we have redemption through His blood, the forgiveness of sin." Eph. 1:7. We are free indeed, because the Son has made us free. "He that believeth shall be saved." Mark 16:16.

"THE WORLD'S ONLY HOPE"

Man without Christ is without hope in this life. Eph. 2:12.

Heathen writers in doleful strains bear witness to this truth.

Cicero says: The best thing is not to be born; the next best to die soon after birth.

Epicure of old advised to eat, drink and be merry, to be like the animals and not to bother about the morrow. When you get tired of that, you may end it all by suicide.

Zeno, the Stoic, advocated hardening the mind so as to make it unfeeling against pain and pleasure, and when tired of that, to commit suicide.

Some try to comfort people by telling them that sin and death do not exist. But such a flat denial does not remove sin and death.

Indeed, man without Christ, is without hope in this life.

Christ Jesus is the world's only hope.

He—the savior of the world, tenderly offers the comforting invitation: Come unto Me all ye that labor and are heavy-laden, and I will give you rest. Matt. 11:28. The blood of the Son of God, shed upon the cross cleanses us from all sins and makes us heirs of the bliss of everlasting life in heaven. He that believeth on the Lord Jesus Christ shall be saved. I am come that ye might have life, and that ye might have it more abundantly. John 10:10.

THE VALUE OF A SOUL

"What is a man profited, if he shall gain the whole world and lose his own soul?"—Matt. 16:26.

This is the world's greatest problem. And Christ Jesus is the only one to solve it.

The whole world on one side —man's own soul on the other. Which is the greater, the more valuable?

Jesus answers emphatically: "The Soul."

And yet, what is held cheaper than a human soul? Some like the heathen Romans and Greeks believed that only men like Cicero and Socrates had souls, but not the common people.

But the Bible teaches that every man, woman, and child has a soul. Yes, even the malefactor on the cross and the woman taken in adultery.

But the Bible tells us more than this. It says that the soul of the thief and the harlot is worth saving, even at the tremendous cost of the life and death of the son of God.

The God of all mercy and grace sent Jesus into the world to save sinful mankind from eternal damnation. The blood of Jesus Christ shed on the accursed tree cleanseth us from all sin. I John 1:7.

In Christ we have redemption through His blood, the forgiveness of sins. His precious and potent blood is the price of our salvation. "Believe on the Lord Jesus Christ, and thou shalt be saved." Acts 16:31.

Hotel Advertising

DURING the early years of the American Lutheran Publicity Bureau's history the usefulness of hotel publicity was energetically stressed and we were laboring under the delusion that the question had been sufficiently agitated to need no further comment. Extensive traveling during the last year has convinced us, however, that surprisingly few of our churches are making use of the hotels as an advertising medium. All the better hotels in larger cities and even medium sized towns present a framed Church Directory. Very often all the local Lutheran churches are conspicuous by their absence. In other cases two or three churches of our denomination are listed out of a possible twenty or thirty. The churches of almost all our larger cities are failing to see the value of helping the Lutheran traveler in his desire to worship with people of his own faith, or of stimulating the impulse to worship by a clear and informative advertisement. Lutheran travelers are continually complaining that the churches in the cities they visit give the hotel guest no information as to their whereabouts. Some of the travelers from our own church now secure from the pastor as much information as he can give regarding the churches in the cities they intend to visit. But naturally he can give no information regarding the time of services and very often he has no knowledge of the geography of the city. The American people have become great travelers. The automobile has stimulated the native "Wanderlust" until it has become almost a national mania. Many pastors, when the summer exodus begins, admonish the prospective tourists to attend a church of their faith while on tour and yet fail to provide information for the tourist who comes within reach of their own bailiwick.

The installation of a suitable hotel advertisement is connected with a little expense and many churches consider the expense unwarranted and tantamount to waste. We have no time to argue the point. Personally we are convinced by our own experience that they are wrong. But if the congregational treasury cannot be tapped for the cost of such an ad, the matter might be taken over by one of the church organizations. We believe it to be a question for lay action. If the pastor is disinterested, let the laymen agitate the question. The larger cities run a syndicated, classified church directory for hotels. See to it that your services are listed. Some hotels permit separate advertisements by individual churches, and usually the only requirement is that the advertisement be attractive and suitably framed. Take up the matter at the next congregational or Walther League meeting or that of the Men's Club. Help the bewildered traveler and silence his justified grumbling.

From Coast to Coast
LUTHERAN CHURCHES
Listed on Hotel Bulletin Boards

✠ ✠ ✠

DID YOU KNOW THAT:

1. The Lutheran Church is the largest Protestant Church in the world, numbering 80,000,000 adherents?
2. Ours was the first church to send missionaries to the American Indians?
3. The first Protestant pastor to land in North America was a Lutheran, coming eight months before the Pilgrims landed at Plymouth Rock?
4. The first book translated into any American Indian language was Luther's Small Catechism?
5. The first president of the Continental Congress was a Lutheran?
6. The first man to unfurl the Stars and Stripes was a Lutheran—General Herkimer?
7. The first American Naval flag was made by a group of Lutheran women?
8. Washington's army at the battle of Trenton was composed largely of Lutherans?
9. It was a Lutheran boy who called a Lutheran sexton to ring the Liberty Bell?
10. A Lutheran was the first speaker of the House of Representatives?
11. The first Protestant hospital in America was built by Lutherans? Today 29% of the hospitals in America are Lutheran.
12. The Lutheran Church in America maintains 116 colleges and other educational institutions, of which 27 are theological seminaries?
13. The Lutheran Church has outstripped all Protestantism in moving toward union? At present 97% of Lutherans are found in three great groups: The United Lutheran Church, the American Lutheran Church, and the Synodical Conference (Missouri Synod).
14. The two principles of the Lutheran Reformation are these: (a) The just shall live by faith; (b) The authority of the Scriptures.

Why Synodical Publicity?

The most serious business in the world is the Business of our Father. The carrying on of this business connotes an intelligent knowledge of that business. Whoever claims to be a Christian must be not only a mildly interested spectator but an active participant in that business. Active participation presupposes an intelligent conception of those things which a Christian ought to know and to do to lead souls to Christ.

Here is where Synodical Publicity takes a rightful place in the curriculum of religious education. Synodical Publicity lays the facts of "Your Synod at Work" before us. No one is fully qualified to decide the "where" and "how" and "how much" until he is fully informed as to where his help is needed, how he can best help, and how much is necessary to carry on the work of the Church.

It is unfair and unworthy of a Christian not to become informed about the work of the Church and then decide the question of his participation in that work from the stand-point of his ignorance.

There is no evading the fact that many Christians of the Missouri Synod are woefully ignorant of the work of our Church. Herein lies one of the causes of our missionary poverty both in men and money.

We give to what we care about. We care for what we know about. Often we give, not according to our ability, but according to the degree of our interest. Information arouses interest, interest arouses inspiration; inspiration arouses expression and action. Synod must give this information to its members. It is endeavoring to accomplish this by means of its periodicals and Department of Publicity.

But the Church members now owe Synod the courtesy of a hearing. Synod is striving, not so much for money to carry out its program as for a hearing. Synod is perfectly content to leave the issue of "how much shall I give" to the awakened Christian conscience if only this conscience allows itself to be informed. The tragedy of the world's need is hardly greater than the tragedy of blind eyes and deaf ears and numb hands of professing Christians who are bland and deaf and numb (and dumb) to the work which their Synod is carrying on for God.

Right here is the real need for work in Synod at present. To a great extent some are unaware of the great needs of the Church and therefore make such uninspired efforts to meet them.

Christianity is a meaningless term unless it incorporates in it the obligation, rather privilege of leading others to Christ. This can best be done through the Church at work. And to do it intelligently a thorough knowledge of the work Synod is carrying on is essential. The means to gain this knowledge are at hand.

SYNODICAL PUBLICITY

First, every family ought to have the *Lutheran Witness* or *Lutheraner*. In most instances the objection of cost can be overcome by a look at the library table. There are usually a goodly number of periodicals there, good, bad, or indifferent; but the Church paper is conspicuous by its absence. One must, of course, draw the line somewhere, but why draw the line on your Church paper?—The Church paper is an essential piece of literature in every Christian home. The business of being a member of your church is fully as important as the business of being a farmer or banker, and neither would think of getting along without his trade journal. Yet many Christians want to be intelligent members of their Church without reading the Church papers which contain the latest news from our fields of work far and near. Often it is these same people who wonder why the Church is in debt and so slow in the work of extending the Kingdom of God.

This applies also to Synod's free literature published by the Publicity Department of the Fiscal Office. Free literature would solve the problem if expense were the real reason why our people do not read Church literature. But the failure to read uncovers a much more serious condition than that of poverty. During the last six months the Publicity Department has issued eight pieces of literature containing a volume of information. For various reasons some did not order it at all; others ordered it but it remains under the desk in the vestry; others report that often it is not read when delivered into the hands of people; that its subject matter is uninteresting; that it is too long or too short.

None of these objections touch the heart of the matter. The real factor is that our people are too little interested in Synod's work and will not take pains to read the literature in order that they may become interested. Or have the tastes of our people become so jaded that their church literature must compete in style and makeup with our present flamboyant newspapers and magazines?

Our Synodical periodicals and free literature are informative. They equip us with facts which cannot but awaken a live interest in a Christian for the work of saving souls. If our publicity materials are distributed, read, they will be a great assistance in arousing an intelligent interest for the work of our Church. And until we know the facts upon which the appeal of our Church are based, we cannot be in a position to fully administer the great trust Jesus imposes upon us.

Hints for more and better publicity in our Lutheran Church as sent out by the Press Committee of the Western District

1. Let each church set aside a definite amount in the annual budget for publicity. Many pastors are handicapped in this work, because they have no fund to draw from. Make a beginning with a publicity fund of $50 or $100.

2. Paid advertisements are a good means of publicity. Regularity counts. A small ad every Saturday is better than a large ad every three months.

3. Do not overlook the opportunity to get free publicity for your church by means of news stories concerning your church in the daily press. This field of church publicity is sorely neglected by the average Lutheran church.

4. News stories must be prepared in newspaper style. Let the first sentence or first paragraph tell the chief point of your story. Succeeding paragraphs are to bring in detail and related facts. Names of people and personal facts always make an article more newsy.

5. The news story should be typed on one side of stationery only and double spaced. Get your story to the editor in plenty of time. An article which is to appear on Sunday should be in the editor's hands Friday evening. Always mark date of release.

6. Be sure that you send or take your news story to proper party at the newspaper office. A personal call now and then will prove helpful.

7. Many happenings in your congregation have news value. Here are a few suggestions that may help you:

  1. A building program, building plans, financial drive for new church, groundbreaking exercises, corner stone laying, dedication of church or school.
  2. Anniversary of pastor or teacher, of congregation or church society.
  3. Unusual services.
  4. Unusual speakers, such as foreign missionary, synodical official.
  5. Special contributions to certain funds for congregation, denomination or nation (flood, tornado).
  6. Death of prominent member of church.
  7. Baptism of large number of children or adults at one time.
  8. Unusual features at school graduation or confirmation (such as very large class, etc.).
  9. An innovation which gets results.
  10. Special Sunday School news.
  11. Special musical program for Christmas, Easter, Thanksgiving.
  12. Brief notes each week on sermon topic, time of services, speakers for church notes in Saturday editions of newspapers.

PLEASE TURN TO PAGE 359

How Cachet Publicity Pays

L AST YEAR on the occasion of the 450th anniversary of Luther's birth, the A.L.P.B. ventured into the field of publishing a cachet. Stamp collectors everywhere wrote us for these envelope jackets. About 10,000 tracts found national circulation by means of this mailing.

This year in commemoration of the anniversary of the publication of the Luther Bible, the second cachet was prepared. Newspaper announcements brought over 3,000 inquiries. These came from all states with the exception of three. Six foreign countries were represented in the list. More than 12,000 tracts were inserted in these envelopes.

Results: Many letters reading like these: "Luther Bible Cachet received. Just wonderful. May I have a few more of the tracts which were enclosed?" Another, "Bible Cachet received. The best I have seen in a long while. Please send a few more of your excellent tracts." From New Hampshire a correspondent writes, "fine cachet, excellent tracts—please accept the enclosed $.......... and send me twenty-five more leaflets 'Search the Scriptures'." We could print a long list of such favorable comments.

The publicity value of cachets: Newspaper write-ups, contacts with non-Lutherans, thousands of mail clerks handle these cachets, the opportunity to make a mass mailing of tracts, articles in stamp magazines, permanent Lutheran publicity in the exhibition of stamp collectors for many years to come and the general opportunity of presenting a Lutheran message to the general public.

Visualizing the Institutional Appeal

V ISUAL education and descriptive advertising is the par excellence of institutional publicity. The value of maps, charts, graphs, posters, motion pictures, lantern slides, models, cannot be over-estimated in presenting the work of missions and benevolent enterprises. Visualizing the work of an organization by actual pictures or suggestive illustrations makes the appeal reach the eye, arrests attention of the mind and prompts the heart to action. Pictures tell the story. Brief texts and interesting captions are read, while the "long story" is laid aside for future reading. "One picture is worth 10,000 words," reads an old Chinese proverb. A child-placing agency in New York City secures its funds by mailing to a large list of contributors neatly printed folders carrying pictures of babies placed in foster homes. The monthly magazine,

Orphans Gift Sunday--

The Bethlehem Orphan and Half Orphan Asylum
Fingerboard Road at Hylan Boulevard   Fort Wadsworth, Staten Island, N. Y.
Bethlehem Orphanage is a Charity Organized and Supported by Lutheran Churches of New York and Vicinity

Dumb Animals, has done much to prevent cruelty to animals by graphic presentation of its work.

Hospitals, homes for the aged, orphan homes, and kindred institutions, would increase their regular contributions and receive more and larger bequests if they would constantly by word and picture keep the good work they are doing before the people who have helped to open these institutions and are interested in their existence.

We have seen annual reports or year books that compel attention and which are never laid aside, but read. But we know also many institutions that are wasting good money by poorly gotten up literature which is not saving money but a rather waste of funds.

We are reproducing on these pages a number of electrotypes used by our Lutheran Bethlehem Orphan and Half - Orphan Home, Fort Wadsworth, Staten Island, N. Y. Space permitting, we would show many more from other parts of the country. These pictures carry out the ideas advanced in this article. Tell the story with pictures.

How many pairs of shoes per month, per year, do the children of your institution need? Show picture of a pile of shoes and cobbler at work repairing them.

Do your children like jam? Illustrate your appeal for home made jellies and preserved

BRING YOUR GIFTS TO YOUR CHURCH OR SUNDAY SCHOOL

fruits, by having a child receive its afternoon "jelly bread." We know of a children's home in which every birthday is remembered.

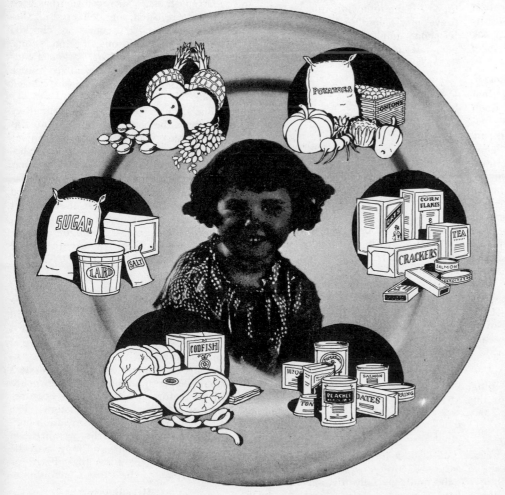

The name of the child is announced, the age given, the birthday cake is distributed. How many patrons of this institution know of this little incident in the family life of this home? Yet such little human stories have a strong appeal.

What is the among of money needed for food, for salaries, for clothing and other maintenance disbursements? Show these expenses with illustrated graphs and pictures. Use cuts and plenty of them. Brief text is better than a long drawn out description of the work.

We know of one institution which sends out its Christmas letter printed in the shape of a Christmas Tree with this pointed appeal: "When you have finished reading our story—please put your name as a gift at the foot of this Christmas Tree and send it with your check or money order, in order that we may spread cheer among the little ones entrusted to our care."

This letter, printed in red and green ink, with cuts of tree and children, brought good results.

(Editorial Note) The cuts reproduced show some of the publicity and advertising material issued by the Lutheran Bethlehem Orphan & Half-Orphan Home, Ft. Wadsworth, S. I., N. Y. We believe other institutions may be benefited by these suggestions for their publicity plans.

Planned Publicity for Conventions

NO HIT AND MISS POLICY will bring about successful publicity for large gatherings, such as conventions, joint Mission and Reformation Festivals, Lutheran Days, etc. Things must be well planned and carried out on schedule. The Press Committee must never be elected or appointed as the event gets under way. At least two weeks before a well-organized Publicity Committee prepares for its duties. This article proposes suggestions and plans, all of which have been tried out and found to be practical.

Advance Publicity

One week or ten days before the date of the event an advance news release is issued. This news release gives the name of the organization, the place of meeting, names of prominent officials, speakers, visitors expected to attend. A general outline of the program may also be given. Most newspapers will be glad to accept photographs to use with the advance announcements. A personal call on the Editors to seek their cooperation will help matters. It also "pays" to insert some paid advertising, probably the Saturday (Church News page) before the date of the event.

The Day Before the Convention

The Press Committee holds its final meeting the day before the event. Each member of the committee assumes responsibilty and direction of certain duties. One person is the "News Agencies" (Associated Press, United, etc.) man, another serves the local newspapers, another directs the taking of pictures. Final contact is also made with the press. All members of the committee exchange address and telephone numbers of their lodgings. A number of sets of envelopes are addressed for newspapers (e. g., City or Desk Editor, New York Times, 316 West 46th Street, New York, New York. In lower corner write COPY FROM LUTHERAN CONVENTION.) In the selection of a room for the Press Committee we suggest space near the stage or platform.

The Convention Opens

As soon as possible after the opening of the convention, the chairman of the Press Committee introduces the following resolution:

WHEREAS, the Press Committee of this convention is responsible for all news printed about this convention, it is therefore desirable that all announcements be prepared and released from the Press Room, therefore be it

RESOLVED, that no members of this body make statements to the press, grant interviews to reporters, or issue statements unless a member of the Press Committee has been informed to such statement, interview, or news release. In all events such announcements should pass through the Press Room of the Convention.

Equipment of the Press Room

A cardboard sign PRESS ROOM on the door will keep out persons having no business with the committee. The typewriters are for the use of the Press Committee, its staff and reporters, and not for members of other convention committees to prepare their reports. Facilities for other committees should be provided elsewhere.

For each newspaper a wire basket or tray lettered with the name of the paper is provided. Reporters will then find copy at the same designated place each day.

Posted on the wall a typewritten directory with the following information will prove very helpful: Names, addresses, telephone numbers of all local newspapers. If morning paper, indicate with "M"; if evening "P.M."; if weekly, "W." Also the same of news agencies; reporter's home and office data; location of telegraph office; map of the city, and transportation folders.

A number of cards size about 12 x 15 should be at hand. Suggested copy: PRESS ROOM, RESERVED FOR PRESS, PRESS ROOM LOCATED ON NEXT FLOOR, etc.

* * *

If a banquet or luncheon is held in connection with the convention, reserved seats are set apart for the Press. A member of the Press Committee is seated between every two reporters. At the noon hour meals a table is reserved for the Press and the staff of the Press Room, since work, sometimes prevents appearance "on time."

All reports are written in at least five copies: one each to (a) presiding officer, (b) secretary of the convention, (c) press table, (d) committee files, (e) reserve copy. All copy should be double spaced. Carbon copies must be legible.

* * *

A display of clippings, the publicity secured is always welcomed by the delegates and especially the convention visitors. Several large sheets of heavy cardboard or soft wood is provided as a bulletin board.

Convention delegates welcome "ready to use news copy" for their home newspapers. These convention bulletins should be especially prepared for that purpose. Two issues per week lettered "News from the convention of the —— in session at ——." In lower corner, "submitted by ——, a delegate at this convention, representing —— Lutheran Church." These bulletins should contain all the important news "boiled down."

Working Plans

Representatives of the Press report to the Press Room, not at the Press table (in convention). Copy given to the Press should have an okay followed by initials of a member of the Press Committee, e. g., OK/JFEN. Date of release should be on all copy thus, December 15, A.M.

As soon as a report, resolution, essay, address, etc., is received in the Press Room, ten or twelve copies of the same are typewritten and placed in basket, "HOLD."

If report, essay, or resolution has been adopted, rejected, or delivered, it becomes news, and the copies are checked for changes, additions, or omissions, etc., then transferred from basket "Pending" to "Release." Material for future consideration is held in basket labeled "Hold."

The member of the Press Committee on duty in the convention hall (seated at Press table) keeps the Press Room informed by messages of the business before the convention. After the vote has been taken or the address (essay) delivered, copy is marked with a notation and sent to the Press Room. If an important matter (result of election, etc.) is announced a special messenger is dispatched to the Press Room with memo: *IMPORTANT, TELEPHONE AT ONCE.*

Members of the Press Committee attend important hearings and committee meetings. Advance information will help in the preparation of the news copy.

The presiding officer should give a daily program of "expected business" to the Press Committee. Photographers should be given an opportunity to secure "shots" before sessions, during noon recess, or after the close of sessions. The taking of pictures in the convention during sessions is only to be permitted on exceptional occasions, and only with the permission of the presiding officer, or the chairman of the Press Committee.

Miscellaneous

MESSENGERS. Boys and girls with arm band or badge lettered MESSEN-

PLEASE TURN TO PAGE 361

Honesty in Advertising

CONVENTIONS of advertising men have for years been giving us the assurance that the days of hood-winking and bamboozling the general public by extravagant and mendacious advertising are over and that absolute truthfulness is the basic principle on which modern advertising constructs its appeal. One wonders, however, if particularly the radio advertisers are not drawing upon their imaginations rather than upon facts. Certain tooth pastes seem to be the most marvelous benefactions ever bestowed upon mankind. By reading the label on certain mouth washes all microbes flee in dismay. By smoking a certain brand of cigarettes one is on the verge of developing a lyric tenor voice and operatic tendencies. The pleasant habit of chewing yeast will banish all the ills of man. The regular use of certain razor blades will prevent wives from leaving their husbands and will throw a monkey-wrench into the machinery of the divorce courts. If modern advertising is truthful, the millenium is at hand.

However much commercial advertisers may draw upon their imaginations and play upon the gullibility of the people in the presentations of their advertising matter, church advertising must always be scrupulously truthful. The public properly resents with unforgiving vehemence any extravagance of claims on the part of a church. If a church advertises under a slogan, that slogan must be true. A church which breathes the atmosphere of spiritual refrigeration and is torn with dissension has no business to advertise itself as "The Friendly Church. "The Church with the Warm Welcome" often confines its welcome to carefully suppressed mental reservations. "The Homelike Church" is often a living demonstration of the reasons why men leave home. Before it advertises at all a church should set its house in order. Let it pay scrupulous attention also to externals, to the condition of its church property, to cleanliness and ventilation, to the appearance of pastor and deacons and ushers, to the efficiency of the organist and the choir, to the condition of the hymn-books, to the courtesies it extends to the stranger. Let it start its services on time and show in every detail that the service is a thing of careful planning and thorough preparation. Of course, as someone recently felt called upon to remind us, "the Word must do the work," but we have no right to present that precious Word in a slovenly package or in repulsive wrappings. Especially if a church through advertising appeals to the general public it must eliminate conditions that would neutralize any response to the advertisement.

Be honest! Advertise your message. Give it the proper setting. You may incidentally advertise the setting, but here again strict truthfulness is in order. It is not truthful to advertise "beautiful music" and then present an organist whose heart may be golden but whose musical endeavors should be confined to turning a radio dial, or a choir whose intentions are excellent but whose renditions belong to the burdens that we bear. If we have such afflictions, let us carry them with patience, but don't let us mendaciously advertise them. Let us be honest!

Printing Attractiveness

AN unsolicited item of commendation has come to us from the president of the Buxton-Westerman Company, book publishers and distributors of the New Analytical Bible. Mr. G. C. Buxton writes us: "I like your magazine because you do not economize on paper. This is really a change from the way in which some religious magazines are sent out to the reader Your magazine stands at the top of the list so far as typography and general appearance are concerned."

Telephone Book Publicity

ONE of the prominent laymen of the church, whose work compels him to do much traveling, recently made a suggestion which we consider worth passing on. He claims that when a traveler gets to a city hotel, and, as is usually the case, finds the Lutheran churches not listed on the hotel church directory, his next resort for information is the telephone book. He may be in a strange town and is not familiar with the personnel of the local clergy. Neither does he know the official titles of the local churches. In the haste of packing he has neglected to put a Lutheran Annual into his grip. He wants to go to church on Sunday morning. The newspaper of the previous evening gives him no information as to the whereabouts of the city's Lutheran churches. So as a last resort he takes up the telephone directory. But here again he is at a loss because he does not know under what title the Lutheran churches may be listed, if they be listed at all. Our lay friend makes the suggestion that all Lutheran churches of a certain community be listed in the telephone directory under the one word "Lutheran:" This word "Lutheran" is then to be followed by the respective titles of the churches, as, for instance, Lutheran, St. John's, 8th and Locust Sts. We consider this an excellent suggestion. There may be twelve churches listed in a certain hotel directory, Christ Lutheran Church under the C's, Jehovah Lutheran Church under the J's, Messiah Lutheran Church under the M's, etc. The brother's suggestion is not only for listing in the classified section of the directory, but in the very body of the ordinary telephone listings. We pass this suggestion on for immediate consideration in every city in the country.

It may be contended that most of our churches have not installed a church telephone and therefore would not be listed in a telephone directory. In such cases it is advised that the church be listed under the Pastor's address. In most cities no extra charge will be made for the additional listing of the Pastor's telephone under the church address. We are living in a traveling and touring age and every possible convenience for our wandering fellow Lutherans should be provided.

BETTER CHURCH PRINTING
F. R. WEBBER

The trouble with most of our church printing is that it is too commercial in appearance. If one were to look over a great pile of samples, collected from the four corners of the land, he would find this to be the case with nearly all of it. It is not always good commercial printing, either. Too often it is stuff from some back-street shop, taken there because that printer is the cheapest in town. And in order to save a few pennies, we ruin the impression that printing is sure to give.

Printing makes a certain impression upon those who receive it. Just as the appearance of a man, or the lines of architecture of a building, make certain impressions upon people, so does printing. For instance, if a man is slouchy in appearance, unshaven, with dirty linen, and finger-nails in deep mourning, we conclude that he is a man of slouchy mental traits—if he is a business or professional man. His outward appearance is an index to his inner nature.

So it is with printing. Big business houses pay high salaries to men who have studied just this little thing. They recognize the fact that certain impressions may be conveyed to the public simply through the outward appearance of their printing. We know of an Art Museum that has hired a printer of refined taste, and several assistants, and has installed quite a complete print shop, just for the one purpose of experimenting in this matter of typographical expression. They want every piece of work sent out by them to convey the impression of refined taste, and artistic skill.

Advertising men have long known that the very selection of type styles carries a message. One type-face gives the impression of strength, another of virility, another of graceful beauty, another of whimsicality, another of old style, another of conservatism. The big banking house invariably selects a certain style of type. A leading New York jewelry house selects quite a different kind. Each style conveys at the first glance, a characteristic impression.

In church printing we have paid entirely too little attention to this fact. The average church announcement, printed on a card to send through the mails, is in the same class, typographically speaking, as the corner butcher's shop, or the new Jewish cut-rate clothing store. There is nothing that gives a first impression of churchliness about most of our printing.

Take, for example, the first page of the average monthly parish paper, or weekly church bulletin. In the majority of cases, the title is printed in some sort of a common, commercial style. Much better would it be to select something of a churchly character. The type-founder has not much to offer us in this respect, so we will have to fall back upon a hand-lettered title. A favorite style is what is known as American Black-Letter. These headings, or titles, are designed by hand, laid out first with a pencil on a large scale, then painted in with a brush and India ink, and finally reduced by the photo-engraving process to a small zinc etching. Such a title costs about two dollars to produce. The effect is much better than commercial type. Its one weakness lies in the fact that American Black-Letter is apt to make a page look top-heavy. The nearest approach to this face that the type founders have, is what is known as Chaucer Text.

For a program, Engraver's Old English is often used for titles. It is a useful face, found in almost every printer's cabinet, and is more churchly in appearance than a Cheltenham or a Century Bold.

For a printed announcement, we must select a neat, graceful face, giving the impression of both dignity and refinement. The Goudy Old-style works well for a short announcement card. It may be set entirely in caps, giving a classic effect, or may be used in caps and lower-case. An announcement card, 5 x 6½, set in 14-point Goudy Old-style caps and lower-case with the initial letter in red, printed on a card of good quality of a delicate gray or India-tint, with a liberal margin, makes a most beautiful appearance. The Cromwell Series also lends itself well to such an announcement, but the effect is a trifle less neat than the Goudy Old-style. The Packard Series, while somewhat quaint and informal, really composes well for some kinds of work. Our own congregation uses it for their pledge-cards and envelopes, and the effect is quite good.

A dozen years ago the influence of the Roycroft movement was still abroad in the land, and printed matter in those days gave a very black impression. Heavy faces, such as Cheltenham Bold, Roycroft, Post, etc., were still in use, and presses were heavily inked. But to-day the pendulum has swung to quite the other extreme. Type-faces to-day are more slender, more refined, and infinitely less dry and stiff in appearance. Irregular outlines, giving the effect of hand-lettered work, are popular,—or at least have been. Pabst, Avil, Goudy, Rugged Roman, Packard, Penprint, and many other artistic faces have appeared. Then we have the beautiful Caslon family, which is popular and good at all times.

Permit us to digress a moment, and speak of type-ornaments. The catalogues are full of them, but what is there in these huge books of specimens that is really churchly? One looks in vain for even a good cross. We have some most charming initial letters, such as the Cloister Initial. These are particularly suited to dignified church work, and may be used together with Cloister Ornaments—headpieces and tailpieces. But if we wish to put in the little ornaments indicating breaks in the reading matter, or to fill a white space on the front of a program, what have we? Who has not seen the printed program of an Easter service, embellished with the familiar surpliced choir-boys marching three abreast! Or, who has not seen a shaded sea-shell, a terrible dragon, an hour-glass, a full-rigged schooner, or a meaningless floral design, on the front of a church dedication program? Have you not noticed them? Look over your samples of church printing and you'll find many of them. The field of church symbolism is so vast that we wonder why some enterprising type foundry does not produce something suitable, and with a meaning. Maltese crosses may be had in almost any size, and are used the world over in church printing. But a big ledger, lying on a book-keeper's desk is a poor substitute for the Bible. However, who has not seen it on a church folder?

The choice of stock is important. Good cards and paper cost very little more than cheap stuff. If we were printing in hundred-thousand lots, the choice of stock might be an important thing. But in getting out say 500 programs, parish papers or cards announcing a mission festival, the difference in cost between good stock and poor stock is slight. A card of good quality, with a delicate gray or creamy tint, and with just the suggestion of a rough texture, looks much better than the common white card.

The color and kind of ink makes all the difference in the world in church printing. We invariably print our Lenten announcements in violet, for this is the proper Lenten color wherever civilization is known. But it must be neither royal purple nor lavender, such as most Lenten printing turns out. Neither may Lenten printing be green or red, if we would observe good taste and appropriateness. Sometimes it adds to the attractiveness of church printing to "run" the initial letters in red. In case of a printed liturgical program, with rubricated parts, these rubrics look very well if done in small italics, and run in red, the body of the program being black, with a very narrow "litholine" border.

Even for common announcements, it might be well to cut down the dead-black appearance of the ink, and use some tint. A deep sepia on India-tint stock looks quite well indeed. A dark gray ink, on a light gray card of slightly rough surface texture makes a good impression.

In closing, permit us to say a word in defense of the parish press. Really we cannot see how an enterprising congregation can get along these days without one. It has become almost a slogan with us that "every parish ought to buy the pastor a Ford." But as a help to the pastor, and every branch of a live parish, what could be better than the slogan, "a printing room in every modern church?" A small printing plant costs less than a Ford, and we believe that it will reach many more people. A good press, either run by a small motor or by foot-power, may be picked up second-hand for as little as $50. A dozen or two cases of well-selected type do not cost a fortune. And these days every city high school, and many of the township high schools teach printing to the boys. But even though the pastor may have to stick type himself, he will find it a great saving.

PLEASE TURN TO PAGE 247

Color in Printing

G. E. HAGEMAN

COLOR printing is increasing in our midst. Many of the samples of printing which now reach our Bureau are in two colors. No doubt we are being influenced by the large amount of color printing which appears on billboards and in magazines. We are learning to know the value of colors in attracting and holding attention to our printed matter. For we are not merely having folders, cards, papers, etc., printed to spend our money, but we want people to read our message. We are discovering that black ink on white paper is not always efficient. A little color, even if it is only in the initial letter of the first word, is an attention-getter. So we are experimenting more and more in our printing with color combinations. But which colors are we to use? What color in ink and what color in the paper stock? Most of us do not know. And we rely upon the judgment of our printer. If he knows his business, we get very fine printing in color. If he is a mediocre man, we get poor color effects. And many of us are looking around to find out the "trick." But there is really no "trick" in this game. The subject of color in printing has been the subject of much discussion with some agreement and much disagreement. But none of us has the time to spend on a study of the subject. So it may prove helpful to reproduce a few common sense ideas which we have found in "The Inland Printer," in an article entitled "The Knowledge of Color," by Faber Birren. We also reproduce his chart.

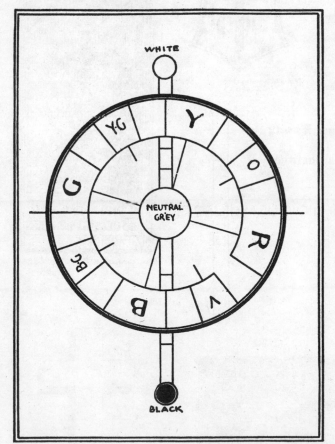

The Visual Quadrad Spectrum. Showing the four psychological primaries, red, yellow, green and blue, with their relationship to black and white. Copyright, 1923, by Faber Birren.

He maintains that it is impossible to set down any fixed rules to obtain harmony in color schemes in printing. And he offers no rules, merely findings and suggestions: "The effect of color is psychological. We judge its beauty solely through emotion, regardless of standard or formula. To say certain combinations are beautiful is useless. Beauty and appeal are obtained through emotional sanction, not through reason." The reason why we can not lay down any rules or laws is because our emotions are not subject to formulas.

"There are three distinct aspects of the subject (of color). In physics the three primary colors are red, green, violet . . . The artist with his red, yellow and blue pigments can also produce all hues. However, from the standpoint of physchology the eye demands four colors, red, yellow, green and blue." And this latter aspect is the important one in printing. We are interested "in knowing the influence of color—how people see it, how it is reacted to, how it pleases, and how it may be used to best advantage." The advantage we wish to gain through our printing is the attention. We want people to read our message. The author's chart which we reproduce is of great interest and will prove helpful to many of us. It is based on investigation and research. We need not go into detail as to the individual and general preferences or masculine and feminine tastes in colors, though these are of very great interest to the business man.

Of his chart he writes: The chart herewith represents a diagrammatic explanation of the psychological relationship of color to the eye. It is based on the four primaries with their opposites. Red is antichetical to green, and yellow to blue. Greatest contrast is secured by using hues that are opposite as indicated. Yellow is the color nearest white, and blue nearest black. No attempt has been made to include harmony, as this would not be possible. Color, though it is decided and positive in its appeal, yet does not create emotion according to rule. There are no laws of color harmony other than personal and individual sanction. Green may be pleasing to one and displeasing to another; and the only safe method to follow is to base all decisions on investigation and research."

Passing by his discussion of the futility of making rules for color harmony and his tables of preferences masculine and feminine for different shades and colors, he makes a few suggestions which may prove serviceable in his discussion of the relationship of colors. "A glance at the illustrated chart will show that yellow is followed by orange, then on to red, violet, blue, and so around the circle. From a standpoint of harmony it has been found through investigation that related colors are deemed considerably more harmonious than hues that are haphazardly chosen. Yet there are few who show any knowledge of this simplest arrangement of color. Red may go well with green, or blue, or yellow. It is difficult to decide. But place red with violet and immediately it will be found that the colors blend more pleasantly. Perhaps there may be a lack of contrast. Exactly! Harmony has been secured due to the congeniality of the two colors. The average person will find red and violet harmonious. With red and green some may find such combination agreeable, and others displeasing. The trick is simple. In brief, the most successful and generally acknowledged harmony in color is obtained through the use of adjacent hues.

Nb. 1720. Size 2½" x 2½" - - - - - $1.50

LUTHERAN PRESS
1819 Broadway,
New York, N.Y.

No. 3241,   size 1″x¾″......................... $1.00
No. 3241A, size 2″x1½″......................... 1.25

No. 3270, size 1″........... $1.25
No. 3270A, size 2″........... 1.50
No. 3270B, size 3″........... 2.00
No. 3270C, size 4″........... 3.00

No. 1602—Size 1¼″x1¾″ 1.75
No. 1602-A—Size 2½″x3½″ 2.50

No. 1390, size 1½″x2″........ $1.50
No. 1390A, size 2″x2¾″........ 2.00
No. 1390B, size 2½″x3½″.... 2.25

No. 3470—Size 1½″ $1.00
No. 3470-A—Size 2″ 1.25
No. 3470-B—Size 2½″ 1.50

No. 3460—Size 1″ $0.75
No. 3460-A—Size 1½″   1.00

New Catalog Ready

[Prices plus postage]

OTHER DESIGNS OF RELIGIOUS SUBJECTS

No. 1590, size 1½″x3½″.. $1.50

No. 1940. Size 3″x 2″   - - - - $1.75
No. 1940A. Size 4″x 2¾″ - - - - 2.50

★

No. 2850M. Size 1½″ x 1⅛″ - $1.25
No. 2850. Size 3″x 2″ - 1.75
No. 2850A. Size 4¼″x 2¾″ - 2.50

No. 2740. Size 3″x 4½″ - - $2.25
No. 2740D. Size 2¼″x 3½″ - 1.50
No. 2740A. Size 1″x 1½″ - 1.00

★ All Electrotypes shown here and in our Catalog are now obtainable in "miniature size," approximately
1½″x 1″. Price, $1.25 each. When ordering this size place letter "M" after number.

PUBLICITY HELPS

Easter Mimeographed Folder No. 213

Size 5½ x 8½
Printed in Gold and Green on Mimeograph Paper.
Price per 100.......$1.00 Postage Extra

"TRIUMPHANT ENTRY" No. 41-A

Size 6 x 9 — $1.40 per 100
No. 41-0, size 3½ x 6¼ — $ .75 per 100
Printed in black and purple on white coated paper. Art finish.
This design is also obtainable in a Mimeograph Folder, size 5½ x 8½. If Mimeograph Folder is wanted specify **Folder No. 58**
Price per 100....$1.00
Postage Extra.

Invitation Reply Post Card No. 103

This card is addressed to an individual who is invited to attend a specific service, the writer to call at a specified time. The return card states that the addressee accepts the invitation.

100	$1.00
250	2.25
500	4.25

Postage extra

Altar Flower Card No. 33-N

Size 5⅜ x 3⅜. Cross and Lilies design with wording: "These flowers come to you from the altar of .... Church and are meant to convey our most cordial greetings." Envelope to match.
Prices, including envelopes:

1 doz.	$ .50
2 doz.	.85
4 doz.	1.50
8 doz.	2.75

Postage extra

Not At Home Card No. 117

Size 1⅞ x 3½. Symbols of the Evangelists and Apostles. Die stamped in blood red in upper left hand corner. This symbol identifies the name of the Church as "St. Luke," "St. Matthew," etc. For the present only symbols of the Apostles and Evangelists are available. Such names as "Immanuel," "Redeemer," "Grace" will be added as we receive requests. When ordering, state name of Church.

These cards are also available without the message, to be used as personal calling cards. Your local printer will print name and address. If this style is wanted order No 117-X.

Luther Bible Post Card

Size 5½ x 3½. Printed in brown ink. Bust of Luther resting on panel containing cut of Bible and historical data of Luther's life, on address side of card. Luther Seal on reverse side with open space for your messages.

100	$ .75	500	$3.25
250	1.75	1000	6.00

Postage extra

Luther Mailing Card No. 450-A

Size 5½ x 3½. Printed in brown ink. Luther Seal and historical data of Luther's life on address side of card. Bust of Luther above panel with space for your announcement on reverse side.

100	$ .75	500	$3.25
250	1.75	1000	6.00

Postage extra

Luther Window Card

Size 10½ x 13½. Printed in dark brown ink on buff 6-ply board. The bust of Luther is die cut. For announcing Reformation Festival or Luther Day services.

Single Card	$.10
6 Cards	.50
12 Cards	.90

Postage extra

Canvass Card No. 107

Size 3 x 5. All the data to be gathered require only checkmarks. A convenience and time-saver.

100	$.50
500	2.25
1000	4.25

Postage extra

No. 1650,	size 5½"x9",	$6.50
No. 1650A,	size 3¾"x6¼",	4.00
No. 1650B,	size 3"x5",	2.50
No. 1650C,	size 2"x3½",	1.75

The Electrotypes illustrated on this and other pages are recent additions not previously shown.

These electros are for sale only. The prices quoted are net, plus postage.

For our complete line of Electrotypes, Folders and other Publicity Material, ask for Catalog No. 30

Electros shown on this page will print equally well on rough or smooth paper

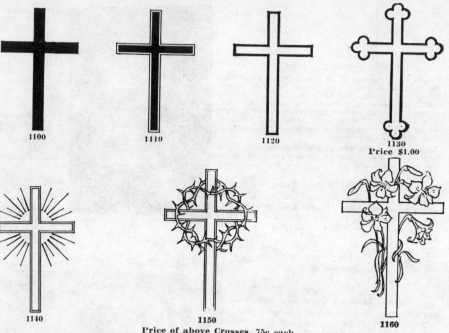

1100   1110   1120   1130
Price $1.00

No. 1040............ $1.00

1140   1150   1160

Price of above Crosses, 75c each

The above crosses may also be had in size 1 inch high and ¾ inch high. When ordering 1 inch size put letter B after number. Price 60c each. When ordering ¾ inch size put letter C after number. Price 50c each.

Two and three inch sizes of above crosses can also be supplied. When ordering 2 inch size put letter E after number, price $1.25. When ordering 3 inch size put letter D after number. Price $1.75 each.

No. 1310............ $1.00

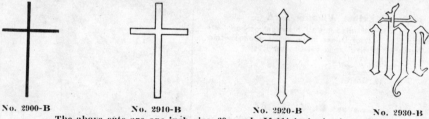

No. 2900-B   No. 2910-B   No. 2920-B   No. 2930-B

The above cuts are one-inch size, 60c each. If 1½-inch size is desired, put letter A after number, price 75c each.

When ordering 2-inch size, put letter E after number, price $1.00 each. For 3-inch size, put letter D after number, price $2.00 each.

No. 1080............ $1.00

No. 3000A, ¾".......... $.75
No. 3000B, 1"........... 1.00
No. 3000C, 1½"....... 1.25
Also supplied in 2 colors:
No. 3000B, 1".......... $2.00
No. 3000C, 1½"........ 2.50

No. 1030,   size 1½"x1⅞"...... $1.25
No. 1030A, size ⅝"x¾".......... .75

No. 1020,   1¾" high........... $1.25
No. 1020B, 1¼ in. high.... $1.00
No. 1020C, 1 in. high........ .75

780,   size ½".... $.75
780A,   size ¾".... .75
780B,   size 1"..... 1.00
780C,   size 1¼".... 1.00
780D,   size 1½".. 1.25
780G,   size 2".... 1.50

Supplied also in 3 colors
780E,   size 1¼".. $3.75
780F,   size 2½".. 4.50

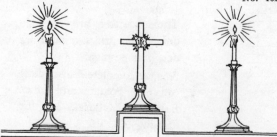

No. 1010,   1½" high.. $1.75
No. 1010B, 1" high...... 1.00
No. 1010C, 2¼" high.... 2.00
No. 1010D, ⅝" high.... .75

A new line of Folders for Mimeographing, also Letterpress Printing is now in preparation. Size of these Folders is 5½x8½. Ask for sample assortment.

Stock Electros

No. 440—Size 2½"x3¾" $2.25
No. 440-A—Size 4"x5¾" 4.00
No. 440-B—Size 1"x1½" 1.25
No. 440-C—Size 2"x3" (Coarse Screen) 2.00

"And a superscription also was written over Him in letters of GREEK, and LATIN, and HEBREW, This is the King of the Jews." LUKE 23:38

No. 880—Size 3"x3¾" $2.50
No. 880-A—Size 4½"x5½" 4.00
No. 880-B—Size 2½"x3" 2.25

No. 3360

No. 3370

No. 3380

No. 3390

No. 3391

No. 3381

No. 3371

No. 3361

Size 1"x1" — $1.00
Symbols of all Apostles in stock.

No. 10A, size 4½x6, $4.00   No. 10B size 3x4, $2.50
No. 10C, size 1½x2, $1.50

No. 1750.
size ⅞"x2¾", $1.25
No. 1750, size
⅞"x2¾", 2 colors $2.50

ALTAR FLOWER CHART
17 x 22 in.
This handsome chart, on card, admits of five lines under the heading of each month, in which the names of those who have promised to supply flowers for the altar are to be written in. Posted in the vestibule of the church, it is a constant invitation to the people to volunteer to supply the flowers for particular dates and an expression of appreciation to those who have volunteered. Obtainable from the American Lutheran, 1819 Broadway, New York, N. Y., at $1.00 post paid.

"A CHANGELESS CHRIST for a Changing World"

No. 1920—Size 2" $1.00
No. 1920-A—Size 3" 1.25
No. 1920-B—Size 4" 1.50
No. 1920-C—Size 5" 2.00

No. 2550—Size 4"x1¾" .... $2.25   No. 2550-A—Size 5"x2¼" 2.75

Chips of Thought

GLEANED FROM HERE AND THERE

Your soul cannot afford to take a vacation.

* * *

The devil never takes a vacation. He works hardest when others loaf.

* * *

Spiritual sustenance is needed in hot weather as well as in cool.

* * *

Let your auto take you to church first. You will then be able to enjoy the rest of the day with a good conscience.

* * *

Remember, it is probably cooler in church than under a blazing sun on a country road.

* * *

The commandment: "Thou shalt sanctify the holy day," does not disappear out of the Bible during the summer season.

* * *

You expect God's grace during the summer. Has He not the right to expect your devotion?

* * *

You cannot put your religion in cold storage without having it suffer severe damage.

* * *

What if God were to take a vacation in His care of you?

* * *

In this actual world, a churchless community, a community where men have abandoned and scoffed at or ignored their religious needs, is a community on the rapid down grade.—Theodore Roosevelt.

* * *

Some men are hiding their light under a bushel, when a pint measure would answer just as well.

* * *

Don't throw mud; you might miss your mark, but you are bound to get your hands dirty.

* * *

The child mind is wax to receive impressions, and adamant to retain them.

* * *

Nothing is easier than fault-finding; no talent, no self-denial, no brains, no character are required to set up in the grumbling business.—Robert West.

* * *

The less of it they have, the more people seem obsessed with the inclination to speak their mind.—Newcastle Courier.

* * *

The man with a perpetual grievance is suffering from ingrowing selfishness.

While the learned are fumbling to find the latch, the simple and poor have entered into the kingdom of heaven. —St. Augustine.

* * *

Never bear more than one kind of trouble any time. Some people bear three kinds—all they have had, all they have now, and all they expect to have.—E. E. Hale.

* * *

What a man earns he puts into his pocket; what he spends he puts into his character.

* * *

When we become partners with God in his work he becomes a partner with us in our work.

* * *

The holier-than-thou attitude may be caused by virtue, but usually it is caused by a poor memory. — Austin American.

* * *

It is an art to say the right thing at the right time, but far more difficult to leave unsaid the wrong thing at the tempting moment.—The Churchman.

* * *

A church of one hundred workers is far more efficient than a church of three hundred members with two-thirds of them sleeping partners.

* * *

Some people are always mistaking the voice of their inclinations for the voice of God.

* * *

A conscience throttled in the vacation season takes a long time to revive.

* * *

A grouch means either a disordered stomach or a case of ingrown selfishness.

* * *

A bird in the hand is worth two in the bush. An envelope deposited is worth a dozen in the carton.

* * *

A person who will enjoy the facilities of a church for years without assuming any of its responsibilities is a religious cheapskate.

* * *

Religion cannot be hung into the closet with the Sunday coat.

* * *

The devil agrees with the argument that one can worship God in nature from behind a steering-wheel as well as in church.

* * *

The boy who sticks is the one whose dad brings him to church instead of sending him.

* * *

Vacation does not mean that we ask the Lord to vacate the premises of our heart for the summer season.

```
THE                              P
    C                            TRUTH
    R                            R
CROSS                            I
    S                            T
    S                            Y
        IS IT                            THY
        NOTHING                          WORD
        TO YOU                           IS
        ?                                TRUTH

C                                THE
THE                                  B
U                                    I
R                                    BIBLE
C                                    L
H                                    E
    A                                        ROCK
    WITNESS                                  OF  •
    TO THE                                   AGES
    TRUTH
    OF
    GOD

THE                              WE
    HAPPY                            P
    H                                R
    O                                E
    M                                TEACH
    E                                C
        WHERE                        H
        CHRIST                               CHRIST
        REIGNS                               CRUCIFIED
        SUPREME

A                                    W
    M                                GOD
    I                                R
    G                                JESUS
    H                                H
FORTRESS                             I
    Y                                P
        IS OUR                               I AM
        GOD                                  THY
                                             GOD

EARTH                            OUR
HAS NO                               C
    S                                STONE
    CROSS                            R
    R                                N
    R                                E
    O                                R
    W                                        IS
        THAT                                 CHRIST
        HEAVEN
        CANNOT
        HEAL

    PRAISE                       THE
    G                                O
    GOD                              ONE
    D                                L
    FROM WHOM                        Y
    ALL                                      SAVIOR
    BLESSINGS FLOW.                          FROM SIN
                                             JESUS
```

```
F                                G
MARRIAGE                         GOD
M                                JESUS
CHILDREN                         P
L                                E
Y                                L
        GOD                              EVERLASTING
        THE                              TREE OF LIFE
        AUTHOR

L                                    O
U                                    HOLY
DOCTRINE                             CHILD OF
H                                    BETHLEHEM
E                                    DESCEND ON US
R                                    WE PRAY. O COME
A                                    TO US ABIDE WITH US
N                                    OUR LORD
        SAVED                            C
        BY                               H
        GRACE                            CHRIST
        THROUGH FAITH                    I
        IN                               JESUS
        CHRIST JESUS                     T

S                                    THE
C                                    WAY
R                                    THE
I                                    TRUTH
DIVINE                               AND THE
P                                    LIFE
T                                        J
U                                        JESUS
R                                        S
E
        SEARCH
        THE
        SCRIPTURES

    ☆
    THE                          THE
    BEST                             L
    NEW YEAR                         CHURCH
    RESOLUTION                       L
    FOR TIME AND                     U
    ETERNITY                         T
    !                                H
    JESUS                            E
    THINE FOREVER                    R
                                     A
                                     N
                                             THE
                                             OPEN
                                             BIBLE

E                                    C
T                                    R
FOREVER                              E
R                                    CREATOR
N                                    T
I                                    U
T                                    R
Y                                    E
        WHERE                                I'LL
        WILL                                 PRAISE
        YOU                                  MY
        SPEND IT                             MAKER
        ?                                    WHILE I
                                             LIVE

ALL                                  L
    H                                GOD
    GLORY                            R
    N                                D
    O                                        TRUST
    R                                        IN THE
        UNTO                                 LORD
        GOD
```

2571

Ten Wayside Pulpits

OSCAR E. FEUCHT

NEVER before in history has the street and highway been as important as today. Travel has increased in the last decade to an extent undreamed of a quarter of a century ago—except possibly by some Jules Verne. The automobile, shorter working hours, the trend to the city, more leisure, more vacations, greater prosperity, and the marvelous net-work of highways has lured people into the open and out on the streets of the world. Fathers and mothers, who had never dreamed of seeing the west, have seen not only the west, but the east as well. They have seen sections of their native state which were unknown to them scarcely a half dozen years ago. People are seeing more in a year than they saw in a decade before the advent of the motor car. It is much more difficult to find people at home than it ever was.

Consider the matter of roads alone. The United States is spending more money for roads each year than are the thirty-three nations of Europe combined. In the last four years Iowa, West Virginia, Louisiana, and Missouri have voted a total of 240 million dollars for state highway systems. Roy D. Chapin, chairman of the highway commission, is authority for the statement that in less than ten years the public has virtually voted 10 billion dollars for the construction and maintenance of roads, or enough to defray our cost in the world war, excluding foreign loans. The department of commerce estimates that there are 6½ million miles of highways in the world, of which more than half are in the United States. New York State alone has 11,000 miles of hard-surfaced roads, while Illinois has 6,000 miles of cement pavements, not considering the other improved roads.

And our granite-faced, steel-ribbed, rubber-tired civilization is here to stay. The investment in motor cars proves that. One million four hundred thousand more cars were registered in 1928 than in 1927. When one branch of the General Motors Corp. alone puts out about a million in a year, and the streets are crowded with many other makes that seem almost as plentiful then we have reason to deal with a fast moving, much traveling people. At the end of 1928 there were close to 28½ million cars in our country alone. Placed end to end they would require 45,000 miles of road. In 1929 not less than 5,000,000 cars were manufactured by the motor car industry of America.

Shall we then go in for highway publicity? The question is answered before it is asked.

The world has an urge to go and it goes. Business knows it must not only go, but go fast; and so business has speeded up in the past decade until efficiency and speed are the standard of the day. It gets out on the highways. It must go or perish. With business it is a matter of self-preservation. The Church has a command from the Lord—to go, to go into the highways and hedges, to go into the whole world. It too must go if it would succeed. It has no selfish motive to use as a propeller. God's command, the welfare of human souls, the blessings it has for mankind, these are far greater incentives than business ever had.

Business aids the world, even as science improves economical conditions. But business often exploits its trade and robs mankind. Business, as it actually exists, has a message. It reads: "Make money. Make it honestly if you can. But make money!" The Church is here to spend and be spent in the service of mankind. It has a message: "Come unto me and be ye saved, all the ends of the earth!" It offers for nothing blessings compared with which the satisfactions of the world are but fleeting shadows.

Shall we compete with business by placing our announcements, and, better still, the heart of our message, in the busy marts of the world? Shall we go out to win the world, with a fire such as no salesman ever had in his eye? The question is answered before it is asked.

The other day I saw a policeman making a check of the traffic that passed a certain intersection in the city. Signs and safety signals are now installed there to reach the billowy waves of humanity that surge too and fro all day long. They are placed there for the protection of the people. When Woolworths locate their stores they usually make a check of the traffic that passes a certain location before leasing a building and setting up their business. They display their wares profusely where the most of the public will see them. Shall not the church go to the streets where the crowds are, place its signals, and display its wares for the protection and for the welfare of mankind?

There is a highway near your church, an arterial traffic way, a through street. Hundreds of cars pass it every hour, and a thousand pass by when day is done and the workers from the city stream out to their hamlets and homes. A street car line with direct connections to the business district runs along that avenue. Hundreds of men, women, and children ride the cars each day, many of them looking out of the windows, and having nothing more to do than view the varied scenes of life, reading signs, and noting the changes that occur from day to day along the car line. There is a junction of the car lines where many people each day wait and look around until their car comes along. It may be a suburban shopping center, a waiting room, or just a bus stop. But the people pass there each day in numbers far surpassing those that gather at your church for all of your Sunday services.

What if you could stand there and reach those throngs every day for a week preaching the Word from five in the morning until the theatre crowds return late at night? Some would pass you by. Some would have no time or inclination to listen. But many would hear the words. Some would hear them, only to forget. Some would try to remember them, but fail. Some would remember them for a day. Some would remember, never to forget. With some these words would slumber until like sharp barbs they pierce the membrane of the conscience in later life. With others they would be daily memorized and treasured up in believing hearts.

You cannot stand there all day and utter a ceaseless flow of words. It is physically impossible. It is uneconomical as far as manpower and money is concerned. But you can place a wayside bulletin in your stead that preaches your message, day in, day out, for weeks and months, at a small cost of money and manpower, and with possibly a bit more dignity than so often attends the street preacher. What if you knew of a plan that would reach the thousands who never darken a church door—part of the unchurched 60%—and reach even such as would not welcome you to the doors of their homes and tenements? What if you could come to them morning after morning and drive a certain text home until it would turn up in their minds when they eat their lunch at noon, and whenever they pass the spot they read the message? You would say: Let's have the plan. The wayside pulpit will accomplish just this. There is a gasoline refining and sales corporation which puts trite sayings on wayside bulletins every day. At no small cost it has salaried a man who composes the proverbs of the day, epitomizes wisdom, giving it a turn or twist that will make it stick to the mind. The sayings are pat and pithy, and to the point. This man once read the statement: "The reason most people write long letters is because they do not take time to write short ones." It set him to thinking, and he concluded that much can be said by a few well-chosen, concise terms. His sayings are repeated each day all over the nation because of their homely truths and humor. An editor once returned a voluminous manuscript with the remarks: "Boil it down. The story of the creation is told in 80 words." The Bible contains the world's greatest truths. And in many instances it tells it in a terse way that sticks to the mind, and with an elegance that makes modern English seem like a lot of balderdash. What can be more striking than Jesus' "I am" sayings: "I am the Light of the World," etc. Who can devise sentences with more dash in them than those found almost everywhere in Paul's epistles? Where will you find more beautiful literature than in the Sermon on the Mount? Consider only the saying: "Sufficient unto the day is the evil thereof." And what a wealth of Gospel verses can be used. Matt. 1, 21 is a real gem: "Thou shalt call His name Jesus for He shall save His people from their sins."

What if you could dominate your community somewhat like the apostles and first Christians filled the city with their doctrine? The setting up of a number of wayside pulpits will not *alone* accomplish this end, but it will help. They will assist the pastor, so that when he calls on the unchurched they respond with: "Oh, you are the minister who gets out those wayside pulpit messages." They will place the name of your church before people who otherwise would know nothing of it. There are many people in the section of the city served by my church who have never seen our chapel, but they know our church is here. They go down town and tell their fellow-laborers who happen to be Lutherans about the church that does wayside preaching. After all a congregation can have but one church to preach its mute sermon at some conspicuous corner. Only those who pass that church spire can be impressed with the church's existence. If in addition the church has ten wayside pulpits, there are ten additional locations where the church exerts even more influence than the mute testimony of a stone or brick church edifice, for the wayside pulpit opens a page of the Bible to the view of the passersby. People will not go to a church about which they know little or nothing. They will view it with suspicion unless they have had some favorable contact with it. The wayside pulpits help to make your church known as one that is active and alert. Nowadays people want a church that is doing things. And since the messages on the bulletin boards are restricted to the dictums of God's Word, the people of the community are going to have a definite opinion of the church that so advertises. They will get the impression that it is a Bible church. They can soon sense the difference between pious platitudes or philosophic half-truths and the words of Scripture.

What if you had an opportunity to tell Christians who are looking for a church that takes the Bible seriously where to find such a church? You would do so, would you not? A lady who is a Sunday school teacher in another denomination often passes our wayside pulpits. A year ago we received the following letter from her: "Will you allow me the privilege of having a part in paying for your 'Wayside Pulpits?' For many years I have felt that the thing in God's service that I must do more than any other, is to help send out God's Word. And I do think that you are

doing a fine thing with the Book, where you put parts of it along the highways, so that 'he who runs may read.' I pray that our Father may bless you in your work for our Lord." With the letter was a check for twenty-five dollars. This Christian woman was unknown to the pastor or any of the people. We had never met. Six months later another letter containing the same amount was received from this same woman as an unsolicited gift.

The wayside pulpits leave an impression. One evening the telephone rang. A woman's voice was heard inquiring for the

pastor of the church that puts up the wayside pulpits. After identifying myself, she told me that her husband was looking for some deserving man for a certain position, and that she had immediately thought of our church, having seen the wayside pulpit messages. The result was that a member received employment.

The splendid chapel of the University of Chicago has just been completed. It has an outside pulpit for open air services. Other churches also have such outdoor pulpits. But these are used only a few times each year. Only a comparatively small number of sermons are preached from them. Most of the time they have no message for the people who pass by. The Wayside Bulletin preaches its sermon daily and thus is of greater service than the stone pulpits of excellent design surrounded by some fine cloister garth.

Calvary congregation in Kansas City is only a mission, organized some four years ago. But it has ten wayside pulpits in that territory of this city that it serves. Seven of these are of the canopy type, while three are plain bulletin boards. The idea is not an original one but was suggested by the various makes of bulletin boards on the market and especially by the wayside pulpit put out by the Beacon Press, Inc., 25 Beacon St., Boston, Mass. Their boards are plain, however, having no gabled "canopy."

Our Wayside Pulpits are built of wood. The plain board without a roof has a frame of two by fours and two panels made by nailing galvanized tin over the frame and then covering the joints with battens. The top panel bears the words: "Wayside Pulpit of Calvary Lutheran Church, 75th and McGee." These words are painted in white on a background of black. The lower panel receives the large paper sheets that bear the Scripture passages in black letters painted on by a sign writer. These sheets are changed every two weeks. We tried glass in the lower panel to keep the paper in but it was broken. When merely tacked on the wind would tear the signs off. So we resorted to small gauge twisted copper wire. Three strands are run across and three or four up and down, equally spaced apart. They are hardly noticeable from a distance, and even where visible do not detract from the dignity of the bulletin board. The frames receive a coat of creosote which gives them a rugged appearance with a touch of old English. It is cheaper than paint, yet more serviceable.

The canopied pulpits are built with 4 by 4 uprights, joined together with two by fours, which are mortised into the posts. The arms (braces) holding up the roof are also two by fours mortised into the posts and cut so as to fit around the purlins that hold up the exposed rafters and the roof. The roof is slate left over from our church building. A creosoted wood shingle would also be quite fitting.

A light frame fits around the lower panel which receives the Scripture sheets. This frame is fitted with hinges on the lower side and is let down when the sheets are changed. Screen door hooks hold it up when in place.

The following material is used in the construction of the canopy type wayside pulpit:

    2—1 x 2 x 16 red wood or white pine for trim.
    2—2 x 2 x 14 for the purlins and rafters.
    2—2 x 4 x 16 for the frame work.
    2—1 x 12 x 14 for the sheathing.
    2—4 x 4 x 12 for the posts.

One pair brass hinges, one pair screen door hooks, creosote, paint for upper panel, two sheets of galvanized tin, one 18 x 52 inches for the upper panel, the other 32 x 43 inches for the lower panel. The large paper sheets measure 32 by 44 inches and can be had in this length at any large paper house. It is a standard size used in printing shops. A stencil cut out of oiled parchment will help you make your top panel. Stipple thick flake white paint with a stiff, stubby brush into the openings of your stencil. A sign painter can prepare your stencil for you. For your Scripture signs use ivory black, an automobile color ground in japan. It is a paste that is thinned down with turpentine and a few drops of varnish. It paints easily with a sign writer's brush. Make your letters about five inches tall. Use lower case letters (not capital letters) because they are more easily read. These paper signs will stand up for six weeks amid rain and snow. After being up a few weeks many are fit to be used over again at another time. Find someone in your church who is a sign writer or handy with a brush. After a year's practice the writer was able to paint a sign in about eleven minutes. Be sure to change your signs every fortnight, or at least at definite intervals.

The locations for the wayside pulpits are secured by seeing the owners of vacant property that is located at good intersections or along prominent boulevards. Make your selections with great care. Describe the nature of the wayside pulpit to the owner of the lot. Show him a picture of one if you can. Promise to keep it in paint. If you can keep the grass mowed in front of it, or, what is better, have a flower bed arranged in front of it, your street preacher will be the more effective. Assure the owner of the location that only Scripture passages will be displayed on the board, not human philosophy, not sentence sermons—Scriptures only. Men do not like to lend their influence and their property to any propaganda. Often a letter to the owner will get his consent. We have been able to place our wayside pulpits into the most restricted home section of Kansas City by going about it in this way.

Can you afford it? The Beacon Press sells the Wayside pulpit (plain type) with two panels and no roof for $25. For 52 Wayside pulpit sheets it asks $7.50. But these sheets cannot serve us since they do not contain Bible passages but the statements of men. We have built all of our pulpits by volunteer labor. Men of the congregation worked for nights to get them finished. The materials for each canopy wayside pulpit, including the roof, hardly exceeded ten dollars. By having someone in the church who paints the signs, this medium becomes a very economical means of publicity. The plain type of wayside pulpit such as is shown by one of the cuts accompanying this article can be built for much less.

A pastor from New York, who saw a cut of one of our wayside pulpits, some time ago wrote me as follows: "I think it would be a fine thing if such a board could be placed on the main roads leading into every city where we have a church." Metal bulletin boards with changeable letters are quite expensive. Many of them cost as high as $100. For the same amount many wayside pulpits of the canopy type could be built, and if given prominent locations in the territory served by your church should serve you many times better than a single bulletin board in the church yard. Many a mission church will probably welcome this idea. Would it not be possible to get one hundred of our congregations interested and have them construct as many such highway preachers as possible? If a number of congregations would adopt the plan the large Scripture sheets could be printed and mailed out much the same as a periodical is sent. If a sufficient number of subscribers for the sheets could be gained the cost would be reasonable and we could do away with the painting of the signs. I shall be glad to list such churches as desire the sheets and give suggestions for the construction of the boards. Kindly address the writer at 400 West 73rd St., Kansas City, Mo. In order to pay for the instruction sheets kindly enclose stamps.

Editorial Musings

Some people come back from their vacation with a festering conscience.

* * *

The regular thumps heard during the next twelve months will be caused by the new crop of college and high-school graduates coming down to earth.

* * *

Mission festivals are in season. Many a man will again contribute a tear for the heathen and a nickel for the Lord.

* * *

It is well to remember that Christ's missionary command does not read "Send" but "Go."

* * *

You cannot be a Good Samaritan by proxy. A check can never take the place of personal contact.

* * *

A man calls himself "economical." His friends call him "stingy." Chances are his friends are right.

* * *

A good friend is one who says to you what the bad friends say behind you.

* * *

To the wanderers on the church premises during the prelude: "If you want to roam, join the navy."

* * *

A churchless week-end is a spiritually weak end.

* * *

A man will have to give himself first before he really starts to give his money.

* * *

The devil sounds no claxon to announce his approach. We now know where many a modern motorist gets his training.

THE CHURCH BULLETIN BOARD
FRED. WAMBSGANSS

"Pure Goods in Slovenly Packages," was the title of a very timely and pointed editorial in the January issue of the AMERICAN LUTHERAN. Applied to the church bulletin board and church bulletin service we would say, that whatever we do in the line of this particular phase of church publicity, let us do it in a dignified and attractive way. A weatherbeaten, ill-kept, in-need-of-repair bulletin board, or a bulletin board empty part of the time or carrying out of date material, as for instance the announcement of the time of last Sunday's services, is worse than none. Don't let people look at your board expecting to see something worth while and then be disappointed.

When purchasing a bulletin board three factors ought to be taken into consideration. First the size of the board. The largest is not too large and will permit the printing of lengthy Scripture passages and sentence sermons. Large bulletin boards will also permit the use of large letters and thus increase the legibility of the announcements, etc. The next point is the style of the board. The best is not too good and is the cheapest in the long run. The storms of winter are hard on bulletin boards. Buy a board made of material that will stand the weather. The third point which should be taken into consideration when purchasing a bulletin board is the place where the board should hold forth as a silent announcer and preacher to the passer-by. Conspicuous ess and attractiveness are to be taken into consideratio. A board the message of which one cannot read until one stands directly in front of it, loses much of its value. Opinions may differ whether the board should be attached to the church or placed on the church lawn. According to the opinion of the writer the lawn is the proper place because it will enable us to add an important feature, i.e., attractiveness. The writer has seen such silent lawn preachers in most unattractive surroundings. The frame in which the board is hung ought to consist of more than two uprights and one cross piece of gas piping painted black. The picture on the cover page shows a bulletin board housed in an artistically designed pergola overgrown with vines and decorated with flowered plants. In front of the pergola is a bed of ornamental plants so arranged that they form the name of the church, "Emmaus" on a background of green. A fountain will be placed in the center of the pergola as soon as warmer weather sets in. Of course, not all churches are financially able to place their bulletin board in such elaborate housing. The church which owns this board has been particularly fortunate in having both its board and attractive housing donated to her by one of her members. With much less money and with a little inventive ability frames and housings for bulletin boards may be made by progressive committees who are entrusted with this work. Bear in mind that your bulletin board is to advertise good things. Do not offer the people passing by, "pure goods in slovenly packages."

After the bulletin board has been satisfactorily placed, the next thing to bear in mind is to keep it functioning as a publicity agent of the church. It is an axiom among experts that only persistent advertising pays. The writer knows that bulletin boards are read. He was told by a woman from another church that she purposely took a car which led past his church to go to town in order to read the new sentence sermon of the week. Do not disappoint people by letting them turn their gaze to your bulletin board only to find it empty or to read an announcement which is out of date. They will then soon forget about your board. The reading should be changed at least once a week, better still twice a week and still better three times a week. To make the reading attractive and legible one should have a good supply of letters on hand of different sizes. To enhance the attractiveness of the announcements, etc., one should also have on hand a supply of ornamental designs such as crosses, stars, torches, anchor, crown and other emblems, vignettes and the like.

The most important feature of the church bulletin service are the announcements, sentence sermons, epigrams, etc. The Sunday announcements should of course be made as attractive as possible. The most important things should be in large type, the less important in smaller type.

A very well written article full of good suggestions with regard to sentence sermons in bulletin boards was published in the Walther League number of the AMERICAN LUTHERAN last summer. The writer fully agrees with what is said in that article. The AMERICAN LUTHERAN, by publishing every month a few sentence sermons for bulletin boards is rendering a very valuable service to busy pastors who are frequently at a loss what to suggest. Perhaps the following suggestions will also be helpful: Make your message very personal and pointed as follows,

JESUS SAYS:

"I AM THE WAY"
ARE YOU WALKING UPON THAT WAY?

or

JESUS SAYS:

"I AM THE DOOR"
HAVE YOU ENTERED THROUGH THAT DOOR?

A long series of such personal questions may be worked out and published.

Here is another series which may be used:

OUR WEEKLY BIBLE READING SUGGESTION
BEST BIBLE CHAPTERS
No. 1
GENESIS 1
THE CREATION CHAPTER
READ IT!

or

OUR WEEKLY BIBLE READING SUGGESTION
PARABLES OF CHRIST
No. 1
LUKE 15:3-7
THE LOST SHEEP
READ IT!

A series of best Bible chapters or of parables will immediately suggest themselves. In conclusion, we would say: Make the most of your Bulletin Board. It has a missionary value.

Sentence Sermons

The Gospel is unchanged and unchanging, but it changes men.

The Christian is free, but not free to sin.

He who waits on God loses no time.

A Christian has no excuse for going incognito

If you are a Christian, remember that men judge your Lord by you.

It is the Word of God that does the work of God.

God's Word provides comfort for every circumstance except that of remaining in sin.

Salvation is not of, by, and for the people; but of and by God for the individual.

Put your faith, not in changing circumstances, but in the changeless Christ.

A man's action is but the picture book of his creed.

The Gospel is not a problem to be solved but a gift to be received.

All things are yours but one thing, yourself. "Ye are not your own."

On the cross Jesus took my Hell and gave me His Haven.

```
OLD                 NEW
         T
         E
  JESUS  S
         T
   B.    A    A.
    C.   M      D.
         E
         N
         T
PROPHECY    FULFILLMENT
```

```
         T
         R
  FAITH  U
         M
         P
         H
         A       LORD
         N        I
         T       BELIEVE
```

```
       P
  GRACE A
       R
       D
       O
       N
         FOR
         EVERY
         PENITENT
         SINNER
```

```
       W
  DEVOTION
       R
       S
       H
       I
       P
         COME
         AND
         WORSHIP
```

```
 IN
       C
  CROSS O
       M
       F
       O
       R
       T
         HE
         CARETH
         FOR YOU
```

```
       F
       E
  MISSION
       T
       I       HE THAT
       V       WINNETH
       A       SOULS
       L       IS
               WISE
```

```
THE
       C
  CHURCH
       U
       R
  SCHOOL
       H    OUR
              NATION'S
              REAL
              ASSET
```

```
       C
       R
  CROSS
       W
       N
       E
       D
         CALVARY
         MY CONSOLATION
```

Editorial Musings

The Bible passage: "The Lord is in His holy temple, let all the earth keep silence before Him," does not mean that worshipers are not to join in the singing.

* * *

Many people spoil today by worrying about what may happen tomorrow.

* * *

If you have an aim in life, don't fail to pull the trigger.

* * *

Religion is not a fur coat to be put away in moth-balls during the summer months.

* * *

Judging by the renditions over the radio, the prime requisite for a jazz singer is catarrh.

* * *

Why is it that to one "worker" in the church there are ten "shirkers"?

When church members "knock," their spiritual machinery is out of order.

* * *

A preacher who wanted to vividly illustrate a sermon on evolution recently took a monkey into the pulpit. He at least proved an intimate relationship with his partner.

* * *

A man who will knock his church is apt to speak sneeringly of his mother.

* * *

The most liberal givers in the church are those who give advice. We do not even need a committee to collect it.

* * *

Many a man's idea of "worshipping God in nature" is to have his place in a solid row of automobiles on the highway, fuming with expressed and unexpressed maledictions on the fellow who is holding up the parade.

* * *

A preacher recently remarked that "some people are like buzzards, they never go near a church until somebody dies."

* * *

Jumping at conclusions almost invariably leads to injustice.

* * *

There is evidence that many a "self-made" man has made a poor job of it.

* * *

Business troubles are no excuse for grouchiness at home.

* * *

The greatest handicap for the spiritual development of many a boy is his unspiritual father.

* * *

A silly mother cannot raise a sensible daughter, as little as a chicken breeds swans.

* * *

When a man begins to realize that he knows little, he is showing the first signs of wisdom.

* * *

When a man begins to stay away from church, hell gets ready for a celebration.

* * *

Many a girl manipulates the lipstick much more dexterously than the broom.

* * *

Many a man dies spiritually because he is choked with gasoline fumes.

* * *

When a Christian has nothing but friends, it is high time for serious self-examination.

* * *

Many people are willing to work in the church in an advisory capacity.

* * *

It's cooler to sit in church on Sunday morning than to change tires by the roadside.

* * *

Many a vacationist needs a month to recover from the effects of the vacation.

Bulletin Board Sentences

CARL H. NAPIER

1. What you don't use you lose. Go to Church regularly.
2. Have you an hour to spare for eternity to prepare?
3. Dollars for Christ; not one cent for sin.
4. When angry, fight anger, not people.
5. Your motives determine your motions.
6. Resentment is the source of unhappiness.
7. To cure a bad temper learn to love others.
8. When you yield your opinion you make a friend.
9. Conviction is unyielding sincerity.
10. Stubbornness is infantile resentfulness.
11. You get a dollar when God takes it from someone else.
12. Everything you have is a gift from another.
13. You are as old as you'll ever be when you are born.
14. You grow younger when you become older.
15. Giving in is saving your face for forgiveness.
16. When you say confound it, not it, you, are confounded.
17. To have hope is always to see a way out.
18. You suffer less disaster when you have a pastor.
19. It is easier to wear than to bear a cross.
20. The things which never happen worry men most.
21. Cross-bearing is active patience.
22. Never be afraid to be afraid.
23. Why be afraid of a man when he must die?
24. God is as close to you as your heart.
25. To have one bosom friend is to have as many as Jesus had.
26. To follow Christ means to do what He allows.
27. When you love a person you are forever free from his tyranny.
28. Pride never rides in the back seat.
29. There is no gain without pain.
30. There is no pain without gain.
31. There is no success without progress.
32. The only way to escape trouble is to pass through it.
33. Fiery speech is the flame of ire.
34. Success always has ups and downs.
35. Damnation is permanent separation from God's face.
36. Forgiveness cannot be bought with love or money.
37. Wherever you may be, God is.
38. You cannot go forward and look backward.
39. To go forward you must have the upward look.
40. Believing is seeing.
41. When you build a house, don't lose your home.
42. From faith in God comes courage, strength and hope.
43. The hardest thing to learn is to say No.
44. Who is willing to fight, never takes flight.
45. When a storm blows over it always leaves wreckage behind.
46. Your tongue can make or break you.
47. Trouble is never troublesome.
48. Christ is the shortest distance between earth and heaven.
49. If you are depressed it is because you are oppressed.
50. Giving is living; living is giving.
51. A little with love is like heaven above.
52. When you face reality, you'll not imagine things.
53. Your soul is your essential self.
54. Have you thought of God today?
55. God never does anything in a hurry.
56. Worry is merely getting ahead of God's providence.
57. Be as good to yourself as unto others.
58. Take time out for your soul.
59. You may walk about and your soul be dead.
60. This Church loves you—do you love it?
61. See a minister before you see a lawyer.
62. To win an object be objective.
63. You'll need at least six people when you're dead.
64. You can weather any storm when you are free of debt.
65. The Bible is God's doctor book.
66. It is better to lay aside than to be laid aside.
67. Christ's love is the best tonic.
68. Divorce breaks at least two hearts.
69. Don't orphan your children with divorce.
70. A baby can make or break your home—be careful.
71. Your greatest problem is solved when you forgive.
72. Your soul is genuinely happy when you are forgiven.
73. Awareness of God's love is the secret of happiness.
74. You can see Christ when you believe in Him.
75 There is no self-made man.
76. Self-confidence is another form of self-conceit.
77. Whoever has confidence in self is a moral coward.
78. You can absolutely trust God to keep His promises.
79. You can't get anything without first giving.
80. If you must fight, then fight sin.
81. Morale is a matter of having more of God in life.
82. You have only what you can carry with you.
83. Every human being has a past—be charitable.
84. You remember only what is emotionally toned.
85. A happy life brings a happy death.
86. When you have the peace of Christ you'll never go to pieces.
87. You are sure to lose faith if you fight it.
88. You fight the fight of faith when you fight with it.

Open your eyes and the whole world is full of God

Do somethings with your religion and your religion will not die

Happiness is the product of habitual right thinking

Keep your mental kingdom holy and you will be whole

Shun doing in secret what you would not do openly

The gift of patience is akin to genius

Your mental assets should be as real to you as your material things

Pay more attention to the quality of your work than to the desire to be noticed

The Kingdom of God is within you

Whatsoever thy hand findeth to do, do it with thy might

As you think, so will your life be

Your character is the sum of your actions

Self-pity is selfishness

Our faith is built on nothing less than Jesus Blood and Righteousness

For a better world tomorrow we preach Christ today

The Lutheran Church takes God at His word

A good word, like a good deed, never dies

Put your principles into practice

Do justly, love mercy, and walk humbly with thy God

Progress comes from not making the same mistake twice

Change your good intentions into good deeds

"Because I live, Ye shall live also," John 14,19

"Man shall not live by bread alone," Deut. 8,3

Remember the Week Day to keep it holy

This church does not try to bring Christ down to man's level, but to lift men up to Christ's level

A selfish Christian is a contradiction

Quitters never win—winners never quit

Our faith is built on nothing less than Jesus' Blood and Righteousness

For a better world tomorrow we preach Christ today

The Lutheran Church takes God at His word

A good word, like a good deed, never dies

Put your principles into practice

Do justly, love mercy, and walk humbly with thy God

Progress comes from not making the same mistake twice

Change your good intentions into good deeds

"Because I live, Ye shall live also," John 14,1

'Man shall not live by bread alone," Deut. 8,3

Remember the Week Day to keep it holy

This church does not try to bring Christ down to man's level, but to lift men up to Christ's level

A selfish Christian is a contradiction

Quitters never win—winners never quit

A weak religion is strongest only when its owner is sick
Godliness with contentment is great gain
The fear of the Lord is the beginning of knowledge; but fools despise wisdom and instruction
My son, if sinners entice thee, consent thou not
Trust the Lord with all thine heart; and lean not unto thine own understanding
As a jewel of gold in a swine's snout, so is a fair woman which is without discretion
A soft answer turneth away wrath; but grievous words stir up anger
A good name is to be chosen rather than great riches
What shall it profit a man, if he gain the whole world and lose his own soul
Like as a father pitieth his children, so the

Lord pitieth them that fear him
He that loveth not knoweth not God, for God is love
Unto whomsoever much is given, of him shall be much required
The Lord is my light and my salvation, whom shall I fear?
God is our refuge and strength, an ever present help in trouble
Whatever a man soweth, that shall he also reap
Create in me a clean heart O God and renew a right spirit within me
Search others for virtues; yourself for vices
Use your head, don't lose it
You can if you will
Nothing of importance is ever done without a plan
More men rust away than wear out
Every day is a "New Year" and gives you another chance
Waste less, give more
An hour in church—a small investment with a big dividend
If the Bible is the Word of God, let's stick to it; if it isn't, then Christianity is just a joke
A Christian life is the church's best advertisement
Life is but a school, and death its graduation day
Our church can bring you peace, happiness and security
Choose you this day whom ye will serve, God or self
Christ is equal to your need
God forgives, do You?
He travels safely who travels with God
Choose: the attainment of man or the Atonement of Christ
Happiness comes from within
The Christian who worries needs overhauling
Would you care to have God treat you as you treat Him?
The hearse is a poor vehicle in which to go to church
No man ever got lost on a straight road
The victims of unbelief are not the readers of the Bible

Revenge is savagery
Gentleness is strength
Happiness is perfection
Purity is consecration
Love is unselfishness
Be a constant help to others
Faith is the masterkey to achievement
Become master of your moods.
Dare to know the true motives for your actions
Your mind grows through use. So does religion.
Nine-tenths of the things you worry about never happen
Avoid the common habit of undertaking too many things at one time
Make this a day of blessing to me, and make me a blessing to others
Educate men without religion and you make them only clever devils
Repentance is being sorry enough to stop
A day of worry is more exhausting than a week of work; trust in God
Character is what a man is in the dark
As thy days are, so shall thy strength be
You cannot whitewash yourself by blackening others
Profanity is a sign of a small vocabulary
Religion that costs nothing is worth nothing

Live your noblest life TODAY

Choose a definite purpose in life

Look to God for everything

Let your work speak for itself

THIS IS A PLACE
where YOU may
MEET GOD

HE promises to receive you, to reveal Himself to you, to explain LIFE to you, to give strength to you, to quiet the unrest of your soul.

"COME . . . . APART and REST AWHILE!"

YOU HAVE BEGUN
another week's toil
IT WILL BE HARD
unless
YOU HAVE GOD'S HELP
BEGIN each day with Him!
"I can do ALL THINGS thru Christ."

YES, TIMES are hard! And they are still more difficult when we try to meet them without God. His WORD has the secret of meeting each day's troubles and trials. Do YOU read YOUR BIBLE these days?
"Thy Word is a lamp unto my feet and a light unto my path"
LIFE'S DAILY ROUTINE
has a monotony which is dull and deadening unless it has a relieving pause.
SUNDAY
is God's gift of "the pause that refreshes"
"THE SABBATH WAS MADE FOR MAN"

THIS CHURCH
has a
RESPONSIBILITY
for
YOUR WELFARE!
It offers you: A Place to Worship
An Unchanged Gospel
An Unchanging Saviour
A Fellowship of Faith

ONLY ONE MORE DAY!
For your weariness, your exhaustion, your sense of failure, your heartache, your disappointment.
SUNDAY
offers a grateful relief.
Are YOU not ready to say with a weary heart of long ago:
"I WAS GLAD WHEN THEY SAID UNTO ME, 'LET US GO INTO THE HOUSE OF THE LORD' "
YOU LIVE daily in an atmosphere of confusion, stress and strain. How wearisome and worrisome to one's soul it becomes!

THE LORD'S DAY offers us a grateful change from all of this exhausting demand upon us. The rest and refreshment of God's House is a beckoning haven from life's storm.

STEER YOURSELF
TOWARD SUNDAY

Sentence Sermons

THE WAGES OF SIN IS DEATH, BUT THE FREE GIFT OF GOD IS ETERNAL LIFE IN JESUS CHRIST.
ROM. 6-23

YOU NEGLECT YOUR SOUL AND SAY: I MUST LIVE, BUT FORGET YOU MUST DIE.

THE CHURCH'S BUSINESS IS NOT TO PROVIDE AMUSEMENT BUT TO SAVE AND FEED SOULS. HOW ABOUT YOUR SOUL?

YOU MAY SCOFF AT RELIGION BUT YOUR FOLLY WILL COME HOME TO YOU IN THE CHILDREN YOU RAISE.

THE CHURCH SERVICE IS NOT A POLITICAL CONVENTION. DO NOT SEND A DELEGATE. COME AND BRING YOUR FAMILY WITH YOU.

THE PRIVILEGE OF PRAYER IS A BLANK DRAFT ON GOD ALMIGHTY TO BE FILLED OUT BY THE BELIEVER.

AMERICA'S GREATEST NEED IS MORE OLD-FASHIONED RELIGION. IT IS YOUR NEED, ALSO.

THE CHURCH WANTS YOU BECAUSE IT HAS A MESSAGE THAT YOU NEED.

TRUTH IS NOT OF MAN'S MAKING, BUT OF GOD'S REVELATION. HEAR IT IN THE HOUSE OF GOD!

AN IMPORTANT QUESTION

CAN YOU BE A CHRISTIAN WITHOUT GOING TO CHURCH? YOU MAY SAY YES, BUT THE BIBLE SAYS NO.

GEORGE WASHINGTON SAID: "I AM NOT ASHAMED TO CALL MYSELF A CHRISTIAN, AND I TRY EARNESTLY TO BE ONE."

ABRAHAM LINCOLN SAID: "GOD BLESS THE CHURCHES, AND BLESSED BE GOD WHO GIVES US THE CHURCHES."

"IS IT NOTHING TO YOU, ALL YE THAT PASS BY?"

"BEHOLD AND SEE IF THERE BE ANY SORROW LIKE UNTO MY SORROW, WHICH IS DONE UNTO ME."

DURING HIS PASSION OUR SAVIOUR SUFFERED FOR YOU—AND WILL YOU FORGET?

REMEMBER CHRIST'S DEVOTION FOR YOU DURING THE PASSION SEASON, BY DEVOTING YOURSELF FOR HIM.

CHRIST DID NOT GRUMBLE WHEN HE CARRIED YOUR CROSS. WILL YOU GRUMBLE TO CARRY THE CHRISTIAN CROSS?

COME AND LEARN HOW "THE MAN OF SORROWS" CAN BRING JOY INTO YOUR HEART.

HOW MANY SUNDAYS IN YOUR LIFE? JUST THAT OFTEN GOD CALLED YOU.

IF YOU WANT TO RISE ABOVE THIS WORLD'S FOGS ASCEND THE MOUNTAIN OF CHRIST-FAITH.

CHRIST HAS DIED FOR YOU. GOD IS CALLING YOU, COME.

THE CROSS IS AN EMBLEM OF JESUS' LOVE

COME AND HEAR THE MESSAGE OF THE CROSS

JESUS DIED.
THAT'S HISTORY
JESUS DIED FOR ME.
THAT'S FAITH.

BEFORE
YOU DOUBT
READ THE BIBLE
YOURSELF.

THE RIGHT WAY TO START ON THE RIGHT WAY IS TO START RIGHT AWAY.

THE QUESTION IS NOT: WHERE ARE YOU? BUT WHERE ARE YOU GOING?

ONLY IN THE DARK NIGHT DO THE STARS SHINE.

THE RIGHT PLACE TO FEEL FOR THE POOR IS IN THE POCKET.

WE NEED NOT FEAR JESUS AS THE JUDGE IF WE KNOW HIM AS OUR SAVIOR.

YOUR QUIET INFLUENCE WILL INFLUENCE YOUR CHILDREN MORE THAN MANY WORDS. COME TO CHURCH!

THE MAN WHO LAUGHS AT RELIGION USUALLY DOES IT TO DROWN OUT THE VOICE OF HIS CONSCIENCE.

THE GREATEST QUESTION IN LIFE:
"WHAT THINK YE OF CHRIST?"
HAVE YOU FOUND THE TRUE ANSWER?

IN SPITE OF ADVANCED CIVILIZATION YOU ARE AS GREAT A SINNER AS YOUR GRANDFATHER WAS. YOU NEED A SAVIOR.

A SOUL WITHOUT THE WORD OF GOD IS LIKE A LAMP WITHOUT OIL. IT HAS NO LIGHT OR FIRE.

THE MAN WHO IS TOO "ENLIGHTENED" TO BELIEVE THE BIBLE IS USUALLY AFRAID OF BLACK CATS AND THE NUMBER THIRTEEN.

BEFORE YOU DOUBT—READ THE BIBLE YOURSELF.

"ALL SCRIPTURE IS GIVEN BY INSPIRATION OF GOD."

SIN IS A REALITY AND REPENTANCE A NECESSITY.

THE LAW DAMNS THE CHIEF OF SAINTS, THE GOSPEL SAVES THE CHIEF OF SINNERS.

GOD'S CLOCK KEEPS GOOD TIME, THOUGH IT BE NOT YOUR TIME.

THERE IS NO HALF WAY CHRISTIANITY. YOU FULLY ACCEPT OR CLEARLY REJECT.

TODAY THOU LIVEST, TODAY REPENT. PERHAPS THY LIFE WILL SOON BE SPENT.

FAITH IS BELIEVING
WHAT WE DO NOT SEE
THE RESULT OF FAITH IS
SEEING WHAT WE BELIEVE

✠

DAILY PRAYER IS
THE BEST REMEDY
FOR DAILY CARE

COME

UNTO

ME ALL YE THAT

LABOR AND ARE

HEAVY

LADEN

AND I

WILL GIVE

YOU REST

IS IT NOTHING TO YOU

ALL YE THAT PASS BY? BEHOLD, AND SEE IF THERE BE ANY SORROW LIKE UNTO MY SORROW, WHICH IS DONE UNTO ME?

IN SPITE OF ADVANCED CIVILIZATION YOU ARE AS MUCH IN NEED OF A SAVIOR AS YOUR GRANDFATHER WAS.

THE MAN WHO LAUGHS AT RELIGION USUALLY DOES IT TO DROWN OUT THE VOICE OF HIS CONSCIENCE.

THE MAN WHO IS TOO "ENLIGHTENED" TO BELIEVE THE BIBLE IS USUALLY AFRAID OF BLACK CATS AND THE NUMBER 13.

THE MAN WHO PLANS ONLY HOW BEST TO LIVE IS USUALLY AFRAID TO DIE.

Seeking true Happiness? Try the Bible Church.

The Word of God, no more, no less,

The world's redemption and redress,

The Word of God, no more, no less,

We Lutherans teach, also confess.

Get peace for your soul through Christ.

Save your soul first.

Christ came to save sinners.

Christianity centers about Christ Crucified.

We have it! We believe it! We preach it! We teach it!—The Bible.

Live right that ye may die right.

We Preach: Not human wisdom, but God's truth

"He that followeth Me, walketh not in darkness."

Pray and Prosper

More of striving, less of strife,

Unconscious service, makes the Christian's life.

What kind of a church would any church be,

If every member did just like me?

Help, lift and save for Christ.

Be never ashamed of the Gospel of Christ, which is the Power of God unto Salvation.

Jesus Saves!

A Mighty Saviour is Our God.

Our Aim: To Save Souls; Our Means: The Gospel.

The Open Bible—Christ—And The Cross.

Our Only Aim: To save Souls; Our Only Means: The Gospel of the Crucified.

Founded on the Faith that makes men Free.

The Old Gospel for the New Day

Keep the Reformation Fires Burning

The Church with the Open Door and the Lifted Cross

Built on the Bible and Centered in the Christ.

An Unchangeable Christ for a Changing World.

We Teach and Preach a Living Christ.

The Faith that moved a World.

He travels Safely who Travels with God.

It is better to live right than to die wrong.

In God we trust, but we should know God; Go to Church

Unyieldingly for the Life everlasting

Unyieldingly for the everlasting Gospel.

The Balance of the way with Christ

The Lutheran Church holds fast to Christ and moves forward with Christ.

Builded and Building on the Gospel of the Crucified, Risen and Redeeming Christ.

Balm for the Sorrowing, Health for the Soul-Sick.

I Am The Church—I Offer—Love—Joy—Service.

Everybody's Church, Everybody's Christ.

Godliness for Godlessness.

Hell or Heaven, Which? You Choose,

Souls for Sale! What Is The Price Of Yours?

Christ Came To Save Sinners—Not The Righteous.

We Point The Way To Rest For The Soul.

New Lives For Old.

A Living Christ For A Dying World.

Where Will You Spend Eternity?

A Saving God For Sinful Souls.

Christ For All—And All For Christ.

A Savior For The Unsaved, A Friend For The Friendless.

I Offer Happiness And Peace For Grief And Unrest.

The Old, Old Gospel in the Old, Old Way.

The Gospel Of Jesus Christ—It Fully Satisfies.

The Gospel of Jesus Christ in all it's Beauty, Purity and Truth.

A Savior For All Men, Everywhere.

A Gospel For Everybody That Fully Satisfies And Endures Eternally.

We are Witness unto Him at home and abroad.

"The King's Business Requireth Haste."

We are here on business for the King.

We are laborers together with God.

We must be about our Father's Business.

Christ the Saviour in the church, the home and the school.

Not riches, nor vain glory, but eternal salvation in Christ our Lord.

"Come Unto Me all ye that are weary and heavy laden and I will give you rest."

Throw yourself on God.

The world wants Jesus, and Jesus wants you.

We seek your soul for Christ.

Service for Souls.

We come to you that you might come to Christ.

The Church—A Mighty force for God and Man.

The Church with the everlasting and ever new Gospel.

God leads, we follow.

The Old Gospel still saves.

The Church with the Gospel Message.

The Church of the Open Bible.

The Lutheran Church is the Bible Church.

An American Church with a message for all nations.

Clinging to Christ.

Teaching Christ Crucified for sinners.

A Church with the message of Christ.

With Christ, for Christ, to Christ.

God's love in Christ our message to men.

The Open Bible, the Old Gospel, the Only Christ.

We Preach the Christ of Scripture.

Christ in all—and all in Christ.

Where will you spend Eternity?

Nothing to lose—everything gained.

The World Needs Christ.

All creeds are colorless except the Christian creed.

One Light never fails—the eternal Gospel of the Living Christ.

FAITH MAKES THE CHRISTIAN
LIFE PROVES THE CHRISTIAN
SUFFERING CONFIRMS THE CHRISTIAN
DEATH CROWNS THE CHRISTIAN.

CHILDREN OBEY YOUR PARENTS IN ALL THINGS, FOR THIS IS WELL PLEASING UNTO THE LORD. —COL. 3:20

NOT TO HEAR CONSCIENCE IS THE WAY TO SILENCE IT.

EVIL EYES NEVER SEE A GOOD THING.

YOUR BUSINESS MAY MAKE YOU A LIVING, BUT CHRIST WILL MAKE YOU A LIFE.

ETERNITY WILL FIND YOU WHERE YOUR SUNDAYS FOUND YOU: WITH GOD OR WITHOUT.

ONE MORE SUNDAY ONE MORE OPPORTUNITY WON OR LOST.

HOW MANY SUNDAYS IN YOUR LIFE? JUST THAT OFTEN GOD CALLED YOU.

IF YOU WANT TO RISE ABOVE THIS WORLD'S FOGS ASCEND THE MOUNTAIN OF CHRIST-FAITH.

CHRIST HAS DIED FOR YOU. GOD IS CALLING YOU. COME.

TAKE CHRIST WITH YOU INTO THE NEW YEAR!

TOO LATE TO MEND THE OLD YEAR, BEGIN THE NEW WITH GOD.

THE NEW YEAR WILL BE HAPPY IF YOU FOLLOW CHRIST.

A GOOD RESOLUTION—" EVENING, MORNING AND NOON WILL I PRAY."—PSALM 55:7

DO NOT WAIT FOR A "MORE CONVENIENT SEASON." THAT SEASON MAY NEVER COME. COME TO CHURCH NEXT SUNDAY!

THIS IS PALM SUNDAY
Do you wear a palm on your coat
or in your heart?
Were you CONFIRMED on a
PALM SUNDAY?
Then this is a holy anniversary for you.
SPEND IT IN CHURCH

Man asks—
"When will things be better?"
God answers—
"Humble yourselves in the sight of the Lord, and he shall lift you up."

Man asks—
"Why doesn't God send us prosperity?"
God answers—
"Ye ask and have not, because ye ask amiss, that ye may consume it upon your lusts."

Man asks—
"What shall I do with my troubles?"
God answers—
"Cast thy burden upon the Lord, and he shall sustain thee."

Man asks—
"What must I do to be saved?"
God answers—
"Believe on the Lord Jesus Christ and thou shalt be saved."

Man asks—
"Who is this Jesus?"
God answers—
"This is My Beloved Son in Whom I am well pleased—"
"He saves from sin."

Man asks—
"Everything is going wrong. What's the matter?"
God answers—
"SIN!"
"There is none that is righteous . . . . They are all gone out of the way."

Christian character is appropriating what God has provided, not the patchwork struggle of our own efforts.

Faith fears no famine.
Wait on God in weighty matters.
It is better to walk by faith than to talk of faith.
Living without God means dying without hope.
Hope is never ill when faith is well.
Every lock of sorrow has a key of promise to fit it.
Christ has made us kings. Why do we live as beggars?
Pray as if everything depended upon God. Work as if everything depended upon you.
Hell is wages: Heaven is a gift.
He gains a loss who shuns the cross.
God's delays are not God's denials.
Be all for Christ since He is all for you.
Prayer is the pathway to power.
Faith goes in where finances cannot enter.
Unbelief is the mark of all men's failure.
It is a great sin to love a small sin.
Faith accepts: Hope expects.
Faith appropriates: Hope anticipates.
Christ is our adornment as well as our atonement.

Hell is truth seen too late.
Do your earthly tasks in a heavenly way.
Work, but trust God, not your work.
God's will is that we should not do our own will.
If the outlook is dark, try the uplook.
The only thing God has ever forgotten is the sins of those who believe in His Son.
He who is heaven bound must be heaven born.
Live as though the Lord were coming today. Work as though he were not coming for years.
Little faith may enjoy great promises.
Christians should be both seen and heard for Christ.
A true believer loves not the world, yet loves all the world.
Disgrace may be a means of grace.
If sin were not deceitful, it would never be delightful.
He who made man, was made sin for us.
His heart cannot be pure, whose tongue is not clean.

Remorse is repentance that does not know what Christ is.

Trials do not weaken us; they show us we are weak.

Christians never meet for the last time.

No matter what your problem is, God is undismayed.

Suffering borne for Christ is always borne with Christ.

The Gospel breaks hard hearts and heals broken hearts.

To be much like Christ you must be much in Christ.

The pleasures of sin are for a season; its wages for eternity.

It is better to suffer for speaking the truth, than that the truth should ever suffer for the want of speaking.

Gasoline is the devil's most effective conscience soporific.

* * *

Why do people forget the first principles of arithmetic when filling their church envelopes?

* * *

The urge to work in the church is like a disease frequently mentioned in magazine advertisements. One out of five has it.

* * *

The only safe time to drop the exercise of one's religion is when the devil takes a vacation.

* * *

Many a church will begin to thrive when it eliminates gossip as an indoor sport.

* * *

Why must a church service be shorter than a moving picture show?

JESUS DIED.
THAT'S HISTORY
JESUS DIED FOR ME.
THAT'S FAITH.

BEFORE
YOU DOUBT
READ THE BIBLE
YOURSELF.

THE RIGHT WAY TO START ON THE RIGHT WAY IS TO START RIGHT AWAY.

THE QUESTION IS NOT: WHERE ARE YOU? BUT WHERE ARE YOU GOING?

ONLY IN THE DARK NIGHT DO THE STARS SHINE

THE RIGHT PLACE TO FEEL FOR THE POOR IS IN THE POCKET.

"HOLY MEN OF GOD SPAKE AS THEY WERE MOVED BY THE HOLY GHOST.

THE BIBLE IS GOD'S BOOK. EVERY PAGE. EVERY WORD.

Outdoor Advertising for the Church

J. F. E. NICKELSBURG

CO-OPERATING WITH THE Outdoor Advertising Association of America and its affiliated organizations, the American Lutheran Publicity Bureau is pleased to offer the following plan for national publicity. Outdoor advertising offers an immense circulation for its message. Automobiles by the thousand crowd the highways of our nation. Poster advertising like no other medium of publicity arrests the attention of the man on the street. Pictorial display and large lettering, and in many cases, displayed on illuminated poster panels, prompts attention, is read, produces results.

What to Do

1. Look about your neighborhood and secure the name of the local Poster Company. The Outdoor Advertising Association of America, Incorporated is a national organization operating in various parts of the country through local branch or auxiliary companies and in some cases by authorized individuals doing posting.

2. Call on your local firm and show them the telegram printed on this page with approval of our design and offering co-operation. Ask for gratis space and posting of the Lutheran Lenten Poster.

3. After arrangements have been made with the local billposting agency, order from

American Lutheran Publicity Bureau
1819 Broadway   New York, N. Y.

For local imprint, use name of church, full address, name of pastor, hours of services. The cost of the poster will be $5.00, and 80¢ for local imprint.

4. It is suggested that wherever space permits, the *Lutheran Hour* broadcast be advertised in part of the local announcement panel. The nearest radio station of the Mutual System may be given, hour of broadcast, etc.

THE ELECTRIC CROSS

A new advertising medium, recently brought on the market, is the electric cross. Its size varies according to the area of space available and local building conditions. These electric lighted crosses, the trade-mark of the Christian religion, have a publicity message and an invitation for the residential population of the community, and they reach the traveling public. The December, 1932, AMERICAN LUTHERAN had this to say: "We insist upon giving the cross the central place of worship inside of our church.

Being consistent, let us insist that it be given a place of prominence outside of our church. The illuminated cross today is within the reach of every congregation. In busy sections of the large city it is usually advisable to place the cross over the church entrance or on the corner of the church edifice where it may be seen from four directions. If the church is advantageously situated the illuminated cross may be placed high upon the building and seen for miles in every direction."

NEWSPAPER PUBLICITY IN RURAL PAPERS

Before the days of the automobile, the "country church" felt itself exempt of real advertising and publicity problems. Not so today. The rural church should make weekly announcements in local hotels, boarding houses, tourist camps, Y.M.C.A. and Y.W.C.A. halls, reading rooms, etc. Every Lutheran church should be represented in the Church columns of its home newspapers. The editor needs the cooperation of the Pastor, and the Pastor has a rightful claim for space in the home town paper. List the name of your church in the telephone directory. Out-of-town visitors come to the cities, towns and villages, from everywhere.

Lutheran Highway Poster

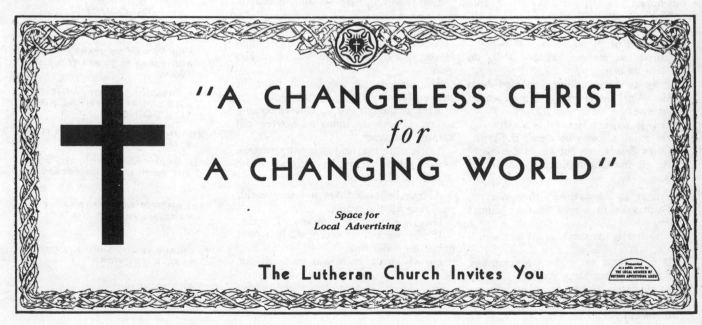

117

Religious Bill Board Advertising

The Outdoor Advertising Association of America, Inc. (formerly the Poster Advertising Association), through its 8,000 associate members agrees to arrange displays of church posters throughout the country on the following plans:

1. Upon request of any church, group of churches, or any responsible organization, the Association member will post free one or a number of these posters, according to the size of the city, the available space, and the arrangements made.

The posting will be on regulation standard poster panels and all services contributed.

2. The church or organization shall pay for the cost of the posters. Regulation size, 24-sheet, which is the American standard, approximately 9 feet high by 20 feet long; price, $1.80 for the "Nativity Poster" printed in 12 colors, "First Award," (so named because it received first prize for best design in national contest), in 12 colors, $1.80; "Third Award" in 12 colors, $1.50; "Church Invitation," in two colors, $1.00 each.

The poster, "First Award," makes ideal Lenten advertising on account of its text. On top, "Righteousness Exalteth a Nation." on bottom, "Come Unto Me and I Will Give You Rest."

The Outdoor Advertising Association of America, Inc., 165 W. Wacker Drive, Chicago, Ill., will send an illustrated folder, with all details, on request. Mention the American Lutheran.

Outdoor Posters

SPACE FOR IMPRINT

Lutheran Welcome Posters printed on white paper, size 18 x 22. Prices 6 for 25c, 15 for 50c, 25 for 75c and 40 for $1.00. Prices for imprint of local advertising on request, also cost of adding extra paraffin solution which will preserve poster against weather conditions. Address, Rev. Fred Stein, 906-A-L Walnut St., Chillicoth, Missouri. Mention AMERICAN LUTHERAN.

The Old Complaint

WRITING in the *Lutheran Church Herald*, a layman writes:

"Last summer while on my vacation I looked for a Lutheran church on Sunday where we could attend and worship. As Lutherans we wanted to attend Lutheran services, because there is where we feel at home, and to us no church service can take the place of our beautiful and edifying Lutheran service. One Sunday morning far away from any acquaintances we decided to go to a town in which we knew there was a Lutheran church. The churches can ordinarily be seen, so there is no difficulty in finding a church provided the town is not so very large. This town had four churches, and not a single one of them had a name that could be seen. After some asking we finally located the church. However, there were no services. We decided to go to the next town, as there also was a Lutheran church. There we had the same experience in locating the church, but after some asking we found the place.

On the following Sunday we were only about 25 miles from a fairly large city, a place having several thousand inhabitants. We knew there was a Lutheran church, and set out to find it. But even there we had the same experience, no name on the church, and after much driving and asking we finally located it.

In our days, when people travel both often and far, the churches are looked for. A road sign telling direction is welcome and refreshing to the traveler, we know we are on the right road. A church sign is just as much needed and very welcome to the one who is looking for a church home while he is away from home. Let us publish our church and its location so that it can be found with the least difficulty. The individual congregations will reap much joy and happiness in having strangers worship with them in their own church. We are again nearing another summer, May it be easy to find your church, because it has the name in big letters placed on it.

This is an old complaint. Almost every traveling Lutheran churchman has reasons to join in the chorus. Not only are the small town churches guilty but the city churches are gross offenders when it comes to neglect in publishing even the whereabouts of their houses of worship. Usually the latter do bear some sign of their denominational character on the outside, but most of them have made no provisions for the convenience of traveling fellow-Lutherans. The hotel bulletins, bringing the advertisements of local churches, very often do not list a single one of our own churches. The Saturday evening papers with their columns of religious advertisements usually bring no enlightenment to the inquiring traveler as to the location or the time of worship of our own Lutheran churches.

There are perhaps two main reasons for the neglect of our churches, both city and rural, to accommodate themselves to the changed conditions of our day. The one reason is the general policy of parsimoniousness which characterizes the life of most of our congregations. The failure to provide for the convenience of the traveler is due in a large measure to the mistaken notion that the investment of money for publicity purposes is a waste. It may, however, be contended and very definitely proven that the investment of such money yields abundant returns even in dollars and cents. The other reason is what we might term the prevalent congregational provincialism and clannishness, based on the idea that a Christian congregation is an organization sufficient unto itself and without any obligation towards the non-member, be he a resident or a traveler. We have been directly told, "Our church is for our members. We are not conducting services for travel-

PLEASE TURN TO PAGE 365

The Week-Day Bible School

KARL GRAESSER

THE NEED FOR ADDITIONAL RELIGIOUS INSTRUCTION for the children in those congregations which have no parochial school is hardly debatable; we should take it for granted. One way in which this additional instruction may be supplied is through the medium of the week-day Bible school. The purpose of such a school is revealed in its name. It is to be a BIBLE school. The methods offered below have been successful in our week-day Bible school, which meets every Friday afternoon from 4 to 5 o'clock, from the middle of September to the middle of June.

Program

4—4:05—Opening service. A hymn is sung, followed by a prayer or a Psalm recited in unison. The entire school meets together for the opening.

4:05—4:20—Hymn Work. In the lower grades the children learn hymns by rote. In the upper grades the hymns are learned by constant repetition. Let those who have had a birthday during the week choose a hymn for the class to sing. A birthday hymn may be used in the lower grades.

4:20—5—The lesson for the day. This includes, as a rule, memory work, a Bible story, and handwork.

Division of Classes. Our school is divided as follows: Beginners, all children up to and including kindergarten; primary, school grades 1A to 3A; junior, school grades 3B to 5B; senior, school grades 6A and over.

Attendance. Keep accurate attendance records. An inaccurate system of recording attendance is worse than none. Let your children know that you are interested enough in their attendance to keep careful records. We use a card system. Since our school meets but one day a week, we use Concordia Sunday school attendance cards. At the end of the year gold lapel crosses are awarded for perfect attendance. Those who are absent with good excuse are not counted absent if they bring a note. Those who have been absent two sessions receive a reminder in the form of a card. Those who miss three sessions are placed on the "suspended list" and are visited. The position of attendance secretary is by no means an unimportant cog in the machine, yet it may be filled by any faithful and intelligent girl of confirmation age. The attendance secretary sends out also the birthday cards.

Memory Work. Some memory work is done in all grades. Little children who cannot read are taught by rote. Older children are given a few minutes to commit the assignment to memory, either from the blackboard, or from their books. In the lower grades the 23rd Psalm is learned by easy stages; also prayers and Bible passages correlated with the Bible story for the day. In the upper grades Bible passages suggested by the story, Psalms, and the books of the Bible are committed to memory. Prayers are reviewed in all grades.

Bible Stories. The Bible stories should be carefully chosen before the beginning of the term. The chronological order may be used, or the stories may illustrate a central theme such as the heavenly Father's mercy. In the beginners class it is wise to choose stories which may be worked out on the sandtable.

Handwork. It is impossible to spend much time on handwork in the week-day Bible school, yet it may be included in the curriculum with profit. Handwork for handwork's sake has no place in a school of religious instruction. Handwork should never be an end in itself, but always a means to an end. Our handwork is correlated throughout with the lesson for the day. Perhaps the most profitable type of handwork is the note book. Provide a picture for the story of the day to be pasted on a sheet of loose-leaf paper. Under the picture let them write a pertinent Bible passage which they have committed to memory, or a brief synopsis of the story. We have also the note books supplied with the vacation Bible school course for the primary grades published by the Lutheran Book Concern. The pictures supplied with the vacation Bible school course for the senior grade, published by the Lutheran Book Concern, are used to make loose-leaf note books. The Outline Picture Study of the life of Christ, a set of fifty-two outline drawings by Lillie A. Faris, is excellent for the loose-leaf note book in the junior grade. The Scripture citations printed below these drawings are not given in the King James Version.

We overcame this difficulty by having the children cut off what was printed below the picture before they pasted it into their books, and having them write in the Bible passage which they had learned as their memory work for the day. It is wise to supply the children with an ordinary filing folder to keep the sheets of their loose-leaf note book neat until the end of the term. Spend the last handwork period in making a cover for the note book. If a short supplementary course in the geography of the Holy Land is given, the children will enjoy locating cities, mountains, etc., on outline maps, and coloring them. It will be false economy to use cheap wax crayons for any coloring work done in the school. Excellent maps may be purchased at a surprisingly nominal price from the David C. Cook Publishing Company, Elgin, Ill. When the course includes committing the books of the Bible to memory, the children may letter and color an outline drawing of a bookcase containing the books of the Bible in separate volumes. These Library of the Bible Charts may be had from Concordia Publishing House. (1932-33 catalog, page 880).

Visual Instruction. It may be taken for granted that pictures will be used with all Bible stories as they are taught. The large colored picture rolls issued by Concordia Publishing House are excellent. A stereoptican machine is a great asset to any school. We have the machine manufactured by the National Pictures Service, Inc., of Cincinnati, Ohio, including also their film slides with pictures for the entire Bible. The stereoptican machine is used every week in our school, the various grades alternating. This picture period takes the place of the regular lesson for the day in that particular grade.

Closing Exercises. If your school has done good work, you owe it to your school to advertise that fact. Invite all who can and will come to the closing session. Do not waste time preparing an elaborate program. Show what you have done in your regular course during the year. Let the little ones recite some of the memory work they have learned. Give one class an examination on the stories they have covered during the year after the manner of a spelling bee—those who cannot answer take their seat, until only one is left. Let the children in groups sing hymns which they have learned. Display the handwork. Award prizes to those who have done the best work, and also to those who have a perfect attendance record.

SPIRITUALITY IN TEACHING THE CATECHISM

RICH. HOPE

One of the greatest needs of the Church is spirituality. The old Adam is a formalist, who is very prone to make religion a matter of mere ceremonies, observance of custom, and routine.

It is for this reason that we find so many "Lutherans" who imagine that when they have once been confirmed and have partaken of their first communion they need not maintain any further connection with the Church than simply retain their Lutheran name and refrain from joining another communion. Others regard the preparation which they have undergone for their confirmation as such a tedious matter that they soon turn their backs to the Church. Still others, who remain within the fold of the visible Church, sink into a state of carnal security and appear to have been "overfed" on religion.

Without doubt these sad circumstances are in most cases due to the individual himself, or to the fact that there is little or no religious atmosphere in the *home.* Yet the reason may also be sought in *mechanical methods of instructing the young.* Next to the Word of God itself, which we have, parents, pastors, and teachers in school and Sunday school need the trait of *spirituality* in order to solve this difficult problem of the religious instruction of the young. That is a quality which only *God* can give us, for while man may be able to produce a certain kind of religionism like artificial flowers, God alone can create the natural, fresh, sweet-smelling flowers of true religion, and He has promised to do that through His Word and Sacraments and in answer to our prayers.

Nevertheless there are also certain principles by which we may be guided in preserving and promoting proper spirituality in our instructions.

I

One of these is to *keep in mind the goal* for which we are aiming.

This is not merely to train the children for participation in the activities of the congregation, or to keep them within the fold of the visible Church, or to give them an intellectual understanding of the fundamental doctrines of Christianity, but to lead them to a saving knowledge of the Lord Jesus Christ as their personal Savior and to keep them with Him, to make them realize more and more that they are the blood-bought property of their Lord, and that He is theirs and they are His.

Jesus said, "Suffer the little children to come *unto Me,*" and in the book of Proverbs we read: "I love them that *love Me,* and those that *seek Me* early shall *find Me.*"

Luther kept this purpose in mind. For in the first chief part of the Catechism he shows our need of a Savior; in the second he speaks of the love of God, the redemption of Christ, and the application of salvation through the work of the Spirit; in the third He directs us to exercise our childlike relation to God and to obtain His blessing through prayer; and in the rest He teaches us the right use of baptism, absolution, and the Lord's Supper.

Not only in the outward arrangement of its chief parts, but also in the very nature of its contents he made the purpose of his Catechism evident. Have you ever noticed how easily his explanations may be turned into prayers and thanksgivings? The whole Catechism may be *prayed* from beginning to end, for it treats of the very things for which we ought to pray.

It expresses in well-chosen words the *inner faith* of every one who adopts it as his own. Note especially the "I" and "me" and "my" in the three articles of the Holy Christian Creed. Can there be a more beautiful, simple, tender, and devout expression of personal heartfelt experience and apprehension and appreciation of the saving love of Jesus Christ than we have in Luther's explanation of the Second Article?

It must become evident throughout our instruction that the entire Christian doctrine pulsates with the warm life blood of the love of Christ. To this end the Lord Jesus must be made as real to the children as, and they must be given a consciousness of as vital a relation to Him as they have to, their own fathers and mothers. Thus their lives will be "hid with Christ in God."

II

If we wish to avoid handing down our instruction in a mechanical manner we must also *preserve a spiritual tone* in our instruction.

Short, simple prayers may open and close the lessons, but they must be couched in such language as the children themselves will be able to understand. Their own thoughts and desires must be expressed in a way in which we would teach *them* to express them.

We must, above all things, avoid the impression that we are going through some form of drudgery or a lesson-period similar to those in a school. The members of a class studying the Word of God are sitting down to a heavenly banquet and treating their souls to a spiritual feast. The instruction must therefore be lively, concrete, and interesting. The teacher must be a whole "curiosity shop" and always have something worth while to say. One must be able to catch the enthusiasm which he feels in teaching, for there is always something exhilarating about imparting information to others, is there not? And what better, more interesting, and more valuable information can we impart to any one than that relating to Christ and to his own soul? If we ourselves are enthused about the subjects of religion and bent on creating a similar interest in others, we ought not find much difficulty in holding their attention almost spellbound throughout.

A good lesson in religion is one in which there is an opening of heart unto heart; one in which the children are made to feel that the teacher knows and loves Jesus and wants to lead those who are sitting at his feet to the fullness of life which he enjoys in Christ Jesus; one after which the pupils will be so enthused that they will want to tell others what they have learned and that they will almost be constrained to exclaim with the disciples of Emmaus: "Did not our hearts burn within us while He talked with us by the way and while He opened to us the Scriptures?"

III

The right use of the Catechism will also prove helpful toward making the teaching and learning of its truths the real spiritual affairs they ought to be.

This excellent little handbook is not to be employed as a mere textbook to be learned by rote, but as a *guide to spiritual life and growth.* The dried flowers pressed between its leaves must be awakened to life again in the hearts and lives of its students, and that in their original beauty of purity, truth, and love. We dare not lose our sense of the perennial freshness and of the life-giving power of the Word of God.

The art of *illustration,* which Christ used so successfully, will be of tremendous assistance to us in making the truths of the Catechism stand out as realities with spirit, life, and power. The *application* must always be considered the main thing, which everything else must serve. We must seek to drive the lesson home, to grip the heart and the conscience with the truth. Even the *memory work* is of value chiefly because the Word of God which has been stored in the memory will prove to be an instrument by means of which the Holy Ghost operates upon the heart. We cannot calculate what a great accomplishment it is when the Catechism has been taught so successfully that it works out through our spiritual pores in *prayer.* If *this* has been accomplished, we may be confident that our children have not merely a *form* of godliness, but have experienced the *power* thereof. Neither teacher nor pupils ought to rest satisfied with anything less.

Concerning the first chief part of the Catechism, it may be said that if the scholars do not long to hear the Gospel after having studied the Ten Commandments the instructor may as well begin all over again. The Law of God must give even children a keener sense of their sinfulness with a view to deeper repentance and firmer apprehension of the grace of God in Christ. In the study of the Second Article the Lord Jesus Christ must be made real to the children, and a real appreciation of, and trust in, and love to, Him must be implanted in them, together with a fervent longing for His return. In the Third Article the Holy Ghost must be made so real that the scholars will be led to thank God that they *have* the Holy Spirit as their Abiding Companion and Comforter and that they have been "sealed with that Holy Spirit of promise." The spiritual way of teaching the Creed is to show that only those have a right to confess it who have a share in the blessings it enumerates. Children become greatly interested and quite enthusiastic when they speak about the *new birth* and *life* they have received as Christians. The tendency toward the very prevalent thoughtless use of the Lord's Prayer must be counteracted in youth. The meaning of Christ's words must be made plain, a heartfelt longing to have and to use the blessings for which we pray must be created, and the ability to apply each petition to our own personal needs and to the needs of others must be awakened. Then, too, the children should be diligently taught to pray in their own words. There is hardly a better way to impress the entire subject of Baptism upon the minds of the children than by having them memorize and catch the spirit of the hymn "I was made a Christian when my name was given." In treating of the Lord's Supper we have a splendid opportunity to speak of the preciousness of our belief. Such teaching will be anything but unspiritual and will certainly be owned by God.

IV

Particular emphasis must be laid upon *perfect clearness with regard to the ceremony of confirmation.*

This sacred rite is not a sort of graduation from the study of the Catechism, nor is it to be regarded somewhat as a brand which the Western ranchman puts upon his cattle. It is not administered simply because a confirmand is old enough, has come to the instructions of the pastor, and ought to be a member of the Church like his parents.

But in confirmation we confess our personal faith in the Lord Jesus Christ by renewing our baptismal covenant and are admitted into the privileges of a communicant member who has been prepared worthily to receive the Lord's Supper. For that reason those only are to *present themselves* for confirmation who are *ready* to make the self-surrender, which is to be made in this beautiful rite, from the bottom of their hearts.

PLEASE TURN TO PAGE 70

Technique of the Annual Roll Call—and Reunion Service

MARTIN STRASEN

WITHOUT sacrificing one little iota of his sincere reverence for and glad obedience to Article VII of the Augsburg Confession, the writer feels that in matters like the Annual Roll Call and Reunion Service uniformity would make for progress; and we do need progress. The ideal method in his opinion, therefore, would be to have our Synodical Board for Young People's Work outline a flexible and workable technique, pass it on to the District Committees for Young People's Work, have them suggest it to the pastors of the congregations in their Districts, and they to their Congregation Committees for Young People's Work.

While still continuing to hope for the attainment of that ideal, a status quo method can nevertheless be suggested for those of our congregations who see the need, yet seek in vain in our synodical literature for directions, unless they are already so youthminded that they own and use the Walther League Manual (a basic guide to the work of the local society), which gives workable suggestions to the young people concerning the assistance they may lend their pastor and congregation in conducting the Annual Roll Call and Reunion Service (p. 241). The International Walther League will hardly consider the present article and the copious use which has been made of their suggestions an infringement on their copyright.

Something that should go without saying but usually doesn't must be said at the outset: The Annual Roll Call and Reunion Service is not a one-man job, just as any other important piece of church work requires the cooperation of faithful members of the congregation. The pastor must, of course, be the guiding spirit, but should enroll the Congregation Committee for Young People's Work, if any, a committee of the Young People's Society, or any other group of willing helpers for the task. With their help the work of preparation, of conducting the Reunion Service, and of following up may be outlined as follows.

The Preparation

1. Prepare a list of the last ten years' confirmation classes from the church records.

2. From each class choose wisely a secretary, whose duty it shall be to supervise the preparatory work of the Roll Call for his or her class.

3. Prepare duplicate filing cards for each member of each of the ten classes; 5" x 3" cards are practical and can well be filed in the little metal U. Y. E. filing cases. (See sample card.)

4. Compare the lists of the classes with other records and lists of the congregation, communion record, roster of Bible Classes, Young People's Societies, Men's Clubs, Ladies' Societies, Sunday School Teachers, etc., to ascertain the status of those who are still members of the congregation.

5. Instruct the class secretaries to gather all possible information, above all concerning the present address and church connection of those who are no longer members of the congregation.

6. Check the membership roster of the congregation for such young people of this age group who were confirmed elsewhere, and include them in the file. If they have moved in from sister congregations, notify those congregations of their membership in your congregation, unless this has already been done.

7. Enroll a group of young people from the congregation (the chosen secretaries if the classes are small), who will agree to look up personally each member included in the Roll Call if still in the community.

8. Obtain for each of these workers a copy of "Lessons in Soul Keeping" by Pastor Oscar E. Feucht, issued under the auspices of our Synodical Board for Young People's Work by the Walther League (5c a copy), and if time permits conduct a training class with these workers, using this excellent booklet as textbook. This is especially important because of the attention which must be given by these workers to those of their fellow youths who have strayed or in danger of straying.

9. With the class secretaries as leaders, make contact through these workers with every member of every class, preferably in person, but at least by a personal letter from some classmate when a personal visit is impossible, mentioning the Roll Call and Reunion Service, and the social gathering, which takes place after the service to renew old friendships and cement new ones, which should be of service in soul-keeping. At least three weeks prior to the service the workers should report in person to their respective secretaries on the results of their visits or letters, who shall make exact notations on their cards and report to the pastor, so that his file may be brought up to date and to give him time to make further suggestions on individual cases.

10. Immediately following this check-up the committee should send announcements or invitations for the Roll Call and Reunion Service to each person on the list. Card No. 1374, C. P. H. Catalog @ 15c a dozen may be used. A better method would be to have a return card included with space for acceptance of the invitation, reason for inability to attend, and notification of present church connection.

11. The Committee should see to the mimeographing of the order of service and prepare the program for the social gathering which follows the service.

The Reunion Service

The Reunion Service (the liturgical part of the service as local custom dictates. After the Offering of Gifts the Roll Call of Confirmation Classes by year and name may take place, immediately after which should come the Reaffirmation of the Confirmation Vow. (See Sample.))

Follow-up Work

1. At social gathering following service try to get promise from inactive ones to attend Bible Classes or other organizations of the congregation.

2. Send information to congregations whose former confirmands attended, or whose members (your former confirmands) came for the reunion.

3. Tabulate results of Roll Call on specially prepared sheets (see sample sheet) File filled out individual cards permanently.

4. Give duplicate cards of those who did not come to U. Y. E. Committee for further work. (The secretaries may take over this work where no U. Y. E. Committee exists).

5. Give duplicate cards of those delinquent members who attended to the individual or secretary who brought them for further soul-keeping work.

6. Send names and addresses of those in other communities from whom no answers were received to the pastors of Synodical Conference

congregations nearest their home.

7. Fill out and return the duplicate card sent to every pastor by Synodical Committee on Roll Call.

Suggested Form for Reaffirmation of Confirmation Vow

Dearly Beloved: When you were little children you were received into God's covenant of grace in Holy Baptism. After due instruction in the Word of God you made public profession of your faith in the Triune God, renewed your covenant with Him, and dedicated yourselves body and soul for time and for eternity to your God and Lord. Kneeling at the Lord's altar you gave your hand as a pledge of your promise, received His blessing, were welcomed by you Evangelical Lutheran Church into communicant membership and invited to participate in all the rights and privileges of the same.

But since without your Savior you can do nothing, must grow weary on the road of life, and be utterly defeated in the perilous battle against the powers of darkness, you do well to come at regular intervals to reconsecrate yourselves to your God and Lord, rededicate yourselves to the cause of your Evangelical Lutheran Church, and pray God to continue unto you His grace and the guidance of His Holy Spirit.

In the name of the Lord Jesus Christ and as a minister of His holy Church I, therefore, ask you:

Do you this day, in the presence of God and of this Christian congregation, reaffirm the solemn vow which on the day of your Confirmation you made with the Triune God, to renounce the devil, and all his works, and all his ways, to remain faithful to your Evangelical Lutheran Church and its true confession of the Word of God, to conform all your life to the rule of the divine Word, to walk as it becometh the Gospel of Christ, and in faith, word, and deed to remain true to the Triune God, even unto death? Then declare so by saying, "We do."

Answer: We do.

Join me, therefore, in making confession of our holy Christian faith in the words of the Apostles' Creed.

Confession of faith.

Prayer from Agenda (Anniversary of Confirmation).

Lord's prayer in unison.

Filing Cards

Name..

Address...

Class of 19....... Class Secretary.........................

Corrected Address...

*Membership...

Assigned to..

Remarks...

*Suggested Code for pastor's file
M—Member of Congregation: ☐ A—Active ☐ I—Inactive ☐ D—Doubt
S—Member of Sister Congregation
N—No church membership
O—Member of other Denomination

Sample Tabulation Sheet

Name	Present	Absent	Class	*Code	Remarks

*Suggested code for tabulation sheet
U. Y. E.—Has been referred to U. Y. E. Committee
W—Has been referred to worker who was instrumental in bringing back
S—Has been referred to sister congregation
L—Lost or unknown

Reunion Reply Post Card

This is a Reply Post Card. Invitation side as shown above. Reply side has a picture of Open - Church - door and printed lines for checking: ☐ Coming— ☐ Not Coming. Reverse of this side should be self-addressed. Make card as complete as possible, so recipient has only to check and mail. If possible affix stamp to reply card to assure greater returns. The price of these Reunion Reply Post Cards is $1.25 per 100. Ask for free sample.

Confirmation Robes

WILBUR N. PALMQUIST

THE FACT that the catechumens in the early Christian Church were dressed in white suggested to us the idea of a white-robed Confirmation Class. Our young women's Guild cheerfully provided materials, and willing hands plied busy needles. As a result, the Class of 1925 (10 years ago) entered the Church on Confirmation Day robed in spotless white. The words from Rev. 3:5 naturally suggested themselves for a text: "He that overcometh shall thus be arrayed in white garments;..." This class of fifteen girls, confirmed at the Trinity Lutheran Church, Omaha, by Pastor Wilbur N. Palmquist, was probably the first class confirmed in the white - confirmation robe.

When first introduced 10 years ago the confirmation robe was an innovation. Today, the robe is used in Churches from coast to coast. The advantages of the white robes may be stated as follows:

They are Churchly. They add to the dignity of one of our most beautiful services They conform to the historic symbolism of the white robe used in the early Church.

They are practical. The entire class presents a uniform appearance. The girls are all equally well dressed. The poor girl is not handicapped by the "banker's daughter" who otherwise might appear in an elaborate "party dress" and whose interest may be more on clothes than on the significance of the day. The boys appear also in uniform dress. The boy of Confirmation age is usually in the "sweater and corduroy pants" stage and the robe makes unnecessary the purchase of a special suit of clothes.

They are inexpensive. The robes can easily be made by the ladies of the Church, the only expense being the cost of materials. White broadcloth is commonly used. The robes are patterned after the common "academic" choir robe, without any attempt to duplicate the elaborate yoke. Ours have been in use for 10 years and are still in good condition.

Wherever the white confirmation robe has been introduced only the most favorable comments have been heard. Not one adverse criticism has reached our ears. If one is to judge by the number of Churches which introduced them last year, the custom will soon become universal.

Robed Confirmation Class of Trinity Lutheran Church, Omaha, Nebraska.

Blackboard Diagram of Christian Church Calendar

An interesting blackboard diagram to depict the plan of the Christian Church calendar. In sketching the illustration the pastor should use colored chalk for the various church seasons. The diagram may be enlarged to include every Sunday of the church year with their appointed Gospel and Epistle lesson.

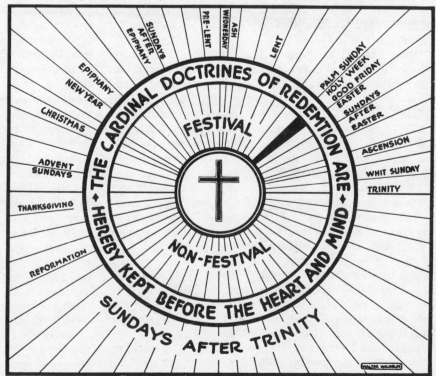

Crisis in Rural Missions

UNDER this heading THE LUTHERAN has published a searching article by Dr. Martin Schroeder. We take the liberty of reprinting some of its paragraphs, because our own synods are just as heavily involved in that crisis as those of the U.L.C.A. Individuals here and there may have given prayerful thought to the problems raised by this crisis, but we doubt whether the bulk of our people really are aware of the seriousness of the situation. Dr. Schroeder's paragraphs will be an eye-opener to many and should move all to fervent prayer that methods and means be 'found to meet these new conditions in the rural field.

The opening paragraphs of the article are a report of a conversation with one of these dispossessed farmers who had hitched a ride with Dr. Schroeder. We go on from there.

"There is yet another story in that farmer's life not yet published, a sequel to 'Grapes of Wrath,' which must be written by the Church—by you and me. If religious forces fail to do so—don't be shocked—the forces of evil will provide that other and concluding volume. I asked the man about church. Yes, he had been a member, even a Lutheran—until his suit gave. out. With that went his church connection. Both fell apart at the same time. Some churches are like that. Clothes make the man and the church member.

"His baby had not been baptized, but they were going to look after it as soon as they were settled again—if and when. One pastor whom I know found in his rural parish fifty-four children whose baptisms had been neglected for that and similar reasons and the error was soon corrected. Our friend of the road, typical of thousands, unconsciously revealed some weaknesses in the church's mission work. One is her losing the dispossessed; another is her inability to react spontaneously to a new situation that now exerts a stranglehold upon rural life and its vital religion.

"What has led to the new situation, the undermining of the country church, is well known. For some farmers it is repeated crop failures, drouth, grasshoppers, and for others a case of 'gone with the wind,' better known as dust storms. Not only have nature's afflictions depressed entire communities and made church work difficult in heretofore normal areas, but new problems have been raised by the change in membership from owners into tenants and accelerated mobility among them. . . .

"There is hardly a country pastor in the midwest area who has not seen some of his flock breaking up home and biding him farewell. Those migrants hope to better their lot somewhere in the West, all the way from Arizona to Washington, with California getting first choice. Several pastors whom we picked at random to give an idea of their losses reported two-thirds to the West Coast, the rest to cities. Reliable estimates place the total of migrant farm labor, not including those who found permanent work and location, California 300,000; Washington and Oregon 50,000; and Arizona 35,000. Among these unfortunates are Lutherans who once upon a time made up the strength of our central states' rural congregations, but now are homeless even as far as the Church is concerned. The Church did not follow as in pioneer days, nor has she stations where they could turn for counsel when they get there. To be sure, some of these wanderers have struck root again in or close enough to a city, where most of our churches are located, to be ministered to. However, we cannot escape the indictment that our Church is not prepared to take efficient care of most Lutherans who, almost penniless, left the corn belt in search of a new home 'out there.'

"Some of our districts have sidestepped rural life consistently. They must now realize their helplessness to act as missionary outposts for our brethren in the country. Through this attitude a fertile field has now been opened to all kinds of erratic sects with less training but more zeal than we have. American church history teaches that any religious group, synod or denomination, which during crucial periods ignored the farming population, has thereby slowed its growth, while the reverse is true of church bodies that took their start among the tillers or in small communities.

"The burden of responsibility rests with the Church at large, with her temper and vision, rather than with any particular section. While our group cannot be charged with having allied itself with great wealth, neither can we claim to be much at home for missionary purposes in the social jungles. We have confined ourselves for the greater part of our work to the cultivation of a middle class Christianity; in other words, to that which is nice and clean. If our members are so unfortunate as to stumble over the economic precipice and collect in substandard groups, they remove themselves thereby from the reach of our influence and through no one's fault in particular. There are, I hasten to say, exceptions. . . .

"So much is certain; that the Church is today confronted with a new missionary obligation in the home field which formerly was not thought of, as there was no special need. That a crisis exists is still not recognized by all who should be aware of it. The unnecessary disintegration of rural work in certain sections of our nation, together with the obligation that 'the poor have the gospel preached to them,' call for strong missionary measures and unavoidable sacrifices. When we speak of 55 per cent of the American people as being unchurched, let us not forget that many of these belong to that group who cannot pay for the privilege under our present system.

"As the problem of the rural church is really the problem of the rural pastor, next to 'statesmanlike generalship' (as Dr. A. R. Wentz puts it), on the part of denominational leaders, the situation calls for men and women who can vision glory in serving the landless and haunted workers of the soil. Colleges and seminaries will have to make their contributions to cultivate the spirit in achieving that end. As things stand, the need is imminent. Scores of rural pastors live on the fringe of bare existence, along with the people whom they serve.

"Does the Church have a helpful answer for our brethren in the faith? Must pleas for rescue continue unanswered with accompanying increase of difficulties?"

Keeping Prospects Contacted

C. H. NAPIER

WITH more than 32,000 Protestant families in Dallas and with less than 10% of Lutheran persuasion, mission work in our city must not only be personal, it must be educational. Tens of thousands of people living within the city know nothing of the history of the Church and they know little of the doctrine of the Church.

Mission work under such circumstances must be chiefly educational. Before any individual or before any family can be won for membership, the individual and the family must first be made conversant with the doctrines and with the practice of the Lutheran Church. When offering a series of membership lectures we have accordingly made it a point to extend an invitation to the general public to attend.

The following notice was given to the press together with a personal cut:

"Beginning Friday night at 8 o'clock and continuing each Friday thereafter, the Rev. C. H. Napier will deliver the first of a series of fourteen lectures on the chief doctrines of the Christian religion. The lectures, which are free to the public, will be given in the auditorium of the Grace Lutheran Church, Centre and Adams Streets, in Oak Cliff. (Oak Cliff is part of Dallas, but is known after the original incorporate name.)

"The series answers every question which one may ask in connection with the Christian religion," the Rev. Mr. Napier said. "It is prepared especially to serve the interest of the many who are confused by a multitude of conflicting religious claims and who have no point of contact where they may hear a frank and an intimate discussion of the Christian religion without cost and without obligation to themselves.

"The subjects of the series is as follows: "The Book of the Ages," "The Divine Will Simply Expressed," "A Sinner Before Sinning," "Unity in Trinity," "The Godhead Incarnate," "The Reality of Jesus Christ," "The Holy Spirit and Sanctification," "Pure Christianity," "The Kingdom of God," "Death's Fatal Blow," "The Model Prayer," "The Keys of Heaven," "The One-Time Sacrament," "Symbolism or Communion—Which?" "Ritualism and Practice."

The press invitation is to the unchurched public. It is a general invitation. We usually have a number of people on a prospective list and to these a government card invitation is sent three weeks preceding the date of the first lecture. To those who attend the first lecture a series of cards is sent. This series helps to maintain interest and it helps to establish the night of meeting in the mind of the prospect.

The following three cards are sent to individuals on the prospect list, one each week for three weeks preceding the night of the first lecture.

YOU OWE IT TO YOURSELF

PEOPLE of today are asking many questions today including, Am I doing right? Will I be saved? What must I do if I want to be prepared to die? Great questions—and there are many more.

The free membership lectures scheduled to open Friday, JANUARY 30, at 8 o'clock, at Grace Lutheran Church, Centre and Adams, are helpful in every way. "I would take no amount of money for what I got out of this wonderful series," one has said.

SAVE YOUR FRIDAY NIGHTS—
IT WILL PAY YOU

YOUR CHANCE COMES THIS WEEK

WITH thousands of people looking for a place to get answers to their questions, you are invited FRIDAY NIGHT to hear the first in the series of lectures touching upon every question which you may ask in connection with the Christian religion.

Remember it will cost you absolutely nothing to hear these lectures. Come! Surely, if you learn more about yourself and your destiny your hour is well spent. So don't forget—

SAVE YOUR FRIDAY NIGHTS—
IT WILL PAY YOU

The above cards are sent out at the beginning of the week so the individual or the family will receive each card not later than Wednesday. The name of the Church and its location is given prominence as is also the night of meeting. The heads are progressive developing thoughtfulness, interest, and decision. The slogan at the bottom of each card is intended to impress the meeting night on the mind, and at the same time to make the prospect feel that he is going to miss something worth while if he passes up the opportunity to attend.

The cards which follow are to be sent only to those who have attended the first lecture. They are built around a lecture delivered or a lecture to be delivered.

A LIFE-TIME OPPORTUNITY

A SERIES of informal talks on subjects of interest to you as a man or woman will be presented at Grace Lutheran Church, Centre and Adams, beginning Friday, JANUARY 30, at 8 o'clock.

These membership lectures are free, instructive, elevating, profitable, never-to-be-forgotten.

"I have never spent 14 hours so profitably in all my life," said one who heard a previous series.

SAVE YOUR FRIDAY NIGHTS—
IT WILL PAY YOU

A TRULY GREAT BOOK, ISN'T IT?

EVERYONE who gets to studying the Bible agrees that it is a great book, a "book divine."

Did you ever get to eating a certain kind of candy— you know the kind I mean, the kind that just melts in your mouth—and how you found you could not get enough of it?

Studying the doctrines of the Bible creates a similar craving. Once you start to study you just want to keep right on and on. But that brings me to say

SAVE YOUR FRIDAY NIGHTS—
IT WILL PAY YOU

EXAMINATION REVEALS BEAUTY

IT was a poet who said: " 'Tis distance lends enchantment to the view." That is true sometimes, but not always.

Of course, a mountain side is more beautiful if viewed from a distance, a river, too, but the beauty of the rose is discoverable only at close sight.

God! I believe you will agree that we can only see the loveliness of God when we see Him as one close at hand. God becomes beautiful and lovely to us as we see him in Jesus. Now don't forget to

SAVE YOUR FRIDAY NIGHTS—
IT WILL PAY YOU

CRIME WAVE SWEEPS OVER WORLD

THERE are literally millions of people who today sit behind prison-bars. They have done wrong and they are suffering for their wrong-doing.

From the beginning of time a crime wave has been in the world. Sometimes it has been violent, sometimes less violent, but the wave has been.

Whence comes it that there is so much sin and wickedness in the world? God's word gives answer.

SAVE YOUR FRIDAY NIGHTS—
IT WILL PAY YOU

WADING IN DEEP WATER

AT all swimming pools warnings are posted to plead with the inexperienced not to take a chance on life by plunging into deep water.

In the free membership lectures being delivered each Friday night at Grace Lutheran Church the listener wades into deep water. Instead of discouraging this, God encourages it. He wants us to learn and learn and learn.

The deeper you get into the waters of Christian doctrine the surer you feel of your footing. Don't fail then to

SAVE YOUR FRIDAY NIGHTS—
IT WILL PAY YOU

THE MIST IN MYSTERY

WHEN a warm and a cold current of air meet with each other the result is a fog or a mist.

In misty, foggy weather trains run on slow schedule, automobilists use more precaution, ships continually sound their fog horns.

Fogs and mists are dangerous because they make VISION difficult. Vision is better as the fog lifts.

As you study God's Word systematically the mist in the mystery of its doctrines lifts. So remember

SAVE YOUR FRIDAY NIGHTS—
IT WILL PAY YOU

CHURCH-GOING A PLEASURE

THERE are many people who get no pleasure out of going to Church. That is easily understood.

If the minister speaks on the subject of sin, regeneration, justification, sanctification, and the hearer is unfamiliar with these scriptural terms, of course, there is little pleasure had.

I believe you will agree that the membership lecture series is informative and explanatory. The more you learn the more you will enjoy going to Church. That's reasonable, isn't it? So let me ask you to

SAVE YOUR FRIDAY NIGHTS—
IT WILL PAY YOU

THE LIGHT OF THE WORLD

THERE is an electric beacon on the top of the Wrigley building in Chicago. The beams from this light may be seen for many, many miles.

Where there is light there is safety. This is true of physical light, and it is true of spiritual light.

Jesus, the Bible says, is the light of the world. We are learning many things of Him and of his doctrine. As we learn we see better where we could not see before, and we get safety too, for safety comes with knowledge. So make it a point to

SAVE YOUR FRIDAY NIGHTS—
IT WILL PAY YOU

GOING DOWN THE HOME STRETCH

WE are getting close to the end of the present series of membership lectures.

What have you thought as you heard them? Have you a better understanding of the Christian religion today than you had ten weeks ago?

We have covered much material. Your knowledge of Christian doctrine therefore should be greater than it was. Your faith should be stronger.

Have you been baptized? Have you ever attended the Lord's supper? You'll learn more of these two sacraments if you will continue to

SAVE YOUR FRIDAY NIGHTS

This "contact" series of cards may be typed, mimeographed or multigraphed. The cards not only serve the purpose of keeping in touch with the prospect, but they serve this purpose too, that they leave a weekly spiritual thought with the prospect. Even though the series does not prove 100% effective, personal invitation even does not bring such results, it serves to keep the name of the Church and the message of the Church with the prospect.

We have seen people go from department to department in a 5 and 10 cent store without buying a penny's worth of merchandise. The people, however, were getting impressions. They will have seen many things on their walk through the departments and yet have bought none of them, but a few days later some of these people will be back in that store buying some of the things which they had seen on the previous visit. And so it is with an invitation series of cards such as the above. They may be sent out regularly to each prospect and a comparatively small number of the prospects may actually come to hear the lectures, but usually it is so at any rate that those who come not will attend the services, and that attendance is a mark of interest. The individual who gets an impression of the Church which sticks is a prospect as long as he attends the service, or as long as he is favorably disposed towards the particular Church.

The Occasional Service Practically Considered

THE RITE OF CONFIRMATION

F. R. WEBER

ALL Lutherans prize most highly the Rite of Confirmation. The significance of the rite lies in the fact that it follows a long period of religious training. Where there is a parochial school, this Christian training may extend over a long period of years, with an hour of religion every day. Where one must reach certain standards with the makeshift of one or two hours a week, the task is quite difficult. In the writer's own experience extending over some seventeen years, we have become convinced that a four year course preparatory to confirmation, is the best solution of the difficulty. The children are divided into four classes. The younger ones meet for a full hour once a week, and the older children meet twice a week for periods of one to one and one-quarter hours each. It is far from the ideal method, but it is better than the hopelessly inadequate plan of meeting one large group but once a week, from late in the fall until Palm Sunday. The older children ought to get not less than sixty to seventy lesson periods each year.

However, we are concerned in this series of papers with the ceremony itself, rather than the more important method which is employed to prepare for it. The extended course of instruction is everything; the ceremony itself is only incidental. And yet the Rite of Confirmation ought to be made as impressive as possible, and ought to be carefully planned from a liturgical standpoint.

The Public Examination. Within the past few years we have become convinced that the public examination and the Rite of Confirmation ought to be two entirely separate services. The experiment has been tried in many places, and its value has been proved beyond cavil. Where the two are combined in the form of a single Sunday service, either the examination is a hurried, formal affair, or else the service is prolonged almost beyond the limits of human patience.

The Friday evening before the date of Confirmation is about the most suitable time for public examination. Let the examination be held within the church. It ought to be raised to the dignity of a service, and not be looked upon as an exhibition night. Let the church be lighted and the bell rung, as for an evening service. The choir ought to be present. If there be a vested choir, let them lead the way into the church in procession, with the confirmation class following, two by two, the pastor coming last. This, I understand, is the proper order nowadays in processions. Let the altar be adorned with cut flowers, and with whatever vestments the season of the Christian Year may require.

The service will begin with a suitable hymn, and with the usual Order of Evening Service, or Vespers. To give fitting dignity to the occasion, let the pastor appear in his robe and bands, or in his cassock, surplice and stole in congregations where these are used. The proper Psalm for the day ought to be sung, and not read responsively in the Reformed fashion. The proper lessons for the day ought to be read.

The entire service is followed down to the place for the sermon. The front pews will be occupied by the confirmation class. In-

stead of mounting the pulpit steps, the pastor will go to the lectern. He may address the congregation and class stating briefly the nature of the occasion. Then, taking up his Catechism and Bible History, he will examine the class on the Six Parts and the Bible History, together with the proof texts. He will select the most important parts, since even with a two hour service, it will not be possible to cover every detail.

It is not necessary to say that this will be an honest examination, and not a hypocritical frame-up, if the reader will pardon this vulgarism. Young children are not slow to realize the hollow mockery of an examination that is staged to deceive their elders. Children have often said to the writer, "Oh, some of the other church bodies confirm the children, and they have examinations too. But what do you think?" And with fine childish scorn they will add, "They give out the questions in advance! They don't learn anything, and they have to give out all the questions in advance!"

After the questions have been asked and answered the service will be closed by following the proper order in the hymnal. We have found that such a service, on the Friday evening next before Confirmation, is attended by a large portion of the congregation and their friends. It allows sufficient time to question the children thoroughly and without haste. Likewise it avoids the liturgical anomaly of a combination of public examination and confirmation on Sunday morning, with the temptation to mutilate the service in the interest of time. A well-conducted examination will consume two hours, including the opening and closing service. A properly conducted Confirmation service will require almost two hours. It is too tiring for all concerned, if the two are combined, and something is sure to be hurried through in a perfunctory manner.

The Sunday Service. The Rite of Confirmation will take place on Sunday morning. Palm Sunday is the traditional date, although in recent years there is a growing sentiment in favor of Whitsunday. Much is to be said in favor of this newer idea. It gives the pastor almost two months more time to instruct the children. It removes Confirmation Sunday, which ought to be somewhat of a festive day, from Holy Week. It allows the congregation to observe Palm Sunday undisturbed, instead of trying to divide the attention between Our Lord's triumphal entry and confirmation. It is more soundly symbolical, for the reception of the three thousand believers into the Apostolic Church on Pentecost suggests the reception of the class of children as members of the congregation.

On the day of confirmation the church will be prepared. While it is decidedly unliturgical to permit a lavish display of flowers during the Lenten season, yet we usually stretch a liturgical point on Palm Sunday, and the church is adorned in a festive manner. Great masses of fresh palms, lilies and other cut flowers adorn the chancel. There are church supply houses specializing in fresh palm leaves. These are much fresher and more beautiful than the pseudo-palms of dull green color that come in tubs and pails. One may buy a surprising display of fresh palm leaves for two or three dollars. These come in 25 pound bundles, and sell at the rate of about 25 for three dollars. One bundle will be enough for a small church, and two or more bundles for a larger one. The palm leaves are delivered wet, and they must be unwrapped immediately and spread out on the floor, and held open by means of tacks. They will dry out enough in a day and a night to permit them to remain open. Palms of this kind, not artificially colored a morose olive green, possess a surprising beauty. Their natural colors are rich greens and tans, of an unusually decorative quality.

The liturgy for the occasion is that properly used on Palm Sunday. The proper Introit, Collect, Gospel and Epistle for Palm Sunday (or Whitsunday, in case confirmation is on that day), will be used. White vestments must not be used on the altar. No local event, be it a confirmation, marriage or funeral, must be allowed to disturb the propria of the Christian Year.

If there be a vested choir, and if processions are the custom of the parish, the choir will lead the way into the church, approaching the chancel through the center aisle. The class will follow, two by two, with the pastor in the rear. All will remain standing while the pastor goes to the altar and begins the Order of Service.

After the sermon, the children to be confirmed may rise, facing the altar, and sing their confirmation hymn. "Let me be thine forever" is the hymn most often used. At the close of this hymn they may move slowly to the chancel rail. Careful preliminary drill must not be overlooked. The words of the Agenda will be read deliberately by the pastor.

There are two ways of performing the act of laying on of hands. If the class is a small one, all may kneel together at the altar rail. If the class is large, it will be necessary for them to kneel in groups. In some congregations they follow the old custom of kneeling one by one, as their names are called. Whatever method be used, it is well to follow the rubrics in the Agenda, which direct that the catechumens shall come forward "one by one, or in groups, as the pastor may have appointed, and, giving the pastor their right hand, kneel down before the altar."

After the laying on of hands, and the pronouncing of the Confirmation Benediction, (five different forms of which are provided in the Agenda), the pastor addresses the Invitation to the class, making the sign of the cross over them at the mention of the Holy Trinity. Then, the class still kneeling, the pastor will mount the altar step, indicate with a gesture that the congregation shall rise, and, facing the altar, he will read one of the prayers at the close of the order of service. Then follows the closing hymn and the benediction.

A friend in a distant city has written a thoughtful letter, in which he expresses the fear that some of us are following what he terms a distinctly Romanistic tendency, because we would follow orderly liturgical custom rather than the free-and-informal fad which flourished in some localities some years ago. This is the stock argument of the individualistic type of mind. We have every respect for the individualist, and we are certainly tolerant enough to admit that he has a right to exist unmolested.

No greater calamity could happen than to compel every congregation in our Synod to wear the same liturgical straightjacket. Some pastors and some congregations might find it quite uncomfortable. We will find the traditional type of mind in every community, and likewise the individualistic type. The traditionalist will prefer a dignified, orderly type of service, with due (and yet not legalistic) respect for churchly decorum. He will prefer an aesthetic background of good architecture, however simple its form, harmonious color, a dignified altar, churchly music, and a devotional type of service. He will strive to conform as much as possible to the liturgical traditions of his ecclesiastical group, in the interest of uniformity.

The individualistic type of man will be unhappy under such surroundings, and no greater injustice could be done him than to force him to conform to a traditional order. He may be, and invariably is, just as sound in faith as his conservative brother. But he will prefer to worship in a church that is less dignified in its design, he will like music of a more lively character than the old chorales and Gregorian chants, he will respond more readily to rhetorical free prayers, unexpected variations of liturgical form, and more informality all along the line.

Both tendencies have a right to exist. The writer of these lines is simply stating the case, without comment, of the conservative Devotional School of liturgical thought. We cannot and dare not overlook the fact that liturgical practice must be purely voluntary, and dare not be legalistic. The Word and Sacraments must always come first. We dare not shift the emphasis from the Means of Grace to the church furniture. Only a traitor would use aesthetic things as a smoke screen to hide laxity of doctrine and practice.

Since there are two ways of doing everything—the way of good taste and the way that isn't so good—we prefer to follow the former as much as possible. It is as easy to do things devotionally as to do them informally. If there are customs that are distinctively and historically Lutheran, there is no harm in following them, rather than trying out novelties, or imbibing the ways of Reformed sectarianism.

The individualist is only too ready to raise the cry of legalism and Romanism, regardless of whether his arguments are well founded or not. Years ago the individualist declared that a black robe and white bands are Romish, forgetting that black robes and white bands come from Geneva, not Rome, and a Roman priest in a black robe and white bands would create as much of a sensation as the Reverend Billy Sunday in a cope and biretta. If legalism is the argument, it will be found that the moderately advanced churchman is much more tolerant than his right-of-private-judgment brother. It is a curious bit of psychology that the liturgical-minded churchman will worship peacefully in a chapel that is as bare as a barn inside, and will tolerate without a murmur the most poverty-stricken liturgical practices. But it is equally curious that the individualist cannot possibly worship in a church with a rich liturgical background without a vigorous protest. We have never yet, after many years of careful observation, heard of a voter's meeting compelling a pastor to use candles, chant the service, or use Lutheran chorales and Gregorian Psalm Tones. But there are unnumbered cases on record where voter's meetings have been known to legislate against these very things. Legalism comes from the individualist camp, and not from the Devotional School. There are parishes where clerical vestments, the Common Service and the chalice were once prohibited by formal resolution, and the conservative group forced to submit. But whoever heard of a group of artistically inclined persons compelling a pastor to wear vestments that he was unwilling to wear, or use Plain Chant when he preferred music of the popular sort? Many of us of the aesthetic school have suffered through services that are liturgically wretched, have listened to crude singing, have read Psalms responsively like a sectarian, and have used hymns of the most shallow, pietistic sort, and all for the sake of the Word of God, which we prized more highly than aesthetic distress. But let the individualist sit through one service of the churchly sort, and he has quite enough. He will either unite with the "evangelical" type of church farther down the street, or if no such church exists, he will remain, with much complaint and protesting, and will work continually to change things to suit his particular views.

Organized Mission-Endeavor in the Rural Church

THE AVERAGE CHURCHMEMBER is not an outstanding success in mission work until he gets a new vision of what it means *not* to be saved. As long as the average church remains dull and lifeless toward personal mission work there can be no great progress. What blessings would accrue if a whole congregation could be persuaded to take an active interest in the endeavor of personal soul-winning!

A certain pastor in a rural community looked back on years of successful mission-work, but saw that more could be done by the people of the congregation. He marshalled all his facts, compiled statistics, laid plans and studied his present field thoroughly. With these he went before his executive-board. The board gave it's whole-hearted support to a planned personal soul-winning endeavor. With a prayer in his heart and a well-prepared plea the pastor stepped before his congregation. Much enthusiasm was aroused. The plan was accepted.

Centuries ago the Lord had said: "Go YE." Many of our people have forgotten their great privilege given to them by the Master and have come to look to their pastor as the only soul-winner. This idea is fundamentally wrong. The pastor is the field manager, the people are to be the sales-crew. The people are to present the Gospel. The pastor is to be called in after the prospect becomes too difficult for the average man to handle. The pastor may through a personal call and through instruction finally close the deal, so that the man has his name on the dotted line, namely in the Book of Life.

Many a pastor-missionary realizes that many more souls could be won for Christ, if more men and women in the community were willing to do the personal mission work. House to house canvassing has been tried, but such efforts have at best been only spasmodic. Could not some means be found to engage the rank and file of the members in a sustained effort in personal soul-winning, directed by the pastor and a staff of workers?

A Plan Put In Motion

A. A large map was made of the entire territory held by the three congregations served. Each congregation had its own map designed. On this map were listed all the families belonging to the church. These were shown by green thumb-tacks. Next all unchurched people were listed and shown with red tacks. As soon as a prospect wished to receive religious instruction the tack was changed to blue. Thus the congregation knew at a glance where its opportunities lay.

B. The home congregation of about fifty voters was divided into four districts. Each district met once each month.

C. Following materials were needed. 4 steel files with index (at Woolworth's for 20 cts.) Cards to record names of the unchurched and calls made on them. Pledge-cards to be given the members on which the name of the person to be called on was written. Post cards were printed, to be sent out to the unchurched at the rate of one each month. Each month's card carried a new message and invitation.

D. Young people were drafted to do the clerical work, such as taking care of the files, sending out cards keeping maps up-to-date, etc.

E. A series of sermonettes was prepared on the subject of personal soul-winning.

Form of Gatherings

Hymn. Prayer Sermonette. Hymn.
Business:

1. Pastor reports on the progress made in various groups.

2. The group reports on calls made. Certain prospects are viewed as to the best method of winning them. Difficulties are gone over and solved. Results are recorded. Pledge cards are then called in and filed under correct names. In time the record of a man once unchurched may look like this:

Mr. J. Jones	Unchurched	*Remarks*
Jan. called on	by W. Schultz	Was Methodist
Feb. " "	" H. Millier	Friendly
Mar. " "	" M. Wright	Went to church twice
		Regular in church,
		wishes to speak to pastor

April. Pastor called; will be in next adult class.

Thus the history of each case is recorded. The object is, of course, to get a new man to call on the prospect each month. Thus the man gets the impression that the whole church is interested in his welfare.

3. New prospects or unchurched found during the month are placed on the map and names filed for future work.

4. Names of the unchurched or prospects are now read, and one by one the various people in the group take certain names of people whom they will endeavor to bring to church.

5. Blessing, a hymn and the Lord's Prayer in unison.

The young people in their society and the children in the Saturday and Sunday School are using the same system in a simplified form.

Results

The people, the men, women and children, have become mission-minded. The joy of gaining a soul is unspeakable. It is remarkable how some of the old staid Germans in the congregation have caught the spirit and are doing fine work. When they have once gotten a soul, they become possessed by the passion for more souls. They got one and now they want a crowd. The people themselves come to church more regularly, for they must see if their calling has had results. So each member is drawn closer to the church. Much of the former spirit of criticism toward pastor, congregation, and individuals has fallen away, for the people are now interested in winning new souls for Christ.

There have been also, by the grace of God other tangible results. Many of the invited have been baptized or confirmed. Many have again at this time asked when the next classes will be formed. The whole community notices that the church people are interested in the unchurched, one and all. Unchurched people who have sometimes failed to respond at first, on meeting the pastor on the street, often stop and say they have received the cards and will soon try and come. The community has become Lutheran conscious.

This has been done in a community where our Synod has been preaching for 50 years. As Jowett says: "Never despair over any church or any community. PRAY a cloud no bigger than a man's hand, out of the sea of God's grace, and there will come out of it enough to break a drought of years and deluge all ISRAEL".

C. Austain Miles says aptly:

If to Christ our only King
Men redeemed we strive to bring,
Just one by one may this be done—
We must bring them one by one.

NOTE: The pastor using the above plan furnishes us with the following statistics for 1934:—

127 families, involving 422 souls have been contacted in the period of 3½ months of this year, 637 calls were made by the people. 381 cards have been sent out inviting these unchurched.
RESULTS: 7 adults were confirmed, 3 adults and 3 children over 7 years were baptized. 39 adults have again applied for instructions. 17 children have been won for the Saturday and Sunday School. 18 families have become regular in their attendance at the services. 12 adults, who had been confirmed more than 10 years were regained for the church.

Methods of Gaining Adults for Confirmation

John F. Schulz

The pastor of a well-organized congregation has a wonderful opportunity for missionary work. He has advantages above those of a missionary in a new field. He has a church building with all the necessary facilities, church machinery, including the many organizations within the congregation, an efficient Sunday School staff, able leaders, and in general, people with a knowledge of Christian fundamentals and willing to do something for their Savior and their Church. Unchurched people will more readily interest themselves in a well-organized congregation than in a small mission station. It is true, not all localities offer the same opportunities, but there are not many fields that offer no missionary possibilities whatever.

The writer has found conditions in his field of labor especially favorable, and by using local facilities and by interesting the congregation in a well-outlined and systematic program, a certain number of adults have been added to the congregation every year. In this work he has received many valuable suggestions from the American Lutheran, and now that the request has come to him from the Managing Editor to outline the methods which were used in gaining these adults for confirmation, he can cheerfully comply in the spirit of "give and take", and if some of the suggestions offered will help to gain souls for Christ and for His Church, he will consider his efforts well repaid.

I. Difficulties in Organizing a Class

People are usually hesitant in joining a regular class for confirmation. As a rule only such can be readily confirmed who have already made up their minds to join the Lutheran Church. This includes relatives of members in the congregation or people that have some knowledge of the Lutheran Church and its teachings and have, perhaps, for some time attended Lutheran services. We are in this article concerned more especially about the large number of those in the community who are not interested in the Lutheran Church or in any other church. Our first work with such people consists in proving to them the value of the Church, church work, and church services, and, if we have been successful in this, then it will be necessary to interest them in the Lutheran Church and to make clear to them why they ought to join the Lutheran Church in preference to any other church.

Common Arguments Against Church

1. They have no time;
2. It costs too much;
3. There are so many hypocrites and dishonest and bad people in the church;
4. There are too many church denominations, and they are constantly fighting against each other;
5. There are hundreds of people outside of the church who are just as good or even better than many people in the church;
6. We do what is right, and God will surely not expect more.

Common Arguments Against The Lutheran Church

1. Other churches are just as good;
2. The Lutheran Church is too strict;
3. It does not accept lodge members;
4. It demands instruction, and other churches do not;
5. The Lutheran pastor has refused to bury some one who was a good man.
6. Lutheran pastors never join with other pastors in joint patriotic and other services;
7. Lutherans are too much like the Catholics.

Of course, it is possible by private instruction in a number of cases to remove such prejudices and to persuade them to join the class, but the fact remains that this method requires a large amount of private advance instruction on the part of the pastor which demands more time than the average pastor of a congregation is able to contribute. The average unchurched individual has certain preconceived notions and ideas about the Christian religion to which he clings for his own justification. He has read religious articles in papers and magazines which stress external morality and character as sufficient for this life and the life which is to come. He has listened to many funeral addresses delivered by representatives of the Christian religion and has come to the logical conclusion that church connection and church activity are not essential factors in gaining an entrance into the kingdom of God. He declares: "If Mr. A has gone to heaven as Rev. X has declared at the funeral, then surely I have as much if not a greater chance to reach heaven without the church and its services." The public press, public religious demonstrations, funeral sermons, the lodge and modernism all combine to make morality the essential requisite for Christianity, to produce among the unchurched self-sufficiency and self-righteousness. . Christianity is confounded with mere civilization; external goodishness has taken the place of that genuine goodness required by God's Law; and, in general, there is evident everywhere a great deal of superficial religiousness with little or no conception of the true religion revealed in the Holy Scriptures. The average unchurched individual is not a publican but a Pharisee. He has no inclination to join the church and, therefore he has no inclination to join a class for instruction. There are certain barriers which must be broken down before entrance can be made into the heart for true religion. These barriers cannot be broken down by human reason and arguments,—they can be broken down only by the power of God's Word.

Since mis-information about the Lutheran Church and misconception of the Christian religion constitute the chief difficulties in gaining adults for confirmation, the writer has in the past seven years offered every fall a series of public lectures on the fundamentals of the Christian religion, and through such lectures,—which give the necessary information and dispel the many prejudices by the power of God's Word,—it has been possible to gain a class every year.

II. Public Lectures

Question: How many lectures do you deliver?
Answer: Eighteen.
Question: On what days are these lectures delivered?
Answer: Every Sunday, Monday and Thursday.
Question: What was the average attendance in the past two series?
Answer: Two hundred twenty-five.
Question: What percentage of your audience is unchurched?
Answer: About thirty-five per cent.
Question: How do you divide the doctrines of the Catechism into these eighteen lectures?
Answer: Following is an outline of the last series:
Lectures 1 to 6, "The Ten Commandments"; Lecture 7, "Sin"; Lecture 8, "The True God"; Lecture 9, "Creation"; Lecture 10, "The Person of Christ"; Lecture 11, "Redemption"; Lecture 12, "The Holy Ghost"; Lecture 13, "The Church"; Lecture 14, "Death, Heaven, Hell, Eternity"; Lecture 15, "Prayer — The Lord's Prayer"; Lecture 16, "Baptism"; Lecture 17, "Essence of Lord's Supper"; Lecture 18, "The Worthy Communicant".
Question: If a person attends all lectures, does it make him eligible to membership?
Answer: No. A class is organized immediately after the lecture series is concluded, and those who are interested either in further instruction or have already decided to join the church are asked to join this class. It is emphasized that the joining of this class will involve no obligations, and no pressure will be brought to bear upon people to join the church.
Question: How many periods of instruction do you give in this organized class?
Answer: From eight to twelve depending upon the amount covered in the eighteen lectures.
Question: How do you get the unchurched to the lectures?
Answer: That brings us again to the beginning of our article.

III. Canvass

A systematic house-to-house canvass is absolutely essential for any concerted missionary endeavor. If we are to gain the unchurched we must know who they are and where they live. If the lectures are held in the fall, this canvass should be made in the early spring. It is not necessary to explain the house-to-house canvass in this article, since a number of articles have appeared in the American Lutheran on this subject in the past. A very exhaustive treatment and detailed explanation of this canvass will be found in the January issue, 1928, of the AMERICAN LUTHERAN, Volume XI, Number 1, Page 7, by O. F. Feucht under the heading: "How to Conduct a Missionary Canvass".

IV. FOLLOW UP

A canvass is of little value, if it is not followed up. The success of the lectures in the fall depends upon the advance work during the summer on the basis of this canvass.

V. ADVANCE WORK

Calls, calls, calls, and more calls. Distribution of literature. Mailing lists. Thorough outline and preparation of lectures. Preliminary advertising of lectures. Setting the date and giving people the following information:

1. Attendance at the lectures costs nothing..
2. No memory work is necessary.
3. Attendance involves no obligation.
4. If after attending the lectures they do not care to join the class, no effort will be made to compel them.
5. These lectures are held to give the necessary information, to offer you an opportunity to learn what the Lutheran Church teaches and what it stands for. When the lectures are concluded, you can do as you please.—

Advance announcements in the local paper. If possible, a few paid ads should be placed.

VI. ADVANCE WORK WITH THE CHURCH

Every opportunity should be used to emphasize local missionary work in the congregation. It is possible at various group meetings, Ladies' Aid meetings, Young People's meetings, and other activities to explain in detail to members the entire missionary program including the lectures and appeal to them for their cooperation. Members of the congregation will know of relatives or friends or neighbors that are not connected with any church. They should be encouraged to speak to them about the lectures and give them the information listed in Paragraph V.

This must be emphasized: That such a missionary program is not the program of the pastor alone, but it is the program of the entire congregation, that active participation on the part of the members is essential to the success of the undertaking, and such active participation includes:

1. That they attend these lectures themselves and
2. That they invite the unchurched,—better still,—bring the unchurched to these lectures.

VII. GUARANTEE AUDIENCE

Pastors have hesitated in conducting such a series of lectures, because they feared that the attendance would be very small and thus the attempt would prove a failure. It is possible for a period of six weeks with three lectures a week, to hold the interest of the people? So much is true, if we depend on mission material alone for an attendance at these lectures, the audience will not be very large. Let us suppose that a certain number of unchurched, on whom we depend, actually made their appearance, the size of the audience would be of such a nature that it would be decidedly discouraging for those prospects who happen to be present. The impression leaves them cold. They will conclude that if the members of the congregation are not interested in these lectures, then these lectures cannot be of such vital importance for them.

Accordingly, it is advisable for the success of these lectures to obtain in advance a "guarantee audience", namely, members of the congregation who have promised that they will, if possible, attend every one of these lectures or at least as many of them as possible. In my present field I have always requested a guarantee of at least one hundred and fifty communicant members. It must be explained to them that outside of the benefits that will accrue to them from these lectures, they are actually participating in the church's missionary program. The mere fact that they are occupying a seat in church during the lectures will help to gain souls for Christ. This drive for a membership audience should begin at least a month in advance. Appeals should be made to the Young People's Society, the Ladies' Aids, or any other smaller group within the congregation. A special appeal should be made to the voting members of the congregation. In two or three Sundays previous announcements of these lectures should be made in the church with a special appeal to the members to attend.

VIII. SIGNATURES

It is not sufficient to receive from the members a verbal promise, but this promise should be made below their signatures, (Fig. I). In my experience I have found that such promises on

---

I herewith declare my willingness to support the missionary program and to attend, if possible, all the eighteen lectures on "The Fundamentals of the Christian Religion."

Signed...

Figure I.

---

the average have been kept, and, when I enter the church for the first lecture I am confident in advance that there will be at least one hundred and fifty people present and perhaps more than two hundred. The attendance at these lectures is bound to increase as the series continues. A large crowd is an incentive to the general public and will produce a larger crowd. Other members of the congregation who have not made any special promise are attracted and will begin to come. However, the greatest value of a good audience for these lectures is the impression it makes upon the unchurched who attend the lectures and the general publicity they will give these lectures throughout the community. They will tell others of these meetings with the result that in the course of time many other visitors make their appearance who have not been on the pastor's list of prospects. It may be stated here that in every class of adults confirmed in the past seven years a certain number of people have been confirmed who were not on the pastor's list of prospects before the lecture season opened. When people have missed a number of lectures in the beginning and are anxious to be confirmed with this particular class, such people are given the necessary private instructions before the regular class is organized.

IX. ADVANCE WORK OF PASTOR

Have a complete outline of every lecture ready at least a month before the lectures begin. It is important that these lectures are well-prepared. A special effort should be made to make these lectures as simple and interesting as possible. Stories and examples, especially, Bible stories, should be used to illustrate. The lectures are primarily directed to the unchurched and prospects who have little or no conception of the fundamentals of the Christian religion.

Arrange the congregational work in such a way that the three or four weeks previous to the lectures can be devoted to making calls. It is at this time that the greatest amount of work can be done. The parish paper can do much to advertise the lectures and to arouse interest and enthusiasm among the members of the congregation. If there is no parish paper, it will pay at this time to print or mimeograph special circulars for mailing and general distribution. Arrange a program for every lecture and have the materials ready in advance.

X. MATERIALS

The following material is distributed at every lecture: a mimeographed copy which contains a resume of the lecture of the evening for people to take home and study privately; penny catechisms and memory sheets containing important passages of the catechism, the general confession, etc., a portion of which is read in unison at every lecture. It will be found that those who intend to join the church have committed to memory a large portion of the small catechism and other passages by the time the lectures are concluded.

XI. LECTURE PROGRAM

Time: 7:30 to 9:00 P. M.
1. Organ prelude.
2. Hymn.
3. Scripture, prayer, and Creed in unison.
4. Distribution of materials.
5. First part of lecture.
6. Hymn, or choir, or quartette selection.
7. The reading in unison of a chief part of the catechism.
8. Question box.
9. Hymn, choir, or quartette selection.
10. Second part of lecture.

11. Collection of questions.

12. Closing service.

Special selections by the choir or a quartette for numbers 6 and 9 will make the lectures more attractive. These numbers should be well prepared in advance. No collection is taken during the lecture. An offering plate is placed at the rear of the church, but people are informed at every lecture that contributions are not necessary. The proceeds of this offering have always been sufficient to cover the cost of all materials and a portion of the advance advertising.

XII   QUESTION BOX

An attractive feature at these lectures is the Question Box. People are anxious to ask questions if they can do so without revealing their ingnorance. The answering of the questions of the Question Box has done more, I believe, to hold the interest of the people in these lectures than the lectures themselves. Most of the questions involve some doctrine of the catechism. The answer to a direct question is naturally more interesting to the audience than any objevtive presentation of the same doctrine, and thus the Question Box can be used to explain as fully as possible the doctrine involved. If the lecture of the evening is on "Sin", and a question is received on "Baptism", it is not advisable to hold that question to the particular evening when "Baptism" is the subject of the lecture, but to answer the question at once as fully as the time permits, and on the evening when the subject of "Babtism" is treated, to briefly refer to the points already covered through the Question Box. The lectures, although well outlined, must be sufficiently flexible to allow more time for the Question Box when necessary.

During the last series a total of two hundred forty-three questions were received through the Question Box. One hundred eighty-two of these were simple questions of the Catechism; Commandments 17· Original Sin 3; The Person of Christ 26; Church, including the various denominations 33; Baptism 18; The Office of the Ministry 15· Heaven 1; Catholic Church 28; Lodge 11; Conversion 3; Everlasting Punishment 17; Confession 1; Prayer 5; Evolution 4.

XIII.   HOW TO OBTAIN QUESTIONS

Few people will contribute questions unless they can do so without being found out. There are some who care not if they are seen writing a question, but they do not want people to know what particular question they have asked.

At the beginning of the lecture distribute to every person present a pencil and a slip of paper. Explain the purpose of these slips and announce that all slips will be collected at the close of the lecture. When the time arrives, tell them to fold the papers once and to place them into the collection plates when they are passed.

XVI.   MISSION BOARD

After the regular house-to-house canvass has been completed, advance calls can be made by certain members of the congregation more especially qualified for such work. Such calls will save the pastor much time and thus give him an opportunity to follow up the more prospective material. Such members can be organized into a Mission Board or a Mission Society. This organization can do much of the routine work of the canvass and have an accurate record kept of all calls made and the information received. It can also stimulate interest among the other members of the congregation for personal mission work. The most active and competent workers are usually found in some organization within the congregation and, accordingly, it is wise to include on this board the following people: Two elders of the congregation selected by the church council; the hospice committees and the president of the Ladies' Aids, Young People's Societies; and the Superintendent of the Sunday School. This board can be permanent throughout the year with regular meetings at least once a month, and before any special missionary program or previous to a lecture course, once or twice a week.

XV.   COUNTRY CANVASS

It is usually difficult to obtain canvassers for country districts. The following method may be used: Make a map of every township. Maps of the county can be obtained at the Court House with the names of the land owners. Arrange a meeting of members living in one township or a number of connected townships.

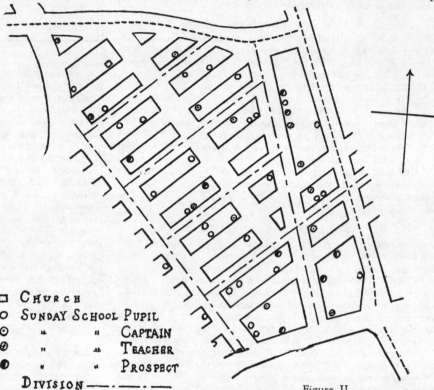

□ CHURCH
○ SUNDAY SCHOOL PUPIL
⊙ "   " CAPTAIN
⊘ "   " TEACHER
◕ "   " PROSPECT

DIVISION —·—·—·—

Figure II

These members will know all people living in the township and the exact location of every residence. Mark such locations on the map. Obtain the same information required on a regular canvass card. More information may be obtained in such meetings than through a regular canvass, and with some one present to take down the most important statements concerning a family, it is possible to place much additional information on the rear of the card. The church connection may also be indicated on the map through colors. (Fig. II)

XVI.   SMALL CITY CANVASS

It is difficult to obtain canvassers for a small city with two thousand or less inhabitants, because everybody knows everybody, and it is somewhat awkward for canvassers to approach one whom they really know and obtain the necessary information for the canvass card. The following system can be used: Divide the city into sections, with ten to twenty families belonging to the church in each section. Arrange meetings of all families living in one, perhaps, as a surprise to some family not so well acquainted in the congregation. It is well to have them bring lunch, to make such meetings more sociable. The meeting is opened with Scripture reading and prayer. A short address is given on personal mission work, stressing the responsibility of every Christian to reach out among the unchurched in missionary endeavor. A map has been prepared for that particular section of the city with the numbers of the houses placed in their respective place. The evening is devoted to placing names on the map, taking each block separately. Use the city directory if one is available. When the name is placed on the map it is at the same time also placed on a regular canvass card before proceeding to the next name. (Fig. III). Many statements are made by the people concerning certain families, and it is well to have some one in the meeting who is able to take down the most important of these remarks in shorthand. It is possible also to use each of these groups to make calls in their immediate neighborhood. Cards of prospects may be distributed among the group present, urging them to make a call and, if possible, to bring them to church services. If a meeting of each of these groups is held

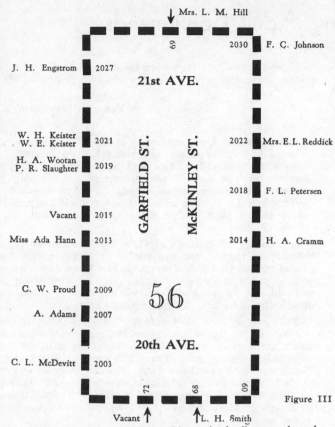

Figure III

↓ Mrs. L. M. Hill

J. H. Engstrom 2027
21st AVE.
69   2030   F. C. Johnson

W. H. Keister
W. E. Keister 2021   2022   Mrs. E. L. Reddick

H. A. Wootan
P. R. Slaughter 2019

2018   F. L. Petersen

Vacant 2015

Miss Ada Hann 2013   2014   H. A. Cramm

GARFIELD ST.   McKINLEY ST.

C. W. Proud 2009   56

A. Adams 2007

20th AVE.

C. L. McDevitt 2003

72   68   60
Vacant ↑   ↑ L. H. Smith

every three or six montns, it is possible to check all removals and arrivals and thus keep the map and the canvass cards up to date.

Such meetings bring the pastor into contact with almost all of his members every year for the purpose of personal missionary work. They help to strengthen Christianity, to increase interest in church work and church attendance, and, above all, make the members of the church mission minded. This method has tremendous value even though no unchurched were gained.

XVII. FOLLOW-UP CANVASS

The best plan is to have a house-to-house canvass every year. It is, however, in many congregations difficult to obtain enough people for this work every year. If the first canvass has been sufficiently thorough, the records can be kept up to date for a Make map of one ward and number each block in that ward. Then make a large map of every block and with the aid of the city directory place the number of every residence on the map in its exact location. Sort the canvass cards of the previous year and group them according to blocks. The new directory will give all changes made since the last canvass, and these are compared with the canvass cards. When the card harmonizes with the directory and the information is complete, mark "No Call" on the map. The result will be that only a few calls for each block are necessary to bring the canvass up to date.

If this work is done by a group of people, the Mission Board, or the Mission Society, much additional information may be obtained in these meetings, prospects discussed and people encouraged to make missionary calls.

XVIII. MAILING LIST

On the basis of the canvass a live mailing list should be kept. The cost of mailing is very insignificant compared to the results obtained. Such mailing judiciously done will more than pay for itself in actual coin. At certain times, as for instance before Lent, Easter, Christmas, or before the lecture season begins the entire mailing should be used, while at other times special letters of invitation to a certain division or the more prospective members on the list may be sufficient. The mailing list should always be kept up to date.

XIX. PARISH PAPER

The parish paper is especially valuable in gaining adults for confirmation, and previous to the lecture season can be placed entirely into the service of the missionary program. The weekly paper is to be preferred. It gives the pastor an opportunity to reach the people every week, and the members are informed regarding all activities of the week and the Sunday services. Appeals can be made when they are still warm. Such a paper should be made as attractive as possible with an appeal to the "outsider" both in contents and make-up.

Methods and church machinery are of no value in themselves and cannot take the place of consecrated personal evangelism. The gospel "is the power of God unto salvation", and the command of Christ reads: "Go . . . . and preach the gospel!" The fact remains, however, that our churches are surrounded by thousands of people that never attend church services and, therefore, cannot be affected by the proclamation of the gospel. Our great purpose and desire must be to bring the unchurched into contact with the Word of God that the Holy Spirit might kindle faith in their hearts, and when methods and church machinery accomplish this purpose, they become valuable agencies in the service of Christ for the salvation of souls.

Commissioning Service for a Missionary Canvass
OSCAR E. FEUCHT

Since this day has been set apart for a systematic missionary canvass, and a goodly number of our fellow-Christians have declared themselves willing to do this noble work, it behooves us to take encouragement from the command of our Lord as laid down in the Holy Scriptures.

Hear then the Word of God as recorded in St. John chapter 20th (19-21): Then the same day at evening, being the first day of the week, when the doors were shut where the disciples were assembled for fear of the Jews, came Jesus and stood in the midst, and saith unto them, Peace be unto you. And when he had so said, He showed unto them His hands and His side. Then were the disciples glad, when they saw the Lord. Then said Jesus to them again, Peace be unto you: as my Father hath sent me, even so I send you. Also in St. Luke chapter 10th (1-2): Now after these things the Lord appointed seventy others, and sent them two and two before His face into every city and place, whither He himself was about to come. And He said unto them, The harvest indeed is plenteous, but the laborers are few; pray ye therefore the Lord of the harvest, that He send forth laborers into His harvest.

Dear Fellow-workers in the cause of Christ: You have volunteered to make a house missionary visitation in the interest of the upbuilding and extension of Christ's Kingdom. In accordance with the Scriptures which you have heard, I as pastor of this congregation do now commission you to do your Lord's bidding and bring to those who are outside of the pale of the Christian Church the soul-comforting message of the gospel, that Christ's kingdom may be advanced among us and precious souls may be saved. Go, then, in His name; and may the Holy Spirit direct you in presenting the blessings of Christ's kingdom and abundantly crown your labors with success. Go in the Saviour's Name and for His glory. Amen.

Since it is the Lord alone that giveth the increase, let us arise and unite in prayer to Almighty God for His blessing upon these, His co-workers and upon this missionary undertaking:

PRAYER.—O Lord, our God, Thou hast made us a royal priesthood, that we should show forth the praises of Him who hath called us out of darkness into His marvellous light. Thou hast given to Thy Holy Christian Church, to every true believer, the privilege of seeking souls in error and sin. Fill us with a due appreciation of the glorious gospel we possess. Pour out the quickening power of the Holy Spirit into our hearts that we may be efficient witnesses of Christ. Accompany these Thy messengers as they go through the highways and streets of this city. Grant that those whom they meet may be touched with the Church's invitation. Lead them through repentance and faith to the foot of the cross and thus into Thy kingdom. Consecrate and hallow us all to the service of winning souls, and make us worthy workmen upon the temple of Thy Church. Grant this O Lord for the sake of Jesus Christ our King, who reigneth together with Thee and the Holy Ghost in equal majesty and glory forever and ever. Amen.

133

The Art of Keeping Adult Confirmands

PHILIPP LANGE

THE ADULT CONFIRMATION CLASS brings the unchurched men and women under our influence but for a short time. Its sole function is to instruct. If by a course of lectures we can ground the adults in a clear apprehension of the cardinal doctrines of the Christian religion as taught by our church, and added to this bring them to a sense of a personal, individual responsibility to God, to an acceptance of Christ, and to an intelligent expression of loyalty to the church, the end of the class is accomplished.

What becomes, then, of these new converts? Their confirmation has launched them, as it were, and now they must sail as best they can. But surely this is not a pastoral training of these people. It has been held that a truly converted man will work out his own training. And so the great energy of the church has been directed to the conversion of souls. The converts have been brought into the fold and left pretty much to shift for themselves. Now if all men were converted like Paul, this plan of Christian culture, or rather, no plan, might have good results. But in an established church like ours of today, the great bulk of adult membership comes into the Christian life as a plant grows to maturity: "First the blade, then the ear, after that the full corn in the ear." And if, from year to year, we postpone the work of giving our adult confirmands the special care and culture that they need, because we see nothing tangible that we can do at once, the majority of these people will never attain to a stage of full maturity, but may even wilt and die in the "blade" period.

FOUR CLASSES OF ADULT CONFIRMANDS

There are, first of all, those regenerated adults who, within a short time, ripen into full Christian manhood or womanhood. They attend the Sunday services regularly. They take an active interest in the affairs of the congregation and the church at large. They thoroughly enjoy their church affiliation. They are enthusiastic workers, and not a few of them more appreciative of the privileges and opportunities of the church than those who have been under the sanctifying influence of God's word all their lives. Some of them develop into most efficient leaders and are elected to the most important offices of the church.

Others remain at a standstill in their state of conversion, never advance beyond the "blade" stage. They make diligent use of the means of grace, but there is little or no growth in their spiritual life. One of the most pathetic statements in the New Testament is the declaration of Paul to the Corinthians (1 Cor. 3, 1-3) that they were still "babes in Christ", in that they had made so little progress in the Christian life since they accepted Jesus as their Savior. In too many cases of adult confirmands there is a feeling that when once a person has received a course of instruction, has made a public profession of faith and been received into church membership, they may rest satisfied. But the Christian life should be just beginning its experience of growth and fruitfulness with this enlistment. If the soldier were to imagine that he has nothing more to do after having been recruited, there would be no victories for him.

In our next class of adult converts, we find those who prove faithful during the period of instruction, but who are easily tempted to be drawn away from the influence of the Word of God and the members of the church. They are the backsliders. They need immediate attention, and are easily won again to resume their Christian duties. In many of these cases we find that, in the hour of affliction or on their death bed, they repent of their unfaithfulness, recall the training they have received at one time, and reëmbrace their Savior and His atonement for their sins.

Here's an example of a woman confirmed as an adult in 1927, breaking her confirmation vow, hitting the old trail of sin and shame, stricken with mental affliction, and now seeking peace and comfort for her sin-disturbed soul, viz:

State Hospital,
Mendota, Wisconsin,

Dear Rev. Lange:

Six years ago I was confirmed as one of your adults. Then I had Jesus in my heart and I loved to go to church. But now, Rev. Lange, I am away from God and church and home. I am writing to you for help. Do you still remember me? Please, write to me and tell me how I can come back to Jesus again. I am very sorry that I have drifted away from the church. Is there still hope for me?

The final group consists of those who soon after their confirmation neglect the reading of their Bible and the habit of prayer and public worship. The Word of God was not deeply rooted in their hearts. They have returned to their old life of unbelief and worldliness. They resent admonition. Their hearts have become hardened.

"Well, pastor, it is all over now," said an officer of the congregation to the writer after the confirmation of an adult class a few weeks ago; whereupon he received the reply, "All over now, did you say? The work has just begun. The foundation has been laid. The superstructure of spiritual culture and growth must now be erected. Having won these men and women, we must now try to keep them. The campaign of campaigns is now on, the most important work of all."

Quite naturally any pastor who has prepared a class of adults for church membership seriously considers the danger of losing them. He knows that they are exposed to the same temptations and trials as the rest of his parishioners. He is painfully sensible that they are not indoctrinated as well and not fortified as strongly against the onslaughts of the devil as those who have been born and reared in the church, and may soon fall away. The parable of the sower teaches him that he cannot expect to keep them all. Is it possible, however, with proper care to render the defections less numerous? We believe it is if we plan definitely for the training of those who have united with the church as adults and are just beginning the Christian life. We must observe the following factors in keeping these young converts within the fold of the church.

MAGNETIC POWER IN THE PULPIT

So much depends on the impressions that the new church-goers gain from our sermons. The church service must present, in its simplest, most direct form, the great verities of our faith. If we are to train our new adult converts through the instruction of the pulpit, we must have in view their special wants and weaknesses. They are young Christians. They have just entered the fold. We dare not take too much for granted. Our subjects and material must be carefully chosen. We often complain of the fickleness of the adult confirmands. Today they are all fire and enthusiasm, tomorrow they are cold and dead. We are then apt to become discouraged. We need to study the character of these people to see in it the natural order of development, and really find encouragement in it. This is not always fickleness and instability, but often the very nature of these people. A careful and continual study of this immature phase of the Christian life must be made to know it and to treat it accordingly. It is for us, dear brethren, to stand by the young and faltering converts. While we set a lofty standard before them in the pulpit, let us make them feel that we understand their own peculiar frailties and follies.

Generalities must be avoided in any sermon and especially in messages designed to indoctrinate adult confirmands. There must be an appeal to the heart. The Gospel must be proclaimed in a vigorous and stimulating manner, so that our adult friends may come regularly and eagerly to hear the word of salvation and thus grow in their knowledge of the Savior and in their zeal to help others.

Let us employ the simplest style possible. That is, after all, in any pulpit the most forceful and effective. There are preachers in our church who use one vocabulary in the pulpit and quite another in daily intercourse, in the discussion of daily happenings, and in the statement of their own feelings and purposes. It was said of Henry Clay that he made his friends with one vocabulary and lost the presidency with another. To strengthen the faith of new churchgoers we must avoid high-flown and bombastic preachment. Our age will have none of it. It knows that the language which a man uses when he talks about the things which interest him in daily life is the language that reveals the man. If a pastor thinks that simple, soulful words are easily spoken, and that they are the sign of lack of preparation, let him try to use them and he will discern his mistake. The form that will have the greatest success in the pulpit is the simple story of the cross translated into the terms familiar to the most illiterate and most irreligious. There is a constant danger of a pastor coming under the category of the Scottish clergyman who was said to be on week days invisible, and on Sundays incomprehensible.

The pulpit, indeed, plays an important factor in winning and holding adult confirmands. A pastor that is trying to do thorough and earnest work at the adult class meetings is very much buttressed in his position if the pulpit gives evidence of the same kind of work. On the other hand, an adult group may become, entirely against its will, an element undermining his influence, if the people, having learned from the class lectures what sincere and practical Christianity is, discover that his treatment of Christian truths in the pulpit is self-centered or slipshod.

Following Up Absentees

Absenteeism must be nipped in the bud. Very often a small misunderstanding is the cause of an absence. It may be that one feels slighted because no one has spoken to him at the church. Perhaps he does not fully understand the financing of the church and has not, for some unknown reason, used his church envelopes regularly, and the financial secretary has mailed him a statement showing the amounts he has up to that day contributed to the church and specifying also the needs of the congregation. They want only his money, he feels. Countless other slight objections may arise. We must be sure that these men and women are never absent for a long period of time without being written to, called up on the telephone, or visited in person. We must adopt a fixed custom to inquire into all absences.

The best way to reclaim the backsliders is to point out to them in an earnest way the error of their ways, to prevail upon them to return to the fold, and also to seek, with quick and unhesitating determination, to help them at the first sign of their slipping away. A special handbook to use in this form of service is the Epistle to the Hebrews. It was written to help weak Christians of the early church, many of whom were slipping because of the hardships involved in being faithful. As intimated at the beginning of the second chapter, some of them were drifting away. The writer of this letter sought to strengthen their faith by picturing what the Lord had done for them and the salvation of the world, also by picturing Him as now interceding for them at the mediatorial throne of God. He sought to show how through the Old Testament times God's servants had made a real contribution to the welfare of Israel and the race had been true to their faith in Christ, as the coming Messiah, though that meant suffering and even death. The special appeal is then found in the first part of the twelfth chapter, followed by many practical suggestions about how to be steadfast as true Christians to the end. Let us get the spirit of this epistle, and God will bless its use as we seek to press home the thought therein upon the hearts and consciences of those who are slipping back to the old life out of Christ, or are considering the temptations to do so, and thus hope to keep them from falling away, or to encourage them to return to their former allegiance to Christ.

Letter to Absentees

Dear fellow-member:

The church has been a potent factor in your life in bringing you to Christ and teaching you the Gospel of your eternal salvation. You have publicly professed your faith in the Lord and loyalty to the church. We know that, for a short time at least, you have worshipped with us and shown a lively interest in the work of the church.

Lately we have missed you at our church services. Your absence is deeply regretted. It is just during these modern times when the world is filled with indifference and materialism that we Christians need the regular weekly visit to the holy courts of the Lord. It is just when all the world is chasing after worldly amusement that Christians should give their souls a feast of the "milk of the divine word."

The result of irregular or non-church attendance is a decline in spiritual life, which, in many cases, terminates in spiritual and eternal death. As surely as you would starve to death physically if you did not partake of food, so surely your spiritual life, engendered by the Holy Spirit through the Word of God, will decline and weaken if you remove yourself from the life-sustaining influence of the Sunday services.

God is not under any obligations to you. That He has called and enlightened you with His gifts is purely a work of grace. And you have His promise that He will keep you in His grace if you remain under the influence of His Word. Therefore, do not take the risk of forfeiting His grace and salvation by neglecting to hear the preaching of His Word. Look upon every Sunday as though it might be your last chance to hear the gospel of Jesus Christ on earth, and our pastor will be inspired by your presence and happy to note that the instructions you have received from him some time ago have taken deep root in your heart and are bringing forth abundant fruit.

It is our aim, dear friend, to make our church services and also the mid-week meetings so full of interest and helpfulness that no one will stay away unless prevented by some unusual cause. If sick or in trouble, please, notify us that some one may call.

Cordially yours,

Hope Lutheran Church.

Systematic Study of the Bible

Most of our adult confirmands have never been Bible readers. They must be trained to read the Book intelligently and systematically. They must be shown the great importance of attending the meetings of the Bible Class. These sessions may be made the means of increasing their love for God's Word and of deepening and strengthening their spiritual life. We must see to it that the atmosphere at these meetings is such that it will seem the natural thing for significant spiritual decisions to be made. Religion takes on a more tender and engaging aspect to these new members. The truths that are taught seem to come home closer. Prayer and song very often are more fervent and hearty. Our dear friends learn more effectually in this way how practical a thing religion is. And it is the best school to learn the exercise of whatever gifts they may have.

Private devotional study of the Word of God should be emphasized. Nothing so nurtures and strengthens faith and zeal as daily Bible reading. It will help to inculcate an ever increasing measure of readiness to deny self and to put Christ first.

At these meetings we may also draw attention to the history of the Lutheran church. It is one of the shining pages in the record's of Christ's kingdom. Her heroes, her achievements, her landmarks, her place in the church's program and progress, are all worthy of recognition and study. Let us remind our newcomers that they belong to a great church and are expected to walk worthy of her history. Once give these people a history, and give it enthusiastically, and we have welded still another bond of allegiance to hold them together in the fold.

SENSE OF RESPONSIBILITY FOR OTHERS

Let us show our new converts the place Providence has marked out for the Lutheran church in this country. When we get them to think of the countless number of churchless men and women that surround them in every city and rural district and to remember that they too can get the truths of Christianity in the Lutheran church in purer form than in any other, it is enough to stir all the Christian zeal that's in them.

We have seen repeated in the case of adult confirmands, over and over again, the scene in the first chapter of John, where Andrew brings Peter, and Philip Nathanael, to Christ. It seems the most natural thing in the world for young converts to look around for some relative or friend or mere acquaintance to make them find the same peace and joy. Perhaps we do not encourage that natural tendency in them as much as we ought to. If we make these folks feel that we expect them to take charge of those over whom they have influence, and inquire after their success, we are training them for personal work and gaining an ever firmer hold on them. Having been won in a missionary way, and now being trained in the art of winning souls, they will become inspired with an evangelistic zeal.

Furthermore, our adults, in the very process of winning others to Christ, establish associations between themselves and those won that go on forever. They are now not only held to the church by their devotion to Christ, but also by a number of precious heart ties. Now we do not define the Christian life by our teachings alone; but those people define the Christian life in the most eloquent way possible —they live that definition. Let us do everything we can to encourage in our newly converted members the sense of responsibility for those who are still without the pale of the church.

THE SOCIAL ELEMENT

A social or reception for the new members may be planned soon after the day of their confirmation. An interesting program should be arranged for this fellowship evening. The key note of this reception should be friendliness. Let everyone get acquainted. And now that the newcomers have been welcomed into the church by pastor and people and their names learned by all, there should be a continuation of this friendly feeling.

It is something very pleasant to see how the newly confirmed adults are attracted to members of the congregation in the various organizations, and it is surprising, at times, to see how strong these attachments are. But it will not do to leave it there. If no provision is made to perpetuate these associations, we shall find other interests drawing them away from the church fellowship. If most of the people in the congregation are failing to render the service of Christian companionship to these fellow members, then it is quite difficult for the pastor to hold them. The chill of indifferent members is too much of a handicap. It doesn't make any difference how warm the weather is during the day, if a killing frost bites the flower at night. So it is in the church. The pastor may radiate a boundless amount of spiritual warmth and energy, but he cannot keep the chill of aloofness away from the new converts. "Well, let us see how these adults will hold out!" What a greeting for young timid Christians! That sort of cold, critical attitude towards the untried is enough to freeze the faith clean out of new members. We must use, as a means of training, the association of the parishioners with the proper age and type of the new accessions. We must be very frank and earnest in pointing out to our members their God-given duties towards these new brethren in Christ. We must with their assistance furnish the necessary material for intimacies and companionships, so that our adult confirmands will never be tempted to form these outside.

That the gospel of Jesus Christ is "the power of God unto salvation" is still true, and in this truth lies the hope in nurturing and strengthening regenerated adults and in stopping the leakage among these souls. Through the tidings of grace and peace there goes forth an actual energy of God to make new creatures of sinners and to keep them on the path of righteousness. Missionary reports bear out this statement every year that God has renewed and fortified the life of men, where the gospel has been proclaimed. According to the power that is already working in us, God is able to do exceeding abundantly above all that we ask or think. This exceedingly abundant power of God is our reliance in the service of winning and keeping adult souls.

Make Phonograph Records of Your Sermons

IT IS being done. Ministers of large parishes, who have a long list of shutins, make recordings of the Sunday sermon or portions thereof. These recordings are delivered from one shutin to another. Their own pastor is heard speaking to them every week in the sanctuary of the sickroom.

A recording was made recently from a radio broadcast of the Lutheran Hour. It was later played to a group of Walther Leaguers who were studying a topic in connection with Dr. Maier's address. In any topic study, recordings can be especially valuable. Public school and music teachers have for many years emphasized the advantage of repeated record playing to properly illustrate and emphasize a certain point. Why should not this teaching principle hold true in religion?

The possibilities of the phonograph recording are tremendous. With the more general use in the homes of the automatic electrical radio-phonograph instrument it is high time that the Lutheran Church awaken to the possibilities of this preaching and teaching instrument for Christ.

Presidents of Districts, visitors of circuits, notables within the church, distinguished visitors, could have the words spoken upon special occasions recorded to be passed on to larger audiences.

Various combinations of phonograph publicity are being marketed by firms of established reputation. We remember an illustrating machine which throws slide film pictures on a screen and speaks a running explanation to the audience by the use of synchronized phonograph records. This combination holds possibilities for Lutheran educational institutions, missions, child welfare organizations, hospitals, etc.

The thing is being done. Why not by our Lutheran churches? Reader, what is your reaction?

Church Publicity and the Parish School

WHAT has the parish school to do with church publicity?

For one thing, the parish school, to maintain itself, needs a great deal of church publicity.

For another thing, the parish school can in turn be made a very effective church publicity medium.

In other words, advertise the parish school and it will advertise the church.

I

The Christian parish school possesses greater intrinsic merits and a larger number of good selling points than any other subsidiary department of the church. But, strange to say, it has received much unfavorable publicity and is, therefore—if it is to endure at all—in greater need of intelligent selling propaganda than even the church itself.

It was not always so.

For many centuries there was no other educational agency in the Christian world than the church or parish school. Even in our own country, where private schools are rare and public schools are everywhere, it has hardly been more than 75 years since the state took over the education of children in an official manner.

It had always been generally acknowledged that the children of a Christian nation needed Christian culture and that only the church, or individuals imbued with the church spirit, could impart that most important element of character building. Private and semi-public religious schools were not merely tolerated, they were highly thought of, generally encouraged, and sometimes even subsidized from community treasuries. They needed little, if any, advertising.

But times brought their changes.

The education of children in our country—owing to circumstances which need not be discussed here—has now passed almost wholly under the authority of the civil government. Where church and other private schools still exist, they are as a rule merely tolerated and sometimes even, if they do not conform to certain fixed standards of efficiency, regulated out of existence.

It is strange that the churches generally not only permitted the development of this situation, but even encouraged and supported it, having apparently regard solely for the alleviation afforded their treasuries in the growth of the state school system. This attitude on the part of the churches amounted practically to the sale of the spiritual birthright of coming generations for the mere mess of the pottage of financial relief. And what at first seemed a good thing became in the course of time a rather vexing problem. For now, in order to gain the privilege of giving their children even only a fraction of the religious training so necessary in character building, the churches must content themselves with the crumbs of time that fall from the table of the public school system, must do their work on a day on which no child wants to go to school, and must humbly apply to the school authorities for additional time in the interest of more thorough religious instruction and training.

Only the Catholic Church, some Lutheran bodies, and a few of the smaller denominations still maintain Christian parish schools —and this in almost every case under difficulties unheard of in former ages of Christianity. Often today the parish school is branded a foreign, un-American element in the "body politic," and some even accuse it of fostering narrowness and bigotry.

The very denominations whose founders in this country established and maintained excellent private schools now repudiate the faith and the educational convictions of their fathers. Even though they have gradually come to realize that their children are sorely in need of a more thorough religious training than these little ones are now receiving, they apparently find the parish school impossible. They point with pride to their denominational high schools and colleges; but they seem to view with horror the project of giving their little children the same privilege which they so earnestly desire for their adolescent youth. To them a denominational college is a desideratum, but a church school, which is merely a denominational college in embroyo, is an abomination. Explain the logic of this who can!

Strangely enough, this state of mind affects even the members of churches which still maintain parish schools, and moves some of them to oppose the educational policies of their own congregations. They seemingly would rather sacrifice the spiritual welfare of their children than be thought out of date and un-American by their social and religious neighbors.

This is the situation in which the parish school finds itself today, a situation which is at the same time a reason why an educational system maintained by a church is in need of intelligent, systematic, and persistent publicity, if it is to maintain itself and function satisfactorily.

Parish school publicity should set forth—

1. A definition of the character and the aims of the parish school; 2. A "bill of rights" justifying the existence of private religious schools in self-governing church bodies and in a democratic country; 3. The importance of a thorough Christian training for all children, whether within or without the church; 4. The superior excellence of an educational system which trains the whole child—soul, mind, body.

It is not difficult to substantiate these propositions. In fact, there is really so much to be said in favor of Christian parish schools and so little against them that we do not hesitate to challenge the denominations to show good and sufficient cause why they are not now maintaining Christian parish schools in connection with their churches.

The parish school is a full time educational institution affording —what cannot be found in any other establishment of its kind— a balanced cultural program, education and training for the soul, mind, and body of the child.

In working out its program the ideal parish school does not merely add a daily hour's work in Catechism and Bible History to the usual curriculum of a secular education; neither does it merely append a few necessary secular branches to the daily instruction in religious knowledge. It is not a compromise, a hybrid, or a makeshift. It is a real school with conscientious regard for the intellectual needs of the child; and a soul-winning agency seeking to fill the pupil's heart and life with "knowledge unto salvation" and the regenerating influence of the Gospel. But its purpose is single, not divided. Its one product is the character of a man of God who is "thoroughly furnished unto all good works" in every walk of life.

Upon its basic program of religious indoctrination is built up the elaborate system of training through which the consciousness of God's presence is carried into every activity of the school, all secular branches are presented in the light of Christian truth and in relation to soul life, all contacts and activities of the pupil are charged with a spiritual atmosphere, school discipline is maintained in a truly evangelical manner, and character is molded on that greatest of all patterns of spiritual excellency, the God-man Jesus Christ.

The parish school really needs no more elaborate and convincing justification for its existence than does the congregation itself. The Sunday school is in no fuller sense a legitimate child of the church than is the parish school; in fact, while the former is still and always will be but a child in the educational realm, the latter is a fully grown adult educational system.

Besides, the future of the church depends largely on the kind of children that are being raised in every generation. The more thoroughly these are trained in Christian doctrine and life the better it will be for the church of the future. Can the church of today be made safe for the generation of tomorrow without the kind of Christian education that only a parish school can give?

And if the state demands to know a good reason why the parish school should be given leave to exist, it need only be said that children who have been raised in the fear of God and the appreciation of Gospel blessings will make better citizens and build a better democracy than will those who have not enjoyed these educational advantages. If the church is hampered in its activity of raising up a generation of well indoctrinated, God-fearing, law-abiding citizens, the state itself will be the loser, and its institutions, including the public school itself, will be affected by the evil consequences.

Not "Americanism," but Christianity is the safeguard for the prosperity and safety of our nation. If Christianity ever goes down, Americanism will not long survive.

We do not hesitate to state emphatically that if all churches established truly Christian parish schools, the benefits and blessings issuing from them upon parents and children, homes and churches, communities and states, would be immeasurable.

But what about the objection that too many parish schools are inefficient and inadequate?

That there have been and still are parish schools which are far from being what they ought to be no one can deny, even as, for that matter, there are secular as well as Sunday schools of the same sorry sort. But does anyone think of disparaging our public school system, or the Sunday school as an institution, simply because there are inefficient public schools and incompetent Sunday schools? Why, in the face of the soundness of the parish school principle and in view of the existence of many good parish schools, there should be so much widespread opposition, not only to the inefficient parish schools, but to the parish school system itself, is hard to understand. When public or Sunday schools show themselves inadequate we do not destroy them, we strive to improve them. Every intelligent Christian church member will admit that the same policy ought to apply, and can be applied, to the Christian parish school.

The parish school is decidedly worth selling, but it will take much patient and persistent publicity to sell it.

II.

One of the most interesting reasons why the parish school deserves general and sustained publicity is this, that *it can in its turn be made a very effective church publicity medium.*

Anything done by a church in an unusual way will attract attention to that church.

The fact that the Roman Catholic Church maintains a great system of parochial schools is one of its outstanding characteristics and is giving that denomination wide publicity.

The same is true of those Lutheran bodies which still have parish schools and which, because of this very circumstance, in many localities are put into a class with the Romanists.

The publicity occasioned by the parish school may be, often is, adverse to begin with. But there is nothing abnormal in that. The church has always received a great deal of unfavorable notice, from the days of Nero, when it was accused of being un-Roman, to our day, in which Christian parish schools and the churches that foster them are charged with being un-American. Nor has adverse propaganda ever really done the harm to Christianity intended by its instigators. As a matter of fact, the church usually thrives on unfavorable criticism, while praise and general good-will do not benefit the church, but hurt it, when gained by compromise of the truth. The words once uttered by Jesus are still worth heeding, "Woe unto you when all men shall speak well of you." If the Christians of the first centuries or of the Reformation had stopped doing all those things for which they were adversely criticized there would be no Christian church today. If there were no persecution of the parish school we could not be sure that it is part of the Kingdom of God.

The question at issue is not as to what people in general think of the parish school. If it can be shown that this institution is an important and necessary factor in the life of the church, that it is doing work which the Lord commanded, and that there is under present-day conditions no better way for doing this work—and all this can be shown—the parish school has amply justified its existence. And it need not fear for its future. Gamaliel's famous dictum still stands, "If this counsel or this work be of God, ye cannot overthrow it."

Moreover, in the censure which the church and its institutions must suffer there is usually the seed of some blessing. That which the enemies intended for evil usually works out for the good of the Kingdom. Human curiosity is often more strongly aroused by censure than by praise. The most loyal friends which the parish school has today have become so through adverse criticism which they found to be maliciously untrue. The writer, whose congregation at great cost maintains a well equipped and efficient parish school, has frequently noted that unfavorable publicity caused more discussion of the parish school among people not connected with the church than any other method of advertising had been able to bring about. Inquiries following such discussions often led to personal investigation, and this in turn revealed the fact that the parish school had been basely slandered. Opportunity was thus given to sell the school issue to these inquirers, some of whom in time became the staunchest supporters of the school. Adverse publicity never really hurts a good thing; on the contrary, it usually does the very opposite, and, in addition, it eventually falls back upon its authors like a boomerang. Jesus says, "Blessed are they which are persecuted for righteousness' sake, for theirs is the Kingdom of heaven. Blessed are ye when men shall revile you, and persecute you, and shall say all manner of evil against you falsely, for my sake. Rejoice and be exceeding glad, for great is your reward in heaven."

One other consideration must be referred to in this connection. A great problem of every age is the child problem. Never has this problem had a more perplexing phase than it is passing through today. Parents everywhere are deeply concerned about the moral welfare of their children; school authorities are seeking more effective methods for the disciplinary control of pupils; churches and Christian people generally are uneasy over the realization that their children are not receiving a sufficient measure of religious education and training.

What these agencies and institutions are vainly seeking, the church with a parish school already possesses. For if there is any other and better solution for this problem than the Christian parish school offers the world does not yet know of it.

A congregation which takes advantage of the situation and can offer its community a well managed and efficient parish school is not only conferring a blessing upon its neighbors and their children, but is giving itself at the same time most impressive and effective publicity. People who do their own thinking cannot otherwise but argue that a church which will go to the length of maintaining its own parish school is worth investigating. Winning a child often leads to the winning of a whole family. A good parish school is worth much more than the money it costs to maintain it, not only in publicity, but even more in effective soul-winning.

If Christian parish schools ever go out of existence it will not be for lack of merit or of possibilities; it will be because their supporters surrendered to the enemies of the Kingdom of God.

What Others Say

"Nobody knows how to teach morality effectually without religion. Exclude religion from education and you have no foundation upon which to build moral character."—Charles W. Eliot of Harvard.

"Nothing will be of greater service to us and to our descendants than the maintenance of good Christian schools and the training of the young."—Martin Luther.

"The time will come when no town or city congregation will be regarded as even moderately equipped for its work without a week-day school for even the smallest children."—Charles M. Jacobs.

We Believe in the Christian Day School

AUGUST W. BRUSTAT

1. We believe in the Christian Day School because "a wise law prohibits crossing the line of demarcation between Church and State." That means that the public schools are not permitted by law to teach the most important subject of all—RELIGION—and rightly so. Religious instruction does not belong to the province of the State, but to the province of the Church. And so it remains for the Church to provide for its children a thorough religious education.

2. We believe in the Christian Day School because though the public schools dare not teach religion, many of them nevertheless do teach a philosophy contrary to the Word of God. "Some of the textbooks purchased by public officials with public funds for public schools, openly picture the world as an accident instead of the masterpiece of divine creation, and man as the product of evolution from the lower animals instead of the handiwork of Almighty God," as Dr. Walter A. Maier so forcefully expresses it.

And if for five hours a day, five days a week our children attending public schools are oftentimes subjected to doctrines so diametrically opposed to the Word of God, we can scarcely hope to overcome such an influence when we have the child for only one hour a week in Sunday School.

3. We believe in the Christian Day School because "the soul of education is the education of the soul." An education directed only to broaden the intellect or the mind, without reaching down into the heart and the soul, is inadequate. Such an education may enable our children to acquire wealth, and prestige, and social standing, but these things are short-lived and with it all they may be lost eternally. If, on the other hand, the Lord Jesus is enthroned in their hearts, they will be rich toward God, and prepared for an eternal habitation with Him in glory.

4. We believe in the Christian Day School because the child was not designed primarily for the home, or for the church (that is incidental), nor for the state (as many false philosophies of government today insist), but for GOD.

One of the finest definitions of education is perhaps the one written by John Milton. Milton was an educator as well as a statesman and poet. In his definition of education he sounds the note that the child was designed for God when he says, "The end of all education is for the child to gain the knowledge of God in Christ, and out of that knowledge to love Him, to imitate Him, and to grow like Him." That object of education can obviously not be attained through the public school system which is not permitted to teach religion. It can be attained only through Church-supported and Church-supervised schools.

5. We believe in the Christian Day School because such a school best serves the interest of the child. Solomon sounded that important note when he said: "Train up a child in the way he should go, and when he is old he will not depart from it." (Prov. 22:6). So much in the adult life depends upon the religious education during youth. "The child is father to the man," says the proverb. We wish our children to grow up to be happy and successful and God-fearing. They will never be that fully without Christ. That is why religious education is more important than secular education, important as secular education may be.

The highest object of education must be to teach the child that he is a lost creature, saved by the blood of Jesus. To have found Jesus is worth more than all else in the world combined—and Jesus cannot be found through the secular education of the public school system.

6. We believe in the Christian Day School because it will insure, under God, the future of the Church. The church that does not thoroughly prepare its children for intelligent church-membership has one foot in the grave. The children of today must carry on the work of the Church tomorrow. If they are not thoroughly indoctrinated when they are young, they will oftentimes have little interest in the Church when they are adults.

According to the synod-wide roll call, the losses to the Church are only half as great where the children attend a Christian Day School.

7. We believe in the Christian Day School because we are vitally interested in the preservation of our American democracy, we are vitally interested in the United States of America.

The future of our country or any other country, under God, lies in the hands of the children. The Jewish Talmud says, "Jerusalem was destroyed because the education of the children was neglected." What our country will be in the next generation is being decided by the kind of education our children are receiving in this generation. If we do not train our children with a sense of true devotion and dependence on God, the days of our nation's greatness will soon be numbered, and its light will go out in darkness.

For our country's greatness is not assured by its frenzied flag-waving citizenry, who today wave the Stars and Stripes. Many of them would just as soon wave the Red flag of Sovietism tomorrow in the same enthusiastic manner.

Our country's greatness is not assured by its street-parading, band-playing organizations which today play the Star Spangled Banner. Many of them would about face tomorrow and play the Third Internationale.

No, our country's greatness is assured only by its Christ-centered, Bible-loving, law-abiding citizens who recognize the truth of St. Paul's words: "Let every soul be subject unto the higher powers. For there is no power but of God; the powers that be are ordained of God. Whosoever therefore resisteth the power, resisteth the ordinance of God: and they that resist shall receive to themselves damnation" (Rom. 13:1, 2).

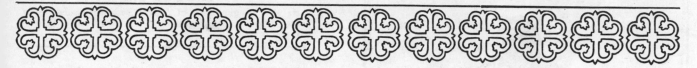

By Rev. F. W. C. Jesse
Chairman Lutheran State Board Education

Why do you maintain your Christian Day-Schools?

Our children will have to die some day. Then comes eternity. And eternity is a long time. It is necessary that our children should have an education for their life on earth. It is even more important that they should learn how to find happiness in eternity. "What is a man profited if he shall gain the whole world, and lose his own soul?"

Does not the Public School teach those things?

The Public School teaches those things which are needed for this life. But the Public School does not teach religion.

But could we not introduce religion into the Public School?

No one who is a true American at heart will want such a thing done. The Public School is an institution of the State. For the state to teach religion is just as un-American as for the church to preach politics.

But in Europe they have state schools teaching religion —in fact, they have state churches. Do you consider that improper?

Most assuredly, it is improper, and destructive besides. For in that case, either religion is controlled by politics, or politics is controlled by religion, and history shows so clearly that the result is corruption for both the church and the state. No higher ideal has ever been found than the American principle of absolute and honest separation of church and state. Let the state provide for peace and security to all its citizens, irrespective of their faith or unbelief. And let the church teach all who will listen how to find peace and security for their souls.

Would you say the same thing if the Lutheran religion were to be taught in the Public Schools?

No man worthy of the name of a Lutheran would want even the Lutheran religion introduced into the public schools. We believe in absolute separation of church and state.

But do you not think that much good could be done by teaching religion in the public schools?

The end does not sanctify the means. Besides, the thinking man will remember that, if the principle is wrong, promising prospects are but deceitful chimeras.

Do you think the public schools should be abolished?

Oh, no! Positively not. Self-preservation demands that the state should make provision for training its future citizens so that they can perform their civic duties intelligently. The public schools provide such opportunity for all.

But do your Christian Day-Schools offer their pupils the same opportunities?

They certainly do. They follow the state course of study— in most cases in every detail, in all cases in substance.

But do they teach patriotism?

Certainly. By all the means at the disposal of the public schools. They do more. They teach the children that God who looks into their very hearts, demands loyalty to their country not only in deeds but in their inmost thoughts.

But do not your schools tend to promote clannishness?

Certainly not. No child is turned away if it is willing to conduct itself as decent pupils should, and wants to learn the Word of God. That is not clannishness, is it?

But does not your church have foreign connections— with state churches of Europe, or the like—which would draw the hearts of the children away from America in a measure?

I am glad you mention that point. No. I claim for our particular Lutheran Church body—not necessarily for all Lutheran church bodies—that, as far as European connections or influences are concerned, it is more absolutely free from them than any other denomination in America. When the founders of our church body—the Lutheran Missouri Synod—came to this country in 1839, they came here for refuge from religious persecution in Europe. All connections with European state churches had been cut at that time. And no connections have ever been re-established, not even for a single day. And today, there is no church body in America which is so fully determined to shut out from their midst every influence of modern European religious thought as is the Lutheran Missouri Synod. We do not accord the hand of fellowship to the leaders of modern religious thought even in countries of Europe which are nominally Lutheran. If any church body in America is free from European entanglements, it is the Lutheran Missouri Synod.

How many pupils are there in your Lutheran Day-Schools in Kansas?

Last year there were 2,131. This year there may be a few hundred more.

Do you take the position that, since your schools relieve the state a great deal of expense, the state should give you a part of the school funds?

Positively not. As citizens, we are glad to vote for every necessary public school tax in order to make the public schools as efficient as possible. But we will forever oppose any movement which would give public funds to any school teaching religion. We are in favor of everlasting, honest and clean-cut separation of church and state. Of course, we want schools for our children in which the Bible is taught and set fourth as the verbally inspired Word of God. But we will pay for these schools out of our own pockets, and will feel that the money is well invested.

You mean to say, then, that the only reason why you have your own schools, is that you may teach your children the Bible?

That is the only motive which any church has a right to have in any of its activities—the spreading and propagating of God's revealed truth. And in maintaining our schools for this purpose, we are doing our children a good turn, and are not harming anybody. We believe with Daniel Webster that, whatever will make a man a better Christian will make him a better citizen.

Lutheran School Work on Exhibit at Free Fair Grounds

Reprint of Paid Advertisement in Topeka Daily Capital—Wednesday, September 15, 1926

Spare the Rod and Spoil the Child

"A false love blinds parents, so that they regard the body of the child more than his soul. Hence the wise man says, 'He that spareth his rod hateth his son; but he that loveth him chasteneth him betimes"—(Prov. 13. 24.). . . . Hence it is highly necessary that all parents regard the soul of their child more than his body, and look upon him as a precious, eternal treasure, which God has entrusted to them for preservation, so that the world, the flesh, and the devil do not destroy him. For at death and in the judgment they will have to render a strict account of their stewardship."

* * *

Popular Education

"It is a sin and a shame that we must be aroused and incited to the duty of educating our children and of considering their highest interests, whereas nature itself should move us thereto, and the example of the heathen affords us varied instruction."

Luther Believes in Spending Money on "Schoolmasters"

"If we must annually expend large sums on muskets, roads, bridges, dams, and the like, in order that the city may have temporal peace and comfort, why should we not apply as much to our poor neglected youth, in order that they may have a skilful schoolmaster or two?"

* * *

A GOOD AD

Here is a good school advertisement issued by a Seattle, Wash., congregation in the form of a blotter, 6 x 3½ inches.

"Repent and be converted, that your sins may be blotted out."

Whose Child Is It?
YOURS? TO BE SURE

What are you going to do for it?
    Care for the Body? Good.
        Care for the Mind? Better.
            Care for the Soul? Best.

Patrick Henry said in his last will:

"I have now disposed of all my wordly property to my family. There is one more thing I wish I could give them, and that is the Christian religion. If they had this and I had not given them a shilling, they would be rich. But if they had not the Christian religion and I had given them all the world, they would be poor."

It is this Christian religion we inculcate in our Sunday School and Christian Day School.

Your child is welcome.

Sunday School opens second Sunday of September.

Christian Day School opens September 6th.

TRINITY EV. LUTHERAN CHURCH

Cor. E. Union St. & 22nd Ave.
OSCAR FEDDER, Pastor
Phone East 6777

"Christ has blotted out the handwriting of ordinances that was against us."

SUGGESTION FOR SCHOOL ADVERTISING

Postage Will be Paid by Addressee

No Postage Stamp Necessary If Mailed in the United States

BUSINESS REPLY CARD
First Class Permit No. 976 (Sec. 510 P.L. & R.) San Antonio Texas

MR. WALTER H. VOTH, Principal
2815 Buena Vista Street
SAN ANTONIO, TEXAS

For

YOUR CHILD'S

Welfare

This card is our doorbell. Mail at once and we will be glad to tell you how we have helped solve the child problem of many parents in the past and how YOU may also have these advantages for YOUR CHILD! Remember, school starts September 9.

MOUNT OLIVE LUTHERAN SCHOOL
3111 Buena Vista Street
Elementary and Junior High School Departments
Phone: Garfield 9597

Name ....

Address ....

Why Send

YOUR CHILD

to Mount Olive

WE AFFORD
    CHARACTER TRAINING
    INDIVIDUAL ATTENTION
    PERSONAL INTEREST
    DEVELOPMENT OF THE *WHOLE* CHILD
    "FOR TIME AND FOR ETERNITY"

BUS TRANSPORTATION   CAFETERIA SERVICE

Personalized Rally Day Invitations

Pastor M. H. Lobeck of Canton, Ohio, has used with much success a card mailed to all pupils of the Sunday School also the prospects and indifferent. These cards carry the picture of the teacher each teacher mailing a card with her or his own picture to the members of the class. The card with the picture of the church, may be mailed to new names. The cards measure about 3½ by 5½. Cuts made for the cards may be used again in the parish paper or otherwise.

CANDLES IN LUTHERAN RITE
from p. 337

ceeds, one light after the other is extinguished, symbolizing Our Lord's gradual yielding to the mortal pain of His Passion; after all the lights on the herse are put out, the candles on the altar are extinguished, the lights in the Church are extinguished or dimmed, and only the feeble flicker of a single candle in the sacristy or behind the altar may be faintly seen. In the solemn darkness Psalm 51, a verse, and the Collect for Good Friday are recited, a noise is made to call to mind the earthquake of Resurrection morn, and the congregation departs in silence.

7. *The Paschal Candle.* This is likewise a very ancient symbol, for a Paschal *Praeconium* is ascribed to St. Jerome. A tall, thick candle is set on the Gospel side of the sanctuary and lit on Easter Eve. It is relighted for all celebrations of Holy Communion during Paschaltide. Finally, on Ascension Day, at the words "a cloud received Him out of their sight" it is put out for the last time. The symbolism is as appealing as it is obvious.

8. *Sanctuary lamps.* Sanctuary lamps are of very ancient origin in the Church and antedate by centuries the custom of lighting a lamp before the Reserved Sacrament. As a matter of fact, the use of the lamp before the Reserved Sacrament probably was not often found before the days of Eustace, Abbot of Flay, about 1200 A.D. (Atchley, *o.c.*, in Legg, *Some Principles, etc.*, page 32, note 5), and in Italy, as late as the sixteenth century, the Sacrament was often reserved without a light (*Tracts on the Mass*, Bradshaw Society Texts, 1904, page 215). While the use of seven sanctuary lamps before the altar is peculiarly an Anglican ostentation, a lamp may properly be hung before any altar or any image or picture to mark it out as an incentive to devotion. Such lamps should, however, be provided with colored glass shades, since a white—the widespread and unrubrical use of red in Roman Churches to the contrary notwithstanding (*Ritual Notes*, 7th edition, 1926, page 4) —lamp implies the presence of the Reserved Sacrament.

Luther Believes in Spending Money on "Schoolmasters"

"If we must annually expend large sums on muskets, roads, bridges, dams, and the like, in order that the city may have temporal peace and comfort, why should we not apply as much to our poor neglected youth, in order that they may have a skilful schoolmaster or two?"

* * *

Popular Education

"It is a sin and a shame that we must be aroused and incited to the duty of educating our children and of considering their highest interests, whereas nature itself should move us thereto, and the example of the heathen affords us varied instruction."

Lutheran P.-T. A.'s

CARL A. GIESELER

IT MAY BE TRUE THAT "we have too many societies in our congregations," but there may be some which do not foster the essential work of the church as much as Lutheran School Parent-Teachers Associations.

Where there is a church school in a congregation, it is of great value to the teacher that he meet the parents of his pupils. This he will do in home visiting, but he may not have the time to see his pupils at their homes as often as he would like. Also the pastor will want to become acquainted with the parents of his school-children. This is especially true in the case of "outside", non-congregational parents. He, too, may not find time to go into these non-Lutheran homes as often as he would in order to gain the parents for the church.

Meetings of the parents of the children and of friends of the school will give both teachers and pastors opportunity to meet and deepen the acquaintance with those who are entrusting their children to our Christian school.

In some cases informal gatherings are held from time to time. In other congregations regular parent-teachers associations are formed. Circumstances will help decide whether an organization is called for or not.

In the writer's church and school a P.-T.A. was organized a number of years ago, and has been very helpful in the development of the school, which has grown from a one-room school at the beginning of the present pastorate to a three-room school, and has been expanded to nine grades, six elementary and three junior high school grades, the system followed in the Denver public schools.

Not only the parents who have children in the school but all friends of the school are invited to attend the meetings of the P.-T. A.

The constitution is very brief. There is only a President and a Secretary-Treasurer. Besides there is an entertainment committee. Nobody joins the association. All parents of school children are considered members, and all parents present, whether members of the church or not, may vote.

It may be well to specify in the constitution that the principal officers must be members of the church. But the association should endeavor to draw in non-church members on the committees.

Some P.-T. A.'s meet without the children. It may be well to consider parents' evenings. But experience teaches that a brief program by some of the children will bring the parents. Put a child on the stage and you draw father, mother, aunt, uncle, grandfather, grandmother, and many others.

One way in which some of the evenings are arranged is the following: The children meet in their respective class rooms. Only the parents are in the hall for a brief business meeting. After the conclusion of the meeting the children give their numbers on the stage. After the program is finished the pupils are served a little refreshment in their class room while the parents go to the dining room in the church basement or wherever the church kitchen and dining room are located. There the informal visiting takes place.

But we may have forgotten the most important question: What are the dues in the association? In ours there are none. But there is an offering at the close of every business meeting. Some of the money in the treasury of the association is used to provide the school with equipment which the congregation would probably not supply. Playground equipment might well be purchased by the P.-T. A. The writer's association bought a fine slide for the little ones.

We have been approached to join the city and state and national confederation of P.-T. A.'s. But so far nothing has been done in that direction. It is possible that we may use some of the material offered by those who have been in this work for quite a long time. A more closely organized association may be able to accomplish greater things. But it is well not to attempt too much. Rather have a number of occasional but well attended meetings during the school year, than to attempt a meeting every month which in time will "peter out."

HOW TO UNDERSTAND YOUR SCHOLARS

Grade: Age:	Primary	Juniors	Intermediates	Seniors	Bible Classes
BODY:—	Rapid Growth Restlessness	Growth in Weight and Height "Steam-Engine" Period	Rapid Growth Awkward Age	Developed Life and Joy	Finer Interests and Feelings Develop
MIND:—	Imagination "Make Believe" Interest in Stories Imitation Inquisitiveness	Mind Develops Interest in Reading (Provide Good Books)	Hero Worship Self-Centered Keen Sense of Humor	Investigating Period First Contacts with Life's Realities	Judgment and Reason Executive Ability Individual Responsibility
SOCIAL:—	Centered in Home Self-Interest	School Interests Loyalty to Friends "Gang" Spirit	Shyness Team Play	Interest in Sex Clothes Larger Social Life	Love of Home Lasting Friendships Public Affairs
SPIRITUAL LIFE:—	Habits of Prayer and Helpfulness	Center "Hero Worship" of Jesus Lead by Comradeship Church Attendance	Decision to Follow Christ and Join the Church	Interest in Church, Societies, etc. Consciousness of Right and Wrong Definite Tasks	Church's Duty to the World Missions Unselfishness Christian Service

(Outline for talk at Sunday School Teachers Meeting)

At Work In Sunday School

LEE G. EGLOFF

Facing the Problem

IT IS A SAD but very true fact that the Sunday-schools are not as efficient nor as effective as they should be. Proof for this rather sweeping statement is so evident to every church worker that it need scarcely be mentioned. Suffice it to say that the Sunday-school children gradually fall away as they grow older, so that comparatively few of them ever become active church members.

The person who is confronted by this state of affairs for the first time is apt to be amazed and wonder what the cause may be. But, after looking into the matter, his attitude is sure to change, so that, instead of being amazed at the number of children who drop away, he is quite likely to be astonished at the number who remain true to the church.

The average Sunday-school labors under immense handicaps. The available time is all too short, and the intervals between lessons are all too long. The pupils are in church about one-sixty-eighth of a week, and are taught for about one three-hundred-thirty-sixth of a week. Christian home instruction is practically non-existent, so that this one hour in a hundred sixty-eight make the odds about a hundred sixty-eight to one against the children becoming Christians. That solitary hour each week would be too little to make much of an impression on the children even if the best of conditions for study and concentration were to be found.

As a rule, in Sunday-school there is too much of a crowd, too much noise, and too many things to divert the attention to permit the teachers to work effectively. That holds true in spite of the fact that the teaching staff usually labors heroically to keep order and to impress the lessons upon the minds of the children.

All credit must be given to those who are willing to accept such a gruelling and frequently thankless task as working for the Sunday-school. The time and effort they expend receives precious little appreciation here on earth. Their reward is in heaven.

Besides, it must be admitted that, in spite of their evident sincerity, an unduly large number of Sunday-school teachers are not properly fitted for the task. The greatest fault to be found with them is usually nothing more than immaturity. They simply have not lived enough of life to fit themselves to prepare others for it. And intensive training courses are practically out of the question.

Although the disadvantages here listed have been the subject of a great deal of thought by very many people, it must be admitted that no real solution has been found, and the average Sunday-school is forced to get along as best it can under the circumstances. In most churches teaching conditions cannot be improved without entailing too much expense for new or overhauled quarters. Trained or even middle-aged teachers are at a premium, since the young folks seem to be about the only ones willing to give of their time and ability to the Sunday-school.

Yet some few churches, realizing their Christian obligation to bring the Gospel to the children as well as to the adults, have gone to considerable expense and labor to overcome these detriments to the efficiency of their Sunday-schools. And they have had the satisfaction of seeing a larger percentage of the children grow up without dropping away from the church. Still, the results often fell far short of their expectations.

Therefore, it is not to be wondered at when we discover that an ever-increasing number of church members are actually advocating the discontinuance of the Sunday-schools. They claim that the children of faithful parents remain true to the church and the children of unchurched parents fall away from the church regardless of the Sunday-school. In most cases, it must be admitted, cold facts bear out their contention. But, since they have not been able to suggest any reasonable substitute, the churches logically insist that the little hold they have on the child in Sunday-school is better than none.

Although such thoughts are very discouraging, and although the odds are against making the Sunday-schools produce a respectable number of church members in proportion to their enrollment, we have no right to throw up our hands and say that the case is a hopeless one. Rather, we should give continued thought to the matter and endeavor to help the Sunday-school with constructive advice, suggestions and personal assistance. Unchurched parents frequently send their children to Sunday-school though they will have nothing to do with the church themselves. As Christians we are obligated to do our best to make Christians of such children in spite of their home environment. The lower grades in Sunday-school have many such youngsters. The trouble is that they trickle away as they grow older and become more and more independent. Our problem is to stop that leak.

In order to do that, we must always keep clearly in mind the objective that is desired, namely, to hold the children in the Sunday-school till they grow up and join the congregation.

Unfortunately the average teacher is convinced that this will automatically take place if the assigned lessons are learned by the children. The result is that in too many cases, too much is demanded and the children are all too glad to take advantage of the first opportunity to drop away.

Now, it is, of course, very praiseworthy for the teachers to try to inculcate as much Christian knowledge into the heads of the children as possible. Yet it must be remembered that the first object of the Sunday-school is a different one.

The children cannot be expected to learn very much during the one short session each week, interrupted as it is with all sorts of diverting noises and incidents. But they can be expected to absorb a whole-hearted interest in the Bible and the church will cause them to stick fast and join the congregation as they advance in years.

Therefore, the Sunday-school teachers should not be too much concerned if their charges do not learn the lesson very readily. On the other hand, they should be very much concerned if the children lose interest and indicate that they only attend because their parents force them to do so.

The main efforts of the teachers should not be expended in teaching the details of the assigned subject. It should not bother them very much if they have to say, "I don't know," to some freak question asked them, although a fairly complete knowledge of the Scripture is undoubtedly a most necessary part of a teacher's equipment.

It is our firm conviction that if the Sunday-school staffs will only recognize the main purpose of their work and strive, first of all, to create a friendly spirit in the children toward the church, the Kingdom of God, their labors will be crowned with a far greater measure of success than has heretofore been attained.

That this should be done in a Christian way, using the means which the Bible provides and suggests, needs hardly be mentioned. Yet it is a fact that in many churches Christianty and the Bible are relegated so far into the background that they are lost sight of entirely. But that difficulty can be easily overcome if the teachers will only stop to realize that the children who become church members without having a Christian attitude will not be of any use to the church but will rather hinder its God-pleasing activities.

Thus the teachers are confronted with the difficult but quite soluble problem of making their Sunday-school classes interesting and attractive without departing from the Bible in order to do so. More power to them. God will bless their efforts, and will not permit His word to return unto Him void.

Duties of Teachers and Officers

The following list of duties is by way of suggestion only. It should be amended to fit the circumstances and requirements of individual Sunday-schools. The point is that each member of the staff should have a clear conception of his responsibilities. Unless steps are taken to that end, inefficiency, harmful friction and needless duplication will result.

The Superintendent

1. He should frequently visit the various classes with the object of improving the work of the individual teachers and the Sunday-school as a whole.

2. At each staff meeting he should make remarks on his observations and present matters which have come to his attention, such as: Individual pupil problems, sub-normal attendance, sub-normal collections, etc.

3. He should speak to new pupils, assign them to classes, and see to it that their names, ages, addresses, etc., are recorded.

4. He should handle unruly children for the teachers, if necessary assigning them to different classes.

5. He should be empowered to remove chronically absent pupils from the roll, after assuring himself that proper efforts to reclaim the child have been made.

6. He should have a list of these duties, and call individual members of the staff to account for laxity in their work.

7. He should see to it that all records are kept properly, and are available.

8. He should assign substitute teachers to classes.

9. He should interview all visitors and strangers, get them acquainted, and, in general, make them feel at home.

10. He should okay all disbursements.

11. He should lead the Sunday-school ritual service.

12. He should give the awards to the children.

Treasurer

1. He should keep an accurate record of all receipts and disbursements.

2. No disbursements should be made unless upon presentation of the bill signed by the superintendent.

3. He should report once a month to the staff, in a regular meeting, itemizing all expenditures and giving the total balance on hand.

4. He should receive the collection after it has been counted by the librarian.

Librarian

1. In general, the librarian should have charge of all things owned or controlled by the Sunday-school except the records of other officers. He should have a complete list of all Sunday-school property and its location.

2. He should receive the collection, count it, keep a record of the same, and turn it over to the treasurer.

3. He should see to it that the hymn books are distributed and collected.

4. He should obtain and distribute all Sunday-school lessons and literature to the teachers or children.

5. He should see to it that the chairs are properly arranged before and after Sunday-school.

6. When the need arises, he should see to it that the staff supplies, replaces or repairs Sunday-school property.

7. He should be in charge of and responsible for the Sunday-school library.

Secretary

1. He should keep and be responsible for the record of the staff meetings.

2. He should keep and be responsible for the Sunday-school attendance records.

3. He should call the attention of the staff, at meetings, to motions which were passed and not carried out.

4. He should supply the teachers with a list containing the names, addresses and telephone numbers of the pupils in the respective classes.

5. He should read this list of duties each year when the election of officers takes place, or see to it that a copy is placed in their hands.

6. He should comment on the attendance of the pupils—individually and collectively—in the staff meetings.

7. He should provide the pastor and superintendent with copies of the minutes of each staff meeting.

8. He should inform the superintendent when certain pupils are to receive attendance awards.

9. He should handle all general correspondence for the Sunday-school, including the mailing of birthday and absentee cards.

All Officers
(Executive Committee)

1. They should hold regular meetings a half hour previous to the regular staff meeting, to plan the sessions and see to it that the meetings progress with a minimum of confusion and wasted time.

2. They should arrange social affairs for the combined Sunday-school.

3. They should make suggestions for individual class social affairs to be conducted by the teachers.

4. They should be empowered to recruit assistance and assistants, as needed, from the members of the Sunday-school.

5. They should be given regular assistants as the Sunday-school expands and their duties become too burdensome.

All Teachers

1. They should attend all staff meetings or present valid reasons for not doing so.

2. They should be present every Sunday—ahead of time. In case they find it necessary to be absent, they should inform the superintendent in advance so that the substitute teachers are not forced to take classes while unprepared.

3. They should do everything possible, in a Christian manner, to make their classes interesting and pleasant.

4. They should contact by mail, phone, or (best) with personal visits absentee children of their classes and the parents.

5. They should remember that they cannot hope to lead others into the Heavenly Kingdom until they have led themselves there, that they will not be able to improve the practical Christianity of the children until they have improved their own, that they cannot hope to have the children benefit from the lessons unless they have benefitted themselves.

6. They should faithfully prepare the lessons and have their teaching procedure definitely outlined in advance.

7. They should remember that the future of the congregation is in their hands. They can make or break the church.

8. They should, as much as possible, arrange social gatherings for their classes, parties, outings, picnics, etc. In other words, give the children a chance to really know and like one another.

Preparation for Teaching

1. As a general rule, prepare twice as much material as you think you will need. Then the class period will never seem too long and it will be relatively easy to hold the attention of the children.

2. Set aside at least an hour each week for preparation. Make it a habit.

3. Always look up the lesson in the Bible.

4. Keep your objective in mind—to hold the interest of the children and make them like Sunday-school.

5. Remember what isn't important. Don't let it worry you if the children seem to forget the lesson. If they are interested in what you say, they'll remember it all right.

6. Remember what is important—to have the children eager to come back next Sunday and hear more of the Gospel message.

7. Ask yourself the following questions each Sunday morning. If you can't answer them with a positive "yes", don't teach.

   a. Did you prepare the lesson and check it with the Bible?
   b. Did you find something(s) in the lesson which will make your life more Christ-like?
   c. Do you consider it an honor to be permitted to teach the Gospel?

8. Remember that the Bible teachings and their practical application should concern you more than the story which, after all, is just an illustration or example.

9. Try to list at least half a dozen ways in which the children can put into practice the teachings of the lesson.

10. Plan your classes in advance. Know how you will begin the lesson, discuss it, apply it, and end it.

11. Prepare some fillers in case you have extra time after having covered the lesson, as:

   a. Drill the children in finding Bible passages in the Scripture.
   b. Drill the children in spelling Biblical names and words.
   c. Drill the definitions of Biblical terms.
   d. Do some additional memory work.
   e. Explain and apply the hymns that were sung, or portions of the Creed, Lord's Prayer, the liturgy, etc.

Teaching the Class

1. Remember your objective: to hold the interest of the children.

2. See to it that they know they are saved (by faith). Basically that is all that is necessary. Everything else you teach is subordinate and should be in line with the above objective.

3. Avoid bribery for learning or memorizing (gifts, stars, pins, etc.). That is not a Christian means of teaching the Gospel.

4. Never use ridicule or sarcasm. It doesn't work. It only hurts the feelings of the children and drives them out of the Sunday-school and church.

5. Never "bawl out" a child who seems ignorant or dense. He may know the lesson without being able to express himself. You can show disapproval of poor work just as effectively by refusing praise and giving the odd jobs to others. If a child actually needs disciplining, turn him over to the superintendent.

6. Remember that the superintendent visits your class to help you, not to find things wrong.

7. Never let good pupils go on ahead of the rest, especially in memory work. It will discourage those who are left behind. Rather give such children extra work not included in the regular lessons.

8. Use pictures in every possible way.

   a. Maps.
   b. Blackboard or tablet drawings. You don't have to be an artist to illustrate what you are saying. If you draw an off-balance circle and tell the children it's a boat, they'll see a boat.
   c. Use word pictures and comparisons. Compare every statement, occurrence, etc., mentioned in the lessons, with its present-day counterpart.
   d. Comment on the lesson pictures. It's a good way to start the class.

9. Use color. Colors have a magnetic appeal to children as well as to adults.

   a. Use colored chalk, crayons, or pencils to illustrate.
   b. Use colorful adjectives. Practice it. Try putting an appropriate adjective before every noun you use.

10. Be careful with your questions.

   a. Mix them into the lesson. It is best not to save them for the end. Remember, you don't care if the children forget the story. If you hold their interest your teaching is a success no matter how much they do or do not learn.
   b. Use the questions to hold attention. If a child starts to cut up or doze, throw a question at him.
   c. Be fair. Ask only such questions as the children can reasonably be expected to answer.
   d. Avoid fact questions. It's not important for them to remember the facts. What is important is that they are interested in trying to think things out in a Christian manner. Ask the children "how", "why", "what

do you think about it", or "what would you do in that case?"

e. Use the questions to assist the children to take part rather than to extract information.

11. Never lecture—always discuss. Ask for the opinion of the children. Let them take part. You will find that you will learn as much from them as they learn from you.

12. Keep a straight face. If you must laugh at a ridiculous remark or antic—smile. If you become boisterous, the children will go out of their way to outdo you, and you'll wonder why the class is so unruly.

13. Achieve as much variety as possible. Nothing disgusts a child as much as monotony. Use your ingenuity. Start the lesson in a different way, approach its teachings from a different angle, and conclude it in a different vein each Sunday. That means preparation!

14. Define all words. Do you know for sure the definitions of "faith", "communion", "charity", "saint", "love", "trespass", etc.? Do your children? Never take it for granted that they know the meaning of any word. They usually don't. And be sure you use a dictionary before you try to tell them!

15. Never read the lesson to the children, nor have them read it during the class. For the youngsters, that's sure proof that you don't know the lesson. And they are usually right!

Memory Work

1. Its value should not be lost sight of. Memorized Bible passages and hymns will become prized possessions in later years.

2. If a choice actually becomes necessary, it is better to drop the memory work entirely than to have it cause the children to dislike and shun Sunday-school.

3. The memory work should be taught in class. This can be done easily and painlessly if the teacher is a bit clever and persistent.

a. Set aside five minutes, more or less, of the class session.

b. The best time for it is at the beginning of the class, not last. Then the children will be eager to get through with it in order to get at the lesson.

c. The secret of success in this field is constant, patient, but not monotonous repetition.

d. Divide the portion to be memorized into sensible phrases or sentences. Say the first phrase slowly and clearly. Then have a good pupil repeat it after you, then another and another, etc. Treat the next phrase likewise. And finally the whole.

e. Let the children know that you do not intend to take up the lesson until they have memorized the passage or verse selected.

f. Don't let the child get away with laziness. If he refuses to learn it, make him painfully repeat it after you, word for word. Usually such treatment will show up his laziness in an unattractive light, and encourage him to apply himself.

g. Review what has been previously memorized. You'll be surprised how fast you and the children forget it if that is not done.

4. Avoid giving the children overdoses. There is no need for tackling lengthy portions. Stay within reason in your demands. The memory work will do far more harm than good if it causes the children to dislike your teaching.

Keeping Order

1. Try rearranging the seating of the children. Separate boisterous youngsters with quiet ones.

2. Do not hesitate to ask the superintendent to sit in on your classes. If you can't handle a particular child, tell him about it.

3. If possible, insist on a permanent seating arrangement, having the children take the same seats each Sunday.

4. Keep the children busy.

a. Pepper the lessons with questions. Make them think. (See questions.)

b. Have the children use pencils or chalk as much as possible. But avoid anything that looks like a test. Rather have them draw or color portions of the lesson.

c. See "holding interest".

d. Assign permanent jobs as a recognition of attentiveness. Turn the jobs over to others if they are not done well. Use your ingenuity in finding such odd jobs.

Some are:

1. Arranging the attendance cards.
2. Taking the collection.
3. Distributing and collecting hymn books.
4. Arranging chairs.
5. Distributing lesson sheets.
6. Keeping order—monitors.
7. Etc.

5. Never get angry at a child. He will either laugh at you or intensely dislike you for it.

6. Always speak softly—so softly that the children have to be quiet to hear you. Never try to talk over their voices. They'll out-talk you in the long run.

7. Speak distinctly. If you don't, you will not be understood no matter how loud you talk.

8. Insist upon and demand that only one person speak at a time in the class. Let the children know that they can talk all they want to—but only one at a time. If you can't enforce this rule, don't teach. The resulting hubbub will not only destroy the effectiveness of your teaching but also that of the other teachers.

Redeemer Lutheran Sunday School —Rules for Teachers

REALIZING THE GREAT RESPONSIBILITY of Sunday School teachers in leading souls to Christ and by accepting the position of teacher in Redeemer Sunday School, I pledge myself:

1. With the help of the Lord to fulfill such duties as may devolve upon me in such capacity to the very best of my ability.

2. To live in close contact with my Savior through daily prayer and diligent study of His Word.

3. To study my lessons each Sunday conscientiously with the helps provided and endeavor to present same in an interesting way to the class.

4. To be present every Sunday unless prevented by circumstances beyond my control or to provide a substitute to take my place, notifying the superintendent or pastor of such a substitute.

5. To be on time and at my place with my class before the Sunday School begins, preferably five minutes before time.

6. To make every effort to maintain discipline in my class before the session and during it.

7. To attend divine worship regularly, every Sunday, for my own spiritual welfare as well as for example to the pupils of the Sunday School.

8. To assist in the preparation and presentation of special programs by the Sunday School.

9. To visit before Rally Day each pupil of my class, to visit sick and delinquent pupils throughout the year, and to take a personal interest in each individual of my class.

10. To attend all scheduled meetings as announced and to make every effort to increase the efficiency of the Sunday School.

Rally Day Suggestions

Select a Sunday when all pupils and teachers will have returned from vacations. Allow one or two weeks for giving the event the necessary publicity.

Each teacher should visit the pupils of his or her class before Rally Day to make sure that all will be present. At the same time a check up of pupils will be made as well as any new prospects for the Sunday School which might be reported in the course of such visits.

Rally the teachers before Rally Day at a supper previous to Rally Day, possibly during the previous week. Plans for the coming year will be discussed, reports will be given on visits made. If the pastor will rally the teachers first at such a supper the Rally of the Sunday School will materially benefit.

A suitable postcard or letter should be mailed to each pupil a few days before as a final reminder of Rally Day.

There are many Rally Day souvenirs on the market which may prove helpful. If it is a custom to give a badge or button to those present on Rally Day each year it may be suggested that pupils who were present on previous Rally Days wear their badges from former years.

A special Rally Day program should be arranged. One of the prepared programs which are on the market may be found adaptable. An informal program of well known hymns, short inspiring talks by the superintendent, department superintendents and pastor, or some outside speaker, special musical numbers, catechism recitations, etc. may be arranged. The lesson for the day may be presented in the form of a story told to the entire Sunday School by the superintendent or pastor.

Program for Rally Day.
Prelude by Piano or Organ.
Hymn by the Sunday School. "Holy, Holy, Holy".
Remarks by the Superintendent.
Prayer by the Pastor.
Responsive Reading of Psalm III followed by Gloria Patri.
Hymn, "Savior, I Follow On".
Talks by Superintendents of Departments.
Vocal or Instrumental Selection.
Talk by Guest Speaker.
Brief Review of Portions of Catechism Memory Work.
Presentation of Awards for Perfect Attendance.
The Story of the Lesson for the Day.
Announcements.
Hymn, "Onward Christian Soldiers".
Lord's Prayer.
Doxology.

In some churches the regular Sunday School period is set aside and the entire Sunday School attends a combination Rally Day Service with the adult Congregation.

Five Rules

For Bringing the Sunday School
Into the Worship Service

1. No one is elected to serve as an officer or teacher in our Sunday School who is not a regular attendant upon the church services. The teacher who carelessly disregards this obligation suggests by his example that he does not consider the church worship hour as essential to a Christian. No amount of good teaching in the class can counteract the destructive influence of a thoughtless example by a teacher whom the individuals in the class admire.

2. We stress the fact that the Sunday School period is solely for teaching and Bible study and that the church hour should be regarded by everybody as the time for worship.

3. We carefully avoid the use at the close of the Sunday School hour, of any form of dismissal which is, in effect, an invitation to the pupil to go home. On the contrary, we try to impress upon the children the thought that, in going from the Sunday School into the church service, we are simply passing from the study period into the worship period, and that the second part of the program is just as important as the first.

4. In our efforts to draw the children into the church service we do not harangue them and constantly remind them of their duty to attend church; nor do we scold them for failure to attend. Rather, we try to locate the natural class leaders, and through the influence of these key-pupils and the teachers we seek to win the co-operation of all the pupils and to draw them into participation in the worship service.

5. We give the worship service careful preparation, admitting nothing which does not tend to create an atmosphere of reverence, and striving to make the service a definite means of spiritual development. We recognize that the needs of the children as well as those of the adults, must be met. The service is never allowed to drag or to run overtime.

As a result, our Sunday School children and young people do attend our church service. Understanding that they are wanted, that the church service is as much for them as for the older people, they accept it and enjoy it.

Copyright: The Duplex Co., Richmond, Virginia.
Reprinted by permission.

Why Should My Child Have Religious Training?

Because—The Courts report that 80% of our criminals are under 25 years of age.

Because—During the past five years 4,000 children between the ages of 5 and 18 have committed suicide.

Because—Without religious education my child must face a great handicap in the fight against the evil forces in the world.

Because—It is not fair to deprive my child of the strength, hope and consolation that I have received from religious training.

Because—"Prison chaplains tell us that the great majority of those brought to court for wrongdoing have had little or no religious instruction."—Judges Thomas Crain, Otto Rosalsky, Alfred Talley.

Because—"The strength of our country is the strength of its religious convictions."—Calvin Coolidge.

Because—"No nation can prosper, no nation can survive, if it ever forgets Almighty God."—Warren G. Harding.

Because—"It is impossible to rightly govern the world without God and the Bible."—George Washington.

Why Should I Send My Child To The Lutheran Bible School?

Because—It will hear and read a good and interesting Bible story every Sunday.

Because—It will be taught to commit to memory some important Bible text every Sunday.

Because—It will learn Psalms and Christian songs and prayers.

Because—It will be instructed in genuine Christian doctrine at the hand of the Bible.

Because—It will receive weekly Christian periodicals full of wholesome reading matter.

Because—It will be warned against sin and wickedness and encouraged to walk in the footsteps of Jesus Christ.

Because—The Lutheran Bible School has a splendid corps of capable, devoted officers and teachers, and my child will enjoy it.

Because—The Lutheran Church has not only retained the beauty of historic forms of worship but has, through the Reformation, restored the pure teaching of the Church of the apostles.

Because—The Lutheran Church, the oldest and largest Protestant Church in the world, after 400 years is still teaching and preaching *straight religion*.

Opportunities in the Sunday School
For Developing A Christian Pattern of Conduct
Educational Contests as Motivating Devices
G. A. KUHLMANN

ALL ORGANIZATIONS within the church exist primarily for the purpose of guiding, directing, and training individual members for a more consecrated personal service to our Lord and Master. Briefly stated, our one purpose is to develop a Christian pattern of conduct in the life of every member of the church. All the organizations within the church contribute to this Christian pattern of conduct through the dissemination of Christian knowledge, the development of Christian attitudes and ideals, and in the performance of those activities which make up normal Christian life.

Of the organizations within the church contributing to this pattern of conduct, the Sunday School has the widest scope of contact, since its teaching departments extend from the pre-school period in the primary department to old age in the adult Bible classes.

The development of a "home study" program through the use of "work books," presenting assignments and projects for use in the various classes, is, in the opinion of the writer, at least a partial answer to the ever-growing problem of utilizing the Sunday School as a more effective agency of Christian training. A mere knowledge program, stressing memory work and knowledge of facts, has a tendency to emphasize unduly the subject matter that is being presented from week to week, rather than the Christian habits and general pattern of conduct that should follow as a result of our teaching.

Too frequently we are prone to forget that the Sunday School has for its purpose to prepare boys and girls and men and women for those activities which make up, or which should make up, normal Christian life. We are satisfied with teaching mere facts as so much knowledge; and we overlook entirely the result which should follow: namely, that Christian knowledge should bear fruit in the form of Christian activity. "Wherefore by their fruits ye shall know them." (Matt. 7:20.)

MOTIVATING DEVICES NECESSARY

Failure to provide proper motivation accounts for much of the lethargy in our church today. Testing devices of various kinds are necessary for a constant check on our teaching in the Sunday School. We should more frequently test our pupils to determine what specific abilities they are developing as a result of our teaching. We must be sure, not only that we have a broad scope of specific objectives, covering both Christian knowledge and Christian life, but also that there is a well-balanced growth and development constantly taking place in the formation of a Christian pattern of conduct.

The following outline presents an experiment in educational contests which were held recently in connection with the annual picnic of Trinity Lutheran Sunday School in Winfield, Kansas, in an effort to provide a motivating device in a wide range of activities. With parents, pupils, and teachers devoting the major part of an afternoon together in educational contests, we feel that new doors were opened for the realization of a number of our specific objectives, which are designed to play an important part in the weaving of an intricate and delicate pattern of Christian conduct. We submit the outline of the educational contests in these columns upon request, in the hope that it may serve as a nucleus around which others may build a larger structure of motivating devices:

EDUCATIONAL CONTESTS FOR PICNIC, JUNE 13, 1937
Trinity Lutheran Sunday School, Winfield, Kansas

PURPOSE: The purpose of the educational contests sponsored by the Sunday School is to stimulate interest and leadership in a wide field of activities which make up normal Christian life. The contests are therefore designed to foster a greater interest in various activities which are included in the aims and objectives of the Sunday School.

ELIGIBILITY: Any one who is enrolled in Trinity Lutheran Sunday School is eligible to participate.

TIME AND PLACE OF CONTESTS: The contests will be held in the large Tabernacle in Island Park on Sunday afternoon, June 13, beginning at 2:00 o'clock.

REGISTRATION: Registration of contestants will be under the supervision of class teachers. Registration in both the "display" contests and the "active" contests should be completed not later than Sunday, June 6, in order that a schedule may be prepared and arrangements made for the displays. Contestants may take part in more than one contest event.

"ACTIVE" CONTESTS

1. BIBLE STORY TELLING. The story, as told by the contestant, should be from 2 to 4 minutes in length. (Time limit does not apply to Primary Dept.) Each contestant shall draw for the story which is to be told, and shall have thirty minutes for special preparation. Contestants shall be prepared to tell any of the following stories:

BIBLE CLASSES	SUNDAY SCHOOL DEPT.	PRIMARY DEPT.
1. The Story of Ruth	1. The Birth of Jesus	1. Jesus Blessing Little Children
2. The Story of Esther	2. Christ's Resurrection	2. Zacchaeus
3. The Story of Daniel	3. Abraham's Sacrifice	3. Feeding the 5000
4. My Favorite Psalms	4. The Syrophoenician Woman	4. David and Goliath
5. The Crucifixion of Christ	5. The Prodigal Son	5. The Good Samaritan

2. BIBLE GEOGRAPHY.

(a) PALESTINE. Contestants will be given mimeographed outline maps of Palestine, together with a list of important cities, mountains, seas and rivers. They will then be required to indicate the correct location of important cities, mountains, etc. Time limit: 7 minutes.

(b) ASIA MINOR. Contestants will be given mimeographed outline maps of Asia Minor, together with a list of important cities, mountains, seas, and rivers. They will then be required to indicate the correct location of important cities, mountains, etc. Time limit: 7 minutes.

NOTE: PRIMARY DEPARTMENT AND JUNIOR CLASS contestants will be given mounted maps of either Palestine or Asia Minor. Time limit: 6 minutes.

3. BIBLE REFERENCES. Each contestant will be given a list of references which are to be found in the Bible. The first four words of each reference are to be written in the space provided with the reference. Time limit: 8 minutes. Separate contests for Bible classes and Sunday School groups.

4. MISSIONARY BIOGRAPHY. The lives of three missionaries (Livingstone, Moffat, Mackaye) should be studied in preparation for this contest. At the time of the contest each contestant will draw for one name. Thirty minutes

PLEASE TURN TO PAGE 154

Objectives for the Sunday School

G. A. KUHLMANN

WHAT EDUCATIONAL RESULT do you expect from your Sunday School teaching? What is the scope of the general Christian knowledge you wish to impart? What habits and abilities and what attitudes and ideals are you trying to develop in the child? In short, what changes do you look for in the child as a result of your teaching?" A discussion of questions of this type by our Sunday School teaching staff led to an enumeration of specific objectives for our local Sundal School.

We agreed that the various organizations of the local congregation have one common end; namely, to prepare boys and girls and men and women for those activities which make up, or which should make up, normal Christian life. The Sunday School should provide thorough instruction in the essentials of Christian belief with Christ as a personal Savior, and it should also provide situations for the growth and development of Christian attitudes and ideals and for the performance of Christian service in the every-day life of the individual.

When this working principle was applied to specific pupils, we recognized that we could not be satisfied with the teaching of factual and doctrinal material as so much knowledge. We must provide, wherever possible, for a full expression of the Christian principles that we are teaching. Each teacher must sponsor a knowing and doing program, in which there is developed a Christian pattern of conduct that is in conformity with the standard expressed by Christ when he said, "wherefore by their fruits ye shall know them." (Matt. 7:20)

In formulating the objectives that are set forth in the following section, our teaching staff has for its own guidance endeavored to list desirable outcomes of learning, as we may look for them in the development of habits, abilities, knowledge, and attitudes and ideals.

By means of special assignments that are carried out in home reading and study during the week, the teacher strives to stimulate the members of the class to reach definite standards of knowledge and ability for a more efficient life of Christian service.

Report Cards and Achievement Contests

A report card system has been developed on the basis of our Sunday School objectives. This brings before the teacher, the pupil, and the parent a periodic check-up and thus provides a medium for an evaluation of the work that is being done in each class.

A further activating force has been found in our annual achievement contest, which provides participation similar to that of the Walther League talent quest in such activities as Bible story telling, Bible geography, use of concordance, Bible references, memory work, Bible characters, Christian hymns, Christian art, etc. A total of fifteen active contests and nine display contests recently brought much youthful talent into the foreground and concentrated attention on many of the fields included in our Sunday School objectives.

Another device, designed to stimulate leisure time activities, has been found in the form of an annual exhibition in

---

TRINITY LUTHERAN (BADEN MEMORIAL) SUNDAY SCHOOL
WINFIELD, KANSAS

PUPIL'S REPORT CARD

PRIMARY, JUNIOR, INTERMEDIATE, AND SENIOR DEPARTMENTS

◇

PUPIL

DEPARTMENT

YEAR ENDING

PROMOTION ASSIGNMENT

TEACHER

NAME OF PUPIL

(A) Means rapid progress.
(B) Means normal progress.
(C) Means slow progress.
Unmarked squares indicate that improvement should be made.

	QUARTERLY GRADES				
	1	2	3	4	Final
BIBLE STORY LESSON					
Studies lesson in advance					
Is attentive during lesson					
Tells story effectively					
Grasps lesson of story well					
Takes part in class discussion					
Applies lesson to life situations					
MEMORY WORK					
Recites memory work well					
Explains meaning well					
Applies meaning to life situations					
BIBLE GEOGRAPHY					
Can locate places on map					
Remembers significance of places					
Reads about places mentioned					
USAGE OF BIBLE					
Reads Bible voluntarily					
Reads sections assigned in Bible					
Can find passages quickly					
Can find cross references quickly					
Uses concordance with understanding					
MISSIONS AND CHURCH HISTORY					
Knows location of Lutheran Foreign Mission Fields					
Knows kinds of Home Mission work of Lutheran Church					
Reads Missionary Biography					

	QUARTERLY GRADES				
	1	2	3	4	Final
Reads about church work in Children's Hour, Lutheran Witness, Kansas Lutheran, or Walther League Messenger					
PRAYER					
Memorizes prayers well					
Makes own prayers well					
SINGING OF HYMNS					
Memorizes Christian hymns					
Sings readily with group					
Sings in Junior Choir					
Reads about hymn writers					
CHRISTIAN GIVING					
Contributes Regularly					
Earns money for giving					
SUNDAY SCHOOL ATTENDANCE					
Attends regularly					
Is regularly on time					
Shows reverent attitude					
Is willing to assume leadership					
CHURCH ATTENDANCE					
Attends regularly					
Shows reverent attitude					
Takes part in worship					
NUMBER OF BOOKS READ					
NEW PUPILS BROUGHT TO SUNDAY SCHOOL					
VISITORS BROUGHT TO S. S. OR CHURCH					

NOTE TO PARENTS

In the Sunday School we are striving to assist you in developing in your child a sound understanding of Christian doctrine and a Christian pattern of conduct. Our teachers are therefore endeavoring to help your child enjoy the blessings of a Christian life by giving it thorough Christian instruction in the essentials of Christian belief with Christ as its personal Saviour. They are trying to provide situations for the growth and development of Christian attitudes and ideals and for the performance of Christian service in the every-day life of your child.

In this report card are listed a number of items which the Church considers important in the education and training of your child. It is being sent to you in order that you may know the teacher's estimate of your child's progress.

Please examine this report carefully and acknowledge its receipt by signing your name below. Kindly return at once.

SUPERINTENDENT

PASTOR

SIGNATURE OF PARENTS

First Quarter

Second Quarter

Third Quarter

twenty leisure time recreational and handicraft activities in connection with the annual Sunday School picnic.

All of these devices provide excellent opportunities for the wide awake teacher to form closer contacts with individual pupils for the development of a general pattern of Christian conduct in line with our Sunday School objectives, which are herewith presented.

I. Christian Knowledge and Ability Objectives

1. Purposeful reading of the Bible.

2. Ability to find selections in the Bible quickly.

3. Ability to use cross references and the concordance with ease.

4. A knowledge of chief Bible characters.

5. A knowledge of Bible events and historical periods.

6. A knowledge of the chief doctrines of the Bible and an ability to prove them from the Bible.

7. Ability to locate on a map the most important places connected with Bible history.

8. Ability to tell Bible stories effectively.

9. A knowledge of the history of the Bible.

10. A knowledge of the early development of the Christian church.

11. A knowledge of the missionary commands of the Bible.

12. A knowledge of the history of the Lutheran church.

13. A knowledge of the home and foreign mission activities of the Lutheran church.

14. Ability to sing from memory a large number of Christian hymns.

15. Ability to appreciate and interpret Christian painting and art.

16. Ability to recite from memory Christian prayers and longer selections from the Bible.

II. Christian Life Objectives

1. Ability to make original prayers, fitting them to the circumstances and problems of daily life.

2. Habits in Christian giving, making personal sacrifices to give regularly for church and Sunday School purposes.

3. Habits in Christian helping.

4. Proper attitudes, ideals, and habits with reference to church attendance.

5. Proper attitudes, ideals, and habits with reference to inviting and bringing others to church and Sunday School.

6. Proper attitudes, ideals, and habits for pleasant and congenial Christian fellowship.

7. Proper attitudes, ideals, and habits in dealing with the unfortunate.

8. Proper attitudes, ideals, and habits of leadership in recreation and entertainment.

9. Proper attitudes, ideals, and habits of reading church periodicals and wholesome Christian literature.

10. Proper attitudes, ideals, and habits for a continued and deep interest in home and foreign missions.

11. Proper attitudes, ideals, and habits for a continued and deep interest in nature.

12. Proper attitudes, ideals, and habits for a continued and deep interest in various types of handicraft.

The Bible in the Sunday School
CLAUDIUS S. KULOW

BEGINNING WITH THE DEPARTMENTS in the Sunday School where the children are able to read, the Sunday School service calls for responsive readings of selected Psalms as found in the hymnal. The familiarization with the "Hymnal of the Old Testament" is indeed a valuable asset in the religious education of a child. As the young people, however, take part in the activities and worship of the Senior Department or in Bible classes they are apt to grow somewhat matter of fact about the reading of a Psalm each Sunday morning. Then, too, with quarterly leaflets and outlines in use throughout all grades of the Sunday School, we are aware that in all too many cases people today read many books *about* the Bible, but do not actually know the Bible itself.

To this end, in our present pastorate, where the Senior and Bible Class departments of the Sunday School meet apart from the rest of the school, instead of reading mere portions of the Psalms as printed in the hymnal, we have taken our responsive readings direct from the Bible. Bibles are distributed at the beginning of the school hour along with the class envelopes and quarterlies, and a chapter or portion of a chapter is read responsively. We have essayed to give no extensive comment along with the reading, but at its close have given one or two minutes to driving home one or two thoughts.

No attempt has been made to fit the Scripture reading to the lesson or the day, but we have merely desired to acquaint our young people with great portions of God's Holy Word. Now many of our young people testify to the helpfulness found in passages hitherto unknown and unfamiliar.

In a period of four years we have read together through the Gospel of Luke, the prophecy of Isaiah, the Gospel of Matthew, the book of Proverbs, the Pauline epistles, Ecclesiastes, the Gospel of John, and the Psalms. Each week the reading is taken up at the point the previous reading was closed. Looking back, it is remarkable at the amount of ground that can be covered in this way with only the few minutes allotted each Sunday.

A Proposed Liturgy for the Installation of Sunday-School Teachers

UNDER this caption Dr. Geo. A. Fahlund, chairman of the Augustana Synod's Board of Christian Education and Literature, writes as follows in "*The Lutheran Companion*":

"Churches who have acted on our suggestion to have their Sunday school teachers installed into their respective offices seem to like it well enough to continue this practice. They have felt that installing Sunday school teachers in connection with the morning services and before the congregation lends dignity to the office of the Sunday school teacher and further impresses the congregation with the fact that after all there is something of importance to the work of the Sunday school. This importance is brought home in a direct manner to every one who is present at such a service.

"Acting on the suggestion of several, both pastors and Sunday school superintendents, that we offer something in the way of a liturgy for an installation service of this kind, we beg to submit the following, which with but a few changes by us have been used by at least one pastor:

"(Call names of teachers, who present themselves before the altar.)

"In the name of the Father, and of the Son, and of the Holy Spirit.

"*Dear Congregation.* Do you desire to set these persons apart as teachers of the children and youth of this church? If so, answer yes.

"*Answer: Yes.*

152

"*To Congregation.* Some of you are parents of these boys and girls and others of you have stood as sponsors at the time of their baptism. Do you now pledge to these teachers your hearty cooperation in the Christian training of our children so they may be reared in the nurture and admonition of the Lord? If so, answer yes.

"*Answer: Yes.*

"*To Teachers.* The Christian church of which you are members has called you to be teachers in its Sunday school and has pledged to support your efforts. In so doing, it has given you the highest recognition which any congregation can confer upon its members. The fathers and mothers here present are committing into your care the dearest that they have. They are asking you to feed these little ones with the Bread of Life, to take hold of their trusting hands and lead them in the way that they should go, and by both word of mouth and godly example to bring them into the fulness of the blessing of Christ. Unto that end do you here dedicate your intellect and hearts, your time and talents; and do you promise to discharge the duties connected with this high office, God helping you, to the best of your ability? If so, answer yes.

"*Answer: Yes.*

"*To Teachers, continued.* Hearing this, your solemn promise, on behalf of this congregation I declare you to be regularly set apart as teachers of the boys and girls of this church, in the name of the Father, and the Son, and the Holy Spirit, Amen.

"Incline your hearts unto God and hear His Word: 'They that are wise shall shine as the brightest of the firmament; and they that turn many to righteousness as the stars for ever and ever. Go ye and make disciples of all nations, teaching them to observe all things whatsoever I have commanded you. And lo, I am with you always, even unto the end of the world.'

"*Prayer:* Almighty, Merciful God, Heavenly Father, Thou art the Author and Perfector of all that is good within us. We ask for Thy blessing upon these men and women as teachers of boys and girls in our Sunday school. Grant them the assurance that Thou art with them, ready to bring to fruitage the Word which they shall plant. Grant them also a lofty conception of their great task as teachers of these little ones, whose angels do always behold the face of the Father in heaven. And when they are tempted, do Thou help them to be true. When they are perplexed, do Thou give them counsel. When they are discouraged, do Thou cheer their hearts and quicken them with a new vision. Give them a glad sense of the eternal worth of faithful service and make them to know that Thou art with them always, even unto the end of the world. We pray in the name of Jesus Christ, our Lord. Amen."

—*Lutheran Herald*

The Sandtable in Sunday School
FOR THE TINY TOTS
By
GLADYS ZINIKER, Eugene, Oregon

NOTE:—The following is a talk given by the author at the spring meeting of the Willamette Lutheran Sunday School Teachers' Association, offered for publication at the pastor's request.

I HAVE THE BEGINNERS CLASS, and I must say that they are very small beginners, and also very restless. The oldest pupil in my class is four years old, and the youngest about two and a half, ten of them altogether. We have from thirty-five to forty minutes for our lesson period.

The first thing I do is to get them all seated. Sometimes some of them are afraid to sit down and I have to hold their hand or let them sit on my lap to keep them from crying. We have little benches for them to sit on, each bench holding two pupils. Next I take the roll and their collection,—if I don't do this at the beginning pennies will be rolling all over the floor. After this we have a short prayer, and then comes the lesson. At the end of the lesson we have our sandtable work and memory verse, sometimes we have primary hymns for memory work.

Our sandtable is about three feet square and about two feet high, just high enough for my class to be able to see into it well.

For the characters in the story I use dolls cut from paper, but if there are only about three characters I use small dolls from the fifteen cent store. For trees I use pieces of fir boughs and dried straw flower foliage. The temples, houses, chariots, etc., are made from paper, with windows and doors cut out. For water I use tinfoil; it can be rolled back easily for such lessons as "The crossing of the River Jordan." For fire I use real fire or sparklers, such as are used on July 4th. Caves and tombs are small cardboard boxes with one end out, covered with sand and "trees." The animals are small tin or porcelain figures, again from the fifteen cent store. Stars are cardboard covered with tinfoil, hung from the ceiling on threads. Birds are cut from paper and are also hung on threads.

I always try to follow the general character of the land where the story takes place, because impressions made on the mind in this manner are very lasting. I always have the story worked out in detail before class time, and never do I let the children help or touch the objects on the table: for the object is to teach them the lesson and not to teach them to play.

Of course the sandtable means much more work for the teacher, but it surely pays well. It keeps the attention. In my class it has "saved the day" more than once. Several Sundays ago one little girl in my class, a newcomer, began to cry. Then a little boy started to cry, too, in sympathy. But when my own little girl began to cry also, I was about frantic. Remembering the sandtable, I said: "Oh, let's see what we have on the sandtable!" Everyone was attention at once, and even the little newcomer forgot herself and talked.

Another thing, then, the sandtable does is to help the small bashful child to forget himself. Children who never talk in class or answer when spoken to, will forget themselves completely and talk when we are at the sandtable.

Then, too, the sandtable stimulates attendance. It certainly did in my class. The first Sunday I used the sandtable was the last Sunday in August. I had just taken over the Beginners Class, and the enrollment was three,—our minister's little boy, my little girl, and another teacher's little girl. In other words, just those children of teachers, who had to come, because their parents had to come and could not let them at home. After the sandtable was installed other children began to see it and talk about it. Then they began to bring little brothers and sisters to see it. Parents came and brought their children. The class began to grow and soon we had to divide it. We had sixteen children from two years to six years of age. Since it is divided I have those from two to four, and another teacher has those from four to six. During the sandtable and music periods I have them all.

Let me tell you about a few of the stories, and how I worked them out on the table:

Elijah and the Prophets of Baal. The sand was arranged to be a large hill. On the hill were two tiny stone altars. On each altar were sticks, and a small animal made of cotton. Many dolls cut out of paper were on their knees around one altar, and Elijah and a few people—also paper dolls,—were on their knees around the other altar. At the climax, when fire came from heaven, I lit Elijah's offering and burned it.

Elijah Taken to Heaven. The sandtable was arranged with a city and a river of tinfoil, with a mountain in an opposite corner. I had Elijah and Elisha leave the city and when they came to the river I rolled back the tinfoil so they could pass over on dry ground. After they were on the mountain, I brought the chariot down from heaven to get Elijah. The chariot was made of paper with a small metal horse hitched to it. I had two sparklers fastened to the chariot, and when I was ready for the chariot I lit the sparklers. Of course, these sparklers do not burn anything, so they are perfectly safe.

David and Goliath. I had two armies of soldiers, paper dolls of course, lined up on each side of the sandtable. Behind the soldiers were their tents, also paper. In the center of the table were David and Goliath. David was a small paper man with a sling, and Goliath was a large paper man with a sword and shield.

The Flood. For this lesson I had a large shallow pan from the gas oven of the bakery. It was only an inch deep, and about three fourths as large as the sandtable. At one side of the pan I piled the sand to resemble a mountain. The ark was made of cardboard with windows and doors cut out. Noah and his family were of paper; the birds were paper, and we used all our animals.

I told the story on two Sundays. The first time I had the ark floating on the water. The next time it was on top of the mountain while Noah and his family were gathered around an altar.

These few descriptions will show how the stories can be worked out on the sandtable. In this way the lesson truths can be brought home to the pupil, while at the same time he is entertained and amused. It is best to use the less expensive objects for the work. It is surprising what can be done with paper, scissors, paste, and of course imagination. Primary children have an active imagination so that you do not need anything elaborate.

The following are some of the points I have observed while using the sandtable during the past eight months. Some of them have been touched on already, and all of them have been learned through experience:—

1. It stimulates attendance. My class grew from three to sixteen members in four or five months. Every Sunday I have from four to six visiting parents. About one third of my class are children of non-Lutheran parents. Mothers tell me that their children cry if they have to stay home from Sunday School.

2. It insures good order.

3. It holds the pupil's interest and attention.

4. It makes the bashful child forget himself.

5. It gives the child a picture of the lesson for his mind's eye. As everyone knows this is the best and easiest way to reach small minds, or any mind, for that matter.

6. The general character of the land in the story should be followed. It is said that eighty-five percent of what we remember comes through the eye. Since these impressions are lasting, they should be as accurate as possible.

7. The lesson should be worked out on the table in detail before class. It takes too much time to do this during class, and it distracts attention.

8. It is never wise to let the children assist in sandtable work, because it brings the play spirit into action, in spite of all one can do.

9. Teach the children not to touch the objects on the table; it disrupts order.

10. The sandtable makes more work for the teacher. Much time is spent in preparing the lesson, for the geography of the land must be known, too. It takes time to prepare the table, and in my case I prepare my own objects.

11. Inexpensive rather than expensive objects should be used. I find that for characters paper dolls are best, because you can have any number of them any size and put them into almost any shape.

And last, but what is really most important,

12. Never should the beauty of the table overshadow the vital truth of the story. If the objects on the table are too pretty, the truth of the lesson will be lost. If too much attention is given to the objects, the lesson truth will be lost. The table should be used as a means to an end; and that end is to bring out the lesson in the story and to have that story make a lasting impression on the children's mind. I think the sandtable accomplishes this with the primary pupil much better than words or pictures. I'm sure that lasting impressions have been accomplished in my class. I have observed most of my pupils at play and have talked with their mothers on the subject, and every one of them uses the Sunday School stories in his play.

I have taught the story from the sandtable in two ways, in what I call *active* and *still* teaching.

Active,—for instance, when David beheaded Goliath I had David tear the head off Goliath and carry it back to Saul. When Noah let the dove out of the ark, I had a paper bird on a thread and let it fly around over the water.

Still,—where nothing is touched on the table, not even by the teacher.

I like both ways for my class. They respond better to the active way. However, a person must be careful not to be too active, or the play spirit will be introduced and the lesson truth lost. For this reason I only have the class at the sandtable for about ten minutes or so.

OPPORTUNITIES IN SUNDAY SCHOOL
from p. 150

will be given for special preparation. The contestant will then be given from 2 to 4 minutes in which to tell the story of the missionary's life. Separate contests for Bible classes and Sunday School groups.

5. MEMORY WORK. Each contestant will be given a sheet of paper on which are given a number of Bible passages and hymn stanzas for completion. The material will be selected from the GRADED MEMORY COURSE in accordance with the classification of each contestant. Time limit: 10 minutes.

6. HYMN RECOGNITION. This contest will be open to ALL WHO ARE PRESENT. Parts of fifteen hymns will be played. Those participating in the contest will list the names of the hymns that are played.

7. NATURE STUDY. IDENTIFICATION OF TREES. Twenty trees in the park will be numbered. Contestants will list these numbers and write the name of each tree on a sheet of paper provided for that purpose. This contest will be opened to ALL WHO ARE PRESENT.

"DISPLAY" CONTESTS

1. ORIGINAL PRAYER BOOKLET. Each contestant will submit five prayers, which he has written and neatly arranged in booklet form.

2. RELIGIOUS PICTURES. Each contestant will submit a scrap book, not less than 12 pages in length, in which religious pictures are neatly mounted and titled.

3. LIBRARY READING. This contest will be in the form of class displays. The names of the books drawn from the Sunday School library and read by individual pupils to be arranged for a display. Awards to pupils reading most books. (Reading time from October 1 to June 6.)

4. NEW PUPILS BROUGHT TO SUNDAY SCHOOL. The names of pupils who have brought new pupils who enrolled in the Sunday School will be listed for display. Awards to pupils having brought most pupils. (Time from October 1 to June 6.)

5. VISITORS' RECORD. The names of pupils who have brought visitors to Sunday School will be listed. (Time from October 1 to June 6.) Awards to pupils having brought most visitors.

Copy for Your Rally Day Printed Matter

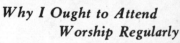

Why I Ought to Attend Worship Regularly

My Father calls me to His House and where His special Presence is, that I may learn and worship.

I must visit His Temple and love to linger there.

I must give my mind work in laying up store of divine truth, and seek grace where God promises that it shall flow.

If Christ could not but do this, how shall I without loss, neglect?

No earthly work, no human friendship or kindred must stand in the way.

I must be about my Father's business.

God has the first claim on my love and on my duty.

Only so can I prepare and make my whole life acceptable to Him and blessed to myself.

Electrotype No. 194—Size 1½ x 3½ inches.—Price, $1.75   **Let's begin on Rally Day!**

Visualizing the Sunday School Lesson

(A Study in Sunday School Methods)

H. W. PRANGE

THERE are five avenues of approach to the human mind, and five only. They pass through the Eye-gate, the Ear-gate, the Nose-gate, the Mouth-gate, and the Touch-gate. The highway which leads into the mind through the Eye-gate is the widest and most congested. On this thoroughfare a multitude of facts and fancies jostle one another and crowd forward with great speed to reach the inner man. In point of traffic and speed, the Ear-gate is second, but more facts enter into the mind through the Eye-gate than through the other four avenues combined. Through the Eye-gate there march armies, through the Ear-gate regiments, through the other gates straggling individuals. When the Eye-gate and the Ear-gate compete, the Eye-gate wins, for the average mind pays attention to what it sees often to the exclusion of what it hears. You may place on a platform the world's most brilliant orator, but if you will allow me to stand at his side and do something that appeals to your eyes, I will defeat him, because you will inevitably look before you will listen.

In view of this fact, the teacher is exceedingly unwise, who omits the Eye-gate approach and limits himself to that of the Ear-gate. The skillful teacher is he who is qualified to attack the Eye-gate as well as the Ear-gate and thus uses the two divinely ordained gateways to the mind and heart of his pupils. This evidently is the method of Christ, the Master-teacher, whose examples of teaching are unsurpassed in the whole history of pedagogy, and who taught with such power that Gennesaret's beach was overcrowded with attentive hearers and a fisherman's boat became the pulpit of the world. Unlike the scribes who labored to teach proper Sabbath observance by formulating rules regarding the most trivial and insignificant acts, Christ visualized His teaching on this question by sketching the merciful man, merciful to his unfortunate beast on the Sabbath day, and by restoring the withered hand and the palsied body. While the scribes wrangled over the precise meaning of the word "neighbor," Jesus taught the truth for all time by painting the immortal picture of the Good Samaritan, by delivering the devil-haunted daughter of the Syrophoenician woman, and by healing the servant of a Roman Centurian. In a word, the scribes were dry-as-dust hair-splitting dialecticians who took delight in talking words to men. Christ was a master artist who drew from life, moulded living forms, and thus taught truth objectively. It was this direct appeal through the eye and the imagination, that fascinated his peasant hearers, and has held the attention of the world for nineteen centuries.

In preparing its curriculum to train efficient Sunday School workers, the CHICAGO TEACHERS TRAINING INSTITUTE has had in mind to lead its students back to the visualizing method of teaching. Assuming that in its teaching function, the church is to teach ideas rather than words, this Institution has endeavored to avoid the soulless method of the scribes, which reduces instruction largely to a mere drill upon words, and to really prepare its students for practical work, by encouraging them to adhere closely to a system of instruction characterized by this more rational method of presenting truth objectively. A number of examples in visualizing a lesson, which follow, have been drawn directly from these Institute lessons; others have been added to indicate how this method of teaching lends itself to the treatment of nearly every subject of Sunday School study.

The advantages of visualizing a lesson are too numerous to mention. The following four reasons for employing this method extensively will appeal to the reader without further reflection.

(1) *We gain time.* Visualizing is always an educational short-cut. Four hours of mere oral teaching will scarcely equal one hour spent in vizualizing the lesson. Try it and be convinced. How large this factor of time looms in our Sunday School work, and what a boon it is to find a short-cut, when the very thought of the brevity of the lesson period dismays us, is evident.

(2) *We make lasting impressions.* We have the saying: "In one ear and out the other," but not: "In one eye and out the other." What you have heard is soon forgotten. Hence the need of endless repetitions. But what you have seen is your lasting possession. The gnawing tooth of time makes slow progress in devouring a mental pitcure.

(3) *We compel the teacher to master his lesson.* Among all the workers for the coming of the Kingdom of God, none, perhaps, ought to be held in higher estimation than faithful Sunday School teachers. As a rule they are among the busiest people in the world, every hour of the week filled with crowding duties, every vult of energy required to do that which their hands and brains are forced to do by the conditions of our congested life. It would be cruel to add one straw to the burden such men and women are carrying, and harsh criticism of their efficiency would be altogether out of place. But sympathetic criticism is never unkind. We are painfully aware that many willing and enthusiatic teachers often appear before their classes unprepared. Too tired to listen at times, they do not always master the thought of the lesson even when it is presented to them in the Teacher's Meetings. But if the lesson is visualized to them, it arouses their own interest, holds their attention and fires them with a new enthusiasm, which cannot fail to show results. And being compelled to visualize the lesson to others, they realize they cannot perform their work with a slipshod preparation.

(4) *We in a large measure solve the question of Sunday School discipline.* Attention depends upon interest. Interest may be developed in many ways, but there is no surer way than to make use of a blackboard. To the average boy only a man with a live animal is more interesting than a live man with a blackboard. You may defy that boy who has come with the seductive pin, if you have the attention of his eyes and his ears. For he will forget his pin. If you have his ears only, he will remember his pin.

To substantiate what has been said about the advantages of visualizing the lesson, and at the same time to open the way for a practical demonstration of this method of teaching, let us visualize the familiar story of Zacchaeus and Jesus. Zacchaeus, the prominent character of this story, claims our attention first. Write upon the blackboard:

Zacchaeus
seeking
Jesus

After drawing out the details of the story, let us proceed immediately to the second fact of the narrative, that Jesus was seeking Zacchaeus. For when the Master came to the foot of the tree, He looked up, and it was apparent that He was seeking Zacchaeus as much as Zacchaeus was seeking Him. This second fact induces us to read the foregoing words upward and we now have:

Jesus seeking Zacchaeus

You perceive at once that we have now come to the very climax of the story. For Jesus says: "Zacchaeus, come down, for today I must abide at thy house." But never mind about Zacchaeus and Jesus. Bring the lesson home to your class. Wipe out the word "Zacchaeus" and substitute the word "You."

You
Seeking
Jesus

But if that is true, read upward once more and you will find that like the Good Shepherd, Jesus has gone out long ago to seek you.

Now consider for a moment what we have accomplished through analyzing and visualizing this familiar Bible story. In the first place, we have brought out definitely the paramount truth, around which the whole narrative revolves—the truth expressed by the prophet in the words: "Ye have not chosen me, but I have chosen you."—that truth which is usually conspicuous by its absence, when this story is related. In the second place, this truth has been indelibly fixed upon our mind. No reader of these lines, we venture to say, will ever be able to listen to this story in the future, without recalling this scheme by which this great lesson was pictured to his eye. Thirdly, the attention of every student was held throughout the lesson, through our mode of presentation, and through the wiping out and the substituting of words, which brought the truth home to us individually; and finally, one of the greatest and most difficult truths of the Bible was taught in comparatively few moments. This illustration naturally leads us to consider in a general way—

The Visualizing Function of All Bible Stories

Not all stories will lend themselves to such a treatment as that of Zacchaeus. Neither is it necessary nor even desirable that they should. For ordinarily, the story itself, properly prepared and told, will visualize in the best possible way the truth which it is meant to convey. In fact, a story is nothing more than a word picture, drawn from history, experience or nature, which presents to the eye of the mind, a faith or character forming truth. When Paul informs us that all Scripture, given by inspiration, is profitable for doctrine and for instruction in righteousness, he can only mean that the stories of the Bible are not to be read merely as history, but that they are to present to us in a concrete form, taken in by the senses, what the abstract statements convey to our reasoning powers. But this is only another way of saying that the story is not to be taught for the sake of the story. The teaching value of the story is not to be found in the historical data which it furnishes, but rather in the truth which it visualizes.

Viewed in this light, story telling becomes an art, which must be mastered through hard study and continued practice. For the effective story teller must habituate himself to analyze the Bible narrative carefully, to find the truth which it visualizes, and having found this truth, he must so construct his narrative, that his pupil will perceive it without further moralization on the part of the teacher. Should it be possible to draw two or more truths from the story, it will be necessary to determine upon one truth to be presented, since it is only confusing to the child to present two truths in the same lesson. Take for example the story of Daniel. Selecting the truth that God hears and answers prayer, we will have the following sequence:

(1) The development of the story material, consisting of the following series of word pictures, so vivid, so full of action, that the child's imagination will make them live and breathe: Daniel's prayer; the plot; Daniel's confidence and loyalty to God; Daniel cast into the lion's den; the King's sorrow.

(2) The climax, which brings out with great force the truth to be visualized: the King's visit in the early morning; the great surprise; the divine deliverance in answer to Daniel's prayer. Failing to bring out this climax with convincing force, you fail in the entire lesson.

Employing the Bible story after this manner, as the visualizing agency of a given truth, the Sunday School lesson material will be correspondingly affected, both as to the subject matter and its chronological arrangement. For—

(1) The lesson leaf will be so arranged that the one thought to be presented will stand out prominently for both teacher and pupil; and the story itself will be so arranged that everything in the lesson will work up to the climax, which brings out that truth.

(2) The chronological order of the lesson will be regarded a secondary matter, and the truth to be taught will determine the choice of the story. It is well known that to the younger child chronological order has no meaning whatever. History as personal biography and Bible stories as such, have a very large educational function for the little child, but not as history. To the older boys and girls and especially to young people, history itself in its chronological order becomes a topic, since it reveals the thoughts and acts of God in his dealings with the nations. When the child has advanced sufficiently to be able to observe God at work in carrying forward his eternal plans and purposes in the building or wrecking of nations, then and not until then, will it find an interest in chronology.

(3) The repetition of the story will not become a mere repetition, but rather the employment of an old story to teach a new lesson. The story of the Flood, for instance, may be used to visualize three truths: the protection of the good; the punishment of the wicked; and the preservation of the creatures. This fact enables the teacher to repeat the story three times, and yet to teach three lessons.

(4) The child will receive proper recognition in the choice of lesson material. Beginning where we find the child, the story will be selected with the view of bringing to him the truth which he needs. Unhampered by any consideration of chronological order, the child will receive his portion in due season, to meet his needs.

Having mentioned the chronology of the Bible a number of times, it would be in place here to say a few words about visualizing it to the pupils. It is a notorious fact that when it comes to the chronology of the Bible, many teachers are all at sea. If you ask them about when Elijah lived, you would be surprised at the brilliant flash of silence that would follow. They are not posted; indeed a good many of them do not know where to find Elijah in the Book, much less in history. For this reason it becomes necessary to localize the great persons and periods of the Bible in the minds of our teachers and children alike, so that the chronology of the Bible will fasten itself on their minds indelibly. To accomplish this purpose, nothing will be so effective as visualization. Note the following diagram:

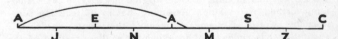

Let that line represent the four thousand years from Adam to Christ. At the beginning we will put down the letter "A" for Adam, and at the close the letter "C" for Christ, and between the two the space represents forty centuries. If you should subdivide in the middle and ask the average teacher what great men lived at that time, he would say, "I don't know." It is worth our while, however, to put down the great man, the father of the faithful, Abraham. If we divide again, making periods of one thousand years, and once more call for names, very few would be able to give us the name that falls between Abraham and Adam. We will simply put it down, so as to expedite matters—Enoch falls there; and Israel's great king falls half way between Abraham and Christ. Now, we have millenniums—Adam, Enoch, Abraham, Solomon, Christ. Once more we will subdivide and make it half millenniums. On the one side we have an unimportant name—Jared, yet we will put it down for a landmark. On the other side we place the great man—Noah. On the other half of the line we will place Moses and the builder of the second temple—Zerubbabel. How greatly this diagram localizes chronologically the great heroes of the Old Testament. And what a surprise comes to us when we realize that the Book of Genesis covers that much of the Old Testament history which is included under the arc in the diagram—more than one-half of that history is covered by that one book. Whatever, therefore, is before Abraham, must be in Genesis.

How perfectly this diagram will serve its purpose for every individual lesson of Old Testament history. Just now we may be studying about Aaron,—Where is he? Well, he is a brother of Moses; he must come near the letter "M." Next Sunday we find ourselves in the time of the Judges,—Where are we then? Between "M" and "S," of course, somewhere. At another time the days of the Kings, in the divided monarchy, occupies us. Of course, we are then between "S" and "Z." In that way the teacher can get at least a bird's-eye view of the Word, and is able to somewhat intelligently localize the actors in this great drama of divine revelation and divinely guided history.

In a similar way, the informed teacher will visualize to his pupils all the great facts concerning the Bible. We know it took sixteen centuries to write the Bible and thirty-six authors were at work in completing this task of writing the sixty-six books. What an educational shortcut and an aid to memory will not the following diagram be—

$\begin{array}{l} 1 \\ 3 \\ 6 \end{array}$ **6** CENTURIES AUTHORS BOOKS

Likewise, we know that thirty-nine books are found in the Old Testament and twenty-seven in the New. How can we better enable our pupils to retain these numbers than by throwing this diagram upon the blackboard—

OLD TESTAMENT
3   9   = 39
NEW TESTAMENT
3   X   9   = 27

Explaining to the pupils that these figures are arrived at by counting the letters in the words, and by inserting the "X" between the figures under the New Testament, because "X" or the "cross" is the prominent factor in the New Testament.

From direct Bible study, let us proceed to the Catechism, that book of abstract teaching, which seems so dry and forbidding to the average boy, and which is usually regarded by the teacher as a handy compendium to provide the school with fundamental memory work and convenient drill material over against the needs of a future day. Of course, the Bible story may be pressed into service to reduce its abstract doctrines to a concrete form, but even dispensing with this device, the skillful teacher who has mastered the art of visualization will find the Catechism itself a book of most attractive pictures, full of color and life, which cannot fail to hold the undivided attention of the child. Following the divine clue, furnished by the two Sacraments, where the facts of our salvation are visualized with such exquisite beauty—Baptism picturing the cleansing power of the blood of Christ, and the Holy Supper speaking of God's great family table, where his children congregate to be fed and strengthened with the bread of life—every chief part of the Catechism may be made to pulsate with life. Space forbids that we linger where there is much to tempt us, yet a few references to the first and second part of the Catechism will almost be necessary for the sake of completeness.

THE TEN COMMANDMENTS VISUALIZED

Four words are used to denote the breaking of the Law: Sin Transgression, Trespass, and Iniquity. Concealed within their bosom these four words harbor pictures which, when brought to the surface, will make the study of the Law a most delightful and interesting exercise. Take for example, the word "trespass." It recalls to the child a very familiar sight: the enclosed field with the forbidding sign, "No Trespassing." The child understands that within the fence there is something which the owner seeks to protect, and that the sign is meant to furnish that protection by keeping out an intruder. Applied to the Law, this expression immediately converts the Ten Commandments into ten protective fences, which God has erected. Visualized to the eye, they will appear as follows:

1ST COMMANDMENT   5TH COMMANDMENT   6TH COMMANDMENT

With such an approach, few boys or girls will be found who will not feel an inward urge to discover for themselves, according to the separate commandments, the things which God is so anxious to protect. And many pupils, perhaps, will be ready to compete with one another in an attempt to find through individual home work, the proper word for each square. All that will be required of the teacher is to work out with his class a pattern square of one commandment. And who will be able to measure the enthusiasm of the teacher in discussing in detail with the class the nature of the divine institutions and the human privileges which are so precious with God that He surrounds them with such a strong, protective wall. And finally, how spirited will not the drill be which naturally results, when all pupils with the Catechism in hand are asked to select the words from each commandment which are descriptive of climbing over the fence and disregarding the sign. Even the dullest pupil will participate in such class work with keenest interest.

Even greater interest will possibly be aroused through the study of the word "Sin," which signifies: "Missing the Mark." For what child can remain disinterested and inattentive when the attractive shooting gallery, with its target and bull's eye, and its riflemen, who hit or miss, succeed or fail, takes form before his eyes? It is now that the positive side of each commandment can be pointed out, since the bull's eye to be aimed at is the "Image of God," or holiness. Along side of the negative drill suggested by the term trespass, you will now have the positive drill, thus covering the entire commandment. How much livelier and more profitable such a study of the Law will prove to teacher and pupil alike, than the customary dull repetition with the possible addition of an explanation of the difficult words.

In this connection, the various kinds of sins will claim consideration. How can this part of the Catechism be studied to the best advantage? Why not after the following manner:

THE TREE OF SIN
Sin is like a Tree, with roots, branches, twigs and fruit.

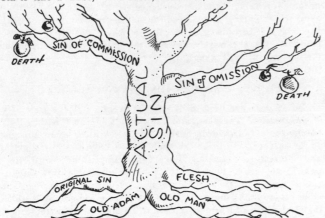

Original (first) Sin, also known as "Old Adam," "Old Man," and "Flesh," is the root of sin—under-ground, hidden in the heart. It is the natural inclination in man to sin. (A ball on a hillside has the inclination to roll down.)

"Out of the heart proceed evil thoughts."

Actual Sin is the trunk of the tree—the inclination of the heart breaking out in thought, word or deed.

"Sin is transgression (walking over) the Law."—1 John 3,4.

Sins of Omission are neglect of duty, leaving undone what we are commanded to do.

Not to fear, love and trust in God—1st Commandment.

Not to pray, praise and give thanks.—3rd Commandment.

Not to defend our neighbor, or speak well of him.—8th Commandment.

Sins of Commission are thoughts, words and deeds which are forbidden:

To have other Gods.—1st Commandment.

To curse, swear, lie.—2nd Commandment.

To slander or defame our neighbor.—8th Commandment.

Death, the fruit of the Tree of Sin is "God's wrath and displeasure, temporal death and eternal damnation." See Christian Questions and Answers in Catechism—Question 4.

"The wages of sin is death."—Rom. 6,23.

"The soul that sinneth it shall die."—Ez. 18,4.

When it is made plain that this Tree of Sin is growing in every life and putting forth the fruit of death, the second part of the Catechism—the Creed—will come to the child as good news indeed. Visualizing the creed, we might follow the following suggestion, because of the post-war age in which we live:

THE CREED—THE CHRISTIAN FLAG

Every nation has a flag. The church has a flag. Our flag—the Stars and Stripes. The Church's flag—The Creed.

The Creed is a flag of three colors and the cross. For 2000 years the Church has been marching behind this flag. We learn the Creed to become flag bearers of the Church.

We draw up our flag at the beginning of every public service, by beginning in the name of the Father, the Son, and the Holy Ghost (The Holy Trinity). We salute and swear allegiance to our flag by reciting the Creed at all public services (a solemn and impressive moment.)

THE QUALIFICATIONS OF A TEACHER
Term I, Semester I, Subject "C"
THE TEACHER'S CONSECRATION
Reference: "The Devotional Life of the Sunday School Teacher," by Dr. J. R. Miller

The foundation for successful teaching in the Sunday School is the personal *consecration* of the teacher. "You cannot throw a stone, until you have first grasped it."

Qualification to assume the grave responsibilities of teaching and capacity to attain and enjoy its precious compensations can be gained only through humble, sincere, heart-felt personal consecration and devotion to the Saviour.

Bible References: Compare Matt. 26, 30-35, 58, 69-75; Mark 14, 26-31. 50, 54, 66-72; Luke 22, 31-34, 54-62; John 13, 36-38; 18, 15-18, 25-27 *with* John 21, 1-19.—The story of the Fall and Raising of Peter.

WHAT IS PERSONAL CONSECRATION?
I. *Consecration in Character.*

1. Demands honest realization of personal sinfulness and unworthiness; sincere contrition and humble repentance; clear recognition of the sinfulness of sin.

The teacher cannot impress the class with their desperate *need* of a Saviour from sin and the unspeakable joy of the accomplished salvation, unless he has first felt that need and experienced that joy in his *own* heart.

Peter was solemnly reminded of his great fall and made to look at it and to think about it and to feel it in all its shamefulness. Then came the commission: "Feed"—"Follow Me."

2. Demands sincere love and heartfelt devotion to the Saviour. Christ asks every teacher: "Lovest thou me?"—Compare Luke 7, 47. Without sincere love in the heart *for* the Saviour, the teacher cannot present to his class the great love *of* the Saviour *for* them.

3. Demands firm faith and trust in the Saviour. "Feed MY lambs." He is the Supreme Shepherd. "Follow ME,"—He leads and shows the way. Promise: Matt. 28, 18-20; note *"therefore"* in v. 19 and its relation to vv. 18 and 20.

Faithfully doing his Master's work, the consecrated teacher has the comforting and encouraging assurance of his Master's presence, guidance, help and strength.—Phil. 2, 13.

II. *Consecration in Service*

1. Genuine love for souls, true compassion for the unsaved. Christians are messengers of Christ, therefore *soul-winners*. As soul-winners they must have the mind which was in Christ Jesus.

2. Genuine love for children. This is not mere matter of emotion or sentiment, but the recognition of every child as a personal object of Jesus' love, however unlovely and unattractive they may be personally.

3. Hence, genuine love and enthusiasm for the work itself as a privilege of service for the Master.

ABOVE WE GIVE A SAMPLE LESSON SHEET AS USED IN THE CHICAGO TEACHER'S TRAINING COURSE.

Installation Service, Sunday School Visitors

A CHRISTIAN congregation comprises a group of people who by profession are servants of the Lord God. This being the case all members of the Church are to willingly use their talents in the service of Jesus Christ.

When a Christian joins the Church he is not satisfied merely to be a member of it. His desire is to glorify his Savior as he labors for the extension or for the strengthening of the kingdom of God.

You have consented to serve the interest of Christ's kingdom in the office of a Sunday School Visitor. In this office you shall serve as a co-laborer with your Pastor to visit the sick in the Sunday School and by visitation of those who are absent from the Sunday School to keep the youth entrusted to this congregation under the influence of the Gospel of Christ.

As you visit the parents of the children living within your district you shall bear in mind that you are to serve the interest of Christ and of His Church. This being so you will, of course, not go beyond the peculiar function of the office to which you are (called, elected, appointed).

In co-operation both with the Pastor and with the Sunday School superintendent, as well as with the teachers whose children you serve, you will find great joy in your work and the blessing of Jesus Christ.

I now ask you in the name of God and in the presence of this Christian congregation do you intend faithfully to perform the duties of the office of Sunday School Visitor,

First, by regularly visiting the absentees in your district,

Secondly, by co-operation with the Pastor and with other workers and officers of the School and of the Church, and,

Thirdly, to limit your activity to the duties prescribed for your particular office, then answer—Yes.

Upon this confession of intention so to serve I give unto you to hold, except for cause, the office of Sunday School Visitor. May the Spirit of God, who only can make us sufficient for work in the kingdom of God give unto you wisdom and understanding, and faithful heart, and a daily spirit of prayer.

Let us pray.

O Almighty God, the Father of our Lord Jesus Christ, because Thou art pleased with the response of Thy people to consecrate and to dedicate themselves to Thy service, we pray Thee to bless these Christian women in the work which they begin in Thy name. Endow them with wisdom and with understanding and enable them by the timely word of the Gospel to bring little children under the influence of Thy Word and thus to assist them and their parents to become worshippers of Thee with this congregation. Inasmuch as Thou only canst make us sufficient to Thy work give to these servants whatever is necessary to enable them to serve this congregation and to serve the interest of Thy great and glorious name. Give ear, O God, to this supplication, for Jesus Christ, Thy dear Son's sake. Amen.—Submitted by Carl H. Napier, Dallas, Texas.

THE LUTHERAN CHURCH USES 100 LANGUAGES

1. Amale, New Guinea
2. Amharic, Ethiopia
3. Apache*
4. Arabic
5. Aranda, C. Australia
6. Assamese, E. India
7. Assyrian*
8. Asu, N.E. Tanganyika
9. Bali, Fr. Eq. Africa
10. Barum, Fr. Eq. Africa
11. Blackfoot*
12. Chaga, Tanganyika
13. Cherokee*
14. Chinese Colloquials*, China
15. Chinese Mandarin*, China
16. Chinese Wenli, China
17. Chippewa*
18. Cree*
19. Croatian*, Jugoslavia
20. Czech (Bohemian)*
21. Danish*
22. Dieri, Australia
23. Duala, Fr. Eq. Africa
24. Dutch, Holland
25. English*
26. Eskimo*, Greenland, Alaska
27. Esthonian*
28. Faroeic, Faroes Is.
29. Finnish*
30. French
31. Frisian, N. Germany
32. Ga, Gold Coast
33. Gal'a, Ethiopia
34. German*
35. Grebo, Liberia
36. Hausa, Sudan
37. Haya, Tanganyika
38. Hebrew*, Palestine
39. Herero, Damaraland
40. High Malay, India
41. High Hindi, India
42. Hungarian*
43. Icelandic*
44. Italian*
45. Ituri, Congo
46. Japanese
47. Kanarese, S. India
48. Karanga, S. Rhodesia
49. Kate, New Guinea
50. Konde, Nyassaland
51. Kuanyama, Ovamboland
52. Kuama, Eritrea
53. Kurdish
54. Landsmaal, Norway
55. Lappish, Finland
56. Lettish*, Latvia
57. Lithuanian*
58. Malagasy, Madagascar
59. Malayalam, India
60. Manchu, Manchuria
61. Masai, Tanganyika
62. Mombasa, Kenga
63. Mongolian, Mongolia
64. Mundari, India
65. Ndonga, Ovamboland
66. Nobonob, New Guinea
67. Norwegian*
68. Nyamwezi, Tanganyika
69. Nyika, Nyasaland
70. Pedi, Transvaal
71. Polish*
72. Portugese, Brazil
73. Quanian, Norway
74. Ragetta, New Guinea
75. Ruanda, Congo
76. Rumanian*
77. Russian*
78. Santali, India
79. Sakalava, Madagascar
80. Shamba, Uganda
81. Shambala, Tanganyika
82. Slovak*
83. Slovenian (Wend)*, Germany
84. Spanish*
85. Suto, Basutoland
86. Swedish*
87. Syriac, Syria
88. Tamil, India
89. Telugu, India
90. Tigre, Eritrea
91. Tigrinya, Eritrea
92. Toda, India
93. Tulu, India
94. Ukrainian (Ruthenian) Poland
95. Urdu, India
96. Venda, Rhodesia
97. Winnebago*
98. Xosa, Cape Colony
99. Yiddish*
100. Zulu, Natal

A LETTER TO PARENTS

Suffer the little children to come unto me and forbid them not, for of such is the Kingdom of God. Verily I say unto you, Whosoever shall not receive the Kingdom of God as a little child he shall not enter therein.—Mark 10:14,15.

Whoso shall offend one of these little ones which believe in me, it were better for him that a millstone were hanged about his neck and that he were drowned in the depth of the sea.—Matt. 18:6.

Dear Friend:—

Our Sunday School is organizing for a new season of work. We deeply realize the importance and responsibility of our work and in order that your child may get the full benefit of our labors we want to enlist your support and co-operation. We want to impress upon you the preciousness of your child's soul and the grave responsibility which rests upon you of equipping your child spiritually for this life and the next. Parents are accountable to God for the welfare of the tender souls entrusted to their care. The root and cause of the present unruliness and frivolousness of our youth lies primarily in our American homes.

The Sunday School is a force for the spiritual training of our children, but it cannot operate successfully without the earnest support of the parents. Help us to increase the effectiveness of our work by faithfully carrying out the following suggestions:

1. SEND YOUR CHILD REGULARLY! Irregular attendance disrupts the school and breaks the continuity of the teacher's efforts.

2. INSIST ON PROMPTNESS! The time of instruction is too short to condone tardiness.

3. REHEARSE the coming Sunday's lesson with your child! Insist on home preparation! The teacher's painstaking efforts are almost useless unless the child studies at home. Go over the lesson with your boy or girl! It will do you good.

4. Insist not only on Sunday School attendance but also on church attendance! Church going habits must be formed in youth. A child old enough to go to Sunday School is old enough to go to church and get something out of the service. The only effective way to teach your child veneration for the house and worship of the Lord is to COME TO CHURCH YOURSELF. A good example speaks louder than words.

We feel certain that you will follow out the above suggestions and thus enable us to do the Lord's work more efficiently.

We furthermore extend to you a cordial invitation to become a member of the Sunday School by joining the Adult Bible Class which is conducted in connection with the school by the pastor.

Feeling assured of your cordial cooperation we are

Respectfully yours,
THE SUNDAY SCHOOL
of
THE EVANGELICAL LUTHERAN CHURCH OF THE REDEEMER
St. Paul, Minnesota

Bible Poster Stamps

WE HAVE SEEN
HIS STAR

DOGS
KINDER THAN MEN

DIVINE WISDOM
SPEAKS

LET'S GO AND SEE

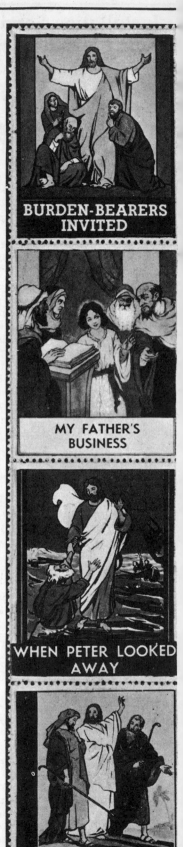

BURDEN-BEARERS
INVITED

MY FATHER'S
BUSINESS

WHEN PETER LOOKED
AWAY

THE HEAVENLY
COMPANION

What are Poster Stamps

THE Poster Stamp originated in Germany early in the twentieth century. Originally Poster Stamps were drab in color till the French introduced vivid and flaming colors. Poster designs were reproduced in miniature on gummed paper, making them available to the general public at little expense, in a form which could be easily collected.

Poster Stamps should have a degree of subtlety, a simplicity of composition and a boldness of execution. The artist may be pardoned for using a little license. There should not be too much detail, as in pure illustrations. Above all, the dash and daring of the artist should be expressed in flashes of brilliant, flat color. People love color. A picture tells more than a page of words and speaks a universal language. The message on the poster stamp may well follow the slogan: "The less you say the more they will remember."

Adoption As An Advertising Medium

The Publicity value of the Poster Stamp was soon recognised. Manuacturers, Exhibitors, Museums, Governments and Charity Organizations soon made use of the Poster Stamp as an advertising and propaganda medium.

The Poster Stamp in America

Getting off to a rapid-fire start in America, the poster stamp vogue swept the country, but experienced a set back during the World War. A few dauntless collectors continued their hobby with the collection of Charity Stamps, such as Anti-Tuberculosis seals, Red Cross seals, etc. The Hobby spread, collectors increased in numbers finally organizing the National Poster Stamp Society.

The Collector's Instinct

The popularity of a hobby of this kind is due to the natural collector's instinct which is latent in most persons. Early in life children begin to collect dolls, balls, marbles, pictures, bottle tops, etc. With people who can afford to indulge the desire for collecting, it is quite natural for this hobby to develop into an interest in postage stamps, old coins, rare books and antiques. There are millions who are eager to build up collections of some kind, but who cannot afford to spend much money to satisfy this desire. At various times they have collected cigar bands, pictures of baseball players, pictures of movie stars, postcards, Indian pennies, covers of match boxes, pictures of aviators, etc.

Having been recognized as an advertising medium of great value, manufacturers are leading the way with outstanding, attractive, well-executed designs. Considerable advertising value will accrue from constant handling, bartering and exhibiting to friends and other collectors. While this is desirable with persons of all ages, it is probably of greatest importance where one wants to make an impression on the minds of children. When children start collecting poster stamps they will press many into service helping them build up their collection. This is particularly true of educational stamps.

The Bible Poster Stamp

Stamp series featuring famous paintings, historical scenes and events, trees, fruits, flowers, birds, animals, fish, insects, flags, safety subjects have been used for educational purposes. The use of Bible pictures for poster stamps as an educational medium has, so far, not been exploited.

The BIBLE POSTER STAMP Co. of New York in collaboration with the American Lutheran Publicity Bureau has had executed paintings of 96 biblical subjects in colors and is reproducing these drawings in full colors in poster stamp form.

27-96

THOUGHTS OF MOTHER

A FRIEND TURNED TRAITOR

A CROWN THAT OUR SINS WOVE

ALONE WITH GOD

They come in sheets of 24 stamps, gummed and perforated. 24 different subjects on a sheet, 4 sheets to the series. The back of the stamp has a Bible verse. For the collector an album is provided with space for 96 stamps.

The Album

The format of the Album is 6½ x 9¾. It has 16 pages and cover. On each page space is provided for 6 stamps. Thus 16 x 6 gives space for 96 stamps. Under each rectangle for stamp a Bible verse appears. This verse is visible after stamp has been pasted.

Relying on the natural instinct of collecting of children as well as adults, it is assumed these stamps will be preserved in the album. The stamps are not pasted haphazardly into the book, but a proper place has been provided for each stamp.

By comparing the Bible verse on back of the stamp with the Bible verse appearing in the album the right place for the stamp will be found. Consequently the Bible passages will have to be read over and over again till the right place is found, which may be on any page of the album. This will prove an educational pastime for children as well as adults.

Bible Poster Stamps and Album are published in the following form: One Envelope containing Album, Four Envelopes of 24 Stamps each (total, 96 stamps, all different). They may be ordered separately or all five parts together. For the present only 48 Stamps are available. We understand they are moderately priced and within the means of any Sunday School or Bible Class.

How to Use Bible Poster Stamps

1. Stamps and Album may be sold by church or Sunday-school at cost or at a profit.

2. In Sunday-school and Bible classes the stamps may be used as a reward. If used as a reward we may suggest the following procedure:

   The Album is handed out first, explaining to the recipient how to use it. There are 96 stamps, to cover a school year of 48 weeks. One stamp to be given for attendance and another stamp for merit. The stamps do not follow the lesson of the day and it is immaterial which stamps are detached. Each sheet of 24 stamps has printed on the tear-margin line for inserting name and class of scholar. Thus each sheet becomes individual and provides an attendance record. Each sheet of 24 stamps comes in an envelope. The Album also comes in an Envelope. In the lower grades the child may require assistance in finding the proper place for the stamps in the album.

   This assistance will undoubtedly be supplied at home. Father, mother, uncle or aunt will be asked questions and will give their help by reading the bible verses.

   This method has been tried by the author and has proven to be a most fascinating pastime.

3. Stamps may be used for attaching to letters, envelopes or printed literature. Such stamps have been looked for and and will supply an existing want. Bible Poster Stamps tipped on all correspondence will encourage larger attendance at services, meetings, conventions, etc.

4. For Radio broadcasts the Bible Poster Stamp Album may be offered as a check up by program sponsors with a possible profit. Album may be offered at 25c. Stamps in full sheets of 24 at 25c. or sheet may be divided in 8 stamps each and offered at 10c. which will net handsome profit.

5. For collectors of poster stamps the Bible Poster Stamp will prove a valued addition to any collection. According to the National Poster Stamp Society there are over a 100,000 collectors of poster stamps in the United States. How many of these might never have heard or read God's word.

ON THE CROSS FOR ME

THE GUEST WHO RICHLY BLESSES

SAFE IN THE STORM

THE VICTORY COMPLETE

Bible Stamp Club
ELMER A. KETTNER

IT WAS QUITE A COINCIDENCE. I had just been telling the good wife that I had a bright idea. I had been trying to get children of pre-confirmation age into a week-day class of religious instruction at our church. Without much co-operation from the parents, it was not going so good. Schemes, awards, lures of various kinds, admonition, nothing worked. They came, they saw, they concluded.

But now I had a bright idea. Children like to collect stamps. If I could interest some company in printing Bible-picture stamps, give the children one stamp each time they came, and give them an album to put them in, perhaps I could induce them to come again. But would any company be interested in the plan? While I was talking about it, the mail came, and lo and behold! a pre-announcement of the printing of album and stamps, just what I wanted, from the Lutheran Press. This was before they got out their first issue.

At first, I was a little peeved that someone had stolen "my" idea. But the new man conquered and I gave God thanks that my problem was so easily and hastily solved. I ordered, before they were even printed.

When they finally arrived, I placed them all in position in an album, brought the finished product into the Sunday School, and enthusiastically described and showed the completed album to the whole Sunday School, telling them of the value of ordinary stamps, of the especial value of these stamps, and that they could have a complete album with stamps free of charge. We would soon be giving them away in our "Bible Stamp Club." I purposely avoided calling it a Bible Class or School. I never use the term learn or teach in connection with the class. For several Sundays I continued to arouse their interest until they could wait no longer. Then I told them that next Thursday at 4 P. M. we would have the first meeting of the Stamp Club, at which we would give, free, the album, and one stamp. They could add one stamp each week after that until the album was filled.

Half the Sunday school turned out.

That was a year ago. They still come every Thursday, and while some parents thought it wise to give their children tap-dancing lessons instead, and while others took up the banjo, and still others tired of walking two miles for one stamp, discontinued, new members came in, and on the whole, the club holds out well.

What do we do? I just came from the Stamp Club now, so that's easy! "On page 3, children, you have a stamp entitled, 'The Smallest is the Greatest.' When did Jesus say that something small was greater than something large? (Answer). Would you rather have a dime or a dollar? (discussion). Why did Jesus say that this quarter of a penny was greater than the thousands of dollars? Recite the memory verse. (Review two or three other stories similarly.)

"Now turn to page 7. Do you find the Bible passage, 'Come unto me all ye that labor and are heavy laden, I will give you rest'? That is an invitation. Ruth, what is an invitation?"

"O when you get a letter asking you to come to a party."

"Did you ever get an invitation to a party?"

"Yes."

"What did it say?"

"Well, it told you where to come, and when, and what for."

"Yes. Let's write down the essential parts of an invitation."

By questions and counter questions we get this outline:

AN INVITATION
I Where to come
II When
III Whom addressed
IV Who invites
V What for

VI Who brings the message

"Now to this invitation. Let's see if we can find all these things in this invitation. Which words in the text tell us where to come, when, etc.—until we have this opposite the blank outline on the blackboard:

I. Where? Heaven (Explanation, "eventually"; to Jesus, in faith, now).

II. When? Now (Get all answers from pupils if possible).

III. To Whom addressed? (All ye. Explain labors and heavy laden as sickness, cares, worry. Did your mother ever cry? Yes, when my brother Charlie was very sick in the hospital. Is your mother invited, then? Can you think of anyone who is not invited? Discussion. "All invited."

IV. Who invites? Jesus. (Shall we offend Him by refusing?)

V. What for? "I will give you rest" (from labors, worries, etc.)

VI. Who brings the message? WE are the postmen. What a pity if the letter stayed in the mailbox and the one invited didn't get it! How terrible, if WE don't deliver that message to those who don't know they are invited.

Now memorize the verse, "Come Unto Me," etc. 3-5 minutes. In the meantime I have erased everything except the outline, "Essentials of an Invitation." Each member of the class now recites the verse. Then for review I ask questions to fill in the outline a second time. Each pupil is graded. Stamps are then given to all pupils who know the verse well and who answer the questions asked them in review of the story. They are dismissed. It is five o'clock.

Where the idea? Well, on the stamp it says: "Burden-bearers Invited." That suggests an invitation. Children are familiar with invitations which they have received. The fill-in material comes from a knowledge and application of Christian doctrine, graded to the child's mind.

Will they study? They don't get the stamp if they refuse. We have no trouble on that score. It is different from any other class I have ever had in just that respect.

Suppose some are absent! I tell them which story they have missed, the album tells them where to find it in the Bible, and they have to get whatever information the Bible gives on it, with classmates or parents and then they may stay after class any time, answer my questions, recite the verse and if I am satisfied they get the stamp. For competition I occasionally ask in class to see who has the most stamps.

Ordinarily, the stamp suggests a story. Most of them do. That makes it easier. I dramatize the story, act it out for them, so as to make it realistic, use modern simple language, the vernacular for the child (except when quoting the words of Jesus).

When they are finished they will have 96 pictures in color, neatly pasted into an album, 96 Bible verses in mind (for we drill them for weeks in review) and the moral of 96 stories. The Club never ends. When one has his album full he is finished. But in the meantime new members have entered and they can start anywhere in the book (we do not take the stamps consecutively) and they go on with us until their book is finished. In this way no stories are duplicated for anyone in the class.

The Bible Poster Stamp Album may be good as an award. I do not know. But as material for a Stamp Club it has solved a real problem for us. They come. They see. Christ Conquers.

THE GUEST WHO RICHLY BLESSES

An Outline on Vacation Bible Schools

I. What Is The Vacation Bible School?

a) A summer school for the children of the congregation and community to teach the fundamentals of the Christian faith.

b) What the Lutheran Vacation Bible school does (see folder)

II. The Aims Of The Vacation Bible School

1. Teach the Bible.
2. Show what sin is and how children sin.
3. Teach Christ, His Person and Work, so that the child realizes that Jesus is the child's Personal Savior.
4. To teach that we become God's children through faith in His Son.
5. To teach the child that true faith shows itself by a God-pleasing life.
6. To memorize gems from the Bible.
7. To memorize the first and second articles of the creed with explanations.
8. To memorize Christian hymns.
9. To acquaint the child with the great work of missions.
10. To teach the child to play, study, and work as a child of God.

III. The Vacation Bible School As A Mission Institution

1. What the records show: whole families gained for church. (120).
2. It enters many homes and opens them for future work.
3. It establishes the church in the minds of the people and gains the good will of the community.
4. It is a fine spiritual service to the community.
5. It broadens the missionary spirit of the congregation.
6. It has a peculiar appeal to almost all children, which the Day and Sunday schools do not have.
7. It is a feeder for Day and Sunday schools.
8. It is effective for teaching the Gospel.

IV. General Plan Of Vacation Bible School

1. Time: Begin week after public schools close for summer vacation. It is important to begin the Monday following close of schools. Course: Four weeks, Daily, Monday to Friday. Each morning from 9 A.M. to 11:30 A.M.
2. Daily Schedule:
   9:00 Devotional opening.
   9:10 Bible story told by principal of school to assembly.
   9:20 Classes assemble. Bible story retold by teacher.
   9:35 Or 9:40 Application of Bible story to everyday life. illustrate with examples. (Total time for story: 40 minutes).
   9:50 Memory work for the day; brief review.
   10:00 Hand work period; relating to the Bible or work of the church—Or: Project period: Some problem of life which demands the application of the principle learned.
   10:30 Recess with supervised play. Daily play programs.
   10:45 General assembly: Joint, short review of lesson of day Bible story; Memory work; Things to remember impressed.
   10:55 Story period: Missionary stories; Stories illustrating lesson; Stories from everyday life which apply; Stories from church history.
   11:10 Singing and memorizing Christian hymns.
   11:25 Devotional close.
   11:30 Dismiss school.
3. Departments of school: Senior, Intermediate, Junior. Primary or: Senior (and Intermediate), Junior, and Primary.
4. Teachers: Pastor or Christian Day school teacher as principal. All teachers should have teaching experience: (Sunday school or public school work). Supervisor for handwork; Playground work to be taken over by one of the staff. Attendance records kept by some responsible older student.
5. Plan of course for week: four lessons and a day for review. "Non multa sed multum." Friday after recess special program employing talent of all children. Picnic about the end of third week. Closing exercise on evening of last day with all parents, neighbors and members invited.

V. Courses Of Study

General theme or aim for the entire course (unified and organized plan with a definite purpose in view. Test your work by having children answer a questionnaire on doctrine on first day and answer same questions on last day).

Weekly theme: (theme for each week, related to general theme). Aim for each day (related to aim for the week and course).

Teach justification and sanctification.

Bible stories basic. Draw doctrines from them. If possible select stories not used in Sunday school course.

The need of a graded course so that pupils who return next year may be advanced by getting a new series of lessons.

VI. Teachers' Helps

Outline of course: Daily Lesson sheets, prepared by pastor or teacher.

Teacher's Notes: The lesson. Difficulties explained.
Approach (introducing lesson; get attention).
Lesson in outline (five or six points).
Application (to life of pupil).
Illustrations.

Daily Teachers' Council.

VII. Pupils' Helps

The pupil's Notebook.

Materials: covers; mimeographed sheets; (See samples or dictate essentials).

Book constructed in handwork period.

Daily lesson outlines: (What is on them? Sample).

VIII. Correlated Handwork

Important but not essential. (Vacation time—play instinct)

Only handwork which relates to Bible and church.

Very useful as a teaching agency.

Correlation of handwork.

1. Books of the Bible: a) blocks; b) pill boxes.
2. Bible maps: a) Colored; b) Relief; c) Electric.
3. Bible houses: architecture of Palestine: a) soap houses; b) paper. Put houses together for a village.
4. Bible objects: Waterpots, Nativity scene, etc., Bible People, scroll.
5. Missionary Objects: Huts of heathen, Heathen village with missionary's home and church, also mission school.
6. Religious Posters for church, etc.
7. Pupil's Bible School Note Book Illustrated.
8. Making Bible story books or hymn leaflets for shut-ins.
9. Kindergarten projects of religious nature for Primary class.

IX. Supervised Play

15 minutes daily.

Work out play schedule.

Games and contests.

Practice for picnic contests (field day).

Get suitable games for rainy days (Bible Baseball).

X. Equipment Needed

Colored manila cardboard for covers. Construction paper.

Paper fasteners (brass staples).

Illustrative material (old S. S. literature, Christian periodicals with pictures; general magazines).

Hectograph or mimeograph.

Publicity folder.

Application cards or blanks (mimeograph).

Mission leaflets.

Blackboard.

Bible maps.

Penny catechisms.

Attendance and registration blanks.

Sign in front of church.

Scissors. Brushes. Paints. Tools. Paste, etc.

XI. Promotional Work

Special folder to mailing list and all homes of community.

House to house canvass for children.

Follow up visits the first week of the school to get those who PLEASE TURN TO PAGE 282

Suggestions for An August Summer School

THE MAY (1934) ISSUE of the AMERICAN LUTHERAN presented a detailed plan for a Summer School. This is an alternate plan which takes for granted the principles and purposes expressed in the previous article; however, these suggestions call for a minimum of time, teachers, and money.

Points of Difference between this and the previous plan:

1. *It is held only during August,* which makes it popular with mothers who are eager to find another month of diversion for their children after the other Summer Schools have closed. It also increases the potential number of entrants.

2. *Its sessions are held three days a week,* on alternate days (Monday, Wednesday, and Friday). Children tend to tire of the regularity of the five day plan. This plan allows for an intervening day of play which has a tendency to bring them back on session days. When this plan was tried, there was no confusion on the part of the children: they came on the required three days. —Mission churches which use this plan will find that it is comparatively easy to get teachers for this three-day-a-week proposition whereas it may have been impossible previously to get them for a five day school.

The School that chooses to make use of Tuesday and Thursday may allow the children to come on those days for additional handiwork, supervised play, or mass drills: no attempt should be made to teach on these days.

3. *Rotating Class System for the Juniors and Intermediates.* The teacher who has the Life of Christ assignment is prepared to present this same material to both the Juniors and the Intermediates on alternate hours (see schedule for day), with the usual difference in presentation, that to the Juniors one still emphasizes the story, and to the Intermediates one emphasizes the practical application and value for life.

4. *Daily Schedule.*

Theme: Christ, our Savior and Friend

A.M.	JUNIORS	INTERMEDIATES	SENIORS	PRIMARY
				Separate Schedule Entirely
9:00—		Morning Devotion		9:30 Session Begins
9:15	....	Combined Classes	....	9:35—9:45 Devotion
9:20—Mission		Life of	Y.T.T.	9:50—10:20
10:00 Stories		Christ	(Pastor)	Story Period
10:05—		Combined Singing		10:20—10:35 Recess Period
10:30	....	Period	....	
10:35—Life of		Mission	Y.T.T.	10:40—11:00
11:15 Christ		Stories	(Pastor)	Song Period
11:20—Handi-		Handi-	Handi-	11:05—11:30
11:50 work		work	work	Story Period No. 2
11:55—		Devotional		11:35—11:55 Handiwork
12:00	....	Close	....	12:00 Devotional Close

5. *Spectacular Closing Exercises,* to mark your Summer School as "different" with resultant good advertising for your Church.—Procure your local theater if your Church has no hall with a stage and curtain. Since theaters are in use evenings, a *Saturday morning* closing exercise is necessary. Sufficient advance advertising overcomes the various disadvantages of such a morning program, and it has proved possible to attract twice the usual crowd for such a program by emphasizing that it was something "different" and new. (Write A.L.P.B. for sample publicity material).

Suggested program for Closing Exercises

NOTE: This type of closing exercise requires only one rehearsal and makes use of the subject matter previously memorized in story and song at the school.

The "costumes" used in the various tableaux are not cut out and made up as is usually done: they are simulated by either draping or pinning the various pieces of uncut materials about the children. This is possible because no movement is required in any of these tableaux.

ALL ANNOUNCEMENTS BEFORE STARTING. *Take Collection at exit at end of program.*

1. *Hymn by the entire assembly*—in place of the usual mimeographed program Hymn Film-slides are obtainable from the SVE in Chicago. See under "Source of Materials". (During the time that the assembly is singing, the teachers are arranging the children backstage for their first song.)

   —Appoint a stage-manager whose duty it is to see that the proper groups of children are gathered and brought on to the stage just as the previous group leaves. Assistant stage-manager to see that children leave stage in orderly fashion and gets them back to their seats. A "property man" is appointed who sees that the proper costume material and setting is ready for the next tableau. Another does nothing but tend to the curtain.

2. *Songs by the Entire Summer School*—mass the entire group on the stage. Begin singing as the curtain opens. Choose songs for the opening with a fast tempo. In this grouping have Primary children in the front so that at the conclusion of the group of songs they can walk forward before the curtain for their part of the program, while the curtain closes on the rest and preparations are made for the setting of the first tableau.

3. *Primary Recitations and Songs* (before the curtain)—even if it is not possible to assign something to each child, have them all on the stage for this grouping.—At the moment the last song or recitation is made by them, let the "Page-boy" appear to announce the first tableau: his announcement will cover the break made when the children are leaving the stage.

4. *Page-boy announces the theme of the coming tableau by the recitation of an appropriate scripture passage of Bible story. Have a different page-boy for each tableau. First boy recites the Christmas gospel to announce the Nativity tableau.

5. *Tableau No. 1: The Nativity.* Characters stand still throughout. Silent for half a minute, then either they or a group back-stage sings: "Silent Night". As the curtains close for the end of the hymn, page-boy No. 2 steps out before the curtain.

6. *Page tells the story of the Twelve Year Old Jesus in the Temple.* At conclusion, curtain opens for the second tableau.

7. *Tableau No. 2: Jesus in the Temple.* Show only a group of "doctors" looking toward a brilliant light off-stage. (Do not attempt to portray the character of Christ.) After a short pause, voice off-stage says: "What think ye of Christ?" Group off-stage sings: "I love to tell the story."

8. *Page recites Twenty-third Psalm,* to introduce third tableau.

9. *Tableau No. 3: Shepherd Scene.* Shepherds with sheep-crook with his back to the audience. Around him, on all-fours are the "sheep". Primary department children dressed in white nightgowns with paper sheep-ears pinned to their baby-caps; white crepe-paper tails—these are the most effective sheep. Group sings "Savior I Follow On".

10. *Demonstration of the Electric Map.* Three boys. One steadies the map, which is placed on a chair. Another asks: "Where is Bethlehem, etc.", while another operates the elec-

trical device. Teacher comes out with boys and explains that if the boy gives right answer, light lights.

11. *Page announces last tableau.*
12. *Guardian Angel Tableau.* After the usual moments pause, entire group recites: "He shall give His angels charge over thee. . . . ." Group the entire Summer School—street clothes—in attitudes of play. One group playing "Ring around the rosie", another "London Bridge". Boys playing catch. Some with hoops. Girls with Jacks, etc. If an angel is included as the central figure, dress her in flowing white. Make no attempt to put wings on her.
13. *Solos by talented local Children.*
14. *Memo pictures of various Summer School activities and of each child in the school.* These Memo cameras and projectors are described below.
15. *Closing Hymn.*

The secret of an impressive program is to have no pauses or gaps in the entire presentation. People are accustomed to ill-prepared childrens' programs, but give them one in which there isn't a single moment of waiting and you amaze them.

Note: Do not break the unity of this program by taking up a collection or by any announcements. Tell all you have to say before the opening hymn or put it in writing on your program. Introduce your teachers and thank them before your program begins, and tell the audience they can meet these teachers in the lobby after the close.

BIBLE-RELATED HANDIWORK THAT IS DIFFERENT

A. Model scenes from the Parables of Our Lord in clay. Or use scenes from the Life of Joseph, if that is on your teaching curriculum. (Missionary stories can also be dramatized in clay. Scenes from the Life of Christ are usually omitted because that would necessitate making figures of the Lord, which, when done by children, are anything but reverent.)

Parables adaptable for modeling:
1. Sower and the Seed (Four Kinds of Soil)
   a) The pathway—soil stamped down hard, with seeds laying on top; possibly models of birds eating seed.
   b) The stony soil.
   c) Thorny ground
   d) Good ground—plant grass seed so that by the time this model is put on display, grass will be sprouting.

Fo all model-background, obtain cardboard from old store-windo. displays. Make the base of each model about 3 ft. deep and 4 ft. wide. Use painted background if desired, otherwise stand for display with a white sheet as the background.—For the above model, have pathway leading irregularly on the left, and divide the rest of the base into three equal parts for the different kinds of soil. Let children gather thorns or thistles from the field and bring to school. In background have figure of a sower and his seed.

2. *The Dragnet and the Fish:* section of an old tennis or volley ball net for the net portion. See encyclopaedia for types of fish. "Good Fish"—let children use their imagination. "Bad Fish"—eels, octupus, horned fish. Paint fish fantastic colors after clay dries a bit. Background consists mainly of blue sky if cardboard back is used. Several small models of fishing boats look well in the rear. Lake-sand pounded around a mirror makes very effective water.

3. *The Good Samaritan* — reproduce the rocky gulch in which these robberies usually occurred. Donkey, Samaritan, prostrate figures are in center. Spondes dipped in green water color make good trees and shrubs.

4. *The Return of the Prodigal** reproduce picture as shown in the Bible histories. Country estate. Trees. Son coming down crooked lane. Father standing with outstretched arms.

5. *House built on Sand—vs.—House built on Rock.* Make two houses of clay and wood, identically the same. Drop or otherwise demolish one. Place the wrecked house upon a heap of uneven earth. Place the other upon a slab of rock. Put these two side by side upon one base.

Note: Be sure to use nothing but pure modeling clay, not any trademarked product.—Figures may be dressed by the girls like little dolls in the costumes of the times. The models will take paint after they have dried for a day.—For the bodies of the figures, to get uniform size, take a clothes pin with a piece of wire wound around the top with ends sticking out to serve as arms. Embed this in the clay. It serves as a base as well as a guide for the children.

Regarding Teachers of Art: Local Art Schools have a list of art-teachers who are eager to give their services free in order to get in their required number of hours of "practice teaching". It can be arranged that these teachers do nothing but give instruction in clay-modeling or in some other phase of art and have absolutely nothing to do with the religious education of the pupils.

Alternate Group of Models: Life of Joseph, to be produced similar to above group. Suggested scenes from Josephs life for clay dramatization: 1) Joseph tells his dream. 2) Sold by his brothers. 3) Joseph in Prison. 4) Joseph before the Pharaoh. 5) The cup is found in Benjamin's sack. 6) Joseph makes himself known to his brothers.

For Egyptian Art background see Encyclopaedia Britannica, any edition; or "Wonders of the Past."

B. *Wood-burning* (Pyrography)—trace Bible pictures on soft wood. Electric burning sets can be purchased in the large department stores (toy department) in many cities. Priced from $1.00—$3.00 per electric pen.

C. *Electric Map*—consists of a paper map to be mounted on beaver board, later to be colored and electrified in such a way that when the proper location of any of the Biblical cities are pointed out, a light lights. Order paper map from Methodist Book Concern, 150 Fifth Avenue, N. Y. C. Price 50 cts. with complete directions. (Price of the map when completed in Summer School, including all materials, about $2.00).

SOURCE OF MATERIALS

VISUAL INSTRUCTION EQUIPMENT

The Memo Camera: takes pictures on 35mm. movie film—still pictures. The finished pictures cost about 4 cts. a frame, and so is very inexpensive to use. These pictures are the ones referred to in the outline of the closing exercises, under point No. 14. This camera costs from $12.50 up depending upon the lens. Projectors price from $19.50. For full information on their use and possibilities, see your leading camera supply house or write Willoughby Camera Shop, 110 W. 32nd Street New York.

For the Church that is seriously considering slide equipment, as well as the use of the above mentioned Memo (film-slide) outfit, we recommend Bausch and Lomb projector model ABM together with the slide attachment. This is the more expensive equipment.

Other sources for visual instruction material are: your local library and Y. M. C. A.

For a comprehensive list of all free movie films—standard and 16mm.—for amateur and professional projection, write to the Society for Visual Education, 327 La Salle Street, Chicago, Illinois. Ask for their book "1001 Films", price 75 cts.

For free lists of free films, write American Museum of Natural History, 81st Street at Central Park West, New York City. Address Extension Department.

For free list of glass slides available write: Metropolitan Museum of Art, 82nd Street and Fifth Avenue, New York. User pays postage both ways.

Text Books:

These books give a definite day-by-day plan, together with all stories to be told. Saves the pastor the work of preparing his own course. These books judiciously used, can be used in a Lutheran Summer School.

For Primary Department, First Year Group:
Vacation Days With Jesus, by M. P. Athy, $2.50
The Heavenly Father and His Children, by M. J. Baldwin, $1.00
Primary Department, Second Year Group:
Vacation Days With Jesus No. 2, by E. B. Schulz, $2.50
Serving the Heavenly Father, by M. J. Baldwin, $1.25.
(Each book is accompanied by supplementary pictures at $1.00 per set extra. The "Heavenly Father" booklets are also accompanied by a book of memory work based on the text. 10 cts. each extra).
Books for Juniors:
Vacation Days With Jesus, by M. P. Athy, $3.00
Stories of Jesus, by M. J. Baldwin, $1.25
Stories of Early Church Heroes, $1.25
For Seniors: Suggest the use of Y.T.T., by F. Nolde $1.25. This book, Yesterday, Today, and Tomorrow, groups the Bible stories which the children have already learned and shows how the Church of today is the continuation of the Old Testament Church, if one may call it that. The material will have to be condensed if it is to be used in this plan.

Incidental Equipment and Supplies:

Art Supplies—School Supplies—Clay: Milton Bradley Co., 120 E. 16th St., New York City—offices in principle cities.
Attendance Cards—Enrollment Cards: 60 cts. per hundred.
Buttons (Celluloid) $1.50 per hundred.

Bible Blocks—Bible Alphabets from 10 cts. up. State what you want this equipment for and the Service Department of A.L.P.B. will furnish you your wants at the lowest market price.

Cut-outs· for general illustration or for sand-table work. Enough for 140 Bible stories, covering all subjects in print. Complete $2.50 (in color) Individual stories 10 cts. set—state which.
Poster Cut-outs—which are much larger—50 cts. a set.
Mission Story Cut-outs (order by naming land of mission endeavor) 10 cts. each.

Muslin Poster to announce Summer School, 36/42″ $1.00—weatherproof.

Printing—Window Cards, 14/28″—three colors, $3.50 per hundred. Write for catalog. Metropolitan Printing Company, 1323 Vine Street, Philadelphia, Pa.

Scrap-book pictures: order old Primary leaflets from Concordia Publishing House, St. Louis, Missouri. Price, 10 cts. per lb. About 80 colored pictures (together with printed material) to lb.
Scissors, blunt tops—$1.25 dozen.

The Cost of Running a Summer School—runs around $8.00 per department. This includes the price of texts and all supplies. Allow at least $10.00 for publicity. The net cost is about $20.00 since in a school of about 100 children they bring in with their offerings, and the collection at the closing exercise, around $25.00.

A good plan for collecting money is to ask each child to bring 2 cts. each day it comes.

Books and material listed above may be obtained through the American Lutheran Publicity Bureau, if you order direct please mention the AMERICAN LUTHERAN.

PUBLICITY HELPS

Publicity on the August Summer School should be handed out the second week in July. The neighborhood should be circularized once each week until the opening day. Sample promotional literature to arouse local interest, together with the advertising material designed to arouse interest in the Saturday morning closing exercises with instructions for proper use will be sent, upon request. Address Service Department, American Lutheran Publicity Bureau, 1819 Broadway, New York, N. Y.

VACATION BIBLE SCHOOL

**Four Weeks
June 13 to July 8**

Bible Study

Mission Stories

Christian Hymns

Bible Hand Work

Supervised Play

**NO
ENROLMENT
FEE**

✠

CALVARY LUTHERAN CHURCH
Seventy-fifth and McGee

VACATION BIBLE SCHOOL

DAILY—MONDAY to FRIDAY

Mornings 9 a. m. to 11:30 a. m.

DEPARTMENTS

Senior—Junior—Intermediate—Primary

TEACHERS

The Pastor, The Parish Worker and others who have had teaching experience.

COURSE

A four weeks course in the chief Teachings of Christianity is offered. Only carefully selected Bible stories are used to teach the fundamentals of the Christian Faith. The lesson is applied to the life of the child. Choice Scripture verses are memorized. There is no home work required.

AIM OF THE COURSE

The aim of the school is to teach the Bible. The child is told that Jesus is the Saviour from sin, that we are saved by believing in Him, and that we are to show our faith with a God pleasing life. There is a definite aim for the whole course, for each week, and for each day.

VACATION BIBLE SCHOOL

HANDWORK

Only such handwork is used as impresses some Bible lesson. In the past years our school has made its own notebooks, Bible relief maps, Holy land houses, Mission villages, Bible blocks, etc.

SPECIAL EVENTS

Special Programs each Friday—A Picnic—A Missionary Pageant—and Closing Exercises, at which the work of the school is displayed to the parents and friends.

ENROLMENT

All children from five to fifteen years of age may enroll. The lessons are planned to supplement the work done in Sunday-Schools. Children are requested to be at the school at 8:30 on the opening day for advance registration.

Further information about the Vacation Bible School may be had by calling the pastor of the church, Rev. O. E. Feucht, Jackson 3251.

VACATION BIBLE SCHOOL

WHAT THE VACATION BIBLE SCHOOL DOES

It teaches only Bible truths.

It puts the child into the daily company of Christ and the Church.

It helps to balance the child's education.

It familiarizes the child with the best Christian hymns.

It introduces the child to the missionary heroes of the world.

It gives to each pupil a treasure of gems from the Bible.

It helps to impart reverence toward God.

It teaches the child that religion belongs to every day life.

It utilizes the vacation play spirit.

It takes the child off the streets.

It makes the summer vacation count for Christ.

It helps parents to be better stewards of their children.

It makes work seem like play.

OBSERVATIONS ON BIBLE CLASSES

FRED H. LINDEMANN

Over a period of several years we have heard numerous complaints in regard to adult Bible classes. In some cases every attempt to organize a class was fruitless, the response on the part of the people was discouraging. In other cases the initial response was excellent but in the course of time the interest waned, the attendance fell off, so that, if the class was not discontinued it was ever on the verge of expiring, requiring constant and heroic treatment to keep it from complete dissolution. In still other cases the attendance was good and there was considerable interest, but the leaders felt that the class somehow was not serving its purpose, for, while the classwork was faithfully done by the majority, independent, private reading and study was not on the increase, people were not learning to read and study with profit, to apply what they read to the problems confronting them in their daily lives. In every case we suggested some changes and asked that we be kept informed as to the results. In practically every instance there was a decided change for the better and a number of brethren waxed most enthusiastic after a trial of the suggested method extending over a year and two years. The few instances in which no improvement was apparent have not shaken our confidence in the method we proposed, for we feel convinced that certain conditions were responsible which are beyond the reach of any method and had better not be discussed here.

Let's begin at the beginning. If a truly helpful Bible class is to be organized it is necessary in the first place that the person who is to act as the leader, usually the pastor, be absolutely sold on the idea that a class is a vital thing, an essential thing. And if he is firmly convinced that he must have a Bible class, let him make up his mind that the only way to get one and keep one is by constant hard work. If a thing is vital and essential it is worth while putting a good deal of effort into it. You cannot step before your class without thorough preparation. For one thing, if you have not carefully planned that particular hour, you are sure to talk too much. Poorly prepared people always do. Do not hesitate to put as much time and effort into your Bible hour preparation as into your sermon work. You have the time. If not, make time. There can be no more profitable occupation than the study of the Scriptures, and it is a sad state of affairs if a pastor does not make time to be spent at his real workbench and with the tools of his trade. The greatest benefit from an essay read before a conference is always derived by the essayist himself. And the pastor who faithfully prepares for his Bible hour will find that in the end he profits most.

But your willingness to work is not enough. Make up your mind what kind of a Bible class you want. What is it that you want to accomplish? The work done by the class when it meets with you ought never to be considered the end but only the means to an end. The final purpose ought to be to make and train independent students and readers of the Bible, to teach how to study and read with enjoyment and profit, to develop an intelligent, consecrated membership who in their private reading find the Bible to be a constant source of help and comfort, people who have a working knowledge of the Scriptures. Your aim must be to lead your class to understand and love and read the Bible. So you must lead them into the Bible. We heard of a "Bible class" some time ago which studied a number of Scripture passages, proof texts, carefully picked by the pastor. The word "studied" must be taken with a grain of salt, for the class listened passively while the pastor lectured on the doctrines of the Lutheran Church. To call such lectures a Bible class is rather misleading. And it certainly did not serve the purpose the class should serve. Another class had a gospel harmony inflicted upon it for a full year. The Holy Spirit never intended the gospels for a biography of our Lord; in divine wisdom He gave us no chronological record, and although our intellect and reason is darkened by sin, we ought to possess enough "horse sense" to shun a harmony when our aim is what it is. After flitting about in the gospels and lighting here and there the class had a vague idea that there was some controversy whether a certain event had taken place prior to another, but of the Holy Spirit's purpose and aim in any of the four gospels they had not the slightest conception. So take up an individual book, preferably a gospel, for beginners. Teach how to find the author's aim, what he is driving at, how to follow him in building up his case, how to apply the truths in daily life.

After you have decided upon what gospel you will take up first make a thorough study of the book. Pay no attention to chapters but treat the book as a whole. Find the author's purpose, if possible the key verse, and divide the book into sections irrespective of chapters. Follow the author in his presentation and see how he puts his case. Make notes and more notes. Read your notes frequently. You might change your mind after you see your thought black on white. And after you have thought and worked a book through thoroughly, get ready for your class.

But you are not going to lecture, you are not going to stand before your class and tell them what you found. Too many classes have been lectured to death. No, the class is going to do the lecturing. All you do is to give them a number of questions and hints at the close of each hour to be answered and reported on in the following meeting. Lead them to finding things and to report in their own way. There may be a little hesitancy at first, but that will soon wear off. Prepare a set of questions and hints and make the class work.

But why not give the class a commentary or study helps or a printed explanation with perhaps a number of review questions attached? Once more recall the purpose of a Bible Class. A class studying at the hand of helps which bring in detail what other men, or the Lutheran confessions, or present leaders in the Church, or the particular authors say on the subject and telling how the passage is to be understood and what it means in the opinion of the writers, be they right or wrong, will be trained to depend upon such helps and will expect little or no profit from independent study unless done with a commentary open beside them. The object of a course in Bible study ought to be to teach the student to swim, to enjoy swimming, to glory in the exercise, and to develop through the energetic use of his limbs. Study helps, which as a rule are nothing but commentaries, place the student in a wheelchair upon soft cushions, while another swimmer performs before him. What the Church needs is that the passive spectator be taken out of the invalid's chair and be taught to swim himself. He may be perfectly content to leave the swimming to others, but that is because he has been led to believe that he can never learn to swim, that others must do the swimming for him. He must be placed in the water and shown how, must learn to go through the various motions, must be instructed with the object and end of learning to swim independently. The student ought not to have his meals served ready for consumption, yes, masticated and predigested, to be given the impression that he is not capable of preparing his own meal, that others must prepare and cook for him. He ought to be taught how to cook. But he never will learn if he sees the dish only after it is fully prepared. This holds true whether the commentary is issued in one, two or ten volumes, or the mailman delivers the material for the studies every month or quarter; whether the predigested canned goods are delivered

by the barrel and truckload or handed out by the can or spoonful. Throw the students of your class into the water and give them only the necessary guidance for them to learn to swim. Do not lecture to them, do not permit the use of commentaries and helps and studies prepared by others. This would be like telling them: "Now sit there and watch how I swim. No, you must not enter the water yourself, it is too deep for one who cannot swim. There, now, surely you enjoyed watching me. And you even had some water splashed on you, you are wet in spots. Just come back next week and we will repeat the performance." No, but tell them: "See here, you must learn to swim. Come into the water. Do this, do that. Try again, and again. Tomorrow come back and swim ten feet, and the next day ten yards." As Lutherans we ought not to feel satisfied until all our members ask: "But why all this prepared food, fed into the mouth. Why should we only swallow? Why should we be only spectators and content to have a little water splashed on us? Why cannot we all learn to swim? To be and remain able bodied Christians we need the exercise, and if we ever find ourselves in difficulty we could hold our own rather than call for the expert, professional swimmers to fetch us out of the water or to try and recall what kind of motions they made when holding forth." So if your Bible class is to serve a real purpose put the ban on all commentaries, helps, and the like. But place a Bible dictionary, a cross reference Bible and a concordance within the reach of all, and teach the class how to use and when to use these books.

And now, after we are clear as to what we want, we are ready to do some preliminary publicity work. By this time you will be full of the subject and it will be possible to preach at least one sermon on the need for and the blessedness of Bible study. Let your sermon be an illustration of the method you intend to employ. Take the story of Aquila, Priscilla and Apollos at Ephesus, Acts 18, or the example of the Bereans, Acts 17, rather than some text that will require a long exegetical introduction. Bear in mind that you are firing the opening gun in a campaign to convince people that the Bible is easily understood. Furthermore, if Bible study is vital and essential it is worth spending a little money. Prepare a folder or a letter telling your people about the course you have planned. Let it ooze enthusiasm, be optimistic, forget about the past disappointments. It might be well to inclose an enrollment card to be signed by the individuals stating that they contemplate or expect or promise to attend the classes unless prevented by circumstances beyond their control. The mere fact that people sign their name will make them think twice before letting other things interfere with their attendance.

But do not have your class run on indefinitely. Limit yourself to a course of so and so many hours. After the summer up to Christmas you may be able to have twelve or fourteen hours. If you have midweek Lenten services it might be advisable to arrange a short course from New Year to the beginning of Lent. Another longer could be given after Easter. But make it clear to your people that they are obligating themselves only for a definite period. If your class went on forever people will not mind missing an hour here and there, but if they know that there will be only a certain number of hours and they see the end not too far off, they will be more apt to put aside all other things for a definite period and attend regularly.

And now we are ready to begin our course. Let us say we decided on a course of ten hours, not ten evenings, but hours. An hour is long enough for people who have worked all day. Send them home while they are still hungry for more. The hints and questions for each hour have been multigraphed. The first assignment has gone out with the folder or letter advertising the course. You have a certain number of enrollment cards returned to you signed. Your attendance will probably be twice as large. Ask those who have not done so to sign a card that you may know who and how many attended. Keep accurate count of your attendance. You want to know if there is a falling off.

As you step before the class keep these things in mind:

1. Don't talk so much. You may talk well and know much but keep it a secret for the time being. A Bible class is soon talked to death. Your task as leader is to state the question, to hold the discussion to the topic, to see that one or two do not monopolize the discussion at the close. If you must talk, ask good questions and wait.

2. The following questions must always be asked in this order: What does it say? What does it mean? What does it mean to me? The first question asked first will prevent many nonsensical applications.

3. The function of a Bible class is to lead the student to direct contact with the Bible itself and to show him how to find in it values for the practical needs of life.

4. Do all in your power to have the class avoid a mere historical and literary study of the Bible, making the mastery and appreciation of the book an end in itself. Remember you are endeavoring to lead Christians to loftier heights and to open to their vision new glories and spheres of greater usefulness.

5. Do not try to have the class familiarize itself with all four Gospels or the whole New Testament. The intelligent grasp of even one of the gospels will go far to-

ward furnishing a background of biblical fact and teaching which thus becomes available for a variety of practical use.

6. Leave Luther and the catechism and the confessions and all so-called authorities in your study when you meet your class. So far as your purpose is concerned it makes not a particle of difference whether you are a Lutheran or what any man said or thought. Be honest with your class and find your own solutions to difficulties. Do some independent thinking.

We Use the "Bible Book of the Month" To Open Our Society Meetings

WE HAVE ALWAYS OPENED the various society meetings of our congregation with prayer. Besides talking on some missionary project of our Lutheran Church we have ofttimes given a short exposition of some Bible reading. For the the past two years we have used the "Bible Book of the Month Club" in opening all of our society meetings. Immediately after the opening prayer a mimeographed sheet carrying the outline of the Bible Book of that particular month is distributed to all members of the organization. Together with the study sheet each person is presented with the compliments of the congregation a penny Gospel of the book to be studied. The pastor then does not make the mistake of taking the entire time of the society for a complete study of the entire outline, but rather selects various interesting paragraphs of the Bible Book of the Month Club study so as to arouse sufficient interest in every person to take their Bible portion home and to complete the study of the book at leisure time throughout the rest of the month. After this short presentation of the principle points the pastor then welcomes questions from persons present as to the outline or the book itself or any question which might come into their minds concerning further study. It is remarkable how this direct approach month after month with its unusual appeal for home Bible reading and study will have upon the devotional life of the congregation. Many people who formerly were strangers in the Word of God, not knowing where or how to begin the study of the Bible, are made to feel that Bible Study, book by book, is not only an easy possibility but also a joyful privilege which will strengthen and inspire them to a more useful Christianity. Over a period of years, the pastor is able to give a direct approach to all books of the Bible.

Since in the Old Testament it is more difficult to get the Bible portions printed in separate books, our congregation has purchased a sufficient number of small Bibles which are conveniently at hand in the parish house. These Bibles being all of the same edition, (incidentally, they are purchased from the American Bible Society at the cost price of approximately thirty cents per copy) have their pages numbered alike and make it very convenient for the pastor to refer to various books by page rather than by chapter and verse. We have found that many of our older people do not like group Bible study because they are *embarrassed* when the pastor asks them to look up some Old Testament Bible reference by naming the book, chapter, and verse because they have never learned the rotation of the books and do not know where to find them. On the other hand, every person finds it easily possible to look up the page number and in this way they know the joy of finding the passage to prove the point, together with the other members of the class.

May we repeat that if the "Bible Book of the Month Club" is to be appreciated as an opening to the various society meetings it should not be made too long but only given for an "appetizer" and incentive for the individual to taste and study further in God's inspired Word when he or she returns home.

STUDY COURSE IN MARK

Any dictionary of the Bible will give the necessary information for the class to report on the author and time and place of, writing. Mark's is the gospel of "Jehovah's Servant the Branch," Zech. 3:8. A study of the word "Nezer" in connection with Is. 4:2 and particularly Is. 7:14, as referred to in Matth. 2:23, will prove most profitable in the light of two statements in Mark, one at the beginning by the demon, 1:24, the other by the angel at the close, 16:6. Read also Acts 10:34-43 for an excellent summary of Mark, and take note of "Jesus of Nazareth" and "who went about doing good," v. 38. Here is the story of "the Nazarene who made the coffin in which was buried the Roman Empire."

For practical purposes the book had best be divided into three portions, I. the public work in Galilee, 1:1—7:23; II. the exile in parts beyond, 7:24-9:50; III. the final crisis in Judea, 10:1-16:20.

The public work section may be divided as follows: 1. Preparatory events, 2. typical happenings, 3. opposition of the Jews, 4. sifting and training men, 5. works developing faith, 6. final proclamation and rejection. The exile tells of the training of the Twelve by private revelation. The final crisis could be divided: 1. On the way to Jerusalem, 2. the final clash with the Jews, 3. a message for the future, 4. passion and resurrection.

As chapter headings could be suggested: 1. Beginnings, 2. Enemies, 3. Followers, 4. Parables, 5. Jairus, 6. 5,000, 7. Defilement, 8. Confession, 9. Transfiguration, 10, Rich man, 11. Entry, 12. Questions, 13. Prophecy, 14. Gethsemane, 15. Crucifixion, 16. Resurrection.

The key or summarizing verse is 10:45. Bear in mind also 16:20: "The Lord working," and 11:22: "Have faith in God."

An outline for the study of Mark in twelve lessons follows:

Of the material presented only the questions are intended for the class.

LESSON I.
Preparation, Mark 1:1-20.

Previous preparation hinted at in 2 and 3. "The time is fulfilled," 15. Hopes of Jews for a new era, delivery from foreign yoke, restoration of ancient national glory. All Palestine feverish with this hope. Note how crowds flocked to John and how they thrilled to the message of Jesus: "The kingdom of God is at hand." But new day a day of spiritual renewal. John emphasizes repentence and confession of sins, predicts baptism with Holy Spirit. Jesus' opening command: "Repent and believe." Not "get armed," but "get right."

In His baptism Jesus commits Himself to the "cause" which John represented. His clear-cut step is followed by the divine stamp of approval, but also by the Spirit-enforced struggle in the wilderness. With the imprisonment of John He makes a second step in undertaking a campaign of proclamation in Galilee.

The last preparatory step is the association with himself of a small group of followers, men with no qualifications, but "I will make you."

Study Questions

1. Write a biography of John Mark according to Col. 4:10; Acts 13:13; 12:12-25; 15:37; 2 Tim. 4:11; Phm. 24.
2. Read the entire book and underline the word "straightway" or its equivalent. How often is it found?
3. What characterizes the Servant's work according to this word?
4. Was there any preparation for the Kingdom before John?
5. What was the general conception of the Messiah's work?
6. What was the effect when the message came: "The Kingdom is at hand"?
7. How did John make the paths straight?
8. Was there anything disappointing to the Jewish hopes in John's message?
9. What was the meaning and significance of Jesus' baptism?
10. What do you conclude from Jesus lining up personally with John's movement instead of sending a letter of endorsement or a contribution?
11. Who saw the Spirit descending according to Mark?
12. For whom was the Father's declaration mainly intended? Why was it so important just at this time?
13. How was the temptation a preparation for the great work?
14. Why did not Jesus work alone instead of associating with Himself men who might prove only a drawback?
15. What qualifications did the first disciples have for their new calling?
16. How did Jesus assure them of success?
17. What could we conclude from the fact that Zebedee is never mentioned again after the statement in verse 20?

Do you know of similar cases today?

LESSON II.
Healing Body and Soul, Mark 1:21-2:12.
Study Questions

1. In what part of the Jewish land do we find Jesus? Where do we read that he left?
2. Put yourself in the place of the disciples during this typical day in Jesus' life described in 1:21-35 and consider how each episode would have affected you.
3. What feature most impressed the crowd?
4. What did Jesus emphasize, healing or teaching?
5. Why did He show such interest in the physical condition of men?
6. Can churches justify their interest in the physical and social welfare of their community?
7. Is this religious work or simply a method of getting hold of people so that you can save their soul?
8. What would be the effect on the cause of the church if it undertook a greater work for the physical betterment of people? What steps in this direction would you suggest?
7. Is this religious work or simply getting hold of people so that you can save their soul?
8. What would be the effect on the cause of the church if it undertook a greater work for the physical betterment of people? What steps in this direction would you suggest?
9. If there is value in combining physical betterment and religious work when approaching people, how may the religious element be introduced without seeming to be "lugged in"?
10. Under what circumstances is it best to meet a man's physical need before "talking religion" to him? And vice versa?
11. When Jesus was so rushed, why did He not pray at His work instead of getting up before day for a special season of prayer? What was the relation of prayer to His daily ministry?
12. When very much rushed would you prefer to work in the spirit of prayer rather than to "take time out" for seasons of prayer alone? Give your reason.
13. Why would Jesus not permit the unclean spirits to testify? 1:25, 34?
14. Why was it difficult for the leper to obey, 1:44 and why the charge?
15. Answer Jesus' question, 2:9.
16. What new element is introduced in the case of the palsied man?

LESSON III.
New Standards for Old, Mark 2:13-3:6.

The incidents of this section illustrate the new teaching and the consequent opposition. The new standards are set forth not in formal discourses but in typical actions and practices of Jesus and His disciples. Offense had been taken, 2:7, the climax comes 3:6. No sooner is Galilee awakened with the joy of the new evangel, than jealousy of the "old guard" prompts the challenge of the innovations.

Study Questions

1. Imagine the shock given a high-caste Hindu by the breaking of caste, or if a cultured lady of the Old South should have sat at table with a Negro. Now read 2:3-17.

2. Is there a bit of irony in 2:17?
3. Was fasting an injunction of the Mosaic law?
4. What did Jesus mean to teach in 2:21, 22 in regard to the new movement and the old traditional rites?
5. Read I Sam. 21:1-6. What did David make of more importance than formal rules?
6. Why did Jesus withdraw before the threat of force at this time rather than face the issue?
7. Read in a Bible dictionary who the Herodians were.
8. Are scribes and Parisees necessarily the same people? Explain.
9. Why is it so difficult to inaugurate a new standard?
10. How did Jesus go about setting a new standard?
11. How did Jesus show that people who work for better standards do not have to take the joy out of life?
12. How would Jesus justify His disregard for customs sacred to His people? Why did He disregard fasting? Why did He "break" the Sabbath? Did he forbid to fast?
13. Why did He not now expose the falsity of the Pharisees as He did later?
14. What religious customs of our day would Jesus criticise? How?
15. How may we tell when a custom is good and when it becomes harmful? Illustrate.

LESSON IV.

Personnel and Growth of the Kingdom, Mark 3:77-4:34

Sifting men for the growing Kingdom. Jesus selects a special group of twelve and calls for another picked group who will "do the will of God." In the face of opposition more rapid progress must be made. Among a seething multitude, curious, or superstitious, or needing physical healing, few grasp the central purpose. So Jesus organizes for more effective work. A few must get His cause, there must be a group on which He can count.

Study Questions

1. Do you see any connection between the threat of destruction by the Jewish leaders and the organization for more effective work by the selection of the Twelve, 3:13, and between the overwhelming but misunderstanding response of the multitudes and the call for another picked group, 4:1-10?
2. How would the parable of the four kinds of soil and the call to produce have the effect of sifting the multitudes? Note 4:10, others besides the Twelve.
3. Could any one have joined the group to whom He explained later?
4. Note the privilege accorded 4:11. What does Jesus demand of these people in 21-25? What responsibility does the privilege bring?
5. What Jewish notion as to the coming of the Kingdom which might still linger should 4:26-34 dispel?
6. What and how much responsibility for bringing in the Kingdom is thrown back upon Jesus' followers?
7. Has the progress since then justified Jesus' confidence in the growth beyond all proportion and expectations?
8. What evidence, if any, do you see that the Kingdom is making progress at present in our social order, national life, community, congregation?
9. What factors at present furnish the most dangerous opposition?
10. To what extent did Jesus count on the first three kinds of soil for help?
11. In expanding the effectiveness of your church, would you emphasize popularizing the church so as to get a larger number to attend or raising the standard so as to enlist a smaller number who have a better purpose?
12. What proportion of your church are really producers, sufficiently for their loss to cripple the church?
13. Why 4:33, 34?

LESSON V.

Development of Faith, Mark 4:35-5:43

Four works of Jesus and men's response. The fear and questioning of the disciples, 4:40, 41, show that they were not yet sure of their leader, who He was, or how far they might trust His interest in them and His ability to handle difficult situations. Following the selection of an inner group on whom He could count to stand by His cause, Jesus' next step was to strengthen their confidence. Mark develops this not by discourses but by presenting

actual experiences. The unique authority is exhibited in four spheres. Before the Twelve were ready to be sent out to represent Him and His cause, there must come a strengthening of their own confidence.

Study Questions

1. What is meant by "other side," 4:35?
2. What does the questioning of the disciples, 4:40, 41, reveal as to their faith?
3. In how many and which spheres does Jesus reveal His authority to them?
4. Note the extreme attempts made in every case at other remedies.
5. How would the fishermen be impressed by the fact that He who was no sailor was a better master in a storm?
6. If you had been one of those who tried to bind the madman, what would have been your impression of Jesus?
7. Why did men laugh when Jesus spoke of sleep in Jairus' house?
8. Why did the confidence of Jairus hold steady?
9. How did the woman come to think that Jesus could help when others had failed?
10. How do you explain that only when the woman, of all the multitude, touched Him, power went forth?
11. What leads people to have confidence in a doctor, lawyer, minister?
12. What grounds had Jesus to be disappointed that His disciples had not yet faith?
13. Why did the people of Gerasene lose confidence?
14. Why does the same experience often affect different people in different ways?
15. If Christ is such a wonderful Leader and Helper, how do you account for the fact that in your home town so large a proportion have not lined up for Him?
16. Would you give any weight to testimony of others as to the trustworthiness of Jesus as friend and leader?
17. What in your own experience causes you to doubt or have confidence in Christ? Would you trust your own experience if it were contrary to the testimony of others? Why?
18. Upon the whole, does your observation and experience with Christianity give you confidence in its power? Why or why not?
19. Suggest some changes you would expect in the lives of people you know, if they had confidence that Jesus could help them meet life situations.
20. Why should no one know of the raising of Jairus daughter? Imagine the result of publicity at this time.

LESSON VI.

Failure and Success, Mark 6:1-7:23

Jesus' failure at Nazareth came at the height of His popularity in Galilee. In spite of this setback, perhaps because of it, He organized His disciples for the evangelization of Galilee on a greater scale than ever before. Supported by these six teams His work must have created a profound impression, so much so that King Herod heard of the new movement and was troubled. The account of John's fate is parenthetical, the event having taken place long before.

Study Questions

1. Why could Jesus not exert His power in Nazareth, 6:5?
2. What effect of His failure in Nazareth do we note in His Work?
3. How did He meet the discouragement presented: (a) by the fate of His forerunner? (b) by the failure of Galilee to respond to His spiritual message? (c) by the misunderstanding of His own disciples? (d) by the opposition of the Jewish leaders? (e) by the seeming impossibility of success for His cause?
4. Why did Jesus withdraw for prayer in the hour of discouragement, 6:46?
5. How do you account for 6:16?

13. How does one get the poise which Jesus felt in the face of discouragement? To what extent does prayer help?

14. Who is to blame when a person gets discouraged?

15. It is claimed that a Christian can get the upper hand in discouragement better than others. What is your observation and experience in this?

16. Compare the treatment of the Pharisees on their first and second visit to Galilee, 3:22ff and 7:1ff.

LESSON VII.
Training and Testing, Mark 7:24-9:50.

The apostles returned a bit elated over their success and Jesus puts them to a test. "After all your great wonders, give this multitude food." From Mark's account Jesus' popularity and fame here reaches its height. There is no indication why He stopped the splendid work in Galilee so soon, 7:24 and left the country. For an explanation see John 6:15ff. Rejected in Galilee and the Pharisees from Jerusalem renewing their hostility He leaves the country after a final word to them.

Study Questions

1. Trace Jesus' travels on the map.
2. Where are we told of His return to Jewish lands?
3. What do you draw from the fact that Jesus could not be hid even here?
4. Bearing in mind what had happened in Galilee can you picture the disciples' state of mind at this time?
5. How do you explain the disciples' failure to stand the same test a second time, 8:3, 4? What did they not understand v. 21?
6. Why could they not cast out the dumb spirit, a thing they had done before? See 6:7.
7. What training value did each story of this section have for the disciples?
8. Is there any evidence that their convictions became more settled as a result?
9. Why the strict charge 8:30? What would have been the effect of this disclosure upon those favorable to Him? (John 6:15ff) upon the enemies? Were the disciples at that time ready to proclaim this truth and all it implied?
10. What new thing did Jesus reveal to the Twelve after they became sure of His deity?
11. What part of this new revelation puzzled them?
12. What Jewish hope did they still cherish according to 9:34?
13. How did 9:36, 37 settle their argument? Think it through, taking the child as symbolizing humility. Although the three in question said nothing, can you imagine that the Transfiguration had anything to do with the argument?
14. Do you think the disciples were better prepared for what was to come when after these things Jesus set His face toward Jerusalem?
15. Can you name some characteristics which He attempted to eliminate because they were not worthy of His true disciples?
16. Were the disciples Christians at this time? Why or why not?
17. In 7:27 read "loaf" for "bread." Notice the contrast in woman's answer.
18. Why all the action of 7:33?
19. Does what you know of John later in his history agree with 9:38?

20. If you were to insert "anything as useful as" before hand, foot and eye, would 9:43-47 seem any plainer?
21. To grasp 9:49, 50 see I Peter 4:12 and Matth. 5:13. Compare 9:40 with Matth. 12:30. How about applying the former when sitting in judgment on others and the latter when on ourselves?

LESSON VIII.
On the Way, Mark 10

After the crisis and the feeding of the 5000 and the seeming failure in Galilee, the disciples were struggling hard for their faith in Jesus. Some features of His work as it developed did not coincide at all with their conceptions. Jesus led them patiently, allowing them to form their own conclusions on the basis of what they saw. Occasionally He was constrained to shake them awake, as in 8:17-21. Only when they were sure, 8:29, did Jesus begin to tell them of His inevitable fate. Still, not understanding His talk about a resurrection, they could not reconcile Messiahship with defeat and death. Six hard days go by, then comes the Transfiguration for three, and the others, after vainly trying to work in the power of former days, are told where their trouble lies. But not understanding, and being afraid to ask after Peter's experience of 8:32ff, the disciples fall into that narrowness and jealousy which is the foe of all pioneers who lose their spiritual vision.

Study Questions

1. Where do we find Jesus throughout the rest of the book?
2. Does Jesus condone any act on the part of married people which would violate the marriage vow?
3. Where the marriage has been dissolved by one party, does Jesus forbid the other party to marry again?
4. Does any act dissolve the marriage?
5. Is it wrong for the government to suffer and grant divorces? verse 4.
6. How does a little child receive the Kingdom? Does the "as" in verse 15 refer to the time or the manner of reception?
7. Why did Jesus love the rich man?
8. Why could he not follow Jesus without selling all that he had?
9. Jesus does not ask all His followers to give away all, but what does He ask of all regarding their possessions?
10. How do Jesus' followers receive an hundredfold in this life?
11. Name some of the life ambitions you have known persons to set for themselves? Which of these do you consider worthy and which unworthy?
12. How about the attainment of wealth as a life goal?
13. How about the establishment of a business which would give a square deal to employes, competitors, and the public?
14. How about the view that the big goal of life is to get to heaven in the next life? What is the "chief end" of man?
15. What was wrong with the goal James and John set for themselves?
16. Judging from 10:32-34, 38, 45, what was Jesus' big goal in life?
17. Why is the big goal which Jesus exemplified rejected by so many?
18. What practical program would a business man, a bricklayer, a doctor, a clerk, a college student or schoolboy have to adopt who wished to strive towards the true goal of life?
19. What would you say as to the relation of verse 45 to the whole book?

LESSON IX
The Question of Authority, Mark 11 and 12.

The beginning of the last division of the book. Four or five months probably elapsed between the departure from Galilee and the arrival in Jerusalem. The Perean ministry is treated more fully by Luke in about ten chapters. The Jewish leaders are now closing in on Jesus. He left Galilee partly to escape them, and no sooner does He return from exile into Jewish territory than the Pharisees are again upon His trail. Travelling towards Jerusalem the disciples believed that Jesus would somehow establish the kingdom. Ignoring His threeford announcement (8:31; 9:31; 10:32), they clung in desperate hope to an earthly rule. In this chapter we have Jesus' efforts to turn their minds from such a goal to the cross and to point them to the true road to His spiritual kingdom. Note that the key verse of the book is found here.

Study Questions

1. What claim did Jesus openly express by the circumstances of His entry into Jerusalem?
2. What authority did He assume by cleansing the temple?
3. Of what did He accuse the priests by this act?
4. Was Jesus a victim of circumstances beyond His control when He suffered and died? Give your reasons.
5. How often and where do we find Him declaring His fate in Mark?
6. How does the parable of the husbandmen answer the question of His authority?
7. What would have happened if He had answered Yes to the question as to paying tribute? What if He had said No?
8. Was Jesus' answer fair, or a clever way of avoiding a difficulty?
9. Can you give a stock question used by opponents of the Bible to-day similar to that of the Sadducees?
10. In regard to 12:35-37 ask yourself: Who was greater among the Jews, the ancestor or the descendent?
11. Why were the common people glad that Jesus won in the clash with their leaders?
12. What were Jesus' chances of rallying the populace about Him in successful opposition to the Jewish authorities? Note 12:12; 14:2.
13. What do you think of Jesus' proof, 12:26, 27? What is direct or by inference?
14. On what matters can Christians (a) compromise so as to avoid a conflict? (b) not compromise? What decides?
15. How far should Christians use the courts and legislation to further and protect their cause?
16. What are the best methods of meeting opposition to the cause of Christ?
17. What authority has Christianity to displace the other religions?

LESSON X
Troublous Days, Mark 13.

The final conflict with the Jewish leaders. Two authoritative acts, the openly expressed claim of the Messiahship by Jesus' entrance as the Son of David and the challenge of the priests' right to their sacred office by the cleansing of the temple. He could not have stirred up the hornets' nest of Jewish officialdom more thoroughly. If anyone thought that He withdrew too easily earlier in His ministry, all fears for His courage are here set at rest. Two challenging questions by the Jews. The Sadducees come with a stock question like the modern: "Where did Cain get his wife?" Jesus carries the war into His opponents' territory and with an exposure of their spirit closes His public work.

Study Questions

1. What was it about the stones and buildings that impressed the disciples?
2. Take each of the two questions asked by the disciples and see how Jesus answers it?
3. What four warning admonitions does Jesus give?
4. Do you think they were intended only for the disciples at that time? Give your reason.
5. Compare verse 30 with 32. Are "all these things" to happen on "that day?"
6. If Jesus had looked upon the destruction of Jerusalem as the beginning of the judgment of God over the world which, continuing through the centuries, should reach its final climax in the complete destruction of the whole world, would that solve the difficulty you experience in this chapter?
7. In what way was the destruction of Jerusalem typical of the end of the world?
8. Read Dan. 2;27, Luke 21:20-24. Also "Jewish Wars" by Josephus, column 11, 12, 13. Tell what you know

of destruction of Jerusalem.
9. In what respect are present times like those described in Mark 12?
10. Do Christians show more confidence than others in facing such troublous times? If so, in what respects? If not, why not?
12. Specifically, what work can the individual Christian undertake to help in these troublous times?

LESSON XI
The Way of the Cross, Mark 14 and 15.

This chapter is parenthetical. The plot to kill, 14:1,2, follows at once upon the failure of the Jewish leaders to cope with Jesus in fair and open play. That this discourse should find a place in such a short book may have the following reasons: Its immediate and practical value to the first-century Christians; the vindication of Jesus as a prophet; the picture it gives of Jesus facing His own sufferings and death with a calm confidence in the final success of His kingdom.

Study Questions

1. What do you think decided the Jewish leaders against their plans, 14:1,2,?
2. Who was the woman? John 12:3?
3. Is it possible for her to have been conscious of the significance of her act, 14:8? Perhaps Luke 10:39 will help you.
4. Would you say that Jesus fought the real battle in Gethsemane and having made there the final gift of life, bore with equanimity the passion proper?
5. Is 14:51,52 perhaps "the signature of the artist in a dark corner of the picture?"
6. To what time does 14:25 refer?
7. Under what circumstances would the cross have been the proof of importance and failure?
8. Can you mention cases where men did not consider a cause worth dying for?
9. What happens to a cause when men cease to think of it as worth dying for?
10. What made Judas feel that Christ's cause was not worth that sacrifice?
11. What caused the change in the disciples, so that fleeing here they later went into death gladly for Christ?
12. What is meant by the statement: "The blood of the martyrs is the seed of the church?"
13. Why is it still necessary that one who becomes a Christian must be willing to die for the cause?
14. Which wins men more for the cause of Christ, the argument that it costs very little to be a Christian, or the challenge that it is worth dying for? Why?
15. Do you remember another occasion when Peter, James and John were alone with Jesus?
16. Does the death of Jesus for His cause differ from the death of any other who dies for a cause?

LESSON XII.
Triumph of Endless Life, Mark 16.

The Jewish leaders planned to wait until after Passover feast, but the treachery of Judas played into their hands and decided them against any delay. The story of the anointing at Bethany is probably told because it partly explains the defection of Judas, John 12:4.

Study Questions

1. Find passages in Mark in which Jesus refers to His resurrection and meeting His disciples in Galilee?
2. Do you think the disciples were familiar with a general resurrection on the last day? See John 11:24.
3. How do you account for their amazement and disbelief on Easter?
4. How many appearances are mentioned?
5. Do you recall when and by whom Jesus was called "Jesus of Nazareth" at the beginning of His ministry?
6. Why did the angel mention Peter particularly?
7. Why was so much made of the Resurrection in early Christian preaching?
8. What would the disciples have preached if Jesus had not risen?

JOIN THE
"Bible Book of the Month Club"
"Fifteen Minutes A Day"
For A Sound Spiritual Education

THE EPISTLE TO THE PHILIPPIANS was written by Paul, probably from Rome between 60 and 64 A.D. The Church in the city of Philipi was ideal in many respects. It was very appreciative and benevolent. See. ch. 4, 15, 16; 2 Cor. 8, 2.

It was founded by Paul on his second missionary journey, in the midst of a storm of persecution. The beginnings of the work were small, among a few women at the river side. Lydia, a seller of purple, was the first convert, and she was soon joined by the Philippian jailor and his Family. These, and perhaps a few others, became the nucleus of the church. Read Acts 16, 12-40.

Characteristics of the Epistle. It is a spiritual love letter to the church. It contains outbursts of warm affection and gratitude. Written under hard circumstances, while Paul was a prisoner, he strikes the keynotes of victory and joy.

Find the CHAPTER and Verse in Philippians where Paul "rejoices": 1) in prayer; 2) in the gospel; 3) in Christian fellowship; 4) in sacrifices for the cause; 5) in the Lord; 6) for the loving care of the church for him.

In Chapter One. FIND VERSE or Verses: Where Christ is the source of spiritual fruit. Where Christ is the theme of preaching. Where Christ is the highest motive of Christian service.

In Chapter Two. Find Verse or Verses: Where Christ is shown as exhibiting the only perfect spirit and example.

In Chapter Three. Find Verse or Verses: Where the knowledge of Christ is the supreme prize for which to struggle in life. Where at Christ's appearing, believers' bodies shall be fashioned anew.

In Chapter Four. Find Verse or Verses: Where Christ's Power is limitless in Christian lives. Where Christ is the channel of Divine supplies for every need.

Find Chapter and Verse of the following quotations: "the Lord is at hand"; "what things were gain to me, those I counted loss for Christ"; "for all seek their own, not the things which are Jesus Christ's"; "beware of dogs"; "do all things without murmurings"; "having a desire to depart, and be with Christ; which is far better"; "salute every saint in Christ Jesus"; "be careful for nothing, but in everything by supplication and prayer let your requests be made known unto God"; "I press toward the mark for the prize of the high calling of God"; "work out your own salvation with fear and trembling"; "let your conversation be as it becometh the gospel of Christ"; "he that hath begun a good work in you will perform it until the day of Jesus Christ"; "for I know that this shall turn to my salvation through your prayer"; "who mind earthly things"; "but my God shall supply all your need"; "that at the name of Jesus every knee should bow"; "for me to live is Christ, and to die is gain"; "he humbled himself, and became obedient unto death, even the death of the cross."

I WILL JOIN

BIBLE BOOK OF THE MONTH CLUB
EVANGELICAL LUTHERAN CHURCH
(Your Church's Name)

If you are willing to read *this book at least once* during the month, please tear off this stub and give it to the pastor or drop in envelope collection box.

Name..

Address...

"Bible Book of the Month Club"
"Fifteen Minutes a Day"
For A Sound Spiritual Education!

The EPISTLE of PAUL to the ROMANS is the greatest of his four doctrinal epistles, was written about 58 A. D. during Paul's three month stay at Corinth during his Third Missionary Journey, and was addressed to the Christian congregation in Rome. Ch. 1,7. Key Verse: ch. 1,16 or ch. 5,1.

1)—Divide the book into two major divisions: I. Doctrinal, chs. 1-11. II. Practical, chs. 12-16. In your first rapid reading, notice that Part I. sets forth "The Plan of Salvation" as Justification by Faith and Sanctification through the Holy Spirit. Part II. is mainly exhortations concerning Christian duties.— Also note the *three walls* with which the apostle surrounds the human race: a) The wall of universal guilt, chs. 1-3 (find a gate leading to salvation in ch. 5). b) The Wall of Sinful Tendencies, ch. 7,15-24 (find a salvation gate in ch. 8.). c) The Wall of Sovereign election, 9,7-18 (find a salvation gate in ch. 10).—Work out the following *Key Chain* of Thought: ch. 1,16; 3,22.23.28; 4,3; 5,1.18; 9,31.32; 10,3.4.6-9.

2)—Work through the entire book a second time checking the following outline: *The Plan of Salvation. 1. The need of,* proven by universal guilt of man: a) of Gentile world, ch. 1,18-27. b) Likewise Jews, ch. 2,8-3,20. c) ALL sinners, 3,23. *2. Illustrated by Abraham* in ch. 4: a) Apart from works, vs. 1-6; b) Apart from ordinances, vs. 9-12; c) Apart from the law, vs. 13-25. *4. The Blessings of,* made effective by love of God, manifested in Christ's atonement, ch. 5,1-11. *5. Scope of free gift* of salvation expounded, ch. 5,12-21; 6. Does not permit continuance in sin, ch. 6,1-23; 7. *Struggle with Sinful Tendencies,* ch. 7,7-24; 8. Find Culmination of *Divine Plan,* in ch. 8; 9. ch. 9,1-5 is a *Parenthesis;* 10. *Mystery of Divine Election,* ch. 9,4-33; 11. *Misapprehension by Jews* of Divine Plan, ch. 10,1-3; 12. *Divine Plan Expounded,* ch. 10,1-18; 13. *God's Dealings with Israel,* ch. 10,19-11,12; 14. *The Gentiles warned not to boast,* ch. 11,13-22; 15. *Restoration of Israel Predicted,* ch. 11, 23-36.

3)—II. PRACTICAL. (Exhortations on Christian Duties) *Chapter 12 is one of the Finest Chapters in All Scriptures Summarizing Christian duties.* COMPARE:—*v.*1 with ch. 6,13.16 and 1 Cor. 6,20; *v.*2 with 1 Pet. 1,14 and 1 John 2,15; *v.*3 with Luke 22,26; *v.*4 with 1 Cor. 12,12; *v.*5 with Eph. 4.25; *v.*6 with 1 Cor. 12,4; *v.*7 with Gal. 6,6; *v.*8 with Heb. 13,7; *v.*9 with Amos 5,15; *v.*10 with 1 Pet. 3,8; *v.*11 with Proverbs 18,9; *v.*12 with Rom. 15,13; *v.*13 with 1 John 3,17; *v.*14 with 1 Pet. 3,9; *v.*15 with 1 Cor. 12,26; *v.*16 with Phil. 2,2; *v.*17 with Matt. 5,39; *v.*18 with Rom. 14,19; *v.*19 with Heb. 10,30; *v.*20 with Matt. 5,44; *v.*21 with Revelation 2,7.7.26.; ch. 3,5.12.21; ch. 21,7.

4)—In Chapter 13 *apply Paul's advice to our present day.* a) Civic and Social Duties, vs. 1-10. b) Duty of living as "children of the day" vs. 11-14. *Apply chapters 14 and 15 to our own congregation:* 1) Charity in judging, ch. 14:1-13. 2) Carefulness not to give offense, ch. 14,15-23; 3) Bearing infirmities and not pleasing self, ch. 15,1.7.

CLOSING THOUGHTS: ch. 15,8-21, Reasons for Thanksgiving; ch. 15,22-16,16, Paul's Desire to visit Rome and personal greetings; Ch. 16,17-27. Final words and Benediction.

I WILL JOIN

BIBLE BOOK OF THE MONTH CLUB
Evangelical Lutheran Church
(Your Church's Name)

If you are willing to read *this book at least once* during the month, please tear off this stub and give it to the pastor or drop in envelope collection box.

Name..

Address...

9. How did the disciples' belief in the Resurrection affect their belief in what Christianity could do for the world?

10. Why were signs of healing and helpful ministry added to the message they were to preach?

11. What has made the progress of Christianity so slow through the centuries?

12. How do you account for the more rapid spread of Christianity in the past century?

13. What right have Christians to seek to spread their religion where other religions already exist?

14. Draw a diagram of the entire book showing three main divisions; name these; show twelve sections and give a name to each chapter.

These Studies are also printed separately, one lesson to a sheet, for distribution in Bible classes. A set, covering the whole course, 12 lessons, cost 10 per set. Remit money with order. Address Business Department, A.L.P.B., 69 Fifth Ave., New York, N. Y.

The World's Debt to the Reformation

TEN JEWELS FOR WHICH WE GIVE THANKS

By Charles L. Fry

The Church of the Reformation calls her friends and her neighbors together, at this festival time, to rejoice with her at the recovery (after the lighting of the candle and the sweeping of the house) of these ten jewels, more precious than rubies, which are her priceless heritage, to be handed from generation to generation.

1. **THE OPEN BIBLE**

The inalienable right of every human soul in all the wide world is to have the open Bible. The very first thing a Protestant missionary does upon entering a new country is to translate the Bible into the language of that people, — the last thing that Rome would ever think of doing. This is the guarantee of Protestant permanence. The Protestant Reformation put the Bible in the hands of the people. Every time we find consolation, inspiration and blessing in its precious pages we are in debt to the Reformation.

2. **JUSTIFICATION BY FAITH**

What a gracious thing it was, in God's Providence, that Luther was allowed to find this key, which unlocks all the Scriptures, before he became a translator! He found it amid his inward struggles during his stay in the monastery. The fakirs, sitting on beds of spikes to obtain peace, the poor widows of India measuring their length to a shrine to propitiate the gods, the mothers casting their children into the Ganges, millions who do penance and make gifts to obtain pardon for sin, would give all they possess for the assurance we have of justification through faith.

3. **THE UNIVERSAL PRIESTHOOD OF ALL BELIEVERS**

This means doing away with all the false distinctions between the clergy and the laity. During the Apostolic age every Christian was a missionary. The evangelization of the world dare never be limited to a select few. Whatever obligation belongs to one, belongs to all.

4. **THE RIGHT OF PRIVATE JUDGMENT**

We deny that the only authority to decide our religious belief is the Pope. Every believer decides it for himself, with God's own Word as his absolute rule. Luther claimed this right in his immortal answer before the Diet of Worms, and in this he was the spokesman of all Protestants.

5. **THE PEOPLE'S PART IN PUBLIC WORSHIP**

What a priceless privilege it is that we have of taking part in public worship. Now, practically all Protestants have some form of service in which all the people join. In Old Testament days even the High Priest himself could go into the Holy of Holies only once a year. We have access every Sunday.

6. **UNIVERSAL EDUCATION**

The principle of Protestantism is the general enlightenment of the people. Every public school system on earth is the gift of the Reformation. How much would North America take for it! How much would South America give for it? Or Mexico, or Spain, or Italy, or Porto Rico?

7. **AN UNMUTILATED SACRAMENT**

This is another of the ten treasures which had been lost, and which were found again, in the Reformation. The withholding of the cup from the laity is a high-handed usurpation of Rome, to bolster up the caste distinction of the priests.

8. **CHRISTIAN HYMNS**

The Reformation was literally sung into the hearts of the people. In Romish countries there are no hymns, either in the Churches or in the home. Without Bibles, without hymn-books, without schools such as we know on every hand, how dark and cheerless were those days compared with the light in which we rejoice.

9. **PROTESTANT PARSONAGE**

How much does North America owe to the Protestant parsonages which are another gift of the Reformation? Name the senators in our halls of legislation, the judges of our courts, the statesmen, the lawyers, the physicians, the surgeons, the merchants, the ministers, the men eminently useful in every walk of life, who have come from Protestant parsonages. What hospitality is there dispensed; what cheer is given to help those who come for advice and strengthening; what example of Christian home-life in our own and in non-Christian lands!

10. **CIVIL AND RELIGIOUS LIBERTY**

In Luther's day the States of Europe were chained to the chariot of the Emperor, whose driver was the Pope. Into their hands Luther placed the sword of the Spirit, which is the Word of God, and States which have wielded that sword have severed the chain and become free. Modern freedom is the fruit of the tree planted by Martin Luther. "The priceless blessings of liberty and the rights of conscience recognized, enjoyed, and guaranteed in our own great republic, and working like a leaven among all people who do not enjoy them, are, directly and indirectly, the result of the truths and principles so clearly and so forcibly proclaimed by Martin Luther four hundred years ago."

Behold the priceless value of these ten lost jewels, recovered in the Reformation, remembering without a single exception that each one has come to be the common heritage of Protestantism as a whole, whatever its differences and divisions, and say whether, in these ten foundation principles, we have cause for united thanksgiving.

1949

Reformation Day Publicity

In an article published in the *New York Times Magazine* for July 4th, 1926, William E. Dodd, Professor of History at the University of Chicago, makes the following statement:

"This appeal (in the Declaration of Independence) to the reason of men everywhere and the assertion that all men are created equal, and not the mere secession of the American Colonies from the British Empire, made of the American Declaration of Independence a universal challenge that gives it rank with Martin Luther's similar challenge of Oct. 31, 1517. And the forest philosophy put forward 150 years ago in the little city of Philadelphia has proved to be as wise and as revolutionary as that of the bold monk of Wittenberg who risked his life in the promulgation of his platform of religious independence. The two challenges make the most important documents of modern history."

October 31 thus is a date whose tremendous significance is recognized also outside of the Lutheran Church. The Synodical Press Committee is convinced that wherever proper efforts are made this date will have a distinct publicity value. It will present to our churches an opportunity to step before the public. Hence the suggestions printed on the cover of this issue of the AMERICAN LUTHERAN.

Pastors and congregational publicity committees would do well to get in touch with local editors some time during the middle of October and to give advance information concerning the Reformation Day services. Brief news articles elaborating on the points mentioned by the committee might be written and submitted to the editor. The points to be emphasized were chosen with a view to the present-day situation. Rome has of course always played a political game and continues to do so. But Protestant churches too are becoming more and more guilty of such practices. In fact, Calvinism was based on the old theocratic idea of the State and that mistaken idea influences the attitude of most of the Reformed bodies toward the State. The Lutheran position on the strict separation of Church and State, our insistence that the chief business of the Church is the proclamation of Christ's everlasting Gospel, has already received editorial approval in various parts of the country. Reference is made to editorials that were written in connection with the recent synodical convention at St. Louis and the Walther League convention at Baltimore. We want more such publicity and ought to be able to get it.

Advance copies of the Reformation Day sermon or sermons might also be sent to the editorial offices. Newspapers will often quote or even run complete parts.

Naturally the services themselves must be carefully worked up, both extensively and intensively. By *extensively* we mean proper publicity in parish and community. For that purpose Concordia Publishing House has printed special invitation cards that may be utilized to good advantage. Circularize the whole mailing-list and endeavor to get the names of as many churchless people as possible so as to invite them too.

Intensive preparation refers to efforts aiming at attractive Reformation Day services. Special music by choir, school children and others ought to be included. An order of service, ready to be used, has been worked out and may be ordered from the Concordia Publishing House.

Joint Reformation Day services might be conducted in larger cities. Needless to say such services possess splendid publicity value. But the main interest of the Committee is in the local congregations. Conditions differ widely. So do editors and editorial policies. But possibilities there always are and with tactful effort and work valuable publicity for our Lutheran Church may be obtained.

He still lives an antagonistic spirit to Rome, and a purifying and preserving spirit to Christianity at large.—Coleridge.

* * * *

He is the chief figure in an historic picture which will be contemplated by the thoughtful of all lands to the end of time.—John Jay.

* * * *

It is impossible to solve equation complicated by factors so immeasurable as a great personality and the spirit of an age; but if it can be said of any man, that without him a mighty revolution might have been postponed, or, perhaps might have totally miscarried, this may be said of Martin Luther.—The Sun.

* * * *

Luther is the most deserving man the world has ever seen; and although four centuries have elapsed since the time he began the good work of reform, his star has not waned; and as his name goes thundering down the countless centuries yet to come, it will gather increased glory in exact ratio to the increase of his following. His work in the past four centuries shows four hundred millions of converts to his ideas.—Nebraska State Journal.

* * * *

It was the merit of Luther that he set free the Word of God; and because that is a Divine agent and touches the main-springs of individual, social and national life, his influence has gone farther and struck deeper than that of any other man in modern history.—Dr. W. M. Taylor.

* * * *

It was the sense of the Divine commission and the profoundness of the struggle that created Luther, who shook the throne of the Caesars and made Europe anew. He is the prophet and priest of human nature at once. To take Luther out of the Reformation is to take the sun out of the sunshine.—Dr. Phillips Brooks.

* * * *

By this man more than by any other man for eighteen centuries, our own century drinks the living waters of Christianity at its fountain source. To Luther, more than to any other man since St. Paul, the Church of Christ is indebted for its grasp of two essential principles: The first is the fact of justification, or forgiveness of sin, by faith and not of words. The second is that the Divine Word is supreme in all faith and practice, and in all organization of the Church. More today, than to any other man of eighteen hundred years, men owe to Luther freedom of thought, of speech, of conscience, of action; the right to worship God according to what conscience dictates.—Dr. Leech.

* * * *

"Luther's influence still lives in the world today, and is probably felt ever more powerfully by English speaking people than by those who belong to the race in which Luther was born."—The United Presbyterian.

* * * *

"So stands Luther (like Bont Blane), a hero, growing more and more the mark of reverence through succeeding centuries—a real author of modern liberty of thought and action, and the giant founder of modern civilization and pure religion."—

The monarch's sword, the prelate's pride,
The Church's curse, the Empire's ban,
By one poor monk were all defied,
Who never feared the face of man.
Half battles were the words he said,
Each born of prayer, baptized in tears;
And, routed by them, backward fled
The errors of a thousand years.
—J. F. Clarke.

LUTHER SAID:

"When respect for the Word of God is at low ebb, then honesty and morality is also."

A Remedy Without Rival

"When habitually reading and hearing the Bible, you will find there is nothing like it as a source of comfort and patience in any troubles of conscience, and even in death."

"The welfare of a city does not consist alone in great treasures, firm walls, beautiful houses, and abundant munitions of war; indeed, where all these are found, and reckless fools come into power, the city sustains the greatest injury. But the highest welfare, safety, and power of a city consists in able, learned, wise, upright, cultivated citizens, who can secure, preserve, and utilize every treasure and advantage."

Married People

"Married people should know that they can perform no better and no more useful work for God, Christianity, the world, themselves, and their children, than by bringing up their children well. . . . It is the peculiar work of parents, and when they do not attend to it, there is a perversion of nature, as when fire does not burn, or water moisten. On the other hand, hell can not be more easily deserved, and no more hurtful work can be done, than by neglecting children, letting them swear, learn shameful words and songs, and do as they please."

Children

"Children should be brought up in the fear of God. If the kingdom of God is to come in power, we must begin with children, and teach them from the cradle.

"See to it that you first of all have your children instructed in spiritual things, giving them first to God and afterwards to secular duties."

Domestic Training

"If we wish to have proper and excellent persons both for civil and ecclesiastical government, we must spare no diligence, time, or cost in teaching and educating our children, that they may serve God and the world, and we must not think only how we can amass money and possessions for them. . . . Let every one know, therefore, that above all things it is his duty (or otherwise he will lose the divine power) to bring up his children in the fear and knowledge of God; and if they have talents, to have them instructed and trained in a liberal education, that men may be able to have their aid in government and in whatever is necessary."

Publicity

"The press (publicity) is the summum et postremum bonum (the best and last gift) by which God would advance the cause of the Gospel."

Obedience to Parents

It is obvious that God attaches great importance to obedience to parents. And where it is not found, there can be neither good morals nor good government. For where obedience is lacking in the family, no city or principality or kingdom can be well governed. Family government is the basis of all other government; and where the root is bad, the trunk and fruit can not be good.

* * *

Good Government Based on Family

What is a city but a collection of houses? How then can a city be well governed, when there is no government in the separate houses, and neither child nor servant is obedient? Likewise, what is a province but a collection of cities, towns and villages? When, therefore, the families are badly controlled, how can the province be well governed? . . . Where father and mother rule badly, and let the children have their own way, there neither city, town, village, district, principality, kingdom, or empire can be well and peacefully governed.

* * *

Stewardship

"Christians are to know that they are in duty bound to serve God with the gifts (opportunities) God supplies. And you serve God by devoting such gifts to the service and benefit of your fellowmen, to the end that they be benefited, and come to the knowledge of God."

* * *

"Children should be instructed in which pertains to God. They should be taught to know the Lord Jesus Christ, and constantly to remember how He has suffered for us, what He has done, and what He has promised. Thus were the children of Israel commanded to relate to their children and successors the miracles God had done for their fathers in Egypt. And when children have this knowledge, and yet do not learn to love and adore God, and to follow Jesus Christ, the punishment of God should be held up before them—His fearful judgment and anger at the wicked. If a person learns from youth up to recognize the benefits of God, and hence to love Him, and likewise, the punishments and threatenings of God, and hence to fear Him, he will not forget it afterwards when he is old."

* * *

"We might thus train our youth in a childlike way and in the midst of their plays, in God's fear and honor, so that the First and Second Commandments might be familiar and in constant practice. Then some good might adhere, spring up and bear fruit, and men grow up in whom an entire land might rejoice and be glad. This would be the true way to bring up children; since, by means of kindness, and with delight, they can become accustomed to it. For what must only be forced with rods and blows will have no good result, and at farthest, under such treatment, they will remain godly no longer than the rod descends upon their backs."

Filling The Pews During Advent

It is not a difficult task to fill our churches during the Lenten season. Our services need no special embellishments to draw the people, for our Lutheran people are pretty well Lenten-minded. But this is not the case in the Advent season. The Lenten season still belongs to the Church, but Christmas has become secularized, and what is worse, commercialized. This is the psychology behind the poor church attendance. People are too busy with the commercial part of Christmas during Advent to go to Church.

The problem therefore becomes a challenge. What can we do to get Christ back into Christmas? What can we do to make our people Advent-minded? The following programs are offered as a suggestion for the Advent Evening service problem. These services have been successfully held. Not only have the attendances been gratifying but also the people attending have become more Christ-minded concerning Christmas.

Many details of presentation are left to individual initiative of the pastor. The following material is presented in outline only.

SERVICE I.
The Holy Night
"In our Service tonight we will tell in song and word what happened on that Holy Night, 1932 years ago.

I. The Town
Prophecy of Micah. David's city. Why not Jerusalem?
Organ (softly).
Children sing: "O Little Town of Bethlehem."

II. The Time
The fullness of time. The prepration which had been made.
Why did God call Abraham? Christ was the matchless blossom which bloomed out of all the growth from Abraham to Mary. The roots to the tree: Priests, prophets, tabernacle, temple, gorgeous ritual and streaming altar, sacrifice and psalms, kingdom and captivity.
The time had come.
Hymn: 146

III. The Angels and the Shepherds.
Angels the servants of God. Angel Gabriel, Zacharias, Mary, the Shepherds.
The first Christmas sermon.
Hymn: 150. or "While Shepherds watched their flocks at night."

IV. The Angel's Song
An angel the first preacher.
Angels also the first choir. A song that thrills us today.
Hymn: 154—Hark the herald angels sing.

V. The Manger
Where will the shepherds go?
What will be the sign?
Their resolve.
They worship.
In a manger: No soft, downy bed; no great palace. A stable, the dark, smelly stable. Thus Christ came into the stable of this world, where men lost their divine image and wallowed in the dirt and filth of sin.
How we love this manger. But the manger means nothing without the Cross.
Choir: "In a Manger." Carols of all nations. Fischer.

VI. The Magi
The story.
The star. The Gifts.
Choir or Children: "We Three Kings."

VII. Call to Worship
Let us go to Bethlehem.
Our duty: Worship and gifts.
Offering.
Benediction and closing hymn or Recessional.

SERVICE II.
A Candle Light Service
Seven Candles placed in a row, or on a candlestick. Same size. In back of these seven candles one large candle slightly elevated.
Behind this candle, raised still higher a cross or Crucifix.
Each of the seven candles stands for a prophecy. The large candle symbolizes Christ.
Hymn 71.
Vesper Service.
Psalm 24, chanted.
Prayer.
I. Candle. Gen. 3:15. Choir: "O come, Emanuel". Gregorian. S. S. hymnal. (words) While choir sings the first candle is lighted.
II. Candle. Numbers 24:17.
Hymn 77. Candle lighted.
III. Candle. Is. 11:1-10. Solo: A Branch so fair. 3 candle lighted.
IV. Candle. Is. 9:6.
Hymn: 69. Candle lighted.
V. Candle. Is. 7:14. Hymn: 116. Candle lighted.
VI. Candle. Micah 5:1-3. "O Little Town of Bethlehem." Candle lighted.
VII. Candle. The Annunciation. Luke 1:26-38. Choir: The Magnificat. Candle lighted.

II Part
Fulfillment
Solo: Silent night.
Luke 2. 1-18. Choir: "Angles We have Heard." Large candle lighted.
The Symbolism of the Cross. Christmas means nothing without Calvary.
The manger has no significance without the Cross.
Offering.
Prayer. Hymn: 101. Verses 1 and 8.
This service can be elaborated depending on the ambition of the choir and Pastor.

SERVICE III.
The Christmas Service of All Nations
This service is a symposium to bring out the universality of Christmas and the Christmas Spirit. The various nations are to be represented by children dressed in the costumes of the particular country. The parents will be willing to cooperate with the Pastor in this work and the children will take quite an interest in the serivce.

The theme of the service is: "Jesus, the Savior of the World."
Music: "Christmas Carols of All Nations." Fischer.
Children march into the church singing a processional hymn. Opening Service. Prayers, or the Vesper Service.
After each legend a carol is sung by the choir, or the children.
If the French carol is sung, for instance, then the girl dressed in the French costume stands in the center, etc.
At the close of the service the children representing the various nations kneel at the entrance of the chancel as the congregation joins in the hymn, "Come hither ye faithful."
The following sources are suggested:
1. The Legend of the White Gifts—by Phebe Curtiss.
2. Her Birthday Dream—by Nellie King.
3. The Fir Tree—by Anderson.
4. Little Jean—by Francois Coppe.
5. How the Fir Tree became the Christmas Tree.
6. Babouscka—by Caroline Bailey.
7. The Shepherd Who Didn't Go—by Jay Stocking.
8. The True Christmas Story—by St. Luke.
These are to be found in "Christmas Stories and Legends". Phebe Curtis. Meigs Publishing Co., Indianapolis, Ind.
This Service can also be used with some changes by calling it

a "Christmas Journey through Many Lands." In this case the legends need not be told, but the Pastor serves as guide for the journey.

Other Suggestions

"The Christmas Cycle" by Peter Cornelius. An exceptional organist and good soloists are needed.

The Christmas Section of Handel's "Messiah." An ambitious program for the choir.

SERVICE IV.
Christmas Pageant
B. VON SCHENK
PROLOGUE

Anxious Voices are heard inquiring of the Watchman when the Prince of Peace shall be born. The Old Testament and New Testament appear and take their places on either side of the stage; they are the pillars which frame and support the entire story of the birth of the Saviour.

Choir: Watchman, Tell us—

Old Testament.—I symbolize the Old Testament, the oracles of God's prophesy. In me is the New Testament Hidden. Out of the dim past come records of faith in One Who was to come, sent of God, to save men.

New Testament—In me are all things fulfilled. The oracles of the Prophets. The Old Testament is revealed in the New Testament.

SCENE I.

Various Prophets of the Old Testament are seen. They utter their messages concerning the Saviour. Prophecies of Moses, Balaam, David, Isaiah, Ezekiel and Jeremiah are heard. The people are heard praying that Emmanuel would come. "O come, O come, Emmanuel."

Action of Scene I.

Moses—The great Jehovah hath spoken to me, His Servant Moses: "The Lord thy God will raise up to thee a Prophet from the midst of thee, of thy brethren, like unto me: unto Him ye shall hearken."

Balaam—I Balaam speak: "I shall see him, but not now: I shall behold Him, but not nigh: there shall come out a star out of Jacob, and a sceptre shall rise out of Israel."

Isaiah—I, Isaiah, have had this vision of the Lord of Hosts: "For unto us a Child is born, unto us a Son is given; and the government shall be upon his shoulder, and His name shall be called Wonderful, Counsellor, The Mighty God, The Everlasting Father, The Prince of Peace."

Jeremiah—Behold, O people as I Jeremiah speak: "In his days Judah shall be saved, and Israel shall dwell safely: and this is His name whereby He shall be called, The Lord our Righteousness."

Ezekiel—The Lord God speak thru me, Ezekiel: "Therefore I will save my flock. I will set up one shepherd over them, and he shall feed them, and he shall be their shepherd."

SCENE II.
Zacharias in the Temple

Zacharias is seen in the Holy place of the temple offering incense and prayer to God. While he is in the midst of his prayer the angel Gabriel appears and tells him that his wife Elizabeth should bear him a son, whose name would be John, and that he was to prepare the way for Christ. All things pointed to the coming of Christ. Therefore the people rejoice and sing: "Hark the Glad Sound, the Saviour Comes."

Action of Scene II.

Zacharias before the Altar. Burns incense.

Gabriel—Fear not, Zacharias, for thy prayer is heard, and thy wife Elizabeth shall bear thee a son, and thou shalt call his name John. And thou shalt have joy and gladness, and many shall rejoice at his birth. For he shall be great in the sight of the Lord.

Zacharias—Whereby shall I know this?

Gabriel—I am Gabriel, that stand in the presence of God; and I am sent to speak unto thee, and to show thee these glad tidings. Behold, thou shalt be dumb, and not able to speak, until the day

that these things shall be performed.

Note:—Zacharias is struck dumb. He stretches out his hand in benediction to the audience.

Curtain

Audience: Hymn No. 77. Hark the glad sound.

(The audience is requested to join in the singing of the hymn):

SCENE III.
The Annunciation

Mary is seen in her home at Nazareth. Her thoughts are expressed in words of Scripture and in the voice heard backstage, "Come thou long expected Jesus." Suddenly the angel Gabriel appears to her and tells her that she should be "The Mother of God." Mary is amazed that she, a humble maiden, should be so highly favored by God, and she kneels in silent prayer, while a voice backstage sings the beautiful Magnificat, which well expresses Mary's thoughts at this time.

Action of Scene III.

Mary sits in her home. Reads: O, that God would redeem Israel. (pause). Behold, a virgin shall conceive and bear a son, and shall call his name Emmanuel. (Muses)

Gabriel enters.

Mary shrinks back in awe and fear.

Gabriel—Hail, thou art highly favored, the Lord is with thee. Blessed art thou among women. (pause).

Fear not, Mary, for thou hast found favor with God. And behold, thou shalt conceive in thy womb, and bring forth a son, and shalt call his name Jesus. He shall be great, and shall be called the Son of the Highest; and the Lord God shall give unto Him the throne of his father David. And He shall reign over the house of Jacob forever; and of His Kingdom there shall be no end.

Christmas Suggestions

Set up one or two outdoor Christmas trees with colored lights. Have an organization of the church take care of such tree. Full sized electric bulbs may be used for the lights. Wiring should be weatherproof.

* * *

Try a new method of decorating the large tree in church. If you have been using the customary ornamentations, try an entirely white tree. Spread cotton or asbestos wool along the top of each branch, then string tinsel "icicles" over each branch. Use all white lights.

* * *

Arrange a cluster of smaller trees around the larger tree or in the corners of the church.

* * *

If the tree sits on a pedestal or table, a Christmas Transparency may be used to advantage under the tree.

* * *

A different method of decorating the tree has been used by spraying shellac on the tree before it is put up. After the shellac dries it looks like frost. The tree may be left without further ornamentation or "icicles" may be thrown over the branches.

* * *

Make use of small trees or branches from evergreens in decorating the church. Such branches may often be obtained without cost from a dealer in evergreens.

Children's Christmas Services

SAMPLE COPIES of certain Christmas Vesper services have been coming in lately, and suggest these lines. The subject is so simple that we hesitate to discuss it. However, there are a few sound principles that are commonly overlooked, and a little serious thought might remedy matters.

In the first place, a Vesper service for the children of the Sunday-school or day school must be exactly what it purports to be, namely a Christmas service. This sounds trite. And yet it is a point missed by some of the printed orders of service that have been coming through the mails. Before us is such a service that seems to be more of a festival for bell-founders, or perhaps change ringers, than a Christmas service, for the theme, from start to finish, is about bells. We fear that the rhymesters are intrigued by the threadbare "ringing—singing" rhyme, which one of our authorities on hymnody has just told us is as overworked as the "sadness—gladness" one.

Much as we love good bells, yet at Christmas time it is the Holy Christ Child, and not the music of the bells, that ought to be our theme. Much as we all love a peal of bells, or even a carillon at Christmas time, yet sentimental things must not crowd the Holy Child of Bethlehem into the background. Bells are fine, but they can become a bad thing if we allow them to take the place of the New Born Saviour. Just note such titles as these: "Christmas Bells are Ringing," "Hear the Bells," "The Music of the Bells," "Ring, Ye Merry Christmas Bells." When four bell songs compete with four Christmas hymns, the order of service is hardly a good one.

A good children's Vesper service will begin, continue and end with the Christmas story, and the Christ Child will be prominent in every hymn, every Psalm, every Scripture lesson and every incidental number. The Lutherans have never permitted Santa Claus to intrude, neither ought we to allow bells, yule logs, Christmas gifts and snow-clad landscapes to become our theme, or even to appear too prominently. There is great temptation to give bell recitations and yule log dialogues to children at Christmas time. This ought to be watched.

In a good Christmas Vesper service for children, the story of the Nativity of Our Lord will be told simply and completely. There must be something progressive about it. Too many such services lack this element of consecutive story telling. There is a bit of the Nativity story here, then something about angels singing, then a lullaby, then some shepherds watching their flocks, then the Tannenbaum with its many lights, and possibly a fragment of the Epiphany Gospel. There is no progress. We ought to limit ourselves with the incidents directly leading up to the Nativity, and clustered round it. The simple story, as told in St. Luke 2, 1-19, is the best possible outline, and everything ought to be planned carefully, so that the incidents of the inspired record are presented in proper order.

A properly planned Christmas service will not do violence to the Christian Year. Christmas and Epiphany will not be confused. Every Christmas service that we have examined this year confuses the two events. We have found that it is very difficult to get the children in the weekly instruction classes to tell the Christmas story correctly. Try any child at random, and here is about the confused picture that you will get: "Jesus—I mean our Lord Jesus—was born in a manger. Some shepherds were watching some sheep, and they saw a bright star in the sky and they followed it to the manger. Then the shepherds opened some boxes and gave Him some gifts of gold and frankincense and myrrh. Then they got on their camels and went back to their country."

It seems a hopeless task to mention such matters, for our Christmas services, printed annually, are filled with references that cannot help confusing the story of the Nativity, and of Our Lord's Epiphany, in the child's mind. Many a picture shows shepherds following a star, shepherds riding on camels with long crooks in their hands, and shepherds and wise men kneeling side by side at the manger.

We would not think of saying to a child: "In a little village of Nazareth was a young virgin called Mary. The Angel Gab-riel appeared to her and said, 'Why seek ye the living among the dead?'" It would seem highly improper to mingle the Annunciation Gospel and the Easter Day Gospel. Why then mingle the details of the Christmas Gospel with those of the Epiphany? But it is done so very commonly that even trained men have been known to confuse the details of the two incidents.

A good Christmas Vesper service ought to follow at least the general outline of a true Vesper Service. Few congregations are ready for the historic and orthodox Vesper Service, with its opening versicles, its five Psalms and their Antiphons, its Kyrie, Collects, Magnificat and other traditional parts. For a children's service, it might be necessary, due to the long customs of the congregation, to use the opening versicles, and reduce the Psalms to one or two. But these ought to be selected from one of the five traditional Psalms appointed for the First Vespers of the Christmas Festival. And there is no reason why they might not be chanted. If the singing of a hymn is much more devotional than the reading of a hymn in unison, why not apply the same principle to the Psalms. They are hymns of praise. Why read them? At the closing service, certainly the traditional Magnificat is more appropriate for Christmas than the comparatively modern substitute, the Nunc Dimittis. And the closing Collect (or Collects) ought not to be omitted, just to save time.

A good Christmas service for children will have a festive ring. The bad habit of singing hymns at funeral tempo must be laid aside on this glad occasion. Imagine "Hark, the Herald Angels Sing", sung in half and whole notes, as we have all heard it done! However, a festive spirit must not be confused with hymns of the revival tent character. In one printed order of service that appeared this fall, the hymns all have the jazzy rhythm of the revival tent. It is entirely possible to be festive without being jazzy.

It is a most unfortunate mistake to set secular melodies to weak verse that is supposed to be of a Christmas spirit. But here is a printed order of service in which we find Dvorak's "Humoresque" used as a melody! The composer intended "Humoresque" to picture a tipsy man reeling homeward. Again we find a German drinking song, only too familiar in the beer gardens, set to words which attempt to tell the sacred Story. And here is "Twinkle, Twinkle, Little Star," words, music and all; and here is "Flow Gently, Sweet Afton," set to "Let us Welcome Our Christmas."

The chief motive in a Christmas service for children ought to be that of praise and adoration. We have, to some extent lost the art of praise, and forgotten the meaning of adoration. There are some who believe that a children's service at Christmas ought to be an entertainment, or sort of exhibition day. There is nothing that may be said in defense of that theory. The idea of "entertainment," "exercises" and "program" is foreign to the Lutheran spirit. Others insist that a children's service ought to to be primarily instruction. But instruction, if not carefully handled, may crowd out the idea of praise and adoration, while the latter, if planned carefully, may be highly instructive. Others declare that a children's Christmas service ought to be largely a catechization. While they are able to present strong arguments, yet in actual practice, a catechization is in danger of becoming too dry and intellectual. Catechization is of great value in the school room, but it is a debated subject as to whether it is just the thing for a church service. It is the school master's method rather than the clergyman's. Some irreverent wag has said that a school master, were he to conduct a church service, would open it with a roll call, and then ring the tardy bell. To which a school master replied that were a clergyman to try to teach school, he'd reach instinctively for the offering plates and make a plea for the deficit. So that's that. A good solution of the problem might be to decide whether we want to have a catechization this year, or a Vesper service, and decide upon one or the other, and then keep the two distinct.

Many a good order of service is spoiled by "decorations." This always looms large in the minds of the people. They must meet at the church and "decorate" the tree. This includes hanging red paper bells from the roof trusses, a red paper wreath in the

CONTINUED NEXT PAGE RIGHT COLUMN.

Using Slides In A Christmas Service

HERMAN BIELENBERG

WEARIED BY THE ORDINARY, banal type of Christmas programs, we resolved a few years ago to present something different and more attractive. Dispensing as much as possible with the recitations and the tiresome question and answer feature, we worked out an original program which utilized the stereopticon and colored slides in an effective manner. Involving an additional amount of thought and work, this type of service-program has compensated us, however, in impressing upon the minds of children, especially, the truths of the Christmas story. Rehearsals, too, have been eagerly attended for the colored slides and community singing of the Christmas carols have attracted our pupils. Incidentally rehearsals have been cut down to a minimum by our slide presentation.

The Christmas story has been presented from numerous angles. We have taken the prophecies of the Old Testament, the Biblical story of Christmas, the celebration of Christmas in many lands and other themes for these services. The church was darkened throughout and by means of colored slides, carefully selected from a nearby depository, usually from their miscellaneous stock, the story was developed. The hymns, too, were flashed upon the screen, and the entire congregation was invited to join in singing the well known Christmas carols, which also were carefully selected to work out the theme of the service. Never have we heard more wholehearted singing of the Christmas songs than during these services. It seems that everyone catches the spirit of Christmas. Hymn slides can be selected from various sources. Usually we make our own, using a piece of cellophane, colored green or red, etc. and by means of double carbon paper type the hymns, and then bind them between two pieces of glass of the proper size. This makes a very acceptable slide.

A reader (usually the Pastor) accompanies the pictorial slides with the narrative. Occasionally while certain beautiful slides are flashed upon the screen, the choir or selected groups accompany the slide with their soft, appropriate melody, or the organist plays softly as a background for the reading of striking Scripture passage. In the interlude between stanzas of the hymns, while the organist repeats several lines of the melody, appropriate slides are flashed upon the screen.

To illustrate let me outline a typical program. The introduction was a dramatization of a Sunday School class the week before Christmas (lights were still on). Six selected pupils asked their teacher about Christmas, gifts, Santa Claus, toys, etc., and she skillfully guided their minds from the externals to the real meaning of Christmas. The final question of the children, "Won't you tell us more about this wonderful Child?" furnished the transition to the central theme of the program, which was introduced by several scenes of the Creation, the Fall and Temptation, and the first Gospel promise. "The Prophet" then appeared and in answer to numerous questions by the reader concerning the birthplace, time of birth, etc., of the Saviour, he slowly read from a scroll numerous well-known prophetic portions. The

hymn slide "Come Thou Precious Ransom" followed. Describing the fulfillment of the prophecies, the narrator read the simple, beautiful account of Luke, while appropriate slides showed Nazareth, Bethlehem, Mary and Joseph refused admittance to the inn, the manger bed, etc. Three stanzas of "Silent Night" were sung by the congregation and Sunday School. The organist, with program at hand, can easily and unobtrusively lead into the singing of the hymns. Then followed the story of the preaching and miracles of Christ, and His last week briefly depicted by three or four slides completed the service.

The selection of the slides offers some difficulty. It is often hard to get uniform and consistent slides. Mary's cloak may be colored red on one slide, purple on the next, etc. (Incidentally, I might give expression to a wish of long standing that a series of artistic, correct and consistent slides might some day be produced which would picture the stories of the Bible.) The office of the Board of Foreign Missions of the United Presbyterian Church in Pittsburgh has granted us the use of slides for a period of three weeks —for rehearsal—at the regular price for a single showing (from 5 to 7 cents per slide).

If you are looking for something new this Christmas, give this plan a try! In addition to the above, we have worked out the visit of the Wise Men (while this is, strictly speaking, in the province of Epiphany, nevertheless I feel there is some justification for it in the celebration of Christmas), the flight into Egypt, etc. Increasing congregations have voiced their appreciation of our impressive Christmas services.

CHILDRENS CHRISTMAS SERVICE *from p. 179*

window, and in cutting some block letters out of cardboard so as to read "Merry Christmas," and stringing these on a line across the chancel. When the place is "decorated," it may be festive, but it's no different from a bedecked grocery store or show window. Everything is too common, and the associations are not distinctively religious. Sometimes there is a tin star hung aloft, with an electric bulb in it.

A better way is to get a few things that give the place a distinctively religious touch. For half a dollar, a commercial artist or a sign painter will make a nicely designed IHC and XPC in the traditional forms, some of which we printed in these columns a few months ago. These may have pointed rays proceeding from them, and may be covered with silver or gold tinsel flake. A good IHC, rayed, is a better termination for a Christmas tree than a tin star. And permit us to say a word in defense of the old-time Christmas creche, or crib. Years ago these used to be quite common in our Lutheran churches, and the stable, with the Infant Saviour, surrounded by the Blessed Virgin, St. Joseph, the shepherds and the traditional ox and ass, had a place of honor on Christmas Eve. But when it was discovered that the sects didn't do these things, many a crib was stored somewhere in the belfry and never used again. Why not revive this old custom? A crib ought to be of good size, say about three feet long, two and one half feet high and two feet deep, with figures at least 10 inches high. Concordia Publishing House lists some small ones, and could provide larger ones, if requested to do so.

Putting Something More Into Christmas Baskets for the Poor

O. H. SCHMIDT

WE SUPPOSE that in every larger congregation in the cities Christmas baskets will be carried to the poor. Frequently, perhaps, this may be done in rather a hasty, cold manner, almost like throwing a bone to a dog, and in the very manner in which it is done tending to wound the feelings and sensibilities of those whom one meant to help. The Walther Leaguers of our congregation here have developed a system of carrying out Christmas baskets which gets away from that coldly impersonal and often repellant manner of simply setting down a basket on the door step, ringing the bell, and saying: "Our church collected some money for the poor, and we bring you a basket." A description of the method developed here might be of interest to others.

The Walther League Society undertakes this work in our church. They get up some large charts, and on them mark off a number of spaces. Carefully the amounts are worked out that will be needed: so many pounds of coffee, beans, etc., so many cans of this or that, or whatever is to go into the baskets; a certain amount of cash is asked for, and for this the meat is bought in one order and then divided. Several weeks before Christmas these large charts are posted in the church vestibule, and then people will sign up. In one space there is written: two pounds of butter, and Mrs. Geo. Bernhardt will put her name down behind that. Another space has: two cans of peaches, and Miss Nolte will sign up for that. Another space has: one dollar cash, and Mr. Kueffner will sign up to donate that. Usually the large charts are quickly signed up, and the committee of the Walther League knows they will have their material at the appointed time. It will not be a haphazard collection, but will contain the proper articles in the proper proportions. The committee then, a day or so before Christmas, assorts the material and fills the baskets. At the mid-December Walther League social everybody brings a ten cent toy, and most of these also later go into the Christmas baskets, for families with little children.

But the most important part of this: for each two or three baskets a captain is appointed, and all our young people are divided into groups, and every one is assigned to some captain. The captain gets up a little speech, perhaps with the help of the pastor. Each captain gets his group together, and they practice a few simple Christmas carols. These groups then carry out the baskets assigned to them; they step into the rooms of the people to whom they are bringing a basket, the captain makes his little speech (in which he, of course, stresses the love of God, and invites the people to come to church, to think mainly of the spiritual side of Christmas), the group sings their songs, and thus the whole matter of bringing a Christmas basket is put upon a much higher plane and invested with much more dignity than might be the case otherwise. And all our young people are drawn into this work, all are given something definite to do in this scheme, and all are given a practical demonstration that it is more blessed to give than to receive, are taught to think of others and not only of themselves. They are thus taught really to grasp through practical participation the spirit of love and good will that should characterize the celebration of Christmas, to find deep satisfaction in doing something for others, and to find deep room in their hearts for the sweet Christian virtue of pity and sympathy. And attention is focused upon the main thing, upon the spiritual, the gift of God to men, the Savior come to bless, and the young people are drawn into confessing their faith.

Our young people like this manner of carrying out Christmas baskets, and consider it a privilege to help in this way, and are effectually being trained for church work.

Christmas Publicity

J. F. E. NICKELSBURG

In all the world's history no publicity or advertising message stands comparison with the greatest publicity message of the ages, *"For unto you is born this day, in the city of David a Saviour, which is Christ the Lord."*

Millions are spent by large business concerns for electric signs for advertising, but when the heavens opened over the fields of Bethlehem and that first anthem, "Glory to God in the highest," filled the air, the message was "sold" to the shepherds because they said one to another, "Let us now go even unto Bethlehem, and see this thing which is come to pass, which the Lord hath made known to us." The Church's business today, as it ever has been, is to "sell" to a sin-sick world the message of pardon.

Modern devices to attract men are numerous and "advertising pays," but for this life and the life to come, only the first publicity message, "a Saviour is born," means a happiness after all the other things "pass away."

A few more weeks, then another season of Christmas joy, another opportunity for the Christian Church, more direct, our Lutheran Church, to proclaim the old, old Christmas message of the Saviour's birth, or to do as did the shepherds on that first Christmas, "and when they had seen it, they made known abroad the saying which was told them concerning the child."

Christmas publicity means by word of mouth and the printed word, to call to the attention of the unchurched and indifferent fellow human beings the message of Christ's coming and His suffering and death for human souls. How can this be done?

A few hints and suggestions:

Help to distribute the printed announcements, sample copies of the parish paper; invite others.

If your church does not insert paid advertisements in the local newspaper, perhaps you or your society can contribute a special sum that this be done.

You may be able to assist your pastor or other church officers to prepare the news items for the newspapers. Stenographers, especially, take notice.

Christmas means special festive attire for your church. Help to decorate. Some churches have found an electrically illuminated tree on the church lawn a new publicity device to attract new people to the services.

Young men are needed as ushers to assist the deacons and regular ushers for the holiday attendance.

Tracts on timely subjects should be distributed at all the services, "for those that come only at Christmas."

The stranger should receive a cordial welcome, a word of appreciation and an invitation to come again. The man and woman in the pews must do this, not only the pastor.

Has your church a modern outside Bulletin Board? Every one makes presents at Christmas. How about a bulletin board for your Church this Christmas?

Christmas carols early on Christmas morn. What better way is there to confess our Christmas joy in a public way to the world?

Visit the public institutions and bring the Christmas joys to the poor and unfortunate, the "sick, the lame and the blind." Be sure your gift of flowers or fruit, or whatever it may be, is accompanied with a "penny gospel," or a copy of the New Testament, or a Scripture text card.

Don't use "Holiday Greeting Cards," with a Santa Claus decoration, but a real Christian Christmas card with a scripture verse.

Make your Day and Sunday School exercises a Children's Christmas Service and not a "Christmas Entertainment by our Children." The Christ Child, *not* Kris Kringle or Santa Claus.

Christmas Publicity

We decorate our churches and make our services attractive with special music for the beautiful festivities that commemorate the Nativity of Our Lord. To be in keeping, the invitations that we send out should be equally attractive and beautiful.

A variety of means may be employed. On a special letterhead, inserted in a corresponding envelope, a Christmas greeting may be written by the pastor, emphasizing the services in which through the Gospel the real joy of this happy season is brought to men. Or a tastefully designed card, of which there are a number on the market, may list the various holiday services. Another, perhaps the best, method will furnish more information than a bare schedule of services: a brief description of each service is added. For this a folder is used, the first page already printed in colors and the three remaining pages blank for local use. As a sure suggestion how these three blank pages may be employed, we submit what was printed on them by one of our churches for last Christmas.

(The material needed for this Christmas publicity — Letterheads, cards, folders—may be obtained from the

AMERICAN LUTHERAN PUBLICITY BUREAU

1819 Broadway
New York, N. Y.

GLORY TO GOD IN THE HIGHEST

Saint Paul
Ev. Lutheran Church

PAGE ONE

A Christmas Message

ONCE MORE THE HOLY NIGHT FALLS when in spirit we gather around a lowly manger-bed in Bethlehem and adore the Child that is bedded there. We lift up our hearts in jubilant gratitude to praise God for this wondrous gift.

WE HAVE REASONS TO REJOICE. Unto us "is born a Saviour which is Christ the Lord." God's good will now is assured to us. We sinners are at peace with Him whose righteousness we have offended.

Now WE NEED NOT FEAR. That Babe is God's pledge of unfailing love. He is with us and for us. Neither sin nor sorrow can separate us from Him.

SUCH A GIFT must make warm our hearts and urge us to respond in kind. God has forgiven us; no grudge will we bear. God has made us glad; by sharing with others we endeavor to bring gladness to all, especially to those who otherwise might be sad.

MAY GOD'S GRACE make it for you and for all men

A Merry and a Blessed Christmas

JOHN SMITH, *Pastor*

PAGE FOUR

SERVICES at
Saint Paul Ev. Lutheran Church
78 Sherman Avenue, New York, N. Y.
CHRISTMAS DAY, DECEMBER 25th
6:30 A. M. Matins

A service whose popularity proves its attractiveness. Christmas comes but once a year. And so does this service. The Gospel always is the same; it is the glad tidings of God's grace in Christ Jesus. But the Christmas setting makes that Gospel particularly effective and heightens the joy it in itself bestows. Add to that all the external elements that move our hearts—the darkness of the morning hour, the beauty of the church, the festival music—and this service becomes the beautiful beginning of a joyous holiday.

9:45 A.M.—German Festival Service
Deutscher Festgottesdienst

Ein Freudenfest ist dieser Tag. Das Kindlein in der Krippe nimmt auf sich all unsere Sorgen und Bürden. Das Licht der ewigen Liebe verklärt die dunkelste Nacht. Das süsse Weihnachtsevangelium die trauten Weihnachtslieder — hört und singt man die, so kann man fürwahr ein fröhliches Weihnachtsfest feiern.

11:00 A.M.—English Festival Service

Crowded conditions in the Matins made necessary the introduction of this additional English service on Christmas Day. As far as possible the matin service is duplicated. The later hour has its advantages. Members living at a distance and dependent upon uncertain transit facilities will find this service a convenience. Where there are small children both father and mother are able to attend the one or the other.

Attend one of these services and worship The Blessed Child—without the Christ no Christmas is complete

PAGE TWO

SUNDAY, DECEMBER 27th

9:30 A. M.—Sunday School
9:45 A. M.—German Service
11:00 A. M.—English Service
7:30 P. M.—Children's Christmas Service

This is the service of our Sunday School. The children will sing and tell the Christmas story. The program, "Even Unto Bethlehem," will be used.

NEW YEAR'S EVE, DECEMBER 31st

8:00 P. M.—German Communion Service
10:00 P. M.—English Communion Service

There is no more fitting way of concluding a year than by gathering in God's House and partaking of the Holy Sacrament which He has instituted to give us refreshment and strength. The past with its sins and failures is cancelled. The future, dark though it be, cannot terrify. Come and receive the pledge of God's love, the Body and Blood of His Son.

There will be no special preparatory services. Announcements will be received on Wednesday, December 30th, 3-5 and 7-10 P. M.

NEW YEAR'S DAY, JANUARY 1st

9:45 A. M.—German Service
11:00 A. M.—English Service

Only as we begin it in Jesus' name will the new year be what we wish it for ourselves and others, a Happy New Year. These services are arranged to help us begin in such a way.

PAGE THREE

Christmas Suggestions

GLEANED FROM HERE AND THERE

By Erwin Kurth

The Christmas Tree

THE anticipatory tree is set up in Advent. On the first Sunday in Advent one candle beams brightly; on the second, two; then three, then four, and lo! Christmas has come.

The tree may be plain or, according to German custom, decorated with roses. "The Rose of Sharon."

Gew-gaws and baubles are being supplanted by other decorations, as asbestos snow with glass icicles, or the plain strips of silver. White lights give a dazzling effect, especially if by means of a string attached to the tree the silver strips are made to tremble. Blue lights give a wondrous effect.

The tree may be sprayed (beforehand and out-of-doors) with shellac, then set up against a background of black and flooded with blue lights from above and below. No ornamentation or electric bulbs are hung on the tree. The shellac when hardened gives a frosty appearance. Some use also red lights.

The golden rain effect is gotten by stringing the tinselled cord from the top to the bottom.

Some churches prefer to have plain trees of various sizes massed in the chancel.

Matins

Pre-service suggestions

Trumpeters in the belfry. Or carollers around the lighted tree on parsonage or church-lawn.

In the church only the candles in the windows and on the tree are lighted. Possibly colored lights in the chancel arch.

Carols by the choir invisible.

A lovely custom is this, that at a certain time, and at stated places old and young people meet and walk down to the church singing carols in the frosty air.

The Service

1. Pastoral Symphony from the "Messiah" by F. Haendel
2. Processional: The First Nowel   Tr. English
   (Some churches garb the choir in white, ornamented with golden rope. Some churches use rheostat to get a gradual lighting effect.)
3. Opening Versicles:
   Pastor: Glory be to God on high! (Chanted)
   Cong.: All glory be to God on high. (Hymn No. 261, stanza 1)

   #### Dominus vobiscum
   Prayer (all kneeling) Response: Amen
4. Choir: Break forth, O beauteous, heavenly Light—J. S. Bach
5. Scripture Reading: The Shepherd and the Angels.
          Luke 2:8-14
6. Chorus, grouped around tree: "Angels sweet we heard on high."   Tr. Flemish
   "Quem pastores laudavere" XIV Century Latin
7. Scripture Reading: The Manger-bed.   Luke 2:15,16
8. Chorus: a. In a manger He is lying   Polish Carol
   b. Stille Nacht (in German)
   Hush Thee, Child   XIV Century (German)
9. Congregation: Praise God the Lord. No. 157
   Come hither, ye faithful. No. 159
10. Sermon
11. Congregation: Joy to the World. No. 158
    From Heaven Above. No. 150

12. Nunc Dimittis. Lord's Prayer. Benediction
13. Recessional: Let us all with gladsome voice. No. 153
14. Organ Postlude on Christmas Hymns   Hosmer

The Carols used in this service may be found in "Traditional Christmas Carols," Howard D. McKinney, and ordered through Concordia Publishing House from J. Fischer & Bro.

The Hymns and Chants are found in the "Evangelical Lutheran Hymn-Book," C. P. H.

THE CELEBRATION OF HOLY COMMUNION

1. Hymn: "O Morning Star." No. 103, 1, 2, 7.
2. The Liturgy, chanted by Pastor. See Agenda
3. Choir: The Te Deum Laudamus (used here as the Gradual)
   Sung antiphonatim in the Gregorian manner. (See "Manual of Plainsong," Novello)
4. Gospel: Luke 2:1-4. Response
   The Nicene Creed
5. Women's Chorus
6. Hymns (sung responsively by young people and congregation)
   a. Hark, the Herald Angels. No. 154
   b. Come hither, ye faithful. No. 159
7. Sermon: Votum
   The Offertory
8. The Communion Liturgy, etc.

CHRISTMAS CAROL SERVICE

1. Prelude "In Dulci Jubilo"   Bach
2. Processional Hymn: Adeste Fideles
3. Versicles (chanted, p. 49 of Agenda)   Gloria Patri
   Venite Exultemus (Ps. 95) No. 575 in Hymn-book (chanted)
   Prayer
   Scripture Reading: Isaiah 40:1-3
        Isaiah 11:1; 35,1; Canticles 2.1
4. Christmas melodies based on O. T. Prophecies:
   a. Comfort ye my people. Aria from Handels "Messiah" Solo
   b. Behold a Branch is growing. Praetorius (Sung by Congregation) or
   b. Lo, how a Rose e'er blooming. Praetorius (Sung by choir)
5. Our Earliest Christmas Hymns:
   a. Magnificat. The Virgin Mary (Antiphonal chant, p. 18 of Hymn-book)
   b. Benedictus. Zacharias (Read responsively, or chanted, No. 570)
   c. Gloria in Excelsis: Hymnus Angelicus (By Congregation, page 3)
   (Nunc Dimittis is reserved for the close)
6. Hymns we increasingly love to sing each Christmas:
   a. Joy to the World
   b. O Little Town of Bethlehem
   c. Silent Night
7. Cantique de Noël   Adolphe Adam
   (In program "Venite Adoremus" By F. R. Webber, C.P.H.)
8. Offertory: Weinachtspastorale   Rheinberger
   Offering
9. Christmas Hymns born during the Reformation Period:
   a. O rejoice, ye children loudly
   b. O Jesus dear, Thy manger here
   c. From heaven above to earth I come
   (First five stanzas sung by "angel")

10. Closing Portion:
Nunc Dimittis, Simeon's Christmas Chant (Page 14)
The Lord's Prayer. Gregorian Chant (347 in S. S. Hymnal)
The Benediction
11. Doxology: 592 (melody 3 in S. S. Hymnal)
12. Postlude: Hallelujah   Beethoven
(Note: The program may be interspersed with remarks and explanations of the hymns)

CHRISTMAS CAROL SERVICE
By the Choir
Program
Organ Prelude: Bethlehem   Malling
Processional: Hark, the Herald Angels Sing
Carols:
Cherubim Song   Bortnianski
Angels and Shepherds
Traditional Bohemian, arranged by Dickinson
How far is it to Bethlehem?   Shaw
Silent Night   Gruber
O What Happiness   Bach, arranged by Becker
(Men's Voices)
The First Noel   Traditional
Sing we Noel   French Carol in 16th Century, arranged by Harvey Gaul
Offertory:
a. Noel Ecossias — Ancient Christmas Carol in Scotch Style   Guilmant
b. Christmas Evening   Mauro-Cottone
Carols:
When the Sun Had Sunk to Rest

Traditional English, arranged by Knight
Come Hither, Ye Faithful   McCollin
O Leave Your Sheep   Arranged by Hazlehurst
When I View the Mother   Voris
(Carol for Sopranos)
On This, The Christmas Morn   Job
God Give Ye Merry Christmastide   Bishop
(Unison Voices)
Recessional: As With Gladness Men of Old
Postlude: The Holy Night   Buck
"From the Redeemer Record"

"A Mystery for Christmas"
This "Mystery" although modern in origin, is based on an old XV Century Scriptural Play. It will not appeal to all, but it may appeal to some. The actors do not speak, they only act; the theme is carried by the Choir. This play contains, among other selections, Luther's "From Heaven Above." Praetorius' arrangement of "Behold, a Rose," Adeste Fideles Bach's arrangement of "Wie schoen leuchtet der Morgenstern." The music was arranged by Howard D. McKinney. F. Fischer & Bro. is the publisher.

Christmas for the Shut-ins
The shut-ins of the congregation may want to receive Holy Communion during the Christmas season. The pastor will attend to that.
The pastor may wish to remember them with a little gift.
After the Dawn Service the young people may go a-carolling and thus enable the shut-ins to hear the Christmas story in song.

Bulletin Board Suggestions
Keep Christ in Christmas
God is love
Christmas is the birthday of our King
The Star still calls the wise
What difference the birth of Christ has made
Let us Christianize Christmas
The whole world was lost in the darkness of sin
The Light of the World is Jesus

The Christmas Gospel
God so loved the world that he give his
Only begotten
Son, that whosoever believeth in Him shall not
Perish, but have
Everlasting
Life.
Jesus, for us men, and for our salvation, came down from heaven, and was incarnate by the Holy Ghost of the Virgin Mary, and was made man.
Blessed is He that cometh in the name of the Lord. Hosanna in the highest!
In the mystery of the Word made flesh, Thou, O Lord, hast given us a new revelation of thy glory.

Prayer
Grant, we beseech thee, Almighty God, that the new birth of thine only begotten Son in the flesh may set us free who are held in the old bondage under the yoke of sin, through Jesus Christ, Amen.

Invitatory
Unto us the Christ is born:
O come, let us worship Him.
Christ the Lord, our Savior, Everlasting God and Mary's Son: we praise Thee evermore.
At even ye shall know that the Lord will come:
And in the morning, then shall ye see the glory of the Lord.

Unto you is born this day a Savior: Hallelujah.
Which is Christ the Lord. Hallelujah.

Thou art the King of glory, O Christ;
Thou art the everlasting Son of the Father.
When Thou takest upon Thee to deliver man thou didst humble Thyself to be born of a Virgin.
The Star will stand over our church tonight. Follow it and you will find the new-born Prince of Life and Lord of glory.

Come hither, ye Faithful
Hear the wonderful message!
Ring it out with joyful voices:
In Bethlehem the
Savior is born;
The Lord is come.
Merry, merry Christmas to
All.
Sing His praise! Hallelujah!

Thou wilt keep him in perfect peace,
Whose mind is stayed on Thee.

Merry Christmas
or Merely Christmas.
Which?

I
AM
THE
LIGHT
of
the
world

Help to put Christ into the Christmas of your friends by inviting them to our holiday services.

STORE-WINDOW PUBLICITY
The Desert Scene
The background is a beaver board painted blue; stars are coarse grains of sand or silver dust sprinkled on dabs of glue. The Star of the East is much larger, illuminated by a flashlight through tiny holes. The floor is covered with sand. The only figures in a space of about 12 by 6 feet are the solitary figures of the wise men and their beasts,—none higher than ten inches. At night the scene is dimly lighted by a shaded flashlight.

Nativity Scene
About ten dollars will purchase the figures of the Christ-child, Mary, Joseph, shepherds, Magi, animals, and the stable. Moss may be used for pasture on hill-top, sand for paths, mirror for lake, etc. If the setting is under the Christmas tree, angel figures may be attached to the branches. The open Bible should be placed in the foreground, with the story of the Nativity marked.

Christmas Carols
Every now and then a person likes to introduce into the service a carol not sung before. Something different, something new. It is surprising how many of the old carols are intriguingly new to us. Why not use them? You can find them in the books listed below:
"Glad Hosannas," compiled by Walter Wismar. Concordia Publishing House.
"Traditional Christmas Carols," H McKinney. J. Fischer and Bro.
"The Christmas Song Book," Adolf T. Hanser. The Sotarion Publ. Co.
"Fifty Christmas Carols of all Nations," Eduardo Marzo. The Willis Co., Cincinnati.
Ungemach's Responsive Service is a lovely piece of liturgical work.

A White Christmas
Have a white Christmas Service the Sunday before Christmas. The plan is simple. Everyone attending Sunday School brings an article of clothing, or a toy, or food, wrapped in white. Each class marches to the platform and presents, individually, its gifts. A committee takes charge of the gifts and distributes to the poor.
A small tree about six feet high, stripped of its leaves, and with the trunk and limbs painted white, will give an opportunity for the men to furnish the "green" in the form of dollar bills which may be pinned to the tree as they are contributed. (Church Management).

Christmas Lighting

KARL SCHLEEDE

AT Christmas time nearly all business houses make a special effort to attract shoppers to their stores by the use of attractive colored lighting effects. In some cities at Easter time a few churches have used lights to illuminate a cross, but very little has been done in most places to make the exterior of our churches carry a message of Christmas to those who pass by. Since our church is on a side street, about 500 feet from the main highway between Albany and Schenectady, several of our laymen decided to make an effort last year to attract the unchurched to our church by lighting up the exterior.

The work was done by members of the church, who are electricians; the planning and placing of lights was arranged for by a lighting expert also a member of the church; the cost of extra lights and electricity was borne by the general fund of the church and the fund did not lose any money, because of the increased attendance and increased offerings during the holiday season.

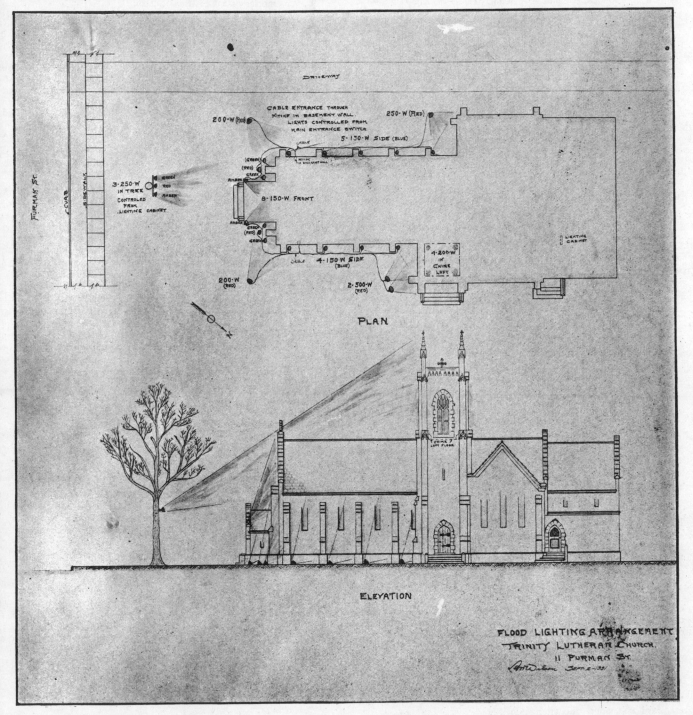

A reporter of the local paper was invited on December 23rd to see the display and his account of what he saw follows as it appeared on Christmas Eve. The carol singers sang in front of the church under the lights before they visited all of our institutions of mercy and closed their singing tour also in front of the church.

LUTHERAN CHURCH ON FURMAN STREET BATHED IN LIGHTS

Magnificent Effects Produced by Reflected Lights in Colors

A mantle of beautiful white snow today added the one touch of magic needed to finish off the hundreds of Christmas lighting display throughout this city and Scotia. And no outdoor display was enhanced more than the one at Trinity Lutheran Church on Furman Street, of which Rev. Karl Schleede is pastor. Those who enjoy driving around the city to look over the many attractive lighting displays, should not miss this one.

Taking advantage of the natural beauty of the Gothic style architecture, built of Weymouth granite, with half split face and half seam face granite, Walter Matern, who supervised the lighting, decided to bring out the real spirit of Christmas with the true holiday colors of green, red and blue. No artificial decorations are used in this display, which will be turned on for the first time tonight. Only the natural shrubbery and trees surrounding the edifice are included in the scheme.

The principal entrance to the church, through an open stone porch having wood beam ceiling above and stone traceried openings on each side, is flooded with a mellow yellow, the designer's idea of a warm color tone that invites all who see it to enter. The entire front of the church is illuminated by a small battery of reflectors that cast red, green and blue shadows on the various shades of light gray to deep pink stone, giving a particularly rich, warm effect. The cross on the apex of the roof stands out vividly against a dark background under the glare of an intense red lamp.

The buttresses on each side of the entrance are outlined in green and amber. A white light behind the big central window above the entrance relieves any tendency toward a dark spot in the picture as viewed from the street. Incidentally the beautiful colors of the window are revealed from various angles.

Both sides of the church are treated with blue shadows against the buttresses, with splashes of red to break the monotony of the tone, and providing an excellent harmony of colors.

The high tower to the rear on the right side of the church is treated with a glowing red, while hidden green reflectors inside the belfry cast their rays out of the traceried openings in a decided and picturesque contrast.

Throughout the entire lighting the artist has succeeded not only in bringing out the beautiful architectural features of the edifice, but in securing shadow effects that are extremely strong where he wanted them or are completely faded where they are not desired.

As a result of the article and the lights Furman Street became a main thoroughfare from seven to eleven in the evenings from Christmas Eve until after the new year. We do not exaggerate when we say the street was crowded nights with cars not only from this city, but also from Troy, Albany and Saratoga.

The cost for wires and reflectors was about $80.00. The cost for electricity was about sixty cents per hour. Reflectors, wires, lamps are all available for this year. Some difficulty was experienced in getting reflectors that would stand the snow and rain, however since then a standard commercial outdoor reflector can be had at a cost of about $7.00. It is hardly necessary to have many lights. Properly placed three or four colored lights will very likely be sufficient to attract attention to the church.

The lights will attract attention to the church. Because a church has stood on a certain corner for fifty years does not mean that all who pass really see it. Some times just because a church has grown old in the service of a community it will not be noticed. Just this week a representative of a vending machine showed the writer that his company had three colors for their machines, that after three months his company noted that sales fell off at every location, that therefore a different colored machine was placed

in the old location and sales were brought back to the old standard as soon as the change was made.

With a little ingenuity an altogether different scheme of lighting will be used here this coming year with the same reflectors and the same colors.

Suggestions for Candle Light Services

Time—Christmas Eve or the evening of the Sunday preceding Christmas or early Christmas morning.

Length of Service—Some Churches prefer to conclude a regular service with the Candle Light Service. When this is done the program must of necessity be brief, but used as a complete Service, many interesting features may be introduced which add to its effectiveness.

Object—The Candle Light Service is one of deep religious feeling. There is something inspirational in the lighted candles and in the entire Congregation unitedly taking part in the service. It is one of the most cherished memories of a Christmas Season.

Some Churches use the Service as a Memorial Service for the Members of the Church who have "Passed On" during the year and this serves to make it even more impressive.

Typical Candle Light Service Program.—Each worshipper is given a small candle and card as he enters the church. At the proper time the candles are to be fitted into the little cards to avoid candle dripping over clothing and woodwork. At the Chancel there is a large candle burning and the windows of the church are also lighted with large candles. If candlesticks are not available, the candles may be set in holes bored in wood blocks.

Usually the service begins with Christmas Anthems followed by a prayer. A talk or Sermon on the Birth of Christ, or the Story of Christmas from the earliest prophecies of the Coming of Christ is next presented. At its conclusion the Pastor lights a candle from the large one burning at the Chancel. The ushers then light their candles from the Pastor's lighted candle at the Chancel. The electric lights are now extinguished in the church. These ushers then pass down the aisles with the lighted candles and at each pew the person in the end seat holds his unlighted candle to the usher's candle. Then in turn the person next to him lights from his neighbor's candle and so on until all the candles are lighted. This procedure eliminates danger in tilting the lighted candles. The Congregation then rises and hold their burning candles shoulder high while the Pastor either offers prayer or discourses on Christ as the Light of the World. An appropriate hymn is then sung while the Congregation remains standing. At its conclusion the Service is ended and the candles extinguished to be taken home to form a part of the celebration there.

(May we suggest as a word of extra caution that several persons be delegated to watch for carelessness by children or for any possible dropping of lighted candles.)

VARIATIONS OF FORM OF SERVICE

Young Peoples' Organizations are particularly enthusiastic about this form of Service. They prepare songs, anthems and a program culminating in the congregation gathering at the Chancel and singing or praying while holding their lighted candles shoulder high.

The average price for the complete service is less than two cents for each member of the congregation. This is indeed a small investment for the required material for such an impressive Service.

Write the Atlantic Refining Co., 260 So. Broad Street, Philadelphia, Pa. Mention the *American Lutheran*.

Epiphany

Sin is darkness. Evil is darkness. Death is darkness.

Where there is darkness, there is fear. Because men are sinners they do evil and they are doomed to death. Therefore they are afraid.

They are afraid of themselves, of the future, of numberless possible dangers. Most of all they are afraid of death. All their lifetime they are subject to this awful bondage.

Usually they manage quite well to cover up their fear. They frolic and make merry. They sing and dance. They pretend to themselves. They are good actors.

But deep down in their heart it is lurking: dread, terror, ghastly fear. And when it breaks through they are pitiful to behold. They weep. They whine. They cringe. They curse. They despair.

Jesus Christ is the Light of the world. He shines and the darkness disappears. Sin is pardoned. Evil loses its power. Death holds no terrors. Fear is cast out. Worry is banished. The future is in God's hands. And God is a loving Father.

Jesus Christ can so hearten and fortify men. Only Jesus Christ. There is salvation in none other.

Let Jesus Christ shine into your heart. More and more His Light should brighten its recesses. One after another the specters hiding there will go.

Walk in His Light. Darkness and light have no fellowship. Conduct should be radiant with the glory of His holy love.

Let His Light shine into other lives. Men need Jesus Christ. Without Him they remain in darkness. Without Him they remain victims of fear. Show them the path that leads to Him. Be yourself such a path.

Epiphany suggests these thoughts. Make it an Epiphany in your life, in many lives.

THE TEN COMMANDMENTS IN RHYME

I am the Lord thy God, saith He,
And thou shalt worship only Me;
Take not My holy name in vain;
Nor dare the Sabbath-day profane;
Obey your parents, lass and lad:
Kill not, nor hate, it's just as bad;
In tho't, in word, in act be clean;
Steal not, for thou of God art seen;
Of no one say an unkind word;
Nor covet, Always love the Lord.
—Author Unknown.

Window Display

Obtain the use of a store window either in a vacant store or one which is occupied. Often storekeepers will gladly grant the use of the window for a display for the advertisement which it brings the store. Dress up the window with two small Christmas trees in each corner. In the center arrange a small manger scene. If it is impossible to set up a manger scene, one of the large Christmas transparencies might serve the same purpose. There may be room for both. Use a flasher socket for the light in back of the transparency. There will, of course, be room somewhere in the window for a sign directing the people to the church and the special Christmas services.

* * *

The Dawn Service

If you have a Dawn Service, have a trumpeter play some of the well known Christmas hymns before the service. He might play from the tower of the church or from the front door.

Some churches have been able to conduct the Dawn Service by candle light entirely. Where this is impossible, candles might be placed to give enough light until the service begins, then the regular lights could be turned on for the singing and again turned off later to leave only the candles burning during the sermon. Suction devices such as ash trays for the windshield of cars have been used satisfactorily for candle holders where it was impossible to place enough candles in the windows. Glycerine is used to make sure that they stick. Candle light will add much to the Christmas atmosphere of the Dawn Service.

* * *

Opportunities of the Christmas Season

Fred H. Lindemann

Lent is a season in which the life of a congregation is quickened, a time of deepened spirituality. For the drifting and lukewarm it is the time for an annual revival of religion. Any spark of religious consciousness which may still survive under the ashes of worldliness and indifference is prone to be rekindled into a flickering flame, though of small and fleeting duration, and there is a tendency to appear in the services during the weeks preceding the Easter Communion. Even people who have cut loose from the church entirely and cannot any longer be classified as "Easter Christians" are not entirely oblivious of the fact that Lent has come again, seem to be more approachable and more inclined towards religion than at any other time. Much as we Lutherans decry a religion which comes in spasms, a Christianity which can be stripped off on the day after Easter and put away in camphor until the next February; suspicious as we are of anything that even distantly approaches the usual "revival" methods, we are availing ourselves of the opportunities offered during this season of awakened religious consciousness. Special services in the churches, noonday services in public places, neighborhood canvasses, special missionary endeavors and the like, have become annual features of the Lenten season.

This annual revival and quickening of religious consciousness did not come spontaneously, but can be accounted for only by the emphasis placed upon Lent by the Roman Catholic, Lutheran and, in a lesser degree, by the Episcopalian Churches. This phenomenon is not independent of the past and present influence of the Church of which she now simply avails herself. It is a thing created by her. Persistent emphasis on the part of the Church accounts for the fact that the announcement of the approach of Lent brings to life memories of special services and weeks of consecrated efforts in the heart of those who have drifted, yes, that even the irreligious and pagan feel something of the appeal of Lent.

If the Church has accomplished this in regard to the Lenten season, would it not be possible to do something similar in regard to the Christmas season? Easter must ever remain the greatest festival of the Christian Church and the weeks of preparation preceding it will always hold their place in the hearts of God's people. Yet the ancient church made much of the Advent season. It too was a closed season, the same as Lent. And it would seem a much simpler and easier task to make the Christmas season something approaching Lent in consecration, intensity and service, for people in general are far more disposed to make more of Christmas than of Easter. True, the general observance of Christmas has degenerated into a purely carnal celebration, an orgy of buying and spending and feasting. But is that not all the more reason to emphasize the Advent season as a time of preparation for a right and true observance of Christmas? All other things being equal, it would seem that our congregations could be readily won for a movement to make the Advent season one of intensified evangelistic work and the general public would be far more inclined to fall in line than is the case in regard to Lent.

The suggestions made in this article in regard to the Advent and Christmas season may bring nothing new to the majority of readers. We incline to the belief that everything is self-evident, but the editors insist that it is not. They ought to know. In any case, if this is old stuff to you, blame the editors. That's what they're there for. Let us start at the beginning. To make the Advent season one of intensified evangelistic and missionary endeavor, there must be preparatory work. Much of this should be done, Advent or no Advent. There should be a house-to-house canvass in October or November. Every house should be visited and the name and address of every unchurched family taken. The fall of the year seems the logical time for such a canvass. The probability is that people will not move again until May and there are at least seven months for follow-up work. If the canvass is made in spring or during Lent the summer months with the disorganization of the congregational forces are upon us before much missionary work can be done upon the people unearthed through the canvass. It must be remembered that the real work only begins after the canvass is ended. If contact is established in fall the Advent season affords a splendid opportunity for intensive follow-up work, provided you make those weeks what they could and should be. The end of November and beginning of December is the time to make the first follow-up call. With special sermons preached in special services the people doing the follow-up work and inviting to the services have an added talking point and something to offer which is bound to appeal more than the usual invitation to a usual service. And if then the prospects see evidence of your church's existence in storewindows and the newspaper and are thus reminded again and again, they are more inclined to give your church and services a trial. So have a house-to-house canvass in the fall and use the Advent season for intensified follow-up work.

When upon your invitation strangers visit your services you must deliver the goods as advertised. Plan for special services and make your usual services attractive. Advertise your features and then deliver the goods. The midweek Advent service need not be made to appear as an added burden to the preacher, to be carried with much sighing and complaining, or a form of penance and a test of patience for the few of the congregation whom a strong sense of duty compels to be present. The sermon need not be a half hour's dry exegetical performance on the horizontal bar of some Old Testament prophecy. The service need not be dead and colorless. A brief address with the stranger in mind and the evangelistic note ringing through, the singing of the beautiful Christmas hymns by the congregation, and of the countless hymns and carols not found in our hymnal by the choir and soloists, with perhaps an occasional instrumental solo, can be combined into a truly attractive service. The morning services too can be made to meet the requirements of a service with strangers present who are to be won. In the evening services a series of character studies of men and women connected with the Christmas story will prove interesting.

But if the members of the church are to use the special services and sermons and added features as a talking point in their missionary efforts, it is necessary that they be given all necessary information. The parish paper makes a splendid medium, but if a copy is to be left with every prospect it might be advisable to print a special pulpit program for wide distribution, an attractive folder in two colors, if possible. As the members go out during or shortly before the Advent season to call on every family found unchurched through the canvass, give them an ample supply of these folders. It is good policy always to leave some printed matter in a home you visit for missionary purposes.

Another excellent means of advertising the special services of the Christmas season is the window display. An empty store in a busy street, with a fairly roomy show window, or a window in some occupied store can usually be procured with a little work and determination. The display itself is a matter of imagination, ability and funds. One within the reach of every congregation's financial ability consists of the scene of Christ's birth. The stable and figures of the Christchild, Mary, Joseph, the shepherds, the magi, and animals may be bought for about $8.oo. These may be arranged on a landscape. Moss for the pasture of hillsides, sand for paths, and a mirror for a lake or stream, mixed with a little imagination, can be made into a most attractive scene. Arrange the whole outlay under a large tree, decorated only with asbestos to represent snow, tin foil as ice and some electric lights, and people are bound to stop for a look. A large Bible, open at the Christmas story, should be placed so as to make reading possible from the outside. Cards and smaller placards with the necessary announcements may be placed wherever possible. Keep the announcements in such a window down to the minimum.

The most artistic and beautiful, as well as the most attractive display we have ever seen consisted of a desert scene with the wise men following the star. The background, covering the entire window opening and shutting off the view of the store, was a large piece of beaver board painted an exquisite blue. The stars in this sky consisted of coarse grains of silver dust sprinkled on dabs of glue and twinkled quite naturally. The leading star was much larger than the rest and was illuminated by a hidden flashlight focused through a tiny hole in a piece of pasteboard. The floor of the show window was covered with sand. Pasteboard hills covered with sand served as desert dunes. The only figures in a space of about twelve by six feet were the solitary figures of the wise men and their beasts of burden, none over ten inches high. At night the scene was very dimly lighted by a shaded flashlight in each of the front corners. It caused a sensation in the neighborhood. At times people were standing before the window five and six deep. Thousands were attracted to gaze upon the scene and to read the brief invitation, printed in small, sedate lettering on a card on the side of the window: "Trinity Lutheran Church invites you to the Christmas Matin Service at 6.15. Join us in rejoicing over the Savior's birth."

The climax of all the work and services of the Advent must of course be the Christmas festival service. With every ounce of persuasion at our command we recommend the early matin service. The Easter Dawn service probably has more historical reasons for it, but somehow it does not even approach the early Christmas service in atmosphere and sentimental appeal. The latter is bound to become the most popular service of all the year. We distinctly remember when years ago we introduced it in a former charge. The first time we broached the matter the men were so skeptical that we abandoned the project for the time being. The following year we asked for the use of the church for a service at six o'clock in the morning. The congregation gave us permission to use the church with unexpressed sympathy for a man who could have such a wild notion as to expect anybody to appear at such an untimely hour. Attractive window cards were placed throughout the section of the city, invitations were sent out drawing attention to the features of this service which was to proceed as the light of the blessed Christmas Day gradually broke upon a worshipping congregation. Curiosity brought out the men who had been so skeptical. They wanted to see if anybody else would turn out. They found not only the usual congregation, not only every pew occupied, but they worked harder that morning than ever before at that hour, carrying chairs and placing people on stairs and into hallways and anterooms. And the attendance has increased from year to year and the service is becoming more and more popular. Our experience in our present charge has been similar. But this time we did not permit the general skepticism to put us off a whole year. We asked for permission to have the service, which was granted with much expression of sympathy and pity. The Sunday School teachers were prevailed upon to procure a store window and to arrange a display, posters were placed in two hundred stores and windows of homes. The choir was cajoled into agreeing to sing for the occasion. Announcements were sent broadcast, the newspapers carried a few paid ads and more free matter. Early that Christmas morning it began to snow. By five o'clock the earth was covered with a white blanket and the flakes were still coming down steadily. For fifteen minutes before the start of the service carols were played from the church tower by a cornetist. For weeks after people told of the chills running up and down their spine, not from the cold, but because of the feeling created by their walking through the quiet streets in the darkness, illuminated only by the reflection of the snow, while the clear notes of familiar hymns came floating through the snowfilled air.

The church was decorated by the young people of the church. All had come directly from work for a supper in the church two days before. After supper everybody set to work putting the church into holiday attire, while singing carols. The main Christmas tree carried none of the colored and senseless five and ten cent store ornaments, but presented a most natural appearance under the load of snow and ice, asbestos and strips of tin foil, with a hundred electric lights hidden away in the branches and shedding a soft and subdued light. Pine branches from dozens of trees, discarded by merchants or bought at ridiculously low prices because deformed were used profusely. In every window recess a large wreath was placed carrying a large candle with electric flame. During the prelude all lights were extinguished with the exception of the candles in the wreaths. The young men had concocted a rheostat of an old barrel, two plates of zinc and salt water. This ingenious invention enabled them to have the lights on the Christmas tree and the holly-trimmed cross above the altar to come up very gradually while the choir sang: Silent night, holy night, in the vestibule, and then proceeded up the aisle to the hymn: Come hither, ye faithful. By the time the hymn was concluded all lights were shedding their full light and the service was under way. An orchestra of violins and brass instruments accompanied the congregational singing. And the most satisfying fact was the church was packed to the doors with hundreds of people who became walking advertisements for the next year's Christmas service. We have long since discontinued intensive advertising of our matin service, we no longer invite by means of posters, because we have been turning people away every year. We endeavor to avoid everything which might induce outsiders to attend and yet they come, members of sectarian churches, unchurched from localities ten miles removed, and members of other Lutheran churches who do not offer this beautiful service. We know of cases by no means isolated, of people getting out of bed at 3:30 and 4:00 in the morning, travelling for an hour and a half and two hours on the subway and trolley car, so as not to miss the service.

Another high point of the Christmas season is the Watchnight service on New Year's Eve. Of course, Maundy Thursday and Easter remain outstanding Communion days, but our heaviest Communion is on New Year's Eve. Yet it is a service most popular with the strangers, who do not seem to mind the lengthening out of the service by celebrating Holy Communion. We begin this service at 10:30 P.M. without a preliminary confessional service, since the sermon is adapted to serve the same purpose. The confession and absolution is included in the main service. With due care and a little ingeniousness it is possible to finish the Communion service a few minutes before twelve o'clock, which makes it possible to go over from the old to the new year with the entire congregation uniting in prayer. People have told us that so long as they live they will not want to miss that moment when, while the congregation is engaging God's ear in prayer, the whistles and bells announce the departure of the old and the coming of the new year. We have built up a considerable clientele of persons who first attend the services of their church earlier in the evening and then come to enjoy ours.

MATIN SERVICE AT 6.30 A.M.

The service beautiful. Darkness, decorations, the illuminated tree, the shades of night retreating at the approach of the most joyous day of all the year, dawn stealing gradually over a worshipping congregation, anthems by the choir, carols by the congregation, and, above all, the old but ever new story of the blessed Christchild's coming. Join us and bow in adoring worship over the infant form of Him Who came to be the world's Redeemer.

ST. PETER'S LUTHERAN CHURCH

(Card announcing the Dawn Service)
Cut. No. 1830

Our Welcome

To all who mourn and need comfort—To all who are lonely and want companionship—To all who pray—To all who love to sing God's praise—To all who sin and need a Saviour, this church opens wide her doors and in the name of Jesus bids you welcome.

(Copy for Parish Paper)

Noonday Services During Lent

ALFRED DOERFFLER

NOONDAY SERVICES have become quite prevalent in Lutheran circles. Is there a real need for these services? Are there any tangible results?

The need exists as long as sin-sick men and women, without hope in this world, need the Gospel of Jesus Christ. These Noonday Services give to the church an opportunity to reach just this class of people. It is rather difficult to persuade them to come to church, but during the Lenten season they are, if we may coin the phrase, Lenten-minded and will go with their friends, over the noon hour, to downtown services where men and women gather for meditation and prayer. It is a strange bit of psychology that unchurched people will listen to preaching as long as the service is not conducted at the regular church hour nor seem to affiliate with the church. Therefore a real opportunity presents itself to us at these Noonday Services.

Then there is a real need for these Noonday Services because of the church members. During the Lenten season they, too, are giving more thought to the central theme of Christianity, the Cross of Christ, and really desire to meditate upon the great things which mean so much to their spiritual life. They are ready to hear this Word of Reconciliation daily.

Opportunity for Personal Evangelism

The Noonday Services also offer to the church members an opportunity to do personal work. They feel free to invite their associates and co-workers in the shop and in the office to go with them, over the noon hour, to a Lenten Service, especially if these services have been properly advertised in the daily papers. Our Christian people find their unchurched friends do not so easily refuse to go with them and, therefore, have much more courage to invite people from office and shop to go with them to these services. Now whenever Christian people intensify their service for the Lord it reacts upon their own spiritual life, makes them more consecrated and devout, and strengthens their faith. Thus these Noonday Services serve to awaken a stronger Christian consciousness in our own people.

Location

These Noonday Services should be conducted for this reason downtown. As a rule some hall or theatre can be secured where these services can be conducted. If our church should happen to have a church building downtown, this may also be used. We have observed that one of the denominations, which has Noonday Services, conducts them in a downtown church, and is doing so with success. However, very few of our churches are downtown in a desirable neighborhood which can be easily reached over the noon hour and, therefore, in most instances, it will be necessary to secure a theatre.

The Theatre

The services in a theatre can be conducted in a very dignified manner. Nothing must be done to detract the attention of the people who attend. For that reason the setting on the stage should be as simple as possible. The drop-curtain serves as the most suitable background, if it has no advertisement on it. Personally we believe that no one should be on the theatre platform except the speaker and the chaplain. To have the choir and others on the platform while the speaker is addressing the audience often detracts. The setting should be such that everyone's mind is set upon the speaker and thus he can hold the attention without being compelled to overcome detracting surroundings.

The Service

The service should be simple and dignified. The chaplain begins the services in the Name of the Father, and the Son, and the Holy Ghost, and then announces a hymn. It is of the greatest importance that the hymns are familiar, not only to Lutheran people but to our mixed audiences. We realize that the Lutheran Church has real treasures in its hymns, but the stranger does not feel at home if he is not familiar with the hymn tune. Therefore, even though we conduct services for six weeks, we should limit ourselves from ten to twelve hymns. The singing of the hymn should be followed by the reading of a Scripture Lesson which, because of the brief service, should not go beyond five to six verses. The Scripture reading should be followed by a Confession of Faith in the words of the Apostles' Creed. Then, if desired, a quartet or choir may sing a simple selection, some devotional and tender song, that will touch the heart-strings of the people. This should be followed by the message of the day. If the services are conducted for more than one week it might be well to alternate between doctrinal sermons and sermons on practical questions of Christian life. But no matter what the topic may be, the speaker *must* in the message of the day bring to his audience the atoning Savior. If a person is there for the first and last time he must have learnt from that message how to be saved. This must be impressed upon every speaker who addresses a Noonday audience during Lent. If he fails to do this, to bring to his audience

Christ crucified, he has failed in his message. He may speak on the Law, on the Home, on Divorce, on the Trinity, or any other theme, but he must in the end present Christ as Savior. Even if he is the speaker for the entire week he must not think that he can bring the message of the atonement on the next day, because his audience is not that of a Christian congregation which regularly worships at his church, but is made up of people who come and go and among them may be some who will never come again.

The Speaker

In selecting the speaker we believe that it is advisable to get someone outside of the community. The people will feel that this is the only chance that they have to hear him. If you have a local man the city people will always feel as though they have plenty of opportunity to hear him, whereas a man coming from some other locality will attract the members as well as the non-members. We also believe that the preaching of this Noonday Speaker should be limited to the Noonday Services. He should not dissipate his energies nor be called upon to split up his audiences. It is a mistake to have him preach at local congregations in the evening. It is important that he will get audiences and, therefore, he should be limited to speak at the theatre at noon. It is important that he have *large* audiences from an advertising standpoint. If the unchurched comes to the Noonday Services and finds the auditorium filled to capacity it impresses them. It also impresses the members of the church. Then it helps the speaker. He can preach a much better sermon to packed houses than to a half-filled house. Thus everybody goes back to shop and office to tell what wonderful crowds are attending the Lutheran Noonday Services.

Because of the advertising value it is a mistake to have a different speaker every day. If people will be impressed on Monday with the message and the man does not speak again the next day or the rest of the week, then all they can say to their friends who were not there that they missed a real speaker and wonderful message. If, however, the speaker is there for the rest of the week they can urge their friends to attend, telling them that there are some more opportunities to hear this man. In this way a real audience can be built up.

If services are conducted in such a dignified manner, always keeping in mind that we are trying to bring Christ the Savior of sin to the people, these Noonday Services will also show tangible results and no one will say that it is time and energy misspent. God has promised that His Word shall not return void. Therefore we can be confident that there are tangible results.

Organization

To conduct Noonday Services requires a real organization. It must not be done in a slip-shod manner. In communities where there are many Lutheran Churches a different organization is required than in a community where there are only one or two churches. In communities where there are many Lutheran Churches each congregation should appoint or elect two delegates to a central committee. The duties of the central committee should be to gain memberships for the Noonday Services. It might be well to have a membership due of $1.00 or $2.00 a year. The entire membership meets once a year to hear reports and elect officers. We would suggest the following Executive Board: President, Vice-President, Secretary, Treasurer, Chairman of Pulpit Committee, Finance Committee, Membership Committee, Usher Committee, Tract Committee, Music Committee, Publicity Committee. These form the Executive Board which plans and makes the arrangements for the Noonday Services. We believe that each committee should consist of one member. If, however, a locality wishes to have each committee to consist of three it might also serve the purpose. Committees of one demand no meetings and, therefore, can function quicker and without delay.

If the community has only one or two Lutheran Churches it will not be necessary to have a central committee which secures memberships. The Membership Committee on the Executive Board can take care of this matter.

Publicity

To conduct Noonday Services successfully the organization must realize the value of advertising and, therefore, its Publicity Committee must make every effort to get into the local papers.

The advertising in the local papers should be of two kinds, paid and news items. It is important that the paid advertisements are seen. For that reason it is well to leave a good deal of white space. Some may think that white space is valueless, but they will soon discover that white space attracts. Again making use of a cross which necessitates white space is a very attractive way of advertising. If those who conduct Noonday Services wish every advertisement for which they pay to attract, place a cross into the advertisement and they will soon discover that everybody reads and sees their paid ad.

The news items should be prepared for the local paper by the Publicity Committee. This means that the committee must have the manuscript of the speaker in their hands two or three days prior to the time that he delivers his message. From this manuscript the Publicity Committee should prepare a news item giving some of the salient points of the message in about two hundred to three hundred words. The committee may inquire of the editor after some time whether he wants more than three hundred words. This news item must be sent in a day before the address is made. A news item should be sent in every day, even though it does not appear every day. Some years ago an editor said to us that one minister in our community sends in his sermon every Saturday. Then the editor added: "Of course we do not print his sermon every Monday, but many a time that pastor's sermon has been printed in Monday's paper because we happen to have room and his manuscript happened to be on the desk." So we believe that we should send in news items every day even though they do not appear daily. And if the Publicity Committee has paid ads regularly the editor will feel that he must also run some of the news items.

Another thing that the Publicity Committee can do is to place a Lenten folder in the offices in the downtown territory. In larger cities there are agencies which do this for you. They will see to it that your folder is placed on every desk. This brings the Noonday Services to the attention of every office.

In smaller communities posters may be placed in the windows, especially in the windows of unrented stores.

If the Noonday Services during Lent are to serve their purpose, then the public must be made aware of them. For this reason every means must be used to tell the people that these services are being conducted and every effort must be made to make the services themselves attractive. For this reason also it is imperative that the services do not go beyond the time set. The people must get back to their offices and, therefore,, the speaker must limit himself to the time given him. Where Noonday Services are carefully planned and then conducted according to plans they will prove to be a real blessing to the church and also show tangible results.

Suggestions for Lent, Holy Week and Easter Publicity

LENT is a time of quiet and devotion, when the soul longs to commune with God and to dwell upon His Passion. During these days come often to your Father's House and meditate upon His love to you!

A LENTEN PRAYER

Oh thou merciful and loving Saviour, my precious Jesus, thou wast slain for my offenses and bruised for my iniquities, that Thy blood might cleanse me. Give me grace to be truly thankful. Help me to believe and trust in Thee. Guide me ever to follow in Thy steps, willingly to bear my cross, and give me strength and courage to speak of Thy love to those who know it not. Let me love the habitation of Thy House, that being faithful unto the end I may enter that eternal Home prepared for Thine own. Have mercy upon me! Amen.

DAILY DEVOTIONS
7:45 P.M.
Holy Week, April 3-7, 1939

Monday—30-Minute Devotion
Tuesday—30-Minute Devotion
Wednesday—30-Minute Devotion
Thursday—Communion Service
Good Friday—Memorial Service

The hour is so arranged that everyone may attend each evening.

There will be Lenten music beginning at 7:30 o'clock. Come at this time if you can, for meditation and prayer.

Copy for Folders

QUIET AND SACRED are the days of Holy Week, when the Christian remembers the suffering and death of his beloved Saviour. Some moments each day he must spend at the cross, to express the devotion and gratitude of his heart.

The brief evening devotions for this week invite you to pause each busy day, and to give a thought to Jesus in His House of Prayer.

Come each night, will you not? Be early or late, leave when you must—but do not live through this holy week without giving thanks to Jesus, and gaining rich blessing for all your life.

The Saviour says:
"All this did I for thee;
What hast thou done for me?"

St. Paul's Lutheran Church
Park Avenue, Amityville

"And when they had platted a Crown of Thorns they put it upon His Head."
Matt. 27. 29

No. 3470,   size 1½".... $1.00
No. 3470A, size 2"...... 1.25
No. 3470B, size 2½".... 1.50

Wednesday Evening Lenten Service

Eight O'Clock, preceded for fifteen minutes by a Lenten Organ Program

Lenten Theme:
"They Crucified, and Crucify"

February 22—"The Indifferent"
March 1—"The Unfair"
March 8—"The Prejudiced"
March 15—"The Envious"
March 22—"The Slanderers"
March 29—"The Greedy"

Come Every Wednesday—
Bring Others to Christ!

St. Paul's Lutheran Church
of Amityville

SO MUCH IS GAINED by the quiet, devout meditation upon the Cross. Here is the tragedy of the ages, yet here alone may we find peace and comfort, in this One crucified for humanity's sin.

Come with us, come all, to look again upon our adorable Saviour, as He walks to Calvary for us.

Keep this Lent holy. Think about your Saviour. Praise Him. Love Him!

Suggestions for Observing the Forty Days of Lent

1—**Daily Devotion.** Use faithfully the Devotion furnished by the Church, or the Calendar Bible Readings.

2—**Daily Offering.** Deny yourself in love for Christ, each day, and bring a Lenten gift on Good Friday.

3—**Daily Thought of Others.** Share the comfort and peace of Christ, by seeking every day someone who may be brought to the Saviour.

LENT is a time for quiet thought, reflecting upon our own life, its conduct, its aim, a season of looking up to Him Who gave all for us. Oh that we might love Him and serve Him!

HOLY WEEK DEVOTIONS

The Most Sacred Week of the year, for which Lent has prepared us, will be observed at a brief Devotion in our church each evening.

We bid you pause after each busy day, and stand with us at the Cross of Jesus these few moments—before the evening really begins.

Come late or early, leave when you must. Commemorate with us the last days of The Redemption, and receive a blessing as we bow in adoration before the Saviour!

EVERYONE IS WELCOME!

DAILY DEVOTIONS
7:45 P.M.
Holy Week, April 3-7, 1939

Monday—30-Minute Devotion
Tuesday—30-Minute Devotion
Wednesday—30-Minute Devotion
Thursday—Communion Service
Good Friday—Memorial Service

The brief addresses at these services will be on "The Friends at the Cross." Let us take our place with them.

Meditation and Organ Recital
(7:30 to 7:45 P.M.)

Come and Go When You Like
The Door Offering is Optional

Copy for Lenten Folders and Cards

THE EASTER OFFERING

EASTER is soon upon us, with its message of hope and comfort.

We bid you to rejoice, and to express your joy in the Risen Christ by a special offering for the extension of His Kingdom.

An offering envelope is enclosed, or may be obtained in the church vestibule.

An Easter Blessing
Awaits You!

THE THREE-HOUR SERVICE

Three-hour services, from noon until 3 p. m.. on Good Friday, are amazingly popular nowadays. One modernistic church has just had one, and it was composed of seven addresses by seven "neighborhood ministers." Their subjects were: The Religion of a Smile, The Gospel from an Aeroplane, Fencing Our Social Cliffs, The Folly of Capital Punishment, etc. The musical "performances" between each number were equally foreign to the occasion.

It is quite proper to conduct a three-hour service in one's own church, as a silent testimony. After a number of experiments along this line, one of our men finds that the following is about as good as any: Make a careful list of all the Passion Prophecies and read them. Read the entire Passion History, the Litany and the Good Friday Reproaches. The last will have to be modified somewhat to suit our needs. Arrange all this material in such a manner that it may alternate with Passion hymns. For example, the Prophecies may be divided into three groups, and the Passion History into seven or more sections. Between each group of Prophecies, and each section of the Passion History sing a good Passion hymn, followed by a carefully selected Collect, read at the altar. After the Reproaches and the Litany let there be a confessional prayer.

The people ought to be allowed to come and go, as circumstances require, but this ought to be done during hymns, and not during the Scriptures or prayers. Few can come for the entire three hours, especially if some must get back to offices or to school.

The Good Friday noonday service ought to be of utmost simplicity. The altar and all chancel furniture are stripped of hangings and colored ornament. The altar cross is veiled. Candles are unlighted. Organ playing is reduced to the very minimum, and of course there are no solos or choir singing at such a service.

The sermon is reserved for the usual Good Friday evening service. Let the inspired Prophet's and the Holy Evangelists do the preaching undisturbed. This is the Word of God pre-eminent, and there are few things in this life more profoundly touching than the Prophecies of Our Lord's Passion and the Passion History, if read from beginning to end, with only carefully selected hymns and prayers from time to time, where they are most effective.

This is not a substitute for the usual Good Friday preaching service, but a noonday service in addition to it, planned for the people in the nearby shops, stores and offices, and in the nearby homes. Almost everybody will go to church on Good Friday. Many of them have never heard the Passion History read throughout, at one time. There is no reason why we may not supplement our usual preaching service with Devotions of the right sort. Make a note of this for next year, try it and be convinced.

Advertising the New York Noonday Services

Holy Week Printing

HOLY WEEK will soon be here. Almost every congregation issues some sort of an announcement for their Holy Week services. It is important that such printing be as neat as possible, and upon the very finest stock. The difference in cost, on a few hundred copies, is trifling.

If a cross be used, there are certain principles that must be observed. We have recognized rules for hanging the American flag, the emblem of our country. There are rules for the use of the emblems of Redemption. A cross, for example, must always stand upright. It is bad form to use a cross that seems to be teetering unsteadily at an angle of forty-five degrees to the horizon. Such crosses are common. A cross must stand upright, and it must appear to be squarely in front of the beholder. A cross that seems to be turned to one side, so that its thickness shows, is bad form, as though one were trying to pass the cross by some detour, instead of facing it squarely. If a cross be used together with another symbol, the cross must be above it, and not beneath; and superimposed upon it, if the two happen to overlap. Thus a cross with a crown above it is incorrect. A cross thrust through a crown is incorrect. There could be no crown (eternal life) except for the cross. For this reason the cross must, even in symbolism, predominate in the design.

It is important that the cross be properly proportioned. Most crosses are much too clumsy and crude. Especially is this the case when one tried to set type in the form of a cross. The two examples given on page 19 of our January issue are good, although one must use exactly the same type-face (Copperplate Gothic Regular) or this wording will not space properly. An extended type-face would not do.

We are printing a few new Holy Week designs. Electros of these may be ordered from the American Lutheran Publicity Bureau at prices given. The first is the Cross Outlined, which is neater than a solid black cross, although for Good Friday a solid black is generally used. The second is the Passion Cross, its sharp points representing the sharpness of Our Lord's suffer-

ing. The third design is the familiar IHC abbreviation, properly drawn. The fourth example is the ordinary form of the Ascetic Cross, and it is much neater and more vigorous than the ordinary fat, stubby forms that are so common. Heavy, black type is long since out of date, and with the present-day neat Caslons and Goudy Lightface, we ought to use a slender cross.

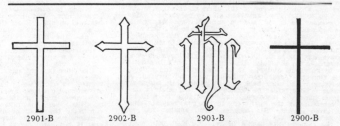

| 2901-B | 2902-B | 2903-B | 2900-B |

Electros of the above crosses come in four sizes; 1″, 1½″, 2″ and 3″ high. When ordering designate size by putting letter after number. For 1″ size use letter B, for 1½″ size use letter A, for 2″ size use letter E, for 3″ size use letter D.

The prices of these electros are as follows:
1″ size $0.60; 1½″ size $0.75; 2″ size $1.00; 3″ size $1.25.

In using the IHC and XPC abbreviations, one must avoid the common blunder of using periods. I.H.C., I.H.S. and X.P.C. are incorrect, for the IHC does not stand for *Iesus Hominum Salvator*, which was the invention of a very eccentric preaching friar, St. Bernardine of Siena. Neither does it mean "I Have Suffered," as some believe. To read these fanciful meanings into it is to rob the IHC of its true significance. I.H.S. or IHS are both wrong, because here we are destroying the meaning by using two Greek and one Latin letters. J.H.S. or JHS is worse of all, for in this case we are combining an English, a Greek and a Latin letter, and the whole thing becomes meaningless. IHC is the Greek uncial abbreviation for "Jesus" and XPC for "Christ," and nothing else.

PARISH PAPER COPY SUITABLE FOR LENT

ONCE MORE THE LENTEN JOURNEY

It is a way that we have taken so often. Year after year we hear the announcement of the Saviour: "Behold, we go up to Jerusalem." And year after year in a series of special mid-week services we follow Him through the scenes of His Passion.

Of course, we are familiar with the details. We have heard and read the story so often. Yet unless we regularly refresh our memories, what we know today may not be our possession tomorrow. Nor can we ever know the story of the Passion well enough. Every new approach will add something to our understanding and appreciation of its extraordinary significance. As the years roll on and our own experience of life is enriched, we see many an incident in a new light and can make new applications to ourselves.

The plan of the ages, evolved by the Blessed Trinity before the foundations of the earth were laid and extending in its results through all eternities after this world shall have come to an end, reaches its climax in the events that the Passion History presents. The redemption of humanity is tied up with them. History records no more momentous period of time than the hours during which the Son of God was "delivered unto the Gentiles, and mocked, and spitefully entreated, and spitted upon, and scourged, and put to death." So all that was written by the prophets concerning the Son of Man was fulfilled and so the glorious truths of the Gospel became facts, on which we now may confidently stake our very souls.

On this Lenten journey we see black and white, evil and good, in such sharp contrast. All the evil passions that lurk in the hearts of men come to the surface and engender a storm of fury, that is positively appalling in its diabolical vileness. And the guilty ones were men, even as you and I! All the unspeakable love of God is so vividly manifested in the patience, the kindness, the spirit that endures and pardons and ever seeks to win, which characterize the conduct of the Son of God. And He is the same today, our loving Saviour!

A contemplation of these Passion scenes, a devout and prayerful contemplation, cannot but increase our faith and thus intensify our hatred of sin and our desire for a more Christ-like life.

So let us take the Lenten journey with our death-doomed Lord and with all His holy saints!

PASSION PLACES—Gethsemane

The Passion of our Blessed Lord opens with a mysterious scene of agony and struggle. The place was a garden on the slopes of the Mount of Olives, where "Jesus ofttimes resorted." He went there "in the night in which He was betrayed" in order to pray; and while He prayed a terrible cup of suffering was pressed to His lips. Or was it that this suffering had begun to come upon Him and that therefore He went to Gethsemane to pray? We cannot tell. In either case it remains gloriously true that in the garden scene we see our Substitute and our Example.

The sufferings in the garden are indescribable and unimaginable. The terms employed by the inspired writers indicate that. He was "sore amazed." His soul was "sorrowful unto death." He was "very heavy." He was "in an agony." His customary composure left Him. He was down on His knees one moment, the next up again and speaking to His disciples. Nowhere else in the gospels is such agitation recorded. "His sweat was as it were great drops of blood falling down to the ground."

What are we to make of this? No explanation can be complete and exhaustive. The accepted view certainly points in the right direction. Our Lord's sensitive conscience was crushed under the burden of the world's guilt. The sins of humanity in all their horrors were made His own. Once again Satan crossed swords with the Captain of our salvation. It is easy enough to write or to read these words, but to get down to the bottom of their meaning remains an impossibility. Our own experiences with sin and the devil, fierce as they may be, cannot even approach this agony. We can only pray that God may help us to understand ever better what a hell our Lord endured for us and because of our sins when He prayed in the garden.

And surely, in our own encounters with an accusing conscience, with temptations and with sins what better example is there to follow than that of Him who suffered in Gethsemane? He prayed and so He survived and so He won the victory. Looking unto Jesus, praying with Jesus and like Jesus, will assure the victory to us.

PASSION PLACES
2. "The High Priest's Palace"

Unholy memories are connected with this place. It was here that the plan was hatched to put Jesus to death. It was here that the innocent prisoner was sentenced to death. It was here that the cruellest indignities were heaped upon the Son of God.

After Jesus was arrested—past midnight it was—the members of the highest Jewish court were hastily summoned to the palace of Caiphas. The trial was a farce. The very time of it was illegal, as were the entire proceedings. False witnesses were called. Their testimony made confusion worse confounded. There was no case. The prisoner was called to the stand. He was asked point-blank: "Art Thou the Son of God?" He gloriously confessed His divine origin and nature. His statement was condemned as blasphemy. His death was decreed.

Then followed a ghastly scene. It was necessary to keep the prisoner until morning in order to affirm the verdict and make it legal in a daylight session. His enemies whiled away the hours by subjecting Him to mockery and torture. "Then did they spit in His face, and buffeted Him; and others smote Him with the palm of their hands, saying, Prophesy unto us, Thou Christ, who is he that smote Thee?"

Unjust judges, unholy priests—such were the men who gathered in the high priest's palace. Jesus was a threat to their authority and power. Therefore it was necessary to get rid of Jesus by hook or by crook. But before throwing stones at them we might well ask ourselves: "Have we ever disposed of Jesus in a similar summary fashion, when He interfered with our program or stood in our way as we sought some fancied treasure?"

In marked contrast to these godless men stands the Son of Man who is also the Son of God. His "great confession lifts the whole scene. We no longer see those small men and their sordid proceedings; but the Son of Man bearing witness to Himself in the audience of the universe." Let those Jewish judges condemn Him to death! We rejoice in Him as the Godman who is our Saviour, because He willingly submitted to torture and death in order to redeem us from sin and death. He has our heart's highest and deepest trust.

PASSION PLACES
3. The Praetorium

The Jewish court had condemned Jesus to death. But it lacked the power to execute the sentence. Only the Roman governor could decide a capital case. And so "when the morning was come . . . they led Him away and delivered Him to Pontius Pilate the governor."

Pilate interviewed the accusers. He interviewed the accused. He was quickly convinced of the latter's innocence. He so stated his opinion, as well as his intention to release him. Then followed a pathetic exhibition of shilly-shallying on the part of the Roman governor. The Jews howled down every suggestion to give Jesus His liberty. They threatened Pilate with Caesar's displeasure. The governor did not dare to risk their wrath. He tried by one means after another to placate them. Every cleverly conceived plan failed. Over and over again the blood-curdling shout was raised: "Crucify Him!" When he "saw that he could prevail nothing, but that rather a tumult was made, he took water and washed his hands before the multitude, saying, I am innocent of the blood of this just man: see ye to it. Then answered all the people and said, His blood be on us, and on our children. And when he had scourged Jesus, he delivered Him to be crucified."

Of course, Pilate's conduct was most reprehensible. Justly his name is preserved in the ancient Creed of the Church as the author of our Lord's sufferings. The power was his to do justice, and he was too much of a coward to do his duty. Unfortunately, the Pilate type is by no means extinct. It is found within and without the Church. Jesus stands before men and demands a decision. And they back and fill, they shift and they dodge. They refuse to clome clean. Ultimately a decision must be rendered, and inevitably it will be a repetition of the final scene in the Praetorium: Jesus is given over to His enemies. And another soul is doomed.

The responsibility cannot be evaded. Each man must decide for himself. Hands may be washed, but that is only a futile gesture. The blood of Jesus Christ clings to every man who will not recognize that only by that blood he is washed clean from all his sin.

What will you do with Jesus?

PASSION PLACES
4. The Via Dolorosa

The final sentence was spoken. Jesus was delivered into the hands of His executioners. Through the streets of Jerusalem a sad procession marched. "And He bearing His cross went forth into a place called the place of the skull, which is called in the Hebrew Golgotha." "And there were also two others, malefactors, led with Him to be put to death."

The condemned were compelled to carry their crosses. That was a crowning touch of ignominy. Our blessed Lord was unequal to this task. Willing the spirit indeed was, but the flesh was weak. The harrowing proceedings of the preceding hours had sapped His strength completely. Not one moment of rest did He have. The burden of the cross proved to be too heavy. So "they laid hold upon one Simon, a Cyrenian, coming out of the country, and on him they laid the cross that he might bear it after Jesus." This Simon became the first of a numerous and honorable company, the company of cross-bearers. No doubt, he was most unwilling to assume this load and chafed under it. Crosses hurt. But in reality a magnificent honor was bestowed on him. Every Christian would have regarded it as such. To have a chance of doing just a little bit to ease the pain of the Saviour—what a priceless privilege that would be! Well, God still bestows such honors upon His chosen ones. Do we see the honor connected with cross-bearing, or do we only think of the ugliness and the discomfort and the pain?

One other incident along the via dolorosa is recorded. Women wept over this man of sorrows. But our Lord wanted no sympathy. Tears which testify only of stirred emotions mean nothing to Him. Tears of honest repentance, grief for the sins that brought such woes on Him, these He values. Nothing but repentance can make the cross a blessing to us. Without repentance we may sentimentally view it, we may weep over it, but never can it be to us the tree from which life and healing come to our sin-stricken souls.

With such tears of repentance let us accompany our suffering Lord along the via dolorosa!

PASSION PLACES
5. Calvary

A howling mob is gathered on that "green hill far away, without a city wall." The air is filled with curses and taunts, with ugly epithets and jeers. Jesus of Nazareth is dying on the cross.

Today a hushed multitude in spirit assembles on that same green hill. Men and women, who have learnt the secret of the cross, stand there with bowed heads and repentant hearts. Confessions and prayers, worship and adoration ascend to the heavens. Jesus of Nazareth has died for their sins.

No mortal mind can measure the extent of the woes that on Calvary gripped the Saviour. Physically and mentally His sufferings were unspeakable. No death was so painful and so shameful as crucifixion. But the supreme agony was in the soul of Jesus. He died for the sins of the world. He died as humanity's Substitute. And therefore that awful cry of His which came out of the bowels of hell: "My God, my God, why hast thou forsaken me?"

Unimaginable as are the torments of the Lord on Golgotha, so also are the blessed results that accrue to men because of them. Some we can grasp, at least in part, and appreciate. Forgiveness of sin is such a one. Conscience cannot accuse. The memory of past transgressions cannot terrify. We look to the cross and a great peace is ours. Reconciliation to God is another. The stern Judge now is a gracious Father. We can trust Him so absolutely. Nothing can separate us from His love. The faith we learn on Calvary is a faith to live by and to die by. But the fulness of the blessing that shall be ours because Christ died on the cross lies far beyond our reach. "It doth not yet appear what we shall be." A glorious, never-ending experience awaits us.

But even amid the splendor and the bliss of heaven Calvary cannot and will not be forgotten. The song of eternity, chanted in jubilant chorus by the hosts of the redeemed, shall be: "Worthy is the Lamb that was slain to receive power, and riches, and wisdom, and strength, and honor, and glory, and blessing."

Should Appeal to Every One

I consider the Sunday-school one of the most important parts of the church work; through the teaching of the Bible it has been instrumental in bringing many souls into the kingdom of God.

I have been connected as pupil, teacher and superintendent of the Sunday-school practically my entire life and cannot too strongly emphasize the importance of this organization in the development of the Christian citizenship of the nation.

I believe that the Sunday-school should appeal to every one who believes in the Christian religion and enlist their sincerest interest.—John G. Richards, Governor of South Carolina, (May 7, 1930).

(Copy for Parish Paper)

"I have long felt a very deep interest in the work of the Sunday School Bible classes, because of the conviction that this sort of serious and continuous study is not only of the greatest spiritual and character-building value, but the means of familiarizing people with one of the splendid monuments of all literature, the Bible."

President Coolidge

Some Suggestions for Lenten Publicity

The copy herewith presented may be used in Parish Paper, Special Lenten Folder, Sunday Announcement Bulletin or otherwise. Pack~~es of Church Printing Samples are available from the American Lutheran Publicity Bureau, 1819 Broadway, New York, N. Y. Enclose twenty five cents to pay postage and packing.

DAILY LENTEN PRAYER

Almighty and everlasting God, who dost govern all things in heaven and on earth; mercifully hear our prayers and grant to the parish with which we are connected, all things that are needful for its spiritual welfare; visit and relieve the sick; strengthen and confirm the faithful; turn and soften the wicked; arouse the careless; recover the fallen; restore the penitent; remove all hindrances to the advancement of Thy truth; and make all to be of one mind and heart within Thy Holy Church; to the honor and glory of Thy great Name; thru Jesus Christ our Lord.   Amen.

YE KNOW THAT YE WERE NOT REDEEMED WITH CORRUPTIBLE THINGS, AS SILVER AND GOLD, FROM YOUR VAIN CONVERSATION RECEIVED BY TRADITION FROM YOUR FATHERS BUT WITH THE PRECIOUS BLOOD OF CHRIST AS OF A LAMB WITHOUT BLEMISH AND WITHOUT SPOT
I PETER 1, 18, 19

DO SOMETHING DURING LENT 1933 to Show Christ that You Really Care!

ALL PUBLIC entertainments will cease during Lent at Messiah Lutheran Church. This is nothing new. Such has been custom with our people for many years. It is well. When we stop to consider that our Savior gave up everything for us during the period of His Passion, it seems trivial for us to make so small a sacrifice. Every Christian should do more. Therefore let us rededicate ourselves anew to Him, and this year again take as our Lent slogan: *"Do Something During Lent 1933 to Show Jesus that you really Care!"*

First of all let us attend all Lenten Services if possible. There are many ways of showing Jesus that you Care. It goes without saying that we would care little if we were afraid to give ourselves to His worship. Again, there are many people during Lent who deny themselves shows, candies, and other luxuries and turn over an additional sum of money as their Lenten Denial Offering. This year such offering will swell our Building Fund. Such self-denial is commendable.

Others make it their business to pay additional visits to the sick, help certain poor, etc. All of these works are splendid and the pastor knows that such actions performed in Love to the Savior must gladden His heart.

We are convinced, however, that the greatest thing we can do during Lent 1933 to show Christ that we care is to bring other people to the foot of the Cross. *To bring friends to church so that they might know Christ, is the Greatest Work on Earth.* If we can do that, then we can first call ourselves "disciples." For the first work of Christ disciples was and still is to be fishers of men.

(Copy for Parish Paper)

DAILY PRAYER FOR LENT

O Christ, Thou Lamb of God, that takest away the sins of the world, have mercy upon me; cleanse me from all sins by Thy precious blood. Grant me Thy spirit, that I may now truly trust Thee, love Thee, and serve Thee; and hereafter may live with Thee in glory. Amen.

LET US MAKE THIS SEASON A BLESSED ONE BY ATTENDING EVERY CHURCH SERVICE; BY READING THE WORD OF GOD DAILY; BY MEDITATING ESPECIALLY UPON THE HOLY PASSION OF OUR BLESSED SAVIOR JESUS CHRIST; AND BY PRACTISING SOME FORM OF SELF-DENIAL F. J. MUHLHAUSER, PASTOR OF CHRIST LUTHERAN CHURCH

Messiah Lutheran Church
42nd Street and Fourth Avenue

A Pledge to My Crucified Savior for Lent 1933

I hereby enroll as a Worker for Jesus during His Passion Season, and I SHALL

1. Make a most conscientious effort to be *present* at all the midweek services.
2. Attempt to bring at least *one stranger* to these services.
3. *Advertise* the services by word of mouth and by distributing the literature supplied by the church.
4. Earnestly *pray* that the Lord may bless these services and bring many to the knowledge of the truth.

Signed..

"Do SOMETHING During Lent 1933 To Show Christ You Really Care!"

(Kindly drop this card in the offering plate)

(Pledge Card for Lenten Personal Evangelism)

LENT

The purpose of our Lenten Services is twofold: To strengthen and deepen our own spiritual life, meditating upon the great love of Jesus for us and, deeply repentant of our sins, seeking forgiveness in Christ crucified; to win others for Christ and His Church.

Give these hours of worship precedence over all other engagements. Certainly we ought not deny our Savior this hour!

Pray Daily—for yourself, for your pastor, for your church, for someone who is still unsaved and unchurched.

Read Daily a chapter in your Bible; meditate upon the things you have read. Read the Passion Story. Psalms 6, 22, 32, 38, 51, 102, 130, 143, Isaiah 53.

Sacrifice Make some special offering for the Kingdom. Increase your weekly offerings.

Come to the Lord's Table Assure yourself of the peace and forgiveness of God through the Blessed Sacrament.

(For Lenten Folder)

RANDOM SUGGESTIONS FOR LENT

In place of the more usual Lenten folder sent out by many churches announcing the Lenten program some churches send out a card listing the sermon topic which may be hung upon the wall as a daily reminder.

The *silent* processional and recessional by the choir at the Lenten services is very effective.

For variation the Litany may be used in the service on Wednesday or Friday without departing from true Lutheran liturgies.

When the seven words from the cross are used for the texts of the sermons, it is very effective to have the choir sing the appropriate stanza of the hymn "Seven Times Our Blessed Savior Spoke" immediately after the Votum. Or it may be used in place of the hymn before the sermon. In such case the choir should always begin every service with the first verse of the hymn, sing the appropriate verse with the correct Word from the Cross and conclude with the last or the two last verses. To be most effective, the choir should sing these stanzas in four parts, and a capella.

Conducting Noonday Lenten Services in a City with Only One Congregation

HENRY BLANKE

THE question: How to conduct Noonday Services in a city with only one congregation, I answer, It must be done in very much the same manner as in our larger cities with five, ten, or more Lutheran churches. Many believe that the task of holding such services successfully is too large an undertaking for one congregation, but I firmly believe that it is not nearly as difficult for one church to hold these services as it would be for several churches. One church can do just as it pleases in making the arrangements, deciding on speakers, and carrying out the advertising campaign. The wishes and desires of other congregations need not be considered. When I write about the method of our conducting these services and about their apparent success, I want it clearly understood that this is not written in a boastful spirit but rather with the desire to strengthen this laudable custom and encourage others to fall in line.

Leavenworth is a city of about 20,000 inhabitants, not considering the 6000 or more inmates of the various penal institutions which are located here. Our St. Paul's Lutheran Church numbers 460 communicant and 104 voting members. Services are bilingual, German and English, every Sunday. We maintain a Christian Day School with two teachers.

During the Lenten season of 1925 we conceived the idea of conducting noonday services during Holy Week at a down-town theatre. The American Lutheran was instrumental in reaching this decision. The matter was brought before the congregation which gave its enthusiastic approval. Only four weeks remained to prepare but the services were a great success. Prof. O. Wismar from our College at Concordia, Mo., Prof. J. W. Werling from St. John's College, Winfield, Kans., and Pastor C. W. Harre, St. Joseph, Mo., were our first speakers. For three days the weather was very unfavorable, still the services were attended by about 2000 people. Our own people were urged to attend 100% strong the first two days so that a packed house could be truthfully reported by the papers. We knew that a large crowd of our own people would attract others and it did. The very first evening our local paper carried in large headlines: *"Lyceum theatre packed today noon for first of series of brief noonday services conducted by local Lutheran Church—Prof. Werling eloquent speaker—Subject: Christ Dying for Men."* On that first day perhaps only 5% of the audience were strangers but by Good Friday fully 20% were non-Lutherans. Strangers would often invite others. The services advertised our Church and were the talk of the town. They deepened the Lutheran consciousness of our people which resulted in a greater interest in Sunday-school and Church services. We make it a rule to open a new adult confirmation class during the week after Easter and several members were gained for each class as a result of the noonday services.

For noonday services in 1926 plans were made earlier, and the services would have been better attended even than in 1925, but the weather was against us. Some fifteen inches of snow fell during Holy Week, which is very unusual for this part of the country. One snowdrift followed another, the highways were impassable, the trains were hours late, the local busses stopped running, and many of our people found it impossible to attend. The total attendance was not more than 1200. In 1925 we had one dollar left after all expenses were paid, but in 1926 we had to write $75.00 in red. Still we maintain that these services in 1926 were successful, for while only 1200 *heard* the addresses, thousands were able to *read* them. By special arrangements with the editor of our paper and with the speakers, a typwritten copy of the address to be delivered was taken to the newspaper office on the day before it was to be delivered. We would return to the office the next morning and do the proofreading; and the address which was delivered at noon would appear verbatim the same evening always on the second page with large headlines. Since Leavenworth has only one daily paper which reaches practically every home, the blessings of this arrangement can hardly be overestimated. The editor told us that people had come to his office and asked for back numbers containing these Lenten addresses in order to send them to relatives.

We firmly believe that in order to make these services successful it is essential to have the good will of the newspaper men. There are various ways of gaining the good will of these men; we found that placing a good cigar on the editor's desk and extending to him an invitation for dinner each day brought 100% dividends. A short news item is of greater publicity value than a large advertisement. Of course, you will have to advertise in order to get into the news column.

Our speakers in 1926 were Pastor F. Worthman, Dean John H. C. Fritz, Prof. Martin Graebner from Milwaukee, and the local pastor. When soon after Easter a report of these services was read to the congregation and the question came up as to what should be done for 1927, it was unanimously decided to hold such services each year. Noonday Lenten services during Holy Week have become a fixed institution in Leavenworth. For this coming season Dr. W. Dallmann from Milwaukee and Prof. W. G. Polack from St. Louis have already been secured as speakers.

The first thing to do is to get the speakers and secure a prominent and conveniently located theatre or auditorium. We pay $5.00 a day for the use of the theatre. 6000 attractive folders are printed and distributed by our school children on the two Saturdays previous to Holy Week. These folders are handed out on the streets and placed in all the parked autos. The folders should be attractive. Our folder has a beautiful picture on the first page, either "Gethsemane" or the very touching scene entitled "The Way of the Cross of Sicily." The second page contained several Bible passages and the following invitation:

DEAR FRIEND:

You are hereby cordially invited to attend the special services which will again be conducted during Holy Week every noon from Monday, March 29th, until Friday, April 2nd, at the Lyceum Theatre, 519 Delaware St., Leavenworth, Kansas. All services will begin promptly at 12:20 and end promptly at 12:50. Every day different speakers with different messages, but each speaker and each message will tell you of the Man of Sorrows and the Way of Life. Each discourse will be based on Scriptural teachings. Any questions in regard to the teachings and practices of the Lutheran Church will be cheerfully answered after the services. Also free literature will be distributed. If you have no church connection, we want you to give Our Church a chance. We have a message for you. Attend the first service and you will attend all. Please accept this folder as a personal invitation.

Cordially yours,

HENRY BLANKE,
Lutheran Pastor.

The third page gave names of speakers and subjects and also a cross. On the last page we had sentence paragraphs on what the Lutheran church stands for. During the week previous a letter was sent to each one of our families. Window cards were placed into the windows of stores and of the homes of our people. We distributed these cards on Friday before Holy Week and naturally had to omit not a few stores, but on Saturday morning the managers or owners of three stores called by telephone and requested that cards be placed in their windows. For ten days an advertisement with the invitation to spend a half hour with God appeared on the screens of every theatre. Several sidewalk advertising stands were placed at prominent corners with different announcements each day. Paid advertisements were placed in the newspapers.

A beautiful window display announcing our services attracted considerable attention and much favorable comment. It represented a miniature altar with Bible, crucifix, candles, flowers, pictures of passion scenes. A window decorator, who is a member of our Church spent hours of his time without any charge. All pictures and flowers were loaned and replaced without charge. The window space was donated by a prominent store. This form of publicity proved to be effective.

The services started promptly at 12:20 and closed promptly at 12:50. Attractive programs were distributed having on the first page a large cross, names of speakers and subjects, and a prayer. The second page contained the order of service. The third page had five generally known hymns. On the last page we featured great truths about God and Man and finally an invitation to attend the services at the local Lutheran Church. Nothing was said about an offering, but an opportunity to contribute was given at the door. The ushers would count the people as they left each aisle. Tracts were distributed at the close of each service.

It is, of course, impossible to give an exact proportion of strangers in attendance, but we know that during these two weeks hundreds of strangers attended these services. Among these were bankers, lawyers, doctors, and ministers of other churches. These services have advertised our Church immensely; but what is more, they have brought the doctrines of our Church, its great truths and principles, to the attention of many non-Lutherans. It gives our church an opportunity to preach the good old Gospel of salvation to many who otherwise would not hear it. God surely will bless such efforts. For that we have His command and promise. We feel that the opportunity of placing, by means of the newspaper, all five addresses verbatim into the homes of over 20,000 people is alone worth more than all the money and efforts spent.

What Leavenworth has done any other city of from 5000 to 50,000 inhabitants can do. We dare not idly stand by while thousands of thousands around us are going to damnation and destruction. Don't hesitate but start right now in the name of the Lord and your labor will not be in vain. Your church will ultimately reap the greatest benefit. Soon these services will again be conducted throughout the length and breadth of our land. May God bless them to the honor and glory of His name and to the eternal welfare and salvation of many immortal souls.

A Pastor's Outline for a Missionary Campaign During the Lenten Season

OBJECT

SINCE every unconverted soul within our reach is a distinct challenge to the Church, and since our Savior's commission to the Church is to preach the Gospel unto all creatures, it is thoroughly in harmony with our Master's will that we utilize every possible means to bring souls into touch with the saving truth.

I therefore suggest that the lenten season of 1933 be utilized for a concentrated and systematic effort to reach as many of the unchurched of the city as possible with our message, and that the Wednesday evening Lenten services be of an evangelistic character with a special appeal to those outside of the Church.

THE CAMPAIGN

1 *Among our Members*
I suggest:
(a) That the plan be presented in detail to the various organizations of the church in their January meetings and their interest aroused.
(b) That the choir be enlisted for wholehearted cooperation and written pledges be secured from every member to be present at every service.
(c) That an attractive letter explaining the campaign be sent to every communicant member on February 2, asking for full cooperation.
(d) That this letter enclose a card on which the member pledges himself or herself 1, to attend all the services unless detained by sickness; 2, to attempt to bring at least one stranger; 3, to distribute as effectively as possible our literature; 4, to make special plea in prayer throughout the Lenten season for the success of the campaign.

(e) That this letter enclose a sheet for the insertion of names and addresses of people to whom literature might be advantageously mailed.

2 *Among the Non-Members*
I suggest:
(a) That in February a special edition of the parish paper be issued in 5,000 copies with a plain statement of Lutheran principles and a direct appeal to the unchurched. This edition to be distinctly evangelistic in character.
(b) That this edition of the parish paper be sent to all the addresses submitted by our members in addition to our present mailing list of unchurched.
(c) That this edition contain a complete program of our services and an earnest invitation.
(d) That this edition be distributed at all the church services preceding and during the campaign.
(e) That our people be urged to distribute this edition through every means at their disposal.
(f) That special folders be printed advertising the organization of the class on Christian Fundamentals on the Friday after Easter, and containing an enrollment blank.
(g) That a sufficient supply of penny Gospels be on hand on the tract table.

ADVERTISING

I suggest:
(a) That 300 window cards be printed and distributed partly by our own people and partly by the Acme Posting Co.
(b) That special ads be placed in the newspapers every week during the campaign.
(c) That the various neighborhood papers be used for advertising purposes.
(d) That cards be sent out to our enlarged mailing list every Saturday during the campaign advertising the coming week's service.
(e) That our members be given supplies of these cards for broadcast distribution.

THE SERVICES

I suggest:
(a) That the campaign proper begin on Ash Wednesday and culminate on Good Friday
(b) That the services be carefully planned also regarding their musical features.
(c) That a special plea be made after the sermon for an interview with the pastor, and opportunity for such interview be announced.

MISCELLANEOUS SUGGESTIONS

1 That a special effort be made to reach those of our members who have become lax in church attendance and communion.
(a) These names are to be given to the Membership Committee for visitation during the first weeks of February.
(b) These delinquents are to be urged evangelically to be more faithful in their church duties and to begin by pledging to attend all the Lenten services.
(c) These delinquents are to be urged to bring others and to become active in furthering the campaign.
2 That the arrangements for the campaign be left in the hands of the Publicity Committee, this committee to be augmented, if necessary, by the chairman of the church.
3 That the follow-up work on the names secured through the campaign be done by the Membership Committee.
4 That about 400 copies of the AMERICAN LUTHERAN be purchased for distribution. This will be a special edition gotten out for missionary purposes.

NOTES

The expected results of the campaign are as follows:
1. A revival of spiritual life and activity among our own members.
2. Winning back the careless and drifting.
3. Accession of new members through the adult class and by confession of faith.
4. Larger church attendance, particularly at the Lenten services.

There is little doubt that the increased collections will more than pay for the cost of the campaign.

(Suggestion for Parish Paper)

Suggestions for Holy Week and Easter

Noonday services during Holy Week need not be restricted to the larger cities. They may be the means of acquainting the people with the Lutheran Church also in smaller communities. Choose a central location. If the unchurched are to be attracted some other place besides the church may serve better. Arrange for special speakers and special music. Advertise well in advance through the local newspaper, by means of blotters or other throw aways, and by direct mail where possible. Emphasize the "half hour" and keep within that limit.

* * *

Where Noonday services are out of the question, the holding of a whole week of evening services is becoming increasingly popular. Some of the above suggestions apply also to such services. Choirs sometimes render an appropriate Cantata on one of the evenings. Have members call on special prospects and bring them along to these services.

* * *

In some communities the business houses close on Good Friday from noon until 3 P. M. A service at this time may prove more satisfactory than the customary morning or evening service.

* * *

The outdoor sunrise service is gaining in popularity every year. Where there are several congregations in one locality they may join in such an undertaking. Some of the congregations of southern California meet on some convenient hill top. Individual churches may find it possible to conduct such a service on the church lawn. A large wooden cross should be erected, around which the worshippers gather. With appropriate hymn, Scripture lesson, and sermon, such a service can be made very impressive. Should weather not permit, the service may be held in church.

* * *

The churches are usually crowded on Easter. Sometimes it is impossible for the pastor to greet all of the visitors or have them register in the guest book if the church has one. Cards may be handed out with the hymnals on which all present may give their names and addresses. Pencils should be provided by the ushers. If there is a weekly bulletin or announcement sheet, space should be provided for such registration.

1732-1799
George Washington
"Let us cherish the memory of the man * *"
Bi-Centennial 1732-1932

One of George Washington's Prayers

ALMIGHTY God, we make our earnest prayer that Thou wilt keep the United States in Thy holy protection; that Thou wilt incline the hearts of the citizens to cultivate a spirit of subordination and obedience to government; to entertain a brotherly affection and love for one another and for their fellow citizens of the United States at large. And finally that Thou wilt most graciously be pleased to dispose us all to do justice, to love mercy, and to demean ourselves with the charity, humility, and pacific temper of mind which were the characteristics of the divine Author of our blessed religion, and without a humble imitation of whose example in these things we can never hope to be a happy nation. Grant our application, we beseech Thee, through Jesus Christ our Lord. Amen.

Electrotype used is No. 2585. Price $2.00

We are glad to welcome you to our service this morning. If you have no church home we invite you to make Redeemer Church your church.

Will you kindly fill in your name and address whether you are a member or a visitor so that we may have a record of all who were present at this service. Thank you!

Name ....

Address ....

(Kindly leave at your seat or hand to usher)

(Suggestion for card or bulletin for Easter service)

A Lenten Series

"THE PRAISE OF HIM WHO DIED" by G. E. Lenski is a book of eight addresses on the suffering and death of our Lord, each address illustrated with a reproduction in halftone of master paintings by Hoffmann, Geiger, Harrach, Munkacsy, Ciseri and Zimmerman. Freshness of thought and a vigorous and pleasing style are characteristic of these addresses. The volume is printed on a good grade of eggshell stock and is bound in royal blue with gold markings on front cover. Price, $1.25.

Order from THE AMERICAN LUTHERAN PUBLICITY BUREAU.

The pictures for use with this series must be ordered direct from Perry Pictures Inc., Malden, Massachusetts. The price is two cents for each picture. No order less than 25 copies can be filled.

Check or money order must accompany order. A catalogue may be obtained from the publishers. The following are the titles and catalogue number of the pictures treated in "The Passion of Him Who Died".

Christ in the Upper Room	No. 280
Christ in Gethsemane	No. 798 E
The Kiss of Betrayal	No. 834
Peter's Denial	No. 3250
Christ Before Pilate	No. 831
Ecce Homo	No. 1102
Christ on the Cross	No. 797 X

Pictures of the Passion
Reproduced from paintings by Gebhard Fugel

Copies of the famous paintings of Christ Passion by Hoffmann, Munkacsy and others have been used with good success in many of our churches to illustrate a series of Lenten sermons by the pastor. The pictures are distributed with the hymnals before the service. During the sermon the pastor has occasion to refer to the pictures to illustrate certain points. The pictures, besides serving to impress such thoughts upon the hearer, are usually taken home and preserved.

Those who have used such a series and are looking for something which is different as well as those who have not used any such series will find that the paintings by Gebhard Fugel lend themselves very well to this purpose. The business department of the American Lutheran Publicity Bureau is prepared to furnish a set of seven pictures of these paintings at prices quoted below.

The pictures are printed in Sepia Ink, on heavyweight Ivory Coated Paper, Art Finish. Paper size 3½"x5¼". A sheet with copies of these pictures will be sent upon request.

The titles of the paintings are as follows:

THE VERDICT
THE ASSUMPTION OF THE CROSS
"WEEP NOT OVER ME"
THE COLLAPSE
THE CRUCIFIXION
ON THE CROSS
THE BURIAL

A mimeographed set of seven sermons which have been preached with these pictures is available from the American Lutheran Publicity Bureau at fifty cents per set.

Prices of Passion pictures:

100	sets	of	seven pictures	$5.00
200	"	"	"	9.00
250	"	"	"	10.00
300	"	"	"	11.00
500	"	"	"	15.00

From a Painting by Gebhard Fugel   ON THE CROSS   No. 2830

(Sermonette or paid advertisement for newspaper)

To the Unchurched

Get this straight! The Church is interested in you. Why? Not because the Church has any ulterior motives regarding you, not because it wants to "rope you in," not because it wants to "put one over on you," but, believe it or not, because the Church has an utterly unselfish desire to confer upon you an infinitely precious and eternal benefit. The Church will manage to get along without you, but you are in a desperately unfortunate condition so long as you are trying to get along without the benefits and blessings of which the Church is the custodian. The Church claims that it has something which represents to you a positive, personal need, and it would be delinquent in its duty if it failed to tell you about it. The Church claims that you, as a rational, immortal being, have no right to drift on to eternity without answering definitely questions like the following: Where am I from? What am I here for? Where am I going? Is there a God? What is His attitude towards me? What is my relationship towards Him? What is life? What is death? What is there beyond the grave? Where shall I spend eternity?

Are these questions vital or not? Can you take a chance by leaving them unanswered? Can you risk postponing their consideration? You owe to yourself to find out whether or not the Church can answer these questions. You may have a superficial and rather disparaging idea of the Church. But what do you know about it and its teachings? How can you be fair in your judgment when it is based on ignorance? Because of the importance of its message and its pertinence to your own person we come to you with a frank invitation to attend our services.

(Newspaper advertisement for Lent)

A Word to the Unchurched

Electro No. 1040

We extend a special invitation to you to attend our services during the Lenten season. We make no excuses for inviting you and will not admit that you are making any concessions to us by coming. We believe we have what you need and you personally will be the gainer.

We invite you because we are certain that you need the Church and not because the Church needs you. There are certain fundamental questions which you cannot afford to leave unanswered. Why are you living? Is there a God to whom you are accountable? What are you doing with your life? Where are you going? Are you taking a chance on eternity? Is the religion of the Bible true? We can only ask you to come and see.

We offer you no bait of sensational pulpit "stunts." We preach the old Gospel story. We are "fundamentalists" without equivocation. We preach Christ and we preach Him crucified for the sins of men. On the basis of this One Thing Needful we extend an urgent invitation to you to attend our services. Attend to the needs of your soul. It is high time.

Sunday Services: Midweek Lenten Service,
Morning, 10:45; Evening, 7:45   Wednesday Evening, 8:15

Trinity Lutheran Church
(ADDRESS AND NAME OF PASTOR)

A Lenten Missionary Program

A. R. G. HANSER

The program here outlined proposes the organization of a group of consecrated members of the congregation to visit in this Lenten season a definite number of people in a given area of the parish territory with a view to bringing them to the services and eventually into active membership in the church. In this effort the visitors are to be supported by weekly letters sent out to all prospects they are to call on and by specially arranged services which the prospects are invited to attend.

LISTS

Compile a list of

1. Indifferent members.
2. Parents of Parochial School children (not connected with congregation)
3. Parents of Sunday School and Cradle Roll children (not connected with congregation).
4. Periodical church attendants.
5. Members of societies who are not affiliated with congregation (Home Department—Boy Scouts—Girl Scouts, etc.)
6. Unaffiliated relatives of members.
7. Families in which pastor has in some way officiated.
8. Any non-members with whom some contact has been established.

* * *

A card should be written out for each prospect, giving name and address.

Under "Connection" should be noted how the prospect is connected with the church; for instance—"member" or "member of Home Department" or "Have child, Sunday School," etc.

Under "Report" the visitor should give all information he has secured in his visit, what the prospects are and what action should be taken.

Sample Card

```
Name

Address

Connection:

Report:

Date of call
```

This list should be written in duplicate so that check up can be made, whether folks have been called on or not.

These cards are later to be assorted geographically to facilitate visitation.

* * *

VISITING ORGANIZATION

Select from the roster of your congregation a sufficient number of the most faithful members to call on this list of prospects during the season of Lent.

Each visitor will be able to make between 3 and 5 calls a week. In the 6 weeks of Lent each can make between 18 and 30 visits. Let us make the average 25. For every 100 prospects you need 4 visitors. Look for quality rather than numbers.

The visitors are to be formed into groups and each group is given a certain territory. It is their duty to visit the prospects living in this assigned territory. The number of the groups will depend on the number of prospects in this territory.

Each group is headed by a leader or captain who is responsible for his group. He must see that each visitor in his group has a sufficient number of prospects, that he does his visiting, that he attends all meetings and makes his reports on his cards properly.

It is well to choose these group leaders in advance rather than to leave them to the selection of the groups themselves.

If you have a man with sufficient executive ability and earnestness of purpose instruct him and put him in active charge of the whole venture.

Reserve your officers for the follow-up work and have them attend every meeting of the visitors.

Write each one you select as a visitor a personal letter stating the plan in general and invite them to engage in it and attend the first meeting.

When all have received their letters call them on the phone to make sure they will come to the meeting and serve. Do not depend altogether on the letter. Besides, if any should decline, you could still substitute others and have a complete organization at the first meeting.

Thereafter meetings should be held every week, the second meeting for final instruction and distribution of lists and material and the subsequent meetings for reports. They could, for convenience, be held after the Lenten services. Each meeting should be planned and prepared in detail. A devotional character should mark every meeting. A general outline is suggested.

LETTER TO VISITORS

Dear Friend:

Lent is again approaching. The cross, that symbol of sublime sacrifice, invites us not only to refresh our faith in its contemplation but to follow its example by some special service.

During this season of Lent we propose to carry the meaning and message of the cross to those who have been touched by our church life and activity but who have not as yet made a declaration of our faith. Will you be one of these messengers of the cross? If so will you come to the meeting to be held Wednesday evening, February 23, in our Parish House at 8:15 o'clock.

It is a fine old custom to abstain from some innocent pleasure as a special discipline during Lent. It is still better, however, to render some special service during Lent; that will profit others as well as discipline ourselves and honor our Savior.

Confident that you will not fail in this opportunity, I remain,

Faithfully yours,

* * *

FIRST MEETING—WEDNESDAY, FEBRUARY 23
Program

1. Prayer or Devotional Exercises
2. Election of Chairman or Leader. See that right man is elected; otherwise appoint him; he should assume responsibility for the whole undertaking.
3. Submit the whole plan of campaign:
   a. Purpose
   b. Plan to be followed—3-5 calls a week
   c. Attend weekly report meetings
4. Nomination of Captains for each section
   They are responsible for all workers in their group and for their territory
   Each captain should have approximately 4 workers
5. Choice or assignment of each one present to a group or captain (If not enough present plan to fill vacancies by next meeting)
6. Appointment of Captains to act as Committee
   a. to arrange prospect cards by districts.
   b. to supervise composing, printing and mailing of letters (all workers should be on mailing list and get copies of what is sent out)

7. Roll call
8. Adjournment with prayer

SECOND MEETING—WEDNESDAY, MARCH 2
Program

1. Devotional Exercises
2. Report of Committee on geographical grouping of prospects
3. Assignment of districts (Groups meet for distribution of cards and material after meeting)
   a. Distribute calling cards for visitors but no polemical tracts
4. General explanation—Pastor or chairman
   a. Explain prospect cards
   b. How many calls a week, etc.
   c. What to report on cards
      1. Complaints
      2. Criticism
      3. Prospects
      4. Family conditions
      5. Number in family, and age
5. Sales talk—What to say to each group. Do this in form of discussion or conference but be prepared to make practical suggestions to them
   a. Indifferent members
   b. Parents of Parochial School and Sunday School children
   c. Former Lutherans—etc.
   Urge each to make special mention of this work in their prayers.
6. Stress ultimate objective
   a. To win back the indifferent to faithful membership (Services and Communion)
   b. To bring in the stranger by bringing him to services and to adult class (if not confirmed)
7. To be faithful in all Christian duties themselves
8. Adjourn for group meetings for distribution of cards
   Have everything prepared and all facilities at hand so that meeting may be short and run smoothly.

MEETINGS THEREAFTER EVERY WEDNESDAY FOLLOWING LENTEN SERVICES
Program

1. Devotional Exercises
2. Report of each group—called for by Chairman
   a. How many calls
   b. Results
      Promises
      No response
   c. Cards visited to be enclosed in envelope and given to Chairman by captain
3. Special experiences
4. Discussion as to method and best approach
5. Adjournment

The officers are to go through returned cards and determine in each case the course to be pursued. The good prospects are to be visited by the officers and finally by the pastor. Much of this work will be futile unless officers follow it up appropriately and faithfully, to get the strangers into Adult class and careless members back into the fold. Officers should keep account of progress of visitation—who have been called on and who remain to be visited so that in the end every person on the list will have been visited and reported on.

PRINTED MATTER TO PREPARE

1. Letters to visitors for meetings
2. Calling card for visitor—
   SAMPLE

   Introducing Callers from
   St. John's Lutheran Church
   Fourth and Hamilton Avenues
   Brooklyn, New York

   (Leave space below for callers to write names)

   ---

3. Letters—to be sent to entire mailing list—(Communions should be noted in postscript on letters to members and attendance urged)
4. Envelopes for enclosing visited cards
   (No. 10 envelope—printed or mimeographed)

REPORT OF GROUP NO.

Number of cards returned

Favorable receptions

Unfavorable receptions

Leader ....

---

5. Selection of tracts, if it is decided to use them.

* * *

CALENDAR

Feb. 16—Mail letter to workers inviting them to come to first meeting.
Feb. 23—First meeting of visitors
   Mail first letter No. 1
March 6—Sermon subject:—"Christ's Self-Revelation"—Mark 10, 46
March 9—Lenten Services
   Third meeting of visitors (for report)
   Mail Letter No. II
March 13—Sermon subject:—"Bondage and Liberty"—Is. 52, 3
March 16—Lenten Services
   Fourth meeting of visitors
   Mail Letter No. III
March 20—Sermon Subject:—"A Home Thrust"—II Sam. 12,13
March 23—Lenten services
   Fifth meeting of visitors
   Mail letter No. IV
March 27—Sermon subject:—"What to do to be Saved"—Acts 16,20
March 30—Lenten services
   Sixth meeting of visitors
   Mail letter No. V
April 3—Sermon subject:—"The Purpose of Affliction"—Job. 48,11
April 6—Lenten services
   Meeting of visitors
   Mail letter No. VI
April 10—Sermon subject:—"Christ and Children"—Matt. 20, 20-23
   In this week all calls should be finished
April 12—Mail letter No. VII
April 14 or 15—Last meeting and report of visitors
April 17—Easter—Sermon subject—"Why Seek Ye the Living Among the Dead "

NOTES

A series of letters have been prepared for those who have not the time or inclination to do this work themselves.

LETTER No. 1

Dear Friend:

   It is the purpose of Christ Lutheran Church to serve its members, friends and the whole community in every possible way; we invite you to command the service of our pastor in any need or trouble.

   A series of special services will be held Sunday mornings at 10:45 o'clock for which the pastor has prepared a list of subjects of particular interest. The first sermon Sunday March 6, deals with "Christ," on whom our whole Christian faith rests.

The subject will be "The Self-revelation of Christ."

The services will be made as attractive and brief as possible and we trust we may have the pleasure of your fellowship with us.

LETTER No. 2

Dear Friend:

We disavow and repudiate the interference of self-appointed leaders in the Church with the personal liberties of the community. We have no sympathy with the Blue Laws or any attempt of the Church to govern the life of the whole community by the laws of a few. That is tyranny and violates the fundamental principles of our government and national life.

But there is an infinitely worse bondage; one which has much more to do with a man's real happiness and enjoyment of life, that is the bondage of sin. From this we would deliver men in the only way it is possible to deliver them, -- by the Gospel.

We invite you to attend the services Sunday morning March 13, at 10:45 o'clock, in Christ Lutheran Church, where the pastor will preach on the subject: "Bondage and Liberty." We would be pleased to have you join us in this service.

LETTER No. 3

Dear Friend:

Do you believe in God? Do you believe in divine providence in your life? Do you acknowledge your dependence on God?

Do you express your belief in any other way than by mere languid, meaningless avowal?

We invite you to unite with us in our worship of God and return thanks to Him for all His countless mercies.

We know you can read your Bible and pray at home. What if you CAN? DO YOU? That is the question.

The man who reads his Bible and prays at home almost without exception goes to church also. If you really pray at home you will also surely soon come to church.

Begin now. Come to church Sunday morning March 20, at 10:45 o'clock, and join with us in worship and song.

LETTER No. 4

Dear Friend:

Is there anything like "heaven" or "salvation"? If there is, is it likely to come to us without effort or condition? We get nothing else that is worthwhile without corresponding effort, why should men expect salvation upon other terms?

Yet the majority of men go from day to day so complacently, almost indifferently, as though they took their salvation for granted.

"What must I do to be saved?" is a serious question. It effects us all and is worth a half hour's consideration. If we find that all is well we can rest back easy again; IF NOT it is time to attend to the matter.

The subject of the pastor's sermon Sunday morning, March 27, at 10:45 o'clock, is: "What must I do to be saved?" Come and think on this question with us?

Sincerely,

....
Chairman of Service Committee

LETTER No. 5

Dear Friend:

I sincerely trust that you have been able to attend our services and that you have found them attractive and helpful. If you will introduce yourself to me or to one of the ushers or to the pastor we will be glad to make your welcome more personal.

Next Sunday morning, April 3, at 10:45 o'clock, the pastor will speak on the subject of sorrow. What is its purpose? Why pain and sickness and losses? Why are hopes and castles so often shattered?

The answer is simple, certain and comforting.

Will you join us on Sunday?

LETTER No. 6

Dear Friend:

Our Public Schools render eminent service to our country and contribute more to the welfare and safety of our national life than any other public institution. However, without the religious training of our children the Public Schools cannot attain their best results. This part of the task falls to the parents and the Church. If you have a family let us recognize each other as partners and cooperate with each other.

The Church teaches the children in Sunday School, week-day religious instruction and Confirmation Classes their duty to God, their neighbors and country on religious and moral grounds; we seek to instill those high ideals and that sense of reverence and responsibility to God which alone will enable them to use their education for their own and our national well being and advancement.

Our services Sunday morning April 10, at 10:45 o'clock, will deal with the problem of training our children. The pastor will preach on the subject: "Christ and Children" and we invite you to be present.

Teach your children to respect the Church as we teach them to respect their parents; take as much interest and cooperate with the Church as you do with the Public School in the training of the children.

LETTER No. 7

Dear Friend:

The joy of Easter is at hand. In the faith of its message of resurrection and life everlasting we find the joy that no sorrow can take from us.

To hide the facts and banish the thoughts of sorrow from our minds will not help us. Our Christian faith enables us to face life's tragedies with calm confidence and a blessed hope. Our Lord's resurrection from the dead is the pledge that the "dead in Christ" live and shall rise on the last day and we will see them again. Our faith is the victory that overcometh the world and all its sorrow, and brings that peace which the world cannot give.

The sermon Easter morning, April 17, at 10:45 o'clock, will bring the comfort and joy of the season in the subject: "Foolish Tears." We invite you to be present and rejoice with us.

In order to acquire a personal touch these letters should, wherever possible, be typed and addressed individually on the pastor's personal stationery.

Sermon outlines and letters are of course only suggestions and each will have to modify them to suit special local conditions.

Avoid polemics in letters and sermons.

Do not attempt to bring out all subtle distinctions in doctrine and practice between the Lutheran Church and others. Be positive, not negative. Hold as much as possible to that which Christian Churches have in common—the simple gospel. Remember, milk for the children. The plan is to preach the gospel, not to give a course in dogmatics or Lutheran Confessions. The first object is to make Christians — afterwards you make Lutherans.

The program outlined employs the Sunday morning services. Strangers are more likely to attend it than the evening or mid-week Lenten services.

Make the service as attractive as possible. A good sermon —short—special music—a word of welcome from pulpit—a tactful reference to the stranger in your prayer. Be careful not to frighten the stranger away with extravagant attention and wholesale introductions, after service. Be a wise fisherman— play the fish—don't jump in and go after them with your bare hands.

The definite results you are after are—

1. Revival of spiritual life of the membership
2. Winning back the careless and drifting
3. Bringing in new members

The tests of success are—

1. Larger church attendance
2. Larger communions
3. Return of backsliders
4. Revival of poor and dead accounts
5. Larger adult class
6. Accessions
7. General revival of the spiritual—social—and missionary life of the congregation

Electro No. 1150

A Declaration and Invitation

To the vast majority of men Easter means nothing. It is to them merely a seasonal festival indicative of the arrival of Spring and an opportunity for a display of fashionable finery. To us it means that He who bore our sins on the tree has come forth from the grave bearing in His hands our victory over sin, death and hell. For us the significance of the Easter festival is summed up in the words: "If Christ be not raised, your faith is vain, ye are yet in your sins." With jubilant hearts we gather around the open tomb. "Now is Christ risen from the dead and become the first fruits of them that slept." In the face of the wondrous fact of His resurrection, all petty trials and troubles of life fade, and even the burdened and heavy-hearted can join in the victorious jubilation of the children of God. In this spirit our church will again celebrate the Easter festival.

If you are without a church home, we extend to you a cordial invitation to worship with us on Easter morning. But we warn you that you will hear no learned and high-sounding dissertation which by feat of mental gymnastics might be remotely brought into connection with the Easter fact. You will hear a proclamation of the glorious blessings which come to man from out of the open tomb. You will be in the midst of people whose hearts and mouth are singing forth the praises of Him who is our soul's Redeemer. But come! You will be brought into contact with the most stupendous issues of your life. You will be in the presence of Him who wants your soul's salvation. We shall be glad to welcome you in our midst.

Easter Cross Decoration

THE accompanying illustration represents a striking Easter decoration which is easy to install by amateur hands. A few boards, a hammer, some nails and a saw and the most elementary knowledge of carpentering are all the things necessary for the fashioning of the cross proper. The height of the cross will naturally be proportioned to the size of the church. A large church will need a six-foot cross placed on a two or three-foot

base. The cross in the illustration measures seven feet in height and stands on a pyramid base three feet high. The foot of the cross is bolstered by a few rough braces. After the frame is finished the decorators can get busy. The cross is first covered with twigs of southern smilax or some other small-leaved decorative greens. The twigs are tied on with green twine and should be used profusely enough to form a solid background. Artificial Easter lilies are then inserted at intervals all over the cross. These lilies can be purchased at a low price and from a distance cannot be distinguished from the real thing. Natural lilies wilt quickly. Artificial flowers can be packed away in some dust-proof container and can be used again and again. The pyramid base of the cross is made by the use of wooden boxes. Ferns and potted plants are then placed in profusion on these boxes until the base looks like a little hill of blooming plants. The bare spots should be filled in with twigs of greens. This beautiful decoration is, of course, proper right in the sanctuary of the church and should be fashioned in proportion to the size of the sanctuary. The tendency is to get the cross too small. Being the principal decorative feature it should stand out even from the rear of the church. Such a floral cross costs little and its construction calls for nothing more than a little patient labor and a degree of good taste.

Rules for Weddings

This is the House of God. A reverent SILENCE is expected of all who enter here.

Throwing rice or confetti within the church is forbidden.

When the Bridal Procession enters, the congregation shall rise. At the close of the Wedding March all shall be seated.

When the Bridal Couple kneels for prayer all shall rise and remain standing until the procession has left the church.

Friends and visitors shall remain in their pews and give the parents and relatives of the Bridal Couple an opportunity to leave first.

(Leave this Card in the Pew)

[Submitted by Rev. Paul G. Sander, New York]

(Parish Paper Article)

EASTER

If you want evidence of the religious bankruptcy of the element which still exists on sailing under the banner of Christianity and calls itself "modern religion," we need only observe the pitiful and labored efforts of its exponents to make something of Easter. They have done away with the deity of Christ, with His vicarious atonement and, of course, with His resurrection, and now they are confronted by the difficult problem of finding an excuse for celebrating a festival which has through ages of observance become such a fixture in Christian circles that it cannot be ignored or eliminated and which has as its reason and basis the risen Christ. Their efforts to find something to celebrate would be ludicrous if they were not so sad. In flowery verbiage and ringing periods they tell of the coming to life of a "new idealism", the rising of our "better nature", the budding into being of noble "dormant faculties," the coming forth from death to life of a "blessed brotherhood", a "spirit of love and tolerance", the awakening of "divine impulses." These and other glowing phrases of meaningless nonsense depict the hopelessness of a religion from which the living Christ has been banished. Hopelessness is its outstanding characteristic.

On the other hand real, well-founded joyousness animates the hearts of the true believers as they gather around the tomb of their resurrected Lord. To them the open and empty grave signifies freedom from the curse and punishment of sin and the wide-open gates of heaven for all who in faith accept the accomplished redemption. The risen Lord is the very foundation of our joy in life and our hope in death. Religion without the essential fact of the Lord's resurrection loses all life and power. Without it we might as well close our churches, burn our Bibles and turn our various congregations and religious organizations into agencies for making a hopeless existence in this world as bearable as possible and for suppressing as much as possible the despair of our lost souls.

But the resurrection is an established fact. The triumphant news rings through all Christendom: "The Lord is risen!" and millions of jubilant hearts greet the great Victor over death and the grave as the surety of our own everlasting life in heaven. Our joy is not labored. We do not try to work ourselves into an Easter spirit with all sorts of fanciful phrases and manufactured emotions. Our Easter happiness is the spontaneous emotion of redeemed souls, rejoicing in their established and divinely attested salvation.

(Copy for Parish Paper)

HOLY WEEK

440C, Size 2x3..$2.00   440A, Size 4x5½ 3.25
440B, Size 1x1½ 1.25   440, Size 2½x3¾ 2.25

Very properly the week which is ushered in by Palm Sunday is so designated. A peculiar sanctity attaches to these days. They recall the events that constitute the climax not only of our Lord's earthly ministry, but also the Triune God's eternal plan of salvation.

The week opens with our Lord's royal entry into Jerusalem. It is a march of triumph. The days that follow are marked by a series of vehement verbal assaults made upon Jesus by His enemies. He parries every thrust. In graphic parables He exposes their evil plans and the doom that their course will bring upon them.

On Thursday evening He gathers with His disciples in the upper room. He institutes the Blessed Sacrament. He speaks so tenderly to these men who will soon experience one shock after another. He crosses the Kidron and enters Gethsemane. His Passion begins.

He is arrested. He is dragged from one tribunal to another. The night is made ghastly by the physical, mental and spiritual tortures to which He is subjected. The scene shifts with kaleidoscopic rapidity. At last the insistent demand is satisfied. The sentence of death is confirmed. Jesus is led away to be crucified.

On Calvary the last act of the Passion occurs. The Son of God dies after hours of agony on the cross. As Good Friday, the anniversary of that day is remembered. So the ransom was paid for a humanity dead in sin and lost to God. So God and man were reconciled. We are verily bought with a price.

Before Good Friday's sun sets His body is laid to rest in Joseph's tomb. Saturday is the one quiet day in this momentous week.

Then on Sunday morning the glad tidings are heard: "He is risen; He is not here." No power of earth or hell could hold that mighty Lord. His prison bars He bursts. The Resurrection is the crowning miracle of His redemptive work.

(Parish Paper article for Good Friday)

THE CROSS OF CHRIST

All Christian religion centers around Calvary. The events that transpired on that memorable Good Friday form the basis of the whole system of Christian doctrine. The work of atonement is the heart which gives life to the

2590D—Size 3" ... $1.75
2590A—Size 1½" . 1.25
2590 —Size 2" ... 1.50

various teachings of Christian theology. In our day and time the cross is being eliminated from religion, even by such as still make profession of being followers of the crucified One. The dying Jesus has become merely an unjustly maltreated martyr, giving up His life because He was misunderstood, and because there was no national response to the ideas He represented. He is in many circles no longer the Son of God sacrificing Himself for the sins of the human race. So-called modernism has stripped His death of any meritorious qualities so far as we are concerned. The old question, "What think ye of Christ?" is still being universally debated.

So far as we are concerned the question is settled. We answer with Peter: "Thou art the Christ, the Son of the living God." Our whole hope of heaven is built upon the deity of Christ and the effectiveness of His substitutionary sacrifice. When we assemble under the cross on Good Friday, we gaze, not upon the agonizing death of a mere human martyr or an unjustly treated moral leader, but upon the death of the Lamb of God that taketh away the sin of the world. Unless He is that, our visit to Calvary has no significance and our whole system of religion is built upon sand. We see on Calvary not merely an example of patient human suffering and of devilish heartlessness and iniquity, but we see our Burden-bearer, upon Whose innocent soul were heaped the iniquities of us all. On Golgotha our eternal fate was settled. Let us, who are so deeply involved in the tragedy and the recipients of all the blessings that the suffering Christ brought out of that frightful struggle, assemble once more beneath the cross with bowed heads and with grateful hearts, praising God for the immeasurable love there revealed.

Stewardship

E. J. GALLMEYER

"There is hardly a hobby, certainly not a habit, which does not cost us more than what we offer for church."

STEWARDSHIP is the act of administering. When we talk of a man or of ourself as being a steward we acknowledge thereby that we are handling the affairs of another. There is a growing appreciation among Christians that we are but stewards here, that all we have and all that we are is not ours to use as we see fit, but rather that we must give an accounting of our earthly goods and talents, just as an earthly steward must do.

I say that there is a growing appreciation in this regard, for the development of thought of stewardship has been receiving more and more attention of late, but the progress has been and is very slow.

The reason for this is obvious. There has been a woeful lack of education among our people on this point. True, sermons and admonitions have not been wanting, but habit development has not been fostered. Among other Christian church bodies, the real facts about stewardship have been on their educational programs for generations.

The importance of stewardship is inculcated into the child and it grows to manhood understanding his responsibility. Among our people there has been a listlessness in this regard. People have been told that they should give according to their means, and with no example to follow, have given as little as they could get by with. Some a mere pittance. Even among the rich. Merely because their contribution was greater than that of some day laborer, they feel they are doing their share. It is not a matter as easily disposed of as that.

Render unto God that which is God's, is just as much a law for a Christian to observe today as any law of the decalogue. Just why so many people must be admonished and importuned to do their duty in this regard is difficult to understand. Either there is a God or there is not a God. Either he expects us to render an accounting of our stewardship or he does not expect it. Either there is a hereafter or there is not a hereafter. Either we need the saving grace in Jesus Christ or we do not need it. Make your choice. Where have you arrived? If you are not a believer, then stewardship is idle prattle. If on the other hand you hold with the Lutheran Church and its confessed doctrine of creed, then you are vitally concerned with stewardship.

You cannot on the one hand really and truly acknowledge yourself as a follower of Jesus Christ and at the same time ask someone else to do your labors in the vineyard. There are a lot of church-going people who believe that they are Christians, who when it comes to using their treasures and talents, are inclined in the vernacular of the street "to let George do it." Those two conditions are not reconcilable. When there is real faith and not a generous hand, then there is a lack of understanding of the responsibility of stewardship.

If a man does not believe that God has had anything to do with his success and earthly accumulations, then such a one is not yet a true Christian. He has as yet not fully recognized his relationship toward his God and Saviour. Knowing that out of the generous hand of God comes all that we are, have, and hope to be, generates the love which actuates a man to the proper kind of stewardship.

What shall I give? When the subject of stewardship is discussed the question arises, "What should I give?" The answer to this is "you should give all that you can afford to give." In the Old Testament, tithing was the law. Giving one-tenth of the income was the law of the Old Covenant. In the New Testament we have no such prescription. Some men give all that they have, they give their whole life to God.

How much shall I give? Answer, "How much do I love God?" The Christian giving of the New Covenant is a reciprocal love toward Jesus for all that He has done for me. He has left that to each Christian to decide for himself, but with this admonition, "As the Lord has prospered you."

The cheapest thing we have today is our religion. There is hardly a hobby, certainly not a habit, which does not cost us far more than our church connection. All too frequently the church

What Is Money?

Of course, money is only one factor in our stewardship. No man can cover the whole of his stewardship in the columns of his cash-book or his ledger. Much of our stewardship has to do with the common duties of life, in our business, in our homes, among our friends, in the various relationships towards our fellowmen. It consists in a large measure of service and influence and prayer. It embraces our whole general conduct. But money is a factor and an important one. It possesses extraordinary power for weal or woe. It is a dangerous factor, for "the love of money is the root of all evil"; yet, rightly used, it may be an instrument of great good, and most of all in the molding and shaping of the man who handles it.

Money is a measure of value; it serves to measure things. But money not only measures things but it affords a measure of those who handle it. Money measures a man. It is a measure of his time. It is a measure of his skill or talent. And the making and spending of money reacts upon the man. It leaves its mark upon him. It may spoil and possess him and finally ruin him. If money be not kept in the place of a servant it will become the master. Money talks: it expresses what its possessors actually are. Listen to the conversation in a railroad train—"stocks," "bonds," "shares," "dollars" "acres," "crops," "dividends," "house," and the like. These words have a metallic ring and give evidence of the dominating thoughts and tendencies of the average man. Yes, money talks.

Money may be part of myself. It is coined personality. The laborer who gets $4.00 a day puts $4.00 worth of muscle, of physical effort, into his pocket, or $4.00 worth of himself. When a clerk gets $30.00 a week he puts $30.00 of himself in his pocket on pay-day. The merchant with a higher brain power, a higher grade of intelligence, has a greater worth in dollars and cents. Whatever we are or whatever we do, we are getting the result of our labor in the shape of cash. The point is this: When you get money into your pocket, it is not merely silver and gold, but is something human, something with power, because it represents power expended. The proper expenditure of this power is outlined by God. We are His, our powers are His, there is nothing we have or are that we have not received from Him, and for the use of which we are responsible to Him. And because money is such a dangerous element for man and so often ruins his character and his soul, the Bible is full of warnings as to its acquisition and use.

Money and the Church

God has made the expenditure of money a test of Christian character. He has chosen human beings as instruments for the spreading of divine truth. Here is where our partnership comes in practically. He blesses us that we might now become blessings to others. Thus, the possession of money immediately becomes a grave responsibility. It may, according to God's direction, be used for our own needs, but a certain proportion is to be devoted to the needs of others, particularly to the spiritual needs which God desires to alleviate through His Church. This giving to the cause of the Lord is the acid test of Christian character. It is motivated by gratitude to God as the great Giver. He is indeed the constant Giver to us. "He Himself giveth to all life, and breath and all things." (Acts 17:25). "He gave you from heaven rains and fruitful seasons, filling your hearts with food and gladness." (Acts 14:17). "It is He that giveth thee power to get wealth." (Deut. 8:18). "God so loved the world that He gave His only begotten Son." (John 3:16). "And He spared not His own Son, but delivered Him up for us all, how shall He not also with Him freely give us all things?" (Rom. 8:32). The verse in John 3:16 gives us the divine standard of true giving. The motive is *love*. "God so *loved* the world." The test is its *cost*. "He gave His *only begotten Son*." The scope is the *world*. "For God so loved the *world*." The end and outcome of all true giving is *Life*. "That whosoever believeth in Him should have *everlasting life*." That is why God expects *cheerful* giving and *liberal* giving. It is to be an evidence of our love and gratitude.

205

A Three-Point Program for Spiritual, Physical and Financial Success

WHEN we go out on the every-member canvass to meet the budget, we usually take for granted the personal devotion and consecration of the individual. We likewise take for granted that the individual will do his share of church work. Consequently, we look to each member only for his pledge of money.

The program herewith outlined takes none of these for granted, but brings to our individual members a specific opportunity for growth in grace under the guidance of this program.

Where this program is adopted, the method outlined in the Every-Member Canvass (likewise printed in this edition of the AMERICAN LUTHERAN) is used. The only change is that the following program is included as part of the booklet containing the budget —which merely becomes section three in that booklet.

These booklets are to be in the hands of each member—one copy for each member—about one week before the every-member canvass is to take place, to give ample time for the individual to fill out the questions.

These booklets properly filled out —or at least the pages in question— are then collected by the canvasser in his rounds for pledges of money.

The Program—Introduction

A church which wants to carry out the ideals of Christ to become a true spiritual force in a community needs something more than merely a large group of people to attend church.

Nothing of value is gained without *sacrifice*. The logical sacrifices of a Christian are:

The Sacrifice of Self

The Sacrifice of Service

The Sacrifice of Substance
(Money and Goods)

It is important to your church to know that it can count on you to make this three-fold sacrifice. For that purpose this pledge list is presented to you so that you can check the things which you will want to do to make your church of real value to yourself and others.

Instructions: Check those items by placing (X) in the ( ) marks which *you* will want to do.

1. The Sacrifice of Self

As visible evidence of my faith in the God who created me; in Christ, my Lord, who redeemed me; and in the Holy Ghost, who has given me the power to believe, I shall:

( ) Attend public worship regularly

( ) Bring others to worship with me

( ) Give the Pastor or the Sunday School Superintendent the name and address of any child who is not enrolled in any Sunday School.

2. The Sacrifice of Service

I likewise pledge to give some of my free time to my Lord through the various fields of activity which I have checked:

(a) ( ) Office work. (State kind which you can do.......................)

(b) ( ) Music. (State whether choir, instrumental......................)

(c) ( ) Visiting. (State whether your preference is among the sick and shut-ins; Sunday School absentees; prospects to attend our church; or service on official every-member canvasses ....)

(d) Women's Work

( ) Sewing

( ) Other charity work

( ) Cooking

( ) Wait on tables at any function

( ) Will care for a baby if its mother is sick

( ) Will help with the housework if anyone needs emergency help

( ) Will take part in the official program of the Women's Group

( ) Will serve as a Sunday School teacher, if I am able

( ) The thing I like to do most is

....

(e) Men's Work

( ) I am handy as a carpenter, painter, ...

( ) I am willing to serve on any committee on which I might be of service. I promise to finish any job I begin

( ) Ushering, if there is need for me

( ) Outdoor work

( ) I will take part in the official Men's Club Program

( ) The thing I like to do best is

....

(f) Young People's Work

( ) I am willing to serve where you think I will best fit

( ) I will be willing to take part in the official Young People's Program

( ) I shall be glad to volunteer as a Sunday School teacher

( ) The thing I like to do best is

....

3. The Sacrifice of Substance (Money and Goods)

( ) Knowing that the church needs money to carry on its physical and spiritual work, I shall give regularly each week, a portion of what I have, as God has prospered me. The exact amount I will declare to the member of the every-member canvass committee when he visits me.

Fill in your name.............................

Address ....

Stewardship

gets the nickels and dimes, whilst gas and oil, theatres and movies, the superfluities and relaxations of life, get the lion's share without a murmur. *Why Should This Be True?*

Why should Lutheran Christians with God's revealed truths preached to them, unadulterated Sunday for Sunday, be less responsive than many who receive only the husks. When the Bible says "Ye are the light of the world," it does not mean that we should be the light payers. It means we should be leaders and to be leaders we should recognize our responsibilities toward our church in a financial way.

Your religion gives you your greatest comfort. It reveals to you the saving grace through Jesus Christ. *It Is Over All.* If this be not true, then there is nothing in religion. Should we then give niggardly to that which we recognize as *Our All* while the passing fancies and trivialities of life are to and do take our major considerations and our larger contributions. No, certainly not. Let everyone take account of his condition. Let us all resolve to study this matter of stewardship.

Let us analyze ourselves, and put this most important matter on a basis which it deserves. Resolve that we will form a new habit, and regularly lay aside that which is God's and apply it to the work of His kingdom. No one ever blamed a pauper as the result of his gifts to God and to his charities.

"As God has prospered you."

The Stewardship of Life

PAUL LINDEMANN

Preface

THE term "stewardship" has been prevalent in Lutheran circles during recent years, but in very many cases the word is being used in its narrower sense, as applying only to the stewardship regarding our monetary possessions. The Scriptures, however, make a much wider application of the term than this. The Biblical conception of stewardship involves all of life. Our time, our physical and mental faculties, our friends, our social contacts; as a matter of fact, it lays claim upon our whole being. Unless this wider sense of stewardship is understood, the application of stewardship in its narrower sense as pertaining to money will never be properly realized or applied.

The following brief studies on stewardship are offered to our people to be used as a part of an educational campaign to create amongst our people, and particularly among the young, a recognition of the general stewardship principle. The material offered may be used as the basis for a series of lectures or it may form the subject matter for study in Bible classes or church organizations. The American Lutheran desires to stimulate a more aggressive spirit of church interest and activity, and for the awakening and maintenance of such a spirit a vivid realization of the principles of the stewardship of life is necessary.

I.

THE SCOPE AND SOURCE OF STEWARDSHIP

Genesis of the word "Stewardship"

The word "stewardship" may probably be traced back to the Anglo Saxon "stigweard" or "stiweard," from "stig" (a sty, or pen, for cattle) and "weard" (a guard). The word apparently has a humble and unpromising origin and yet the position indicated was even in oldest times one of definite responsibilities. These responsibilities became more significant as time went on, especially in old England, where the steward finally became the most valuable and trusted helper, "the chief officer of the manor, who on behalf of his lord transacted its legal business." The first of the great officers of state in England is that of the "Lord High Steward." The Hebrew word "Sar," commonly rendered "prince" in the English Bible really stands for an honored steward, one who manages or superintends the household of another. Eliezer (Gen. 15:2 and Gen. 24) was to Abraham "the elder of his house that ruled over all that he had," "having all goodly things of his master's in his hands." In Titus 1:7 Paul tells us that "The bishop shall be blameless as God's steward." Peter (1 Peter 4:10) thinks of all disciples as "good stewards" who have at their disposal "the manifold graces of God." In Jesus' parable (Luke 16) "the unjust steward" had been completely entrusted with his lord's affairs. Dr. Harvey Reeves Calkins says, "A steward is the loyal partner and trusted representative of another. Stewardship is alive with personal meanings. The word comes out of the vivid life of the orient. There is color in it, and the glow of living things." "A steward may be a servant, but only in a high and exalted sense." The word "steward" is the best word to designate our relationship to God. Other words are used, such as "partner," "employe," "manager," "agent," "superintendent," "director," "executor," "trustee," but the word "steward" is most definitely significant of God's connection with and His expectations of us. A steward is absolutely trusted with his master's property, plans and reputation. He is trusted when his master's back is turned, when he is absent, when he cannot trace the action. He is trusted with the interests, safety and welfare of his fellow-servants. He is trusted to carry on confidential and diplomatic affairs of high impotance. The position calls for integrity, initiative, independence, energy and loyalty.

The position does not imply a sacrifice, does not entail any burdens. It indicates a position which is exalted and to which we must measure up. It signifies a privilege to be welcomed, an honor, a desirable and sacred trust.

No Recognition of Stewardship without Recognition of God's Ownership

God is the absolute owner of everything by right of creation. "The earth is the Lord's and the fullness thereof." (Ps. 24:1) God says, "Every beast of the forest is mine"—the cattle, the birds. (Ps. 50:10-12) "The silver is mine and the gold." (Hag. 2:8) "All souls are mine." (Ez. 18:4) The complete ownership of God by right of creation and preservation is generally granted in Christian circles.

Man as Steward of the Heavenly Owner's Goods

(Read Ps. 8:3-9) "No man liveth to himself." "Whether we live or die we are the Lord's." Our very life is a trust. To have anything is to owe, not to own. If we admit that God is our Maker, our common Father, for all are brethren, then our stewardship obligations involve all human values and contacts. We have been made stewards of our body, our mentality, our talents, our days and hours and years, our temperament and influence, our friends, strangers, even our enemies, our accumulations and possessions, all our spiritual resources, and since we are stewards of these things we shall be held responsible for them.

Israel was never allowed to forget that God was the Owner

Our present conception and laws of property show distinct signs of pagan origin. They are based upon the conceptions of the Roman law, where possession meant ownership and might meant right. God told the Jews, however, "The land shall not be sold forever, for the land is mine. I am the Lord your God." Every year the people were required to set apart as an acknowledgment of divine ownership, a portion of their increase, a tenth, for the support of one of their tribes whose duty it was to instruct the people and maintain the worship of Jehovah.

Again they were required to tithe their annual increase in order to provide the annual expense of certain great religious and social festivals.

They were obliged to take care of the poor and unfortunate.

Every third year a tithe of the crops was set apart for the poor, and every seventh year (when the land "rested") the poor were permitted to gather the natural produce of the fallow ground, together with the grapes and olives.

In the fiftieth year, the year of jubilee, liberty was proclaimed throughout all the land, unto all the inhabitants, in order that every man of every generation might have at least one complete opportunity to secure the blessings of prosperity. Every debtor was discharged of his debt and every bondman returned unto his own family.

The corners of the fields and the gleanings of the harvest were always to be left for the poor. In years of distress and famine the worship of Jehovah was an insult unless the poor had first received special consideration. In such a striking and practical manner was this ancient people taught the meaning of ownership and the duties of possession.

Property and the Early Church

The book of Acts tells us of the early Christians that "Not one of them said aught of the things which he possessed was his own." This was not communism. There was no compulsion in this arrangement, neither was there any general conversion of possessions and goods into money for the purpose of general distribution. But only "as every man had need." The arrangement was not a wild experiment of misguided enthusiasts. It was a stupendous manifestation of a proper conception of stewardship.

Sources of our Stewardship

We New Testament Christians are the property of God not only by the right of creation, but also by right of accomplished redemption. The redemptive work of Jesus Christ has made us

The Stewardship of Life

peculiarly God's own. "Ye are bought with a price." "Ye are not your own." Jesus indicates the proper incentive for all our life in His question, "Wist ye not that I must be about my Father's business?" Unless we, the redeemed children of God, are with all our life and all our facilities and all our possessions about our Father's business, our life is being mislived. We must be able to join our voice in Jesus' statement, "My Father worketh even until now, and I work."

God's Great World Scheme

The world has no other purpose or excuse for existence except to be the scene for the carrying out of God's great plan of grace. The world stands and continues because "God would have all men to be saved and come unto the knowledge of the truth." Our life is misapplied and misdirected unless we find and occupy our definite place in this world scheme of our Lord. The filling of this place is the real purpose of our life. We are to work out our own salvation with fear and trembling and then we are to yield ourselves as instruments of God for the salvation of others and the building of God's kingdom. No independence of God is possible. As servants of Jesus Christ we have a commission of ministration just as did our Lord, who said, "The son of man came not to be ministered unto but to minister." Unless this complete and general stewardship of all our life is recognized, our life is bound to be aimless. We must yield ourselves as instruments in order that God's object may be fulfilled: "They shall come from the east and west, north and south, and shall sit down in the kingdom of God."

The Motive

The motive of consecrated stewardship service is not compulsion but love. Our love of God and the consequent love of our fellowmen is kindled at the fires of God's love for man. Jesus gave up His life for His friends. We are the beneficiaries of His glorious work of salvation. He has won us and bought us at a tremendous price. Our love for Him must now lay claim to our complete life. Thus stewardship can never be self-calculating. Jesus said of Himself, "I came to do the will of my Father and to finish His work." We have no other purpose in life but to do the will of our Father and to finish the work which according to His divine guidance we are called upon to do. There is not a single phase of life in which we are not constrained to ask of our Redeemer, "What wouldst Thou have me to do?" Our rule of life must be, "Whatsoever He saith unto you, do it."

II. THE PHYSICAL LIFE

Our Bodies a Trust

ST. PAUL admonishes us, "I beseech you therefore, brethren, by the mercies of God, that ye present your bodies a living sacrifice, holy, acceptable unto God, which is your reasonable service." (Rom. 12:1). Again he says, "Know ye not that ye are the temple of God, and that the Spirit of God dwelleth in you? If any man defile the temple of God, him shall God destroy; for the temple of God is holy, which temple ye are." (1 Cor. 3:16,17). The same apostle exclaims, "What? know ye not that your body is the temple of the Holy Ghost which is in you, which ye have of God, and ye are not your own? For ye are bought with a price: therefore glorify God in your body and in your spirit, which are God's." (1 Cor. 6:19,20). There was a time when the human body was regarded as an unfortunate and troublesome encumbrance to the soul. Some misguided fanatics looked upon it as a necessary evil of this earthly life and as a moral weight, whose nature was constantly to submerge and destroy the spirit. Men spent much time in keeping the body under. Good men struggled against it, and the better the man the more fiercely he fought. He punished his body, abused his body with lashings and fastings, believing that by the castigation of the body he would be furthering the health of the spirit. Today we properly think of the body as one of God's most priceless gifts.

The Body is the Medium of the Soul

The body is the organ of all our human activities. Our mind has no means of communicating with the world except through the body. Without the eye there is no light, no vision, no beauty. Without the ear the world of harmony round about us would be silent. Without these senses and those of touch, taste and smell the presence of any object would be unknown. The body is therefore an important factor in our life.

Stewardship of the Body

Our body, with its various faculties, is part of the capital which by our God has been placed in our hands for investment. God expects us to make the most of it, to protect, preserve, develop and use it. He expects us to produce returns on the capital for the benefit of ourselves, our fellowmen and our divine mission. Our bodies are not our own to use as we please. We are sinning against God's divine intention when the body is pampered, indulged, mistreated, neglected, overworked, or destroyed. Our body belongs to God as part of His creation. It is in every sense a miracle of His divine production and it is to be held by us in trust for God's wise purposes.

Interaction

Our body is not only the instrument of physical achievement but it measurably conditions even our mental processes as well as our moral character and our spiritual experiences. There is an interrelation between our physical and our mental life, and the two functions are interdependent. The shape of a skull in a measure determines at least the mental powers and moral capacities of a man. A physical disarrangement, such as abnormal pressure on the brain, a sharp blow upon the head, a tumor, a bullet wound, may induce a marked intellectual impairment and may be responsible for a condition of melancholia or insanity. It is a generally recognized medical principle that mental incapacity and moral delinquency may often have physical causes. Criminal tendencies may be the result of disease or accident.

Care and Preservation of the Body Important

Health and vigor are very important factors in the battle of life. A disregard of the needs of the body may prove a severe handicap in the attainment of our ambitions and even in the performance of our common duties. The handicap of missing or wasted vitality is beyond estimate. The extended service of God or the intensive labors in the vineyard call for bodily vigor accompanied by sound mentality. The prodigious labors of the apostle Paul must have called for a terrific expenditure of physical vigor. This is true of all missionary leaders. It is said that David Livingstone had a very wiry body. But even if we have physical handicaps we nevertheless are stewards of these diminished powers. As a matter of fact, some of the finest achievements in the kingdom of God have been wrought in spite of ill health. Paul refers to the "thorn in the flesh." Livingstone had a crushed arm. Milton kept on laboring in spite of his sightless eyes.

Our Duty Towards Our Bodies

The duty of seeking to keep healthful is divinely imposed. No doubt the restrictions placed upon the diet of the Jews in the Old Testament were not only of symbolic and religious significance, but were at the same time commonsense health laws. In order to keep our bodies fit the amount and character of our food must receive our watchful attention. The same care must be exercised regarding sleep. No human being has the right to deprive himself of the refreshment which sleep affords. Inordinate sociability undermines health. Furthermore, it is not too bold a statement to claim that exercise is a Christian duty and not merely a matter of taste. Recreation is a human requirement. "All work and no play makes Jack a dull boy." Now the Christian in order to keep his body fit for God will refrain from contracting

The Stewardship of Life

pernicious habits and will be careful in the selection of his companions. Anything and anybody that would drag us down from our lofty Christian ideals must be avoided. The Christian will shun base sensual thoughts, words, and images. He will cultivate the habits of temperance, chastity and self-control. The injunctions of the sixth commandment are especially applicable right at this point. Not only is our body a temple of the Holy Ghost, but it is the actual tool of God for the carrying out of His designs.

Our Accountability to Human Society

"None of us liveth to himself, and no man dieth to himself." We are "members, one of another." Our obligation to the past and to the present are beyond computation. We shape the future. Our physical, mental and moral traits are passed on. There is a perpetuation of our personal qualities no matter whether we believe in heredity or not. We have a very solemn duty to posterity. We must bequeath to our children and children's children healthy bodies, healthy minds, healthy ideals, healthy character.

The watchfulness over our physical welfare is incumbent particularly upon youth in order that they might be spared the vain after-regrets with which so many of their elders are afflicted. They have the duty of the fullest development of their physical powers. This preservation and development must not be actuated by selfish reasons, but by the desire to be of the highest possible service to God. Our health comes from God. It is to be consecrated to His service. Otherwise it is bound to be a snare. Thus also our physical powers are a vital part of our Christian stewardship.

III. THE MENTAL LIFE

THE mental powers of man are, because of the perversion of the human heart, naturally evil. Paul ascribes it to the grace of God that a man is enabled "to think soberly." Sound thinking is to be patterned after Christ. Paul says, "Let this mind be in you, which was in Christ Jesus." (Phil. 2:5). He describes a Christian as "Casting down imaginations, and every high thing that exalteth itself against the knowledge of God, and bringing into captivity every thought to the obedience of Christ." (2 Cor. 10:5). At this point we might read with special profit the parable of the talents as we find it in Matthew 25:15-19. A thinking mind is the point of distinction between man and the animals. In many respects animals are physically superior to man. The elephant is larger, the horse is stronger, the bird is swifter, the monkey is more agile, the tortoise longer-lived. In all but mental equipment man is surpassed by a score of other creatures. But mind has placed man so far above them all that he thinks of them only in terms of personal convenience. They are of interest to him only as they interfere with his more ambitious plans or contribute to his welfare. Man is nature's masterpiece. He is the lord of creation. All the creature world was made subject unto him. The other creatures were made for his convenience. His supremacy is entirely that of the mind.

The Mind as a Trust

Our mind is one of the most sacred items of stewardship with which we have been entrusted. For its use and its development we are again accountable to God. It is very important to consider by what means we may best protect, most fully develop, and most wisely direct the mind in order that our high stewardship may be faithfully discharged. God commands us, "Thou shalt love the Lord thy God with all thy mind."

Our Mind Must Grow

The normal, healthy mind should be a growing mind, and God has so gifted it that it may continue to grow. In this it differs from the body. The body reaches its full size early in life. The mind keeps on growing and developing and should continue to do so as long as we live. But just like the body, the mind must be fed. The food of the mind is thought. No one has the right to permit his mind to lie fallow. The duty of mind training is again a divine commission. God wants the human being to develop to the greatest degree of usefulness, and this development is primarily the development of the mind. A trained mind has great advantages over the untrained mind. It is certainly not improper that the human being have certain intellectual ambitions which are based upon personal reasons. But these personal reasons must not be supreme. We are to develop our mind for greater service, since service is the object of our living. Our talents have been entrusted to us for investment. It is for this reason that the Church has ever encouraged education. The Lutheran Church has fostered it throughout its history and it is today one of its chief concerns.

Reading

Our mind is furthered or retarded in its development by the things we take into it, by the books, papers and magazines we read, by the lessons we learn, by the stories we hear, by the conversations to which we listen, by the sermons, lectures, concerts, pictures, landscapes, statues, fields and forests; in fact, by everything which enters as a new and stimulating experience into our lives. All this is food for the mind. In the care of our bodies we refrain from taking poisonous food. We also refrain, if we are wise, from overstimulation. A man who overeats physically may be troubled with indigestion. There is something like mental indigestion due to the unwise choice of mental food.

Exercise

There is a tendency to feed the mind haphazardly, although perhaps pleasurably, without any intellectual exertion. The lurid magazines of the day are a case in point. Frothy novels, tabloid newspapers, are not conducive to true mental exercise. They touch only the high spots, and usually the high spots of sensuality. Most Americans are inclined to let others think for them. Edison says, "What America needs is more solid thinking." The mind must not only read but analyze. The mind must not only listen but ask why. Problems must be attacked and solved. Lessons must be mastered. Mental laziness must be avoided. We must develop a dread of superficiality. The reading of magazines constitutes a waste of mental energy if they only entertain. For all who desire to progress mentally a course of *systematic reading* is suggested. It is good to form the habit to read something worth while every day, if it be only a page or two. Increasing mental vigor begets mental independence and self-confidence. Our minds must not be an undisciplined power over which we have no control. One of the great requirements for successful work in the Church is sound thinking and the power of independent decision. For this reason the mind must be protected from poisonous, debilitating and disintegrating forces. There must be a thorough examination of the mental food which the market offers. The Christian should learn to avoid books that waste the hours without conveying thought. Books and articles that teach untruth, that with more or less subtlety suggest unworthy ideals. The child of God will be careful of what kind of songs he sings, what kind of stories he reads, what kind of pictures he sees, what kind of places he visits, what kind of pleasures he indulges in, what kind of companionships he forms. He will seek with a growing power of discrimination to eliminate as a mental influence everything that weakens the will or stimulates impure and unhealthful emotions.

A Sound Mind Can Serve Best

A healthy, well-stocked, thoroughly disciplined mind is ready for constructive service of God. It is rich in potentialities. It has almost unlimited possibilities for moral and spiritual helpfulness. An untrained and undisciplined mind lacks the power of concentration and is constantly inclined to run off into byways, into harmful paths, and to accept counterfeit products for

The Stewardship of Life

reality, and to even prefer the poisonous to the wholesome. A thinking mind is trained in its judgment, whereas the untrained mind is untrustworthy in its judgment. Furthermore, the untrained mind is prone to lack stability and in the battle of life is apt to stagnate, to dwarf and shrivel. It permits all sorts of weeds to grow up in its mental garden, and the weeds are apt to overgrow it completely.

Marvelous attainments are possible to the human mind. But these attainments are so very often placed in the service of sin whereas they should be placed in the service of God. All the mind's powers should be at God's disposal. As a matter of fact, this service of God should be the very purpose for which the mind is being trained and developed. The glorious mental distractions and the previous emotions which are at our disposal through the cultivation of the mind are indeed part of the stewardship with which we have been entrusted. The glories of music and art and literature are gifts of God and should be employed to His glory. Wherever they are utilized for merely personal aggrandizement they become abased and the divine Giver is dishonored. Any talents which we may develop along these lines belong to God.

Mental Gifts and the Church

It is a sad fact that very often the best mental talents are weaned away from the Church. It seems that there is a tendency to become selfish and worldly-minded and conceited as the mind is developed. The devil is very active in developing amongst the educated classes an intellectual conceit which holds the religion of the cross in contempt. The Church needs, however, the best minds of the human race for its tremendous and glorious tasks. Let every educated person remember that his sharpened faculties are part of the stewardship for which he must give an accounting before the judgment throne of God.

IV. SOCIAL RELATIONS

WE have very distinct duties towards our fellowmen. Paul says, "I am debtor both to the Greeks and to the barbarians, both to the wise and to the unwise." (Rom. 1:14). He gives very definite advice regarding our relationship towards our fellowmen in the 12th chapter of his letter to the Romans, verses 10 to 21. Jesus beings out the Christian's duty towards his fellowman in the wonderful parable of the Good Samaritan. (Luke 10:29-37).

Man's Social Nature

The interrelationship of man to his fellowmen is a divine arrangement. At the very outset of human history God gave the command to the first human beings, "Be fruitful and multiply." It is generally true of men what God says of Adam, "It is not good that man should be alone." In His arrangement of the universe we read that "God setteth the solitary in families." The word "friend" is a common one in Scriptural language and also on the lips of our Saviour. "There is a friend that sticketh closer than a brother." "I have called you friends." The tendency of human beings to herd together and live together in groups is inborn. A child longs for companions and even as a human being advances in old age he never outgrows the desire to associate with his fellows. The presence of another life is sweet and necessary to our wellbeing. Even the lower animals flock together in a friendly community of life. We speak of swarms of bees, of flocks of birds, of herds of cattle. The human being by nature is a social creature.

Influence of Environment

The individual as he lives upon earth is a composite product of the past and the present. He comes into the world with a natural endowment bestowed upon him through heredity and his ultimate self is fashioned and determined by these hereditary tendencies plus the environment in which he moves. We human

beings every hour of our lives are being molded by the social contacts that we form. These contacts provide the ruling motives and the restraints of life. As we associate with others we are constantly gaining impressions and making them on others. The impatient young person who says "I will live my own life," is stating an impossibility. We cannot live our own lives. We cannot live among others without influencing others and being influenced by others. As a matter of fact, even if we were to isolate ourselves, our very isolation would influence those with whom we have been in contact. The whole spirit of the Word of God makes voluntary isolation wrong. Hermits and recluses are evidently not fulfilling the divine purpose. God has placed us into this world, and in this world of men He assigns to us a very definite place, a definitely appointed sphere of influence. We may therefore properly speak of the stewardship of our social contacts.

These contacts begin in infancy. Every moment of our baby life was stimulated or controlled by others. We were not permitted to grow up wild, but we were compelled to fit ourselves into the plans of others. At the proper time we were given encouragement or were guided by those who had charge of us. There was the necessity for the repression of certain tendencies and impulses. We were trained along a certain program which others had determined. As a matter of fact, self-determination in those years was reduced to its lowest terms.

Then came our school life. Here again we were thrown together with and made dependent upon others. We imbibed new ideas. We were confronted with new inducements. We were restrained with new personalities. We were urged onward with new proddings. Even on the playground we were surrounded with certain incentives and were subject to a certain discipline. Other

social influences were provided by the Sunday School and the Church. As we developed and grew we were placed into new surroundings when we went to college. We formed new friendships. We conceived new ideals. We saw before us new examples and also new temptations. There were groups of new elements providing either a stimulus or calling for self-repression. In our adult age new contacts with others were formed in our daily occupation. We came into the influence of office life, or of the discipline in factory or shop; or we submitted ourselves to the routine of the farm, the store, or the kitchen. Wherever we went there were certain circumstances which told us, "This you must do," or "This you must not do." We have been compelled to conform to certain standards of life even in our speech, in our clothing and in our manners. Our thoughts and our acts are very often influenced by that great force which we indefinitely call "they." The person who would insist on complete independence of all social influences would soon become a social outcast. Custom and convention are the great autocrats of human society. If we are to live with a certain degree of peace and happiness we must mold ourselves to others.

Duties Imposed by Social Contacts

The fact that we live lives that are interwoven with the lives of others naturally imposes upon us certain duties and obligations. We have a very distinct duty not only to the age in which we are living, but to the generations that are to come. Paul says, "I am a debtor—both to the wise and to the foolish." The responsibilities that we have towards society cannot be avoided. Those duties involve in a measure all mankind, even those human beings with whom we have no direct connection. As Christians our duty must be animated by the sentiment of love. This love for our human brethren is a natural result of our love for God. "He that loveth not his brother, whom he hath seen, how can he love God, whom he hath not seen?" In his adaptation to the demands of men upon him Paul says, "I have become all things to all men that I may by all means save some."

Motives

The motives that animate us in our contacts with others may not be merely curiosity, pleasure, or material gain. The social contacts in our time are animated by a ruthless cold-blooded philosophy. The irreligious philosophy of the day leaves God out of the picture. It is the philosophy of "Every man for himself, and the devil take the hindmost." Actuated only by godless

The Stewardship of Life

sentiments man feels justified in using others for his own selfish purposes. He find himself confronted by every possible situation with the question, "What can I get out of it?" He sizes up his fellowman with the inner query, "Will he be useful to me?" The Christian, however, sees in man a creature of God, saved with him by the precious blood of Christ. He knows that God has the purpose to seek and to save that which is lost, and that our contacts with our fellowmen must carry out this fundamental purpose of God. The Christian feels himself constrained to make his contacts spiritually constructive and helpful to others. He feels that in these contacts he must build God's kingdom. Therefore he seeks instead of avoids human contacts. To him the most interesting textbook in the world is man. He finds that the most absorbing study of mankind is man. He is convinced that the knowledge of men is necessary in order to develop the greatest degree of helpfulness. The men in history who have been helpful to mankind have always been men who really knew men. The English genius Shakespeare shows an astounding knowledge of the human heart. The same may be said of men like Lincoln, Roosevelt, and others. No man, however, ever knew men like Jesus did. We read of him that He "knew what was in man." So the true servant of Jesus Christ must not and cannot withdraw himself from men but must have an unfeigned interest in all men.

Opportunities for Influence

The first and perhaps the most powerful social influence that we can exert is right within the confines of the home. The intimate relationships of the family offer the most glorious opportunity for effectively building the kingdom of God by our influence upon the souls of others. In the vast majority of cases character is formed through home influences. The impressions of the home, the parental example, the ideals formulated in youth, are the powerful forces that mold the individual life. Children are a mighty factor in the stewardship life of parents. The Scriptures are full of admonitions to train the children in the fear and admonition of the Lord. The duties of parents towards children are explicitly outlined. Earnest warnings are issued against the offensive influence which might be exerted upon the tender souls of little ones. The contacts of our family relationships in every case form the most immediate opportunity for the exercise of our stewardship in carrying out the fundamental world purpose of God. Brothers and sisters are mutually stewardship obligations, and so down the line through all the various degrees of blood ties.

Further social contacts are offered man in his daily occupation. He usually does not work alone. He has companions and fellow workers. The Christian employer is to feel that his employes are a stewardship obligation. A salesman may beneficially influence his customers, and vice versa. The Christian must always be about his great work of winning lives for Christ. That is the final objective of his social contacts. He must never forget the personal influence which he is bound to exert. His attitude in any situation must be a living testimony of the great cause that he represents.

This responsibility which we bear is brought out in the Scriptural warnings regarding the watch which we are to place upon our words and our acts. Adults are called upon to exercise special watchfulness over against children, since children are imitative. The Christian is required to exercise those graces and qualities which Christ and His apostles emphasized as the true fruits of faith. There must be in the Christian's conduct a reflection of the Saviour's love. That love naturally creates a constant courtesy and consideration. The Christian will even watch his dress in order that it might not become offensive. He will keep a strict guard over his habits. The arrangement of being compelled to live among others imposes upon us a very stern responsibility. I am indeed my brother's keeper, and the various situations which my contact with him is bound to call forth constitute a very distinct part of my Christian stewardship.

V. THE STEWARDSHIP OF POSSESSIONS

Money

MONEY is a general medium of exchange. It has taken the place of the primitive form of barter and exchange. Money is the expression of the worth of a thing. The great buildings that surround us, the ocean liners that cross the seas, the automobiles and airplanes that transport us from place to place, the radio station which transmits its messages through the air, the suspension bridge that connects two bodies of land, the tunnel which saves us hours of time, the university which contributes to our mental development, the hospital which takes care of our sick, the great churches in which we worship, are all material testimony to the essential importance of money, to the welfare and progress of men. Money has in our day become the standard of measurement of success in life. It is regarded as an index of talent. It is considered the condition for domestic contentment, the goal of personal endeavor, the proof of fitness for survival.

Money a Sacred Trust

Like all things, money is a gift of God. Its possession is a sign of divine confidence. It must be emphasized that its possession is not a sin. We have the stories of good rich men in the Bible, men who were directly enriched by God's blessing. In His teachings Jesus does not make the possession of riches a sin, but He warns against the perils of covetousness, against the danger that lurks in undue love of wealth and an unwarranted trust in material things. This warning is repeatedly echoed by the apostles. Three New Testament authors caution against the peril of "filthy lucre." In some circles there is a spirit prevalent that there is something essentially defiling about money and the expression "tainted money" is used. As a matter of fact, there is nothing like tainted money. There may be tainted hands that presume to use money to which they have no right or to use it for unholy, vicious purposes. But naturally money in itself is an insensate thing and incapable of possessing any moral quality whatsoever. Money in itself is absolutely lifeless and colorless. It displays and reflects the color of that with which it is associated. In the hands of evil men money becomes a powerful instrument of evil. In the hands of good men it acquires infinite possibilities for good.

Origin of Money

Money, or wealth, is a product of a great partnership between God and man. In the form of rich, abundant, raw material it comes forth fresh from the hand of God. in sunshine, showers, waving grainfields, bending orchards, grazing cattle, mines bursting with ore, seas sparkling with pearls, and every conceivable bounty of nature. On this unlimited store of raw material the sweating brains of thinking men and the calloused hands of toiling men set to work. The result by God's direction is wealth. Money is a combination of the generosity of God and the toil of men. Sometimes in the perverted life of a man a third factor enters in and that factor is Satan. But the devil is never a producer of anything useful. He has never produced a dollar, though he has perverted and destroyed the use of many. Only God and man working together have ever produced anything worthy to be dignified as wealth. Money is life minted into tangible form. Money may be called coined personality.

Perils of Money

Money, or wealth, according to God's intention is to be a blessing. It is intended for the beneficial use and the happiness of man. But under misdirection it often becomes poison with which men destroy themselves. This is due to the misuse and abuse of money. It is bound to be a disastrous influence when placed in the devil's service. It becomes a most pernicious power when it is used for the fostering of selfishness. That is why the Scriptures claim that "Love of money is the root of all evil." Again and again the divine admonition comes to us, "Beware of covetousness."

Money represents stewardship in its concretest form. That is why when stewardship is mentioned most people at once think of money. This is a natural reaction. The one possession we have which passes current in every market, which we can with

The Stewardship of Life

the greatest facility trade, accumulate, increase, squander, and convert to a variety of uses, is money. Money is the form of our possessions which can most easily be given to God. It is the medium through which we can most easily express our devotion and acknowledge our obligation.

What does the Stewardship of Money mean?

Since God is the giver and the sustainer of wealth, money belongs to God. Like all our other physical and mental possessions we do not own money. It is part of our stewardship and belongs to God. It is given us for temporary handling, and in the handling of it we must always have in mind the fundamental purpose of God in giving man his gifts. For His great world cause God asks that man set aside a definite proportion for its advancement. In the New Testament He does not definitely designate the proportion which the Christian should directly invest in God's kingdom. That proportion is to be fixed by the means with which we have been provided. But a steward's first consideration is the service of his master, the promotion of his master's interests and true service naturally involves exertion, self-effacement, devotion and sacrifice. The due proportion of the offering cannot be left to the judgment or caprice of the steward. The first consideration of stewardship is mutual agreement. The criterion must not be the individual's inclination. The proper proportion is not what he himself happens to be willing to offer. He must give the proportion of the income which he has full reason to believe will be in accordance with the will of his God. The matter is plainly one of conscience.

The proportion given by the Jews was legally prescribed. The principal passages relating to tithing are found in Leviticus 27:30, Deuteronomy 14:22, Numbers 18:20,21. Read also Lev. 27:30-34, Deut. 14:20-29; Num. 18:20-32. It may be safely asserted that Jesus' gifts amounted to a far larger proportion than the tenth part of His income.

New Testament Giving

Love and gratitude are the sentiments which should prompt our gifts to the cause of our Lord. We are daily recipients of

God's abundant mercy. God "left not himself without witness, in that he did good, and gave use rain from heaven, and fruitful seasons, filling our hearts with food and gladness." (Acts 14:17). We cannot dispose of our temporal possessions by leaving God out of consideration. "For in Him we live, and move and have our being." (Acts 17:28). "Every good gift and every perfect gift is from above and cometh down from the Father of lights." (James 1:17). Jesus brings out the unfailing character of divine provision in the well-known passages found in Matthew 6:19-34 and Luke 12:22-34. The blessed results of free and unselfish devotion of our temporal possessions to the cause of God is brought out in the words of Jesus, "Give, and it shall be given unto you; good measure, pressed down, and shaken together, and running over shall men give into your bosom. For with the same measure that ye mete withal it shall be measured to you again." (Luke 6:38). Paul brings out our dependence on God's grace when he says, "God is able to make all grace abound toward you; that ye, always having all sufficiency in all things, may abound to every good work." (2 Cor. 9:8).

The New Testament gives us a glorious exalted conception of human life. Jesus calls His followers "The light of the world." He says, "Ye are my friends." In reference to our body He says, "Know ye not that your body is a temple of the Holy Ghost?" Peter tells the Christians, "Ye may become partakers of the divine nature." Paul exults that "Whether we live or whether we die, we are the Lord's." We are called "the children of God," "a royal priesthood," "a chosen generation," "the sons of God." Because of the marvelous blessings bestowed upon us we are admonished, "Freely ye have received, freely give." Paul's admonition is directed to the Christian world, "I have showed you all things, how that so labouring ye ought to support the weak, and to remember the words of the Lord Jesus, how he said, It is more blessed to give than to receive." (Acts 20:35).

At another time He says, "Every man according as he purposeth in his heart, so let him give; not grudgingly, or of necessity: for God loveth a cheerful giver." (2 Cor. 9:7). In Cor. 8:9 we read, "For ye know the grace of our Lord Jesus Christ, that, though he was rich, yet for your sakes he became poor, that ye through his poverty might be rich." The ideal relationship between man and his possessions was attained by the Church at Jerusalem of whose members we read, "And the multitude of them that believed were of one heart and of one soul: neither said any of them that ought of the things which he possessed was his own: but they had all things common." (Acts 4:32).

Accountability to God

Man's accountability to God for the use and investment of his money is brought out very forcibly in the parables of the talents and the pounds. (Matt. 25:14-30; Luke 19:11-27).

Our possessions here upon earth are only temporary in character and a strict accounting will be required when the period of our temporary possession terminates. With great earnestness Jesus admonishes the Christians to watchfulness and warns against the preoccupation with merely temporal affairs which would make man unprepared for the sudden summons into the presence of God. Christ delivers a very impressive discourse on the necessity of this watchfulness in Luke 12:35-48. Paul's striking warning to Timothy is always timely. We refer to the warning found in 1 Tim. 6:6-21. The apostle realizes the insidious temptation which lies in the possession and use of money and his solemn words should be frequently read by Christians in these times where money has become the world's idol. In the consideration of the question of the stewardship of possessions we might also profitably read the parable of the unjust steward (Luke 16: 1-13), that of the rich young ruler (Mark 10:17-31), of the rich fool (Luke 12:13-21); also Paul's exhortation to the Corinthians, (1 Cor. 16:2), and the story of Ananias and Sapphira, (Acts 5:1-11).

The question of the stewardship of money is one which needs the most thorough discussion in our Christian circles. There is the most widespread misconception regarding the question. Our whole attitude in the application of our temporal possessions for the needs of God's kingdom requires drastic revision. The fruits of years of mistraining along the lines of giving are being reaped today in Christian circles. The human being seems to be averse to the admission that his money belongs to God and is very unwilling to admit that the prime use of money is the carrying out of the heavenly purpose which God has in mind with the world. It is in the use of money that the whole structure of Christian stewardship in the life of the individual usually falls down.

Christian Stewardship Sentiments

To have is to owe—not to own.

Systematic earning makes an industrious man; wise spending a well-furnished man; thoughtful saving a prepared man; conscientious giving a blessed man.

Unconsecrated wealth in the hands of Christians is one of the greatest hindrances to the progress of the Church.

The Kingdom of God can never be established merely by the raising and expending of money, but money is greatly needed for its world-wide extension.

Jesus Christ teaches that a man's attitude toward God and His Kingdom is revealed by his attitude to the property committed to his trust.—*Missionary Review.*

Stewardship is the recognition and fulfillment of personal privilege and responsibility for the administration of the whole of life —personality, time, talent, influence, material substance, everything—in accordance with the spirit and ideals of Christ.
—*Julius Earl Crawford.*

* * * *

Giving to the Lord's Work

Dr. O. M. Norlie

"IT is more blessed to give than to receive," says the Good Book. Now, many people do not think so. It may be worth while for every one of us to meditate a little while on this question in the light of God's Word. The Bible is our only source and rule of faith and works. It states the principles and practice as to giving better than any other book. What it has to sa yabout giving is given by inspiration of God and is authoritative and profitable (2 Tim. 3:16-17). Only two aspects of the question will be considered—the reasons for giving and the manner of giving.

I. REASONS FOR GIVING

We shall briefly state six Scriptural reasons for giving under the following headings:

1. God's Ownership—Our Stewartship
2. God's Commands—Our Obedience
3. God's Example—Our Imitation
4. God's Work—Our Partnership
5. God's threats—Our Woe
6. God's Promises—Our Weal

I. God's Ownership—Our Stewardship
a. God's Ownership

God is the Creator and Owner of all the land (Lev. 25:23), the silver and gold (Hag. 2:8) the cattle upon a thousand hills (Ps. 50:10), every soul (Ezek. 18:4;1 Cor 6:20). Therefore we sing: "We give Thee but Thine own" (Deut. 8:18; I. Chron. 29:14; Joh. 1:16). If he is Owner, He can demand His property back. Citizens of a country must pay taxes, borrowers must pay interest.

b. Our Stewardship

That everybody must sometime give an account of his stewardship is the sure teaching of Christ in His parable of the Unjust Steward (Luke 16:1-13). Paul has stated the well-known principle, applicable to secular affairs as well as religious life: "It is required in stewards, that a man be found faithful" (I Cor. 4:2). In the light of stewardship it should be a great pleasure to give to the Lord's work.

In the light of stewardship, it makes one sad to think of the ill spent riches of professing Christians—of the needless purchases, the amazing extravagances, the risky speculations, the shameful wastes, the unholy indulgences, of some church members in good standing. A woman, for example, who had spent $20,000 on the draperies of her house alone and was planning on spending several thousand dollars on landscape gardening, fretted about the high cost of living and remarked that they would have to cut their church subscriptions in two this year. The average yearly individual church contribution is less than $5.00. We do not know what this woman contributed, but we can easily imagine that she was not an ideal steward. An ideal steward makes all he can saves all he can, and gives all he can. He takes as little as possible for his own support, and gives as much as possible to God's work.

2. God's Commands—Our Obedience
a. God's Commands

God has commanded His people to give, "Bring ye all the tithes into the storehouse," is the Law of giving in the Old Testament (Ma 1.3:10). "Freely ye have received, freely give," is the Gospel of giving in the New Testament. In both He commands. His commands are not grievous—His yoke is easy, and His burden is light (Matt. 11:30). His commands are wise and good, are right and righteous altogether.

b. Our Obedience

When He commands, we should obey. We have to obey our civil magistrates and do it gladly. It is expedient, and it is right as long as they do not command us to sin. The present income tax calls for the payment of up to 63 per cent of one's income. This tax has to be paid. All taxes have to be paid. If we refuse, our property is seized and sold and our title to it is forfeited.

3. God's Example—Our Imitation
a. God's Example

Giving is a trait of God. He gives every good and perfect gift (Jas. 1:17). He gave us life, and richly and daily provides us with all things to enjoy (1 Tim. 6:17; 1 Cor. 1:5-7; Matt. 6:19-33). He gave His Only-begotten Son (John 3:16). He gives His Holy Spirit (Luke 11.13). The Son gave His life for us that we might be saved. "Tho He was rich, yet for our sakes He became poor, that we through His poverty might be rich" (2 Cor. 8:9). The Holy Spirit is constantly giving Himself to us through the Means of Grace.

b. Our Imitation

We should be imitators of God. Jesus says: "Be ye merciful, even as your Father also is merciful" (Luke 6:36). Peter tells us that "Christ suffered for us, leaving us an Example, that we should follow in His steps" (1 Pet. 2:21). Jesus also points to Himself as an Example to be imitated (John 13:15).

4. God's Work—Our Partnership
a. God's Work

The work of a ruler or a government is urgent and takes precedence over every private enterprise. The Lord is King of Kings and the work of His Kingdom is the one thing needful. It consists in saving the lost and protecting the saved.

b. Our Partnership

The work of the Church is God's work. The Almighty wants men to be laborers in His vineyard (Matt. 20: 1-16), ambassadors in Christ's stead (2 Cor. 5:20). They are His stewards and servants, but are regarded by Him as friends and sons (John 15:14-15; Gal. 4:7). In 1 John 1:3 we are told that our partnership, or "fellowship, is with the Father, and with His Son Jesus Christ." In the business world it sometimes happens that some industrious and honest servant gets a share in the business, becomes a partner of his employer. In the Church God makes the humblest servant His child and partner, a co-worker and a co-heir with Christ.

5. God's Threats—Our Woe
a. God's Threats

God s gracious commands were given to be obeyed. They contain a threat either expressed or implied (Gen. 2:17; Ex. 20:5; Lev. 26:14:39).

b. Our Woe

These threats are not idle words. They mean woe to us and our posterity if we disobey. In Adam's fall we sinned all. Through the neglect of bountiful giving a billion people now living are still sitting in spiritual darkness. At least one person dies every second who has never heard of the Savor. Our expenses for war and wastes are sufficient to evangelize the whole world many, many, many times. The Jews returned from the Babylonian Captivity, but neglected to build the house of the Lord. They were very busy working in the field and the market. Making money? Yes, but, as Haggai puts it: "Putting it into a bag of holes" (Hag. 1:6). Later on, after the Temple had been restored, they refused to give their tithes. Then grasshoppers and drought and hard times resulted. Malachi states the situation thus: "Ye are cursed with a curse; for ye have robbed God" (Mal. 3:8-9).

6. GOD'S PROMISES—OUR WEAL
a. God's Promises

God has made many promises. Some one has counted over 20,000 of them in the Bible. They are all yea and amen in Christ Jesus (2 Cor. 1:20). They include also blessings resulting from obedience in giving. Says Malachi: "Bring ye all the tithes . . . and prove Me now herewith, saith the Lord of hosts, if I will not open the windows of heaven, and pour you out a blessing, that there shall not be room enough to receive it" (Mal. 3:10; Prov. 3:10). Says Jesus: "Give, and it shall be given unto you; good measure, pressed down, and shaken together, and running over, shall men give into your bosom" (Luke 6:38; 2 Cor. 9:6).

b. Our Weal

Christianity has come about by giving. If there had been more giving, the Christian Church would now have reached farther. Christian nations are the richest and most enlightened. These very blessings, if not passed along, may become a woe instead of a weal. "They that be rich," says Paul, "fall into a temptation and a snare" (I Tim. 6:9-10). The Church is exposed to all the dangers that wealth can bring—self-sufficiency, worldliness, covetousness, and miserliness, love of pleasure and luxury, stagnation. Liberal giving, as stated before, becomes a safeguard against these many woes. Liberal giving does not diminish one's possession. If we subtract from our income and give to the Lord's work. He will add to our weal and our wealth, our pleasure and our profit. If we divide with the Lord, He will multiply for us. This was David's observation (Ps. 37:25). This was the widow of Sarepta's experience (1 Kings 17:16). The little fountain gave up its fresh water to the streamlet, watering the fields and satisfying the thirst of man and beast. The slough kept its waters and made the neighborhood sick with malarial fevers until dried up by a providential wind.

"A man there was, though some did count him mad,
The more he gave away, the more he had."

II. MANNER OF GIVING

The Church employs many methods of raising money. Some of them, such as charity balls, card parties and lotteries, are wicked and wrong. They are a disgrace, while right giving is a grace 2 Cor. 8:7). The best that can be said about some of the other methods is, that they are weak and wasteful, inadequate and unbiblical. In the following an attempt is made to outline the right method and attitude in giving. The argument is grouped under four points, corresponding roughly to the intellectual, emotional, volitional, and moral-religious sides of man. These points are:

1. Proportioning—Accounting
2. Lovingly—Gladly
3. Freely—Regularly
4. Conscientiously—Believingly

I. PROPORTIONING AND ACCOUNTING
a. Proportioning

By Proportioning is meant the setting apart regularly of a definite proportion of one's income for the Lord's work. What per cent this separated portion shall be, is, to a considerable extent, a personal question in the Christian Church. That it should be according to one's ability is evident from such passages as 1 Cor. 16:2: "Upon the first day of the week, let everyone of you lay by him in store, as God hath prospered him." In view of the urgent reasons for giving outlined above, the Lord's portion should be as large as possible whereas now it is too often made as small as possible Compare, if you please, the liberality of one of the "boys" in a saloon and at a church collection. A young man regrettingly put 5 cents into the contri-

bution basket and then after service gladly paid 39 cents for soda and over $1 for cigars. We should make all we can, save all we can, and give all we can.

There is no positive command, no legal requirement, in the New Testament as to how much to give. Nevertheless, a Bible student may find in the New Testament, as well as in the Old much guidance on this vexed question. In the Old Testament the Jews were required to set apart as a minimum one tribe out of twelve for the Lord's work, one day out of seven, and one tenth of the income. This tenth is known as the tithe (Lev 27:20; Deut. 14:22; 2 Chron. 31:5-6; Neh. 10:29-37; Mal 3:7-12). In Matt. 23:23 Jesus commanded the paying of the tithe while rebuking the hypocritical spirit of the Pharisees. Men ought to do at least as much under the Gospel as the Jews did under the Law. The Christians have received more from the Lord than did the Jews, they have a larger field and a more urgent program. They should therefore give more. Jesus has said: "For unto whomsoever much is given, of him shall be much required; and to whom men have committed much, of him they will ask the more" (Luke 12:48). Zaccheus gave half of his possessions. The early Christians gave all. Multitudes of Christians down through the centuries have proved the Lord by freely setting aside a tenth or some larger portion of their income for His work. They have found that it is not harder for them to give a tenth than it was to the Jews. They believe that it is God's financial plan, and know that it is businesslike, safe, sure, adequate, and economical. There is nothing legalistic about it, for they chose of their own free will to give the tenth or more. They hold that there is far more bondage under the old hit-and-miss systems, that there are laws that make men free, and that this is one of them. They feel sure that if men everywhere would come with the tithes, the financial problem of the Church would not cause much work and worry, as it does now. Strong, in his book, "Our Country," estimates that the church members in America are giving only 1-16 of 1 per cent to the Lord's work. McConaughy, in his book, "Money the Acid Test," relates that in one church 11 per cent of the members gave 82 per cent of the contributions, but these most generous givers were also proportionate givers. Proportioning is a sensible, Biblical method of giving.

b. Accounting

Proportioning implies accounting. We are stewards and shall have to render an account of our stewardship both to Caesar and to God (Matt. 22:21; Luke 16:2; Rev. 20:12). We have to keep account with our grocer and government and why not also with God? In keeping accounts we have to face the facts, we discover what amounts are necessary for living expenses, for self-improvement, for pleasure, for the Lord's work. We learn to be more saving and systematic. We have a chance to plan as to how to distribute our gifts, to what objects we shall give. We get to realize more and more that we are accountable for not only the separated portion—the first fruits—but also the rest—what is spent and what is saved—is to be treated as no less a sacred trust.

2. LOVINGLY AND GLADLY
a. Lovingly

God has given much and continues to give much, because He loves much. Jesus ate at the house of Simon, a Pharisee. A woman came and anointed His feet with oil. This woman was praised for loving much. Simon was rebuked for loving little. Our giving should spring from a loving heart (1 Cor. 13:3). Love opens the hand and fills it with good gifts. We never tire of doing good to those we love. If we love Christ, that love constrains us, compels us, to give (2 Cor. 5:14). And we know that what we do unto one of the least of His brethren, we do unto Him (Matt. 25:40).

Giving to the Lord's Work

b. Believingly

The best method of giving springs from faith and increases faith. "By faith Abel offered unto God a more excellent sacrifice than Cain" (Heb. 11:4). Christian faith is a firm conviction of the truth of what God has revealed in His Word. It accepts as trustworthy every precept and promise about giving. Luther, like the patriarchs of old, walked by faith, and not by sight. He was a bountiful giver. On one occasion, when chided by his good wife for being too liberal, he replied: "Never mind, for He is rich and has plenty who has let us have what we have had."

c. Gladly

We should give gladly, for it is written: "God loveth a cheerful giver" (2 Cor. 9:7). Some people give with deep felt pain. Giving is no joy or blessing to them, although it may bring joy and blessing to others. Here is a story of a Selfish Fool who was of this attitude. He had received a rice field. It was covered by irrigation water which flowed over to his neighbor's field, bringing much fertility and fruit to both. He determined to prevent the neighbor from getting free water. By damming up his field he robbed his neighbor of a crop and turned his own field into a stagnant marsh. Flowing water is full of life. Gladsome giving brings grace abounding. The more we give the more we live.

3. FREELY AND REGULARLY

a. Freely

Freely implies an act of the will, a choice of one's own accord. "Freely ye have received, freely give," is the New Testament rule. "Every man according as he purposeth in his heart, so let him give, not grudgingly, or of necessity" (2 Cor. 9:7). Paul praises the churches of Macedonia because they willingly gave to the support of the poor at Jerusalem as much as they were able and beyond their power (2 Cor. 8:1-5).

b. Regularly

Regularly implies an act of the will in putting a purpose and plan into execution. Paul's direction was that everyone should set apart for the Lord's work a portion every first day of the week. A sermon may inspire one to make a generous resolve, but it is not saying that the resolve will hold out until the next Sunday. Such resolutions like watches, have a tendency to run down. In his book, "The New Christian," Cushman tells of a campaign to secure proportionate, regular giving. Cards were received from 314 people: 1 pledged 7% of his income; 6 pledged 5%; 1 wrote 3%; 10 hovered around 1%; and 296 named no percentage at all. These represent no doubt the average giving—spasmodic, irregular, sad, "sacrificing," small, inadequate. The Church needs a steady flow of revenues, which can easily be supplied by regular giving.

4. CONSCIENTIOUSLY AND BELIEVINGLY

Conscience serves everybody, even the heathen (Rom. 2:15) It may be practically silenced by secular and heretical teaching and by the unwillingness of a person to listen to it. It should be kept untainted by false teachings. It should be obeyed. It often reinforces the Christian giver so that his plan becomes more definite, his zeal more holy, his purpose more set.

The Three Sacrifices

HOWARD L. HALTER

THE Every Member Canvass is merely a systematic method used to remind Christians of their financial obligation to their Lord.

That's part of Christian Stewardship. But not all.

So wouldn't the Every Member Canvass be more complete if it included the opportunity for the church member to pledge something more than merely money to his church?

To that end we suggest a pledge form for the canvass which might include the three-fold sacrifice of (1) Self, (2) Service, and (3) Substance.

MY PLEDGE—1942

Check those items by placing (X) in the ( ) marks, which you will do, WILLINGLY:

1) The Sacrifice of Self

( ) I shall do all within my power, with the help of His Spirit, to give visible evidence of my faith in the Triune God by leading a Christian life in word and deed.

( ) I shall attend Public Worship Regularly.

( ) I shall try to bring others to worship with me.

( ) I shall try to bring children to our Sunday School who are not enrolled elsewhere.

2) The Sacrifice of Service

( ) I pledge to give some of my free time to my Lord through the service of the church in its various fields of work.

( ) hours a month is about the most I could possibly spare for the work which I have checked below.

NOTE—fill in the number of hours you can give in the space above; below list, by checking, the work which you like best.

Office Work

( ) Typing—I do/do not have my own typewriter

( ) Hand work, such as stamping, sealing, mailing

( ) Mimeographing

( ) Operate an addressing machine

( ) Other work I can do in the office of church ....

Music

( ) I prefer choir work. If I join the choir I promise to attend rehearsals regularly.

( ) I can play (name of instrument)
....

Visitation—this work is open to both men and women

( ) The sick and shut-ins

( ) Sunday School absentees

( ) Prospects for church

( ) Willing to serve on any official church campaign

Women's Work

( ) Sewing ( ) Other charity work

( ) I shall take part in the official program of the Ladies Aid

( ) Sunday School teacher

Men's Work

( ) I am handy as a carpenter, painter
....

( ) Ushering

( ) I shall take part in the official program of the Men's Club

( ) Sunday School Teacher

Young People's Work

( ) I'm willing to help wherever you think I will fit in

( ) I shall take part in the official YPS program

( ) Sunday School teacher

3) The Sacrifice of Substance

( ) I recognize my Christian obligation to share with my church a just portion of my income, as God has prospered me. To that end I have filled out the pledge card which is herewith attached.

(NOTE—the pledge card used in your church for the every member canvass should be attached.

This pledge list on the Threefold Sacrifice is not complete. Revise to meet the needs of your own church.

No. 1730. Size 3⅜"x 3⅜" - $1.50
No. 1730A. Size 2⅛"x 2⅛" - 1.25
No. 1730B. Size 1½"x 1½" - 1.00

Reducing Debts

by O. A. Geiseman

REDUCING DEBTS . . . The generally prevailing building fever and the hilarious prosperity of the late 1920's caused many congregations to venture forth on ambitious building programs. The depression which immediately followed in the wake found a large percentage of such congregations still burdened with a sizable debt. The years intervening from the fall of 1929 to this time have found most congregations shifting along on financial programs dictated by expediency and intended to solve problems only for the moment. Interest rates have been cut down, bond issues have in some instances been decreased through the good will of bond holders, and others things have been done to ease the burden for the individual congregation and make possible a modus videndi. Congregations tend very rapidly to become victims of custom and to ride along contentedly in deep ruts and grooves; hence it might help to arouse some to action were we to say that the time for a definite attack on the capital debt has come and that any congregation burdened with a load which has not as yet undertaken a genuine campaign for the reducing or wiping out of its obligations ought to do so without needless delay. The financial outlook for our country seems to be very good for the next year or two to come in the opinion of professional economists and statisticians. Certainly this much is true that we are presently riding a wave of rising and returning prosperity and every congregation ought avail itself of the opportunity thus afforded to cut down the dead weight of a capital debt and to decrease the fixed non-operating overhead cost by such an effort.

Such efforts if they are to be successful must, however, be based on more than wishful thinking. No church will achieve attainable results unless it plans very carefully and then aggressively carries through the plans which have been formed in any debt reduction effort. Since all campaigns have at least in a measure the same fundamental requirements we should like to list the more important items which dare not be overlooked if a campaign is to be carried through with gratifying success:

1. First, last and all the time, pray. Get all of the members within the church through your Ladies' Organization, Men's Club, Voting Members group, and Young People's Societies to pray for the success of the effort.

2. Get a hand-picked committee, not one which is selected and elected by off-hand nominations from the floor. Be sure to have enough young men on your committee. Men who have suffered severely as a result of the last great depression have in many instances not as yet recovered anything like an undaunted spirit of victory and conquest. They are more or less defeated and see the black side of life. One or two such defeated men ought be on the committee so that the committee will be prepared to meet their type of thinking when the program is presented to the voting members. The controlling strength on the committee should, however, rest with the young men who are eager to go forward and who still believe that success lies out ahead.

3. A definite goal ought be established. This ought be done by considering both the needs of the congregation and the ability of its members to give. If several members of the committee who are reasonably well acquainted with the individual constituents of the congregation will go over the list it may be possible to reach some reasonably reliable conclusions as to the financial abilities of the membership.

4. Each item in the campaign should be carefully outlined so that specific dates are set for all necessary meetings and all detailed items with reference to pledge cards, methods of collection, period of time during which the collections are to be made and the like. All of these things should be carefully determined by the committee. The fullest measure of congregational support may be expected if the committee will submit its ideas to the church council for criticism, improvement or approval. Then if supported by the board they should also be submitted to the voting members so that these may be well informed and feel that they are playing an active part in the program.

5. The chairman and the secretary of the Executive Campaign Committee ought together with the pastor also select the individual members who are to serve as workers on the larger committee so that the best material available from the congregation may be called into service in such an effort. It is a shame to think that sometimes men are used for work like this just because they happen to be elected to some other office. They may not be the least bit qualified for the task even though they may have splendid abilities for some other type of congregational work.

6. All items in the program should be given the widest possible publicity. Every detail ought be made known to all of the organizations within the church and a number of letters ought be carefully formulated setting forth the program. The preparatory labors by way of education and inspiration might well reach their climax in a special service in

which the songs and prayers and the message will all deal with the same subject, and in which the workers of the committee who are to solicit pledges may well be formally charged with their task. Publicity which can be secured in local newspapers ought, of course, also be employed.

7. Should the campaign meet with success it will be inescapably necessary to secure as many advance pledges as possible. The first people who must commit themselves must be the members of the Executive Committee. Then persons within the church who are able to make larger contributions should be approached. This work can be done either by the pastor or by some able member of the Executive Committee. Finally every worker who goes out to solicit pledges from others must be held first to make his own pledge before he is allowed to go, assuming, of course, that he is in a position to make such a pledge. Inability to pledge should not disqualify anyone from serving if he has other abilities. If one-third or one-half the goal has already been reached through advance contributions and everybody in the congregation is well informed as to both the needs and the pledges already made by others, then the soliciting committee will find its task quite easy.

8. All workers who it is assumed have met once or twice previously and been thoroughly instructed as to what should be done and the manner in which they should do it should be held to complete their task within a few days if the congregation is large, and possibly on one Sunday afternoon and evening if it is small and its members are not too widely scattered. All workers should be required to make a preliminary report if it cannot be a complete one at a dinner meeting held possibly on a Tuesday evening if the campaign was started on Sunday. Such a meeting is important because it will give those who have succeeded an opportunity to encourage those who have not been so successful. It will enable the officers of the committee and the pastor to give additional encouragement and it will give all the workers a chance to join once again in prayer for divine blessing upon the effort.

9. Opinions will probably vary as to the period of time within which pledges should be paid up. It is our opinion that a five year period is too long, particularly in times such as these when it is so difficult to look ahead. One year, we believe, is too short a period for people are not able, generally speaking, to find room in their budgets for any additional large sums. We would say that if possible a three year period would perhaps be the most ideal. Local conditions must, of course, in every instance be given consideration.

If your congregation is not burdened with a debt you might do well to remember that Synod is and the method outlined above can be made to prove just as successful in the interest of Synod's treasuries as in the interest of your own congregation.

Checking The Budget

C. S. KULOW

I. The basis upon which the budget should be prepared: actual needs and possible expansion ventures in relation to the congregation, synod, district, and other benevolent enterprises.

II. Preliminary Procedure: a tentative budget drawn up by Trustees or Finance Committee together with the Pastor on the basis of requirements rather than resources. All interests should receive careful attention.

III. The Local Church Budget.
  A. The Pastor.
  1. His Salary. Is it in keeping with his needs as a leader of the church in its relation to the community?
  2. His Associates. The Assistant Minister, Parish School Teachers, Secretary, Student Assistant. If the church cannot provide adequate volunteer workers, should not the question of employing a theological student for a year be considered?
  3. His Vacation. Stipulation for supply pastors.
  4. Conference Expenses.
  B. The Music.
  1. Salary of the Organist. The choir and its music. The Organ. Extra services.
  C. The Caretaker. The ultimate economy in paying enough for the services of a good workman.
  D. Religous Education. Literature and Supplies.
  1. Parish School.
  2. Week-Day Religious School.
  3. Confirmation Classes.
  4. Vacation Bible School.
  5. Sunday School.

  E. Office Expense. Stationery and postage. Telephones.
  F. Publicity. Advertising. Bulletin Board. The Church Paper. Special programs—Confirmation, Easter, Christmas. Expense of postage and stationery for circularizing.
  G. The Church Plant. Interest on mortgage. Insurance—fire and liability, charge up premiums on yearly basis. Fuel—coal or oil, check up on safety and adequacy of heating plant. Light and power. Water. Repairs and maintenance—possible needs for painting, flooring, roofing, concreting, landscaping, and replacements.
  H. Reduction of Capital Indebtedness. Amortization of mortgage, retirement of notes, redemption of bonds.

IV. Benevolences. Synod, District, special appeals of Home and Foreign Missions, wiping out Synod's Debts, Inner Missions, Valparaiso, American Lutheran Publicity Bureau, etc.
  A. The importance of assuming a definite obligation.
  B. The ideal to be perpetuated: as much for others as for ourselves.

V. Contingent Reserve or Sinking Fund.

VI. Plate Collections—stipulate the purposes.

VII. The question of annual pledges. Encourage members not only to pay towards, but to pray for the financial needs of the church.

VIII. A suggested slogan: Every member caring,
Means every member sharing.

To practise a paralyzing economy and a policy of retrenchment where a deeper consecration and harder work would make possible a fearless program of advancement even in these trying days is a sin of omission in the eyes of a generous-hearted God.

How to Keep the Treasurer's Book for A Congregation

LOUIS HENZE

I DO NOT PRETEND to be a bookkeeper. There were times in my life when I had to keep books, and I have to deal a lot with figures today. There are other people who must keep books, and I know that they are not all bookkeepers. I refer to congregation treasurers. I happen to know that many treasurers would like to keep better books. For that reason I consulted about treasurers' books with a number of men who keep books well: Mr. E. Lundell of the American Smelting and Refining Co., New York City, Mr. H. M. Mahlstedt, a retired expert bookkeeper, Mr. C. Vincent of the Union Carbide Co., New York City and Mr. A. H. Kirchhoff who has kept the books of the Atlantic District for many years. All that I have to offer in this article is the result of the consultation with these men. Mr. Lundell is the treasurer of a small church and Mr. Mahlstedt is the treasurer of a large church, and we have tried to devise a system which may be used in any church, large or small.

How often does it happen in a Church Council meeting or in a meeting of the voting members that questions of finance occur: How does our fuel bill compare with last year? How do our plate collections compare with last month? How are the subscriptions for current expenses and for Synod coming in? These and similar questions take the floor and the harassed treasurer gets out his pencil and begins to page his book and, hoping that he has found all the items, makes a hurried calculation. He announces the result with some trepidation and then when he gets home and goes over the figures, he finds that one figure eluded his hurried quest. And at last comes the time for the annual report and the hours of agony to get it correct. The simplified system analyzed below should solve many problems and make the treasurer's work easy and enjoyable, and the annual report just a routine matter quickly accomplished.

The necessary requirements are nothing more than a book with a number of columns to a page, commonly known as a Cash Book. There are a number of such books on the market. You may buy, if you wish, a Universal Multi-Column Book which may be had from stationers all over the country. The columns run from 6 to 16 and you will find such books with 150 pages and up. We advocate the use of a bound book and not a loose leaf book from which pages may be taken out.

One page is headed Receipts for a given month. Mark your columns in harmony with your general receipts. Here is a sample:

RECEIPTS

Receipts – January 1938

Date 1938	Description	Total	Envelopes Current Expense	Envelopes Benevolence	Plate Offering	Misc. and Special Offerings	Debt Reduction
Jan. 2	10:45 A.M. Service	81 65	44 20	15 10	12 35		10 00
9	" "	76 55	40 20	12 60	15 25		8 50
	Orphan Home	5 00				5 00	
16	10:45 A.M. Service	79 10	41 55	14 25	13 50		9 80
23	" "	84 60	40 00	16 20	17 55		10 85
	Am. Lutheran Pub. Bureau	4 00				4 00	
30	10:45 A.M. Service	80 80	43 15	13 65	12 80		11 20
	Totals	411 70	209 10	71 80	71 45	9 00	50 35
	Balance from Dec. 1937	225 70					
		637 40					

DISBURSEMENTS

Disbursements – January 1938

Date 1938	Payee	Description	Ck. No.	Total	Salaries	Janitor Service & Fuel	Telephone Gas and Electric	Stationery and Supplies	Maintenance and Repairs	Misc.	Mortgage Amortiz. & Interest	Synodical Budget	Sundry Contrib.
Jan. 1	Rev. J. Smith	Salary	101	150 00	150 00								
3	A.B.C. Coal Co.	4 Tons Coal	102	48 50		48 50							
6	City Telephone Co.	Jan. Service	103	7 25			7 25						
	Printing House	Pamphlets	104	2 20				2 20					
10	Gas & Elect. Co.	Jan. Service	105	6 45			6 45						
11	A. Jones	Janitor Salary	106	10 00		10 00							
15	Nat'l. Bank	Mortg. Int.	107	200 00							200 00		
17	Oak Lumber Co.	Lumber	108	12 00					12 00				
21	A. Jones	Janitor Salary	109	10 00		10 00							
25	Paper Co. Inc.	Paper Towels	110	1 50						1 50			
31	Atl. Dist. Treas.	Synodical	111	80 80								71 80	
		Orphanage											5 00
		Tract Fund											4 00
		Totals		528 70	150 00	68 50	13 70	2 20	12 00	1 50	200 00	71 80	9 00
	Balance Carried Forw'd. to Feb.			113 70									
				642 40									

Head the opposite page for the same month Disbursements. Head your columns in harmony with your church budget. Draw a line down through the large space on the left and mark the one side Account and the other Description. Use the little columns on the far left for your check number and date. We take it for granted that every treasurer pays bills always by check.

You will note that the total paid out is entered in the first column under Total and this amount is analyzed in the columns across the page. At the end of the month all columns are totalled and the balance from the previous month is entered below the total figure in the Total column and added. The difference between this new total and the total disbursements is the amount to be entered as the balance carried forward to the next month. Naturally when disbursements are always made by check, the bank balance will not always agree with the cash book balance due to outstanding checks and perhaps undeposited receipts.

See sample on preceding page. You may have special columns which you require for the needs of your church. These may be added to meet requirements. There may be some in the sample which may be omitted.

Use the last two pages of your book for a Recapitulation of Receipts and Disbursements for each month of the year. The columns are headed the same as those for each month and the totals of the columns for each month are shown in the respective columns. These columns may be totalled at any time to arrive at the present standing of receipts and disbursements. Totals are added for the entire year.

From this set-up it may be readily seen that a treasurer is in a position to answer, at a glance, the usual questions put to him provided he keeps his book up to date. The annual report is a pleasant task. Add to this that the income of the church is such that he can pay all bills promptly and remit monthly a check for the work of the church-at-large and the treasurer ought to be a happy man.

RECAPITULATION—RECEIPTS

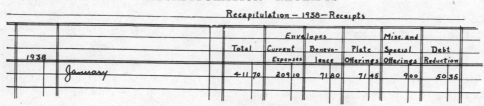

Recapitulation – 1938 – Receipts

1938		Total	Current Expenses	Envelopes Benevolence	Plate Offerings	Misc. and Special Offerings	Debt Reduction
	January	411 70	209 10	71 80	71 45	9 00	50 35

RECAPITULATION—DISBURSEMENTS

Recapitulation – 1938 – Disbursements

1938		Total	Salaries	Janitor Service & Fuel	Telephone Gas and Electric	Stationery and Supplies	Mainten. and Repairs	Misc.	Mortgage Amorit. & Interest	Synodical Budget	Sundry Contrib.
	January	528 70	150 00	68 50	13 70	2 20	12 00	1 50	200 00	71 80	9 00

"Don'ts" For Ushers

1. Don't be late! Your work begins when the church doors are opened.
2. Don't delay ushering until the church begins to be filled up. Even the early comers should be ushered to a seat.
3. Don't give up the attempt to train people to move over and give up end seats to others.
4. Don't be gruff or resentful, whatever the provocation. Courtesy is one of the prime requisites of your office.
5. Don't fill up the church from the rear. Begin from the front. Gradually you will train the people to cooperate.
6. Don't look disgusted if someone you have escorted deserts you and leaves you to parade along the aisle alone.
7. Don't fail to hand the late comer, after he or she has been seated, an open hymnal and to designate the verse which is being sung.
8. Don't get excited! Try to handle every situation quietly and efficiently.
9. Don't usher people to their seats during the responsive service or Scripture readings or special musical numbers.
10. Don't fail to courteously inform them why the doors are closed during the opening service.
11. Don't, either by dress or demeanor, attract attention to your own person. The best usher is he who does his work with self-effacing efficiency.
12. Don't look glum! The church attendant is to feel that you consider it a pleasure to usher him to a seat.

Spiritualizing The Canvass

IN A RECENT BOOK entitled "The Every Member Canvass," Dr. H. C. Weber, director of the Every Member Canvass Department of the General Council of the Presbyterian Church, issues some very sane statements regarding the every member canvass, which is perhaps becoming an annual institution in most of our congregations. This, of course, is not the season for the every member canvass, but a few of Dr. Weber's statements might be passed on for the consideration of those who are responsible for the every member canvass in their respective congregations next fall. Dr. Weber properly claims that the every member canvass should be directed to the people and not to their pocketbooks. He says,

"The canvass, rightly conceived, is a problem in human relations, and not a plan for raising money. It is a major contact adventure in the task of personalizing people in and toward religion. It is even more than this. It has great spiritual possibilities. It furnishes an expressional release for the religion in a man.

"The canvass that has become or is a drudgery is a handicap and not a help. The right sort of canvass will add very tangible Christian assets to a congregation's store, —more consecration, more power and joy to sacrifice, more sympathy and understanding, larger ideals and ambitions. Instead of a weight to carry and offset in some way, the good canvass provides wings by which the congregation may rise to a higher level."

He says again, "Giving is a grace, not a grind. It is a grace around which the real canvass should be built, and of course that means that its impact, its method, its content must be spiritualized. Graciousness, not grasping; a tonic, not a taxing; happiness and not snappiness, should be its atmosphere."

Another pithy statement is, "The canvass committee has a high vocation within the church. Its members should be stewards of the manifold grace of God, not stewards of temporalities, or methods, or programs. . . . To everyone the gate of stewardship should be opened not so much for the profit of the church as for the profit of the individual soul." The author then gives in the course of his book very valuable suggestions as to how the canvas may be "spiritualized."

We agree with the author. The mere mechanization of giving in a congregation, the mere systematization of the church's machinery, will not solve a church's financial problems. In many cases the every member canvass has become merely a necessary and much-dreaded chore. Annually the congregation goes through the same congregational gestures, which have no higher objective than that no member of the church should be overlooked. Without the cultivation of the spirit of Christian stewardship every member canvasses may be merely a part of a congregational machinery which perpetuates systematized penuriousness. When once our people begin to realize that their contributions to the kingdom of God are a means of Christian expression and an exercise of Christian graces rather than an assessment to keep the external machinery of the church going, our financial problems will begin to be solved. There has been altogether too much begging, too much importuning for money in our circles, and far too little education as to what money is and for what purpose God supplies it. We have had far too many drives and emergency collections and hole-stuffing campaigns, and not enough steady, persistent training along the principles of the stewardship of life. Throughout the Church our financial affairs need to be spiritualized.

ORGANIZING THE CONGREGATION

Geo. H. Siebern

To successfully carry out any undertaking, organization and system are necessary. In the financial endeavors of a congregation an organized and systematic effort must be made. Experience has taught that lesson. The sooner every congregation realizes this the better it will be. The object of this article is to show HOW a congregation can be organized.

Let us assume that the fiscal year ends December 31st. During the month of October the Finance Committee should prepare a budget showing the financial needs and requirements of the church for the coming year. This budget should then be presented, discussed and ratified by the voting members at a meeting held prior to the middle of November. On the second or third Sunday in November the Pastor should preach a sermon on stewardship. Now the necessary literature should be prepared. The literature should include a copy of the budget, a pledge card and a folder explaining the needs, etc. An attractive folder will be more effective than a mimeographed letter. Canvassers should also be selected at this time, and one or more meetings should be arranged for their inspiration and instruction.

Some evening before the last Sunday in November a meeting of the entire congregation, young and old, men and women, should be held. At this meeting the budget should be presented and explained in detail. Have printed copies of the budget distributed. Give everyone an opportunity to ask further questions. A talk on the duties and privileges of giving would also be very much in order. The talking at this meeting should be done not by the Pastor but by the laymen of the congregation. A stereopticon lecture on stewardship will prove very helpful. A congregational meeting of this kind could also be held on a Sunday immediately after the regular services. In this case, of course, the illustrated lecture would be omitted due to lack of time.

On the last Sunday in November, an even stronger sermon on stewardship than the previous one should be delivered.

About the middle of the following week the necessary literature should be mailed out and the members should be informed that on the first Sunday in December the subscription cards, or pledge cards, will be gathered. Some people object to the word "pledge"; "subscription" may be substituted.

For the leader of an undertaking of this kind the following suggestions might be useful.

Secure a list of the names and addresses of every member of the congregation. Ask the Pastor if any of these should *not* be approached, then arrange this list alphabetically. Number this list consecutively, the first name being number 1, the second name number 2, etc. We shall call this list the Master List.

Now take some index cards and write the name and address of each member on a separate card, with the corresponding number, as found on the list, in the upper left hand corner of the card. After this has been done, arrange your cards according to districts, so that all those living in the same vicinity can be visited by the same canvassers. Some members might need special attention.

Remove these cards for special attention. Do not make districts too large. Ten to twelve should be the limit. If at all possible, send out your canvassers in pairs or teams.

It is essential to know what members are being visited by each team. Try the following method. Number each team, as for instance:

Team I—John Jones and Henry Schmidt
Team II—Edward Adams and Arthur Mann.

Then assign Team I to one of the districts. Take the cards representing that district and on another card (Team Cards) put this information: Team I is visiting cards numbered 1-3-6-8-9, etc. Then, on your Master List, to the right of numbers 1-3-6-8-9, place the team number I. And so on with each team.

On the Sunday of the canvass a special consecration service may be held in the morning, and all canvassers should be asked to report at the church at 2 P.M. Before they start out give them the cards they are to visit and be sure to give them a supply of pledge cards. Also impress upon them that they must return every card given to them with some remark written thereon. Tell them to return to the church not later than 6 P.M. for a luncheon, and report. Upon their return, all cards noted "Not at Home" should be given back to them with the request that they visit again during the week. The merits of all other remarks should be discussed with the Pastor at some subsequent meeting of the Finance Committee, and suitable action taken. The returned pledge cards should be arranged alphabetically, and the amounts recorded on the "Master List." After this has been done, place all the team cards before you and then check on your Master

List the number to the left of each member who has pledged, and also check the corresponding number on the team card. After every member has pledged or the remarks of every member has been acted upon and disposed of, you will have before you on your Master List a complete and exact record. At all times you will have before you what canvasser visited any and every member, what canvasser is delinquent, what members have not responded, etc., etc. The completed Master List will look something like this:

No.	Name Address	Team	Amount Pledged	Remarks
✓ 1	Adams, Henry, 585 E. 178 St.	I	$100.00	
✓ 4	Weber, John, 3133 Third Ave.	IV	....	Wants Env.
✓ 2	Jones, Thos., 735 E. 176 St.	III	....	No Pledge
✓ 3	Smith, Jas., 716 E. 180 St.	II	....	Cannot contr.
	etc., etc., etc.			Moved

After every name on the Master List has been checked, take all the pledge cards and arrange them alphabetically, number them consecutively in the upper right hand corner, and from them put the name and address on the corresponding envelope boxes. Ask your canvassers once more to make the rounds and distribute these boxes some time between the last Sunday in the old year and the first Sunday in the new year.

The work has now just started. The contributions of every member should be carefully recorded and regular statements and receipts issued at least quarterly, if not monthly. Should any member fall in arrears with the contributions, special inquiry should be made.

No claim is made that the above method is the only and the best one to pursue. However, the plan outlined has been tried and has proved to be successful.

Money-Raising Without Entertainments

IN FACE of a possible loss of revenue from the bazaars, cake sales, and entertainments which were held in our church, we decided upon an experiment which was to last for one year: In the event that the experiment failed we were to revert to the old order of things. This is what we did: we decided to try financing our church entirely on the New Testament Plan, which is based on the Bible principle of the free-will offering. In other words all monies for the support of the church and its varied activities were to come only through free-will offering, envelopes and plate collections. Societies were not in any way to be assessed for the running of the church.

Money was not to be mentioned from the pulpit for the period of one year. However, in order to educate the people to the seeming radical change of the financing of the church, a series of 5 letters, which are reproduced at the end of this article, were sent out to each communicant member. These letters were mailed so that they would receive one letter every third day. The members were reminded how their church was to be financed and why the change was brought about.

On the face of it, it might sound as though social life in the church were to come to a standstill. Not at all—socials, plays and get-togethers were to be continued—only bazaars, cake sales, and the so-called social functions, which are but thinly veiled money-raising devices—were to be banned. However these social functions were to be given only in the name of sociability and not for money-making. No tickets were to be sold. The parties that cost us money were also to be financed by variation of the free-will offering. Sometime during the course of the party an announcement was made of what the individual refreshments cost the church. A plate was placed somewhere in the room and those who could afford and wanted to pay their share knew well enough what to do. Expense money for the various other activities was taken from the regular dues of the members.

This plan automatically cut out the party nuisances which so annoy the merchant of any community. No longer were they dunned for prizes to be given at card parties, no longer would they have to donate tea, coffee, and sugar for the various social affairs.

From the very outset, the idea of a church being self-sufficient and self-supporting, not depending upon outsiders and upon the methods of the commercial world for financial support, appealed to the imagination of the people. Naturally there were a number of flarebacks. Particularly from the hardest working, but short-visioned members of the organizations who foresaw bankruptcy in cutting off these lucrative avenues for church finance.

On the Sunday following the 18th day after the explanatory letters had been sent out on the system, an every-member canvas was made. Basing their argument on the fact that no one would be pestered for money, donations, or special gifts during the entire course of the year each member was urged to double his previous years' pledge. The men had facts and figures to back them up—no longer would the women have to pay for dishcloths at double their value, no longer would they have to witness amateur performances simply because they had been railroaded into buying a block of tickets, no longer would they have to stand over a hot oven baking a cake, giving it to the church and buying back another cake for $1 not nearly so good as the one they gave. (Incidently the added time which the women's societies now had on their hands was used in charitable work; doing sewing for the local hospital and helping the local relief agency with the unfortunate.) Nothing succeeds like success. Despite the prophets of doom our church ended the year with $300.00 more than we had the previous year. In addition to that we had earned the good will of the various merchants of the town who appreciated our understanding of their problems.

But one of the most amazing single incidents of the first year of this system was that our local mortician called us to his office one day and told us how much he liked our new idea. He ended his commendation by handing us an envelope containing a check for $50.00 which he asked us to accept in sincere appreciation of what we were doing to bring the church back to its position of honor and respect in the community. He also asked that his name not be connected with the donation.

Money raising
#1 of a Series

At the Church Office,
Thursday

Dear Member:
From our very beginning this church has always been proud of the fact that it tried to pattern its doctrine and its life after that of Christ, our King. And now this year we are attempting to go one step farther and even pattern our church finances after the principles of the Master which He set down long ago in the pages of the New Testament.

So this year, before we ask you to make your pledge, we want to tell you a bit more about the way this Plan operates, and briefly bring to your attention where the money goes.

As you have already heard, this year we are financing our Church on the New Testament Plan. That means that we support the church entirely through voluntary contributions. It will not, hereafter, beg, gamble, or use the many commercial methods of money raising.

Your pledge and mine support the church. But when you make a pledge, the church also makes a pledge to you: no one will annoy you by trying to sell you tickets, nor beg for donations and gifts for sales and bazaars. You make one pledge, and that holds good for the entire year. And when you make your pledge you don't have to hold back, for our church pledges to you that it will not ask you for another penny all the rest of the year. if you live up to your weekly pledge.

Sincerely yours,
In the Lord's Service,
THE FINANCE COMMITTEE
per: John Smith, Chairman
Next: "Why an Envelope has Two Pockets".
FC

Money raising
#2 of a Series

At the Church Office,
Saturday

Dear Member:
Do you know why an envelope has two pockets? — The left hand pocket is used to meet the expenses of our own church.

The money received in the right hand pocket is used to carry on mission work in our own country and in foreign lands, to support colleges and seminaries where young men are trained for the ministry, and to publish Christian literature and periodicals.

Incidentally, it was money from the District office of the Lutheran Church which made this church possible. The District not only lent us money when we were getting started, but they have also guaranteed several loans made by us to complete the church building and to pay for the land. Your pastor's salary is still paid by the District.

So if other Lutherans throughout our District had not given liberally in this right hand pocket, our church would not have been possible. Likewise, unless we give regularly and generously through this right hand pocket, it is not possible for either Synod or District to carry on their work of bringing our church to others.

Sincerely yours,
In the Lord's Service,
THE FINANCE COMMITTEE
Next: "How our church actually saves you money through the New Testament Plan"
FC

Money raising
#3 of a Series

At the Church Office,
Monday

Dear Member:
Here are a few questions you will never hear at our church — and, incidentally, a few reasons why our church actually saves you money:

"Will you take a couple of chances on this blanket?"

"Will you bake a cake for our Cake Sale?"

"Can you spare a dollar for our Coal Fund?"

"Will you donate something for our Bazaar?"

"Will you buy a few tickets for our play?"

Such devices cost church members money. You can't afford to buy things you neither want or need and still have money left to give to the church in your envelope.

By running a church on the New Testament Plan the way we do saves you money. It protects you from this everlasting begging. No part of your money goes to the butcher, the baker, or the candlestick maker; for every cent you give through your envelope goes for just one thing: Church! Furthermore, you know at the beginning of the year about how much you can afford to give, and you aren't expected to give one cent more. So it is only natural that the pledge you make this year will be larger than any you have ever made before. For there are not going to be any unexpected "Touches."

It is dignified and Christ-like, too, this method of running the church in accordance with the New Testament Plan.

Sincerely yours,
In the Lord's Service,
THE FINANCE COMMITTEE
Next: "How much shall I give?"   FC

Money raising
#4 of a Series

At the Church Office,
Wednesday

Dear Member:
"HOW MUCH SHALL I GIVE TO THE CHURCH?" — The amount you give to the church is entirely up to you. But it is a good plan to set aside a certain percentage of your income each month.

Let's say a man gets $100. a month (the total amount earned before the bills are paid.) If he gives 5% of his income, he will contribute $5.00 a month or $1.25 a week. (Of this we suggest splitting the money between the two pockets of the envelope as follows: $1.00 for Current Expenses; and 25¢ for Missions and Outside Purposes. 4-1 is the suggested ratio.)

We feel that the idea of giving a certain percentage to the church each month is the best way to give. Here's how it works out: if a man's income is suddenly cut in half, he simply continues to live up to his pledge. Let's say he is giving 5% and got $100. a month. If his income were cut in half he would just give 5% of $50., or $2.50 for that month. On the other hand, if he got a $50. increase, the church, too, would get its "raise". The percentage system is most fair — both ways.

If you are very much in debt, perhaps you can afford to give only 2% or 3% of your income. But that's up to you. We believe that the Lord remembers those who are willing to sacrifice for Him.

Your pastor gets $110. a month salary. Of this $110. he gives $11. a month to the church, or about $2.75 a week — that's 10% of his salary.

What percentage are you willing to give?
Sincerely yours,
In the Lord's Service,

PLEASE TURN TO PAGE 224

Helping the Treasurer

C. H. NAPIER

INASMUCH as each congregation is free to establish whatever financial system will best meet local contingencies, we would have it distinctly understood at the outset that this article must not be construed as propaganda in favor of any particular system. After all we are not concerned with the manner in which any congregation takes its contributions, our plan is to follow repeated suggestion to submit an outline of simplified congregational book-keeping to lighten the burden of the treasurer.

The local congregation formerly used the triplex system of envelope collection. A special envelope was used to take the contribution for district and for synodical work, while another with a duplex pocket was used for charitable and home purposes. Although the communicant membership was not large, this system laid a real burden upon the treasurer.

A triple entry of the names of the communicants was required. In order to keep record of the monies for home and charitable purposes the treasurer ruled off fifty-two squares after each name to take care of the possible number of envelopes in a year. Twelve squares were ruled off for the monthly synodical contributions.

This triplex system literally consumed hours of the treasurer's time, and in the audit of the book several hours were required. The nickels and dimes and quarters had first to be added separately and then the total amount of all communicants added together to discover the whole. The treasurer was a slave to his work and he felt the burden of it.

Thereafter the congregation discarded the special synodical envelope and used the pocket on the duplex envelope, hitherto designated for charity, for district and synodical purposes. With one envelope less the treasurer's work was lessened, but the difficulties of keeping a perfect record were not eliminated. The system of book-keeping was complicated and a new treasurer found it hard to understand.

Five years ago the congregation began the use of a single envelope and with it came a simplified system of book-keeping. The envelope in use, printed by the Concordia Publishing House, is given below:

140   Jan. 4, 1931

GRACE EV. LUTHERAN CHURCH
Budget for 1931, Including
Current Expense, Salary, Light, Heat, Etc.
Payment on Church Debt
District and Synodical Needs
REMEMBER TO BRING YOUR GIFT

Regular deposit of your envelope will enable your church to do its work efficiently.

Every man according as he purposeth in his heart, so let him give; not grudgingly or of necessity, for God loveth a cheerful giver.—2 Cor. 9, 7.

C. P. H., ST. LOUIS, MO. MADE IN U. S. A.

With this envelope in use the treasurer writes in the names of the communicants but once. Two thirds of the work required under the triplex system is eliminated.

The treasurer uses one of the Paramount series of record books. This book, while its printed headings do not always serve the system of the congregation, is nevertheless satisfactory for its purpose. At the beginning of the book there are pages printed with the following ready-made entries: Credit, Debit, Number, Name, Address, Telephone Number. Three full ruled columns are found on the credit and the debit pages.

The system in vogue uses three columns as follows:

Credit Page		
Current Expense	Debt Fund	Synodical
Debit Page		
Current Expense	Debt Fund	Synodical

All monies received by the congregation whether by envelope, by cash in the plate, by special contribution appear on the credit page, which, let us say, is page one. Page two is the debit page. In our congregation each page will permit a record for three months, so that the amount of income and the amount of disbursements for any quarter of the year is contained on the two pages.

The amounts which are entered in any one of the three columns is determined on a percentage basis. Let us say that the congregational budget calls for $3000. Of this amount $600 is to be applied to the payment of a note at the end of the year. Another $600 is the congregation's synodical apportionment. In either case the amount is 20% of the total budget. The two items together would be 40% and the other 60% would include contributions for salary, and such other current expenses as light, gas, coal, etc.

Now then, if the treasurer finds at the end of the month that the income by envelope was $250, the average on the month necessary to meet the budget, then after the system he would divide $250 by 5 which would give him the amount to be set down in the "Debt Treasury." Again dividing by 5 he would also have the amount for the "Synodical Treasury." With $100 applied to these two treasuries, he would have remaining $150 and this sum he writes in in the column designated "Current Expense."

A separate page is maintained for the plate collections. Half of the page is headed "A.M." and the other half is headed "P.M." In the book which is used approximately a half year's morning and night plate collections can be entered. The page is filled as follows:

PLATE COLLECTIONS, 1931

	A.M.	P.M.
January 1	New Year	4.30
4	5.25	4.80
11	6.75	6.45

The month of January is completed, each column is added, thus giving at sight the morning collections and the night collections. In the same line with the totals but under the date on the "A.M." side the total of the two collections is placed.

A separate page is also used for special contributions, a contribution for some charity or otherwise which is not included in the congregational budget, but which is remembered by a communicant.

With the amount of plate collections determined, and with the amounts of each envelope entered after the name of the communicant, and having percentaged the synodical and the debt items the treasurer is ready to complete his credit and debit pages. We let the exhibit follow:

CREDIT PAGE					DEBIT PAGE			
Date		Current Exp.	Debt	Synodical	Date	Current Exp.	Debt	Synodical
Jan. 1	Balance on Hand	$175.00			Jan. 1 Salary to Minister	$125.00		$50.00
	By Envelope $250.00	150.00	$50.00	$50.00	5 Power and Light Co.	5.00		
	By Cash (Plate)	55.00			7 Water Department	2.00		
	By Special, see page	15.00			9 Church Stationery	6.00		
					10 Telephone	5.00		
Jan. 31	Total	$395.00	$50.00	$50.00	31 Church Cleaning	15.00		
	Disbursements	165.00		50.00	31 Insurance (Hail)	7.00		
Jan. 31	Balance	$230.00	$50.00		Total	$165.00		$50.00

The above items and figures, of course, are assumptive. When making up his credit page at the beginning of the year the treasurer first writes in the carry-over balance. Then he indicates the total envelope contributions. He arrives at this amount by totaling the contributions by each communicant for the month. This done he enters the amount of plate collections, special contributions, etc., and having percentaged his envelope collections—we are using the budget of $3000 and $600 for debt retirement and $600 as the synodical apportionment—he adds the amount in each column. Having already completed his disbursement entries he brings the current expense items to the current expense treasury column on the credit page. Inasmuch as the synodical monies are sent off each month he transfers this item from the debit to the credit page. The amount in the debt treasury accumulates unto the end of the year.

In making his report to the congregation the treasurer states the facts as they are before him. "We had a carry-over of so much," he says. "Our collections by envelope were so much." The plate collections were—and then the amount. Our disbursements for the month totaled so much. Of the contributions by envelope this amount, let us use the figures above, of $250.00 was appor-

tioned as follows: $150 for current expenses, $50 for the sinking fund, and $50 for synodical purposes. This latter $50 by congregational resolution is immediately sent to the district treasurer. The balance on hand as of January 31 is therefore $230 in the current expense treasury, $50 in the debt treasury, and nothing on hand for synodical purposes, the amount of $50 as stated having already been remitted to the district treasurer.

This system which is an application of the unified budget system claims these distinct advantages.

The Synod is assured of a contribution each month depending on the income of the congregation.

A certain amount is regularly laid aside for debt retirement.

The congregation knows the amount sent to the district treasurer each month and they know the possible consequences of any lapse of envelope contributions.

The treasurer has a compact record. He keeps a record which if he should be retired in favor of another, the new man will not have to spend much time to learn the system. But more than this the treasurer finds joy in his work and this makes him to be a willing and an efficient servant to the congregation..

MONEY RAISING *from p. 222*

Money raising
#5 of a Series

At the Church Office,
Friday

Dear Members:

Sunday our canvassers come to your home for your personal pledge. Please feel free to ask them any question not covered in the letters you have received during the past weeks.

Here, briefly, is a resume of this year's budget. You will notice that the entire sum must be raised this year on the basis of the free will offering. None of the societies have been asked to pledge their support or to underwrite any part of the current expenses. All money must come in through the envelopes or other such free will offerings.

This plan for raising money is as old as the Christian Church. Yet we, by having the courage to adopt this old method in a time when churches have largely turned to the commercial methods of money raising, are seemingly pioneers. This plan calls for faith, and faithful giving.

Budget adopted for 1936
CURRENT EXPENSES
(Left hand pocket of the envelope)

Advertising	$300.00
Debt Reduction	300.00
Interest on Loans	300.00
Light, heat, water	500.00
Office Expenses	200.00
New Equipment and unforeseen exp.	300.00
Rent (parsonage)	500.00
Salary (pastor)	1500.00
	$3900.00

MISSION AND OUTSIDE PURPOSES
(Right hand pocket of envelope)
All budgeted purposes   900.00

Submitted by
THE FINANCE COMMITTEE

P.S. Our next letter will give you a resume of the total pledges made for the budgets.

Stewardship is the heart of Christianity. God is counting upon all we have for His work, for we are His stewards. He does not want us to waste our TIME, LIFE, TALENTS or POSSESSIONS.
—*Lutheran Herald.*

* * * *

The practice of stewardship is the ultimate goal of all Christian preaching and teaching. To use *all* one's time and talents, *all* one is and has, in accord with the will of God, that is surely to reach the ideal. That is truly to love God with all the heart, mind, soul and strength, and one's neighbor as oneself. That and nothing less is Christian stewardship.—*W. E. Henry.*

* * * *

Stewardship emphasizes the element of obligation that inheres in the Gospel. It takes into account every phase of human living. It is the personal responsibility of the individual to God in the matter of possession of all kinds—life, time, talent, energy, money, and all forms of power or wealth.—*Julius Earl Crawford.*

---By ROGER BABSON---

"The tithing system, if adopted by the churches, would give astounding figures. A compilation shows that the annual business turnover in this country amounts to more than five hundred billion dollars. It is estimated that of this amount four-fifths pass through the hands of the church people. One per cent of this amount would mean five billion dollars a year. Assuming that there is a profit of ten per cent on this turnover, it would mean that there is coming each year to the church people of this country an income amounting to forty billion dollars. If the tithing process were in operation, this would give the Church in tithes about four billion dollars a year. These figures seem very extraordinary, but on checking them up no flaws can be found. The facts are that the church people of the country are giving less than 1 per cent of their income to Church and missionary work. If this were increased to 10 percent the Church would become the most powerful organization and the wonderful results which have been indicated could eventually come to pass. Then the Church could come into its own in a great big way that heretofore it has been able only to talk about."

"Up-to-Daters Club"
A Successful Plan for Loyal Giving
CLAUDIUS S. KULOW

THE GREAT CHALLENGE to a responsive church membership is that of loyalty to the enterprise. That which claims our affection demands our loyalty. It is no less true when it comes to the pecuniary support of the church.

In times past, at the close of the fiscal year, some congregations have published a list of the membership with the financial support of each member listed alongside. True, those who gave little may have been shamed by seeing their niggardliness presented before them "black on white." But very often the eye would run down the list of figures for the name of the contributor with the highest amount behind his name. Many congregations abolished such statements since the motive was misinterpreted. Outside of the matter of record, finance boards have felt the weakness in the presentation of such a statement but once a year. It was soon forgotten and the contributions, like water running down the hill, soon again sought their lowest level.

The challenge to loyalty, however, remains. It holds true whether the giver be able to place much or little in his envelope. It is required of stewards that they be found faithful. Experience has repeatedly demonstrated that what counts in answering the financial needs of the church is the regular, weekly envelope contribution based on a definite weekly pledge procured through the Every-member Canvass or Annual Stewardship Enrollment Campaign. But, here again, John Doe, filled with new resolutions at the beginning of the year, challenged by the pressing needs of his church, the literature distributed and the visit of the canvasser, often lapses into his lackadaisical and spasmodical method of giving.

How can we challenge our membership to make a pledge and THEN KEEP IT UP? If your church possesses financial officers who are willing to spend a little time and energy each week for the welfare of your church, we believe we have the answer. Each week, after the envelopes are turned in, enter the amounts on the quarterly statement. Then review the statements and list each member who is "up-to-date" in his contributions on the basis of his pledge. On the following Sunday distribute a printed or mimeographed list of such members under the title "Loyalty Group" or "Up-to-Daters Club." Such a list, passed out each week, is a tremendous challenge to CONSTANT loyalty.

Note, especially, that the enrollment on the loyalty list is not based on HOW MUCH—that is a personal question between man and his God—but rather on HOW REGULAR. Thus, the school boy who in his small way is systematic in his attendance and contributions is placed on a par with the largest giver. The challenge to loyalty reaches down to every member of the church.

Some of the tangible benefits of the "Up-to-Daters Club" in the church have been: (a) A twenty-percent increase in envelope contributions. (b) Many who made no pledge at the time of the stewardship enrollment, but took and used the envelopes, wanted to know why they were not included in the loyalty list. When told they could not be "up-to-daters" unless their gifts were based on a definite promise for comparison, most of them brought in their pledges and now keep them up. (c) Envelopes came to church each week with a resultant increase in church attendance. (d) When the contributor was to absent himself from services the following Sunday he began to think of his church contribution before he went away instead of after or never, with the result that the church had just that much money to work with in the meanwhile. (e) Some who paid by check each month or quarter felt it was unfair that they were not included in the list. They were simply asked to pay their pledges each month or quarter in advance and their names would be carried on "Up-to-Daters" for the entire period. (f) Especially during vacation periods the challenge to loyalty meant payments before rather than after, thus enabling the church to better carry on during the summer season.

When the "Up-to-Daters Club" is inaugurated in the church, some of the officers are apt to look at it askance lest some be offended. The challenge to "come up higher" always does that. But the fact that people begin to wonder why their name is not included in the list is the MOST HEALTHFUL BY-PRODUCT of the entire plan. The finance committee and pastor should welcome the opportunity to talk about this matter. The beauty of it is that the members will come to the committee rather than necessitate the visit of the committee to the member. The challenge to loyalty in this way puts the burden squarely upon the shoulder of each member. In every case, the fact that the challenge is to loyalty rather than an amount of money makes the case simple yet impersonal. One church of five hundred members increased its contributions fifteen hundred dollars the first year the plan was used, and five hundred more the second year.

"Up-to-Daters" is a method of keeping church finances before the congregation each week in a dignified, quiet way. It talks in terms of men rather than money. It does not permit the "let George do it" attitude, but places definite responsibility upon every boy and girl, every man and woman in the constituency.

We have presented, at the request of the editor, the most exacting and, we believe, successful operation of the loyalty challenge in church current finances. Some churches without the stringent demands of the financial officers available have issued a list but once each month. Others simply require that each envelope be turned in without reference to the pledge. Such a plan might be pressed into service in the Sunday School where no pledges are exacted from the children. In any event, "Up-to-Daters" with its challenge to loyalty will mean a healthful improvement in the financial status of any church.

JUST A PENNY

I cost only a penny;
  BUT
I bring joy in the midst of sorrow,
I help the shattered body to regain health,
I pay for doctors, nurses, and medical care,
I provide food and shelter;
  AND, FURTHERMORE,
I give opportunity to preach the Gospel,
I make possible Christian comfort for the afflicted,
I help point sin-sick souls to the Great Physician,
I bring peace to the dying in their last hour.
I AM THE WHEAT RIDGE CHRISTMAS SEAL.

Buy Me!

Policies Relative to Money-Gathering in Harmony with the New Testament Plan of Church Financing

HOWARD HALTER

In dealing with church finances many of us have difficulty in making clear to our congregations the differences between the right and wrong way of gathering money; and particularly in dealing with things which are not wrong in themselves, such as bazaars, cake sales, and the like, but which are actually not the methods which Christ intended for support of His Church.

It is difficult and dangerous to formulate rules by which any and every church can be guided, because of individual differences and problems with which we all have to contend. But the following rules have proved effective through actual use. We pass them on to you for what they may be worth, and for the elements of truth which they contain.

General Policies

1. The New Testament Plan of Church Financing has as its basis the Free Will Offering, as it is expressed in the envelope system, the plate offering, and other types of free will collections.

2. By its very nature, the church depends upon gifts or offerings since it has no physical commodity to sell. Therefore, the church has no reason to enter into competitive buying and selling for the purpose of maintaining its physical organization. For a church which is obedient to its Founder will maintain its physical structure and its educational services through the three-fold sacrifice of self, service, and substance.

3. Consequently the church must look to those who receive a direct or indirect spiritual benefit from it for its support on the basis of their free will offering. And, conversely, the church must not look to any one group of people, be it a society or group of wealthy individuals, either to meet the current obligations of the church, or to depend upon them for funds, should special need arise.

4. When an individual has made a pledge to his church through the every-member canvass, and has obligated himself for a specific sum to be paid each week through his envelopes,

he has fulfilled his financial obligation to the church and the church must, therefore, protect him from any form of solicitation which might tend to void this former obligation. Where no such obligation to support the church exists, as in the case of the non-member residents of the community, or of the tradesmen within the community, the church has no right or reason to solicit aid in any form for the church.

5. When a group of individuals within the church voluntarily band themselves together to form a society to accomplish as a group what they could not do as individuals, they may, by virtue of the potential church work which they can thus do, gather additional free will offerings from within that group in their effort to carry out a program and maintain the society. But such gathering of funds shall be carried out on the basis of the free will offering. Dues.

Can a Society Raise Money?

6. If in the course of its work, any society performs a public service either for the individual members of the congregation or for others, without offering such service to the individual by personal solicitation, and accrues a cash profit thereby, such funds shall be their own to be utilized by the society in any churchly way; preferably for charitable causes not covered by the budget. Important it is, so that the principle and spirit of the New Testament plan be not violated, that funds so raised shall not be used by the church to meet any current obligations or budgetary expenditure.

   a) Under the head of "public service" is included the sale of religious articles, without personal solicitation
   b) Also included are parties, dinners, and the like, which tend to make for good will and fellowship among the members.

How About Tickets?

7. The sale of tickets within a church is generally one of the worst forms of personal solicitation which soon gives the impression that the

church is always begging. Consequently, when it is necessary to determine in advance the attendance for a certain function, such as a church dinner, the use of the reservation form, listed below shall be used, to avoid the danger involved in "high pressure" ticket selling.

The Reservation Form

Please reserve ——— plates for me at the dinner to be held at the ——— church on the ———, 1940.

Signature ....
Address ....

8. This reservation form is to be signed by the individual who wants to attend the function, and the form retained by the group giving the function. No money shall be accepted in advance, so that no accusation can arise that a ticket has been sold.

A reminder may be sent to the individual who signed the card a few days before the function, reminding him of his reservation. If a reservation is made and is not cancelled prior to the function, the maker of the reservation shall pay the sum involved. Price expected may be stated.

The use of this reservation form generally excludes people who would normally buy tickets "to help a good cause." It brings only those people who actually want to attend. It likewise takes away the excuse from those who do not pledge a weekly amount in their envelopes since they support the church through parties, and the like.

In General, No Ticket-selling

9. There shall be no ticket selling in connection with any church affair. Neither shall there be general solicitation in connection with the signing of the reservation form.

10. The sale of tickets for affairs *outside* of the church shall be permitted subject to the following limitations:

   a) Providing that these tickets are sold for some accepted charitable cause, or that they somehow further the cause of Lutheranism, such as the sponsoring of a sacred concert, rally, etc.

b) That some individual member of the society which is sponsoring the sale is appointed as agent to collect the money and deliver the tickets.

11. The sale of lottery tickets in any form is forbidden, no matter what charity is sponsoring the sale, be it within or without the Lutheran church.

Commercial Methods of Raising Money Forbidden

12. There shall be no bazaars, lotteries, card parties, cake sales, rummage sales, nor any similar commercial method of money-raising which tends to lower the dignity of the church. Likewise is forbidden any such similar venture on the part of the individual for the benefit of the church or any society.

13. There shall be no personal solicitation among members of the residents of the community for articles of their own handiwork of whatever sort for the purpose of sale. Neither shall there be any solicitation for money or goods from the tradesmen of the community, nor the sale of program advertising of any sort, nor solicitation of donations by any means whatsoever.

14. No congregational membership or address lists will be released for any commercial use, be it a private individual or a company which promises commission to the church.

Purpose of These Policies

The purpose of these policies is to restrict the gathering of money to the free will offering. Adherence to these policies pays, as experience has taught.

Hidden Talent of Gold

We also pointed out to them that almost every cent which they contributed through their children's envelopes was returned to them in the form of books, leaflets, presents, trained teachers, picnics, and the like. And that they were in no way contributing to the support of the church which made this fine Sunday School possible.

It was our experience that about 75 percent of these Sunday School parents were happy to contribute—and that their contributions were, for the most part, on par with the contributions of our own communicant members.

Incidentally, the children still retained their own envelopes—their contributions still went to the support of the Sunday School. But the church gained, in addition to this, about 20 percent of its total budgeted expense through this hidden talent of gold which had been in our midst all along—and just found in this manner!

Commissioning Service

FOR USE IN SETTING APART MEN FOR THE EVERY MEMBER CANVASS

HEAR the word of God as recorded in St. Luke 10:1-2. Now after these things the Lord appointed seventy others, and sent them two and two before his face into every city and place, whither he himself was about to come. And he said unto them, The harvest indeed is plenteous, but the laborers are few; pray ye therefore the Lord of the harvest, that he send forth laborers into his harvest. Also in Acts 13:2,3. And as they ministered to the Lord, and fasted the Holy Spirit said, Separate me Barnabas and Saul for the work whereunto I have called them. Then, when they had fasted and prayed and laid their hands on them, they sent them away.

Dear brethren: You have been asked to make a visitation in this congregation in the interest of the upbuilding and extension of Christ's Kingdom. I ask you, therefore, in the presence of the assembled congregation whether you are now ready and willing to carry out the instruction given you, depending upon the gracious help of God? If so, then answer, I AM.

In accordance with the Scriptures which you have heard, I, as pastor of this congregation, do now commission you to visit among the members and friends of this congregation, soliciting for greater loyalty, liberality, devotion and consecration, that Christ's Kingdom may be advanced among us and that this congregation may become a greater power in the world's evangelization. Go, then, in His name, and may the Holy Spirit direct you in presenting the claims of Christ's Kingdom and abundantly crown your labors with success. Go in the Saviors name and for His glory. Amen.

Then shall the congregation be addressed as follows:

And now, brethren and friends of this congregation, as we are setting these men apart for this definite service, I ask that you receive them kindly and sympathetically. They are your brethren and workers together with God. Prepare yourselves thoughtfully and prayerfully that you may give a prompt and favorable answer to their questions and requests.

To this end let us arise and unite in prayer to Almighty God for His blessing upon them and us, in the work we are undertaking.

Let us pray.

Then shall follow a brief prayer of definite petitions.

Go then, in the name of your Lord and Master and do your utmost to promote His Kingdom.

A Layman's Business

THE WORK OF THE CHURCH is a layman's business. Mr. Armour used to say that his business was serving the Lord and he packed pork to pay expenses. The development of a special class of workers, set apart and trained for the business of the Kingdom of God, has taken the responsibility and obligation off the shoulders of the layman and put them on the shoulders of a few men who alone are considered to be called to the Lord's work. "Them He also called" is the suggestion of one inclusive class, and every individual who has taken upon himself Christ's name has been called to Christ's service. The Protestant Church in the United States for its successful advance to-day demands the active cooperation in its work of every layman. If this cooperation is not given, we may see a tremendous loss of prestige and power.

The plan of group supervision as followed in many churches has engaged the activities of the laymen. One church in Newark Presbytery has put its laymen to work in the supervision of a neighborhood asking the group representative to call upon the sick and the stranger and to relate himself to every church member living in the area assigned to him. The same leadership is employed in the Kernahan plan of personal evangelism and then also in the every-member canvass.

Concrete cases are only examples of the application of a principle. The principle is lay activity and lay co-operation in the promotion of the Kingdom of God—the laymen's business.

"Give"—Is His Command; Not—Buy and Sell

(The New Testament Stewardship Plan of Church Finance)   AUGUST W. BRUSTAT

BY "New Testament Stewardship Plan" we mean, briefly, the support of the local Church and the Kingdom of God at large entirely by free-will offerings, without the selling of tickets for any function or the running of money-making or money-raising schemes of any kind.

Some of the reasons that have been advanced against money-making schemes are the following. The reader may be able to add others.

1. The Church that enters any business except the business for which it is chartered by the State is sailing under false colors. The Church is chartered to proclaim the Gospel of Christ —AND NOTHING ELSE. The Church is called to do that one thing, and it ought to bend all its efforts and energies, all its gifts and talents in doing that one thing well. The Church is called to witness to the whole counsel of God under the leadership of the Holy Spirit. And if we follow His leadership He will never lead us along the lines of worldly activity.

2. The Church has no moral right to compete with bakeries, haberdasheries, restaurants or casinos. Your cake sale will not induce the baker in your town to feel kindly disposed to your Church because you are a competitor, even if only once or twice a year. The business people in your community are tired of giving out one prize after another for your bingo or bridge. If you don't believe it, just ask them about it sometime.

3. Money-making schemes cast an odium upon the Christian Church.

This afternoon we visited a family that recently moved into our community. Before deciding to join our church they wanted this one question cleared up: "Do you have money-making schemes in your Church?" They were determined not to join a Church which would prove a repetition of their former experience when they were asked to purchase one ticket after another and to serve on this luncheon, and that bingo committee. They felt that the Church should be supported by free-will offerings only.

Last week we had a similar experience. Duplications abound. People who are really interested in the Lord's work are becoming a bit tired of getting anything but spiritual benefits from the Church.

Oftentimes we have heard the charge hurled against the Church: "The Church is too commercialized, it has become a racket." We actually heard a man ask a clergyman to whom he had just been introduced: "How's your racket?" And sad it is, but in all too many instances it is true that that the Church has become a racket.

We heard a story the other day. Perhaps you have heard it too. It is supposed to be authentic. But if not, it serves as an illustration and a lesson. A man was lying unconscious by a street curb after an automobile accident. The police officer was looking over his personal possessions to determine his name and address. Eventually he called the local priest to administer the last rites. While the priest was officiating the man regained consciousness and reported that he was a Protestant and not a Romanist. When the priest questioned the officer he found that he had been called because a bingo card was found in the man's pocket. Bingo has been associated with Romanism to such an extent that it has been called the "Bingo Church." But sadly enough, the same appellation may be applied to many Protestant Churches. All of this casts an odium upon the Church which seriously hampers its real purpose.

4. Attendance at Church functions salves the consciences of non-church goers.

When we first came to our present parish we visited some whose names appeared in the Church records but who had not attended the services since our installation. When we inquired about it we received the answer: "Why, I come. I've attended every affair at the Church for the last few years." But they did NOT come to the SERVICES. They came to affairs—and no doubt they thought that in buying tickets they were duly supporting the Church and incidentally acquired a sort of invisible ticket which would assure entrance through the Pearly Gates. Money-making schemes are undesirable because they have the tendency to salve men's consciences into a false security regarding their salvation.

5. To arrange money-making affairs diverts the attention of the Church members from the REAL WORK of the Church.

The Ladies' Aid Society or Men's Club that, like Martha, is everlastingly busy in the kitchen or in the committee meeting arranging for the next bazaar, or bingo, or bunco, will not, like Mary, have much time left to sit at Jesus' feet to hear His Word and then DO it. Time spent in planning and then executing such Church affairs seems to us a case of "Much Ado About Nothing."

And please, people are NOT won for the Lord Jesus by attending card parties and bazaars. They are won only by attending to the things of the Lord. But you say, here is a chance to meet the unchurched and invite them to the services. But now really, are you much in the mood to speak of Christ and His great salvation over the card table? Are the unchurched inclined to listen if you should suggest the subject? The amount of time consumed by many church members over church affairs seems a misuse of the stewardship of time.

Free-Will Giving

Free-will giving has been advocated for the following reasons:

1. It is Scriptural.

Nowhere do we read that the Lord or His people in the Old Testament, or the Apostles and Evangelists in the New Testament advocated any other kind of church support than free-will offerings.

The Lord Jesus tells us how to secure money for the Church's support when He says: "Give, and it shall be given unto you; good measure, pressed down, and running over, shall men give into your bosom. For with what measure ye mete withal it shall be measured to you again." (Luke 6:38). And it might be well to study the words of St. Paul in 2 Cor. 8:7. 12-15; 9: 1-7.

In the Old Testament we read numerous passages which insist that the Lord's work be supported by the tithe. That same principle should be the basis of our giving in these New Testament times, for the tithe was never, to our knowledge, revoked. In fact Jesus commended tithing (Matthew 23:23); and St. Paul inferred it (1 Cor. 16:2).

Can you imagine the risen Jesus, after the Cross and the Resurrection, standing on the brow of Olivet, momentarily to ascend to the Father, giving the disciples the great Mission Command, and then adding: "To do this world-work money will be needed. Suppose you get it from the heathen (for you are only a small, poverty-stricken group), by giving a card or bingo party once in a while, hold an annual bazaar, and raffle off an automobile, and you will have the necessary funds to carry on my work.

Can you imagine St. Paul encouraging his congregations in a similar manner to help the poor in Jerusalem? No, rather they encouraged giving from a generous and grateful heart. They encouraged free-will offerings. "Freely ye have received, freely give." For all the blessings of Cavalry we should be willing to give, if need be, our all, to carry on the great work of our Lord.

2. Free-will giving allows the members of the Church more time in which to do the real work of the Lord. It relieves them of the time-consuming preparations required to devise and execute ever new methods of wheedling money out of people. It helps to make church members realize the importance of the stewardship of time as well as the stewardship of money.

3. When the members of a Christian congregation do the Lord's work and stick to that one job, that congregation will command the respect of even the unchurched in the community. If the churches of America would universally follow the free-will giving plan, the Church would, we believe, regain much of the dignity and prestige it has lost during the money-making era.

4. Free-will giving will be an incentive to have people BRING their offerings to the CHURCH SERVICE, if they love their Lord at all. And once in the service they will hear the Word of God and find soul-strength in the Church's ministrations. By the money-raising plan people can conveniently absent themselves from the service, for did they not attend that function at the Church on Friday night? There they paid their fifty cents and saw the pastor. That ought to do for a while. In fact, it ought to do until the next Church function is announced. The free-will offering plan will cause people to realize that their connection with the Church must and can be only through the Church's God-appointed ministrations. In other words, people will begin to realize that they come to church for purposes of worship, not for purposes of entertainment.

5. The free-will offering plan is the best to balance the church's budget —to keep the church out of the red. Generally the money-making churches are always short of money and in debt. We have often wondered why this is when they are always making money. Is it perhaps because it costs real money to arrange money-making schemes? Is it because the ticket-buying constituency have begun to feel that such is the only way to support the Church, or that ten cents in the weekly offering envelope ought to be enough because the Ladies' Aid just gave the Church $100.00, which represented the proceeds from the last bingo party? Is it because money-making schemes kill the spirit of real giving? Is it, perhaps, because the Lord can't use and bless that kind of money? Perhaps money-making schemes do not really make so much money after all. These are only suggestions, perhaps someone can find the real answer.

6. Free-will offerings, even though these may not be as generous in many instances as they ought to be, will, nevertheless, be blessed of God, and will give both the pastor and the members the satisfaction that the work of the Lord, as far as they are concerned, is done in the Scriptural manner. It is done with the funds received according to the New Testament plan of stewardship.

These are some reasons in favor of free-will offerings. Others may suggest themselves to the reader.

Some Objections Answered

1. "We have in our congregation a poor widow who can barely manage to live on her meagre earnings, but would like to help the Lord's work with her baking. She is an exceptionally fine baker of pies. Why should she not be able to bake her pies and sell them at the bazaar, and thus dedicate that talent to the Lord and so contribute to the Church?"

We would suggest in the first place, that she might secure a number of customers privately without bringing her business into the church. Better perhaps would be the suggestion that she just put the cost of making the pies on the collection plate.

Furthermore, if such a case arises, perhaps the church ought to be helping the poor woman and not she the church. The comparatively few folks who are in such a position ought not be a veil for the others who are too niggardly to give generously to the Lord's work and salve their consciences by "working so hard" for the bazaar.

2. Another asks: "What can we do to keep the ladies busy if we eliminate the money-making program with which they have been occupied since their inception?"

If it is really true that the Ladies' Aid can do nothing else than sell tickets and arrange money-making schemes, they ought to be dissolved without further ado. No organization has a right to exist as a society of the Christian Church without a good missionary and educational program. Let's make Priscilla's and Tabitha's out of our ladies. Get them busy visiting the poor and the sick and the missionary prospects. Get them busy sewing gratis for the hospital and orphanage. It will give them a real thrill when they get into it. Give them some real Bible study and make it interesting and you can keep the ladies busy until Jesus returns to take His Church into glory. And your church will grow and prosper and have sufficient funds for its local work as well as that of the far-flung empire of the Church.

Christian Sociability

This consideration does not mean, of course, that we are to have no Christian sociability in our churches. Far from it. Social events which enable Christians to rejoice in the company of fellow-Christians are very much in order.

Let the Seniors give their Biblical drama in the Parish Hall. Let the ladies celebrate that church anniversary with a congregational supper. Let the Juniors have that beach party. Let the Men's Club sponsor that Ladies' Night. But remind them that no tickets are to be sold for the occasion. Only a free-will offering will be taken. The event is not sponsored for the purpose of making money for the church, but for the fellowship of Christian believers. The church's expenses are taken care of by the free-will offerings of the worshippers on Sunday. The functions are held only for an evening of fellowship with Christians. And that purpose is accomplished without the sale of tickets, or with the idea of making money for the Church. The expenses of the Church should be met by the free-will offerings of those who receive the spiritual benefits of the Church.

We may add that in eight years of experience with free-will giving, we have never had any social event that did not more than pay for itself.

We conclude with this quotation: "In a marriage the husband is supposed to take care of the expense of the wife. But there are times when we read notices in the papers where a husband announces that he will no longer be responsible for the debts of a wife who has been unfaithful.

The Every Member Canvass
A Brief Summary of the More Important Steps in the Canvass
HOWARD L. HALTER

THE majority of our churches conduct an every member canvass annually. But many canvasses do not bring in the maximum support because of inadequate preparation or because of an untrained personnel. Both steps are relatively simple. The purpose of this paper is to outline these various steps. Not that anything new will be presented—merely the restatement of principles which have been proven sound by the experiences pooled from many churches.

The Budget

The foundation of the successful canvass starts with the preparation of an adequate budget. The best way to set up the budget for the ensuing year is, at a regular meeting of the church council, preferably at the September meeting, to appoint a budget committee, consisting of the Pastor, the church treasurer, the financial secretary and, if he is a member of the church council, the Sunday School superintendent.

It is the duty of these men to report at the October meeting and to be able to justify every expenditure which they list in the budget.

Courage Essential

For a truly successful canvass, it is essential that this budget committee forget any past deficits or past failures and to start out fresh as though the church has had no financial problems (as haven't we all).

The actual needs and expenses of the church are to be listed. And the budget should not in any way be limited merely because it has hovered at such and such a figure during the past year or years.

Rewards

Few of us know what our congregations, poor as they may be, are capable of until we present them with a challenge in the form of a materially increased budget—providing that budget can be justified. We know of one instance where a church had been raising $3,500 annually, and where the pastor was convinced that his congregation was actually not capable of raising more money.

He tried this thorough every member canvass, and started out with a budget of $7,500—more than twice the previous year's figure.

He brought in $6,300 in actual subscriptions, which, together with the plate collections met this new budget. The editors of this magazine will give you the name and address of this pastor, upon request. He is anxious to share his experience with others since his "conversion" to the courageous way of meeting a financial problem through an adequate and systematic canvass.

THE BUDGET 1940

1. CURRENT EXPENSE

A. Ministerial Service
Salary	$0,000	
Parsonage Rent	000	$0,000

B. Administrative Expenses
Church Supplies	000	
New Equipment	00	
Postage—All Dept.		
Printing		
Paper and Mimeo. Supplies	000	
Special Services	00	
Organist	000	
Advertising	000	
Car Allowance	000	
Conference Expenses	00	
Insurance	000	
Sexton	000	
Telephone	00	0,000

C. Plant Operation
Gas and Electricity	000	
Fuel Oil	000	
Water	00	
Building Maintenance	00	
	000	0,000

2. DEBT REDUCTION

Synodical Church Extension Fund Loan (No Interest)	$00,000
District Church Extension Fund Loan (No Interest)	00,000
Mortgage at Bank at 5% Interest	00,000
Total Indebtedness	$00,000

Synodical Church Extension Fund Repayment	0,000	
Synodical Church Extension Fund Administration Fee 1% (annual)	000	
District Church Extension Fund Repayment	000	
District Church Extension Fund Administration Fee 1% (1st year)	000	
Interest on Bank Mortgage at 5%	000	0,000

3. MISSIONS AT HOME AND ABROAD AND BENEVOLENCES

To Synod and District	000	
American Lutheran Publicity Bureau	00	
Tract Fund	0	
American Bible Society	00	
Lutheran Inner Mission	00	
Queens Service Centre	00	
Bethlehem Orphan Home	00	
Adirondack Mission, Saranac, N. Y.	00	
Chinese Mission, N. Y. C.	00	
Lutheran Hospital, Brooklyn, N. Y.	00	000

	$0,000

Presentation

The budget is presented in three subdivisions. (See facsimile page).

1. Current expenses—which is redivided into:
   a) General administrative expenses.
   b) Plant operation.
2. Debt reduction—also repairs.
3. Missions and benevolences.

Items one and two come from the left hand pocket of the envelope. Item three is a listing of the expenditures from the right hand pocket.

It is essential that if there was a deficit from the previous year that this will be included in the budget. If there have been any salary cuts, it is well that they be restored. Any anticipated expenses, such as painting and repairing, money for a new organ, etc. must also be listed in their proper category. This is much better than trying to run a special drive later in the year.

This budget is then to be presented and explained at the October meeting of the church council, where, having met with approval, it is next presented to the congregation for the approval of the voting body.

Faith Needed

Faith and courage to pass upon a budget which may be materially higher than the previous one is the prime factor for the beginning of the successful every member canvass.

The Budget

1. Note that sections 1 and 2 (Current Expense and Debt Reduction) constitute the left hand pocket of the envelope, while section 3, (Missions at Home and Abroad and Benevolences) covers the right hand pocket.
2. Note that under section 2, Debt Reduction, the total indebtedness is listed in detail, so that the congregation will have a full background of the church's financial condition when they make their subscription.
3. And most important of all, notice that *anticipated offerings* and subscriptions are not to be listed in any way. The principles behind publishing the full budget is to get the congregation to raise that full amount of money. In the above budget, about $1,000 will be received in plate collections over and above the envelope subscriptions. If this money comes in, it will be used to pay off the indebtedness. Ladies' Aid and Men's Club contributions, if expected, should likewise not be listed, otherwise those who could do more in their envelope contributions will hold back, privately feeling that, after all, they have to contribute through this

body, too. Get 'll the money in the envelopes through subscriptions. Anything else that may come in through any other source, you will be able to find ample use for.

The Workers

Since success in getting the subscriptions for the budget depends upon the workers and especially upon the one who guides them, it is essential that a chairman of the canvass committee be appointed who is both able and willing to undertake the task.

This chairman is to be selected and appointed by the budget committee with the approval, of course, of the church council.

Lists

Before selecting any of the workers, this chairman shall be provided with a complete membership list; likewise, a list of all of the parents of the Sunday School children who are not members of the congregation. A list of all "dead wood" may also be included.

These lists are then converted into "workers cards" (see illustration) which lists the members according to families, thus materially reducing the number of calls to be made later.

It is understood that all information on these cards is confidential. In cooperation with the financial secretary or treasurer, the weekly gifts of each member of a family is to be listed on these cards under their proper heading. The column headed "Subscription" is not filled in until later.

The task of making out the worker's card will again familiarize the chairman with all individuals within the church. It will give him a bird's eye view of the entire financial situation, and will at the same time bring to his mind the people with whom he has to deal.

Selecting the Workers

The Chairman, together with the other members of his committee selects the workers on the basis of the workers cards, which have now been filled out.

He will naturally choose those who themselves have shown an interest in their church by the adequacy of their own gifts. But even more important, he will choose those who have the ability to meet people; those who are pleasant and affable and will be able to influence others. He will try to choose enough canvassers so that no worker will have to make more than ten calls.

Having chosen the workers on paper, the next step is to interview them individually and "sell" them on the proposition if they are in any way hesitant about serving. The usual excuse given by prospects for not serving is that "they would not know what to do or say." Tell them that all will be cared for in the workers meetings.

Assigning the Cards

A duplicate set of each of the worker's cards is now to be made either by the chairman or his staff.

Next the chairman procures a large map of the community and divides the entire parish into as many small sections as there are to be canvassers, figuring 10 calls or less to each canvasser. The purpose of this is to allocate all calls so that all cards given to any one canvasser will be in reasonably close proximity to one another.

Each section is numbered on the map, and all calls within this section receive the section number. The ten or less calls in each section are placed in an envelope, marked only with the section number. And this entire section is then later assigned to one of the workers.

It is important not to put the name of any worker on the cards themselves.

Facsimile of a "Worker's Card"

Worker's Confidential Record

Prospect's Address: 719 Spruce Ave.   Section Number 2

Individuals in this Family	Status	Previous Weekly Sub.	Suggested Sub.		Envelope Number
			C.E.	B	
Husband: Stein, Louis	SSP	——	$1.00	.25	188
Wife: Minnie	C	——	——	——	——
Children: Mary	SS	.05	.10	.01	189
Robert	SS	.05	.10	.01	190
Others:					

Code "C"—Communicant SSP—Unchurched Sunday School parent "SS"—in Sunday School "A"—attend services, but not a communicant member of the church. C.E.—Current Expenses, left pocket of envelope. "B"—Benevolences, right pocket.

If a worker drops out, it means that a new name has to be written on each card, with the result that someone feels he is doing what someone else did not want to do. Put the name of the worker on an envelope means a switch of sections to another man is easily accomplished by simply filling out a new envelope. The section number remains the same.

Cards are not to be given out until the second meeting of the canvassers. And just shortly before this meeting, after you know whom you can depend upon by their presence at the first meeting, actual assignment of cards is made to the individual worker.

Don't for the Chairman

Don't assign relative to each other, neither close friends. Don't assign the 10 best prospects to the workers, but to the chairman himself. Don't assign distant points to a man without a car. Don't allow the telephone to be used in any phase of your work. The whole system is based upon personal contact.

Anticipated Subscription

Either before or after the worker's cards have been divided into sections on the basis of a map study, the amount of the anticipated subscription should be placed upon the worker's card under the heading, "Suggested Subscription." Consult your chart on "Proportionate Giving to see whether or not, in your opinion, the individual contributor is doing his share.

Let's say that Mr. Louis Stein has an income of $30 a week. His dependents are Mrs. Minnie Stein, and their two children, Robert and Mary. Our chart on proportionate giving shows that Mr. Stein's gift should be $1.50 per week. Naturally, since He is the only wage-earner in the family, his gift is subdivided among the other members of the family, as suggested on the Worker's Confidential Record previously shown. Proper subdivision has here been made according to the family members, and according to the two pockets of the envelope. The gifts credited to Mary and Robert may go to the Sunday School department of church.

Training the Workers

First Meeting

It is essential that the workers approach their task with enthusiasms and understanding. Both of these objectives can be accomplished by several dinner meetings.

This meeting ought to begin with a dinner at the expense of the church to be given either at the church or at a good local restaurant. When given at the church, none of the members of the canvassing staff is to help with the preparation—they are the guests.

The practical reasons behind this dinner are to get the people in question to attend the meeting. And there is nothing like a good dinner to put a man in a receptive frame of mind.

This first meeting is devoted almost entirely to the presentation and explanation of the budget. Where a budget booklet is printed, this dinner is the first time it is used—and then confined to this group of future canvassers.

The Usual Objections

If the budget for a church of 200 communicants amounts to $10,000, someone present is certain to figure out that this means the average gift per communicant member of $50 per year— a contribution of $3.00 per week for a family of three communicants. And the same individual is certain to point out that, with so many families on relief, and with so many of the communicants of high school age and not self-supporting, that this is an impossible high average—hence that there is no hope in meeting this budget.

This is your opportunity to point out the principles of proportionate giving. Point out that these statistics are interesting, but that they are not to be mentioned by the workers to their prospects, since individuals who could afford to give ten times the average amount will hold themselves to the average. Each communicant must give in proportion to his income. And this means success in reaching the necessary amount.

Card Showing Proportionate Giving

To Meet the Budget, Each Member Must Give In Proportion to His Income

If Your Weekly Salary Is:	Your Total Contribution Will Be:	This Sum is Divided between the Left Pocket C.E.	Right Pocket B.
$10.00	$ .50	$ .40	$ .10
$15.00	.75	.60	.15
$20.00	1.00	.80	.20
$25.00	1.25	1.00	.25
$30.00	1.50	1.20	.30
$35.00	1.75	1.40	.35
$40.00	2.00	1.60	.40
$45.00	2.25	1.80	.45
$50.00	2.50	2.00	.50
$55.00	2.75	2.20	.55
$60.00	3.00	2.40	.60
$65.00	3.25	2.60	.65
$70.00	3.50	2.80	.70
$75.00	3.75	3.00	.75

Note: Where there are children in the Sunday School Department, money is placed in the child's envelopes from this Total Contribution on the basis of 10c deduction for each child.

Example: Mr. Stein, whose income is $30.00 weekly and whose total contribution amounts to $1.50, has two children. He will redivide this gift as follows, $1.00 in C.E. (left pocket), 30c in the B. (right pocket), and 10c in each of his child's envelopes. Total, $1.50 weekly.

Stewardship

Proportionate giving is nothing more than the principle of stewardship practically applied. The Bible standard of true stewardship has always been 10% of a man's gross income—we do not even propose this Bible minimum, but a lesser amount—just enough to meet the budget successfully, which comes to about 5% of people's gross income in the average church.

The proportionate share cards which were passed out at the beginning of the meeting will now be referred to. It is essential that the five per cent basis be adopted since in the average congregation there will be those who will not be able to keep their pledges, those who move away, and those who, through neglect, do not keep their pledges—not to mention those who are not self supporting or who have no income whatever other than relief. Actually, 5% still does not enter the class which the Bible encourages—that of "sacrificial giving"—giving which really hurts.

Booklet Essential

The presentation of the budget will be made much easier if it is made an integral part of the congregation's annual report to the members. It is highly essential that printed matter in this booklet be kept at a minimum, and that it be illustrated, otherwise it will not be read.

Reports of each society with emphasis on work done rather than on money raised, together with reports of the educational committee, the elders, the deacons, and the pastor, will insure reading of the booklet itself.

The cost of such a booklet is an investment rather than an expenditure. For it is all too true that our people do not give enough because they are not well enough informed as to the need. Neither do they generally understand where the money goes, or why it is necessary to spend so much for this and that.

So instead of a mere budget presentation, where this booklet is used, you are giving your workers—and later on your congregation—a complete survey of work accomplished during the year, and are preparing them for the ready acceptance of the budget itself. Chances are your congregation does not know what your church—any you—have accomplished.

232

Addenda—The Budget

Frankly most churches are in a bad financial condition because they depend upon false premises to raise their money. It seems to be the New Testament principle that those who benefit by the church are the ones who must support the church.

It is evident that Our Lord had money to pay expenses incurred in His work. Obviously He received this money in the form of free will offerings from those who had received some benefit from His Word and work. He had nothing to sell.

So it is evident that the church which depends upon commercial methods of raising money is doing its work the hard way. It is training its members to look for some physical exchange on the part of the church for money received by it.

Other Beneficiaries

The unchurched parents of your Sunday School children are obviously receiving an indirect spiritual benefit from your church. Go to them, give them the opportunity to share in the expenses of the church which makes your Sunday School possible by giving them the opportunity to make their subscription to the church even if they, themselves, never enter it.

If it is the custom of your church to run various affairs to make money, either use that money for purposes not in the budget, or get the society to pledge this money for outside purposes —also not in your budget. And depend upon your budget subscriptions to run the church.

A Powerful Argument

It's worth hundreds of dollars to you to be able to say to a member, "We hope that you will find it possible to raise your subscription this year, because we have no other means of raising money. For the only money we get comes in the form of free will offerings from those who receive some benefit from this church."

"Pledge" vs. "Subscription"

Never use the word "pledge." You will find that many will not "pledge," but they will "subscribe." The church isn't going to sue a man who doesn't keep his "pledge." All you are after is a statement—signed, if possible—as to that individual's *intention* of giving.

"Subscribe" means just that. And if a man has to change his subscription to less during the course of the year, he will not, somehow, feel so self conscious as he would had a "pledge" been made.

The Worker's Subscriptions

It is essential that the workers make their subscriptions before they go out to interview others. A man who has made his own committment is in a better frame of mind to tell another of his duties if he has already fulfilled his.

The time to take this subscription from the workers is at the second meeting. But, to prepare the workers, announcement should be made of this intention here at the *first* worker's meeting to give them opportunity to make up their minds on the basis of the budget presentation here made.

The Second Worker's Meeting

Again, the best meeting takes place after a dinner.

We previously mentioned the advisability of having a large staff. This serves two purposes. It instructs a larger group of the church in the principles which really all ought to know; and it allows for a natural decrease in the number of workers who will finally do the work. It also cuts down the number of calls the individual has to make.

The purpose of this second meeting is:

1. To provide the workers with their materials, subscription cards and working kits.
2. To instruct them how to meet people to obtain larger pledges.
3. To overcome natural objections toward increased giving.
4. To arouse mass enthusiasm.

The Worker's Kit

Following the dinner, engage the group in a few community songs. Get away from the serious purpose of the meeting for fifteen minutes.

Open the second meeting by giving out the envelopes which contain the section to be visited by the individual. You have had the opportunity during the dinner or during the singing of reassigning any envelope previously assigned to a worker who did not appear. Assign all envelopes to the workers present. Do not hold them and hope to give them out later. Now is the time.

Together with the envelopes a working kit is also given out which contains a duplicate copy of the "Catechism of Objections," a share card, and the new packets of church envelopes, the numbers of which were copied on the workers card by the Financial Secretary or the chairman of the committee. Likewise, subscription cards.

A copy of the "Catechism of Objections to Giving" should be sent to the workers a few days before the second dinner meeting, so that they can familiarize themselves with the material.

They will ask questions about it.

Following the discussion of the objections to giving which people will naturally raise, go into your instruction of the workers on their approach.

Don't Visit

Tell your workers to get down to business immediately after the usual salutations. Simply say, "I am one of the workers in the Every Member Canvass, and I came to talk to you about the church budget for this coming year." If the party being interviewed is one from whom a definite increase is expected, simply hand him the card on Proportionate Giving and say, "Mr. Stein, I thought you would be interested in seeing this card, which has been worked out on the basis of proportionate giving so that our church can meet its budget this coming year. As you know, there are many in our church who are not in a position to contribute liberally, so we who can must do our full share."

Mr. Stein will, no doubt, counter with some objection as to why he cannot give more than he has in the past. What ever the answer, don't argue.

A Catechism for the Worker
Objections to Giving—and Their Answers

(Write out a catechism which particularly fits your own circumstances— these are merely suggestions to show the general principle. Answers must be brief and factual—never argumentative. If they do not turn aside the objection, the worker is to report the name of the individual in question to the chairman, who, in turn will visit them personally).

1. "I can't afford to give now"— Answer: The idea of the subscription is that you don't have to give the entire amount now. You spread it over a long period, in amounts that you can afford.

2. "I'll take envelopes, but I will not make a definite subscription." Answer: What would happen if everyone in the church did not state what could be expected of him?

3. "I can't afford to give much." Answer: Our church never expects a man to do more than he is able to. We only ask that you give what the church is worth to you.

4. "I don't see why a definite subscription is necessary." Answer: We have to know in advance how much is coming in so that we don't obligate ourselves beyond our ability to pay. It's a strange thing, but the church which doesn't bother with definite subscriptions is generally the one which is forced into Bingo and bazaars to pay its bills.

5. "We give through our child's

Sunday School envelopes. I do not care to take envelopes from a church which I do not attend." Answer: The money which you give in your child's Sunday School envelopes is given back to you in the form of books, trained teachers, gifts, etc. Little of that money goes for the support of the church which makes this Sunday School possible. Now we merely ask you to support that church, for we believe that those who share in the benefits of the church, directly or indirectly, are the ones to whom we can look for support since we have no other means of raising money.

6. "The church is always begging." Answer: Yes, some are. That's because the members and friends of those churches do not support theirs the way we ask you to do through this every member canvass. We come once a year. You fulfill your subscription through your weekly envelope and you will never hear us talk money during the rest of the year.

Answer him on the basis of the "objections to giving" sheet. Simply emphasize the amount of good which is being done with any money given.

Workers should stick to the point of their call. They should not "visit."

Confidential

Never, under any circumstances, are the workers to show the prospect the confidential worker's cards.

The worker is to refresh his memory from this card before he enters the house in question. Once inside, his card remains in his pocket.

The workers must likewise be impressed with the damage they will do if they discuss the amounts received by them through the subscriptions. It is a breach of faith to tell Mr. Smith how much—or how little—Mr. Stein gave.

Inspirational Address

Following this formal instruction and the answering of any questions on the part of the workers, either the pastor or the chairman will make an inspirational address, again covering the highlights of the budget, emphasizing what it will mean to the church to get the people to subscribe this higher amount.

Following this address, the subscription cards are passed out to the workers, who are now asked to make their own subscription, bearing in mind all that has been said.

If secrecy is desired in subscribing each worker may be furnished with a blank envelope into which he places his signed subscription card. This can be done so that no one but the chairman, the pastor, and the financial secretary will know the actual amount contributed.

Following the signing of the cards,

another community sing is held, during this period, it is a good plan to tally all the cards so that just before the prayer at the end of the meeting, announcement can be made of the total amount subscribed that evening, and its proportion to the entire budget.

This announcement acts as an incentive for the workers to go out and finish the job successfully—particularly if the response of the workers has indicated an increase in their own pledges over again the previous year's amount.

Subscription Card

In gratitude for all that God has done for me, for my salvation, for the gift of life and health, it is my desire to show my appreciation to Him by my support of the Church's work.

To that end I herewith subscribe the following amounts to the 1941 Budget of the Lutheran Church of the Resurrection.

Name	C.E. (Left Pocket)	B. (Right Pocket)
Louis Stein	$1.00	25c
Mary	8c	2c
Robert	8c	2c

Signed: L. Stein
Address: 719 Spruce St.

It is my intention to give this sum weekly. I shall raise or lower the amount subscribed if my circumstances become better or worse, in my attempt to give proportionate to my income, as God has prospered me.

Publicity

The Budget Booklet

The budget is best presented to the congregation in the form of an illustrated booklet not illustrated with stock religious cuts, but drawings or photos which tie in with the purpose of the campaign and give background material from and of the church.

Or the booklet may be merely an amplification of the budget. In either case there ought to be as much illustration as type.

The campaign—and naturally the booklet—ought to bring home a definite theme like "Let's Become Self-Supporting this Year" or "We Burn Our Mortgage" or "The Story of My Church." And each page in the booklet must carry forward that theme to the logical acceptance of the budget.

The Church Studio, Fox Chase, Philadelphia, Penna., will prepare such a booklet, provide drawings, prepare the copy, and furnish up to 1,000 completed copies for about $95. It can be done for less, if you do all the work. But whatever the cost, it is worth the

money if it is well done—for people still read—and get the message—of a well-prepared booklet.

Mailing

Where such a booklet is prepared, it is well to send it out about eight days before the start of the canvassing. This booklet is usually accompanied by a letter, preferably only one paragraph long, stating again, the purpose of the booklet. This letter should be signed by hand by the chairman of the worker's committee.

Second Letter

Three days later another letter should go out telling of the Every Member Canvass, giving date of the Consecration of the Workers (Loyalty Sunday) and the date the canvass is to end.

This letter might be accompanied by a tract which can be purchased from the Duplex Envelope Company at 50c a hundred called, "Is Yours a Guess Work Church?" This particular tract again tells of the importance of the budget and of the subscription through the weekly envelope.

Some churches even include a mission booklet from our Synod office, such as "Beyond the Clouds, a Star" to back up the plea for the right hand pocket of the envelope.

As a final means of reminding the people of the Every Member Canvass, a paragraph is inserted in the church-paper giving details and dates of the Every Members Canvass, listing the entire staff.

The Canvass

The work usually begins on a Sunday afternoon. To make certain that the workers will not have to travel needlessly, some churches serve a luncheon immediately after services. A brief service is held, and the workers are sent out into the field.

In your last minute instructions to the workers, insist that they do not stay at any home more than 15 minutes, that they get down to the purpose of their visit as soon as they enter the home.

Impress upon them that if they run into any unusual difficulty, that they merely report the incident in writing to their chairman for further action either by him or the pastor.

Don't Leave Envelopes

The workers should not leave the church envelopes at any home which says, "I cannot subscribe, but leave the envelopes anyway. I'll give what I can." Neither are subscription cards to be left at any home on the promise that they will be turned in later. These instances are to be reported to the chairman who will himself make another call on these people.

Only a Penny

When a family of doubtful loyalty or doubtful financial circumstances states that they are not in a position to make any subscription because they cannot afford it, simply say, "I know that times are hard. We don't expect much from anyone who doesn't have it, so why don't you take the envelopes and subscribe only 5c to be given every week. Or if you can't afford 5c, give only a penny in each pocket of the envelope. But give regularly. Because even these small gifts mount up. So far as our Lord is concerned, He values a gift from the poor, however small, as much as any gift from the rich."

But under no circumstances leave envelopes if the family refuses to subscribe.

Alternate Canvass Plan

Some churches, on Loyalty Sunday after the consecration of the workers, hold a congregational meeting at which the chairman speaks on the budget.

Those present are then given subscription cards to fill in at that service.

Dinner Party

A better plan is that of the congregational dinner party, at which a dinner is served to the congregation by one society (charge is usually made) which is followed by an entertainment, brief, but good.

Following the entertainment the chairman addresses the congregation on the budget, gives an inspirational address asking for increased pledges. Cards are then distributed and signed by the individuals.

No Substitute

These plans, though, are weak. There is no substitute for the good old house-to-house personal contact proposed in this canvass outline. No other plan can successfully cover all members of one family but the member to member visitation.

Report Meetings

At five o'clock Sunday afternoon and at approximately 9:30 on each evening during the week of the canvass, a report meeting is held in church.

The moment a worker returns from his section, he hands over his subscription cards to the chairman for tabulation.

Exchange of Experiences

Over coffee and cake experiences are exchanged. Each member present is called upon to tell his most difficult case, never naming names. Successes and failures are discussed, and encouragement given for the next evening's work.

Some churches distribute the next day's quota of calls at these report meetings instead of giving them all out in one envelope at the second Worker's meeting.

Display Totals

On a large blackboard or in any other way, display the number and amount of subscriptions received to date. The number of refusals, the number not at home, and in a general round-up the total amount subscribed and amount yet needed.

Workers are often divided into two teams, each with a captain, to add the competitive spirit to the proceedings.

It is a good plan to engage the group in a community sing before the blackboard is unveiled.

Report to the Congregation

If the budget has been fully subscribed, a Service of Thanksgiving is in order the following Sunday morning at which this announcement is made by the pastor. Formal thanks can then be made to the chairman and to the staff.

Letter of Thanks

It is likewise well for the pastor to send out a letter under his signature thanking all those who subscribed. For though people have given to the Lord's work, all of them, without exception, will appreciate a word of thanks and appreciation from the Lord's vicar.

The Campaign Continues

The campaign to meet the budget does not end with the canvass. It continues with the appointment of a man who will visit the delinquents, and whose duty it is to find out the reason that individual is not fulfilling his self-imposed obligation.

Monthly Statements

It's a tremendous lot of work for the Financial Secretary to issue and mail monthly statements to each and every subscriber, but it pays.

This system provides a quick check on all accounts, and reminds people who are in arrears before it is too late for them to catch up. That, incidentally, is the one great reason many fall down on their subscriptions. No one reminds them of their obligation for a period of three months—and by that time they owe so much that it is impossible to pay. And, instead of starting anew, they drop the whole idea of paying at all—particularly if they are "fringe-members" or the unchurched parents of Sunday School children.

The Visitor

If someone is made responsible for

the task of visiting these people who fall behind, he can be given the monthly statements of those in arrears. His visit will bring in 95% of all subscribed money—not by force, but by the very courtesy of his visit. This has been experienced by those who have used this system.

You Get Out . . . .

As usual, you get out of a canvass what you put in. Take the time to do it right—follow principles which have proved successful in other cases, and you can't help but increase your potential gifts many times more than you thought possible.

Incidentally, another valuable reference book on this work is called "Your Budget and Your Canvass," put out by Duxplex Envelope Company, Richmond, Va.

For the Pastor

Creating the psychological background for the every member canvass is up to the pastor. During the month prior to the canvass itself—often termed "Loyalty Month"—the pastor

1. Addresses each organization within the church on the spiritual background of giving, pointing out that worship, prayer, and giving are the three demands which the Christian must fulfill if he would have God's blessing. Also explanation of the budget.

2. A special Sunday School lesson on giving.

3. At least two sermons on the Stewardship of Time and Money. Remember that the greatest favor you can render your members is to teach them to give proportionately. God makes giving a condition for blessing His people. "Give and it will be given unto you."

4. The pastor visits all his members, especially the marginal members. Money not to be discussed on this visit, merely a pastoral call to bring all people closer to their church.

5. Editorial for the parish paper, announcement of Loyalty Month or Loyalty Sunday.

Following the canvass, it is up to the pastor and the chairman of the canvass committee chairman to institute a definite follow-up system for delinquent subscriptions. A group of men are to be assigned to this work who, at the end of the first month, when it is noticed that this or that one is falling behind, make a call on the individual and tactfully find out the reason. If a subscription cannot be met, it is best for these men at once to recommend a reduction, lest the individual stay away from church entirely because he feels he owes something which he cannot pay.

A Budget for the Christian Steward

A Personal Budget

A BUDGET is simply a statement of estimated receipts and expenditures for a given period of time, usually for the ensuing year.

No thoughtful business man and no responsible board of directors of any corporation or institution would think of entering the year without a budget.

While the average individual, who earns and spends money, may not bother about writing down on paper an estimate of his income and expenditures for any given period, yet he forms some idea of what his income may be and what he may want to spend it for.

But why not go a step further and carefully prepare and write down one's personal budget for the year? As stated, a budget is an estimate of income and outgo. One may not be absolutely sure of receiving all the money anticipated, and the calculations of one's expenditures may be upset to a certain extent by unforseen circumstances, and yet a personal budget has definite value.

Benefits of a Budget

1. In the first place a budget may help us to see more clearly whether or not we are giving as God has prospered us. We are stewards of God, accountable to Him for the manner in which we spend the money He has given us. To many, who, for the first time, prepare a budget for themselves, it may be somewhat of a disturbing revelation when they see how small their expenditure for church purposes has been in comparison to what they have been spending for all other purposes.

2. The second benefit of a budget will then follow if we are sincere Christians who are willing to be led by God's Word and moved by the Church's needs. In other words, when our own budget has shown us that we have been practicing anything but proportionate giving, it will lead us to readjust our expenditures in such a way that God will not only receive a fair share of our income, but that we will also spend the rest of our money more wisely.

Mr. X's Budget

Mr. X's income was $125.00 a month. For years his own and his wife's contribution to the Church totaled $1.50 monthly or $18.00 a year. Until their pastor began stressing proportionate giving, they thought they were doing as well as might be expected of them. Mr. X and his wife were Christians, and when they realized that proportionate giving was, indeed, the New Testament precept for Christian giving, the thought immediately occurred to them that they might not be giving God a fair share of their income. But let us permit Mr. X to tell his own story:

" 'Mary,' I said to my wife one evening, 'let us make up a budget and see where our money goes and what percentage of my salary we are giving to the Lord.' She agreed enthusiastically, but although we both labored to produce a budget, it was no easy task, for we had never before prepared one, nor had we ever kept an account of all our expenditures for an entire year. However, after some hard thinking and figuring, we arrived at the correct figures in some items and closely approached those of all the others. And this is what our budget looked like:

1. Income: $125.00 a month
2. Expenditures:

Rent	$ 30.00
Food	35.00
Clothing	8.00
Payment on Auto	18.00
Coal	4.50
Light and Gas	6.00
Cigars	4.00
Insurance	2.00
Gas and Oil	8.00
Amusements	3.00
Miscellaneous	5.00
CHURCH	1.50
	$125.00

"It did not take us long to notice that some of the figures were altogether out of balance. Why, our church contribution was the smallest expenditure! It was only 1⅕% of our income, and it made us both feel ashamed of ourselves. We therefore immediately decided to make some readjustments. Some items, we knew, could not easily be reduced, but there were others that could. That smoking expense must be cut down, so must the expense for gasoline and for amusement. Perhaps a few other savings could be effected. We would try

We did try, and soon we found that we were giving the Lord $7.50 a month, instead of only $1.50. And this is how our revised budget looked after about a year:

1. Income $125.00
2. Expenditures:

Rent	30.00
Food	35.00
Clothing	7.50
Payment on Auto	18.00
Coal	4.50
Light and Gas	5.50
Cigars	2.00
Insurance	2.00
Gas and Oil	7.00
Amusement	2.00
Miscellaneous	4.00
CHURCH	7.50
	$125.00

The rest of the story is simply told. Mr. and Mrs. X did not miss a thing they had given up. They felt happier and experienced that keen satisfaction which comes from knowing that one is doing the Lord's will and helping to spread the Gospel in all the world. To show Mr. and Mrs. X's increased sense of stewardship, it may be added that the first thing which they did when he brought home his salary was to take $7.50 of it and put it in a special purse, which they called "The Lord's Purse," and they never permitted themselves to use this money for any other than church or benevolent purposes. As time went on and Mr. and Mrs. X learned more and more the meaning and joy of practical Christian stewardship, they not only made more readjustments in their finances, but they also became ardent and successful supporters of proportionate giving in their circle of Christian friends, and thus became a blessing to others, also.

Pamphlet sent out by Western District Stewardship Committee.

✠ ✠ ✠

The Gideons have just placed the largest order for new Bibles in all their history— 250,000, the greatest number in forty-four years of Gideon endeavor. These Bibles have been distributed in hospitals, hotels, schools, and jails. It is the opinion of the executive committee of the Gideons that the tension created by the present European war has stimulated increased interest in the Bible.

The Hidden Talent of Gold

An analysis showed that contributions from the children in our Sunday School amounted to about six cents per child per Sunday.

This money paid the running expenses of the Sunday School department, but in no way helped share the burden of the church's budgetary expenses. Moreover, according to the policies of our church, even if there were a surplus in the Sunday School treasury, it would not be available for church purposes.

So on our last every member canvass the non-member parents of each Sunday School child was visited, and a subscription was asked of them. They were asked to take the weekly envelopes, state the amount that they felt that they could give during the course of the year, just as any communicant member would be asked.

This was done in harmony with our policy that "those who receive the benefit from the church are the ones to whom we look for support" since we have no other source of revenue other than the envelopes and the plate offering.

Even those Sunday School parents were approached for a pledge who were totally unchurched and never attended our services. We went to them, too, on the premise that they were receiving a definite spiritual gift—in the form of a child who was under instruction in the word of God—and these, too, ought to share in the church's budget. For were it not for the church, the Sunday School would not exist.

An Illustrated Budget

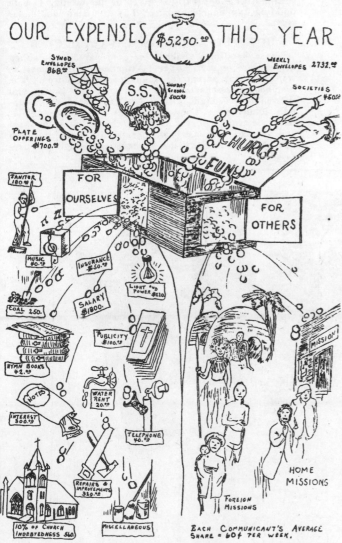

GIVE AS THE LORD HAS PROSPERED YOU!

mind. When Christ's people *see* and are convinced of the needs of Christ's kingdom they will give. Not only have we met our local budget, but the past several years we have also been on the synodical honor roll. This latter accomplishment of our people will stand out still more when I tell you that six years ago we not only gave little or nothing to Synod, but our District held several notes against us. This present year our budget was increased by $1,200 over the past year, and at this date all indications are that we shall meet that.

The picturization of our budget was distributed and explained by teams of our church-councilmen as they went out in November to distribute the sets of envelopes to the various households."

A Permanent Bulletin Board

MANY ANNOUNCEMENT BOARDS have a mechanical appearance which adds nothing to the beauty of the church property. Believing that the readers of the Service Department will

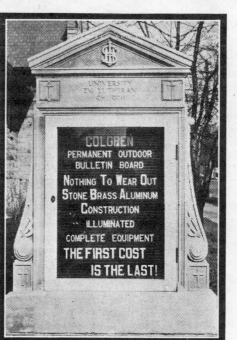

welcome information regarding a new bulletin board which contributes to the beauty of the church property, increases the efficiency of this form of publicity, and defies exposure and obsolescence, we call attention to a bulletin board which is constructed of Indiana limestone, attractively carved, and fitted with imperishable brass and aluminum equipment.

The Colgren Permanent Outdoor Bulletin Board, illustrated on this page, is the product of Charles A. Colgren, Bloomington, Indiana, and represents the best features of monumental design and fine craftsmanship. An installation of a Colgren Board solves for all time the bulletin board problem of the church; there is nothing to wear out, nothing to replace. The equipment includes three hundred letters in two and three inch sizes and complete electrical equipment for illuminating the sign panel.

The cost of the Colgren Permanent Outdoor Bulletin Board is very reasonable and competes favorably with mechanical devices now widely used for outdoor announcement purposes.

The above cut of an illustrated budget is from a copy furnished by the Rev. L. Buchheimer, Jr., of Lancaster, Pa. The illustration was made and reproduced on his mimeograph. Concerning the results of this illustrated method of presenting the needs of Christ's work, Pastor Buchheimer writes:

"The practical and main question with regard to this method of presenting our annual budget is, no doubt, Did it bring results? There is no longer any question of that kind in my

A CAMPAIGN THAT WENT OVER THE TOP

Geo. C. Koenig

Congregational campaigns for sums which a decade ago would have seemed preposterous are being attempted today—and successfully. Nor is there any reason why this should not be the case. Our Lutheran Christians have shared in the prosperity that accrued to the nation at large during the past years. Another element that must not be overlooked is the decreased value of money. $50,000 today represents roughly only $25,000 of pre-war money. Our congregations can raise large sums of money. The one thing necessary is the demonstration of need for larger expenditures. Lutheran church members are Christians and as such will follow along avenues of bigger faith and deeper consecration. In any campaign of this sort preparation, organization and, above all, information are indispensable. We want to tell the story of such a campaign. It may prove to be encouraging and stimulating.

WHY A CAMPAIGN WAS UNDERTAKEN

The congregation in question numbers about 700 communicant members. It is worshipping in a frame church built thirty-five years ago. During the past few years the section of New York City served by it has undergone a complete transformation. Houses sprang up by the hundreds and thousands. The old facilities proved to be inadequate. A large corner-plot, adjoining the old property, had been purchased three years ago. The problem that confronted the congregation was: How shall we get the money to erect a new church?

A shabby, flimsy, brick-veneer structure might have been built for a comparatively small sum. Cheaper it would have been, but its cheapness would have shouted to the heavens. Fortunately such a proposition was not entertained. The building committee wisely engaged a reputable firm of architects. The church as drawn up by them promised to be a monument of beauty, a worthy temple of the living God. But the estimated cost reached the $200,000 mark. Hence the campaign.

HOW THE CAMPAIGN WAS OPENED

A mass meeting of the entire congregation was called for a Sunday evening last February. A detailed description of the new church was given. Slides showing the floor plans, elevations and perspectives were flashed on the screen. The building committee presented a novel plan for securing the necessary funds: Individual sections and parts of the church were to be *sold*. The altar was to cost $2,500, the chancel arch $1,000, a clerestory window $500, a column under the trusses $250, a buttress $100, a front step $50, etc. The invitation to this meeting consisted of a beautiful piece of printed matter which forcibly brought home to the individual members the need of at once doing something toward making building operations possible.

Enthusiastic aproval was given at this meeting to both building and financial plans. The campaign was under way.

HOW THE CAMPAIGN WAS CONDUCTED

Three handsome booklets were prepared and mailed at regular intervals to every communicant member as well as to the parents of Sunday School children. The first booklet emphasized the need of a new church and showed by word and picture how the old plant was totally inadequate. The second gave a complete and detailed description of the proposed church, again in word and picture. The last booklet featured the financial plan and presented a long list of items that might be pur-

PRINTING THAT WON HEARTS
Used in the Campaign Described

chased. The prices ranged from $2,500 to $50.

Much time and thought was devoted to the material offered in these booklets. The resources of modern printing were made to cooperate so as to make the finished product both beautiful and inspiring. In this connection we would permit ourselves a fling at the penny-wise, pound-foolish policy of so many church committees. For the sake of a few dollars they will permit a shoddy piece of printing to go out in the name of the church, thereby at once stamping a proposed undertaking as cheap, as worth very little. In order to get money it is necessary to spend money, not foolishly, but wisely. A handsome folder, costing more, but bringing an important message in a dignified guise, will more than repay itself.

One month after the mass meeting mentioned above a group of canvassers was commissioned in a solemn church service. For two weeks these canvassers made visits, reporting their results every night at the church. Every canvasser had received a list of individuals (not families) to be visited. These lists were most carefully prepared so as to send the person best suited to every prospective contributor. Each canvasser was also equipped with a numbered list of articles to be sold, the list containing 520 items. As reports were rendered evening after evening the sold items would be checked off on every list. A feature of the campaign was the growing enthusiasm at these meetings.

WHAT THE CAMPAIGN ACHIEVED

No definite amount had been set as goal. The subscriptions received totalled $86,000. The money is being paid on installments running over a period of two years.

But this large sum was not the only result. Throughout the congregation there is a live interest in the new church. Everybody knows all about it and nearly everybody is telling all about it to every possible victim. These people will see their plans through.

A CONCLUDING WORD

Only the practical side of the campaign has been sketched in this article. Our readers will understand, we take that for granted, that every step of it was accompanied by much prayer. Nor did the pastor neglect to prepare his people months in advance for such a venture of faith. The need of stewardship as an essential element of practical Christianity was brought home time and time again. Without faith—faith in the promises of God, faith in the efficacy of the Gospel, faith in the message of the Cross as a power that *will* transform selfish and stingy hearts,—any such undertaking is impossible. The congregation which has been described is an average congregation. It has no really wealthy members. The largest amount contributed was $2950. But everybody, young and old, participated in the campaign. The young people especially are bringing some remarkable sacrifices. Many a one is taking a considerable amount out of the weekly pay-envelope in order to pay the promised contribution. All this can be achieved only by the Spirit of God, working through the Word and the Sacrament. But the point is that it *can* be achieved. We want to repeat it: This is not an exceptional congregation. What has been done there can with Gods' help be done in hundreds of other congregations.

Church Money-Raising

AT THE CONVENTION of the Lutheran Synod of New York held during the month of June some noteworthy resolutions were passed regarding church financing. A special committee appointed at a previous convention presented recommendations strongly condemning the raising of church money by means of card parties, bazaars, etc. While making clear that the morality of card parties, dancing, and similar matters was not the point at issue, this report went on to say, "A search of the Scriptures certainly will not reveal a single phrase in support of any commercial method of supporting the religion of Jesus Christ. The report also discusses the question from another standpoint, that of tax exemption and aptly states, "For a congregation exempt from taxation on its property, without a license from the sanitary department or a license from the city to give a supper is certainly unfair competition with the restaurants, which are paying taxes on their property and which are inspected by the sanitary department and must pay for a license." The report adds "It is no wonder therefore that the communistic element despises the Christian Church for its unethical methods."

The point of the resolution was not, of course, to condemn all social activities of the Church. Even banquets and suppers and the like may have as their objective the fostering of Christian sociability, the cementing of the bonds of Christian fellowship. But all too often these social events are completely commercialized and are inaugurated and perpetuated as a source of revenue on which a local church counts heavily for the raising of its budget. The money-raising methods to which many congregations have stooped have brought the Church into merited disrepute. Pretentious bazaars and elaborate card parties for the express purpose of filling a depleted church treasury are all too prevalent also in Lutheran circles. Whatever arguments may be offered in their defense, it cannot be denied that these money-making schemes are a distinct hindrance to the development of the spirit of Christian stewardship and there is not a single piece of evidence at hand that they have contributed anything to the spiritual life of a church. Churches where such methods are in vogue are usually at a low ebb spiritually. Five hundred at the card party and a hundred at the church service—that may be about the ratio.

The churches that seek to develop the spirit of Christian giving according to the principles laid down in Holy Writ do not have to resort to questionable methods of the world to carry on the Lord's work and are usually also financially in a fairly healthy condition. Where the unwary dollars must be coaxed and dragged forth by clever cajolery and by all the commercial artifices of the world, there the spirit of worldliness is bound to prevail. The very proponent of and participants in such means of raising money for the Lord's kingdom are themselves bound to hold the Church in low esteem and naturally degrade it in the estimation of the outsider. The resolution of the New York Synod was in order. The Church must rid itself of this unhealthy excrescence. It is high time that the tables of the money-changers and card sharps be kicked out of our churches to make room for Christ and the methods which He sponsored for the support of the Kingdom of God.

One of the tragedies of the low economic level on which so many of the clergy are compelled to live is the inability of these clerics to build up their libraries with worth-while books. There is probably no profession that demands more continuous and diversified reading than that of the ministry. Many of our pastors are perforce compelled to suffer from intellectual malnutrition. This starved condition is bound to affect their professional life and particularly their pulpit work. Congregations seldom take this factor into consideration when determining the economic status of their pastors.

Consolidation of Congregational Funds

ARTHUR A. RAUF

BY CONSOLIDATION OF THE FUNDS of a congregation, we mean the actual merging of all monies received by the treasurers of all organizations within the Church, into one Treasury and administered by the Treasurer of the congregation.

The Plan

On the premise that the Voting Body is supreme in the congregation and that all societies exist and function by its sufferance, it seems only proper that the Trustees should supervise, control and safeguard monies that flow into the church regardless of the origin of its entry. After all, the Trustees are recognized as "The Church" in a community and outwardly, are in a position of authority and responsibility. The fiscal reputation of a congregation should not be placed into immature, careless or irresponsible hands whose acts might very easily prove embarrassing to the congregation.

Its Advantages

There are several arguments favorable to the plan, among them being:

1. All monies being deposited in one account at the bank, has a tendency to swell the daily balance, thereby increasing the congregation's credit rating and proportionately its lending power in the event of the necessity of making a bank loan.

2. The larger daily balance makes possible the opening of a checking account at the bank or, when there is one, eliminates the payments of service charges for failing to maintain the minimum daily balance required by some banking institutions.

3. Payment by check provides a receipt for every remittance in the form of a voucher returned by the bank and constitutes a more business-like policy than the handling of cash.

4. Society Treasurers dislike the practice of taking money entrusted to them into their homes and risking loss by fire or robbery.

5. Under this plan the administration of any organization would not stand accused of laxity of supervision in the event of misuse or misappropriation of funds. An organization Treasurer may be authorized to retain a maximum sum of say, $10 to $15 for petty cash expenditures thus minimizing possible losses.

6. In congregations embracing six or more organizations it must become necessary annually at election of officers, when Organization Treasurers are superseded, to change two or three Signature Cards at the bank. This bothersome practice may be almost entirely eliminated, bringing that eventuality down to but one, the General Treasurer. He, being a more or less stationary figure, a change of signatures is made necessary only at infrequent intervals.

From an accounting viewpoint, the procedure entails no elaborate or involved mechanics in bookkeeping and the forms necessary for efficient conduct of the system are very inexpensive. Forms A and B are bound in books of 50 and Form C is put up in pads.

No. 288 193

I have this day deposited for your account and hereby acknowledge receipt of

.................................Dollars

$.......... ....
General Treasurer

No. 288 193

General Treasurer:
  Please Deposit and Credit our account

with the sum of...................Dollars
and acknowledge receipt.

$.......... ....
Treasurer

"A"

No. 290 193

Creditor........................

For...........................

....

$.................

No. 290 193

General Treasurer:
PLEASE PAY TO THE ORDER OF

........................and Charge to Our Account

the sum of...............................Dollars

$...................

Approved................ ....
Committee President   Treasurer

The Procedure

The procedure follows:

The Treasurer of the congregation is to be known as the "General Treasurer"; the others as "Organization Treasurers."

Whenever the Organization Treasurer accumulates a sum in excess of his authorized petty cash allowance, he uses Form A to transmit such monies to the General Treasurer direct or through the Financial Secretary who, in turn, receipts the stub which remains in the book as part of the Organization Treasurer's records.

When the Organization Treasurer wishes to pay a bill, he uses Form B as a draft upon the General Treasurer mentioning the payee and the amount. This form provides for approval of the Committee Chairman or anyone responsible for the commitment, thus establishing a protective feature for both Treasurers.

Both Forms A and B are perforated for easy separation and spaces provided for matched serial numbers similar to the ordinary bank check book.

Form C is used by the General Treasurer to issue monthly statements to each Organization Treasurer, showing the status of his account. This is checked, approved and returned to the General Treasurer.

The Bookkeeping

The Organization Treasurer may use the stub of Form B exactly as he would a bank check book, posting deposits with the General Treasurer and deducting withdrawals as he progresses and balances each month with the Form C Statement, regarding the Office of the General Treasurer in every way as one would a bank.

The Financial Secretary simply adds a column in his books for each organization, parallel to those of other collections he is called upon to report separately each month. A breakdown of his total receipts should itemize monies received from each organization as well as Plate Collections, Envelope Collections, Mission Collections, etc.

The General Treasurer will open a separate account for each organization and treat them as he would any other monies he is called upon to keep intact, such as contributions for Synodical Purposes or Outside Charities. Such

		DR.	CR.
..........................193			
OFFICE OF			
GENERAL TREASURER			
To...................................			
.... Treasurer			
Following is a Statement of your account for the			
month of			
Please check and return.			
Balance (Date)...............			
Deposits Nos..........to......			
Withdrawals Nos......to......			
Balance (Date)...............			

The above Statement of our account has been checked and found correct.

"C"

amounts need not necessarily be reported, however, at the congregational meetings.

This plan may, of course, be modified or amplified to suit circumstances that may obtain in any given instance. By and large, it should effect efficiency in the handling of money entrusted to fiscal officers of the Church, to the utmost satisfaction of the donors who, after all, have the right to expect an orderly administration of their gifts.

This system has been in actual operation in a New York Congregation for a period of ten years and its proven success lends encouragement to pass it on to any church feeling the need of such a plan.

from p. 278
GIVING THE CHURCH A SETTING

...r a tree in the middle of a lawn space must be resisted. The place for flower beds is along the borders of a lawn. Do not break up a lawn space.

A compost heap is an essential part of every garden. In some out of the way corner all grass cuttings, leaves, etc., are placed on a heap where they are permitted to decay. The next year another pile is started. The following year the first pile will be ready for use as good humus for the garden.

Do not hesitate to transplant or even discard a plant that no longer fits into the plan either because it has lost its good form or because it has grown too large.

If there is a flower garden or rock garden, follow a different plan of flowers occasionally. Introduce new flowers and discard those which do not prove satisfactory. In that way the gardener's interest is kept as well as the interest of those who watch the garden for new things.

Raise perennials and annuals from seed. It is fascinating and saves money. A few seeds sown indoors in pots will enable the gardener to be ahead with flowering annuals.

The above suggestions have been tried out. The writer started out with practically no knowledge of plants or flowers. He did not know the difference between a spruce and a cypress but he learned to know and love plants, shrubs, etc., besides for their beauty also because they mean something to his church. We do not say that this is the only way to give the church a proper setting. It is merely one way that has proved successful.

Tithing

1. Ten Reasons Why I Prefer Tithing
ERWIN KURTH

I AM in favor of tithing, because it does away with bazaars and all the clap-trap devices and schemes for money-making to which many of the churches today are given. Tithing forever settles the financial problem of the church. It is the only method which always and everywhere collects itself.

Tithing makes a church more mission-minded. As Dean Fritz says, "If the Christians of our day would give ten per cent of their income, as the Jews did in the Old Testament,—or if the Christians of our day would support the Church to the extent of their power and even beyond their power, as did the poor Macedonian Christians,—the treasuries of the churches would always be filled to overflowing, and there would no longer be the proverbial church deficit."

2. I am in favor of tithing, because it offers a distinct challenge. It challenges me to attempt big things for the Kingdom. I am tired of such talk as, "If everybody in our Synod gave TEN CENTS a week, we should have a lot of money." Or, "Can't you raise your weekly pledge a NICKEL?" Or, "At every meal put a penny in the bank. Surely, you won't miss a PENNY." Or, "Our mission needs old clothes. Give your OLD CLOTHES to Jesus."

Tithing offers a distinct challenge to adventuresome youth, and you will find most of your converts for tithing among the youth. You remember the famous appeal of Garibaldi. When you become a tither, you KNOW it. You don't say, "I think I am a tither." You know it. Every pay-day you are exhilaratingly God-conscious. You thrill to the challenge of the tithe.

3. I am in favor of tithing, because it is the most satisfactory way of giving that I have found. I am almost tempted to say, it is a painless way of giving. There is only one battle to fight, and that is when you reach your first decision to become a tither. But once that is over, the rest is easy. You always have money for any worthy appeal, for it is a foregone conclusion with you that the tenth is not yours; it is sacred unto the Lord. You do not grumble and growl when, for instance, you are apprized of any special need to which the surplus in the Lord's Treasury can be devoted. The practice of tithing makes one a cheerful giver.

4. Tithing brings blessings. The Scriptures affix many blessings to liberal giving. A paradoxical law is at work, namely, that the more you give away the more you have. This line of argumentation is altogether unreasonable; the only thing that can be said in its favor is that it works; it is true.

The blessings one receives are not always of a material nature. Nor need they be. There are blessings higher than an influx of worldly prosperity. Tithing is not an insurance against the trials and testings of life. Tithing is not expected to deprive us of the chastenings of the Lord, those visitations which make us more chaste and pure. But of this we can be certain, that nine-tenths with the Lord will go farther than ten-tenths without God.

There are many examples from modern life which show how the promises of God have been also literally fulfilled. The question is not whether we can afford to tithe, but whether we can afford not to tithe.

5. Tithing helps people to a rather full understanding of what is meant by the stewardship of life. Too many people are imbued with the idea that we owe everything to God in general, and nothing in particular. But get them to tithe, and you will see how they understand your language when you speak to them of the stewardship of time, of talents, of personality, of influence.

6. Tithing, I feel, is fair to rich and poor alike. It has often been said that the rich do not give in proportion to their income. Tithing will remedy this. To be sure, the rich should learn to go beyond the tenth. But usually they do not learn to do so unless they first get the tithing habit fixed as a life principle. How about the man who has six children to support and the man who has none, yet both receive the same salary? Should the former be expected to tithe? The answer is, Both begin with the tenth, but the man without children should go beyond the tenth.

7. I am in favor of tithing, because the tithe was God's law to the Jews, and, in the full exercise of my Christian liberty, I wish to take that as a SUGGESTION for my proportionate giving. I sincerely believe that I should give as God has prospered me, and, when I cast about for a percentage, I prefer to be guided by the percentage God established for his people in the Old Testament, and that is the tenth. After all, the one and only definite financial system which God Almighty gave to his children in the Old Dispensation was the tithe. Of course, since I am living under the New Dispensation and enjoying larger blessings I shall earnestly strive and struggle to manifest my appreciation by giving more than the tenth. But the tenth is to be my minimum.

This is the argument of Dean Frit[z] in his Pastoral Theology. On pag[e] 259 he says in a footnote: "If the Je[w] of the Old Testament could give te[n] per cent. of his income, there is no rea[son] why we cannot do so; and consider[ing] the greater liberty and privilege which we New Testament Christian[s] enjoy, why should we not give at leas[t] AS MUCH as the Jew of the Old Testa[ment] did?"

This is also the argument of Dr. [F.] Pieper in his "Die Gaben der Chris[ten]." "Some one remarked that th[e] weakest Christian should begin wher[e] the Jew left off, namely, at ten per cen[t.] and then, once again in the exercise o[f] Christian liberty, seek to increase th[e] percentage."

8. I incline towards the percentag[e] of the tenth because from times im[memorial] the tithe has been regarded a[s] a just proportion to set aside for th[e] honoring of Deity. Tithing was prac[ticed] before the Mosaic law was pub[lished]. This proportion of the tenth com[mended] itself to the consciences o[f] men as being good.

Abraham, the father of the faithfu[l] gave the tenth to Melchizedek, King o[f] Salem. Jacob vowed, the morning afte[r] his wonderful dream, "of all that tho[u] shalt give me I will surely give th[e] tenth unto thee."

Where did Abraham and Jacob ge[t] the idea to give one-tenth? Was th[e] principle of tithing deeply imbedded i[n] the human race?

9. So far as I can ascertain, Jesu[s] did not speak unfavorably of tithing. I[n] Matthew 23:23 he said, "Woe unto yo[u,] Scribes and Pharisees, hypocrites! fo[r] ye pay tithe of mint and anise an[d] cummin, and have omitted the weightie[r] matters of the law,—judgment, mercy and faith; these ought ye to have don[e] and not to leave the other undone." O[n] the one hand he upbraided them fo[r] their sins of omission. They failed i[n] matters of judgment, mercy and faith while punctiliously observing the tithe even down to the little garden vegetable[s.] Regarding judgment, mercy and fait[h] he told them: "These ought ye to hav[e] done." But, on the other hand, regard[ing] the tithe, he told them, "and not t[o] leave the other undone."

Dr. P. E. Kretzmann says in com[menting] on this passage: "It was wel[l] and good in itself to pay tithes, if th[e] interpretation of the teachers include[d] even the garden herbs, but what wa[s] punctiliousness in this small matter i[n] comparison with the far more importan[t] necessity of cultivating the greatest vir[tues?" Page 129. Popular Commentary[.]

Is it not interesting to note that th[e] Pharisees and Sadduccees and Herodian[s] never once criticized Jesus in any ma[tter]

ter pertaining to the tithe? They dogged his steps constantly. They were ever on the alert to find something whereof to accuse him. They accused him of THIS alleged infringement of the law of Moses and of THAT. But they never once accused him of violating the law of the tithe. Did Jesus observe this law, even as he fulfilled all others? Did Jesus tithe? To say the least, it is an interesting question.

10. Finally, I am in favor of tithing because the person who tithes definitely learns to put God and the Kingdom first. When week after week you put aside the tenth that you declare is sacred unto the Lord, somehow it gets into the pith and marrow of your bones, this truth, that God comes first in your life. With many professed Christians, self, home, business come first; and the Kingdom last. God takes last place instead of first. The order should be reversed.

When a man is asked to become a tither, he is asked to establish as a life principle the habit of putting God first. This, of course, gets the tithe, but it gets more; it gets the tither. It gets the man.

God's finance system for the Jews was this: "Bring ye all the tithes into the storehouse, that there may be meat in mine house, and prove me now herewith, saith the Lord of Hosts, if I will not open you the windows of heaven, and pour you out a blessing, that there shall not be room enough to receive it." Malachi 3:10.

Shall we of the New Testament voluntarily adopt this suggestion?

II. Objections to Tithing Considered

TITHING IS LEGALISTIC. That is the first and foremost objection commonly raised.

Certainly it is legalistic, if you insist that man is conscience-bound to tithe, if you insist that every non-tither is violating an express command of the Lord. But who has said that a man is under moral compulsion to tithe?

The Jews had to tithe. For them there was a "must" about it. We have no such law in the New Testament. However, we have a higher law that constrains us to support the work of Christ. It is the law of love. If anything, we wish to be more liberal than the Jews. The statement has often been made: "If the Jews under the law gave one-tenth, for a Christian under grace to live less is a disgrace." Assuredly, Jesus did not come to make duty smaller or to scale life down to a lower level. In order to prove that we are free from the Mosaic law it is not necessary for us to give less than the Jews; we can give more. When it comes to supporting the work of Jesus, there is a "must"

that controls us. It is not the "must" that proceeds from S i n a i, but the "must" that flows from the five wounds of Calvary.

A second popular objection against tithing is: *I Cannot Afford It.* This is a very ancient objection. It is an objection that will never die as long as men and women place a higher value upon things material than spiritual. What! The Christian cannot afford to put God first in his life? Babies are born with their hands tightly closed, and often life itself is not long enough to teach man the lesson of the open hand.

Back in 1928, when the church appealed for a more generous support of Synod and District, we heard the be-whiskered excuse: "I cannot afford to give more than I am giving. Ten percent! Why, the suggestion is outrageous." But these self-same people could afford to take a twenty, thirty, fifty percent cut in salary. They had no choice. If the prosperous B.C. (Before the Crash) days were to come back in 1940 and people again received the same salary as of yore, I wager the cry against tithing would once more be heard in the land, and this would be the cry, "We cannot afford it." Thus the heart of man is slow to learn the grace of giving.

"But I am in Debt," says one, in voicing the third objection. "In debt?' I ask. "To whom?"—"To man."—"That is the everlasting trouble. You think first of your obligation to man, and then if anything is left, you think of your obligation to God."

The tither adopts as a life principle the habit of putting God first. No matter what other expenses he has, no matter what emergencies arise—(and, after all, are not emergencies the normal thing in this life?)—the tither says, God comes first.

The tither has this philosophy, God has set me up in business, and I wish to pay him dividends. I may owe others rent, grocery bills, and the like, but first of all I owe God my body, soul, reason, strength, everything I have and am. My partner must be paid first.

The tither says God is my possessor and my possession. He is my Shepherd, my staff and stay, my recompense, my rock and fortress, my high tower. He is my covert from the wind, my hiding-place from the tempest, my bright and morning star in earth's night. He is my pearl without price, my everlasting God, my Redeemer and my Lord. And I? I am his child and heir, accepted in the Well-Beloved. I draw my life from him, my strength and health, my heaven, and my all. I am his own, purchased and paid for. I want to serve Him in everlasting righteousness, innocence, and blessedness. To this end I place my time,

talents, personality at his disposal. And, among other things, I also want my money to turn Christian. Money is a part of myself, of my brain and brawn. I want to use my money for the furtherance of His cause. Nine-tenths I shall use for myself, but one-tenth *at least* I shall invest in His work. The only thing I can take with me beyond the grave is what I have given away.

What About the Ministers

The men of the cloth, I believe, are by and large liberal contributors. Here and there in the annual report of a congregation we do notice, however, that not a red cent has been contributed to Synod and District, not even by the minister, that is, according to the report. But I believe this is a rare exception to the rule. Certainly, no minister will refuse on the ground: "Shall I contribute towards my own salary?" He knows and every one else knows, there are expenses in a church besides the minister's salary. Surely, the minister esteems it a privilege to support the church which offers the means of grace, the Word and the Blessed Sacrament, which offers facilities for giving his children additional religious education, the church which does so much for the community. And certainly no minister wishes to be behindhand in supporting the missionaries along the far-flung battle-line of the Lord. It is a blessed privilege to give. In fact, according to Jesus, "it is more blessed to give than to receive."

And, if a minister should ask, "How about tithing? Should I tithe?" I would answer, "If you are looking for a suggestion along this direction, why not consult Numbers 18.26. There we read: "Thus speak unto the Levites, and say unto them, When ye take of the children of Israel the tithes which I have given you from them for your inheritance, then ye shall offer up an heave offering of it for the Lord, even a tenth part of the tithe." The people were to tithe, and the Levites in turn were to tithe the tithe. They gave their tithe to the priests. The principle of tithing was universal in the Old Testament. The tithe was the minimum. The poor should not give less, and the rich should give much more.

Finally, a person may object on this wise saying, "I believe no definite ratio should be stated; I believe a person should give what he feels like giving."

I wonder who voices this objection,— the man who gives fifteen per cent, or more, or the man who is disinclined to give as much as the tenth?

Is it not true that most of our people give by impulse, without any definite principle to guide them? One says, "I give what I think is right." Another,

"I give as much or as little as the next person." A third, "I give enough to save my face and keep the financial committee from my door." A fourth, "I give what I gave when I was confirmed." A fifth ought to say, "I give not according to my means, but according to my meanness."

Suppose our country had to depend upon the impulses of its citizens for raising taxes,—how much would be gathered in? Suppose each autumn the collectors were sent out among the people, with instruction to make patriotic speeches and then to pass the hat around for a free-will offering,—how much would be collected? Now, of course, we realize the church cannot have any legalistic system, such as the state, but, at the same time, we must bear in mind that the Church of the living God cannot be satisfied with any haphazard, go-easy, hit-or-miss, give-when-you-like-it method of supporting the cause which is dearest to the heart of Jesus, our God. God is a God of law and order. His definite instruction to us is: Give as I have prospered tnee. In other words, we should give proportionately.

Now, can you suggest any reason why we should give less than the Jews? Can you suggest any reason why we should be less systematic in our Christian giving? Is there any percentage better adapted to the rank and file of our people than the percentage which God himself set for the people in the Old Testament? If it is a suggestion that we want, can we improve upon this: "Bring ye all the tithes into the storehouse?"

The Motive

THE MOTIVE for Christian giving, whether such giving is in the form of impulsive giving, proportionate giving, or paying the tithe, is love to Christ and to his Church. This love is nurtured in the heart by the Gospel. The appeal for supporting the work of Jesus must ever remain an evangelical one.

Paul made an evangelical appeal when he wrote to the Corinthians, saying, "I speak not by commandment, but by occasion of the forwardness of others, and to prove the sincerity of your love. For ye know the grace of our Lord Jesus Christ, that, though he was rich, yet for your sakes he became poor, that ye through his poverty might be rich." 2 Cor. 8:8, 9.

Dean Fritz says in his Pastoral Theology, page 257, "The stewardship of money must have its roots in the consecration of the Christian to his God and to his Saviour."

How Much?

The New Testament does not lay down any set rule. The general principle is: Give as God has prospered you. Freely ye have received, freely give. The love of Christ must constrain us to give liberally, cheerfully, and proportionately. The Macedonian Christians "first gave themselves to the Lord," and then they gave alms "to their power" and "beyond their power." No coercion was brought to bear upon them, but they gave willingly, out of hearts surcharged with love. They gave in accordance with their means, and even beyond.

The "thin piece" of the poor, if given out of a cheerful, loving heart, is just as acceptable to God as the handsome gift of the devout among the rich. God looks not merely at the gift, but at the giver. He looks not merely at HOW MUCH is given, but FROM how much it is given. Our giving should be liberal, cheerful, and proportionate.

What Tithing Means

In previous articles we wrote about Reasons for Tithing, and Objections to Tithing. Let us now consider what tithing means, as commonly understood today.

Tithing means to set apart one-tenth of your NET income for Church and Charity.

What constitutes the NET income?

If you are a minister of the Gospel, your net income is what you receive by way of salary, perquisites, free parsonage, free light and heat and coal MINUS expenses incidental to your work, as the purchase of supplies, books, surplices, the purchase and upkeep of a car for congregational use, and so forth.

Example:

Salary	....
Perquisites	....
Parsonage (usually computed on the basis of one week's salary	....
Dividends, interest, if any	....
Total income	....
Minus expenses incidental to your work	....
Net Income	....

This Net Income is tithed.

If you are a mechanic, or employee and wage-earner in any capacity, whether by day, month, or year, your net income is your total income less legitimate business expenses connected with your work, such as carfare, tools, and the like. (Not lunch-money)

If you are a merchant, or a manufacturer or a banker, of course you keep accurate accounts. Your net income is the gross profits of your business less strictly business expenses. (Not family or personal expenses.)

If you are a landlord, your net income is the rent-money you take in, minus taxes, insurance on property, the cash outlay for repairs and decoration, and janitor service.

If you are a farmer, your net income is your gross receipts minus all farm expenses, wages to farm hands, depreciation on farm machinery and implements.

So then, by way of example, let us suppose that your NET income is two hundred dollars a month. One-tenth of this is the tithe, or twenty dollars. You keep account of this in a book, or you place the money in a separate box or purse known as the Lord's Treasury. You never touch the Lord's money for personal use. You do not even borrow from it. Out of this Lord's Treasury you pay everything for church and charity. In other words, all the money you expend for purposes which net you no material gain comes out of the tithe. For instance, out of the tithe you will pay:

a. Your weekly contribution to Church and Synod through the regular envelopes. This will be the largest part of the tithe. About 75%.

b. Your contributions through the special envelopes, as Christmas, Easter, Thanksgiving, Missions, Coin-a-Meal Banks, and the like.

c. The money your children give to Sunday School.

d. Society dues, as to the Hospital Auxiliary, the Orphanage, Home for the Aged and Infirm, the Lutheran Education Society, American Lutheran Publicity Bureau (not the dollar which brings you the magazine, but the dollar which is used in the Free Tract Fund), the Altar Guild, the Home Department with its charity work, the Poor Fund, the Ladies' Aid and Men's Club, provided the money is not used for your entertainment, for coffee and cake, for a bus ride, or a dinner.

e. The money you or your family place on the offering-plate.

f. Red Cross annual enrollment fee. Flood relief. Unemployment relief. Finnish relief.

g. National Tuberculosis Seals, Wheatridge Seals, Hospital Seals.

h. The money given to the beggars at the door.

Etc., etc.

To repeat, all the money you expend for purposes which net you no material gain comes out of the tithe. The tithe is expended for church AND charity.

When tithing is thus explained, some people will say, "I have always been a tither and never knew it." (Rara avis.) Others will say, "I am so close to tithing, that I might as well go all the way." Again others will say, "I have never been a tither, but I am willing to become one." And finally, some one will say, "The tithe has revealed to me what a tight-fisted person I have been all my life. I shall at least quadruple my present contribution."

How to Introduce Tithing

TITHING is not to be introduced into a congregation as another method of raising money, but as a phase of Christian stewardship. We should at all times be more interested in men than in money.

Tithing, or, for that matter, any kind of liberal giving, presupposes a fervent consecration to the Lord and his Church, a measure of His grace. Note how frequently the word "grace" occurs in connection with giving, as found in II Cor. 8.

Winning people as tithers calls for four things:

1. Thorough instruction in what the Bible teaches about the grace of giving. The grace of God in Christ Jesus should move us to abound in this grace also.

2. Thorough information as to where the Saviour has need of money. (Presentation of the work and needs of the local Church, the District, the Synod, and charitable institutions.

3. A comprehensive explanation of tithing and all that it implies.

4. The canvass.

For six weeks before Stewardship Sunday the pastor should improve every opportunity to stress stewardship in general (Cf. Christian Stewardship and Its Modern Implications, Rev. Paul Lindemann) and the stewardship of money in particular. By means of talks in the services, and in the meetings of the various societies, by means of such tithing literature as he may choose and order from the Layman Company, 730 Rush Street, Chicago, by means of special literature prepared by himself, and sent out at intervals of a week, and by means of a sermon or two, the congregation can be rather thoroughly informed. The pastor and the finance committee should not go haltingly into a tithing campaign, saying, "Let's try it. If it fails, it will do no harm." No, they must be enthusiastic. And the pastor must be ready for a lot of personal work. He must figure, it may be, on doing the task almost single-handedly. It is taken for granted that the pastor is a tither before he asks his people to become tithers.

Next, I suggest that the pastor personally interview all his officers and confront them with the question: "Are you willing to tithe?" Those who declare their willingness to become tithers may sign the tither's enrollment blank. Later on they may be given a certificate of membership in that spiritual union known as the Tithers.

Next, the pastor should personally visit all the canvassers, and put before them the same question. Since the canvassers are to visit the bulk of the members, it is important that they *are* what they ask the others *to be.*

On Stewardship Sunday, after the special sermon on the grace of Christian giving, an opportunity may be given the members to sign the tithers' Enrollment card. The results, we warn you, will not be amazing; best results are achieved through personal visitation.

The subject of tithing should be presented often, particularly to the young and to the catechumens. The long-range view is important. Big results can be expected only after years of training.

I close with a quotation from the article on Christian Stewardship in Dr. Fritz' Pastoral Theology: "In view of the great and glorious opportunities and responsibilities of the Church it is more than a pity that the progress of the Gospel is being hindered by a lack of money—*not in the pockets of our people, but in the treasuries of the Church.* Shall we stand in the way of the Church's progress by withholding that from the Lord which rightly belongs to him? We know that if the whole case is put before our Christian people and they are prevailed upon by the mercies of God and the grace of our Lord Jesus Christ, they will respond nobly in supplying the financial needs of the Church."

WANTED

WANTED—Every Member of St. John's to realize his or her duty in the matter of church attendance and worship.

WANTED—At least several hundred of our members to become active in the work of our congregation in the matter of our Societies and Organizations.

WANTED—Fifty per cent of our members who have not come to the table of the Lord this year to carefully plan to come to our next Communion service on October 8th.

WANTED—About one hundred of our non-contributing members to make up their minds to give to their church an offering of about ten cents a week.

WANTED—As many as possible of our members who are regular in their attendance, communion and contributions to give just a little bit more to their church each week.

WANTED—All of our YOUNG PEOPLE to realize that we have one of the finest Young People's Societies you can wish for and that realizing this, to join us at our regular meetings.

WANTED—Still more of the Fathers of the children in our Sunday School to come to the Men's Bible Class with their children and then to BRING their children to the church service which follows.

WANTED—Information as to how your Pastor and your church may be able to be of greater service to you as an individual or a Family.

WANTED—A CONTINUATION of the fine Spirit of Love and Friendship which has existed between your Pastor and you during the ten years of his Pastorate.

WANTED—The names and addresses of your friends and associates who might become interested in uniting with our congregation.

WANTED—Those folks who attend our church services to make up their minds that they will get to know at least one additional fellow member each time they come to church.

WANTED—The more than 100 "silent" sets of 1939 Duplex Envelopes to say something to the Church Treasury in the line of Good News.

WANTED—About 50 of the fine Ladies of our congregation to come and participate in the fine women's Bible Class which meets in the church every Sunday at 9 A.M.

From Parish Paper of Ev. Luth. St. John's Church, Buffalo, N.Y.

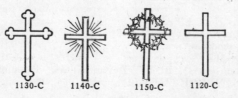

1130-C   1140-C   1150-C   1120-C

The Lord's Acre Movement

H. F. Meyer

WHAT IS THE LORD'S ACRE PLAN?

At present it is peculiar to Western North Carolina. The movement was begun in 1930. Six churches began it then. The movement is now in its seventh year. At the last annual meeting, held in Asheville, N. C., January 13, 1936, it was announced that 250 congregations, with 12 denominations represented, now constitute the Lord's Acre Movement.

It is not a new plan. God is the Originator, for we read in Exodus 34:26, "The first of the first fruits of thy land thou shalt bring unto the house of the Lord thy God." God certainly expects as much from His own chosen people in our generation. We dare not insult God with our *left-overs*. God does not ask for our surplus—in this a good steward and a poor steward are alike, they have no surplus. God wants our *first*.

The Plan. The Lord's Acre plan is that each member of the Church, Christian day school and Sunday school shall set apart and dedicate to the Lord a part of the farm land, or some farm animals, and on the land raise some crop, or rear the animals. The project may be an acre or a quarter of an acre of corn or potatoes: or a pig, a brood of chickens, a calf, or Sunday eggs—just what each member resolves to undertake and so pledges.

I am giving a practical plan, a plan which is operating successfully today. It is for this reason that the plan is very limited as given above. Our Western North Carolina mountains are not adapted for a diversified crop. Cotton, peanuts and some wheat should be added as we enter farther into the Piedmont section. At no time did I hear tobacco mentioned, although in our section the highest priced tobacco of the entire South is raised.

Director Dumont Clarke has set forth the following reasons for the Lord's Acre Movement:

(1) "It is a most practical proven means of church support; gives every one in the church and school (Sunday) the opportunity to have a self-respecting part;

(2) "Sets aside the Lord's portion at the beginning and does not depend upon a late and indefinite 'left-over';

(3) "Greatly increases the total contributions to the church; supplements and stimulates other methods of giving;

(4) "Builds Christian character by giving all in the church a definite daily work for the Lord; is the highly valued project method of education with a Christian application;

(5) "Is an ideal method for training both the older members and the children in Christian Stewardship;

(6) "Brings the satisfaction of religion naturally into daily farm life; unites the work of the week effectively with the program of the Kingdom;

(7) "Makes an added and pleasing bond of interest between the pastor and his people;

(8) "Greatly increases interest in the church and raises up leaders for the church—'folks who work for the church are interested in the church';

(9) "Increase fellowship within the church and between Christians of all denominations (the movement is perforated with *unionism*; but it can readily be stripped of such trappings and adapted for use in our church);

(10) "Has years of successful experience behind it and is rapidly spreading to many parts of the world (Native converts of the Presbyterian Church in Africa are using it successfully and enthusiastically)."

At all the meetings I attended and in conferences with men directly interested in this movement this was the continual refrain:

THE LORD'S ACRE MOVEMENT IS NOT MEANT TO TAKE THE PLACE OF WEEKLY CASH GIFTS WHEN THESE CAN BE GIVEN (many of our mountain people have practically no cash turnover during the entire year; they are still more or less dependent on the barter system), BUT TO PROVIDE MANY CONTRIBUTIONS WHICH WOULD NOT OTHERWISE BE POSSIBLE; AND ALSO TO ENABLE EVERYONE TO GIVE SUPPLEMENTARY AID FOR SPECIAL CAUSES.

THE PLAN WILL WORK, so says a Presbyterian minister. I will let him speak:

"From my own experience I know that the plan really succeeds. Three years ago our group of churches was getting an annual appropriation of $700 from Presbytery's Home Mission Committee. For the past two years we have been *self-supporting*. Last year our Lord's Acre projects amounted to about $375.00. Six pig projects brought a total return of $63.54. One of our most destitute families (the south and especially the mountainous regions must be known to really understand that word 'destitute') gave, through cotton and chicken projects $15.61. The head of the family told me they would have had nothing to give if they had not had a Lord's Acre project. Another family in very poor circumstances paid $10 to the church. Both of these families have projects again this year. One non-resident family of tenant farmers paid last year, through a Lord's Acre cotton project $35.71 and enjoyed doing it. One family not financially able to make any contribution last year has dedicated one-third of an acre in sweet potatoes."

ANOTHER INSTANCE. A tenant farmer has been on his place for seven years. The first three years (bear mind that cotton brought a good price at his beginning, 18 cents at least) he gave only two or three dollars to the church, so I was told. And he was always in debt. In 1932, through the Lord's Acre project, he paid $15. Last year he paid $25, settled up his debt and had a balance left.

ANOTHER MINISTER HAS THIS TO SAY:

"I had a tenant farmer in my congregation who last year paid $45 through a cotton and pig project." He remarked that if I were to turn to the minutes of the General Assembly, I would find that the total membership of some of his churches (the denomination he belongs to) has not paid more than this one tenant farmer. Our own Statistical Yearbook will reveal the same and worse conditions.

MORE PROOF. A church after introducing the Lord's Acre Movement for the first time in its history met the benevolent budget in full and overpaid the current expense budget.

Pastors using this project are unanimous in the following opinion, *THAT THE COUNTRY CHURCH THAT WILL FAITHFULLY USE THE LORD'S ACRE PLAN MAY NOW FACE THE FUTURE WITH COURAGE.*

THE THING THAT CLINCHED IT FOR ME—A LUTHERAN PASTOR. I was present at the annual meeting held in Asheville, N. C., January 13, 1936. My admission was by card. This I got through the good offices of a friend interested in that movement. The auditorium held but 1900. Hundreds were turned away. During an intermission of the session which lasted all day I tackled a typical mountaineer farmer and plied him with many questions. He volunteered answers to all and he had the answers. I then took the negative side of the movement and fired at him many objections. He had but one answer which fit all objections:

"Cap," he said, "you gotta have a good religion afore hit'll work." After he found out I was a Lutheran he left me with this parting shot: "Hit mought not work fer the Lutherans, but hit shore works with us Baptists, Methodists and them thar Presbyterians. You heered what I said, you gotta have a good religion afore hit'll work."

Now, if anybody has a good religion, the Missouri Lutherans have it. And if it takes a *good religion* to make this God's Acre plan work, then Missouri Lutheran congregations (rural) need look no farther to hitch the power generated by the preaching of the pure Word of God.

HOW CAN THE PLAN BE PUT IN OPERATION?

A GENERAL DIRECTOR is appointed by constituted church authorities. He must be a consecrated man, sold on the Lord's Acre Plan, live with it and sleep with it.

He in, turn, with the help of constituted District officials, appoints KEY-MEN in various Districts. It will take persistent and intelligent leadership.

LOCALLY the pastor must be interested and must seek to enlist all his officers, teachers in day schools and officers and teachers in Sunday school. In local congregations a DETER-MINATION COMMITTEE is appointed at the beginning of the calendar year. The committee is composed of three or five members. As the plan is now in working operation one woman is always on this committee. The committee in turn appoints a SUPERVISOR. He is expected to encourage all in their projects during the year and to supervise or cooperate in every possible way.

EVERY MEMBER CANVASS. (Emphasis is always placed on this: the movement is not meant to take the place of weekly cash gifts.)

THE LORD'S ACRE PLEDGE CARD

(Recognizing God's goodness to us and His claim upon us and especially upon our farm life, because without His sunshine and His showers all our efforts would be in vain.)

WE HEREBY AGREE TO BEGIN, TO DEDICATE TO THE LORD, AND TO TEND FAITHFULLY IN 193...... THE PROJECT LISTED OPPOSITE MY NAME AND TO GIVE THE PROCEEDS FROM EACH PROJECT TO MY CHURCH..........................FOR THE EXTENSION OF CHRIST'S KINGDOM HERE ON EARTH.

Name Project Goal Started Inspected Yield

....

(Suggested projects: Potatoes, wheat, corn, chickens, a pig, a calf, Sunday eggs, etc.)

The plan is not dependent on a 100% participation. To have six participants is enough to begin the movement. Every effort should be made to interest the women and children of the congregation. It is suggested that two-thirds go to Synod and one-third be used for local building fund, new hymnals, etc. Synod's president and his advisors are the ones to regulate the proportion of distribution. Pictures should be made of projects and slides made of these pictures. Lectures based on slides are to be held wherever possible. In rural Lutheran communities the radio, if possible, is to be used. Stations seem to be willing to put their facilities at the disposal of this project without cost to the organization sponsoring it. An annual meeting is to be held at a central point. Short reports are heard, progress noted, but the chief emphasis must always be on the spiritual side.

The Lord's Acre plan offers wonderful spiritual opportunities. A dedication service in the early spring, and a harvest or thanksgiving service in the fall, should be carefully and inspiringly conducted. Rogation Sunday will have a deeper meaning when observed in connection with the Lord's Acre work. An out-of-doors service on this project can be made spiritually memorable.

The Pastor, the Determination Committee, the Teachers, the parents, by enthusiastic sustained leadership, by supervising the projects, above all by earnestly and persistently bringing out the spiritual values, can make the Lord's Acre plan an immeasurable blessing.

The plan has demonstrated that individual projects are strongly recommended. Such a project serves as a daily reminder of God in the home and on the farm. This plan also develops personal responsibility. The GROUP PROJECTS could be an added feature, but they are to be encouraged only when there is good leadership and the spirit of cooperation.

The best cash crops should be selected for the project.

According to laymen and pastors, the GENERAL DIRECTOR should be a pastor. The reason they give is that the spiritual emphasis should never be forgotten.

The plan itself is most flexible. It is true that it takes in only rural congregations. Let somebody else come forward with a plan for city congregations—there are plenty of such plans. The denominations sponsoring the movement, aside from the spiritual value received, are strong in their assertions that future church leadership must come from the rural sections of our country. Incidentally, their budgets for Rural Missions (Home Missions, they call it) are large while with our church the reverse is the case.

This is humbly and prayerfully submitted to you for your perusal. For four years I have watched with interest the growth of this movement. Next to the men active on the field I know the difficulties encountered. Unless personally on the field and personally acquainted with the psychology of mountain people one cannot begin to estimate the potentialities, both spiritual and financial, in this movement—also for our Church. God knows that the hour has struck that something Biblical and practical must be done at once if our Church is to hold what it has.

For our own honor as Christian men, for the sake of our missionaries at home and abroad, who represent us at Christ's front and who are breaking down under their burdens, for Christ's sake, whose we are whom we serve, let us get together and do something NOW.

BETTER CHURCH PRINTING
from p 98

With a parish press, the older boys or men of the congregation will be able to print several thousand cards in an evening, explaining the various activities of the church. In another evening the same boys or men, by arranging the territory, will be able to get these cards into several thousand mail-boxes, by going from house to house. We know of a mission Sunday-school that gained 74 new members through this simple expedient. The cards cost them nothing, being "trim" from a print shop. A few lines of well-written advertising, a church press, and a few boys to distribute the cards to front doors, and into every automobile parked before certain picture shows, did it.

With a parish press, one may experiment in producing really attractive printing, which will make a good impression upon those who receive it, and which will be read, as many a commercial-looking printer's job never will. A 10 x 15 press in good shape, does not cost a fortune, if bought second-hand. And it will pay for itself very quickly, if properly used.

One of our pastors has served three congregations, and in every instance he had no trouble at all to make the people see the value of a parish press. The congregation he serves prints its own parish paper, at a cost of exactly fifty cents for 250 copies. True, it's a good day's work to set up the type by hand, but a parish paper, mailed to 250 families—members and prospective members—every month is a good stroke of publicity. It keeps occasional attendants and outsiders in touch with the very life of the parish. And if something "special" is going on, such as an anniversary or a mission festival, the parish paper, printed exactly as you want it, and not as some busy printer wants it, mailed to 500 families, will surely bring a crowd.

And to get a large congregation on short notice, nothing is more useful than a parish press. We recall an occasion when a mission was applying for a loan. A certain official sent word at the eleventh hour that he wanted to meet the congregation, preach to them, and size them up. It was too late to get word around to a hundred families, even with a flivver. So the missionary spent just one hour in buying 100 common post-cards and printing an urgent announcement, asking every member to be present. Before the ink was dry, these were in the mails. The result was a packed church, a surprised synodical official, and of course, a loan. This was some years ago, so the identity of the mission official doesn't matter now.

A parish press may be used in countless ways. It takes several hours to write letters to even 25 people, announcing a special meeting of a church society, or a choir. But within 30 minutes a few lines may be set up on a post-card and sent through the mails. Thus one will be able to do work that no one would think of sending to a printer.

"Imitate"—Not Legislate the Tithe

AUGUST W. BRUSTAT

SCORES OF LETTERS have been received from all parts of the country in response to the articles on tithing that have appeared in the pages of the AMERICAN LUTHERAN during the past year. These letters wholeheartedly endorse the tithe. "I'm with you 100% on tithing," writes a Seminary professor. "The tithe would assist greatly in solving our candidate problem," writes one of our pastors. Other sentiments might be summarized in this statement from still another letter: "God grant that our people soon generally follow the principle of the tithe. Our Church, with its doctrinal purity, would, under God, then become the powerful missionary agency it ought to be."

One voice expressed itself to the contrary, and in harmony with the policy of the AMERICAN LUTHERAN to publish both sides of an open question, that expression was voiced in the previous issue of this magazine.

The Cry of Legalism Again

The objection is briefly summarized in this statement: "Yes, we are raising the cry of legalism."

We must remember, however, that just because some have advocated the tithe in a legalistic manner, is no reason why the advocacy of the tithe in itself need be legalistic.

Moreover, we ask: Just what is legalism? Is it legalistic to strive toward the ideal of having our members attend church every Sunday? Pastors have repeatedly told their people that as good Christians they will attend worship every week unless prevented from doing so by circumstances beyond their control. Surely there is not a single clear-cut Bible passage to which these pastors can point. Yet we would not think of calling such admonition legalistic.

The same holds true of Holy Communion. How often should we encourage our members to commune? Is Synod's average of 2-plus the ideal? Should we be satisfied with that? Would it be legalistic to express ourselves somewhat along Luther's lines and say it is to be feared that unless a person communes at least four times a year he is not a Christian? Would it be legalistic in view of this sentiment by Luther to encourage our people to attend Communion once a month, or better yet, as we believe, every week?

Now it seems the same reasoning may be applied to the tithe. Surely it cannot be called legalistic to strive toward the Old Testament ideal of gathering the tithe from Christians for the Lord's work in this New Testament dispensation. Is the 1% or so that our people give to the Lord ideal? Would it be legalistic if now we tried to raise that to 2% or 5%? Is it legalistic to raise additional funds which are so greatly needed by high pressure thank-offerings? Why then should it be called legalistic to encourage the tithe as the basis of giving?

To say that unless a person gives the tithe he cannot remain a communicant member of the church would conceivably be called legalistic. To make tithing mandatory or compulsory would be legalistic in our opinion. But no such thought has ever intentionally appeared in our literature on the tithe. We cannot see how it can be called legalistic to encourage, in an evangelical manner, the giving of that percentage of one's income which all races of men from time immemorial have considered the proper proportion due the worship of deity and which was specifically advocated under the Old Dispensation.

Dr. Theodore Graebner has crystalized just this angle in his usual cryptic style: "It is not right to condemn tithing as legalistic simply because there has been legalistic tithing. Nor can we say that because it was part of the Old Testament Law, tithing should not be urged upon Christians."

What Is Proportionate Giving?

Another point. Paul's statement in 1 Cor. 16:2, "Upon the first day of the week let every one of you lay by him in store as God has prospered him," is repeatedly advanced as referring to proportionate giving, and we believe correctly so. But now, just what is proportionate giving? Is the proportion which our people generally give the proportion which Paul had in mind? He must have had some concrete proportion in mind. And surely the Corinthians did likewise. Otherwise Paul's statement just does not make sense. Is the average of about $1.80 per communicant per year which our people give for all of Synod's world-wide activities the correct proportion? Just what do we mean by proportionate giving? The only answer is, that secular as well as biblical history points to the tithe. Should we, who are now "free from the ceremonial law," as our correspondent expresses it, to use our freedom "as a cloak of maliciousness" and salve our consciences by denouncing the tithe as a guide for our giving? Let us not be heresy-hunters just for the sake of argument.

Listen again to Dr. Graebner. "It has been aptly said that if one dislikes to tithe because it is Jewish, he can make his giving Christian by raising it to 11%."

"The Love of Christ Constraineth Us"

It seems that sometimes in our zeal to avoid abuses we almost lean backwards. We have repeatedly encouraged our people to greater liberality by appealing to the suffering Christ with all the emotion at our command, concluding with:

All this I've done for thee,
What hast thou done for Me?

But it leaves our people cold. They seem to have heard it so often that it no longer moves them. And they continue to give 1%. But now, if we appeal to that love of Jesus Who gave Himself into death for us and our sins, and couple it with a BASIS for proportionate giving—the time-honored tithe—perhaps we would get somewhere.

What do the "fathers" say?

In all of our thinking on the subject of the tithe, it might be well for us to pause and search the writings of the fathers.

"Imitate"—Not Legislate

Let us start with Luther. Luther thought that paying the tenth was "the fairest way of raising money." "Though not compulsory in the New Testament, paying the tenth is a fine institution, and it were well could we agree among ourselves to give it in order to pay the preacher." Again listen to Luther: "IMITATE Jacob's example, vow and pay to the Lord the tenth of all He giveth you." (Vol. 53, p. 245; Vol. 33, pp. 302 and 303, Erlangen edition.)

From the St. Louis edition we again quote Luther: "The tenth is good and *should be retained*." (Vol. 21a, p. 626), and, "The tenth is the *best proportion* and from the very beginning of the world has been in use." (Vol. 10, p. 854.)

Statement by Dr. Pieper

And here are Dr. F. Pieper's words from his "The Gifts of the Christians." "It is a terrible abuse of Christian liberty, however, if the Christians use their freedom from the tithe in such a manner that as little as possible or nothing at all is given Christ for His kingdom . . . They are then doing that against which the apostle wars with the words, 'as free,

"Thinking Through the Tithe"

AUGUST W. BRUSTAT

OUR attention was recently called to an interesting statement in John Gunther's "INSIDE ASIA," which we quote: "The wealth of the Aga Khan is, as everyone knows, almost inconceivable. He is probably one of the four or five richest men in the world. His revenue is derived in the first instance, not from land, but from the offerings of his Ismaili followers. These, who are for the most part fanatically loyal, are supposed to *PAY HIM TEN PERCENT OF THEIR INCOMES EVERY YEAR,* as a faith offering and fee for religious services which the community provides; of course by no means all of the ten million pay him so much, but the amount is nevertheless very considerable."

These words as we read them again and again set us to thinking. The phrase, "These are supposed to pay him ten percent of their incomes every year" began to burn in our soul and that inner burning, if any would have been present to perceive, was reflected in the flush of our cheeks.

Many of these Mohammedan Indians, for the most part poor people, poorer than perhaps the greatest poverty known in the United States, give ten percent of their meager annual income to a mere man as a "faith offering." They give it to him without complaint. And what for? So that he, "one of the four or five richest men in the world," may travel the capitals of Europe and spend money like the proverbial "drunken sailor," so that he might squander his people's hard earned money in self-gratifying pleasure.

And the thought came home to us with double emphasis: We American Christians, admittedly living in a land showered with the benedictions of heaven as perhaps no other nation, we American Christians with our plenty, to say nothing of our luxuries, we would give less than the tithe to Jesus Christ for the furtherance of His glorious Kingdom. We would give less than ten percent of our incomes for the promulgation of the everlasting gospel of salvation so that sin-stained but blood-bought souls may hear the only message this side of heaven which can prepare them for heaven.

Chiengmai, Siam

We hardly recuperated from the physical weaknes caused by the shock of con-

(Italics our own.)

trasting the Ismaili Indians supplying the Aga Khan with a tenth of their meager incomes to make him one of the wealthiest men in the world, and American Christians grudgingly giving a mere pittance to the "Kings of Kings and Lord of Lords," when another shock weakened us as we were perusing the September 1939 issue of the RELIGIOUS DIGEST. There we read: "A Church in Chiengmai, Siam, is said to have 400 members and every one a tither. Their income is less than twenty cents a week per capita, but they support their own pastor and have sent out two missionary families. They look after the unfortunate of their own community."

We reflected on the faithfulness of these Siamese whose "income is less than twenty cents a week per capita" but who so willingly give ten percent of their poverty for the Lord's work. And we considered again the faithlessness in this regard of untold thousands of American Christians. We have statistics from several sources which tell us that the average contribution of Americans is one percent of their incomes a year for the Church. If we Christians in America would give as these Siamese Christians give, we could evangelize the whole world in a very few years. What a challenge these Asiatics hurl at us!

"The Love of Christ Constraineth Us"

If we love Jesus we will most assuredly manifest that love by giving the tenth, and more than the tenth, if possible. Love always manifests itself in giving. A husband's love can usually be estimated by the amount of self he spends upon his wife. A mother gives life to her baby. Nestling in her arms she gives it sustenance. Parents manifest their love for their children by giving them an education, the luxuries as well as the necessities of life, oftentimes by practical slaving. The love of a citizen for his country finds expression in service, if need be, service unto death. The love of the Christian for Jesus will manifest itself in sacrificial giving of time, efforts, energy, talents and money for the extension of the glorious Kingdom of the Lord.

John Howard said something on Christian giving that is well worth repeating: "We must learn to give of our luxuries to supply the comforts of others; our comforts to supply their neces-

sities; and even our necessities to supply their extremities."

Perhaps you have read of Arthington, of Leeds, England, who lived in one room and cooked his own meals, but gave to missions at least $25,000,000.00. Or you may have read of that humble Scotch woman who lived for many years on porridge that she might give to missions the cost of her comforts and luxuries. That's SACRIFICIAL giving, and God honors it.

I Corinthians 16, 2

There are some who have argued against the tithe on the ground that St. Paul never speaks of it in his New Testament writings. On the surface the argument seems valid for Paul does not mention the tithe by name. But a deeper reflection of Paul's statement to the Corinthian Christians (1 Cor. 16, 2) presents an argument which dare not be overlooked. Paul's statement reads: "Upon the first day of the week let every one of you lay by him in store as God has prospered him."

Paul is here speaking of PROPORTIONATE GIVING, i.e., giving according to one's means or ability. But what is the proper proportion? Paul does not here state it. On the surface this would seem to be a grave omission until we analyze Paul's unquestioned thinking.

Since Paul was a Jew, "A Pharisee of the Pharisees," schooled in Gamaliel's University at Jerusalem, it would not be amiss to take it for granted that Paul had the tithe in mind which every Jew knew to be the correct and accepted proportion due to God.

But Paul, it will be argued, was not writing to Jews. He was writing to Gentiles who had no Old Testament background. How were they to know that Paul had the tithe in mind? But they DID KNOW, for archaeology has established the fact that from time immemorial the Gentiles recognized the tithe as the portion due to the worship of deity.

So Paul did not have to mention the tithe as the proportion of giving even to those Christians at Corinth of Gentile background because they knew all about it. Paul could simply take the tithe as the proper proportion for granted.

Why Not Try Tithing?

AUGUST W. BRUSTAT

SOMEONE HAS ESTIMATED that the Protestant people of America have robbed God of $350,000,000 annually, if we assume that the tithe is the fundamental principle of our support of the Lord's work. Surely this ought to provoke and invoke conscientious thought in the minds of all leaders of the church.

The problem of receiving monetary donations from the church's constituency must be a perpetual headache and heartache to all financial officers in our church as well as in Protestantism generally. We are told that in the Protestant churches of America receipts for religious purposes have fallen off 32% in 1938. Most churches are far short of the monies required to meet the necessary missionary and educational requirements. Eleemosynary and educational institutions under the supervision of the church are hard pressed financially to meet even their current expenses.

America and Money

We feel that the mounting church deficits in America are inexcusable and unpardonable despite the "depression" pleas we hear almost constantly. Depression? Let us see:

Americans spend $200.00 per year for luxuries and pleasure—50 cents per person per year for all religious purposes.

For every dollar spent for church Americans spend 8 times that amount for motor up-keep—4 times that amount for motion pictures—An equal sum for beautifying the female figure—Twice as much for candy—Jewelry purchases mount to the staggering figure of one billion dollars annually.

America spends more for chewing gum alone than she does for God. In a recent year our American people spent $15,000,000 for chewing gum and $8,000,000 for foreign missions.

If the church could have only one-tenth of the money spent for tobacco in America she could put missionaries in every nook and corner of this lost world.

Last year (1937) the liquor interests spent $25,000,000 for ADVERTISING ALONE. We doubt if all of Protestantism spent as much to take the gospel of Jesus Christ to the millions of souls all over the globe.

These figures, if they do nothing else, point to a symptom. America has forsaken the God of her fathers and has gone out after false gods. America is worshipping the god of pleasure—she has given herself over to luxuries—the movies—the radio—the automobile.

Thousands of American men and women are ashamed to offer a pullman porter as little as a dime for a tip; but many of these same people will lay that dime on the Lord's plate without any compunction whatsoever. A quarter for the porter and a dime for the Lord—think of it!

We realize that in our day a dime or a quarter may be real sacrificial giving for some. God knows about that and we would not condemn these people. But there are many with sufficient incomes who, when dining in a restaurant, would timidly leave a quarter as a tip for the waiter, who, when in church, will nonchalantly toss that quarter on the plate, then throw out their chests and lustily sing, "Praise

God from Whom all blessings flow." Somehow a quarter assumes marvelous proportions in the church! How can we remedy this financial delinquency in the church?

God's Solution

God has a system for giving. We believe that system to be the tithe. The child of God is to set aside one-tenth of his

net income as soon as he receives it, and to honor God by distributing it for the extension and maintenance of His glorious kingdom. WE ARE TO HONOR GOD WITH OUR FIRST-FRUITS. If a man's net income from his business is $100 per week, then he owes God $10.00. If a workman receives a salary of $25.00 a week, then, if he tithes, he sets aside $2.50 per week for the service of God.

Pre-Mosaic Tithing

Many people imagine that the tithe is an institution of the Jewish law and has no place or part in the Christian dispensation. This is a grave mistake. The law of tithing definitely antedated Jewish institutions. Four hundred years before the law of the tithe was given to the Jews, Abraham was a tither. In Genesis 14: 18-23 we read: "And he (Abram) gave him (Melchizedek, priest of the Most High God) a tenth of all." This is not the first time Abraham tithed, evidently. It appears that it was a principle in his life.

In Genesis 28: 19-22 we read of Jacob: "Jacob vowed a vow saying . . . I will surely give the TENTH unto Thee." Jacob evidently knew about this principle of giving and practiced it all his life.

The fact is that the ancient world as a whole knew the principle of the tithe. One has said: "This principle is not only as old as Eden, but universal with the race." Clay tablets unearthed by archaeologists in the ruins of ancient cities show that the nations as far east as Babylon and as far south as Egypt were tithing in Abrahamic times. Here are the conclusions of men who have made a study of this matter. Dr. Adam Clark says: "Almost all nations of the earth have agreed to give one-tenth to religious use." The learned Grotius says: "From the most ancient ages one-tenth was the portion due to God." And Montacutius remarks: "Instances are mentioned in history of nations that did not offer sacrifices, but NONE that did not pay tithes." It is surely not necessary to elaborate on the fact that tithing was included in the Mosaic law.

Christ's Commendation of the Tithe

We find that when Jesus graced the earth with His physical presence He commended tithing when He told the Pharisees: "For ye pay tithe of mint, and anise, and cummin and have omitted the weightier matters of the law, judgment, mercy and faith: this ought ye to have done and NOT TO LEAVE THE OTHER (the tithe) UNDONE." (Matthew 23:23).

Christian Stewardship

But the objection will most certainly be raised: The

Christian is not under the law. It is necessary to insert this here, lest some should think that we are becoming legalistic. True, the Christian is not under the ceremonial law. The Christian is above the ceremonial law, and consequently is one who surrenders ALL to God. He presents, or ought to present, his BODY as a living sacrifice, holy, acceptable unto God. (Romans 12:1). And this implies that the Christian gives HIMSELF to the Lord first of all, and in turn means that if he is sincere and true, all things that he possesses, even life itself, are at the disposal of God. This is what we understand by stewardship. The practice of tithing is the experience-demonstrated way of reminding a man that not he, but God, is the owner of his possessions. The habit of tithing, as we see it, has this unspeakable value to the Christian's soul, that it keeps him from forgetting his immeasurable debt to God.

The tenth is by no means all that a man owes God. The Christian should *start* with the tithe, but we do not think he should stop there. If possible, he will go beyond that in his generosity to God because he is above and beyond the ceremonial law. The example of the poor widow who put ALL HER LIVING into the treasury of the temple (Mark 12: 41-44), teaches us that the Christian should START WITH THE TITHE, but not stop there. But, the pity of the matter is that so many Christians are giving the Lord so much LESS than the tithe. We wonder if the average in our Lutheran Church is as much as two or three percent.

The Early Christian Church

It is worthy of note too, in considering the history of the tithe, that the EARLY CHURCH lived by this principle of tithing and was richly blessed. We could quote rather extensively from the writings of the early Church Fathers, like Jerome, Ambrose of Milan, and others, but let us content ourselves with just one quotation, and that from St. Augustine who lived A.D. 354-430, who says: "Our ancestors used to abound in wealth of every kind for this reason that they used to give tithes and pay the tax to Caesar. . . . We have been unwilling to share the tithes with God, now the whole is taken away. The scribes and Pharisees gave tithes for whom Christ had not yet shed His blood. . . . I cannot keep back what He who died for us said while HE was yet alive, 'Except your righteousness shall EXCEED the righteousness of the scribes and Pharisees ye shall in no case enter into the Kingdom of heaven.' They gave a tenth. How is it with you?"

Modern "Churches" and the Tithe

And what of today. It is not a little astonishing to note that the Mohammedans, the Latter Day Saints, the Christian Scientists, the Seventh Day Adventists and others advocate tithing as a fundamental principle of their religious practice. It seems strange to us that Lutherans who acknowledge the superior blessings of the religion of Jesus Christ to any of those mentioned, should give less than that percentage widely accepted as a minimum by people of other faiths which have not the validity and fullness which our faith has.

If we were to continue the study of this history we would learn that most of the great saints who were blessed of God in material and spiritual ways followed this principle of the tithe and honored the Lord with the first-fruits of their substance. I doubt if any man has been fully blessed of God who has been negligent in this matter of tithing. As leaders in the Church we will of course always mention and emphasize the MOTIVE for tithing, namely, the boundless love of God and the atoning sacrifice of the Lord Jesus on the Cross through which the crimson stains of our sin are washed away. "The love of Christ constraineth us." (2 Cor. 5:14).

Think It Over

Mounting deficits—Perennial indebtedness—Constant appeals for money from every needy and worthy source—The bane and blight of unsanctified money-making and money-raising schemes in many churches—we could avoid it all. Let us restudy this matter of tithing and advocate it to our people as the foundation of their giving to the Lord. Let us advocate it to our people soon—let us advocate it to our people now—Experience from time immemorial proves that God blesses the tithe and the tither.

"Thinking Through the Tithe"

The Cry of Legalism

The cry is often raised that tithing is legalistic. We claim however, that it is no more legalistic than to tell people they ought to go to Church or to Holy Communion if they would be members of the Christian Church. If there is any compulsion about tithing it is the compulsion of the Gospel, the compulsion of love, love to Christ for all He has done for us. "The love of Christ constraineth us" . . . also to tithe.

There is only one thing that comes under the category of MUST as far as the Gospel is concerned, and that is "Ye MUST be born again." While there is only one MUST, there are many OUGHTS of the Gospel applicable in the Christian life. For example,

1. We OUGHT to attend Church every Sunday.

2. We OUGHT to attend Holy Communion very frequently.

3. We OUGHT to consecrate our lives to the service of God.

4. We OUGHT to be faithful missionaries. And we may add

5. We OUGHT TO TITHE.

And a Christian will approximate or exceed the tithe "As God has prospered him."

"Imitate"—Not Legislate

and not using your liberty for a cloak of maliciousness.' (I. Pet. 2:16.)

"God has removed from the New Testament Christians the yoke of bondage, of force, of the tithe for the purpose and with the expectation that they serve Him not less, but more.

". . . God has His troubles with the Christians today. He freed them from the tithe with the intention that they might serve Him more diligently in this freedom. But they abuse the liberty. Instead of giving God 11% of their own free will, they use their liberty to satisfy God with 1% or less.

"Someone has said, and not incorrectly, that the weakest Christian should begin where the Jew stopped, namely, with 10%, in order, according to his Christian liberty, to strive continually for a higher goal."

And these are also our sentiments. "IMITATE" — NOT LEGISLATE THE TITHE.

"And the Things Which Thou Hast Prepared, Whose Shall They Be?"

ROGER SEIDEL

TRULY DOES THE PSALMIST DECLARE, "For when a man dieth he shall carry nothing away" (Ps. 49:17) and again, "Wise men die; the fool and the brutish alike perish, and leave their wealth to others" (Ps. 49:10). Yet many in our day, who worship at the idol "Success" as it is currently expressed in terms of wealth, power and position, spend tedious years in toil, attempting to acquire a fortune without ever seriously considering what they are going to do with the fortune when they get it, or what will become of it when they die. "He heapeth up riches and knoweth not who shall gather them" (Ps. 39:6).

Both Old and New Testaments are crammed with warnings against covetousness and trusting in riches. The lesson of Jesus' parable of the fool who amassed a fortune and trusted therein (Luke 12:16) has echoed through our churches for generations. But economic conditions have so changed that possessions which would have been considered fabulous riches in Jesus' day are now accepted as part of the normal American standard of living. Our Lutheran Church has attempted to arrest the development of worldliness by laying emphasis in its preaching upon Christian stewardship. It is evident that if our concept of riches has been enlarged, our attitude toward our use of the same must likewise undergo a proper development. So by our stewardship emphasis we hope to convert the rich fool of whom Jesus speaks into a devout Christian who conscientiously shares his possessions with God.

Let us suppose our preaching has been entirely successful. The parable has so changed that its chief actor has spent his life charitably sharing with God and his fellowmen in a manner exemplary of Christ. His life has been a notable achievement. When his soul is then required we shall have no fear as to the outcome. Yet his barns are not now depleted. On the contrary, despite his partnership with God, or, rather shall we say, because of his partnership with God, they are now supplied more bountifully than ever. When the question is now asked, "The things which Thou hast prepared, whose shall they be?", we shall not fear the dread answer which Jesus must have anticipated. But unless our subject has made some testamentary disposition, the answer must inevitably be that God who has been his partner through life will be completely divested of any share in his estate. There can be nothing for philanthropy without a will. Doubtless the estate will soon be squandered by thoughtless relatives.

It would therefore seem to follow that when our pastors speak of stewardship in life, they are not discharging their full duty unless they occasionally also allude to stewardship in death. As pointed out by Pastor Paul Lindemann in a recent editorial in this magazine, the Presbyterian Church through its Stewardship Department has already drawn attention to this "posthumous stewardship."

Experience clearly indicates that most people do not make wills More than half of all persons whose estates pass through the Surrogates' Court fail to make their wills. One reason, of course, is natural inertia. Many people never do today what they can put off until another time. An exposition of the many benefits to be derived from having a will and the serious consequences of not having one together with an explanation of how easy it is to make

a will should be sufficient to arouse such from their lethargy.

Again, many refrain from making a will because they associate it with death and there is aroused the fear of death. Many persons cultivate the habit of continually shutting out of their minds any thought of death. Surely this reason can have no weight with the true Christian and the pastor, through his training and experience, is excellently equipped to dispose of this argument.

For a third reason, many allege that they have nothing of importance or value to leave, consequently a will is unnecessary. If we die intestate the law will distribute our estate in accordance with certain established principles. No effect will be given to our individual wishes and, as we have already seen, we must necessarily leave God without any part of what we in our lifetime have acknowledged to be His. However little we may have, we should therefore consider it sufficiently important to personally fix during our life its disposition at our death.

In the fourth place, many are loath to approach a lawyer on the question because they fear he will charge an exorbitant fee. If we had time to review the countless incidents where far greater expense and inconvenience was occasioned by not having a will, by having it inartistically drawn by the corner drug store notary or by attempting to do it oneself on a blank purchased at the stationers, this objection would soon vanish. Doubtless the reader has had contacts or experiences which would amply bear out this point.

Still others may feel that legal procedure is cumbersome and they do not want to become involved in anything they do not understand.

Let us see just what a will is. By definition, a will is a written instrument legally executed by which a man makes disposition of his estate to take effect upon his death. The right to make a will is not a natural, inalienable, inherited, fundamental or inherent right, or a right of citizenship, nor is it guaranteed by the constitution. It is a privilege conferred by the various states. Therefore a will must be made in conformity with the formal requisites of the statutes of the state where the testator resides. Usually these statutes provide that the will must be signed at the end by the testator, who must sign, seal, publish and declare it to be his last Will and Testament in the presence of two or three witnesses who also sign in attestation. Contrary to popular belief, it is rarely necessary that a will be acknowledged before a notary public. In most jurisdictions it is not necessary that the witnesses know the precise contents of the will. It is sufficient if they are satisfied that the testator knows what disposition he has made and that he has duly acknowledged to them that such is the disposition he desires made of his estate after his death. Inasmuch as these statutes vary, it is not possible here to give precise information with regard to any particular state. Mention is made of these facts merely to point out in a general way the method of making a will in order to remove some of the mystery surrounding the procedure and demonstrate how really simple it is.

Nevertheless, the drawing of even a simple will is a task calling for the experience of a competent lawyer. Formal requisites of the execution of a will may normally be mastered by a layman after careful consideration of the statutes of his state. But the language used in a testamentary disposition must be carefully chosen inasmuch as many words in common use have acquired a technical and restricted meaning when employed in wills, as a result of judicial interpretation. The law libraries of our country contain row on row of decisions interpreting the legal effect to be given such common words as "children", "heirs", "descendants" and the like.

In this connection, it is interesting to note that where a bequest is made for charitable purposes, the Courts strain to hold the gift valid if at all possible. If the nature of the gift is definite and the beneficiary named with sufficient clarity to enable its identification, the gift will not fail because the proper legal name of the beneficiary has not been used, or if irrelevant portions of the language are not applicable. For example, if one died today leaving a will containing the following clause, "I give and bequeath the sum of One Thousand Dollars to the Lutheran Publicity Bureau at 69 Fifth Avenue", the gift would take effect to the American Lutheran Publicity Bureau whose present offices are at 1819 Broadway, for the organization intended to be benefitted is made sufficiently clear for identification. Similarly, a gift to the "Lamprecht Fund" would take effect, even though the correct legal designation is "Theodore Lamprecht Memorial Endowment Fund." Of course, if the language used is susceptible to two different interpretations, the gift may fail because of indefiniteness.

An interesting decision was made by the New York Court of Appeals on November 23, 1937. Because of the unique situation, quotation is made at length from the opinion:

"The construction of the ninth paragraph of Alice E. Wilson's will is involved in this appeal. It provides: 'I give and bequeath to the Minister's and Missionary Benefit Board of the Northern Baptist Convention, New York City, sum of $2,000 as an annuity, the income from same to be paid to my brother Albert C. Wilson during his lifetime.' Prior to the execution of this will, correspondence occurred between Miss Wilson and the Ministers and Missionaries Benefit Board, in the course of which the secretary of the board wrote: 'Loved ones should of course be remembered. And Christ and His cause should share with others in direct bequests. You may also make the same bequest benefit a loved one for life and provide for a definite Christian service thereafter each year in perpetuity. * * * That which is left to this board by will or otherwise is never lost. Therefore many people are specifying in addition to direct bequests, that certain other bequests shall be used at their decease to secure annuity bonds from this board in favor of relatives or friends. Those so remembered receive generous incomes for life without danger of loss. The principal is kept intact as an endowment fund and after the decease of the one remembered the full principal sum continues to bear interest for the cause of Christ. It is true benevolence to give income to loved ones rather than responsibility. * * * It is the settled policy of the Ministers and Missionaries Benefit Board to place in permanent funds the total principal sums given on the annuity plan. A high annuity rate is paid for life and then, the full original amount continues to bear interest for the benefit of our Baptist Ministry. Thus your life is projected into the future in a gracious Christian service. * * * Perhaps you can help us. Many have made wills remembering this cause. Some of them possess very little, but they are happy that they can make even small bequests which will be placed in permanent funds bearing their names. The income will be used forever to provide the necessities of life for our aged ministers

and missionaries. * * * Some must make provision for loved ones by will. In such cases a bequest may be made to this board with the understanding that an annuity will be paid for life to a son or daughter or to husband or wife or friend.'

"The courts below have held that the ninth clause of the will directs the purchase of an annuity for the sole benefit of the brother without any valid gift over, and that, therefore, he has the right to elect to take the capital sum instead of having it invested for the purpose of purchasing an annuity. As we interpret the language of that clause, the bequest is to the board subject to payment of an annual income to the brother during his lifetime. We think such an intent was clearly expressed."

Both courts below had held that inasmuch as this clause of the will did not specifically state that the use of the money was to go to the Ministers Board after the death of the brother, it was a direction to purchase an annuity for the sole benefit of the brother and that therefore he was entitled to receive the two thousand dollars outright, the Ministers Board thus receiving nothing. The Court of Appeals decided that there was a clear intent to make the bequest to the Board subject to the payment of the annual income to the brother during his life. One not initiated in the theories of testamentary construction and jurisprudence would be inclined to say, "Well of course that was the intent, there can be no doubt about it." Nevertheless two courts in passing upon this will had held the very opposite. The costs of printing, filing, attorneys' fees and incidental expenses involved in these two appeals would have been sufficient to amply compensate any attorney for drawing perhaps a dozen wills. And what if the Court of Appeals had not reversed the decision of the lower courts?

But if the gift in this case had been to the U. S. Steel Corporation, for example, instead of to the Ministers Board, it is safe to predict that the decision of the Court of Appeals would have been otherwise. Thus the services of an attorney are necessary for the protection of loved ones and charities alike.

There is also the public policy of the state to be considered. Most states have adopted rules designed to prevent the tieing up of estates over long periods of time. These statutes are usually referred to as the "rule against perpetuities." It is useless to attempt a discussion of this matter within the confines of a brief article, not only because the law varies from state to state but chiefly because this branch of the law is one of the most difficult even for legally trained persons to understand, due to the many conflicting decisions and the technicalities of the matter involved. As the good physician simply proceeds to cure his patient without attempting to instruct him in pharmacology, perhaps we should here simply refer the reader to his attorney for solution of his particular legal problems in connection with testamentary disposition.

One further point will be of interest to the layman, and that is the matter of taxation. By making bequests to charities it is possible to substantially reduce the amount of inheritance taxes payable. Thus not only does the testator make a gift, he forces the government also to contribute to the cause he wishes to foster. To give a specific example, let us suppose the testator dies a resident of New York leaving a net estate of $1,100,000, which is to be divided among his four sons. Figuring the total tax liability under Article 10-C of the New York State Tax law and the Federal Estate Tax under Revenue Act of 1926 and additional tax under Revenue Act of 1932, we find that after allowable exemptions for four sons, the tax to be paid New York amounts to $39,440, The Federal tax amounts to $96,700, or a total tax of $136,140. The law of New York also provides that not more than one-half of the net estate may be left to charities where the estate passes to a husband, wife, child, descendant or parent. Let us suppose the same testator makes charitable bequests to the extent of $500,000. Such bequests are tax exempt under New York and Federal law. When we now figure the taxes on the same basis we find the New York tax to be $14,600 and the Federal to be $40,900 or a total tax of $55,500. Comparing the figures, we find that he has saved $80,640 in taxes. To put it differently, instead of contributing $500,000 to charity, he has in effect contributed only $419,360, the Federal and State governments having supplied over 16% of the gift.

Here again, the taxes assessed by the various states will differ and the rate of Federal taxation is often changed. Nevertheless this principle will generally be found to be operative. In passing, it may be noted that this principle also applies to income taxation. The following table gives indications as to how Federal income taxes may be reduced by giving the full quota of 15% of net income for charitable uses.

I. If your net taxable income is	II. Your tax on net income will be	III. You can give away up to 15% to Church
$ 1,000	$ 40	$ 150
4,000	160	600
10,000	700	1,500
20,000	2,060	3,000
50,000	9,700	7,500
100,000	34,000	15,000
250,000	130,000	37,500
500,000	306,000	75,000
1,000,000	681,000	150,000

IV. Your income tax after making your gift would be	V. Actual cost to you of your gift would be reduced to	VI. Tax saving and percent of gift which U. S. virtually gives to Church through full use of your 15% deduction privilege
$ 34	$ 144	
136	576	
550	1,350	
1,570	2,510	$ 6 4%
7,420	5,220	24 4
25,350	6,350	150 10
105,250	12,750	490 16.125
252,000	21,000	2,280 30.4
567,000	36,000	8,650 57.66
		24,750 66
		54,000 72
		114,000 76

The American Lutheran Publicity Bureau is in receipt of a letter from the Treasury Department, Washington, containing the following paragraph: "Contributions to your organization by individual donors are deductible by such individuals in arriving at their taxable net income in the manner and to the extent provided by section 23(o) of the Revenue Act of 1936 and the corresponding provisions of prior revenue acts. The deductibility of contributions by corporations is governed by section 23(q) of the Revenue Act of 1936." We have therefore the official ruling that contributions to the A.L.P.B. are deductible as charitable gifts under Federal taxation laws. No doubt this ruling will also be followed by a majority of the states.

If one feels that he cannot make large bequests to his favored charities, the suggestion of Rev. George C. Koenig is worthy of note. We quote from "My Church": "You have been supporting some charity in which you are especially interested, say, Inner Mission. Every Christmas you have sent Five Dollars. Once you are dead that contribution stops. Inner Mission will certainly miss it. Yet a bequest of $125 would permit this annual contribution to be continued for 25 years. * * * A long list of splendid causes might be mentioned—your home church, the various missions of the church, the Church Extension Fund, Bronxville Concordia, Wheat Ridge Sanitarium, the American Lutheran Publicity Bureau, hospitals, orphanages, old people's homes, etc."

It is hoped that the foregoing remarks will serve to spur the reader on to a serious consideration of his testamentary disposition and also supply pastors with a bit of material which may perhaps be used in presenting this subject to members of their congregations.

Theodore Lamprecht Memorial Endowment Fund

DURING September, 1921, Dr. Frederick Pfotenhauer, president, Synod of Missouri, Ohio and Other States, endorsed the work of the American Lutheran Publicity Bureau in these words:

"The American Lutheran Publicity Bureau is carrying on a noble work worthy of commendation, since it lends a helpful hand in the spreading of the Gospel and in bringing the saving truths of Scripture to many who otherwise would not be reached."

The receipt of this endorsement gladdened the heart of our president, Theodore H. Lamprecht, who wrote Dr. Pfotenhauer the following:

"As I happen to be the president of the American Lutheran Publicity Bureau, in whose work I am very much interested, I feel like adding a few personal lines of appreciation of your recent endorsement of our Bureau. The official letter of thanks will reach you in the regular way.

"My own connection with this Bureau is only a recent one, but I have been so impressed with the cheerful, undaunted and efficient work which its founders, the editorial and office staff have been doing these years, under great difficulties, financial and otherwise, and are still doing in a most unselfish and even self-sacrificing way, that I know words of such commendation as yours will gladden their hearts and strengthen their hands. They deserve them in every way and they deserve substantial support from everyone in our Synod. As you truly say, the Bureau is "bringing the saving truths of Scripture to many who otherwise would not be reached," and that fact once generally recognized in our circles should bring a steady flow of funds needed for further developing this work. We need both financial and moral support. Contributions from congregations or societies within congregations would seem particularly appropriate. We are getting quite a number, ranging from $5.00 to $50.00, and I would indeed appreciate it if you, whenever opportunity offers, would not only say words in the Bureau's favor, but help along such contributions by suggesting them in whatever manner you judge to be proper.

"The earnest, consecrated men who do all this work—(I do not count myself among them because I do practically nothing)—certainly do not merit unfriendly opinions. They are working for the welfare of our Synod and the Lutheran Church, as unceasingly, conscientiously and efficiently as any men of our church. This ought to be publicly recognized and words like yours are extremely helpful to this end."

We have taken this old correspondence from our files for a purpose. Our president, Mr. Lamprecht, has gone to his reward. He has passed from the "Church Militant to the Church Triumphant."

But the work remains to be done. Once more, we will let Mr. Lamprecht speak. In one of the last letters received a few days prior to his death, he said, *"The Work Must Go On."*

The Theodore Lamprecht Memorial Endowment Fund has been created by the A.L.P.B. for the purpose of giving perpetual financing to plans of dignified Lutheran publicity, such as was suggested in the letter quoted above. The income from this fund will enable the trustees to carry on certain plans which for lack of funds have been long contemplated, but always postponed, because no money was available.

We appeal to our congregations, church societies and interested Lutherans to support this fund with contributions. Interest-bearing securities are just as welcome as cash donations.

The purposes of this fund should appeal to every wide-awake Lutheran. Its aims demand support. May those who read take it to heart and with a substantial check aid "in bring the saving truths of Scripture to many who otherwise would not be reached."

A SHORT DISCUSSION OF CHURCH ARCHITECTURE

E. Donald Robb

Without a thorough understanding and a sincere love of the church-builders of the Middle Ages, it is difficult to solve successfully the problem of the church as we find it today. Knowledge of the methods and conditions under which these churches were built always leads to a fuller appreciation of their charm.

The professional architect of the Middle Ages was a person unknown. In those days he was the "master of the works" or "master mason." He drew plans, usually very crude affairs, laid out the work, bought the materials, hired and paid the workmen and worked on the structure in person. In the earlier Middle Ages workmen were sometimes members of some monastic order. The master mason was at once a craftsman and an artist. He understood not only the technique of masonry but the way to produce architectural effects. Moreover he had the conviction and the resulting impulse of his religion behind him. The works he produced were wholesome and natural expressions of his devotion to his Church; and he had this advantage over the modern architect, his entire corps of assistants down to the humblest workman were wholeheartedly in sympathy with the project. The spirit of devotion which the medieval builders worked into their churches has been radiating from them ever since, and has stirred the same spirit in the hearts of countless multitudes.

The church architect of today has a very different set of conditions to contend with. Assuming that the architect has a deeply religious nature, and a desire to produce a church which will be a constant benediction to future generations, combined with all the necessary technical knowledge and training, his child, alas, is the offspring of many parents besides himself, and when fully grown, will, in spite of all he can do, often show the effects of its heredity. In this day and generation he is working against odds, and it is small wonder that the precious spark of religious spirit which is to become the soul of the building, should so frequently be prematurely extinguished. And yet in spite of everything, our church architecture has shown a steady improvement during the last two or three decades, which has equalled that made in secular work.

Ecclesiastical architecture has always occupied a prominent place in the great art movements in history, quite as conspicuous at the low water mark as at the high. We are all too familiar with the cheap and tawdry structures that masqueraded as churches during the period of artistic depression through which we have just passed, with their foolish wooden buttresses and pinnacles, galvanized iron cornices and crockets, and contemptible ornamentation of every kind. These fraudulent imitations that we have on every hand are rapidly being relegated to the scrap heap, or are being transformed, without much difficulty, into moving picture theatres.

Compare these flimsy makeshifts with those matchless little buildings scattered so plentifully throughout the length and breadth of England; with their very intimate and human qualities which command so much of our wonder and admiration; and the result is certainly a sad commentary on the religious sincerity of the years just behind us.

A SMALL PARISH CHURCH IN ENGLAND

An ancient church, built in the days when art was yet instinctive in every country workman. The thousands of tiny churches which dot the landscape of Great Britain, built in the Middle Ages, inspire and tantalize the architect of today.

Whatever the form of worship for which the church is to be built, from the simplest to the most elaborate, it must be dignified inside and out. It must bespeak the purpose for which it is erected—the worship of God—and should be characterized by a solemn reserve and dignity.

Dignity does not necessarily call for symmetry, although a certain balance is desirable, but restraint is absolutely indispensable. Anything forced or overdone will ruin it, and above all, any attempts at "picturesqueness" should be avoided. Nothing should be allowed to spoil that influence which we like to think a properly designed building of any kind has on the community. On the other hand, a too apparent striving after dignity sometimes produces quite the opposite effect, and the designer spoils his work by disclosing his tricks.

As the Church in its broadest sense is undeniably a permanent institution, its outward and visible form, as embodied in its architecture, should be as enduring as it is possible to make it, and only those materials which have stood the test of time should be used in its construction. We can surely learn much from the builders of the Middle Ages; for while their masonry was not always the best, at least they built solidly; and their work, which has now been standing five centuries and more as a memorial of their sincere devotion to their Church, will still be in active service long after our flimsy structures, built to the minimum allowed by buildings laws, will have been forgotten.

As the majority of small churches with which we have to deal usually demand the maximum seating with the minimum cost or space, it is sometimes a problem to combine these two factors in a good design. The Gothic style is one that lends itself to inexpensive building, for it is content to appear in humble clothing and, in fact, is much more attractive in common sandstone, brick or limestone, with perhaps a simple plastered interior free from pretence or false pride, than it is when bedecked with expensive marbles, imported woods and costly but tawdry decorations.

It is needless to say that in carrying out a scheme for the decoration of a church the architect should have supreme command. This should be, and usually can be, arranged at the very beginning of negotiations, and should be so stated in the contract between architect and client. In this way the decorative scheme can be controlled, and each feature, when it is executed, can be made to take its proper place as a part of the whole. The subjects included in the decorative scheme whether they be for painted work, stained glass, carving in wood or stone, hardware, tiles or embroidery, can then be arranged in an interesting sequence; and, as each memorial is to be presented, its donor selects the item and subject from the prearranged scheme, and adheres to the restrictions laid down by it.

This is of especial importance in the question of the memorial windows, for the reason that of all the decorative features in the church, the windows, being the source of light, are by far the most conspicuous; and, of all the arts and crafts that go towards the making of the church, no single one is so likely to make or mar the interior effect as the glazing of the windows. And no one of the arts of the church has sunk so low since the age of good church building as the art of stained glass. In no other art is is quite so easy to disregard the limitations imposed by the materials and transgress the rules of good design. In this, as in other crafts, the workmen have become too expert. Inasmuch as anything can now be accomplished in glass, they argue that they are at liberty to do anything their fancy prompts.

But this policy is sure to lead to disaster, for artists must learn restraint if they would excel. Donors of windows should not insist on too much sentimentality or prettiness in stained glass. This is only obtained by a sacrifice of sublimity and grandeur. Sentimentality, or effeminate prettiness, to the large majority of the untrained public, especially to those whose better judgment has been recently dislocated by some bereavement, is the acme of beauty. This fact is thoroughly understood by many stained glass purveyors, who play on the overwrought feelings of their prospective patrons, and introduce into their designs lovely maidens with dove-like expressions, resembling that of the departed, perhaps floating in graceful curves, or accompanied by sad-eyed cherubs and fleecy clouds. That sort of art should not be allowed to disfigure the tracery of a real church. In the same class with this is the copy of the Hoffman picture,—shades, shadows and all,—or the wholly unreligious subject, a good example of which completely counteracts the good influence of one of our best known modern churches. The subject—an apple tree with wide spread branches—fills the upper half of a five-light window; in the lower half is a winding stream, ending in a gorgeous sunset, without doubt the identical place where the wealthy donor went swimming as a boy.

A revival of the use of color in the decoration of woodwork, walls, vaults, etc., after the manner of the ancients, has begun to take form in this country, following the example of the modern English work. If this work is done by some one familiar with the rules governing the use of color in heraldry, the result will repay for the cost thereof; but chaos is liable to follow if these simple rules are not observed.

Much could be said on the subject of chancel furniture,—the dimensions, arrangement, and design of each piece,—but space will not permit of anything like the detail of which such a comprehensive study would demand. There are many indications that the two types of chancel—the liturgical and the non-liturgical—will some day become one, the shallow chancel with portable communion table giving place to the more ancient and dignified arrangement now in use by the churches having a more formal service. There is one thing of vital importance throughout the church, and especially in the chancel—dignity. The design of each article of furniture, both here and in other parts of the church, should assist towards this end—to attain that dignified solemnity which is the making of the church.

The artificial lighting of the church is a problem which the builders of the Middle Ages were not concerned; the result is that we have very few lighting fixtures that may be spoken of as strictly Gothic.

INTERIOR: ST. PAUL'S CHURCH, KITTANNING, PA.

Brazer and Robb, Architects. In this small parish church, Mr. Robb and his former partner have succeeded in creating a fine sense of dignity through their use of height, and a fine deep chancel. Contrast this interior with the wide, low, restless interiors of many modern churches of today!

Closely allied to the lighting fixture problem is the question of hardware. Here again the commercial artist has supplied us with page after page of Gothic designs in cast brass or bronze, rich in crockets and tracery, but meaningless when considered in the light of an architectural accessory. These should by all means be scrupulously avoided, and the hardware, at least that operating the principal doors, should be hand wrought. This is by no means a financial impossibility, even in the inexpensive church. It would be ideal to have the hardware and lighting fixtures made by the same artisan—in any case they should be of similar materials and finish. The churches of the Middle Ages are rich in examples of hardware, from the very simple to the most elaborate, and these are easily adapted to our modern mechanism without loss of character. We have in this country a few craftsmen of a very high order, who are capable of executing this work in the real spirit and with much the same enthusiasm as the worker of the Middle Ages.

Of the craftsmen who are working today in the real spirit of the old work, we have conspicuous examples in the field of furniture and joinery, in wrought iron and hardware, in stained glass, painted decoration (which, however, is still little explored in America,) and ecclesiastical tile work.

It may some day be realized that the mason, the carpenter, the roofer, the plasterer, and the painter are craftsmen, as much as the workers in the more ornamental lines. The building trades will then surely be elevated to the level of the crafts, and the art of building will be even more deserving of her title, "Mother of the Arts."

AN APPRECIATION OF THE FRENCH GOTHIC STYLE

J. W. C. CORBUSIER, A.I.A.

The following article does not profess to be an exhaustive study of French Gothic. The writer merely wishes to record his impressions and the inspiration he has received from studying the buildings themselves and drawings of those who love Gothic Architecture for its beauty and feeling of life both ecclesiastical and secular.

A brief study of Romanesque Architecture which immediately preceeded Gothic would give one a greater appreciation of the latter style. Romanesque at its best was heavy and massive. The next step forward was to find some better way of counteracting the thrust of roof and vaulted stone ceiling in order to lessen the effect of weight and enhance the grace and beauty of line.

Such means were at length discovered in the use of the pointed arch together with a new adjustment of ceiling ribs and a new form of abutment. Once these principles were discovered and put in practice, the first step in Gothic Architecture was taken.

As time went on proportions were perfected, mouldings and carvings were refined, heavy walls between the heavy columns and piers were eliminated, giving more space for glass, until, at the height of its glory, the Gothic Church was a marvelous framework of stone enclosing delicate tracery and beautiful glass. The cruciform plan of the church building reached its highest development during this period, typifying the body of Christ; the head was the chancel containing the altar and sanctuary and choir. The transepts represented the arms and the nave the body.

In many instances the nave or body of the church was divided into five, seven, nine or more bays, these numbers having an ecclesiastical significance. This form has come down through the ages and prevails among the better class of churches today.

After the ground plan of the church was perfected, the Gothic builders began to strive after height and the result was the world's first skyscrapers.

"I will lift up mine eyes." was a phrase of some significance which has been quite forgotten in our day of church buildings with a 15 or 20 foot ceiling.

Generally speaking, Gothic Architecture was conceived in the neighborhood of Paris and the surrounding country and from there spread to Normandy and other parts of France, from France it spread to England, Germany, Italy and Spain.

France, England and Germany are the only countries where Gothic is a living vital art, that of Germany being modeled after France more than England.

In the other countries it is attractive but generally superficial and weak.

But of them all, the French builders were the ones who expressed the greatest and most profound religious aspirations in churches of awe-inspiring magnificence. They strove more than those of any other country to give a feeling of height even greater than actual measurements.

Even in the small parish churches they would emphasize the vertical lines and diminish the horizontal ones. Their churches were all rather narrow and long as well as high, and these properties are the only ones which will lead the eye and soul alike up to the throne of our Heavenly Father.

The vaulted ceiling of Beauvais Cathedral is 153 feet from the floor, that of the Cathedral of Amiens is 147 feet. In buildings like these the rumble of the organ and the voices of the choir boys ascend to mingle with the spirits of that dim and vaulted height and one's eyes and soul are drawn upward to Him who dwells in the High Places, with a feeling of true worship.

The Gothic builders proved that music is heard at its best in a room that is higher than it is wide. In their churches the singing of the choir marching toward the altar is a paean of praise which once heard can never be forgotten.

The interior of the Gothic church is also noted for its vistas through aisles flanked by slender columns and glorified by the warm and harmonious colors of stained glass; the finest the world has even known. Rarely did they build a church where the eye could not look through a side aisle and not infrequently through two adjoining side aisles separated by columns, each sup-

Exterior: This downtown church, now under construction, is designed in such a way that it will not be smothered by the high buildings in the immediate vicinity. The style is based upon the French Gothic.

porting a cluster of stone ribs which in their turn supported the stone-vaulted ceiling.

These stone columns at first were large round ones and the ribs of the vaulted ceilings were large with rounded edges. As the style grew towards perfection, these columns were so changed that they appeared like a cluster of small columns, the rib mouldings were elaborated, until at the end of the Gothic period the columns and ribs formed one continuous line of mouldings from the small bases at the floor to the point of intersection of the arch at the ceiling, thus giving an unbroken line from the floor to the highest point in the interior.

The exterior of the French Gothic church was fully as magnificent and beautifully proportioned as the interior.

In the vicinity of Paris and including Picardy, the majority of large churches had two large towers in front, and a very light, tall fleche or spire at the junction of the nave and transept roofs, this being a strikingly beautiful composition.

In Normandy a tall, massive, square or octagonal tower took the place of the fleche. These towers were beautiful in themselves, but unless handled skillfully, tended to dwarf the two front towers.

Other noticeable features were the flying buttresses. These were exterior supporting arches helping to hold the roof and stone ceiling in place. They were strong supports but gave a very light and graceful appearance to the exterior. The same general plan of subordinating the horizontal lines to the vertical was typical of the exterior as well as of the interior.

An interior based upon French Gothic proportions. Impressiveness is gained by stressing height, and by accentuating the vertical lines.

placed along the parapets and other points, while gargoyles were numerous and useful. In carving vines and flower ornaments, local flora were used as models and many beautiful specimens have come down to us.

We have already mentioned the increased glass area of the Gothic over the Romanesque, and the stained glass of the Gothic period was as far ahead of that of the Romanesque as was the structural design.

The art of designing in stained glass reached its highest development during the 13th century. The glass makers of that period did not try to make a picture with colored glass but used it more as a translucent mosaic. Each small fragment, jewel-like in its coloring, with the rich reds and blues predominating, gave the windows a brilliance and harmony of color never equalled before or since.

The interior walls of the church were painted in color and gold to harmonize with the windows.

Some architects and writers contend that English Gothic is more adapted to our American needs than the French, but if our churches are to hold their own with the skyscrapers we must adopt the French idea of vertical lines predominating over the horizontal.

We cannot hope to have our churches stand out in isolated magnificence the way they do in European towns, but we can at least design them that their beauty will stand out in contrast to the utilitarian architecture by which we are surrounded.

In order to accomplish this the modern church building committee must

An important detail of Gothic Architecture was the sculpture. The French sculpture of the 12th century was always severely conventional, though not entirely lacking in realism, but the artists of the 13th century gave more animation to their figures without diminishing their architectural value.

On the western facade of the church were placed the more important carvings, though other parts of the exterior were more or less richly adorned with statues and carvings.

Grotesque stone figures, both large and small, were

select as an architect one having the training and vision that inspired the builders of those glorious cathedrals of old France which still stand as the finest examples of a living faith. But the architect must have a committee which is in sympathy with his ideals and has confidence in his ability to carry them out.

In concluding let us say that modern French Gothic architecture in no wise interferes with the requirements of the modern church and its work, but is a monument to our religious faith which will contrast favorably with those so-called "dark ages."

A Pleasant Surprise

IT IS ALWAYS a risky thing to write an extended description of a new church building. One's mail is likely to be full of letters asking why just that church was described, and certain other ones overlooked. It is evident that we cannot give a detailed description of a church just because it is new. Too many new buildings follow so closely a fixed type that if we have seen one, we have seen twenty of them. The description of one will fit a score of others, with nothing different except the name, and a few minor details.

There is a new church that was built during the years 1932-1933, that is so different from the usual, rubber-stamp type of thing, and so full of pleasant surprises, that it merits description. It actually exists in three dimensions, and it was built by a widely-known architect. Externally it is a bleak, painful thing, therefore we beg leave to say nothing in regard to its location, the name of the congregation that built it, or the name of the architect, for the superficial observer will accuse us of describing a mediocre building. Externally it is all of that. Except for the fact that it is built of a rather interesting, mouse-grey brick, with stone window tracery and trim of almost the same shade, it is not a church that one would look at more than once. The average person may admire the texture of its brickwork, but he will not take the trouble to look inside its doorway, even though the door is always invitingly ajar, seven days a week, from early morning until dusk. It would seem that the distinguished architect tried to make it as unpromising as possible externally, as a protest against the pomp and swagger of our day, which so often lavishes money on vulgar exterior ornamentation, and is content with an altar of ply-wood. Such a church is like the Cockney girl, all dressed up for a party, with finery and cheap jewelry bought from the push-cart merchants in the side streets. Frankly one is shocked when told that the bleak, mouse-grey building, with a square doorway exactly like a garage, is so surprisingly good within, that it embodies so many original features, and above all, that it is the work of a great architect.

The Church's Interior

The church of which we speak is a Latin cross on plan. The long arm is 120 feet 5½ inches from east to west (for it is correctly orientated), and the cross arm is 71 feet. We quote inside dimensions, of course. Take a piece of paper and try to make a rough drawing of its plan. The sanctuary is 24 feet 6 inches wide by 16 feet 7½ inches deep, and contains the altar. The choir space is 33 feet wide and 16 feet 4½ inches deep. Thus the entire chancel, including sanctuary and choir, is 33 feet deep. The nave is 73 feet 10½ inches long by 33 feet wide. The vestibule, at the west end of the nave, is 24 feet 6 inches wide by 13 feet 7½ inches deep. The south transept is 33 feet from east to west and 15 feet deep. The north transept is 33 feet from east to west and 20 feet deep. Just off the south transept is a very low addition with a flat roof. This contains three rooms: a clergy vestry 13x14 in size, a choir vestry 14x21 in size, and a ladies' vestry (whatever that may be) 13x14 in size. All dimensions are external. The church seats 450 persons.

The first unusual thing that one notices is that the roof is supported mainly by four great arches of masonry. An arch divides the sanctuary from the choir. A second arch divides the choir from the nave. There is a third arch midway between the chancel and the vestibule. A fourth arch separates the nave from the vestibule. There are arches opening into each transept. These four lateral arches, and the two opening into the transepts, are all of a uniform width of 23 feet 6 inches. They are constructed of solid brick, and the thickness of their walls is 3 feet 4½ inches, except the sanctuary arch and the vestibule arch, which are 2 feet 7½ inches thick. All side walls are 27 inches thick.

The central space, from which radiate the chancel, the two transepts and the nave, rises somewhat higher than the other parts of the church, and has a flat ceiling of timbers. Over it is a central tower. The chancel, transepts and nave are covered with roofs of a pitch somewhat steeper than 45 degrees, bell-swept at the eaves. The exposed rafters are solid pieces of timber about 4″ x 6″ in size, as we recall them. The ceiling proper is of matched planks, with rafters and purlins exposed beneath, and finished in a light grey tone. The whole interior has a pearly grey cast, with a very sparing use of gold.

Another unusual feature is the choir. One of the evils of the present day is the chancel choir. If one puts it just in front of the altar, the altar is obstructed, and the choir is the focal point. If we put it in one corner of the nave, the whole interior of the church is thrown out of balance, and the choir is still the focal point. In the church of which we are speaking, the problem has been solved by making the sanctuary 24 feet 6 inches wide and the choir space 33 feet wide, and five steps lower than the altar. The vertical portions of the chancel arch project about four feet, and there is a stone parapet as high as the choir stalls. Thus the singers are concealed, until they stand up. From the nave one is hardly aware that the choir exists at all. The altar is entirely unobstructed. The first impression is that of a spacious chancel, entirely free of choir stalls.

Another pleasant surprise is the location of the organ. It is almost out of sight, in the south transept, and against its east wall. No pipes are in sight. The case is of oak, and looks like a paneled screen, with some perforations at the top. And yet the organ is entirely in the open, with no chamber to bottle up the sound. Forty years ago an architect cried out against our custom of featuring organ pipes. He said that we not only feature these things, but paint them red, black and gold, as though to proclaim that the human flesh, the devil and the god of wealth are the gods to be worshipped in that particular church. The building of which we are speaking is free of all such things, and one is not aware that an organ exists. Its tonal value is not impaired at all.

The seating is another agreeable surprise. In olden times, in all churches, the people all stood. Later on, the peasants got together and constructed rude benches of wood, and the men sat on one side and the women on the other. Realizing their frightful ugliness, the thick oak slabs which formed the bench-ends, were carved, in later ages, in all manner of intricate designs. Some of the ancient bench-ends would cost from $100 to $200 each, if produced today under modern conditions. And yet, they are frightfully awkward and uncomfortable. We have said, again and again, that the chapel chair is the correct solution. This is not an opera chair. It is a low-backed chair, somewhat like a simple dining room chair, with a rush seat, a wide rail at the top, and a device for holding hymnals. For some curious reason, these cannot be made for less than $10 to $15 each in America, so they have never gained in popularity here, because of their cost. There are two or three English chair factories who have been turning out good, sturdy chairs at from $2 to $3 each. Transportation across the ocean is from $60 to $65 per hundred. By the time one pays transportation and duty, they will run $4 to $5 each. Even so, they cost less than benches, they are much more comfortable, and they look vastly better than the solid lines of pews.

The vestibule of the church which we are describing *is not* separated from the nave by means of a partition and swinging doors. A partition and swinging doors not only cuts off all of one's west light, which is the most effective of all our natural church lighting, but it encourages the usual group who stand about and chatter. Where there is no such partition, there is no chatter. Somebody has said that the surest way to prevent the robbery of a church is to keep the door unlocked, for no thief will attempt to steal the pennies in the poor-box, if there is the possibility that he will be interrupted at any moment by somebody entering the unlocked door. Just so, the surest way to stop the buzz of conversation in the vestibule before church, is to do away with the partition. And yet the vestibule is there, with its usual tract case, its desk with the visitors' book, its shelves for hymnals, its compartments for church papers, and its bulletin board. In case the church is crowded, 30 to 40 more people may be seated in this particular vestibule. To prevent draughts, there are little porches at each end of this vestibule.

Simplified Quality

Throughout this church, a quiet feeling of quality is apparent. There is nothing flashy, no gim-crack ornaments, no ostentation. The parson is a quiet, modest chap, and as he takes one through this new church, there is nothing for which he need apologize, and nothing to encourage boastfulness. The altar is a simple table about 10 feet long, made honestly of oak, its mensa and panels of genuine slabs, well-seasoned, and honestly mortised, tenoned and pegged. There is no gradine or candle-bench. A simple crucifix, and a pair of candlesticks stand immediately upon the mensa. At either end of the altar are floor candlesticks, each holding a single candle. The reredos is a simple, straight-forward affair, with a carving of the Crucifixion in its center panel. The other five panels are blank. All is finished in a pewtery-grey color, without shine or varnish. The beauty of the fine, comb-grained white oak is not ruined. There are no harsh contrasts of dark oak and white plaster walls, no gaudy steam radiators flanking the altar, no fancy clergy chairs, no exit signs. The windows have well-designed stone tracery, and humble diamonds of ordinary antique glass, set in wide leading. The organ is not large, but every stop has a row of genuine pipes back of it. There is no camouflage and no unifying. The tone of the organ is that of quiet, dignified quality. It is one of the few organs of recent years without the usual vulgarity of "vox, harp, chimes and echo," that have turned so many churches into motion picture houses in atmosphere. The lighting fixtures are of oak, entirely without stain, but with a sort of lime finish. They are remarkable. There is a central, vertical, hexagonal piece of oak about four feet long, with three projecting brackets, holding three small, shaded lights. These are over the seats, not over the passageways. The walls are painted in one uniform tone of soft, pewtery-grey. Some vandal got in his deadly dado, the one thing that mars a perfect interior. It is a band of dark grey, about four feet wide, around the base of all the walls, and it reminds one of some of our Pittsburgh churches, after the flood waters subsided a year or two ago, and left a band of muddy color about the base of the walls. If the church people could have the courage to remove this unsightly band of color, the interior will be all that one could wish. Every visitor notices

this one discordant note, and it is likely that it will be corrected.

It is a real pleasure to describe this church, but since we have been truthful in regard to its external bleakness, and the ugly dado inside, we prefer not to mention its name, nor the name of its well-known architect. And, since we have told absolutely all we know about it (unless we might add that it *does not* have horrid wash rooms just inside its main doorway), we decline to answer any inquiries about it. It actually exists, but beyond what we have said, we know nothing more.

Even its unpromising exterior is a point in its favor. Too many churches have everything on the outside and very little inside. At long last an architect has come forward and has reversed this vulgar swagger. Perhaps he has overdone it. One comes away with the feeling that he has made the outside of the church unduly plain and ugly. It is almost like the man with carefully-studied humility. The beautiful, quiet, devotional interior will remain long as a pleasant memory. It is a place where one may sit undisturbed, and concentrate upon the beauty of Word and Sacrament. Everything is solid, genuine, beautiful, excellent in design, honest in materials and careful in workmanship in that interior. Moreover, it is all church and no clubhouse. There is no basement. The little, low building attached to the south transept, contains only the choir room, the clergy sacristy and the so-called ladies' vestry. Under it, one presumes, is the heating apparatus. The impression upon the world is powerful. One goes there to worship, and nothing more. The Word and Sacraments are the only attractions. Those who wish to find recreation and other such activities will be disappointed. We presume that there is a day school somewhere nearby.

STRUCTURAL HONESTY IN CHURCH BUILDING

A. F. Bernhard

Above all, a church building should be honest and truthful, even if it must be plain. No shams or subterfuges of construction should be permitted. A church is built to the glory of God and as a lasting tribute to the Creator. To build cheaply of imitation or inferior materials is not economical except for temporary structures. Generally the average church building is not as well cared for as a private building, and hence the construction, particularly on the exterior, should be adapted to withstand the elements and ravages of time without repairs or special attention. In brief, build honestly, beautifully, and permanently.

It is not style nor ornament that makes a structure Christian, but rather the manner in which the architectural features are used. Still, it appears to be easier to give a religious impression to a building by means of the Gothic than by any other style. Gothic architecture was developed among Christian people whose thoughts were upon their religion in a fuller way than ours are. No other style has the distinction nor has any other style so accurately and beautifully expressed man's faith in his Creator.

The typical Gothic church or cathedral consists of a skeleton of piers, buttresses, arches and ribbed vaulting, all held in equilibrium by the combination of oblique and vertical forces neutralizing each other. The walls were thus merely required to enclose and not to support the structure, and indeed they principally consisted of glazed windows with vertical mullions and traceried heads. Gothic architecture, in common with Greek, relies on the evident truthfulness of its structural features, which in both styles are component parts of the artistic scheme. Thus in Gothic architecture the features were not left to mere artistic caprice, but were in the main determined by stern structural utility, as exemplified in the novel shape of a capital specially designed to support a novel superstructure, and in the ribs of vaults which accurately express their function to support the vaulting panels. Although most of the forms were founded primarily on structural necessity, others were the expression of artistic invention; thus the spire fulfilled no structural requirement, but it served as a symbol and formed an outward and visible expression of the religious aspirations of the time and directed the thoughts of men heavenwards.

The use of a truthful style still does not always make a church an honest Christian structure. The materials and methods of construction must also be taken into consideration. Cheap and imitative materials now flood our building market, and their use for church buildings in particular should be avoided. Most of the building materials are equally good when used honestly each for the purpose for which it is best adapted; they all become bad either when employed for a purpose for which they are not appropriate, or when one material is substituted in the place of, or to imitate another.

In present day practice, concrete in almost universally used for foundations. Concrete always consists of a hydraulic cement, a fine and coarse aggregate,—which generally are Portland cement, sand, and crushed stone or gravel. Trap rock makes an excellent coarse aggregate, while a cinder concrete is lighter, more porous and thus not impervious to water.

The use of concrete blocks to face a concrete or rubble wall below or above grade is sham. Concrete or rubble are legitimate building materials and when used should not be hidden or disguised. In stone work there is an individuality and interest in the wall surface, in that no two stones are alike; while in concrete each piece is like its neighbor, making a rather monotonous effect. A concrete wall surface is often tooled to imitate real stone. Such practice is usually deceiving only temporarily, for the surface cracks and chips upon exposure to alternate freezing and thawing, and the dishonesty becomes apparent.

It should be remembered that a high and long wall needs to be thicker than one that is frequently braced by floors and partitions, and in the average church the roof construction usually imposes a considerable weight on the wall, and often a slight outward thrust. The walls whether of brick or stone should be of ample thickness, solidly and honestly built. When a building is roofed with trusses it is almost necessary to place buttresses against the walls, opposite the trusses, not placed haphazardly. A wall may be made more stable, with the same amount of material, by the use of buttresses and a thin wall between buttresses than by making a wall of uniform thickness. Buttresses are structural features of a building, placed logically along a wall to abut or strengthen a surface which has been broken, and naturally weakened, by window or door openings.

Walls of Gothic churches are generally built of stone, or of brick with stone facing or with stone trim. The considerations effecting the choice of stone are practical and aesthetic. The practical consideration includes strength, cost, and durability, while color and texture make up the asthetic consideration. Today terra cotta and artificial stone are being used extensively in place of stone. Although apparently just as durable as stone, these materials do not appear the same as stone. Artificial stone, made of a finer quality of concrete, is of comparatively recent manufacture and, even when made in a first class manner, cannot well claim equality with the natural product as its weathering qualities have not yet been sufficiently tested. Terra cotta manufacture has been greatly improved in recent years. It will withstand more heat than stone or granite, in case of fire, but when its surface is chipped from any reason the damage becomes apparent and cannot be repaired, as its exposed surfaces are only skin-deep. It must also be made in comparatively small pieces to avoid warping and twisting due to the process of its manufacture. Wood-framed churches are not adaptable to Gothic design, but should be rather of the New England type of picturesque colonial designs.

Maple, oak, or quarter sawed yellow pine are suitable woods for flooring when tile, slate, or stone flooring is not used. Cement floors covered with cork carpet or with other suitable sanitary and noiseproof covering for comfort are also considered good construction.

The manner in which a church is roofed has much to do with both the appearance and the cost of the building. The narrower the building, the cheaper it can be roofed, and if the funds for building the church are very limited, the facility for roofing should to a considerable degree determine the arrangement of the plan.

The French medieval architects favored the stone vault with a wood framed roof over the same to protect it from the weather, and its use is excellent for it is truthful and permanent. The more recent Gustavino tile vault construction is of similar character and has produced splendid results. These are, however, expensive and an honest open-timbered roof generally is more economical and usually gives a very handsome interior. A timber roof becomes dishonest when it is hidden from view by means of a false plaster ceiling hung from the trusses. Such a ceiling is sometimes arched and painted to imitate a stone vault. Moreover, the height of the church is also materially reduced by this experiment. The English developed as no other nation the construction of various types of open-timber roofs, which culminated in the elaborate hammer-beam variety, often gaily painted in gold and colors. With elaboration goes expense, and a church of limited means should be satisfied with a simple tie-beam truss exposed to view in all its truthfulness. The most desirable shape for a truss will be determined to a considerable extent by the span, the strength of the walls, and by the degree of economy that must be practised.

At times members carrying no load are introduced in the truss design for appearance sake alone. Such practice is to be condemned for it is structurally dishonest and the cause of unnecessary expense. Steel trusses encased in wood are also objectionable for a church building of ordinary construction, as they are strictly speaking, a disguised material. Unless fireproofed, steel trusses offer no greater protection from fire than wooden trusses, as the steel will twist and bend under heat so as to destroy the roof.

Occasionally in open timber construction, the rafters, the purlins and the underside of the roof sheathing, as well as the truss members are dressed, and left exposed to view. This requires heavier timbers and regular spacing of the rafters to give a good effect. The slight thickness of wood separating the interior from the outer air also permits much loss of heat. This loss can be overcome considerably by laying a good insulating mat on the wood sheathing before applying the roofing materials. Another method to conserve heat in the church is to leave the rafters rough, ceil the underside and plant mouldings on the ceiling to divide it into panels, leaving the trusses and purlins exposed below.

In the larger churches, and where building regulations require it, fireproofed steel construction for roofs is necessary and perfectly logical. Where no stone or tile vaulting is used to form ceilings under such roofs, the fire-protected members can be decorated directly on the fireproofing or on plaster finish covering same.

There is scarcely any feature of a church edifice which does as much to give the building a churchly appearance as honest, well designed tracery windows. For the more expensive stone or brick churches the tracery should be of stone. In the smaller and medium-priced churches it may be necessary, on account of the cost, to make the tracery of wood, but of less intricate design. Many churches make the mistake of sanding and painting wooden traceries in imitation of stone work. Needless to say this never appears the same as stone and the effect is displeasing and cheapening. It is better not to use wooden tracery at all in exterior windows, but to have moulded mullions instead, or to simply fill the large openings with properly designed ornamental glass reinforced with solid metal bars placed to harmonize with the design.

An important item to be considered when designing a church is danger from fire. Few churches have the means to construct a fireproof building; however much can be done to prevent the rapid spread of fire, in the event that one should be started from the inside. All vent and hot air ducts and ceilings of rooms generally should be made of incombustible material, and especial pains should be taken to protect the boiler room so that fire cannot originate there.

A Scheme for A Small Church

WE ARE INDEBTED to Mr. J. A. Fichter, of Akron, Ohio, for the church design printed in this issue. Mr. Fichter is a Lutheran of our Synod, an able church architect, and a member of our synodical architectural committee. We are proud of the fact that three or four really high class church architects have been developed within our own circles. Only one other church body is suffi-ciently fortu-nate.

The design shown herewith solves the prob-lem of a small, yet excellent church building, which may be built for a mod-erate sum of money. The building is ex-tremely simple. There is a chancel 16 feet wide by 27 feet deep; a nave 21 feet wide by 42 feet long; a west tower, a sac-risty and a choir room. To the left of the church, and somewhat back of it, is a small parochial school. The dimensions which we have quoted are, of course, all internal.

To the left of the chancel is an organ chamber large enough for a two manual organ with about ten stops, which is sufficient for a church seating 140 people, as this one does. The choir room is 11 feet by 21 feet in size. The walls of the church are of solid stone, and two feet thick. The tower walls average 32 inches in thickness.

The most striking exterior feature is the tower. Professor J. Prower Symons who was here a few days ago, said that a church without a good tower is like a man without a head. This tower is 18 feet square, and it rises well above the peak of the roof. It is centered squarely on the end of the nave, as every tower ought to be, now that the horrible corner tower fad is decidedly a thing of the past. The tower stands forth honestly from the building, and is not a compromise tower, retreating half its area within the nave, to the utter ruination of both tower and nave. The most unusual feature of the tower is its gabled termination. The tower walls, to the north and south, are carried up into gables, with a roof somewhat more than 45 degrees in steepness.

This device is not only a striking one, but it effects a considerable saving in stone masonry, and yet there is proper height.

Upon entering this church, the chancel impresses us immedi-ately. A chancel may make or ruin a church. If the chancel is trivial, the whole church is trivial. This one, 16 feet wide by 27 deep, is about the minimum for good effect.

About 16 years ago, your writer had a church thrust upon him. The chancel is a mere raised platform, bounded on the north by a row of organ pipes and on the south by an organ con-sole and clergy seats. The choir boys and the men sit in make-shift stalls on the same level as the congrega-tion. The organ was built by a firm whose work costs consider-ably more than any other build-ers in the country. We have spent time and money getting carv-ings, furnishings, altar hangings, linens, candlesticks of all kinds, a true tabernacle, and a great many other things which scarcely show. All of this fails to redeem a chancel which is much too shallow. The people of the town call it "the church that doesn't look like a church," and all because the chancel is inadequate. Were it 27 feet deep, as Mr. Fichter's is, it would save the day.

Many a very beautiful little English church owes everything to the chancel. Patrixbourne, New Haven and scores of others are possessed of very ordinary and uninteresting naves. But their fine chancels save them from mediocrity.

We all know people whose bodies are unshapely, hands and feet awkward, but whose faces are possessed of both beauty and character. We forget about their poor, misshapen bodies, their large feet and their awkward hands, because their beautiful, in-telligent faces attract us. So it is with a chancel. A good chancel is the secret of a good church interior.

In the case of this design, both chancel and nave are well pro-portioned. The ground-plan itself is beautifully proportioned. With a chancel of good proportions, and sufficiently deep to be

CONTINUED

dignified, the next consideration is its furnishings. We dare not vulgarize it with cheap, shoddy furnishings, as a beautiful girl might cheapen herself by using an overdose of rouge, and lip-sticks too bright and crude in colour. A good rule is to allow the architect to design, or at least to pass upon, everything that goes into the church. Thus all will be in harmony.

A church of this sort ought to have a proper setting. It dare not be crowded against the sidewalk. Even though the church is a small one, yet it ought to stand back at least fifty feet from the street, and there ought to be plenty of green lawn, blooming shrubs and trees around it. This particular design ought to be done in stone for stone looks decidedly better than brick, and lasts longer. Engineers have declared that the best type of stone construction, such as the Cathedral of St. John the Divine, will last for 5,000 years. An ordinary brick job lasts about 50 years. There are European churches over 800 years old, built of stone,

and little the worse for wear today. Good stonework is the sec-ret. Of course one must examine the pointing about once in ten years, and repoint the mortar joints, if necessary, so that mois-ture has no chance to work in and freeze

Mr. Fichter's design is extremely simple, but its fine effect is due to its good proportions, careful scale, its thick walls and the fact that it is built of stone. He does not rely upon ornament to conceal bad planning and bad proportions. We had a very famous architect who used to do that. His planning was poor and his structural sense rather terrible. But his magnificent hand-ling of ornament saved the day. He reminds us of the man whose rich voice and dramatic mannerisms serve to conceal a lack of preparation in the case of a public address. Mr. Fichter uses al-most no ornament, but he studies his planning and his propor-tions with great care. This is why his simple, inexpensive little churches are so singularly effective. And with it all, he insists upon good thick walls and lasting construction.

HELPING TO MAKE OUR CHURCH SERVICE BEAUTIFUL

F. R. WEBBER

(This article was written for our Walther League number, and hence addresses itself immediately to the young people. We were prevented from using it in the special issue, but since this number also will reach a large circle of young people, it still is most appropriate. Incidentally, the principles here enunciated are such as we, who are older in years, also need to learn ever better. The article is written and printed for all of our readers, whatever their ages, even though the specific application in this case is to the young people. —Ed.)

The Managing Editor has asked us to say something to young people, along the lines of church art. Now don't refuse to read any farther, for we are not going to discuss technical problems of church building. It is our intention to indicate a few things that the young people of the average congregation may do to make things more attractive.

Our religion ought to be beautiful. There is no reason why we ought to worship in ugly surroundings, sing sectarian music, or get along with a crippled liturgy or a wheezy old organ. Neither need we sit and gaze sadly at violently colored windows, or an abominable color scheme, which really is not a scheme, but a conspiracy!

The Christian religion is the most beautiful thing in all the earth. Our teachings are beautiful. Hence their outward expression ought to be beautiful. While beauty does not make truth, yet there is no good reason why truth ought not to be surrounded with beautiful things, rather than things that are repellent. The stock argument of the man who gives not according to his means, but according to his meanness, is that "we can worship the Lord in a barn." True enough. But why should we? We try to make our homes attractive. Why not also the Lord's house?

Some years ago, when the heavy cloud of Calvinism hung over the land, it was imagined by many denominations that churches ought to be as bare and unattractive as possible. That was the unwritten Sixth Point of Calvinism. But, like the other five points, it was based on false argument. The past few years have seen a most amazing change.

The writer is not yet forty, but he remembers the day when even a cross, or a preaching robe, might be relied upon to throw the sectarian denominations (and here and there a Lutheran congregation) into a panic. Horrors no! Such things were considered "Cath'lick." In many places church bells were ruled out for the same reason. Church music, in those days, was not all what it ought to have been. The liturgy was usually a short, mutilated thing that began with the Long Meter Doxology and ended with nothing much at all.

Surprising changes have taken place lately. We could mention several churches of the Congregational group where true altars, elaborate altar crosses, colored vestments, deep chancels, octagon pulpits, and concealed organs and choirs are in use. In our own town the Presbyterians and Methodists have introduced vested choirs in some of their leading churches. Many of the sectarians have restored the clerical robe and bands. Some use Gregorian chants and elaborate liturgical forms.

Among the Lutheran congregations similar changes are taking place. A growing appreciation for all our old, traditional treasures is apparent. We have churches today, both finished and under construction, that compare favorably with any in beauty of design and furnishing. We are appreciating more and more the treasures that we possess in church music. The Episcopalians, with all the stress that they lay upon church music, are using our Lutheran *chorale*. Their latest American hymnal includes a number of our standard Lutheran hymns. Their latest and most expensive English hymnal has many fine Lutheran hymns. If others appreciate our Lutheran treasures, why should not we also?

The St. Olaf Choir, and such men as Director Christensen, Mr. Rechlin and Teacher Wismar—to mention only three—are doing much to make our grand Lutheran church music known and appreciated. The congregation that lags far behind the procession and sings hymns of the Billy Sunday type, or is content to worship in a theatre-style building, is very much out of date, nowadays.

There are many things that our young people may do to make the outward surroundings of religion more beautiful. For one thing, a local Walther League society might set as their goal a new organ. We do not mean a cheap, harshly-voiced thing like a circus calliope, but a real organ of true merit. When we buy an organ, *tone*, pure, refined tone, is the thing to be kept in mind. The amusing notion that an organ is to be judged by its length, width and height, or by the number of stop-knobs on the console, or the number of pipes on its wind-chests, is dying out. We ought not to buy mere bulk, but rather refinement of tone. A high-grade organ may cost a trifle more sometimes, but if we wait a year or two longer and save our money, it will come. But in this, the pastor and vestry, the organist and music committee must be consulted, and the smooth trade-talk of oily-tongued organ salesmen taken with several grains of salt. If a salesman tries hard to induce you to buy his make of organ, beware. Good organs, like a genuine five dollar gold piece, do not need much persuasion to cause them to meet with approval.

Then the young people might work hard for a better choir. We do not mean just a group of people who sing "easy" catchy music. We mean a choir willing to work hard; and with genuine musical principles back of them. There are good and bad principles back of church music and church building, just as there are good and bad principles back of everything else. Here's a hint: most things that "take well" are to be regarded with more or less suspicion. While it is true that many good things take well, yet the same is true with many bad things. A catchy deistic anthem published in a small Ohio town, by an unknown composer, may "take" better than one of real merit with some people. But that is no indication of its worth. A wavery, quavery, shivery tremolo style of choir singing may "take" with the uninformed, but I have noticed that one hears no tremolo in the case of the matchless St. Olaf choir or the famous choirs of our leading eastern cities. If our Lutheran young folks work hard in order to stir up an appreciation for high-grade Lutheran music, both vocal music and our matchless organ treasures, it will be a grand work well done. In this age of jazz, of rag-time and of trashy church music on every musical counter, hard work is needed in this respect.

While the week-day musical and dramatic entertainments of our young people are in no respect a part of the church service, yet much good work may be done here. A few coarse people may laugh boisterously at a song or a one-act play making light of the holy estate of matrimony, or at some jest with a double meaning, but our young people ought to cater to the better element, rather than the worst. Dramatics in which girls appear in masculine clothing or in scanty costume may draw a crowd. But it cheapens the church in the eyes of all. Raffles, games of chance, cane-racks and doll-stands may delight some folks, but since the law prohibits such things, our young people will do a real service by substituting something more elevating instead.

Then the church building itself may be beautified. Have you a baptismal font that is badly designed and old? Why not save money and present the church with a beautiful new one, not selected out of a catalogue, but designed by some architect of real reputation? Does a deacon carry the water to the font in a white pitcher and thus arouse one's sense of humor, making one think of the bell-boy with his pitcher of ice water? For $75 to $100 even Mr. Cram himself will design a beautiful hammered brass ewer, made by some eminent metal craftsman, such as Mr. Wolley. The whole thing, designing, workmanship and all, will not cost over $100.

Are the altar hangings dull and dingy? Are they of cheap velour, with tarnished, imitation gold fringe?

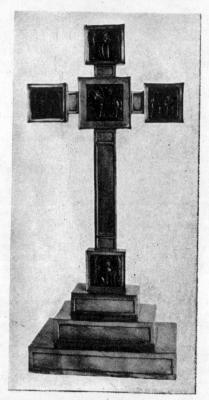

Altar Cross owned by the Rev. J. F. Pfeiffer's Congregation, Roslindale, Boston, Mass. Designed by Cram, Goodhue & Ferguson. Carved of precious woods by Mr. I. Kirchmayer. Overlaid with beaten silver by J. T. Woolley. The panels show the traditional symbols of Our Lord and the Four Evangelists.

Are they wrong in color? Fifty to sixty dollars or more will get a beautiful set of hangings for altar, pulpit-desk and lectern, made of handsome brocaded silk of the proper liturgical color, and hand-embroidered most exquisitely by some such skilled needlewoman as Miss Mackrille, whose card appears in every AMERICAN LUTHERAN, and whose work is so beautifully done.

But why go into further detail? The principles upon which to work is to get things little by little, and get only the best. Whatever we put into a church, whether it be our time, our talents or our gifts, ought to be done to the glory of the Triune God, and hence the very best obtainable. If we get fewer things, we will be able to get things better in quality.

Are the church windows old? Are the designs and colors bad, and the lead-lines thin, so that the windows bulge and leak? Why not start a fund, and replace them gradually, getting glass of real merit? Here again, stock designs and catalogue goods are to be regarded with extreme caution.

There are scores of other things that we might mention: A set of properly designed candle-sticks, with genuine candles, to replace the cheap, Renaissance ones on the altar; or a beautiful altar cross, or a crucifix, designed by an able designer, and hand-carved, with an overlay of hammered silver, such as the beautiful cross designed by a noted office, and carved of hollywood, overlaid with silver, now in Pastor Pfeiffer's church in Boston.

With it all, let the gifts be the reflection of a loyal spirit of true Lutheranism. We are told by the worldly, and in thunder tones, that our beloved Synod must let down the bars, yield on such things as lodgery, union services, etc., and become a sect among sects. But this dare not be. There are over two hundred sects as it is. Why should we add another to the list? And in the final analysis, the most beautiful things that we can do, after all these other things are done, is to maintain the greatest of all adornments, and really the only things that matter spiritually: the pure Word and Sacraments.

The Wood Ceiling

F. R. WEBBER

"THE CONGREGATION has insisted upon having a false ceiling at the height of either 13 or 15 feet," writes a young pastor. "I should certainly hate to see that false ceiling, since I know what a difference an open ceiling means. I should therefore like to beg of you to help me by giving the arguments in favor of an open ceiling."

It is most unfortunate that such things as this are left to the whims and prejudices of a majority vote. We have seen many a case where a bank clerk, a salesman, a cobbler, a printer, a railway mail clerk, a grocer, a jeweler, a dry goods man and a proof-reader constituted the building committee, and were armed with a deadly majority vote. Each was a good enough man in his line, but not one of them had ever mixed so much as a pail of concrete. And yet these men most solemnly determined the constituency of cement mortar, the thickness of walls, the construction of roof trusses and the size and location of windows. The architect and the pastor had no voice in the matter, except as more or less the part of spectators. Unfortunately this is exactly the set-up the average congregation thinks necessary in order to build "as economically as possible."

Later on the same committee bewail the fact that they got so badly "gypped" on the work. It was the building committee, not the architect or the contractor, who decided to omit waterproofing the foundation, who thinned the side walls to 13 inches, who insisted that guttering be of ordinary sheet tin and who imagined that a false ceiling of plaster is the proper thing.

Irrespective of the majority vote of a building committee or a voters' meeting, what are the merits of a wood ceiling?

The average building committee is absolutely sure to decide that a false ceiling of plaster is warmer in winter, cooler in summer, and more economical in every way than the open timber sort. Their decision reminds one of the student who defined a lobster as a red fish that crawls backward. "Splendid!" exclaimed the professor. "Your observations are quite admirable, except for the fact that a lobster is not a fish, he is not red, and he doesn't crawl backward."

The open ceiling, with exposed timbers, wood roof boards and open to the very peak of the ceiling, has every argument in its favor.

A ceiling of this sort is warmer in winter. Uninformed people jump at the conclusion that a church with a ceiling of this sort is hard to heat. This is not the case. If one uses a false ceiling of plaster, it creates a large pocket of dead air, which becomes chilled when the fire gets low. It takes longer to heat a pocket of dead air than the same quantity of live air. The Thermos bottle is based upon this principle. A fire must be kept going for half a day before this big pocket of dead air, between the false ceiling and the roof, is warmed. People sit in some churches and shiver, even with a roaring fire in the furnace, because the big pocket of dead air is chilled, and chills the room below. Even in a small chapel, this pocket of air isn't warmed up until mid-afternoon.

To heat a church quickly and economically, it is necessary that air currents be created. The air must circulate. Warm air from the heating plant tends to rise, and cool air comes down and mingles with the warm air until all is warmed to a proper temperature. The pocket of dead air in the space between the ceiling and the outer roof cannot circulate. Air currents cannot be set in motion, so that the chilled air may be brought down and mingle with the warm air below. The real test is to climb up into the attic of a church, even when the room below is warm.

A false ceiling means a waste of fuel, for the sexton must keep a hot fire going for hours before this pocket of dead air is slowly tempered by radiation. Churches with false ceilings actually mean that one burns up several more tons of coal in a given period than in the case of a church of the same size with a ceiling open to the highest point of the roof.

A church with an open ceiling is cooler in summer for the same reason. Where there is a suspended ceiling of plaster, there is a pocket of dead air, which heats up in summer to a point considerable greater than the room below. This acts as a huge radiator all through church. This is why one must go into a church and throw open all the windows, and give the stagnant air a chance to circulate. Even then the church is hot, for the dead air above the ceiling cannot circulate.

We all know that the attic of a house is unmercifully hot in summer, and that this attic keeps the upstairs rooms warmer than the downstairs rooms. Throwing open the attic windows does not seem to help a great deal.

If a church has a false ceiling, the pocket of dead air becomes heated by 10 a. m., and by 11 o'clock the church is unpleasantly hot. A church of the same size and type, but with an open ceiling, is cooler in summer, because air currents are started as soon as the windows are thrown open, and every cubic foot of the air is set in motion, and tempered. There is no big pocket of dead air to act as a huge radiator overhead.

An open ceiling is more economical than a false ceiling. True enough, there must be roof trusses. But if these be made of solid timbers, as they ought to, they are not excessive in cost. Such trusses are costly only when one builds them up of four or five thicknesses of plank, and then tries to box them in with seven-eighths yellow pine. An honest timber truss, if properly designed and carefully made, is not at all bad in appearance, and its functional honesty is much more pleasing than the more expensive, boxed-in sort. If one desires a safe roof, trusses are necessary in any case. It is only a badly designed, carelessly made truss that is unsightly.

An open ceiling is very much more economical in the 3nd, because its first cost is the last cost. If entirely of wood, as it ought to be, and no plaster panels between, it may be given a light coat of stain, and it needs no further attention. But a plastered ceiling must be painted frequently. Where a wood ceiling is used, the expense of interior decorating is reduced by almost two-thirds, because it is not necessary to erect scaffolding. The side walls may be reached from painters' ladders and planks, and the end walls, in many cases, from ladders.

An open ceiling does away for all time with water stains and falling plaster. There are no lath streaks with which to contend. We have quite an assortment of 8" x 10" photos, sent in by churches where plaster has fallen from the ceiling, or where stains appear, due to a leaky roof. Leaks will not cause patches of wood ceiling to fall, neither will such a ceiling show ugly stains.

An open ceiling gives one much more interior height, and does away with the unsightly, squatty interior which is almost sure to result if a false ceiling be used. With a ceiling open to the peak, the side walls of the church may be a little lower, and yet with good proportions. If a false ceiling be used, the side walls must be made higher, if a low, squatty interior is to be avoided.

An open ceiling enables one to get a much higher chancel arch. If a false ceiling be used, the height of the chancel arch is reduced by at least six or eight feet. No arch can possibly be pleasing in appearance if it is about as high as its width, or even wider than its height. With an open ceiling, one may carry the chancel arch well up into the gable, producing an opening at least twice as high as wide.

An open ceiling results in a higher chancel. A low chancel is absolutely sure to dwarf a church interior. Some of Mr. Cram's exquisite little churches owe much of their effect to the fine, high chancel ceiling. A chancel, whose ceiling is as high as that of the nave, or very nearly so, is very impressive. With a false ceiling, the chancel ceiling is likewise crowded down. We know of no case where men of such recognized ability as Mr. Cram, Mr. Frohman, Mr. Robb, Mr. Goodhue, Mr. Corbusier, Mr. Vaughan, Mr. Bodley, Mr. Klauder, Mr. Little, Mr. Foster (to mention but a few), used false ceilings suspended below the roof trusses.

An open ceiling results in better acoustics. With a suspended ceiling of plaster, or of patented acoustical devices, there is too large an area of sound-absorbing material. A wood ceiling, if left unvarnished, seems to provide just about the proper acoustical results. One must beware of too much sound-absorption. We have gone to absurd extremes in this country, and our recent churches are frightfully dead within. We have tried so hard to get rid of possible echoes and reverberations that we have eliminated every shred of resonance. It is like talking into a blanket. Music, both organ and vocal, gains most decidedly in effect if there. is a reasonable amount of resonance to the building. To the average American, "good acoustics" means a complete lack of resonance. A varnished wood ceiling might produce bad results, but if wood be left unvarnished, the effect cannot be bad, but is quite likely to improve the acoustics by adding a slight amount of resonance.

To construct a wood ceiling, one must use trusses, purlins, rafters and roof boards. The scissors truss is cheap and strong, and is the thing for an inexpensive frame chapel. However, it is more utilitarian than graceful, and must not be used in the better class of work. It looks out of keeping with cut stone columns, rich stained glass and beautiful chancel wood-work. But in the case of a simple, inexpensive frame building it is the thing to use. For permanent churches of the better sort, some form of the arch-braced truss may be used. This is more graceful, but the walls must be of stone or brick, must be rather thick, and must be strengthened by means of exterior buttresses of sufficient width and projection.

If rafters are to be exposed within, which is the best practice, they must not be the ordinary 2" x 8" or 2" x 10" sort, for these are rather unsightly when left exposed. It is about as cheap, and certainly better in effect to use 4" x 6" rafters, spaced 20" or so on centers. These may be exposed to the nave of the church, and the effect is very good.

Roofing boards must be at least an inch and a quarter thick, and a little more if possible, both for strength, and to keep the slater's nails from coming through. Tongued and grooved, V-jointed boards are used. These are generally ordered in three widths, and laid at random. If roof boards are all of uniform width, the effect is rather mechanical and uninteresting below.

A wood ceiling of this sort is quite pleasing in appearance. The honest timbers of the trusses, with a few real wind-shakes to show that they are genuine timbers; the solid purlins that stiffen the roof and take up the sag of the rafters; the exposed rafters and the ceiling boards all give the church a much more interesting interior atmosphere than a monotonous expanse of uniform plaster. One instinctively feels this, and that is why money is squandered in some places painting imitation beams on a plastered ceiling, or dividing it into painted panels. The genuine thing is no more costly than the imitation, and is certainly more pleasing in appearance. Moreover, it has every advantage, and none of the disadvantages of the plastered ceiling.

A wood ceiling ought to be stained a light grayish brown. If too dark in color, it is gloomy, and the church is apt to be cold in effect. Two young ladies said just last night, "Have you ever been in .... Church? You'll never want to go a second time. Why it's so frightfully cold looking! Cold white stone columns, a black wood ceiling, black beams overhead, black furniture in the chancel, and great patches of white plaster." Neither of them knows the first principles of church building, but each was very sure that a first visit to that particular church will be the last. Stone of slightly creamy cast, plaster side walls tinted a warm gray, roof trusses and ceiling boards of quite a light shade of grayish brown, chancel furniture and pews with but little stain and no gloss would remedy matters amazingly, and pull the whole thing together into a mellow ensemble, where now it is a patchwork of clashing whites and very dark browns.

COMMON MISTAKES IN CHURCH BUILDING

F. R. WEBBER

The False Ceilings. In addition to his curious delusions regarding acoustics, his love for high basements, pseudo-transepts, corner towers with their middle stage lacking, and shallow chancels, the Old Adam is very partial to the false ceiling. Partial? He fights for it with a determination worthy of a better cause. For once he has no argument whatever to justify his position. In despair he must fall back on the word "a-koo-sticks," blissfully ignorant of the fact that acoustics are *improved* by doing away with the false ceiling of lath and plaster.

A false ceiling is constructed by nailing furring strips and lath to the under side of the roof trusses, and plastering the ceiling. Such a ceiling is often called a suspended ceiling. There is a space containing dead air, between this ceiling and the actual roof.

Such a false ceiling is bad because it is false. It is a structural sham. If there is anything that is irritating to the architect it is a thing that is structurally false. A church ought to be structurally honest.

A false ceiling is bad because it is extremely inartistic, and architecturally intolerable. It destroys the proportions of the interior. It exaggerates the width of the church, and reduces its interior height. It takes away the churchly effect of the interior, and makes the building look like a theatre, or an assembly hall. The quiet, reverential feeling is completely destroyed. It is also bad, because the congregation that insists upon having a false ceiling, usually makes it doubly hideous by painting imitation beams upon it, and filling in the panels with great, crude scrolls, and stenciled ornaments in decadent Renaissance patterns, or even Rococo and Baroque patterns, with all their unsavory suggestions!

A false ceiling is bad, because it soon becomes very ugly because of black streaks. About a year after it is painted, dark streaks begin to appear, showing the location of every lath, every batten and every rafter. Water stains are also common. Unless we have a roof of high grade, thick slate, nailed with the best copper nails, our roof will leak. The best cedar shingle, creosote-dipped, is of limited age. Nails rust through, and shingles decay around the nail holes. Asbestos and asphalt shingles are of limited durability. A driving rain will go through even the best of roofs, with the possible exception of heavy, graduated slate. Even where the roof is sound, the flashing soon leaks, unless made of copper, and of generous size, and well put on. Driving rains cause leaks, and leaks cause unsightly stains on the plaster ceiling.

A false ceiling of plaster is very expensive in the long run. It contains more actual square feet of area than the side and end walls. Hence, when the interior of the church is painted, it takes more paint to cover the ceiling than the side and end walls. The church must be filled with scaffolding, which is a costly process, and the chances are that services must be dropped for two Sundays. The work goes slower, for it is harder to paint a ceiling than to paint side walls. Figured over a term of ten years, a false ceiling of plaster means quite an outlay of money, for painting and repairs.

The false ceiling is out of style. Architects gave it up as a bad job long ago. Not a single one of the best known examples of good church building have such a ceiling. It is also out of keeping with the Gothic style, which, if consistent, must have an honest vault, or else a timbered ceiling.

The most artistic ceiling, and the most architecturally honest one, and the most economical as well, is the true Gothic ceiling, with the roof trusses exposed, and the panels filled in with matched boards. Such a wood ceiling, with no plaster whatever, is not costly. If the trusses and the boards are stained a warm brown, wholly without varnish, the first cost is the last. We have in mind such a ceiling, installed 38 years ago, and as good today as the day it was built. In all those years it has never needed paint or stain, and has never showed a leak.

Such a ceiling must be run up to the very peak of the roof, to be architecturally correct. "But is it not harder to heat such an interior?" somebody is sure to ask. Not at all. It is *easier* to heat. A false ceiling contains a pocket of dead air between ceiling and roof. In winter this dead air is cold, and it requires five or six hours, and plenty of coal, to heat such a pocket of dead air. With a wood ceiling, running up to the peak of the roof, heating is easier than in the case of the false ceiling. Good insulating roof-paper or felt, laid under the slate, will prevent heat leakage. A fine, honest effect is obtained by letting the purlins and rafters show. In this case the rafters are made about 3 x 4 inches in size (instead of 2 x 6), and spaced evenly. In summer it is decidedly cooler, because there is no pocket of dead, heated air overhead, to act as a great radiator, and make the interior insufferably warm.

The Bungalow Roof. A man walking down the street with a woman's hat on his head attracted a great deal of attention lately. He was noticed, and people laughed at him because his hat was so ridiculously out of keeping with his other clothing. The same is true of a Gothic church, with a roof of low pitch. There is only one type of design where the roof of low pitch is admissible. That is the Gothic church with very high side walls. If the side walls are less than the width of the nave, the low-pitched roof is an absurdity. There is no such thing as a bungalow type of Gothic. We see that term in print frequently. But there is no such thing. Bungalow design and Gothic design are mutually antagonistic. A bungalow roof on a Gothic church is as absurd as a windmill on the tower of the county court house.

A roof of slightly more than 45 degrees pitch is not expensive, if properly designed. Many people think that a great deal of money can be saved by using a low-pitched roof. This is not true, unless the church is about 20 to 24 feet wide. In such a case the span is small enough to use a truss of three timbers: a heavy tie-beam at the plate, and two beams supporting the roof, with a heavy bolt in the center. But—mark this well—if such a roof is to look in proper proportion, the side walls must be somewhat higher than the width of the church. If the church is 24 feet wide, the side walls ought to be 30 feet high *inside the nave,* not outside, in order to have proper Gothic proportions.

THE "HIGH" BASEMENT AND STEEP FLIGHT OF STEPS THE CORNER TOWER AND MISPLACED BUTTRESSES THE FALSE TRANSEPT AND BADLY PLACED TOWER THE SMALL, CROWDED CHANCEL AND BAD FENESTRATION

Pointed Arches in Frame Buildings. We have mentioned this point again and again, in this series of papers on church building. And yet the Old Adam is more persistent than ever. Committees simply demand pointed, rounded or segmental arches, whether the building is of stone, brick or wood. A pointed arch, over a window or a door, is structural, not ornamental. It goes with stone or brick construction. It is entirely out of place in a building of wood construction. More than that, it is a structural sham. It is classed by all honest architects as a violation of the fundamental principle of truthful design. The only proper and truthful form of window or doorway in a frame building, is that with the square head.

Let it be the rule that if our proposed church is of Gothic style, and built of stone or brick, the doorways and windows may have pointed arches. If in the Romanesque style, these may be round. But if we are building of wood, or wood covered with stucco, the only proper type of doors and windows are those with the square heads, unless we wish to make our church the laughing-stock of the town.

Overdoing Things. It has been pointed out many times by various noted authorities, that a small church dare not be a shrunken cathedral. A small church (say one seating 450 or less), is a distinct problem of its own. In building a small church or a chapel, we cannot hope to have all the accessories of a great metropolitan foundation. Fourth Presbyterian, Chapel of the Intercession, and other large parishes may have a complete array of features which the humble Trinity Lutheran, or St. Paul's Chapel never can hope to have.

And yet, we have had to argue times innumerable with folks who have but $40,000 to spend, and want a large church, a tower, a basement under the entire plant, a Sunday-school unit, sacristies, guild halls, parish houses, and so on.

One word must be kept in mind, and that is *simplicity.* Simplicity need not mean ugliness. Good proportions are no more expensive than bad ones. But simplicity means that we must hold to simple, unbroken lines and a few broad masses of surface. Transepts are very fine, and a beautiful apsidal chancel is very fine on a church of some size. But as Cram points out at length in his *Church Building,* these things are not essential, and often are absurd in the case of a small church. A tower is splendid, if large enough to be dignified. But it is very expensive, and unless it can be done properly, it had better be left undone for a few years. The same is true of elaborate stone trim and tracery. Plenty of such trim is essential, but in a small building it need not be elaborately carved. And the tracery may be reduced to a very simple form. In the case of windows, it is best to stick to simple diamonds, in the case of a small church, and use an amber glass and heavy lead-lines.

Completeness. Completeness is not always a virtue. Mr. and Mrs. Archibold Whitehouse (names fictitious), had about $900 to spend for furnishings for their new home. They went to a dealer on Prospect Street, and bought everything complete to the last tin dipper, and the last Wallace Nutting picture for $898.88. But they had to skimp on every point. Mr. and Mrs. Stanley Hollinger (names also fictitious) had the same amount to spend. They invested it in a few pieces of furniture of the most necessary kind, and of *good quality,* and then added a little from year to year. Who was the wiser?

It's precisely the same in building a church. It is not necessary to have everything complete to the last colored window in the sexton's dust-brush room. A better way is to spend whatever money is available for honorable construction, and let many things go, to be added from year to year. An excellent plan is as follows: Retain an architect of highest ability. He costs no more in the end: often less. Lay out a complete group of buildings, asking him to make *preliminary drawings,* for which he will charge but one per cent. Then erect a small portion, doing the work thoroughly well, getting *working drawings* of the portion to be built. It may mean a chancel and three bays of the nave, with the street end of temporary wood and stucco. The remainder of the nave and the tower may be added later. The Sunday-school may meet in the church for the present. Thousands do this. Sacristies and club rooms may have to find temporary quarters for a time. A day-school of two or three rooms may be built, also with the idea of future expansion, as needed. The windows of the church may be of temporary amber glass. There may have to be folding chairs for a year or two. The interior may be wholly undecorated. A small, second-hand organ may be used until a *good* new one is possible. Then, many things, such as windows, a permanent lectern, pulpit, font, reredos, organ case, etc., may be given gradually as memorials, by families, or parish organizations. (Conspicuous name plates are in bad taste.)

Lowest Bids. It is not necessary to select the lowest bidder. In many cases it is unwise to do so. The matter ought to be mentioned in the specifications. A congregation ought always to reserve the right to reject any and all bids. We know of one church,—a beautiful building in its general lines,—that falls completely flat, because of an unwillingness to spend a few hundred dollars more. It would not even have been necessary to spend this money. Less costly fixtures in the social hall would have saved enough to have made the church proper what it ought to have been.

The same holds good with the selection of furnishings. It is rarely safe to buy lots of things, and select the lowest bidder each time.

Too Much Advice. Too many cooks spoil the broth, and too many designers spoil the church. The most chaotic results are sure to follow if the building committee imagine that it is their function to do the planning and designing. Get a good architect, state frankly the requirements, and the available money—and leave matters of a technical nature to him. An architect does his best work when given a free hand in matters of design.

We had a great many other things in mind, when we approached the subject of common mistakes in building. We might have discussed pew ends, showing that the type with low, square ends, is to be preferred nowadays. But these, and many other things, must go back into the vertical file until some time in the remote future.

WOOD BUTTRESSES & POINTED
ARCHES ON A "FRAME" CHURCH

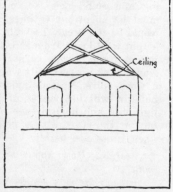

THE FALSE CEILING
AND SQUATTY INTERIOR

THE "BUNGALOW" GOTHIC
HORROR & "HIGH" BASEMENT

TOWER TOO THIN
AND NAVE BADLY DESIGNED

More About the Church That Expands

WE CANNOT ANSWER the large number of letters received in response to the article in the January issue on the church that expands. We started to answer them all individually, succeeded in writing to 32 inquirers, and then had to abandon the task, hoping that some additional information in this column may satisfy those who are yet awaiting reply. Here are the questions most frequently asked:

Question: Could that church be built in wood, for about $5,000 to $6,000?

Answer: It might prove difficult. Observe that the side walls must be 22 feet high in order to add the necessary side aisles later on, and yet have room for clerestory windows above. The first unit is shown in the lower left-hand corner of our illustration. To do such a design in wood might result in a building that would look like the two-story house that your grandmother lived in, back in 1890. A clerestory church, in wood, seems a bit impractical. It couldn't be done for the price you mention. Select a different design.

Question: Is your idea practical? Has such a church ever been built in this country?

Answer: It isn't our idea. It is standard practice in many countries abroad. It hasn't been done here so often, because building committees lack humility. They want the biggest thing possible, and a church much too large for average needs. This results in a killing debt, and an inability to meet the missionary budget. St. Mark's, Mt. Kisco, a few miles out of New York City, began with a simple chancel, nave and low wing for sacristies in 1909. It has been added to from time to time until now it is an imposing complex of stone buildings. St. John's, West Hartford, was originally a little chancel and nave. It has grown to a church almost 100 feet long, seating over 500, with a whole group of subsidiary buildings. St. John's, Buffalo, may be enlarged in Mt. Kisco fashion. There are several other examples which prove that the plan is eminently practical; as well as hundreds, if not thousands, overseas.

Question: Could the chancel and nave be built first? If so, what would it cost?

Answer: It has often been done. St. Ignatius', New York City, is a case in point. Another is Laira, a suburb of Plymouth. There they built a chancel 22' wide by 37' deep, a nave also 22' x 37' and side aisles about 12' wide. The nave seats 88 and each side seats 72, or 232 all told. The festival capacity is 300, since they use chapel chairs. This imposing stone church, with thick walls and 30" x 42" interior columns of stone, cost $24,000. When finished it will have cost $53,325, according to estimates given us by the Incorporated Church Building Society. This organization, by the way, has reduced church building to an exact and business-like science. They permit no over-building and no shoddy work. They have powers to enforce their requirements, and their staff does not change from year to year. The Laira church is to be extended westward, by lengthening the nave. The west front is temporary.

Question: Why the round arches in the side walls? Aren't you mixing your styles?

Answer: By using round arches and short spans, we have reduced the height by five feet, and saved $6,000. A pointed arch 8' wide will have to be at least 15' high to look right, while a round one may be 8' wide and but 10' high. The former calls for a 27' side wall, and the latter a 22' side wall, if clerestory windows are used. Pointed clerestory windows may safely be placed over a round-arched aisle arcade, but it is bad design to place round-headed clerestory windows over pointed arches in the aisle arcade.

Question: Could the church be widened to 35 or 40 feet?

Answer: Yes, if you increase its height in proportion. You will increase its cost enormously if you widen and heighten it. A clerestory church 35' wide must have side walls at least 40' high, and if you make it 40' wide, the side walls will have to be at least 45' high. There's a definite relation between width and height that may not be violated. Keep the span narrow, and you keep the cost low. We built scores of clerestory churches previous to the depression. Most of them were 27' to 30' wide, with side walls 30' to 35' high, and their average cost was from $125,000 to $150,000.

Question: Why do you suggest chapel chairs? I like pews better.

Answer: To keep down the cost. Good, sturdy chapel chairs cost $8 to $10 each in America, and but $2 each overseas. Two hundred chapel chairs, imported, will cost you $685, counting customs duty and ocean transportation. Well-made benches to seat 200 will cost at least $2,000. Save $1,315 and spend it for more important things. Chairs are more comfortable, they may be spaced to suit changing needs, and by using them one gets rid of the succession of strong horizontal lines that tend to make an interior look small. All post-depression churches abroad use chapel chairs. We are still in the hitching-post and buggy-whip stage in America, in church seating.

Question: Is such a design strictly Lutheran?

Answer: Just as much so as your motor car or electric ice box. We should lay stress upon a strictly Lutheran loyalty to the teachings of the Bible, and not waste time trying to evolve some odd type of design. We don't attempt a strictly Lutheran design for our homes or our shop fronts.

Question: May one use a roof lower than 45 degrees?

Answer: Yes, if your side walls are high. A church with low side walls and a roof of low pitch is ugly. High side walls and a roof a little lower than 45 degrees is not bad at all. Pastor Stein's church is very good, within and without. It is about 30' wide inside, it has no structural side aisles, the window sills are 10' above the floor, the side walls are about 30' to 32' high, and there is a roof of comparatively low pitch, with a horizontal tie-beam at the plate. The length of the church is perhaps 100 feet.

Question: How about a 12' x 12' tower on one corner?

Answer: A tower of that size is too small for this building, and would look like an asparagus stalk. Since a tower must be about three times as high as its width, its cost would be too great. To build a tower of sufficient bulk and height would cost from $15,000 to $20,000 additional. Never put a tower on one corner if it can possibly be avoided. Never push a tower part way into the building. Never build a wood spire. A stone spire is fine, but any construction bulletin will list scores of wood spires either struck by lightning and burned each month, or blown down. Be content at the start with a bell-cote, and let the tower come when times are better.

Question: How about an altar niche and a mother's room?

Answer: Nobody builds niches nowadays. A niche is a recess in a wall for a statue. Today we build chancels of proper depth. It is fine to take the service for Pastor R. G. Long, because of his beautiful chancel, 22' wide by 24' deep,

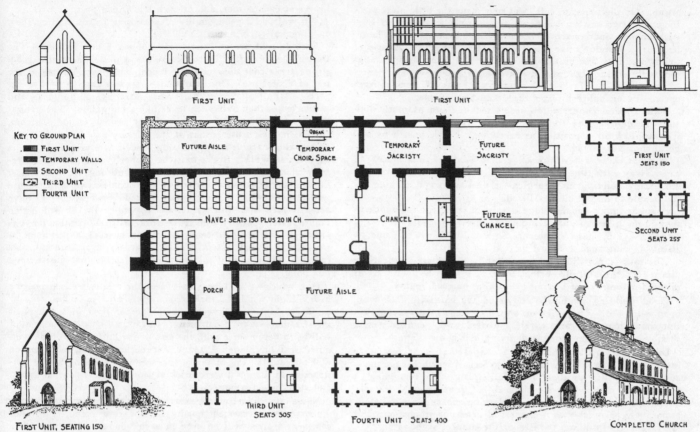

KEY TO GROUND PLAN
- FIRST UNIT
- TEMPORARY WALLS
- SECOND UNIT
- THIRD UNIT
- FOURTH UNIT

FIRST UNIT

FIRST UNIT

FIRST UNIT SEATS 150

SECOND UNIT SEATS 255

FUTURE AISLE

ORGAN

TEMPORARY CHOIR SPACE

TEMPORARY SACRISTY

FUTURE SACRISTY

NAVE: SEATS 130 PLUS 20 IN CH

CHANCEL

FUTURE CHANCEL

PORCH

FUTURE AISLE

FIRST UNIT, SEATING 150

THIRD UNIT SEATS 305

FOURTH UNIT SEATS 400

COMPLETED CHURCH

entirely unencumbered by choir stalls. The addition of this fine chancel to an older building gave great dignity and character to the church in question.

Question: Would this church eventually have to have inside pillars? People object to such things.

Answer: Interior columns are structurally necessary in some churches. In our design, but 12 people have to sit behind columns, and only then when the church is jammed to utmost capacity. With chapel chairs, sittings may be arranged so that none need sit behind columns. I myself prefer to sit back of a column. One is not so conspicuous, if in a strange church, and he may slip out if the sermon is poor, or if the music is bad. Rows of columns and arches add magnificently to the beauty and atmosphere of an interior, and one gets many an interesting vista through arches, impossible in the hall-type church.

Question: Could we put Composyte in the ceiling, for acoustics? Or would you stretch wires?

Answer: There is much more danger of deadening an interior with too much patented acoustical treatment than to get too much resonance by omitting it. Our churches are usually too dead. Listen to one of Palmer Christian's brilliant recitals at Ann Arbor, which are now being broadcast, and imagine the effect were the interior treated so as to eliminate all resonance. It is only the man who does not articulate distinctly, and who speaks with a drawl, who is afraid of a little resonance. Stretching wires is totally worthless.

Question: How dark would you stain the wood-work?

Answer: Not dark at all. Dark "mission" finish is another relic of buggy-whip days. A church must have tone, and that depends upon avoiding harsh contrasts of dark wood-work and light walls. Dark stain takes all the life out of woodwork, and ruins its natural beauty of grain. A very little stain, with a waxed finish—not varnish—is proper. The magnificent new wood-work of St. Mark's, in Exeter, was ruined by the stupid device of dark finish, demanded by an unintelligent building committee.

Mission Chapels

F. R. WEBBER

A MAN visited one of our big manufacturing plants the other day and applied for a position. He posed as an executive, and demanded a salary that would take one's breath. He boasted of a brilliant past, and was not at all modest in regard to what he could do. The man was shabby in appearance. A seedy coat hung over his ungainly frame like a phosphate sack on a fence post. His trousers were baggy, and had not been pressed in a month. He hadn't shaved in three days. His neck was not clean, his collar was wilted, and his nails seemed to be in deep mourning. It is hardly necessary to say that he didn't get the job.

We visited a mission chapel that reminded us of that man. It stands somewhat back from the street. In front of it is a weather-beaten sign, with the text of last Sunday's sermon still

on it, although today is Friday. Weeds as high as one's knees cover the lot. A walk of loose planks placed end to end, leads up to it. The chapel needs paint, and the guttering is rusted out. Imitation shingles bristle up, reminding one of the hackles of a growling dog.

The interior is even worse than the exterior. Four dozen shabby folding chairs are arranged in hit and miss fashion. There is a tiny altar, passed on from some other mission chapel. It is made of common yellow pine boards, and painted a muddy brown. A felt hanging, once a vivid green, hangs crookedly upon it. A tarnished brass crucifix, two glass candlesticks, two empty china vases, a hymn book, a pile of Sunday-school literature, and a small bell complete the fittings of the altar.

To the right is a small pulpit, and beside it a wheezy "reed" organ. On the opposite side, and very near the little altar plat-form, are two sewing machines and a rickety table piled high with ancient Sunday-school literature and hymnals of the loose-leaf sort. Windows are filled with opalescent glass. A strip of grimy matting lies in the center aisle. A hymn board hangs crookedly on the right of the altar, and a Sunday-school register of attendance and fares paid hangs on the left. A Rock of Ages chromo-lithograph completes the decorative scheme.

This mission congregation seems to have just as much diffi-culty in gaining the confidence of the community as the man who applied for a position as executive. People pass it by and go to churches far away.

"I went there a few times," a man said not long since. "I came away each time feeling as though I hadn't been to church. An untidy building, no liturgical service whatever, nothing for the people to do but sit and listen."

A great many people judge a mission congregation much as they judge a restaurant or a butcher shop. If it looks neat and attractive, they have confidence in it. But how shall one go about building such a chapel as that?

The task is not difficult if we spend our dollars in the right place. It's the old, old, principle of being satisfied with fewer things for the sake of having everything of good quality.

Good building materials and good workmanship look well, even when old. They take on added charm as the years go by. But cheap materials and careless workmanship soon take on a shabby look, and no amount of fixing can better matters.

Let us start with a plan for a chapel that is 25 feet wide inside by 65 long. We will allow 50 feet of length for the nave, and this will give us about 180 adult sitting. The remaining 15 feet will be devoted to the chancel. If funds permit, we will make the chancel 20 feet deep. Nothing makes for a religious atmosphere so quickly as a chancel of generous proportions, and the larger the building, the deeper the chancel ought to be.

The foundation of our chapel will be of solid brick. Cement blocks are apt to be damp, and soon discolor. They are too coarse in texture for the work in hand, and if they have an artificial "rock-face," they offend against good taste. Bricks backed with hollow tile may be a good talking point, but in the end solid brick will prove just as economical, so why not do it right while we are at it?

We will make our foundation wall 13 inches thick, and will see that it is thoroughly waterproofed outside, that a line of field tiles are laid around the footings, that the backfilling is properly done, and all precautions taken to get good workmanship.

Good design, whether in church work, residential or commer-cial, calls for as few steps as possible. Stores were built several steps above grade years ago, and so were residences and churches. People who had never been to England called such things "English basements," blissfully ignorant of the fact that English churches and houses are invariably built but a step or two above grade. We will turn a deaf ear to the man who argues for "five feet in the ground and five feet out," and we'll place our basement where basements ought to be—in the ground. To get light, we will build generous light-areas around the windows, the bottoms of which will be a foot below the win-dow sills, and provided with a drain in each area. This is the modern way. Better yet, we will save from one-fourth to one-half of our building fund by having no basement at all. With the money thus saved we will build a low wing above grade for the housing of those activities usually relegated to the basement.

On top of our foundation walls we will lay wood sills of 6 x 8 inch timbers, halving them together at the corners and at joints. These sills will be bedded in good cement mortar, and long bolts will anchor them to the foundation walls.

At each corner of the chapel we will erect an 8 x 8 inch post the exact height of our side walls. These we will brace by using 6 x 6 inch timbers, carefully framed into the sills and the up-right posts. At each interval of ten feet along the side walls, we will erect a vertical 8 x 8 inch post, bracing it into the sill. Then we will fill in with 2 x 6 inch studding. One chapel in North Platte, Nebraska, is being built with 8 x 8 inch posts and 2 x 8 in. studding. This is ideal.

The plate will be made of 6 x 8 inch timbers, with diagonal braces at each corner, and at each 8 x 8 inch post.

We will use a good quality of sheathing board, nailing them on diagonally, of course.

For our roof, we will use trusses of 8 x 8 inch timbers. The Committee on Church Architecture has a detail sheet of a good, strong truss that does not cost much, but which has stood the test of actual use. Our roof will be steeper than forty-five de-grees. A half-pitch roof is not very attractive on a church, and a roof lower than half-pitch looks like a bungalow. The bunga-low fad is a thing of the past, both for residences and churches.

The simplest truss is that of the scissors type. If made with painstaking care, it is very strong, and exerts very little thrust on the side walls. But it must be properly designed, and care-fully made. In the case of a frame building we are almost limited to the scissors variety of truss, unless we want to use iron tie-rods, which are extremely wicked. Several chapels have actually met with disaster lately because of the absurd notion that a rafter roof, with no truss-work, will do. Unless one has plenty of interior partitions, as in the case of a residence, a truss is absolutely essential. In view of several recent roof failures, we hope that all our mission boards may insist upon this point.

Our windows will be small, and their sills well above the floor. Eight windows, each with a glass area 32 inches wide by 44 inches high will give an abundance of light in a chapel of the size that we are considering. In fact, an inch or two smaller will be in better scale with the size of the building. These win-dows will have square heads, for no intelligent congregation will tolerate the fad of thirty years ago, of treating frame con-struction as though it were brick or stone, even to pointed arches and sham wooden buttresses!

Nowadays chapel windows are hung casement style, swinging outward, with casement hardware to anchor them. Two such casement frames will be used in each window opening, with a slender mullion between, and not one of the brutal sort. If we use weights and pulleys, we must have thick mullions. But with a casement window, a slender mullion is the rule. The same is true with window casings. A double-hung window, with weights and pulleys, calls for casings inside and out, to hide the weight boxes. But if we use the modern casement type, then we will not be so unintelligent as to use a wide frame around the window. A narrow strip of wood is much neater. An inch in width, or even less, is used today in best society. The windows will be set nearer the outside wall-surface than the inside, and the jambs splayed a little, and merely plastered inside. The glass will be deep amber rectangles, of the "ham-mered cathedral" sort, set in half-inch leads, with panes not larger than 4 x 7 inches.

The exterior will be covered with common siding, rough side out. It will be all siding, and not half siding and half shingles, which was an unhappy fad a few years ago. Nowadays the gables and the eaves project very little. Many good architects allow the roof to project two inches or less at the gables, with narrow board, and a small moulding under the shingles. A projection of a foot or more, verge boards, and heavy cornices are things of the past, except where an historic sort of design calls for these things.

The chapel will be painted with as few colors as possible. There will be not horizontal stripes, no corner-boards, no dividing of colors. Side walls and trim will be of one color, and perhaps the window sashes, (but not the frames), of a different color.

The interior will be plastered, and merely tinted. Stenciled borders are shocking. The ceiling will be of wood, the trusses and purlins showing. All interior wood work will be stained a warm nut brown, using as little stain as possible, and keeping varnish and filler off entirely.

By omitting useless interior casings, we will save enough money to get a beautiful cross. By leaving off the silly scroll-work and stencils, we will save enough to get a pair of fine candlesticks. We'll forget about a roll-top desk for the sacristy, and get a nice altar desk instead. With the $75 given for a fine rug for the sacristy, we will, with the consent of the donor, get a set of beautiful silk vestments for the altar.

A Building That Expands

IT IS a simple matter to build a small church in such a way that it may grow to the north, the east, the south, the west, and even upward. One may start with a seating capacity of 100 or so, and end with a seating capacity of 500 to 600. The method is so extremely simple that a small boy can grasp it, but in all these years we have succeeded only once in getting somebody to adopt it. That was last Summer.

The usual method is to waste considerable money on a makeshift structure. About the year 1900, it was considered quite the thing to spend $20,000 for a basement, hoping to add the upper part later on. Many a congregation buried itself for a long term of years in such a basement, and when they came out of their hibernating, styles had changed radically, and the $20,000 basement was often a complete loss. About 1910 the two-family-flat idea was developed by some crack-pot. There was a chapel on the first floor and apartments for the parson on the floor above. The thing looked exactly like all the other two-family dwellings on the street, and few ever noticed it. It proved a $20,000 blunder. Other fantastic devices followed, the most recent of which has been to build the recreational rooms first, and hope that the church may come later on. It is like the man who spends so much money on a garage on the back of the lot, and a motor car to put in it, that he has no money left to build his house. The most sensible of all these incomplete schemes is to build a parochial school, with a school hall, either as Professor Polack did at Evansville, or as Pastor Walter Obermeyer has done.

The new idea that we have so often suggested is really the most ancient of all, and it may be traced back almost to the beginning of the time when men began to build churches.

The scheme, in brief, is to build a small part of the permanent church and build it well. It is designed in such a way that it may expand readily to the four cardinal points of the compass, and, if really desired, in an upward direction. This may be done in either of two ways: 1). By building the chancel first; and 2). By building the nave first. The vast majority of the churches throughout Europe have been built in just this way, and have grown with the centuries. Only prejudice and bigotry prevents us from doing it,—that and our fantastic belief that anything done in Europe or England is about 25 years out of date.

Were we to be given a few thousand dollars and told to start a church, the money would never go for a temporary chapel, to be pulled down a few years later at a total loss. We would build the chancel of the future church. It would be about 20 feet wide, 35 feet long and the side walls 25 to 30 feet high. Twelve feet of the eastern end would form the sanctuary, and the 23 feet to the west would be a temporary nave. Our measurements are all internal. This would seat about 60 people. It could be built in such a way as to expand to the north, the west and the south.

Should one have more money to spend, and wish to seat twice as many people, then one could build the nave of his future church. This could, *for economy's sake*, be 20 feet wide by 55 feet long, with side walls 25 to 30 feet high. Dimensions are internal again. It would seat about 120 people. Fifteen feet of the east end would form the chancel, which would be the same height as the nave. In the east wall we would build an arch 12 feet wide by 28 feet to the peak. This would be walled up again with a thin curtain wall. It is our future chancel arch. In the north and south walls we would have arches, five to each wall. These arches would be 10 feet on centers and about 12 feet to the peak. We would wall up each arch with a thin curtain-wall, leav-

ing shallow recesses inside, as we did with the chancel arch. The walling on the outside would be flush throughout. The west wall would be of hollow tile, stuccoed on the outside, perhaps.

Everybody can see quickly the beautiful possibilities of such a church. Its initial cost would not be great. It would seat 120 people. It could be made as long as we wish, in any multiple of 10 feet. If we outgrow the 120 sittings, our next step is to knock out the curtain-wall to the east and add our permanent chancel. We would now have a building composed of a chancel 20 feet wide, 20 to 30 feet deep, and a nave 20 feet wide by 55 feet long, seating 160 people. When that is outgrown, we will knock out the curtain-walls of the north arches and add a side aisle 10 feet wide and 55 feet long. Our seating capacity is now 240. When that is outgrown, we will knock out the curtain-walls in the south arches, and now we build our south aisle, also 10 feet wide, and find that we can seat 320 people. Finally we will pull out our west wall, of hollow tile, and extend the whole thing westward. If we add 10 feet to the west, we will seat about 380 people. If we add 20 feet, we will seat over 450. If we add 30 feet, we will seat over 500.

Our little 20′ x 55′ chapel, seating 120, has grown with the congregation over a term of years. Not a brick or stone has been wasted. Not a single church service has been missed, for in actual practice one would build his new unit first, and then pull out the curtain-walls.

It is the old, time-tested method almost 2,000 years old, and is standard in every civilized country except America. It meets with furious condemnation in this country, for some vague reason. We designed a church of this sort less than a year ago, and it is going ahead. Within a few months it will be pictured in the church papers. People tell us that such a church would prove to be too narrow at the outset. If they have more money we will make it wider, but for every foot one widens a church, he must add 14 to 16 inches in height, and costs begin to skyrocket.

It is a synod-wide scandal when one recalls the millions, literally, that are dumped into more or less temporary buildings, that must be pulled down in a few years. The Lutherans build 6,153 new churches each decade, the U. S. Census reported a few years ago. At least 3,000 of these are temporary buildings. Assuming that each such temporary building costs only $5,000, we are guilty of spending $15,-000,000 for structures that must be wrecked, at a total loss, perhaps before the end of the decade.

In normal times, the Lutherans spend a *minimum* of $123,000,000 for new construction of all kinds. Government figures show that only 28% of the seating capacity of the average church is occupied, while 72% is represented by vacant pews. Among Lutherans this condition may be a little better. But assuming that every Lutheran church is 50% filled on an average Sunday, we are guilty of spending at least $60,000,000 for empty pews! Our bill for patching up bad construction runs to something like $12,000,000 every ten years. Thus, on three items alone (each one wholly unnecessary) the Lutherans misuse and squander $87,000,000 every decade!

This is not visionary guess-work. These are hard facts, based upon actual construction reports. Is it to be wondered at that Europeans tell us that we are a nation of madmen? It is a waste that can be prevented. The type of church that we have suggested will stop at least two of the big scandals, that of squandering money on a church twice as large as need be, and that of building a church and tearing it down in a few years. If we use good materials and construction methods, we will avoid the third item of waste.

The Modern Organ

By WALTER HOLTKAMP

IN THE DESIGN OF A CHURCH ORGAN, the necessity for original planning cannot be too strongly urged. Not only do the acoustic qualities of the church and the location of the organ dictate the design, but the denomination of the church and the form of service have a distinct influence on the design. Since of all places the church should be devoid of all useless or meaningless ornamentation, it is essential that the organ contain only those tones which are necessary and suitable to the service.

The successful organ planner must be a man of musical appreciation, as well as esthetic appreciation, in order to suggest or build that which will tie into the particular church service. To sit down and design an organ on paper, as ideal from the musician's standpoint, and then try to adapt this specification to the particular church, seldom if ever is successful. There are literally hundreds of golden opportunities for original and suitable planning gone to waste when organs are installed according to specifications rather than dispositions. It is commonly believed that such and such organ stops placed together and adapted to the building will produce a musical instrument. Often they will,—but more often they will not. If, however, the organ planner be a person of organistic mind and has a fair knowledge of musical requirements, the results are generally good. To such a person the feel of the church auditorium for certain tonal effects is of most importance. Each church has a certain tonal reaction differing from every other church, and the duty of the planner is to recognize this reaction. Just as the architect must plan his church according to the needs and requirements of the congregation and the landscape of the neighborhood, so must the organ-builder plan the organ. Certain tones or combinations of tones go well in certain buildings and are complete failures in others.

All organ tones are assisted or retarded by their surroundings; an orchestral violin is a great fighter of acoustics but an organ pipe is seldom better than its surroundings. It is therefore vitally important to choose those tones which are sympathetic to the particular building. A European cathedral with its magnificent proportions is favorable to tone and a comparatively poor organ sounds well under such conditions, while our smaller and acoustically unfavorable American churches, with their carpeted, cushioned and felted interiors, present a problem many times as difficult.

The position of the organ is a large contributing factor. At present there is a vogue for having the organ in a cruciform type of church speak into the chancel only. The theory is that the tone will mix with the voices of the choir and then as if by magic rush out into the nave in one glorious homogenious entity. As a matter of fact, however, the tone is usually bottled up in the chancel to such an extent that it is either hardly audible in the rear of the church, or if it is audible in the rear of the church, the tone sounds like an explosion in the chancel. Another reason for this mistaken notion is that if the organ speaks into the transepts or nave, as well as into the chancel, the people nearest to the openings will hear the organ in a distorted form. This is fully true in a small, shallow church where the chancel is out of proportion to the nave and partly true even in a church of fair proportions, but why spoil the organ for 900 people to please 100, when the 100 seats are usually the last ones to be occupied anyhow?

The ideal position of the organ in the cruciform type of church, or the church with a long high nave, is at the edge of the chancel or choir. In this position it is of course necessary that the organ be elevat d above the line of vision,—between the pews and the altar. This can be accomplished nicely by placing the organ on a rood-loft. The choir may also be on this loft or in the chancel immediately below. The console should be placed with the choir but so located that the organist is in touch with the nave for processions and congregational singing. The advantages of this position for the organ from a tonal standpoint are many. The organ is then open on four sides and top and a magnificent effect is assured. The tone can grow like a living, beautiful thing and prevade the entire church without undue effort. An organ in this position need not be large, since each pipe has an opportunity to speak a free and natural tone without forcing. Actual speaking pipes should be used to decorate the case work. These pipes may be in wood or metal. The case-work must be well proportioned and in harmony with the architecture of the church, where, funds allow carved and polychromed case work this adds to the general richness so much desired in or near the chancel.

The gallery or west wall of the church provides a good sound board or reflecting surface for organ tone and this position must be recommended as almost as good as the rood-loft position. The west gallery position for the organ is the traditional location for all churches where the choir may also be in the balcony. When the choir must be in the chancel, a small choir or chancel organ is placed convenient to the choir and the grand organ may occupy its traditional place in the west gallery. Both organs may then be played from either position. Many charming antiphonal effects are possible with such an arrangement and are far better than when the main organ is placed in the east and a so-called "echo-organ" in the west. An echo-organ has really no function in a church service and is only useful for creating melodramatic and highly emotional effects.

In connection with the main west gallery organ a very beautiful and useful addition is an organ built into or onto the balcony rail. The Germans called this a Ruckpositiv and the English a chair organ. The name comes from the fact that the organ was placed at the back of the player and near his bench or chair. The present name Choir Organ is derived from the chair organ of the 17th century. This Ruckpositiv or choir organ has all the advantages of the rood-screen location and also can serve as a very nice decorative feature. Here again actual speaking pipes should appear in the casework.

The whole question of the location of the organ can be summed up by likening organ tone with any other tone and affording the organ just as good a chance to speak as the choir or the pastor from the pulpit. Architecturally this is not always possible but the closer this ideal is approximated the more successful the organ will be. The present practice of hiding the organ away and treating it as a necessary evil in the planning of the church is unsound in more ways than one. The tone of a buried organ must be forced if it is to be heard at all and forced tones are not musical. If the organ has a function in a church it must be beautiful to be admitted into the service or ritual, and forced tones of any kind can hardly be said to be as beautiful as natural tones. Another distinct loss resulting from the buried position is that the enclosure dampens down the fundamental tones and so robs the organ of its very nature as a vibrating immensity which you feel as well as hear. With the fundamental tones reduced by too much enclosure the upper partials stick out in undue proportion and the organ sounds reedy and shrill. Its granduer and compelling dignity is lost. It is then a nervous type of tone instead of the calm, soothing and protecting thing suitable for a sanctuary. Part of the dignity of an organ lies in its impression of reserve strength. These buried organs give the impression of yelling at the top of their lungs at all times.

On the economical side, the musical value of an organ is in direct proportion to its free standing position. A buried $25,000 organ is not as musically valuable as free standing $10,000 organ. It takes a greater volume of tone dollars to fight their way out to the listeners. Millions of dollars have been wasted in mammoth organs which could have been saved by a little judicious planning and a study of organ requirements. The watch word should be smaller organs, of finer quality, in advantageous positions. They are more of a pleasure to build and certainly more of a pleasure to listen to. The mammoth thing satisfies the ego of the purchaser and organ builder but sins against all dictates of good taste. The church is the last place for ostentation.

Seven-tenths of all our impressions are said to come through our eyes. It is also said that the more senses we can bring to bear upon the appreciation of any given thing, the greater will our impression be. If this be true there is every reason why an organ case should be a finely designed and beautiful piece of cabinet work. A church organ is erected to the glory of God and should be as beautiful to the eye as it is to the ear. It is sad but true that many organs are installed long after the architect has finished his work and the church authorities do not recall him into consultation. The usual result is a nightmare of homely pipes covered with radiator bronze, and entirely out of keeping with the architecture of the church. The poor organ builder is up against it because the committee insist upon a simple case or worse yet a grille. The purchasing decision is usually made by comparison, of "numbers of pipes" balanced against numbers of dollars asked. All thought of the organ case is lost in a desire for a great quantity of interior speaking pipes. An organ pipe in itself is good to look at if it is honestly made of good material. It is good practice both from a musical as well as an architectural standpoint to incorporate actual speaking pipes into the organ case. This is true of the smaller as well as the larger pipes. The average organ loft or chamber is usually too small and if a number of the pipes can be placed in the case they will not only speak better themselves but afford the interior pipes a better chance to speak. It is a coincidence that the two best placements of the organ, namely west gallery and rood-loft also allow for the greatest number of speaking pipes being placed in the case. The gallery organ is usually a very wide construction and in the event of a rose window many smaller pipes may be incorporated to advantage. The rood-loft position has four sides to embellish and hence offers the greatest opportunity for the designer.

Why hide the organ? Its use is a part of the service. Some say that an organ should be heard but not seen, but the result is that it is also not heard when the desire has been to keep it from being seen. No one would think of drawing a curtain in front of a symphony orchestra. If functional design is one of the fundamental laws of architecture, there is every reason why the organ should be seen prominently. The organ should, however, be so placed and treated that it does not detract from the altar or pulpit. The design should be such as to convey the impression that the organ is really part of the original plan of the church and not an afterthought, so to speak. Where pipes are placed in the front without crowns, it is recommended that their lengths be restricted to their actual speaking or tonal length instead of attempting to obtain symmetry by adding a perfectly useless amount of material overlength. The speaking or tuning length lends itself to a graceful treatment of towers and removes cold, hard outlines. The field is wide for the serious and able designer of organ cases.

Pipes may be made in various materials. Zinc or wood are the usual practice today but copper, tin, brass, pewter, monelmetal may also be used. Domestic woods such as poplar, maple, pine, oak, beech, etc. afford ample opportunity to vary the monotony and add interest. Paintings may also be included into organ case design. Usually musical subjects are best for these paintings. A mine of inspiration may be found in the panels of Fra Angelico. While it is recommended that pipes be left in their natural metal, it is not wrong to decorate them in color. Very rich effects may be obtained by an artist. Wood pipes, while not attractive to the eye in their natural state, may easily be made so by a clever wood carver without damage to the tone of the pipe.

In general, the hand of the craftsman should be evident in well executed organ case work. A feeling of strength suits the casing for organ tone far better than a too lacy or polished effect. Carving should be bold and if the organ case is high up, the detail quite rugged. Great care must be exercised in keeping the design open enough for free agress of tone. Pipes should be spaced well apart. Large wood panels should be avoided if possible, but where necessary they should be pierced for the sake of ventilation as well as tone agress.

The organ is essentially an ensemble instrument. Good taste in organ tone dictates that all ensemble-disturbing tone be eliminated. The well trained and appreciative architect considers his building as a mass before he works out the details. Then he blinds the details into a homo-genious structure. Each detail plays an important part in the general effect. Good design possesses unity.

All the evidence centers on the fact that an organ is like every

Exeter Cathedral

artistic endeavor, and its production must obey the natural laws of harmonic proportion if it can be said to possess unity and beauty.

The attainment of perfect harmonic proportion in an organ is an acoustical problem which varies with the acoustics of every church or auditorium interior. Let us assume that we have four classes or families of organ tone to deal with; Diapason, Flute, String and Reed. Each group begins with the harmonic development of one family and gradually works up or down according to the harmonic development until it reaches the borderland of another group and then merges into it. For instance a Diapason may be flutey or stringy or any degree in between and still be a Diapason. Certain Flutes may be reedy in quality, and Reeds may be stringy. Painters also employ many hues and values in color. To say "Diapason" to an artist organ builder or to say "blue" to a painter conveys only a vague meaning. What kind of a Diapason? What kind of a blue? What function is to be filled? Which other registers will the Diapason speak with? How many registers? What 4's and 2's are there? How are they voiced? Are there any mutations? A thousand questions immediately suggest themselves.

Diapason tone has caused more discussion than any other class of organ tone, and this largely because the real function of a Diapason is so little understood. "All argument resolves itself into a discussion of definition." With the misunderstanding of the function of the Diapason and the various qualities of Diapason tone available it is little wonder that so much confusion exists. So often have we heard about the predominance of Diapason tone. In the past 25 years it was almost a religion to push the Unison Diapason for all it was worth. Pipes were scaled larger and larger in an attempt to force the Diapason to predominate. The old saying "You can lead a horse to water but you cannot make him drink" applied nicely because the forced Diapasons became Grosse Flutes and the traditional foundation of the organ was gone. Diapason tone is the foundation of the organ, but it must not predominate any more than the foundation of a building predominates. In fact it is impossible to have it do so. Diapason tone is foundational only in its peculiar ability to enfold and absorb the other tonal families with its rich but flexible harmonic development. There must be only enough Diapason tone in an organ to furnish a junction for all other tones. The Diapason is the most unselfish of all organ tones. To say of a Diapason that it has a refined tone pays that Diapason no compliment for it should really be rather rugged and almost primitive in nature.

It is important to consider Diapason tone in the light of a chorus of ranks and pitches matched together rather than as a single unison stop. The number and proportion of these ranks and pitches must be governed by the size and resonance of the church and the size of the organ. Resonant churches allow the use of a more complete series of harmonics than non-resonant or so-called "acoustically treated churches." The size of the organ or the number of stops to be supported by the Diapason chorus, and the nature of these stops, is the second governing factor. It is lamentable that the average American church has so little resonance or ring. Few architects or church building committees have considered resonance as of value. Emphasis has been put on the voice from the pulpit rather than the voice from the organ or choir.

For the sake of structural build-up each unison registers greater in power than *piano* must have its companion octave to assist and beautify the parent unison. It follows logically as well as artistically that a group of unisons and octaves greater in power than *mezzo* should have associated with them their proper Fifteenth, Twelfth and Sub. Great care must be exercised in the Sub. This pitch is not nearly so important as is usually believed and is responsible for much of the organ's present reputation as a grave instrument. The continental European manuals were founded on 16′ tone and the effect is grand and impressive for short whiles. Heard too long or too often, this predominant low pitch produces the same oppression as a heavy, low ceiling. The organ is a joyful, happy instrument too seldom, and to burden its manuals with heavy 16′ tone increases its dreariness.

Any considerable weight in manual 16′ tone indicates 32′ tone in the pedals to support the weight, and only a few American churches have taste, money or space enough to desire, afford or allow genuine 32′ installations. It is almost always a safe rule to decrease the power and enrich the harmonic development as the pitch descends. Booming tone in the Pedal is unmusical and too resistant to join on to the manual upperwork. The ideal Pedal tone is quite rich and flexible.

All possible tone colors should appear in the Pedal because as the vibrations decrease in number all pipes become more alike. A Pedal Organ for instance, composed of Double Open Diapason, Bourdon and Lieblich Gedeckt is an abomination. Three degrees of power in the same color! What chance has the Lieblich Gedeckt and Bourdon when the Double Open is on? The Bourdon is a necessary register but the Double Open should be in metal with a slight Geigen character and the Lieblich should be Quintaten or Dulciana. Then the three augment and color each other. These three, together with soft reed from Swell, together with a proper proportion of Octave, Twelfth and Fifteenth produce plenty of Pedal for an average three-manual organ. The old Cello 8's of Johnson and Roosevelt provide the most essential first octave tone. Weighty 8′ Flutes in the pedal destroy its clarity and point, and tend to raise the pitch. Pedal Octave dare not be as strong in proportion as manual Octave because of the lack of overtones in pipes of slow vibration. The parent 16′ will not absorb the octave. An admirable Pedal Twelfth is a Wald Flote and the super-octaves are never better than when Gemshorns or Dulcianas. The balancing up of the Pedal department must be done in the church on account of the acoustics, and difficulty in giving the larger Pedal pipes a free speaking position.

The organization of the color and mass of octave and mutation ranks calls for rare judgment and artistic perception. There is no reason under the sun why each octave and mutation should not beautify as well as augment. In fact, beautification is often more important than augmentation. The octave should be so chosen and voiced that it flows into the unison without appreciably raising the pitch but materially altering its color. The two together form a cushion for the reception of the Fifteenth and Twelfth. If these registers are so formed and voiced, they become

of even greater importance than unisons since their combinational use is many times greater and their coloring possibilities various. Two 8's never join so well as when a proper 4′ is in between.

The conception of a pipe organ as a concert instrument need not worry us since a good church organ is at the same time the best concert organ. An organ is in a tonal class of its own, and as long as it remains in its own field it is supreme. The moment an organ begins to rival a band or an orchestra, or take on the color of any other musical instrument, something ludicrous or unsound is bound to result. The fiddle player in the orchestra does not try to imitate trumpet tone, and no more should an organ try to imitate. The tone of a strictly built organ is musically satisfying. Its office in the world of music is sacred and its boundaries well defined. The present unpopularity of organ concerts is due to a hybrid tonality which is not in itself musically satisfying.

This does not mean that orchestral transcriptions may not be played on a pipe organ. Far from it. The orchestral transcription will, however, sound better if we use only typical organ tones. For instance, a Salicional 8′ and Violina 4′ put a Viole d'Orchestre to shame as a colorful tone. The Viole d'Orchestre is too intense and concentrated a tone and is like a white light or flame. Furthermore, a Violina 4′ occupies a definite niche in the tonal structure, whereas a Viole d'Orchestre is only ornament and hence interferes with the tonal structure. The Violina 4′ is useful in combination with practically all other registers in the department if it is properly voiced while the Viole d'Orchestre is limited to use alone. The Violina 4′ costs less than the Viole d'Orchestre, stays put and is in every way a much wiser investment. Similar comparisons may be drawn with the majority of orchestral-organ tones.

The case against the imitation tone is particularly strong where reeds are concerned for here the question of tuning comes in. The majority of imitative reeds are forced tones and hypersensitive to dust and thermometric changes. Why spend money for an occasional semi-musical effect when the real thing is so much better and the tuning bills practically nil?

A Real Organ for Small Churches

THERE can be no doubt as to whether or not a church wants an organ because even the smallest congregations have ambitions of some day owning one. For hundreds of years the pipe organ has been the recognized musical instrument of the Church. Its origin, of course, dates back to great antiquity; the flute, which is a component part thereof, is one of the most ancient of musical instruments. It is pictured on the walls of early Egyptian tombs; specimens of it, still in playable condition, have been unearthed and can be seen in our museums. The organ of today represents the development of over two thousand years and the skill of countless inventors, designers and artists. In recent years special effort has been put forth to give the small churches the same musical advantages as those enjoyed by large congregations, with the result that high grade organs are being produced at prices heretofore unheard of. One leading American builder is actually offering a standard two manual and pedal pipe organ for $820.00.

Never in history has there been such tremendous interest displayed in small organs. Builders have come to realize that EVERY church wants an organ and not all of them can afford to invest thousands of dollars. Hundreds of organs are being sold, yet thousands of churches either know nothing of these creations, or they feel that the price is too low to make possible the production of a good organ. Proper publicity will make known the fact that quality organs are available at attractive prices and a demonstration will convince the most skeptical that these instruments are well built, finely voiced and in general ideal for the church service.

There are several questions which should receive particular mention because they are raised in many instances:

Q. Are these organs expensive to operate?

A. Only a ¼ H.P. motor is required to supply the wind, therefore the operating cost is very low—about the same as burning a 200-watt bulb.

Q. If the church is not heated during the week, will the organ be harmed?

A. There is available today an organ action which eliminates the thin pneumatic leathers generally used so that temperature has no effect whatsoever upon the mechanism. It will withstand the cold equally as well as any other furnishing in the church. If one felt disposed to play this modern organ in zero temperature, it would not fail to perform as efficiently as under normal conditions.

Q. Will the cold affect the tuning?

A. An organ goes out of tune because the materials of which pipes are made contract and expand, but when considering that services are not held in cold churches, there is no need to be concerned. The moment the temperature is somewhere near normal, the organ is again in tune. In very large organs costing thousands of dollars, there are sensitive sets of pipes included and these of course call for greater care, but this does not hold true with smaller organs. They are designed so as to keep tuning and maintenance costs down to a minimum. A vast number of organs have been in use for three and four years without the slightest attention.

Q. Is the maintenance expense an item to be considered?

A. Due to the very simple construction employed, action and other troubles are almost unknown.

Q. How is it possible to get a good instrument at such low prices?

A. This is where the ingenuity of the organ builder enters into consideration. He simplified his action and the general construction to such an extent that costs were greatly reduced.

Q. Is the quality of material and the voicing equivalent to that of large organs?

A. Yes, providing you are dealing with a responsible builder who has only one quality.

Q. For what sized churches will these smaller organs be adequate?

A. Much depends upon the acoustical properties, but the following will serve as a general guide:

Seating capacity	Cost of organ
75-150	$ 820.00
150-225	$ 995.00
225-350	$1195.00
350-400	from $1375.00 to $1545.00
400-450	from $1575.00 to $1750.00
450-500	from $1750.00 to $2000.00

Q. Must our organist be an accomplished musician to play it?

A. No. If he or she has played a piano or reed organ, no difficulty will be experienced in becoming acquainted with the organ. Moreover, there is an easy book of organ numbers available now, showing the registration for small organs exclusively.

Q. Is much space required for placement?

A. Very little indeed, in fact about 5′6″x5′6″ will suffice for the smaller organs. They can also be fitted into an odd room, tower or special chamber and the console detached.

Q. Is the blower noisy and hard to locate?

A. The blower is very quiet, in fact may be enclosed within the organ. Connections are made with a regular cord, as one would connect an electric iron or extension cord.

Pages could be written on the subject; however, the foregoing will provide some general idea of what has been accomplished in the building of pipe organs which will serve every need. Briefly, the important things to bear in mind are:

1. An organ is NOT expensive.
2. It is easy to install.
3. Keeping it in tune is NOT a problem.
4. Cost of upkeep is low.
5. Installation is simple.
6. Easy to play.

Finally, see and hear one of the new small organs and judge for yourself whether or not it has any merit.

Code of Ethics for Organists

Unethical competition and alleged unfairness on the part of churches have caused the American Guild of Organists to appoint a committee to draw up resolutions to abate existing evils. The committe made the report given below to the Council of the Guild and the Council adopted the report on October 23rd. Here is the report:

To the Council of the
American Guild of Organists

Your committee on a Code of Ethics for the Guild, herewith submits the following report:—

We carefully have considered the reports of unfair practices, which have been brought to the attention of the Council, and the suggestions as to the means to be taken to abolish these practices.

We therefore present for the consideration of the Council, the following rules and recommendations:—

RULE 1. No organist shall apply for a position, nor shall any teacher or school of music seek to place anyone in a position, unless a present or prospective vacancy, definitely has been determined.

RULE 2. When demanded, churches should give organists a yearly contract, which may be terminated upon expiration, at ninety days notice.

RULE 3. None but the regular organist of a church shall play at weddings or funerals, except by arrangement with said organist.

THE COMMITTEE RECOMMENDS:—

A—That a bureau (or committee) be established at Headquarters, and in each chapter, to receive complaints of irregular and unfair practices, on the part of both organists and churches. Such complaints shall be kept on file, and notices of protest may be sent to the offending organists or churches.

B—That organists be cautioned against these unethical practices, and advised to be ready to cope with the situation, by preparing themselves for all possible requirements of their positions, thus making themselves invaluable to the churches.

C—That churches appoint as "Minister of Music," an organist who has proven his worth, with full power to carry out the policies in regard to music in the church, as the pastor and music committee may authorize. That such a "Minister of Music" shall be protected in his tenure of office, and hence be free to do his best work.

Your committee does not think it desirable to unionize the Guild. Nor do we recommend any effort to fix a minimum rate of pay, either in amount on in its relationship to other expenditures of the church. In our opinion, owing to the varied conditions in churches throughout the country, any such effort would be futile. We do, however, strongly recommend, that at Headquarters and in all Chapters, steps be taken to strengthen the Guild, by bringing into its membership, a larger proportion of the organists of the country.

In conclusion we wish to emphasize the fact, that a large majority of churches need no code; that in them music has its rightful and highly honored place. But we deplore the increasing number of cases brought to our attention, of organists who have been discharged without adequate notice, and of efforts by organists and others to supplant another organist in his position.

Dr. George W Truett, the great Baptist preacher in Dallas, Texas, whose ministry in the field of Christian stewardship reads like a romance, puts it this way: "We emphasize stewardship, not for the purpose of getting the money, but for the purpose of developing Christian life in the giver. To give is to live. To withhold is to die."

* * * *

Chimes

A PASTOR WRITES US, saying that much has been said in the past in regard to bells and peals, but nothing in regard to chimes. By this he means a progression of bells arranged for hymn playing. We realize that this subject has been overlooked.

In order to play hymns on an assemblage of bells, it is necessary, as a rule, that the bells be hung "dead," that is, bolted solidly to a steel beam or framework of steel or wood. The clappers must be held in a position so that they may be brought quickly and crisply against the sound-bow of the bells. There must be a keyboard of wooden or of metal bars, about two inches on centers, and with a fall of one and a half to two inches or so. These are connected to the playing mechanism by means of wires, with some provision for adjusting the tension of the connecting wires. A small chime of this description, capable of playing a number of simple hymn-tunes, may be had at a price ranging from $3,500 upward, complete.

The minimum number of bells will be an octave of eight bells, the largest weighing about 450 pounds and the smallest about 100 pounds. With a straight diatonic scale of eight notes, simple hymns may be played, provided they lie within the octave. If there be an augmented fourth note, or a diminished seventh, as is often the case, it is better to buy the extra F♯ and B♭ bells than to mutilate well-known hymns, to the annoyance of the neighbourhood. With a progression of ten bells a number of additional hymns are possible. However, the ideal might be a progression of twelve bells, with not only the added F♯ and B♭, but with two notes below the scale as well. Almost any hymn written may be played upon such a chime.

American friends are doubtless extremely impatient with our repeated comments on English bells and certain articles of chancel equipment. But it will be noticed that we have never suggested going to England for organs, for lighting fixtures or for several other products. But it does happen that there are certain bell founders in England who supply the world with *tuned* bells today. The art of tuning was long a lost one, and most of the bells made by previous generations were merely rough castings. Efforts at tuning were seldom successful. They did not know that a bell yields a compound tone of five or more notes, and when this fact was at last rediscovered, few bell founders had the slightest idea as to how these notes are produced. Just how true it is we cannot say, but there is said to be but one tuning machine in America!

We do know that there are one or two bell founders in England who understand the art perfectly, and whose product is so widely recognized that they have virtually a monopoly of the business. Untuned bells may, now and then, turn out tolerable to the ear if there be but one. But as soon as we try to ring two or more of them, their discordant character is at once evident. A Detroit pastor, now deceased, journeyed far to hear a peal of bells famed in song and story. He came back disgusted, saying that he never heard so discordant a jangle in all his life. The bells happened to be untuned. We recall many a Sunday, in a certain town, listening to a chime of bells, one of the upper notes of which was a full semi-tone out of proper pitch. Try playing "Old Hundredth" on your piano, always striking the top note a full semi-tone higher than it should be. Just how the neighbours can endure such mutilation of hymn tunes is a mystery.

The bells supplied by the English founders in question are not only in perfect tune with themselves, and with one another, but chords of two or three notes may be played on them with complete satisfaction to the most exacting ear. However, the harmonics of bells differ somewhat from those of a piano, and chords with minor thirds are more agreeable than those with major thirds. We would plead with certain friends who like to play hymn tunes in major thirds: try minor thirds instead.

Although it is almost actionable to mention it, yet one must not be misled by what high-pressure salesmen may say in regard to substitutes for bells. Such substitutes cost almost as much as real bells. Their tone is thin, tinny and of limited range, and when two or more of them are struck together, a sad jangle is the result, for they possess harmonics that seem to defy proper blending.

It is possible to produce bells more cheaply in England than in America, it is true. Unfortunately there is a 45 per cent duty on bells, and by the time import duty and freight is paid, no money is saved. The only advantage is that of a chime of bells properly tuned, and with a playing mechanism that is virtually perfect. With all due respect to Yankee ingenuity, most of the playing mechanism produced in America is rather crude and heavy.

We are quite aware of the sales arguments on the other side, but the fact remains that four-fifths of all the carillons in America are British made. Bells and sets of chimes are going over on every ship, and have for years. Most Americans, upon investigation, believe that British bells are best.

Question: "You speak of change ringing. I'd like you to say in your department of *The American Lutheran* whether we could play such changes on our church bells. These we operate with hand levers. Also please give us direction for change ringing." —C.S.

Answer: Peal ringing from hand levers is but a substitute for the real thing. The only really satisfactory way is to have one's bells hung properly for peal ringing, with one man to each bell. But the effect of change ringing may be approximated by means of the hand clavier. Mr. Frank Naisby, a skilled ringer, has given me the following "rows" of Stedman Triples:

12345678	41752368	54621738
21354768	14725638	45612378
23145678	17452368	46521738
32416578	71425638	64512378
23461758	17246538	65421738
24316578	12764358	56247138
42361758	21746538	65274318
43216578	27164358	62547138
34261758	72146358	26574318
43627158	71264358	25647138
46372518	17623458	52674318
64327158	71632548	25763418
63472518	76123458	27536148
36427158	67132548	72563418
34672518	61723458	75236148
43765218	16732548	57263418
34756128	61375248	52736148
37465218	63157428	25371648
73456128	36175248	52317468
74365218	31657428	53271648
47356128	13675248	35217468
74531628	16357428	32571648
75413268	61534728	23517468
57431628	16543278	32154768
54713268	15634728	31245678
45731628	51643278	13254768
47513268	56134728	12345678
74152368	65143278	(etc.)
47125638	56412378	
(see next column)	(see next column)	

No. 1 is the smallest bell, No. 2 the next smallest, etc., down to No. 8, which is the largest, or tenor. We have added the eighth bell as a "cover bell" for each row. Play the changes rapidly, with little or no pause at the end of each row. Transcribe these rows to notes on a musical staff, and it may make it easier.

With a pencil trace a line through the figure sevens, down each column, and note the course of the seventh, or "observation bell."

Giving The Church A Setting

WILLIAM F. BRUENING

IT MAY BE A TRUTH that hardly needs stating that the beauty of a precious stone is lost without a proper setting. The same is true of a church. Drive along the highways of the country and you will find beautiful churches set on a plot of ground without a single tree or shrub. What a pity! Go along a little farther and you will find a mail order house or a tractor factory set off with evergreens, flower beds, etc.

The plea that costs of landscaping are prohibitive does not hold. The only thing required is a pastor who will interest himself in what can be done to beautify the setting of his church which stands as symbol of the living Gospel

proclaimed within. If he learns to love plants and flowers (and that can be learned) then his church will not long be without such plants and flowers.

Fabulous sums quoted as being paid by the rich for the landscaping of estates or perhaps even estimates given by landscape gardeners at the time of the erection of the church sometimes frighten congregations into believing that nothing can be done.

Building committees should never make the mistake of feeling that landscaping is one of the places where costs can be cut. When counting the cost of the building, its

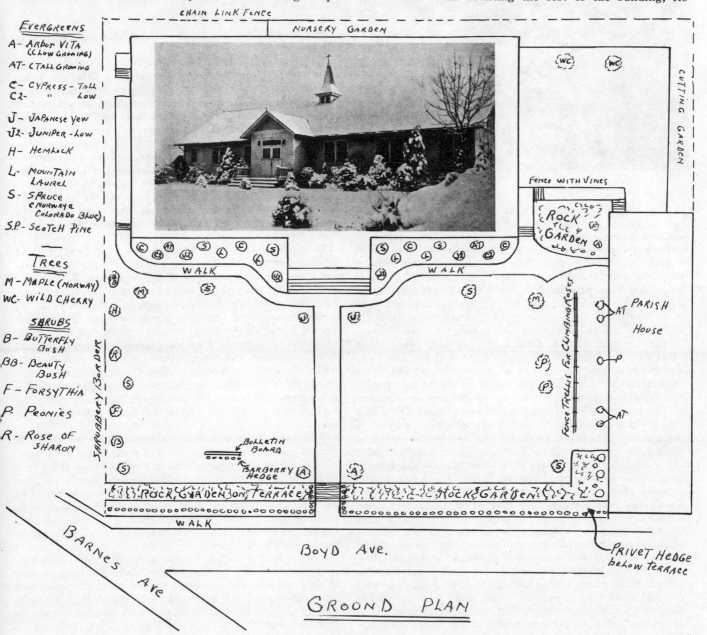

Evergreens
A- Arbor Vita (Low Growing)
AT- (Tall Growing)
C- Cypress - Tall
C2- " Low
J- Japanese Yew
J2- Juniper - Low
H- Hemlock
L- Mountain Laurel
S- Spruce (Norway & Colorado Blue)
S.P.- Scotch Pine

Trees
M- Maple (Norway)
WC- Wild Cherry

Shrubs
B- Butterfly Bush
BB- Beauty Bush
F- Forsythia
P- Peonies
R- Rose of Sharon

GROUND PLAN

Rock Garden

furnishings, etc., a sum should be included for this most important item. Too often the attitude is taken that landscaping will come "later on." Too often it does not come later on. A sum of $100 will go a great way in beginning a landscape plan to give a beautiful church a beautiful setting.

For those who contemplate landscaping a plan is essential. Such a plan can be furnished by a competent landscape gardener. The entire plan need not be completed at one time. The most essential plantings can be put in first. Some inexpensive temporary fast-growing shrubs can be put in first with the view to replacing them later with permanent evergreens, etc., if the plans call for such.

Perhaps it would be best to tell how we developed such a plan successfully. Our church is a simple white frame portable structure. If it had been left without planting it would not have presented a very inviting appearance. The first work that was required was proper grading, etc. That work was included in the original estimate for excavation. A layer of top soil about six inches deep was also included in the contract for excavation. The grounds were ready after such work for the planting of the lawn and the foundation shrubbery. The first order for shrubs cost $50. Since that time very little has been spent on shrubs and plants. Every spring an appeal is made for the garden. Members of the congregation are invited to bring in needed plants and shrubs to the church which are no longer wanted in their home garden. A florist of the neighborhood took a special interest in our garden and one spring donated twelve evergreens for spots where they were needed. Members of the church took a special interest in the church garden and donated plants and special trees where they were needed. Two large maple trees were planted in memory of a departed loved one. Such who wished to make donations were always requested to consult with the pastor as to what type of flowers and plants were still needed. Not every offer of a plant or shrub was accepted if it did not fit into the plan. A small rock garden was put in one spring to "treat" a certain slope where it was difficult to grow grass. The rock garden became so popular that the next year one of the members contributed the amount necessary to provide the rocks and labor to plant a rock garden along the entire front terrace of the church yard. Very few plants had to

be bought. Plants existing in other gardens were "divided" and new plants were donated from the gardens of members. Our rock garden has actually become a beauty spot of the community and people can be seen who come to the church just to look at the garden. The garden, lawn, shrubbery, etc., is now maintained at the cost of $25 per year for materials, an amount included in the annual budget.

For those who may be planning church gardens, landscaping, etc., who may not have had previous experience, perhaps a few general suggestions might be made which have proved helpful to us in our plan.

Get a few seed catalogs, attend a garden show where that is possible, or buy a practical book on garden and begin by studying. (Such a book that has proved very helpful is "The Practical Book of Outdoor Flowers" by Richardson Wright, published by the Garden City Publishing Company, Garden City, N. Y.)

For the lawn buy the best grass seed available. Such seed usually costs about 60c per pound but it is far superior to cheaper grades.

Do not expect a lawn or garden without spending some money on fertilizers. A commercial "complete" fertilizer may be used for the lawn. For evergreens the best is manure. Bone meal is the safest to use for flowers although slower in action. Caution must be exercised in the use of commercial fertilizers, bone meal will not "burn" the plants.

Have a nursery somewhere in the back where evergreen or shrubbery seedlings may be planted and used to complete the landscape plan when they have reached the proper size. Small evergreens can be purchased for as little as 10c to 25c and will serve very well after several years in the nursery garden. Any landscaping plan should be a "long term" plan.

A cutting garden from which flowers may be cut for the altar or for the sick should be planted in some inconspicuous place where appearance is not important. Flowers for such a garden may be the well known zinnias, snapdragons, marigolds, coreopsis, African daisies, cosmos, larkspurs, etc.

Appropriate rock garden plants are the perennials: arabis, mountain pink, candytuft, violets, sedums (many varieties), ivy, thyme (several varieties), golden alyssum, snow-in-summer and many others. Annuals that do very well are: portulaca, petunnia, dwarf marigolds, ageratum, and snapdragons, begonia, geranium, sweet alyssum. Daffodils, tulips, and iris as bulbous plants find their use in the rock garden. Dwarf evergreens and hardy azaleas are also very useful.

When shrubs or hedges are planted do not be afraid to prune them severely and continue to prune them every year. Directions for such pruning can be obtained from the manufacturers of pruning tools. Evergreens should also be pruned regularly for proper shaping and to encourage full growth. The different types need different treatment in pruning but they should be pruned. A good time for such pruning is usually just before they make their most vigorous growth in the spring.

The habit of growth of any shrub should be known before it is planted. Tall growing evergreens should not be planted in front of windows unless there are plans to move them later. In general tall growing trees should be planted in the corners or between windows with smaller shrubs in front of them or grouped around them.

The almost ever present temptation to plant a flower bed

PLEASE TURN TO PAGE 241

What Is the Greeting at Your Church Door?

IDA WHITE PARKER
Director, National Plant, Flower and Fruit Guild

As they were in November, 1923

"The exterior of a church and the grounds that surround it create the first impression of what the interior has to offer. If these are 'right' not only the members of that particular church but 'the stranger within the gates' will be drawn more warmly to enter and partake of what has been prepared for them."

With this thought in mind the National Plant, Flower and Fruit Guild a few years ago started its campaign to encourage the beautifying of church grounds in rural and suburban districts. The progress of this campaign has been splendid with the result that many churches have benefitted by the advice and help of the Guild.

It is not a difficult matter to have attractive church grounds. There are great varieties of native trees and shrubs to be had, and local gardens will gladly furnish the desired flowers.

Today one of the most attractive rural churches in New Jersey has green lawns with artistic groupings of native cedar trees near the church building, with native ivy already beginning to weave its delicate tracery over the field stone of which the church is built, while a simple hedge of clipped privet sets it a little apart from its neighbors. A few years ago this church stood bare and bald in a roadside lot, dusty and hot in summer, wet and bleak in winter; a most uninviting edifice, that tempted no one to enter. The seeming miracle was brought about with little labor and almost literally no expense.

A somewhat similar story is told of a church in a New England factory town. The church and church house stood on a street corner in the midst of a bare lot with no sign of green or living thing about it. To-day that corner, thanks to the minister of the church, is a beauty spot. A privet hedge three feet high and four feet across the top encloses the two church buildings in a charming and intimate way. A fine lawn covers the ugly vacant lot of four years ago; a native cedar tree—used for Christmas and other festive occasions—stands in a corner of the lawn; shrubs and flowers are growing and blooming in appropriate places on the church grounds. All this has been accomplished in a little less than four years and at an expenditure of only One Hundred Dollars.

Many other instances might be cited of the possibilities for beautifying our church grounds if space permitted.

A booklet called "Beautifying the Church Grounds" is issued by the Guild; churches are encouraged to form Church Garden Clubs to undertake the work of beautifying their own grounds, in which the Guild is prepared to offer the expert help and advice of a well known New York landscape architect, free to the Church Garden Clubs affiliated with the Guild.

The headquarters of the National Plant, Flower and Fruit Guild are at 70 Fifth Avenue, New York City, and a letter addressed to Mrs. Ida White Parker, Director, will be answered promptly and very gladly.

As they are today, after four years of care and an expenditure of only $100.

Cuts furnished by courtesy of National Plant, Flower & Fruit Guild

Stained Glass

An Artist's Medium in Light and Color

CHARLES J. CONNICK

THE INTEREST in stained glass windows has grown to a remarkable degree within the last ten or fifteen years. In view of this growing interest it may seem absurd for one who has chosen it as his favorite medium of expression to say that the craft still suffers through the dominance of realistic painting as the medium of visual expression in the arts.

The nature of the craft itself,—simply expressed as bits of glass held in place by grooved leads and iron supporting bars, —dictates its adherence to principles of design.

For years design was sacrificed, especially in American windows, to pictorial expression. Our churches throughout the country have been influenced by the pictorial idea, and few that were built before 1910 escaped the picture window altogether.

It may seem unimportant to the casual observer whether or not a window is a sympathetic architectural unit. To students and lovers of architecture the matter is of first importance.

Windows are designed to function in light; therefore, to blanket them, or to curtain them so that much of the surface is opaque, is seriously to impede their honest service. Obviously, whatever is done within the limitations of a window surface should be controlled by the idea that it is designed for light. Light, even though it be translated into various colors and symbols, should be an active and vital force in every unit. Light is the glory of the stained glass craft, and it is the vibration of light, as it plays through various colors, that most powerfully distinguishes the medium.

A window "comes alive" in light, and is at the mercy of the light it receives. A window designed for a north light might be extremely beautiful in that position, but if it were changed to an eastern exposure it would probably dazzle the eyes of all beholders in the brilliant light of a morning service. Similarly a window designed for a southern exposure would probably be too dark if it were changed to a northern window. Good windows have been ruined through the erection of a building in gray stone or red brick nearby. I have seen an aisle window suddenly flush to an ugly red through the appearance of a red delivery wagon on the street outside.

The problem of the worker in glass is complicated, and the hazards increased by the power of light and its action through transparent colors.

The laws governing light in transparent glass are but little understood, and I know of but one really significant work on the subject. It is by Viollet le Duc, and it comprises his chapter on stained glass in his famous Dictionary of Architecture, published many years ago in France. In consideration of this fact it is surprising that so many really good windows are now being made for our American churches.

An interesting example of the consideration given the effects a varying light is in the great group of choir windows erected to honor the Blessed Virgin in the Cathedral of Notre Dame, Chartres. The lancet on the right of the center opening was made darker than the center to allow for the brilliance of the southeastern light in the morning. On a brilliant forenoon it takes its place in the group, but on a gray day, or in the afternoon it is noticeably darker than the central opening. Similar realization is to be found in the color schemes of the north and south transept windows. The lancets of the north window are extremely warm with a predominance of red, while the lancets of the south window are much cooler. This understanding of the varying qualities of light on the part of the old masters in glass may be discovered in many of the great churches and cathedrals where the windows have their original positions.

The question of scale is almost equally important, and the great windows have been so fitted to their distinctive positions that it seems as though they might have grown there.

The influence of color upon color and the devouring or dissolving power of light are subjects that may sound technical but a study of almost any transparent window at varying distances and in different lights will reveal their real significance.

Committees or donors or architects who have the problem of stained glass before them should recognize the importance of a

"THE GLORIFICATION OF CHRIST THE LORD IN HEAVEN AND ON EARTH"

Photograph of the Cartoons for The Great West Window in The Mercersburg Academy Chapel, Mercersburg, Pennsylvania. Installed September 1926. (Footage is 286 square feet.)

Designed and Made by Charles J. Connick, Boston.

Inscription surrounding the figure in the rose: "I heard a great voice in Heaven saying, "Alleluia, Salvation and Glory and Honor and Power unto the Lord Our God."

In the base of the center lancet the following inscription occurs: "The kingdoms of this world are become the Kingdoms of Our Lord."

point of view that is unique and directly opposed to one with which we are most familiar in considering works of art.

Reproductions of windows in black and white, like those that accompany this article, are in themselves misleading. I am always reluctant to publish them, for I realize that they have a tendency to suggest the lingering comparison between windows and opaque forms of expression.

When they are reproduced in color this confusion is less marked, but I sometimes think that if windows were known only through examples in place, the appreciation of the craft would grow more normally.

It is interesting to consider, for example, the tendency we have had, more or less consciously, through the development of painting, to magnify the importance of expression in faces.

THE GREAT ROSE WINDOW IN THE WESLEY METHODIST EPISCOPAL CHURCH, WORCESTER, MASSACHUSETTS
The chief theme of this window is found in the expression, "I am the Vine, Ye are the Branches," and a decorative use of the vine and grapes runs through the sections in the six great divisions of the rose.
Designed and Made by Charles J. Connick, Boston.
Installed February 1927.
Footage approximately 184 square feet.

When so appreciative a critic as Henry Adams singled out for eulogy the head of the Blessed Virgin in the famous "Notre Dame de la Belle Verrière" of Chartres, there is certainly ample excuse for the rest of us to look for the significant power of that composition in the face of the dominant figure.

The truth is that a careful study of that great window in the ambulatory of Chartres is bound to lead to the conviction that it is the entire design, and most of all, the glowing color throughout, that gives it that thrilling quality of beauty and serenity we all love. The face is only incidental to the great symbol of the Mother holding the Christ Child, and the one that Henry Adams saw was probably painted early in the

THE HUNT MEMORIAL WINDOW IN SAINT PAUL'S CHURCH, TIVOLI, NEW YORK.
Installed in May, 1926. (Footage is 44 Square Feet.)
Designed and Made by Charles J. Connick, Boston.
This window is dedicated to Children and to the great place they occupy in Christianity. The entire composition is dominated by the large medallion in the center lancet which symbolizes the spirit of the text from the nineteenth Chapter of Saint Matthew, "And He took them up in His arms, put His hands upon them, and blessed them."

eighteenth century by a glass craftsman of Chartres to replace a broken one which may or may not have been the original.

The great masters in glass did their work before painting had reached anything like its present development, and fortunately they escaped the influence of photography altogether. Therefore, their figures are eloquent throughout in terms of design, not of realistic pictures. They made every gesture and every fold of drapery tell toward their presentation of ideas and ideals,—not of narrow or accidental "facts." Consequently, if we look for subtle expressions in faces we are disappointed. If on the other hand, we have imaginations trained to discern

the significance in line and color through symbol and design together, we will not fail to get the full message of a great window. Of course, we do get from all the best early windows a definite emotional appeal in color that may well be their noblest distinction.

The fundamentals of the craft that produced those great masterpieces have not been lost, but there is a mellow quality of serenity and low vibration accumulated naturally through centuries of changing seasons, wind and dust and rain that cannot be reproduced. There are skilled modern craftsmen who deliberately and thoughtfully attempt to copy those windows and their unique charm, line for line, and color for color. There is something grotesque, of course, in placing copies of old windows in our modern churches with their atmosphere of present day spiritual problems and messages. They do, however, help toward one important realization: that windows are designed symbols, not pictures. While such work may not develop the artist and craftsman who thus surrenders his own urge toward expression of the beauty he knows, it undoubtedly does help toward the education of those who see them from day to day in varying light.

Some prominent church architects probably have some such point of view when they encourage the direct copying of old forms, but we should be grateful to have in America men like Ralph Adams Cram, Charles D. Maginnis, and the late Bertram Goodhue, who are not content with the multiplication of precedents.

I am often asked by interested people in all sincerity what one should do in order to judge wisely when faced by bewildering problems of interior decoration in stained glass. I suggest that one should know stained glass windows well enough to appreciate the vast distinction to be made between them and all artistic expressions on opaque surfaces. When you have a conscious recognition of the power and beauty of color alive with light, you will probably feel a kinship with the worker in glass who revels in its splendid potentialities.

You may safely make demands upon the sincere artist in glass whose ideals are related to the beauty and significance of color and form in light. He should have the spirit of a poet and the scientist's respect for natural laws. With this he will be handicapped in his sustained efforts unless he has a realization of "the power within us, not ourselves, which makes for righteousness."

VACATION BIBLE SCHOOLS
from p.163

have not fully decided. (Relate first days' success).
Letter to all scholars of previous years.
Get members to talk about the school.
Ora et labora.

XII. Workers Needed

Canvassers, Distributors, A Principal, Attendance secretary, Teachers, Handwork Supervisor (optional), Intercessors, Follow up visitors (the teachers), active help of the pastor, Moral, physical and financial support from church and Sunday school.

XIII. Bibliography And Textbooks

The Community Daily Vacation Bible School, by E. C. Knapp.
Dr. Lathem's folders, (Presbyterian) Chester, Pa.
Bibles.
Penny Catechism.
Missionary Stories: Pfeiffer.
  "   "   P. E. Kretzmann.
Mission leaflets (Fiscal office).
Stewardship stories (Fiscal office).
Favorite Christian Hymns: Polack
Bible History References: Rupprecht.
Bible Story Book: Egermeier.
Missionary Stories: Appelgarth.
Religion for Primary Grades: Kraeft.
Things to make: Jones.
God's Wonder world: Cobb.

The Occasional Service Practically Considered

II. HOLY BAPTISM

F. R. WEBBER

THE Sacrament of Holy Baptism is one of the two great Sacraments of the church. Theologically considered, a Sacrament is a sacred act, instituted by Our Lord, in which a visible, earthly means, accompanied by God's Word, conveys a heavenly blessing. Liturgically considered, a Sacrament must always be celebrated in the church, in the presence of the congregation, unless weighty reasons make it necessary to do otherwise. In cases of actual illness, either Holy Baptism or the Lord's Supper may be administered privately, but he who would be true to sound Lutheran tradition will not celebrate a Sacrament except in the presence of the congregation, unless necessary.

This principle seems so sound that one would hardly question it, yet the sad fact remains that there are whole communities where it is customary to administer Holy Baptism privately, and under circumstances that are not at all dignified. In some places looked upon as strongholds of Lutheranism, Holy Baptism has been degraded into little more than a convivial gathering of relatives. People speak of "going to a christening" much as they would speak of attending a party.

In a certain parish well known to us, the people at one time took it for granted that a baptism in the home was the rule, and a church baptism the exception. This condition obtained in a number of other congregations in the same city. It was discovered that these christenings were anything but devotional. The pastor arrived at the home of the parents and found the house filled with relatives and neighbors. Thick layers of cigar smoke hung like somber clouds in every room. Somebody handed the pastor a cigar, and offered him a chair. He was expected to sit down for a social chat. After a time one of the women appeared with a glass dish of water and a napkin. The child was brought in, and amid more or less good natured banter, the sponsors took their places. The pastor laid aside his cigar and proceeded with the baptismal service. The moment the benediction was said, there was once more a ripple of amused laughter, and more facetious conversation as to the conduct of the child. Then somebody appeared with a tray of wine, and all must drink to the health of the heir apparent. Usually foaming glasses of beer followed, with the announcement that it was the host's best home brew, made with greatest care in the family wash boiler, or other equally smart comments. We will say to the credit of that community that it took very little admonition to persuade the people that all baptisms must take place in the church, with the congregation present. They realized that a home baptism was not the proper thing.

In other communities it is customary to baptize in the church, but the congregation is dismissed, and only the sponsors remain, together with two or three relatives. Some pastors have been known to remove their robes and bands, in order to give the ceremony as informal an appearance as possible.

These are abuses that have crept in. There is almost nothing in connection with religion that was not sadly degraded a century or so ago, when Rationalism wrought such sad havoc. Calvinsim and Puritanism had little respect for the Sacraments. To show their contempt for these alleged relics of popery, the Puritan often did not baptize at all, or if he did, there are instances where the water was actually carried in a common pail, or a tin pan.

Fortunately we are living in an age of restoration. There is a growing respect for decency and order. Conferences and private study groups are searching forgotten records in order to discover the true practice of our Lutheran forefathers. They realize that sound doctrine and laxity of liturgical practice are incongruous yokefellows.

In order to carry out a baptismal service in a churchly manner, there must be a font. The presence of a font of dignified size and design is a perpetual reminder of the importance of Holy Baptism. It recalls to the worshiper his own baptism, and reminds him of his baptismal covenant. It is likewise a silent reminder

that Holy Baptism ought to be administered in the church.

If at all possible the font ought to be of stone. The cost of a stone font is not great. Even the smallest congregation can afford it. The trivial sectarian type of font must be avoided. As a rule they are too small to look dignified, and the mail-order house type of font is almost always very bad in design. If the font is made of wood, or if it be a small stone or marble font, there is too much temptation to treat is as an incidental bit of furniture, and move it into a corner on the slightest pretext. A stone font of proper size is more apt to find a permanent place in the church, and will not be pushed aside in order to make way for Christmas decorations, wedding parties, funerals, or to obtain a place for folding chairs when there is a large attendance.

If the font is of wood, it is usually provided with a good sized basin of copper or hardened lead. This is usually arranged so that it may be lifted out, and the water poured into the piscina. There is no reason why even a wooden font ought not to be provided with a drain, and permanently connected with clean earth. In the case of a stone font, such a drain is almost essential.

The most satisfactory font is one that is designed to order. Several good books of designs exist. The best one is possibly Francis Bond's exhaustive work entitled "Fonts and Font Covers." It shows fonts of every possible style and type of design. F. A. Paley's "Baptismal Fonts" is an excellent work with 120 full-page plates. It is quite out of print, but second hand copies are easily found, and the current price for a good used copy is but $1.50.

Every font must be provided with a good sized ewer. This must be designed and made to order, for the mail-order designs happen to be very bad, and entirely too domestic in appearance. The ewer may be of hammered brass or hard pewter. It ought to hold at least a gallon of water. When not in use it ought to stand close to the font.

Neither the font nor the ewer must be used for anything other than the purpose for which they are intended. To place flowers in the font or in the ewer is not devotional at all, and if such flowers are allowed to remain even for a short time, they are quite likely to discolor the basin of the font or the ewer.

The proper place for the font is in the nave of the church, and not in the chancel. In olden times the font was placed just within the door of the church, to emphasize the fact that Holy Baptism is the entrance into the Kingdom. In the Anglican Church and her American and colonial derivatives, this custom is carried out to this day. In a Lutheran church the font is usually found somewhere near the entrance to the chancel, and usually to the left of the center aisle as one faces the altar. It is in accordance with sound tradition to provide kneelers at the font, so that the sponsors may kneel at the proper place in the service.

The parents and sponsors are informed by the pastor in regard to the exact time of the christening. If the hour of service is 10:30, and the Common Service is used, the hour for baptisms may be set at 11:20, and yet allow time for the liturgy, hymns and sermon. If the sponsors and child arrive during the sermon, they are given seats inside the church door. During the offertory hymn, one of the church deacons conducts the baptismal party to the font. Another deacon carries the water to the font in the ewer, and quietly pours it into the font. The full order for Holy Baptism, as found in the Agenda, ought to be used. If the pastor so desires, he may follow the ancient custom of dividing the water in the font with his extended thumb and two fingers, in the form of the cross. This very ancient custom was practiced by our forefathers, although it is not found in our modern liturgies.

It is well to have both parents and sponsors stand at the font and to let all of them answer the questions addressed to the child. It is not necessary to say that sponsors must be devout people, and of the same faith as the child. If two sponsors are used, one may be a man and the other a woman. If there be three sponsors,

PLEASE TURN TO PAGE 334

Baptismal Certificate

Herewith you are being handed your child's baptismal certificate.

You will note that both the text and the format mark it out as a document to be *framed*. We hope that you will have it framed and that you will hang it in a prominent place in your child's room. One of the greatest theologians of the Church in America used to tell his classes at Seminary: "Next to a crucifix, the best thing that can be hung in a child's room is a framed certificate of Holy Baptism, that the child may grow up with a constant reminder of his rebirth in the Spirit ever before his eyes." We believe that the advice is good. For your convenience in framing this certificate, we have had it printed with extra wide margins, so that it can be framed in the most economical fashion in frames of a great variety of sizes.

Under the Seal of the Parish are two ribbons, one violet, the other white. Violet is the color of repentance, recalling the first of Blessed Martin Luther's Ninety-Five Theses: "When Our Lord Jesus Christ says, 'Do penance.' He requires that the whole life of a Christian be one of repentance." Similarly the Small Catechism reminds us that Baptism "signifies that the Old Adam in us should, by daily contrition and repentance be drowned and die with all sins and evil lusts." White is the color of forgiveness and of purity, proclaiming that they who have been baptized into Christ have washed their robes white in the Blood of the Lamb of God, and enjoining those who have received the Sacrament of Regeneration to "see that they keep unspotted their Baptismal purity."

Should you have no crucifix for your child's room, the Pastor will be happy to secure one for you, that Christ may be set before your child evidently crucified for him. An attractive and unobtrusive ebony and nickel crucifix of good design can be had for about seventy-five cents.

Through Holy Baptism your child has become a member of Faith Church. The Pastor is there to feed the lambs of Christ's flock as well as their parents. In the event of illness the Pastor should be called, even during the child's infancy. Intercessions for the sick are offered by the congregation at any public service for old and young alike; requests for such intercessions should be addressed to the pastor the evening before the service in question, if possible. As your child grows older, feel free to consult with the pastor about any problem that may present itself. At Christmastime and in anticipation of birthdays, the pastor will be happy to recommend suitable gift books and pieces of religious art which will be of assistance to you in rearing your child "in the fear and admonition of the Lord," according to the Apostolic admonition.

Should you change your address, please notify the pastor at once. If you move out of the community, the pastor should be requested to issue a letter of transfer for your child, placing him or her under the care of the pastor of the parish into which you remove.

The facilities of the Sunday school are available to children of all ages from two and a half up. An excellent set of Beginners' Leaflets containing Bible stories, Bible pictures, and religious poetry suitable for a pre-school and nursery school child may be had from the Sunday school at forty cents for a set of fifty-two.

Your child's name has been placed upon our Cradle Roll. All children upon this roster are commemorated by name at the periodic Cradle Roll services, of which notices will be sent to you from time to time. (Submitted by Arthur Carl Piepkorn, Cleveland, Ohio.)

Anniversary of Your Baptism

NO DAY of our life is greater and more meaningful than the day of our baptism. In holy baptism we receive the greatest blessing which God can give, even the forgiveness of our sins and the promise of our eternal salvation through our Lord and Saviour Jesus Christ. May God's little children ever remain in the love and service of God, and keep their baptismal covenant unto the end!

Our prayer for you is this:

"Lord Jesus Christ, our Lord most dear,
As Thou wast once an Infant here,
So give this child of Thine, we pray,
Thy grace and blessing day by day.
O Holy Jesus, Lord divine,
We pray Thee guard this child of Thine."

H. von Laufenburg
Cradle Roll of Faith Lutheran Church
South Broadway and 95th Street
Los Angeles

Emma T. Bostiom,
Superintendent.
(Text for Cradle Roll Card.)

𝔊race and ℘eace in 𝔍esus 𝔠hrist our 𝔏ord. 𝔄men. 𝔎now all men that

born on the   day of   𝔄nno 𝔇omini 19

the child of

and of   his wife,

having renounced the devil and all his works and all his ways, was by me baptized in the ℕame of the 𝔉ather and of the ℭon and of the 𝔥oly 𝔊host, according to the 𝔈vangelical 𝔏utheran ℜite, in 𝔉aith ℭhurch, 𝔥ayden 𝔄venue at 𝔊lenside ℜoad, ℭleveland, 𝔒hio, on the   day of   being

𝔄nno 𝔇omini 19

𝔖ponsors:

𝔓astor

The Bible Foundation of All Learning and Truth

(1)

Baptism Certificate

Name_____

Date of Birth_____

Father_____

Mother_____

Date of Baptism_____

Name of Church_____

Sponsors or Witnesses _____

_____

_____ Pastor.

✝ ✝ ✝ ✝

My Baptism

IN HOLY BAPTISM I was made a child of God. Here the heavenly Father granted me the mercy and love which my Lord and Saviour Jesus Christ won for me by His death upon the cross. The sins which stained my soul even from my birth were cleansed away by this gracious water of Life. My soul is now clothed with the holy garment of my Saviour's pure holy righteousness. I believe this because God Himself has said, "As many of you as have been baptized into Christ have put on Christ" (*Galatians* 3, 27). Heaven is now open to me, for I am one with the Triune God into Whom I was baptized. My Baptism shall ever be my surety for this. God's great love to me shall now inspire my love to Him. With His help I shall be faithful to Him even unto death. That I may continue as a member of His Kingdom I am resolved to walk according to His Word in His church on earth.

I will now endeavor to keep my baptismal promise by daily putting off things that are evil, and striving for the things that are good in His sight. I will guard myself against sin, and give myself to the guidance of the Holy Spirit. All my life I will strive to walk as a child of God that I may enter into the joys of my heavenly home-land.

(2)

A Word To Parents

YOU have brought your child to the font of Holy Baptism according to the Saviour's direction. Your child has been committed into the gracious keeping of a loving Saviour in Whom "we have redemption through His blood, the forgiveness of sins." What a true and constant comfort and happiness this ought to bring to you!

A great responsibility now rests upon you, parents. Yours is now the solemn duty, as you have also acknowledged before God, to lead your child, at each stage of development, into the realization of the meaning of Baptism and the Christian life.

How far-reaching and eventful is your responsibility! It may be said that the eternal weal or woe of your child is to an extent in your hands. If you become careless and neglectful in your Christian instruction and example you will contribute to a loss which may be irreparable in later years. But if you faithfully assume your divinely imposed duties by caring for the spiritual welfare of your child, you will assist and strengthen it to keep the Baptismal covenant unto the end, and thus be saved.

IT HAS been said: "The home is the greatest school of Christian living," and "A mother's heart is the greatest schoolroom." What the children learn in the home from the example and precept of their parents will be woven into the character-design of their life. Jerome, a towering personality of the ancient church, used to say: "As water follows a finger drawn through the sand, so one of soft and tender years is pliable for good or evil." To Chrysostomus this beautiful statement is credited: "Higher than every painter, higher than every sculptor and than all other artists, do I regard him who is skilled in the art of forming the soul life of children." How far-reaching, parents, is your influence! Your example, your life, your words, will be the open Bible which your children read.

Therefore let your home be a Christian home. Make Christ the Head of your home, the unseen Guest at every meal, the silent Listener to every conversation. Make yours a home in which the Bible, our Saviour, the Church, and the Kingdom of God are held in prayerful esteem. Make yours a home that fears God and loves Christ; a home in which children are taught to pray, to strive for pure, honest lives, to love and obey their parents, to cherish their country and its institutions, their Church and its teachings.

THE PASTOR who baptized your child will at all times be ready to assist you in the selection of a course of Christian instruction in the home. Also, the facilities of the Sunday school are open to you. Attend the Sunday school with your children, and the services of the church.

A blessed reward will be yours if you keep these responsibilities. Your child and eternal life are worth the cost.

(3)

The Good Shepherd

"I think when I read that sweet story of old
When Jesus was here among men;
How He called little children as lambs to His fold,
I should like to have been with Him then."

THE thought of God as a loving shepherd is an old, old one. David, in one of his most tender moods, used it in the immortal **Twenty-third** Psalm. "The Lord is my shepherd, I shall not want." Isaiah carries it even further when he writes, "He shall feed his flock like a shepherd, he shall gather his lambs with his arm, and carry them in his bosom."

Jesus used this same picture in his preaching. He was the Good Shepherd—one who was willing to lay down his life for his sheep. He was eager to protect his charges from ravening wolves and other dangers. Literally, he took the little lambs to his bosom. All he asked in return was that they enter this security through him.

"I am the door . . . I am the shepherd."

Shepherd of tender youth,
Guiding in love and truth
  Through devious ways;
Christ our triumphant King,
We come Thy name to sing,
And here our children bring,
  To join Thy praise.

Ever be near our side,
Our Shepherd and our Guide,
  Our Staff and Song;
Jesus, Thou Christ of God,
By Thy enduring Word,
Lead us where Thou hast trod,
  Make our faith strong.

CLEMENT OF ALEXANDRIA, 211 A.D.

(4)

[Suggested Copy for individual Baptismal Certificate]
[Above reproduction half size]

Holy Communion

FRED. H. LINDEMANN

ANOTHER reason for the general neglect of Holy Communion is undoubtedly the attitude that an infrequent doing of this is sufficient. The term "frequent" commonly used is relative. Is four times a year frequent? Is twelve times? How often did the Lord intend His disciples to do it? To keep love burning in their hearts towards Him and their fellows, to keep them ceaselessly and hopefully active, a remembrance of Him once or four times a year or even once a month would not suffice. The Early Church felt this and celebrated every day and later every Lord's Day.

We want to keep love burning brightly and expect, or say we expect, ceaseless service of the Christ, but should be content if our people received the Lord's Supper four times a year. Yes, we celebrate every month, even every two weeks, but when the Communions become more frequent, all are given to understand that this is to reduce the number of communicants and the time consumed. The idea that every member commune at every opportunity and that opportunity be given at least once a week, has long since been abandoned. And yet we are disturbed that our people forget Christ, that He is crowded out of their lives, that there is so little evidence of brotherly love, that the Lord's work is disregarded.

The sum of all reasons for the general neglect of Holy Communion must be that we have not given it the place in life which the Lord intended. That must be the reason. Our people are Christians. They want all their Savior offers. Their neglect must be due to their not expecting to find all. And they do not expect it because they have never been told or taught to receive.

The remedy is to make Holy Communion truly a celebration, so rich in the loftiest experiences, so helpful in the weekday life, so sweet and precious, that our people will look longingly to the next opportunity. That is what the Lord had in mind for His people when He instituted it and pleaded that it be done always. We must teach our people to meet their Lord in the Sacrament, the Lord in all His grace and love. To meet Him is to love Him. He must be the object of devotion, the Christ, who gave His Body and shed His Blood for love of us, and tenderly gives us that very Body and Blood as the seal and earnest of His abiding, unchanging love.

That is what the Lord meant when He voiced the yearning of His heart and pleaded: "This do in remembrance of Me." Why do we ignore and shy away from these words? We seem to see only the words, "This do." All we seem to find in His plea is that He wants it done until the end of time. But He did say that we should do it in His remembrance. Why permit Calvin to rob us of the remembrance? Surely, our Lord meant that His disciples needed to be reminded to remember Him. There would be so many things crowding in between. To prevent this, they were to do this and be reminded to remember Him, His love for them which led Him to give His Body and to shed His Blood. They needed to be reminded constantly. They were never to forget Him for a moment. He sent them out into the world with the shadow of His Cross falling on their way.

Our young people today need nothing more than to be reminded to remember Him. If they will not permit themselves to forget Him, all will be well. They need to be reminded, not twice a year, or every month, but every week, yes, every day. They need to exercise their faith constantly that it might grow stronger. They need to be united with Christ constantly in Holy Communion. Ceaselessly they must be reminded to remember that there is partnership between them and Christ and with each other through Christ. Then their love for Christ will not cool and they will love each other. They need to be reminded to remember that with the price they receive in Holy Communion Christ bought them that they might be His own and serve Him. That will make and keep them consecrated workers.

But they must be taught to find all this in Holy Communion. It is not necessary to slight the chief purpose of the Sacrament. But the scope must be widened to include the fruits which presuppose forgiveness. In doing this we cannot go far wrong if we endeavor always to reconstruct the scene in the Upper Room and the mental processes of our Lord that night. There is little need of restating here what is usually said in our circles in regard to Holy Communion. We are looking for a new approach. We have in mind particularly our young people. We want them to receive all Christ intended for them, not only the forgiveness but all that is implied. And then it becomes impossible to ignore the plea: In My Remembrance.

Is the Sacrament one of the answers to our problems? Having given them knowledge and the necessary training for service, the answer to our remaining problems is the Sacrament. All that we want for our young people, they may find in the Sacrament, provided we teach them how. All we need now is to teach them how to apply the Sacrament and its blessed fruits in a practical way.

Can they forget the Christ and cease to love Him if every week they meet Him in Holy Communion and are reminded to remember Him in all His love, eat and drink His Body and Blood and exercise their faith in believing acceptance of the words, "which is given for you, which is shed for the remission of your sins?" Meeting the Christ so, they cannot forget Him. Meeting Him, they must love Him.

Do we wish to keep a confirmation class together or all young people with each other? We need but to reconstruct the scene of the Upper Room as we invite them to Holy Communion. On that night the Lord said, "This is My commandment, that ye love one another as I have loved you." In the Sacrament they experience His love. There is nothing higher, holier, and more divine. This is the tie which is to unite the young people, the bond which is to tie them into a new unity. It brings about a two-fold union, between Him and His disciples and between one disciple and each 'ther. Christ's people are one with Him because He has loved down and loved out of existence every dividing barrier. Christ's people are one with each other because they love each other as Christ loved them. This two-fold union finds expression in Holy Communion. It is to help us love down and love out of existence all the barriers which separate Christ's people from one another. If one has any load to carry, if in peril or need, if his soul is in danger, if he becomes careless, indifferent, sluggish, that is as much ours as his. As they kneel together at the Table of Him who loved them to the death on the Cross; as the old story fills their hearts with its blessed peace, they will pray that they may comprehend with all the saints what is the length and breadth and height and depth, and to know the love of God which passeth understanding, that they may love one another as Christ has loved them.

Do we want our young people to consecrate themselves with all they are and have to the Master and His cause? Then let them experience every week the union with the Master. They are one with Christ. If He has any merit, any standing with God, any fortune, it is as much theirs as His. If they have anything, it is as much His as theirs. They have a life to live, time, strength, possessions and money. These are as much His as theirs. They have the same purpose in life as Christ. In Holy Communion they declare that they consider themselves one with Him. Joyously they lay hold of the assurance that all Christ has is theirs for time and eternity. But at the same time they must be conscious of the implication that all they have is His. Lovingly they give Him the assurance that they do not consider themselves or anything they are and have their own but as a joint possession with Christ.

Do we want our young people to live a Holy life? The Lord's death which they proclaim in Holy Communion was the pronouncement of God against sin. It was made necessary by sin. There is no more awful revelation of the damnableness of sin. Sometimes we make a truce with sin. We forget how deadly it is. We will be roused out of our forgetfulness when we come to the Sacrament, for it cries out against sin. When the Christian sins, it is because he forgets. To be reminded every week to remember Christ's death for us, is to be kept from forgetting.

Do we want our young people to live an unselfish life? The death on the Cross was only the climax to a life spent in the service of others. Christ's death was the greatest proof of His devotion to others. They need to be reminded to remember that. It is so easy to forget. We forget to be kind and considerate, and become grasping and self-centered. Then the Sacrament speaks. It proclaims the lasting glory of service.

Do we want our young people to be active missionaries? In Holy Communion they declare that they are people whom Christ purchased to be His own, upon whom He depends for the salvation of the world. They are apt to forget that. So the Lord calls them to His Table and reminds them not to forget that they belong to Him, not to self, not to the world. They remember Him, how fully and completely He gave Himself to the work for which He was sent. "As My Father hath sent Me, even so send I you." He insists that His work is as much ours as the Father's work was His. As He gave Himself and His very life for the advancement of God's cause, so are we. Young people, in particular, are so apt to lose sight of their life's purpose. In the Sacrament they are reminded to remember Christ's earnestness and devotion.

Do we want our young people to be loyal to the Church in the face of disagreeable experiences and manifest weaknesses? Then remind them to remember Christ every week in Holy Communion. Conditions in the Church, as it presented itself in its human aspects, were far from ideal in His day. The leaders were scoundrels. Once when He dared to speak in church, they wanted to kill Him. His enemies were always watching Him in the synagogue. Yet He went regularly. He loved the Church, with all its human failings and abuses, so much that He gave His life for it.

Do we want our young people to be filled with the spirit of optimism? Again we reconstruct the scene in the Upper Room. The Master says, "I will drink it new with you in my Father's kingdom." This is not the last time. The day is coming when we shall meet again around the table in the Kingdom. I am going into death this night, but that is not the end. The Kingdom, life, glory lies ahead. As He said that, the atmosphere of the Upper Room changed. It became an antechamber to the courts of glory. The little street outside was no longer a blind alley, ending in the shame of a malefactor's death, but a royal avenue winding to a throne. As the disciples listened, the cheap room became a palace of the King. Fear faded from their hearts. The transfiguring light of immortal victory fell on their faces, and the fires of an enthusiasm that was never to be quenched flared into flame. St. Paul caught this spirit. He says, "Ye proclaim the Lord's death till He come." Jesus is not a dead Savior. He lives and works and will come again. The Church has a future and the believer an immortal hope. We need to be reminded to remember that. Sometimes we grow discouraged. Doubts confuse us. We are afraid. Appearances seem against us. Then once more our Lord assures us, in the Sacrament that He is not dead. He is on the throne. He is ruling the world. He is mightier than ever. And some day He will return visibly and in the fulness of power. We shall eat and drink with Him again in the Kingdom. There is no defeat for truth. Victory is assured even now. No uncertain hope, but the definite assurance. I shall drink again with you. Nothing can defeat that.

Corporate Communion

F. R. WEBBER

There is no reason why the members of a choir intending to receive the Blessed Sacrament ought not to go in a group. This is quite customary in some congregations, and, we believe, encourages more frequent communion. We read a day or so ago of a Sunday-school teacher and his entire class, who attended the Lord's Supper in a group. It happened that all had announced, and what was more natural than, when this fact was discovered, that all should go together, as we have seen entire families commune together?

An examination of the statistical report of a certain District reveals the fact that in a great many congregations the average number of communions per year is slightly more than two. Certainly it is not a healthy sign when the average church member attends the Eucharist but twice a year. Do we stress the spiritual value of more frequent communion as much as we ought? Some may say that corporate Communion may encourage some to attend who are unworthy and unprepared. That may happen occasionally, but the danger is not nearly so great as is the danger that many who really ought to go, do not go. There are good arguments pro and con. But where it can be done properly by all concerned, we see little danger in corporate communion. We have known of entire confirmation classes, numbering sixteen or eighteen, attending in a group, without any suggestion from the pastor. "It makes a fellow more careful about his thoughts and conduct," one of the boys remarked. Certainly this is much more wholesome than a sweet young thing who remarked lately, "I hope you'll excuse me for not coming to Communion last Sunday. I was to a dance Saturday night." When asked why she didn't stay away from the dance and attend the Lord's Supper, she smiled in a silly manner and said "I guess I could have done that, maybe."

Young People and Holy Communion

FRED H. LINDEMANN

A MOST SIGNIFICANT sentence written by one of our Church's leaders in young people's work may well serve as an introduction of our subject: "The more I think about the present state of the Church, the more I believe that perhaps one of the answers to our problems lies in the Sacrament."

There is much thinking about the state of the Church, and in the thinking our young people are naturally the chief consideration. If the Church is to have a future, we must keep the young loyal to the Christ, their Saviour and Lord; we must keep them together as a flock and members of the body of Christ; we must lead them to become whole-hearted, unselfish workers in the Kingdom of the Master.

To accomplish our purpose we instruct and train our young people. Beginning at an early age, this instruction and training is continued through adolescence into manhood and womanhood. We insist that after the more intensive instruction preceding confirmation, our children join the young people's societies, where instruction and training is continued. We have prepared a splendid program. We offer ample opportunity for sociability. Continued attendance upon church services and Bible classes is required. Much is done for our young people.

Yet, thank God, none of us are satisfied. We feel that we are not accomplishing what we should like. We are not succeeding in the measure we wish. The problem is still with us: How can we keep our young people with the Christ, with each other, and with the Church? How can we make of them consecrated workers for the Kingdom?

It is not a new problem. Modern conditions and the world's redoubled efforts to lead this generation astray may have aggravated the problem, but it has always been there.

It is the problem which confronted our Lord in the Upper Room nineteen hundred years ago. For the last time before His death, His Disciples were gathered about Him, and He was saying farewell. In that hour of sweet companionship, He looked into the future to the time when He would no longer be with His friends. Days of sorrow and sadness lay immediately ahead, and beyond stretched years of trials and persecutions. Will these men continue to love Him after He has gone? Will they remain true to Him? Will they continue to love each other and remain united as they were now? Would they dedicate themselves to the work of salvation and give themselves wholly to the continuation of the Father's business?

The Master had conducted a Department of Christian Knowledge for over three years, day and night, and the disciples had learned many things. Some of the Master's teachings they did not understand at this time, but upon His return to the Father, the Master would send the Holy Spirit, and He was to teach them all things and lead them into all truth. There was no need to be uneasy as to their knowledge.

Neither had the Department of Christian Service been neglected. There had been much opportunity for practical

instruction as the Master journeyed with His pupils. They had even served as missionaries, and upon their return expressed high elation over their accomplishments.

And yet the Lord felt that imparting and acquiring knowledge and efficiency in practice had not equipped the disciples for the dangers and troubles which lay ahead. He felt that there was something still lacking. In this last hour of fellowship He would supply that need.

Would these friends always love Him? Would the memory of Him become faint as time went on? So many things would clamor for their attention and affection. He must give them something to keep Him always in their thoughts, to keep the memory of His love for them fresh through the years. He must unite them to Him in the years that lay ahead. Knowledge and training were not sufficient. This yearning for their continued love was so strong that He was not ashamed to voice it.

Would these men continue to love each other after He had gone from them? They had left all when the Master called them. They had been happy in their companionship. But it was most necessary that this brotherhood be continued. If their love for each other cooled, all hope for the triumph of the Gospel would vanish. How could He keep them united in a loving brotherhood? The love for Him had first united them. This love must keep them united. This love must outlast their petty differences and fuse them into a unit. Weak and strong should be bound together in this bond of their common affection for Him. They must be made to feel at all times that they were still members of one body even after the Master's visible presence had been withdrawn. He must devise some means of drawing them together and keeping them in sweet communion with each other. Knowledge and training was not enough.

Would these men forget all else, and give themselves solely to the continuation of the work which had brought Him to earth and occupied Him during the past years? Would they put aside all considerations of person and selfish ambitions and apply themselves unstintingly to telling men what He had done for all in a little corner of the great world? Everything depended on them. Again and again He had seen indications of a spirit which would ruin His plans for the world. Even that night, Judas, realizing that nothing was to be gained for himself by remaining loyal to Him, disappointed and outraged at the turn of events, had resentfully betrayed Him. On the way to the Upper Room the strife as to who should be the greatest had broken out afresh, and the sight of basin, towel and pitcher at the entrance, beckoning to humble service, had caused the monster pride to lift its ugly head anew. None of them would stoop to wash the others' feet, lest this be construed as a renouncing of his claims on greatness. He must leave them something which would serve as a constant reminder that they must forget self in an unswerving devotion to Him and His cause. They needed to remember the Master in His unfaltering devotion to the work which

His Father had given Him to do, how in utter disregard of self He had given Himself to the task of salvation, how He had willingly gone to the Cross, given His Body, shed His Blood. The memory of His unselfish love would compel loyal devotion to the same cause. He must keep Himself and His sacrifice of love always before their soul's eyes, they must never be permitted to forget even for a moment. He must leave them something to accomplish this. Knowledge and training, teaching and guiding was not enough.

So, knowing the disciples would be fully instructed theologians after the Holy Spirit had increased their present knowledge, knowing that with the power and help of the Spirit their training was ample and sufficient, knowing that the Spirit would fill them with divine enthusiasm on Pentecost, the Lord nevertheless felt that something more was needed to keep the disciples in communion with Him, with each other, and with His cause.

He took bread, gave it to His disciples, and said: Eat, this is My Body, that Body broken and given for you on the Cross out of love for you. He took wine, gave it to them, and said: Drink, this is My Blood, that Blood which is shed for the remission of your sins on the Cross. Do this always, take bread and wine and eat and drink My Body and Blood. And whenever you do it, do it in My Remembrance.

That was the Lord's solution of the problem which confronted Him that night. How could He keep their love for Him fresh and living? How could He keep His disciples united in blessed communion with Him and with each other? How could He keep them working unselfishly and wholeheartedly for Him? They must eat His Body, drink His Blood. They must exercise their faith by believing that they were eating the very Body given for them, drinking the very Blood shed for the remission of their sins. They must eat and drink the very price paid for forgiveness. They must taste the love which prompted the sacrifice. They must ever be reminded by eating and drinking to remember Him, to remember all He did for them and all men, and how He crowned all by dying on the Cross.

Strange, that with the Lord's solution of our problem ever before our eyes, we should not have seen it clearly long ago. But thank God that a man with a fine program for young people and a Department of Knowledge and of Service in operation, should write: "Perhaps one of the answers to our problems lies in the Sacrament." Is it beginning to dawn on us that we have neglected, perhaps, to make that use of the Sacrament which the Lord intended? that we have failed to use this blessed means of keeping our people united to the Saviour in fervent love, failed to use it in the measure even approaching the wide and glorious sweep which the Lord had in mind?

It is not that we have ever abandoned the administration of the Sacrament. It is not that we have failed to administer it according to Christ's institution or permitted false teaching to rob us of intended benefits. But have we given it the place in our lives which the Lord intended for it?

Holy Communion is a means of grace to us. We instruct our people in the doctrine and they know the difference between the Roman and the Reformed and the Scriptural teaching. They know that in, with and under the bread and wine they receive the Lord's Body and Blood with the mouth of the body. They know that in the Sacrament forgiveness of sins is given and sealed. They may even be aware that the words, "which is given for you, which is shed for the remission of your sins," calls for a conscious exercise of faith. They have also heard that the words, "This do in remembrance of Me," means that the Lord wants this done unto the end of time. They have learned that the Sacrament is to be received for the strengthening of faith, for furtherance in holiness of life, and in testimony of the communion of faith. They have memorized the Christian Questions which tell us we wish to go to the

Sacrament that we may learn to believe that Christ died for our sins out of great love, and that we may learn of Him to love God and our neighbor.

And we are agreed that the imparting of forgiveness is the chief object of Holy Communion. All other fruits depend not only partly but wholly on the fact that the Sacrament is the means of remission. All other fruits can be enjoyed only by such as have forgiveness and know that they are reconciled to God. All other fruits dare not be coordinated but must be subordinated to the forgiveness.

And yet these subordinated fruits dare not be slighted or disregarded if the Sacrament is to be to us all that our gracious Lord intended. There are reasons for believing that we have not taught our people how they may derive the many benefits which flow from forgiveness or are held out to him who has remission. It would seem that spiritual and mental processes by which all the intended benefits are derived, are an unfathomable mystery to most. That forgiveness is sealed by eating and drinking the price, is a known process. Also that by the exercise, faith is strengthened. But when it comes to the furtherance in holiness of life, the thinking becomes vague. How they should learn in the Sacrament to love their neighbor requires deduction and conclusions beyond many.

Or have we made the most of the Sacrament? What have we held out to our people as benefits? Have we kept it the sweet, comforting, uniting, glorious thing the Lord gave us? How have we taught our people? In our sermons we have taught the doctrine of the Real Presence over against Transubstantiation and the Memorial Theory. We have assured that forgiveness is received. And then we absolved them in the name of the Trinity even before they came to the Sacrament, which cooled the eagerness considerably, for they were already sure of forgiveness. But this forgiveness is only for the penitent. And this brings us to the point we were aiming at all along. St. Paul said something about eating and drinking unworthily. How fortunate! Even where respect for all other holy things is at a low ebb, the Sacrament is still reverenced and regarded with awe. None would partake unworthily. For does it not say he eateth and drinketh "damnation" to himself? He is lost in time and eternity. And so we proceed to harrow men: Are you worthy? Are you truly sorrowful for your sins? Will you put them away? Then follows a recital of all the preacher's grievances. For once he has the upper hand. You have announced for Holy Communion, you must partake, now repent or eat damnation to yourself.

Transfer that preparation to the Upper Room on the night before the Lord's death! Can you imagine or picture the Master injecting such thoughts into the celebration? Little wonder that so many feel no desire to have their conscience stretched upon the rack at frequent intervals and put off a similar experience as long as possible. This will account, at least in part, for the wretched record of two communions per year as the average for an entire church body. Christians are not made on Sinai but on Calvary.

The Sacrament A Means of Grace
FRED H. LINDEMANN

WHEREVER I go the pastors are talking about Holy Communion." In these words a man who travels extensively and is in personal touch with a large number of pastors in every section of our country gave expression to a conviction which must come to every one with open eyes and ears. There is a widespread and pronounced trend toward greater emphasis on the Sacrament. Everywhere there is dissatisfaction with the flagrant neglect of a means of grace indicated by the communion record of our Church. If the communion record is the spiritual thermometer, the spirituality has reached an alarming low. And so conscientious pastors everywhere and thoughtful laymen too are concerned with ways and means of remedying this grave weakness.

This revived emphasis on Holy Communion is not surprising. It was to be expected as a natural, historical, inevitable development. No organized effort, no movement, no propaganda was needed. Any endeavors on the part of groups or individuals may have accelerated and stimulated in a measure but were only symptoms in themselves. Essentially the movement is spontaneous and natural.

Sooner or later the confessional Lutheran Church would find itself compelled by circumstances and the pressure of isolation to stress the means of grace in ever greater measure as the only instruments of operation. Purified and sobered by affliction it would be led to emphasize exclusively its Sola Scriptura. Conscious of its unique position in a modern world it would learn to appreciate its historic scriptural principles. This would result in a careful restudy of the subject of the means of grace. Upon a careful reexamination of Scripture would follow the restudy of the means of grace in the Early Christian Church and the Church of the Reformation. This would lead to the rediscovery of the Sacrament as the seal upon the preached Word. It was bound to come. It would be surprising therefore if the entire program for the observance of the Centennial now in preparation were not to resolve itself simply into a renewed emphasis on the means of grace. That the Sacrament should not be emphasized as the seal of the Word, inseparably united with the Word, is unthinkable.

A restudy of Scripture, of the Church's history in apostolic, post-apostolic and Reformation times, will result in the realization that the word "means" is not a singular but a plural. It will result in the discovery that we today are far from according Holy Communion the place in our church life which our Lord clearly intended for it and which it occupied in the Church of the first centuries and after the Reformation. There will come the disquieting conviction that we have not inseparably united the means of grace, Word and Sacrament, but in a measure have restricted ourselves to the Word without applying the seal of Holy Communion to the preached Word. Our deep regard for historic Christianity and our firm conviction that the Lutheran Confessions truly set forth the doctrine and spirit of the Scriptures will not permit us to be content with the preaching of the Word minus the seal. If it is the grace of God we want, the Sacrament must not be neglected as it has been in the past, for it is a means of obtaining and enjoying that grace.

We have with us then a new awakening to the practical inclusion of Holy Communion under the means of grace. Now that it has come, what are we going to do about it? There is always the temptation, which may become a habit and a mania, to see countless dangers and therefore to frown upon and discourage and oppose, to view with alarm, assume a negative, passive attitude, and when mistakes are made for lack of proper leadership to spend the rest of one's life in deploring and bemoaning and denouncing the mistakes. That there are dangers which must be clearly seen and avoided no one will want to deny. But shall we continue in our neglect of a means of grace and withhold from our people the priceless blessings of a frequent communion merely because there are dangers to be avoided? Dangers are always with us. There is danger in everything we do. There is a danger lurking even when we preach justification by faith without the deeds of the law. Men might draw a false conclusion and neglect good works. If ever a doctrine has been abused and misinterpreted and falsely applied it is that we can do nothing toward our salvation. Yet the danger of abuse does not keep us from preaching the doctrine. Some of the dangers which may be conjured up and seen in the trend towards a more frequent use of Holy Communion are purely imaginary and do not exist. The dangers which actually exist the Lord probably foresaw also and yet gave us the Sacrament. It might be well to do simply what He commanded. He considered Holy Communion of such importance that we cannot afford to assume any other attitude but that of enthusiastic helpfulness over again any effort in its behalf.

On the other hand, there is an attitude which may prove just as harmful as paralyzing overcarefulness. It is the attitude which leads to action and changes without previous careful consideration and study. To curb this false enthusiasm one is tempted to say that it would be unwise to give this movement too much impetus, lest the advance be too rapid and grave mistakes be made. Our one concern at present must be to keep the movement within safe and sane bounds. A careful restudy of the Scriptures, of historic Lutheranism, of the post-apostolic age, and of our confessions is in order before any action is taken. No changes or innovations should be made without reading and heeding Luther's opinions. He was compelled to make quite a number of changes in his day and he made them against the background of a thorough knowledge of history. His experience will prove valuable and his advice extremely wise.

At the very outset we must see clearly and never lose sight of the fact that this is not a matter of ceremonial or liturgics. Essentially it is a question of restoring the Sacrament to the place which was intended for it by our Lord, which was given to it in the Early Church, and which it occupied long after the Reformation. Its restoration is rightly accomplished only by patient teaching of spiritual truths. Luther tells us we "are to preach in such a manner that of their own accord, without our law, they will urge themselves and, as it were, compel us pastors to administer the Sacrament."

The introduction of more frequent celebrations and the participation of a larger number present practical problems to our churches. If there is only one service on Sunday and all communicants present commune, the service becomes lengthy in larger congregations. The correct solution of this problem is certainly not the introduction of celebrations without the preaching of the Word, either before or after the "main service". This arrangement may reduce the amount of time consumed and prove less strenuous for the pastor, but that is about all one can say for it. The "main service" has always been the Communion. It was the chief and main service for no other reason than that the Sacrament was administered. Luther had excellent reason for insisting that the congregation should never assemble only for the reading of the Word and that there should always be preaching. He knew from history to what the omission of preaching is apt to lead. And from the beginning the Sacrament was always used as the seal upon the preached Word and followed immediately upon the exposition of Scripture. It is when innovations of this kind come to one's attention that doubts arise as to the wisdom of efforts to accelerate a spontaneous movement. Things might be done hastily, without sufficient thought and study. And so the last state of that church shall be worse than the first.

The oldest description of a Christian service after Bible days is given us by Justin Martyr, who died 166. He tells us that on Sunday the Christians gathered for the reading of portions from the prophets and from the letters of the apostles. Then followed an exposition and application of what had been read. Finally all present received the consecrated elements.

At the beginning of the fourth century, in the time of St. Augustin, the Sacrament was still celebrated every Sunday and received by the entire congregation. It was at this time that the main service was divided into the Missa catechumenorum, the preaching service, and the Missa fidelium, the communion service.

At the time of the Reformation the weekly communion was general. The Apology of the Augsburg Confession states: "With us many use the Lord's Supper willingly and without constraint every Lord's Day." Article VIII, Triglot, page 325. The German version has "das Volk" for "multi", many. Again: "We do not abolish the Mass, but religiously maintain and defend it. For among us masses are celebrated every Lord's Day and on other festivals, in which the Sacrament is offered to those who wish to use it." Article XII, Triglot, page 384.

The same article states: "Epiphanius writes that in Asia the Communion was celebrated three times a week. . . . And indeed he says that this custom was handed down from the apostles. For he speaks thus: Assemblies for Communion were appointed by the apostles to be held on the fourth day, on Sabbath eve, and the Lord's Day." Triglot, page 386.

In Lutheran orders of service published between 1540 and 1594 we find the weekly communion still prescribed for the main service. However, a place is given for formal or extemporaneous admonition when no communicants came forward. The absence of communicants and the lack of desire for the Sacrament was deplored and the people were admonished and encouraged to commune frequently.

How in the course of time the celebration was dropped from the main service and the liturgy adapted to a service without Holy Communion is a long story. All that need be said here is that conditions which are responsible were not enviable and the process is not worthy of imitation. Thank God for the indications that the means of grace are no longer to be separated, that the Sacrament again is coming into its own as the seal upon the preached Word. Our chief concern must now be to keep this development in the right channel, that it be not a development away from the Word but along scriptural, apostolic, historically Lutheran lines.

The Visitor and the Communion Service

The visitor in our churches must be put at ease, if he is to be impressed by gospel preaching and dignified worship. Uncertainty as to the customs of the congregation makes for confusion and distress, which places the Church and its message in an unfavorable light. Particularly at the celebration of Holy Communion is the visiting worshipper ill at ease. Here are questions which repeatedly arise. Must one register before partaking of Communion? Can one partake and register later? When does the congregation kneel during the service? Must everyone present kneel? May one leave the service just before the celebration of Communion?

The following folder, "Considerations For The Communion Service," placed in the hymnals on Communion Sundays has proved helpful in informing the visitor and new additions to the membership.

1. REGISTRATION FOR HOLY COMMUNION is the custom of this congregation. Please observe the rule of registering your name personally in the Sacristy at the appointed hours, in advance of the Communion Service.

2. KNEELING for the Confession of Sins is a commonly observed and long standing custom of the Lutheran Church. The practice is encouraged by such numerous Bible statements as Psalm 95, 6: "O come, let us worship and bow down: let us kneel before the Lord our Maker," as well as by the Prayer-example of Our Lord. If you find this custom useful in expressing your humble penitence and respectful devotion before your God, you are invited to kneel with us, facing toward the altar.

Do not rise from your knees until after the questions, and the final Absolution are spoken by the Pastor. Kneeling is also recommended if you are not partaking of Holy Communion today, since no one present wishes to exclude himself from the Confession and the Absolution spoken by the Pastor. Your compliance is, of course, purely voluntary.

LEAVING THE CHURCH in the midst of the Service is irreverent and disrespectful to the Saviour who approaches His disciples in the Sacrament and it is an inconsiderate disturbance of other people's devotions. Please remain to the end of the service unless urgent considerations compel you to leave.

Communion Prayer

Lord, Jesus, Who callest unto Thee all those that labor and are heavy laden, to refresh them and give rest unto their souls, I pray Thee, let me also experience Thy love at the heavenly feast which Thou hast prepared for Thy children on earth. Keep me from impenitence and unbelief, that I may not partake of the sacrament to my damnation. Take off from me the spotted garment of the flesh and of my own righteousness, and adorn me with the garment earned with Thy blood. Strengthen my faith, increase my love and hope, and hereafter make me to sit at Thy heavenly table where Thou wilt give them that are Thine, to eat of the eternal manna and to drink of the river of Thy pleasure. Hear me for Thine own sake. Amen.

(Submitted by Walter A. Reuning, Westfield, N.J.)

Making the Most of Communion Announcement

ARNOLD H. GRUMM

WHAT CONSTITUTES progress in church methods? A pastor writes in his parish paper, "Announcements for Holy Communion during the holiday season are permitted at any time, by any method: Personal—card—telephone; those who commune for the first time in this church should see the pastor personally." Another pastor tells a new member received by transfer, "It is not necessary to announce personally for Communion. That's old-fashioned and takes up too much time. Use the cards you find in the pews." If the purpose of announcement is merely to register names so the pastor can exercise control over the attendance at the Lord's Table in that way . . . and that is what announcement has become in many congregations . . . aren't those pastors right? Why not save everybody's time by making use of cards or telephone? Why not streamline our old method of personal announcement for the benefit of all concerned?

The writer would find no fault with the conclusion, if he could let the premise stand. He believes that making announcement for Communion a mere registering of names is the vital mistake. That is the step backward, because it represents the loss of a blessed opportunity for the cure of souls.

Progress in church methods is not to be measured principally in terms of minutes saved but of opportunities offered to bring the Word of God to bear more effectively on hearts and minds and lives of as many people as possible. Paul uses the word progress in this sense, when he urges Timothy (I Tim. 4, 15) to let his progress be manifest by practicing himself in study, exhortation and teaching. Personal announcement for Communion offers the pastor an excellent opportunity for just such exhortation and teaching applied to the individual. There the pastor is face to face with the soul that is entrusted to his care and that at a time when spiritual matters are uppermost in the mind and heart. There he is in a position to practice "Seelsorge," so sorely needed in our churches, to get to know more about the spiritual life of the individual, the level of his thinking and the actual needs of his soul. There he has an unparalleled opportunity to help deepen this spiritual life and solve the problems of the troubled soul, help the communicant receive the maximum of divine blessings obtainable in the Lord's Supper.

"Splendid in theory," you say, "but how is all this to be accomplished? A few words of exhortation will usually not bring about the desired results; besides, it takes considerable time, which is not always available, to get the communicant to speak about his spiritual problems. Often too it becomes necessary to receive a number of people at one time for announcement because of the rush so that the necessary privacy is lacking."

There is truth in that objection. Let's not minimize the difficulties; they are considerable. It would seem however that the problem presented should serve not as a proof that nothing can be done about it, but as a challenge to be met.

Have you ever tried to introduce your discussion with a well-prepared question? Some time ago the writer of the "While it is Day" column of the AMERICAN LUTHERAN suggested such a question, "What progress have you made in your spiritual life?" Try putting that question the next time. Help the communicant member get the full implication of the question by showing him briefly but concretely what such progress involves: greater faith, a more devotional life, happy service of God and man, etc. Point out to him, if necessary, how God in and through the Sacrament can and will make such progress real in his life. Ask him to think this over until Sunday, when he goes to Communion. If he does only that you should have a well prepared communicant. In a number of cases he will begin discussing his spiritual problems.

For years the writer has used this question method with encouraging results and with the conviction that the majority of his communicant members are receiving a decided benefit from it. He has used questions like this:

"What rule do you follow about the frequency of your communion attendance?" To help the discussion along certain customs in this connection were mentioned as examples. Many had never given the matter any particular thought. Others discovered they were slaves to a custom for which they could give no reason. Their attention was called to the fact that if they had to have a rule they could set up one like this: Why *shouldn't* I go to Holy Communion this time? This discussion as all others was kept on a free and easy level; every effort was made to avoid embarrassing anyone with a too direct question. The results have become apparent in increased Communion attendance.

"Have you ever tried examining yourself according to one or more of the petitions of the Lord's Prayer?" was another question asked. As example the second petition was taken, its meaning briefly reviewed; then attention was directed to the fact that God's Spirit brings us the answer to that petition through the Sacrament and assures us of the answer to every true prayer. With some individuals and with some groups . . . four to six at a time if necessary . . . the discussion became quite animated. A related question was: "Has the use of the Sacrament helped you in your devotional life?" This form of question can be varied to read: "To bear your troubles with joy? To forgive and speak well of your neighbor? To become a more ardent soul winner? etc."

Other questions were: "What would it mean to you, if you were in a place or in a position where you could not go to the Lord's Supper regularly? Much or nothing?" . . . "Have you ever noticed any appreciable difference in the blessings received from the Sacrament, when you prepared conscientiously and when you did not prepare so conscientiously?" This led to a discussion on how to prepare. A similar approach was made at another time, when one of the series of devotional books was used to show how certain prayers and daily readings could be used to help prepare the heart for the Sacrament.

No direct answer was ever demanded, though sometimes answers were volunteered. The member was always asked to think his question through carefully and give the Lord a frank answer. That would lead to an honest self-examination and a greater appreciation of the blessings offered in the Sacrament. In this manner scores of other questions can be prepared, but they should actually be *prepared,* if they are to be applied effectively.

This is offered not as a cure-all for but as an approach to the problem of making the most of announcement for Holy Communion to practice "Seelsorge." Here is an opportunity to reach a large part of the congregation personally with a minimum of effort and a distinct saving of time. Why throw it away?

Reunion Communion

Instead of holding a Reunion Service of those who have been confirmed in the local congregation on Palm Sunday evening or upon some other appropriate occasion, Pilgrim English Lutheran Church, St. Paul, Minn., has a Reunion Communion on Maundy Thursday evening. Last year 95% of all the young people, still residing in St. Paul, who were confirmed in the past eighteen years of the congregation's existence partook of Holy Communion in this service. Of the 5% not present, 3% were absent because of illness or absence from the city and only 2% were absent for unaccountable reasons.

The classes of the past five years partook of the Sacrament in class groups while the rest approached the altar in groups of their own choosing. The class groupings are not insisted upon and some of the members prefer to partake of Communion in their family groups.

In preparation for the service announcement cards are mailed to all members of the confirmation classes and the young people register by returning the cards to the pastor after the Palm Sunday service. A telephone follow-up is used to get in touch with those who do not register on Palm Sunday.—Submitted by Edgar F. Witte.

Nameless Churches

In the Lutheran Herald a pastor tells us of a trip he made by auto with his family from Canada to the Gulf of Mexico. He relates:

On this trip we passed scores and scores of churches; frame churches, brick churches, rock churches, concrete churches, old churches, new churches, large churches and small churches, churches of many faiths. But who could tell which? Only in the cities, with few exceptions, were these churches so marked or named that the traveling public might read and know. Some had the usual bulletin boards readable from the sidewalks, but hardly from passing autos.

Christian Science churches were invariably well marked, but in the smaller towns and rural districts extremely few churches bore any identifying marks. Undoubtedly many of these were Lutheran. But, why in the name of common sense don't we Lutherans mark our churches better, especially in the rural districts?

The world is passing by our church doors in ever increasing numbers today. Why hide our identity?

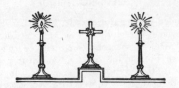

Communions During Holy Week
April 13, 16.

The Communion Record shows that it has been some time since you have partaken of The Lord's Supper. Will you not come on Maundy Thursday and make our congregational family not only one in the faith but also in showing forth our Lord's Death.

The Board of Elders

BETHLEHEM LUTHERAN CHURCH

Fourth and Ovington Avenues

Brooklyn, New York.

The Rev. A. F. Bobzin, Pastor

The proper spiritual relation of a Pastor to his people is that of a shepherd and his sheep. Our blessed Lord pictured this relation by this figure many times. The true Pastor, who is not an "hireling," but indeed an undershepherd of his Lord, will ever be mindful of the huge responsibility this Shepherd office imposes upon him. He prayerfully watches over those entrusted to his care. He is grieved when he sees that some of the flock do not partake regularly of spiritual food and hence grow spiritually weak. He is happy when he sees them often in God's pasture and notices the unmistakable signs of spiritual growth in their life.

Your Pastor is fully conscious of the responsibility of his Shepherd-office, and desires only that his flock be nourished and yet many others be brought into God's fold.

It is in this spirit that I call your attention to a very vital matter, the record of our individual attendance at Holy Communion. The Church record shows that during the year 1933 you knelt at your Lord's table..........times.

Our attendance upon the Lord's Supper is a pretty reliable thermometer of our spiritual life. It shows whether our love for Christ and His Kingdom is warm, lukewarm or cold. May our congregation realize this.

Dear Christian, come often, very often to the Table of your Lord to receive His blessing. Kneeling there is the very highest of our Christian privileges.

Your faithful Pastor and friend,

A. F. Bobzin

P. S.—HOLY COMMUNION will be celebrated in your Church this Sunday, Feb. 25. The Preparatory Service begins at 10:30. Registration for Holy Communion may be made Saturday afternoon and evening. In this season of Lent there is so much to urge us toward a closer Fellowship with JESUS.

(SUGGESTION FOR PASTORAL LETTER)

The Pastor As A Performer of Marriage Ceremonies

FREDERIC NIEDUER

ONE OF THE MANY functions that are included in the duties of ministers is that of performing marriage ceremonies. The pastor is called upon to render this service to members of his congregation and to such people as are not under his spiritual care; in most cases the pastor's duty in the matter is clear, but in some cases he is confronted with situations that constitute problems for his conscience. It is the purpose of this article to discuss briefly a number of things connected with the performance of marriage ceremonies.

It should be recognized that the pastor performs marriage ceremonies both as an agent of the civil government and as a servant of the church. Marriage is an agreement or contract between the two parties; and while it was instituted by God and continues to be a divine ordinance, yet its character of an agreement between two parties makes it a civil matter, "weltlich Geschaeft" as Luther puts it. Marriage, therefore, is subject to such regulations as the State may enforce; and in designating the parties who may legally perform the ceremony of marriage, the State includes ministers. In the United States there are about 130,000 religious officiants and about 30,000 civil officiants; about 75% of the marriages in our country are performed by the clergy.

However, the matter has another aspect, especially when the persons to be married are members of the pastor's congregation. The members of his church have called the pastor as their spiritual adviser and teacher and are bound to hear and heed his admonitions and inculcations that are in accord with God's Word. And since the Holy Scripture contains many things about marriage that must be taught to Christians, the pastor who arranges for a marriage ceremony, explains the meaning of Christian marriage, and finally reads the marriage rite is performing the functions of a teacher of Christian doctrine and life. We may, therefore, readily declare that the pastor, as a performer of marriage ceremonies, is acting as an agent of the state and as the servant of the church.

This dual nature of this prerogative of the pastor gives rise to the problems that sometimes confront the minister when he is asked to perform a marriage ceremony. A man who transacts this business merely as an agent of the state, such as a Justice of the Peace, needs only to observe the state laws and is not bound to consult his conscience beyond that. He may perform marriage ceremonies from which a Lutheran pastor would recoil with horror. The writer has on more than one occasion refused to perform a marriage ceremony for strangers on account of the previous divorce of one or both parties, and the couple proceeded immediately to the nearby Justice of the Peace, who is a member of the writer's church, and were married, without in the least affecting the standing of the Justice as a member of the church. The Lutheran pastor, however, is bound to observe the restrictions contained in the Bible when he is asked to unite a couple in marriage.

As indicated before, the conscientious pastor may find it necessary at times to refuse to perform a ceremony that is requested. He will not reach for his Agenda immediately upon the production of a marriage license. In cases where the parties to be married are both members of his church there

is little possibility of the necessity of a refusal, unless there was a misstatement concerning their age when the license was issued, or the pastor has reason to suspect that the parents of a youthful prospective bride or bridegroom may object to the marriage, or the marriage would be one prohibited by Scripture on account of blood relationship existing between the parties asking to be married.

Pastors have declined to aid in uniting in marriages such members of their congregations to whom the law of the state accorded the right to marry, but of whose right to become husband and wife the pastor had serious doubts based on his study of Scripture. The question of whether marriages involving "Schwagerehe" are permissible has agitated the minds of many pastors and the refusal to swerve from the path designated by conscience has caused much difficulty in congregations. Stories that are interesting, but perhaps apocryphal, are told about pastors who squirmed at the thought of performing a marriage ceremony involving "Schwagerehe" and advised the parties in question to go elsewhere for the tainted ceremony and then return for a premeditated confession of sin and the reception of forgiveness from an offended congregation.

In cases where one or both parties to be married are not members of the congregation, the pastor will exercise the great caution that his conscience demands. He will have a number of questions to ask. He may not feel inclined to ask as many personal questions as are contained in the question schedule of a certain large metropolitan Lutheran Church, where prospective brides and grooms are required to give information concerning their education, interests, tastes, health, family background, social life, finances and the like; it must be said, however, that a pastor has an opportunity to discuss matters vital to a happy marriage when a wedding ceremony is requested and he may be doing the couple to be married an invaluable service by calling to their attention the factors that make marriage happy or unhappy. A thoughtful reading of an article in the May number of the Reader's Digest will suggest to the pastor the benefits of such a practice on the part of the pastor; it should be added that the article also contains parts which are entirely unacceptable. One thing the pastor will want to know above all things, and that is if there was a previous marriage, and if so, how it was dissolved. If it is apparent that one or both parties have been divorced for a reason not sanctioned by Scripture, the pastor will not soil his hands by blessing such a union. The pastor will see clearly that by helping such people to enter a second marriage he would be aiding them to commit adultery. Pastors situated in small communities near large cities have frequent occasion to perform marriage ceremonies for strangers. The writer could add a dozen highly interesting anecdotes concerning people who waited an hour or two for his return, only to be told that the pastor would not officiate. Their anger was violent, but not less strong is the resentment of the suburban pastor who is called from his bed at three in the morning by a tipsy couple of divorcees bent on receiving a divine blessing upon a second or third attempt to find an elusive happiness in the bonds of matrimony.

The pastor will also exercise due care lest he unite in marriage people who are under the required age and who have evaded the necessity of obtaining parental acquiescence by lying to the license clerk. In some places license clerks are notoriously lax in the issuance of licenses; they will accept a girl's statement that she is over 18 when a moment's glance will arouse the suspicion that she is only 15.

In general, the pastor will guard himself against being a "marrying parson". Social workers, whose daily duties bring them into contact with unhappy homes, deserted brides, disillusioned husbands, abandoned children, and the many and varied problems of domestic infelicity inveigh vehemently against the marrying parsons, the Marriage Marts, the Gretna Greens and other agencies and factors that make it possible for thoughtless people to rush into clandestine marriages that bring about no happiness but only misery and ruin. The laws of some states shoulder a good deal of responsibility upon the officiating minister. In 12 states the minister can be punished if he performs a ceremony that is illegal; in 2 states he must examine the candidates to ascertain if their marriage will be legal; in 22 states he is obliged to refuse to officiate if he knows of any valid objection to the marriage.

The pastor might, to save himself any and all qualms of conscience, make it his undeviating policy to refuse to perform any marriage ceremonies for strangers, restricting his services to members of his flock or to such people who come duly attested by their own pastor. Whatever may be said of the safety and desirability of such a policy, the fact is that it probably does not exist generally throughout our church. Pastors often do not observe parish lines meticulously when the performance of a marriage ceremony is required. We know that if we refuse to officiate the couple will in all probability go to the nearest Justice or pastor of another church. And it is the prevailing thought among us that we prefer a marriage performed by a Lutheran pastor, even if the circumstances are not all as they should be, to a marriage performed by another officiant. Without a doubt it would be a step in the right direction if a more rigid practice could be adopted and enforced, making it obligatory upon the pastor performing a marriage ceremony for members of a sister Lutheran congregation to assure himself of the respective pastor's assent to his officiating.

Perhaps this is impossible of achievement, but the whole matter of marrying strangers or members of sister churches might be given renewed thought. They may be perfectly legitimate reasons why a couple should want to get married at some other place and by some particular minister, and these reasons can always be respected. But we must not lose sight of the fact that the reasons prompting a desire to marry elsewhere are not always unobjectionable. For a married woman to continue to pose as a single woman, after her marriage at another place, to hold her job, may be called an economic necessity, but it is certainly a kind of deception; and such a marriage will, from its very inception, disregard the first purpose of the ordinance of matrimony.

We rightly deplore the ever growing tendency to mixed marriages; yet when such a marriage is to take place, we must make the best of the situation by trying to win the confidence of the non-Lutheran party at the very outset, so as to pave the way for future church membership.

A time-honored custom in our congregation is to have marriages performed in church, before the altar. This practice lends solemnity to the rite, and the recollection that their vows were given before the altar of God may in some instances serve to accentuate the seriousness of the marriage obligation. Of course, a ceremony performed in the pastor's parlor or in another home has no less binding effect. It is only to be observed that the solemnity appears increased through a church wedding; and where the couple fears the expense entailed by a wedding in church, the suggestion may be made to have it

perfectly private with no one at all present except those concerned. When weddings are to take place in church in a public service, a variety of precautions might be observed. The prevalent custom of practicing for the wedding should not become an occasion for engaging in boisterous hilarity in the church. Even at this occasion the participants should be reminded that they are in God's House and that reverence is also expected when the church is empty.

A custom formerly considered vital to a Christian marriage, but now often omitted, is the public prayer for the couple in connection with the banns. The value of such an ancient institution as the banns is evident when it is considered that there is more and more agitation in our country for greater and more prolonged publicity of a forthcoming marriage. Some states have passed laws providing for an intervening space of several days between the procuring of the license and the performing of the ceremony. It is a sad thing that those about to take the serious step into marriage do not always feel the desire for the prayers of their fellow Christians. The couple to be married should be encouraged to have the prayers said; if they object to the public proclamation of their coming marriage, a compromise may be affected by having a suitable prayer on the Sunday *after* the ceremony.

Occasionally a young couple that ran away to get married come to their senses a short time later and, ruefully admitting that they should have come to their pastor for the sacred ceremony of the church, they ask whether they cannot be married over again. The Lutheran pastor will carefully explain to the couple that they are really and truly married already; but he may readily go through a ceremony with the couple, omitting such parts as would be out of place, but pronouncing a blessing upon the marriage.

In the ceremony itself the pastor will observe all proper decorum. He will employ a marriage form that reflects Lutheran usage, and he will not be led to ape every digression that may have pleased the eye or ear of someone at some time. The writer has never been requested to omit the word "obey" from the marriage service, and does not know whether such a request is frequently made; but if a bride who objects to that word is shown from Scripture that it is not the obedience of a servant that is required, but an obedience of love, then the Christian bride will probably drop her objections to the word "obey". The wedding address, where it is customary, affords a fine opportunity to give instruction in matters that the world has forgotten and that Christians are in danger of disregarding.

It happens occasionally that a pastor is called upon to officiate at the celebration of a Silver or Golden Wedding Anniversary, not to mention a Diamond Anniversary. When God has preserved the union begun in His name for 25 or 50 years, this is truly cause for rejoicing, and the blessing of God may be pronounced upon the couple anew by a repetition, with needed changes, of the marriage ceremony. On the other hand, the pastor who has a realization of the solemnity of the marriage ceremony, will shun any participation in a Mock Wedding, as well as any connection with a marriage performed in such a way or in such a place as will provide a sensation, such as a wedding ceremony in an airplane, waist-deep at a popular bathing beach, as the crowning feature at a carnival or walkathon, etc.

The Lutheran pastor does not consider himself as celebrating a Sacrament when he performs a marriage ceremony; but he also does not minimize the gravity of the function that he is performing. He will at all times remember that he is dealing with a divine ordinance, and a matter that deeply concerns the welfare of the state, and that produces either the greatest earthly happiness or the most fearful earthly misery. Let it be his constant care and prayer that his words "I pronounce you husband and wife" shall promote the glory of God and the welfare of those who are united by him in marriage.

Questions Before Marriage

A NOTEWORTHY LIST of questions for those contemplating marriage has been prepared by the Rev. Frederic C. Lawrence, rector of St. Peter's Church, Cambridge, Mass., with a view toward bringing into the open before irrevocable steps have been taken some of the conflicts and tensions which if unresolved are apt to lead to unhappy or spiritually deadening marital life, even to broken homes.

The following 28 questions are given to each intending bride and groom with the admonition: "Consider these questions. Talk them over together. If I can help in any way to answer them, let me do so":

SECURITY

1. Do you both know what your total income will be?

2. Do you expect it to continue as it is, increase, or diminish?

3. How much of this income will be spent in starting housekeeping, your wedding, or paying off debts?

4. Have you budgeted your income so that you know how much you will need for rent, food, fuel, clothing, doctors, recreation, "good will" (that is, hospitality, gifts, donations, club dues, etc.), and savings?

5. How much can you afford to put aside for sickness, for increasing overhead expenses, for children, for education?

6. Have you any relatives who are, or might become, wholly or temporarily dependent on you? Does the other realize this?

INTERESTS

7. What interests have you in common? Have you considered how you will develop them?

8. What separate interests, hobbies, or obligations have you which might take time (evenings and holidays) or money from which you might otherwise spend together? Have you considered together the continuation of these activities?

PARENTS AND IN-LAWS

9. Are either of you over-dependent on your parents or inconsiderate of them or of your in-laws?

10. Is there any feeling of tension with parents or in-laws which could be cleared up at this time with a friendly, frank talk?

11. Does either of you feel restrained by the other one in carrying out what you feel are your rightful and loving obligations to your own family?

12. Are there any particular circumstances of sickness, loneliness, or isolation that will necessitate either of you being with your parents a great deal? If so, does the other realize this?

13. Are conditions such that at any time you might have to live with relatives or they with you? If so, do you both understand this?

RELIGION

14. Have you ever talked together of your ideas of God?

15. Are you a Christian? What does it mean to be a Christian?

16. Do you find reality in prayer?

17. Will you start, with your marriage, an adventure in prayer beginning with prayer together the night that you are married and learning more of it continually together?

18. Are you members of the same Church?
19. Does the Church meet your spiritual need?

20. What part will the Holy Communion and the worship of the Church play in your lives?

21. If you are not members of the same Church have you seriously studied each other's religion to find out if you might unite on one Church? Or, have you counted the cost of a divided loyalty and intelligently faced it?

PERSONAL

22. Is there anything in the life of either of you which you have concealed, or intend to conceal, from the other?

23. Is there anything in marriage which you fear?—yourself, the finality of marriage, fear of each other, fear of having children, or of any of the physical aspects of marriage?

24. Is there any information which you do not possess, and feel you should have before you are married?

25. Have you, to your own knowledge, any disease or likelihood of disease, which might affect your future? Have you seen a reliable doctor in regard to this?

THE SERVICE

26. Have you read the service, so that you know what you are to promise?

27. Have you planned your wedding as you, yourselves, wish it, so that you will always cherish the memory of it?

28. Have you considered others, particularly your parents and relatives, in deciding who will be present at it?

Items from "Planning the Church Wedding"

By HELEN BARTLETT, Etiquette Editor, *Chicago Tribune*.

"A SHOWY, inexpensively staged wedding is in poor taste for persons of modest means. It is far more dignified to have a wedding in scale with the mode of life of both families.

"Selecting the date is technically, the bride's privilege, but she should confer with the groom to make certain that the selected time for the wedding trip is convenient to his business plans. The time of day also must be considered.

"Expenses, to the average family, are the most important items to be considered in this preliminary planning of a wedding. And weddings are expensive. The greater part of the expense is borne by the bride's family, or, if she is of independent means or orphaned, by the bride herself.

"These are the usual expenses met by the bride or her family: The trousseau, invitations and announcements, bride's gown, etc., fee for the use of church or other place where the wedding may be held, fee for the choir, organist, etc., canopy if one is used, floral decorations of church, home and place of reception, all expenses of reception or breakfast, motors for bridal party to church and return, and the bride's gifts to her attendants. It is customary for the bride's family to provide the flowers for the bride's attendants but the groom may do this if he wishes. The bride's family also pays for the photographs.

"The groom's expenses are: The marriage license, wedding ring, flowers for bride, bride's mother and his own mother, gift to the bride, clergyman's fee, ties, gloves and boutonniers for the best man and ushers, motor for himself and the best man to church or wherever ceremony is performed, and all expenses of the wedding trip.

"The left side of the church is reserved for the family and friends of the bride, and the right (facing the altar) for the family of the groom. When a wedding guest arrives at the church door, he tells the usher whether he wishes to be seated on the bride's or the groom's side of the church. If the guest does not state which side, the usher asks the question and then proceeds up the aisle with the guest and seats him accordingly. If a man and woman enter together the usher offers the woman his arm and the man walks on the other side of her.

"The family of the bride sits in the front pew on the left, of course, so that it is easy for the bride's father to return to his seat after he has taken his daughter to the altar.

"The best man is intrusted with the ring and should produce it speedily and surely at the moment the minister needs it. The bride should have removed her left glove, if she wears any—

and long sleeves make them unnecessary, and give it to the maid of honor. She should, before the ceremony, put her engagement ring on her right hand until after the wedding so that when the groom puts the wedding ring on her finger she will not have to stop and fuss about taking off the diamond.

"It will be observed that the best man does not appear in either processional or recessional. At the conclusion of the ceremony, he goes out the way he came in, following the minister. He retrieves the groom's hat and wrap, and his own, and brings them around to the front door of the church, where he meets the wedding party.

"The use of children in a wedding party is not always recommended, especially if they are too young to behave well. However, if flower girls are used, they precede the bride in the processional, walking just after the maid or matron of honor.

"Bridesmaids and ushers never walk into the church or leave it arm in arm.

"The amount of the fee for the clergyman varies from $5.00 to $100.00 or more, according to the means of the groom. The best man presents this money or check to the minister."

(The above is printed from "The Order of the Marriage Ceremony" as issued by Rev. A. R. Kretzmann, Chicago. The American Lutheran printed the marriage ceremony as conducted by Rev. Kretzmann in the *American Lutheran*, November, 1932. Back numbers are available at ten cents.)

Marriage With Music

Pastor George R. Seltzer, Hartford, Connecticut, Offers Sound Advise to Organists and Brides for Church Weddings

WITH THE APPROACH of the time when we shall be "knee deep in June" there arises the perennial problem of proper music for the marriage service. It is a question which annually confronts many pastors, organists, and church people. It is not to be dismissed lightly. But following the course of least resistance, there are always those who desire, or suggest, the use of music that is secular, or, to say the least, unchurchly. The desires and suggestions frequently arise out of a mistaken impression that there is little music for organ or voice that commends itself for use at a wedding. Such is not the case, as a glance at the catalogues of any good music publisher will show. In other cases there is the definite purpose to make the ceremony as "gay" and a religious as possible. The types of frivolous music used at many marriages range anywhere from selections from the operas to the songs borrowed from modern musical comedy. The most unobjectionable type of secular music is probably the love song, the principal objection to which is, that it has nothing in common with a religious service. Pastors and organists will be able to overcome the use of objectionable music if they are able to make positive suggestions. To this end the present writer has compiled a selected list of music suitable for weddings, consisting of selections for the organ, hymns, and choral pieces.

It is frequently convenient to have the music sung or played before the beginning of the service. The Common Service Book recommends the use of a hymn, or of Psalm 67 or 128. If a Psalm is sung, the latter one will commend itself in most cases. It would not be improper to substitute an anthem-setting of one of the Psalms, if the services of a choir were available. It is generally undesirable to interrupt the service for vocal or other music. But if this must be done, "to allow a friend of the bride to sing," it might be after the blessing of the couple by the minister, and before the Collect.

There are a number of beautiful hymns in the Common Service Book which may also be used. They may be sung by the choir and congregation, or by the choir alone. In some cases a hymn is sung as a solo before the service begins. At a recent wedding in one of the finest churches in America, the hymn, "Now Thank We All Our God," was sung as the couple departed from the church—an original and beautiful use of that hymn.

The field of selections for the organ is particularly rich, and should commend itself to organists who wish to be progressive and to get away from the hackneyed in wedding music.

MUSIC FOR THE ORGAN

Guilmant, A., *Nuptial March in A Major*, Book 8, No. 21.
 Postlude Nuptiale, Book 13.
 Epithalame in C, "The Practical Organist," Book 11.
Loret, Clement, Opus 40, *Marche Nuptiale I*.
Dubois, Th., *Cantilene Nuptiale in A flat*,
 also, *Nuptial Mass*, five pieces for organ.
Parker, Horatio, Opus 20, No. 1, *Wedding Song in E*.
Henselt, A., *Ave Maria*.

Woodman, R. Huntington, *Epithalamium* (wedding hymn).
Faulkes, William, *Marche Nuptiale in E*.
Saint-Saens, C., Opus 9, *Benediction Nuptiale in F*.

The above selections for organ may be secured from G. Schirmer, Inc., of New York.

ANTHEMS FOR THE WEDDING SERVICE

Stainer, Sir John, *Love Divine, All Love Excelling*.
Barnby, J., *O Perfect Love*.
Mann, *God Be Merciful Unto Us* (Psalm 67).
Wesley, *God Be Merciful Unto Us* (Psalm 67).
Elvey, *Blessed Are They That Fear the Lord* (Psalm 128).

These anthems may be secured from Novello & Co. Sir John Stainer's setting of "Love Divine" is also arranged as a duet for soprano and tenor (Schirmer, G.)

HYMNS SUITABLE AT WEDDINGS (COMMON SERVICE BOOK)

"Lord, Who at Cana's Wedding Feast"—Thrupp, No. 414.
"O Perfect Love"—Gurney, No. 415.
"O Blessed House"—Spitta, No. 416.
General hymns which are suitable:
"Lead Us, Heavenly Father, Lead Us"—Edmeston, No. 274.
"Father of Heaven, Whose Love Profound"—Cooper, No. 165.
"O Light, Whose Beams Illumine All"—E. H. Plumptre, No. 373.
"Through Good Report and Evil, Lord"—Bonar, No. 259.
"Love Divine, All Love Excelling"—Wesley, No. 276.
"Now Thank We All Our God"—Rinkart, No. 283 (after the service).
"O God of Mercy, God of Might"—Thring, No. 237.
"O Lord of Heaven and Earth and Sea"—Chr. Wordsworth,
 No. 385. (Stanzas 1, 2, 3 and 8 of this would be suitable).

Other music which might be used at the marriage service might be added to the foregoing, such as Psalm 37: 3-7, and these hymns, "The Voice That Breathed O'er Eden," John Kebel (No. 348 in The English Hymnal), and "How Welcome Was the Call," H. W. Baker (No. 351 in Hymns Ancient and Modern). Sometimes one of the fine settings of the final Amen of the service is used to bring a festive note at the close: the Dresden Amen, and Stainer's "Sevenfold Amen" come to mind here.

This list of wedding music does not pretend to be complete. But even a brief selection such as this will show that it is quite unnecessary for church people to be deprived of proper music at the wedding service. The wealth of material available should be an incentive to every one who has to arrange such services. The wedding service, where it is conducted under the auspices of the church, is a religious service, and as such deserves the finest type of religious music that can be brought to it. The purely secular is "out-of-place."

—*The Lutheran*

Shall We Have a Men's Club?

MARTIN WALKER

Shall we have a Men's Club? That is still a debatable question in many Lutheran congregations. And since my congregation has had a flourishing Men's Club for fourteen years, which is still "going strong," the Editor of this magazine has requested an article from me on Men's Clubs. May the use of the first person and constant reference to our own club therefore be pardonable.

As Lutheran congregations are constituted, a Men's Club might seem an "unnecessary evil." Theoretically and ideally, every male communicant over twenty-one years of age should become a voting member of the church. These voting members meet anywhere from four to twelve times a year. What better Men's Club could there be? Well, as a matter of fact not all men who are communicants are willing, or even should be urged, to become voting members. Moreover, the meetings of voting members are fully occupied with "the King's business," and leave little or no time for developing Christian fellowship. Especially in our larger cities, where our membership is recruited from many sources and lives widely scattered, the men would have little opportunity for becoming acquainted with each other and developing friendship without a social organization. This fact led to the organization of our Men's Club in 1913.

THE OBJECT of our Club, as stated in the constitution, is: To foster the spirit of Christian fellowship; to secure the associated service of the men of the parish in educational, social and philanthropic work; also in such religious work as does not properly belong to the congregation as such; to edify and entertain its members. This triple object of the Club has been steadfastly adhered to and fairly well achieved.

MEMBERSHIP.—"Eligible to membership in this Club shall be any man eighteen years of age and over (as a matter of fact we prefer to have them twenty-one years, keeping them where possible in the Young People's Society until that age) who is either (a) a communicant member of Calvary Church; (b) an attendant at the services of the church; (c) a member of any other Lutheran congregation and making application of his own accord (thus enabling men of sister congregations to join where they have no social organization); (d) any man of good moral character known personally to at least three members of the Club.—This latitude in membership is to give the Club a missionary opportunity to bring men into the church. However, "only such members as are also communicant members of the congregation shall be eligible to hold office in the Club." A membership committee, composed only of communicant members, is on the lookout for new members, and is provided with printed application blanks. The applications must first be submitted to the Executive Board, of which the Pastor is an ex-officio member, and must receive his endorsement before being voted on at a meeting of the Club.

OFFICERS AND COMMITTEES.—The Club has the usual officers who with the Pastor constitute an Executive Board that meets monthly, and takes care of petty routine, and submits recommendations to the Club on larger matters. The first Vice-President is Chairman of the Entertainment Committee, that secures speakers for meetings, furnishes music and other entertainments and refreshments. The second Vice-President is Chairman of the Membership Committee. There is also a Visiting Committee, whose duty it is to visit members when sick or in distress, or when irregular in attendance or in arrears. An Employment Committee and a Publicity Committee have functions readily understood.

MEETINGS.—The Club meets monthly, nine times in the Parish House, and during the three summer months outdoors. In June the Club joins the general Church Picnic. Either the July or August outing is for the families of members. Ball games and other athletic contests feature the summer outings; and there are at least two "stunt nights" during the winter. For at least six of the indoor meetings a speaker of ability is secured. The topics covered have been religious, educational,

social, civic, and even political. Since we rightly and rigidly keep all political discussion out of our pulpit, the Men's Club furnishes a fine agency for discussing live political problems. We have permitted candidates for office to appear before the Club and make their pleas. Members of the Club have been drawn on for trade and travel talks. In this way the Club serves to develop latent talents. There have been comic nights with mock trials; and such serious nights as a debate with a team from a sister church on the question of establishing a central parochial school. This meeting was open to all and a Judge of the City Court presided. A stereopticon, owned by the Club, is sometimes used with lectures, and is loaned without charge to other church organizations. As a rule, light refreshments are served at the close of the indoor meetings.

OTHER ACTIVITIES.—Near the time of the annual election of officers a special service is held for the Men's Club on a Sunday evening. Then there is the annual banquet, for which we have facilities in our own Parish House; and this is the outstanding social event of the year, for which tickets are sold to all. As a rule we have two main speakers: a minister with a strong message and some other man prominent in public affairs. Music with lively singing is strongly featured. The Club also holds an annual Father and Son Supper, when boys of the Sunday School whose fathers are not members of the church either bring in their fathers or are provided with "fathers" by the Club. Our Club publishes its own little monthly called The Club Visitor, spiced with news and good humor. Furthermore, our Men's Club has also sponsored a baseball club and a basketball club, both entered in the local Walther League of Clubs; and silver loving cups in the cupboards of the meeting rooms are eloquent trophies. While the annual dues of three dollars pay for the current expenses of the Club and allow for some benevolences (such as Christmas gifts to our students preparing for the ministry and contributions to the libraries of young men who have entered the ministry from our church) the proceeds of entertainments and special donations are used for purchasing equipment for the athletic clubs, and the like

BENEFITS OF SUCH A CLUB.—From the foregoing it must be apparent that a Men's Club can be made to serve very good purposes in the church. I do not believe that attendance at Men's Club meetings has had an adverse effect on attendance at monthly meetings of voting members. On the other hand, at the social meetings of the Club, on the bowling alleys, and at the outings, a splendid spirit of Christian fellowship has been developed which has undoubtedly helped to tie the men to the church. Of course, the spirit of the Club depends very much upon its leadership. A wise pastor will seek to exert his influence rather through the Executive Board than directly in the open meetings.

IS THERE SOMETHING BETTER? "Yet show I unto you a more excellent way" (1 Cor. 12:21). Good as a Men's Club is, useful as it can be made; the more excellent way would be to start with a Men's Bible Class, to meet Sunday mornings before service. Thus the fathers could bring rather than send their children to Sunday School. The fathers or older brothers need such a Bible class to "grow in grace and in the knowledge of our Lord Jesus Christ," to become more intelligent Christians and more loyal Lutherans. Stewardship, the missionary work of the church, and other special topics could be studied, either under the Pastor, or better yet under a competent layman, if such can be found. Such a Bible Class could then hold regular monthly business and social meetings along the lines of a Men's Club and accomplish all that was outlined above, in addition to securing the great spiritual gain of systematic Bible study. For such a Bible study and social group I would suggest the name "Brotherhood" as a more churchly term than "Club."

Lutheran Women's Societies

OSCAR E. FEUCHT

IF THERE HAS BEEN one organization that has gotten the right of way in our congregations more than others it is the Ladies' Aid. Before there were youth organizations of any note these women's groups were well established. The history of the Frauen-verein of many an octogenarian congregation goes back almost to the founding of the parish. Anniversary booklets of our churches, almost without exception, bring graphic accounts, well illustrated, of the ladies' societies.

And why not! Shall not the church use its womanpower? Have not our Christian mothers and sisters of yesteryear shown a deep piety and wonderful consecration to the cause of Christ? Indeed, it has been observed thru the centuries that the finer feelings and the tenderer sympathies of womanhood have rallied as only woman's heart can to the Gospel of the living Redeemer and to the Church He founded with His blood-stained, cross-torn hands. That followers of Jesus are listed by name and sex in the Bible is not without significance. The retinue of women who followed Jesus to Calvary, who were the last at the cross and the first at the tomb, the pensive Mary at the feet of the Master, the Magdalene, the one person of the Bible who vies with the thief on the cross as a recipient of mercy, the Syrophenician whose faith evokes the greatest expression of praise our Lord ever spoke, the widow whose giving of all she had has made her sacrificial love immortal, the woman whose tears bathed Jesus' feet, — all these indicate that there is something holy and deep in woman's religious devotion. Glance thru the inspired writings of so virile an apostle as St. Paul and note the references to women in the church — Lydia, Priscilla, Phoebe, Tryphena and Tryphosa, Eunice and Lois. St. John writes a whole epistle to one of the godly women of his day. But it is the erudite, consecrated Paul who strikes that most democratic note of the New Testament Church so symbolic of the fullness all have in Christ. — "There is neither Jew nor Gentile, there is neither male nor female; we are all one in Christ Jesus." —

If there was ever a time when woman's work in the church was needed, it is now. The most constructive, and certainly the most difficult project our church can and should undertake is the rehabilitation of the home. Major difficulties in the church are traceable to the breakdown of the Christian home. How reconstruct the home so that it again becomes a strong influence for piety in this modern, urbanized civilization? It is the mother who often gives the highest ideals to her children, who moulds their characters, who gives the home its atmosphere. Will sons and daughters become mission-minded if mothers are not interested in missions? Shall the church use one or two additional contacts a month with its women who otherwise run off to bridge-parties and let the inconsequential consume the energies and talents the Creator has intended for His glory?

The opportunities of the church have never been greater. True Christianity stands out in bold relief to the world of today like in the early Christian era. Today the Christian who is true to the Bible is strikingly different. The great work of home missions with its new task of community mission work fairly shouts to our women, who have the necessary time and better opportunities than the men to make good contacts in the neighborhood. The challenging missions abroad suggest a hundred tasks for women to do from an informational program of mission-study to supporting a Bible Woman in India, or gathering supplies for the new Mission in Africa.

The home congregation always the most important field of service suggests projects in soul winning and soul keeping. The whole field of Christian charity, especially as attached to community missions, institutional missions, settlement missions, our Lutheran hospitals, orphanages, Altenheims and similar homes needs the continued support of our women. And these need service much more than they need money!

The development of parish workers, case workers, visitors, is such a crying need when the congregation wishes to individualize the great commission that we need not only women's leagues in our churches, but some sort of program, training courses, and stimulation that is national that is, synod-wide.

The lesson of the depression should not be lost to our womanhood. The social approach as well as the implications of the Gospel call for more hearts and hands that will prove to a community that Christians are twice-born, remade men and women, here in the world on a great mission — the quest for human souls. If Jesus and Paul in their world found the aid of women very helpful, can we ignore this great power in the church today?

This brings us to the question whether we should encourage any organizations in the church. Already self-centered living and false notions of an indolent Christianity have made thousands of church-members believe that there is nothing vital and life-absorbing in Christianity. To them church-life is a more or less joyless experience filled with inhibitions and fears instead of a glorious adventure into the highest life and greatest service possible on this earth. Shall the church offer an alternative to womanhood at a time when women's lives are pretty much fashioned by the magazine ad, the billboard, the materialism and vanity of the movie and radio, and the beauty-sex propaganda of the drug-store There is only one real contact left — the sermon — and that has become an ever-decreasing quantum as far as results are concerned.

In the face of all this shall the church constructively utilize another channel already existing to reach into the lives of its wives and mothers?

Organizations in the church are a defense measure against a world that is heavily organized into clubs, unions, lodges, societies, etc. With radio, entertainments, teas, magazines already asking for 100% of our women's time shall the church claim its place?

But organizations are more than defensive. They can supply church-workers, trained for efficiency, helpers for the ever-increasing duties and opportunities of the local pastor. They can become one line of attack on a mere passive Christianity. They can be useful in assimilating new adult members of the church. They can assist in expressing Christian fellowship. They can be organized especially for soul-keeping. They can help build up the spirituality of the women.

To accomplish all of this the program must be spiritual and kept on a high plane. Unfortunately this is not always the case. In fact, the absence of a program and distasteful experiences have made objectionable even the name "Ladies' Aid." Money-raising devices have wholly demoralized many a society and undermined the stewardship of the whole congregation. It is another example of the church dissipating its powers. When the enthusiasm for the annual sale and bazaar overshadows the enthusiasm for the annual mission festival, when a ladies' aid takes out a vending permit from the city government to legalize its selling activity, it is time to ask — whither? These things hurt the church wherever they are done. The spiritual damage always wipes out any financial profit. They leave a congregation and community as desolate as a fire-scarred forest. They make the next conversion only so much more difficult because they fortify the one great objection to the church in the minds of the unchurched masses: "All the church wants is your money." It is positively damaging! Think of it—while we could be training in salesmanship for the Lord, we are allowing society after society to consume thirty minutes at most every meeting on the next money raising scheme. New converts say, "We thought church life to be prayer and praise, learning and reading the Word, spreading the Gospel, but it seems to be merely pots and pans!" Anyway, whoever told organizations that they must pay for pews, organs, costly altars, and bowling alleys? Who blighted their lives by saddling a debt on them?

A writer on Church-Management speaks of the decision his church made to outlaw merchandising and describes excellent results during a three-year moratorium on such money-raising. He closes with this sentence:—"We truly believe that we are making progress in becoming a church." In this article he replies to a clergyman that bemoans the fact that while such a decision *improves* the treasuries, it makes the church a little less active. As though mere activity is a sign of spiritual life. Only that which helps in terms of deepened faith, and a definite expression of that faith in Christian life, actually helps the church. This writer then lists the following projects of his Women's Society: (1) *Giving* a penny a day for missions above the regular offering and extending participation in this sacrificial, year-round plan to 430 members of the congregation; (2) well planned, excellently balanced programs; (3) monthly sewing in conjunction with local charitable endeavors; (4) visitation of every home in the congregation once each quarter; (5) helping to promote fellowship by serving suppers for congregational gatherings; (It should be borne in mind that fellowship suppers, even where a charge is made, need not be a money-raising device, but can be a worthy project in Christian service.) (6) adopting needy families of the congregation for year-round aid.

We need a constructive program for all our women's societies that can be used in replacing the program which most ladies' aids still have. A program that will help build the "superstructure" on the Foundation of confirmation instruction; a definite program of Christian Knowledge and Christian Service; a program that continues the work begun in good young peoples' societies.

In fashioning such a program for Calvary Church in Kansas City, we could find no better plan and guide than the program of the Walther League. The idea was suggested to us by a young brother-pastor. The W. L. program was revised to fit the possibilities and opportunities that would arise from time to time and worded in such a way that the program can be undertaken in part or in its entirety as time and talent dictate, by a small circle of only a few members as well as by a society of hundreds of members.

In the hope that this program and organizational plan will stimulate the work of our women's societies, enlarge their vision, and increase their usefulness to the congregations of our Church, the following constitution and plan, produced by a committee with no little prayer and perspiration, is submitted.

Constitution Of The Women's League

ARTICLE I—NAME
The name of this society shall be "The Women's League of Calvary Evangelical Lutheran Church, Kansas City, Missouri."

ARTICLE II—PURPOSE
The purpose of this League shall be to carry out under the auspices of the congregation and the leadership of the pastor as much of the following program of activities as time and talents permit.

A. CHRISTIAN KNOWLEDGE

1. Topic Study
(General Christian subjects)
Discussions
Talks

2. Mission Study
Discussions
Group study
Program

Lectures
Readings
Question Box

Plays
Book reviews
Methods in soul winning

B. CHRISTIAN SERVICE
a. General service to the congregation and its auxiliary organizations.
b. Specific service.

1. Soul Winning
Visitation
Christian education
Missionary offerings
Greeting strangers
Special projects

2. Soul Keeping
Promoting attendance (church, Bible class, League)
Fostering Christian love
Gaining members
Christian education

3. Christian Welfare
Care of the sick, poor and unfortunate in community, city and synod
Visitation Sewing Handwork
Cooperation with welfare agencies and institutions

4. Altar Care
Linens
Vestments
Chancel furnishings
Flowers

5. Christian Fellowship
Social programs Plays
Refreshments Dinners
Recreation Picnics

6. Earning Projects
Personal enterprise
Group enterprise

ARTICLE III—SCRIPTURAL AUTHORITY
In carrying on its work this League shall be governed by the Word of God and shall do nothing contrary to the doctrines and practice of the Evangelical Lutheran Church.

ARTICLE IV—MEMBERSHIP
1. All women who are communicant members of Calvary Evangelical Lutheran Church may become members of this League.
2. Such members as are unable to attend the meetings of the League may at the discretion of this society be organized into a home department engaging in as many of the activities of the League as is deemed feasible.

ARTICLE V—OFFICERS
1. The officers of this society shall be: President, Vice-president, Secretary, and Treasurer.
2. All officers shall hold their offices for the term of one year and may succeed themselves whenever re-elected.

ARTICLE VI—DEPARTMENT DIRECTORS, LEADERS, AND COMMITTEES
1. There shall be a Director of Christian Knowledge and a Director of Christian Service appointed annually by the Council.
2. The execution of the League's program shall be entrusted to such Leaders or committees, standing and special, as shall be deemed feasible from time to time, all such Leaders and committees being appointed annually by the Council.
3. There shall be a Home Department Director if the League deems it advisable, said director to be appointed annually by the Council.
4. All of the above appointments are to be ratified by the League.

ARTICLE VII—THE COUNCIL
The President, Vice President, Secretary, and Treasurer of this League shall constitute the Council, with the Director of Christian Knowledge, the Director of Christian Service and the Home Department Director as advisory members.

ARTICLE VIII—MEETINGS
1. The meetings of this organization shall be held at such times and places as the League deems necessary for an efficient administration of its business and execution of its program.
2. Special meetings shall be held when deemed necessary by the president or when requested in writing by five members of the society.
3. The regular business meeting held in the month of January shall be the annual meeting.

BY-LAWS

ARTICLE I—PARLIAMENTARY RULE
Robert's Rules of Order shall govern the parliamentary procedure at all meetings of this League in all matters not specifically stated in this constitution and by-laws.

ARTICLE II—DUTIES OF OFFICERS AND COUNCIL
1. It shall be the duty of the President to preside at all meetings of the League and to perform all other duties pertaining to her office. She shall advise the department directors and be ex-officio member of all committees. She shall see to the observance of all rules and regulations and to the execution of all resolutions. She shall call special meetings of the League when deemed necessary or upon the written request of five members. In case of a vacancy she may make a temporary appointment.
2. The Vice President shall perform all duties of the President in her absence, and at her request, and shall be of such help and assistance to the President as may be required from time to time.
3. The Secretary shall keep a record of all meetings of the League, in a book suitable for such records, furnished her by the League and remaining the property of the League. She shall keep a correct and complete list of all members. She shall notify the pastor as to the time and place of all meetings, so that proper announcement may be made. She shall perform such other duties as may pertain to her office, and which she shall be required to do from time to time.
4. It shall be the duty of the Treasurer to collect all contributions and receive all money. She shall make disbursement by order of the

League only. An accurate record of all receipts and expenditures shall be kept by her in a suitable book furnished her by the League and remaining the property of the League. She shall make a financial report at each regular business meeting, balance her books on the day preceding the annual meeting, submit same for audit, and perform such other duties as may pertain to her office, and which she may be required to do from time to time.

5. The Council shall assist the President in planning and carrying out the League's program and work and submit its recommendations to the League.

ARTICLE III—DUTIES OF DEPARTMENT DIRECTORS, LEADERS AND COMMITTEES

1. The director of Christian Knowledge shall arrange and be in charge of a program of Christian Knowledge and training in harmony with the purpose of this organization as stated in Article II of the Constitution. All reports to the League on Christian Knowledge are to be arranged by the director. A topic study leader and a mission study leader, with their assistants, shall help the director in planinng and conducting educational programs, assisting in the selection of topics, deciding on the presentation methods, and making the assignments. They shall at all times maintain a high standard of worthwhile programs, working in close cooperation with the congregation and its pastor.

2. The director of Christian Service shall arrange and be in charge of a program of soul winning, soul keeping, Christian welfare, altar care, Christian fellowship, and earning projects, as outlined for opportunities for Christian service to the congregation and its auxiliary organizations, to the community, and to the church at large, and shall propose same to the League. She shall plan the monthly Christian service project and announce it at the business meeting, and in a general way keep Christian service as a joint work or as a personal enterprise before the League. All reports to the League are to be arranged by the director.

3. The leaders in Christian Service that may be appointed from time to time, such as leaders in soul winning, soul keeping, welfare, altar care, fellowship, and earning, with such assistants as they may choose, shall study their assignments of work and seek its promotion by the League in a wholehearted way. They shall work in close cooperation with the congregation, and the pastor, the director of Christian Service, and with each other, and shall help to maintain a consecrated spirit in the Christian service projects of the organization. The leader of soul keeping shall also take care of the enrollment of new members in the League.

4. Such special committees as shall be appointed to some general service shall also be under the Director of Christian Service and shall report through that office.

ARTICLE IV—NOMINATION AND ELECTIONS

1. At the regular business meeting in October a nominating committee of three shall be elected by acclamation. The election shall take place by ballot in the November business meeting after the nominations have been duly approved.

2. All vacancies shall be filled in a similar manner.

ARTICLE V—Quorum

A meeting of the League shall be legally qualified to conduct business providing one third of the members (exclusive of those considered in the Home Department) are present, and the meeting is held according to the provisions of this constitution and by-laws.

ARTICLE VI—AMENDMENTS TO THE BY-LAWS

These by-laws may be amended as follows: The proposed amendment must be read and recorded in the minutes of a regular meeting of the League and voted on in the next regular meeting. Two thirds of the votes cast shall be required to pass the amendment.

ARTICLE VII—ORDER OF BUSINESS

When two sessions are to be held during the month, the schedules given below shall govern the meetings. When more or fewer than two meetings become desirable, the Council shall formulate the program and order of business.

FIRST MEETING

1. Devotional opening by the pastor or his substitute
2. Roll call followed by minutes of the past month
3. Welcome to visitors and enrollment of new members
4. Report of the Department of Christian Knowledge
5. Report of the Department of Christian Service
6. Topic Study
7. Recommendations of Council
8. Report of Secretary and Treasurer
9. Unfinished business
10. New business
11. Election of officers and ratification of appointments
12. Announcements
13. Adjournment and devotional close
14. Fellowship

SECOND MEETING

1. Devotional opening by the pastor or his substitute
2. Roll call and welcoming of visitors
3. Mission Study
4. Christian Service Plans
5. Announcements
6. Adjournment and devotional close
7. Christian Service project

Editorial Gleanings and Musings

A MID-WESTERN pastor has carbon copies made of his Sunday sermons and sends them to the church's chronic shut-ins. The service is much appreciated and in the coming year will have to be extended.

* * *

A Walther League society in the northwest publishes a monthly mimeographed paper with much interesting material of a serious and a humorous character. It is helping to build up well-attended and profitable meetings.

* * *

Another church reports the establishment of a photographic history of the church. All photographs of past events have been gathered and fashioned into uniform size and henceforth all outstanding church events and personages will be photographically immortalized for the benefit of future generations. The photographs are preserved in specially made large loose-leaf volumes. A good idea.

* * *

A Men's Club in Illinois annually donates a respectable sum of money toward the extension of the pastor's library. We venture to remark that not only the pastor but the whole church is reaping benefit from this laudable custom. The practice deserves widespread emulation.

* * *

Protests against the vesting of our Lutheran church choirs continue to be heard, but it is noteworthy that choir vestments are being rapidly introduced all over the country. We have never heard of a vested choir going back to the vari-colored dress parade and millinery show of former years.

* * *

According to the Statistical Year Book the Missouri Synod is now 57 per cent English. In 1919 it was 62 per cent German. The transition period is progressing slowly. The year 1929 showed a gain of only 1 per cent for the English language over the year 1928.

* * *

In going about to different churches we notice that cards in the pews and invitation folders contain disturbing misspellings and other errors which indicate slipshod proofreading. Such printed matter deprives itself of fifty per cent of its possible effectiveness.

* * *

There are evidences that the taste for and the appreciation of good choral music are on the up-grade in our circles. One hears surprisingly fine renditions here and there. Recent experiences of our own include a splendidly trained mass choir in Milwaukee, a fine church choir in a bi-lingual church at Akron, and a good children's choir at the same place, all singing worth-while Lutheran music. May the day come when our churches will give no patronage to the publishing houses that flood the market with hurdy-gurdy religious music.

Circle Meetings for Lutheran Women

OSCAR E. FEUCHT

THE request from the AMERICAN LUTHERAN to share with the church at large our most recent experiences in woman's work in the modern church, comes at a time when the Synod's resolution has focused new attention on our hidden woman-power.

There are a good many reasons why the organization of our women should be undertaken at once and with the utmost care, drawing on the best experiences in this field, already well developed by other branches of Christendom.

Perhaps we will get an altogether new viewpoint of the importance of the issue before us when we consider some of the reasons for a Christian woman's movement in our church.

1. The believing woman had a definite place both in the ministry of our Lord and of His apostles. The list of women in their following and their acts as given in the New Testament are imposing. The passages of St. Paul that restrict somewhat woman's function in the church must never be interpreted in a way that militates against the Apostle's own practice.

2. For centuries the tenderer sympathies and finer feelings of Christian womanhood have rallied as only woman's heart can to the Gospel of the living Redeemer and to the church He has founded with His blood-stained, cross-torn hands. Martin Luther rightly said: "Earth has nothing more tender than a woman's heart when it is the abode of piety."

3. The new task of our churches for which there seems to be an ever greater awakening is personal mission work. In the fulfilling of the community mission of the home (local) church lies our chief success, present and future. Our women have the necessary time and better opportunities than the men to make good contacts in the neighborhood.

4. Both Christianity and modern civilization have done much to liberate woman and give her a new status. If this new freedom has gone too far it can be counteracted by nothing I know of but a greater faith and consecration produced by closer and more frequent contact with the Gospel. Woman wields an unprecedented power today. She spends most of the nation's payroll, is the beneficiary to most of the insurance policies, and controls much of society. A district president of our synod a few years ago said: "A man can only give

as much or save as much as his wife lets him."

5. Present day society with its clubs, teas, magazines, book reviews, and its radio is already asking for every spare moment of the woman's time. Time-saving devices and smaller families have increased leisure. However lamentable some of the results of modern trends may be, it behooves the church not to stand by and take the left-overs but get in with demands for time that exceed those of the world and with a program that not only is a defense measure but forms a mighty offensive for victory.

6. "Civilization is breaking up," we are told, by leading thinkers in Europe and America. There have been frantic efforts to prevent this, but to no avail. A new order is in the making. If it is to be Christian, it must rise out of the hearts of twice-born men and women. And these again will come out of Christian homes. Whatever weaknesses we have traced in our own church are almost all traceable to the home. It is the mother who gives the ideals her children possess, ideals which include or exclude a Christian pattern of thought and either train for active Christianity or against it. The father has his specific place in the Christian family, but no one will gainsay the position and importance of the mother. What specific help is she getting from us for her great work?

Our experience has shown that the woman's society of the congregation needs three things: First, an adequate, well planned, thoroughly spiritual program with a fine balance between Christian knowledge and Christian service. Secondly, an organizational plan that gives the individual woman her place, and breaks the program down so that it is close to the small neighborhood group. Thirdly, a plan that builds up around the Christian home and puts its chief emphasis there.

In 1936 the former Ladies' Aid of the congregation reorganized under the name of Calvary Women's League. The chief change was in regard to the program. This was built up under the two departments of Christian knowledge and Christian service. From year to year the women chose general discussion topics for the business meetings and mission studies for the monthly missionary meetings. A wide variety of subjects and methods was used. The Christian service department also was

organized into six fields of endeavor: soul-winning, soul-keeping, Christian welfare, Altar-care, Christian fellowship, and Earning projects.

This was a great improvement and brought new interest. It definitely spiritualized the meetings. Many of the topics were led by the women themselves and while the "Readers' Roll of Honor" project was carried out more missionary books were read in our homes than ever before or since. Strong on the educational side, the new program became top-heavy until this was remedied by connecting work projects with the missionary meetings. Those who liked welfare work were led by the welfare chairman. Those who were interested in Sunshine work made booklets and cards for children, the sick, and shut-ins. The Mission group made Bible School posters, collected and trimmed stamps for missions, made missionary scrap books, planned the annual party for foreign women workers. One group encouraged earning projects as group or private enterprises.

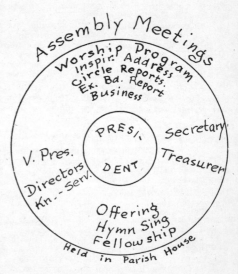

An Altar Guild was formed about this time. Its balanced educational program covered the study of Christian doctrine, history, worship, architecture, symbolism, and music. This group has given valuable service, especially in the past year when a chapel too small for our congregation has made three services a Sunday necessary. It was stimulating to note the fine devotion of these women and how readily they took charge of many details. The guild gave a worthy outlet to the energies of a dozen or more women. This showed us again that our women are willing. Just give them something worthwhile to do and "put some intelligence into it," as L. H. Schuh, Ph. D. so nicely elaborates in his "Enjoying Church Work."

So far, so good. But not good enough! Only thirty percent of the women were attending meetings. The Guild and the League felt they needed some common denominator—some one thing to bring all women into the picture. A fairly large committee of women was formed, some of which were members neither of the Guild nor the League. At one of the first meetings of the committee the "Neighborhood Circle Plan" was suggested. It took root. The committee met almost every week right through a Kansas City summer. Point for point the program was developed. Sample circle lists were drawn up strictly by neighborhoods. We checked every item again and again. We couldn't afford to experiment with some fantastic brain child. Would the circles work out? Could we find enough competent leaders?

The church must live where it is, in its own community! There are some things that cannot be taught well to crowds. They must be learned in the retreat of a small group where one person talks to another out of the fullness of a heart where Christ is enthroned. Christianity must be deep, strong, personal, if it is to have value and power in today's world. Persons are won for Christ not in droves, a herd at a time, but individually, one by one, through personal witnessing to the power of Christ. If this can be done in the many neighborhoods of the same community the church would grow, as never before. And so we adopted the circle plan as our pattern of organization.

All women of the church were assigned to one of eleven neighborhood circles. (Why not make active church-membership the rule rather than the exception!) These lists were revised three times until they were satisfactory. All circle chairmen were carefully chosen, and then called in at once to help us fashion the rest of the program. A letter was sent to all women informing them of the plan. The circle chairmen chose their own assistants and made personal contacts. The first circle meetings were held in September. Each circle elected its own secretary-treasurer and appointed its own visitation chairman and stewardship (penny-a-meal-bank) chairman. Each circle was also given a list of prospective members to be gained for the circle, for the Adult Bible Class, and eventually for the Church.

We decided on six mission topics and six Parent-Home topics for the twelve

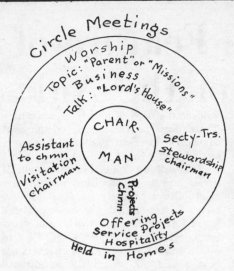

Circle Meetings

Worship
Topic: "Parent" or "Missions"
Business
Talk: "Lord's House"

CHAIR-
MAN

Assistant to chmn
Visitation chairman

Secty-Trs.
Stewardship chairman

Projects Chmn
Offering
Service Projects
Hospitality

Held in Homes

circle meetings. These were prepared months in advance. At the close of each circle session one person makes a three minute talk on "The Lord's House," closing with a hymn verse and a silent prayer for the pastor and the congregation. This closes every circle meeting with an "invitation" to be in the Lord's House on Sunday. There are twelve Lord's House talks for the year. Here are a few of them: "The Church Building," "The Altar," "The Cross," "The Liturgical Colors," etc.

The circle meetings are held in the homes once a month (first two weeks). The programs follow this pattern: Hymn or Poem, Scripture Lesson, Circle Prayer, Topic, Business, Talk on the Lord's House, Project Period, Offerings, Hospitality. Sometimes they are simple luncheon meetings, sometimes afternoon meetings.

On the third Wednesday of the month, alternately on afternoons and evenings (to help mothers) the Women's League Assembly takes place. Its program is strongly inspirational. Here is the pattern: Call to Worship, Hymn, Scripture, Prayer for Some Specific Cause, Handmaiden's Pledge, Address by a guest speaker, Business, Offering, Hymn-sing, Fellowship.

On the fourth Wednesday evening the circle chairmen, League officers, and directors of Christian knowledge and service meet in executive council. Here the next month's program is previewed and all plans and administrative problems are worked out. This is the "drafting room" for the organization.

The third specific requirement I would make of a Christian Woman's organization is—It must do something definitely tangible for the home. The home is the bulwark of society and the church. We shall succeed in our church plans when once we find a way to rekindle the fires of faith on the altars of our homes. "The school and the church

must be taken back into the home again," said a teacher who recently helped write a philosophy of education for our city school system.

We had tried Parent-Teacher meetings years ago. They failed. How could we take the vital subjects regarding the Christian home into the homes and let the mothers work them out under our guidance? We had no topics of this nature on hand, nor an outlet for them. God supplied both. We wrote a number of persons in our church. They gladly consented to write the topics and the Christian Parent Magazine gladly offered space and so is giving the Ten Parent-Home topics wider distribution. (We use six of the ten.) Thus the Circle Plan led to the inauguration of a new, in my estimation very vital, topic series on the Christian Home. If you doubt the possibilities in this field look at a partial list of the subjects below. In this way we began a really effective parent-guidance, home-building program that goes into eleven neighborhoods six times a year—a physical impossibility for the pastor alone.

A PARTIAL LIST OF TOPICS

Church Attendance of Children
The School and the Home
Devotions for Children
Solving Home Problems
The Place of the Father
The Place of the Mother
Character and the Christian Motive
Sex Education of the Christian Child
Building Christian Attitudes
Emotions and Christian Education
Parent-child Relationships
Correcting the Child
Behavior Problems
Christian Discipline
Understanding the Adolescent
Parental Self-Control
Methods of Child Training
Christian Child Psychology
Learning by Doing
Stories and Story-Telling

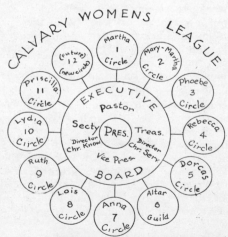

CALVARY WOMENS LEAGUE

EXECUTIVE
Pastor
Secty   PRES.   Treas.
Director Chr. Know.   Director Chr. Serv.
Vice Pres.
BOARD

(future 12 new circle)
Martha 1 Circle
Mary-Martha 2 Circle
Phoebe 3 Circle
Rebecca 4 Circle
Dorcas 5 Circle
Altar 6 Guild
Anna 7 Circle
Lois 8 Circle
Ruth 9 Circle
Lydia 10 Circle
Priscilla 11 Circle

PLEASE TURN TO PAGE 308

The Service Feature of the Work of the Aid

THAT THERE is legitimately a service feature in the work of the Ladies Aid Society is readily understood. In fact, the ladies will grasp this much quicker than they will fall in with the idea that there should be an educational program in the Society. It is motivated readily by our Christian principles of stewardship and by all the passages of Scripture that call upon us by love to serve one another. Just in these modern times where the woman in the home has so much more time, what with labor-saving devices, more compact homes, less canning and cooking and sewing, with the children's time usurped by their school far beyond their ordinary school hours, there is much opportunity for service on the part of the women. And many of them are skilled, trained in former office, school, or shop experience, accustomed to activity, and just "rarin' to go" if only we show them what to do. Probably some persons' antipathy against or fear of a Ladies Aid Society was occasioned by this, that they recognized there was a certain restlessness and urge to engage in activity and the leaders in question were helpless over against this, because they did not know what to tell them that they should do. Prof. R. told me that in his early years in the ministry he had several times experienced a rather peculiar feeling. He is quite an eloquent speaker, and he said that repeatedly he had his people all steamed up and eager to do something, and then there was a letdown because he was at a loss how to direct and use this eagerness to serve.

Now, if the Ladies Aid Society is to function properly and carry out also the service end of its organization, there must be a clearly outlined program of work; there must be a well-understood purpose; they must know what there is to do and have the spirit and the organization to attack that work and strive for the attainment of that goal. Care must be exercised that the Society is kept steering for that goal, is preserved from veering off at a tangent, from dissipating its powers and opportunities upon minor and insignificant matters to the neglect of its greater objectives. And always the motive must be: love for Christ and His Gospel, gratitude for God's blessings, a self-forgetting service to the Lord. This motive must receive nourishment constantly from God's word.

Speaking of the service end of it, we will see the need of proper organization. There must be the proper complement of officers. The Society must not be over-staffed and over-organized, nor under-staffed, with an equitable distribution of duties and responsibilities, and the responsibilities properly fixed. If the Society is over-staffed, there would be a lot of lost motion and working at cross purposes, or in a milder form, a lot of effort would be expended in channels not related and not effectively coordinated with one another. If the Society is under-staffed, much will remain undone because it rests upon the shoulders of a few. That is a danger to avoid, anyway, letting a few do all the work. It is not at all a compliment to say of Mrs. Jones: "Oh, she is such a hard worker for the Aid. She is in everything and does everything!" She would have served her Aid better if she had permitted some one else to do some of the work once in a while.

Aside from the usual officers, the Society might then have a number of committees, with the chairman of each committee responsible for the work her particular committee is to do, and the president responsible for making each chairman carry out her particular assignment. Committees might be as follows: a topic or educational committee; a committee for visiting the sick; a committee to visit new members, mission material, follow up delinquent Sunday School pupils, etc.; a house committee; a relief committee: a membership committee; a social committee; an auditing committee; other committees may be appointed as occasion demands, or committees may function under different names than those listed above.

Speaking of the separate items of service, let us take up mission work first, since that is so definitely in line with the work of the church in general. While we certainly want to see the ladies engaged in mission work, we are not so keen about having them undertake house-to-house canvasses, or drives, or promiscuous efforts at collecting funds. We believe that this is preeminently the work of the voters' body, of the men. It is easy enough to get the ladies to do it, but the men do little enough as it is, and it would be a mistake to let them dodge work of this kind. Furthermore, much of the house-to-house canvassing and promiscuous calling may be unsuited for women workers. You might expose them to rather unpleasant, embarrassing and even dangerous experiences, for instance in a tenement district such as we had surrounding Concordia Church in Cincinnati or a rooming house neighborhood such as forms the immediate field of First St. Paul's in Chicago.

Nevertheless, mission work should loom large upon the calendar of the Ladies Aid, and there is enough for them to do. The mission committee may have a general chairman serving for the whole year, with teams of two each serving three months at a time. The members should be chosen with great care for this work, as it consists largely in making contacts with new people where the first impression, if an unfavorable one, may spoil everything. These committees may be used to visit new prospects, or to follow up such, to make visits of condolence after a death in a family, or to see delinquent Sunday school pupils if their teachers are not able to see them. Usually, the names, with pertinent information, are furnished by the pastor, and the committee reports in detail at the meeting of the Society, and the pastor keeps track of the work done upon his card index or master sheet, or whatever system he may use to keep record of such work. Efficiency calls for careful preparation of these lists, of instructing the members of those committees as to how they are to go about their work, of the rendering of reports in a proper manner, and of keeping record of the work accomplished. This committee would also make it a point to meet newly-confirmed adults and possibly arrange a reception for them, getting the last class to act as hosts for the new class, thus drawing the last class promptly into some form of service and making the new class at once feel that they are tied up with the church in a special way and establishing bonds of friendship with certain groups right off the bat.

Just as the members of this committee should be chosen with care, so they should be trained for their work. The pastor will probably have a good meeting with them at the beginning of the year and endeavor to instruct them for this work: how to approach people, what to say and what not to say; literature that may be left with prospects, how to meet objections and complaints, how to make reports, etc.

This committee would also be in charge of arranging for concerted mission efforts by the entire Society. We like to think of the entire group engaging in some specific mission project once or twice a year. For instance, about ten days before the annual mission festival of the church, the members of the Ladies Aid, going out two by two, visit every home in the parish and distribute the mission booklets published by our fiscal office, with perhaps a special letter written by the minister, and mission offering envelopes for every communicant in the several families, with a word of personal invitation: "Now, be sure and come to church next Sunday to hear our pastor's sermon preparatory to the mission festival, and then come to church on mission Sunday, when we shall have as guest speakers Missionary X and Rev. Z." They are not to collect money, but deliver a personal invitation to the mission festival and get the pertinent literature into the hands of the people. Quite spontaneously, there usually ensues a fine conversation, and the members of the Ladies Aid can put in many a fine word for the work of the Church, and they themselves will profit exceedingly from this effort. I know from experience that congregations doubled the collection and practically doubled the attendance at their mission festival in this manner. Similar projects may be carried out just before the Lenten season, before a special undertaking of the congregation, say for a special effort for clearing the debt resting on their church, just before Rally Day, etc.

Another mission project that can be engineered by the mission committee is the arranging of neighborhood or pyramid parties: they secure a number of women who volunteer to be hostesses; a party is first given for the hostesses at which the plan is explained to them and the program and the items of the menu are decided upon; then on a given day every one of the hostesses serves the same thing and has the same program arranged and makes the same speech (which the pastor probably has to write out for them). But the real value lies in this: that a concerted effort is made to reach every lady of the church not yet a member of the Society, and every good prospect for membership in the church (new people just moved into the neighborhood from a parish in another city, members of the present adult class, etc.) and to have these people meet in a smaller and more intimate group with a number of members of the Society. Again, the matter of personal invitations will play a large role and prove a precious bit of mission work if properly carried out.

Even if there is a special mission committee, that should not excuse the rest of the members from doing mission work wherever opportunity offers. All the Society should be alive to their mission obligation and it is important that they consider this as definitely their work and are ever interested in it.

Visiting the Sick

This is very properly a part of the service program of a Ladies Aid Society. The Bible tells us that is a good work, to visit the sick. Here a real service can be rendered. After all, there is no spiritual gain to be recorded if Mrs. Brown's cake was a masterpiece of the art of baking or a great loss if it sank a little and the frosting was a bit gooey; but there is a decided spiritual gain if Mrs. Brown and Mrs. Jones executed properly a series of visits with patients at the hospitals or at home, called upon invalids and shut-ins, or lonely old people. People who are sick are in need of spiritual comfort and encouragement, will desire the kind offices of their Society's committee, and will be grateful for this attention, or resentful if they should have been slighted and neglected. The main spiritual attention should come from the pastor, and from members of their own family, but this can be supplemented by visits on the part of the Ladies Aid's committee. The committee to visit the sick may consist of two members, or of several such teams if the congregation is very large. They may be appointed for a month at a time, alphabetically, with only the very old and infirm excused, so that as much as possible all ladies of the Society share in this work. The pastor will probably supply them with names and addresses of those to be visited, aside from persons they may already know, adding pertinent remarks as to information this committee may need. From time to time the pastor instructs the ladies as to the manner of making these calls. The ladies must learn to make their visits properly, at the right time, short, not to interfere with doctors and nurses, with a cheerful spirit (no "death-watch-Mary" lugubriousness, "My goodness, you look awful!"—"My cousin's father-in-law had just what you've got, and he lasted only four days"); no exciting them with gossip or getting into arguments with them. Don't think this is far-fetched; we could cite day and name for the above.

At the next meeting of the Society, this committee gives its report, and the pastor keeps track of the visits made on his master sheet. It is well, also, to have a standing rule about flowers: to whom they are to be sent, under what circumstances, and in what amount, and who is to take care of this.

Relief Work

What a blessing there is in this department of the work of the women in the church! Here many women find new interests and outlets for their love and energy, especially if they have gone through some loss or sorrow themselves, and much blessing will flow over into the whole life of the congregation if this part of the work of the Ladies Aid functions well. The work of the relief committee is sufficiently characterized by its name. It has a blessed task, indeed, and one that should loom large in the consciousness of any Ladies Aid Society, but withal a task that calls for much of sympathy and tact. The pastor will confer frequently with this committee, call attention to this or that worthy case, and advise with the committee as to the best way of extending relief. Perhaps jobs can be found; perhaps there is some sewing to be done for needy families; perhaps some things can be made ready for the foreign mission fields, orphan homes, or other institutions; perhaps some used clothing can be gathered and distributed; a poor boy or girl fitted out for baptism or confirmation; baskets made ready and carried out for Thanksgiving and Christmas, or whatever else there may be found for the relief committee to attack. Whenever necessary, the relief committee augments itself; and whatever work is to be done, is planned and managed by this committee, and reported on by them.

How much of relief work can be done depends upon circumstances. Some localities are so well blessed that it is difficult to find persons to whom relief should be extended (it was impossible to find a washer-woman in Chaska; nobody needed to do work of that kind!) In that case, not to permit the Aid to forget about doing relief work, this might be directed beyond the boundaries of the congregation, say in the gathering of clothes for Western Canada, as relief for people in the dust bowl, etc., but it would be well to let the relief committee handle it.

Much of service is possible for the women of the church in connection with the physical property and equipment of the church. The usual Ladies Aid Society may have a *house committee* whose particular duty it would be to think on these matters. For this committee, ladies should be chosen who have good judgment and who are thoroughly familiar with the work of the church and the needs of the congregation. They would have charge of the physical equipment of the Society, make needed purchases and replacements, perhaps through a sub-committee they take care of flowers for the altar, or take care of the altar hangings, and concern themselves about the outward appearance of things, as far as that lies within the province of the Ladies Aid Society. Some fine things have been written on the work of an altar guild by Pastors Weidmann and Otte, published in the Ecclesia Lutherana.

In the interest of order and efficiency, all proposals that have to do with the physical equipment of the church and Society should come before the meetings of the Society through this committee. This gives them an opportunity to discuss very thoroughly any plans along that line, and if necessary to confer with the trustees of the church. It is a good rule never to have larger purchases or expenditures undertaken by any Society in the church except upon the sanction and approval of the trustees. If this plan is followed, the committee and the Society know what they are doing, whether a certain plan is advisable and feasible, whether it would conflict with some other undertaking of the church and put too great a strain on the financial resources of the church, and concrete recommendations will be forthcoming. And again, much embarrassment may be avoided as when some member suddenly arises with a proposal that cannot possibly be carried through or that would be all out of line with what is desired, and her feelings would be badly hurt if she had to be set down right there in the full meeting.

THE SOCIAL COMMITTEE. This committee also has a very important place. As the name indicates, they would plan and arrange everything in the nature of social gatherings, suppers, receptions, picnics, serving meals for conferences, and matters of that general nature, probably also an annual family night for the whole congregation. This committee should be large enough, with an experienced and level-headed chairman. And again, the trick of efficiency is in the painstaking preparation, the planning, the distributing of work and fixing of responsibility. If you had a conference scheduled for your church, and you arbitrarily assigned six different groups of women to serve, with no coordinated planning, the brethren at the conference might be regaled with wieners six times in succession—not a pleasing prospect for any one who abhors wieners with the fervency of deponent. For church suppers, quite a lot depends also upon the attractive appearance of the tables, tasty decorations, smoothness in handling the crowd and serving the guests, and a careful and systematic accounting for tickets and other money dealings.

The present speaker is not greatly enthused about apron sales and bazaars and similar affairs, believing that the church fares much better if the people are trained to out-and-out giving, without taking recourse to this that people must kid themselves into giving or be fooled into contributing, with the thought that they ought to get their money's worth every time they give something for a church purpose. Of course they are getting their money's worth, and much more, incomparably more, every time they hear the Gospel, but we mean to counteract the tendency that a man wants his stomach filled first before he will contribute a dollar for the church. Still, one cannot just say that an apron sale, or a sale of baked goods, or of fancy work prepared by the ladies, or whatever it may be, is wrong in itself, provided a reasonable price is asked, which leaves a reasonable profit. At any rate, all objectionable features, charging exorbitant prices, wheedling prizes out of the merchants, or all games of chance, must be strictly excluded. Similar views would obtain as to card parties.

Educational Feature

THE LADIES' AID SOCIETY ought to have a strong educational program. That lies within the scope of proper stewardship. That is in accord with the call of the Apostle: Seek that ye may excel. That follows from the Lord's admonition that we search the Scriptures. That would be deduced from the praise bestowed upon the Berean Christians for their diligence in comparing the Scriptures. That is embraced in the desire to continue steadfast in doctrine as well as in fellowship, breaking of bread, and of prayer. Any Society within the Church must justify its existence, must offer a worth-while program, must deepen and galvanize the spiritual life of its members, otherwise it is an imposition to ask people to give up their time and attend those meetings. We must mean it when we tell people: Come thou with us, and we will do thee good. If a Society were to exist only for the purpose of promoting sociability among the members, although that is one purpose, and a very legitimate one, especially in larger city congregations where people so frequently do not get to know one another at all even if attending the same church, the danger is that the Society will not endure or will not amount to much. Teaching the pastor to balance a cup of coffee on one knee and a plate of cake on the other while manipulating a sandwich and conducting a conversation with three different ladies at the same time, may be quite an accomplishment, but it really contributes nothing to the life or work of the church. The late Pastor Paul Lindemann, dynamic editor of the American Lutheran for almost a quarter of a century, used to grow quite vehement when speaking on the point. I think we will all agree on this, that the Society must offer more than merely to regale the members and visitors with coffee and coffee cake, or a detailed report as to how many doughnuts were sold at the last bake sale; there must be more body to the meetings, otherwise there will be no real appeal, no truly compelling power to bring the members to the meetings and to command their time and serious attention. We all need advancement in Christian knowledge and instruction in Christian living. By advancing in Christian knowledge we become better members of the church and better qualified to serve.

You may find that the ladies do not always appreciate the need of an educational program for their Society. Many of them have not learned a thing since they graduated from grade or high school, and one shall have to be forever vigilant lest the educational feature of the Society's work is side-tracked or otherwise accorded rather shabby treatment. The best way to keep it alive, of course, is to make it so good, so interesting and helpful that the ladies look forward to each meeting's educational feature with keen anticipation.

The Scope of the Educational Feature of the Aid

Since we are treating of church societies it would seem reasonable that also the educational features of the Society should confine themselves, in the main, to the work of the Church, although every once in a while some other topic may be given consideration if it has a beneficial purpose and sufficient appeal to warrant granting it a place upon the program. First of all, we would place Bible study, the Bible itself and its precepts and characters. Then, lessons from church history, talks on the work of the local congregation in its various phases, the work of the circuit, of Synod, her educational institutions, Valparaiso University, the various charitable institutions and enterprises, liturgics and hymnology, or whatever would be of interest and benefit in the home church and in general. This might take the form of addresses by the pastor, by guest speakers, through illustrated lectures, motion pictures, playlets and tableaux, by members of the Society or groups within the Society. Occasionally other topics may be given consideration, if they have a beneficial purpose and deserve the time of the Society and if they can be competently presented, something in the line of home economics, music especially as related to the work of the church, of general cultural interest, of civic interest such as county welfare, public health, travel, wild flowers of the vicinity, or whatever might be mentioned.

We would favor giving missions a prominent part upon the program of this educational side of the work. Perhaps one might designate each third month as a mission meeting, with addresses, discussions, and presentations of a "mission" character, typing in, if you wish, with the Women's Missionary Endeavor launched by the Central District or similar movements in other Districts. So much of the work of a Ladies' Aid Society is so definitely pointed at the missionary endeavors of the Church that it should prompt giving a good portion of the educational program of the Society to that phase of the work.

Carrying Out the Educational Feature of the Work of the Ladies' Aid Society

Probably a good way to carry out this feature would be to have a topic committee appointed at the beginning of the year. This educational committee would have a meeting right at the beginning of the year and would try to map out a program for the entire year: talks by the pastor on this or that topic at this or that meeting, this or that outside speaker to be invited for that and that meeting, a little mission tableau or playlet given at that meeting, meeting of this or that month to have such and such a general character, etc. This program is then submitted to the Society, and accepted by them, and then it is the duty of the topic committee, under the friendly and sympathetic direction and supervision of the president and the pastor, to see to it that it is carried out. And after the Society has accepted the program, they are committed to it and should not be permitted to shelve or disregard it. The topic committee makes all further arrangements, secures the speakers and prepares whatever is needed for each feature, and introduces the speaker or the respective feature at each meeting. It serves a good purpose if the pastor permits the committee to wrestle, under his supervision, with the problem of building up the program and securing the speakers, etc.; even if he could do it more rapidly himself, it is a good thing to let the members do this work.

A good deal of the work connected with the educational feature of the Ladies' Aid will fall to the lot of the pastor, and we should like to encourage the pastors to devote enough time to this

department and to give it sufficient dignity; take the necessary time for preparation of talks expected of you, and give them freely and in a manner that says: Now, here is something important! We have little patience with the reading of stories culled from various sources, as was formerly often done, that the pastor read continued stories from the Abendschule—well, if he read Jack Roostand, that may not have been so bad! But in our day the reading of namby-pamby stories will not go over so well, and it must be a pretty poor stick of a pastor who cannot deliver an attention-arresting talk to his Ladies' Aid Society after he has given the necessary time to assembling his data and mapping out his line of presentation or argument.

But we are speaking not so much to pastors as to members or prospective members of Ladies' Aid Societies, and we here ask them to give the educational feature its proper place and to afford the speaker of the day, whether it be the pastor or some one else, the proper courtesy and attention. Give this feature its appropriate spot on the afternoon's or evening's agenda, where it comes as something of a climax, not a grudging fifteen minutes at the very tag end when everybody is getting restless, when the ladies are beginning to sniff the enticing aroma of the coffee, and when many of them are getting a bit uneasy about getting home on time. Much can be done by the president and other officers of the Society to make the educational feature seem important and to induce the members to listen to it respectfully. No whispering among the members, or other by-play, should be tolerated while the speaker has the floor. It may not be particularly flattering to the ladies, but many of them are atrociously poor listeners, almost as poor as pastors, who are the poorest listeners on earth. I don't mean that in respect to their pocketbook, though goodness knows that may be flat enough.

If persons other than the pastor are to lead the educational feature, make sure that they understand their assignment and that they are prepared and try to assure yourself, as much as this can be done in an unobtrusive and tactful manner, that nothing will be said or done which would conflict with the work of God or with the standards, aims, and ideals of the Society. If physical apparatus is needed, see to it that all such properties are ready before the ladies arrive for the meeting. It is extremely disconcerting and can well spoil the entire effect of an otherwise worthy lecture to have last-minute preparations intrude upon the time of the Society and then possibly go wrong, just because they are hurried. If the person giving the talk

has come from a distance, arrange beforehand that someone is authorized to take care of the expenses, and to do it generously.

All educational features should be well prepared and competently presented, and should be kept within the proper time limits. A quick way to kill the educational feature is to have a scheduled fifteen or twenty minute talk drag out to forty-five minutes, with everybody getting more and more anxious for the talk to end. One has to play fair. If you induce the ladies to attend a meeting, the implied understanding is that they will be able to get home for their household duties, and one must respect that tacit agreement. Twenty minutes is a good time for a lecture; half an hour may be granted occasionally to a guest speaker; but that should be the limit of the time allotted for this feature.

Sample Programs

What we mean with the educational feature can perhaps be illustrated with sample programs taken from actual experience. We know very well that they would not fit all cases and that they are not perfect. Nevertheless, for purposes of illustration we give you these sample programs. We are not citing programs of systematic Bible study, as you can secure these quite readily or they can be built up by each pastor. The line-ups we give here grew out of the circumstances of this particular parish; to make use of the talent at hand and to serve the needs of this particular parish.

Schedule A

January—The Christian Clock, a reading by several members with an alarm clock in another room.

February—Introduction to Matthew, by the Pastor.

March—Prof. Wehling, playing records of Bach's St. Matthew Passion.

April—Address by Rev. Isadore Schwartz, on Jewish missions.

May—Plans for the new hymn book, by the Pastor.

June—Miss Eliz. Rechenberg, Spring Flowers.

July—Outing.

August—The Centennial of Porter County, bringing in the early days of our church, material gathered and presented by several of the local ladies.

September—Making Rally Day Count.

October—Address on Mission Work in the State Reformatory for Women at Shakopee, Minn.

November—How Synod Works, by Dr. O. C. Kreinheder.

December—Address on "Elizabeth."

Schedule B

January—Things New and Old (every member bring some antique and explain it) ; the pastor makes the application with a ten minute address: The Gospel is always new and fresh.

February—Address: How to Reach the Deceived and Deluded—explaining the difficulties of institutional mission work.

March—Biographical talk on Dr. Heinrich Wunder (pioneer Chicago pastor, who was instrumental in founding our congregation).

April—Address by Rev. M. N. Carter, colored Lutheran pastor.

May—Talk by the pastor on Liturgics.

June—Cradle Roll party, with talk by Mrs. Jox (a former nurse).

July—Outing.

August—Address: The Adolescent Youth, Prof. Lindberg.

September—Jane Addams, described by Mrs. Koch (a local lady).

October—Preparing for our Mission Festival (the members of the Aid were organized and sent out two and two, to carry literature into every home of the church, instructed what to say).

November—Dr. Schwiebert: A Map of Whittenberg of Luther's Day.

December—Question Box (written questions had been handed in the meeting before; some very interesting questions were raised).

Schedule C

January—The Saxon Immigration.

February—Hannah as a woman church member.

March—The Christian Questions in the Catechism.

April—What the Saxon Immigration meant for mission work in America.

May—Early days in Fort Wayne (connecting up with the Centennial of that college), Prof. W. M. Miller.

June—Music, girls' trio, illustrating the old style of sitting around a table and singing parts.

July—Outing.

August—Demonstration of foods, by representative of Reid, Murdoch & Co.

September—Liturgical Colors.

October—Address on "Andrew."

November—The old Valparaiso, Prof. Chaffee.

December—The Madonna in Art, Mrs. Stoner (a local woman).

Schedule D

January—Talk on the Work of the New Year.

February—A Day in Wittenberg, Mrs. E. G. Schwiebert.

March—The Legal Aspect of the Trial of Christ, Prof. Jox.

April—Play: The Woman Who Turned Back (on mission in Corea).

May—Rev. Vandre describes his work in Crown Point jail and sanitarium.

June—Introduction to St. Luke.

July—Outing.

August — Cathedrals in Southern France, Mrs. Wise.

September—Preparing for the Neighborhood Parties (these were a mission project of the Aid).

October—Reading: The Mission Command, led by Mrs. Harms, with a number of the members reading pertinent Scripture passages.

November—Motion picture on the school for deaf-mutes at Detroit, Rev. Kempf.

December — S o m e little-understood customs and principles of the Lutheran Church (such as close communion, announcement, etc.).

Other features that were given: Starting Under Difficulties, by Candidate Hessler in East Gary; tableaux in connection with Mother's Day of different ages in the life of a woman; lecture on home economics by a former teacher; mission studies according to topic outlines furnished by Central District Mission Board; Rev. H. H. Kumnick: the reading matter that comes into your home; interpreting the Lutheran Witness, with the pastor discussing each item in a given number, adding personal touches and the human interest angle; a number of lectures on liturgics, common faults in the services, on hymns, etc.; at various times musical programs by local people or university students; playlet: the case of the mite box, "Eye" (I) trouble; lecture by Dr. Kaufmann on lessons from botany; address by Dr. Schwiebert on the Reformation; addresses on Christian homes, Christian Schools, the work of the Church today, recruiting an adult class (describing actual cases from a former parish), talk on congregational finances, and a great many other topics.

· · · ᕲ · ᕲ · · ·

CIRCLE MEETINGS from p 303

The Use of the Catechism
Good Books
The Use of Pictures
Developing Your Child's Prayer Life
Child's Use of Money and Property
The Child and Missionary Education
Directing Home Play
Value of Encouraging the Child

Meanwhile the interest in projects not only continued, but flourished. Many more hands at work, began and completed five or six times the number of projects formerly finished.

And now after five months, what are the results?

1. Participation of the women in the congregation has increased three hundred percent. Whereas formerly we had thirty women in the meetings of our Guild and League we now have seventy or more in the circle meetings and an average of over forty in the assembly meetings each month.

2. This plan is creating a wonderful leadership in the way leadership is best developed, "by doing." Instead of one president we have twelve (eleven circle chairmen and the League president) ; instead of one topic leader we have eleven; instead of one secretary we have eleven; etc. And yet all form but one women's group, one organization. Not only does this plan create leaders; it makes every woman feel that she, personally, has an important place in her church.

3. The Circle program brings the church's message down to life in the home. It individualizes and personalizes the Gospel in its own way. When seventy homes a month get the benefits of a topic on personal mission work or parent education, then the results in spiritual improvement are bound to come. Educationally and psychologically the plan, we believe, is sound. Instead of taking the women out of the home as most plans do, this one takes them into one home after another until all homes of the congregation are covered.

4. The Circle plan is a natural plan for effective neighborhood (personal) missionary work. One circle of eleven members has had no less than eleven visitors, mostly prospective members, in its first five circle meetings. The Adult Bible classes show the results of the home visitation work of the circles.

5. The Circles are creating a fine congregational unity and feeling of fellowship. There is absent in most modern churches that closeness that sends Christian to Christian to the hour of need. In this we are victims of urbanization and secularization. City congregations find it difficult also to properly assimilate new members and give that feeling of close fellowship which our times especially demand. Through the circles which are the "table-talk" of the homes closer Christian friendships between the men as well as the women are being built up.

6. Many busy hands are also bound to bring many cheerful gifts. The budget of the Women's League has been quadrupled almost overnight. And yet —there are no dues! The money comes from free will offerings and service projects.

7. Never in my ministry have I sat back and looked on as much as I am doing now. It is a great stimulus to the minister to see his people smoothly operating the Lord's business. The pastor originates, guides, controls in the best sense. The members do the work. This is my idea of the priesthood of all believers.

Christian Knowledge Topics for the Ladies' Society

A. H. SCHLEEF

BECAUSE THE MEMBERS of the Dorcas Society believed that they were not making the best of their meetings without the discussion of topics pertaining to Christian knowledge and service, the executive committee of this society, aided by the pastor, selected the following list of topics for the year September, 1938—June, 1939:

September: The Mission Booklet, "Forward for Jesus." The pastor reviewed the book, gave a few side-lights, and asked a few questions which were designed to get everyone to read the booklet carefully.

October: "The Attitude of Christian Women Toward Lodges, Boys' and Girls' Clubs, Civic Organizations, etc." The purpose of this topic was to discuss those features which make an organization objectionable to a Christian. The members came to this meeting with prepared questions, which we endeavored to answer.

November: "Biographies of the Old Testament." Three Old Testament books were discussed in this series, and the pastor drew word pictures of the persons after whom these books were named. The aim was, of course, to urge everyone to read the book in question at home. "EZRA" was the book and biography for October.

December: "Good Church Manners." First the fundamental ideas underlying public worship were presented by the pastor. Then the members suggested things which, as they thought, should be avoided; and which should be cultivated.

January: "Biographies of the Old Testament." The book and biography for this month was "NEHEMIAH." Studied in much the same manner as the November topic.

February: "Bible Quiz." Questions pertaining to Christian doctrine, and a few regarding Bible knowledge in general, were mimeographed, and each member was given a sheet and asked to check the correct statements. Nearly all of the questions were taken from the Walther League "General Bible Knowledge Contest."

Instead of collecting the papers, the answers were given in the same meeting, and each member checked her own paper.

The following are planned for the months to come:

March: "Biographies of the Old Testament." Continuing the series of November and January. "ESTHER" is the book and biography for this month.

April: "Preparation for Holy Communion." We plan to confine this discussion to the following: (a) Helps for self-preparation. (b) Making the most of announcement and registration. (c) How our Communion service may be made more quiet and dignified.

May: "Regain the Drifting." Since this meeting will be held during the week following April 30, the "Family Plan" of the "Centennial Call of the Cross" will be discussed. Members will be asked to prepare special questions with regard to social problems as they affect our congregation.

June: "The Family Altar." The "how" rather than the "why" will be the topic. The method, material, and time of home devotions.

The general plan of presenting these topics is about as follows: Introduction of the subject by the pastor. Then the members are asked to present their questions or suggestions. Since most of these topics were suggested by members particularly interested in them, they discuss these things with the pastor before the meeting, and he helps them in the preparation of their material. Frequently the entire thing becomes a round-table, free-for-all, talkfest.

However, toward the end of the meeting a few minutes are always reserved by the chairman, in which the pastor is asked to sum up the discussion, and point out certain errors which may have been made.

For material we are indebted to the educational topic sheets of the Lutheran Laymen's League, in the following: "Lodges and Organizations, etc." May and October, 1935; "Church Manners," June-July, 1937; "Preparation for Holy Communion," January, 1938; and "Family Altar," October, 1936.

Though Dead They Serve

The American Lutheran Publicity Bureau recently received a bequest from the estate of the late Mary D. Gauss. The money helped considerably to change the financial picture of the Bureau. Deficits have a depressing effect on initiative and enterprise. Directors' meetings, that should be devoted to planning new methods for making known the saving Gospel, are frittered away on financial calculations. Now the slate is almost clean and with the continued support of its loyal members the Bureau can forge ahead.

Mr. Gauss, whom God called home some years before his wife, had made generous annual contributions to the Bureau. After his death his widow continued what he had started. And in her will she saw to it that the Bureau would not suffer by her death.

So Mrs. Gauss, though dead, is rendering a splendid service to Lutheran publicity. That is the point which we wish to emphasize.

The American Lutheran Publicity Bureau is not the only undertaking that keenly feels the death of faithful and regular contributors. Missionary projects, charitable institutions, social agencies—all will sorrowfully verify that statement. Yet there is no need for such a loss. A clause in the last will and testament can provide continued support for any cause in which the testator is interested. The bequest need not be large. If the annual contribution was Five Dollars, $165.00 (figuring interest at three percent) will bring an equal return. $3300.00 would provide an annual income of One Hundred Dollars.

We do not mean to suggest that the bequest should be so tied up as to permit the use of only the interest. We believe that the controlling board of the cause to which the money is left should be allowed to use its own good judgment as to how it should be put to work. But we do strongly urge upon all who are interested in any particular cause to make some provision for that cause in their last will and testament. So of them too it will some day be true that though dead they continue to serve.

- - ◯ ◯ ◯ ◯ - -

The influence of the Lutheran movement viewed from whatever angle has been so far reaching, that it is difficult to attempt to measure it. The cause of religious freedom was set forward immeasurably by the said movement."—Charles Summer Burch, Bishop Suffragan, Diocese of N. Y.

* * * *

Flowers in Church

J. M. BAILEY

JESUS noticed flowers when He walked this earth in the flesh. He used flowers to teach spiritual truths. From the way in which He referred to flowers we may infer that Jesus loved flowers. One of His favorite resting places was a garden. Does it not follow that Jesus still loves to see us adorn the places where we worship Him with flowers? We use flowers in church for a twofold reason: first, because it is pleasing to Jesus, and second, because of the lessons which the flowers teach.

Is It Possible to Use Too Many Flowers?

The answer is a categorical "YES." The first group of pictures with which this article is illustrated shows a use of flowers which we shall do well to avoid in our churches. It is a Lutheran principle

holidays *only*, you make the price of flowers higher on those days. Therefore we say that the spasmodic use of flowers is neither wise nor economical.

Convince yourself of this principle before you start to agitate or work for a large use of flowers in your own congregation, "A regular use of flowers, every Sunday, the year round, is the most desirable and the most economical." When you are convinced of this fact, and we feel that you shall be after you have read this article, then consult your pastor before you take the matter any further. You can depend on his support. He will assist you to work out a plan something like the following, or one that is better suited to your local conditions. Remember it is impossible for us to make one Sunday by Sunday list of flowers for altar use that

1   2   3

that the organ, the choir, and even the Christmas tree, never should be the central part of any scheme of church decoration or interior. The altar and the pulpit should stand out in bold relief, above the organ, the choir, the Christmas Tree and even above the flowers.

This is a story attached to the picture at the right of our first group. A prominent florist's son was married in this beautiful Lutheran church. The decorations, ornate though they were, did not overshadow the pulpit and the altar. The effect of this gorgeous display of floral beauty was such that when the faithful, conservative members of this church convened in their regular meeting they passed a resolution against ornate decorations of their place of worship. The use of flowers can be overdone in our churches.

Good Lutheran Practice is a Moderate Use of Flowers

Our churches use flowers for special occasions. There are flowers on the altars of most churches on Easter, Palm Sunday, Confirmation Day and on such occasions as dedications and anniversaries. This use of flowers is very spasmodic. It is not a wise use of flowers. The tremendous demand for flowers on the special days mentioned makes the price of flowers very high at such times and many people come to think that the use of flowers on the altars of churches is so expensive that no economically conducted church would ever put the item "altar flowers" on its budget. We suggest most strongly a regular use of flowers every Sunday the year round instead of this spasmodic use of flowers on special occasions. Some churches will find that if they take the sum spent for floral decorations on special occasions and go to their florist and tell him we want to use flowers every Sunday the year round, or every Sunday from November 1st until May 15th, that they will get a price not very much above the price that they have paid for their special decorations. Remember that when you use flowers on the special

will fit Florida, California, Minnesota and Canada conditions.

Your pastor will aid you to make a list of this sort, keeping in mind the spirit of the church season and the altar covering colors for the various seasons of the church year. We shall start with Advent when the altar covers are purple.

First Sunday in Advent—White Chrysanthemums
Second Sunday in Advent—Pink Roses, White Pompoms
Third Sunday in Advent—White Carnations
Fourth Sunday in Advent—Deep Pink or Talisman Roses
These flowers can be arranged for use either in baskets or vases. Two vases and two tall baskets should be the property of every church.

Christmas has come to have a flower of its own, the beautiful California Poinsettia. The bright red flower and the brilliant green foliage make this a splendid bloom for Christmas. Poinsettia may be used for altar decorations either as a cut flower or as a potted plant.

After Christmas, cut flowers usually are very scarce and exceptionally high priced. Cooperate with your florist and let him provide a foliage plant, such as a fern, or a draecena, or a pandanus for your altar decorations. Possibly he may have a beautiful blooming begonia, primrose or cineraria sufficiently large to make a true ornament for any church altar.

February brings the first of the early spring flowers and you may now have daffodils, tulips and hyacinths for your altar. These again may be obtained either as cut flowers or potted plants. If you get them as cut flowers they will be most attractive when used as a part of a mixed bouquet.

For Palm Sunday the Calla Lily and for Easter Day the Easter Lily are the accepted flowers everywhere.

After Easter the flower problem becomes very simple. The altar coverings are shades of red and green which will blend with almost

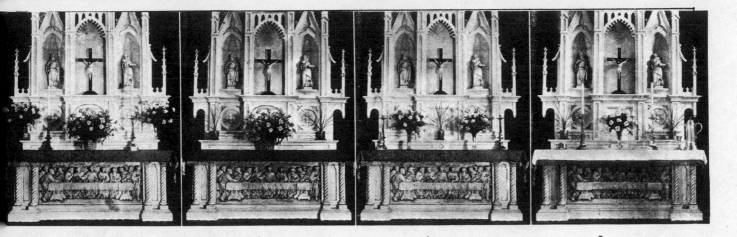

4   5   6   7

any of the spring flowers that now flood the markets, and you will find the carnations and roses are also obtainable in abundance and of splendid quality.

Pictures 4, 5, 6 and 7 show simple types of altar cut flower decorations.

After May 30th the home gardens should provide the flowers for your altar every Sunday. Look at this list of available flowers.

June brings tulips, hyacinths, iris, peonies, roses and candida lilies.

July finds the home garden flooded with the riotous colors of roses, daisies, calendula, gaillardia, zinnia and the tiger, rubrum and regal lilies.

August brings the gorgeous gladiola and the dahlia to add their flaming colors to the other summer flowers.

In September you will be able to gather cosmos, marigolds, gladiola and the early pompoms and chrysanthemums.

How Shall We Get the Flowers to Use on Our Altar?

Grow Your Flowers

We have already intimated this in the preceding paragraphs. It can be done easily. One pastor grew flowers for his church altar every Sunday one summer. It took only a little care and forethought. Remember the garden's greatest pleasure comes when you see the flowers that you have grown adorn the altar of your church. You committee and your pastor will but suggest it. The garden and flower lovers in your congregation will be happy to grow flowers for your altar. Be concrete, however. Make a list of the flowers that you need and of the time that you need them. Look about and see which of your garden lovers grows the varieties which you want to the best advantage. Then ask them to grow some of these simplest kinds of flowers for your church altar. Success

is bound to come if you ask for tulips, peonies, tiger, rubrum, regal and candida lilies, daisies, calendula, zinnias, gladiola, cosmos, gaillardia, marigolds and dahlias.

Buy Your Flowers

Do not expect the florist or the commercial gardener to donate the flowers for your altar. Buy your flowers and buy them wisely. It may seem best for you to shop around and buy here and there wherever you may get flowers the cheapest. In the end, we feel safe in saying, that you will find that the most satisfactory arrangement is to make a yearly verbal agreement with one florist, with the understanding that he is to furnish your church with all the flowers that are bought during the ensuing year. Promise him all your business and try to get a flat rate for bouquets and pot plants for your altar for every Sunday during the winter at a set price. If you have two florists that you desire to patronize, make this arrangement with one for one year and with the other man for the next year. Tell him about the entire plan which you have in mind. He will not only be glad to sell you flowers, but he will undoubtedly help you to buy the best bulbs and seeds for your home gardens and he can give you many an invaluable hint about the growing of blooming plants outdoors. Your florist knows what grows to best advantage in your community. In addition, you will be surprised at the FLOWER VALUES that you will get from your florist just as soon as he learns that you will give him all your flower business for the year.

A Successful Plan

One church has tried this plan for getting flowers for their altar. It has worked very successfully for several years. A flower committee was appointed. It consists of two ladies. The pastor let them have the church records and they looked up forty families who had suffered bereavements

9   8

during the recent years. They asked each of these forty families to promise to pay for the altar flowers on the Sunday nearest to the anniversary of the death of their dear one. After the church services, some of the donors desired the flowers and they took them to decorate the graves of the departed. Others requested that the flowers be given to the sick committee and that they be taken, by the sick committee, on Sunday afternoons to the sick and the bereaved in the congregation.

This committee also used the birthday idea. They needed a few more flower donations and so they looked up birthdays. They went to the younger members of the church and used the slogan, "On Your Birthday Send Your Mother Flowers."

These flowers usually were sent first to the church for Sunday and then home to the mother. The exception was when the birthday came on Saturday. Then the flowers went to the mother first and she was requested to send the flowers to church on Sunday. Illustrations eight and nine show some of the work of this committee. Picture number eight is a donation of two baskets of outdoor flowers which were given as a memorial altar decoration on the anniversary of a mother's death. Picture number nine shows a basket of flowers which was given by a young man to his mother on his birthday.

Use flowers regularly in church. Let their brightness adorn the altar every Sunday. After the Sunday services are over *take* the flowers into the home of the bereaved and to the bedsides of the sick as a sanctified messenger of your Christian love and sympathy.

Altar Flower Chart

This handsome chart, on card, size 17 x 22 inches, admits of five lines under the heading of each month, in which the names of those who have promised to supply flowers for the altar are to be written in. Posted in the vestibule of the church, it is a constant invitation to the people to volunteer to supply the flowers for particular dates and an expression of appreciation to those who have volunteered. Obtainable from the AMERICAN LUTHERAN, 1819 Broadway, New York, N. Y., at $1.00 post paid. If wanted in water color by the artist who designed the chart, we can have this done at an additional charge of $2.00. In water color this chart is very attractive.

Flowers On the Altar

THE custom of having flowers on the altar has become quite general in Lutheran circles. It is perhaps superfluous to say that artificial flowers are out of place, just as everything spurious and unreal must be avoided in church furnishing or adornment. But flowers from the garden are eminently appropriate. They not only offer a beautiful means of decoration, but they speak of life and of the providing love and care of the Almighty God.

A custom which is growing in favor is that of placing flowers on the altar in memory of some departed loved one instead of taking flowers to the cemetery to wither quickly in the heat of summer, and to be almost immediately nipped by frost in winter. In many churches families observe the anniversary of some departed relative by placing flowers on the altar on the Sunday nearest the anniversary. Usually the pastor mentions in his announcements that flowers have been donated by So-and-So in loving memory of So-and-So. The announcement, of course, is optional on the part of the donors. The custom seems to us infinitely better than the periodical grave decorations. Through the floral altar donation the memory of the departed one is kept fresh also in the minds of friends and church members, and it seems much more fitting to pay our respects to the deceased children of God at the place where He is proclaimed who has brought life and immortality to light than at the grave, the place of death.

The custom also serves a practical purpose. As a decorative feature flowers bring cheer to the assembled congregation, whereas at the cemetery they are left to wither or freeze unnoticed. Many churches have the laudable custom of taking the flowers after the service to some sick member of the church or to some unfortunate shut-in. We have found the results of this practice most delightful. The letters and expressions of joyous appreciation are worth a hundred times over the little inconvenience the delivery of the flowers entails. There seems to be a sentimental value attached to the fact that the flowers were on the altar in the church service and enjoyed by the whole congregation. We send the flowers to the sick as a message of sympathy and hope from the congregation. We add sentiment to the floral message by enclosing a card of greeting. For the benefit of those who might be interested in introducing a similar custom we are reproducing the card in this issue of the American Lutheran. Try out the plan. These little touches of Christian sentiment are very valuable in maintaining congregational morale The ushers take care of the delivery

Dear Friend:—

These flowers are from the altar of our church and are sent to you with the hope that they may bring you a measure of good cheer and with the assurance of our best wishes and prayers for your spiritual and physical welfare.

With cordial greetings,

THE EVANGELICAL LUTHERAN CHURCH OF
THE REDEEMER ::   :: ST. PAUL, MINN.

Minde Kranz

RECENTLY, we officiated at a funeral. There were flowers,—of course! But in this case there were many flowers . . . so many in fact, that the entire room was filled to overflowing with floral pieces. When the undertaker began to carry them from the house, he filled a special flower car. He filled a second flower car to overflowing, and still there were many floral pieces to be crowded into the hearse. As we watched this gorgeous floral display being taken to wilt upon the cemetery ground, we could not help but wonder how much the flowers cost, and so we asked the undertaker. He made a hasty estimate and said, "Why, speaking conservatively, the flowers here cost at least $2,000.00."

TWO THOUSAND DOLLARS SPENT ON FLOWERS WHICH WOULD WILT WITHIN A FEW HOURS!!

A few days later we happened to talk to the widow about the way in which her husband had been so generously remembered. She said, "Pastor, I don't want you to think that we did not appreciate the good intentions back of the flowers which were sent, but it was really a shame. My husband would not have wanted it so. While living, he always tried to help whomever and wherever he could. If he could have spoken, I am sure that he would have requested only a few flowers and urged that these two thousand dollars be applied to some persons in real need. It is a shame to think that this money spent on flowers did no real good!"

This sentiment of the widow is precisely the point in question concerning the Minde Kranz—or Memorial Wreath.

For many years the AMERICAN LUTHERAN has approved the intelligent use of the Minde Kranz. Whenever we read in our Church papers of sums which had been left to missions and deserving charities by means of a Memorial Wreath we felt that if the dead could speak they would say: "It is well. I could wish for nothing better than to have food given to hungry, medicine to sick, Christ's gospel to heathen—in my memory."

We are so convinced of the right value of the Memorial Wreath idea that we are perfectly willing to apply it to our own selves. When God takes us from this earth, we would feel a distinct satisfaction if we could know that God pleasing deeds were being carried on in our memory. If we would be able to have any voice in how the money was to be spent in our memory we would be sure to see that it was used for something really useful.

We are glad to say that we do not stand alone in our opinions.

During the past summer we have received communications from various parts of our Lutheran Church urging a wider publicity concerning the Minde Kranz idea. Different men spoke enthusiastically of the important part which the Memorial Wreath—or the Minde Kranz—was playing in their congregation's charitable work.

A pastor in the Middle West has the Minde Kranz idea so well implanted in the mind of his people that it is a custom which is simply taken for granted at every funeral in his congregation. When the pastor makes the official announcement of the death, he also announces "Mr. So-and-So is in charge of the Minde Kranz which will be devoted for the ....(charitable purpose)........ This custom has become so favorably known in this congregation that the people would feel at a disadvantage if Memorial Wreath idea were dropped. For instance: If Mr. A.'s death is announced, his friends Mr. B and Miss C. and Mrs. D. wish to show their sympathy in a fitting Christian manner. They do not wish to spend a great sum of money for large floral pieces, and yet they do not like to appear miserly by sending only small sprays of flowers. But in a joint congregational Minde Kranz these individuals can give their sums of $2, $3, and $5 to the general fund and have their names added to the card of "In Memoriam" which is sent to the bereaved family.

This brings us to the card illustrated on this page. For years many pastors have been looking for a card which is sufficiently ornate and fittingly composed in a spiritual way to warrant the functions of a Memorial Wreath. We are therefore glad to announce the new "In Memoriam" card folder, of the LUTHERAN PRESS. The first page of the folder carries the greeting "In Memoriam" together with a cross with lilies and palm leaves. Underneath we find the familiar quotation from John 11, 25, "I am the Resurrection and the Life."

The second page reproduces the victorious message of St. Paul as taken from 1 Cor. 15:54-57 in the form of a cross. The third page gives the words of the Memorial Wreath as follows, "To the Glory of God and in Loving Memory of (name of deceased) a bequest of .... dollars has been made to (name charitable purpose) by (names of donors). The last page carries a reproduction of the beautiful funeral hymn "When the Day of Toil is Done," embellished with notes of the Capetown melody as found in our hymnal.

The folder is printed in three colors, black, purple, and gold. The edges of the card are heavily gilded. A purple lined envelope gives a fitting touch of loving refinement to the message of the card. This envelope and card is then placed in a second envelope for mailing.

"Mindekranz"   Pastor H. Daib

This word is a newcomer among us. But it has come to stay. So let us get acquainted with this late arrival and give him a place at our hearth and in our heart.

"Mindekranz" is Norwegian by birth. The English equivalent would be "memorial wreath."

However, among our Norwegian brethren the word "minde-kranz" is connected with an established church custom and has thus received a peculiar meaning in church language, as will readily be seen from the following quotaion from one of their church papers:

"One of our young mothers, Mrs. ...., died last week, leaving her husband and five little children.

"Instead of decking her casket with costly flowers, several of her relatives send $30.00 for foreign mission, and a number of her neighbors, friends, and fellow-members of the congregation donate $51.00, also for foreign mission, as a "mindekranz" for her grave."

"Mindekranz," then, in its peculiar, or narrower, sense means a gift, or bequest, for some religious or benevolent purpose, given in place of a floral piece at the death and funeral of a relative, friend, or neighbor. In this sense we have adopted the word and wish to recommend the general use of the "mindekranz" in our circles.

In the past, we have used flowers for this purpose. And certainly, flowers are not out of place on such occasions. They are a true picture of the vanity of our lives, as David says in the 103 Psalm: "As for man, his days are as grass; as a flower of the field, so he flourisheth. For the wind passeth over it, and it is gone; and the place thereof knoweth it no more."

However, the matter of sending flowers at funerals has been greatly overdone, running into senseless and wasteful luxury, and the meaning of the flower as a picture of the vanity of life has been lost entirely. On this point, Prof. Fuerbringer (Luther-aner, vol. 79, p. 12) writes as follows:

"Who among us has not been present at funerals where the measure of the floral gifts exceeded all proper bounds? We at least must confess that we have often been offended on this score. There was absolutely senseless waste. No one, least of all the mourners, could notice each separate floral piece and ap-preciate them all.—Then these flowers lay in the cemetery, un-noticed, and on the following day even the casual observer saw nothing but withered waste. For this reason, even worldly minded mourners often request their friends by way of the public press to "omit flowers," because such practice strikes them as foolish and bad taste. In all this, we do not advocate that the casket which contains the earthly remains of a dear brother or a cherished friend should not be decked with flowers at all; but we are very emphatic against overdoing the matter. If the world knows of no better custom and tries to hide the darkness of its despair "beneath a wilderness of flowers," Christians at least should show that they are of a different mind and think of higher things."

Many of our Christians, who had no delight in such wasteful luxury, nevertheless continued to practice this custom, because they knew of no other way in which they could show and express the high esteem and regard in which they held the deceased.—Now, we hold that the "Mindekranz" is another, and a better way. Listen once more to Prof. Fuerbringer, who continues and con-cludes his article as follows:

"Therefore, we look with favor upon a custom which some of our congregations have adopted and others would do well to follow. In the "Messenger" of the North Wisconsin District, which is a regular caller at our office, we find, among other news items from the congregations of the District, some obituary notices under the heading "Mindekranz." These obituary no-tices contain the name of the deceased, his birth-place and date, the day and place of his death and the funeral, the name of the officiating clergyman, and the text of the funeral address. Following these data, we read in three obituary notices in the last number of the "Messenger":

"Instead of a short-lived floral piece, Concordia Choir, of which the deceased was a member, made a bequest of $10.00 to our Wauwatosa Kinderheim in his memory. The Y. P. S. hon-ored his memory by giving $5.00 for missions."—'In her memory her grandchildren gave $20.00 for missions. Another bequest of $2.00 by———and one of $1.00 were also made for missions.

"Surely, this speaks a better language and serves a better pur-pose than excessive floral tributes.

"In our circles also, flowers are played up at funerals at an expense of many thousands of dollars annually, which could and should serve a better purpose, especially since the treasuries of our Synod and charitable institutions are always laboring under a heavy deficit. In the year 1921, there were 12,328 funerals within our Synod. Figuring each funeral at only $10.00 for flowers, that would make a not insignificant total of $123,280.00. How much good could be done with this money among those who are suffering from material or spiritual poverty! Every year, thousands perish in body, because they lack bread, clothing, or shelter; thousands are eternally lost, because they do not know the Bread of Life, the Savior Jesus Christ.

"Some of our church members are beginning to feel that the money spent for elaborate floral pieces is practically thrown away. And we can say from experience that they take kindly to the idea of the "mindekranz." From three congregations in which the matter was merely mentioned (not published and pushed) the "mindekranz" yielded a revenue of $70.00 for church and benevolent purposes in the very first year.

"In this respect, we may also learn from others. The Roman Catholic church, which has always had a keen eye to its own financial interests, has long since substituted "mass" gifts for floral gifts. The person who wants to honor a deceased friend and express his sympathy to the mourners pays for one or more masses to be read for the person deceased. For this he receives a receipt from the priest, called a "spiritual bouquet card" (mass card), which he sends to the bereaved family. We have reliable information that at the funeral of one man, who could not be classed as prominent or popular, at least 20 such "spiritual bouquet cards" were delivered to the family, which meant a goodly sum of money paid to the priest for the cause of the church."

The North Wisconsin District furnishes a simple "mindekranz" card free of charge to all members of the District. Any person within this District wishing to donate such a "mindekranz" is in-structed to give his pastor the money and to designate the purpose for which it is to be used. He will then receive a "mindekranz" card properly filled out and signed which he takes or sends to the bereaved family. The pastor will then send an obituary notice, containing the data mentioned above to the Editor of The Mes-senger.

It may interest our readers to learn how the memorial wreath idea has gained ground in the North Wisconsin District from year to year. The number of such bequests and the amounts thus given for missionary and charitable purposes follow:

Year	Number of Memorial Wreaths	Amounts
1921	1	$ 5.00
1922	5	70.00
1923	13	143.25
1924	47	439.00
1925	85	683.40
1926	108	1,438.85
1927	149	1,524.10
1928	181	2,065.91
1929	197	3,694.43

Church Music

THE PRESENT-DAY TYPE

WALTER SASSMANNSHAUSEN

HAVING thus reviewed the Church Music of the ancient, the early Christian, and the Reformation periods, let us now center our attention on our present-day type of church music as commonly employed in our Lutheran Church Service. Are we still bent on retaining the high standard of hymn tunes and church music as outlined to us by our religious and staunch forefathers, such as Luther, Bach, Mendelssohn, and many others,—or are we drifting into the trivial, meaningless, and jiggy music generally employed in churches of other denominations?

Hymn-Singing

You will all agree with me that nothing is more inspiring than good hearty congregational singing. The hymn-singing of a congregation is almost an unfailing barometer of its spiritual condition. Good hymn-singing is a sure sign of a wide-awake and energetic parish, while poor congregational singing, on the other hand, is generally a sign of spiritual indifference and stagnation. Let us also remember that hymn-singing is not an artistic exercise. It is merely the outpouring of the soul in heartfelt religious emotion. The members must be taught what Luther maintained, namely,—that they are participators in, and not observers at, public worship and that it is their right and privilege to take active and audible part in the proceedings.

How can good hymn-singing be accomplished?

Use the very best tunes available and ample interest will be returned upon the investment. It is a mistaken idea that good tunes are more difficult to learn than poor tunes; that the congregation will enter more heartily and readily into the singing of trashy tunes than worthy melodies. Needless to say that the text must always be of prime importance in the practical consideration of hymn-singing.

What constitutes a good hymn tune?

A good hymn tune is judged by the same standards as the text of a good hymn. The thought must be worthy. It is not sufficient to have it appeal to man, for it must also be worthy of presentation to God. If the tune does not respond to the inner meaning of the hymn, it is a misfit and a failure. A good hymn-tune will readily adapt itself to unison singing, especially when a considerable number of male voices are singing the melody. Besides composing their own melodies, Luther and his musical co-workers arranged the celebrated chorales of that period from folk-songs or from the music of the Roman Catholic liturgy. These tunes are marked by devotional earnestness and dignity. The wondrously *beautiful melody of "O Bleeding Head"* was originally a love song to the words, "Mein G'muet ist mir verwirret."

England has always more or less been looked upon as a model in regard to the class of hymnals and hymn tunes. Their latest hymn-book, "Songs of Praise," has excluded nearly all of the so-called better tunes of American hymnals. More than one-half of the 467 hymns are supplied with old traditional melodies, either sacred or secular. Less than one-fifth of the tunes have been written since 1800.

What has been gained by this change?

It has given them melodies full of manly vigor, variety, and a freshness which no modern melody possesses. These fine old melodies may seem strange and uninviting to the inexperienced ear, or to ears that are satisfied with the sentimental ointment of modern tunes. Real tunes cannot be judged by playing them with one finger on the piano or by a casual singing over. They must be

given an opportunity to soak in, and then their sterling qualities will be revealed. We Lutherans have such a rich treasury of tunes that there is not the slightest excuse for lowering our standards or resorting to melodies of questionable character.

The Minister and Hymn Singing

It is a well-established fact that the hymn repertory of the average congregation is appallingly meager. It is said to be some fifty or sixty hymns. Our English Lutheran Hymnal contains 567 hymns. This would mean that about ten percent of the available material is actually in circulation,—surely a sad return on the investment. On the other hand, the members are deprived of an excellent means of spiritual uplift due to lack of interest on the part of the pastor. Why not have a congregational rehearsal occasionally? With the assistance of the choir which has been well drilled beforehand, a new hymn can easily be taught in ten minutes. These congregational rehearsals will prove of inestimable value if conducted with enthusiasm and a well-directed effort. If "Amens" are used, they should not always be sung with a rather sentimental slowing or quieting down, but in the style of the tune, namely,—a brilliant "Amen" with a brilliant tune and a quiet "Amen" following a quiet tune.

Furthermore, the day is rapidly passing in which the minister thumbs over the hymnal at the last moment for a familiar song, and where the choir sings a selection for no more reason than that it is pretty or convenient to sing. The pastor should plan the service well in advance, so that the choirmaster will have ample time to prepare suitable music. Then hymns, anthems, Scripture readings, prayers, and sermon may all serve to emphasize the importance of the service. Such order of services are not easily planned, but they are well worth a good strong effort. The serious worship of the Almighty God should not be a haphazard affair, but be carefully and reverently prepared.

How can Hymn-Singing be improved?

There are various ways of improving hymn-singing, or making it more interesting and effective. The simplest means is probably antiphonal singing, i.e., men's voices against women's voices, choir against congregation, or the like. To have all the stanzas of a long hymn sung by everybody is rather tiresome and wearing upon the voice. By resorting to antiphonal singing, this fatigue can be avoided. However, the first and last stanzas should be always sung by everybody. Furthermore, I do not wish to be understood that every hymn during a church service should be treated in this way, but occasionally one hymn might well be dealt with in this manner. A short history of that particular hymn would also prove very interesting at the same time.

Take the hymn, "Come, Thou Almighty King," for example. The first stanza could be sung by everybody, the second by the men inasmuch as it contains the words, "mighty sword," the third "Come, Holy Comforter," by the women, and the last stanza again by everybody.

The Choir

But music makes other contributions to worship than congregational singing. A fine choir, under the leadership of a God-fearing and talented musician, one who can inspire his singers with full reverence and appreciation of their privileged duties,—can indeed make a joyful noise unto the Lord and move the hearts of the listeners. No music should ever be sung merely to please either choir or listeners. Every anthem should be selected for its worship value and have its proper place and meaning in the service. It is far better to sing a worthwhile anthem more than once than to resort to anthems of a trivial or worthless character.

However, a choir is not only to offer fine anthems, but its primary duty is to lead the congregation in full-voiced, heartfelt song. A conscientious choir director will therefore be bent on rehearsing not only familiar melodies, but also practice new hymn tunes occasionally with his choir, provided the hymns are to be had in time for the rehearsal.

Happy indeed is the congregation where both the choir and congregation members join heartily and fervently in voices of thanksgiving and praise to their Creator and King.

The Christian Day-School

Let us not lose sight of another very important factor in furthering Lutheran Church Music, as well as our congregational singing, namely,—our Christian Day School. Having a regular devotional period, besides two or three weekly singing periods, this precious little garden with the proper care and culture cannot help but blossom into a veritable treasure in promoting good church music. It is therefore not surprising to have members of other denominational churches inquire, "Why is it that all members of the Lutheran Church,—children as well as adults,—join so whole-heartedly in the congregational singing?" There can be only one answer—"It is due to our parochial school."

A few years ago I was asked to give an organ recital in one of our large Lutheran churches. The congregation did not maintain a parochial school, and I was assisted by the local choir. After the recital I complimented the director on the choir's fine singing, whereupon the director who was a very capable musician, remarked, "That may be all true, but I am missing something." "What is that?" I inquired. He then replied,—"A parochial school."

Let us therefore foster and nurture this blessed institution, where our children are not only taught the one thing that is needful, but also are generally taught to know and appreciate good church music.

The Sunday School

In connection with this, I would like to add that the Sunday-School may also be instrumental either in furthering or retarding the trend of good church music. It is therefore of the utmost importance that the superintendent or musical director of the Sunday-School be on the alert as to the choice of tunes and not search the so-called tabernacle song-books or other song-books of questionable character for melodies to be sung in the Sunday-School. Those in charge of this branch would do well to consult with the pastor, organist, or one of the teachers not only as to the proper melodies but also as to the musical part of the Sunday-School service in general, unless they themselves are competent of handling the situation.

The Organist

Then the organist with his instrument can add immensely to the dignity and fitness of a church service, or he may be a sad disappointment. On him rests not only the responsibility of providing good church music, but also of determining the character of the congregational singing in the church in which he is employed. If he is of a careless type, the members will respond in a heedless manner; if he is wide-awake and conscious of his calling, he will immediately strike fire in the hearts of the worshippers and bring about the desired results. The organist should not be asked to play a serenade, a waltz, or some other fanciful pretty trifle that has nothing to do with the worship of the Almighty God. We cannot call music "church music" because it is played or sung in church. If the music is primarily for entertainment or does not further the reverence and spiritual uplift, it is not Church Music.

Imagine the effect an offertory would have if, after hearing a most inspiring and heart-touching sermon, the organ would peal forth a refrain of some love song, or a melody commonly employed in the theatres, or perhaps an excerpt of some well-known opera. If you had at some time prior to this attended a movie or an opera, you would undoubtedly be reminded of the picture or play, leaving the thoughts of that wonderful sermon to vanish. Thus we see that the organist can make or mar the whole situation.

The Laity

But the ideal religious service fails of its purpose if the worshippers are not conscious of its beauty, its fitness, and its lesson. We all are in need of being occasionally reminded of the proper conduct during the church services, in order that we may better appreciate the great act of worship. When we enter the church, let us remember that we are entering the House of God. Also bear in mind that the preludes, offertories, and postludes are a specific part of the service and should not serve as an accompaniment to an interesting conversation or as a means of subduing spontaneous gusts of laughter.

Try Descant

AN ORGANIST asks whether there is any safe and sure manner of promoting good congregational hymn singing. There is. Try descant settings to the hymns. We are printing the well-known hymn-tune "Dundee" in descant form. This is closely allied to the so-called "tenor-tunes" of which Luther wrote so enthusiastically.

In using descant settings, greatest moderation must be observed. At the start, it is well to confine descant to the organ accompaniment alone, and not experiment with choir descant until the congregation is well accustomed to it. It is of utmost importance that very little descant be used. In a short hymn, play descant for the last stanza only. In a five-stanza hymn, the third and fifth may be with descant organ accompaniment. In a seven-stanza hymn, three stanzas may be descanted. Only one hymn, or at most two, should be sung with descant accompaniment at a single service, and it is well not to try it every Sunday. The congregation must be warned in advance, either by announcement, or better by a carefully-made card on the hymn-board, reading "Desc. 2-4," or "Desc. 3-5-7," indicating the stanzas to be thus treated. Of course the congregation sings the melody, in strict unison, while the organ plays the descant.

Nothing is more thrilling than descant, properly done. We have tried it on various occasions, even without a choir. On such

occasions the hymn has been announced verbally, "Hymn 556, with descant on the last stanza." Congregations are delighted with it, but it must not be overdone.

"A Book of Descants" by Alan Gray, comes in two volumes, one for organ accompaniment only, and the other for voices. Both are inexpensive books. "The Descant Hymn-Tune Book," two volumes, by Geoffrey Shaw, and "Hymn-Tunes with Faux-Bourdons" will all prove valuable. All are to be had of the H. W. Gray Co., 159 E. 48th Street, New York.

Special Reading List—Books About Church Music

HERBERT D. BRUENING

"THIS list is not intended to be a complete bibliography, but rather represents those books which are in general accurate in historical matters, helpful in suggestion, and practical."—*Charles N. Boyd*, Instructor in Church Music, Western Theological Seminary, Pittsburgh, Pa.

All titles not of more or less specific interest to Lutheran pastors and directors of music in our churches have been omitted from Professor Boyd's list, which was published in the *Bulletin* of the General Theological Library, Boston, January, 1929, Vol. XXI, No. 2. The condensed list follows:

I
Music in the Church

(The) Art of Public Worship, 2nd Edition, Percy Dearmer.
Mowbray, London, 1920.
Originally delivered as the Bohlen lectures at Philadelphia, and later repeated in London. Chapter on "Music and Ceremonial"; outspoken, and strongly in favor of congregational singing. A thought-provoking book.

Church Music, Edmund S. Lorenz. Revell, 1923.
Intended to treat of the things a minister should know about church music. The philosophy of musical sounds; the psychology of music; the history of church music; the pipe organ. Comprehensive but not always discriminating.

Church Music and Worship, Earl E. Harper.
Abingdon Press, 1924.
A program for the church of today. The problem and the need, music and religion, the musical leadership of the church, congregational singing, choirs (junior intermediate, and senior), choral services. Timely and valuable; the work of a successful leader.

(The) Evolution of Church Music, Frank L. Humphreys.
Scribner, 1896.
Sketches the history of church music. A chapter on the limitations of American church music.

(The) Hymnody of the Christian Church, Louis F. Benson.
Doran, 1927.
"It is the special purpose of this book to furnish the materials for that better understanding of Christian hymnody as a preparation for getting the most we can out of it in life and worship."—*Preface*.
A fascinating book by a master of the subject; should be read by every clergyman.

Music in the Church, Peter Christian Lutkin.
Young Churchman, 1910.
Hymn Tunes (with historical notes), congregational singing, the organ, the organist and choirmaster, the vested male choir, the development of music in the Anglican church. A practical and interesting book by one of America's most distinguished and experienced church musicians.
Lutkin is an ardent admirer of Lutheran hymnody.—*H. D. B.*

Music in the History of the Western Church, Edward Dickinson.
Scribner, 1902.
A valuable and scholarly work, by an authority who was for many years Professor of the History of Music in Oberlin College. Deserves the careful attention of every person interested in church music.

Musical Ministries in the Church, 5th edition, Waldo S. Pratt.
Schirmer, 1914.
"A series of popular studies on selected aspects of a great and fertile subject, growing out of an experience of a church musician and a teacher in a theological seminary for many years."—*Preface*.
One of the most sensible and best small manuals. Price, $1.25.

Report of the Joint Commission of Church Music to the General Convention of the Protestant Episcopal Church.
Secretary, 296 Huntington Ave., Boston, 1922.
Specially valuable for its constructive recommendations on the practical problems of church music.
Remarks about processional and recessional, etc., of interest.—*H. D. B.*

II
Hymns and Hymns-Authors

Annotations Upon Popular Hymns, Charles S. Robinson.
Barton, 1893.
"Paragraphs of incident and exposition, of biography, history, literary criticism, and art suggestion—attached now and then to the data of authorship and composition."—*Preface*.
A book which has found wide use.

Christian Singers of Germany, Catherine Winkworth.
Lippincott, 1869.
Selections (in English translation) of German hymns from the early dawn of German sacred poetry in the ninth century, with historical and biographical note.

Dictionary of Hymnology, John Julian. Scribner, 1892.
The standard, remarkable for scope and thoroughness. A monumental work which should be found in every theological library.

(The) English Hymn; Its Development and Use, Louis F. Benson.
Doran, 1915.
An exhaustive, scholarly and fascinating treatment.

English Hymns: Their Authors and History, S. W. Duffield.
Funk, 1886.
"A compendium of biography, incident, and religious suggestion." A large and fully annotated collection.

(The) Evolution of the English Hymn, Frederick J. Gillman.
MacMillan, 1927.
An historical survey of the origins and development of the hymns of the Christian Church. Written in live and interesting style for the "ordinary reader." Has a chapter on "Quakerism and Hymnody."

(The) History and Use of Hymns and Hymn-Tunes, David R. Breed. Revell, 1903.
The outgrowth of a series of lectures on these subjects before theological seminary students. Practical advice on the selection and use of hymns.

(The) Hymn as Literature, Jeremiah Bascom Reeves.
Century, 1921.
"The hymn as the most ancient type of literature and as a most pervasive and powerful kind of poetry has not had its just dues from the critics."—*Preface*.
A worthwhile study from an unusual angle.

Hymns, Ancient and Modern, Historical ed.
Clowes, London, 1909.
With notes on the origin of both hymns and tunes; an excellent general historical introduction by W. H. Frere; and short biographies of authors and composers. Nine hundred and eleven pages. A most valuable book for any Protestant clergyman.

(The) Hymns of Martin Luther, Leonard Woolsey Bacon and Nathan H. Hodder. London, 1884.
Thirty-six hymns, with the original melodies. German text and English translation. Luther's prefaces to three hymnals. Historical notes by the editor.

Dr. Martin Luther's Deutsche Geistliche Lieder, C. von Winterfeld. Breitkopf, Leipzig, 1840.
In German only. The work of a German authority.

(The) Story of the Carol, Edmondstoune Duncan. Scribner, 1911.
"Hymnology and carolry share an identical source." The progress of the carol down the ages. A readable book by a competent English authority.

Studies of Familiar Hymns, Louis F. Benson.
Westminster Press, 1903.
Twenty-five papers on as many hymns, intended primarily "that groups or societies might be led to think over and discuss the messages of hymns they so often sing, sometimes, it may be, too, thoughtlessly." Fully illustrated, authoritative and a most desirable book.

III
Hymn-Tunes and Books on Composers.

Chorales; Die Entstehung und erste Entwicklung des deutschen evangelischen Kirchenliedes in musikalischer Beziehung, Ph. Wolfrum. Breitkopf, Leipzig, 1890.
A useful single volume on the history of chorales and chorale-melodies.

Hymn-Tunes and Their Story, James T. Lightwood.
Kelly, London, 1905.
A connected narrative in popular style. One of the most useful and readable books on this subject.

(Die) Melodien der deutschen Evangelischen Kirchenlieder, 6 vols., Johannes Zahn. Bertelsmann, Guetersloh, 1889.
The most significant melodies of the German Evangelical Church from 1523. Their sources, composers, variants, and uses in important collections. As useful for this purpose as Julian's Dictionary is for hymns.

IV
Choirs and Choral Music

Choirs and Choral Music, Arthur Mees. Scribner, 1901.
The beginning and development of chorus singing; the origin of choirs; the Mystery and the Oratorio; choral culture in America; practical suggestions. A good book, by an authority.

Choirs and Chorus Conducting, F. W. Wodell. Presser, 1901.
A treatise on the organization, management, training and conducting of choirs and choral societies. Practical and useful, it has gone through several editions. (Note: the seventh edition.) Price, $2.00.

Choral Technique and Expression, Henry Coward.
Novello (Gray, New York).
An excellent book by one of the leading choral conductors in Great Britain. "This book is simply indispensable."—Dr. Harold W. Thompson. Price, $3.75.

Essentials in Conducting, Karl W. Gehrkens. Ditson, 1919.
The author has had in mind his own fruitless search for information upon the subject when beginning his career as teacher.—*Preface*.
Planned for amateurs. A helpful book for beginners in choir or orchestra leading.

Words of Anthems, new edition.
Novello (H. W. Gray, New York), 1898.
A valuable compilation of anthem texts, well classified and with full indexes. Long lists of English anthems appropriate to certain days or seasons.

V
The Organ and Organist

Hints on Organ Accompaniment, Clifford Demarest. Gray, 1910.
One of the best little books for the enlightenment of the average non-liturgical organist.

(The) Organ and Its Masters, Henry C. Lahee. Page, 1903.
A short account of the most celebrated organists, with a brief sketch of the development of organ construction. Chapter on leading American organists.

(A) Primer of Organ Registration, Gordon B. Nevin.
Ditson, 1920.
On the use of organ stops and accompanying. Should be read by all organists.

(The) Story of Organ Music, C. F. Abdy Williams.
Scott, London, 1905.
The story of organists and organ music from the earliest days.

History and Biography

American Writers and Compilers of Sacred Music, Frank F. Metcalf.
Abingdon Press, 1925.
One of the best possible sources of information on this subject, representing years of investigation. About one hundred biographical sketches of the more important figures, and much general information.

(The) Bible and Church Music. S.P.C.K., London, 1898.
A handbook of Patriarchal and Hebrew musical instruments and terms, the Temple service, and a sketch of ecclesiastical music.

Dictionary of Music and Musicians, Sir George Grove.
MacMillan, 1928.
Six volumes, the last being devoted to music in America. A standard English work, not particularly devoted to church music, but containing many articles on church music subjects and composers.

(The) History of American Music, Louis C. Elson.
MacMillan, 1915.
One of the most extensive works on the subject, with chapters on the religious beginnings of American music, early musical organizations, national and patriotic music, organists and choirmasters of distinction.

"A Shelf of Books for the Organist-Choirmaster," Harold W. Thompson, Ph.D.
(Titles and descriptive notes taken from article in "Diapason," August 1, 1923.)

Audsley—Organ Stops and Their Artistic Registration.
Gray. Price, $2.50.
Most valuable for an organist facing the responsibility of ordering and planning a new organ. His scientific knowledge is simply colossal.

Skinner—The Modern Organ. Gray. Price, $1.25.
The work of a great builder and hard fighter.

Dickenson-Thompson—The Choirmaster's Guide.
Gray, 1924. Price, $2.00.
For the first time an attempt has been made to list anthems, solos, duets, trios, responses, canticles and cantatas appropriate to every season of the church year, covering the catalogues of all publishers as far as is humanly possible.

Dickenson, Clarence—The Technique and Art of Organ Playing.
Gray. Price, 5.00.
Has a good deal of reading matter of the highest value, particularly to the organist who has to be self-taught. There are hints on registration, accompaniment, hymn-playing, transcription, and all the problems which the church organist must face.

Nevin, Gordon B.—Swell Pedal Technique. Ditson.
Gives full advice regarding the use of the much-abused swell-pedal.

Ellingford—The Art of Transcribing for the Organ.
Gray. Price, $5.00.

Hull—Organ Playing, Its Technique and Expression.
Augener. (Also Boston Music Co.)
Probably the best-known work on the subject, rather conservative but sane and clear and thorough.

Hall—The Essentials of Boy Choir Training. Gray. Price, $1.00.

Stubbs—Practical Hints on the Training of Boy Choirs.
Dr. Hall's method on training children's voices has been eminently successful. Two books of value not only for those of our choir leaders who have boy choirs, but also a help to our parish school teachers in the training of voices of their boys.

Shakespeare—The Art of Singing. Ditson. Price, $3.75.
His exercises are practical, and his theory is clearly stated.

Miller—The Voice. Schirmer.
Written by a physician who has had the care of famous operatic voices.

Forsyth—Choral Orchestration. Gray.
For those who have occasion to arrange orchestral parts for anthems and other choral works.

Dickenson, Clarence and Helen—Excursions in Musical History.
Gray. $1.50.
An especially interesting section on the development of the organ.

Surette and Mason—The Appreciation of Music. H. W. Gray Co.
A pioneer work in five volumes. Each, $1.50.

Spaulding—Music: An Art and a Language.
Arthur P. Schmidt Co.
A recent publication of high merit.

Richardson, Madelay A.—Extempore Playing.
Schirmer. Price, $2.00.

Wright—Musical Examinations. Gray.
Intended for Guild candidates (American Guild of Organists).

Addenda

Liliencron, R. Freiherr von—Liturgisch-musikalische Geschichte der evangelischen Gottesdienste von 1523 bis 1700.

Kade, Otto—Der neuaufgefundene Luther-Codex vom Jahre 1530.

Herold, Max—Alt-Nuernberg in seinen Gottesdiensten. Ein Beitrag zur Geschichte der Sitte und des Kultus.

Rieschel, Georg—Die Aufgabe der Orgel im Gottesdienste bis in das 18. Jahrhundert.

Sittard, Joseph—Compendium der Geschichte der Kirchenmusik.

Klinkhardt, F. A. T.—Die Kunst, insonderheit die Tonkunst, als Dienerin im Heiligtum.

Bachmann, F.—Grundlagen und Grundfragen zur evangelischen Kirchenmusik.

Eitner, R.—Biographisch-bibliographisches Quellenlexikon.

Koestlin, H. A.—Luther als Vater des evangelischen Kirchengesangs.
The above titles are submitted by Pastor A. Wismar, Ph.D., by request of the undersigned.

Lochner, F.—Der Hauptgottesdienst.
Concordia Publishing House. $3.50.
A scholarly work by an esteemed authority on the liturgy of the Lutheran Church. A book every Lutheran pastor and every Lutheran organist ought to absorb.

Kretzmann, P.—Christian Art in the Place and in the Form of Lutheran Worship. Concordia. Price, $3.50.
Contains extensive chapters on the History of the Liturgy, Hymnology, the Liturgical Content of the Lutheran Services, and many references to such authorities as Kliefoth, Loehe, Jacobs, Fuerbringer, Daniel, Richards-Painter, Neale, Ohl, Srawley, Sehling, Horn, Alt, Schuette, Muehe, Lochner, and Palmer.

Wedgewood, James Ingall—Dictionary of Organ Stops.
Vincent Music Co., London.
The standard work in this phase of organ work. "There seems to be nothing in existence quite like it."—Burgess.

Buck, Dudley—Illustrations in Choir Accompaniment, with hints in registration. Schirmer. Price, $1.75.

Macdougall, Hamilton C.—First Lessons in Extemporizing on the Organ. Schirmer. 75 cents.

Stoessel, Albert—The Technique of the Baton. Preface by Walter Damrosch. 1928. Carl Fischer. $1.50.
A practical, profusely illustrated book by one of the foremost choral conductors in America.

Truette, Everett E.—Organ Registration. Thompson & Co. 1919.

Grace, Harvey—The Organ Works of J. S. Bach.
H. W. Gray Co. (Novello.) $4.50.
A most useful and indispensable volume to any organist who tries to find Bach in Bach's organ works.

Pirro, Andre—J. S. Bach, the Organist, and His Works (translated from the French by Wallace Goodrich). Schirmer. $1.50. 1928.
The aim of this wonderful little volume is to make "easier for the student to play Bach in the Bach spirit."

Bach, J. S.—Organ Works.
Critico-Practical edition of five volumes published by Schirmer. Other editions that supply metronome markings, phrasing, fingering, etc. (valuable for the uninitiated) are those of Breitkopf & Haertel, Novello, Augener, Steingraeber, etc.

Terry, Charles Sanford—J. S. Bach: A Biography.
Oxford University Press. 1928. Price, $7.50.
Among some hundred outstanding works on Bach, this extraordinarily complete and well-documented work rightly claims to be a real biography, and nothing else. Considered by competent critics to be the most monumental tribute to the great Leipzig Cantor. German translation under way; preface by Kantor Karl Straube of St. Thomas, Leipzig.

Schweitzer, Albert—J. S. Bach. Preface by C. M. Widor (translated by Newman). Breitkopf and Haertel. 1911. 2 vols.
Another invaluable work on Bach. Chapters on Origin of Chorale Texts and Melodies, the Chorale in the Church Service, the Chorale Prelude before Bach, the organ works, the performance of the organ works, etc., in first volume; and chapters on the various motifs of Bach and cantatas especially fascinating in second volume. Terry and Schweitzer are two of the foremost Bach authorities of the day.

Terry, Charles Sanford—The Four-Part Chorals of Bach.
Oxford University Press. 1929. Complete edition, $35.00. For prices on separate parts, write publishers.
The most complete collation of Bach's genius in this form. 405 four-part chorals harmonized by Bach, German and English texts, historical introduction, critical appendices, etc., etc. A monumental work for reference. Prices on quantities of single chorals or a selection quoted on request. Volume has been placed in the foremost libraries.

Terry, Charles Sanford—The Mass in B Minor. 1924. The Passions (Books I and II). 1926. The Cantatas and Oratorios (also two vols.). 1925.
Five booklets (75c each), written to provide reliable guides to these classics.

Church Organ Music.

Anthems of Today.
Two pamphlets (25c each; address Diapason, 1507 Kimball Hall, Chicago); results of questionnaires, compiled by Dr. Harold W. Thompson.

While this bibliography is not nearly complete, nor by any means the last word, it is, nevertheless, of sufficient scope to give anyone seriously interested in church music and the Lutheran service in particular more than a passing acquaintance upon having read in part or in entirety many of the volumes listed here.

Some Sources

Plainsong, often called Gregorian music, is not a matter of controversy. It is the historic music of the Christian Church, having its roots in the Old Testament temple worship; and developing in early days, with certain influence from Grecian sources which did not alter its structure materially. St. Ambrose, St. Gregory and others did great work in collecting, editing and elaborating upon what already existed. Plainsong grew in richness, gradually losing its primitive character. Nobody who is familiar with the exuberant melodies of the Introits, Antiphons, Graduals and Offertories, with their joyous "jubilations" and alleluias can possibly look upon it as crude.

Plainsong became the standard music of early Lutheranism, and our finest chorales, especially the earlier ones, are very strongly Gregorian in character. Get a copy of the Great Te Deum of St. Ambrose, and play it on a good church organ, and all will insist that it is some mighty Lutheran chorale. Mr. Arthur Quimby, head of the music department of the Cleveland Art Museum, spoke over the radio recently pointing out the striking similarity between the Lutheran chorale and the earlier music known as Gregorian. Every lover of our matchless chorales is bound to love Gregorian, for our finest chorales are but elaborations of Gregorian melodies. "Wachet auf," for example, is but a festival arrangement of the Fifth Gregorian Tone.

It is true that a number of papers have been read lately before gatherings, on Plainsong, and that they have stirred up heated argument. Men have taken sides, for and against. This is unfortunate, for if one loves the chorale, he must likewise love Gregorian.

The very frequency of the discussion of Plainsong in our circles is proof that it is a subject that has awakened lively interest. We have received a number of requests from readers, including men of half a dozen synods, asking for sources of authentic music for such things as the Introits and Graduals. The extra work of Lent and Holy Week prevented us from answering many of these letters. A professor of music in a well-known Lutheran institution has suggested these lines, hoping that they may be of assistance to the many clergy, teachers and choirmasters who are seeking the correct Plainsong settings for the "propers" of our Church Year.

Unfortunately we have no Lutheran material in print, at present writing. But many people are not aware that the same traditional melodies are to be found in Anglican and Roman Catholic publications. The Easter antiphon, *Vidi Aquam*, is sung to precisely the same melody in the Anglican and Roman Catholic churches, that we use. The same is true of the Easter Introit, *Resurrexi, et adhuc*, and the Easter Gradual, *Haec dies*. The new edition of the Roman Catholic *Liber Usualis*, a book of over 1,600 pages, contains the music and words, but in the Latin language. Antiphons, Introits, Gospels, Epistles, Graduals, Offertories, etc., are listed under each Sunday of the Church Year. For those who would make a critical study of the subject, and comparisons, this book is of value. It sells for but $2.25, and any church supply house can get it. The new, Solesmes edition is the best, by far, for it contains the best musical text.

With rare exceptions, the Antiphons, Introits, Collects, Gospels, Epistles, Graduals, etc., of the Anglican church are identical to our own, and the advantage is that the Anglicans publish all these in the English language.

A large number of our own congregations, as well as those of the U. L. C., the A. L. C., and other church bodies, have been using certain Lutheran publications containing modern musical settings to the Introits. These are sung in place of the old-time anthem. The idea has decided advantages, for it maintains the unity of thought for the day. We were rather startled to read in a local paper that a congregation injected Schumann's "Traumerei," and Rachmaninoff's "Prelude" into their Easter service, and that numerous anthems were sung that had no possible connection with Easter. To sing the Introit instead of a more or less unrelated anthem is a big step in the right direction. And yet there are some of our clergy and choirmasters who prefer the

Plainsong settings to the Introits and Graduals. They say that it takes considerable time and labor to teach a choir a new Introit and a new Gradual every Sunday, in four-part harmony. Where one has a fine choir of 160 trained singers, as Teacher Arkebauer has at Zion's, Akron, the task is not so difficult. But some of our organists and choirmasters desire something a little simpler.

The easiest way is to sing the Introits and the Graduals to the Gregorian Psalm Tones. These may be adapted quickly to the text, and an average choir of volunteer singers will grasp the thing with little difficulty. A better way is to provide oneself with the historic melodies to the Introits and Graduals. For those who have trouble in finding suitable material in print, permit us to call attention to the Plainsong publications of several overseas sources.

The Plainsong and Mediaeval Music Society is an important organization, and they issue a great deal of inexpensive Gregorian material. Inquiries may be directed to the Hon. Secretary, the Rev. Dom. Anselm Hughes, O.S.B., Nashdom Abbey, Burnham, Bucks. Membership in this musical society is but two shillings sixpence per annum for clergymen and organists. This society, which is Anglican, publishes the Versicles and Responses for the Church Year, at twopence per copy, and 1s/8d per dozen, or say 40 cents per dozen in our money. They publish the Gregorian Psalm Tones, with organ accompaniment, at 2s/6d per copy, or about 62 cents in our money. They list the proper Antiphons to the Psalms at 2s/6d, the Great Advent Antiphons at sixpence each and the Litany and Suffrages at sixpence per copy. The Anglican Litany differs somewhat from ours, and adaptations must be made. They list the Paschal Anthems ("Christ our Passover is Sacrificed for Us,") at twopence each, the Te Deum of St. Ambrose at twopence, the Salve Regina at twopence and the Salve Rex at fourpence. They publish a book, "Plainsong Hymn Melodies and Sequences" at 3s/6d, or about 86 cents. This contains the Sequence Hymns which the choir may sing after the Hallelujah. These are appropriate to the season of the Church Year. They publish a booklet of fourteen fauxbourdon arrangements to the Magnificat, in four to six parts, at 2s/, or 50 cents, and eight settings for male choirs at one shilling each, or 25 cents. They list the Laudes in Die Paschae at sixpence. The last named is in Latin, and the others in English.

Another publishing house is connected with St. Mary's Convent, Wantage, also of the Anglican church. They publish the Psalms and Canticles, pointed to the Eight Gregorian Psalm Tones, at 4s/9d, or $1.18. However, the text is English Prayer Book arrangement, I believe, and not the King James translation. Frequent adaptations would have to be made. Among a number of other publications we might mention at random the Antiphons for the Magnificat and Nunc Dimittis, the Great Advent Antiphons, the Order of Compline (a beautiful evening service used now and then in several of our own churches), Tenebrae, a special Good Friday service, a complete set of Introits for all Sundays and Festivals, a book of Graduals, Alleluias and Tracts for the entire Church Year, a service for Ash Wednesday, the Good Friday Reproaches, a service for the Burial of the Dead and the Subvenite. These publications cost from fourpence to 3s/6d each. The Psalter is 4s/9d, or about $1.18.

Nashdom Abbey, Burnham, Bucks., publishes two Plainsong settings to the Communion Service, including Kyrie, Gloria in Excelsis, Credo, Sanctus and Agnus Dei, with the shorter responses, at sixpence each. They list the Rex Splendens setting at fivepence, a Simple Plainsong Communion Service at the same price, a 7th century setting of the Nicene Creed at twopence each, and one shilling for the organ accompaniment. They publish the Asperges Me, a portion of Psalm 51 traditionally used at the Confessional Service, at twopence each, the Good Friday Reproaches at threepence, and a list of eighteen Sequences for Advent, Christmas, Epiphany, Easter, Ascension, Pentecost, etc. at twopence and threepence each.

The Faith Press, Ltd., 22 Buckingham St., Charing Cross, W.C. 2, London, lists a Psalter and Canticles at 2s/6d, a Plainsong Evening Psalter and Canticles at 3s/, a Simple Psalter and Can-

PLEASE TURN TO PAGE 326

What Shall I Play Sunday?

WALTER WISMAR

MUSIC plays an important role in our Lutheran churches. In many, perhaps in most of them, the organ sounds the first and the last note. More and more we hear of choirs who not only sing on festival days and special occasions, but who contribute their song or anthem regularly every Sunday. We also hear that many of these choirs are vested, perhaps this is another good argument in favor of vestments. If it will be a help in making choir members prompt and regular, let them wear vestments. It is all well and good to oppose changes, but he who never organized a volunteer choir and tried to keep it going and growing and improving does not appreciate the difficulties of the task. The participation of the congregation is in most cases a singing participation, unless the Creed is spoken or a Psalm is read responsively. Three to four hymns are sung by the congregation. In many churches the pastor is the only one whose speaking voice is heard during the service, but the participation of organist and choir is a musical one, and in most cases the congregation's share too is largely or entirely a musical one.

Since the organist is the first to appear on the musical program of the service, we shall at this time consider one phase of his important work, the choice of a prelude.

The organist is a church organist, not a concert or concertizing organist, which means that the service is not the time nor the place to show off the organ or the technical skill and brilliancy of the organist. Certainly the church organist should have a good technic, but during the service his skill should not be pushed into the foreground, but rather be relegated to the background. At the same time an ambitious organist should be considered a boon to the congregation. The pastor, the committees, the congregation, should encourage, not discourage, him to give concerts at regular intervals, and not only give their moral support. On the day of the concert the church members should put in their appearance, and they should invite and bring friends and neighbors. The organist has given much of his time to prepare for the concert, may have had many small or large expenses, or both. We hope the congregation will show its appreciation in a remunerative way.

The service is not the time nor the place to concertize. The congregation comes to church to pray, to sing, to meditate, and to hear the Word of God. So does the organist! If he does he will approach his organ and organ work in an entirely different spirit than if he does not come to church to worship.

The numbers of the organist are solo numbers. He plays them alone, he interprets them. Yet they ought not to be considered as solo numbers (nor should the organist consider himself a soloist in the service), rather as parts, more or less important of the whole service. Perhaps it will be well for the organist to consider his numbers of lesser importance.

His first prelude is the introductory number to the service. He should have considered a day or two or three earlier the subject of the sermon, the epistle and gospel lessons, and the hymns. The conscientious church organist often devotes more time searching for fitting and appropriate numbers than for actual practice. What shall the prelude be for the opening hymn or to any hymn, for that matter?

We believe it will be a good rule for a church organist to adopt, to try to select preludes that have a direct bearing on the hymn. It is not possible to find a prelude of this nature for every hymn or choral. Again, for some hymns the number of preludes is rather limited. It is also true that there are many more preludes in existence for the German choral than for the English and American hymn tunes, so we find that there will be many occasions when one is forced to make an exception to the rule. We must always bear in mind that our organist is a church organist that he should put the congregation in mood to sing sacred melodies and to listen undistractedly later to the preaching of the word, that he should ever and always remind his hearers that they are in the House of God, to which they have come to sing and pray and worship.

In secular music, in opera or oratorio, that overture or introduction receives high praise that will put the audience in the proper mood and prepare it for what is about to follow, so the main themes of this or that solo or chorus are injected into the overture, sometimes only "mentioned" or sometimes developed at length. We are thoroughly convinced that the preludes which introduce the melody of the hymn, in toto or in part, will serve as the best introduction for each and every member of the church, musically educated or uneducated. If an organist makes it his rule to play choral or hymn-tune preludes he will have a guiding star for his church work.

Why don't we hear preludes of this nature more frequently? As already intimated, it means a long, careful search of programs, catalogs, and music stores to collect such a library. (It may be well for the organist to index his music, state key, time and signature, number of pages, nature of the composition and where it is found, in what collection, who publishes it, etc. Then, too, these selections are not easy to play, though they may appear so and sound so. The organist must practice and study such music assiduously and plan to prepare the registration carefully. Other compositions are often much easier and more attractive; they will sooner win the admiration of the members and earn a compliment or two. It is not the object nor the duty of the organist to tickle the ears of his audience. He should not cater to the popular in music. Even though it is good and legitimate concert music, it is often secular music and so the effect might be just the opposite from what the church organist intended and he may awaken wordly thoughts and emotions. The hymns and the sermon point to God and heaven, likewise should the organ music. A difficult task, a high ideal, but—why are you a church organist?

The congregation should be willing to supply the organist with the proper music, to pay for the library of organ music, to be, of course, the property of the congregation. It should certainly purchase only church music, naturally! Here again one may have a guide. The music founded and grounded on our hymns and chorals may certainly be counted upon to be more appropriate church music than any other kind.

We believe this is a simple and effective way to develop a taste for church music. The taste may or may not be there, but it must be formed and developed. By and by the organist will learn what is good, appropriate churchly music, what not to select and reject. This cannot be learned overnight. The old organists during and after Luther's time must have worked along these lines, also Bach, whose choral preludes are admired and played by the best organists to this day, even in concert.

Personally we like to term these preludes characteristic preludes, because we are firmly convinced that they help to make our services and music characteristic, characteristically churchly. In adopting the rule mentioned above, one is not following the line of least resistance, it is by no means an easy task. It means searching, practicing, studying, experimenting with the organ and its stops, indexing, compiling! The labor will bring its reward. In the end one will be a better church organist, deserving of the title, respected by colleagues and an honor to the profession.

Psalm Singing

THE Lutheran Church is called the singing church. Not only did she give the world an enormous number of chorales (some place the number at 10,000), but she preserved for all others a most complete liturgy. One smiles at the fuss that some writers in current musical journals are making over the full choral Eucharist. These writers overlook the fact that we have an order of service that, when given in its full form known as the Common Service, is choral throughout, and more complete than any other post-Reformation liturgy. It was the intention of those who compiled our liturgy in the sixteenth century that it should be fully choral, both pastor and congregation singing their parts. Where there is a good-sized, resonant church, this ought to be carried out.

After a period of liturgical mutilation, this old, historic Lutheran liturgy is coming into her own once more. Even in *Gloria in Excelsis*, once omitted for no reason other than liturgical laziness, is used today by most of our congregations.

And yet there is one thing upon which most Lutheran congregations are lame. That is the proper chanting of the Psalms and Canticles. The Psalms are hymns of praise. David and his people sang them, and did not read them responsively. They were sung by our Lord and His apostles. They were sung by the Early Church, and are sung throughout Europe to this day. It is as liturgically absurd to read a Psalm responsively as it might be to read a hymn responsively. The Psalms and the Canticles are hymns, and are the only verbally inspired hymns that we have. Then, why in the name of all good sense do we read them? Why not sing them, regardless of what our Puritan neighbors might say?

It is argued by some that the early Lutheran fathers did not provide musical settings for the Psalms and Canticles. It is said that the chanting of Psalms originated in the Church of England in the 17th and 18th century. These things are not true at all. Our Lutheran fathers had the eight Gregorian tones and the Tonus Peregrinus, to which Psalms had been sung from early times. Why go to the task of composing and teaching the people new musical settings? In the days of Rationalism, a century or so ago, many excellent things were lost to the Lutheran Church, either temporarily or permanently. In England, the singing of the Psalms and Canticles died out. In the 17th, 18th and 19th century the old custom was slowly revived, and many new settings were composed, now known as Anglican Chants. Some were single chants, others double, and occasionally there were triple ones. It is these that one finds today in such books as "The Cathedral Psalter," "The Parish Psalter," "The New Cathedral Psalter," etc.

The Psalms and Canticles ought properly to be sung to one of the eight or nine Plain Chant (Gregorian) settings. And yet there is no harm in learning some of the more familiar Anglican Psalm-tones. Nine tenths of our English hymn tunes come from Anglican or Scottish sources. If we borrow Anglican hymn tunes, why balk at borrowing an Anglican chant? The Anglicans borrowed their liturgies from us centuries ago, and many Anglican organists rejoice when they can teach their congregations to sing one of our majestic chorales. No one religious group gave the world everything.

We ought to teach our choirs one new Psalm-tune a month, and an occasional new setting to one of the Canticles. These could be used at Matins, Vespers in the Sunday-school, at funerals, or wherever the rubrics call for a Psalm. If at all possible, one of the ancient Plain Chant settings should be used. It is likewise proper to learn some of the chants originating in England but now known and used throughout the world. A copy of "The Cathedral Psalter" (H. W. Gray Co.), is inexpensive. We may begin with a simple single chant, such as

Battishill, Goodson or Reinagle, and continue with double chants, such as Crotch, Garrett, Boyce, S. S. Wesley, and others.

In learning a chant, omit the words entirely until the melody is thoroughly learned. Sing it on "la" at first. Then sing it to the words "One, two, three, four. One, two, three, four, five, six," etc., gradually prolonging the reciting note. This is one of the best methods for learning a chant quickly.

In fitting the words to the music, remember that in a chant the words, not the value of the notes, govern the tempo. A chant must be sung precisely as it would be read, with the same stresses as in good reading. The reciting note must not be hurried. Above all things, the pointing must be right. Much of the old-time pointing is very bad, and this is why Psalm chanting was formerly unpopular. Nobody likes to sing such nonsense as: "Gawbemercifulunto US AND blessus, ncausehis FACE TO shineuponus." This is exactly what happens when reciting notes are rushed, and when arbitrary stresses are put upon syllables. Giving each syllable the same value as in good reading, and stressing our chanting exactly as we would stress good reading, will avoid these common faults.

One of the worst mistakes in chanting is the common one of producing a double stress at the end of a line, commonly called the Anglican thump. Dean Lutkin coined that term years ago. The Anglican thump is produced when one sings the last two syllables of a line to a single note. In countless Lutheran churches one hears this musical barbarism: "As it was in the beginning—is now—and ev-ver-rr shall be." The word "ever" is slurred over two or three notes, and the "shall be" sung to a single, concluding note. With proper pointing it is sung thus: "As it was in the beginning, is now, and—ever—shall—be," the last three words each getting a different note. Chants should be avoided if the line finishes with two repeated notes of the same pitch.

Sit down at your piano and learn thoroughly a good Psalm setting. Then point the words properly, and learn to sing the Psalm with animation. After learning it thoroughly, teach it to your choir. If you have never learned to sing a Psalm, a new thrill awaits you.
—*Lutheran Church Art.*

Junior Choirs

By Gunnar J. Malmin

A CHILDREN'S CHOIR, or, as it is more frequently called, a Junior Choir, is a real asset to any church, and one which lies within the reach of almost any church that wants it. The chief requisite is children, and what church does not have children! There will be no lack of interest on their part in such an enterprise, if it is at all properly handled. They will take a real pride in the work of their organization, and, what is more important, they will thus be brought into active participation in the work of the church from their earliest youth.

Of course, there must be a leader. He must have a fairly good ear for music, combined with some knowledge of the art, but need not be a conservatory graduate or anything of the kind. He must know a few simple facts about children's voices, but such knowledge is not difficult to get. The marvellous field of public school music is the best source of information. A prospective Junior Choir leader is urged to read Gidding's "Grade School Music Teaching," for example, or Gehrken's "An Introduction to School Music." In addition, it is well to observe a competent music supervisor at work, and to hear the children singing under such direction. Some of the methods there used may well be carried over into the Junior Choir rehearsal. A congregation may consider itself fortunate, indeed, if its children are under the instruction of a competent music teacher in the public schools. In such a church it should be a relatively simple matter to build up a children's choir, and an orchestra, too, if such an organization is desired. Furthermore, the adult choir, as well as congregational singing itself, will soon benefit by it to no small a degree. All honor to the public school music supervisor! Let us give him every encouragement possible in his noble work.

Without going too deeply into technicalities it will perhaps be well to give a few specific suggestions for the benefit of those who already have a Junior Choir or are considering one. A Junior choir is generally made up of children from six to fourteen. A fairly large group is desirable—forty or sixty, or even a hundred in large congregations. No changed voices will be used. Children below the third grade have little or no reading knowledge of music, but they will easily learn their part from hearing the older children sing it. Children below the fifth grade should all sing 1st soprano. From the fifth grade and up, they should be tested and classified into 1st and 2nd soprano and 1st and 2nd alto. Four-part singing, however, is not advisable. In two-part singing, all the sopranos will sing together on the soprano part and the altos on the alto part. In three-part singing, the lowest of the 1st altos will sing with the lowest part, and the highest of the 2nd sopranos with the melody, while the remaining 2nd sopranos and 1st altos will sing the middle part. In order to get the proper balance, there will have to be more 1st sopranos than any other part, especially if very small children are included.

It is important that the children sing softly and lightly. Tell them their singing should be like ivory soap: it should *float*. But soft singing does not mean that they are to *mumble*, warn them against lazy lips. Tell them that you want to *see* them sing. Soft singing does not mean lazy singing. They must concentrate. They must sit up straight with both feet on the floor, and they should frequently stand while singing. Soft singing does not mean *dead* singing. The voices are flexible, and the director should insist on good crescendos and decrescendos and whatever other contrasts and expression the music calls for—always bearing in mind that a fortissimo does not mean a lot of loud, noisy singing. Some adults, who are accustomed to hearing the children shout forth some favorite hymn in Sunday School may be surprised to hear that that is not the correct way for children to hear at all. It not only sounds bad but it may actually injure the voices. Tell the children to sing with their hearts, not just with their lungs. The fact that they will shout a song does not necessarily mean that they are singing from the heart.

It is necessary from the very beginning to insist that the children not only watch the director but respond instantly to his directions. Insist that they all start together, and that they do not drop a final note until the director gives the signal. In rehearsal it is well to stop the baton occasionally in the middle of the phrase as a signal for the children to hold that note as long as the director desires. If they get out of breath and stop, ask them what they're going to do about it, and someone will surely answer, "Take another breath!" Vary the speed of the song frequently, even in an exaggerated way, so that the children will never take you for granted. Keep them alert by doing the unexpected. They will enjoy that, and you will all have a good laugh once in a while when you do catch them sleeping. Above all, strive for smooth sustained tone all the time. That is the only way to get beautiful part-singing.

Securing the right kind of music is somewhat of a problem. Music written for women's voices may be used, provided the alto part does not go below *a* or an occasional *g*, and the soprano part not above *g*. It is well to warn against the use of cheap, tawdry music, which too often makes up the bulk of the Junior Choir repertoire. We must be careful to distinguish between that which is truly childlike and that which is merely childish and cheap. For the first rehearsal or two, any good hymnal furnishes considerable material. Select hymns whose soprano and alto parts give an easy, pleasing harmony. Such hymns as "Savior, Like A Tender Shepherd Lead Us," "Jesus Loves Me," and "Just As I Am," while not musically all that might be desired, are easy songs for starting the Junior Choir. Have them hum one stanza, with a group of younger children singing the words. Try singing the hymn without piano accompaniment, striving for a smooth, sustained, well-balanced harmony. Singing a fine old Lutheran chorale in unison is very effective, and is certainly educating the children along the right lines. Responsive singing between the children and the adult choir is interesting. Select a song on the type of "Praise Ye" by Palmer (St. Olaf Choir Series) and have the children sing the duet parts alone, with the adults coming in on the four-part harmonies. The same effect

may be obtained with an anthem having a simple solo part. And why not plan a Christmas program in which solos, numbers by the children and by the adult choir, together with the familiar Christmas hymns sung by choirs and audience, present the familiar Christmas story? Surely such a "home-made" Cantata will be much finer and much more impressive than the general run of Christmas Cantatas.—*The Ansgar Lutheran*.

The Junior Choir

THE ideal is the 'Boys' Choir. Lochner, in his Hauptgottes-dienst, advocates it. He seems to be in favor even of salary-ing the boys in a modest way.

But some of us that don't know so much about voice-culture find it difficult to train the boys. Our problem begins even before this—we find it hard to get the boys, and—to control them. Over it all hovers the shadow—"How soon will the voice break?"

The next best thing is a Junior Choir composed of a few boys and a lot of girls, girls ranging in age from six to sixteen. It is surprising what satisfying work they can do. Perhaps their work will not be wholly satisfying to a musical critic, but it certainly is to the congregation.

This was a revelation to me. When I organized the choir a year ago, I said to myself, "We won't be able to render anything ambitious. I must keep out of mind the beautiful works rendered by the boys in St. John the Divine and Grace Church on Broadway as also by our children's choir in Cincinnati. No, just a few chorales and sacred songs, and later on, perhaps, we might branch out and do some two-part singing."

I had the choir sing each Sunday. Each Sunday I was in an apologetic frame of mind. I was ready to say to the congregation, "I hope you will bear with the youngsters. They are just start-ing out, you know. What they have to offer is simple enough, but for the time being try to be content therewith."

After a month I was aghast. The congregation had been thrilled, enraptured, edified. I could hardly believe it. Yet it was so.

I wish some one had told me a few years ago that it is mighty easy to organize a choir, and secondly that it is mighty easy to satisfy the members of the church. In other words, the members will be content, aye, regaled, even if the children sing only the melody,—provided of course that the melody is sung properly. If some one had told me this before, I should long ago have started a Junior Choir. I pass my findings on for some other timid, hesitant soul, some other music-lover who has not advanced beyond the chorale-playing stage.

Some of the readers may welcome a list of the hymns and songs that we have used, or intend using. They are to be found in the G.—Green Book, i.e., the regular C.P.H. church-hymnal with tunes; S.S.—Sunday School Hymnal, also of Concordia Publishing House, St. Louis; S.—Selah Song Book, published by Sotarion Publishing House, Buffalo; S.&H.—Select Songs for School and Home, J. A. Theiss and B. Schumacher, C.P.H.; P.S.—The Par-ish School Hymnal, The Board of Publication of the United Lutheran Church in America.

Advent

G. 131—Jesus came, the heav'ns adoring
G. 133—Hark, a thrilling voice. On 1st S. in Advent after Epistle
G. 549—Wake, awake
G. 551—That day of wrath. 2nd S. in Advent
G. 143—Once he came in blessing
P.S. 1—O come, O come, Immanuel   Ancient Plain Song
P.S. 2—Come, thou long-expected Jesus
P.S. 12—Watchman, tell us (Sung antiphonally)
S.&H. 2—On Jordan's banks. 4th S. in Advent

Christmas

G. 156—We Christians may rejoice today
S. 879—Lo, our little hearts rejoicing   Duet
S. 881—Weihnachten ist da
P.S. 30—God rest you merry, gentlemen
P.S. 35—The first Noel
P.S. 34—Good Christian men, rejoice
P.S. 18—The new-born King
P.S. 24—While shepherds watched
P.S. 42—Carol, sweetly carol
S.&H. 8—Joy to the world   Duet
S.&H. 11—Happy Christmas, for all children   Duet
S. &H. 12—We hail thee with rejoicing
S.&H. 16—Where are you going, children dear?
S.&H. 26—Beside thy manger here I stand   Trio

New Year's Day

G. 172—O God, our Help in ages past
S. 32—With the Lord all things begin
G. 569—I will lift up mine eyes   Chant

Epiphany

P.S. 53—We three Kings of Orient are.
Any of the Christmas hymns

Lent

G. 574—De Perfundis.   Chant for Ash-Wednesday
G. 191—A Lamb goes uncomplaining forth
G. 194—Jesus, grant that balm and healing
G. 198—Beloved Jesus
G. 205—See, world, thy life assailed
G. 82—Jesus, priceless Treasure
G. 87—I leave thee not
G. 416—Lord, to Thee I make confession   Ash-Wednesday
G. 418—With broken heart
P.S. 58—Hail, thou once despised Jesus
P.S. 64—O Lamb of God, still keep me
P.S. 65—Jesus, meek and lowly
P.S. 80—Into the woods my Master went
        (After the reading of Gethsemane lesson)
S.&H. 39—Saviour, Thy dying love
S.&H. 118—The Lamb of Calvary   Trio
S. 361—Mein Heiland nimmt die Suender an
S. 366—Ask ye what great thing I know
S. 411—O, do you hear the Saviour calling
P.S. 69—Jesus, keep me near the cross
S. 43—Kyrie   Spangenberg
S. 413—He, who on the cross did love me
S. 440—O Lamm Gottes   (To be sung in German)
G. 422 and 423—And wilt thou pardon. Out of the deep

Good Friday

G. 215—O darkest woe
G.—Lord Jesus, No. 217

Easter

S. 477—Christ is arisen   Sacred Folksong, XIII. Century
P.S. 83—Christ, the Lord is risen   Medieval Sequence
P.S. 84—Jesus Christ is risen today   Lyra Davidica
P.S. 81—The Day of Resurrection   No. 81
S.&H. 110—There is a tender Shepherd.

        For 2nd S. after Easter

S.&H. 46—We will carol joyfully
S. 480—I say to all men
S. 487—Christ is risen   (Antiphonally)
G. 226—I am content

Ascension

P.S. 97—See the conqueror mounts
G. 238—Hark, ten thousand harps
G. 556—Jerusalem the golden
S.&H. 50—Come, wave your palms

Pentecost

G. 249—Come, God Creator   Veni Creator
G. 257—Veni Sante Spiritus
G. 250—Spirit of mercy — To be sung according to the Tallis' Canon, G. 36 B. Note: The choir is divided into two parts, the first part begins, singing "Spirit of mer-" At this point the second group starts in, singing "Spirit of etc.." In other words, the second group sets in on the second G. note.

Trinity

G. 571—Te Deum
S.&H. 243—Glory   Duet
P.S. 110—Hail! Holy, Holy, Holy Lord   Ancient Welsh Melody
S. 55—German Sanctus
S. 614—Holy is the Lord
G. 271—God the Father, be our Stay
G. 394—The Creed
S.S. 347—The Lord's Prayer

Thus far for this time. If any of the readers believe that a continuance of the list would prove helpful, will you kindly communicate with the A.L.P.B. office. Also state whether you would appreciate a list of chants, the music for the eight or nine Gregorian Tunes, and other liturgical matter which will do much to elevate the service, particularly for those of a traditional bent of mind.

Training The Junior Choir

"WHAT MUSIC SHALL WE USE?" This question comes to my desk regularly for with the steady rise in popularity of the Junior Choir, the problem of what to sing is important. It is to be regretted however, that the writers rarely ask for worship materials. The great demand seems to be for anthems, a sort of piece de resistance as it were.

Yes, an anthem is good and rather desirable. The choristers like it; the congregation expects it; and through its use the director has an opportunity to develop real artistry in tone, interpretation, light and shade. The anthem accentuates the topic, clinches the sermon, and makes for a climatic effect.

But after all, the real music to teach our children is the service-music itself; hymns, chorales, with a variety of effects through the use of descants; the choral responses, the Gloria Patri, the Gloria in Excelsis, the Doxology. Every Junior Choir should be taught to chant well, for chanting betters the diction, and leads to a broader style of Church music.

Let the singing of the children be in unison for a year. In no other way will it be possible to develop a beautiful tone and a fine ensemble, for the most important matter at the start with the young choristers, will be their quality of voice. Is the singing easy to listen to, and is it easy to do? It will be impossible to have one without the other.

Perhaps you are saying that part-singing is necessary. Rather, is it not necessary to the musician who does the training? Of course he or she feels the need of vocal harmony, and it is possible; but in introducing part-music too early, one runs the risk of forcing the tone and undoing all the effort expended in the production of a beautiful quality.

Of course the children will love part-singing, even the lazy ones if they are at all musical. Their parents will also enjoy it for it stimulates their pride to observe the accomplishments of their children. But even so, part-singing is a dangerous undertaking for the beginning choir, and the results will eventually be far better with steadfast work on unison songs. Here one should seek for a tone that floats, and a perfect blend, until the unison anthem sounds as if sung by one lovely voice.

After six months' strict adherence to unison singing, the plan might be changed with the use of a descant. And here avoid any shouting, for the children so enjoy their lusty fashion of singing, and will revert to it at once in their eagerness to keep their "part." And while descant singing is delightful, give the choristers but a taste of it, only enough to lure them to stay in the choir in anticipation of future part-singing in their second year.

Meanwhile the choristers are growing in musical and vocal ability. The second year the introduction of anthems written for first and second soprano will be free from danger. The following year alto singing will be safe, and two-part singing (soprano and alto) will be possible for all the hymns. Later the boy with a changing voice will emerge, and when he arrives the most difficult problem of the Junior Choir is to be met. However, this problem has been met and overcome, so it is not an impossible situation. And it more than justifies every effort expended.

The aim of all Junior Choir training should be an increasing power and a steady development. Only in this way will it be possible to interest and hold the children. Above all avoid music or training that is purile. Try to give the young choristers as wide a view as practicable, and build such foundations that the coming musicians of the Church will truly "worship God in spirit and in truth."—*The New Music Review*

The Vested Choir

FRED H. LINDEMANN

VESTED choirs are on the increase in Lutheran circles. During the past two years at least twelve have come into existence in our own city. From Kentucky comes the word: "We have had a vested choir for a number of years." We find them all over the country in ever increasing number. Some of us do not like this fact, but it remains. Some of us protest against it with every ounce of energy at our command, but the vested choirs keep on increasing. Some think they know good reasons why a choir should not wear a distinctive garb, others believe that there are ample reasons for introducing and maintaining such a thing. The most of us know very little about it, the remainder even less. And the difficult thing is to find some worthwhile information which will be of service to a man interested in the Lutheran angle of the question. Vested choirs are said to be a new thing in America, if a thing introduced about fifty years ago can be called a new thing. Much of what is written does not apply to a Lutheran choir as it is constituted today. Yet everybody seems to go ahead in his own way. When one asks a pastor or choirmaster why and wherefore this or that is done, which happens to be peculiar to that choir, the only reason given is that it was copied from some other choir, introduced because it struck him as impressive, or that it was the creation of his own imaginative mind with no particular meaning attached to it. Things are done because the person responsible "likes" them or for no reason at all. And everybody seems to be doing them differently.

Perhaps a discussion of this subject would not be unwelcome. The esteemed editor of the American Lutheran was positive on this point. Will the reader kindly bear in mind that this is to be a discussion of the problem and not a dispensation of authoritative information. We hope that it will inaugurate a more or less general discussion in the columns of this magazine, that men and women who have some definite information in this matter will come forward. We agreed after some urging to start the ball rolling by setting up a row of wooden Indians and inviting everybody to take a shot and knock them down. This knocking down of wooden Indians set up by another is fascinating sport, and we hope to tempt others to come forward with information and suggestions which they have been hiding under the bushel. And when the smoke of battle has cleared, all of us will have learned something. This paragraph seems to contain a mixed metaphor or two, but let it stand. It is no more muddled that the general conception of the vested choir and so symbolizes a state of mind.

In the ancient church everybody wore the tunica, the common dress of the day. All who took part in the public service, bishops, presbyters, deacons, wore white, as this was the festive color. When the style of dress changed it was felt that the bishop should not follow this change and celebrate the Eucharist in the same clothes he wore in private. It was not sacerdotalism but the consideration of what was fitting which led to the introduction of a distinctive garment for the officiating bishop. More or less naturally the same argument applied to all who rendered official service in the congregation. There are very early traces of deacons and altar boys wearing the surplice.

The choir was originally composed of the minor clergy, who were vested. It is said that before the Reformation the opening part of our Common Service was chanted in the sacristy while the officiating priest donned his vestments. It was meant as a preparation for him alone. During the Introitus he was led into the church and to the entrance of the sanctuary. This was changed for reasons quite evident, and this preparatory part now finds itself in the church proper and serves to prepare both pastor and congregation. Incidentally it might be mentioned that since it is still to prepare also the pastor he ought not to enter the sanctuary before the Introit. He ought not to say or chant this first part of the service from the altar or from behind the Communion rail but take his position outside of the rail in some other part of the chancel. The time to enter the sanctuary and approach the altar would be while the choir sings the Introit.

So the choir was vested in the ancient Church. The reason was that they were part of the clergy. We take it as the Lutheran principle that the choir is part of the congregation. This point could be successfully challenged if the choir were composed solely of men, for all men were vested in the old days if they appeared in an official capacity during the service and performed some task before the congregation. But our choirs are usually mixed, and no one would argue that a woman should be considered part of the clergy or perform official service in the assembled congregation. It would seem that liturgically a woman cannot be vested on the grounds stated. You may vest the boys, the deacons, the organist, the sexton and janitor, the male choir. All have had their vestments in the Lutheran Church. But is there a precedent for vesting a woman?

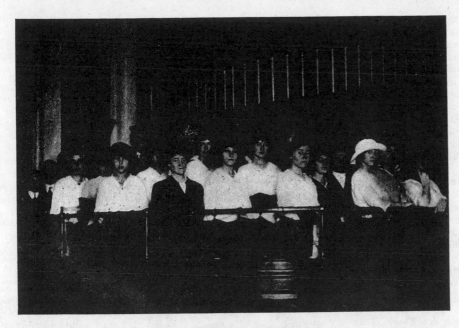

A CHOIR BEFORE ADOPTING ROBES

Having gone so far, we must take the next step and say that mixed choirs would seem to be unliturgical. And yet we have them. If then we are unliturgical enough to have women in the choir what is to prevent us from taking the next step and vesting them? It appears to be the tendency to take the choir out of the narthex balcony and to place it somewhere near the chancel or in the chancel. If that is done and the choir is in full view of the congregation the garb should be uniform. It is annoying and disturbing to have hats and dresses and suits and ties of every shape and color represented. There might even be an apparent effort on the part of one or the other to impress the congregation with a new dress every Sunday of the year. A garb common to all makes any display impossible.

So far we follow. Personally we are willing to violate our liturgical feelings and outrage our sensibilities to the extent of placing the choir somewhere in the east portion of the church and of vesting it. But when it comes to placing a woman in the chancel, that is where we draw the line. It may be only the foolish trick of a liturgical conscience which has already been reduced to a formless, bleeding mass by admitting the possibility of vesting a mixed choir, a conscience which no longer can function properly. But we feel that some other place should be provided. Not in a transept but perhaps to the side of the chancel.

Now that we have yielded to the corrupting influence, stalking through the Church unashamed, to this extent, let us consider what would be a proper vestment for a mixed choir. We put this question to a man who is considered one of the leading authorities in

this country and with a profound contempt he suggested a blue bungalow apron, red silk dusting cap and a rolling pin. This was to convey the idea that there were no rules or regulations, that so far as church usage is concerned everything is permissible and the sky is the limit. That is going too far, however. There are certain fundamental principles which apply also to a mixed choir, even though it is an abomination to the high and mighty authorities.

One fundamental, ancient principle would eliminate an entirely black vestment. At no time did the Christian Church vest in black until Zwingli and Calvin went off on a tangent and a Prussian king compelled the church of Germany to adopt the color of ravens. Let us start right in this respect. That is easier than to correct a mistake after our people have grown accustomed to the wrong thing and get the idea that the wrong thing is "Lutheran." If the choir is to sing the glorious and joyous truths of God's glad tidings into the hearts of men, why in all the world should they appear in depressing, doleful dress? So while the cassock may but need not be black, the cotta or surplice should cover the dark cassock and this cotta or surplice should be white, the festive, cheerful, joyous white. In those Lutheran churches which trace their origin back to Germany and still insist that the clergy appear in the black Geneva gown, the pastor will find himself at a disadvantage if the choir is vested properly. They will seem more important than he. Everybody will instinctively feel that he suffers by comparison while he is in truth the main personage as the messenger of the Word, the mouthpiece of God Almighty. The remedy is simple. Let

THE SAME CHOIR VESTED

Cuts furnished by courtesy of Cox, Sons & Vining

him persuade his congregation to go back to the truly Lutheran vestment and to discard that badge of shameful yielding to Prussian oppression, Calvinistic fury and Rationalism, the Geneva gown.

When choosing the vestment for the choir it ought to be impressed upon the female members that the object is not to make them look "cute," or ridiculous. They are not to insist upon the silly "Buster Brown" collar and tie which was designed for little boys. A "V" shaped neck on the cassock, set off by a soft white collar seems most appropriate and practical. The men ought not be permited to wear soft collars, for these are still considered "undress" and give an indifferent appearance. Shoes should of course be black. Many people feel that the female members of the choir ought to wear a cap. But if this is insisted upon because St. Paul once said something about a woman not uncovering, it would be well to read that passage of his letter very carefully and see whether he spoke of hats and headcoverings or whether he had in mind the veil worn over the face at that time by all women who wished to be considered ladies. If our memory serves us right there was a time when style decreed that the bride's attendents display themselves at church weddings without hats and no wedding was stopped because of this lapse.

And now that we have a vested choir in the east part of the church, what are we going to do with it? There is no reason now why we should not introduce the processional and recessional. Here again things are done fearfully and wonderfully in some of our churches. A little thought would have made many methods impossible. There seems to be but one logical and historical reason for having the choir come and go before the assembled congregation, and that is to lead the messenger of the Word in and out. The processional announces to the congregation that He who is to proclaim to them the Word is approaching and is about to make his entrance. When he enters, the congregation rises. The choir escorts him to the entrance of the chancel. Having fulfilled his office the choir again leads him out. We have been told that in England the choir does not sing at these times. During Lent many choirs in America have the silent processional and recessional, which is very effective. Our hymnal will cause many a sigh where the choir sings while entering and leaving. The processional should be a joyous hymn, set to four-fourths time, for it is to announce to the congregation that once again it is privileged to hear God's saving message of grace and love. The recessional ought to be a hymn of thanksgiving ending an a paeon of exultant praise, and naturally only four-fourths time is appropriate. Some choirmasters insist that the choir take two steps to the measure, one step every two beats. Others pay no attention to time and ask only that the individual pairs keep in step. We profess ignorance as to what is proper and correct.

It is evident then that the pastor should not be at the altar when the choir approaches, for if the choir does not escort him into the chancel there is no earthly reason for a processional. That it "looks nice" is no reason for doing it in the house of God. Neither should the choir disappear through some door during the singing of the Doxology, leaving the pastor in the chancel to pronounce the Benediction. Having escorted him in, they must lead him out. Our order of service correctly prescribes that the Doxology be sung before the Benediction, which may be followed immediately by the recessional. It is idle to argue that our recessional hymns are too short. We have seen a men's choir of 200 voices come down the side aisle of the large St. Thomas Church in New York City and proceed up the center aisle to the chancel. The processional was "The Son of God goes forth to war," and the fourth stanza was begun as the last of the choir approached the chancel. When all were in place the first stanza was repeated. This made interludes necessary, and these were splendidly done by the organist. The

Standard Cassock and Cotta

spirit of the hymn made use of the tuba stop particularly appropriate in mighty calls to battle. The fact that the choir did not sing continuously was not in the least disturbing, on the contrary the martial interludes were very effective.

Another problem confronting the choirmasters of churches not built with the vested choir in view, is the question: From where should the choir make its appearance and where shall it disappear? We have been told that on festivals the choir would enter in front and proceed down a side aisle and up the center aisle. On ordinary days it would enter in front and proceed to the chancel directly without passing through the nave. With most Lutheran choirmasters it is a question of doing the best he can in a church with side aisles too narrow for the choir to pass down. In that case it would seem best to have the choir enter from the narthex on festivals. If there is a convenient door in the east wall of the transept the choir should proceed from here on ordinary days.

Here then are a few things which ought to be considered in connection with the vested choir. Is there some one who has definite information on any of the matters touched upon in these lines and is willing to help us? A frank discussion of the problem can be only helpful and beneficial to everybody.

· · · ⌒ ⁝ ⌒ ~ · · ·

SOME SOURCES
from p 319

ticles at one shilling, and a Choir Missal in two volumes at four shillings. This missal contains twelve different Plainsong settings to the Kyrie, Introit, Gloria, Credo, Sanctus, Agnus Dei, etc. They likewise publish books on The Chorales, The Church Organ, Plainchant, Latin Hymnody, The Priest's Part in the Liturgy and Byzantine Music and Hymnography at 4s/6d each, or say $1.18.

Alexander Moring, Ltd., 10 Clifford St., Bond Street, London, W. 1, publishes "Altar Music," a bound book containing Plainsong music for the clergyman's parts of the liturgy. It sells for 7s/6d, or about $1.86.

These are but a few of many things which may be obtained abroad. For choirmasters who prefer to sing the Introits and Graduals instead of an anthem, here is unlimited material, at low cost. In ordering, it is necessary to enclose an International Money Order, which may be obtained at any local post office as readily as a domestic money order. Firms abroad do not send free samples of music, nor do they, as a rule, send material on credit.

The Choir Institution

F. Melius Christiansen

A CHOIR has a personality of its own particular kind. The character of this personality is formed by its constituency and its object. As a person has a certain spirit and character about him, so has a choir as an institution. Each member is a part of that institution and still the choir itself is far above its membership because of the fact that the object of the choir—that which it aims to do —lies in the world of idealism. The work of the choir is the same as that of the minister—to edify, to instruct, to create atmosphere conducive to worship, to pray, praise and give thanks. On the other hand the strength of character and personality of the choir depends on the character of each member. If the members are superficial and insincere the choir as an institution will be weak in its influence for good; if they are honestly in love with God's Kingdom and in singing of His love and are devoted and loyal to the cause of the choir, the influence of that institution will be strong.

I have seen the change that has taken place of late years in the membership of the choirs and the Choral Union. In former years we could see many more middle aged and elderly people in the choirs. Now they are almost all school children and young people. This is to be regretted. The choir needs the older people to give the institution its proper strength, authority, and weight. A message given by experienced people is of much more value than that given by inexperienced young folks. It is also a fallacy to believe that the voices of young people are better than those of older ones. It has been my experience as director of a school choir that the more mature voices of the upper class people have been of greater value than the voices of the freshmen, not on account of the quality of the voice itself as much as for the reason of a greater personal development. A singer's voice is a reflection of the personal experiences, of the growth and maturity of the individual. A great singer is not so much a great voice as it is a great personality that sings. The greatest singers are around forty-five years old. In the zenith of his physical power and with the greatest power of mind, he can transmit his soul's desire with more force and influence than a younger person. The voice itself is colored by that personal feeling, becomes rich and resonant. This not only because he is a more experienced singer, but also because an older person has more life experiences, more emotional and mental force.

The idea that younger persons do not like the association with older people in the choir is based upon a wrong attitude. The choir is not a social club; it is rather a miniature congregation with the same objects and aspirations as that institution. The rehearsals of the choir are for the purpose of developing its talents in order to sing the praises of God more perfectly than a congregation can do. Members of the choir who have this in mind do not differentiate in the ages of people. They are glad to be given a chance to take part in this fine work and think of the object of the choir as the all-absorbing interest. The choir must be held in respect as an institution to which the members come for instruction and upbuilding of their mental and emotional life. The choir is an educational institution in which the director is the teacher and the members are the scholars. The scholars are of different grades and of different ages, but here they are put in the same class for a special study. Some are slower in learning than others, but they all bear the burden together. Some are older and more experienced and others are younger and lighter in character—they all balance up in one common interest.

It happens often that there are certain pupils who are too little gifted along the line of choir work and hamper the progress of the institution too much. I refer to pupils whose voices are too shrill for blending or whose pitch perception is too dull. In such cases it is up to the teacher to tell them that their gifts are stronger along other lines and that they should try to find their best talents and make use of them for the betterment of themselves and humanity.

The choir as an institution is too significant and important when one considers its real purpose, to be tossed about by the notions of inexperienced youth. The older folks will lend earnestness and dignity to the choir.

As a rule we find the older members too willing to give way to the notions of younger folks. A father who really likes to drive his automobile himself will let his younger son drive because he is afraid to stand in the way of the progress of the coming generation. There is room for both young and old in a choir—they all can drive. The older members will not stand in the way of younger folks. When the main purpose of the choir is held in mind, the smaller matters become very insignificant. Therefore remember the main issue and purpose of the choir and let that be the power that drives the wheel.

Lutheran Church Herald

Headgear for Women

B Y far the great majority of questions submitted to this department during the past month have related to the subject of choirs, choir vestments, church music and church organs. It is impossible to discuss all the questions submitted, or to list the helpful suggestions made. A number of these have been answered by letter, where a self-addressed, stamped envelope has been enclosed, and where time has permitted. Others, of general interest, will be answered in print.

One of the most interesting letters of the month comes from a young lady in Indiana. She says that she is a member of a church choir, and that the singers wear black academic gowns and no caps. The choir is in a west gallery. At Communion the singers must go from the choir loft to the basement, remove their robes, get their hats and wraps, receive the Sacrament, then return to the basement and don their black robes again. She complains that the result is not devotional. She asks whether it might be proper to practice corporate Communion, that is, the singers commune in a group, in their choir vestments. It is an interesting problem.

In the first place, the good folks ought to endeavor to get the correct choir vestments, which are not academic gowns. These ought to be reserved for college people. Church choirs ought to wear black cassocks and white surplices. The men will wear a full length cassock and a white surplice, rather full, and reaching a bit below the knees. The women will wear a skirt cassock designed to slip easily over their ordinary clothing, and falling to the shoe-tops. Over this they will wear the full surplice similar to those worn by the men. The women, moreover, ought to wear either the small, black skull-cap at all times, or else a soft cap with four points—not the stiff mortar-board, which is proper for colleges, but the soft kind sometimes called a Canterbury cap. These caps must be black, never white.

With vestments of this sort, there is no reason why the choir may not commune in their vestments. Since the Scriptures state, I Corinthians 11, that a woman ought to pray with her head covered, and a man with his head uncovered, it is customary for women to wear a hat or head covering of some sort in church. I have seen ushers in European churches remind women of this fact, and request them to keep their hats on. Choir caps are very inexpensive. Mr. Paul Buck, 665 Fifth Avenue, New York, sent a folder a few days ago with illustrations of churchly headgear for choir women. He lists several styles, but the skull cap and the soft black Canterbury cap seem to be the most churchly. Certainly the mortar-board is intended for college choirs only.

The Liturgical Training of the Church Choir

F. R. WEBBER

WHILE, by the grace of God, our branch of the Church has never become sectarianized in doctrinal matters, yet our liturgical practice and our church music suffered sadly. All went rather well until a century or so ago. Then Rationalism and the State-Church abomination in Europe, and a rampant revivalistic movement in America, obliterated many of the old Lutheran liturgical landmarks. The splendid old churches, with their stately ceremonial and their fine music became empty, barren structures. Fine old windows were smashed so as to flood the old churches with light. Liturgical traditions yielded before a Calvinistic influence that had sprung up long before in the south of Germany. The clergy were compelled by strict order to don the Genevan robe and bands. The celebration of Holy Communion was made an appendage at the end of the service. To show contempt for the Sacrament, the people were encouraged to walk out of church after the sermon. Very few remained to receive Holy Communion.

The fine old choirs, with their tremendous libraries of splendid music, gradually disappeared, and what music there was, was furnished by a small band of harsh voiced boys, often from the "ragged schools" nearby. Little effort was made to train them, much less to produce agreeble tone-quality.

Even half a century ago the music in Lutheran countries must have been a terrible thing to people of refined musical taste. Read Dr. J. Spencer Curwen's shocked words in one of his series of books entitled "Studies in Worship Music." The good Doctor found the finest music in the world in Lutheran lands— but the most wretched execution. Things were not much better among the Lutherans in this country some years ago. The musical critic of a large daily, after hearing one of our celebrated Lutheran male choirs wrote, some years ago, "Of noise there was plenty, of music very little," or words to that effect.

Today an astonishing change has taken place, not only in America but in Germany, the mother-country of good church music. After a century of musical barbarism, insofar as the Church is concerned, Germany has returned once more to her old days of glory. Even the great Dr. G. Edward Stubbs, who can see little merit outside his own denomination, devotes much space in the last *New Music Review* to an account of modern church music in Germany, in both Lutheran and State Church circles. Almost overnight Germany has come forth with choirs of men and boys which, a competent musical critic, quoted by Dr. Stubbs, declares may be compared most favorably with the finest Anglican and American male choirs. This was not true even a few years ago. We all have heard most wretched singing in Germany—throaty shouting of boisterous selections that bore but slight relation to a dignified church service. But the musical critic just mentioned finds choirs of men and boys springing up throughout Germany, which not only sing most beautifully from memory and often without organ accompaniment, but which are able to produce clear, beautiful tones, and the most refined sort of shading.

All of this is joy to those of us who have realized that Germany has been in a bad way, artistically, for a long period of years, if not for centuries. The dyed-in-the-wool Germano-American will exclaim, "I always told you so. The critics are only now waking up to the truth that has always existed." Our Anglican neighbors, justly proud of their splendid choirs at the Abbey, St. Paul's, Exeter, Gloucester, York and countless other places, are beginning to write articles expressing astonishment. They have long admitted the high merit of Lutheran music *per se,* and have adopted Bach with undisguised enthusiasm. But to go into artistically crude Germany, and find male choirs springing up, that are even now able to compete with the finest English choirs,

is almost too much for them to realize. Meanwhile a very few of us who can trace a long ancestry to both sides of the Channel, sit back and smile at all the commotion in musical circles. Have a few of us not always said that England and France gave the world the greatest ecclesiastical architecture, and Germany gave us the finest music? And now the descendants of the Lutherans of Germany are insisting upon churches done in the English Gothic manner with French glass, while the descendants of Merbecke, Tallis, Gibbons, Monk and Samuel Sebastian Wesley are waxing enthusiasm over our own Bach, and laboriously teaching their choirs to sing our chorales, and to sing the Psalms to Gregorian Psalm Tones, even as did our fathers on the south side of the North Sea.

Every year sees more interest in choir work in our own land. There was a day when a typical Lutheran choir learned their music by ear, and were content to sing anthems out of a bound book once a month, and a simple *Te Deum* once a year. Today all this is different. Our choirs are taking on a new significance.

There was a brief period of wavering. At the beginning of the transitional period in language, many of our choirmasters imagined that we must, in order to be English, sing the anthems of the Methodists and Baptists. And thus it was that our Lutheran choir lofts were filled with curious village-church collections of music, written last year by some evangelistically inclined organist in Mauch Chunk, Dayton, Newport News or Fargo. Curious things they were, too. We set down a few names, because they represent a definite historic development. There were such titles as "Lord, I'm coming home," "Arise and shine," "Praise ye the Father," "Send out Thy light," "Sweet is Thy Mercy," "Tarry with me," "When we all get to Heaven" and "Jehovah's glorious Name." We refrain from any and all comment, because these things are associated with the tenderest religious experiences of many splendid Christian people. We mention these titles merely to show the trend of modern times.

Today we have all begun to realize that the function of a church choir is not merely to sing an anthem each Sunday, or at less frequent intervals. A choir is an important factor in directing the musical tastes of the entire congregation. They ought to be trained carefully, not only in proper sight reading and in enunciation, but in the principles of church music as well.

If a church has a choirmaster of churchly tastes it possesses a rare treasure, and ought not to begrudge an ample remuneration for his time and labor. But since a Lutheran choirmaster must possess good musical training good taste, good churchmanship, some knowledge of sound theology and be able to train voices as well, it is apparent that the post is not an easy one to fill. He may be a brilliant organist, and yet not be able to teach vocal music to others. Or, he may look upon his choir as a group of entertainers, which is quite bad indeed.

Where a good choirmaster is not available, the pastor ought not to feel it beneath his dignity, or unworthy of his time, to devote some time and money to the task. We include money because very few of our pastors have been trained to teach music. However, a man of average ear and intelligence may learn very quickly. Let him go to a competent vocal teacher of churchly training and state his case frankly. Let him go once a week and take lessons himself. Perhaps he will never become even a fairly good singer, but at least he will learn the theory of correct tone production, and the many faults so natural to untrained voices. After a short period of training, he will be able to pass on much valuable information to his choir. Their interest and rapid improvement will be one of the big thrills of their pastor's lifetime. It will please the choir to know that their pastor is taking a keen interest in their work, and is willing to help them. It will be surprising how hard they will try to show their appreciation by singing according to the principles he lays down.

There are certain traditions followed by the liturgical churches which are not affectations, but the earmarks of good singing. In the matter of correct enunciation and pronunciation we might call attention to a few of the more common faults, and their remedy.

The word "infinite" must not be made to rhyme with "right," as most untrained choirs are apt to do. "Lord," "Father," "glory" and such words must be sung with mouths very wide open, and with very round vowel sounds, and never through half-closed teeth. "Strength" must never be sung with a silent "g" as many choirs fall into the habit of doing. Words such as "renew," "stupid," "new" and "due" must rhyme with "few" and not with "do." To sing these words improperly is much more unpleasant than to pronounce them improperly. The word "night" must have an "ie" quality to the vowel. The word "day" must have an "ae" quality. The final consonants of such words as "defend" and "defeat" must be pronounced distinctly, but without undue stress. "Evil" is pronounced as though spelled "eve-ill," whether in the spoken or the sung parts of the liturgy. "Trespasses," when spoken, must always have the accent on the first syllable, and never on the second. When sung, as in chanting the Lord's Prayer to the Tallis setting, it must be accented on the first and the last syllable. Words such as "creation" and "salvation" must have the well-known "shawn" ending, but without exaggeration. The word "innocency" must have a decidedly long "o" sound, and never a "u" sound. Words such as "creature," "nature," "nurture" and "future" must be sung without a suggestion of a "ch" sound. Thus the choir, trained in correct liturgical diction, will sing "cree-ture," "nat-your," and "fut-your," and never "cree-chur," "nat-cher" or "futchure." The word "knowledge," astonishing as it may sound at first, is pronounced with almost a long "o" in good liturgical reading and singing. "Grant," "commandment," "past," "trespass," and "ask" are sung and spoken with the "a" as in "father" by those liturgically trained, but "and," "hand," "Calvary" and "hadst" are sung and spoken with a moderately short "a" sound. The word "generation" must not be sung "jennie-ration," as is so often done, but "gen-uh-ray-shon," with care not to exaggerate.

One of the biggest difficulties is to cause the singers to open their mouths. Many choirs sing through closed teeth. The mouth ought to be opened wide enough to admit at least two fingers. For certain vowels, more will be necessary.

A second difficulty is to get rid of the burring "r" sounds, and yet avoid the affectation of a decided "ah" sound. The dudes of thirty years ago said, "Ah don't appwove of hawwid wah." Some choirs are equally bad, when trying to avoid the provincial "r" sounds of the rural districts.

A choir must be taught to sing smoothly, without blurting each syllable on the one hand, and without the crude sliding from a high note to a low one on the other hand. Both are vulgarisms that must not be allowed. A good vocal exercise to guard against blurting each syllable is the well-known "Bay-dah-may-nee-poe-too-lah," sung on c, e, g, a, and down again on g, e, and c. Or, in the tonic-sol-fa system on do, me, sol, la, sol, me and do. Learn to sing it very smoothly, without blurting and without slurring. Begin on middle c, and take the exercises on each semitone of the chromatic scale. Then, on do, me, sol, do, and do, sol, me, do, sing the words "The night is past. The day is done," or some such exercise, striving for both smoothness and cultured diction.

The choir must be taught that certain words must be intentionally distorted, in order to make them carry. Ether waves, or whatever the medium may be, distorts certain words. If we sing "earth" and "world" as we say them in spoken conversation, by the time they reach the ears of the congregation they will become "urrth" and "wurruld." Thus we must sing, "All the awth doth waship Thee," and "wald without end." It is impossible to set down the correct sound without seeming to exaggerate. One must simply learn from a competent teacher, or he will go to the opposite extreme, which is silly affectation. The distortion must not be pronounced when heard at a distance of fifty feet away.

The liturgical training of choirs must include much drill on pronunciation, enunciation, diction and shading. The first fifteen minutes of each rehearsal, for one year, is not too much time to spend on this. Then there is drill in correct breathing, in the production of refined tone quality and not hard, throaty tones, on the avoidance of tremolo in chorus parts and on correct tempo.

The work must not stop here. The choir must be taught to appreciate music of the proper sort. They will want to sing anthems from time to time. All choirs do. But certain principles must govern the selection of these numbers. In a non-liturgical church, almost anything is sung. But in a church with any pretentions of liturgical taste, the anthem must be either in the inspired words of Scripture, or on rare occasions a special arrangement of some widely-known hymn. In the former class are those anthems whose words are based upon the Canticles of the Church, a Psalm, a selection from the prophecies, a musical arrangement of the Introit for the Day, and other like material. Some decidedly liturgical churches rule out everything other than anthems in the exact words of the Scriptures, settings to the three Creeds and the *Te Deum*.

Choirs may be taught to sing the Psalms. It is as absurd to read a Psalm responsively as it might be were we to read a hymn responsively. An unexpected storehouse of rich treasures awaits the choir that has never been taught to sing the Psalms and Canticles of the Church to Plain Chant and to Anglican settings. Our Vesper Service is based upon one of the Plain Chant or Gregorian tones. In the back of our English hymnal are a few of the large number of Anglican settings. But more on this point in a later article.

As the choir gains in ability, some of the better settings to the *Te Deum* may be attempted, such as Stanford in B Flat or Willan in B Flat. These are *Te Deums* at their best, while Dudley Buck's arrangements, longer and shorter forms, are illustrations of all that must be avoided.

Due attention must be given to the proper singing of the church service. The fixed parts must be mastered. Variable parts, such as the proper season Hallelujah and Sentence, must be committed to memory. Every choir ought to know several settings to the Lord's Prayer and the Apostles' and Nicene Creeds. Tallis in G is an excellent setting, for the choir and congregation chant on a single tone, while the organ takes the four-part harmony which moves in dignified progression. But it is no easy task to point and sing these things in the traditional manner. Tallis, badly sung, is much better left unsung.

Training of this sort will not only improve the quality of work done by the choir, but it will awaken in them a taste for churchly things as well. This ought to be augmented by an occasional evening spent by the entire congregation in learning to sing properly the church service, and some of the less familiar hymns.

Constitution and By-Laws for a Choir

(EDITORIAL NOTE: The editors of this Department have had repeated requests for copies of a Constitution and By-Laws for choir. We welcome further suggestions.)

ARTICLE I.
Name
The name of this Organization shall be—"The Choir of the English Ev. Lutheran Church of the Redeemer."

ARTICLE II.
Object
The object of this Organization shall be the furtherance of the Kingdom of God by beautifying the services of the English Evangelical Lutheran Church of the Redeemer and fostering the studying and appreciation of good Lutheran church music.

ARTICLE III.
Membership
When an applicant for membership has been recommended by the choirmaster, the proposed member is required to attend four rehearsals before he or she can be accepted into membership, and cannot appear in the choirloft until he or she has become a regular member.

ARTICLE IV.
Duties of Membership
The duties of Membership shall be:
1. Regular and prompt attendance at rehearsals.
2. Regular and prompt appearance at all church services where their services are required.

ARTICLE V.
Meetings
1. The Choir shall hold at least one regular business meeting a month on an evening to be designated by the Choir.
2. Regular evenings for weekly rehearsals shall be determined by the majority vote of the Choir members.
3. Special meetings may be called at any time by the President.
4. Special choir rehearsals may be called at any time by the Choirmaster.
5. Attendance of ten (10) members shall constitute a quorum.
6. All rehearsals shall begin promptly at 8 o'clock.

ARTICLE VI.
Officers
1. The Officers of this Organization shall be, a President, a Vice-President, a Secretary-Treasurer, a Librarian and an Assistant Librarian.
2. The duties of the President and the Vice-President shall be those usually incumbent upon such officers.
3. The duties of the Secretary-Treasurer shall be to keep the minutes of all meetings, to keep an exact record of the attendance of choir members at all rehearsals and church services; also to keep a check of all delinquent members and report same to the choirmaster.
4. The duties of the Librarian and the assistant Librarian shall be the care and distribution of all choir music.

ARTICLE VII.
Election of Officers
1. The election of Officers shall be held at the January meeting of the choir and shall be by ballot.
2. The term of officers shall be the calendar year.

ARTICLE VIII.
Change in the Constitution
Any change in the Constitution must be proposed at one meeting and voted upon at the next. A two-thirds vote of the members present shall be necessary to make the change effective.

BY LAWS
ARTICLE IX.
Section 1. The business meetings shall be held on the first Friday of each month.
Section 2. The Choir rehearsals shall be held on Friday evening.

ARTICLE X.
The Chairman shall appoint the following standing committees:
1. A vestment Committee.
2. An entertainment Committee.

ARTICLE XI
Section 1. It shall be the duty of every choir member to report his intended absence, with proper excuse, from choir rehearsals and church services to the secretary or the choirmaster.
Section 2. Members who have been absent from three (3) consecutive rehearsals without proper excuse, after having received due notice from the secretary of their delinquency, automatically forfeit their membership.

ARTICLE XII.
Section 1. The names of prospective choir members must first be submitted to the Music Committee for consideration.
Section 2. Prospective members must attend four (4) rehearsals before they can be accepted as regular members and cannot appear in the choir loft until they have been accepted as regular members.

ARTICLE XIII.
New Members shall deposit 25 cents for a locker key, also old members who desire duplicate keys.

ARTICLE XIV.
Seating
Section 1. It shall be understood that the Choir Organization is under the jurisdiction of the Music Committee as to seating members in the choir loft or the re-arranging thereof, if in their judgment a re-arrangement should be deemed advisable.

ARTICLE XV.
The Music Committee may on special occasions, augment the choir if it should be deemed desirable.

ARTICLE XVI.
A member, not having attended rehearsals of a song, cannot appear with the choir when such a song is rendered, unless pre-arranged with the choirmaster.

Don'ts for Singers

DON'T think of your choir as a group of entertainers. Their work is solely to assist the congregation in its worship.

Don't think that the anthem is the big thing. It is not. It is an occasional thing, which has come to assume entirely too much importance in recent years.

Don't fail to devote plenty of time to the singing of the liturgical responses. Learn to sing the Introits, too. Learn to sing the Psalms and the Canticles. A well-chanted Psalm or a Canticle is much more churchly than the much-abused anthem.

Don't think that you ought to sing a solo frequently. Any sort of music that pushes individuals into the lime-light causes the spirit of common, congregational worship to recede.

Don't use a pronounced tremolo in chorus parts. A soloist may employ a restrained *vibrato*, not a tremolo, but good blending of tone calls for singing of organ-like character.

Don't expect your director to lead you with a baton. This is necessary in the choir room, but an outrage if done during the church service. It is a cheap sectarianism to be avoided.

Don't clamor for a weekly processional and recessional. It may easily degenerate into a vulgar thing. Reserve such things for appropriate occasions, and then do it in a quiet, churchly manner.

Don't demand cheap, non-liturgical music. Everything ought to fit perfectly the spirit of the Church Year, and the type of service found in our circles.

Don't forget that a poor, discordant choir is worse than none. A choir sang over the radio last Sunday, and its work was an outrage to all good taste, and bad publicity to the reputation of the "singing church."

Don't forget that your presence in church is solely to worship the Lord, and not to attract attention to yourself, or your group.

"Lutheran Church Art"

What Is Lutheran in Vestments?

FRED LINDEMANN

IT is evident that a revival of interest in liturgics is sweeping through a large portion of the Lutheran Church in this country. Any number of late churches would indicate that we are building with the consciousness that ours is a liturgical church. A picture taken at the corner stone laying of an Ohio Synod church shows the pastors in cassock and surplice. In a number of United Lutheran churches the somber black vestment of the pastor has been replaced by a more festive habit. In the Scandinavian churches surplice and chasuble is not an uncommon sight. Also in a few Missouri churches cassock and surplice have made their appearance. A few lines on the subject of vestments which appeared in the *Lutheran Witness* called forth a surprising correspondence. The evidence is that there is a live interest in matters pertaining to liturgics in general and to vestments in particular.

Naturally the idea of a Lutheran pastor appearing in anything but black will call forth opposition. After accustoming ourselves to seeing him in black his appearance in anything else causes a sensation. We can sympathize with people who find it hard to approve of a change in anything connected with the public worship. We can bear with the objector who has no other reason for his opposition but that he does "not like it." But when the claim is made that the black gown is Lutheran and everything else un-Lutheran, that cassock, surplice and chasuble are Roman Catholic or Episcopalian, we feel in us the urge to admonish: "Tread lightly and circumspectly, friend, thou art on thin ice!" We have a feeling that the usual vestment of the Lutheran pastor in this country is anything but Lutheran. We even have a slinking suspicion that cassock, surplice and chasuble are truly Lutheran. Just what is Lutheran? What makes a thing that? Is there any way to determine this? Is a thing Lutheran if Luther did it, or if Lutheran churches after the Reformation did it? Or does it become Lutheran when it has been done for a long time by a large proportion of the Church? Would a thing be considered Lutheran if Luther and his contemporaries approved and urged it, if Lutheran theologians and people treasured it for a long time after the Reformation, if it was defended by them as something typically Lutheran against the attacks of fanatics, princes and rationalists? Would it be any the less Lutheran if after a long and determined battle it gradually disappeared in that portion of the Church which had to contend with these powerful enemies of everything Lutheran? Would it cease to be Lutheran if for 150 years a large part of the Church substituted something else? Does a thing become Lutheran when a daughter continues to do a thing of her own free will which the mother was compelled to do? It would seem that if there is such a thing as a Lutheran vestment it would be that in use before the Reformed fanatics and princes forced their black gown on us, rather than the Reformed gown which the German Lutheran Church was compelled to adopt by sheer brutality.

The subject of vestments belongs in the class of adiaphora. In the New Testament nothing is commanded in this respect. The fact that Luther or Lutheran pastors for two centuries after him wore a certain vestment is no compelling reason for wearing it today. On the other hand, the fact that a certain gown is worn generally today is no reason for continuing to wear it if there are historical or liturgical arguments against it and the individual congregation, after careful instruction, chooses to discard it. The question is simply: Should we call the fifty-seven varieties of black vestments on view in American Lutheran churches today "'Lutheran"? Is any other vestment "un-Lutheran"?

Within the scope of the present article it is possible merely to touch upon certain historical tendencies and trends. Perhaps one or the other of the readers will have his appetite sufficiently aroused by the facts presented to wish for more information on the subject. A few books which will prove helpful in further study are: Joseph Braum, "Die Liturgische Gewandung," Freiburg, 1907; Paul Graff, "Geschichte der Aufloesung der Alten Gottesdienstlichen Formen in der Ev. Kirche Deutschlands," Goettingen, 1921; Hermann Waldenmaier, "Die Entstehung der Ev. Gottesdienstordnungen Sueddeutschlands," Leipzig, 1916; P. Severinsen, "The Proper Communion Vestments." We can bring merely a few expressions of Luther which ought to be interesting and at the same time admittedly "Lutheran." Almost fascinating is to determine the position of the Church in Germany in the days of Paul Gerhardt, when a Reformed king commanded that the vestments used by the Lutherans up to that time must be put away and the Lutherans insisted that these things were so typically Lutheran that to give them up would be to sacrifice distinctive Lutheran features. The Lutheran Church yielded in the end and the pastor became black. Later freedom as regards vestments was granted, but rationalism prevented a return to what had been discarded under pressure. Yet there are people today who insist that it is Lutheran when the pastor celebrating Holy Communion is black as a raven, while all this blackness does not go back even two hundred years, and is found only in that portion of the Church which had to yield repeatedly to influences from powerful Calvinistic quarters. In the lands where Lutheran kings reigned, in Denmark, Sweden and Norway, the black vestment of the Calvinists was never looked upon as Lutheran. To this day many Norwegian and Swedish churches have retained the ancient vestments in this country. It is in the churches which trace their origin to Germany, the land of Calvinistic kings and royal commands, the land of rationalism, that the black gown is considered Lutheran.

Cut No. 1 is intended to show a clergyman with a white linen alb which is the under garment shown; an amice, which is the collar piece; a stole the ends of which can be seen beneath the chasuble; a chasuble and a maniple on the arm. This represents a complete set of Communion vestments. The chasuble illustrated is the Gothic type.

First, then, the question: What was worn by the priest at Luther's time? So far as we can determine the black garb of the priest was properly his private dress at home and abroad, on the streets and in society. The undergarment was the ordinary cassock. Over it was worn the loose flowing gown, which the Germans called the "Schaube." It was open and without buttons. The edge of it was turned back and formed a collar. Being without buttons a person had to wrap it around himself in order to close it. Portraits of Luther show him attired in this fashion. The sleeves of the gown might be short and very wide so that the narrow sleeve of the cassock would show, or they might be very wide and long, especially in the academic gown. The cloak of the common parish priest, worn over the cassock when appearing in public, had no sleeves.

What did Luther wear when

Cut No. 2 shows the back of a Gothic chasuble made of the Agnus Dei Damask with the orphreys of silk outlined in galloon or braid with the same galloon or braid around the outer edge and neck of the chasuble. The design in quatrefoil is the dove emblematic of the descent of the Holy Spirit. This cut also shows the back of the stole with the small neck cross. This is an actual photograph of a chasuble. The front of this chasuble would be the same as shown on cut No. 1, except that on the pillar in the center there is embroidered a Cross.

he celebrated the mass? In the Middle Ages monastic regulations were that the entire clergy should wear fur coats during the daily services in the cold churches. But the services in the sanctuary had to be conducted in white vestments which led to the introduction of the surplice, the superpelliceum, that is, a garment worn over a fur coat. To be practical it was very loose and had wide sleeves. In Germany it was also used without sleeves. Its length varied much at different times. It was worn on all sorts of occasions, both in and out of the church, at baptism, while preaching, at minor services and when the Sacrament was administered to the sick. For the celebration of Holy Communion the alb was used, a long tunic with narrow sleeves, raised to the ankles by a girdle around the waist, made of pure linen. It was usually white, but could be of any other color, except black. The priest was to appear in festive garments at the celebration and black was prohibited. Over the alb the chasuble, called "Messgewandt," often ornamented in the most elaborate fashion, was worn at the altar throughout any part of the Communion service proper, but was removed whenever the priest left the altar to perform some duty as that of preaching, baptising, and the like. All these vestments were at one time the garments of the ordinary man and when styles changed it was considered proper that the priest retain these garments although they too changed greatly through the centuries.

Then came the Reformation and with it Zwingli, who did away with the vestments, together with altar, candles, crucifixes and organs, as expressions of ungodliness. The South Germans followed him generally and constructed the service not along the ancient order of the Communion, but on that of the preaching service of the Middle Ages. Luther built the Communion service on the order of the mass and retained the Communion vestments, which were considered an entirely neutral matter, doing neither evil nor good. In the Order of the Mass of 1523 Luther says that the vestments may be used unhindered when pomp and luxury is avoided, but they should not be dedicated or blessed. This position was the very opposite of that held by the fanatics. Luther was forced to emphasize liberty in these matters by urging the continuation of the vestments. In the fall of 1524 in his pamphlet "Against the Heavenly Prophets" he says: "Here we are masters and will not submit to any law, command, doctrine or interdict. Therefore has the service of the Communion been celebrated in both ways at Wittenberg. In the monastery we have celebrated the Mass without chasuble or elevation, with the greatest simplicity, as is recommended by Karlstadt. In the parish church we have chasubles, albs, altar, and elevate so long as it pleases us." In the German Mass of 1526 he retained vestments, candles and altar. In the Confession of the Communion of 1528 he insisted on the same liberty.

The work of revising and ordering the services in different countries was delegated to Bugenhagen and in full agreement with Luther's stand he retained the ancient vestments. He could take a very definite stand in these matters. In 1528 he had ordered the services in Braunschweig but a fierce dispute broke out a couple of years later. The preachers Rebeling and Hayer started an agitation for the abolishment of the vestments. Hayer was especially zealous. It is said that he arranged with one of the townsfolk to tear the chasuble off him that it might be said that the public wanted the vestments abolished. Martin Goerlitz and the other preachers objected at first but yielded later. So it was announced from the pulpits that in order to show their Christian position all the preachers would in the nearest future omit the use of the chasuble, with the reservation that they could resume the use of it when it so pleased them. On hearing of this Bugenhagen became highly displeased and wrote a letter to Goerlitz dated September 27th, 1530, about "offending neighboring cities with unnecessary things." He says: "There are two doctrines of the chasubles. The one is the truth, viz. that chasubles may be used. This does not offend those who are used to hear the Gospel. The other is a Satanic lie from the doctrine of demons, viz. that it is not permissible to use the chasuble. This offends the community where it hears that kind of lies taught and believed by preachers." He then goes on to wonder whether the church at Braunschweig is "farther developed" than the one at Wittenberg and calls attention to the fact that there are yet organs, bells, yea, church buildings to be abolished.

To close the Wittenberg Concordat the South Germans came to Wittenberg in 1536 and were greatly shocked by the Communion service on Ascension Day. Wolfgang Musculus of Constanz wrote in his journal that there were pictures in the church, candles on the altar, and a priest in "papistic" clothes. While the Introitus was played on the organ and the choir sang in Latin the priest having the Celebration proceeded from the sacristy wearing vestments. The South Germans complained to Bugenhagen, who comforted them by stating that Communion was also celebrated without vestments in the convent and at the early celebrations. They were also much comforted when they saw Luther preach in his academic gown, his common clothes.

So matters continued until 1548 when the Imperial Interim made the use of the vestments together with many earlier ceremonies, obligatory. There were Lutherans who objected, but wherever the Saxon Interim, recommended by Melanchton, was adopted, the vestments became more firmly intrenched. One gains the impression that the use of the Communion vestments was considered typically and distinctly Lutheran as over against the black gown of the Calvinists. The surplice was not only worn over the cassock but also in place of it.

A hundred years later, about the year 1650, St. Nicolai in Leipzig possessed extremely rich vestments. These were the days of strict Lutheran orthodoxy and of Paul Gerhardt. The alb was used with amice, maniple and parurer. The collection of chasubles included five of various colors for ordinary Sundays and sixteen most elaborate ones for festivals. At the administration of the Sacrament four boys held the sacramental cloths over which the Sacrament was handed to the communicants who passed the celebrating pastors. The boys were in black cassocks with surplices over, but on festival days the boys wore "special cassocks of crimson velvet" donated by a widow. Rationalism sold this whole collection in 1776.

In Nueremberg a collection of chasubles was confiscated by the city 1797 and sold as a contribution to the taxes. The surplice was not abolished until 1810. In Ansbach the surplice was discarded in 1798 to save laundry expenses. Until rationalism asserted itself in this manner chasubles and surplices were in general use. In 1705 Caspar Calvor, General Superintendent in Klausthal in the Harz, writes that the surplice and chasuble is used "every where by all ours." The Saxon Chr. Gerber tells us in 1732 that the churches are plentifully supplied with chasubles. People present them as gifts. After the gospel the pastor, standing before the altar, lifts the chasuble off over his head and leaves it at the altar. After the sermon he puts it on again. Gerber is vexed because the pastors complain that the chasubles are worn. He thinks they should rejoice in the prospect that they would soon be worn out.

Typical of the attacks upon the usages and customs of the Lutheran Church is Wagner's "A Legal Dispute about the Sabbath," published in 1702. The author shows strong traces of rationalism and belonged to a circle which got its inspiration from the Mencken of that day by name of Thomasius. After demanding the prohibition of pictures, crucifixes, bells, hymns, chanting, and the like, he comes to the Communion vestments. He insists that they were invented by the priests in order to be different from other people and thus secure their authority. The idea of a special dress is partly borrowed from the heathen, partly from the Jews. If from the heathen it is wickedness. If from the Jews it is superstition. It is God's special guidance that the priest imitate the dress of the Pharisees that it may become evident to all men that the priests as a whole are Pharisees and the services mostly pharisaic. He advises that everything distinguishing the priest be abolished, but if nothing else, at least the chasuble must go, since it is manifestly from the days of the pope.

This book of Wagner was reviewed in most unsympathetic and bitter terms by Loescher's "Unschuldige Nachrichten," the publication of orthodox Lutheranism. When 1732 the book by the pietist Gerber appeared this paper reviewed also this book in anything but friendly terms. The Lutherans attached great importance to their vestments and were not ready to give them up.

But in 1733 Frederick Wilhelm I, a Calvinist, prohibited the "remnants of popery in the Lutheran Church: copes, communion vestments, candles, Latin song, chants, and the sign of the cross." Many pastors sanctioned the step, but conservatism was also very strong. A great number complained and looked upon the event as "a betrayal of genuine and pure Lutheranism." Many reports were also given of the disappointment of the congregations. The brutal King repeated his command in 1737 with the addition: "Should there be those who hesitate or who desire to make it a matter of conscience, we wish to make it known that we are ready to give them their demission." At least one pastor was discharged for refusal to submit. "Unschuldige Nachrichten" called upon its readers to pray God that He turn

Cut No. 3 shows the Roman style chasuble which is used only by the High Churchmen of the Episcopal Church and the Roman Church. As a rule this style chasuble is imported from Europe. These are seldom hand embroidered, the designs being mostly appliqued.

the mind of him who sits upon the throne of honor. We quote in part: "If human presentations and certain ancient ceremonies of our church cannot be reckoned as becoming for pure Christianity, then may the Holy God see to this in His infinite grace. These things are admittedly not of any inner necessity, but they have become no insignificant mark of our church and must therefore be safeguarded under these circumstances." Among the "ancient ceremonies of our church" is included "the solemn clothing of the church's servants." Even the pietists with their dread for externalism protested against the royal command. The only effect was a repetition of the order in 1737.

Frederick II succeeded his father in 1740 and at once issued a cabinet order allowing the churches and pastors full liberty in the matter of religious services. A number made use of the liberty granted. In Berlin and other places the Communion vestments were restored. But it was not the time for pious sentiment. Rationalism flourished and it had an infinite dread of all that was "mystic" or that was handed down from the past. The use of Communion vestments was decidedly "Catholic" to the mind of that age. It is said that the white surplice or alb is still in use in Leipzig and surrounding country, in a couple of churches in Berlin, in Weimar, Koenigsberg, and probably in other places. The chasuble was still used in Dresden in the early part of the nineteenth century. It was discontinued in Nuerenberg in 1810, and about the same time in Hannover, Grimma and Luebeck. A number of Prussian churches as the Maria Church in Danzig and the Cathedral Church at Brandenburg possess even today the greatest collections of Communion vestments in Christendom. Whether they are still in use we do not know. At the outbreak of the great war there was probably no church in Germany where the chasuble was in use.

That is briefly the story of why the German Lutheran pastor appears at present in the black Calvinistic cloak, handed him by the Reformed king of Prussia and kept on him by rationalism. It is a story of one tremendous defeat, a colossal yielding and giving up of typical Lutheran ways and customs. The blackness of the clergy in the Lutheran churches of America today is not only not Lutheran, but it is a remnant and constant reminder of a period of the greatest helplessness and degradation of the German Lutheran people. In so far as externals are concerned, the brutal king followed by the overwhelming power of rationalism shifted the German Lutheran Church from her natural position among the great historical communions of Christendom to a place among the sectarian, Calvinistic denominations. In externals the daughter in America has distinguished herself by continuously yielding in order to make herself acceptable. Lutheran in theory and doctrine and increasingly Reformed in practice. Ever so many splendid customs, full of symbolic significance, have been discarded because they might offend the Reformed neighbor or some ignorant member who might look upon it as "too Catholic."

What is Lutheran in clerical vestments? Who can say? But this much seems certain: The original and typical apparel of the Lutheran clergy when officiating in the sanctuary is not that of blackness and gloom but the festive apparel of the historic church through the ages. When the Lutheran pastor today appears in black he so much as declares to the world that his church is even now, in this land of the free and the home of the brave, too timid or too indifferent or too spineless to shake off the badge of a shameful yielding in time of persecution. But if we continue the Calvinistic black cloak as the vestment for all occasions, let us at least not claim that it is Lutheran. We may not care enough, we may not have enough energy and vitality left to go back to the Lutheran vestments, but let us not add ignorance of what is truly Lutheran to the other, by insisting that anything which comes from Geneva can possibly be Lutheran.

Out Among Them

Dr. Ambrose Hering Writes About Taking the Gospel to the Open-air Crowd in New York

I DON'T BELIEVE A WORD OF IT," was the shattering retort of a young woman as she pushed her baby coach past us the other evening while our open-air preaching service was in progress at Madison Square (Twenty-fourth Street and Madison Avenue), New York City. The remark fell flat. She had failed to reckon with the Holy Spirit.

We are having a genuinely interesting time of it here in Manhattan this summer—confronting the city multitudes with the saving Gospel. It is evident there are grievances, pent up emotions and deep resentments in the hearts of the unemployed and the homeless; for hunger and insecurity do not breed peace and faith seldom blossoms in an atmosphere of despair. The tide has been running in the interests of the evil one.

HECKLERS TURN HEARERS

We were warned beforehand about hecklers and the violence of "those down on religion and the Church." While it has at times been mildly exciting during the after-service discussions, our messages have been accorded a fair, if not sympathetic, hearing. During the first weeks faces could be spotted in the crowd with black opposition and disagreement written over them. From here and there came a defiant fling at the Church (friend of the rich). "Why don't you preachers practice what you tell us?"—one man remarked and walked away.

Increasingly the atmosphere is becoming friendly. As a man put it last week, "The churches aren't any good and the preachers are all alike but your folks must be different or you wouldn't come out here to talk to us."

These are peculiarly opportune times to carry the fight into the enemy's lines. The old order has broken down. Plundering no longer pays. Despair kills. Destructive radicalism in America

HOLY BAPTISM
from p. 283.

then there ought to be two men and a woman if the child is a boy, and two women and a man if the infant be a girl. This is sound tradition.

The sponsors may kneel for the closing prayer. At the time for this prayer the pastor leaves the font and goes to the altar. The congregation will rise, and the concluding prayer is said before the altar, facing eastward. After this prayer a suitable baptismal hymn ought to be sung. Then, if there be no Communion, the congregation is dismissed with the benediction. After the close of the service, one of the deacons will drain the font, if it be provided with a drain. If there is no drain in the font, he will carry the water to the piscina, and quietly dispose of it. It is decidedly unchurchly to pour the water into the common sewer. If there be no piscina, the water ought to be carried out and poured on the earth in the form of a cross, pouring three times, once from east to west, once from west to east, and finally from north to south, in accordance with tradition.

Where these directions are followed, Holy Baptism is made a part of the chief service and is given an importance which it cannot possibly have where it is treated as a minor event, at the close of the service, or where it is administered in the home.

The only argument advanced against this is that it is necessary to wait for two or three weeks until mother and child are able to be brought to the church. But it is better to wait a week or so longer, and to conduct the baptismal service in the solemn surroundings of the church, than to have it done amid the domestic atmosphere of the home.

There are others who say that the congregation will not remain for the entire service, if it is made a part of the chief service. We have yet to meet with an instance where a single person left the church. Congregations are not only willing to remain, but seem glad to do so. Let the sermon be shortened five minutes, if need be. The average thirty minute sermon might be improved by condensation. If a congregation objects to the additional ten minutes necessary for a baptismal service, then it is a sure indication that this Sacrament is held in low esteem, and it is high time that something be done to remedy matters.

• • • 〰 • • •

may get a hearing but it has no following. Is not this a land of free speech and free assembly? Moreover everyone is discussing "the new deal." When new codes and new regulations are being set up for industrial groups by the government, why not a new deal for the human soul by the Church? Why not?

THE ZEST OF ADVENTURING

After all, God has not withdrawn His Holy Spirit from the open-air crowd and the saving Gospel still saves. Have a message and it will be heard. Should someone interrupt, the crowd will register its opinion—often in language more forceful than elegant. This "stumping" for the Gospel is really an adventure which the laymen enjoy as much as the preachers; and how the young folks delight in it!

There is an element of pathos in the open-air evangelistic situation. Men peer with wistful eagerness to catch every word. They know the wreckage of sin and defeat only too well. "Like sheep without a shepherd." No wonder He had compassion on them. Must these depressed souls be left to the scourge of fanatical errorists and professional agitators? Or will evangelical Christianity bear them the good news of redemption and release?

The ministrations of Jesus were essentially open-air ministrations—because there He found the folks who needed Him. To Him the market place became a pulpit. The prophets, and later the reformers also carried the message beyond the accustomed sanctuaries. We are "to go out into the highways and by-ways"; which means the "white-ways," too. Prodigality has spent all and is coming to. The tide is beginning to run the other way.

HOPES AND SUGGESTIONS

How to proceed? It is very simple. Get a permit. Enlist a few earnest friends. Go where the crowd is and never mind the noise. Stand up and tell frankly and simply what He means to you. Announce your next service. Secure a generous supply of devotional literature. A trumpeter, soloists, choir, organ are all helpful but not essential.
—*The Lutheran.*

The Cross As An Ornament

In this connection may we refresh the minds of our readers on an editorial which appeared in the *American Lutheran,* August, 1932:

"It is rather significant and reassuring that just now the cross is coming back as an article of womanly adornment. At any rate we take it for granted that the many crosses which we have noticed among the girls and women of our church are an indication of a nation-wide movement. Such feminine tendencies are usually not just local in character. Of course, the wearing of a cross as a throat pendant or as some other means of feminine adornment may just be a meaningless gesture or a concession to a prevailing fad. It may also be, and probably in most cases is, an unashamed and unafraid confession of Christian faith, an open declaration of adherence to the cause of the crucified Savior. It is a wholesome and refreshing sign when the girls and women of our churches openly wear for all to see the precious symbol of their faith. That cross may be more than a personal profession, however. It may be a silent sermon to the careless and the drifters, a reminder of broken pledges and forgotten vows. It may be a means of protection for the wearer and her companion in times of temptation. When in these days of cynical wordliness and godless scoffing we see a young Protestant girl wearing a cross we feel like shaking her hand in congratulation and commendation. We like her nerve. She is usually a clear-eyed, wholesome youngster with a glint of determination in her eyes and an upward tilt to her chin. She is, thank God, representative of a vast host of glorious American girls growing up in our churches. May her display of the symbol of her faith be not a passing fad but a permanent institution.

But why should the wearing of the cross be confined to our feminine Christians? It is not to the credit of the men that they are as a rule much more diffident about making a public profession of their faith than are the women. There is noticeable among the men a shamefaced reluctance to have their religious connections publicized. This fear of becoming conspicuous among their fellows seems to be an almost general male failing. It was broken down somewhat by the happy idea of the proponents of the Lutheran Hour to give out tiny crosses to the constituents of their radio audience. Thousands of these little

gold crosses appeared on the lapels of men's coats and are still being worn. The practice of such adornment deserves to be encouraged and developed into a permanent custom. There is no reason why the wearing of a gold cross as a watch-charm should be confined to the clergy. A small cross on a stick-pin or in a seal ring is appropriate for a Christian man. Our perturbed times need every form of Christian testimony that can be given. We hope that the cross as a personal ornament has come to stay in our midst."

We have already expressed our joy in the fact that the cross has of late years come into vogue again as an item of feminine adornment. Many of our young women are wearing it as a necklace appendage. Its continued popularity seems to indicate that its use is more than just the passing caprice of an incalculable fashion which ordinarily changes its decrees rapidly and without warning or reason. It may be that we have in the present vogue the evidence of a desire on the part of our young women to make public confession of their Christian faith. It may be said to the credit of our young people that they are showing an increasing readiness to make an unashamed declaration of their faith before the world. May the number of our feminine confessors grow. From the purely practical viewpoint of a mere man it seems sensible to wear an adornment that really means something rather than some nondescript gew-gaw that has nothing to commend it but a flashy design.

But why should the cross as an object of ornamentation be confined to the women? Men suspend from their watch-chains, elks'-teeth, moose-claws, Masonic symbols and other insignia of lodgery. College men proudly wear their fraternity pins and watch-charms. Why should not the Christian man exhibit on his apparel an indication of his connection with the greatest brotherhood on earth, the followers of the cross? We are afraid that our men lack the spirit of courageous profession exhibited by our women. Men seem to shy away from the conspicuousness to which they think the public wearing of the cross might subject them. Or are we doing them an injustice? Many of our men are wearing the little cross secured through the proponents of the Lutheran Hour. The proposition of using the cross for male adornment is worthy of serious consideration. We need open profession of the cause of Christ today. The forces of evil are advertising themselves blatantly. Members of purely secular organizations like the Rotarians and the Kiwanis Club proudly proclaim their membership on their watch-chains and coat-lapels. The Christian man, however, often hesitates to publicize his connection with the body established by Christ Himself and membership in which constitutes the greatest glory that can come to man.

We venture to go a step further. Why should not the cross or the crucifix find its place on the walls of our homes? Among the hallowed places of our childhood was our father's study, but the only ornamentation of its walls which has stuck in our memory is the ornamental crucifix which hung immediately above his desk. To our boyish imagination it seemed symbolic of the character of the work that was done in that sanctum. Why should not the cross be on the walls of our home as well as in our churches? In our own church the junior pastor in late months has experimented with the attitude of the people towards the proposition. Without previous agitation a few crucifixes were placed on sale at the book table. Thirty of them have been sold within a few months. Evidently the spirit of confessionalism is growing. May God grant a rapid growth. In these sin-darkened days our confession must be clear and bold and there must never be any hesitancy to declare where we stand in regard to the crucified Christ. Besides the profession of our lips the silent testimony of our personal and home adornment may oftentimes be effective.

Candles In the Lutheran Rite

ARTHUR CARL PIEPKORN

TRADITIONAL usage in the Lutheran Church calls for two single candles in candlesticks upon the altar. Before the middle of the nineteenth century it would have been difficult to find evidence for any other arrangement, and the employment of either candelabra in place of single candlesticks, or of a multiplicity of single candlesticks cannot be justified on the basis of Lutheran liturgical precedent. The general use of six candlesticks is demonstrably a post-Reformation Roman innovation; at the end of the fifteenth century they were admitted only at masses said by a cardinal or prelate (Cuthbert Atchley, "The Ceremonial Use of Lights," in J. Wickham Legg, *Some principles and services of the Prayer-Book historically considered*, 1899, page 39, note 2). The use of eight candlesticks is a modern Anglican development. Four lights are the mark of a Roman side altar. There is of course nothing heretical or intrinsically inappropriate about four or six or eight or even more lights; these arrangements merely do not represent the traditional Lutheran usage.

The substitution of candelabra for the two single candlesticks is a very modern innovation without any justification at all. The use of candelabra in addition to the two single candlesticks is a matter of individual choice. If the use of ten or fourteen additional lights on the altar incites to greater devotion, no valid argument can be cited against it. But good taste is more liable to concur in the criticism of Morel de Voleine when he complains about the theatrical number of candles recently introduced in his day on the high altar at Lyons Cathedral: *"Il est possible que cette illumination attire de curieux, mais à coup sûr elle est fort opposée à l'ancien esprit liturgique . . . si grave, si opposé aux petits procédés mis enusage pour produire de l'effect"* (*De l'Influence de la Liturgie catholique sur l'Architecture*, 1861, page 15). The use of more than two lights on a small altar—one under seven feet in length—is to be avoided because of esthetic considerations, and even longer altars do not *require* more.

The candlesticks may be made of precious metals, of wood, or of brass, but in any case the best that the size and wealth of the parish admits. Great care should be exercised to keep both the candlesticks and the candles themselves in scale with the altar and with the rest of the chancel. More than one chancel has been dwarfed by oversize candlesticks and overly tall candles.

Liturgical artists prefer candles an inch and a quarter in diameter (Edwin Ryan, *Candles in the Roman Rite*, 1934, page 16). But except on very imposing altars set in very deep chancels the candles may be as thin as three-quarters of an inch without damage to the scale. They should not be allowed to burn down to less than two inches in length. The use of devices to impart a spurious height, such as "candle-stocks," is as reprehensible as any other sham in God's house. Electric lights have neither historical warrant nor any show of justification. They were foisted upon us by commercial-minded Roman Church supply houses. Where they have been insinuated the use of wax candles should be restored as soon as possible. The counterfeit becomes doubly regrettable when an effort is made to disguise the artificial character of the electric lights by using flame-shaped bulbs.

Like the altar crucifix, the candlesticks were originally carried to and from the altar for each service. The custom of removing the candlesticks out of service time persisted in some European churches at least as late as the begin-

ning of this century (Legg, *Ecclesiological Essays*, 1905, pages 33-35, plates II-IV). The statement of Mr. J. N. Comper is *à propos*: "They were there as part of the ceremonial, rather than as forming the decoration of the altar" ("The English Altar," in Legg, *Some principles etc.*, page 93). The custom of removing the candlesticks out of service time is preferable to the deplorable practise of laying the candlesticks on their sides after the service and covering the altar with a black dust-cloth. On a modern altar of the Roman type such as is commonly used among us, with a *gradin*, or step, at the back, the vesper cloth can be spread without interfering with the candlesticks. On an altar of the medieval type, without *gradin*, it would be better to remove the candlesticks (and crucifix) to the sacristy when no service is in progress, if a vesper cloth be habitually spread. Similarly, in climates or seasons where the heat may cause the candles to soften and bend of their own weight, the candles and preferably the candlesticks should be removed to the sacristy, not laid on the altar. Best usage dictates that the candlesticks should never stand empty on the altar, although Dr. F. Bock's book, *Geschichte der liturgischen Gewänder des Mittelalters* (1871, volume 3, plate 14, figure 1), does reproduce a Flemish miniature in the British Museum (*Add. MSS.* 25,698, folio 9) which shows an altar with two empty pricket candlesticks on it.

The place of the candlesticks is at the extremity of the back part of the altar. It is difficult to decide whether it is indirect assimilation to Roman procedure at low mass that has moved so many of our churches to put the candlesticks next to the crucifix or whether some other factor has been operative. It may be that the definitely modern and novel custom of putting cut flowers on the altar in vases is responsible. It would be far better to put flowers in pottery jars or vases around the altar on the floor of the sanctuary, but where flowers are put on the altar, they should be so disposed that the lights retain their rightful place at the extremities.

Except for the reference to "candlesticks" in Revelation i:12.13, there is no evidence for the liturgical use of lights in the Eastern Church before the fourth century or in the Western Church before the fifth. Tertullian (*Apol.* xxxv) and Lactantius (*de Div. Inst.* vi) argued against their use. The Spanish Synod of Elvira forbade their use in cemeteries in the daytime (Ryan, *o.c.*, page 3). The *Admonitio Synodalis* of St. Caesarius of Arles (541) provided for no lights (Archdale A. King, *Notes on the Catholic Liturgies*, 1930, page 16). Not until the days of Constantine the Great can we speak of a liturgical use of lights even in the East (Eusebius, *Vita Constantini*, book 4, chapter 22; St. Jerome in Migne, *Patrologia Latina*, volume 23, column 345). With the institution of the Feast of the Presentation of Our Lord in the West at the end of the fifth century (Ryan, *o. c.*, page 6) the symbolic use of lights in the Western Church may properly be said to have begun.

Before the days of candles, oil lamps were suspended from wall brackets and from the ceiling. Even the introduction of dipped candles did not at first modify the rule that lights were to be placed not on, but near the altar. Candles *on* the altar are not found at all before the eleventh century (Joseph Braun, *Liturgisches Handlexikon*, 2nd edition, 1924, p. 19; *Der Christliche Altar*, 1924, II, p. 173). The general use of candles *on* the altar is difficult to document before the sixteenth century (Ryan, *o.c.*, page 21). It is still customary to supplement the lights on the altar with other lights about the sanctuary.

Thus altars with riddel curtains often have riddel lights. These may be mounted on top of the riddel posts or at the extremities of the riddel-rods, depending on the manner of suspending the curtains. Where there are no riddel curtains, two tall candlesticks are often placed on the floor of the sanctuary somewhat in front and on either side of the predella. Another alternative is to have a light in a sconce on each side of the sanctuary, let into the wall; it is equally correct to have only one sconce with a single candle, in which case it is let into the wall on the Epistle (right, facing the altar) side of the sanctuary. In lieu of a sconce light, a third candlestick may be employed; it is set neither upon the altar nor upon the credence but on a special little table or bracket at the Epistle side of the altar. The use of this third candlestick is very ancient.

The riddel lights, or sconce lights, or the third candlestick are all treated as *Sanctus*-lights, so-called because they were lit at the conclusion of the *Sanctus* (more accurately at the beginning of the *Canon Minor*). These lights are not extinguished until the Sacred Species have been either consumed or removed. In the latter case, the *Sanctus*-lights are extinguished before the altar lights.

To heighten devotion standard candelabra may be set about the altar on the sanctuary floor.

The mode of lighting the candles is properly this: At the beginning of the service, the person appointed to light the candles proceeds to the altar, and, standing before the midst, lights the candle on the Epistle side first, then the light on the Gospel side. In extinguishing the candles, the light on the Gospel side is snuffed first, then that on the Epistle side. If there be more than one candle on each side, those on the Epistle side are lit first, beginning with the one nearest the Crucifix; then the ones on the Gospel side, again beginning with the one nearest the Crucifix. In extinguishing, the order is reversed; the first candle to be put out is the one on the Gospel side farthest from the Crucifix, the last to be extinguished is the one on the Epistle side nearest the Crucifix. Candles standing in the sanctuary should be lighted after the altar candles, extinguished before them.

The candles should be lighted with a taper which has been previously lit in the sacristy not with a match ignited on the deacon's fingernail, shoe sole, or trouser seat. They should be snuffed, not blown out. Candle lighters with snuffers can be purchased for as little as $1.50; any high school manual training shop can produce an eminently satisfactory one for fifty cents. The lighting of the candles is properly done by a server, vested in surplice or rochet over a cassock. In the absence of a server it may be done by a choir-boy, or a choir-man, or by the officiant himself. If the officiant performs this office and habitually wears a stole or scarf over a surplice, the stole or scarf should not be assumed until after he has lighted the candles.

Tradition requires that the candles used on the altar should be at least 51% beeswax, and stearine lights should be used only if beeswax candles cannot be secured. Candles are generally bleached almost white. Unbleached (brown) candles are used during Advent and Lent, except on Feast Days, and at funerals of adults throughout the year.

Where it is customary to veil the images and pictures in the Church throughout Lent or during Passiontide, it should be noted that the candle-sticks should not be veiled.

Certain uses of candles have fallen into desuetude in the Lutheran Church. Some of these, such as the blessing of throats in order to secure the intercession of the quasi-historical St. Blase on the morrow of Candlemass—despite the great advance made in the application of the tapers through the use of the ingenious device patented by Brother Thomas M. Mulkerins of the Society of Jesus!—had best

remain forgotten, but some at least might prove edifying if revived. Certainly it would be preferable to do this than to devote ourselves to the introduction of such sentimental fripperies as "candle-light services." A brief description of these ceremonies follows:

1. *Candles at the Holy Gospel.* Since the days of St. Jerome it has been customary in the Church to signalize the singing of the Gospel at a solemn celebration with lighted candles. The current use is for two servers bearing lighted candles in candlesticks to proceed to the altar. If there be only one sacred minister officiating, they flank him at the singing of the Gospel from the Gospel side; if there be three sacred ministers, they escort the liturgical deacon to the place where the Gospel is customarily sung, either a spot in the architectural choir or from the roodbeam, and stand at either side during the singing of the Gospel. Blessed Martin Luther's *Form of the Mass* (1523) contemplated the retention of this custom.

2. *Candles at the Sanctus.* In place of the riddel lights, sconce lights, or third candlestick, two servers at a *missa cantata*, bearing in opposite hands candle-sticks or standing before the standard candle-sticks in the sanctuary, light their candles in the manner described above under the riddel-lights.

3. *Torches at solemn celebrations.* At solemn choral Eucharists it is customary for two, four, six, or even eight torch-bearers, depending on the dignity of the feast, to proceed to a place before the altar during the Preface and kneel. During the *Sanctus* and at the elevations their torches are lifted up. The torch-bearers then retire after the communion of the people.

4. *Candles in procession.* In any procession with a crucifer, that functionary is generally flanked by two candle-bearers. When the way is too narrow for three to proceed abreast, they precede him.

5. *Candlemas.* On the Feast of the Purification of the B. V. M. (the *Mariä Lichtmess* of our older KOO, the *Mariä Reinigung* of our German *Agende*) the candles to be used during the following year are blessed. The ethos of this benediction is that the primeval curse placed upon creation because of man's sin ought to be removed by the invocation of God's Holy Name before any part of creation is used in the divine service. The ancient benedictions of Candlemas

have been carefully analyzed in Adolph Franz, *Die kirchliche Benedictionen im Mittelalter*, 1909, volume 1, pages 442-460. In honor of the "Light to lighten the Gentiles" lighted candles are carried in procession by the congregation during the singing of the festival anthems. At the end of the procession they are extinguished, to be relighted at the reading of the Holy Gospel, and again during the time the *Sanctus*-lights are (or would be) burning, *i.e.*, from the beginning of the Consecration prayer to the consumption or removal of the Sacred Species.

6. *Tenebrae.* The services of *Tenebrae*, properly the matins and lauds of the *Triduum Sacrum* anticipated on the respective evenings preceding, are remarkably effective, and since the entire service, with the exception of a few paragraphs from St. Augustine's very suggestive commentary on the Messianic psalms, is in the *ipsissimis verbis* of the Sacred Scriptures, they are unexceptionable even to the most critical. The old Continental rite called for twenty-four unbleached candles (in contradistinction to the modern Roman rite, which uses only fifteen) mounted on a large wooden candelabrum called the "herse." As the service pro-

PLEASE TURN TO PAGE 143.

The Three Types

F. R. WEBBER

EVERY large city has three types of department store. The first is the quality type. Aisles are broad, ceilings high and not much merchandise is in sight. Deferential salespeople speak in quiet tones to polite customers. That is one type. In the second type, aisles are narrower, ceilings lower, and much merchandise is on display. Some of it has large price cards nearby. Clerks are more numerous, crowds greater, and there is a certain amount of noise and hustle. It is difficult to create a picture of the third type. Its aisles are very narrow, its ceilings low, and the merchandise is dumped in disorderly array in open bins. Customers trample and elbow one another, everybody is burrowing among piles of shabby, bin-soiled merchandise. Clerks rush about distractedly, there is noise, confusion, loud talk everywhere. Coatless, hairy men, with soiled suspenders, and blowsy, perspiring women jostle one another about the open bins. Crude signs on streamers of white muslin announce that it is the last day of record-breaking bargains, when everything must be sold at half-price to make way for a trainload of new bargains due to arrive next week. It is hot, the air is fetid, and a smell of stale tobacco smoke and the reek of perspiring human beings and not overly-clean bodies is everywhere.

The same thing is true in regard to our church customs. At one extreme we have the "nice peoples'" church. The building may be large or small, but it has a quiet atmosphere of utmost gentility. Quiet sidesmen hand one a hymnal at the door and tip-toe as they show one silently to a vacant seat. The music is quiet, the church uncrowded, the singing somewhat subdued, and the service from start to finish a model of polite worship. The sermon is literary in style, and

delivered in a conversational tone, with positively no attempt at sensationalism.

In the second type of church, there is more hustle and noise. Self-assertive ushers whisper animatedly to one as he enters, hand him a hymnal and a few pieces of printed literature, and stride magnificently before him and wave him to his seat. There is a slight undertone of noise, people moving about on a variety of errands and a certain amount of restlessness everywhere. The singing is hearty, the choir comes in with a swinging stride, and the pastor reads his parts of the service in an animated tone. The sermon is lively, there is quite a bit of gesticulation, word painting and striving to keep up one's interest to a moderately high pitch. After the service the pastor hurries to the door, there is much hand-shaking, and one is taken in hand and introduced to a dozen talkative women of middle age and two or three men, and then asked to sign the visitor's register. One receives a few more pieces of printed literature, and sent on his way with an invitation to come often.

The third type of church is equally well known. Men and boys stand smoking cigarettes on the steps, and as we approach (perfect strangers), everybody speaks to us. Inside two ushers seize us, ask us our name and place of residence, and at once introduce us to everybody in sight. A fussy usher shows us a seat, hands us a book, and bends over us explaining how to get through the service. Here is the Introit. The choir sings that. We must sing the Gloria Patri. The Kyrie is sung responsively. The Gloria in Excelsis is omitted, and somebody will sing a solo instead. The fussy usher leaves us, and we are glad, for his breath smells of onions and a five-cent cigar. He returns, and whispers hoarsely that there is a card-party Tuesday evening, tickets 50 cents, and we must be sure to attend. Mrs. Sensenbrenner and Mrs. Schunkweiler will have tickets at the door, and the pastor will "announce it off the pulpit." The choir comes in. We are aware of its nearness because of an animated buzz of conversation coming up the basement stairs. The singers come in, dressed in the current, bizarre raiment of some small-town mail-order church supply house. Cassocks may be blue, maroon or red. Surplices are extremely short, and there may be Eaton collars, enormous bow ties with flowing ends, and the women may wear mortar-boards in imitation of the local high-school graduating class. They come in shrieking a hymn at top voice, with a wobbly tremolo and a sustained triple-forte from start to finish. The pastor brings up the rear, singing lustily. A boy carries a processional cross, his right elbow at right angles to his body. He wears white gloves, even though the handle of the cross is not of brass.

The pastor reads the service in an oratorical manner. He inserts a multitude of rubrics: "Now, let us all unite in singing the second hymn, which is Number 42 in the old book and Number 326 in the new." "Now, let us all stand and unite in repeating the Creed, found on page 36. Page 36." "Let us all be seated while the choir sings 'How Awful is This Place, O Lord'."

Several parts of the service are omitted, and unrelated anthems and solo work substituted. The sermon is delivered in a uniform fortissimo, with exaggerated gestures, much story telling, and the usual "I was talking this week to a good woman, and she said, 'Pastor, I have often believed—'." The sermon shows signs of hasty preparation, for in these very busy, hurried churches the pastor has too many minor activities to permit study until Friday night after the picnic.

After the closing service a dozen people seize the stranger, we are plied with personal questions, our name, our occupation, our telephone number, our street address, our church connection, and whether or not we wouldn't like to join the church, buy a ticket to the roast pork supper, attend the Men's Club picnic, go with the Walther League on a moonlight steamship ride to Weetasket Beach and whether we know how to sing or play a musical instrument.

We shove through the crowd on the church steps, and walk away with a talkative man at each elbow. In our pocket we have three church bulletins, two copies of the district bulletin, four devotional booklets, a complimentary ticket to a week-night lecture on stewardship, two five-cent cigars, a tract "What Did the Reformation Stand For," tracts on Christian giving, distinctive Lutheran customs and the separation of church and state. All these were thrust into our hands by friendly people at the church door. We accepted them all with thanks, and we declined as graciously as we could, the purchase of three different tickets.

We may be annoyed at the silly antics of a gentleman in a formal coat and bow tie, waving his arms as he directs the choir. We may dislike a sloppy minor seventh at the end of every stanza of the hymn and every Amen. We may not relish being pounced upon by half a dozen people and plied with questions the moment we mount the church steps. Nor may we like to have anthems of the "Praise ye the Father," "Send out Thy Light" and "Incline Thine Ear" sort shouted at us.

However, we walk away with thankful hearts, remembering that there are at least two other types of churches.

We recall with thankfulness that all churches are not like this one. We have other types from which we may choose. One is equally thankful that noisy, fussy churches exist, for many people would feel distressed without them. Some folks are elated if they are laid hold of and gushed over, before and after service. They like noisy, self-assertive choirs, they like tremolo stops and they like the vox humana. There are even people who like electric organs with no pipes. Were we, by some Act of Uniformity, to sweep all this away, it would not seem like church to many people who like this sort of thing. Or, since

such people may be in the majority, should the Act of Uniformity mean that the noisy church is the ideal type what a punishment it would be for us of the minority! Viewed from either angle, we are in favor of allowing the three tendencies to develop normally and to survive, so all may be happy And, to change the subject abruptly, if there must be a change of name, why not fall gradually into the habit of referring to ourselves as the SYNODICAL CONFERENCE, and gradually drop "Missouri." The name will need no explanation and no act of the legislature.

What May One Dedicate?

ONE of our pastors raises an interesting question. What things may one dedicate to the glory of God? He attended an anniversary service not long ago. The Praeses had been asked to come and dedicate a number of things to the glory of God, which he did. The things dedicated were as follows: a new altar cross; two round glass globes for the pulpit lights; two brass vases; a new piano; chairs for the Sunday-school; a new carpet for the church aisle; a new organ bench; chairs for the choir; an electric organ blower and a new hot air furnace. "The President began to read off each item, and in each case dedicated it to the glory of God. In each case the donors were mentioned, and each item was solemnly dedicated to the glory of God." Thus writes the pastor who attended this unusual service. He says that it may be quite proper to dedicate an altar, a lectern, a pulpit, Communion vessels, candlesticks, etc., and of course a new church, a parish house, a bell, an organ, a dwelling and a burying ground; but he questions whether other objects may properly be sanctified by means of the Word of God and a dedicatory prayer. His letter is so full of sound common sense that we should be only too glad to quote it verbatim and in its entirety; but this pastor asks us not to do so. He does not care to be misunderstood, for he did not write in a critical spirit. He attended the service, and the question arose in his mind: How far may one go in dedicating things?

Certainly we all agree that it is a praiseworthy thing to add to the

physical equipment of the church from time to time. Only a shiftless congregation will be content to poke along, year after year, and never make any improvements. Our restless friend, the Rev. Eusebius Snapp, has moved again. He accepted a call to a small town congregation. When he got there, he found a large frame church of the Victorian type, with wooden buttresses, pointed arches in clapboard construction and all that. Wisely enough he began his modernizing with the chancel. The altar was one of those catalogue affairs of the middle eighteen-eighties, and it looked like a small table. The reredos reminded one of three dog houses set side by side. There was an altar guild with about $1,000 "on" the bank, which had been accumulating for many years. Pastor Snapp persuaded them to get a new altar and reredos. The writer designed it for him and full-sized it on paper, and a reputable group of craftsmen built it for him. The Ladies' Aid provided the white, green, violet and black altar hangings, and promised a red set next year. The Sunday-school (also with quite a sum lying idly "on" the bank, provided a set of really fine Communion silver; for the old set was of the electro-plate sort and the plating had long since become extremely shabby. The Men's Club provided a good crucifix and candlesticks. A few Sundays ago Pastor Snapp had a short dedication service after the sermon, and everything that we have described was set apart by means of appropriate Scripture verses and a dedicatory prayer. Nobody will deny that it was a praiseworthy thing to make these

improvements. Money that had been lying idly in the bank was used to replace old and shabby equipment. It was fitting that these things, as a group, be set apart, and a brief dedicatory service held.

Then trouble arose. There was a voters' meeting next night. The Walther League, not to be outdone in any praiseworthy thing, offered to get a new bell to take the place of the old, unmusical thing that had served its purpose for so long. The bell was accepted by the voters, and it was decided to bring it into the chancel whenever it arrived, and dedicate it with a brief service. Upon hearing this, old Simon von Guckenberg, a wealthy retired brewer, arose and offered to present a new motor car to Pastor Snapp. The voting members promptly decided to dedicate the motor car and the thousand gallons of gasoline that old Simon gave with it.

It would not be hard to imagine such a precedent to gain ground, and to be carried to absurd extremes. What is to prevent the Sewing Circle from presenting a new rug for the sacristy, and demanding that it be set apart solemnly with appropriate Scripture verses and prayer? Some extremely curious things have been dedicated, just to keep peace in the family. People simply do not use their heads. If the Sunday-school presented a fine Communion set, and it was dedicated with impressive ceremonies, then who is to prevent the Martha Society from getting busy and buying a new coffee urn for the church kitchen, and expecting it to be duly consecrated to its intended use and us to the Lord's service?

Perhaps a good rule o' thumb might be to dedicate only those things that are associated particularly with the Word and Sacraments. We might extend this to include the bell or bells, for men have dedicated these things since time immemorial, and to fail to do so might offend many people. However, we can see no reason why a stained glass window should be duly "blessed." If the window is an inferior one, not a great deal need be said about it except to thank the people who gave it, and silently overlook their bad taste. If it is really a thing of merit, then it ought to be sufficient to print a beautiful folder of four to eight pages, with a good picture of the window, and an explanation of it, with a few words of appreciation to those who gave it, and of him in whose memory it is given.

An organ may be formally dedicated with an appropriate service, provided it is good in quality and genuine. But if it is one of these miserable unified things, with three sets of pipes extended upward and downward, and twenty-four wholly fictitious "stops" taken from it, then the pastor who remains silent is at least setting an example to all in the matter of charity and forbearance. If it is one of these things composed of a keyboard hooked up to a radio receiving set, from which emanate sounds that remind one of a steel banjo, then it is enough to sing one hymn and there let the distressing matter rest. An appropriate hymn would be the one of the old Puritans:

"Lo, how dreadful is this house
Wherein we luckless wretches dwell."

We can see no good in dedicating a parish house, for it is in no way associated with the Means of Grace. Why "bless" a place that is to be used for eating, drinking and card playing? Some years ago we were shown a newspaper cutting describing, of all things, a Solemn Service of Deconsecration. A certain sectarian church had sent some 200 miles for the bishop of the diocese, and after an eloquent sermon he had proceeded to deconsecrate the parish house so that the young people might hereafter be privileged to dance in it! This was followed swiftly by another incident. The clergy of a certain denomination were hankering for an opportunity to hold a joint service with certain pastors of another denomination. However, the rubrics would not permit such a thing, for they stated clearly, so did their Canon Law, that no ecclesiastic of a different faith could possibly officiate at their altars nor preach from their pulpits. The Solemn Service of Deconsecration gave them their clue. They got their obliging bishop down and proceeded to ordain the consecrated lay-preachers of the Baptist and Presbyterian persuasion. Having been duly ordained by a bishop with water-tight apostolic succession, they went in solemn procession into the church, where the union service was held. At the close of the service they retired to the guild room, where another service was held, and the Solemn Form and Manner for the Deposing and Unchurching of an Unworthy Incumbent was read, and the "converts" who had so recently "made their obedience" to the apostolic procession were formally unfrocked.

When one begins by "blessing" everything in sight, even to the altar vases, the new kneelers in the pews and the new hymnals, it is an easy matter to keep things going until there is nothing left to consecrate. Then, for want of some new stunt to satisfy man's love for Formal Occasions, it is a simple matter to begin deconsecrating things. The two authentic instances cited above will show how far this deconsecration matter can go, if it once gets started.

The wise way would seem to be: consecrate sparingly, and limit it only to those objects connected directly with the Word and Sacraments; with bells and organs, schools and burying grounds included.

The liturgy and ceremonial connected therewith should be brief and simple. We have gone through a folder in our vertical files, and brought forth a few sample copies of such dedication services. Almost all of them are long-winded affairs. The prayers are particularly verbose. There was no valid reason why the Rev. Eusebius Snapp need print a 750-word prayer, beginning "Almighty, Everliving God, we are assembled here today to dedicate to Thy glory a superb new altar and reredos, which have been provided for the use of this Christian congregation through the kindness and generosity of Thy servants the Altar Guild of St. Paul's Evangelical Lutheran Church of ———, ———. We are also gathered in Thy sight to dedicate to its intended use and to Thy Name's honor and glory the beautiful superfrontals for the altar which were provided by the ever faithful and hardworking Ladies' Aid Society of St. Paul's Church; as well as the chalice, paten, silver cruets, ciborium and other vessels given to us by our faithful Sunday-school, and the new Bible on the lectern, which was given by Thy faithful servant Mr. John Josiah Brennenwald and his devoted wife Martha Caroline," etc., etc.

Such informational prayers are idle rhetoric. No prayer need be informational. If we have information to impart, and names to mention, it is certainly worth while to print a beautiful little folder containing this information. It is only the man who likes to hear the sound of his "much speaking" who will pray an informational prayer.

Suggestions for Bulletin Board

WE BELIEVE
-1-
that the Bible
is the
Inspired Word
of God.

WE BELIEVE
-2-
in the Holy Trinity,
God Father, Son
and Holy Ghost.

WE BELIEVE
-3-
that Jesus Christ,
the Son of God,
died for the sins
of all mankind.

WE BELIEVE
-4-
that the Holy
Spirit is true God
and a real person.

WE BELIEVE
-5-
that Jesus Christ
rose from the
dead and lives.

WE BELIEVE
-6-
that "faith"
without works
is dead.

The Structural Outline of the Church Service

F. R. WEBBER

Many people are familiar with the fact that our Common Service is laid out in a cruciform plan. This was done deliberately, long before the Reformation. In many of our churches where the plainest and simplest form of service exists, a vestige of this cruciform structural outline still persists, for the pastor often reads the Epistle from the south end of the altar, the Credo from the middle and the Gospel from the north end. Just why is this?

We are printing a diagram which will make matters clear. It is not an original diagram, for we have merely taken the ancient structural arrangement of the pre-Reformation Mass, and have omitted those parts which Luther omitted, namely the prayers following the Offertorium. Were this structural plan of the Common Service more generally kept in mind, we would hear of fewer mutilations, fewer additions to the service and fewer substitutions of parts.

In order to remind the people of this cruciform structural outline of the service, the priests of old, and our Lutheran forefathers read or chanted the Introit, Gloria Patri, Epistle, Hallelujah and Gradual from the south horn of the altar, the Gloria Tibi, Gospel, Laus Tibi and Sermon from the north, and the other parts of the service from the midst of the altar. Let us study our diagram in detail.

In Volume 2 of the Apostolic Fathers, St. Justin the Martyr, who was born just after the death of St. John the Apostle, describes the service of the Apostolic Church in detail. This is found in his *Apology*. The church service consisted of four parts: Preparation, Worship, Instruction and the Celebration of the Lord's Supper. These four main parts of the service, each with its own secondary preparation, progress and climax, is found in our Common Service today. The Early Church, the Mediaeval Church, and the early Lutherans all assumed that these four parts be used every Sunday and feast day. It was not until the spiritual blight of Pietism and Rationalism spread over northern Europe, with its contempt for the Sacramental element in religion, that the fourth chief part of the church service was the exception rather than the rule.

We picked up a certain magazine lately and read it through in dismay, for again and again we read statements to the effect that our liturgical forms and our customs are products of the Middle Ages. Have we forgotten that almost our entire Common Service has an unbroken history of at least fifteen hundred, and in some cases, almost two thousand years? It is time that certain universally recognized historic facts be restated. And historic facts are not matters of controversy. Let us study the parts of the Common Service in detail, noting the origin and use of each.

The first of the Four Chief Parts of the Common Service is the Preparation, commonly known as the Confessional Service. This is made up of five, and often six parts: In Nomine, a Collect, a Scripture reading, the Confiteor and the Absolution. Often a confessional address is added. The officiating pastor, facing the altar, and standing at its lowest step, says, "In the Name of the Father, and of the Son, and of the Holy Ghost. Amen." Then follows a short Collect (found on pp. 24-25 of the "Liturgy and Agenda"), or some other suitable Collect. Then comes a Scripture Lesson, which custom decrees should be Psalm 51, 7-9. In some parts of the Lutheran Church, the entire 51st Psalm is read at this point. Then follows the Confiteor. The pastor says, "Let us humbly kneel and confess our sins," and here the Confiteor of the Small Catechism is used. Originally this Confiteor was addressed to "Almighty God, to Blessed Mary ever Virgin, to Blessed Michael the Archangel, to Blessed John the Baptist, to the holy Apostles Peter and Paul, and to all the Saints." Luther recast this Confiteor into the form that we have today. After the Confiteor, the celebrant rises and pronounces the Absolution to the kneeling congregation. Then they arise and proceed at once to the Introit.

If there be no Communion, then the opening Collect, the Asperges Me (Psalm 51, 7-9), the Confiteor and Absolution are omitted, and the Lesser Confiteor and Declaration of Grace, found on the first page of our hymnal, are substituted. Years ago, the Confessional Service was held on Saturday evening, and later it was moved to half an hour or so before the Communion Service. In those days the Lesser Confiteor and Declaration of Grace were needed. But where the Confessional Service is followed immediately by the Communion Service, the Confessional Prayers and Absolution are not said twice.

The Introit. The Second Chief Part of the service is that of Worship. It begins with the Introit. This is the beginning of the service proper, for the First Part is merely preparatory.

Liturgical writers almost always ascribe the series of Introits as we have them today to Celestine (423-432 A.D.), but it is the writer's humble opinion that the series did not reach its final form until the time of Gregory the Great (540-604 A.D.), and that it is safer to say that the Introits, as they stand today, date from about the year 430 to the year 550 A.D.

An Introit is composed of the proper Antiphon for the day, a Psalm verse and the Gloria Patri. Up to the 16th century, an entire Psalm was often sung.

The Introit is of greatest importance, for it is the herald that sounds the keynote for the entire service. Its theme is restated in Collect, Epistle, Gradual, Gospel, Sermon and in the prayers and hymns, giving the service an unbroken continuity of thought.

The Introit may be chanted, either antiphonally or otherwise, or it may be read or chanted by the pastor. If no other part of the service be Gregorian, the Introit and the Prefatio ought to be sung to their historic melodies, and in strict unison. Several books of modern musical settings are used in our circles, but none can surpass the traditional Plainchant melodies, with their matchless jubilations. Until a Lutheran book of the ancient Gregorian melodies appears, we will have to borrow from the *"Liber Usualis"* and translate into English. If the traditional Introit melodies cannot be had, the next best thing is to use the Gregorian Psalm Tones. An inexpensive collection of Plainsong Introits, is published by St. Mary's Press, Wantage Berks.

The Kyrie Eleison. This Lesser Litany was known at the time of the Council of Vaison, in 529 A.D., and it is generally supposed, because of its Greek words, to go back to Apostolic days. It is very often sung in the original Greek, *Kyrie Eleison,* for like the words *Alleluia* and *Hosanna,* it seems to resist translation. It is proper to sing it three, six or nine times. In Luther's *Formula Missae,* which all conservative liturgical scholars consider his best arrangement of the Common Service, he retains the old, nine-fold form. In his German Mass it is reduced to a three-fold repetition. Nowadays it is often sung antiphonally by pastor and people, each petition repeated to form a six-fold Kyrie. The finest nine-fold arrangement is that found in the *Missa de Angelis,* which is nothing more than an ancient Gregorian musical setting to the chief parts of the Communion Service. A good English arrangement may be had for a few cents from H. W. Gray & Co., 159 E. 48th Street, New York.

The Gloria in Excelsis. This is the Christian Church's oldest hymn of praise, probably antedating even the Te Deum. The first sentence of it was sung by the angels at the birth of our Saviour. Like the Lesser Creed, it developed gradually, taking its present form before the Council of Nicaea, 325 A.D. In earliest days it was sung only at the Midnight Mass on Christmas Eve. At one time it was chanted first in Greek and then repeated in Latin. Later its use was restricted to bishops only, a priest using it only on Easter Day. About the year 500, it was commonly used every Sunday.

The Gloria in Excelsis is always used at Communion and on all Festivals, even in Advent and Lent. If there be neither Communion nor festival, it may be omitted during Lent. Our "Old Chant" is musically inferior, and some congregations have substituted a familiar Gregorian setting found in both the *de Angelis* and the *Marialis*, which is more joyous than the somewhat dragging "Old Chant." And lest the reader be shocked, permit us to say that the *Marialis* is nothing more than an ancient musical setting to the Kyrie, Creed, Gloria, Sanctus, Lord's Prayer and Agnus Dei.

The Collect. Each Sunday and holy day has its proper Collect, which restates the theme set forth in the Introit. In addition there is a multitude of other collects, some of which are as ancient as the Temple worship, and were repeated, or rather sung, without doubt by our Lord and His Apostles. Most of our present-day Collects are at least as old as the fourth, fifth and sixth centuries.

A Collect is a sentence prayer, made up of a Salutation, a Relative Clause, a Petition, an Antecedent Reason and a Doxology. Often the fifth part is omitted, and occasionally the second part. For a very full and fine discussion of the structural form of the Collect, see Dr. Percy Dearmer's "The Art of Public Worship," found in most public libraries.

The historic Collects of the Church are marvels of beautiful liturgical English, and do not seem to suffer in their translation. They are among the choicest gems of lyric prose in all literature, and some of them have the rhythm of poetry: "Grant us that peace which the world cannot give," for example.

The Epistle. In earliest days the Church read the Old Testament Law and Prophets. But when the Epistles were written, St. Paul gave instructions that they be read in all the churches. This gave rise to a systematic, liturgical reading of the Epistles, as well as the Gospels. St. Justin Martyr, born 114 A.D., says in his *Apology* that at every church service "the records of the Apostles or the writings of the Prophets are read as long as time permits." Tertullian likewise bears witness to this custom. By about the year 150 A.D., a complete series of Epistles and Gospels was in use, which formed the foundation for our present system.

Our present system of Epistles and Gospels is at least as old as the time of St. Jerome (died 420), for in his "Companion" we find the two series just about as we have them today.

From earliest days the congregation remained seated for the Epistle and stood for the Gospel. The former was chanted from the south end of the altar, and facing the altar, and the latter from the north end or horn of the altar, but not facing it. It is likewise a very ancient custom to chant the Epistle in monotone, with a drop of a semi-tone at a question.

The Hallelujah and Sentence. Following the Epistle, the Alleluia is sung, changing with the various seasons of the Christian Year. Seven of these Alleluias are retained in our Common Service. The strange omission of the Alleluia for the Christmas season is an unfortunate thing, and ought to be corrected.

These Alleluias are the congregation's joyful response to the Word of God, and they ought always to be sung to their proper melodies.

Formerly there were certain Sequences, such as the hymns *Victimae Paschali Veni Sancte Spiritus, Stabat Mater, Lauda Sion* and *Dies Irae*. At first there were Sequences (Proses, Jubilations) for every Sunday and Holy Day, some of which developed into metrical hymns. In the 16th century these were reduced to those just mentioned, some of which were retained by the Lutherans in the form of hymns rather than responses to the Epistle. A number of the old sequences are to be had of the Plainsong and Mediaeval Music Society, Nashdom Abbey, Burnham, Bucks.

The Gradual. This is composed generally of two Psalm verses, two Alleluias, another Psalm verse and a single Alleluia, except in Lent, when their structure changes, and Tracts are used. Luther retained the use of the Gradual. It was omitted in the 1877 German Common Service and the 1888 English edition. Recent Lutheran hymnals have been restoring the Gradual. The rubrics of our present hymnal permit a Psalm or a Gradual hymn to be sung instead. It would be desirable to restore these Graduals and Tracts, for they are historic parts of our Lutheran liturgy. St. Mary's Press, Wantage, Berks., an Anglican concern, issues a book of Graduals and Tracts, with Plainsong settings.

The Gospel. Our present series of liturgical Gospels, like the Epistles, is of great antiquity. Some sort of a series came into use in very early times, but our present series developed between

say the years 400 and 600 A.D. There were lessons for the holy days and station days as well, so that every incident recorded by the Four Evangelists, and all the important Christian doctrines, were read publicly every year, and in the course of the Christian Year, the entire life of our Lord was read consecutively, as well as the Christian doctrines found in the Epistles. It would be a splendid thing were all our congregations to restore the "forgotten festivals," such as the Transfiguration, the Presentation (Purification), the Annunciation, the Assumption (*Mariaeheimgang*), All Saints' Day, etc. These are retained in our German hymnal, and "propers" are provided for them in our present English hymnal.

Great importance was attached to the Gospel in olden days.

The Structural Plan of the Communion Service

THE ALTAR

THE COMMUNION SERVICE

I. PREPARATION
1. In Nomine
2. Collect
3. Asperges Me
4. Confiteor
5. Absolution

II. WORSHIP
3. Kyrie
4. Gloria in Excelsis
5. Collect de tempore

1. Introit
2. Gloria Patri

III. INSTRUCTION
5. Gloria Tibi
6. The Gospel
7. Laus Tibi
10. Sermon

8. Credo
9. Cantica de Tempore

1. The Epistle
2. Hallelujah
3. Gradual

IV. SACRAMENTAL
1. Offertorium
2. Prayer
3. Intercessions
4. Thanksgivings
5. Dominus vobiscum
6. Sursum Corda
7. Gratias Agamus
8. Prefatio and Season Preface
9. Per quem majestatem
10. Sanctus
11. (Exhortation)
12. Lord's Prayer
13. Verba
14. Pax Domini
15. Agnus Dei
16. Administration
17. Blessing
18. Deo Gratias
19. Nunc Dimittis

23. Post-Communion Hymn
21. Benedicamus
22. Benediction
20. Post-Communion Collects

It was preceded by the *Gloria Tibi* and followed by the *Laus Tibi*, two joyous ejaculations of praise. It was sung from the north or Gospel side of the church, and at its singing a festive procession of acolytes, bearing torches to symbolize the Light of God's Word, moved to the Gospel station, and surrounded the Gospeller, who first censed the book and then chanted the proper Gospel, first signing the book with his thumb in the form of the cross, then signing himself on forehead, lips and breast. At the reading of the Gospel, all rose to their feet and sang joyfully the *Gloria Tibi*, and later the *Laus Tibi*.

The Credo. The Nicene Creed is, of course, the chief Creed and the one invariably used for Holy Communion and on all festivals. It dates to the year 325 A.D., when some 318 church dignitaries gathered at Nicaea for the purpose of meeting the

Arian heresy and confessing their faith in the Holy and Undivided Trinity and the divinty of Our Lord.

It is a very old custom to kneel at the words "And was incarnate * * * and was made Man." We recall speaking with old people who recalled distinctly this custom among our own grandfathers, in certain Lutheran localities. The Apostles Creed may be substituted for the Nicene, if there be no Communion or festival. The setting known as Credo II is very good.

The Cantica de Tempore. This is an hymn sung just before the sermon. It is the *Hauptlied* of the third chief part of the service, and it must reiterate the thought of Introit, Epistle, Gradual and Gospel, even though the sermon might present some other theme. It must conform to the day of the Church Year rather than to local circumstances. Thus if there be Confirmation on Palm Sunday, this particular hymn must voice the thought of Palm Sunday, and a Confirmation hymn may come later.

The Sermon. Originally this was preached from the north side of the church. When pulpits finally came into use, they were located at first on the north, or Gospel side of the building. Various explanations are given for the southern position of the pulpit in many Lutheran churches, such as greater freedom of gesture where the pulpit is built against the Epistle pier, and the better light on the south, or sunny side of the church. The sermon normally repeats and elaborates upon the theme for the day, first proclaimed in the Introit.

The Offertorium. In early days the Christians brought gifts of bread and wine, presenting them in procession at this part of the service, likewise announcing at this time their names for Communion. In St. Augustine's time, a Psalm was sung as the procession moved around the church with their offerings.

A distinction must be made between the Offertorium and the Offertory. The latter was a prayer which followed the Offertorium, and it reads, "Accept, Holy Father, Omnipotent, Eternal God, this immaculate Host which I, thy unworthy servant, offer Thee." Luther rejected this prayer on the grounds that the Holy Eucharist is not a gift which man offers to God, but a gift of God to man. Likewise he rejected the prayers for the living and the dead which followed it.

It is to be deplored that so many of our choirs substitute an anthem at this place, singing "Create in me a clean heart," and then an anthem. The chief objection to the anthem or solo is that it so often is entirely foreign in thought to the theme for the day. Many a non-Lutheran has complained eloquently in the musical magazines against this practice. One writer states that he visited a church, in this case Episcopal, where the proper Introit, Collect, Epistle and Gospel for our Lord's Transfiguration were used. Then followed a hymn in regard to the duty of prayer. A sermon on stewardship followed, then an anthem which was none other than Kipling's "Lest we Forget," set to ornate music. Then came an "offertory selection" on the organ, a fantasie on "Vom Himmel Hoch." The writer of that article declares he went away with a confused picture of Transfiguration, prayer, stewardship, patriotism and the Nativity in his mind, instead of a powerful impression of a single theme, set forth in Introit, Collect, Epistle, Gradual, Gospel, hymns, sermon and Offertory.

If the choir has ambition to sing a new anthem each Sunday, let them substitute the proper Offertorium for the day, just after the sermon. One exists for each Sunday and festival, and the rubrics of all Lutheran hymnals permit "any other suitable Offertory" to be sung in place of "Create in me a clean heart, O Lord." The task of choir preparation may be greatly simplified, if the traditional Plainsong settings to the Offertorium be used, and sung in unison, with no repetition of the words of the text. If the choirmaster cannot locate readily the proper Offertoriums, there are men willing to assist him.

The Prayers. Our lengthy General Prayer takes the place of the pre-Reformation intercessions for living and dead. It is rather long for the present day, and our rubrics permit any other suitable prayer at this place, as well as special intercessions and thanksgivings. Our St. Louis "Liturgy and Agenda" provides a short Collect repeating the thought of either the Epistle or the Gospel, and one of these may be used instead of the lengthy General Prayer, in congregations where the service must be timed down to an hour or so.

The Prefatio. This begins with the *Dominus Vobiscum* and ends with the *Sanctus.* This is among the very oldest parts of the service, and many liturgical scholars believe that it dates back to the very Apostolic Church, or at least very soon thereafter. Not only the words, but the traditional musical setting as well, are extremely ancient, and are used almost universally, both words and music, in Lutheran, Roman Catholic and Anglican churches the world over. Few have attempted to provide substitute melodies, and few of these survive for any length of time.

Liturgical authorities place the number of Season Prefaces that once existed all the way from 240 to 407. The Roman Catholic Church has reduced the Season Prefaces to twelve, the Anglicans retain eight and the Lutherans but six. It would be desirable to restore an Epiphany Preface, and possibly the one commonly used for the Presentation, the Annunciation and the Transfiguration.

The missing Preface for the Epiphany season reads: "Who, in the substance of our mortal flesh, manifested forth His glory; that He might bring us out of darkness into His glorious light. Therefore with Angels and Archangels," etc. That for Presentation, Annunciation and Transfiguration reads: "Because, in the mystery of the Word made flesh, Thou hast caused a new light to shine in our hearts, to give the knowledge of Thy glory in the face of Thy Son, Jesus Christ. Therefore with Angels and Archangels," etc. That for All Saints' Day is very beautiful, reading: "Who, in the multitude of Thy Saints, hast compassed us about with so great a cloud of witnesses, that we, rejoicing in their fellowship, may run with patience the race that is set before us, and together with them may receive the crown of glory that fadeth not away. Therefore with Angels and Archangels," etc.

No music exists more deeply devotional in its spirit than the traditional setting to the *Prefatio*, beginning with "The Lord be with you," and ending with the *Sanctus*. The great historian, the Venerable Bede, states that St. Cuthbert (died 687), could never chant these traditional melodies without being so deeply moved that he sobbed aloud by the time the *Sanctus* was reached. When he raised his hands aloft at the *Sursum Corda*, he often choked with emotion. St. Augustine could never sing it without weeping. Mozart said that he would gladly have the world forget everything that he ever wrote, had he only been the composer of this music, and that of *Pater Noster*. Other great musical composers have declared these traditional melodies to be the finest and most deeply devotional music ever written. And yet this music is not sentimental. It is extremely simple, much of it monotonic recitation, with certain melodic inflections of strangely haunting beauty. It rises from height to height, and at the *Sanctus* carries the devout worshipper to the very throne of Heaven.

If every other part of the service be read, at least this part ought to be chanted by both pastor and people, as it is in many of our German congregations. The musical text of the German Service at this place is not pure, for banal "la, si, do" inflections have been substituted for the traditional "do, do, do, do, si, la, la, si, si." We would plead for a restoration of the musical melodies of the *Prefatio*, for they have been used by two-thirds or more of all Christendom, for almost twenty centuries.

The Sanctus. The Preface rises from climax to climax, until it reaches the *Sanctus*. This is taken from Isaiah's prophecy, and from the Apocalypse. It is the inspired hymn of praise sung by the heavenly choirs about the throne of the Holy Trinity. The musical setting in our green hymnal is a good one, and fits well with the traditional setting to the Preface. The *Sanctus* is likewise of early origin, having been known to Tertullian, Cyprian, St. Cyril and St. Chrysostom.

The Exhortation. This is regarded by many liturgical students as an unfortunate insertion, because it interrupts the progress of the Communion liturgy at this point, so that a sermonette on the need of self-examination and faith may be heard. It is not found in Luther's first arrangement of the Common Service. It was inserted in his later German Mass, probably to satisfy Hausmann and other friendly critics. So evident is its intrusive character than it is very often omitted, and the admonition in regard to self-examination incorporated in the sermon itself, which is more logical, liturgically.

The Lord's Prayer. Anciently the Prayer of Consecration came at this point, and it was retained by some of the older Lutheran liturgies, particularly Pfalz-Neuberg KO., of 1543. It is, in those Lutheran liturgies which retained it, merely a prayer asking the Lord to bless the bread and wine, and cause them to convey to us His true Body and Blood. But in our present-day Common Service, the Lord's Prayer is used instead. Tertullian,

Cyprian and Origen refer indirectly to the use of the Lord's Prayer here, and St. Cyril mentions it specifically. The ancient musical setting to the Lord's Prayer is much finer than some of the modern, college-chapel settings. This ancient melody, as well as the entire Preface, may be had in the Victor Red Seal gramophone discs, and the traditional rhythmic flow of the music may be learned from these.

The Words of Institution. This part of the service dates from patristic, if not from Apostolic days. St. Augustine taught that here we have the Consecration proper. "The Word is added to the element and it becomes a Sacrament," he said. So likewise Gregory the Great. Luther believed that the Verba is all that is required to validate the Sacrament. Elevation of the host formerly occurred at the words pertaining to the bread, and elevation of the chalice at the close of the Words of Institution. Despite all present-day controversy, Luther retained this Elevation, but he did not regard it as essential, but where good reasons could be shown for its omission, he permitted this. Its use is merely historic, for it was done in early times as a sign to the congregation that the celebrant believed in the Real Presence.

The Pax Domini. This is reminiscent of the kiss of peace in the early Church, at the words "The peace of the Lord be with you." Later this kiss was given "liturgically," the celebrant merely placing his hands on the deacon's shoulders, both inclining their heads slightly, but not actually kissing.

The Agnus Dei. This, like almost all the other parts of the liturgy, is taken from the Scriptures. It is from St. John 1,29 It was used previous to the time of Gregory the Great, and is included in his Sacramentary. Sometimes it was chanted but once, sometimes twice, again thrice. The addition of the final words "Grant us Thy peace" is due to a carpenter, who believed that the Virgin Mother appeared to him and showed him a medal reading, "O Lamb of God, that takest away the sin of the world, Grant us Thy peace." This reputed vision made so profound an impression at the time that these words were added to the *Agnus Dei,* and remain to this day.

The Post-Communion Collects. The Collect found at the close of the Communion Service, like other parts of the liturgy, is ancient. It is read at the south end of the altar, and facing it. It is a thanksgiving to our Lord for the gift of the Blessed Sacrament. Luther permitted two Collects from the Mass at this place. One of these is retained in our present service.

The Closing Hymn. After the Benedicamus and Benediction, a hymn was sung. Custom decrees that this shall be "Holy God, we praise Thy Name," (Grosser Gott, wir loben Dich). This is a majestic old hymn, sung with deep feeling by Lutherans, as well as Roman Catholics and Anglicans. An excellent English translation exists. It is a more fitting conclusion than the Long Metre Doxology, for which there is little historic authority at this particular place.

Usages We Have Found

THE CUSTOMS we have listed below are in vogue in some of the churches with which we are acquainted. They may or may not be in harmony with the ideas of sticklers on liturgical form, but we present them for what they are worth. A number of them impressed us deeply.

1. In a certain western church the pastor prefaces the reading of his text with an ex corde prayer to which the choir sings a four-part Amen. Different Amens are used in accordance with the season. The number of the Amen to be used is posted on a little blackboard in the choir-room. In order to have no awkward break between the pastor's concluding words and the Amen, the last sentence of the prayer is written out and handed to the organist beforehand. Thus there is perfect team-work. The arrangement is impressively effective. Many of the Amens are sung a capella. This, of course, presupposes thorough practice.

2. In a church at St. Louis, after the doxology had been sung and while the congregation is bowed in silent prayer, the organist plays very softly a stanza of some appropriate hymn. The congregations remains in worshipful attention until the stanza is finished. We were impressed by the fact that this arrangement eliminated completely the unseemly haste which characterizes the silent prayer in most churches. There was no bustle of donning coats and wraps, which usually follows about two seconds after the concluding note of the doxology. Not a soul moved until the organist had finished his stanza.

3. In a Minnesota church late-comers are not ushered to seats during the opening service. They are compelled to remain in the rear of the church until the pastor proceeds to the lecturn for the reading of the lessons, when the organist plays for a few moments until all the people are seated. The service then proceeds. This does away with disturbance during the beautiful responsive opening service and permits those who have been on time to retain their spirit of devotion. It also helps to show up the habitual late-comers.

4. Many churches now rope off the rear pews of the church in order to bring the audience up forward. The rear seats are reserved for women with little children and for late arrivals. Usually the ropes are removed during the second hymn. There may be objection on the part of a few people, due to the inherent human instinct to gravitate towards the rear seats, but usually there is no difficulty in persuading the people of the advantages of the arrangement. Late-comers should not be subjected to the embarrassment of being marched up to the front of the church, perhaps even during the sermon. It is painful for them and distracting to the congregation. Ushers should be trained to fill the church up from the front and not from the rear. With a little encouragement most of the people will cooperate. Roping off the rear will be a help. Heavy silk drapery cords should be used.

5. Some churches have flowers on the altar every Sunday. If some individual does not supply them in memory of some departed relative or friend, the church organizations take turns in footing the bills. One church has a standing order with a local florist. Prospective donors notify the chairman of the committee in charge and remit the price. The price is the same for every Sunday, except when otherwise desired by the donor. After the evening service the flowers are taken to some hospital with an appropriate card for some sick member of the church.

6. Some churches reserve the front part of the church on communion Sundays for the communicants. Before the service the head usher inquires of the pastor how many guests are expected at the Lord's Table and marks off the needed number of pews. As the people enter the ushers courteously inquire as to whether or not they are communing and seat them accordingly. The arrangement has obvious advantages.

Conducting the Church Service

F. R. Webber

"I ATTENDED service in St. ......'s Church in ....," writes a Lutheran. "Such liturgical practices in such a fine church! I shudder when I think of it." A day or two later a Lutheran editor wrote, "Very few of our men know how to use their altars and chancels correctly, once they have built them into their new churches."

Far be it from the writer of these lines to pose as an authority on liturgics, for he has very much to learn on this point. The following homely hints are thrown out with the hope that the readers of this magazine may respond, and that a helpful discussion may take place.

ORDER: Everything ought to be ready for the church service half an hour ahead of time. The altar book, hymnal, lectern Bible, pulpit Bible and announcement book ought to be lying where they may be picked up instantly, and at the right place in the service. To cross the chancel needlessly, to retreat into the sacristy after a forgotten book, or to make the congregation wait while a vestryman arranges the hymn board, or the organist his music—all of these things are breaches of good liturgical etiquette. Sunday-school call bells and bulletin boards ought to be put out of sight, and Sunday-school hymnals collected and stored away. Should there be doors into adjoining parts of the building, care should be taken that such things as the sewing circle's quilt, and the day school's blackboards be kept out of the line of direct vision. Empty alms plates ought not to lie on the altar. The sacristy should be arranged in such a manner that persons wishing to see the pastor need not pass through the chancel.

SILENCE: Over a side doorway leading into a magnificent New York church is the word SILENTIA, carved beautifully in oak. It may seem a bit brusque, but silence is a churchly virtue, and whispering, gossiping, running about from sacristy to organ loft, opening and closing windows needlessly, or distributing hymnals at the last minute are disturbing. Catechumens ought to be taught a suitable prayer, and young and old taught in a tactful manner the psychological value of silence as a preparation for worship.

THE USHERS: The ushers ought to be told not to show late comers to a sitting during Scripture reading or prayer. One or two convenient places in the service may be decided upon for admitting late comers, and members of the congregation ought to be sufficiently well bred to know that it is rude to turn and stare at the belated worshipper. The proverbial string that connects every nose with the door knob is a disturbing thing.

LEAVING THE CHURCH: Members of the congregation ought to be asked not to indulge in the rude habit of getting up and walking out of church after the sermon on Sundays when there is communion. In a church in Cologne we saw a good sized congregation straggle into church all through the opening service, and then straggle out again after the brief sermon, leaving the pastor and exactly nine persons to worry as best they could through the communion service. It may be a state-church custom, but it is a bad habit that is easily remedied, if attention be called to it in the proper way. In a certain congregation, the number of persons communing was increased from 456 to 768 within five years, by calling attention to this point. It can be done. It was only the excommunicated and the unconfirmed who were dismissed after the sermon in the early Christian Church.

THE PRELUDE: A quiet prelude, of devotional character, goes far toward creating an atmosphere of worship, but a noisy prelude, with booming pedal-bass, is almost a sure invitation for whispering and gossip.

THE OPENING: The pastor may remain in the sacristy unless he is actually officiating at the altar, or preaching. This is a good old Lutheran custom. A clergyman sitting cross-legged in an ornate chair beside the altar suggests the wholly fictitious popular belief that the priests of the Middle Ages sat in elaborate, throne-like chairs around the apse. A clergyman with humility of spirit will prefer either the sacristy, or else sedilia built into the south wall of the chancel.

The pastor ought to approach the altar from the front rather than from one side. He may carry an open service book rather than let his hands dangle. In turning to and from the altar, he will always turn in such a way that his right hand is nearest the altar as he turns. At the benediction he will turn so that his left hand is nearest the altar as he turns.

Some good authorities state that the service, down to the Introit, should be read several feet in front of the altar, and that the pastor shall mount the altar step proper at the Introit. The service should never be read from the lectern. Only the lessons and the announcements are made from the lectern.

The congregation should always remain standing for prayer, for the Introit, the Gloria in Excelsis, the Gospel, the Creed, the text of the sermon and the Offertory.

READING: The service ought to be read clearly, but without undue force and without "elocution." It is a golden maxim of sound liturgics that attention must be directed to that which is read rather than to the way in which it is read. In other words, elocutionary efforts or exaggerated mannerisms, which attract attention to the reader, are to be avoided. His personality must not assert itself in such a way as to awaken admiration for his skill as a public speaker, but rather should he subordinate any such gifts in order that the undivided attention of his congregation may be focussed upon that which he is reading. To read part of a Scripture verse and to recite the other part while gazing at the congregation is a bad habit.

CHANTING AND INTONING: Since our altar books contain choral settings to the service, it is well to use these where the congregation is not hostile to the custom. If the pastor has a poor singing voice, or if his chanting is nasal, or tends to drop a semi-tone or two, or if he is inclined to chant in a boisterous fashion, it is better to be satisfied with a plain reading of the service. Too much color causes such intoning to become rather florid. Due attention should be given to the sterling old Gregorian settings to both the pastor's and the congregation's parts of the service. Our Lutheran chorales are so often based upon older Gregorian themes that a Lutheran congregation will accept the dignified old Gregorian chants without a question, where other denominations, accustomed to florid Italian themes or the pretty froth so characteristic of modern chants, might find the old Gregorians lacking in the spicy tang that this jazz age demands even in its worship.

ORIENTATING: When ought a pastor to face the altar? We have seen pastors read the entire Vesper Service with their backs to the people. This is incorrect. A good general rule is to face the altar during those parts of the service which are addressed to the Lord, and to face the congregation for the parts spoken to the people. Thus the General Confession is said toward the altar and the Absolution to the congregation. Collects and other prayers are said toward the altar. In some congregations, pastor, choir and people all turn toward the altar for the Gloria Patri.

Some authorities take the position that the Apostles' and Nicene Creeds are confessions of faith which we make to one another, and that the pastor ought to face the congregation. Others maintain that the Creeds are confessions addressed to the Lord, and hence the pastor ought to face the liturgical east. A well-known poem states:

"I turn to the east when I say the Creed,
  For thence the rising sun
Through thousand circling months and years
  His ceaseless course hath run.

"I turn to the east when I say the Creed,
  And my Redeemer bless,
Who rose on this benighted earth,
  The Sun of Righteousness.

"I turn to the east when I say the Creed,
  And look for my final doom;
For thence, the Scriptures seem to speak,
  The Righteous Judge shall come." Etc.

The Creed may be intoned to a good musical setting, such as Tallis' in G, but the custom of speaking the Creed while the organist plays a succession of soft diminished sevenths (barbershop chords), is a vulgarism that is dying out.

PRAYERS: The lengthy free prayer of the Victorian era is losing ground, even among the sects. Free prayers are apt to be lengthy and rhetorical, to say nothing of vain repetitions.

In our Common Service, prayer has an important place. Our prayers are distributed throughout the service, and not heaped up in one spot after the sermon. A pastor ought to be able to compost good prayers for any unusual occasion that may arise, but he should take care that such prayers be in collect form. The typical collect contains an invocation, a relative clause, a petition, a purpose and a Trinitarian ending. "The Art of Public Worship," an inexpensive book by Percy Dearmer, contains a fine chapter on the art of making collects.

Prayers ought to be spoken properly, and not in a hollow, theatrical, radio voice. Affectation should be avoided. To stand with nothing but the whites of the eyes showing, suggests the glory-barn type of evangelist or the faith-healer.

KNEELING: Why do Lutherans turn their backs to the altar when they kneel? No doubt visitors are surprised to see the pastor face eastward and the people face westward during the Confessional Service. In some of our churches kneeling benches are provided, and a recent book issued by our publishing house mentions this as a good custom. There may be a portable Litany desk, brought out before service, for the pastor whenever the Litany is used. Should such a thing be used, its place is at the head of the center aisle, facing the altar, symbolizing Joel 2,17.

A simple rail may be provided for kneeling before the altar at Holy Communion. It is strange that many people have the notion that such a rail is an opening wedge for celibacy, fiddle-backed chasubles of bright scarlet, reservation, and prayers for the dead. But then they was a day when electric organ blowers were denounced as utterly un-Lutheran, and within the memory of men still living a pastor was tried for publishing a parish paper! A writer in a very recent issue of the *American Church Monthly*, after exhaustive study of post-Reformation Lutheranism, has shocked us all by disclosing the fact that our Lutheran fathers overseas retained such wicked things as eucharistic vestments, incense and sanctuary lamps, even down to the days of rationalism!

ANNOUNCEMENTS: In this age of ours a notice-board in the vestibule is a good thing. A cork board, with a well-designed frame, possibly in tryptych form, will serve the purpose. All announcements of an unchurchly character ought to be placed on this. It is not exactly dignified to hear a pastor bring the service to a close by dilating upon the excellency of the sauerkraut to be had at next Thursday's supper, or to announce that a hand-bag containing eighteen cents, a powder puff, and a door key have been found, and may be had after service by speaking to Mr. Karl Kominski.

It is not necessary to announce standing events. Mowbray's issue various kinds of notice-sheets, at very low cost. These are about 8½ x 13 in size, printed in two colors in churchly type, and have spaces for announcements for the coming eight days. If there is no weekly printed bulletin, announcements may be printed on good card stock, and distributed at the door after service.

It is not good taste to announce names. If a churching prayer is desired, it is enough to say that a member of the congregation desires prayer. Begging and urging should be reduced to a minimum. An undue elaboration of coming events often defeats its own purpose. It is better to lay stress upon the importance of a coming event rather than upon the eloquence of the speaker, lest we cause our congregation to become pickers and choosers. In speaking of the sexton, we ought not to call him the janitor, nor should we refer to the congregation as the audience. A church service is not a "services."

THE LORD'S SUPPER: The Lord's Supper is celebrated, not served, or held, or administered. Our leading church papers use the word "celebrated." It is a correct term.

A complete set of sacramental linens ought to be available and used. The old European custom of the pastor using a lavabo basin for washing the fingers immediately before celebrating, is a good one.

Genuine candles are better than imitation ones. They ought to be good beeswax altar candles, about 1¼ x 18 in size, and without elaborate decorations. Poles of any length are to be had, with a lighter and a cone-shaped extinguisher on the end. An extinguisher with a cone four inches in length is large enough. This lighter ought to be lighted in the sacristy. If there be a vested choir, one or two of the choirmen may be delegated to light and extinguish the candles. Where two candles are used, the candle at the right of the altar is lighted first. In extinguishing them, the candle on the left is extinguished first. Where there are five-branched or seven-branched candlesticks in addition to the eucharistic lights, then two men, each with a lighter, are generally used. In this case they begin with the candles nearest the cross. In extinguishing the candles, they begin with those farthest from the cross. If but one man is available to light the candles, then he lights those on the right of the altar first, beginning with the candle nearest the cross. Then he lights those on the left, beginning nearest the cross. In extinguishing them, the reverse of this order is practiced. The men who light and extinguish the candles ought to approach the altar without haste, and ought to do their work deliberately and gracefully. If choirmen in vestments are not available, one of the deacons, wearing a simple verger's robe, may do this work.

In preparing the sacramental vessels, the corporal (a piece of fine linen 21 inches square) is first laid on the altar. The chalice is placed upon this. A purificator (of fine linen, 12 to 15 inches square, and folded lengthwise into three divisions) is placed over the chalice. The paten is placed on top of this, and the pall (a piece of heavy cardboard seven inches square, covered with fine linen) is laid on top of the paten. The ciborium and flagon are next placed upon the altar, and the veil is thrown over the eucharistic vessels.

If there be Communion, the offering plates ought to be placed briefly upon the altar, and then carried to the credence shelf or table. This is an inconspicuous shelf or else a table about 16 x 30 inches in size, located somewhat to the south of the altar, either against the east wall, or against the south wall. The offering plates are kept on this credence when empty, and are carried there from the altar when there is Holy Communion.

To empty the wine remaining in the chalice into a common sewer is unfitting. A picina is used in well-appointed Lutheran as well as in other churches. This is a small block of white limestone, with a bowl about seven inches in diameter cut out of its upper surface. It is recessed into the south wall of the chancel, about 42 to 45 inches above the floor. A drain connects with mother earth—never with the sewer. Into this the wine remaining in the chalice is poured, as well as the water remaining in the font after Holy Baptism, unless the font be provided with a drain, also connecting with the earth.

Sacramental linens, such as the corporal, the purificators and the linen covering the pall, ought not to be washed with the common laundry. Fitness, as well as sanitation, would seem to demand

PLEASE TURN TO PAGE 352

Conducting the Church Service

II. Avoiding Crudities

F. R. Webber

THE Lutheran Church has lost many people of culture, such as John Wanamaker, Jacob Riis, Victor F. Lawson and the Weyerhaeusers. Just why these men found their way into other denominations would be hard to say. However, we could mention two or three men or more or less prominence who ought to be Lutherans today. When approached in regard to the matter they have made no mention of the doctrinal "narrowness" that is so obnoxious to the shallow-minded man. On the contrary, they have expressed admiration for the courage of the Lutheran Church in maintaining a Scriptural position, even in this age when it is unpopular to do so. But they have had something to say about certain crudities, which it is our honest conviction are keeping many people of education and refinement away from some of our churches. It is a most delicate subject, and we approach it with much hesitation.

A man who is quite well known was interviewed several times and seemed to be in full harmony with our doctrine and practice, but his first visit to a Lutheran church was his last. He declared that the church in question was intellectually satisfying, but emotionally irritating to his nature.

A second man, of national prominence in his profession, comes from sterling old Lutheran stock, but is one of the lay leaders in another denomination. Years ago he stated that many churches are driving their members into the lodge in search of the emotional color which the cultured soul craves, even in its worship. Deny a man a legitimate outlet for that emotion, and he will seek a fantastic form in the ritual of the lodge. Incidentally, this man is not a lodge member himself.

The wife of one of our well-known pastors, a young lady of education and culture, expressed herself in strongest terms on the subject of certain crudities of a liturgical and artistic nature which she must endure.

Another loyal Lutheran woman, a graduate of a college with a high reputation, said just the other day, "The Lutheran Church is all that can be desired doctrinally, but I often wonder about some of the things heard and seen in some churches."

None of these people have reference to the burlesque type of emotionalism that is commonly called sensationalism, such as sensational sermon topics, hymns of the tent-meeting sort, frock coats and white lawn ties, sentimental music, Mothers' Days and mourners' benches. They speak of the legitmate form of emotionalism which is created by a churchly place of worship, by the proper employment of color, by artistic lighting, dignified music and by ceremonial of the right kind.

Things that are Irritating. Even the exterior of a church may prepare one for worship, or else give a bad impression in advance. Cheap wit on the bulletin boards, such as "U R Welcome," is as bad as an untidy, run-down exterior. Noise and confusion within the church, the belated arranging of hymn boards; or altar candles lighted by scratching matches, or extinguished by the human breath, are not favorable to good decorum.

An organ prelude of a noisy character, an organist who arranges draw-stops and music with ostentation, and an organ frequently out of tune, or possessing snarly reeds and biting string-tones, are all disquieting to one's finer feelings. A constant, accordion-like see-sawing at the swell-pedal, or too frequent a use of the tremolo stop, are vulgarisms to be avoided. Even a "sung" processional becomes tiresome if one must endure it 52 times a year. A processional is of doubtful value unless one has a good choir and the proper architectural setting. Hymns and chants that are sung intolerably slow, or else unduly fast, are apt to detract from good emotional effect. Too much organ registration is a bad fault. Some of the finest organists shade their hymn playing as carefully as a fine singer shades his singing. Too much fortissimo,

either by organ or choir, is not effective, for fortissimos must be reserved for fitting occasions.

Crude singing, throaty tenor, explosive basses, sopranos who "break" on high notes, and tremolo in chorus parts, are faults that will interfere with refined effcet. Children's voices have a heart-gripping emotional appeal, if the children are taught to sing sweetly, but shouting, forced chest tones, nasal singing, too much alto, or boys who are allowed to sing the melody an octave below written score before their voices are fully changed, will only serve to discourage a devotional atmosphere.

A pastor in a baggy, ill-fitting robe with a V-neck, or in a robe with bands flaring open like a carpenter's square, is awkward in appearance. To read the service in a loud, argumentative manner, to blow one's nose noisily, to expectorate in one's handkerchief, to sway from side to side, or to shake one's head as some do while reading the service, are bad mannerisms.

A man, possibly the most prominent man in his city, went to a certain church, but came away much disappointed. He spoke of the fine sermon, but he had noted some mis-pronounced words, and these had spoiled the sermon for him. Among them were the words "alzo" for *also*, "Jee-suss" for *Jesus*, "wur-ruld" for *world*, "war-ship" for *worship*, "pozzibly" for *possibly*, and such mis-placement of accent as ADult, DIScourse, ADDress, ADministration, orGANization, authoriTATive and tresPASSes. Another man found the expression "Thus far the text" particularly annoying. We mention these things with humility, fully aware of our own shortcomings.

Crudities that will clash with a church service, even though it be beautifully conducted, are observed now and then by many people who find them irritating. Bad colors on the wall might be mentioned. An authority on color wrote an article for a national magazine, and he told of experiments conducted in school rooms, large offices and industrial plants, in which the effect of certain colors was studied. Some colors produced drowsiness, others a sense of coldness, other caused restlessness, and some provoked frequent bad-tempered outbursts on the part of the students or the office workers. Too much cannot be said on this subject, for there are churches in own own circles where the entire spirit of the congregation was most agreeably changed by the simple device of calling in a color expert, and adopting simple, quiet tones.

Even the finest order of service may be marred by the sound-glare reflected from a pressed-steel ceiling. On the other hand, our recent American penchant for a church interior in which every particle of resonance is killed, causes a lifeless sort of service that puts one to sleep. It is ideal for a speaker who does not care to exert himself, but is fatal to a good rendition of the service, and to organ and choral numbers. In such a church many people take part in the service in a most listless manner.

A church service may be done in letter-perfect fashion, but much of its emotional effect may be lost through bad lighting effects. Too much light is bad, and an unduly dim interior is equally unpleasant. Indirect lighting, or semi-indirect, have their legitimate places in commercial buildings, but what is more fatal to churchly atmosphere than batteries of strong lights bombarding the ceiling? A row of lights behind the chancel arch gives the chancel a stagy effect that is not churchly. Spot-lights playing upon the altar are annoying to persons of refinement.

Correcting these Crudities. Any of these things, so fatal to a good emotional background for the church service, may be corrected with little trouble. A good psychological first impression may be obtained by keeping the exterior of the church in good repair, with well-kept lawn and walks. The bulletin board ought to be kept in good shape, the letters frequently washed, and cheap, smart-alex notices avoided.

With a little effort, absolute quiet and good order may be maintained before the service starts, and few things are so powerful in their effect upon the worshipper as a few minutes of absolute quiet.

The organ may be kept in tune without trouble or undue cost. If the reeds are bad (as is so often the case), it is not unduly expensive to discard them and buy new sets of reeds. These may be installed in a few hours' time. If the string-tones are acid-like (a common fault in many an organ), a set or two of new pipes is an easy and not an expensive remedy. The organist can assist by arranging his stop-knobs as unobtrusively as possible. He can soon break himself of the bad habit of keeping his right foot continually on the swell pedal, and jabbing in staccato fashion at the first ten pedals with his left foot. The tremolo should be used sparingly, and stops of the motion-picture organ sort, such as the usual run of Vox Humanas and Voix Celestes, Gross Flutes and Tibias, may be traded in for good, fundamental organ tone. Too many organs are all shrill super-octaves and heavy bass, with nothing to speak of in the middle registers.

The crois may be dressed properly. Now that the fashion for vested choirs has taken strong hold in so many places, we can make the best of the situation by insisting upon churchly vestments. Great harm is done by go-getter commercial houses who insist upon selling nondescript, baggy black robes with V-necks and wide white collars. With proper encouragement the same firms may be prevailed upon to supply the regulation choir habit known the world over, namely the simple black cassock with fairly small sleeves, and a simple white surplice or cotta. These must be kept fresh and clean by frequent laundering. A noted collegiate choir may wear a collegiate style of choir vestment, but there is no reason whatever for a church doing it. The women in the choir must, of course, have some sort of headgear. A simple black choir cap is proper, but a mortar-board is out of place in a church. The simplicity and freshness of a proper choir vestment is always conducive to devotion, but freakish choir outfits are irritating to persons of good taste.

The singers out to be taught to sing the service. A few minutes should be devoted at each choir rehearsal to some part of the liturgical service. They should be taught to phrase and to shade properly, and not to sing it at one uniform rate of speed and degree of force. Careful attention ought to be given to refined pronunciation, avoiding flatting, avoiding tremolo in chorus parts and hymns, not overdoing tremolo effects in anthems containing solo work, avoiding prolonged consonants, nasal vowels (such as short "a" sounds), and avoiding such crudities as "incarnut," "glary," "prize" for *praise*, "mountun" for *mountain*, "saw-vren" for *sovereign*, and avoiding the French style of carrying certain final consonants over into the following word. A fading away on final syllables, or a failure to give a final note its full value must be avoided.

Even the busiest pastor will not consider it wasted time to take a course in public speaking, now that every college has such a course, and every town its private classes. Bad habits, such as the pulpit-tone, shouted delivery, excessive gesticulation where the subject matter does not seem to demand it, rolling the eyes, swaying back and forth, or faulty pronunciation may be corrected speedily.

Careful attention ought to be given to color and to lighting, because of the powerful aid that such things are to the properly conducted church service. Broad masses of restful color should be the rule. Borders, scrolls, texts on fluttering ribbons, symbols painted on the plastered walls, blue skies over the altar, gilt stars overhead, illusions of clouds and aerial perspective, are not considered in good taste. We would not tolerate such things in our homes. Cheap windows of opalescent glass, or gaudy picture windows of the realistic sort are long out of date, and only serve to distract the attention. Ornament and color should be restricted to parts of the church to which attention ought to be directed. Good wood carving is extremely effective, but it must be confined to its proper place, or it will be emotionally distracting and will produce a restless effect that is fatal to a quiet, devotional background for the church service. The same is true of color. No good decorator nowadays would think of painting or gilding the organ pipes, nor would he allow gilt radiators to form disturbing spots in or near the chancel. Artificial light should be subdued, and directed downward, not upward, and should be mellow rather than white.

Altar hangings may be of good silk damask, in the proper liturgical colors, with good hand embroidery and silk fringe. A crucifix of excellent design, massive candlesticks containing real candles with their emotional flicker and cheering warmth, an immaculately white fair-linen, communion silver of the very best quality and design, all contribute to a fitting background. We are in receipt of a letter from a well-known pastor urging attention upon this point. Too many of our churches, he says, have cheap, goblet-like chalices, patens of wash-bowl design and cruets that look like a coffee pot. Likewise many a baptismal font has a white pitcher, when a ewer of brass or pewter is much more refined in appearance. Why insist upon fine equipment for the church kitchen, and then use the cheapest plated britannia ware on the altar?

Acrobatic choir leaders with flourishing batons ought to be kept entirely out of sight. Anthems ought to be of a liturgical character, fitting perfectly into the service, and conforming with the season of the Church Year. The sentimental works of Barnby, Goss, Stainer, Dykes and Buck are giving place to works of a more liturgical character. Jangling chimes of brass tubing, and imiatations of orchestral bells cheapen a dignified Lutheran service, but we ought to use real tower bells that *are* bells. A church that can afford it may have a set of genuine chimes of the best quality, for there are good bells and only too many cheap, discordant things. Our hymns may be played for the benefit of the whole community, and publicity of the most dignified sort is thus possible. It is not too visionary to think of a guild of bell-ringers, playing the age-old changes that thrill the visitor to almost any European town. After all, our highly efficient bells, tapped by electricity, fall short of the fine old bells which possess that peculiar, heart-stirring power that is possible only when bells are swung by hand, and not cut short by a mechanical tapper.

All of these things form a background to the church and her service. The cause of true Christianity is so important that we ought to be willing to utilize every force to make our efforts more effective. If we can provide a suitable background for our church services, we are doing a good thing. Even the most perfect chalice cannot be photographed to any advantage if the background is a brick wall.

A pastor well acquainted with conditions in lands beyond the seas, remarked to us not long ago bout the strong sentimental attachment that the Christian Church has upon so many people abroad. It is significant that this sentimental attachment is never lacking in countries where proper attention is given to these details. At a recent conference, pastors marveled at the appeal of certain sectarian Noonday Lenten Services and radio broadcasting, even where the sermons were intolerably poor, and they attributed it to the skill with which the sectarians in question created a dignified emotional background. Nothing can make up for a neglect of Word and Sacraments, but might not the same attention to the emotional settings made Word and Sacrament all the more effective? Who could appreciate the immortal Ninth Symphony if the setting were antagonistic to the music?

Other denominations have awakened to the value of emotional appeal of the more dignified sort, and it would astonish the average reader to know how far many of them have gone in this respect. If we are to hold the increasing number of cultured people in our congregations, we must realize that man has an emotional nature as well as an intellect, and that this emotional nature demands the right sort of a devotional setting. This may be created at will, or destroyed. The right use of music, of liturgical forms, of color, of churchly arrangement—all of these are most effective hand-maids to the proper conduct of a church service.

Ritualistic Practices of Lutheran Germany

H. B. GROVE

THE Lutheran Churches of Germany and their descendant bodies in America and elsewhere are now emerging from the devastating effects of pietism and rationalism beginning in the seventeenth century and culminating in Prussia by enforced mechanical union with the Reformed Church in 1817. Recent liturgical developments are not merely aesthetic; still less are they an imitation of Roman usages, as one ignorant of our past might imagine. They result from a longing for adequate, satisfactory worship in harmony with our theology. Luther and his followers kept the venerable cult of the Western Church, but rid it of un-scriptural abuses and false Roman notions. The Geneva gown, and other Calvinistic externals may express the doctrines of the Helvetic Church, but they cannot give meaning to our faith.

It is commonly thought that the Scandinavian Churches, at the time of the Reformation, retained more ritualistic practices than did the Germanic Churches. This is not true. Lutherans of German background have a fine catholic tradition of mediæval vestments, ceremonies and customs that were not unique survivals in stagnant villages and isolated sections out of touch with changing ideas, but flourished in all parts of Germany in the important cities, from which they were copied by smaller churches in a surrounding area.

The altars remained as they were before the Reformation, equipped with crucifix and candles and adorned with flowers, paintings and statuary. Some of the finest paraments existing are to be found on our altars in Germany. Often a sacramental lamp hung above the altar.

Many time-honored customs, such as reverencing the altar, bowing at the mention of Jesus and the persons of the Trinity, the sign of the cross and ringing the passing bell, lingered on in Saxony and other conservative sections even in the nineteenth century. The churches were always open. When the Nuremburg Council ordered them to be closed, except during services, it aroused a great commotion among the citizens, and such vigorous protests were made, that the municipal council had to yield and the churches remained real houses of prayer.

The Gregorian tones and modes and the traditional plainsong melodies were sung all over Lutheran Germany. In the eighteenth century, pietism mutilated both the liturgical text and the music to which it is inseparably wedded. But in Bavaria, Mecklenburg and Saxony the Gregorian music has, happily, never been lost.

The most noteworthy feature of conservatism in worship was the persistent use of Latin. It is not strange that this should remain at university services where students understood it, and at matins at schools "that the boys may learn that language." But Latin was also employed at our churches in the large cities and the people apparently did not object to worshipping in a dead language.

At Laccuna the canonical hours were intoned in Latin till the eighteenth century. Until 1690, the entire service was in the ancient tongue at both St. Sebald's and St. Lawrence's Churches in Nuremburg; and the Preface, Sanctus and Consecration continued to be so intoned well into the nineteenth century. In Magdeburg as late as 1692, the Epistle, Gospel, Creed, Preface, Sanctus, Consecration and Pax were always in Latin. Up to 1732 throughout Saxony the Preface and Sanctus were intoned in Latin. In some churches the choir sang the Introit and Gradual in Latin. In a few churches the chief parts of the Liturgy were not sung in the vernacular until about 1750.

In the above cities and a few other places, Lutherans sang Latin hymns till the end of the eighteenth century, and at Halber-stadt until as recently as the middle of the last century. The Gloria in Excelsis was sung by Lutherans in its original Latin form for a long time all over Germany and has often been so used even in the nineteenth century. Occasionally the Te Deum has been sung in Latin. The Kyrie is, and has always been, sung in Greek at German Lutheran, Roman Catholic and Eastern Orthodox services.

Incense was retained by many of our churches in different parts of Germany for more than a century after the Reformation; and in some parishes censers were still used in the early nineteenth century. In Magdeburg, until the end of the eighteenth century, the sacristan hung a silver thurible, full of glowing coals and incense, on a pillar in the chancel. At the Offertory, the deacon with two lectors and two vicars went in solemn procession from the credence table, bearing the sacramental vessels which they placed on the altar, and the thurifer incensed the bread and wine and then the altar.

The cassock, biretta and cloak were worn by our priests till the latter part of the eighteenth century when wigs became fashionable, but in some towns of northeastern Germany, the clerical costume has never gone out of use. Until 1631 the Lutheran monks of Laccuna were garbed in the white habit and black scapular of the Cistercian Order. The beneficiaries of the Augustinian Seminary at Tübingen wore the cowl until 1750. At Closter-Lüne in 1608 the rector wore an alb of yellow gauze and a chasuble on which our Lord's Passion was wrought in needlework; and the abbesses and inmates wore the costume of the Benedictines. By order of the Nuremburg Officium Sacrum (1664) the clergy in white copes stood in their stalls after early mass and sang the hymn, *Erhalt uns, Herr, bei deinem Wort.*

The opening of the nineteenth century found the surplice no longer in use in many parts of Germany. It was abolished in

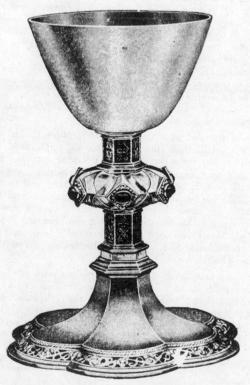

Silver chalice with amethysts in knop

Vested for the Eucharist—amice, alb, cincture, maniple, stole, chasuble

Nuremburg in 1810 to save laundry expenses. However, it is still used in Leipzig and environs, at several churches in Berlin, in Königsberg, Lausitz, Pommern, Slovakia, Weimar, Old Wurtemberg, parts of Austria, and a few other places.

The Brunswick Agenda (1657) authorized celebrants to go to the altar clad in alb, chasuble and other mass vestments. Throughout Saxony until about 1750 priests celebrated mass wearing all the eucharistic vestments. They left the chasuble and maniple at the altar when they preached from the pulpit. Our churches were well supplied with chasubles. Parishioners presented them as gifts. The popular conception was that the historic vestments were typically Lutheran, and the black robe and bands distinctively Calvinistic.

To gain an idea of the richness and beauty of the Ornamenta in the days of strict Lutheran orthodoxy, let us imagine we are visiting the sacristy of St. Nicholas Church, Leipzig, during the pastorate of Paul Gerhardt, the greatest Lutheran hymnographer (1607-1676). There are apparelled albs and amices, lace albs, stoles and maniples of high artistic merit. There are five chasubles for ordinary use, described thus: green satin, red patterned velvet, scarlet velvet crimson satin and violet brown velvet. On Advent Sunday one made of green velvet with Christ's Entry embroidered on it was worn. For the Feast of the Circumcision there was one of gold cloth. On Palm Sunday one of green silk with a design of palm leaves was used. Maundy Thursday had a light green satin one. For Easter Day there was one of white silk with a cross of pearls. Whitsunday had a brownish red velvet one with the Trinity seal wrought in pearls and other gems. Beside these there were a great many other magnificent chasubles. On festivals the altar boys wore red velvet cassocks and lace cottas. These vestments were sold in 1776, due to rationalistic pressure. Our churches in Nuremburg were ordered by the municipal council to turn in their chasubles and dalmatics as taxes. Among those sent from St. Sebald's and St. Lawrence's Churches were eighteen very beautiful ones ornamented with pearls.

Frederick William I of Prussia was Reformed, but the majority of his subjects were Lutherans. By an edict of 1733 he autocratically "prohibited the remnants of Popery in the Lutheran Church: copes, mass vestments, candles, singing in Latin, chanting, and the sign of the cross." Some Lutherans of rabid pietistic tendencies approved of this, but, as a whole, our people were attached to their wonderful heritage and many complained that it was a "betrayal of genuine and pure Lutheranism." In Königsberg, Magdeburg, Halle, Pommern and elsewhere, our priests rightly refused to obey the brutal tyrant. Many pastors were dismissed from their benefices for not submitting. This becalvinization of the Church in Prussia, ruthlessly effected by a despotic king, led other Reformed rulers to similarly humiliate their Lutheran subjects. For a detailed account of this unfortunate affair, see P. Severinsen's *De rette Messeklaeder,* chapters VII and VIII.

Frederick William I was succeeded by his son, Frederick the Great, who allowed the Lutherans full religious liberty. Vestments were restored in Berlin and other cities. The Brandenburg Cathedral and St. Mary's Church, Danzig (the largest Lutheran church in the world), possess even now the greatest collections of ecclesiastical vestments in Christendom. In 1810 the chasuble was abolished in Hamburg, Hanover, Lubeck and Grimma.

Seven years prohibition disaccustomed people to vestments and other adjuncts of worship. Calvinistic compulsion, followed by rationalism, shifted the German Lutheran Church from its natural position as a part of the Holy Catholic Church to sectarianism, where, Lutheran in theory but increasingly Reformed in practice, she has had to repudiate her past in order to prove acceptable. The Church Book had restored the ancient custom of the sign of the cross in the Ritual for Baptism, but even this last remnant of Christian symbolism was omitted from the Common Service Book. It would be too churchly for a fundamentalist and seem superstitious to a modernist.

The tradition of the Eucharist as the normal and principal service for all Sundays and festivals was much stronger in Lutheranism than in Anglicanism. The Divine Liturgy was conceived of as a sacrifice of prayer, praise and thanksgiving. The chief act of worship on all Sundays and festivals was the Holy Communion. Many of our larger churches had daily mass. The Reformers rightly forbade mass to be celebrated without communicants, thus ending that monstrous pre-Reformation abuse, by which mere attendance at mass had been substituted for the actual reception, laymen taking communion only once a year. To encourage more frequent communion our pastors announced: "It is to be feared that he who does not desire to receive the Lord's Supper at least three or four times during the year, despises the sacrament and is no Christian."

Toward the end of the seventeenth century the sermon as a means of intellectual edification was so emphasized that the Eucharist as the main service could not long survive. However, it was felt that congregational worship was not complete if its most vital part, Holy Communion, was lacking and in 1650 our clergy 'll endeavored to be consistent with universal Christian precedent. In some churches there was always a low mass at seven or eight A. M. In other churches this occurred at ten A. M. But High Mass vanished* and "dry mass"† took its place; and this abnormal condition is the rule throughout almost the whole Lutheran Church today.

The sharp class distinctions then prevalent, also worked against the weekly Eucharist. The nobility disliked to drink from the same chalice that others used and had their chaplains give them private communion. The common people, imitating them, also absented themselves from mass. Even in Luther's time some who did not intend to communicate left after the sermon. The

---

*The name lingered on in certain sections. In Sweden, and Swedish Lutheran churches in America, the chief morning service (i.e. antecommunion) is still called High Mass.

†Also called Proanaphora or Antecommunion. From ancient times it has been used on Good Friday, but not on Sundays and festivals.

Cope—worn by the clergy at processions

Devotion to the Blessed Sacrament was extremely fervent among German Lutherans in the early seventeenth century. Holy Communion was everywhere received with deepest humility. Some pastors taught that if a drop of consecrated wine fell on anyone's clothing the spot made must be cut out and burned, and to legitimate this, Luther was appealed to as having done the same thing. In many parishes, men were instructed that if the Blood of Christ fell on their beards it must not be wiped off, and at Hildesheim it was ordered that the hairs to which a drop had adhered must be plucked out and burned; while at Rostock, Pastor Reiche demanded that his men should cut off their beards if they intended to communicate. In Breslau, if a drop of consecrated wine fell from the chalice to the floor, the place was scratched out and carefully preserved. In Hesse the communicants drew the wine through reeds, so that it might not spill. A rubric in the Brunswick Agenda (1657) directed sacristans to hold a cloth in front of each communicant during the administration, that no particle of the sacred species be dropped. If any wafers and wine remained after the communion, our Kirchenordnungen bade the celebrant to reverently consume them, and the clergy were most scrupulous in making the ablution of the chalice. Such intense adoration of the Body and Blood of our Lord really present under the form of bread and wine is altogether consistent with the sacramental teaching of the Augsburg Confession and our other symbolical books.

Exorcism was retained by Luther, and found in all our agendae, except a few which were influenced by Calvinism. In the seventeenth century, rigid adherence to this rite was considered a mark of fidelity to Lutheranism. In Hamburg it was practiced till 1786, while in Saxony it continued to be used as late as 1836. The Berlin Court and Cathedral Agenda of 1822 revived it in Brandenburg after almost two centuries of disuse there. The Churching of Women is another significant rite that rationalism made obsolete.

attempt to have all remain throughout the whole Liturgy was not abandoned till the end of the seventeenth century. The point was made that the entire service was the act of the entire congregation, and that therefore, those who were not prepared to partake of the Lord's Supper should remain and pray for the communicants. But many did not stay through the long service when not communicating. Thus it became the regular thing to celebrate the Eucharist only once a month or even less frequently.

Preparation for Holy Communion was everywhere most thorough. Saturday was set apart for this purpose. There was a Penitential Office and a short sermon on sin. This was followed by compulsory private confession for each individual intending to receive the sacrament, and the conditional absolution was considered effective. But the burden of hearing a great many confessions, and the consequent routine, led to the substitution of a formal confession recited by all penitents, which was the Reformed practice. In Frankfort the confessional boxes were repaired in 1687 and were in constant use till 1783. It was customary to fast communion, except on Maundy Thursday.

In Nuremburg and elsewhere, the celebrant arranged the wafers on the paten in piles of ten, like the shewbread of the Old Covenant, while the choir sang the Introit and Kyrie. In all our churches the worshippers knelt for the Confiteor, Consecration and Communion. Elevation was practised because "it served to stir the hearts of men to deeper devotion." By the eighteenth century it had almost entirely ceased. The sacring bell was used as such in Breslau till 1736, after which it was employed for over half a century as a signal for communicants to approach the altar. The houseling cloth was used in Saxony and Silesia in the eighteenth century, and in some places has never been discontinued.

Altar Boy vested in a Cotta

[Illustrations in above article designed by
A. R. Mowray & Co., Ltd., London, England]

STOLES

The stole is that liturgical vestment which is most generally worn now by Lutheran priests in America. There are very few of the new Lutheran churches whose sacristies do not contain sets of stoles in the proper liturgical colors

Daily matins and vespers, often in Latin, were customary. Here is the list of weekday services at St. Sebald's Church, Nuremburg, at the opening of the eighteenth century:

Daily—mass, matins, vespers
Wednesday and Friday—litany
Saturday—penitential office and sermon

Other large churches had similar schedules. On Fridays in Nuremburg, Magdeburg, and Regensburg the *Tenebrae Factae sunt* was sung, followed by a silent Pater Noster and a versicle and Collect of the Passion. In the Church of the Augsburg Confession, Friday was universally observed as a memorial of the Crucifixion. The Reformers did not object to the canonical hours. Some Kirchenordnungen retained all seven offices. But those chiefly for parochial use kept only matins and vespers.

In addition to the festivals and saints days in the Calendar of the Common Service Book, the Ember Days, Corpus Christi, the feasts commemorating the Holy Innocents, St. Sylvester, St. Mary Magdalene, St. Lawrence the Martyr, and Holy Cross Day were observed in Prussia, Saxony and elsewhere. In many churches the Gloria in Excelsis was not sung during Advent and Lent. The ceremonies peculiar to Holy Week, especially the Blessing of Palms, were retained in certain localities.

The authentic Church of the Augsburg Confession is very different from the colorless thing that pietism, rationalism and sectarian contacts have made it. The morbid notion that services must be somber, bald, unlovely and conducted by someone in a long black robe is utterly foreign to the joyful character of our evangelical religion. Do we owe allegiance to the living Christ as confessed in our symbolic books or to the maukish sentimentality and grotesque individualism of sects that reject, deny and ignore our teachings? As time goes on the beautiful and historic usages of the Church are being revived in our parishes. At last our people are learning to appreciate our former splendor and to "ask for the old paths, where is the good way." (Jer. 6:16). We have fed on the husks of an alien faith too long. Let us return to the excellent things of our Father's house.

Conducting the Church Service
from p. 346

that these be washed in clean hot water by themselves. Bluing and starch are not used.

If there be an abundant supply of purificators, and if the rim of the chalice be cleansed with a purificator after each person receives, there will be little agitation for the (fully patented) individual cup. Would a father hold out an apple to his child and then give the child a stinging slap as he received it? Would our Lord give us His Body and Blood, and give us some germ disease with it? Purificators are not for removing disease germs, but so long as men chew tobacco and women chew gum, cleanliness dictates that the rim of the chalice be wiped after each person receives.

The font should be provided with a suitable ewer, either of pewter or brass. It is used for carrying water to the font. The font ought to have a tight-fitting cover, lest flowers or books be placed in it.

An ancient church rubric states that there ought to be a small crucifix on every pulpit, to remind the preacher and all others that "We preach Christ crucified."

Altar candles may be lighted for baptisms and confirmations, if so desired.

Artificial flowers ought not to be used on the altar. Cut flowers may be used. We bought a pair of vases, of heavy brass, about 10 inches high, and of good design, for about $10 for the pair, at Wippell's, Ltd., Cathedral Close, Exeter, Devonshire, England. There was a small duty on them.

Flowers are not generally used during Lent and Advent, except perhaps on the Third Sunday in Advent and the Fourth Sunday in Lent. White flowers ought to be used, if possible, on Easter Day, Christmas, the Epiphany, Maundy Thursday, Ascension Day and the Annunciation of Our Lord. Red flowers are appropriate for Whitsuntide, and for dedications and anniversaries. No flowers, and no colors whatever, are used during Holy Week, except on Maundy Thursday.

In some parts of Europe, even the altar crucifix and the candlesticks are covered with violet veils from the Fifth Sunday in Lent to the vespers of Easter Day. On Maundy Thursday the crucifix only may remain unveiled. On Good Friday a black veil is placed upon the altar cross or crucifix. If there be a reredos of tryptych form, its leaves are folded shut on Good Friday.

These are a few random notes on the practical side of the subject of the Church Service. Among the readers are doubtless persons who are better informed than we, and without doubt the editor would welcome a discussion of this subject, which is being talked of so widely nowadays.

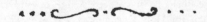

THE HANDMAIDEN'S PLEDGE

We are indebted to the Northern Illinois Lutheran Women's League program for the wording.

"In fervent gratitude for the Saviour's dying love and His blood-bought gifts of redemption, we dedicate ourselves to Him. We consecrate our hands to work for Him, our feet to go on His errands, our voice to sing His praises, our lips to proclaim His redeeming love, our silver and our gold to extend His kingdom, our will to do His will, and every power of our life to the great task of bringing the lost and the erring into eternal fellowship with Him. Amen!"

Altar Vestments

LUTHER D. REED, D.D.

THE public worship of the Christian congregation has certain requirements and has developed certain features not found in the private worship of the individual. The long experience of the Church has produced and preserved practices best calculated to promote dignity, solemnity, edification and uniformity in common assemblies. The usages of influential groups have gradually been combined and unified, art and taste have refined and perfected the conventionalized forms, and thus have developed the great Christian traditions which center in the Liturgy, the Church Year and the church building itself.

THE ALTAR AND ITS VESTMENTS

We all recognize the church building as the House of God, a building set apart for divine worship and holy purposes. The chancel is its head and heart. The altar, as the central feature of the chancel, dominates the entire edifice. It is the Table of the Lord, the place for the celebration and admiration of the Holy Communion. It is the place of benediction, where God's grace is affirmed and bestowed. It is also the place where the united prayers of the congregation are offered and where vows of fidelity and consecration are spoken (as in confirmation, ordination and marriage). As such, our highest and holiest moments of public worship find a common center in this liturgical and architectural focus.

Possessing such central significance, the altar—and in lesser degree the pulpit and lectern.—have ever made the strongest appeal to art, the handmaid of religion. Painting has placed some of its great achievements upon the altar; sculpture in stone and wood has enriched both altar and pulpit; and embroidery, more ancient than either in the service of the Church, has given them warmth and invested them with new life and significance. For it is embroidery, rather than sculpture or painting, that gives a festival character to the altar and the pulpit, and, by its symbolism and color, enables them to unite with the liturgy, the hymns and the sermon in expressing the changing thought of the Church Year and lifting the great Days and Seasons above the monotony of an uneventful order.

The use of embroidered linens, stuffs, etc., in gold, blue, purple and scarlet, was expressly enjoined in the Old Testament (Exod. 28). The early Christian Church employed curtains, veils, coverings, etc. Innocent II in the twelfth century definitely prescribed white, green, scarlet and black as the liturgical colors, and violet was soon added. At the time of the Reformation the Reformed Churches abandoned the use of vestments and colors, as indeed, very generally, the use of the altar itself. The Lutheran Church, however, in all lands retained these as among the usages which "ought to be observed as profitable unto tranquillity and good order in the Church" (Augsburg Confess. XV). The periods of Pietism and Rationalism (17th and 18th centuries) with their loss of historical and churchly consciousness, neglected all liturgical appointments. With the revival of Church life in the last century, the Lutheran Church throughout the world has renewed its interest in all that pertains to the public worship and the arts of the Church. Embroidery guilds were organized and often conducted by women of rank (e.g. Countess v.d. Schulenburg in Lower Saxony); Church Needlework Departments (Paramentenanstalten) were established in important Deaconess Motherhouses (Neuendettelsau, Dresden, Christiania, Hanover, etc.).

Three gifted and godly men gave the movement direction and leadership. Wilhelm Loehe, the founder and head of the institutions at Neuendettelsau, and one of the ablest leaders in Germany in the nineteenth century, who influenced the development chiefly along the lines of the ancient Church tradition; Pastor Moritz Meurer, who awakened general popular appreciation by his books on Church Architecture and Altar Embroidery; and Prof. M. E. Becke, a gifted layman of the Moravian community at Herrnhut, Saxony, who gave his life to the designing of ecclesiastical embroideries, tapestries, rugs,

etc. His designs and their execution in the Deaconess institutions lifted the whole movement to a plane of high achievement in the Protestant Churches of Germany and Scandinavia, and secured a limited appreciation, which is happily growing, in our country.

With these facts as a background, we now consider some of the practical details.

THE SEASON VESTMENTS

1. KINDS. Anciently the altars, whether made of stone or of wood, were perfectly plain and received their decoration from movable frontals. Sometimes these were made of thick plates of gold or silver, studded with gems; but more generally they were of silk, richly embroidered. Less splendid coverings, of embroidered linen, were used for the lesser Festivals and Days.

In our usage today, the front of the altar is covered in one of three ways with embroidered hangings which change with the Seasons and are made in the five liturgical colors. The entire front of the altar may be covered with a so-called *frontal,* the upper part also having a *superfrontal,* extending six to eight inches from the top edge and running the entire width of the altar. The combination secures the richest effect, and is, of course, the most elaborate and costly. The frontal will have a central design embroidered upon it, flanked, often, by broad vertical orphreys, or panels, also embroidered. The superfrontal will also have a few bold embroidered designs, and both vestments will be finished with fringe at the bottom.
(Illustration A.)

A. Altar (and Retable) with Embroidered Frontal and Superfrontal

When the front of the altar itself is of rich carved or mosaic design, and even if it be quite plain,—the superfrontal can be effectively used alone, in which case the embroidered designs should be especially bold so as to be distinguishable from the nave. (B.)

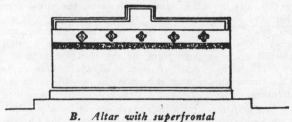

B. Altar with superfrontal

The third kind of vestment is the *antependium,* which is less elaborate and costly than the frontal and yet may be very effective. It is a "fall," covering the center of the altar from the top edge of the table to within an inch of the base, and it is also finished with fringe. This type of vestment, so far as the writer knows, is not found in Roman or Anglican Churches, but is peculiar to the Lutheran use, having been introduced largely by the workers in our Deaconess institutions abroad who used Prof. Beck's designs. It is finding very general acceptance in our churches in America. (C.)

Black should be treated with severe simplicity. Only that which refers directly to the sufferings and death of Christ is admissible, e. g. crosses, the monograms, the emblems of the Passion, as above, with possibly thistles and the passion flowers for decorative detail.

ALTAR LINEN

The season vestments change with the Church Year. The altar linens are the same for all Seasons and Festivals, and are placed over the season vestments. The latter are never removed when the Lord's Supper is administered. Thus the altar, properly vested, suggests to the worshipper the thought of the Church Year and the thought of the Sacrament at the same moment.

If the altar is of stone, a heavy linen cloth stiffened by wax, cut the exact size of the mensa or top of the altar, is first laid upon it as a protecting cloth. Upon this is spread the season vestment, and upon this the altar linens proper. These must be of the finest quality that will bear frequent laundering. The altar linens are:

1. *The Fair Linen Cloth.* This is of fine, white linen (never damask), the exact width of the altar and usually long enough to hang half way to the floor at each end. The ends are finished with linen fringe or fine lace. The cloth may be hem-stitched all around, and five crosses,—representing the Five Wounds,—may be worked upon it, one in the center of the Cloth and the others at each corner of the altar. All embroidery or lace on the ends must be pure in design and refer to our Lord or to the Sacrament,—e. g. the IHS, wheat and grapes, the passion flower, etc. If the season vestment be an antependium, the Fair Linen may be the exact size of the altar table and bordered with very fine lace in good ecclesiastical patterns and five or six inches in depth. *Lace cannot be employed in this manner if a superfrontal is in use.* It should never be used at all unless of the finest quality and in good ecclesiastical designs. *Even then its use is questioned by some authorities.*

The Fair Linen Cloth marks the altar as the "Table of the Lord," and it is placed upon the altar at all services, whether there be a Communion or not. The other linens are only used when there is a Communion.

2. *The Corporal* is a square of fine linen, usually 21 by 21 inches, sometimes 21 by 24 inches in size. It is placed in the center of the altar, over the Fair Linen, and the Communion Vessels are arranged on it. It is hemstitched or edged with fine lace. Its only ornament is a simple cross, not in the true center, but in the middle of one-half or one-third. When laundered and folded in two or three folds lengthwise, and the same number crosswise, this cross comes in the centre, indicating the side to be turned toward the minister when it is unfolded at the altar.

3. *The Pall* is a cardboard square, six inches or slightly larger in size, covered tightly with linen, the edges sewn together and finished with the finest white cord. It is used to cover the Chalice and protect the Wine from foreign substances. The linen on the upper side may have a small embroidered cross or monogram, or the INRI surrounded by a crown of thorns. Another square of plain linen is tacked on the under side, and this may be readily removed for laundering.

4. *The Purificators,* of which there should be a plentiful supply, and which are used to cleanse the rim of the Chalice during administration, are small napkins of fairly heavy linen,—never damask,—11 to 13 inches square. They have a plain, narrow hem and a simple embroidered cross in one corner.

5. *The Veil* is in general use, though in different forms. The Roman and Anglican Churches cover the Chalice and Paten when borne to the altar with small silk veils in the Season colors. The best usage in the American Lutheran Church requires a Veil of most delicate sheer linen, sufficiently large to cover all the Vessels. This will mean that the Veil must be at least 30 or 36 inches square. It may be hemstitched, with a border of the finest lace sewn about the edge. Our Churches abroad frequently embroider the Veil elaborately in red, but the best usage in this country requires that only white linen thread be used, the designs, of course, referring directly to our Lord or to the Sacrament. When removed from the Vessels, the Veil should be carefully folded and laid upon the altar.

6. *The Burse.* This is but rarely found in the Lutheran use, thought common in modern times in the Roman and Anglican Churches. It is a cover or case, 9 inches square, made of cardboard, lined with linen, and covered the color of the season vestments. It is sewn together along one side, and thus shuts flat like a book and lies flat when opened. The folded Corporal, the Pall and the folded Purificators are carried in it to the altar.

The highest ornament which the linens,—or the vestments or vessels,—can possess is their immaculate condition. No starch or bluing is used in laundering.

THE MAKING AND CARE OF VESTMENTS

It is much to be regretted that our Church in America has no Church Embroidery centers connected with its own institutions. In Germany and Scandinavia our Deaconess Mother-houses maintain departments where church vestments of the highest quality in material, design and workmanship are produced. Our Deaconess Institutions here have not undertaken this work, though they might do so with great advantage to the Church. We are dependent chiefly upon commercial houses dealing in Church goods, and of these there are perhaps less than half a dozen in the entire country whose standards in point of quality and taste can be depended upon, and none of these, so far as the writer knows, have any close connection with our Church. The only advice we can give, however, is to purchase materials, embroidered designs and complete vestments only from such first-class firms. Manufacturers and dealers with poor qualities and worse taste must not be encouraged or permitted to furnish Lutheran Churches with inferior supplies, even if some of them have close personal affiliations with our congregations.

When a congregation or a community is fortunate enough to possess women who can bring both talent and time to this work, Altar Guilds or Church Embroidery Institutes can be organized to study this subject and make vestments. The chief difficulties are the securing of competent direction and of proper designs, suitable at once for Church use and for working with the needle. Neither of these difficulties, however, is insuperable, and many good church vestments are thus being made by our own churchwomen.

At all events, each congregation should have an Altar Society or Guild to care for the chancel and its appointments, even if it does not attempt to make vestments itself. These matters should not be left to the pastor or his wife, or to the sexton and his wife. A group of earnest women, some of them mature, and all of them enjoying the confidence and respect of the congregation, should be entrusted with this important work. They should have a working sacristy or room separate from the pastor's sacristy, and with running water, for their use. Here they can keep supplies, clean the altar vases and the Sacramental Vessels, arrange the altar flowers, and care for the vestments and linens. These should be kept in chests with long flat drawers, or in high closets where they may be covered and hung without folding.

BIBLIOGRAPHY

The following literature is suggested:—Moritz Meurer, *Altarschmuck*, Leipsic, 1867. M. E. Beck, *Evangelische Paramentik*, Dresden, 1906. Buerkner, *Kirkenschmuck u. Kirchengeraet.* Paul E. Kretzmann, *Christian Art*, St. Louis, 1921. Maud R. Hall, *English Church Needlework*, 2d. ed. London, 1913. Hinda M. Hands, *Church Needlework. A Manual of Practical Instruction.* London. 1909. Rolfe, *The Ancient Use of Liturgical Colors*, London, 1879. Paul Z. Strodach, *Liturgical Colors.* (Article in *Memoirs of the Lutheran Liturgical Association*, Vol. III.) Luther D. Reed, *Altar Linen, (Article in the Memoirs,* Vol. II.)

*C. Altar with Antependium and Fair Linen Cloth,
edged with Lace*

The pulpit and lectern have falls, corresponding in general form, though smaller, to the antependium. These are dependent in size and shape upon the design and dimensions of the pulpit and lectern themselves, but they are usually nearly as wide as the flat desk of wood or brass which supports the Bible, and they should always be longer than wide. Embroidered designs are worked in the center, and they are finished with fringe. It is not practicable to use a fall on a brass eagle lectern, which is simply supplied with silk bookmarkers, in the season colors or gold, embroidered with small designs.

One other hanging which may be mentioned is the dossal *curtain,* sometimes hung above and back of the altar in place of a more elaborate and costly reredos of panelled wood or stone. It hangs flat, several inches wider than the altar, and higher,—sometimes much higher,—than wide. It is usually finished with a projecting canopy at the top. It is often divided into vertical panels and bordered with wide galoons, or bands, of rich braid.

2. MATERIAL. Nothing but the best materials, the richest in appearance and the most lasting, should be used. Silk brocade or damask, with ecclesiastical patterns, lions, harts, dragons, fleurs-de-lis, crosses, etc.—or fine broadcloth, are the best. Silk velvet may also be used, but never cotton velvet or felt. All the season vestments should be lined with strong dark blue or dark red linen.

The material of the altar vestments need only come to the edge of the altar, an extension of linen or other strong materials passing over the mensa, or table of the altar, and under the fair linen cloth to the back, where it is held in place by strips of lead covered with materials. When the pulpit has a brass desk, the fall is fastened by being sewn to the edge of a piece of similar material covering a Bristol board the exact size of the desk top. A band of broad elastic passes under the ledge and holds the drapery in place. The fringes used to finish the vestments are of silk. Fine silk cord may be used to bind the edge, *but tassels are inadmissible.* To secure the best quality and the exact colors all the materials must be secured from first-class firms which specialize in ecclesiastical goods.

3. COLOR. The five liturgical colors used by the Roman, Lutheran and Anglican Churches are: white, red, green, violet and black. These have been definitely associated with certain Festivals and Seasons for many centuries, and their use at once suggests the thought or mood of these times. The symbolism which lies back of this traditional association cannot be pressed too far, but so far as it pertains to the Lutheran use it may be broadly stated as follows:

White, the "unbroken light," is the color of the Deity and of all in His presence. Luther called it "the color of the angels and all saints." It is the color of purity, glory and victory. As such it is used on all the Festivals of our Lord and their Seasons (Christmas, Epiphany, Easter, the Annunciation, etc.). Also on the Festival of the Holy Trinity and its octave, and on St. Michael's Day.

Red is the color of power and dominion, of love, of fire and blood. It is used on the great Festivals of the Church,—Whitsunday, Reformation Day, Apostles' and Evangelists' Days, Church Dedications and Anniversaries, etc. It reminds us of the tongues of fire on the Pentecost, the Church's birthday, and of the blood of the martyrs, the "seed of the Church"; of the constant presence and power of the Holy Spirit; of the daily sacrifices which we must bring in God's service; and of the love and devotion of the Church, the Bride, for Christ, the Bridegroom.

Green is the restful, every day color of the earth, the color of life and hope. In strong contrast to red, it is used on the ordinary days and seasons when the Church is led quietly through the green pastures of the Word: during Septuagesima to Ash Wednesday, and from the Second Sunday after Trinity to Advent.

Violet is the color of penitence, humility and solemn self-examination, and is used during Advent and Lent.

Black, the color of sorrow and death, is reserved for Good Friday and Days of Humiliation. (For more complete details see the *Common Service Book,* page 282.)

It cannot be too strongly stated that the significance of the liturgical colors is found entirely in their intimate connection with the Church Year and the Liturgy. They reveal the mind of the Church as a whole in glorifying the Festivals of our Lord and of His Church. They must not be made to express the personal experiences of any individual or group of individuals within any particular congregation. Weddings and funerals, then, will not affect them at all. Nor will the celebration of the Holy Communion affect the vestments in use during any Season.

A word should briefly be said concerning the important and difficult subject of the use of colors in embroidery. These must not be employed realistically, but conventionally, in a way that will best harmonize with the color of the vestments themselves. Red vestments may be embroidered in gold, green, olive green, brown, blue and white. Green vestments, in gold, black, crimson, golden brown, silver or white. Violet vestments in red, white or silver, black, gold and brown. Black vestments in white, softened by blue, violet, olive and gold in subordinate lines. White vestments are the most difficult, and call for crimson, dark violet, green, pink and blue with gold to relieve the contrasts. When it is desired to use designs which must themselves be in white, (the lily, dove, lamb,) these may be outlined in darker colors. The silk fringes which finish the vestments are the color of the cloth, sometimes with alternate spaces of gold or some color employed in the embroidery. Black vestments may have silver fringe; violet vestments, gold or silver.

4. DESIGNS FOR EMBROIDERY. These must be simple and not realistically or too minutely worked. Their purpose is symbolical and decorative. They must be flat, without attempt at perspective, though the chief features in the design may be softened and embellished with decorative sprays, etc.

We cannot enter very far upon the rather large subject of ecclesiastical symbolism. But certain general designs, such as the sacred monograms (the IHS, the Chi Rho,) the Alpha and Omega, crosses of many forms, etc., often enclosed in circles, vesicas, etc., may be used practically on any of the vestments. Other designs specially appropriate for the different colors are:

White. The Festivals for which white is used celebrate Christ's work of redemption. The Lamb, trampling upon the dragon; the angels of Christmas and Easter; the monograms surmounted by a crown; lilies, roses and fleurs-de-lis are appropriate.

Red portrays the work of Christ through His Church. The Lamb, again, or the monograms may be used with the symbols of the four evangelists; the dove, the tongues of fire, the vine, the pomegranate, the Greek cross with ornamented ends, etc.

Green reflects the life and growth of the Church. The Good Shepherd; the monograms; symbols of the water of life, with harts and doves; grapes and wheat ears, as symbols of the Sacrament; interlaced triangles and circles, and the pomegranate, again, whose many seeds represent the extension of the Church.

Violet for Advent and Lent, may well have types of Christ, e. g., Aaron, Isaac, Melchizedek; the pelican giving its blood for its young; the Agnus Dei; symbols of the evangelists; the monograms and crosses in many forms, thistles, as a symbol of sin; the passion flower and the emblem of the Passion, encircled by a crown of thorns (the spear, nails, hammer, scourge, ladder, etc.).

Our Experience with the Home Altar

DAVID T. E. HOLLAND

AS OUR EYES FOLLOW the wide bend of the river from the cozy shelter of our log-cabin-on-the-Maumee, a northwest wind, laden with April's last snow flurry, comes sweeping down and spends its full blast upon the sturdy spruce logs of which is built our lodge for the week.

The only result of the storm outside is to increase our appreciation of the crackling logs in the fireplace and of the sense of security which is ours on the inside of the cabin. Here the great stone fireplace is easily the dominant focal point about which all else in the room seems to gather. The oil lamps on the walls with their gleaming, fluted reflectors are like beacons from another age shining still to tell us of some glow that we have lost somewhere along the way in spite of all our gains in the so-called standard of living.

It all leads my mind back to the first family altar scene that I can remember. I recall the quietness and peace which came as the family gathered about just such a fireplace and as the father reached down the great Bible from the walnut mantel and reverently read the divine message for the day. I remember how we knelt at our chairs and were led to unseen heights in simple worship. The focal point was not the fireplace after all, but the open Bible; the Word of God in the center of a family circle—truly an altar unto the Lord.

It must have been partly due to the lingering influence of that experience which led to our attempt to set up a similar situation within the modern homes of our parish. To gather our modern families around the open Bible in daily worship; to make it possible for every member of every family "daily to appropriate grace from God's Word"; to approach the homes of our people from this sacramental point of view has come to be the purpose back of "The Home Altar." It is simply the Word of God as a means of grace in the heart of the home.

How to restore this traditional practice and make it a daily habit in these days of divided family interests presented a difficult problem. We needed a focal point to objectify family worship so as to make it simple and tangible. We needed to help bring out from their hiding places the Bibles that were so common and still so ineffective in every home. We needed to aid in opening these Bibles intelligently and habitually in every home. We needed to create the atmosphere of reverence and worship within the homes of our people. We needed to emphasize the Word as a means of grace and guidance. We needed to encourage the reading of religious literature of the Church so as to furnish an intelligent basis for the work of the Church. We needed to cultivate the active expression of such religious impulses as giving, witnessing and serving. In a word, we needed to integrate the whole program of the Church within the four walls of the home where, in the final analysis, it was to become effective, if ever

THE HOME ALTAR. A silent witness to family worship in the homes of Pastor Holland's congregation at Bowling Green, Ohio

So it came about that the home altar as we developed it became the focal point for the whole program of the Church as it found expression in the home.

The altar itself is finished in walnut and the background of Gothic arches furnishes a setting for "Thorwaldsen's Christ." Attached to this is the devotional calendar pad. The Bible rests upon the altar desk opened invitingly while the magazine compartment, which forms the base of the altar, is, of course, to be reserved for church papers, missionary magazines, hymn book, church school literature and catechism. The offering envelopes and thank-offering box present a daily reminder to "lay by in store as God has prospered" the family. Here in the home, WORSHIP, EVANGELISM, EDUCATION and STEWARDSHIP are all learned by daily practice.

FORM AND PLACE MAKE IMPRESSION

The objective form of the home altar made family worship at once practical, easily understood and easily introduced into the family circle. We found that it did not remain an outward thing, however, as the spirit of reverence and love which springs from the reading of the Word, and from family prayers, soon carried its deeper significance far beyond any outward form. Enough liturgical symbolism was used to create the desired atmosphere of reverence and to indicate the nature and purpose of the altar. The magazine cabinet made it a natural part of the everyday life of the family and led to a more effective use of the religious literature of the Church. The suggested reading on the calendar page with its accompanying exposition and prayer has served as an intelligent and reverent guide in the opening of the closed Bibles of our people and the prominent date on each perforated page has helped to keep them open. The offering boxes and the witness list of possible members for the Church have served to furnish an opportunity for definite expression of the impulses to give and to serve.

Most of our families place the home altar on a side table in the dining room or living room from which the Bible and daily page are carried to the table when the evening meal is set. Here, around the table, after the meal, family worship is conducted. Whether it be in the morning or evening, in the dining room or living room, the method is about the same though every family reports some slight variation in the procedure. Generally the one who has the calendar page announces the Scripture to be read; another reads it from the Bible, after which the explanation is read by one and the prayer by another member of the family. All unite in praying the Lord's Prayer.

FAMILY USES

In a recent survey of the use of the home altar in our parish many interesting variations have been reported. One man and

PLEASE TURN TO PAGE 357

A Correct Altar*

IN SPITE OF ALL that has been said in print by various persons, yet the construction of a rubrically correct altar seems to be more or less of a mystery to many people. The design of an altar is not a matter of controversy. It is not a thing upon which good arguments may be advanced, pro and con. Altars have been used for so many centuries that there is no ground for guess-work, nor for private opinion. Therefore, what we are about to say, is not the personal opinion of the writer, but merely the composite of many centuries of practical experience. Altars are described in detail in books whose pages are yellow with age, and in books fresh from the bindery. Yet these are in surprising agreement.

To strive for a "distinctively Lutheran" type of altar is nonsense. One might just as well undertake to design a typically Lutheran violin, or office chair, or typewriter. A book of dogmatics may be distinctively Lutheran, or a church organ may be planned with Lutheran requirements in mind. But an altar is an altar, and so long as we use it as such, its dimensions are fixed by its function.

A correct altar will be about 40 inches high, and its mensa, or flat upper surface will be about 21 inches wide by about eight or more feet long. It is a mistake to deviate from these dimensions. There is a sound reason for each. Its height is not variable. Since its first function is to provide a suitable place where Holy Communion is celebrated, and since that celebration requires the presence of one or more clergy, its height cannot be a matter of controversy. The average clergyman's height ranges from about five feet six inches to six feet. A man of this height will find that an altar whose mensa is 40 inches above the floor will prove to be ideal.

In one of our churches is an altar but 37 inches high. It was designed for a former pastor who, like Zacchaeus of old, was short of stature. Two pastors have succeeded him, and both have complained that it is very awkward. An altar 42 inches high will seem very awkward to most men. The only safe way is to adhere to the standard height of approximately 40 inches.

The mensa, or flat upper surface of the altar, cannot be much greater or less than 22 inches in width. If less than that, there will not be sufficient room for the communion vessels. If more than 22 inches, it will be difficult to reach the crucifix, candlesticks and flower vases on the gradine. These things are generally cared for by an altar guild composed of women, and women are, on an average, smaller in stature than men. If we adhere to the traditional width of 22 inches, we will find that it is a convenient width.

The mensa ought to be at least eight feet long. Since all of our altars contain a crucifix or cross, two candlesticks, and usually two vases of cut flowers, a length of eight feet will prove ample.

But sooner or later we are sure to reach the stage, even in the simplest of churches, where there will be a desire for a pair of seven-branched office lights in addition to the two communion lights, and where these are used, eight feet is the minimum length. If we build the altar but seven feet long, either the seven-branched lights, or else the cut flowers will have to be omitted. Every properly arranged altar will have a missal stand, or "book rest." This stands a little to the left of the center of the mensa. If the mensa is but six or seven feet long, one will feel crowded at communion time. Then an altar 40 inches high and but six or seven feet long is not good in proportion. A length of eight feet will look better, and is more dignified in every way. It is better to err on the side of generosity of space than to err in the other direction.

Beyond the mensa, and about five or six inches above it is the gradine. This is a shelf upon which crucifix, candlesticks and flower vases stand. It ought to be the full length of the altar,

and ten to twelve inches deep. This width must not be deducted from the width of the mensa. It must be in addition to it. Thus a properly appointed altar will have a mensa 22 inches wide, plus an elevated gradine 10 to 12 inches wide.

In the midst of the gradine is a base of some sort for the crucifix. In ritualistic churches, this is a true tabernacle, with a swinging door. It is really a cedar lined chest ten or twelve inches square, and a foot or so high. This does not call for reservation of the altar breads that may remain after celebration, as many suppose. In churches where reservation is not practiced, it may be nothing more than an orderly place for the ciborium and the altar breads. If placed there, they are always within easy reach, for every pastor has, at some time or other, made a mistake in counting, only to have the supply of altar breads run short, with the delay of going to the sacristy for additional ones, and their second consecration. But if even this is objectionable, the tabernacle may be omitted, and a raised base provided for the crucifix. If the crucifix, candlesticks and flower vases be placed on the same level, a pleasing composition is impossible. But elevate the crucifix a few inches, and the improved appearance is surprising. An old rubric states that the crucifix ought to stand on a higher level than the candlesticks. The most satisfactory artistic composition results if the feet of the Corpus are on the same level as the tops of the candlesticks. • ⌘ • ⌘ •

HOME ALTAR from p 356

The minimum requirements of a Lutheran church call for two candlesticks and a crucifix or cross. In this case, the two candles are lighted only when Holy Communion is celebrated. Within the past decade, a number of our churches have been using six candlesticks of equal height, and lighting them all at Communion. This is not correct. There is no harm in having six candlesticks, but if this is done, they ought to be considered strictly as office lights. Two additional candles must be provided for Communion. If we have two candles on the altar, they are Eucharistic lights, and ought not to be used at any other time. If we have sixteen lights, twenty or thirty, only two of these are Eucharistic lights, and these two must not be used at any other time than at the celebration of the Lord's Supper. All additional candles are merely office lights, and may be used at any time, either at Holy Communion, or at any other service.

Back of the altar there may be a reredos of stone or wood, or a tryptych, or perhaps a dorsal curtain. The reredos may be either a simple paneled arrangement rising eight or ten feet above the floor, or it may be richly carved with traceried canopies and niches, in which are figures of Our Lord, and His Apostles. The reredos proper is about the same width as the altar is long, or slightly greater. In an ordinary church, a height of eight or ten feet above the floor will prove satisfactory. If the church is lofty, more height may be necessary. But a lofty reredos is seldom effective unless the church is extremely rich otherwise, for there is danger that it may become so conspicuous as to detract attention from the altar itself. The carved figures in the richer sort of reredos are often too large. In order to keep the entire composition in good scale, it is better to have rather small figures. These ought to be of stone, if the reredos is of stone, and of wood if the reredos is of wood. Plaster figures seem to cheapen the general effect, rather than add to it.

The tryptych is a very beautiful device, and it ought to be more widely used in our circles. It is a wood arrangement somewhat similar to the reredos. There is a wide center panel and two side panels, each of which is one-half the width of the center one. The two side panels are hinged, and project well beyond the ends of the altar. Within each panel may be a painting. These must be very good paintings, strictly flat and decorative, and must not be of the realistic sort. During Holy Week, the two side panels are swung shut, so that they cover the center panel. The back of each swinging panel is treated with a simple, all-over painted pattern, in order to avoid too much bareness when the leaves are folded shut. The tryptych is common in Europe, and a few good examples exist in our country. There is no reason why many more ought not to exist, for the tryptych

---

* An altar such as described in above article, of dignified proportions with a gradine for altar brasses, and a low, richly carved reredos, was illustrated in the March, 1932, issue of the AMERICAN LUTHERAN. Copy of this number mailed on request.

is very decorative, and very good architecturally. It is entirely a matter of architectural design, and no liturgical or doctrinal principles are involved in any way.

The dorsal (spelled "dorsal" but pronounced "dossal") is used where funds will not permit a more permanent structure. It is merely a curtain about eight feet high, suspended back of the altar. It is made of rich, heavy fabric, and is suspended by loops from an iron rod. In some of the older examples, it is stretched flat on a wooden frame, but more recent and better practice calls for a curtain about one-third full, so that it may hang in folds. The effect is rather more graceful than the curtain tacked to a wood frame. About a dozen years ago, a number of our own churches copied a dorsal curtain that once hung in St. John's Church, West Hartford, Conn. This was a curtain stretched on a frame, and divided into three vertical panels by means of wide braids. There was a box-like canopy overhead, and riddle curtains at the sides. At one time this was generally regarded as the proper and only type. Other good forms have displaced it.

Riddle curtains may be used either with a reredos or with the dorsal curtain. These are vertical curtains about seven feet high, and they project at right angles to the reredos or dorsal. Their width is about three feet. They must hang parallel with the ends of the altar, and must not be swung to an angle of 45 degrees. The riddle curtain is purely decorative, and its purpose is to add a touch of richness to the altar and reredos. Riddle curtains also serve a practical purpose, for they cause the candles to burn a little more steadily. They are suspended from horizontal rods, fixed so as to swing freely. This is necessary when the altar paraments and linens are changed.

A tester adds considerable richness to the altar. This is a carved canopy, often enriched with color and gold leaf, which projects outward from the wall, some feet above the altar. In ancient times it was used to prevent the profanation of the altar by birds which sometimes found their way to the carved roof trusses of the old churches, and likewise to guard the candles from the down-drafts that were common in some of the larger churches of olden times. In our day the tester is purely decorative.

It is really astonishing to recall the old-time utilitarian devices that have been retained purely for their decorative value, or for some use other than the original one. The altar tester is a case in point. The pulpit canopy was used originally to protect the bald head of the priest from down-drafts in poorly heated buildings. The altar rail was used in ancient times to prevent dogs from entering the sanctuary. Altar candles were used to give the priest light to read the missal. Incense was used not only to symbolize prayer, but likewise to purify the atmosphere in the days when even the nobility bathed infrequently in winter. Acolytes with their flaming torches were necessary in order to permit the deacon to read the Gospel in the gloomy churches of ancient times. The organ was used originally to furnish interludes while the priests and their assistants moved from place to place. Only in comparatively recent days has it been used to accompany singing. Chanting by the clergy was used in order to make the voice carry in large churches. Pews were used originally only by the aged and infirm, and the first ones were stone benches against the side walls. And yet we would not think of poking fun at organs, communicant rails, candles or pews, because of their curious and strictly utilitarian origin. Such things are a part of the devotional atmosphere of today.

To return to the subject: A permanent altar, rubrically speaking, is one that is made of stone. It must have a mensa, or flat horizontal slab, and this, rubrically, must be of one piece of stone. It must have five Greek crosses incised in its upper surface, representing Our Lord's five wounds. One cross is incised in the center, and one close to each corner of the mensa. This slab may be supported by four or more vertical pillars, or else (as is more usual) by three to four vertical slabs of stone. Now and then one finds an altar made of a single great block of stone.

A wooden altar, rubrically speaking, is classed as a temporary altar. It may be 50 years old, 100, or 500 years, but if it is of wood it is, strictly speaking, a temporary altar. If we are faithful to the rubrics, we will provide a small slab of stone, if we have a wooden altar, large enough for the sacred vessels. This is inlaid in the midst of the mensa, and it contains the five Greek

crosses mentioned. This is rubrical. And what do we mean by that? A thing is said to be rubrical when it adheres strictly to sound, conservative, and generally recognized tradition. In ancient times, these principles were printed in small red type in the old service books. Not only liturgical rubrics, but architectural rubrics and calendar rubrics were to be found as well. As time went on, many of these things became so well known, and so uniformly observed, that they were no longer printed in red type in the service books or missals. Most of the early Lutheran service books omitted these rubrics, for it was taken for granted that the clergy knew that the Introit, Kyrie, Credo and Epistle were sung from the south of the altar and the Gospel and certain other parts of the service from the north. It was taken for granted that the mensa was of stone, and that the sacramental vessels were placed in the center of the mensa.

If the altar is of wood, it ought not to be dark in finish. During the early years of the present century it was customary to stain the chancel woodwork a dark, gloomy "mission" color, and to add a horrible shiny varnish. Just why people liked dark stain, and why they called it "mission finish" is not clear. Today even the most commercial mail order type of church furniture is almost natural in color. Just enough stain is used to cut down the raw appearance of the new wood, and the finish nowadays is invariably of wax, or else some liquid substitute for wax. This has resulted in an astonishing improvement in our altars and other woodwork. Even the finest joinery suffers if stained too dark. Mediocre work is often made rather presentable if kept light in color, and without gloss.

his wife have their family worship each morning after breakfast, at which time they read the entire chapter from which the reading for the day is taken. They report that friends seeing their altar in their home always inquire about the use of it, and this opens up the whole matter of family worship in quite a natural way. A family of four, including two young people of high school age, take turns in conducting the devotions for the day. One family of five, including three small children, tell of the smaller children using their beginners' department prayers in connection with their daily devotions at the dinner table. Another family of five, with slightly older children, tell of their evening devotions in the living room before the children retire. The enclosed picture tells the story of their evening worship. Each child offers up a sentence prayer after the father's free prayer and the mother's read prayer. This family is learning some of the psalms together and they often add a hymn to their family worship program. On one occasion when, since guests were present, no mention was made of evening devotions and it was suggested that the children retire at their regular time, the five-year-old boy said, "Why, we can't go 'till we've read the Bible." So the guests were invited to take part in the worship for that evening. This same family reports that no matter how boisterous have been the games of the evening after the devotions there is a noticeable quietness which lasts all the rest of the evening. Another family of six, including small children, tell of using Bible stories as a part of their family worship. A family including two small boys report the custom of giving their reasons for thankfulness as they drop their coins into the thank-offering box. Adult families also report some encouraging experiences concerning the comfort that has come in the presence of sorrow and sudden difficulty and tell of the steadying influence of this daily participation in family worship. One family of four has had the joy of seeing this practice of family worship carried over into the new home which has been established at the marriage of their son. When this new home was dedicated by the pastor, the family altar was dedicated to the daily worship of God. At the marriage of every couple this practice of daily worship is stressed as a method of enriching the new life together and strengthening the cords of love.

After two years of daily use of the home altar by our members we may say that, to a high degree, it has accomplished the desired results. About ninety-five per cent of the families of our church practice daily worship and we can see a definite reaction in the congregational life; in increased attendance in family worship at church; in a self-initiated Bible reader's group; in family communion groups; in a growing spirit of evangelism, evidenced by a city-wide church home canvass and, of course, in the general spiritual tone which would result from these developments.

The Sacred Monograms

A READER in Texas writes us, stating that a discussion has developed in a Bible class regarding the correct meaning of the IHS symbol, so commonly used in church decoration. He quotes the popular explanations, namely "*Iesus Hominum Salvator*," "*In Hoc Signo*," "I Have Suffered" and "Jesus, the Saviour of Mankind." He asks for a discussion of this smybol, and for the name of a book "containing explanation of this and other church symbols."

The four interpretations submitted by the Texas reader are the common ones, but none of them are correct from the standpoint of scholarship, for all of them do violence to what is one of the most ancient symbols of the Christian Church. All of these are late interpretations of a very early idea, and all are based upon sentiment, rather than upon sound archaeological research.

The correct rendering of the symbol is IHC, and not IHS, and certainly never I.H.S. In its most correct rendering, it is accompanied by the XPC symbol. Both the IHC and the XPC ought to have a horizontal line over them. This is the correct form, as found almost without variation in early Christian art.

This IHC XPC symbol is found so universally that it would be an impossible task to trace its origin to any particular country. It is certain that it comes from the early Greek manuscripts of the New Testament, where the name of Our Lord was written out in Greek uncials, or what one might nowadays call capital letters. The uncial spelling of Our Lord's name was IHCOYC XPICTOC, or "Jesus Christ." The Greek uncial I corresponds to our letter "J," H to our long "e", C to our letter "s", O to our "o", Y to our "u" and C to our "s". The Greek uncial X is our "Ch", P is our "r", I is the same as our English "i", C is our "s", T our "t", O is our "o" and C our "s". Thus Our Lord's name in Greek, but spelled in our modern letters, is "Jesous Christos," which is almost the same as the modern German rendering.

However, the Greek scribes often used ligatures and abbreviations. Instead of writing out "IHCOYC XPICTOC" in full, they often wrote it "IHC XPC," with a horizontal line over each group of letters, signifying the fact that it is an abbreviation. These so-called monograms are still to be found profusely upon early Christian tombs, on the walls of the catacombs, in early churches, in mosaics and elsewhere.

It remained for an eccentric preaching monk, one St. Bernardine of Sienna, (died 1444), to read a fanciful meaning into the sacred monograms, as they are commonly termed. St. Bernardine, born of noble parents, entered the Franciscan order, and became a famous popular preacher and reformer of his day. Immense crowds flocked to hear him. Somewhat sensational, he changed the original IHC to IHS, in order to permit him to preach popular sermons on the three letters, fitting them to the Latin words "*Iesus Hominum Salvator*," or, "Jesus, the Saviour of Mankind." He lettered these words upon a large sheet of parchment, and at the climax of a sermon he would hold them aloft, calling upon the throngs who followed him to accept the Lord Jesus as their Saviour. A legend states that in later life he lettered these words upon a board, which he wore hung about his neck wherever he went.

Bernardine's rendering of the sacred monogram does violence to its original meaning. In order to accomplish his purpose, he created a curious mongrel, composed of two Greek letters, IH, and one Latin letter S. It is not a good form of the IHC, because it robs it of its original intention. It remained for the ignorance of modern commercial decorators to insert periods, and make it the absurd I.H.S., or the still more absurd J.H.S. of the mail-order houses of our day.

Since all church decoration ought to be truthful, we ought to adhere to the original form, namely IHC XPC. This looks best in decorative black-letter. We are printing an example copied not long since from the pulpit in Canterbury cathedral.

Even more ancient than the IHC XPC symbol is the XP symbol, which is the abbreviation of the Greek word "XPICTOC," meaning "Christ." Numerous examples of this exist upon early Christian coins, lamps, pottery and burial inscriptions. IC XC is another early form of the IHC XPC symbol. IC XC NIKA is another old form, and it refers to the Victorious Christ, triumphant over sin and death. All of these forms are highly appropriate for use in a Lutheran church, whether carved in wood, painted on stained glass, worked on vestments and paraments, wrought in metal, engraved on sacramental silver or used in mural decoration. However, they must not be used in the encaustic tiles now so commonly used in paving aisles and chancel, for it is inappropriate to place any Christian symbol where it is trodden underfoot.

The best book upon Christian symbolism is Pugin's "Glossary of Ecclesiastical Ornament and Costume," published about 90 years ago. Excellent copies, with their beautiful color-plates are still to be had of dealers in out-of-print books, but the cost is beyond the reach of the ordinary person. Geldart's "Manual of Church Decoration and Symbolism," published in 1899, is a very complete and valuable book, but likewise out of print. English dealers ask two pounds for a good copy. "Church Symbolism," published in 1917 by J. H. Jansen, 315 Caxton Building, Cleveland, is a book that needs revision, and correction of many typographical and other errors common to first editions. It is still in print, and sells for $7.50.

SYNODICAL PUBLICITY *from p 93.*

13. Pictures of unusual events or people. Always mark pictures on rear, "Please return to . . . . Name and Address "

14. Sermon manuscripts. Many newspapers are glad to publish sermons or sermon excerpts.

8. Do no become discouraged if your news story does not appear every time. Often more important news matter simply crowds your item out. Each newspaper destroys whole columns of news matter each day. If you fail once, try again and hope for better luck. Remember it is free space the papers are giving you, and for this reason never be unreasonable.

9. Even a little story about your church at frequent intervals will give your church much publicity. Many people read the newspaper from cover to cover and they read also little items in hidden corners.

10. It is best if the news stories are written by the pastor. He knows best what is a credit to his church and what is not. If the pastor is too busy let the publicity work be done by others under the pastor's supervision.

The practice of stewardship is the ultimate goal of all Christian preaching and teaching. To use *all* one's time and talents, *all* one's and has, in accord with the will of God, that is surely to reach the ideal. That is truly to love God with all the heart, mind, soul and strength, and one's neighbor as oneself. That and nothing less is Christian stewardship.—W. E. Henry.

* * * *

"THE CHURCH AND THE LIBRARY"

G. E. Hageman

"It (the public library) is the great neutral public institution, storing and making accessible recorded opinions but favoring none," writes Mr. Arthur E. Bostwick in "The Bookman" for June of this year. "And the odd thing is that in so far as it ignores the church the library is nullifying in one place its latest step in advance, which is to work with, in and for groups within the community; while by turning a cold shoulder to the public library the church is refusing to make use of one of the most powerful aids that could be offered her for the fulfilment of her mission."

Mr. Bostwick is the librarian of the St. Louis Public Library, "a man well known in civic as well as library circles, both as editor and writer." What he has to say on the church's relation to the public library is of interest to us who are just beginning to realize how valuable this public institution is to us in the dissemination of knowledge respecting our Church, her history, doctrines and principles. Some of his remarks are worth quoting here.

"The odd, the almost unbelievable thing is, that most religious groups in this country seem to be as unaware of the public library as we are of them. I will make but two exceptions—The Roman Catholics and the Christian Scientists. The Roman Catholics have been active in public library matters ever since I have known anything about public libraries.

"The Christian Scientists apprehend the library intensively in limited directions. They have committees whose business it is to see that all libraries are well supplied with 'Science and Health,' and they encourage the purchase of some other books. I have never known them to protest against the presence in a library of attacks on their faith, although there are some pretty stiff ones.

"Outside of these evidences of religious interest, I have never known, from my library contacts with readers, whether they were Baptists or Mohammedans, Buddhists or Methodists," continues Mr. Bostwick. Notice that the Lutherans are never mentioned. They are unknown. "I account this a fault of my own. It is strange that the religious group is the only body that the librarian has not gone out to seek with some activity. We long ago ceased to blame plumbers, or manufacturers of textiles, or Hungarians, or business men, if they did not use the library. We are recognizing that such failure is our failure. It may be theirs too; but we can mend our ways rather more quickly than other people's, and so we soon learned to go out after these gentry and to return with more or less willing bunches of them. But who ever heard of a librarian going out after a Methodist, or a United Presbyterian, or a Congregationalist? The very suggestion makes one smile; and yet some of these are quite as good game as engineers, or aviators, or students of Gaelic."

The following criticism of the public library is of value because it suggests a certain line of books which we can readily supply with little expense. "Our libraries are generally deficient in religious reference books. We buy lists of English peers and of American dealers in plumbing supplies, but we neglect the official clergy lists of our churches. Every library of good size should include what I may call the official literature of each church —its year book, with a list of its clergy, its fundamental law, whatever that may be termed in each case, its statements of doctrine, its liturgy if it has any, and its authorized book or books of hymns. If extended to the principal denominations this collection alone would constitute a very respectable library; its limits, of course, will be determined by the necessities of the case. Most of it may be bought once for all; the annuals should be purchased as they appear. To these should also be added, however, considerable unofficial material: the history of the denomination, the lives and chief works of its principal divines, plans and descriptions of some of its noteworthy church buildings, and so on."

Mr. Bostwick believes that the public library may foster the trend towards unity among the various Christian bodies. By that he means that the public library ought to make it possible for all religious bodies to come in contact with one another through their literature. In other words, the public library ought to be used as a public centre or depository of denominational literature, so that each religious group might have the opportunity to study at first hand the religious tenets and history of other religious groups, a clearing house, so to speak. There can be nothing objectionable in this as far as we Lutherans are concerned. We have nothing to be ashamed of and we ought to be only too ready to submit our Church's history, her doctrines and principles to public inspection. We believe that we have the pure Gospel and that all our principles are Biblical.

To continue with Mr. Bostwick—"The first thing that we need, here as elsewhere, is a survey of faith and order; and with all the work done toward unification of Christianity, I cannot see that this has ever been touched, perhaps not even sensed as a necessary element. Yet how can we reconcile Presbyterian and Baptist, Protestant and Catholic—nay, look abroad and ask how we can bring together Buddhist and Mohammedan, Tao and Shinto, unless we know what separates them? Much of this is now on record, but it is nowhere assembled. What Christian bodies believe in justification by faith? Which have more than one order in the ministry? Which are Congregational in government? Which have bishops? Which believe in the apostolic succession? Do all accept the Apostles' Creed exactly as most of us recite it? I need not go on. . . . The first step toward a general intelligent recognition of points of agreement and difference is the assemblage of material, and it is such an assemblage that the library would be making, if it should proceed as I advise. I do not advise for this purpose filling the shelves with controversy, and buying books intended to convert Protestants to Catholicism and Unitarians to Methodism; but I do think that we ought to have the facts. It is a fact that a body of persons believe in a stated thing, whether that thing is true or not, and for purposes of record, of survey, these facts we must and should have somewhere."

Let us supply the facts respecting our Church and her teachings. We have them. We are not ashamed of them. We preach them. We live them. We believe that the world ought to know them. Let us put them on the shelves of public libraries everywhere. The librarians are asking for them. Why not grant their request?

Lutheran Books in Public Libraries

QUESTION: Where does a person go if he wishes authentic information?

Answer: To the public library.

But if a person goes to the public library in his community and comes away with a misconception of the Lutheran Church because of insufficient information available in that particular library, whose fault is it? The fault is our own!

Obviously, it is the duty of the Lutheran Church to see that books containing authentic Lutheran information be found upon the shelves of every public library so that all who seek may find.

suggestions:

First: Go to your local library and examine the books on the shelves and the index cards. Note the titles lacking.

Second: Get acquainted with the librarian and have a frank talk together. Explain that you wish to cooperate with the library in bringing the book collection of the religious department to a higher state of perfection. Suggest that books of a general reference character, such as Davis' "Dictionary of the Bible," should be purchased from library funds, while books dealing with purely Lutheran fields might be furnished by your own church. Get the librarian's promise to accept the gift of Lutheran books and place them on the shelves should you furnish them free of charge.

Third: Get the Walther League or any other society or individual to provide the necessary funds for purchasing the important Lutheran books which the pastor would select.

Fourth: Create the DEMAND. As the librarian of the New York Public Library told the writer, "We will be glad to place any reliable books upon our shelves, providing you can prove that there is a sufficient demand for it. . . ." It is the pastor's duty to help create that demand among the people. People, as a rule, do not appreciate good music and other fine arts until they are interested in them. It is the same with religious topics. Arouse interest!

Fifth: Do not give up if the librarian should give you a cold reception. INSIST that the American reading public is entitled to the true facts of the Lutheran Church just as well as it is entitled to the facts of our American history, and at the same time point out that our own Lutheran authors are the best qualified to give these facts.

In answer to our appeal of 1926 we are glad to say that many Walther League societies gave this matter their earnest consideration. Our Lutheran Walther League office at Chicago cooperated by giving the cause publicity in their magazine and in the monthly *Workers' Bulletin.* We also wish to thank Concordia Publishing House for arranging lists of books in convenient "sum groups," which encouraged gifts of $5, $10, $15 and $25 from young people's societies for library purposes. It is impossible at this time to give accurate statistics as to the number of libraries listed, but we do know that thousands of dollars have been expended and that hundreds of good Lutheran books have been placed in the various libraries throughout the country.

During the past three years, our committee was very successful in inaugurating the special $1.80 Club Subscription Plan, which includes THE AMERICAN LUTHERAN, the *Lutheran Witness,* and the *Walther League Messenger.*

We are convinced, however, that many libraries of our country are still unrepresented by a Lutheran magazine. We are furthermore convinced that practically every library would welcome a free subscription to any magazine listed in the special Club Subscription Plan. This thought should be a challenge to every Lutheran Church society!

Even though the individual pastor may have many duties to attend to, still we feel our appeal of placing Lutheran books in public libraries is of sufficient importance to our Lutheran Church and to the Kingdom of God at large as to merit his attention and perhaps a bit of his own time.

Let our motto be—*A Representative Lutheran Shelf in Every Public Library*

A Public Address System In the Church

OUR PUBLIC ADDRESS SYSTEM was born of a real need. The reed organ was not powerful enough to carry the congregational singing, a pipe organ was out of the question at the present time, so a "Public Address System" solved the problem. Radio had been a hobby, so with the help of a local radio engineer a system was planned which would take care of all our needs.

We began on a small inexpensive scale, building at first a small amplifier with about a four-watt output (three tubes), equipped with an inexpensive carbon microphone and a second-hand loud-speaker. We found so many uses for this system, however, that it was soon improved, so that today it has grown into a complete well-equipped 30-watt amplifier with the best of microphones and loud-speakers, as well as a phono-pickup for playing electrical recordings.

With hotels, theatres, clubs, etc., installing such public address systems, churches, too, should find them profitable investments as ours has proved to be.

Our system has been used for the following:

1. To amplify the reed organ so that it will easily carry congregational singing with a well-filled church.

2. To bring the organ music to the choir room in the basement of the church for the processional, etc. This was impossible without the system.

3. To play some of the best recorded sacred music before the service.

4. To boost the pastor's voice so that he is heard with little effort all over the church. It is surprising how a public address system may be utilized for this purpose without the congregation being conscious of its use. People slightly hard of hearing are especially grateful for the installation.

5. To carry the service to an overflow crowd in the Parish Hall on special occasions.

6. To "broadcast" Christmas music to the neighborhood before the Christmas service.

7. To amplify music and voice at the outdoor service held on the church lawn during the summer.

8. To amplify the speaker's voice at dinners, etc. To make announcements at affairs, etc.

9. To improve the hearing of the children's Christmas Program, plays, etc.

Other uses which come to mind are the outdoor mission festivals held by many congregations, the amplification of organ chimes through a loud-speaker in the church tower, playing of recorded chimes, furnishing music for parades, reproducing sound on film motion pictures, providing an additional outlet for electonic organs, etc.

The equipment of a public address system consists of the following units:

1. The input or pickup device. This may be a microphone for picking up music or voice, a phono-pickup for reproducing recordings, or a photo-cell for reproducing sound on film.

2. The amplifier. This consists of the tubes, transformers, etc., which amplify the sound signal which has been picked up by the microphone or other input device. The amplifier should have a good "frequency response" and should be of sufficient power. Its power (watts-output) will be determined by its use. For merely "boosting" speech or music a small three- or four-watt amplifier may be satisfactory. For general purposes a 15-watt amplifier will serve best. Such an amplifier will even serve for outdoor purposes, although 30-watts output are generally recommended for that purpose.

3. The loud-speaker. The loud-speaker should have a good frequency response (perhaps 50-7000 cycles) and should be capable of handling the full output of the amplifier. In other words a 15-watt amplifier should be equipped with a 15-watt speaker or two or three speakers whose total wattage equals that amount. In general it is best to have several speakers placed correctly rather than one speaker at one place.

Complete public address systems are on the market. Their cost is much lower than usually supposed. We have seen complete systems manufactured by a reliable concern which cost about $40 for a complete 5 to 8-watt system, up to $100 for a complete 30-watt system. Some systems are built to work either from a six-volt storage battery or regular 110 A. C. house current. This is especially valuable where the outfit must be a portable one.

Any competent local radio service man or dealer should be able to obtain either complete units ready-built or to build one from parts.

PLANNED PUBLICITY FOR CONVENTION from R96
GER. These carry messages between committee rooms, press room, press table, in convention hall, deliver telephone messages, etc.

* * *

The Press table should be near the platform or stage. The convention secretary hands a copy of report or resolution before the house to the Press table.

Suggestions for the Distribution of Gospel Tracts

     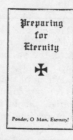  

Introductory

IT IS ESSENTIAL to a successful distribution of gospel tracts that the person supervising the work first of all carefully examine the tracts to be disseminated. Not only should the tract be carefully read, but the argument understood, so that any conversation resulting from the distribution may be intelligently used to strengthen the tract's message. The principal purpose of a tract is to drive the opening wedge. Unless this first advantage is followed by intelligent personal evangelism upon the part of the Christian worker there will be little tangible result. It goes without saying that only those tracts should be selected which can be understood and applied to the readers for which they are intended.

The *name, address* and *time of services* of the distributing church should be imprinted on each tract either by rubber stamp or the local printer.

Methods of Distribution

Which All Can Do

Hand tracts personally to neighbors and friends and relatives who do not attend Church. Where oftimes it is difficult to speak of religion to those we know, it is easy to hand them a tract, which will speak of the matter more completely than we are able or have time for. Take tracts to business and let them lay on desk, etc., where they will be seen and picked up by associates. Enclose tract when writing to friends.

Reaching The General Public

Place assortment of tracts on literature tables of railroad and bus terminals. Christians working in large department stores can see that rest rooms are supplied. When traveling, leave tracts on reading tables of Pullmans and steamships. To and from town leave tracts on seats of street-cars, subway and elevated lines.

Ask your doctor or dentist for permission to leave appropriate literature in his reception room. Through Lutheran members place tracts in station houses of policemen and firemen (especially on reserve duty), state troopers, etc. Take advantage of state and county fairs to erect church booth and distribute tracts to those who will accept them.

Use Tract Racks

Every Church should have a neat tract rack placed conveniently where all who enter must pass, with the words printed above a neat display of the principal tracts, "FREE — TAKE ONE !" Keep tract rack always well filled and literature "looking new." Tracts which have fallen forward due to the wrong construction of the tract rack—or are dog-eared due to curious handling make a poor impression upon the visitor. Tract racks in many instances are the best means of handling the dstribution problem in tourist camps, stores, waiting rooms, Y. M. C. A. and Y. W. C. A. halls, information bureaus. Those wishing to purchase a correctly designed tract rack especially built for the purpose should communicate with the American Lutheran Publicity Bureau.

Use Paid Advertising

The Christian Science Church and the Seventh Day Adventists insert paid newspaper advertisements announcing free literature. In larger cities a small advertisement might well be placed upon the church page reading: "Lutheran Information Bureau" 2116 Main Street. Send stamped, self-addressed envelope for FREE LITERATURE.

Addresses procured by such methods should be carefully filed and given to the City Missionary who may distribute them to the pastors in the prospect's locality for a missionary visit.

Use Tracts In Church Work

Besides distribution through the regular tract channels there are many uses to which the tract can be put in the average church's program.

1. *Hospital Visitation* is never truly complete unless the visiting society or pastor leave some religious material in the hands of the patient. Appropriate tracts should be chosen for hospitals, Old Folks Homes, penal institutions, etc.

2. *In conducting a community survey* a tract explaining some vital principal of the Lutheran Church should be left with each prospect. Some churches believe that it pays them to distribute into the letter boxes of the entire community a tract of general Christian appeal which carries the local church's name and invitation to services.

3. The pastor or church deaconness will find certain tracts a great aid if handed out when making the regular church *missionary calls.* Especially in making sick visits should certain selected tracts be left with the patient. It is at this time that the prospect has time to read and is in a more receptive mood than usual to learn more of Christ.

4. The tract is a wonderful aid in giving "spiritual talks" to the various *church societies.* The mere mention of "tract" and "tract distribution" gives an excellent opportunity for speaking of personal evangelism. Make the subject of a single tract the subject of the short spiritual matter talk, distribute a copy to each member present, ask them to refer to certain important paragraphs and suggest that they take the tract home and show it with similar explanations to the family and friends.

5. Several tracts lend themselves very well to presentation in *the Sunday's sermon.* Slip a copy of the tract into each hymnal. In the sermon refer to the various Scripture passages printed out in the tract as proving the points of the sermon. Urge the people to take additional tracts from the literature rack and carry on personal evangelism with their friends.

6. As *strangers* sign up in the church's "Guest Book" present them with a suitable tract with compliments of the church.

7. When sending out *flowers from church altar* to sick with suitable card from congregation, send also "the Great Physician" or other suitable tract.

8. From time to time *mail out tract* with parish paper. Insert paragraph in parish paper calling attention to important points in tract and why it should be passed on to a friend.

9. *Adult Classes.* When speaking on subjects such as "Forgiveness of Sins," "Holy Communion," "Where and How to Pray," "What the Lutheran Church Stands For," "Why Go to Church" and other practical topics, it will help the pastor to distribute tracts treating the subject *to each* member as supplementary information.

The Untalked of Christ

OUR SAVIOUR has been described by many adjectives. He has been called the forgiving Christ, the sinless Christ, the inspiring, healing, tempted, suffering, betrayed, triumphant, risen Christ. These are all true descriptions of Jesus. The character of Christ is like a gem which reflects many phases of light when turned at different angles. But is it not true that in many respects Jesus is also the "untalked of Christ"?

Undoubtedly, the reason the world is not more Christian today is because we have not told more people about Christ. Why is it that we leave so many people in ignorance of Him? What does Jesus mean to you? What has He taught you? What comfort, strength, courage, faith, foregiveness, blessing, friendship have you received from Him? Then why do we so often leave Him as the "untalked of Christ"? Why not recommend Him to others as their Friend, Comforter, Saviour and Redeemer?

In our cities we at times see a young man wearing an army uniform who is in the enlistment service. He is looking for recruits. He watches the crowds carefully and when he sees a young man standing idly at the corner, out of work, discouraged, lonely, he puts his hand on his shoulder and tells him what the army will give him and do for him if he enters the service. As Christians you and I have something better; can we afford to do less? We know that many people are suffering, sorrowful, lonely, and lost in sin, and we know that Christ has died to save them and give them just what they need. Shall we allow them to live and die in sin and hopelessness? Should we not rather try to enlist them in the host of the redeemed under the banner of the King of kings? To many souls today He is the "untalked of Christ."

Perhaps you will say: "I cannot do that. I can't talk Religion to people." The experiences of the Tract Department of the American Lutheran Publicity Bureau definitely proves that this is a quite general conviction. That is one reason why tracts are so tremendously popular and have been increasing in distribution. Where oftimes it is difficult to speak of Religion, it is easy to hand people a properly chosen tract which will speak of the subject more thoroughly than we are able or have time for. Or we may send these little "silent Gospel-preachers" on their missionary journey to unknown persons by leaving a copy on the street car or train seat, placing them on the table in rest rooms, depots, etc. This certainly is something all of us can do. Sow the seeds of truth. We know that Christ will do His part by blessing the message.

We can feel very confident regarding results when we distribute A·L·P·B tracts. Here are a number of reasons.

1. They convey a Sublime Message. They speak of Christ and Him crucified. They present unanswerable, unimpeachable arguments and passages from God's Word.

2. They have been tested by Experience. Our tracts have been printed by the millions because there has been a steady and increasing demand for them on the part of an ever-widening circle of Christian people. Our tracts have helped thousands.

3. They are Attractive. Many individuals and agencies of the leading Christian denominations have written us to compliment us on the dignified and appealing make-up of our Gospel tracts.

4. They are Free. As long as God supplies our needs in the Free Tract Fund, we print them and send them out free to all those who will carefully and prayerfully use them.

Divinely commissioned to evangelize the world, in the interest of the noblest cause under the sun, possessing that which makes for man's highest welfare in time and eternity, the sinner's only means of salvation, the glorious Gospel of Christ, let us scatter these tracts over the field of humanity where they may yield a plenteous harvest.

What YOU can do:

1. Send for tracts and prayerfully distribute them.

2. Give your financial support to this tested method of bringing Christ to the nation.

How to Use Tracts

THE METHODS of tract distribution are various and manifold. Local ingenuity will find an almost unlimited number of ways of distribution. We mention only a few that are being put into effect.

1. Many churches have instituted tract racks on tables where a goodly number of tracts are kept on hand for the use of church attendants. A dependable person is responsible for the regular replenishment of depleted stock.

2. Tracts are being extensively used in neighborhood house-to-house canvasses. The Bureau publishes a number of tracts that are especially adapted to such use.

3. Some churches periodically enclose tracts in their church bulletins with the request that the members of the church hand the enclosed tract to some unchurched friend or neighbor.

4. The mailing list of a local church lends itself splendidly to the spreading of tracts. They are regularly enclosed in the church's literature.

5. Many thousands of tracts are annually distributed at downtown noonday Lenten services. They are either enclosed in the programs or offered in special tract racks at the exits.

6. Similar use of tracts is made at joint festival celebrations and Luther Day observances. Such services offer a fine opportunity to reach a large number of non-Lutherans.

7. Church membership and visiting committees find tracts very useful. Visitors carry a selected supply with them and use them at their own discretion.

8. Some business men enclose a tract in all their personal mail that goes out from their offices. This is a courageous and effective way of testifying.

9. Some professional men keep a select supply of tracts on their reception room tables. Waiting patients or clients are almost sure to browse through them.

10. In some localities permission has been obtained to have a small tract rack at railroad and bus stations, and it is reported that these racks need continual replenishment.

11. Some church members always have a number of tracts with them, handing them out at opportune moments or leaving them lie "accidentally" at strategic places.

12. Literature sent to Sunday School pupils whose parents are not connected with the church may enclose tracts that have been carefully selected.

Rubber Stamp Your Tracts

 Most of the tracts published by the American Lutheran Publicity Bureau provide a blank space intended for the imprint of the local congregation or society, or individual, distributing the literature. Experience has proven that a local address is of much missionary value. Rubber stamps to be used for this purpose are not expensive and can also be used for other purposes. For those that are in need of such devices, the business department of the Lutheran Publicity Bureau, 1819 Broadway, New York, has made arrangements with a large firm manufacturing the best of rubber stamps at the following charges, one line $.50, two lines, $.80, 3 lines, $1.10, four lines, $1.40. Please send check or money order with plainly written copy, better still, printed instructions.

Appreciation Goes a Long Way

CLAUDIUS S. KULOW

WE have attended many church fellowship and anniversary banquets, but none impressed us quite as did that commemorating the Fortieth Anniversary of the English Lutheran Church of Our Saviour of Brooklyn. All the elements of the successful banquet fellowship were in evidence—a commodious dining hall, festive decorations, tasty food promptly served, prayer and benediction, the salute to the American flag, the national anthem by the audience, the salute to the Christian flag by the recitation of the Apostles' Creed, community singing directed by a spirited song leader accompanied by an able pianist, a printed menu-program and table decorations in keeping with the occasion, a few soloists, timely greetings from well-known personalities, not too many "main" speakers, and a capable layman of the congregation as master of ceremonies who really kept things moving.

"Recognition Makes Labor Sweet"

Most significant, however, was the tangible expression of the motto "Recognition makes labor sweet." It is this element of the fellowship dinner that we herewith commend to the readers of the AMERICAN LUTHERAN. At the psychological moment in the program, the toastmaster said: "A grateful congregation, remembering the inspired and sacrificing service of its many officials to the Church of Our Saviour, to the Church at large, and to the community during the past forty years, wishes to take this opportunity to say 'thank you' in public. Believing that recognition makes labor sweet, we salute them tonight." Many former officers came from far and near to be present on this momentous occasion and were presented with carefully inscribed "Certificate of Recognition." The acknowledgments were categorized as follows: 1) Recognition of officers living; 2) Recognition of officers now deceased; 3) Recognition of wives of officers past and present; 4) Recognition of pastors who have served the church; 5) Recognition of charter members still members of the congregation.

When all past and present officers had been summoned to the platform, the master of ceremonies continued: "We only wish it were possible to give cognizance to the fine and splendid services which all our people have rendered in all the branches of the work—Sunday School teachers, choir members, society leaders and the like—but obviously this is impossible tonight. We do, however, deeply and sincerely thank them for their efforts in every department of our work. Tonight we deem it a great privilege to participate in the presentation of 'Certificates of Service' to the many men who have during the past forty years given unstintingly of their efforts, time and talents. We are grateful to God for the excellent service they have rendered. We also wish to call to mind the splendid records of those men who have served but who have been translated to the Church Triumphant. The work they have done will always remain garden-fresh in our hearts and minds. We pause to salute their memories, and in so doing honor ourselves. Our men have been imbued with a spirit of consecrated service. May God bless them, each and every one."

Note the all-inclusiveness of the above remarks which take in all who labor in the interest of the church. No one was forgotten. After the presentation of certificates, the speaker continued: "Our tribute is only half complete. We now pay tribute to all the women, be they wives or mothers, who gave so freely of their time, efforts and prayers, so that their husbands or sons sould serve the church. We salute them all, past and present, for they also surely served. As a symbol of our love, esteem and respect, we have picked the Queen of the Flowers, a beautiful red rose, to present to every mother, wife or nearest of kin. The rose, being sweet and lovely, gives joy to the beholder." Here, one of the four charter members, a dear lady rich in years, presented the symbolic rose to the men for their wives.

The Certificate

The front cover of the certificate was adorned with a picture of Christ and His disciples with the wording. "Jesus said, 'Follow Me' . . . and they followed Him." The inside pages read: "In Recognition of Service. The congregation and pastor join in this token of good will and sincere appreciation. To ——, for helpful and consecrated service rendered as —— during the period from 19— to 19—. In recognition thereof, we hereby set our hand and seal. ——, Pastor. Presented on the occasion of the 40th Anniversary Banquet, November 7, 1941. English Lutheran Church of Our Saviour, Brooklyn." It is noteworthy that the above ceremony was prepared for the occasion by Mr. Bernhard von Hagen, layman of the church.

Charter Members Honored

Before the presentation of a framed picture of our Lord Jesus Christ to each of the women charter members and a plaque to the one surviving male member of the congregation still active in the membership and work, the pastor spoke as follows: "In the long ago there lived a holy man and humble, Thomas à Kempis, who wrote a book of Meditations. In one of his meditations he wrote that it is remarkable and noteworthy if a person, year-in and year-out, decade after decade, without let or hindrance, serves God and man through the church. Tonight we wish to pay tribute to that type of faithfulness. The four charter members have served God and man for forty years through His Church. They have been faithful in their attendance upon Word and Sacrament. They have been pillars in the Temple of God. With God's grace resting upon them they have manifested their faith in Jesus by a life of consecrated and loving service. It is my honor, as pastor, to present unto them individually a token of our esteem."

Wording of the Testimonials

The inscriptions on the testimonials presented former pastors and the charter laymen are apt to be suggestive to those who feel that appreciation is a beautiful flower and might some day desire to make such gratitude tangible. These follow:

Greetings
to
The Rev. John H. C. Fritz, D.D.
Founder and First Pastor of the Church
of Our Savior
Our Father in Christ, remembered long
A Servant of God, a Prince among men
Theologian, Educator, Author, Dean

This Testimonial is Affectionately Tendered by the English Lutheran Church of Our Savior at the Fortieth Anniversary Celebration.

(Signed by the members of the Church Council, Trustees, Chairman, Secretaries, and Pastor. The seal affixed.)

(Continued on page 22)

In Tribute
to
Mr. Henry Wahlers
An Exemplary Christian
A Loyal Son of the Church
A Gifted and Faithful Worker
Of Sound Judgment and Broad
Sympathies
Respected and beloved by all, etc.

Greetings
to
The Rev. Arthur R. G. Hanser
Pastor of the Church of Our Savior
1914—1925
Eloquent Preacher, Profound of
Thought
Loyal Friend, Generous of Heart
A Leader of Men
etc.

Lighting the Birthday Cake

Ever present at birthday celebrations is the proverbial cake with its candles. We felt that the appropriate words spoken as the birthday cake was lighted were so apropos to the occasion as to make this the highlight of the evening. Since many requested a copy of this ceremony, in the hope that by using the pages of the AMERICAN LUTHERAN greater service might be given to a greater number, we were led to persuade Pastor Erwin Kurth of the Church of Our Saviour to permit their reproduction. Again, note the all-inclusiveness of gratitude and thoughtfulness.

"Greetings to you all, and gladness, thanksgiving and joy.

As one family we are gathered together to celebrate a birthday. Candles adorn the birthday cake. Let them be lighted.

First, we shall light a candle in adoration of the Head and Bishop of the Church, the Lord Jesus, who came as a Light into this dark world, and has enlightened us with the gifts of His Holy Spirit. (The tall beeswax candle at the center of the cake is lighted.) May we evermore walk with' our faces towards this light that all the shadows of sin and death might be cast behind us.

2. We light a candle in honor of the former pastors, the charter members, and all others who have held aloft the torch of the Gospel. We have traveled forward in the light which they shed abroad.

3. We light a candle in honor of those whose lamps were trimmed in our church and who are now shining lights in other congregations. May they ever shine forth the beauty of Him who called them out of darkness into the glorious light of discipleship.

4. We remember those who aforetime walked in the Light but now dwell in darkness and the shadow of death. May they return unto Him Who is the Light of the World.

5. All the members of our happy family cannot be with us this evening. Father thinks of them. We all think of them. We think of our boys in the armed forces of our country. Wherever they are—on land or sea or in the air—may they let their light so shine before men, that others may see their good works, and glorify the Father which is in heaven.

6. We light a candle for the boys and girls at college and university who crowd around the lamp of vision. May they always let the Scriptures of God be a lamp unto their feet and a light unto their path.

7. A candle is lighted for the men who toil at night—the mothers who watch over their little ones—doctors and nurses who care for the sick. May the star of God's love ever shine into their hearts.

8. And for those who have gone to the City Foursquare, where there is no night, where the Lamb is the Light thereof, we light a candle IN MEMORIAM. Rest eternal grant unto them, O Lord, and let light perpetual shine upon them.

9. And for one and all, let now the candles be lighted. It is the birthday of the Church. May love, life and joy evermore be ours. May we be knit together as one holy family in the mystical body of the Lord Jesus Christ until we reach the plateau where shines the Everlasting Light."

The ceremony is concluded with an appropriate song.

As Christians, we are constantly reminded to render thanksgiving to God for all His mercies to us as individuals and as a church. To Him be glory and honor. Yet, to our mind, appreciation of those who, in an exemplary manner, labor long and loyally for the Master is "angel's work indeed." We feel that the Church of our Saviour, its pastor and laymen, have utilized this opportunity.

Gleanings From Wide-Awake Churches

Bus service for Sunday School pupils in outlying districts has been instituted by quite a number of churches. Bus companies seem to be willing to quote very low rates for such service.

A western church has regular Sunday automobile accommodation for the nurses of the city hospital, where rules of punctuality make dependence on street-car service inadvisable.

Another church makes practical use of the gardens of its members by asking for floral contributions to be delivered at the church on Sunday mornings and distributed on Sunday afternoons among the sick.

Many city churches are making use of the school police system to insure the safety of the Sunday School pupils at dangerous street intersections. These youthful policemen are commissioned by the city and have the same standing as public school police.

The practice of sending multigraphed copies of the pastor's Sunday sermon to the sick and shut-ins is growing. The most gratifying results are being reported.

Some of our churches are running attractive standing headings on their weekly church announcement sheets. These headings are usually in the form of cuts. Some have their cuts printed on a year's supply of the sheets used for mimeograph or multigraph purposes. Others use a standing multigraph cut.

One church makes the suggestion that, unless the Sunday announcement sheet is crowded, the text of the choir anthem be printed out in full. If the choir number has been carefully selected and is in harmony with the sermon, such an arrangement will enhance the value of the service.

THE OLD COMPLAINT *from p 118*

ing Lutherans from other parts of the country." And yet a Christian congregation is only part of the larger body of believers and may well regard it as a duty to help stem the growing neglect of the house and Word of God during the summer months brought about by the migratory habits of the present generation. Even from the standpoint of reciprocal helpfulness the need of providing for the traveling strangers should appeal to every congregation. The affixing of a sign onto the church building costs very little. The placing of helpful highway markers will give one of the local church societies a worthwhile objective. The placing of a notice in the weekly paper of the community usually costs nothing. A small-town hotel keeper will usually be glad to hang in his establishment a neatly framed sign giving the location of the church as well as the time of services.

The summer season will soon be upon us again and the time is at hand to make suitable provisions for the many thousands of traveling Lutherans who flit from place to place and who have the laudable desire to worship on Sundays with their brethren in the faith.

Celebrating the Church's Jubilee

ARTHUR E. HOHENSTEIN

LUTHER SAID that the preaching of the Word of God is as a "Platzregen"—that is does not remain long at one place.

It is, therefore, an event of special significance and worthy of extreme rejoicing and of heartfelt thanksgiving when a congregation is privileged, through the grace of God, to celebrate its seventy-fifth or diamond jubilee.

And a congregation which may look back over the seventy-five years and see how it grew from a preaching or mission station, then to an organized congregation of thirty members, until now it numbers 1,800 communicant members—such a congregation is inspired because of the manifold blessings of God, to celebrate its diamond jubilee not for merely one day or even one week. Great are the blessings—great must be the public recognition of these blessings.

This was the spirit which guided the members of Trinity Lutheran Church of Bloomington, Illinois (Rev. W. E. Hohenstein, pastor) in planning and executing its diamond jubilee program during this year of 1933.

The observance of such an important milestone in the life of a congregation should be not only a time of rejoicing and of thanksgiving. It is also a time for reflection and for self-examination.

There are peculiar dangers to the spiritual life of the members of an old established, large congregation. The age of the church brings with it, almost naturally, a feeling of self-sufficiency and self-satisfaction, and the largeness of the congregation results, just as naturally, in a loss of the feeling of individual responsibility for the work of the church. Not that these attitudes necessarily must predominate such a large, old-established congregation, but these dangers are always at hand.

It is, therefore, well for a church to precede the actual day or days of the observance of its founding with a program of reconsecration—an extended period of self-examination, of repentance, and of rededication to Christ and His work.

The actual date of the seventy-fifth anniversary of Trinity Lutheran Church was September 19, 1933. The reconsecration program was begun in January. The program resulted from a report of the church's Publicity Committee. The committee had made a systematic study of church attendance during 1932. Its object was to improve church attendance during 1933, and, its yearly report, recommended the program of reconsecration as, among other things, a method of creating a greater love for and interest in the church, with a resultant increase in attendance at divine services. The committee also recommended that this reconsecration program and the entire jubilee celebration be turned over to a special jubilee committee.

I. ORGANIZATION

The appointment of the jubilee committe was left to the church council. They appointed a jubilee committee of twenty-nine members, representing the following groups within the church:

Pastor	1 member
Church Council	3 members
Board of Education	2 members
Church Visitors	4 members
Church Membership Committee	2 members
Finance Committee	3 members
Publicity Committee	2 members
Lutheran Laymen's League Club	2 members
Senior Walther League	2 members
Berea Bible Class	2 members
Voting Members in General	6 members
Total	29

This committee was also assisted by co-operating committees of the Ladies' Aid Society, Mission Society and Junior Walther League.

At the first meeting of this committee of twenty-nine, the following officers were appointed: chairman, assistant chairman, secretary, assistant secretary, and treasurer. These officers, together with the pastor, formed the executive board. The large committee was of value in getting a cross-section of congregational feeling and opinion on points under consideration and in laying out general plans of procedure. It was up to the executive board then to work out the details and to carry into execution the general plans adopted by the large committee. It is highly important that such a large committee elect a smaller executive board which can function more easily in matters of detail.

Frequent meetings of the executive board are necessary. Occasional meetings should also be had of the executive board with the large committee to make reports of progress and to plan future work.

In addition to the executive board, sub-committees were appointed from time to time to handle special phases of the jubilee work.

II. RECONSECRATION PROGRAM

Its organization being completed, the jubilee committee immediately undertook the all-year program of reconsecration.

The motto for this reconsecration program was the heart-searching words of Christ, "Lovest Thou Me?"—John 21, 15. In this program, each member of the church was urged:

(1) to attend divine services *every* Sunday;

(2) to attend the Lord's Supper at least *four times* during the year;

(3) to invite and to bring others to divine services and to endeavor to win the unchurched for church membership;

(4) to establish or maintain the family altar and to bring up the children in the fear and admonition of the Lord;

(5) to a personal reconsecration of soul, mind, body, and talents to Christ;

(6) to consecrate our earthly goods by placing regularly, *each month*, a gift for the local church and for missions in our church envelopes; and

(7) voting members, to renew their pledge regularly to attend the congregational business meetings, and others, who are eligible, to become voting members.

The points of the reconsecration program were first presented to the congregation by sermons by the pastor and by short talks by laymen toward the close of divine services on Sunday mornings. The pastor delivered sermons on points (2) attendance at the Lord's Supper and (4) establishing the family altar. Laymen presented the points (1) on church attendance, (3) personal missionary work, (5) personal reconsecration, and (6) regular giving.

Points of the reconsecration program were also presented by laymen and laywomen at the meetings of the church societies.

Finally, the entire program was presented to the entire church membership by an every-member visit made by a group of one hundred and thirty Jubilee Workers. A group of adult workers visited the adult members of the church and a group of young people workers visited the young people.

Before the visits were made, separate meetings were held for each group of workers to acquaint them with the entire reconsecration program. The meetings opened with the singing of "Jesus, Thy Boundless Love to Me," followed with a Scripture reading, the singing of "Take My Life, and Let It Be," and a prayer.

The reconsecration program was then considered point by point. Instructions were given on how the visits were to be made. A set of mimeographed instructions were also given each worker. It was emphasized that the visits should be heart-to-heart talks on each point of the reconsecration program and of its desired effect upon the heart and life of each member. Since there were seven points to the reconsecration program, it was definitely mentioned that a thorough presentation of the entire program would take time, that no more than one or two calls could be made in an evening, and that a short social call of ten or fifteen minutes would not bring the desired results.

To assist the workers in presenting the complete program, a portfolio was prepared which contains a set of mimeographed folders* on each of the seven points of the program. Each member was presented with one set of these folders.

RECONSECRATION PROGRAM LITERATURE

The cover of this portfolio shows the Hoffman picture of Christ with outstretched arms and the reconsecration motto "Lovest Thou Me?"

On the inside cover, the following words appear as a scroll, ". . . . Yea, Lord, Thou knowest that I love Thee. To show my love to Thee, I will:—" and here follow the seven points of the reconsecration program.

On the back cover page appear the words "Bless the Lord, O my soul, and forget not all His benefits;" Psalm 103, 2. Following this is a statement that this program is a part of the Seventy-fifth Anniversary of the church, then the name and address of the church, and the name of the pastor.

The reading matter for each of the pamphlets on the seven points of the reconsecration program was prepared by the pastor and by laymen of the church. Each pamphlet is richly illustrated. Christ and an appropriate Bible quotation are used for the picture on the front page of each pamphlet, and scenes from the church or church life are the pictures used for the other pages.

RECONSECRETION SUNDAY

Sunday, May 14, the Sunday following the meetings with the Jubilee Workers, was designated as Reconsecration Sunday.

A soul-stirring sermon on reconsecration was delivered by the pastor. The Jubilee Workers occupied reserved seats in the front pews of the church. During the services they were consecrated to their work by the pastor. For this service, there was placed, in the front of the church (next to the altar), a life-size, hand-tinted picture of Hoffman's Christ with the reconsecration theme, "Lovest Thou Me?"

In four weeks, all visits were to be completed. At the end of this time, separate meetings of the adult and young people workers were again held to check-up on the calls made and to ascertain the reactions to the reconsecration program. All workers reported most favorable responses.

III. SERMONS PREPARATORY TO THE JUBILEE

The actual observance of the diamond jubilee next occupied the attention of the jubilee committee.

The pastor prepared the hearts of his members for this important festival by delivering a series of sermons prior to jubilee week. He used as his text the Letters to the Seven Churches of Asia Minor (Rev. 2, and 3).

IV. THE JUBILEE SERVICES

After months of preparation, the days of the great jubilee arrived.

In order to represent all organizations within the church in the jubilee, a series of nine services were held. Outside speakers were, of course, engaged.

For the services on Sunday, September 17, a public address system was installed in the church, with loud speakers in the church annex and church yard, for the overflow audience. We were concerned that *no one* be turned away from these main jubilee services for lack of room.

The societies sponsoring the week-day services sponsored them to the full extent of selecting their speakers, arranging for the music features, and paying for all expenses of speakers, programs, and floral decorations. It was of special interest that the musical numbers were also by members of the respective societies. This helped to create extra interest in the services. Of course, all programs received the approval of the pastor and the jubilee committee.

The week-day services were for *everybody* and not merely for the men, or for the ladies, or for the young people.

All jubilee services were open to the public and very many "strangers" attended the services.

REUNION SERVICES

The Reunion Services deserve special mention. The task of arranging such a service for a seventy-five-year-old congregation, with many large confirmation classes, was a tremendous one. A special committee of five members (not members of any other jubilee committee) was appointed to take complete charge of these services.

The first task of this committee was to go over the church records and to make a list of the members of the various confirmation classes. They were assisted by members of various classes in finding the present addresses of the various members. This was no small task, especially in the case of the older confirmees.

About a month before the reunion services, a written invitation was mailed to each confirmee, inviting him or her to the services. The left margin of the letter presented five pictures from the lives of "Our Fathers:" Immigration, settlement, church, school, and sacrifice and consecration. The right margin pictured "My Participation:" Baptized, educated, instructed, confirmed, ministered unto, and source of riches, worthy of my love (picture of church).

With this letter was inclosed an addressed one-cent postal card reservation at the Coliseum with the confirmee's class. A badge was also inclosed, giving the year date of confirmation. The badge was worn as the confirmee entered the Coliseum so that he could be quickly placed at the services.

The large corps of ushers had two meetings prior to the reunion services for instruction on handling the work in a prompt, orderly, and efficient manner.

ATTENDANCE

The Lord blessed the jubilee services with fine weather, and each service drew a "capacity" audience. The attendance record follows:

Sunday, September 17	1,440
Tuesday, September 19	826
Wednesday, September 20	830
Thursday, September 21	1,019
Friday, September 22	913
Sunday, September 24 (A.M.)	1,044
Sunday, September 24 (Reunion Services)	2,013
TOTAL	8,085

The average per service was 1,155 (German and English morning services counted as one service).

The number of communicants at the communion services was 660, one of the largest in the history of the church.

V. DECORATIONS

Since our jubilee was an all-year event, a constant reminder of the jubilee in the form of a large scroll was placed high in the chancel of the church at the beginning of the year. This scroll, with a silver background, had the following raised-letter inscription: "Diamond Jubilee; 1858-1933."

For the Reconsecration Sunday in May and for several Sundays thereafter, a life-size, hand-tinted picture of Christ was placed, in a setting of ferns and flowers, in front of the pulpit. A neat card bore, in large, legible letters, the reconsecration theme, "Lovest Thou Me?" The background for the picture was in the form of a large church window. It was covered with silver cloth, with a neat border of lavender and gold ribbon. Flood lights of contrasting colors were played on the background and the picture itself, presenting a beautiful spectacle at night.

The Christ picture was again erected for Jubilee Week (September 17-24), but a new card bore the assuring words of Christ, "Lo, I am with you always." The picture was also transferred to the Coliseum for the reunion services, and added to the inspiration of this great service.

For the annual mission festival (held two weeks later), the Christ picture was again erected in the church with a new placard worded: "Go, Preach the Gospel."

A gorgeous display of flowers, palms, and ferns was arranged for all services by the Ladies' Aid Society. Especially for the reunion services at the Coliseum, many memorial bouquets were presented by individuals and by two of the confirmation classes, so that the front of the large stage at the Coliseum was completely banked with a most colorful array of flowers.

VI. PUBLICITY

Publicity formed an important part in the entire jubilee program. In addition to the reconsecration program literature already described, many forms of publicity were used for the jubilee services in September.

The most effective publicity for the members of the church and for the community were the extensive newspaper write-ups and the many pictures used with them.

The newspaper write-ups, prepared by the church's publicity committee, presented each service in detail, gave sermon extracts, and showed pictures of the pastor of the church, all the festival speakers, the church, the school and its principal, the group of one hundred and thirty Jubilee Workers, the church choir and its director, the Ladies' Jubilee Chorus of seventy-five voices, the Man's Club Chorus of eighty-five voices, the Children's Choir of thirty voices, the oldest living confirmee, and a portion of the two thousand people who attended the reunion services.

And a highly commendatory editorial added even greater weight to the other newspaper publicity.

A four-page folder, giving the dates of each service, speakers, and music features, was distributed to each member as an inclosure to the invitation to the reunion services. Extra copies were distributed at the church doors. This program avoided any possible confusion in the minds of the members as to the date, time, and nature of each service.

Neighboring congregations were invited to celebrate the happy festival with us. Extra copies of the above-mentioned folder were mailed to them for display on their church or school bulletin boards.

Large posters were placed in our school hall and church annex, inviting our members to attend each and every service, and giving an outline of the various services.

During the summer months, a large poster, in the interest of our school, was also displayed.

One of the members took moving pictures of the various events during the year, as a unique and valuable remembrance of this great year in the history of the church.

VII. SOUVENIR JUBILEE BOOKLET

Shall we, during this year of economic stress, issue the customary souvenir jubilee booklet? Surely, our people will want some memento of the diamond jubilee of their beloved church!

The publication of a jubilee booklet was decided upon. A subcommittee was appointed to take complete charge of the preparation of such a booklet. The booklet of forty-four pages contains a history of the church, of the school, and of the various societies,

and thirty-one pictures. The booklet was sold at cost—35c a copy.

A separate committe of two was appointed to take charge of the arrangements for the sale of the booklet. Personal contact with each congregational member was made by the group of Jubilee Workers. The booklets were also for sale at society meetings and after church services.

Complimentary copies of the booklet were presented to the President of Synod, the President of the United States, the Library of Congress, the Historical Society of Concordia Seminary, the American Lutheran Historical Library at Milwaukee, the Lutheran Witness, the Statistical Bureau of Synod, the County Historical Society, the local public library, and to others. A letter of acknowledgment was received from President Roosevelt through his secretary.

VIII. FINANCES

Can a congregation *afford* to celebrate a jubilee during hard times? If the *only* purpose of a jubilee is to raise a large fund for some church project, then the jubilee celebration had best be postponed until better times—although such action seems as much out of order as if one were to say, "Tomorrow is my twenty-first birthday, but I shall postpone celebrating it until next year."

Although I strongly believe that a congregation, in days of prosperity, should, for its jubilee, present its church with a large thank offering, yet I also feel that such a collection is *not absolutely essential* for a jubilee celebration.

For our jubilee, no big collection was undertaken. Some money, however, is needed to carry on a comprehensive, all-year program. Our expenses were met by the following methods.

MELTING POT

A committee of the Ladies' Aid and Mission Societies undertook the collection of old gold and silver. This was turned over to a jeweler of the church and a goodly sum of money was realized to help pay some of the early expenses.

CHURCH COLLECTIONS

The collections for the four week-day services and the reunion services were placed in the jubilee fund. The collections for the Sunday morning services were placed in the regular congregation treasury, although the jubilee fund paid all expenses for these services. The church societies helped materially by paying all expenses for their week-day services.

SURPLUS

It was a happy feeling, after a successful, joyous jubilee, to report a surplus of over $250 in the jubilee fund. This was possible because of the good collections at the well-attended jubilee services and by the committee's exercising reasonable economy. With the surplus, the committee is to purchase a suitable article for the church (bulletin board or the like) in commemoration of the diamond jubilee.

In conclusion, let us always remember that a congregation's jubilee should be undertaken and carried out with constant prayers for God's guidance and blessing. All plans and all events should have as their sole purpose the glorification of the name of God and the giving of thanks to Him to whom honor is due. *Soli Deo gloria!*

Travelers and Tracts

A student at Concordia Seminary, St. Louis, writes us:

"Is anything being done to utilize the tourist or vacationist coming from our congregations in spreading Lutheran tracts? How would it be if the pastors of our churches would be advised to instruct their touring or vacationing members to that effect and furnish them with tracts? It would serve to strengthen the feeling of the duty of personal mission work among the Lutheran laity at a time when they need it most. It would help to bring the Gospel into the most varied sections and much frequented places in our country."

The suggestion is good. The average tourist, stopping off at small-town hotels and tourist camps, will find many a hitherto unutilized opportunity to leave a tract where it may be picked up and read. It is a means of seed-sowing which we probably have not made much use of. We commend it to the general attention of our people.

Strange Missionaries

I PICKED UP THIS PAPER in the street car a couple o' weeks ago," said Raymond Preuss* showing the minister a rumpled tract on *Why Go To Church?* "It didn't bother me much at the time, but when I sent my suit to the cleaner's I found the paper in a pocket although I don't remember putting it there. I haven't been to Church since I came here and I feel that this thing must be meant for me. So here I am. Can I join up with you?"

—There is nothing very exciting about Mr. Preuss' experience, but if he had not found the tract which finally stirred up his conscience and brought him back to the Church, who knows, perhaps the Church would have lost another of its own. Who left the tract on that street car is not known, but again a tract proved its power as a "silent missionary."

Ushering and Its Obligations

(EDITOR'S NOTE—The following rules are taken from the instructions given to the ushers of the Lake Avenue Baptist Church of Rochester, N. Y. In general, the rules are good and most of them are applicable to practically any church conditions.)

FIRST—THE USHER

An usher is a responsible person who holds within himself the power to add or to detract from the atmosphere of a church service. He can make, or lose, many friends for the church by his use of, or lack of, tact and judgment. He should always be alert to serve and ready for any emergency which may occur at an unexpected moment. He should present a neat personal appearance.

SECOND—THE OFFICE

The very foundation of efficiency in this work lies in adopting a right mental attitude toward it. To start rightly one must see its large proportions, weigh its values and ponder is possibilities. If impressed with its importance, each usher will hold the position in high esteem.

Ushering should be regarded primarily as Christian service. It is Kingdom work. An usher's working motto may well be "I serve the Lord Jesus Christ." Such an attitude will call forth the best in each one in order that he may measure up to his opportunity. "Whatsoever ye do, do it heartily as unto the Lord and not unto men, knowing that of the Lord ye shall receive the reward of the inheritance, for ye serve the Christ."

From the usher the guest receives not only his first impression of the church but much of the mental and spiritual tone of the service to come. It is, therefore, well to remember that whole-hearted courtesy adds dignity to this office of receiving guests in the church of Jesus Christ; that a pleasant smile is worth many words and that every expression may convey friendliness and help create an attitude of reverence.

The only limit to the possibilities of service in ushering is the limitation of the personality of each individual usher. While it is imperative that one conform in a general way to the policies adopted by the Boards of Ushers, there is always room for originality and individual expression. The spirit of the usher is a most important factor, for an official or professional attitude is not becoming in a host and, in the final analysis, ushers are just that—hosts for God.

THIRD—SERVING THE GUEST

When greeting a guest at the church entrance or in the foyer the usher should look him squarely in the face for two reasons: first, to stamp the guest's face upon his memory so that he may know him when he returns and second, to impress the guest with the sincerity of his welcome. Generally such personal attention coupled with a smile will claim a smile in return and put the visitor at ease. Calling a person by name, as "Good Morning, Mr. Brown. May I show you a seat?" carries with it a feeling of acquaintance and fellowship that is very attractive to most people.

Ushers should consider each guest's desires, with a view to pleasing, just as a business man would study a good prospective customer. He should always offer to conduct people to seats and never direct them in an off-hand manner. If at any time an occasion demands firmness, authority should be exercised in a kindly way. Under no circumstances should a guest be embarrassed, although the usher may feel that he does not deserve consideration. It is the latter's duty to control his feelings and play the part of a good host, making no exception in courtesy nor showing favoritism in any manner. If people seem unresponsive and cold, it will help the usher to keep in mind that his own physical and mental condition is often not up to normal. Strangers should be seated next to church members, where possible, to assist in acquaintance and for the purpose of fellowship.

FOURTH—THE USHER AT WORK

a. *Punctuality*

It should be considered a solemn obligation to be on time at 10:00 o'clock for the morning service and 6:45 o'clock for the evening service when the latter begins at 7:15 o'clock. On special occasions the chief usher will designate the hour.

b. *His Relation to the Head Usher*

If, for any reason, an usher cannot act on a given Sunday, he should notify the chief usher in advance. If he is unexpectedly delayed and upon arrival at the church finds that someone has been assigned to his place, he should not expect the substitute to retire in his favor without consulting the chief usher.

c. *In the Foyer*

Everything should be done to create an atmosphere of reverence and quiet in the foyer, especially during the service. The sign "Please Be Quiet" means just what it says, and conversation should be discontinued. Those who act as "Greeters" can do a fine piece of work here. They need not feel that they must visit with those whom they meet. A hand-clasp and cheery "Good Morning" or "Good Evening" will serve their purpose admirably.

d. *Closing the Doors into the Auditorium*

In order that the services may be conducted in an orderly and worshipful manner the doors into the auditorium will be closed at certain intervals, to be agreed upon by the pastors, the organist and the chief ushers. Instruction will be given to the ushers regarding the opening and closing of these doors and the seating of persons who arrive after services have begun. When the doors have been closed ushers should remain in the auditorium in a position to open the doors at the proper time. People should not be seated after the signal has been given to close the doors.

e. *Seating the Congregation*

The matter of seating an audience is very important. As soon as one party of guests has been seated, the usher should determine where he will place the next. He will, thereby, avoid embarrassing people by keeping them standing midway in the aisle while he locates a seat. In order to avoid being left alone in the front of the church because someone has taken a seat in the rear when the usher expected him to follow, it is suggested that the usher glance over his shoulder to see if the guest is on his way down the aisle. It is important that each person be seated where he will be most comfortable This can be most easily accomplished by quietly asking if he has any preference. The usher should try to remember any preference so that he need not ask again when that person returns.

Generally speaking, the audience should be seated well forward. Seats in the rear of the center should not be used until later in the service when they will be needed for late arrivals. If it should seem likely that the audience is to be small, guests should be seated in the center, between the two side aisles and as far forward as possible. It is better to put two or three people in each pew instead of filling a few and leaving several vacant ones between those occupied. This will require tact and good judgment; it is best, however, for an apparently filled room creates a better feeling than the sight of empty seats. Such an arrangement will also facilitate the taking of the offering.

On special occasions when large crowds are to be served it will be necessary to use every available sitting. To do this it will be necessary to ask people to move to the farther ends of the pews leaving the vacant spaces next to the aisle. The usher may then ask the number of people for whom he has sittings to come down the aisle. Extra chairs should never be put in the aisles or in the foyer and the stairways and aisles should always be kept open.

During the morning service the ushers in the lower foyer should ascertain whether or not there are seats in the gallery so that people may be sent upstairs and so relieve the congestion in the foyer.

f. During the Service

When the time arrives for the sermon, ushers should find seats, if possible, in the rear of their own aisles, in order that they may seat late arrivals with the least possible confusion and for the purpose of being on hand in case of an emergency. If people arrive late for the service, the usher should go out into the foyer to greet them and seat them in the auditorium as quietly as possible. Guests should not be allowed to stand in the foyer with no attention given to them. In the event of a crowded service ushers should not sit in the Board or Barrett Rooms and allow people to stand in the foyer without attempting to find a seat for them somewhere.

Ushering Hints

THE prime requisite for a successful ushers' corps is an able and faithful head usher. Great care should be taken in selecting the proper person with the necessary qualifications. It is an important and responsible position. Qualities of leadership are necessary. An affable personality is a good asset for the position. Unswerving faithfulness is presupposed. The head usher should be given uncurtailed authority and should not be subjected in his duties to the conflicting notions of the members of the church council. It would be well in every case to clearly define his duties and make him fully responsible for efficiency in the work to which he has been appointed. Make him responsible also for the collection. There is no reason why this function should remain the eternal prerogative of the deacons. A head usher who is imbued with the importance of his job and is given free hand in working out his problems is pretty sure to rise to the necessities of his office.

Equal care should be taken in the selection of the ushers. For obvious reasons comparatively young men should be chosen. They are much more liable to be in sympathy with their work and to adapt themselves to new conditions than the older members. It is also well to enlist men who are not already burdened with other church work. It is not difficult to get men enrolled as ushers who are hard to interest in other phases of church work. A distribution of jobs among as many men as possible is always wise. Candidates for ushers should be impressed with the importance of their office. Slipshod attention to duty should not be tolerated. The ushers should be as dependable as the pastor and organist. Remissness in duty throws the whole church machinery out of gear. Have your ushers function even when the church is not crowded. They are not to stand at the doors and tell people: "There are plenty of seats up forward." There is a degree of satisfaction, particularly to the visitor, in having the courtesy of being escorted to a seat extended, even when the church is half vacant.

Rules and regulations governing the selection and management of the corps of ushers are given elsewhere in this issue. Local conditions and specific needs will naturally prompt a church to formulate the regulations in accordance with local peculiarities. But by all means dignify the ushers' corps with full charge of the physical details of the service. If the office is made worth while, the right kind of men can be secured to accept it.

Rules for Ushers

1. Realize the importance of your office. Strangers receive their first impression of our church from you. Next to the pastor, organist and choir, you are the "keymen" in keeping up the worshipful atmosphere. Be quiet in all your work. Be neat in your personal appearance—clothes pressed, shoes shined, etc. Be polite.

2. Be at your post at least ten minutes before beginning of service.

3. The head usher should always be at the rear of the church at the main entrance, the first to greet the arrivals and to indicate to them which aisle to take. His duties in general are:

(1) Assign the duties to the ushers, placing them in the aisles, etc.

(2) Get an accurate count of the attendance at each service and keep a record of same in the book provided for that purpose.

(3) Have charge of the lighting and ventilating of the church during the service.

(4) Keep a watchful eye on all that is going on during the service and offer helpful suggestions to the ushers for the improvement of their work.

(5) See to it that no one is ushered up the aisle during prayer, the reading of the Scriptures, or special music.

(6) At communion services, station two ushers at head of the entrance aisle to admit 18 persons at a time to the altar rail.

(7) See to it that exit doors are opened when last Amen is sung.

4. Two men will work each of the two main aisles and one man each wall aisle. The two men in each aisle will automatically take turns in ushering the new arrivals.

5. Greet the new arrivals that come to your aisle with a smile and a slight bow or nod. Give them a sign to follow you and then walk boldly up the aisle, not too fast, until you come to the place where you desire to seat them. If you find that you have "lost" them on the way, do not show any embarrassment, but return to the place where they have seated themselves and with a smile hand them the Bulletin.

6. Bulletins should be given to each individual after seating them. Bulletins should not be given at the door. They are the ushers' "bait." See to it that all are provided with Hymnals. In going down the aisles offer Bulletins to those who have "escaped" the ushers, especially those that have come in through other entrances from the Bible School.

7. Study the seating of the congregation. Learn the favorite places of members, especially those that are hard of hearing, etc. Distribute the people in various parts of the auditorium with "salt and pepper" effect. This will give the appearance and "comfortable feeling" of a well-filled church even if it is only half filled. Then the empty seats can be filled later, if church gets crowded. Always give strangers the best seats (usually just forward of center of the church).

8. The secret of getting the front pews filled is to get the folks well forward as early as possible in the service. The older folks usually do not object to the front seats. But after the main body of the church is well filled it is "like pulling teeth" to get people to the front. The aisle then seems to them a mile long, with "everybody staring at them."

9. Keep the rear pews empty until all other space is occupied. Reserve them for the late arrivals, so that they need not disturb the service, and for families with small babies. Never allow groups of children in the rear pews, unless accompanied by parents or other older people.

10. In taking the offering be sure that you know your "marching orders." Know and keep your place. Keep in step and in line. Remember that the offering is a part of the worship and that you are officiating in the same.

(*From Year Book of First Church, Ottumwa, Iowa.*)